TRACE MODEL RESEARCH AND MATERIAL EVIDENCE AUTHENTICATION: MING DYNASTY LONGQUAN KILN SYSTEM CELADON

明代龙泉窑系青瓷迹型研究与物证鉴定

周筱慧　周强　著

南方日报出版社
NANFANG DAILY PRESS
中国・广州

图书在版编目（CIP）数据

明代龙泉窑系青瓷迹型研究与物证鉴定 / 周筱慧，周强著．—广州：南方日报出版社，2016.11

ISBN 978-7-5491-1417-7

Ⅰ．①明… Ⅱ．①周… ②周… Ⅲ．① 龙泉窑—青花瓷（考古）—鉴定—中国—明代 Ⅳ．① K876.34

中国版本图书馆 CIP 数据核字（2016）第 122281 号

MINGDAI LONGQUAN YAOXI QINGCI JIXING YANJIU YU WUZHENG JIANDING

明代龙泉窑系青瓷迹型研究与物证鉴定

周筱慧　周强　著

出版发行　南方日报出版社
地　　址　广州市广州大道中 289 号
电　　话　（020）83000502
经　　销　全国新华书店
印　　刷　广东信源彩色印务有限公司
开　　本　889mm × 1194mm　1/8
印　　张　61.25
字　　数　455 千字
版　　次　2016 年 11 月第 1 版
印　　次　2016 年 11 月第 1 次印刷
定　　价　380.00 元

投稿热线：020-83000503　读者热线：020-83000502
网址：http://www.nfdailypress.com/
发现印装质量问题，影响阅读，请与承印厂联系调换

陶瓷迹型研究系列丛书

《陶瓷迹型学概论》

2013年已出版

《元青花迹型研究与物证鉴定》

2014年已出版

《明代龙泉窑系青瓷迹型研究与物证鉴定》

2016年已出版

《清代康熙彩瓷迹型研究与物证鉴定》

计划2017年出版

《宋代耀州窑青瓷迹型研究与物证鉴定》

计划2018年出版

《唐三彩迹型研究与物证鉴定》

计划2019年出版

《宋代吉州窑瓷器迹型研究与物证鉴定》

计划2020年出版

The Ceramics Trace Model Study Series

Survey of Ceramics Trace Model Study
Published: 2013

Trace Model Research and Material Evidence Authentication: Yuan Dynasty Underglaze Blue Porcelain
Published: 2014

Trace Model Research and Material Evidence Authentication: Ming Dynasty Longquan Kiln System Celadon
Published: 2016

Trace Model Research and Material Evidence Authentication: Qing Dynasty Kangxi Polychrome Porcelain
Planned Date of Publishing: 2017

Trace Model Research and Material Evidence Authentication: Song Dynasty Yaozhou Kiln Porcelain
Planned Date of Publishing: 2018

Trace Model Research and Material Evidence Authentication: Tang Dynasty Three Color Ceramics
Planned Date of Publishing: 2019

Trace Model Research and Material Evidence Authentication: Song Dynasty Jizhou Kiln Porcelain
Planned Date of Publishing: 2020

陶瓷迹型学系列丛书编辑委员会

作者：

周强（化工硕士，高级工程师，曾任职广州市化学工业研究所，现任广州东方博物馆副馆长）
周筱慧（广州东方博物馆研究部部长）

翻译：

周筱慧　马士宁（Matthew Bunney）　戴灵（Debby Bunney）

The Ceramics Trace Model Study Series Editing Committee

Authors:

Zhou Qiang, MA.Chemical Engineering, Senior Engineer, Former Research Fellow at Guangzhou Chemical Industry Research Institute, Current Vice Director of Guangzhou Oriental Museum
Annabelle Bunney (Zhou Xiaohui), Current Head of Research Department of Guangzhou Oriental Museum

Translation:

Annabelle Bunney (Zhou Xiaohui), Matthew Bunney, Debby Bunney

科研项目牵头单位与合作单位
Sponsors and Partners

《明代龙泉窑系青瓷迹型研究与物证鉴定》牵头单位：

Trace Model Research and Material Evidence Authentication: Ming Dynasty Longquan System Celadon Primary Research Project Sponsors

1. 广州市番禺区文物管理委员会办公室
2. 广州番禺博物馆
3. 广州东方博物馆
4. 广东省文物考古研究所
5. 龙泉青瓷博物馆
6. 广东大埔县博物馆
7. 广州番禺职业技术学院
8. 广东省收藏家协会
9. 东方陶瓷迹型物证研究中心

1. Guangzhou Panyu District Cultural Relics Management Committee Office
2. Guangzhou Panyu Museum
3. Guangzhou Oriental Museum
4. Guangdong Provincial Cultural Relics and Archeology Research Institute
5. Longquan Celadon Museum
6. Guangdong Dabu County Museum
7. Guangzhou Panyu Polytechnic
8. Guangdong Collectors Association
9. The Oriental T.R.A.C.E. Research Center

陶瓷迹型研究项目合作单位：

1. 广州市番禺区文物管理委员会办公室
2. 广州番禺博物馆
3. 东方陶瓷迹型物证研究中心
4. 广东省文物鉴定站
5. 广东省文物考古研究所
6. 广东省收藏家协会
7. 广东大埔县博物馆
8. 广东客家博物馆
9. 中山大学社会学与人类学学院
10. 中山大学人类进化与科技考古实验室
11. 广州大学美术与设计学院
12. 华南师范大学公共管理学院
13. 广州番禺职业技术学院
14. 深圳职业技术学院

Research Project Partners

1. Guangzhou Panyu District Cultural Relics Management Committee Office
2. Guangzhou Panyu Museum
3. The Oriental T.R.A.C.E. Research Center
4. Guangdong Cultural Relics Authentication Station
5. Guangdong Provincial Cultural Relics and Archeology Research Institute
6. Guangdong Collectors Association
7. Guangdong Dabu County Museum
8. Guangdong Hakka Museum
9. Sun Yat-Sen University, Sociology and Anthropology Department
10. Sun Yat-Sen University, Human Evolution and Hi-tech Archaeology Laboratory
11. Guangzhou University, School of Art and Design
12. South China Normal University, School of Public Administration
13. Guangzhou Panyu Polytechnic
14. Shenzhen Polytechnic

15. 景德镇陶瓷考古研究所
16. 景德镇陶瓷大学
17. 景德镇景德陶瓷集团有限公司
18. 中国科学院高能物理研究所
19. 龙泉青瓷博物馆
20. 耀州窑博物馆
21. 内蒙古包头博物馆
22. 内蒙古明博草原文化博物馆
23. 鄂尔多斯青铜器博物馆
24. 鄂尔多斯农耕游牧博物馆
25. 陕西省文物总店
26. 台湾鸿禧美术馆
27. 澳门博物馆
28. 金乐轩
29. 泰国曼谷大学东南亚陶瓷博物馆
30. 印度尼西亚国立博物馆
31. 新加坡国立大学博物馆
32. 新加坡国立大学考古研究中心
33. 新加坡南洋大学华裔馆
34. 伊朗国立博物馆
35. 英国苏富比艺术学院
36. 英国格拉斯哥博物馆
37. 英国巴斯亚洲艺术博物馆
38. 美国波士顿艺术博物馆
39. 美国旧金山亚洲艺术博物馆
40. 美国得克萨斯州金贝尔艺术博物馆
41. 美国印第安纳波利斯艺术博物馆
42. 美国洁蕊堂

15. Jingdezhen Ceramics Archeology Research Institute
16. Jingdezhen Ceramics University
17. Jingdezhen Jingde China Group Co., Ltd.
18. Institute of High Energy Physics - Chinese Academy of Science
19. Longquan Munincipal Museum
20. Yaozhou Kiln Museum
21. Inner Mongolia Baotou Museum
22. Inner Mongolia Mingbo Grasslands Culture Museum
23. Inner Mongolia Ordos Bronze Ware Museum
24. Inner Mongolia Ordos Farming and Nomadic Museum
25. Shaanxi Cultural Relics Collective
26. The Chang Foundation, Taiwan
27. Macau Museum
28. Jinlexuan Collection
29. Southeast Asian Ceramics Museum, Bangkok University
30. National Museum of Indonesia
31. NUS Museum, Singapore
32. NUS Archeology Research Center, Singapore
33. Overseas Chinese Museum at Nanyang Technical University, Singapore
34. National Museum of Iran
35. Sotheby's Istitute, London U.K.
36. The Burrell Collection, Glasgow U.K.
37. Asian Art Museum, Bath U.K.
38. Museum of Fine Arts, Boston
39. Asian Art Museum of San Francisco
40. Kimbell Art Museum, Fort Worth
41. Indianapolis Museum of Art
42. Jie Rui Tang Collection

广州番禺博物馆简介
Guangzhou Panyu Museum

广州番禺博物馆坐落于广州市番禺区银平路龟岗东麓，于1997年11月落成开放，是国家二级博物馆，番禺八大美景之一。馆区所占面积240亩，分为多功能陈列大楼、番禺文博园、东汉古墓群景区等三部分。博物馆展览面积8000平方米，内容丰富，形式多样，表现出鲜明的地方特色。番禺文博园占地面积约30亩，古民居、石桥、牌坊、里弄、古炮、传统作坊等遗迹与田园水乡融于一体，景观宜人。墓葬景区规模宏大，并进行原貌展示，独具特色。

广州番禺博物馆是国家文物局首批展示与服务提升项目的试点单位之一。一楼设冼星海纪念馆；二楼设有“番禺古代文明”等三个展厅和多功能临展展厅；三楼设有“馆藏文物”“名家书画”“尹积昌雕塑艺术”等多个展厅，陈列独具匠心，融思想性、知识性、艺术性于一体，充分地展示了番禺灿烂的古代文明和今天的辉煌成就。

Panyu Museum is located in Guangzhou City, Panyu District along the Eastern edge of the Turtle Hill Reserve. Established in November 1997, it is a National Level 2 Museum and one of the ‘8 Scenic Locales of Panyu’. Sitting on 40 acres, the complex is divided into 3 main sections: The Main Multi-Purpose Building, Cultural Garden, and Han Dynasty Burial Grounds. The Main Building consists of 8000 square meters of Display Area with a multifaceted and abundant array of cultural relics from the local area. The Cultural Garden consists of 4 acres and includes: Ancient Peasant Buildings, Stone Bridge, Relic Cannons, and traditional Chinese garden fixtures.

Panyu Museum is one of the first National Cultural Bureau’s experimental projects for an elevated level of Display and Service. The First floor is dedicated for the Memorial Hall for Musical Composer Xian Xinghai, a Chinese hero and musical legend. The second floor is divided in to three ‘Panyu Ancient Culture’ exhibitions as well as one multi-purpose hall. The third floor is allocated to housing Museum Relics, Special Exhibitions, and the Yi Zhichang Sculpture Hall. This Museum is dedicated to showing the wonderful ancient culture of Panyu as well as the modern accomplishments that this fine area boasts.

广州东方博物馆简介
Guangzhou Oriental Museum

广州东方博物馆占地30亩，总建筑面积约8000平方米，由中国建筑设计研究院设计，建筑群体简而不陋、素而不苍，姿横捭阖、藏风纳气。

博物馆按主题展览、专题展览和临时展览之形式分设七个展厅——钟表铜器厅、百砚厅、交流厅、两个书画厅、两个陶瓷展厅以及四个展廊。

博物馆未来的发展方向：科学研究，去伪存真，联合国内权威瓷器研究机构和大专院校，深入展开对陶瓷的量化研究，有效保护、传播、传承中华民族的文化薪火！

Guangzhou Oriental Museum, sitting on over 5 acres of land, includes a usable construction area of 8000 ㎡. Designed by China Architecture Design and Research Group (CAG), the entire construction is simple but not meek; plain but not dull; and appears open and expansive but still catches the wind.

The museum is comprised of main exhibitions, themed exhibitions, and special exhibitions spread across seven halls: Bronze Ware Hall, Hundred Ink Stone Hall, Research Exchange, two Calligraphy and Painting Halls, and two Ceramics Halls; these halls are linked by four Special Exhibition Corridors.

Guangzhou Oriental Museum's main developmental direction is anchored on: Scientific study, the elimination of bogus pieces and holding on to true relics, partnering with international ceramics studies organizations and major universities, thoroughly developing the quantification research of ceramics, and creating a ceramics research group to take in hand, protect, and pass on the torch of Chinese cultural study!

龙泉青瓷博物馆简介

Longquan Celadon Museum

龙泉青瓷博物馆，是国内唯一的以龙泉青瓷为主题的博物馆，系统研究展示龙泉窑起源、发展、鼎盛、衰落、复兴各个时期的历史面貌，以及“人类非物质文化遗产——龙泉青瓷传统烧制技艺”特征和龙泉窑考古发掘成果。该馆集龙泉青瓷的考古研究、展示宣教、学术交流、文化休闲等功能于一体，是龙泉青瓷历史价值和文化创意的重要展示交流平台。

龙泉青瓷博物馆，建筑面积约10000平方米，展示面积4000平方米，共推出“青瓷的记忆”“瓷海明珠”等十多个基本陈列。此外，还配有临时展厅和学术报告厅，适合不定期举办各种展览活动和学术交流。

The only Longquan Celadon themed museum in China, this is an institution where people can carry out systematic study and learn the origin, development, peak, decline, and revival of the historical features of Longquan Celadon. Additionally, patrons can discover the characteristics of this intangible cultural heritage: Traditional Longquan Celadon firing techniques and archaeological excavations of the Longquan kilns. The Longquan Celadon Museum collects, researches, exhibits, holds academic exchanges and provides leisure functions. The Longquan Celadon Museum is one of the most important showcase platforms of Longquan Celadon's historical value and cultural creativity.

The Longquan Celadon Museum has a construction area of about 10,000 square meters, including 4,000 square meters of exhibition area, which consists of a dozen basic exhibitions such as "History of Longquan Celadon", "Ceramic Pearl" and so forth. In addition, the Temporary Exhibition Hall and Academic Lecture Hall are also equipped with various exhibitions and academic exchange activities.

前言

陶瓷迹型物证鉴定及其意义

陶瓷文物鉴定是一项运用传统方法或现代科学技术分析辨识文物真伪、年代、质地、用途和价值的工作。

陶瓷文物鉴定有两种形式：人证鉴定与物证鉴定。

人证鉴定是主观非量化的，具有不确定特征的鉴定，属玄学推理；物证鉴定是科学量化的，具有确定性特征的鉴定。陶瓷文物鉴定中的物证鉴定，是终极鉴定，因为物证是鉴定的终极证据，属于科学实证。

鉴定不是审美，审美讲的是主观感觉，鉴定要讲客观证据。人类的司法取证，经历了从神证、人证到物证的过程，说明了人类社会的进步与文明。陶瓷鉴定证据从主观到客观，从陶瓷的类型证据到陶瓷显微的迹型证据，说明了人类的认识与科学在不断发展。

因此，人证鉴定属于文物鉴定的初级阶段，它需要有物证进一步补充证明，因为物证只有客观性与稳定性。陶瓷迹型物证研究与其他鉴定方法的推广应用，与科学技术发展阶段相关联，它使得鉴定结果具备实然性的终极特征。

经验性的鉴定往往是神秘的，经常听到大师说："有些东西，只可意会，不可言传。"科学的陶瓷迹型物证鉴定是透明的、客观的，强调眼见为实。人人都可以借助陶瓷迹型标准图谱，亲自参与比对。陶瓷迹型物证鉴定有民众效应，易于普及。大数据时代不缺乏数据，缺的是科学数据，传统的主观经验性鉴定，也不乏经验证明，但缺乏科学数据的证明。因此，陶瓷迹型学这门学科的建立，发展、优化、升级了传统的陶瓷鉴定方法，开拓了陶瓷鉴定的新领域。

陶瓷迹型的研究与提取，为陶瓷年代的确定提供了清晰可见的物证，对陶瓷迹型的风化程度与风化速度的研究，突破了政治、宗教、种族、国家的藩篱，它属于全人类的文化研究项目。

该项研究是为国家陶瓷迹型研究建立资料库，为市场的公平、商业的诚信提供技术支撑，类似网球、羽毛球的鹰眼技术，足球的门线技术，钻石科技检测技术以及人类DNA亲子鉴定技术。

它使得陶瓷鉴定从目前经验性为主的人证阶段，迈向了科学的物证阶段。也就是说，陶瓷鉴定从过去主要讲感觉的经验性人证鉴定，进入到讲证据的科学物证鉴定阶段。眼学鉴定知识是宝贵的，我们要尊重传统的眼学鉴定经验，但不能就此满足于经验，认识不能停留在经验上。陶瓷迹型学，是一门新创的科学，它将打破陶瓷鉴定自古以来师傅带徒弟的做法，可纳入大专院校开设学制专业，统一为国家培育人才。

陶瓷迹型学在实践中的应用，有利于规范市场，有助于建立诚信、公平、公正的交易制度，降低收藏风险，降低国家对市场的管理成本。该项技术的运用可提升陶瓷真伪鉴定的准确率，增强陶瓷鉴定的公信力，恢复国人文物收藏传承的自信心。

该项科学研究技术成果，可迅速转化为陶瓷收藏爱好者的鉴定技能，并将陶瓷迹型物证鉴定科学技术与互联网相结合，通过大数据库与国家公共服务网并轨，广泛为民众服务。

广州番禺博物馆馆长　曾昭明
广州东方博物馆馆长　周　勇
广东省收藏家协会主席　陈少湘

Foreword

Ceramics Trace Material Evidence Authentication and Meaning

Ceramic Authentication is the process of utilizing traditional knowledge and modern scientific techniques to determine authenticity, age, production location, use, and value.

Ceramic Authentication can utilize two approaches: Human Witness Authentication and Material Evidence Authentication.

Human witness authentication is qualitative and not inherently conclusive. It is a metaphysical inference. Material evidence authentication is a quantitative and conclusive form of authentication. Ceramic relic authentication, utilizing material evidence, offers ultimate conclusions; as material evidence is an ultimate proof, a scientific verification.

Authentication is not aesthetics, for aesthetics speaks of subjective feeling, authentication needs objective proof. Human's shift of legal proof has moved from divination, to human witness, to material evidence, and speaks to the civilization of society. The move of ceramic authentication from subjective to objective, from noticeable evidence to microscopic ceramic trace evidence speaks to human's unending development in knowledge and science.

Because of this, human witness authentication is seen to be the base level of relic authentication, needing material evidence to offer further authoritative support, as it is only material evidence that has objectivity and stability. The extended use of Ceramic Trace Model Material Evidence Research and other authentication methods is linked to the developmental stage of science and technology, allowing authentication results to possess verifiable and ultimate characteristics.

In the past, authentication was laden in mystery. Experts often offered statements as "Some things, you can only sense, there no way to verbalize it." Whereas scientific trace model material evidence authentication is objective and stresses the importance of visible proof. Anyone can utilize a Standard Trace Atlas Model, and personally take part in comparison. Trace Model Material Evidence Authentication is user friendly, and easily popularized. In this macro data age, data is not lacking, what is lacking is scientific data. Similarly, traditional authentication is not lacking evidence, it is lacking scientific evidence. Because of this, the establishment, development, and evolution of this academic discipline, Ceramic Trace Model Authentication, is an upgrade to traditional authentication, brining ceramic authentication into a new realm.

The research and refinement of ceramic traces offers clearly visible evidence in the determining of ceramic age. Researching ceramic trace weathering severity and weathering speed has broken down political, religious, racial, and national boundaries. It is a cultural research project that belongs to all of humanity.

This research project offers technical support for the establishment of a national ceramic trace database, for market equality, and for business integrity. It is likened to Hawkeye instant replay technology, scientific diamond testing technique, and DNA paternity testing.

This moves ceramic authentication from the current stage of experience based human witness, to a stage of scientific proof. Which is to say, ceramic authentication had primarily been based on feeling and testimony, and can move into the scientific material evidence stage. There is a wealth of knowledge within naked eye authentication, and we need to respect this traditional experience. However, presently we cannot be satisfied with just experience, we must press onward beyond recognition at an experience level. Ceramic Trace Model Study is a newly developed discipline of science, which succeeds the ancient master-apprentice ceramic authentication method, and brings authentication into the higher education system, allowing for unified international talent training.

In practice, Ceramics Trace Model Study is beneficial for market standardization and the building up of a trade that is upright, fair, and just. It lowers collection risk as well as market regulation costs. This technique can improve the authentication veracity rate, strengthen ceramic authentication credibility and return confidence to the generational collection and passing on of cultural relics.

The resulting techniques of this scientific research project can quickly develop the skills of ceramic collection hobbyist. It can also globally connect those with Ceramic Trace Model Authentication skills to the World Wide Web, offering a database that is integrated into the public service network, allowing the service to be enjoyed by all.

Guangzhou Panyu Museum Director: Zeng Zhaoming
Guangzhou Oriental Museum Director: Zhou Yong
Guangdong Collectors Association Chairman: Chen Shaoxiang

目 录

第一章 龙泉青瓷概述 / 2

第一节 龙泉窑发展史 / 4
一、龙泉窑的起源/4
二、龙泉窑在古代的发展/8
三、龙泉窑的衰落/12
四、龙泉窑在新中国时期的复兴/16
五、总结/18

第二节 龙泉窑的历史地位 / 24
一、龙泉窑在国内的地位/24
二、龙泉窑在海外的地位/30
三、总结/36

第二章 明代浙江龙泉窑青瓷与广东余里窑青瓷类型研究 / 42

第一节 明代浙江龙泉窑青瓷与广东余里窑青瓷器型比较分析 / 44
一、明代浙江龙泉窑青瓷器型类别/44
二、明代浙江龙泉窑青瓷器型表/44
三、明代浙江龙泉窑青瓷器型图集/44
四、明代浙江龙泉窑青瓷器型风格分析/66
五、明代广东余里窑青瓷器型类别/66
六、明代广东余里窑青瓷器型表/66
七、明代广东余里窑青瓷器型图集/67
八、明代广东余里窑青瓷器型风格分析/72
九、总结/72

第二节 明代浙江龙泉窑青瓷与广东余里窑青瓷装饰工艺比较分析 / 74
一、明代浙江龙泉窑青瓷装饰工艺/74
二、明早期浙江龙泉窑青瓷官窑器纹饰类别/76
三、明代广东余里窑青瓷装饰工艺/89
四、明代广东余里窑青瓷纹饰类别/89
五、总结/93

第三节 明代浙江龙泉窑青瓷与广东余里窑青瓷胎釉比较分析 / 94
一、瓷胎比较/94
二、瓷釉比较/104

第四节 明代浙江龙泉窑青瓷与广东余里窑青瓷制作工艺比较分析 / 120
一、浙江龙泉窑青瓷制作工艺/120
二、广东余里窑青瓷制作工艺/134

第三章 龙泉窑系青瓷釉层的化学成分、性质与形貌 / 142

第一节 龙泉窑系青瓷瓷釉化学成分 / 144
一、青瓷瓷釉的概念/144
二、青瓷瓷釉的构成/144
三、青瓷瓷釉化学成分/144
四、龙泉青瓷瓷釉的配方/144

第二节 龙泉窑系青瓷瓷釉各化学成分的作用 / 150
一、网络形成剂作用/150
二、助熔剂作用/150
三、着色剂作用/152
四、其他成分作用/152
五、龙泉窑系青瓷瓷釉的化学成分与釉层结构稳定性的关系/154
六、总结/154

第三节 龙泉窑系青瓷釉表面活性 / 156
一、龙泉窑系青瓷釉表面活性概念/156
二、龙泉窑系青瓷釉表面活性产生原因/156
三、总结/156

第四节 龙泉窑系青瓷釉层形貌 / 158
一、龙泉窑系青瓷釉层概念/158
二、龙泉窑系青瓷釉层形貌/158

第五节 总结 / 168

第四章 龙泉窑系青瓷釉层变化 / 172

第一节 龙泉窑系青瓷釉层变化机理 / 174
一、龙泉窑系青瓷釉层与水的反应/174
二、龙泉窑系青瓷釉层与碱的反应/174
三、龙泉窑系青瓷釉层与酸的反应/176
四、龙泉窑系青瓷釉层与CO_2的反应/176
五、龙泉窑系青瓷釉层与盐溶液的反应/176
六、总结/176

第二节 龙泉窑系青瓷釉层变化与环境的关系 / 180
一、地上环境/180
二、地下环境/180
三、水中环境/184

第三节 龙泉窑系青瓷釉层迹型风化特征 / 188
一、玻璃相迹型风化特征/188
二、气相迹型风化特征/188
三、晶相迹型风化特征/188

第四节 总结 / 192

第五章 明代龙泉窑系青瓷典型迹型类别 / 196

第一节 龙泉窑系青瓷斑块类别 / 198
一、龙泉窑系青瓷斑块概念/198
二、龙泉窑系青瓷斑块类型/198
三、总结/227

第二节 龙泉窑系青瓷纹路类别 / 228
一、龙泉窑系青瓷纹路概念/228
二、龙泉窑系青瓷纹路种类/228
三、总结/244

第三节 龙泉窑系青瓷气泡类别 / 246
一、龙泉窑系青瓷气泡概念/246
二、龙泉窑系青瓷气泡种类/246
三、总结/261

第四节 龙泉窑系青瓷鬃眼类别 / 262
一、龙泉窑系青瓷鬃眼概念/262
二、龙泉窑系青瓷鬃眼形成与分布/262
三、龙泉窑系青瓷鬃眼特征/262
四、总结/269

第六章 陶瓷迹型原理及规律 / 272

第一节 陶瓷迹型基本原理 / 274
一、陶瓷迹型量变原理/274
二、陶瓷迹型时间过程性原理/274

第二节 陶瓷迹型规律 / 276
一、陶瓷迹型随机性规律/276
二、陶瓷迹型色差规律/276
三、陶瓷迹型量变规律/276
四、陶瓷迹型层次性规律/276
五、陶瓷迹型多样性规律/278
六、陶瓷迹型差异性规律/278
七、陶瓷迹型分明性规律/278

第三节 迹型出现位置的合理性与变化的同步性 / 280
一、陶瓷迹型出现位置的合理性/280
二、陶瓷迹型变化的同步性/280

第七章 明代龙泉窑系青瓷迹型标准图谱模型建构 / 284

第一节 标本选择与来源 / 286
一、标本选择/286
二、标本来源/286
三、研究合作单位/286

第二节 明代浙江龙泉枫洞岩窑青瓷和明代广东余里窑青瓷迹型标准图谱模型 / 288
一、明代浙江龙泉枫洞岩窑青瓷和明代广东余里窑青瓷迹型标准图谱模型说明/288
二、明代浙江龙泉枫洞岩窑青瓷迹型标准图谱模型/290
三、明代广东余里窑青瓷迹型标准图谱模型/311

第八章 明代龙泉窑系青瓷迹型真品与赝品比对分析 / 336

第一节 龙泉窑系青瓷斑块真品与赝品比对分析 / 340
一、坑点斑/340
二、絮状斑/348

第二节 龙泉窑系青瓷纹路真品与赝品比对分析 / 350
一、C形纹、O形纹/350
二、釉裂纹/358
三、划痕/363

第三节 龙泉窑系青瓷气泡真品与赝品比对分析 / 368
一、色变泡/368
二、壁变泡/374

第四节 龙泉窑系青瓷鬃眼真品与赝品比对分析 / 382
一、真品二维特征/382
二、赝品二维特征/382

第五节 龙泉窑系青瓷釉层形貌真品与赝品比对分析 / 386
一、真品三维特征/386
二、赝品三维特征/388

第九章 建立龙泉窑系青瓷迹型物证的实际操作 / 390

第一节 建立龙泉窑系瓷器迹型物证的方法 / 392
一、迹型物证建立的特性/392
二、迹型比对/392
三、迹型本质论证/394

第二节 龙泉窑系瓷器迹型物证建立操作 / 422
一、迹型观察记录/422
二、迹型形成本质论证/422
三、龙泉窑系青瓷迹型标准图谱模型的局限性/422
四、总结/422

附录1：青釉莲瓣纹碗迹型分析报告 / 428

一、送检器物基本情况/428
二、检验性质/428
三、条件/428
四、方法/428
五、操作流程/428
六、送检器物迹型与龙泉窑系青瓷迹型标准图谱模型比对/429
七、迹型现象比对结果综述/439
八、送检器物物证分析/439

附录2：2013年度广东大埔余里窑址发掘概况 / 454

一、地理位置/454
二、发掘经过/454
三、文化堆积/454
四、主要遗迹/456
五、遗物概况/457

参考文献 / 462

后记 / 466

CONTENTS

Chapter 1: Overview of Longquan Celadon Wares / 3

Section 1: The History of the Longquan Kilns / 5

1. The Emergence of the Longquan Kilns / 5
2. The Development of the Longquan Kilns / 11
3. The Decline of the Longquan Kilns / 17
4. The Rejuvenation of Longquan Wares in Modern China / 22
5. Conclusion / 22

Section 2: Longquan Kilns' Place in History / 25

1. Longquan Kilns' Place Domestically / 25
2. Longquan Ware's Place Overseas / 33
3. Conclusion / 39

Chapter 2: Typical Characteristics Study on Ming Dynasty Longquan Kiln System Celadon: Zhejiang Longquan Kiln and Guangdong Yuli Kiln Celadon / 43

Section 1: Comparative Analysis of Ming Dynasty Longquan Kiln System Celadon: Zhejiang Longquan Kiln and Guangdong Yuli Kiln Celadon Shapes / 45

1. Ming Dynasty Zhejiang Longquan Kiln Celadon Shape Categories / 45
2. Table of Ming Dynasty Zhejiang Longquan Kiln Celadon Shape Categories / 45
3. Zhejiang Longquan Kiln Celadon Shape Image Catalogue / 47
4. Ming Dynasty Zhejiang Longquan Kiln Celadon Shape Style Analyses / 55
5. Ming Dynasty Guangdong Yuli Kiln Celadon Shape Categories / 57
6. Table of Ming Dynasty Guangdong Yuli Kiln Celadon Shape Categories / 57
7. Ming Dynasty Guangdong Yuli Kiln Celadon Shape Categories Image Catalogue / 59
8. Ming Dynasty Guangdong Yuli Kiln Celadon Shape Style Analyses / 63
9. Conclusion / 63

Section 2: Comparative Analysis of Ming Dynasty Longquan Kiln System Celadon: Zhejiang Longquan Kiln and Guangdong Yuli Kiln Celadon Decorative Techniques / 75

1. Decorative Techniques of Zhejiang Longquan Celadon / 75
2. Zhejiang Longquan Kiln Early Ming Dynasty Official Ware Decoration Categories / 77
3. Decorative Techniques of Guangdong Yuli Kiln Celadon / 83
4. Guangdong Yuli Kiln Celadon Decoration Categories / 85
5. Conclusion / 87

Section 3: Comparative Analysis of Ming Dynasty Longquan Kiln System Celadon: Zhejiang Longquan Kiln and Guangdong Yuli Kiln Celadon Body and Glaze / 95

1. Porcelain Body Comparison / 95
2. Porcelain Glaze Comparison / 99

Section 4: Comparative Analysis of Ming Dynasty Longquan Kiln System Celadon: Zhejiang Longquan Kiln and Guangdong Yuli Kiln Celadon Manufacturing Technique / 121

1. Zhejiang Longquan Kiln Celadon Manufacturing Technique / 121
2. Ming Dynasty Guangdong Yuli Kiln Celadon

Manufacturing Technique / 129

Chapter 3 Chemical Composition, Nature, and Appearance of Longquan Kiln System Celadon Glaze / 143

Section 1: Chemical Composition of Longquan Kiln System Celadon Glaze / 145

1. The Definition of Celadon Glaze / 145
2. The Components of Celadon Glaze / 145
3. The Chemical Composition of Celadon Glaze / 145
4. The Formulation of Longquan Kiln Celadon Glaze / 147

Section 2: The Functions of Longquan Kiln System Celadon Glaze Chemical Components / 151

1. The Function of Networking Agents / 151
2. The Function of Flux / 151
3. The Function of Coloring Agents / 153
4. The Function of Other Components / 153
5. The Relationship Between Longquan Kiln System Celadon Glaze Composition and Glaze Stability / 153
6. Conclusion / 155

Section 3: Active Nature of the Longquan Kiln System Celadon Glaze Surface / 157

1. The Active Nature of the LKSC Glaze Surface Defined / 157
2. Causes of the Glaze Surface Activity / 157
3. Conclusion / 157

Section 4: Longquan Kiln System Celadon Glaze Level Appearance / 159

1. LKSC Glaze Level Defined / 159
2. LKSC Glaze Level Appearance / 159

Section 5: Conclusion / 169

Chapter 4 Longquan Kiln System Celadon Glaze Level Changes / 173

Section 1: Mechanics of Longquan Kiln System Celadon Glaze Level Change / 175

1. LKSC Glaze Level Reactions with Water / 175
2. LKSC Glaze Level Reactions with Alkali / 175
3. LKSC Glaze Level Reactions with Acid / 177
4. LKSC Glaze Level Reaction with Carbon Dioxide / 177
5. LKSC Glaze Level Reaction with Salt Solutions / 178
6. Conclusion / 178

Section 2: Relationship Between Environment and LKSC Glaze Level Change / 181

1. Above Ground Environment / 181
2. Underground Environment / 181
3. Underwater Environment / 185

Section 3: Characteristics of Weathered Longquan Kiln System Celadon Glaze Level Traces / 189

1. Characteristics of Weathered Glass Phase Traces / 189
2. Characteristics Of Weathered Gas Phase Traces / 189
3. Characteristics Of Weathered Crystallized Traces / 191

Section 4: Conclusion / 193

Chapter 5 Ming Dynasty Longquan Kiln System Celadon Typical Trace Categories / 197

Section 1: Longquan Kiln System Celadon Mottle Category / 199

1. LKSC Mottles Defined / 199
2. LKSC Mottle Classes / 199
3. Conclusion / 219

Section 2: Longquan Kiln System Celadon Striae Category / 229

1. LKSC Striae Defined / 229
2. Types of LKSC Striae / 229
3. Conclusion / 239

Section 3: Longquan Kiln System Celadon Air Bubble Category / 247

1. LKSC Air Bubble Defined / 247
2. LKSC Air Bubble Types / 247
3. Conclusion / 257

Section 4: Longquan Kiln System Celadon Bristle Pit Category / 263
1. LKSC Bristle Pit Defined / 263
2. LKSC Bristle Pit Formation and Distribution / 263
3. LKSC Bristle Pit Characteristics / 263
4. Conclusion / 265

Chapter 6 Principles and Laws of Ceramic Traces / 273

Section 1: The Principles of Ceramic Traces / 275
1. The Quantitative Change Principle / 275
2. The Passage of Time Principle / 275
Section 2: Ceramic Trace Laws / 277
1. Ceramic Trace Law of Randomness / 277
2. Ceramic Trace Law of Chromatic Aberration / 277
3. Ceramic Trace Law of Quantitative Change / 277
4. Ceramic Trace Law of Gradation / 279
5. Ceramic Trace Law of Variegation / 279
6. Ceramic Trace Law of Disparity / 279
7. Ceramic Trace Law of Distinction / 279
Section 3: Ceramic Trace Location Rationality and Change Congruency / 281
1. Ceramic Trace Location Rationality / 281
2. Ceramic Trace Change Congruency / 281

Chapter 7 Ming Dynasty Longquan Kiln System Celadon Standard Trace Atlas Model Construction / 285

Section 1: Selection and Origin of the Samples / 287
1. Sample Selection / 287
2. Sample Origins / 287
3. Research Partner Organizations / 287
Section 2: Ming Dynasty Zhejiang Longquan Fengdongyan Kiln Celadon Standard Trace Atlas Model and Ming Dynasty Guangdong Yuli Kiln Celadon Standard Trace Atlas Model / 289
1. Ming Dynasty Zhejiang Longquan Fengdongyan Kiln Celadon Standard Trace Atlas Model and Ming Dynasty Guangdong Yuli Kiln Celadon Standard Trace Atlas Model Explanation / 289
2. Ming Dynasty Zhejiang Longquan Fengdongyan Kiln Celadon Standard Trace Atlas Model / 290
3. Ming Dynasty Guangdong Yuli Kiln Celadon Standard Trace Atlas Model / 311

Chapter 8 Ming Dynasty Genuine and Forged Longquan Kiln System Celadon Trace Comparative Analysis / 337

Section 1: Genuine and Forged Longquan Kiln System Celadon Mottle Comparison / 341
1. Pit Mottles / 341
2. Floccus Mottles / 345
Section 2: Genuine and Forged Longquan Kiln Style Celadon Striae Comparison / 351
1. C and O Shaped Striae / 351
2. Glaze Cracks / 355
3. Scratches / 357
Section 3: Genuine and Forged Longquan Kiln System Celadon Bubble Comparison / 369
1. Color Change Bubbles / 369
2. Textured Bubbles / 371
Section 4: Genuine and Forged Longquan Kiln System Celadon Bristle Pit Comparison / 383
1. Characteristics of Genuine Article / 383
2. Characteristics of Forged Article / 383
Section 5: Genuine and Forged Longquan Kiln System Celadon Glaze Surface Appearance Comparison / 387
1. Three-Dimensional Characteristics of Genuine Article / 387
2. Three-Dimensional Characteristics of Forged Article / 387

Chapter 9: Trace Model Material Evidence Establishment: Longquan Kiln System Celadon Methodology and Operation / 391

Section 1: Longquan Kiln System Celadon Trace Model Material Evidence Establishment Method / 393

1. Trace Model Material Evidence Establishment Characteristics / 393
2. Trace Comparison / 395
3. Nature of Trace Proofs / 395

Section 2: Longquan Kiln System Celadon Trace Model Material Evidence Authentication Operation / 423

1. Trace Recording Process / 423
2. Nature of Trace Proofs / 423
3. LKSC Standard Trace Atlas Model Limitations / 423
4. Conclusion / 425

Appendix 1: Longquan Celadon Bowl with Lotus Petal Pattern: Trace Model Material Evidence Analysis Report / 440

1. General Information of Test Piece / 440
2. Nature of Test / 440
3. Evidence Collection Requirements / 440
4. Evidence Collection Method / 440
5. Evidence Collection Operating Procedure / 440
6. Trace Comparison with the Longquan Kiln System Celadon Standard Trace Atlas Model / 441
7. Trace Appearance Comparison Comprehensive Results / 453
8. Trace Valuation and Evidence Collection Result / 453

References / 462

Afterword / 466

第一章

龙泉青瓷概述

阅读提示：

本章论述了龙泉青瓷的起源、发展及衰落的过程，讨论了龙泉青瓷在国内外的历史地位。

主要论述问题：

1. 在我国浙江地区，青瓷是什么时候开始烧制的？
2. 龙泉青瓷起源于哪个朝代？
3. 龙泉青瓷为什么在宋元时期发展如此迅速？
4. 龙泉青瓷在明代逐渐衰落的原因是什么？

Chapter 1

Overview of Longquan Celadon Wares

Text Note:

This chapter covers the emergence, development and eventual regression of Longquan Celadon Wares. It also discusses the historical status of Longquan Celadon Wares within China as well as internationally.

第一节 龙泉窑发展史

中国人对青瓷的喜爱由来已久，浙江龙泉窑是我国陶瓷史上烧制时间最长、窑址分布最广、产销规模最大的青瓷名窑。龙泉青瓷影响深远，窑场遍布在浙江省南部的龙泉、庆元、云和、景宁、丽水、遂昌、松阳、缙云、武义、青田、永嘉、文成、泰顺等十多个县市，现在已经发现各时期的龙泉窑窑址至少达900处。

我国烧制青瓷的历史十分久远，从商代的原始青瓷到南宋龙泉窑烧制的可与翡翠媲美的“梅子青”，历经2000余年，至此龙泉窑达到青瓷烧制的顶峰，受到社会各阶层的喜爱。加之南宋政府推行鼓励海外贸易的国策，使龙泉青瓷走出国门，畅销海外。龙泉窑自宋代起历代行销全国各地，并远销亚、非、欧三大洲，这一情况延续到元代，有增无减，及至明代虽有减弱，但生产一直延续至清代。

一、龙泉窑的起源

龙泉窑属于我国南方的青瓷系统，在我国浙江省龙泉、丽水、云和、遂昌和永嘉等地都有许多古代窑址。从这些窑址堆积的大量遗物特征来看，它们都属同一个系统，因主体遗存和瓷业生产中心集中分布在龙泉县，所以统一命名为“龙泉窑”[1]。而龙泉县古属处州，所以龙泉窑也被称为“处州瓷”或“处器”[2]。

浙江是我国青瓷的重要发源地，从商周时期开始，青瓷就已经出现了。

（一）青瓷在浙江的起源和发展

1. 商周时期

早在商和西周时期，在今绍兴、上虞、义乌、衢州、江山、遂昌、武义、桐乡、德清、长兴、鄞州等县市都已经开始使用原始青瓷。

2. 春秋战国时期

青瓷在春秋战国期间继续发展，在绍兴、萧山、诸暨等地都发现了烧制原始青瓷的遗址，窑场集中，生产量大。

3. 汉代

汉代晚期，浙江的陶瓷工匠们成功烧制瓷器。

4. 六朝时期

进入六朝时期，青瓷业蓬勃发展，越窑形成了庞大的瓷窑体系。

（二）关于龙泉窑起源的不同认识

在越窑的带动下，位于浙江中南部的婺州窑和瓯江下游的瓯窑也都有了很大的发展，浙江的制瓷业呈现一片繁荣景象，青瓷成为老百姓生活中不可或缺的日用品[3]。在这样的历史背景和条件的促进下，地处浙南偏僻地区的丽水、龙泉也开始生产青瓷。关于龙泉窑的创烧年代，学术界有不同的认识，目前通行的主要有三国两晋说、五代说及北宋说。

1. 三国两晋说

20世纪70年代以来，我国陆续发现了一批三国晋代古墓中出土的瓷器，其特征与越窑、婺州窑有差别，具有自己的特色。一些学者认为这些瓷器应该是龙泉窑早期的产品[4]。

对此，任世龙等认为，由于未有证据证明出土器物的烧造窑址就在龙泉县（因找不到有纪年的与之对应的窑址），所以它们确切的生产窑址有待进一步研究判定[5]。而且，这些三国晋代古墓中出土的瓷器主要在松阳、丽水等地，数量少，质量很一般，即便明确了这些瓷器就是产于龙泉地区，它们很有可能属于自产自销的土窑产品，在文化特征上与北宋晚期的龙泉窑青瓷相差甚远，二者之间不存在时间传承上的直接联系，作为龙泉窑开始烧造的证据难免有些牵强[6]。

Section 1:

The History of the Longquan Kilns

China's love of 'Qing' glaze (Celadon) porcelain is long and storied. The Longquan Kilns area of Zhejiang Province is the longest running, largest kiln location, and most vast production capacity of all celadon kilns throughout China's history. Longquan Ware's impact is deep and vast, stretching over 10 plus counties across Zhejiang Province including: Longquan, Qingyuan, Yunhe, Jingning, Lishui, Suichang, Songyang, Luoyun, Wuyi, Qingtian, Yongjia, Wencheng, and Taishun. Currently, over 900 Longquan kiln sites from several different time periods have been found across the region.

China has the world's longest history of firing celadon wares. From the emergence of green glaze proto porcelain of the Shang Dynasty to the emerald green glaze of the Longquan Plum Glaze Celadon wares of the Southern Song Dynasty, over two thousand years of development took place. This marked the pinnacle of Chinese Celadon production, and the point at which it was held in highest regard throughout society. Additionally, the incidental introduction of Song Dynasty's policy to encourage foreign trade led to Longquan Celadon exiting China for the first time and finding a welcome reception internationally. Starting in the Song Dynasty, Longquan Celadon wares found their way throughout all of China, and even as far as other parts of Asia, Africa and Europe. This continued without decline until the Yuan Dynasty, and while slowing during the Ming Dynasty, production continued well into the Qing Dynasty.

1. The Emergence of the Longquan Kilns

Longquan Wares belong in the category of Southern Chinese Celadon Wares, with ancient kiln sites being situated in and around the Zhejiang Province, Longquan area. Due to the common materials and techniques found across these kilns, and as their central location is Longquan County, they are generally known as the Longquan Kilns [1]. Additionally, because Longquan County was formerly known as Chuzhou, the wares are sometimes referred to as Chuzhou Porcelain or Chu Wares [2].

Zhejiang is one of the main starting points of celadon production within China. Beginning in the Shang and Zhou Dynasties, celadon wares had already made early appearances in the area.

A. The Emergence and Development of Celadon Wares in Zhejiang Province

a. Shang and Zhou Dynasties

As early as the Shang or Western Zhou Dynasties; in areas such as Shaoxing, Shangyu, Yiwu, Quzhou, Jiangshan, and other counties of Zhejiang Province; the earliest and rawest forms of celadon wares began to emerge.

b. Spring and Autumn and Warring States Periods

Celadon continued its development through the Spring and Autumn Period as well as Warring States Period, with excavation findings of large amounts of closely clustered early celadon ware kiln sites being discovered through Shaoxing, Xiaoshan, Zhuji, and other counties.

c. Han Dynasty

Late Han Dynasty saw the successful firing of proto porcelain by artisans in Zhejiang Province.

d. Six Dynasties

Entering into the Six Dynasties Period, the development

2. 五代说

（1）宋人庄季裕的记录

龙泉窑始烧于五代晚期的说法，其中一个依据来自宋人庄季裕的《鸡肋编》："处州龙泉县……又出青瓷器，谓之祕色。钱氏所贡，盖取于此。"[7]

"钱氏"即五代吴越国的国王钱氏。由文献记录可见，早在吴越国时期，龙泉县已成为吴越钱王纳贡所需秘色瓷的生产地。

（2）龙泉大窑和金村窑址发现五代瓷片

1960年发掘龙泉大窑和金村两地的古窑址时，发现北宋窑床下面有五代的瓷片堆积层[8]。这证明上文庄季裕关于龙泉窑始自五代的说法是可信的。

（3）五代时期龙泉窑的主要烧造地点

朱伯谦等认为，出土文物表明，五代龙泉窑是继越窑发展起来的（受越窑影响的五代龙泉窑址共发现十余处，主要分布在龙泉县的大窑、金村、王湖、安福，丽水县的黄山、石牛等地），也有一部分产品受到了瓯窑的影响[9]，甚至有可能是瓯窑的手工业者直接到龙泉经营生产的。受瓯窑影响的五代龙泉窑青瓷，在龙泉县金村的窑址中也有发现[10]。另外，处州与婺州接壤，五代宋初时，繁荣的婺州窑瓷业也给龙泉窑带来了一定的影响。

五代吴越钱氏，一直有向北宋朝廷进贡，贡物以丝绸和瓷器为主，数量达十几万。五代中期之后，越窑上林湖地区制瓷业生产所需的燃料和瓷土资源匮乏，数量如此庞大的贡瓷，并不是上林湖一地所能烧制供应的。上林湖地区难以承担钱氏进贡的重任，便转向资源丰富的龙泉地区。

五代时期的龙泉窑主要烧造地点在金村窑隔小梅溪对望的上垟一带，上垟窑初期产品就非常成熟，有浓郁的越窑风格[11]。在上垟窑群堆积层中处于最表层的为北宋早中期瓷片，说明上垟在那时就基本停烧了，而后龙泉的瓷业生产重心逐步移向金村。新发现的上虞县窑寺前的五代窑址和龙泉大窑、金村等地的五代窑址，都应是当时烧制贡瓷的重要地点[12]。

吴越统治85年，始自唐景福二年（公元893年），亡时已是北宋太平兴国三年（公元978年）。因此，所谓五代龙泉窑，也应包括北宋早期。吴越亡后，北宋统治者对浙江的青瓷生产仍然十分重视。太平兴国七年（公元982年）赵光义派殿前承旨赵仁济监理越州窑务。这对于龙泉窑后来的发展有很大的影响[13]。

3. 北宋说

龙泉窑始于北宋一说，着眼于龙泉窑自成体系的烧制活动的开始。

（1）越窑衰落

古代越窑地处丘陵地带。五代中后期开始，越窑大规模的烧瓷活动，加上宁绍平原大量的山地被辟为茶园或开垦为农田，自然植被大面积减少，导致就地取材的制瓷业燃料匮乏；同时，工匠工资的上升和沉重的瓷业赋税等种种原因，都导致越窑逐渐走向衰落。名窑的工匠们不得不另谋出路。龙泉地区山林覆盖率高，境内瓷土矿资源丰富，加上该地区劳动力比宁绍地区廉价，且已经有零星的小范围制瓷活动，而迁移来的工匠带来的制瓷技术和经验，以及市场因越窑的衰落而形成的青瓷产销上的供不应求等各种原因，使龙泉窑迅速发展起来[14]。

（2）北宋晚期龙泉窑的产品与北宋早期产品并无直接联系

通过对比龙泉出土的北宋早期及北宋晚期的青瓷，学者李刚推断：北宋晚期的龙泉窑青瓷并不是从北宋早期的发展而来的，与上述北宋以前松阳、丽水、庆元等地的土窑产品也无渊源关系，判断依据包括分布地域和时间上的缺环，以及器物外观特征和工艺的显著差异[15]。

学者李宝平的发现也与李刚的结论类似。根据比较分析大量带有纪年实据的瓷器遗存，李宝平推定龙泉窑第一期遗存年代应该是北宋宋真宗大中祥符年间到宋英宗时期（公元1008—1067年）[16]。而比这更早的北宋早期太平兴国（公元977年）的粗质碗（出土于浙江龙泉金沙塔基），与李宝平所推定的龙泉窑第一期产品明显不同，却与庆元黄坦村唐代窑址的自销产品相似。

龙泉县位于浙江南部山区，境内崇山峻岭，开发较迟，及至唐代，龙泉地区仍属山区，交通不便在一定程度上限制了龙泉窑的进一步发展。真正意义上的交通改善，要到北宋元祐七年（公元1092年）对龙泉以及缙云等地的险滩进行疏浚，龙泉地区与外界的水路开通。

of celadon continued with the emergence of the substantial porcelain system known as Yue Kiln Wares.

B. Theory Discrepancies of Longquan Kilns Emergence

Spurred along by the influence of the Yue Kilns, the Wuzhou Kilns in Zhejiang's South Central section and Ou Kilns near the lower reaches of the Ou River underwent huge developments, and Zhejiang's porcelain industry flourished. Celadon wares became an irreplaceable part of daily use items amongst all common peoples [3]. It was within this historical context that the furthest southern reaches of Zhejiang Province, Lishui and Longquan, began producing their celadon wares. As to the exact starting date of Longquan production, there are three main theories held amongst academics: Three Kingdoms Theory, Five Dynasties Theory and Northern Song Theory.

a. Three Kingdoms Theory

Since the 1970s, there have been several discoveries of porcelain excavated from a Three Kingdoms Jin Dynasty burial site that were characteristically different from Yue and Wuzhou Kiln wares of the time. Some believe that these may be the earliest examples of Longquan production [4].

In relation to these findings, Ren Shi Long et al have put forth that due to the fact that there is a lack of evidence proving these pieces were made in Longquan County — as there have been no recorded dates or corresponding kiln sites — current findings preclude these pieces from being considered Longquan Wares without further research and discovery [5]. Additionally, the porcelains from Three Kingdoms Jin Dynasty burial site, mainly found in Songyang and Lishui area, are also low in quantity and poor in quality. Even if they were produced in the Longquan area, it is very likely that they were, only produced and consumed locally. From a cultural characteristic perspective, there is a huge discrepancy between them and the Longquan Wares of the Northern Song. As such, there is no direct connection between the two, and for them to be considered as "early Longquan" is quite a stretch [6].

b. Five Dynasties Theory

I. Zhuang Ji Yu's (Song Dynasty) Recording

In relation to Longquan starting during the Five Dynasties Period, there is one record written in the Song Dynasty that reads: "Chuzhou Longquan County… producing celadon porcelain, the color is specifically called 'mi' color, officially for the Qian Family" [7].

This goes to show that during the Five Dynasty Period, Longquan was already charged with making official celadon wares for the Qian family (Royal family of the Wuyue Kingdom).

II. Discovery of Five Dynasty Shards at Longquan Dayao and Jincun Kiln Sites

In 1960, a Five Dynasty Period excavation layer of shards was found below the Northern Song Period strata at the Dayao and Jincun Kiln sites of Longquan [8]. This goes to further prove the aforementioned record that Longquan was started during the Five Dynasty Period.

III. Main Firing Location of Longquan Kilns During the Five Dynasties

Zhu Bo Qian et al, have put forth that according to excavations, Longquan Wares of the Five Dynasty Period are the development of Yue Kiln Wares (with over ten discoveries of Five Dynasty Period Longquan Wares that bear the influence of Yue Wares). These excavations were found in Dayao, Jincun, Wanghu, and Anfu of Longquan County as well as Huangshan and Shiniu of Lishui County. Additionally, there have been some discovered pieces that seem to have received influence from Ou Kiln ware [9]; possibly indicating that artisans from the Ou Kilns were directly involved in the production of early Longquan Wares. The Longquan Wares that were influenced by Ou Kiln were also discovered in the Jincun kiln sites of Longquan County [10]. Moreover, Chuzhou borders Wuzhou, and as such the flourishing Wuzhou kilns of the Five Dynasties to Early Song Dynasty seem to have had a certain influence on the Lonquan Wares as well.

从此，龙泉窑青瓷通过瓯江水路，突破崇山峻岭的屏障，源源不断地运往丽水、温州再转销各地。

所以，自北宋元祐八年（公元1093年）起的生产情况，可作为龙泉瓷业开展的一个指标[17]。这与李宝平推定的龙泉窑第一期遗存年代靠近。

4. 小结

三国两晋说有一定的证据间接指向龙泉窑烧造的开始，但缺乏匹配的有纪年依据的窑址遗存，无法自圆其说。

五代说有窑址遗存证明五代时龙泉县地区已经开始烧制青瓷，但此时正处于萌芽阶段，而且大部分实物及资料都表明，五代时期龙泉窑的烧制基本都属于支援越窑。比如在已发掘的五代吴越国王钱氏家族墓和辽墓中所出的瓷器都是越窑瓷，并没有龙泉窑瓷器；在《十国春秋》《宋史》《宋会要》等书中有关五代吴越国王钱氏贡瓷的记载，也只见“秘色瓷器”“金陵秘色瓷器”“越器”“越瓷”，而不见龙泉窑瓷器[18]。

由此可推论，即使龙泉窑在五代时期已经开始烧制青瓷，但也未被王室看重。由于主要属于支援越窑烧制，继承浙江原有的制瓷传统，还没有形成自成体系的艺术风格，质量也不出众，仅能将其看作龙泉地区早期窑业活动，这种窑业活动，可以理解为龙泉窑系瓷器烧造的萌芽。

经过对比分析考古资料和文献，笔者认为，真正意义上的龙泉青瓷初创期，也就是龙泉青瓷自成体系的优质产品的出现，应该在北宋晚期。

北宋时期龙泉青瓷，在制瓷工艺和文化审美上属于承上启下的阶段，造型品种以百姓日常生活的实用器为主，装饰手法也比较单一，普遍流行刻划花。这方面的考古资料与文献记载基本保持一致。经考古调查与发掘，北宋龙泉窑遗址以现今龙泉的金村、大窑、安福、大白岸和庆元县上垟等为中心，逐渐向南向东沿瓯江流域扩展，瓷窑数量与分布范围显著增加。

二、龙泉窑在古代的发展

（一）鼎盛期（南宋中晚期到元初）

1. 南宋迁都临安

“靖康之难”以后，北宋王朝灭亡，宋徽宗第九子赵构先于靖康二年（公元1127年）在河南商丘建立南宋政权，后于今浙江杭州建都，名为临安。南宋王朝定都临安，使临安迅速成为当时政治、经济和文化的中心，给周边地区的经济发展带来了许多机遇。与临安毗邻的龙泉窑得到快速发展，窑址分布范围广及龙泉、云和、遂昌、永嘉、泰顺、文成六县[19]。

南宋迁都后，大量北方人涌入南方。南迁的北方人除一般百姓外，还有许多贵族、文人、士大夫与大批手工业者。南迁的上层阶级成为高档陶瓷的需求人群，而南迁的陶瓷工匠也将北方的陶瓷生产技术及经验带到了南方，成为南方制瓷业的新劳动力[20]。

2. 南宋官窑的烧制

南宋立国后不久，朝廷在临安自置官窑烧制御用瓷器，“袭徽宗遗制，制窑于修内司造青器，名内窑……后郊坛下别立新窑，亦曰官窑”[21]。

龙泉窑制瓷技艺的进一步革新应该是在南宋官窑建立之后开始的。南宋官窑可谓当时最优质的青瓷，被王室垄断，当时龙泉窑的产品与其无法相比，也不如北方的汝窑、耀州窑等产品。官窑的制瓷工艺成为龙泉窑技术革新的基础，同时北方制瓷工匠的技术与经验也起了很大的作用[22]。

3. 官窑对龙泉窑的影响

南宋后期，龙泉窑产品一部分保存了前期的生产特点，另一部分则受到南宋官窑及北方制瓷工艺的影响，工匠们在原有制瓷技术的基础上对青瓷的造型设计、胎釉配方、上釉技术和成形装饰等方面都做了重大的革新。

首先，龙泉窑在胎质方面做出了改革，出现两种不同类型的新产品：一种是白胎青瓷，这是从原有的制瓷传统中加以改进的代表性产品；一种是黑胎青瓷，这类产品与南宋官窑非常相似，可以说是仿官窑或接受宫廷订货的产品[23]。黑胎青瓷的坯料改用“瓷石和紫金土”二元配方。同景德镇窑的二元配方原理相似，紫金土中氧化铝含量较高，能提高胎体烧成温度，从而可以烧制薄胎瓷器，胎体也不变形。由于紫金土中氧化铁的含量较高，

Five Dynasty royalty, The Qian Family of the Wuyue Kingdom, had a continual tribute relationship with the Northern Song Dynasty. Gifts comprised mainly of silks and porcelain, numbered in the hundreds of thousands. The Yue Kilns of the Shanglinhu area, while trying to supply for the massive required tributes of the Qiansi King, ran into issues of supply of firing timber and porcelain materials. As such, a portion of the burden for these tributary goods was shifted to the rich-in-porcelain-making-resources-area of Longquan County.

During the Five Dynasties Period, the main area for Longquan kiln firing was Shangyang. Even the early Shangyang Kiln wares were very developed, and carried a distinct Yue Kiln influence [11]. The most surface level strata of excavated shards from the Shangyang Kiln site are known to be of the early to mid-Northern Song Period, which means that by this time they had almost completely finished firing activity in that area, and later Longquan production gradually migrated more towards the Jincun area. Recently discovered kiln sites in and around the Longquan area from the Five Dynasty Period are all most likely main production sites used for tributary porcelain production [12].

The Wuyue Kingdom was in control for 85 years, running from Late Tang and eighteen years into Northern Song (893-978 A.D.). As such, "Five Dynasty" Longquan does include some time within the Northern Song Dynasty Period. After the fall of Wuyue, the Northern Song Dynasty court placed the utmost importance on celadon wares coming out of Zhejiang Province; and in 982 A.D., specifically sent officials to oversee the Yue Kiln production. This had a direct impact on the development of the Longquan Kilns [13].

c. Northern Song Theory

The theory that Northern Song was the beginning of production for the Longquan Kilns is primarily focused on the basis of Longquan becoming an established kiln system and such associated activity.

I. The Decline of Yue Wares

The Yue Kiln of old was located deep within the hill country. Towards the middle to late Five Dynasty Period, the Ningshao plains and surrounding hillsides were cultivated as tea gardens or planted fields, and natural vegetation used for fueling the firing of the ceramics industry became scarce. At the same time, increased wages for craftsmen, higher taxes on ceramics, and other circumstances led to the gradual decrease in the Yue Kiln production. Artisans from these kilns had no choice but to look for work elsewhere. The Longquan hills were densely forested, the land rich in porcelain clay, and labor was relatively cheap compared to the Ningshao area. Add to that the small amounts of kilns sparsely scattered throughout the area that had already begun production, the new influx of skilled labor and experience from the Yue Kilns, and the felt lack of supply to meet market demand of celadon wares brought on by the collapse of the Yue Kilns; and the incredibly rapid development of the Longquan Kilns ensued [14].

II. Lack of Relation Between Late and Early Northern Song Wares

Through the comparison of excavated Longquan Wares from the Late and Early Northern Song Dynasty Periods, Li Gang puts forth that Late Northern Song pieces are not the direct development from the earlier Northern Song productions, and there is no direct link between the aforementioned wares to local kilns such as Songyang, Lishui, Qingyuan, and so forth. The basis for this conclusion includes the areas the shards were discovered, lack of periodic link between them, features of the wares, and the techniques used in production [15].

Li Bao Ping's discoveries also seem to support Li Gang. Through extensive amounts of comparative analysis on dated excavations, he has put forth that the earliest Longquan Kiln productions in the Northern Song Dynasty range from 1008-1067A.D. [16]. The pieces excavated from the Zhejiang Longquan Jinsha Pagoda, dated 977 A.D., have very distinct differences from those that Li Bao Ping put forth as the first productions of the Longquan Kilns, and in fact look more similar to Tang Dynasty excavations (locally consumed products) of the Qingyuan Huangtan Village kiln sites.

Longquan County is located in the south of Zhejiang Province, a mountainous region with high elevation,

因此紫金土比重大的瓷器，胎体颜色也较深，因而得名黑胎青瓷[24]。

其次，龙泉窑在釉质和施釉工艺上也有了创新：由前一阶段的厚胎薄釉，变为薄胎厚釉。由于改变了釉的配方，釉层加厚而不流，可以多次上釉，加上对窑内烧制气氛的调整和控制，创烧出了色比青玉、光泽莹润的梅子青和粉青釉，能与官窑、汝窑瓷媲美[25]。

从此以后，龙泉窑进入了其发展史上的鼎盛时期，完全取代了越窑的地位，成为当时全国青瓷生产的领头羊。

4. 南宋龙泉窑的特色

南宋龙泉青瓷在器型风格上也与北宋时期有别，南宋器型品种更加丰富，用途广泛，有日用瓷、文娱用具，还有陈设祭器等。其中每一种类型还包含多种式样，器型小巧优美，结构比例讲究，轮廓线条简练，制作精良[26]。

在纹饰方面，南宋改变了北宋惯用的刻划花纹的手法，更趋向于简单大方，以突出釉色为主，使用浮雕和堆贴花，或者仅用几条凹凸的弦纹。这样的装饰手法配上瓷器薄胎厚釉的工艺，更富有艺术感染力[27]。

装烧方法的改进，主要表现在窑具上。前期所用的喇叭形垫座已经完全被淘汰，坯件都改用匣钵装烧，使窑室空间得到充分利用，提高产量，也降低了生产成本[28]。

5. 南宋政府的外贸政策对龙泉窑生产的影响

南宋时期，虽然国家的国土和人口都丧失了大半，但国家税收反而上升，这与南宋政府大力推动开放海外贸易的国策有很大的关系。在这个时期，龙泉窑产品的出口已初具规模。朝廷先后在温州、宁波等地设立市舶司进行贸易[29]。这使龙泉窑成为当时最有影响力的外销瓷生产基地，从而进一步刺激了该地区的窑业发展。

（二）扩展期（元代中晚期）

如果说南宋晚期的梅子青及粉青釉瓷的成功烧制使龙泉青瓷进入第一个鼎盛期，那么元代繁荣的外销贸易则第二次高峰——龙泉青瓷的生产窑址以及产品类型和数量在此时期都达到前所未有的高度[30]。

总体而言，元代龙泉窑青瓷的烧制工艺整体不如宋代讲究，瓷胎逐渐变厚，釉层逐渐变薄，玉质感有所降低。至元代末期，多次施釉工艺已很少使用。装烧方法也发生改变，垫托常放在坯件的外底，碗、盘等瓷器的外底一圈无釉。更有甚者，为增加装烧量，一个匣钵内叠装两三件同类的碗、盘，因此内底无釉或一圈无釉。

1. 工艺技术创新

元代在龙泉窑青瓷胎釉配方上做出改进：胎中铁含量明显降低，白度进一步提高；釉中钙、镁含量进一步降低，而钾、钠含量进一步提高，使得釉在高温下黏稠度继续提高，烧成温度范围继续拓宽。

元代产品除部分继承了宋代传统以外，在器型和装饰手法上又有创新。如大件器物的烧制成功：在大窑和竹口等地窑址发现大量元代大型瓷器，有高达1米左右的花瓶和口径达60余厘米的瓷盘；安仁口岭脚窑址有口径达42厘米的大碗[31]。大件器物的烧成标志着制瓷技术的新成就。

元代在窑炉烧制技术上也有改进：窑型仍沿用长条形斜坡式龙窑，与宋代窑制无异，只在长度上略有缩短，这有利于提高窑内温度，并使热量分布更均匀，利于烧制大型器物[32]。

此外，龙泉窑由于在元代销售范围扩大和消费群体增加，产品种类及样式不断增多、十分丰富，而且无论器物大小几乎都有纹饰，题材也非常广泛，并在纹饰的结构、形象和刀法上下功夫。元代的装饰纹样采用刻、划、印、贴、镂、堆和褐色点彩等工艺，其中印花、贴花和镂刻是这一时期新发展起来的。尤其是这时期的印花工艺，其精美程度能够与金银器媲美。还有在同一瓷器上同时出现涩胎与青釉两种对比效果的工艺，青色和红色相映生辉，别有韵味[33]。

2. 外贸政策更加开放

蒙元朝廷的对外经济贸易政策比南宋政权更开放。作为游牧民族，蒙古族对贸易的依存度向来就高。统一中原后，蒙元政府将其重商政策贯彻到底，积极推动海外贸易。在这样的背景下，龙泉窑依凭得天独厚的自然资源、发达的水系交通网络及成熟的制瓷工艺，迅速地由交通不便的大窑和溪口、向瓯江和松溪两岸扩展[34]。

inconvenient transportation, and as such was developed relatively late. During the Tang Dynasty, it was primarily an untouched mountainous area with little to no infrastructure, which greatly limited the development of the entire Longquan Kiln area. It wasn't until late into the Northern Song Dynasty (1092 A.D.) that transport into the Longquan area was made readily accessible, and waterway access between Longquan and the outside world was opened. From then on, celadon from Longquan was able to flow out to Lishui and Wenzhou and on to the rest of the world.

Therefore, a major milestone in the opening of the Longquan ceramics industry was during the Northern Song Dynasty (1093 A.D.) [17]. This is very close to the date put forth by Li Bao Ping's research.

d. Summary

The Three Kingdoms Theory has a certain amount of evidence that points to the emergence of Longquan Kilns, but lacks matching dated kiln site excavations to support it as concrete.

The Five Dynasty Theory is substantiated by excavations that show there was indeed kiln activity in the Longquan County area during the Five Dynasties, but admits that these activities were very grassroots and most likely just a supplement to the Yue Kiln productions prevalent during the day. Excavation of Wuyue tombs and hoards contain only Yue Kiln wares, and Longquan pieces have yet to be found among them. Additionally, historical records of the tribute pieces produced for the Qian Family only mention certain colors of specifically "Yue" porcelain or wares, and the term "Longquan Wares" is not to be seen [18].

From this it can be seen that during the Five Dynasty Period, celadon production had in fact started in the Longquan County area but had yet to be recognized by the rulers of the day. Due to its similarities with Yue wares and other Zhejiang productions, lack of its own characteristics, and mediocre quality; these kiln activities can only be considered as early kiln development in the Longquan area and represent the first sprouts of the Longquan Kilns.

Through analysis, archeological excavation, and records, it can be seen that the beginning of the Longquan system of kilns, with its own distinctive characteristics and qualities, can be said to have started during the late Northern Song Dynasty.

Northern Song Longquan Celadon is an important connecting link in terms of ceramic history and aesthetic culture. The main portion of production focused on daily use items for the general public; with the design relatively one dimensional and carved decoration the most common. Additionally, archeological findings as well as historical record both go to support this. Archeological excavations have uncovered Northern Song Longquan Kiln activity primarily based around the Longquan County areas of Jincun, Dayao, Anfu, Dabaian and Qingyuan County Shangyang area, with more sites spreading south and east along reaches of the Oujiang estuaries.

2. The Development of the Longquan Kilns

A. Golden Age (Mid Southern Song to Early Yuan Dynasty)

a. Moving the Southern Song Capital to Lin'an

After the fall of the Northern Song Dynasty (1127 A.D.), Zhaogou established the Southern Song capital city called Lin'an (modern day Hangzhou of Zhejiang Province). This move vaulted Lin'an to the forefront of development and planted it as the political, economic, and cultural center of China, and poured economical gains upon the surrounding areas. As such, the neighboring Longquan Kilns enjoyed escalated development and expansion over six counties including: Longquan, Yunhe, Suichang, Yongjia, Taishun, and Wencheng [19].

After the move of the Southern Song capital, a large number of Northern Chinese moved to the Southern regions. This huge North to South migration saw with it the increase of not only commoners in the South, but also many nobility, scholars, officials, and artisans. These aristocratic migrants became the consumers of high-end porcelain goods. Additionally, ceramic artisans from the North brought with them techniques and experience and became a new part of the

3. 生产规模扩大

龙泉窑中心产区大窑附近的窑场达到50多处，制瓷作坊几近300处，范围由龙泉的大窑、金村、溪口一带逐渐沿水路向外扩展，另外在遂昌、景宁、武义、缙云等地也新建了一批窑场生产青瓷[35]。元代龙泉窑系如此大的生产规模是前所未有的，这段时期其产品遍布世界各地。

三、龙泉窑的衰落

龙泉窑在宋元时期盛极一时，及至明代中期开始走下坡路。

明代龙泉窑的产品在继承宋元时期传统的装饰基础上，又形成自有的特色，以印花、刻划花为主，这种装饰正适合这一时期产品釉层普遍透明度较高的特点，使作品另具有一种美感。尤其是明初的一些精品，纹饰精巧、层层分明、密而不乱。

总的来说，明代龙泉青瓷，无论在釉色方面或是在瓷质方面，都不如前代。但明代早期龙泉窑青瓷依然繁荣，产品质量较高，甚至烧制官窑瓷器。

据《大明会典》一百九十四卷载，洪武二十六年（公元1393年），明朝宫廷供用器皿等物，数少者“行移饶、处等府烧造”。又据《明宪宗实录》卷一载，天顺八年（公元1464年）正月，宪宗皇帝即位“……以明年为成化元年，大赦天下……一江西饶州府，浙江处州府，见差内官在彼烧造瓷器，诏书到日，照数起解，未完者，悉皆停止，差委官员即使回京，违者罪之”。浙江龙泉大窑枫洞岩窑址考古出土的大量供应朝廷的精美瓷器标本，更充分证明了明代龙泉官窑的存在与瓷业辉煌。

明代中期以后，窑口减少，质量下降，龙泉窑瓷业逐渐衰落。据清乾隆《龙泉县志》卷三“物产”记载：“青瓷窑……明正统时顾仕成所制者，已不及生二章远甚，化治以后质粗色恶，难充雅玩矣。”成化、弘治以后，龙泉窑瓷器的胎体更加厚重，釉层更薄更透，刻划花及挖足工艺更粗更草，质量显著下降，生产规模渐渐缩小。

根据2006年9月至2007年1月对龙泉大窑枫洞岩遗址的发掘结果，龙泉大窑遗址所出土龙泉青瓷的年代范围为南宋晚期至明代中期，少见明代中期以后的产品[36]。这说明明代中期是龙泉青瓷发展的一个转折点，至此之后，龙泉青瓷便逐渐走下坡路。

至清代，龙泉窑仅剩下大窑、孙坑等几处瓷窑烧制青瓷，胎骨粗硬，呈灰或灰白色，釉层薄透呈青灰或青黄色。龙泉窑青瓷在清代仍作为单色釉瓷的代表，保持着一定的影响力。

民国初期，龙泉窑业从大窑、孙坑转移到宝溪溪头一带，主要以烧制日用青花瓷器为主，同时还坚持烧造传统龙泉青瓷，并以家族和师徒方式传承青瓷烧制技艺。其中，“李生和”“张义（贰）昌”“龚三兴”等瓷坊是龙泉窑青瓷薪火传承的典范。有识之士徐渊若、陈佐汉为龙泉青瓷文化传承起到了积极的推动作用。民国时期对龙泉青瓷烧制技艺的保护与传承，为新中国成立以后的恢复大规模生产和走向中兴做出了重要的贡献，具有重要的历史意义。

龙泉窑式微的原因，主要有：

（一）国内产品竞争

1. 同类产品竞争

龙泉窑的繁荣带动了周边地区的制瓷业。这些瓷窑竭力模仿龙泉窑的制瓷工艺，充分利用当地的沿海地理优势，与传统的龙泉青瓷产区争夺市场[37]。

位于福建省西北部的闽北地区，与浙赣二省交界，在已发现的20多处宋元窑址中，几乎都有青釉瓷器出土。在福建中部与南部沿海地区的古窑址发掘中，也出土了不少过去被称为“土龙泉”的青瓷，这些青瓷明显受到了龙泉青瓷的影响[38]。

广东潮州东郊的笔架山生产大量瓷器，素有“百窑村”之称，其中不乏青瓷的制作，其中也有许多是作为外销瓷生产的[39]。

近年在广东大埔县发现的龙泉窑系青瓷窑业遗存，为目前广东省境内已知最早的龙泉窑系青瓷窑业遗存，也是同类窑址中罕见保存较好、规模宏大的明时期龙泉系青瓷窑场。

此外，江西的吉州窑、横峰窑、弋阳窑以及湖南、湖北的许多窑场都曾烧制青瓷，这些窑场是否供应外销还有待进一步研究探讨，但它们对龙泉青瓷的内销市场所造成的影响是客观存在的[40]。

根据日本学者青柳洋治的调查[41]，12至13世纪（宋代晚期），福建瓷器广泛流行于东南亚岛屿；13世纪末至14世纪（元末至明初），东南亚地区所出土的瓷器

Southern ceramics production labor force [20].

b. Official Kiln Firing During the Southern Song

During the early years of the Southern Song Dynasty, the imperial court established an official kiln in Lin'an, called Guan or Official Kiln, to make imperial use porcelain [21].

It was this induction of the Official Kiln that most likely brought on the further revolution of the Longquan techniques. Southern Song Official Kiln wares were the ultimate in celadon quality and were made exclusively for the imperial court. At that time, Longquan productions were not even close to the same level of quality, nor did they approach the quality of the Ru Kilns in the North, Yaozhou Kilns, and so forth famous kilns. It was the impeccable production quality of the Official Kiln that became the foundational technique for the Longquan innovations, while the newly infused experience from Northern artisans also brought about a large impact [22].

c. The Impact of Official Kilns on Longquan Wares

In the latter stretches of the Southern Song Dynasty, Longquan productions retained some of the characteristics of its earliest predecessors, but alternately began to take on some of the qualities of Official and Northern Kilns. Artisans, on the already established foundations of ceramic making techniques, brought about innovative changes to celadon shapes, glaze recipes, glazing techniques, and decorations.

First, Longquan clay went through a reform in quality; bringing about the induction of two types of porcelain bodies: The first was a white body celadon, which was representative of further perfection of traditional porcelain production; and the second was a black body celadon, which was very similar to that of Southern Song Official Kiln wares, even to the extent that they could be Official Kiln copies [23]. Black body celadon saw the utilization of the dual base clay recipe (porcelainite plus Zijin) similar to the dual base clay technique common in Jingdezhen. Zijin was rich in oxidized aluminum and allowed for a higher firing temperature of the wares, thus allowing for thinner clay bodies that would not deform during firing. Due to the high iron content in the Zijin clay, the fired clay color was much darker, earning it the name "Black Bodied Celadon" [24].

Secondly, Longquan saw innovation to the glaze quality and glaze application techniques; and a general move from thick body thin glaze to thin body thick glaze. Due to changes in glaze recipe, glaze could be applied in thicker amounts without running off the body. Also, multiple applications of glaze could be achieved. In addition, new understanding of how to change and control the inner kiln firing atmosphere allowed for the creation of jade-like glazes, such as Plum Green and Powder Green, that could rival Official and Ru Kilns in their beauty [25].

From then on, the Longquan Kiln wares entered into the golden era, completely taking the place of the Yue Kiln, and becoming the foremost sought after celadon in all of China.

d. Characteristics of Southern Song Longquan Wares

Southern Song Longquan also had dissimilarities from its Northern Song predecessor in terms of shapes, with a more abundant range of shapes and uses being achieved during the Southern Song Dynasty (i.e. daily use items, entertainment pieces, sacrificial furnishings, and so forth). Each style included many types; their stylizations fine and elegant, compositions very precise, lines simple, and execution exquisite [26].

From the perspective of patterns, Southern Song changed the method of engraving that was utilized during the Northern Song, with patterns more simplistic in nature and the glaze color becoming the main focus of decoration. They began to utilize light engraving and piling; keeping only a few indented or raised lines on an entire piece. This decoration method, paired with the thin body thick glaze technique created a finished product that was markedly reserved in its aesthetics [27].

Lastly, changes in firing technique can mostly be seen in the kiln firing tools utilized. The horn shaped firing cases that were used in the early stages of production completely phased out and there was a shift towards the use of firing sagars for all pieces. This improved the use of kiln space efficiency, increased firing success rate, and lowered the total cost of firing wares [28].

多数都产于福建泉州及其周边地区，青瓷则来自浙江龙泉地区，景德镇青花瓷较少见。从这些调查结果来看，国内其他地区尤其是福建等地的陶瓷生产对龙泉青瓷的影响是不容忽视的。

2. 景德镇窑的不断创新

（1）宋代时期的创新

宋代景德镇窑生产的影青瓷，因其色泽青白透澈如玉，深得王室喜爱，于是宋王朝在景德镇设立了司务所，派遣官员到景德镇监督制瓷，以贡京师[42]。

（2）元代时期的创新

元代时期，景德镇窑烧制出成熟的青花瓷器，色彩明艳，开辟了由素瓷向彩瓷过渡的新时代，成为中国陶瓷史上的一朵奇葩。蒙古人崇蓝尚白，对青花瓷自然钟爱有加。同时，景德镇窑瓷胎的制作引进高岭土的方法（即瓷石加高岭土的制胎法，俗称“二元配方”），这个技术革新成为之后景德镇瓷业生产高度发达的前提，使景德镇一跃成为中世纪世界制瓷业的中心[43]。《元史》卷八十八记载：“浮梁瓷局，秩正九品，至元十五年立，掌烧造瓷器。”浮梁瓷局是元代在地方上设置的唯一督烧瓷器的官方机构，体现了政府对景德镇窑业生产的高度重视。

（3）明代时期的创新

明代在对瓷器的审美上偏好纹饰，赋予纹饰较多意义，如龙凤纹、莲纹、八宝纹以及人物纹等[44]。此后景德镇生产的其他瓷种、釉里红、五彩、斗彩、粉彩以及其他颜色的单色釉等彩瓷，纹饰表现力强，深得老百姓及统治阶级的喜爱。龙泉青瓷在纹饰表现力上明显不如景德镇彩瓷，青瓷逐渐淡出历史舞台也就不足为奇了。从此景德镇窑在中国制瓷业中一枝独秀。而龙泉青瓷则销量骤减，走向衰落[45]。

（4）国外市场对青花瓷的钟爱

从外销市场上看，伊斯兰教从12世纪就已经开始渗入东南亚，在14世纪末到15世纪初基本上建立了伊斯兰文化在东南亚的文化主导地位[46]。伊斯兰文化视蓝色为吉祥色，青花瓷在受伊斯兰文化影响的东南亚地区毫无疑问受到了广泛欢迎。及至15至16世纪初，青花瓷已经成为当时主要的外销瓷[47]。于是传统的青瓷销售逐渐让位于青花瓷，龙泉青瓷外销市场进一步缩小。

（二）国外同类产品竞争

中国制瓷历史悠久。随着古代中国与海外文化和贸易交流的深入，伴随着中国瓷器远走他乡的还有瓷器的烧制工艺，从此世界上其他地区也开始了对中国陶瓷的仿制[48]。

约北宋末到南宋时期，在高丽王朝统治下的朝鲜半岛，成功烧制了高丽青瓷[49]；宋嘉定十六年（公元1223年），日本陶瓷家加藤四郎和左卫门到浙江学习造瓷技术，回国后创建“濑户窑”，并成功烧制模仿龙泉青瓷的陶器[50]；越南历史上的李朝（1009—1225）与陈朝（1225—1400）是其陶瓷烧造的黄金时代。对龙泉青瓷的仿造十分成功[51]；14世纪末至16世纪初是泰国陶瓷业的鼎盛时期，位于泰国中北部的宋克洛瓷窑产品大量外销到东南亚，其中包括不少仿制中国的青瓷[52]；北非与东非这些地区都存在着模仿中国瓷器的制陶业，尤其是埃及，仿制中国青瓷的陶器惟妙惟肖[53]。除了上述地区，印度、波斯、伊拉克也在不同程度上仿造龙泉青瓷。

在东南亚发现的龙泉外销瓷的年代主要集中在南宋以后至明代中期以前，明代中后期以后数量逐渐减少，虽还在东南亚的瓷器市场中占有一定份额，但在数量上已不是主导地位，数量不及国内福建地区及泰国或越南的青瓷。比如：14世纪的图里昂沉船遗址所出水的瓷器中，泰国瓷器的数量占57%，中国瓷器占35%，其中龙泉青瓷的数量仅占中国瓷数量的10%，占瓷器总数的3%；15世纪的巴卡奥沉船遗址中出水有泰国瓷器、越南瓷器以及中国的白瓷、褐瓷、青瓷等，其中泰国瓷器的数量占绝大部分，其余的瓷器品种（包括龙泉青瓷在内）数量较少[54]。

尽管这些国家和地区的仿制水平程度各不相同，但在世界各地人民对龙泉青瓷的热爱与追求的前提下，当地仿制的青瓷迎合了当地人民的消费心理，利用低成本优势获取本地市场，有许多地区的龙泉青瓷仿品还走上了外销之路。这些仿品不仅影响了龙泉青瓷在当地的销售市场，还同其在海外市场展开了竞争，给龙泉青瓷的外销造成了冲击。

e. The Impact of Southern Song Foreign Trade Policy on Longquan Production

During the Southern Song Dynasty, even though the land size and population decreased by more than half, tax revenues increased dramatically. This is primarily due to the foreign trade policy that was implemented by the Southern Song government. It was during this time that Longquan Celadon began production for export. Goods moved to cities such as Wenzhou and Ningbo, and were moved on to ships marked for foreign trade voyages [29]. This made Longquan Celadon the most influential product on the export porcelain market, and in turn increased development of the area's ceramic industry.

B. Age of Expansion (Mid to Late Yuan Dynasty)

If we are to say that the successful firing of Plum Green and Powder Green of the Southern Song Dynasty was the first Golden Era of Longquan Celadon, then the widespread export porcelain production of the Yuan Dynasty would be its second peak. This was the height of Longquan production, with kiln numbers, volume and types all excelling that of the earlier periods [30].

In general, the techniques utilized during the Yuan Dynasty were not as precise as that of the Song Dynasty. The bodies became increasingly thick and the glaze increasingly thin, causing jade-like qualities to slowly wane to the point that by the end of the Yuan Dynasty some techniques, such as multiple glaze applications methods, nearly vanished altogether. The firing process also underwent changes, for example, the firing rings were often placed on the foot of the pieces; as a result, most bowls and plates had an unglazed ring on the outer base. Furthermore, two to three similar pieces could be stacked inside one sagar during firing so that the number of pieces that could go into one kiln firing increased. As such, the inner well of these pieces would be unglazed or have an unglazed ring.

a. New Techniques

The Yuan Dynasty also saw a change to the body and glaze composition of Longquan Celadon. The iron content within the clay body decreased significantly, increasing the whiteness of the fired body. Additionally, the calcium and magnesium amounts in the glaze steadily decreased, while potassium and sodium increased. This increased the viscosity of the glaze under high firing temperatures, and helped to broaden the range of successful firing temperatures.

Aside from continuing the traditional decoration techniques of the Song Dynasty, Yuan Longquan saw considerable innovation in shape and decoration design. For example, the successful firing of very large wares: Dayao and surrounding kiln excavations have produced vases as tall as one meter in height, plates with over 60 centimeters in diameter, and bowls as large as 42 centimeters in diameter [31]. The firing of such large pieces acts as an indication of the successful induction of new firing techniques.

Aside from this, Yuan Dynasty also saw improvements in the control of kiln firing techniques. They continued to use long-shaped, slanted "Dragon" style kilns that were used during the Song Dynasty, but decreased the lengths of these kiln chains, increasing the inner kiln temperature and improving the even dissipation of heat, which helped in the firing of large pieces [32].

Additionally, as the market and number of consumers of Longquan Celadon drastically increased during the Yuan Dynasty, the number and styles of pieces also increased. They were increasingly abundant, and regardless of the size of the piece, almost every ware had decorative motifs. The content of these motifs also increased, as well as the structure, shapes and carving techniques of such patterns. During the Yuan Dynasty, decoration techniques included methods such as carving, incising, impression, appliqué, openwork, heaping and spotting. Of these, impression, piling, and openwork all had new innovations from this era. Specifically, the techniques for impression during this time were particularly innovative, with outcomes rivaling gold and silver wares in their intricate beauty. Furthermore, there was an introduction of bare body and glazing utilized on a single ware; a technique, which created a green and red juxtaposition with particular beauty [33].

（三）政治因素

1. 政府干预

古代龙泉窑的兴起主要是市场经济的结果，但这在中国古代封建社会的大背景下，注定不能持久发展。与同样在北宋兴起的景德镇窑相比，龙泉窑缺少足够的政府干预与引导。明代时期，龙泉与景德镇两处窑场虽然地位貌似平等，但又有不同，景德镇设立的是御器厂，“制陶供上方，称官窑，以别民窑”。但是龙泉窑场可能只是民窑承担了制瓷贡御的任务。在《明实录》中频频提及有诏令命景德镇御器厂生产瓷器以贡御，而关于龙泉窑场的生产则寥寥无几。不可否认，龙泉窑的确承担过烧制贡瓷、官用瓷的任务，但比起景德镇窑得到政府直接在当地设置行政机构执管窑务的待遇，龙泉窑还是缺乏应有的政治支持和保护，其衰落就不足为奇了[55]。

2. 出口政策

明初时期，朝廷对外国贡使带来的贡品一律本着“薄来厚往”的原则回赠，对外的“朝贡贸易”基本上是赔本买卖。久而久之，朝廷不堪重负，从而开始对贡期、贡船数目、随船人数、进境路线及停泊口岸等做出限制性规定。此时，东南沿海倭患不断，进一步促使明朝政府的对外政策趋向保守，最终导致了嘉靖年间的全面海禁。这一政策使得一直以来以私商外销形式进行海外贸易的龙泉青瓷遭遇了前所未有的重创[56]。

3. 严苛税率

明代税率严苛，征税的名目数不胜数，尤其是从明代中期起，凡“肩背之贩无一物不税，绳枢瓮牖无一间不税”[57]。龙泉县所“造青器，粹美冠绝当世……价高而征课遂厚”[58]。由此可见，龙泉青瓷也逃不过被征重税的命运。

4. 社会动乱

始于明正统十二年（公元1447年）的以叶宗留等人为首的处州乡民叛乱也使龙泉窑场的生产受到严重的影响。

《明史纪事本末》载：“处州多银矿……英宗正统七年十二月，丽水盗陈善恭、庆元盗叶宗留合众盗福建宝峰场银冶，命浙江、福建有司捕治之。十二年春二月，叶宗留聚众盗掘少阳坑。”[59]自此之后，处州地区叛乱不断，一直到成化年间，朝廷依然被这问题困扰，《明实录·英宗实录》中于成化五年（公元1469年）、七年以及九年等均有关于处州叛乱的记载[60]。战乱对龙泉窑瓷器的生产造成了极大的负面影响。

（四）小结

综上所述，龙泉窑制瓷业内外交困，缺乏生产动力，导致质量下降，产量陡减。明中期龙泉窑的瓷品质量已极为低下：“上品仅有葱色，余尽油灰色矣，制亦愈下”[61]。嘉靖《浙江通志》亦有记载：“自后器出于刘田者已简陋利微，而课税不减，民甚病焉。”据清乾隆《龙泉县志》记载：“明正统时顾仕成所制者，已不及生二章远甚，（成）化（弘）以后质粗色恶，难充雅玩矣。”[62]

及至清代，龙泉窑虽仍有烧造，但其规模与质量已不可与往日同日而语。清后期至民国，龙泉窑规模和质量继续下降。

虽然龙泉窑在南宋时期创烧出梅子青与粉青瓷器，至元代在产品装饰技术、类型和数量上都有创新和突破，但综看产品总体的发展历程，始终局限在单色釉范围内。景德镇窑成熟的彩瓷生产使国内政治阶级的审美喜好起了变化，从而带动各阶层审美喜好的变化，这种审美变化得到了国内政府的支持和海外市场的认同及推动，加上国内及国外制瓷行业的激烈竞争，龙泉窑最终走上衰败之路。

四、龙泉窑在新中国时期的复兴

新中国成立以后，各级政府对龙泉青瓷的恢复工作给予高度重视。1957年，周恩来总理给出恢复龙泉窑的指示。1959年，在浙江省委、省政府的领导下，省轻工业厅牵头相关科研单位、大专院校和文物考古部门一起组成了“浙江省龙泉青瓷恢复委员会”，联合龙泉制瓷老艺人们在对龙泉产区进行全面系统的考古发掘、科学测试、复制试验和规模生产的基础上，使龙泉青瓷于上垟龙泉瓷厂成功恢复。2006年，龙泉青瓷传统烧制技艺入选“国家非遗”；2009年9月30日，龙泉青瓷传统烧制技艺被联合国教科文组织批准列入人类非物质文化遗产代表作名录，成为全球目前唯一入选“人类非遗”的陶瓷类

b. Opening of Foreign Trade Policy

The foreign trade policy adopted by the Mongolian rulers of the Yuan Dynasty was even more progressive than that of the Southern Song. As they were a migrant herdsman society, trade was of the utmost importance to the Mongolians. After consolidating China under their rule, the Mongol powers aggressively pushed for foreign trade, and opened the floodgates of maritime trade. Under these circumstances, Longquan Kilns received vast natural resources and greatly improved waterway transportation; the less transport friendly kiln production areas of Dayao and Xikou were rapidly expanded to reach as far as the banks of the Oujiang and Songxi rivers [34].

c. Enormous Production Capacity

The central production area of Longquan Celadon, near Dayao, had over 50 kiln sites with over 300 ceramic producing workshops throughout the area. The main areas of production were Dayao, Jincun, and Xikou along the banks of the rivers and expanding out, while new celadon firing kiln sites were also built in places such as Suichang, Jingning, Wuyi, and Jinyun [35]. This scale of Yuan Dynasty Longquan Celadon production had never before been seen, and its products were reaching nearly every corner of the globe.

3. The Decline of the Longquan Kilns

Longquan production flourished during the Song and Yuan Dynasties, and did not start to decrease until the middle of the Ming Dynasty.

Ming Dynasty Longquan Celadon continued on the foundation of Song and Yuan traditions, but also brought about its own distinctive properties. Specifically, impression and incising became the predominant decorative patterns, which were perfectly suited for the particularly clear glazes at that time; giving the pieces a new aesthetic altogether. In particular, several Early Ming masterpieces have decorations that are exquisitely executed and clearly depicted, dense but not overdone.

In general, whether from a glaze color or porcelain quality standpoint, Ming Longquan does not match the overall quality of its predecessors. However, some Early Ming wares have exceeding quality and were executed to a standard of imperial use.

According to text written during the Early Ming Dynasty (1393 and 1457 A.D.), the imperial court specifically ordered Longquan Wares from Zhejiang province. Archeological excavations of a huge number of masterpiece works from the Dayao Fengdongyan Kiln site substantiate these records, and high quality Ming Longquan Imperial wares, in fact, did exist.

During the Mid Ming Dynasty, the number of kiln sites began to decrease and quality dropped with it. The Longquan Celadon industry began to undergo a sharp decline. Qing Dynasty records written in relation to Longquan County history clearly indicate a sharp decline in overall quality, glaze color, and aesthetic design. By the end of the Chenghua and Hongzhi reigns, Longquan Celadon had markedly thicker bodies, thinning and clear glaze, with the inscribed decorations increasingly poor, quality noticeably affected, and the entire industry was in steady decline.

According to the archeological excavation of the Fengdongyan kiln site in Longquan's Dayao, September 2006 to January 2007, the excavated shards from the area included pieces from Late Southern Song through to Mid Ming Dynasty [36]. There were very few examples of pieces later than Mid Ming, which indicates that the Mid Ming period was a turning point for the Longquan Kilns, and production from that point on began a steady decline.

By the Qing Dynasty, the only firing locations left in Longquan were in Dayao and Sunkeng areas. The pieces fired across a few kiln locations were of dense clay body, grey in color, and had thin translucent greyish green to yellowish green glaze. During the Qing Dynasty, Longquan Celadon continued be a representative monochrome glaze, but only held minor importance.

By the early Republic of China Era, Longquan kilns had moved out of the Dayao area and migrated to the Baoxi area. Their products included primarily daily use underglaze blue wares, and some traditional Longquan Celadon. Most kilns were held within single families or run by a master and apprentice system, and the traditional Longquan techniques

项目。龙泉青瓷以其亘古不衰的生命力，延续人类文明。

五、总结

龙泉窑是我国一个文化内涵庞杂、窑址分布广阔、窑业规模空前的青瓷窑业系统，融南北瓷业技术和瓷窑文化，在“官窑”和“民窑”不同文化层的相互碰撞中，博采众长，集青瓷技艺之大成，最后超越其他青瓷窑系，在南宋之际把青瓷烧制技艺推上历史巅峰。龙泉青瓷传统烧制技艺递代相传，明以后又经历清代的艰难维系和民国的复苏、新中国成立以后的传承弘扬和当今的发展振兴，至今仍然保持着旺盛的、顽强的生命力，成为中国陶瓷史上的一棵常青树，并最终成为人类陶瓷文明的代表。

were passed from generation to generation. Several production houses such as "Li Sheng He", "Zhang Yi Chang", and "Gong San Xing"; as well as well-known activists did extremely important work in the preservation and spread of traditional Longquan Celadon techniques. These foundations were invaluable in paving the way for the rejuvenation and rebuilding of traditional Longquan Celadon production that has been seen after the induction of P.R. China.

The main reasons for Longquan Kilns' decline include:

A. Domestic Production Struggles

a. Similar Product Struggle

The flourishing of the Longquan Kilns brought along with it the ceramics industry in the region. These kilns utilized replication of Longquan Celadon techniques, and made use of nearby waterways to wrangle portions of the market from the traditional Longquan Celadon wares [37].

Located in the north western region of Fujian Province, near the border of Zhejiang and Jiangxi, already over 20 kiln sites have been discovered. They date between the Song and Yuan Dynasties and almost all contain celadon wares. In the central and southern coastal region of Fujian, additional ancient kilns have been excavated and shards of Longquan-like wares, known as "local Longquan", are commonly found throughout. These shards clearly were influenced heavily by the Longquan Celadon productions [38].

Bijia Mountain in the eastern section of Chaozhou in Guangdong Province, also called "Hundred Kiln Village", also produced a large portion of celadon productions, of which many were slated as export porcelain [39].

Recently, in Dabu County of Guangdong Province, kilns within the Longquan style have been excavated, and are currently the earliest known Longquan system kiln sites to be found within the province. The kiln site is relatively well preserved, and the production scale of Longquan system celadon wares during the Ming Dynasty was vast.

Aside from these, Jizhou Kiln, Hengfeng Kiln, Geyang Kiln of Jiangxi, as well as many kilns throughout the Hunan and Hubei Province areas undertook celadon production. It is unclear whether they were able to produce porcelain for export, and further research is needed to confirm. However, it is clear that they would have at the very least impacted the domestic market share of Longquan Celadon [40].

According to Aoyanagi Youji's research [41], 12th to 13th century (Late Song) Fujian porcelain was wide-spread amongst the island countries of Southeast Asia. By the late 13th and 14th centuries (Late Yuan — Early Ming), the excavated wares from Southeast Asia primarily came from Quanzhou and surrounding areas of Fujian province, and very few pieces were coming from Longquan or Jingdezhen. These finding go to show that many regional porcelain productions, specifically Fujian, created an undeniable impact on the market for Longquan Wares.

b. Continuous Innovation at the Jingdezhen Kilns

I. Song Dynasty Innovation

The Song Dynasty saw the invention of Yingqing or Shadow Blue glaze at Jingdezhen. Due to its inherent beauty and jade-like qualities, it received the lauded approval of the Song Court. As such, the Song government set up an administrative post in Jingdezhen to oversee the production of tribute goods to be made in Jingdezhen [42].

II. Yuan Dynasty Innovation

During the Yuan Dynasty, Jingdezhen began full scale production of Underglaze Blue Porcelain, a vibrant and beautiful porcelain that thrust the entire industry from the monochrome era into the new age of colored porcelain, and became a crown jewel in Chinese Porcelain. The Mongolian love of blue and white naturally created a deep affinity for underglaze blue. At the same time, Jingdezhen artisans began introducing kaolin clay into the porcelain mixture (This mixture of porcelain clay mixed with kaolin became known as the "Dual Base" porcelain clay mentioned earlier). This technical innovation was the building block on which the flourishing of Jingdezhen was built, vaulted it to the center of world porcelain production, and founded it as the center of the Chinese porcelain industry [43]. Additionally, the establishment of specific government bureaus in Jingdezhen to oversee the production of porcelain goes to show that the rulers of the day placed the utmost importance on the administration of the Jingdezhen Kilns.

III. Ming Dynasty Innovation

The Ming Dynasty ushered in huge innovation to the decoration of Chinese porcelain. Meaningful decorations such as Dragon and Phoenix, Lotus, Eight Treasures, and figures all became staples of porcelain decoration. From then on, all types of porcelain were created at Jingdezhen including: Underglaze red, Wucai, Doucai, Famille rose, and various colors of monochrome glazes. These all had deep inspirational decorations that captured the heart of the common people as well as the nobility and ruling class. Longquan Celadon decorations lacked the expressive power of those from Jingdezhen, and it slowly lost its presence on the world stage. Because of this, Jingdezhen went on to become a one-act show, while Longquan Celadon slowly slipped into relative obscurity [45].

IV. Foreign Market's Love of Underglaze Blue

Islam had already begun to spread into Southeast Asia by the 12th century, and by the late 14th to early 15th century it had become a foundational part of Southeast Asian culture [46]. Islamic culture values blue as an auspicious color, and as such underglaze blue porcelain found a very welcome audience amongst the Islamic culture enriched Southeast Asian markets. By the 15th to 16th century (Early Ming), underglaze blue had already become the primary export porcelain [47]. Due to the shift from traditional celadon to underglaze blue, the Longquan Celadon foreign market decreased correspondingly.

B. Similar Foreign Product Struggles

The history of Chinese ceramic making is extensive. Along with the deepening Sino-foreign trade, and with the wide spread of Chinese porcelain and porcelain production techniques, other regions of the world were slowly able to begin replication of Chinese porcelain [48].

Around Late Northern Song to Early Southern Song Dynasty, artisans in the Korean peninsula, under the rule of the Goryeo Dynasty, first successfully fired Goryeo Celadon [49]. In 1223 A.D. the Japanese ceramic artisans Katou Sirou and Saemon, went to Zhejiang to study porcelain making techniques. Upon their return to Japan they established the "Sedo Kiln" and successfully fired imitation Longquan Celadon [50]. The Chen and Li Dynasties of Vietnam (1009-1400 A.D.), were the golden era of ceramic production, and they were extremely successful at producing Longquan replications during that time [51]. From the late 14th century to the early 16th century was the golden era of ceramics in Thailand. Located in the central north of Thailand, the Kalong Kiln fired many export wares, including a large amount of replica Longquan Wares [52]. Northern and Eastern Africa also took part in the replication of Chinese ceramics. In particular, Egypt produced celadon ceramics that very strictly replicated Longquan Wares [53]. Aside from the aforementioned, other locations including India, Persia, Iraq, and so forth all took part in, to some extent, the making of Longquan style wares.

Of the Longquan Celadon discovered throughout Southeast Asia, the samples date between Southern Song and Mid Ming Dynasty, with very few examples of anything after the Late Ming Period. Even though some examples can still be seen, the number indicates a sharp decline in its position, and samples sizes are smaller than celadon pieces from Fujian, Thailand, and Vietnam. For example: Of the ceramics taken from a 14th century shipwreck, 57% were from Thailand and Chinese ceramics were only 35%, of which less than 10% of them were Longquan Wares (less than 3% of the total stow); within a 15th century shipwreck, pieces of Thai, Vietnamese, and Chinese origin were found (including white glaze and celadon), of which the majority was Thai and each of the other types (including Longquan Celadon) only made up a small portion [54].

Each of these regions' replication ability and styles varied, but they all go to show that the locals of each region had a deep love and appreciation for Longquan Celadon. Local replications show the local consumer psyche as they all attempted to utilize lower priced local materials to break off pieces of the local market, and a substantial number of Longquan replications even made it onto the foreign market. These replications not only impacted the Longquan market share in the local area, but began to erode at the grip that Longquan held on the world celadon market and created a huge market struggle for Longquan Celadon products.

C. Political Reasons

a. Governmental Support

The rise of the Longquan Kilns came about as a result of economic market pull, but under the feudalist society of ancient China, this could only pull development so far. Compared to the Jingdezhen Kiln, which similarly rose up during the Northern Song Dynasty, the Longquan Kilns did not receive enough government support and leadership. The difference during the Ming Dynasty, even though Longquan and Jingdezhen were of similar status, was that Jingdezhen had been established as the location of the imperial kilns, as recorded: "The kiln firing for official use is the Imperial Kiln (at Jingdezhen), the rest are Common Kilns". However, it is possible that Longquan was a common kiln that was utilized for the firing of imperial service. In the Ming Dynasty records, Jingdezhen is listed many times as the official imperial kiln, but not much mention of Longquan is made. As such we can see that even though Longquan did partake in the firing of imperial and official use wares, it was not established as a specific area of governance like Jingdezhen, and lacked overall support and protection from the imperial court. Because of this, it was able to more easily slide into obscurity [55].

b. Export Policy

During the Early Ming Dynasty, the imperial policy on tributes was to bestow more than was received, but over time the imperial court was unable to support this type of tribute policy. As such, gradual limitations were put on the flow of tribute goods including: Numbers of goods, frequency of visits, number of ships, which ports could be used and so forth. At the same time, constant attacks from pirates along the southeast coast of China caused even stricter regulations to be put on maritime travel. Eventually, during the Jiajing reign, all maritime trade was banned. These policies had negative implications on the Longquan Celadon foreign trade [56].

c. Harsh Tariffs

The taxes levied by the Ming Dynasty were heavy and frequent, specifically through the Mid Ming Period. Ancient records indicate that Longquan County goods were heavily levied, and as such the prices for celadon had to reflect these tax hikes [57] [58].

d. Social Unrest

Beginning in 1447 A.D., rebellions within the Chuzhou area greatly impacted the kilns within the Longquan area. These rebellions continued through to the next reign period, and were a thorn in the side of the imperial court. These uprisings had an increasingly negative impact on the production of Longquan Celadon within the area [59] [60].

D. Summary

According to the aforementioned, the Longquan Celadon Industry had struggles both domestically and abroad and lacked production pull, which led to a drop in quality and deflated output. Several official records and documents written throughout the Mid Ming Dynasty, and even into the Qing Dynasty, all made note of the drop in quality seen in Longquan Wares [61] [62].

Through to the Qing Dynasty, even though Longquan Celadon continued to be fired, its quality and proportion never reached the levels it had once seen. This decline in quality and production capacity continued through the Late Qing Dynasty and into the Republic Era (1911-1949 A.D.).

Even though during the Southern Song Dynasty the innovation of Plum and Powder Green glazes appeared, and during the Yuan Dynasty many more shapes, sizes and varieties were created; comprehensively speaking, Longquan Celadon has had a one-dimensional development history limited to the confines of monochromatic glaze. Due to the fact that Jingdezhen brought about the era of polychrome porcelain, it ushered in a new aesthetic taste of the imperial court and changed the affinity for colored porcelain through each level of society. This change in aesthetic appeal gained not only governmental support, but that of foreign ceramic markets as well. This coupled with the continual market battles, both domestically and abroad, caused the long and steady decline of Longquan Celadon.

4. The Rejuvenation of Longquan Wares in Modern China

After the induction of Modern China in 1949, several levels of government poured out support for the rejuvenation of Longquan Celadon. In 1957, Premier Zhou En Lai specifically mandated that Longquan Celadon production should be restored. In 1959, a team of scholars, officials, and archeologists joined together to form the "Longquan Celadon Rejuvenation Committee". In joint cooperation with artisans from the Longquan area, they carried out extensive archeological excavation, research, replication experimenting, and restoration. On the foundation gained through these efforts, the Shangyang ceramics factory was able to successfully replicate Longquan Celadon. In 2006, Longquan Celadon was selected as a "National Heritage", and on September 30th, 2009, Traditional Longquan Celadon Production was added to the United Nations List of Non-Material Cultural Heritage, and is the only ceramic to be registered on the list. Undying production of Longquan Celadon is an important link in the chain of human civilization.

5. Conclusion

Longquan Celadon is one of the intrinsic elements of Chinese Culture. With widespread kiln locations, an amalgamation of Northern and Southern Chinese Celadon techniques, the fusion of Official and Common Kilns, and through capturing the hearts of all who encountered it; Longquan was able to surpass all other celadon producing kilns to become the representative celadon of China. From the glorious golden era of the Southern Song, through the decline of the Ming, near extinction during the Qing, restoration during the Republic Era, and finally rejuvenation during the Modern Chinese Era; Longquan Celadon has proved to be a tradition with unmatched vitality. It is the evergreen of Chinese ceramics, and has become a representative part of human culture and history.

第二节 龙泉窑的历史地位

龙泉青瓷在人类陶瓷发展史上扮演着重要的角色，对世界商贸文化交流史有着深远影响。

南宋时期，龙泉青瓷形成了青釉配制、多次施釉、厚釉烧成、开片控制四大独特传统烧制技艺，窑工们烧制出粉青、梅子青的精美釉色；掌握了素烧和多次施釉的工艺技术，以厚釉装饰来达到如玉的审美效果，龙泉窑登上了青瓷发展史的历史巅峰。

元、明时期，龙泉窑迅速扩张，大量出口至世界各地，还带动了江西、福建、广东、广西等省甚至东南亚国家的瓷业发展。其窑业之盛、分布之广、技艺之精、产量之丰、延续之久、影响之大令人叹为观止。

龙泉青瓷器物造型多种多样，既有各类日用器皿，也有文房用具，还有仿制青铜器和玉器的造型。宗教、植物、动物、人物、文字等各类纹饰，题材广泛、内容丰富，反映出不同时期的社会心理，折射出不同的生活情趣和审美观念。这表明龙泉青瓷工艺上的成就受到社会各阶层的喜爱，反过来也受不同层次审美需求的影响。

窑工们使用多样的支烧和装烧方式，并熟练掌握用肉眼判断窑内温度气氛的火控技术，掌握利用胎釉鼓胀系数的不同控制裂纹装饰的开片控制技术，使材质美、自然美、装饰美达到了完美的结合。

一、龙泉窑在国内的地位

（一）宋代

1. 北宋时期

宋代君王好素瓷，喜欢“类玉”的单色釉。中原汉文化对玉的崇尚有着渊源的历史。东汉时期，许慎在《说文解字•玉部》中总结了春秋时期延续下来的儒家“玉德”思想，提出了玉之“五德”说，并提出了玉乃“石之美者”，指出玉不仅有“玉德”，而且是“美”的，这使玉逐渐从皇室权贵走向世俗，为之后的瓷器代玉以及瓷器“尚玉”提供了理论前提[63]。正所谓“上有所喜，下必好之”。臣子百官、文人墨客、黎民百姓及各大窑口都以君王的审美为自己的审美观，因此，生产青瓷的龙泉窑在宋代发展迅猛，进入鼎盛期。

五代至北宋初期是龙泉窑的萌芽期，它从南方众多青瓷窑场中脱颖而出，生产规模和产品得到世人的关注。早期龙泉窑大量生产日用瓷，虽然器型种类不多，但都是老百姓日常生活的必需品。这彻底打破了过去所谓“供奉之物，臣庶不得用”的局限，奠定了青瓷使用的群众基础[64]。（由第一节的叙述可知，除生产日用瓷之外，此时期龙泉窑也是生产吴越钱氏纳贡所需瓷器的重要瓷窑之一。）

到了北宋中晚期，龙泉窑产品质量提高，龙泉窑的工匠们在原有的基础上改进工艺技术，增加了新品种，许多都是北宋早期所未见的，在纹饰表现方面手法也更加成熟巧妙[65]。同时，北宋晚期对龙泉的龙泉溪、秦溪、缙云的好溪等瓯江上游浅滩进行开凿疏通，水路航行安全畅通[66]。从此龙泉青瓷得以通过水上交通转销各地。交通的便利吸引了更多外来陶瓷工匠前来龙泉窑务工。从此龙泉的生产活动沿瓯江由南向东扩展。已发现的北宋时期龙泉窑址至少有159处，主要生产日用器[67]。龙泉青瓷的地位初步奠定。

2. 南宋时期

南宋时期龙泉青瓷窑址分布广泛，形成了一个规模庞大的青瓷窑系。此期间，朝廷建立了修内司窑和郊坛下官窑，专为宫廷供应青瓷。但是生产规模较小，产量不多，不能满足统治阶级和出口贸易的需要。此时，已经小有名气的龙泉窑在胎釉配方、上釉技巧、造型设计、装饰艺术和装窑烧制等方面均做出改革，提高质量，扩大生产，获得朝廷青睐，从而开始接受官方订制[68]。

Section 2：

Longquan Kilns' Place in History

Longquan Celadon has played an important role in the history of ceramic development, and has impacted trade, culture, and exchange throughout the world.

During the Southern Song Dynasty, traditional techniques of Longquan Celadon achieved four main accomplishments: Celadon glaze recipe, multiple glaze applications, thick glaze firing, and controlled glaze crazing. Artisans were able to create Powder Green and Plum Green glazes, firmly grasp the art of raw and multiple glaze firing, and create a thick glaze decoration with jade-like beauty that vaulted Longquan Celadon to the pinnacle of celadon development.

During the Yuan and Ming Dynasties, Longquan production expanded rapidly and was exported to almost every corner of the globe. With it, it brought along the ceramics industries in Jiangxi, Fujian, Guangdong, Guangxi and so forth Provinces, as well as South East Asian countries. The success, breadth, technical prowess, production capacity, and sheer life-span of this kiln system have had an immense impact and have gained worthy praise.

Longquan Celadon wares came in many shapes and styles. They spanned from everyday use items, to cultural display pieces, and even covered a vast selection of bronze and jade vessel replications. It also included religious, natural, animal, human, and written themes to adorn its beautiful face; the themes vast and content abundant. These motifs reflected the societal mindset and aesthetic pursuits of the day. This goes to show that Longquan Celadon was loved throughout each level of society, and also indicates that it took aesthetic influence and direction from every stratum.

Kiln artisans utilized a myriad of means to create their works, and established naked eye techniques for telling the temperature, atmosphere and fire control. They were also able to understand and utilize the differences in glaze and clay thermodynamics to create and control glaze crazing. These technical achievements allowed them to achieve the perfect composite of material, with natural and decorative beauty.

1. Longquan Kilns' Place Domestically

A. Song Dynasty

a. Northern Song

The Song monarchy court favored simple porcelain, preferring 'jade-like' single color (monochrome) glazes. Central Plain Han culture's advocacy of jade has deep roots in history. *Shuo Wen Jie Zi* (The original Han Dynasty Dictionary) has a section specifically dedicated to the praise of Jade. It is said that the "Jade Virtues" were passed down by Confucian ideology from the Spring and Autumn Period, and talks about the "Five Virtues" of jade as well as lauding it as the "Beauty among stones". This gradually brought jade from within the courts of the royal intellects into the hearts of all the Chinese people. It is specifically these premise principles that directed development of ceramics to become 'Jade-esque' [63]. This value carried throughout each dynasty, and deeply impacted the aesthetic desire of the imperial courts. The aesthetics of the court flowed downward to impact each level of society, including artisans and kilns. As such, the production of Longquan Celadon during the Song Dynasty exploded into a golden era.

The Five Dynasties Period and Northern Song Dynasty were the first sprouting of the Longquan Kilns, and they had to peak out from amongst the many celadon kilns of Southern China to increase to a capacity and product level that would catch the World's attention. Early Longquan production did

正是在这样改革创新的前提下，南宋时期的龙泉瓷窑发展迅猛，窑场数量显著增加，迄今发现的南宋龙泉窑窑址至少316处，主要集中在大窑、金村、溪口、梧桐口、小白岸、大白岸、道太、松溪、安福、安仁口、大棋、黄金坑、武溪等地；除龙泉境内之外，云和梓枋、水碓坑，庆元上垟，遂昌湖山镇，缙云大溪滩、碗窑山，甚至泰顺、文成、永嘉等县市都相继建立了瓷窑[69]。同时此时期用作烧制瓷器的龙窑长度也可谓空前绝后，如安福、山头等地有数座龙窑长度均在60米以上，最长的甚至达97米，单窑装烧量惊人。

南宋时期龙泉窑的成功还促进了浙江省境内各地的青瓷生产，它的影响力还扩散至周边地区，尤其是沿海地区福建等地（见本章第一节同类产品竞争部分）。

3. 龙泉青瓷在宋代宫廷中的地位

（1）北宋时期

从古文献的记载中可以发现北宋时期龙泉青瓷与宫廷的联系。宋人庄季裕《鸡肋编》中记载："处州龙泉县……又出青瓷器，谓之秘色。宣和中，禁廷制样须索，益加工巧"[70]。即早在宣和年间（1119—1125），宫廷便对龙泉青瓷"制样须索"。按此文献所载可推断：龙泉青瓷在北宋晚期的宣和年间已进入宫廷。

另外，南宋人叶寘的《坦斋笔衡》以及顾文荐的《负暄杂录》中有如下记载："本朝以定州白瓷器有芒不堪用，遂命汝州造青窑器，故河北唐、邓、耀州悉有之，汝窑为魁。江南则处州龙泉县窑，质颇粗厚。宣政间，京师自置窑烧造，名曰官窑。中兴渡江，有邵成章提举后苑，号邵局。袭徽宗遗制，置窑于修内司，造青器，名内窑。澄泥为范，极其精致，油色莹澈，为世所珍。后郊下别立新窑，亦曰官窑，比旧窑大不侔矣"[71]。

关于龙泉青瓷，以上文献有一句提及："江南则处州龙泉县窑，质颇粗厚"。对此学术界有不同理解，有人认为这只是对北宋龙泉青瓷质量的一般描述，但有学者却认为不止于此。这则文献论述了当时宫廷用瓷的一些情况："本朝"应是指当时的北宋朝廷，所用瓷器有定窑，有汝窑，有河北唐、邓、耀州窑等地所产瓷器，"宣政"即北宋政和（1111—1117）和宣和（1119—1125）年间，皆为宋徽宗年号，在此年间设置官窑。到了南宋又分别设立修内司官窑和郊坛下官窑。把龙泉窑的描述放在"定窑""汝窑"之后，北宋宣政的"官窑"，以及南宋"修内司窑"与"郊坛下窑"之前，将龙泉青瓷与定窑、汝窑、修内司官窑以及郊坛下官窑等并列比较，可见在北宋时期，龙泉青瓷与定窑、汝窑等瓷器就已在宫廷出现，而且在宣政设立"官窑"之前，即最晚在"宣政"时，龙泉青瓷就已进入宫廷[72]。这种说法从文学角度的理解是可取的，不过缺少考古实物证据的支持。

目前在考古遗址中所见的北宋龙泉窑纪年青瓷有江苏溧阳竹箦李彬夫妇墓（北宋元祐六年，公元1091年）出土的折扇纹碗。李彬为地方富豪，与龙泉青瓷同出的随葬品也皆较为高档[73]。此外还有四川阆中陈安祖夫人墓（北宋崇宁四年，公元1105年）出土的莲花纹盘等。陈安祖为北宋三陈（陈尧叟、陈尧佐、陈尧咨）之后，陈氏家族在当时极为显赫。由此看来，龙泉青瓷在北宋时期就已出现于达官显贵之家，以此类推，龙泉青瓷此时已进入宫廷也不无可能[74]。

（2）南宋时期

龙泉青瓷在几个与南宋宫廷相关的遗址中均有出土。在南宋恭圣仁烈皇后宅遗址以及南宋太庙遗址中出土有一定数量的龙泉青瓷，由瓷器特征来看，其年代为南宋后期产品[75]。由此可见，至迟在南宋中期，龙泉青瓷已经进入宫廷。

在南宋恭圣仁烈皇后宅遗址第四层下水池遗迹当中发现的瓷器品种除了龙泉青瓷外，还有南宋官窑瓷、汝窑瓷、高丽青瓷、定窑白瓷、景德镇窑仿定白瓷、景德镇窑青白瓷和磁州窑白瓷等。经统计，所占比重最大的为定窑白瓷，占总量的64.81%，其次为龙泉青瓷，占20.07%，再次为南宋官窑瓷，占11.03%，然后是景德镇窑青白瓷和仿定窑白瓷，占1.6%。在青瓷品种当中，占比重最大的为龙泉青瓷，占总量的60.90%，其次为南宋官窑瓷，占33.46%。在南宋太庙遗址第四层出土的南宋时期瓷器品种有龙泉青瓷、景德镇窑瓷和定窑瓷等，其中龙泉瓷器所占比重最大，占总量的80.70%，其次为定窑瓷器，占13.43%，再次为景德镇窑瓷，占10.45%。除了以上遗址外，在绍兴六陵所出土瓷器中也主要以龙泉青瓷为主[76]。

not include a wide variety of shapes and styles, but they included primarily daily use items that were needed by the commoners. This broke the mold that had previously limited common use items from being used by the court [64]. As such, Longquan was able to keep its foundation amongst the laymen while, as stated in Section 1, it was also able to be utilized as one of the main kilns for tribute ware production of the Wuyue Qian Family.

By the end of the Northern Song Dynasty, the quality of Longquan had risen to new heights. The artisans were able to use the technical foundations of their predecessors and innovatively create new and numerous shapes and styles that were not seen in the Early Northern Song Dynasty. Additionally, decorative techniques became more refined and polished [65]. At the same time, the Late Northern Song government put effort into the establishment and improvement of transportation and waterway safety measures in and around the Longquan area and its tributaries [66]. From then on, Longquan Celadon was able to be transported over water from kilns to all the markets in which it would be consumed. Ease of transportation also encouraged the flow of additional ceramic artisans into the Longquan area. From then on, the kiln development of the Longquan area expanded south and east along the Oujiang River. Over 159 kilns dated to the Northern Song Dynasty have been discovered, with their main products being daily use items [67]. Longquan Celadon's status was thus already established in its adolescence.

b. Southern Song

The distribution of Longquan Kilns during the Southern Song Dynasty was expansive, and a huge scale system of celadon porcelain emerged. At this time, the Song court established a series of kilns that were firing exclusively for imperial and official use. However, the capacity of these kilns was small and outputs were nowhere near enough to cover the market demand as well as need for tributary exports. Simultaneously, the already somewhat well-known Longquan Kilns underwent improvements in glaze recipes, glaze application techniques, shape designs, motif tastes, and kiln firing controls. These all helped to bring about new innovations, increase capacity, and vault Longquan Celadon to levels of imperial approval. From then on, Longquan was charged with the supplemental firing of imperial and official wares [68].

It was under this type of innovation that Southern Song Longquan blossomed into its golden era. Kiln numbers skyrocketed to over 316 kiln sites from that period discovered so far, primarily centered around Dayao, Jincun, Xikou, Wutongkou, and so forth locations. Kilns outside of the Longquan boundaries including Yunhezifang, Shuiduikeng, Qingyuanshangyang, and so forth surrounding areas also saw the establishment of kiln sites [69]. It was also at this time that the longest of all "dragon" kilns were being utilized. There were a number of dragon kilns that were over 60 meters long, with the longest reaching as high as a staggering 97 meters.

The success of the Longquan Kilns during the Southern Song Dynasty spurred on the celadon industry throughout the entire province. Its impact was deeply felt through all the surrounding areas, specifically the coastal areas of Fujian and so forth (See Similar Product Struggles in Section 1 of this chapter).

c. Longquan Ware's Place in the Song Imperial Court

I. Northern Song

We can see the relationship between Longquan Celadon Kilns and the Northern Song Imperial Court through ancient records. One specific record mentions that in the Xuanhe Reign (1119-1125A.D.) of the Late Northern Song Dynasty, Longquan Celadon had already made an appearance within the imperial court [70].

Additionally, amongst the list of imperial items that were produced for the court, including Ding Kiln and Ru Kiln wares, a small excerpt mentions the quality of Longquan Wares [71].

Some suggest that this is merely a mention as to the quality of Longquan and nothing more. Still other scholars argue that the simple mention of Longquan amongst the other imperial use items, such as Ding Kiln and Ru Kiln, indicate that Longquan had a certain status, albeit after the aforementioned. This record also shows that Longquan

根据以上数据可知，在南宋宫廷所用瓷器当中，白瓷以定窑居多，青瓷则以龙泉青瓷居多。龙泉青瓷占有相当的比重，与定窑、官窑一起，成为当时宫廷用瓷的主要品种。

（二）元代

元代仍是龙泉窑的兴盛时期。此时，中国制瓷业呈现出新的秩序与格局，宋代几大名窑已相继衰落，南方制瓷业主要靠龙泉窑和景德镇窑两大支柱支撑。

蒙古族马背上的文化给龙泉青瓷的生产注入了新的元素。蒙古民族的大气与粗犷使这一时期增加了许多大件瓷器，其颜色并不逊于南宋时期的梅子青和粉青[77]；同时在装饰风格上也发生了变化，由南宋时的重釉色、重造型变为重纹饰[78]。

这段时期，龙泉青瓷的生产更多的是追求数量的增加，而不是质量的提高。由窑址实地考察可见，元代龙泉窑址堆积非常丰厚，器物品种繁多。据统计，元代有龙泉窑遗址至少445处，其中在大窑一带就有50余处。在龙泉东部至丽水瓯江沿岸，新的青瓷窑迅速发展起来，这里水路方便，沿江经丽水、温州等地销售至海内外各地。同时在遂昌、武义、缙云、永嘉等地也新建瓷窑生产龙泉青瓷，盛况空前绝后。

但是，元代龙泉青瓷总体的质量不如南宋。主要是因为它的主要享用对象是老百姓，不再像南宋时期主要针对上层社会[79]。

龙泉青瓷在元代宫廷中的地位

元代统治者并不以瓷器为珍。蒙古统治阶级偏好使用金、银、玉石、漆器，瓷器相对来说，似乎得不到蒙元统治阶级的特别青睐。此外，元大都出土少数品质相对较高的瓷器，像龙泉青瓷、青白瓷、枢府形瓷和青花瓷则作为其他珍贵器皿的补充，而磁州窑器物则更次一级，大部分作为储藏器和杂器。《元史》卷一百六十八列传第五十五“何荣祖”条记载：“荣祖身至大官而僦地以居，饮食器用青瓷杯。中宫闻之，赐以上尊及金五十两，钞二万五千贯，俾置器买宅，以旌其廉”。当皇后听闻身居要职的何荣祖以青瓷杯饮水喝酒时，立即赏赐他以表彰其清廉，可见青瓷地位不高[80]。

元代“国俗尚白，以白为吉”[81]，且“祭器尚纯”[82]。在瓷器使用上，元代统治者偏好青白釉、卵白釉瓷器，对龙泉青瓷的喜好程度相对较低。从考古发掘资料中也可见这一点。在元代皇宫遗址中出土了若干瓷器，其中包括景德镇湖田窑的青花瓷器与青白瓷器、龙泉窑的青瓷、钧窑瓷器和磁州窑瓷器，龙泉青瓷仅占7.4%[83]。

不过，瓷器仍然是元代贵族生活中不可或缺的必需品。龙泉青瓷上出现八思巴文［八思巴文在至元六年（公元1269年）正式颁行以来，元朝政府屡次下令和强制推行，但它的使用仅限于给官方文书和官方造发的东西，是元代的官文］说明龙泉窑还是有一定的政治地位[84]。在与元代宫廷相关的哈拉和林古城遗址、阿里麻里古城遗址[85]以及元上都皇城遗址[86]中均有龙泉青瓷出土。

（三）明代

龙泉青瓷经过宋、元至明代，生产活动继续进行。明初在全国制瓷业中还占有一定的地位。明代龙泉窑除元代遗留下来的窑场多数还在继续烧以外，又在庆元县建立新窑；但窑的总数比元代少，规模也小了[87]。从明中期开始有衰退的趋势。

在国内各地的明代早期墓葬中，龙泉青瓷的出土数量远比景德镇青花瓷要多[88]。在弘治《大明会典》中，所列民间器物的税收条例，关于青瓷的项目特别多，说明了民间用瓷在弘治年间仍以龙泉青瓷为主[89]。

龙泉青瓷在明代宫廷中的地位

根据《大明会典》中的相关记载，“洪武二十六年（公元1393年）定：凡烧造供用器皿等物，须要定夺制样，计算人工物料。如果数多，起取人匠赴京，置窑兴工，或数少，行移饶、处等府烧造。”（此处“饶”指景德镇地区，“处”指龙泉地区）

2006年至2007年间，浙江省文物考古研究所等单位对浙江龙泉大窑枫洞岩窑址进行了考古发掘，发掘出土了大量龙泉青瓷，其中洪武、永乐地层中出土的龙泉青瓷经研究为明代官器[90]，部分与清宫旧藏龙泉青瓷传世品相对应，其精湛做工是普通龙泉民窑无法企及的：精美秀丽的刻花纹饰，主题除了植物花果，还有两角五爪龙纹。这些龙泉青瓷与部分同时期的景德镇青花瓷有惊人的相似之处，从装饰风格到器型样式都如出一辙，规格大小也是不相上下，甚至还能找到二者在纹饰、器型大小上完全一样的实例。这说明龙泉窑和景德镇窑都按照同样的瓷样烧制这类瓷

Celadon entered the court no later than 1111-1125 A.D. [72], but sufficient archeological evidence does not exist to fully substantiate this thesis.

Currently, dated archeological excavations of Northern Song Longquan Celadon have been discovered in the 1091 A.D. tomb of Li Bing, an affluent noble in Jiangsu Province. The dig produced, amongst many other high-end items, a Longquan Celadon bowl [73]. Additionally, in Sichuan Province, the 1105 A.D. dated tomb of Chen An Zu's wife produced a Longquan plate with Lotus pattern. Chen An Zu, the patriarch of one of the lauded Three Northern Song Chen Clans, was one of the most affluent officials in his area. From this we can see that Longquan Celadon had found its way into the home of some of the most influential officials of the Northern Song Dynasty. As such, the presence of Longquan within the imperial court is not improbable [74].

II. Southern Song

There have been several excavations of Southern Song Imperial sites that have contained Longquan Celadon. At both the residence of a Southern Song queen as well as the Southern Song Tai Temple, a substantial portion of Longquan Celadon wares was unearthed; produced in the Late Southern Song Period [75]. From this we can see that no later than the Mid Southern Song Dynasty, Longquan Celadon made its way into the imperial courts.

In the queen's residence excavation, aside from Longquan Celadon, was also a variety of other ceramics including: Official (Guan) Kiln, Ru Kiln, Gorean Celadon, Ding Kiln White wares, Jingdezhen Ding Kiln replicas, Jingdezhen Qingbai (Greenish-white) glaze, and Cizhou Kiln White wares. A survey of the site revealed that the majority of wares were Ding Kiln at 64.81%, second was Longquan Celadon at 20.07%, third was Southern Song Official (Guan) Kiln at 11.03%, and the rest spread over the remaining types. Of celadon wares, the vast majority was from Longquan at 60.90%, and Official (Guan) Kiln at 33.46%. At the Southern Song Tai Temple excavation, pieces of Longquan Celadon, Ding Kiln, and Jingdezhen Kiln wares were discovered. The proportions of these were 80.70%, 13.43%, and 10.45% respectively. Aside from these sites, pieces excavated from the Shaoxing Liuling excavation consisted of primarily Longquan Celadon [76].

From the above statistics we can see that among the Southern Song imperial use items, white glaze items were dominated by Ding Kiln wares, whereas celadon wares were primarily Longquan Kiln produced. Longquan Wares made up a large portion of excavated pieces, and along with Ding Kiln and Official (Guan) Kiln, made up the lion's share of official use items.

B. Yuan Dynasty

The Yuan Dynasty was the second golden age of Longquan Celadon. At this time, the Chinese ceramics industry underwent changes in governance and controls. The five main kilns of the Southern Song persistently declined, and of the kilns in Southern China, all but Jingdezhen and Longquan dwindled to obscurity.

The horseback culture of the ruling Mongolians infused a new element to Longquan production. The boisterous and lively Mongolian people ushered in a market for an increase in large and bold wares, but they retained the reserved color that was seen in the Southern Song Dynasty's Plum and Powder Green glazes.[77] At the same time, the style of decoration underwent change, with the emphasis placed on glaze and shape that was seen during the Southern Song morphing to an emphasis on decoration [78].

The period saw an increased desire to upsurge the numbers produced rather than improve quality. Excavations of kilns sites have shown that levels of Yuan production were extremely abundant with numerous types and styles present. Presently, over 445 sites dated to the Yuan Dynasty have been discovered, of which 50 are centered around the Dayao area. On the eastern edge of Longquan, along the Oujiang River near Lishui, new sites appeared and developed. This area enjoyed increased ease of water transportation that flowed past Lishui on to Wenzhou, and as such wares could be distributed to markets both domestic and foreign. Additionally, new sites in and around Suichang, Wuyi, Jinyun, Yongjia and so forth, constructed Longquan Celadon kilns. Production levels were higher than ever before and would be unparalleled after.

器，印证了明代官窑器是由“内府定夺制样”烧造的事实，也说明了两处窑场供给宫廷的产品在地位上几乎是同等重要的。

到了明代中晚期，龙泉青瓷几乎断供于宫廷。《明宪宗实录》中记载，成化元年（公元1465年）正月乙亥，诏：“江西饶州府，浙江处州府，见差内官在役烧造磁器，诏书到日，除已烧完者照数起解，未完者悉皆停止，差委官员即便回京，违者罪之”[91]。由成化皇帝的即位诏书可知，成化即位前朝廷还曾派官员去龙泉窑监烧瓷器，可见龙泉窑是明代宫廷用瓷的重要来源之一。但也就是从这道诏书之后，相关文献中再未见龙泉青瓷供给宫廷的记载，考古发掘资料中也未见此后与宫廷相关的龙泉青瓷出土[92]。

（四）清代

龙泉窑自明中期开始走下坡路，至明末清初，龙泉境内尚有窑址160余处，清前期仍有70多处，可见进入清代以后，龙泉窑并未停烧，还具有一定规模。1984年版《浙江省龙泉县地名志》“孙坑”条：“清乾隆至民国范姓曾在此烧制青瓷销售全国各地”。20世纪80年代，在文物普查工作中，发现龙泉瀑云埠头村、青溪孙坑村及宝溪溪头村等地有清代青瓷窑址，其中以青溪孙坑窑较为出色[93]。

英国大英博物馆收藏的有“处州府龙泉县……道光二十四年”等文字的青瓷瓶，证明龙泉窑在晚清还产青瓷，但其后产量不断减少。可见，龙泉窑是中国制瓷历史最长的一个名窑。

龙泉青瓷在清代宫廷中的地位

传世宋代龙泉青瓷在清宫中使用或收藏的地点均集中在乾隆皇帝幼儿、成年、亲政及预备归政后居住之所，乾隆御制诗也多次针对宋代龙泉青瓷，说明清宫和乾隆皇帝本人对于龙泉青瓷的重视。

不过清代的龙泉青瓷在清廷中的地位似乎不及宋代。叶佩兰女士曾介绍过故宫博物院所藏带有清代年款的几件龙泉窑青瓷，年代包括顺治、康熙到乾隆、光绪，但件数不多，在清宫旧藏的众多瓷器中可谓凤毛麟角[94]。

二、龙泉窑在海外的地位

龙泉青瓷在我国陶瓷史上占有重要的地位，不仅行销国内，而且远输海外。龙泉青瓷的输出海路之长，分布国家之广，数量之大，产品之精是全国绝大多数窑口无法相比的[95]。

（一）宋代

北宋王朝立国之初就比较重视海外贸易，设立管理对外贸易的机构，在东南沿海的广州、明州、杭州、泉州等处先后设立了市舶司。北宋开宝四年（公元971年）于广州设立，稍后又在杭州、明州设立，泉州设立于北宋元祐二年（公元1087年），负责征税、海货买卖和各国朝贡等事务[96]。

南宋偏安江南，财政拮据，因此更加重视海外贸易。绍兴七年（公元1137年）宋高宗说：“市舶之利最厚，若措置合宜，所得动以百万计，岂不胜取之于民，朕所以留意如此，庶几可以宽民力尔！”绍兴十六年高宗又说：“市舶之利，颇助国用，宜循旧法，以招徕远人，阜通货贿。”[97]

宋王朝还大力发展造船业，能制作远涉重洋的海船，设备齐全先进。这也大大促进了海上贸易。造船技术先进和航海技术的提高，使海运事业和海外贸易有了很大的发展[98]。

赵汝适在任福建路市舶提举时所撰的《诸蕃志》是宋代瓷器外销最详尽的文献，记述了当时我国与亚洲地区50多个国家和地区有贸易往来，其中与30多个国家和地区有陶瓷贸易[99]。

在亚非地区不少国家的古城废墟和沿海地带，陆续发现了很多我国宋代瓷器及碎片标本[100]。由在苏门答腊北部出土的一件南宋早期的龙泉青瓷盘可知，在南宋早期龙泉青瓷就已经开始输出至东南亚地区了。南宋晚期的龙泉青瓷在东南亚地区相对较多，南宋晚期出现在东南亚的龙泉青瓷无论是从数量还是质量上都要优于南宋早期，这也反映了龙泉窑产品自身的发展过程[101]。除此之外，在日本、巴基斯坦、朝鲜等地都有宋代龙泉青瓷出土[102]。

对外贸易的频繁使大量钱币外流，导致了国内钱荒。嘉定十二年（公元1219年）南宋政府下令禁止铜钱外流，规定：凡买外货以绢锦绮，瓷器为代价，不用金银铜交换。这种瓷器就是当时的龙泉青瓷[103]。

（二）元代

到目前为止，在中国境外进

However, holistically speaking the quality of Yuan Dynasty Longquan Celadon was not on par with that of the previous Southern Song Dynasty. This is primarily because of the shift in target market from the higher echelons of society to include everyday use items for more common markets [79].

Longquan Ware's Place in the Yuan Dynasty Court

The ruling class of the Yuan Dynasty did not place the utmost importance on porcelain. Mongolians preferred gold, silver, jade and lacquer, whereas porcelain comparatively did not receive the same favor. The higher quality pieces of porcelain such as Longquan Celadon, Qingbai (Blueish-white) glaze, Shufu glaze and Underglaze Blue excavated in the Yuan Capital Dadu were used primarily as supplement to sacrificial wares of precious materials listed above. Cizhou Kilns wares were one class lower, and used for storage and other miscellaneous uses [80]. One Yuan Dynasty record states that when the queen found out that one of her high level officials was using celadon as his drink ware, she was impressed that he was an upright man for using such a humble vessel for his personal use. From this we can see that celadon's status amongst the court was not particularly high.

During the Yuan Dynasty, there was an affinity towards using white and purity [81] [82]. As such, the court favored the use of Qingbai (Greenish-white) glaze or Luanbai (Egg White) glaze porcelain, and had a relatively low regard for Longquan Celadon. We can see this substantiated by archeological excavations. The Yuan Palace discovery produced porcelain wares including Jingdezhen Hutian Kiln Underglaze Blue, Qingbai Glaze, Lonquan Celadon, Jun Kiln, and Cizhou Kiln; of these only 7.4% were from Longquan [83].

However, porcelain was an obligatory part of nobility possessions during the Yuan Dynasty. Longquan Celadon wares with Basiba Script have been discovered. Basiba Script is writing inducted during the Yuan Dynasty (1269 A.D.) and was to be used only for official government items. From this we can see that Longquan Celadon must have had a certain status amongst government officials [84]. Additionally, excavations of imperial use locations at Halahelin Ancient City, Alimali City [85] and the imperial palace at Shangdu [86] all produced pieces of Longquan Celadon.

C. Ming Dynasty

Longquan Celadon continued its production from the Song and Yuan Dynasties, and continued into the Ming Dynasty. During the Early Ming Dynasty, Longquan held a position of status amongst the Chinese porcelain industry. Aside from the continuation of kilns erected during the Yuan Dynasty, new kilns emerged in the Qingyuan area. However, the overall number of kilns and total production capacity showed regression [87]. From the middle of the Ming Dynasty, Longquan began a steady decline.

Amongst many tombs dated to the Early Ming Dynasty, all throughout China, the number of Longquan Celadon vastly outnumbered that of Jingdezhen Underglaze Blue [88]. Tax records written during the Hongzhi reign list numerous lines of Longquan Celadon projects; further solidifying that Longquan held a substantial part of the common porcelain market [89].

Longquan Ware's Place in the Ming Dynasty Court

According to a Ming Dynasty imperial record written during the 26th year of the Hongwu Reign (1393 A.D.), an edict was written that all official fired articles should follow a specific pattern. Additionally, if the order was of substantial quantity, kilns should be built in the capitol and artisans would come and complete the order there. If the volume was reasonably low, the orders could be sent directly to Longquan or Jingdezhen to be completed locally.

2006—2007 excavations of the Fengdongyan Kiln Site in Dayao by the Zhejiang Provincial Archeology Department produced pieces deemed to be official fired wares that were discovered in the strata of Hongwu and Yongle reign periods [90]. Some of which held resemblance to imperial wares held in the Qing Dynasty Imperial Collection, with quality and craftsmanship exceedingly higher than standard common use Longquan Celadon from that period. Motifs were exquisitely executed and contain patterns of flora as well as a five-clawed dragon (exclusive to the emperor). These examples, surprisingly, have exact matches amongst Jingdezhen Underglaze Blue porcelain. They possess precisely the same dimensions, patterns, sizes, and stylizations as their Jingdezhen Underglaze

行的考古调查中发现的龙泉窑瓷器，年代主要为南宋至明代，其中数量最多的是元至明中期的产品[104]。龙泉窑的外销产量与各朝代实行的对外贸易政策有关。元代统治者宽松的对外贸易政策使龙泉青瓷生产规模在元代继续扩大，窑址和产品的品种及数量都达到前所未有的程度。

元代在中国历史发展进程中是版图最大、疆域最广的。在这样内需外求的社会大背景下，龙泉窑丰富的自然资源和发达的水系交通网络，加之成熟的制瓷工艺，及蒙元朝廷的积极的对外贸易政策，使大批龙泉青瓷畅销国内外市场[105]。

1278年，忽必烈下令推动海外贸易："可因番舶诸入宣布朕意，诚能来朝，朕将宠之，其往来互市，各从所欲。"作为北方游牧民族，蒙古族对商品贸易的依存度向来就高。征服中原后，蒙元民族的重商习俗并没有改变，在推动海外贸易的发展上更积极。成书于元大德八年（公元1304年）的《大德南海志》，著录当时贸易海外之国有142个；晚40年成书的《岛夷志略》，记述泉州远航所至各国，以99国为条目，各条目之中有提到其他若干国家或地区达百余处，书中有大量"青瓷""处州瓷"的贸易记录。此外，《真腊风土记》也有元代瓷器外销的多种记述[106]。

多年来，考古工作者在西亚和南亚地区进行的调查和发掘中，发现了大量元明时期的龙泉窑瓷器。《岛夷志略》《星槎胜览》《西洋番国志》《瀛涯胜览》《明史》等文献中有关于西亚、南亚地区出现中国瓷器的记载。通过考古调查印证，凡古文献中提到有中国瓷器运往的国家和地区，几乎都发现有元明时期的龙泉窑瓷器。如元代汪大渊《岛夷志略》，书中提到当时的商贾以"处州瓷"与"无枝拔""麻里鲁""苏禄""旧港""花面"等地进行贸易，换取当地特产（"处州瓷"即龙泉青瓷，据《岛夷志略校释》考证，"无枝拔"为现在的马来西亚马六甲一带，"麻里鲁"为现在的菲律宾马尼拉，"苏禄"为现在的菲律宾的苏禄群岛，"旧港"为现在的印度尼西亚苏门答腊岛东南部巨港，"花面"则是在印度尼西亚苏门答腊岛北部）[107]。

1975年在韩国西南部的新安海底发现一艘元代沉船，打捞出1万多件瓷器，其中龙泉青瓷占了9000多件[108]。1976年，在韩国木浦附近海域，发现元代满载瓷器的沉船，有青瓷3000多件、白瓷2000多件，多为龙泉窑及景德镇窑产品[109]。除此之外，在东南亚许多国家和地区都有元代龙泉青瓷出土及出水[110]，反映了龙泉青瓷在元代对外贸易中的重要地位和惊人数量。

（三）明代

明代早期龙泉窑青瓷质量还是比较高，依然是我国主要的外销商品之一。

明早期郑和下西洋是我国外交及对外贸易史上的盛举，从永乐三年（公元1405年）六月第一次从江苏太仓刘家港出航，到宣德八年（公元1433年）1月止，前后七次，总计28年，经过30多个国家，最远到达的是红海沿岸和非洲的东海岸。每次出使郑和都准备了大量瓷器、丝绸和其他物品，在抵达海外诸国时，或作为礼物赠送，或作为商品贸易，这使中国的瓷器广泛地流传到东南亚、南亚、西亚和非洲各地，龙泉青瓷就在众多瓷器之列。

从考古资料看，明代时期的瓷器在日本，朝鲜，菲律宾的卡拉塔冈、宿务岛、苏禄群岛、棉兰佬岛、吕宋、马尼拉，印度尼西亚的婆罗洲、苏门答腊、爪哇、西里伯斯、西伊里安、北婆罗洲、沙捞越，马来半岛，中南半岛的真腊、占城国，印度半岛，非洲埃及的福塔特遗址、索马里、埃塞俄比亚、肯尼亚、坦桑尼亚，甚至中南非的津巴布韦、莫桑比克、扎伊尔、赞比亚、马拉维、博茨瓦纳、马达加斯加、南非等大量发现[111]。

《陶说卷三》"明瓷器篇"记载："洪武十六年（公元1383年）占城、真腊（位于今柬埔寨）来中国，朱元璋各赠以瓷器及其他器一万九千件。洪武十九年又瓷器赠真腊，及至永乐二年（公元1404年）琉球山南王求青瓷，冒着触犯海禁之罪，私自至龙泉之处州求购瓷器"。明宣德之后，龙泉青瓷已成为世界性商品。明景泰二年（公元1451年），翻译官马欢在《瀛涯胜览》中提到"中国青瓷碗等品……甚爱之"。明末龙泉安仁、大白岸等地及处州、永嘉等地所烧的青瓷继续出口，在渤纽、苏门答腊等地用以交换香料、琅渭、胡椒等物品[112]。

中国和欧洲的直接贸易始于明代，1517年葡萄牙人到达广州，后在澳门建立商站。1578年，荷兰舰

Blue counterparts. This indicated that Longquan Celadon, along with Jingdezhen Underglaze Blue, both utilized the same imperial patterns for the carrying out of imperial fired goods, and substantiates the imperial decree specifying the governance of such items during the Ming Dynasty. It also indicated that these two kiln areas simultaneously carried out imperial firing, and as such had a similar status amongst the court.

By the Mid to Late Ming Dynasty, Longquan nearly ceased to provide imperial items for the court. According to an edict handed down by the Chenghua Emperor, Jingdezhen and Longquan had been carrying out the role of official firing with government supervision, but any such supervision was to cease forthwith [91]. From then on, no other mentions are found of Longquan firing official wares within the imperial records. Additionally, no archeological excavations have produced imperial quality Longquan Celadon produced after that time [92].

D. Qing Dynasty

From the middle of the Ming Dynasty, the Longquan Kilns steadily declined. By the end of the Ming and beginning of the Qing Dynasty, only 160 kilns were operating in the Longquan area. By the end of the Early Qing, there were 70 kilns remaining in operation. From this we can see that entering into the Qing Dynasty, Longquan did not cease to exist, but retained a certain production capacity. In the 1984 record of Zhejiang's Longquan County, it is written that from the time of the Qianlong Emperor through to the Republic Era, Longquan kilns continued to fire celadon that was consumed throughout China. Excavations from the 1980s further substantiate this. Kiln sites dated to the Qing Dynasty were found throughout the Butou Village, Sunkeng Village, Xitou Village, and surrounding areas, of which the Sunkeng Kiln was of most notable quality [93].

Housed in the British Museum is a celadon vase with the inscription "Chuzhou Prefecture, Longquan County… 24th year of the Daoguang Reign". This proves that even in to the Late Qing Dynasty, Longquan was still producing its celadon wares, but from that point on, the production steadily declined. Through this we can see that Longquan is indeed the longest continually producing kiln area in Chinese history.

Longquan Ware's Place in the Qing Dynasty Court

The use and or collection of Song Dynasty Longquan Celadon occurred throughout the lifetime of the Qing Dynasty Qianlong Emperor, and wares were found throughout areas where he spent much of his time. Additionally, Qianlong often called upon Song Longquan in his poetry. This goes to show that the Qing Court, specifically Qianlong himself, had a strong affinity towards Longquan Wares.

However, the Qing Dynasty court's affinity for celadon pieces made contemporary to their own dynasty paled in comparison to that of previous times. Yei Pei Lan introduced the entire collection of Qing Dynasty dated Longquan in the Palace Museum collection; they include pieces from Shunzhi, Kangxi to Qianlong, and Guangxu. However, the total number of pieces is incredibly small and their proportion amongst the collections' porcelain is miniscule [94].

2. Longquan Ware's Place Overseas

Longquan Celadon's important place in Chinese History is not only because of its domestic consumption, but also owes credit to its prowess abroad. The distance of its overseas reach, breadth of international consumption, sheer volume of production, and quality of wares is incomparable by most kilns within China [95].

A. Song Dynasty

From the very beginning of the Northern Song Dynasty, the court placed high importance on international trade. International trade governance was established, and the Southeastern coastal cities of Guangzhou, Mingzhou, Hangzhou, Quanzhou, and so forth were established as international trade centers. The Guangzhou trade center was established in 971 A.D., to be followed by the establishment of Hangzhou and Mingzhou. Quanzhou was then established in 1087 A.D. These cities were charged with maritime tariff collection, maritime trade, and management of incoming

队到达远东进行贸易。1599年，英国东印度公司成立。他们把数量巨大的瓷器运往他们本国或转卖至世界各地[113]。

龙泉青瓷在世界各地享有不同的称誉，如“麻尔达拔里”瓷器、“箇里”瓷器及“雪拉同”。据《马可波罗游记》载：元代至元十七年（公元1280年）到明代宣德十年（公元1435年）的一百五十余年间，福建泉州成为当时世界最大贸易港口之一。大量龙泉青瓷由泉州港运至世界各地。龙泉青瓷运至缅甸麻尔达海湾的麻尔达萌城（是东西各国海陆交通转运的中心点），所以龙泉青瓷又被称为“麻尔达拔里”瓷器。龙泉青瓷运往印度，是从波斯、阿富汗边境的箇尔城去的，所以又把龙泉青瓷叫做“箇里”瓷器[114]。欧洲将龙泉青瓷称为 Celadon（中文译名为“雪拉同”），传说是因为龙泉青瓷的釉色与欧洲戏剧《牧羊女亚司泰来》中男主角雪拉同的青色衣服颜色相近，所以当时的贵族阶级将其命名为“雪拉同”。

记录西方贸易的《葡萄牙王国记述》称中国龙泉青瓷“是人们所发明的最美丽的东西，看起来要比所有的金、银或水晶都更可爱”，可见龙泉青瓷在世界人民心中的地位[115]。

（四）其他

中国的龙泉青瓷经过数朝数代，以其玉质冰清的釉色受到世界人民的青睐和追捧。目前世界上已发现龙泉青瓷的国家及地区（出土或出水）包括：泰国、印度尼西亚、菲律宾、马来西亚、柬埔寨、缅甸、文莱、越南、日本、朝鲜、伊朗、黎巴嫩、伊拉克、阿富汗、土耳其、巴林岛、印度、斯里兰卡、马尔代夫、巴基斯坦、埃及、坦桑尼亚、阿拉伯联合酋长国、叙利亚、阿曼、也门、红海等[116]。龙泉青瓷的海外流传史也是一部中国古代对外贸易交流的发展史。

下面列举一些影响较大的国家与地区：

1. 东南亚

东南亚诸国地处东西贸易要道，与我国毗邻，在历史上的联系颇为密切，是龙泉青瓷外输的重点区域之一，东南亚几乎到处可见龙泉青瓷的踪迹。近年来在东南亚地区的一些陆地遗址以及相关海域的沉船遗址中发现了许多龙泉青瓷，发现龙泉青瓷的地点已经远远超过了文献记载，年代从南宋早期延续到明代中期。龙泉青瓷在东南亚地区的发现，一定程度上反映了历史上龙泉青瓷对该地输出的情况。印尼和泰国出土龙泉青瓷的陆地遗址较多，另外菲律宾、马来西亚、新加坡、柬埔寨、越南、文莱以及缅甸等国也有相当数量的龙泉青瓷出土[117]。

龙泉青瓷在东南亚的用途主要为生活用器、祭器、随葬器和陈设器等。其中将龙泉青瓷用作祭器，在泰国较多；将龙泉青瓷用作随葬器，在菲律宾较为普遍，但随着伊斯兰教的传入，龙泉青瓷被用作随葬器的逐渐减少；将龙泉青瓷用作陈设器，主要集中在东南亚上层社会。龙泉青瓷大量外输东南亚地区，对当地的制瓷手工业产生了很大的影响，许多国家也开始烧制本土青瓷，带动了青瓷在世界各地的销售和使用[118]（见本章第一节国外同类产品竞争部分）。

2. 土耳其

位于土耳其首都伊斯坦布尔的托普卡比皇宫中珍藏着一万多件中国古代瓷器，跨越了元、明、清三朝。皇宫所珍藏的中国古代瓷器不仅数量众多，造型和纹饰丰富，而且在时间跨度上反映了元至清以来六百年中国外销西亚的各式各类外销瓷器的全貌，是目前世界上关于中国古代瓷器收藏数量最大、品质最佳的博物馆之一[119]。其中有1350余件龙泉青瓷，大多数是元代和明代初期的产品。

这些来自中国的青瓷在奥斯曼人眼中是权势和财富的象征。据托普卡比皇宫档案记载，来自中国的珍贵的青瓷并不可以随便使用，而是专门用于苏丹登基、寿辰、大婚及其他重要庆典。为了装饰、保护和修缮中国瓷器，奥斯曼人会将宝石镶在瓷器上，或在破损瓷器上以镶金装银的方式来修补，表明龙泉青瓷在当时的珍贵程度[120]。

3. 欧洲

明代对外贸易中，欧洲各国一直是主要的海外出口地，约在明代中晚期，龙泉青瓷传入欧洲，价值昂贵，千金难求。1504年英国威尔海主教送给牛津新学院一件精美的青瓷碗，曾轰动英国，据说这是中国传到英国的第一件龙泉青瓷；法国路易十五和萨克森君王奥古斯特

tributes from various countries abroad [96].

The establishment of the Southern Song Dynasty saw an ever increasing importance placed on maritime trade, as it moved to the more rural reaches of Southern China and government funds were increasingly tight. Numerous official records record the importance of maritime trade in the governance of the Southern Song Dynasty [97].

Additionally, the Southern Song government strongly pushed development in the ship building industry; creating a fleet with the capacity to fare the open sea with the most advanced equipment of the day; greatly increasing maritime trade. Along with these advancements in shipbuilding and maritime travel techniques, the shipping industry and maritime trade abroad increased exponentially [98].

The record written by Zhao Ru Shi is the most detailed description of ceramic trade during the Song Dynasty. It records that China had entered trade arrangements of some sort with over 50 countries and regions across Asia, of which over 30 were involved in the trade of ceramics [99].

Many ancient cities and coastal areas across Asia and Africa have had discoveries of Chinese Song Dynasty ceramic shards [100]. One example is a piece of Early Southern Song Dynasty Longquan Celadon uncovered in the Northern reaches of Sumatra. From this we can tell that Longquan Celadon had already made its way to Southeast Asia as early as the Southern Song Dynasty. Late Southern Song Dynasty Longquan Celadon discoveries throughout Southeast Asia are numerous. Whether looking at quantity or quality, Late Southern Song wares far outreach those of the earlier periods. This goes to show the natural development of the Longquan Celadon industry throughout the Song Dynasty [101]. Aside from these, Song Dynasty Longquan shards have also been discovered in Japan, Pakistan, and the Korean Peninsula amongst others [102].

International trade brought about the flow of Chinese currency to markets abroad, as such a shortage of coinage within China occurred. To combat this, the edict was given that all trade should be made with porcelain as payment for foreign goods rather than gold, silver, or bronze coins. The porcelain to be used was Longquan Celadon [103].

B. Yuan Dynasty

Currently, of all Longquan Celadon discovered in archeological excavation overseas, the dates predominantly range from Southern Song to the Ming Dynasty, with the vast majority of productions falling within the Yuan to Mid Ming Dynasty periods [104]. The amount of Longquan Celadon to reach foreign markets was directly related to the foreign trade policy of each corresponding period. The loosening of foreign trade policy during the Yuan Dynasty led to the large expansion of Longquan Celadon production. Kiln site numbers, production capacity, variety, and volume all exceeded previous periods, and the production scale was the largest it would ever be.

The Yuan Dynasty represented the largest expansion in Chinese History, with the most expansive boundaries China has ever seen. It was under this societal structure of domestic supply to meet foreign demand, coupled with abundant natural recourses, development of waterway transportation, progression of ceramic techniques, and the Mongolian policies placing importance on foreign trade that Longquan Celadon exploded onto foreign markets [105].

In 1278 A.D., Kublai Khan put forth an edict to expand foreign trade. As they were a northern herding society, the Mongolians placed great importance on production trade. After the taking over of Central China, this did not change. Official records written in 1304 A.D. indicate that trade was taking place with 142 nations, and a record written 40 years later, of the trade from Quanzhou, included over 99 nations mentioned, some nations including over a hundred different sub-regions. These records have many mentions of "Celadon" and "Chuzhou Porcelain" going to foreign markets. Additionally, other records make regular mention of foreign porcelain trade during the Yuan Dynasty [106].

For many years, archeological excavation throughout West and South Asia have produced numerous discoveries of Yuan and Ming Longquan Wares, and many historical records have noted the presence of Chinese ceramics throughout West and South Asia. Excavations of the areas mentioned in records have almost all produced Longquan Celadon, and Yuan Dynasty records of trade, stated above, include mentions of

二世都喜爱和收藏龙泉青瓷；路易十五时期，法国洛可可风格盛行，流入欧洲的龙泉青瓷受到洛可可华丽、精致、繁琐的装饰风格影响，被改造成别具特色的洛可可青瓷，价值连城[121]。

龙泉青瓷自它登上世界陶瓷史的舞台，就扮演着文化使者的身份，并承担起传播陶瓷文明的重要使命。

三、总结

龙泉窑是一个庞杂、深厚的青瓷文化集成，既担当过官窑的角色，也是国内民窑的领头军。无论在造型还是装饰上都体现出传统思想、宫廷审美、民间文化的相互碰撞和相互影响。

龙泉青瓷为世界陶瓷文明所做出的丰功伟绩，使其成为目前人类非物质文化遗产代表作名录中手工技艺类的唯一陶瓷项目。它填补了人类非物质文化遗产代表作名录中陶瓷项目的空白，彰显了中华民族的文化，也标志着龙泉青瓷将背负更崇高的使命，步入新的发展里程。

Modern Day Malaysia, Philippines, and Indonesia [107].

In 1975, off the Southwestern Coast of Korea, a shipwreck dated to the Yuan Dynasty was discovered that contained over 10,000 pieces of ceramics, of which over 9,000 were Longquan Celadon [108]. In 1976, off the coast of Mokpo, South Korea, an additional shipwreck dated to the Yuan Dynasty was found containing over 3000 celadon wares and 2000 white glaze wares, predominantly of Longquan and Jingdezhen production [109]. Aside from the above mentioned, there are many other land and sea excavations with huge amounts of Longquan Celadon throughout all of Southeast Asia [110], further indicating the overwhelming volume of Yuan Dynasty Longquan trade in the area.

C. Ming Dynasty

The quality of Longquan Wares coming into the Early Ming Dynasty was still quite high, and held a dominant portion of international trade goods.

The renowned sea voyages of Zhenghe, imperial eunuch, during the early part of the Ming Dynasty marked the golden era of Chinese maritime trade. Starting during the Yongle reign in 1405 A.D., his seven voyages spanned over 28 years and reached well over 30 countries and went at least as far as the Red Sea and the eastern coast of Africa. Every voyage preparation included the amassing of huge amounts of porcelain, silk, and other precious domestic products. When these products reached foreign soil they acted as imperial gifts and trade goods; advancing the reach of Chinese ceramics to some of the furthest reaches of the globe including: Southeast Asia, South Asia, West Asia and Africa. Longquan Celadon was included in these huge stows of porcelain.

From archeological records we can find that Ming Dynasty Chinese ceramics have been excavated in places such as: Japan, The Korean Peninsula, The Philippines, Indonesia, Malaysian Peninsula, Indo-China Peninsula, The Indian Peninsula, North Africa (i.e. Egypt), East Africa (i.e. Kenya and Tanzania), and as far as South Central Africa (i.e. Botswana and Madagascar) [111].

According to historical account, in 1383 A.D. the Khmer Kingdom, in modern day Cambodia, sent delegates to pay homage to the Hongwu Emperor (The first of the Ming Dynasty). In return for their tribute, the Chinese emperor bestowed upon them over 19,000 items of porcelain and other goods. Three years later, porcelain tribute goods were again bestowed upon the Khmer Kingdom. In 1404 A.D., during the Yongle Reign, the king of the Ryuku Islands braved the seas in spite of maritime travel bans, to personally visit Chuzhou in search of Longquan Celadon for purchase. By the Xuande reign of the Ming Dynasty, Longquan Celadon had already been established as a world commodity. Toward the end of the Ming Dynasty, wares from Longquan's Anren and Dabaian as well as Chuzhou and Yongjia continued to be exported to the Southeast Asian Spice Islands and Sumatra in exchange for spices and other goods [112].

Direct Sino-European trade also commenced during the Ming Dynasty. In 1517 A.D. Portuguese arrived in Guangzhou and later established mercantile shops in Macau. In 1578 A.D., Dutch fleets sailed to the "Far East" to take part in foreign trade. In 1599 A.D., England established the East India Trading Company. They carried huge amounts of Chinese porcelain back to England and distributed them through other parts of the world [113].

Longquan Celadon received many names in different parts of the world that it reached. As recorded in Marco Polo's travel diary, from the 150 year span of 1280 A.D. (Yuan Dynasty) to 1435 A.D. (Ming, Xuande) Fujian Province's Quanzhou was one of the largest trade ports in the world. Huge amounts of Longquan Celadon flowed through the Quanzhou ports and sailed on to all corners of the trading world. From there, a substantial portion of the porcelain made its way to the Burmese city of Martaban and from there was break bulked and prepared for distribution to other markets. As such, it gained the name Martabanian porcelain. En route to India, Longquan Celadon left land from the city of Gwadar on the Persian-Afghan border also gaining it the name Gwadarian porcelain [114]. Europeans, however, adopted the name Celadon for this green glaze ware. Legend tells that it is because celadon glaze resembled the green color clothing of one of the main characters, Celadon, in the French novel L'Astree, thus earning it that name amongst nobility.

Written in the annals of the Portuguese King, Longquan Celadon was said to be the most beautiful thing imaginable in human history; more lovely than gold, silver, or crystal. From this we can see the sort of place Longquan Celadon held in the hearts of people throughout the world [115].

D. Other

China's Longquan Celadon has spanned across dynasties and centuries. Its fresh jade-like green glaze has captured the hearts of people throughout the world, and made it the desire of nations. Currently, the countries and regions that have excavated Longquan Celadon include: Thailand, Indonesia, The Philippines, Malaysia, Cambodia, Burma, Brunei, Vietnam, Japan, The Korean Peninsula, Iran, Lebanon, Iraq, Afghanistan, Turkey, Bahrain, India, Sri Lanka, Maldives, Pakistan, Egypt, Tanzania, UAE, Syria, Oman, Yemen, and the Red Sea, amongst others [116]. The history of Longquan Celadon's spread throughout the world is an important part of China's international trade history and development.

Below are a few countries and regions with a particularly large impact:

a. Southeast Asia

Southeast Asia was an important conduit for the flow of goods between the East and the West. It acted as an incredibly important middle ground and staging area for Chinese goods, and operated as one of the distribution hubs of Longquan Celadon. As such, Longquan Celadon can be found in almost every part of Southeast Asia. In recent years, excavations on land and in the sea throughout the region have produced copious amounts of Longquan examples, and the number of locations of actual discovery have greatly surpassed anything written in historical record. These pieces range in date from Early Southern Song Dynasty and continue through to Mid Ming Dynasty. The sheer volume of pieces that have been discovered throughout the region speak as to how important this area was within the market of Longquan Wares. With Indonesia and Thailand producing the largest numbers of excavation sites, places such as The Philippines, Malaysia, Singapore, Cambodia, Vietnam, Brunei and Burma also have relatively large amounts of discovered pieces [117].

The primary use of Longquan Wares throughout the Southeast Asian region included: Daily use, sacrificial, burial, and miscellaneous furnishings. Of these, sacrificial use items are found primarily throughout Thailand; burial items have been mainly discovered in The Philippines. With the spread of Islam came the decline of burial wares; and use of Longquan Celadon as furnishing and display items was predominantly seen within the home of the higher echelons of Southeast Asian Society. The huge amounts of Longquan Celadon that found its way to Southeast Asia created an enormous impact on the local ceramics industries. Many nations saw the establishment of local celadon firing, which brought on the world-wide spread, consumption and use of celadon porcelain [118] (See Similar Product Struggles in Section 1 of this chapter).

b. Turkey

Located in Istanbul,Turkey, the Topkapi Palace collection houses more than 10,000 pieces of Chinese porcelain dating from the Yuan, Ming, and Qing Dynasties. The palace collection not only houses an enormous amount of porcelain, but the multiplicity of types and time span covering over 600 years of Chinese exported porcelain to Western Asia helps to holistically create a snap shot of the entirety of exported porcelain. It is one of the largest and most important collections of Chinese porcelain in the world [119]. It contains around 1350 pieces of Longquan Celadon, predominantly dating from the Yuan and Early Ming periods.

Chinese celadon, in the eyes of the Ottoman Empire, was a symbol of power and wealth. According to official Topkapi Palace records, celadon was a valued treasure and could not be used for common occasions, but was reserved for important celebrations such as coronations, birthday celebrations, weddings and the like. In order to protect Chinese porcelain, the Ottomans would inlay the pieces with precious stones, and repair damaged pieces with inlays of gold or silver. This indicates the incredible importance that was placed on Longquan Celadon [120].

c. Europe

Throughout the majority of the Ming Dynasty, Europe was one of the most important markets for Chinese foreign trade. During the middle and late portions of the Ming Dynasty, Longquan Celadon arrived in Europe and was extremely valuable. In 1504 A.D., an English Admiral bestowed to the newly established Oxford University, a beautiful celadon bowl. It impacted the entire kingdom of England, as this bowl is rumored to have been the first ever piece of celadon to enter English borders. Both Louis XV and Augustine II loved Chinese celadon and kept pieces in their personal collections. During the Louis XV era, Rococo style was in vogue, and pieces of Longquan Celadon that entered Europe would be post fitted and adorned with decoration in the Rococo style, creating Rococo celadon, some of the most expensive wares in the world [121].

Ever since Longquan Celadon's emergence onto the world stage, it has held an important cultural role, and carried the important weight of spreading ceramic culture throughout the world.

3. Conclusion

Longquan Celadon is the complex and profound integration of celadon culture. It has taken on the role of official imperial porcelain, as well as being the broad shoulders bearing the consumerism of the popular Chinese market. Whether speaking of its shape or decoration, it has displayed the collision and impact of tradition, imperial aesthetic pursuits, and common popular culture.

Because of its impact on the world's ceramic culture, the Longquan Celadon craft is the only ceramic craft to be inducted to the United Nation's Non-Material Cultural Heritage List. This induction filled the gap of ceramic craft on the list of non-material cultural heritage, is the manifestation of Chinese culture on the list, and expresses the lofty mission Longquan Celadon has assumed along the road of continuous innovation.

第二章

明代浙江龙泉窑青瓷与广东余里窑青瓷类型研究

阅读提示：

2014年，广东省大埔县三河镇余里村发掘出四座明代青瓷窑址，并出土大量青瓷。经专家鉴定，余里窑青瓷无论从类型特征、化学成分还是烧制工艺方面都与浙江龙泉窑青瓷十分相似，属浙江龙泉窑系。本章从肉眼观察的角度，从青瓷的器型、装饰工艺、胎釉特征和制作工艺四个方面，分析比较明代浙江龙泉窑青瓷与广东余里窑青瓷的类型特征。

主要论述问题：

1. 明代浙江龙泉窑青瓷与广东余里窑青瓷主要都有哪些器型？
2. 明代浙江龙泉窑青瓷与广东余里窑青瓷在装饰工艺上有什么区别？
3. 明代浙江龙泉窑青瓷与广东余里窑青瓷的胎和釉各有什么不同？
4. 明代浙江龙泉窑青瓷与广东余里窑青瓷在制作工艺方面有什么差异？

Chapter 2

Typical Characteristics Study on Ming Dynasty Longquan Kiln System Celadon: Zhejiang Longquan Kiln and Guangdong Yuli Kiln Celadon

Text Note:

In 2014, Guangdong Dabu County Sanhe Town Yuli Village, four Ming Dynasty celadon kiln sites were excavated, and large amounts of celadon porcelain discovered. Experts have put forth, whether speaking of topological characteristics, chemical composition, or production techniques, these examples are highly related to Zhejiang Province Longquan Celadon; and belong to the Longquan Celadon System. This chapter takes a look at the four main facets that are observable to the naked eye: Shape, decoration, glaze and body characteristics, and techniques to analyse and depict the typical characteristics of Zhejiang Longquan Kiln and Guangdong Yuli Kiln Celadon.

第一节
明代浙江龙泉窑青瓷与广东余里窑青瓷器型比较分析

一、明代浙江龙泉窑青瓷器型类别

明代时期，浙江龙泉窑青瓷的器型类别主要可分为碗、杯、盘、碟、罐、瓶、尊、壶、炉及其他类别。其中每个类别中还有多个种类。

二、明代浙江龙泉窑青瓷器型表

器型类别	碗	杯	盘	碟	罐	瓶	壶	尊	炉	其他
器型种类	墩式碗	小杯	折沿盘	折沿碟	荷叶盖罐	梅瓶	执壶	凤尾尊	洗式炉	盆
	莲子碗	高足杯	折腹盘		双系小罐	玉壶春瓶		石榴尊	樽式炉	洗
	侈口碗	爵杯	侈口盘		带盖小罐	扁瓶（福寿瓶）			筒式炉	钵
	敞口碗		敞口盘		瓜棱罐	双耳瓶			鼎式炉	卷缸
	高足碗		荷叶形盘		直颈罐	八棱瓶			鬲式炉	花盆
					卵腹罐	葫芦瓶			熏炉	笔山
					长腹罐	长颈瓶				塑像
						筒瓶				烛台
										砚台
										砚滴
										绣墩
										器座
										盏托
										屏风
										觚
										笔筒
										渣斗
										簋
										粉盒
										油灯

三、明代浙江龙泉窑青瓷器型图集

（一）碗类

1. 墩式碗

墩式碗主要见于明代早期官窑器，直口，深壁，垂腹，丰底，矮阔圈足，故称作“墩式”。（见图2-1-1）

Section 1：

Comparative Analysis of Ming Dynasty Longquan Kiln System Celadon: Zhejiang Longquan Kiln and Guangdong Yuli Kiln Celadon Shapes

1. Ming Dynasty Zhejiang Longquan Kiln Celadon Shape Categories

Ming Dynasty Longquan Celadon shapes can primarily be split into the following categories: Bowl, Cup, Plate, Saucer, Jar, Vase, Zun, Kettle, Censer and Other. Each category can be further divided into types.

2. Table of Ming Dynasty Zhejiang Longquan Kiln Celadon Shape Categories

Categories	Bowl	Cup	Plate	Saucer	Jar	Vase	Kettle	Zun	Censer	Other
Types	Mound Bowl	Small Cup	Bent Rim Plate	Bent Rim Saucer	Lotus Lid Jar	Meiping (Plum Vase)	Ewer	Phoenix Tail Zun	Xi Shaped Censer	Basin
	Lotus Seed Bowl	Stem Cup	Bent Well Plate		Small Jar with Double Ringlets	Yuhuchun Vase		Pomegranate Zun	Zun Shaped Censer	Xi (Washer)
	Flared Mouth Bowl	Jue Cup	Flared Mouth plate		Small Lidded Jar	Flat Bodied Vase			Tong Shaped (Tubular) Censer	Earthen Bowl
	Open Mouth Bowl		Open Mouth Plate		Melon Shaped Jar	Double Handle Vase			Ding Shaped Censer	Cylinder
	Stem Bowl		Lotus Leaf Plate		Straight Neck Jar	Octagonal Vase			Li Shaped Censer	Planter
					Egg Shaped Jar	Hulu (Gourd) Vase			Incense Burner	Brush Stand
					Long Bodied Jar	Long Neck Vase				Figurines
						Cylinder Vase				Candle Holder
										Inkstand
										Water Dropper
										Lattice Stool
										Vessel Holders
										Cup Stand
										Screen
										Gu (Beaker)
										Pen Holder
										Residue Jar
										Gui Bowl
										Powder Box
										Lamp

图2-1-1

明代龙泉枫洞岩窑址出土了十余件墩式碗，其器型、装饰完全一致，制作精美，可推测其为官家定制[122]。

明洪武帝朱元璋在开国之初定下“祭器皆用瓷”的规矩，墩式碗是重要的祭祀器，用来盛羹[123]。

2. 莲子碗

莲子碗仅见于明永乐时期[124]，敞口，圆唇，弧腹，内底凹，外底微凸，圈足。（见图2-1-2）

图2-1-2

3. 侈口碗

此类碗侈口，圆唇，曲腹，圈足。（见图2-1-3）

图2-1-3

4. 敞口碗

此类碗敞口，圆唇，弧腹，圈足，内底平，外底尖凸。（见图2-1-4）

图2-1-4

5. 高足碗

高足碗为侈口，圆唇，深弧腹，高圈足微外撇。（见图2-1-5）

图2-1-5

（二）杯类

1. 小杯。

见图2-1-6。

图2-1-6

2. 高足杯

高足杯属于外来文化器型，应是受到了游牧民族文化的影响。游牧民族喜爱马上饮酒，高足易于抓握。

明代沿袭了这一器型，明早期高足杯大多数为侈口（见图2-1-7、图2-1-8），明中期多了八方形，口沿更加外撇。（见图2-1-9、图2-1-10）

图2-1-7

图2-1-8

图2-1-9

图2-1-10

3. Zhejiang Longquan Kiln Celadon Shape Image Catalogue

A. Bowls

a. Mound Bowl

Mound Bowls primarily appeared as official use items during the Early Ming Dynasty. They have a vertical rim, deep and rounded well, a broad base, and short round foot ring, earning it the name "Mound Style" (see picture 2-1-1).

There have been over 10 such bowls discovered at the Fengdongyan Kiln site in Dayao Longquan; the shapes and decorations of which are all entirely the same. Their composition is very fine, and it can be assumed that they were made specifically for official use [122].

The Hongwu Emperor, establisher of the Ming Dynasty, put forth a decree that all sacrificial wares should utilize porcelain. Mound Bowls were important sacrificial use items used for holding stews [123].

b. Lotus Seed Bowl

Lotus Seed Bowls were briefly seen during the Yongle reign of the Ming Dynasty [124]. They have an open mouth, rounded lip, arced well, concave inner base, slightly convex outer base, and foot ring (see picture 2-1-2).

c. Flared Mouth Bowl

This style of bowl has a flared rim, rounded lip, curved well, and round foot ring (see picture 2-1-3).

d. Open Mouth Bowl

This style of bowl has an open rim, round lip, arced well, foot ring, with a flat base and convex outer base (see picture 2-1-4).

e. Stem Bowl

Stem Bowls have a flared mouth, rounded lip, deeply arced well, with a tall round foot ring that slightly flares out at the base (see picture 2-1-5).

B. Cups

a. Small Cup

See picture 2-1-6.

b. Stem Cup

Stem cups are a shape from foreign origin, and most likely received the influence of herdsman culture, which played horseback drinking games, and as such the stem of the cup acted as a handle for better stability.

The Ming Dynasty saw the continuation of this shape. Early Ming Dynasty stem cups primarily have flared mouths (see pictures 2-1-7 and 2-1-8). Mid Ming Dynasty saw the addition of octagonal stem cups, with mouths even more flared (see pictures 2-1-9 and 2-1-10).

In the Ming Dynasty Fengdongyan Kiln excavation site, discoveries of vertical mouth (see picture 2-1-11) and open mouth varieties have been found (see picture 2-1-12).

c. Jue Cup

These are a type of wine vessel, and are also a replication of ancient bronze ware (see picture 2-1-13).

C. Plates

a. Bent Rim Plate

Flat rim plates have an outwardly bent mouth rim and can be split into two sub types: Straight Rim (see picture 2-1-14) and Foliated Rim (see picture 2-1-15); of which Foliated Rim is the more common.

These large plates (or chargers) were important sacrifice use items during the Early Ming Dynasty. They were primarily used to hold an assortment of sacrificial items, but could have also been utilized for an assortment of other uses [125].

b. Bent Well Plate

Bent Well Plates are commonly seen with foliated rims that flare outward. They have a concave well that is bent as it approaches the center. They have a foot ring (see pictures 2-1-

在明代枫洞岩窑址还发现有直口（见图2-1-11）及敞口（见图2-1-12）的类型。

图2-1-11

图2-1-12

3. 爵杯

爵杯属于酒具，也是仿青铜器具而来。（见图2-1-13）

图2-1-13

（三）盘类

1. 折沿盘

折沿盘的口沿向外翻折，折沿口有两种——直口（见图2-1-14）或菱口（见图2-1-15），其中菱口更常见。

图2-1-14

图2-1-15

大盘在明初也是重要的祭祀器，用来盛放各种祭祀物品。当然也不排除祭祀以外的其他用途[125]。

2. 折腹盘

折腹盘常见有菱口，口沿外撇，曲腹，下腹折收，圈足。（见图2-1-16、图2-1-17）

图2-1-16

图2-1-17

3. 侈口盘

此类盘侈口，圆唇，弧腹，下腹收，内底平，外底圆凸，圈足。（见图2-1-18）

图2-1-18

4. 敞口盘

此类盘敞口，圆唇，曲腹，浅阔圈足，外底心微凹。（见图2-1-19）

图2-1-19

5. 荷叶形盘

这类盘口沿呈荷叶形，口沿外

16 and 2-1-17).

c. Flared Mouth Plate

These plates have a flared mouth, rounded lip, reserved curved well, flat inner base, convex outer base, and foot ring (see picture 2-1-18).

d. Open Mouth Plate

This type includes an opened mouth, rounded lip, concave well, shallow and broad foot ring, with a slightly concave center on the outer base (see picture 2-1-19).

e. Lotus Leaf-Shaped Plate

These plate rims are lotus leaf shaped, with an outward flared mouth, rounded lip, slanted concave well, with a slightly concave center on the outer base and round foot ring (see picture 2-1-20).

D. Saucers

Bent Rim Saucer

These saucers have a foliated rim, flat mouth, slanted well, with a foot ring (see picture 2-1-21).

E. Jars

Jars, used as storage vessels, have been a representative shape since the first emergence of ceramic wares. Following the improvements in ceramic technology, the shapes of jars have undergone continual change [126].

The majority of Ming Dynasty Longquan Dayao Celadon jars have vertical mouths, short necks, and broad shoulders that taper towards the base. In general, the shoulders were free of handle decoration.

a. Lotus Lid Jar

Lotus lid jars were popular during the Yuan Dynasty, and were common during the Early Ming Dynasty. The shapes predominantly followed the suit of their predecessors. The pinnacle of the lotus lid could present with an unglazed lion, a jewel, or be flat (see picture 2-1-22).

b. Small Jar with Double Ringlets

These jars have vertical mouths, rounded lips, short necks, rounded shoulders, rotund bodies, and flat bases. The shoulders were often adorned with small ringlets (see picture 2-1-23).

c. Small Lidded Jar

These jars have a vertical mouth, rounded lip, short neck, slender shoulder, restrained body, and have a paired lid (see picture 2-1-24).

d. Melon-shaped Jar

These jars have a vertical mouth, rounded lip, short neck, slender shoulder, restrained body with ribbed melon-shaped exterior wall. They were sometimes paired with a lotus leaf lid (see picture 2-1-25).

e. Straight Neck Jar

These jars have a curled mouth, rounded lip, vertical neck, rounded shoulders, and rotund body with a slightly outward slanted foot ring (see picture 2-1-26).

f. Egg-Shaped Jar

These jars have a flared mouth, rounded lip, short neck, long ovular body, and foot ring (see picture 2-1-27).

g. Long Bodied Jar

These jars have a vertical mouth, rounded lip, short neck, broad shoulders, and long round body that tapers to a slightly outward flared foot (see picture 2-1-28).

F. Vases

a. Meiping (Plum Vase)

Meiping (plum vases) are a shape that was first fired during the Northern Song Dynasty. They have a small mouth, short neck, broad shoulders, and reportedly gained their name from having a mouth the size of a plum [127].

翻，圆唇，斜弧腹，外底心微凹，圈足。（见图2-1-20）

图2-1-20

（四）碟类

折沿碟

此类碟多见菱口，窄平沿，斜腹微弧，圈足。（见图2-1-21）

图2-1-21

（五）罐类

罐，作为盛储容器，从陶器出现时起就已成为一种代表器型。随着陶瓷烧制技术的提高，罐的形制也在不断变化[126]。

明代浙江龙泉窑青瓷的大罐多为直口，短颈，丰肩，腹以下渐收。通常肩部不见耳的装饰。

1. 荷叶盖罐

荷叶盖罐流行于元代，在明代中期多见，基本沿袭前朝风格。荷叶盖罐罐盖顶部有素胎狮纽、宝珠纽或平顶等形式。（见图2-1-22）

图2-1-22

2. 双系小罐

此类罐直口，圆唇，短颈，弧肩，鼓腹，平底，肩部有两个小系。（见图2-1-23）

图2-1-23

3. 带盖小罐

此类罐直口，圆唇，短颈，溜肩，束腹，配有盖。（见图2-1-24）

图2-1-24

4. 瓜棱罐

此类罐直口，短颈，溜肩，束腹，瓜棱壁，有的配有荷叶形盖。（见图2-1-25）

图2-1-25

5. 直颈罐

此类罐卷沿，圆唇，直颈，弧肩，鼓腹，圈足微外斜。（见图2-1-26）

图2-1-26

6. 卵腹罐

侈口，圆唇，短颈微束，长圆腹，圈足。（见图2-1-27）

图2-1-27

Comparatively, Song Dynasty Meiping were relatively thin and elegant (see picture 2-1-29). The Yuan and Ming Dynasties saw Meiping of more robust stature with broader shoulders and wider features in general. In general, the body tapering of Ming Meiping was more evident than their Yuan predecessors, with a smaller foot than the earlier versions (see pictures 2-1-30 and 2-1-31). Some of the Meiping that were excavated from the Fengdongyan Kiln site have matching lids (see pictures 2-1-32 and 2-1-33), and all vases would have had lids originally fitted to them.

b. Yuhuchun Vase

Yuhuchun vases were first fired during the Northern Song Dynasty [128]. They have a flared mouth, thin rounded neck, peach or pear shaped body, and foot ring. They were utilized for alcohol storage, floral vases, and sacrificial wares [129].

The Yuan Dynasty saw the standardization of the Yuhuchun shape, and the Ming shapes closely followed suit. The mouth was larger than the Song Dynasty variety (see picture 2-1-34), the neck longer, body more rotund, and were generally more stout. Compared to Yuan Yuhuchun vases (see picture 2-1-35), the Ming Dynasty versions have a shorter neck and fuller body (see picture 2-1-36).

c. Flat-Bodied Vase

These vases have a square mouth, protruding lip, long neck, two ringed handles, flat round body, and a slightly outward flaring foot ring (see picture 2-1-37).

d. Double Handle Vase

These vases have a flared mouth, rounded lip, restrained neck, double handles, smooth shoulders, obtusely rounded body, flared foot, and concave outer base (see picture 2-1-38).

e. Octagonal Vase

These vases have a flared mouth, rounded lip, short curved neck, broad shoulders, long rounded body, and is composed of eight sides arranged in an octagonal shape (see picture 2-1-39).

f. Hulu (Gourd) Vase

Hulu Vases are in the shape of the hulu gourd, which is one of the auspicious items of Taoist lore that is a close homophone to the Chinese words for wealth and longevity. As such, since the Tang Dynasty, it has been a traditional shape [130] (see picture 2-1-40).

G. Kettles

Ewer

Ewers are an alcohol storage vessel that first appeared during the Sui Dynasty. The Ming and Qing Dynasties saw an expansion in kettle shapes, and the introduction of kettles being used as tea set pieces [131].

Yuhuchun vase shaped ewers were commonly produced as Early Ming Dynasty official wares; one side being adorned with a long curved handle and the other with a pouring spout (see pictures 2-1-41 and 2-1-42). The shapes of kettles in the Mid Ming Dynasty became more abundant, with the mouths becoming wider and bodies more rotund (see pictures 2-1-43 and 2-1-44). There were also melon shaped kettles (see picture 2-1-45).

H. Zun

a. Phoenix Tail Zun

Phoenix Tail Zun are also called peony vases due mainly to the fact that their main decoration motif was peony scrolls (they can also present with chrysanthemums scrolls or lotus scrolls, but peonies scrolls where the most common). Phoenix Tail Zun were created in the Longquan Kiln during the Yuan Dynasty, and became very popular during the Ming Dynasty [132] (see pictures 2-1-46—2-1-50).

From historical records and collections we can see that the firing of Ming Dynasty Longquan Kiln Phoenix Tail Zun, speaking of volume or influence, overtook that of the Yuan Dynasty. Firstly, the Ming Dynasty saw the popularized use of Phoenix Tail Zun as sacrificial use items. Aside from the peony vases given to temples, they were also used as vessels

7. 长腹罐

此类罐直口，圆唇，短直颈，丰肩，弧腹，下腹收，圈足外撇。（见图2-1-28）

图2-1-28

（六）瓶类

1. 梅瓶

梅瓶是北宋创烧的一种瓶式。小口、短颈、丰肩，因“口径之小仅与梅之瘦骨相称”而得名[127]。

相对于宋代梅瓶的修长秀美（见图2-1-29），元代和明代的梅瓶更为雄壮，肩部更丰满，胫部和底足也更宽。大部分明代梅瓶的腹部收束比元代更明显，圈足也比元代梅瓶要小。（见图2-1-30、图2-1-31）明代龙泉枫洞岩窑址出土有梅瓶瓶盖（见图2-1-32、图2-1-33），当时的梅瓶都应配有盖。

图2-1-29

图2-1-30

图2-1-31

图2-1-32

图2-1-33

2. 玉壶春瓶

玉壶春瓶是北宋时创烧的一种瓶式[128]。撇口，细弧颈，桃形或梨形腹，圈足。玉壶春瓶具有酒器、插花、祭祀等多个功能[129]。

元代是玉壶春瓶形制标准化时期，明代玉壶春瓶基本沿袭了元代的风格，口部较宋代（见图2-1-34）更大，颈部更细长，腹部更突出，整体比例更加协调端庄。与元代玉壶春瓶（见图2-1-35）相比，明代颈短腹丰的特征更加明显（见图2-1-36）。

图2-1-34

图2-1-35

图2-1-36

for displaying plum blossoms. This combination was loved by people of the Ming Dynasty [133].

Historical records show that during the Ming Dynasty there were certain customs for displaying flowers, and it was written that in the winter one must use "Large Longquan Vases" for the display of plum blossoms. These large vases mentioned would have been a 60 to 70 cm Phoenix Tail Zun. Thus we can see that the peony vases of the Ming Dynasty were much larger than during the Yuan. It was also recorded that in the winter time when displaying flowers, due to the cold weather, a thicker porcelain body must be used otherwise cracking can occur. As such the Ming Dynasty saw the use of thicker body porcelain in Phoenix Tail Zun.

The bodies of the Phoenix Tail Zun during the Ming Dynasty were composed of several different sections. Specifically, the body was composed of a top and bottom section connected together; this was not seen during the Yuan Dynasty. Some have clearly alleviated discrepancy between a smaller top and larger bottom section that looks like a smaller vase placed inside a larger vase (see pictures 2-1-47 and 2-1-50). These changes in design, aside from being easier to fire, also helped the function of cold weather expansion, and go to show the innovation during the Ming Dynasty in firing Phoenix Tail Zun [134].

b. Pomegranate Zun

Pomegranate Zun were first fired during the Xuande Reign of the Ming Dynasty, with a shape that resembles a pomegranate [135] (see picture 2-1- 51).

I. Censers

Censers are used for the burning of incense, and were utilized as sacrificial items [136].

a. Xi-Shaped Censer

These censers often have an inverted mouth, rotund body, and three feet (see pictures 2-1-52 and 2-1-53).

b. Zun-Shaped Censer

This shape of censer originated during the Han Dynasty. They often have a vertical mouth, flat rim, vertical body, and flat base with three feet. On larger pieces, the bottom often has a hole in the center, and smaller pieces do not present with such hole (see pictures 2-1-54—2-1-56).

c. Tong-Shaped Censer

This is a variation of the Zun Censer, and is also held up by three feet; the vessel mouth and feet having almost identical diameter [137] (see pictures 2-1-57—2-1-59).

d. Ding-Shaped Censer

This censer is a replication of a bronze ceremonial ware shape (see pictures 2-1-60 and 2-1-61).

e. Li-Shaped Censer

This style of censer is a replication of a Shang and Zhou Dynasty bronze ceremonial ware shape (see picture 2-1-62).

J. Other

a. Basin

Basins normally have a bent rim, deep curved well, shallow foot ring, flat inner base, and slightly concave outer base (see pictures 2-1-63 and 2-1-64).

b. Xi (Washer)

These are a washing vessel and used similar to a basin, they have a foliate mouth (see pictures 2-1-65 and 2-1-66) or inverted mouth (see picture 2-1-67).

c. Earthen Bowl

See picture 2-1-68.

d. Cylinder

See picture 2-1-69.

e. Planter

See pictures 2-1-70 and 2-1-71.

f. Brush Stand

See picture 2-1-72.

3. 扁瓶（福寿瓶）

此类瓶方口，凸唇，长颈，双耳勾圆环，扁圆腹，圈足微外撇。（见图2-1-37）

图2-1-37

4. 双耳瓶

此类瓶撇口，圆唇，束颈，双耳，溜肩，扁圆垂腹，圈足外撇，外底凹。（见图2-1-38）

图2-1-38

5. 八棱瓶

侈口，圆唇，短颈微束，丰肩，长圆腹，瓶壁呈八棱状。（见图2-1-39）

图2-1-39

6. 葫芦瓶

葫芦瓶形似葫芦，是道教的灵物之一，唐代以来因谐音似“福禄”，逐渐成为传统器型[130]。（见图2-1-40）

图2-1-40

（七）壶类

执壶

执壶是隋代出现的酒器之一，又称注子、注壶。明清以后，执壶造型增多，也作为茶具[131]。

玉壶春瓶形的执壶多为明早期的官窑器型，一侧以板状流云衔接曲流，另侧按绶带弯柄（见图2-1-41、图2-1-42）；明中期的执壶体型更丰满，口沿增大，腹部鼓起（见图2-1-43、图2-1-44）；还有瓜棱形制的（见图2-1-45）。

图2-1-41

图2-1-42

图2-1-43

图2-1-44

图2-1-45

g. Figurines

Figurines were most commonly seen during the Mid Ming Dynasty. They could be completely covered with glaze (see pictures 2-1-73 and 2-1-74) or with the face and hands unglazed, with lifelike facial features clearly visible (see picture 2-1-75).

h. Candle Holders

Mid Ming Dynasty saw the increase of lampstand styles and varieties (see pictures 2-1-76—2-1-80).

i. Inkstand

See pictures 2-1-81 and 2-1-82.

j. Water Dropper

See pictures 2-1-83 and 2-1-84.

k. Lattice Stool

Lattice stools were a seating furniture that were first fired during the Yuan Dynasty, and popularized during the Ming and Qing Dynasties. The Ming Dynasty stools had a notably convex seating surface (see picture 2-1-85).

l. Vessel Holders

See pictures 2-1-86 and 2-1-87.

m. Cup Stand

See pictures 2-1-88—2-1-90.

n. Screen

See picture 2-1-91.

o. Gu (Beaker)

The Gu or Beaker first appeared during the Early Shang Dynasty. They have a trumpet mouth, a thin body with tall stature, and flat base (see picture 2-1-92).

During the Song Dynasty there was a cultural renaissance which saw the use of the bronze ware Gu as an elegant and high-class item used for decoration and floral display. It was under this influence that the Gu began to be used as a ceramic shape [138].

The Ming Dynasty did not see much change to the shape of the Gu: Trumpet mouth, thin body, and foot ring. Sometimes the neck and leg portion of the Gu would be adorned with flanges (see picture 2-1-93).

4. Ming Dynasty Zhejiang Longquan Kiln Celadon Shape Style Analysis

The porcelain body of Ming Dynasty Zhejiang Longquan Celadon was comparatively thick. Compared to that of the Song and Yuan Dynasties, the porcelain was not as refined in general [139]. The shapes of daily use items were quite simplistic, and follow the style of earlier dynasties. Primarily seen were bowls, bent rim plates, Xi (washers), stem cups, and censers [140].

A. Primary Shapes of the Early Ming Dynasty

The most common shapes of the early Ming Dynasty include: bowls, plates, basins, stem cups, jars, vessel holders, cup holders, lampstands, candle holders, ink stands, earthen bowls, ewers, Meiping (with lids), Yuhuchun vases, censers, planters, and powder boxes [141].

Wares from this time period were comparatively thick. Bowls, plates, and so forth pieces primarily present with a concave outer base. Large pieces usually present with a broad foot ring that is comparatively flat. Small pieces have a relatively narrow foot that have a glazed foot ring, and on bent rim plates a slightly convex circular foot ring was most common [142].

B. Official Use Shapes of the Early Ming Dynasty

Official wares from the early Ming Dynasty had shapes that were specifically calculated and precisely executed.

Official wares from the Hongwu reign period include: Mound bowls, stem bowls, foliate mouth plates, bent rim plates, five-claw dragon plates, ewers, Meiping, and

（八）尊类

1. 凤尾尊

龙泉窑凤尾尊也叫牡丹瓶，以主题纹饰多为缠枝牡丹而得名（也有饰缠枝菊纹或缠枝莲纹者，牡丹瓶只是一种习惯上的泛称）。凤尾尊是元代龙泉窑新创的品种，流行于元明[132]。（见图2-1-46—图2-1-50）

从文献及传世收藏情况来看，明代龙泉窑凤尾尊的烧造量及其影响力较之元代有过之而无不及。首先，明代流行使用凤尾尊作为供器，但除了供于寺庙外，它还有一个重要用途是作为陈设瓷来插梅花。腊梅和龙泉大瓶，曾是明代人所钟爱的搭配[133]。高濂（公元1573—1620）《遵生八笺》“论诸品窑器”中提到“（龙泉窑）立地插梅大瓶，诸窑所无”；又“瓶花三说・瓶花之宜”谓：“冬时插梅必须龙泉大瓶……高三四尺以上，投以硫磺五六钱，砍大枝梅花插供，方快人意。”明代牡丹瓶在形制上普遍比元时更大，高濂提到的龙泉大瓶就应是尺寸高达六七十厘米的凤尾尊。“冬间插花，畏冰冻，瓶质厚者尚可，否则破裂”，所以明代凤尾尊胎体更为厚重。

明代凤尾尊器身分多个部分拼合，其中腹部为上下两段拼合，此为创新，元代没有。有的上下段上小下大十分明显，看似小瓶套于大瓶（见图2-1-47、图2-1-50）。这些设计的改进除了方便成型，还能经受热胀冷缩的考验，体现了明代凤尾尊在制作工艺上的进步[134]。

图2-1-46

图2-1-47

图2-1-48

图2-1-49

图2-1-50

2. 石榴尊

石榴尊始见于明宣德时期，器型类似石榴果实[135]。（见图2-1-51）

图2-1-51

（九）炉类

炉属于焚香用具，也可用作陈设供奉之用[136]。

1. 洗式炉

此类炉通常都是敛口，鼓腹，三足。（见图2-1-52、图2-1-53）

图2-1-52

Yuhuchun vases [143].

Official wares from the Yongle Reign Period were comparatively small to those of the Hongwu period, They include: Mound bowls, lotus seed bowls, washers, five-claw dragon plates, stem cups, Meiping, Yuhuchun vases, and ewers [144].

C. Primary Shapes of the Mid Ming Dynasty

Shapes from the Mid Ming Dynasty include: Flared mouth bowls, open mouth bowls, open mouth lotus petal bowls, plates, saucers with foot ring, basins, planters, lidded jars, ewers, Meiping, Yuhuchun vases, flat-bodied vases, fish handle vases, square vases, Phoenix Tail Zun, jue cups, tong-shaped censers, zun-shaped censers, xi-shaped censers, latticed vessel stands, cylinders, kettles, cup stands, stem cups, candle holders, earthen bowls, shuizhu ewers (water pourer), figurines, Meiping lids, lotus leaf lids, unglazed lion handle lids, octagonal lids, foliated lids, and so forth [145].

An innovation of the Mid Ming Dynasty was the introduction of forming pieces using molds, the shapes include: Yuhuchun vases, lidded jars, lids, saucers, flat-bodied vases, fish handle vases, square vases, jue cups, tong-shaped censers and so forth. Flared mouth bent rim plates, xi (washer), tong-shaped censers, flat-bodied vases, and unglazed lion handle lids where the most popular items during this time, and were pieces that were not seen in the Early Ming Dynasty. Candle holders, vases, lids, stem cups, and so forth items came in many shapes, types, and varieties [146].

D. Primary Shapes of the Late Ming Dynasty

The late Ming Dynasty saw the use of primarily bowls, cups, plates, saucers, zun, earthen bowls, jars, kettles, vases, cylinders, censers, stem cups, pestles, water pourers, and so forth vessels; with large items relatively uncommon. The use of molds in shape forming became very widespread, the shapes included bowls, plates, cups, saucers, and so forth [147].

5. Ming Dynasty Guangdong Yuli Kiln Celadon Shape Categories

The primary categories of vessel shapes of Ming Dynasty Guangdong Yuli Kiln Celadon include: Bowls, cups, plates, saucers, jars, vases, kettles, censers and other.

6. Table of Ming Dynasty Guangdong Yuli Kiln Celadon Shape Categories

Categories	Bowl	Cup	Plate	Saucer	Jar	Vase	Kettle	Censer	Other
Types	Flared Mouth Bowl	Small Cup	Bent Rim Plate	Open Mouth Saucer	Small Jar	Double Handle Vase	Ewer	Zun Shaped Censer	Inkstand
	Open Mouth Bowl	Dou (Bean Shaped) Cup	Bent Well Plate	Bent Well Saucer	Lidded Jar	Straight Neck Vase		Incense Burner	Brush Stand
	Vertical Rim Bowl	Stem Cup	Open Mouth Plate	Flared Mouth Saucer					Vessel Holders
	Flower Mouth Bowl		Chrysanthemum Rim Plate						Candle Holder
	Bent Well Bowl		Octagonal Plate						Lamp Stand
									Water Dropper

图2-1-53

图2-1-56

2. 樽式炉（奁式炉）

樽式炉源于汉代的奁，所以也叫奁式炉，通常都是直口，平沿，直腹，饼底，三足。较大型者底心大多有一孔，较小者则多数没有孔。（见图2-1-54—图2-1-56）

图2-1-54

图2-1-55

3. 筒式炉

筒式炉源于樽式炉，三足支撑。炉口、底直径几乎相等[137]。（见图2-1-57—图2-1-59）

图2-1-57

图2-1-58

图2-1-59

4. 鼎式炉

鼎式炉是仿青铜礼器鼎的形状。（见图2-1-60、图2-1-61）

图2-1-60

图2-1-61

5. 鬲式炉

鬲式炉是仿商周时期青铜礼器鬲而作。（见图2-1-62）

图2-1-62

7. Ming Dynasty Guangdong Yuli Kiln Celadon Shape Categories Image Catalogue

A. Bowls

Bowls were one of the most common shape found at Guangdong Yuli Kiln. There are many excavated samples which in general the variety of shapes is not very large, and can be divided into the following types:

a. Flared Mouth Bowl

This type of bowl has a flared mouth, rounded lip, curved well, and round foot ring. They are primarily the same as the flared mouth bowls of Zhejiang Longquan (see picture 2-1-94).

b. Open Mouth Bowl

These bowls have an open rim, curved well, and round foot ring. There are several differences in the foot ring: Some with a small foot ring in which the foot wall is thick and has a trapezoidal cross-section; others have a large foot ring and the cross-section is straight and thin; still others have a high straight foot ring (see pictures 2-1-95—2-1-98).

c. Vertical Rim Bowl

This type of bowl has a vertical rim, round lip, straight slanted well, and round foot ring (see picture 2-1-99).

d. Flower Rim Bowl

This type of bowl has a flower rim, flat brim, straight well, and round foot ring (see pictures 2-1-100 and 2-1-101).

e. Bent Well Bowl

See picture 2-1-102.

B. Cups

a. Small Cup

Small cups can further be divided into three varieties: open mouth, flared mouth, and straight mouth; they all have a round foot ring.

Some open mouth small cups present with a curved well (see picture 2-1-103), while others present with a straight well (see picture 2-1-104).

The majority of the sample selection included flared mouth small cups, with shapes that were primarily the same; with straight slanted well that is comparatively deep. Only the foot section presented with dissimilarities, some having a round internally concave cake foot, the foot slanted and thick with a small bump in the center; others present with a short round foot ring that has a thin rectangular cross section (see picture 2-1-105).

Vertical mouth cups had a well that is straight and shallow. The well of the bowl is relatively thin, and the base and foot of the bowl is comparatively thick (see picture 2-1-106).

b. Dou (Bean-shaped) Cup

Theses bowls have an inverted rim, an arced well, and a trumpet-shaped solid foot. The foot base can have a concave conical shape, or have a carved round foot ring (see picture 2-1-107).

c. Stem Cup

Stem cups have a vertical mouth (see picture 2-1-108), or an open mouth (see pictures 2-1-109 and 2-1-110).

The cup stems can present as smooth, with bamboo joints, or with two rings. The foot base flares outward in a trumpet shape, and the foot interior is carved out as a foot ring, or can present with a conical shape.

C. Plates

a. Bent Rim Plate

The mouth rim of a bent rim plate is externally bent and flat, it has a shallow well, and a round foot ring. Bent rim plates came in two varieties: straight mouth (see pictures 2-1-111 and 2-1-112), and foliated mouth (see pictures 2-1-113 and 2-1-114).

（十）其他

1. 盆

盆类通常都是折沿，深弧腹，浅圈足，内底平，外底心微凹。（见图2-1-63、图2-1-64）

图2-1-63

图2-1-64

2. 洗

盥洗用具，作用与盆类似，有葵口（见图2-1-65、图2-1-66），有敛口（见图2-1-67）。

图2-1-65

图2-1-66

图2-1-67

3. 钵

见图2-1-68。

图2-1-68

4. 卷缸

见图2-1-69。

图2-1-69

5. 花盆

见图2-1-70、图2-1-71。

图2-1-70

图2-1-71

6. 笔山

见图2-1-72。

图2-1-72

b. Open Mouth Plate

This type of plate has an open mouth, round lip, shallow well, and round foot ring (see picture 2-1-115).

c. Chrysanthemum Rim Plate

This type of plate has a broader rim, shallow well, and round foot ring (see picture 2-1-116).

d. Bent Well Plate

Bent well plates have a large flared mouth, shallow well, round foot ring, with the internal well drastically inclined and a clearly delineated bend between the upper well and the inner base. As such, it assumes a general trumpet shape (see pictures 2-1-117 and 2-1-118).

e. Octagonal Plate

Octagonal or multiple angle piece shapes were common amongst Longquan Celadon during the Southern Song Dynasty. Their popularity continued into the Yuan Dynasty, but dwindled during the Ming Dynasty. Octagonal plates have an eight sided rim, shallow well, and round foot ring (see picture 2-1-119).

D. Saucers

a. Open Mouth Saucer

This type of saucer has an open mouth, rounded well, round foot ring, and flat inner base. Some have a round lip (see pictures 2-1-120 and 2-1-121).

b. Bent Well Saucer

Bent well saucers have a large flared mouth, shallow well, and short foot ring. The internal well has a steep decline, and has a clearly delineated bend between the well and the base. As such, it assumes a general trumpet shape (see pictures 2-1-122 and 2-1-123).

c. Flared Mouth Saucer

Flared Mouth saucers have a clearly flared rim, slanted well, flat foot, and a flat inner base (see picture 2-1-124).

E. Jars

a. Small Jar

Small jars often present with a vertical mouth (see pictures 2-1-125 and 2-1-126), or an inverted mouth (see picture 2-1-127).

b. Lidded Jar

See picture 2-1-128.

F. Vases

a. Double Handle Vase

Double handle vases have a flared mouth, long neck, flat shoulders, tapered body, and trumpet-shaped foot that turns vertically downward near the base. Either side of the neck presents with ‘S’ shaped handles and the vase is not hollow (see picture 2-1-129).

b. Long Neck Vase

See picture 2-1-130.

G. Kettles

See picture 2-1-131.

H. Censers

a. Zun Censer

These censers have a flat rim, slanted body, small cake-like base, and three feet. They come in a variety of sizes, and the cake face is often one layer, with some presenting with two or three layers. A portion of the cake bases present with a hole in the center. The feet usually present as hooves, a small portion present as a simplified ruyi shape, and some can present as beast feet (see pictures 2-1-132—2-1-134).

7. 塑像

塑像更多见于明中期，有满釉（见图2-1-73、图2-1-74），也有脸部及手部露胎，五官清晰可见，栩栩如生。（见图2-1-75）

图2-1-73

图2-1-74

图2-1-75

8. 烛台

明中期开始烛台样式更多样化，品种较多。（见图2-1-76—图2-1-80）

图2-1-76

图2-1-77

图2-1-78

图2-1-79

图2-1-80

9. 砚台

见图2-1-81、图2-1-82。

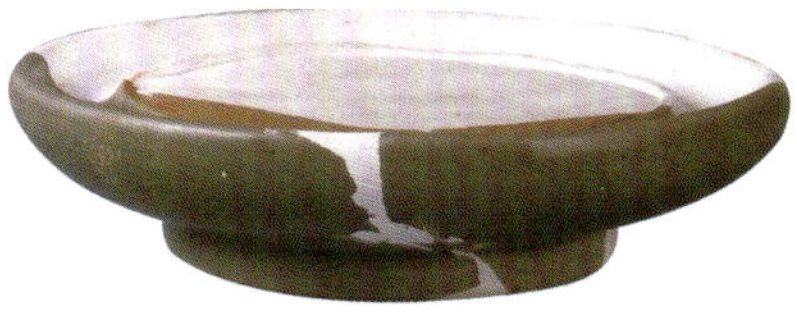

图2-1-81

图2-1-82

10. 砚滴

见图2-1-83、2-1-84。

图2-1-83

b. Incense Burner

The sample selections found, only the base section of this shape exist. It has a round cylindrical shape, flat face, and round foot ring. The base has a long rectangular-shaped hole, and the censer body has four holes on each side (see picture 2-1-135).

I. Other

a. Inkstand

Inkstands have a round shape, arced exterior wall, and round foot ring. The stand face is wide and flat surrounded by a concave trough (see picture 2-1-136).

b. Brush Stand

See picture 2-1-137.

c. Vessel Holder

There was only one such piece excavated at the site. It has an inverted mouth, flat, shallow well, and trumpet-shaped foot with hollow center. This vessel stand is made of clay and is unglazed (see picture 2-1-138).

d. Candle Holder

The upper portion of the lampstand sample has been damaged and only the lamp base remains. The base is solid, foliated, with a slanted body that tapers towards a round foot ring (see picture 2-1-139).

e. Lampstands

Many such samples were excavated, but the shapes are all the same. They have a round lip, arced well, with a small dimple in the center of the flat base. The internal well has a half circle fastened to it that protrudes from the wall of the well used for placement of the wick (see pictures 2-1-140 and 2-1-141).

f. Water Dropper

See picture 2-1-142.

8. Ming Dynasty Guangdong Yuli Kiln Celadon Shape Style Analyses

The amount of varieties of vessel shapes found at the Ming Dynasty Guangdong Yuli Kiln excavation was relatively small, and consisted primarily of small pieces and a few large pieces. Of these, they primarily consisted of daily use items such as bowls, plates, and saucers.

Bowls primarily consisted of flared mouth and vertical mouth; plates primarily consisted of flat rim varieties; and saucers were primarily flared mouth with a concave exterior base, and no foot ring.

9. Conclusion

The varieties of Zhejiang Longquan Celadon are much more numerous, and do not only include daily use items but also decorative items as well. The amount of shape categories was much more abundant than those of Guangdong Longquan Celadon, and there is a clear discrepancy in quality.

The primary category composition of the excavations at Guangdong Yuli Kiln consisted of daily use items. There were relatively few categories, and the shapes were primarily uniform, with small pieces making up the majority, and large pieces rarely seen. Large plates, lattice vessel holders, Meiping, large jars, Yuhuchun vases, and so forth large items that were popularly produced at Longquan Fengdongyan Kiln were not seen at the Yuli Kiln site in Guangdong.

There are some similarities between pieces found at each location, of which a few simple examples will be used for comparison:

The bowl shapes found at the Yuli Kiln site can all be seen at the excavation sites in Longquan, but the variety is less robust than that of Longquan.

Stem cups were a new shape introduced during the Yuan Dynasty at Longquan Kilns. Their mouths were slightly flared out with a body that closely resembled a half globe and a short stem. Entering the Ming Dynasty, the mouth diameter decreased and the well deepened with an introduction of a bamboo joint stem. Stem cups were a common shape found at the Yuli Kiln site, and the styles were very similar to that

图2-1-84

11. 绣墩

绣墩是一种坐具。瓷质绣墩始见于元，流行于明清，明代墩顶普遍隆起。（见图2-1-85）

图2-1-85

12. 器座

见图2-1-86、图2-1-87。

图2-1-86

图2-1-87

13. 盏托

见图2-1-88—图2-1-90。

图2-1-88

图2-1-89

图2-1-90

14. 屏风

见图2-1-91。

图2-1-91

15. 觚

青铜觚出现于商代早期，喇叭口，细腰，高身，平底。（见图2-1-92）

宋代金石学兴起，青铜觚成为文人雅士鉴赏与把玩的雅物，被用作陈设品和插花器。在这种风气影响下，陶瓷中开始出现觚造型[138]。

明代的觚在整体造型上没有太大变化：撇口、细身、圈足，颈部及胫部有时装饰出戟。（见图2-1-93）

图2-1-92

of Longquan Kiln. One of the differences being that the Longquan variety included a protruding lip (see picture 2-1-143) and the Yuli variety has a vertical rim (see picture 2-1-144).

The shapes of plates found at the Yuli Kiln site are very similar to those of Fengdongyan. For example: Broad rim arced well plates, open rim arced well plates, bent well plates, flower rim plates, and so forth. However, the shape and decoration quality of the Yuli examples are relatively simple, and do not come close to those from the Longquan Kilns.

Foliated rim, being the most common of the Longquan flower mouth varieties (see picture 2-1-145), gained popularity during the Early Song Dynasty which continued through the Ming Dynasty. Aside from the foliated rim of the wares found at Fengdongyan, the inner wall of the wares also included floral ribbing; while the Yuli Kiln examples only included a foliated rim, and the interior wall was left unformed (see picture 2-1-146). Similarly, the chrysanthemum rim plates at the Yuli Kiln have only a foliate mouth, and smooth interior wall (see picture 2-1-147).

Censers at the Longquan Kiln came in a large assortment of shapes and sizes. They include: Zun-shaped, xi-shaped, li-shaped, drum-shaped, and so forth censer shapes. The most popular foot styles were hooves, beast, and ruyi style. The censers excavated from Yuli were comparatively simplistic in variety, with Zun-shaped censers being the most common. The three feet varieties seen in Longquan can all be found on Yuli pieces, but the most common was the hoof shape.

To conclude, all the varieties and shapes excavated in Guangdong Yuli Kiln can be seen in the Zhejiang Longquan Kilns, but their types are less abundant. Moreover, the commonly seen shapes of washers, cups and so forth shapes with complex decoration and abundant varieties have yet to be found at the Yuli Kiln site. The shapes from the Yuli excavation are generally more simplistic. Aside from a few examples of foliated round wares, the pieces are quite modest in shape, and there is a lack of life-like or ancient shape replications.

图2-1-93

四、明代浙江龙泉窑青瓷器型风格分析

明代的浙江龙泉窑瓷器胎体厚重，相对南宋及元代，瓷器整体造型制作不够细致[139]。日用瓷的器型趋于单调，仍沿袭前朝风格，多见碗、折沿盘、洗、高足杯、炉[140]。

（一）明早期主要器型

明早期的主要器型有碗、盘、盆、高足杯、罐、器座、盏托、灯盏、烛台、砚台、碾钵、执壶、梅瓶（带盖）、玉壶春瓶、樽式炉、洗式炉、花盆、粉盒等[141]。

这个时期的青瓷造型厚重。碗、盘等圈足外底心多内凹，大型器物足壁较宽，足端较平；小型器物足壁较窄，足端裹釉稍圆[142]。

（二）明早期官窑主要器型

明早期官窑器物大都器型规整，制作精良。

洪武官器有墩式碗、高足碗、菱口盘、折沿盘、五爪龙纹盘、执壶、梅瓶、玉壶春瓶等[143]。

永乐官器尺寸相对于洪武官器偏小，有墩式碗、莲子碗、洗、五爪龙纹盘、高足杯、梅瓶、玉壶春瓶、执壶等[144]。

（三）明中期主要器型

明中期的器型有侈口碗、敞口碗、敞口莲瓣碗、盘、圈足盏、碟、盆、仰盅式花盆、盖罐、执壶、梅瓶、玉壶春瓶、福寿瓶、鱼耳瓶、方瓶、凤尾尊、爵杯、筒式炉、樽式炉、洗式炉、镂空器座、卷缸、投壶、盏托、高足杯、菇芯烛台、高圈足烛台、碾钵、水注、塑像、梅瓶盖、荷叶形盖、素胎狮钮盖、八角形盖、菱口形盖等[145]。

明中期创新，有的器物可整体模制，器型有玉壶春瓶、盖罐、器盖、碟、福寿瓶、鱼耳瓶、方瓶、爵杯、筒式炉等。撇口折沿盘、洗、筒式炉、福寿瓶、素胎狮钮盖等为这段时期的主流产品，这些器物都不见于明早期。烛台、瓶、器盖、高足杯等形式多样，品种较多[146]。

（四）明晚期主要器型

明晚期的器型有碗、盏、盘、碟、尊、钵、罐、壶、瓶、缸、炉、盅、高足杯、碾钵、水注等，大件器物少见。使用整体模制比较普遍，器型主要有碗、盘、盏、碟等[147]。

五、明代广东余里窑青瓷器型类别

明代广东余里窑青瓷器型主要可分为碗、杯、盘、碟、罐、瓶、壶、炉及其他类别。

六、明代广东余里窑青瓷器型表

器型类别	碗	杯	盘	碟	罐	瓶	壶	炉	其他
器型种类	侈口碗	小杯	折沿盘	敞口碟	小罐	双耳瓶	执壶	樽式炉	砚台
	敞口碗	豆形杯	折腹盘	折腹碟	盖罐	直颈瓶		熏炉	笔山
	直口碗	高足杯	敞口盘	撇口碟					器座
	花口碗		菊瓣口盘						烛台
	折腰碗		八棱盘						灯盏
									砚滴

七、明代广东余里窑青瓷器型图集

（一）碗类

碗类为广东余里窑遗址出土器型中的主要器型之一，出土量较大。从整体造型看，碗的形制变化不大，可大致分为以下几个类型：

1. 侈口碗

此类碗侈口，圆唇，曲腹，圈足。与浙江龙泉窑的侈口碗大同小异。（见图2-1-94）

图2-1-94

2. 敞口碗

这类碗敞口，弧腹，圈足。圈足略有不同，有些圈足小，足墙厚，横切面呈梯形；有些圈足大，足墙直且薄；有些圈足高，足墙直。（见图2-1-95—图2-1-98）

图2-1-95

图2-1-96

图2-1-97

图2-1-98

3. 直口碗

此类碗为直口，圆唇，斜直腹，圈足。（见图2-1-99）

图2-1-99

4. 花口碗

此类碗花口，折沿，直腹，圈足。（见图2-1-100、图2-1-101）

图2-1-100

图2-1-101

5. 折腰碗

见图2-1-102。

图2-1-102

（二）杯类

1. 小杯

小杯分有敞口、侈口和直口，均有圈足。

敞口类型的小杯，有弧腹（见图2-1-103）也有直腹（见图2-1-104）。

侈口类型的标本较多，器型基本一致，斜直腹，腹较深。仅足部略有不同，有些饼足内挖空呈圈足，足墙斜直厚重且有鸡心底；有些则为矮圈足，足墙薄直。（见图2-1-105）

直口杯为直腹，腹浅。杯壁胎较薄，杯底及圈足胎厚。（见图2-1-106）

图2-1-103

图2-1-104

图2-1-105

图2-1-106

2. 豆形杯

此类杯敛口，弧腹，喇叭形实足，足底内凹呈圆锥形，部分足部削直呈圈足状。（见图2-1-107）

图2-1-107

3. 高足杯

高足杯有直口（见图2-1-108）也有敞口（见图2-1-109、图2-1-110）。

高足有的光滑，有的为竹节状，也有的为两道弦纹。足底略往外撇呈小喇叭状，足部削直呈圈足状，足底内凹呈圆锥形。

图2-1-108

图2-1-109

图2-1-110

（三）盘类

1. 折沿盘

折沿盘的口沿向外翻折，浅腹，圈足。折沿口有两种：直口（见图2-1-111、图2-1-112）、菱口（见图2-1-113、图2-1-114）。

图2-1-111

图2-1-112

图2-1-113

图2-1-114

2. 折腹盘

折腹盘大撇口，浅腹，圈足，下腹内收厉害，近底部有明显折腹，内底界限明显，整体呈倒喇叭状。（见图2-1-115、图2-1-116）

图2-1-115

图2-1-116

3. 敞口盘

此类盘敞口，圆唇，浅腹，圈足。（见图2-1-117）

图2-1-117

4. 菊瓣口盘

此类盘宽沿，浅腹，圈足。（见图2-1-118）

图2-1-118

5. 八棱盘

八角器型或多角器型在南宋的龙泉窑就较为常见，且流行于元代，明代较少。八棱盘口沿呈八方形，浅腹，圈足。（见图2-1-119）

图2-1-119

（四）碟类

1. 敞口碟

此类碟敞口，弧腹，圈足，内底平，有的有圆唇。（见图2-1-120、图2-1-121）

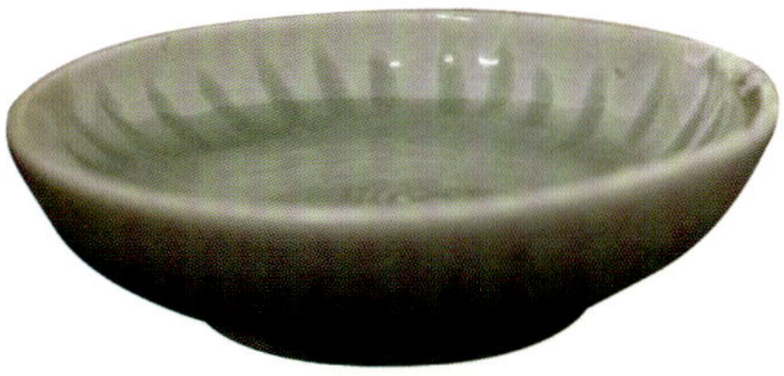

图2-1-120

图2-1-121

2. 折腹碟

折腹碟大撇口，浅腹，矮圈足，下腹内收厉害，近底部有明显折腹，整体呈倒喇叭状。（见图2-1-122、图2-1-123）

图2-1-122

图2-1-123

3. 撇口碟

撇口碟撇口明显，斜腹，卧足，内底平。（见图2-1-124）

图2-1-124

（五）罐类

1. 小罐

小罐常见有直口（见图2-1-125、图2-1-126）或敛口（见图2-1-127）。

图2-1-125

图2-1-126

图2-1-127

2. 盖罐

见图2-1-128。

图2-1-128

（六）瓶类

1. 双耳瓶

双耳瓶撇口，长颈，平肩，下腹内收，喇叭形足，近足底处足壁削直，颈两侧饰长S形耳，通体实心。（见图2-1-129）

图2-1-129

2. 直颈瓶

见图2-1-130。

图2-1-130

（七）壶类

见图2-1-131。

图2-1-131

（八）炉类

1. 樽式炉

平沿，斜直腹，小饼底，三足。形制有大有小。饼足多为一层，少数有两层，还有的有三层。部分饼足中心一圆孔。三足多为蹄形足，少数为简化如意头形扁足，也有兽足。（见图2-1-132—图2-1-134）

图2-1-132

图2-1-133

图2-1-134

2. 熏炉

标本仅存底部，呈圆筒形，平底，圈足。底部一长方形孔，炉身一周方圆形孔。（见图2-1-135）

图2-1-135

（九）其他

1. 砚台

砚台为圆形，外壁圆弧，圈足；砚面宽平，四周一圈凹槽。（见图2-1-136）

图2-1-136

2. 笔山

见图2-1-137。

图2-1-137

3. 器座

在余里窑窑址仅出土一件。敛口，平唇，浅腹，喇叭形足，中空。该器座为陶器，通体不施釉。（见图2-1-138）

图2-1-138

4. 烛台

发现的烛台标本上部残，仅存台座。台座实心，花口，斜腹，近底处内收，圈足。（见图2-1-139）

图2-1-139

5. 灯盏

灯盏出土的标本较多，但形制单一。圆唇，弧腹，小平底内凹，内壁竖贴一半圆，圆顶部有数个突起，可放置或缠绕灯芯。（见图2-1-140、图2-1-141）

图2-1-140

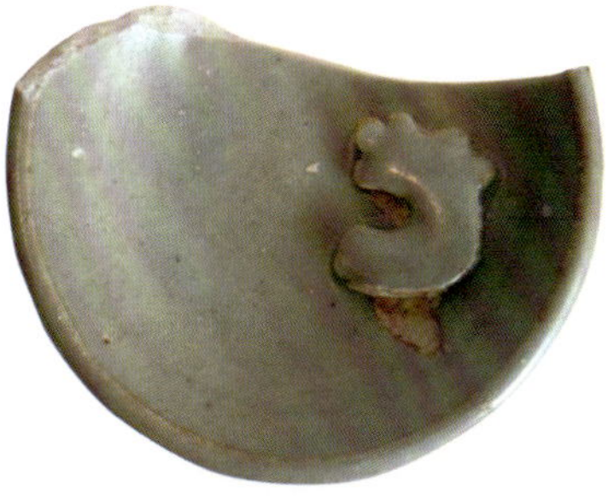

图2-1-141

6. 砚滴

见图2-1-142。

图2-1-142

八、明代广东余里窑青瓷器型风格分析

明代广东余里窑青瓷的器型种类不多，小件器居多，少见大器。其中主要是日用瓷，以碗、盘、碟类为主。

碗类器口多为侈口或直口；盘类以折沿盘居多；碟类多为侈口，卧足，碟外底心内凹。

九、总结

浙江龙泉枫洞岩窑青瓷器型类别比广东余里窑青瓷多，不仅有日用瓷，还有陈设瓷，在质量上也明显更高。

广东余里窑址出土的青瓷以日用瓷为主，器型种类较少，造型单一，以小型器居多，不见或少见大型器物，如龙泉枫洞岩窑流行的盆、镂空器座、梅瓶、各式罐、玉壶春瓶等等，在余里窑址均未有发现。

余里窑址出土的瓷器型制与龙泉窑有很多相似之处，现简单举例进行对比：

余里窑址出土的碗的形制在浙江龙泉窑均有发现，但样式较龙泉窑单一。

高足杯是元代龙泉窑的一种新产品，口沿微向外撇，杯身近似上大下小的半圆形，把手不高；到了明代，口部逐渐瘦小，腹部加深，底部装的竹节形足。余里窑发现有不少高足杯，样式与龙泉窑的相似，但工艺更为简单，龙泉窑高足杯口沿呈圆唇状（见图2-1-143），而余里窑高足杯的口沿则少见此工艺（见图2-1-144）。

图2-1-143

图2-1-144

余里窑址出土的盘类，器型与龙泉窑的基本一致，如宽唇弧腹盘、敞口弧腹盘、折腹浅盘、花口盘等等，但造型、装饰均较简单古朴，远不如龙泉窑精致。

菱口为龙泉窑的典型花口形制（见图2-1-145），早在南宋时期就很是流行，且一直延续到明代。龙泉枫洞岩窑址出土的菱口盘，除口沿为菱口，盘壁也呈菱花瓣式，余里窑的菱口盘则仅口沿为菱口，盘壁并没有做类似处理。（见图2-1-146）余里窑菊瓣口盘也是仅口沿为菊瓣形。（见图2-1-147）

图2-1-145

图2-1-146

图2-1-147

龙泉窑的炉形制多样，有樽式炉、洗式炉、鬲式炉、鼓式炉等，是龙泉窑的典型器物。蹄形足、兽形足和如意头形扁足比较流行。余里窑址出土的炉形制比较单一，以樽式炉为主，蹄形足、兽形足和如意头形扁足等三种形制的足均有发现，但以蹄形足最为常见。

综上所述，广东余里窑址的器物基本能在浙江龙泉窑找到相似或相同的器物，但样式相对较少，龙泉窑大量生产的洗、盏等纹饰繁复、式样丰富的器物均不见于余里窑址。余里窑的瓷器造型相对简单，除少数花口圆器，余皆器型古朴，不见有仿生造型、仿古造型。

第二节
明代浙江龙泉窑青瓷与广东余里窑青瓷装饰工艺比较分析

一、明代浙江龙泉窑青瓷装饰工艺

明代浙江龙泉窑青瓷的装饰工艺，基本承袭了元代的风格，比如刻划花，并在其基础上创造了剔刻花这种新技法。贴花工艺则在明代逐渐消失，其他工艺也与前代略有差异。

（一）刻划花

刻划花是龙泉窑青瓷上比较常见的装饰技法。

明代早期，由于瓷器釉层增厚，刻花工艺由元代的斜刀浅刻发展为斜刀深刻（见图2-2-1、图2-2-2），单线浅划的手法变为单线深划或双线深划。这种单、双线深划的手法常用于绘制双线缠枝、卷草、回纹、莲瓣内的花纹等等。（见图2-2-3）

上述变化在明早期的官器上尤其明显。明代中期的刻划花则深浅不一，纹饰比较随意，多勾勒缠枝莲纹、莲瓣纹等。（见图2-2-4、图2-2-5）

图2-2-1

图2-2-2

图2-2-3

图2-2-4

图2-2-5

（二）剔刻花

剔刻花装饰是明代创新的一种技法，明早期开始出现。明代中期在执壶、盖罐、炉等器物中比较盛行[148]。这种工艺纹饰凸出于器表，题材多为花果枝叶或者吉祥语，纹饰尺寸比例较大。（见图2-2-6、图2-2-7）

图2-2-6

图2-2-7

（三）印花

明代早中期印花盛行，主要装饰一般民窑碗、盘、碟、洗、炉等器物，纹饰题材较多，包括牡丹纹、菊花纹、茶花纹、金刚杵纹、飞马海涛纹等[149]。

Section 2：

Comparative Analysis of Ming Dynasty Longquan Kiln System Celadon: Zhejiang Longquan Kiln and Guangdong Yuli Kiln Celadon Decorative Techniques

1. Decorative Techniques of Zhejiang Longquan Celadon

Ming Dynasty Zhejiang Longquan Celadon essentially continued the use of Yuan Dynasty techniques: This includes carving and incising, and the introduction of deep carving based on the Yuan foundation. Appliqué almost completely ceased during the Ming Dynasty, and other techniques underwent changes.

A. Carving and Incising

Carving and Incising were comparatively common types of decoration used on Longquan Celadon.

In the Early Ming Dynasty, because of the thickness of the porcelain glaze, carving evolved from the use of slanted knife shallow incising into the use of deeper carving (see pictures 2-2-1 and 2-2-2). Single shallow line incising evolved into single deep line incising or double line deep incising. This type of single and double line deep incising was often used in the decoration of double line floral scrolls, classic scrolls, fretted scrolls, and the inside pattern of lotus petals (see picture 2-2-3).

The above-mentioned change was most commonly seen on the official wares of the Early Ming Dynasty. The carving and incising of the Mid Ming Dynasty were not uniform, with deep and shallow cuts, the decorative lines more free-flowing, and dominantly consisted of lotus spray outlines and lotus patterns (see pictures 2-2-4 and 2-2-5).

B. Deep Carving

Deep carving was a new innovation started during the Early Ming Dynasty. It was comparatively more common to be seen on Mid Ming Dynasty ewers, lids, censers, and so forth items [148]. This type of decoration protruded off the face of the porcelain body and decorations primarily consisted of flowers and fruits for auspicious inscriptions, the size of which were all comparatively large (see pictures 2-2-6 and 2-2-7)

C. Impressing

The Mid Ming Dynasty saw the widespread use of impressing, which was primarily used on common use items such as bowls, plates, saucers, washers, censers, and so forth items from common kilns; the content of such decoration relatively abundant, for example: Peony pattern, chrysanthemum pattern, tea flower pattern, golden staff (Vajra Pestle) pattern, flying horse amongst waves pattern, and so forth [149].

Impressed patterns during the Mid Ming Dynasty became more abundant, including all types of floral patterns, figure and horse pattern, lotus and infant pattern, phoenix pattern, blessing and deer pattern, money pattern, golden staff (Vajra Pestle) pattern, miscellaneous treasures pattern, and various types of inscriptions [150] (see pictures 2-2-8—2-2-12).

This period saw the induction of a paper cutting style of impressing patterns, which was often used on the interior of bowls, and the content primarily consisted of stories and inscriptions. This type of pattern impressing increased the production efficiency, but the image composition was rigid, images of people were muddled and unclear, and the handling technique was clumsy.

明中期印花纹饰题材更加丰富，有各式花纹、人物牵马纹、荷下卧婴纹、凤纹、福鹿纹、钱纹、金刚杵纹、杂宝纹以及“金玉满堂”铭、“顾氏”铭、“王氏”铭和“石林”铭等[150]。（见图2-2-8—图2-2-12）

这时还新兴一种剪纸式的印花，常施于碗的内壁，题材以人物故事及文字为主。这类印花生产效率较高，但画面构图呆板，人物形象模糊不清，处理手法拙劣。

图2-2-8

图2-2-9

图2-2-10

图2-2-11

图2-2-12

（四）贴花

贴花是元代龙泉窑盛行的技法之一，题材也十分丰富，但这项技法到了明代已不多见。

二、明早期浙江龙泉窑青瓷官窑器纹饰类别

明代洪武及永乐官器基本上都使用刻划花装饰。纹饰题材也都是照图样定制的。纹饰风格繁密，构图布局有序。

主题纹饰除五爪云龙纹外，基本上都是花果类。许多纹饰如芍药、山茶、枇杷、荔枝、仙桃、葡萄等都是明代才出现的[151]。

上述的花果类题材，如牡丹、菊花、山茶、莲、月季、芍药、芙蓉等很可能为当时皇家园林种植的观赏花卉，符合皇族的审美情趣；桃子、石榴、荔枝、葡萄、枇杷、林檎等果实除了是当时比较珍贵的水果品种外，也有吉祥的寓意，如桃子表示长寿，石榴表示多子多孙等；另外还有园景松石题材的纹饰。这些纹饰可能都与统治者的偏好有关。传说洪武帝朱元璋在建造御花园时就对园林石峰非常推崇[152]。

正因为统治阶级的喜好，浙江龙泉窑青瓷上的刻花工艺在明初的官器上达到了前所未有的艺术高度。刻工娴熟流畅，一般采用“双入正刀法”，每刻一笔，施以两刀，并用斜刀刻法，中间用刀口刮平，凹面平整，兼有线和画的艺术效果[153]。

另外，这段时期的刻花纹饰与上釉技术有完美的配合。要达到青釉之青色与纹饰的完美结合，施釉太薄或太厚都不行，釉太薄呈现不出青瓷的青绿之美，釉太厚则看不见纹饰。此外，这些器物在纹饰表现与构图上也十分巧妙。首先是纹饰细腻秀美，有工笔画的韵味，纹饰层次繁多，但搭配合理，密而不乱。其次是同一主题纹饰有不同表现手法，如最常见的莲花，表现手法或写实或写意或图案化，形式或独枝或折枝或缠枝等。不同器型搭配不同图案，根据器物的尺寸大小纹饰也有所调整。在这些纹饰设计和表达方式上可以看出当时工匠们的巧妙心思，这与民窑刻花的随意草率形成鲜明对比[154]。

下面列举一些常见纹饰。

（一）莲瓣纹

莲瓣纹常见于碗、盘类的外壁

D. Appliqué

Appliqué was in vogue during the Yuan Dynasty, and the subject matter of decorations was extremely abundant, but this technique was almost completely unseen during the Ming Dynasty.

2. Zhejiang Longquan Kiln Celadon Early Ming Dynasty Official Ware Decoration Categories

The official wares used during the Hongwu and Yongle periods of the Ming Dynasty almost exclusively used carving and incising for the application of patterns. The subject matter of the pictures was all made in accordance with sample images. The decorations were stylistically dense, and the layouts were strictly arranged.

Aside from five-claw dragon pattern, the main decorations consisted of floral and fruit patterns. Many patterns, such as herbaceous peony, camellia, loquat, lychee, peach of immortality, grapes, and so forth, were all first seen during the Ming Dynasty [151].

The above-mentioned floral patterns, such as peony, chrysanthemum, camellia, lotus, Chinese rose, herbaceous peony, hibiscus, and so forth were most likely botanical items seen in the Imperial Gardens. They were all in accordance with the aesthetic appeal of the Imperial family. Patterns such as peaches, pomegranates, lychee, grapes and loquats, aside from being relatively precious fruits at the time, also had implied auspicious meaning. For example: peaches were a sign of longevity, pomegranates were a sign of fertility, and so forth. Additionally there were also garden scenes with pine and rocks used as content for patterns. These patterns most likely all reflected the habits and past times of the ruling class. It is said that the Hongwu Emperor highly esteemed the use of forests and stones in the construction of the Imperial Garden [152].

It is specifically because of the favor of the ruling class that the carving technique used in the early Ming Dynasty on official use items reached such heights seen on Zhejiang Longquan Celadon. The carving artisans were adept and fluent, utilizing a new combination of techniques that brought together direct angle and slanted angle carving and smoothing which produced more life-like and artistically appealing imagery [153].

Additionally, the carving technique utilized during this time perfectly matched the glazing techniques. It was necessary to achieve the perfect balance between decoration and celadon glaze application; too thick or too thin would produce unwanted results. If the glaze was too thin, it would lack its beautiful green color; but if the glaze was too thick, the decoration would become obscured. Aside from this, the decoration on these pieces was extremely complex. Firstly, the decoration style was fine and elegant and represented a meticulous painting style. The patterns presented in many layers, but had appropriate composition, dense without being messy. Additionally, different types of patterns could utilize very different types of techniques, for example: The most commonly seen lotus flowers could be seen as life-like or impressionistic, and were drawn independently, in scrolls, or in sprays. Different vessel styles were paired with different images, in accordance with the shape and size of the vessel itself. Through the design and application of these patterns, we can see the level of precision used by the artisans, juxtaposed to the more free hand style that was seen in the contemporary common kilns [154].

Following are a few of the most commonly seen patterns:

A. Lotus Pattern

Lotus patterns most commonly appeared on the exterior of bowls and plates, and on the shin section of jars. In accordance to their shape, they can be further split in to two varieties: Deformed Lotus and Pointed Head Lotus.

a. Deformed Lotus Pattern

The deformed lotus was essentially the same as its predecessors, with a cloud incised within the lotus (see picture 2-2-13).

b. Pointed Head Lotus Pattern

This type of pattern was most commonly seen as a

及罐类的胫部。按其形态可分为变形莲瓣纹和尖头莲瓣纹。

1. 变形莲瓣纹

变形莲瓣纹基本沿袭前朝的风格，莲瓣内刻划朵云纹。（见图2-2-13）

图2-2-13

2. 尖头莲瓣纹

尖头莲瓣纹常常作为辅助纹饰饰于碗、罐或瓶的胫部，甚至是梅瓶盖上。莲瓣顶部为尖形，莲瓣稍微凸起，斜削并有弧度。（见图2-2-14—图2-2-17）

图2-2-14

图2-2-15

图2-2-16

图2-2-17

（二）菊瓣纹

菊瓣纹应该是由莲瓣纹简化而来的，多见于碗外壁或盘内壁。在器身上浅刻划直线或者弧线作为菊瓣，菊瓣细长，分布均匀。（见图2-2-18、图2-2-19）

图2-2-18

图2-2-19

（三）缠枝花卉纹

缠枝花卉纹常见的有缠枝牡丹、缠枝莲、缠枝灵芝等。

1. 缠枝牡丹纹

缠枝牡丹纹常见于罐类的腹部，牡丹纹为侧面牡丹，花朵朝上，花瓣包裹花蕊，花蕊由交叉斜纹画成，花瓣左右各三瓣对称。（见图2-2-20、图2-2-21）

图2-2-20

图2-2-21

supplementary pattern applied to the shin of bowls, jars, and vases or Meiping lids. The top section of the lotus has a pointed shape, producing a slightly convex petal with a general slanted arced position (see pictures 2-2-14—2-2-17).

B. Chrysanthemum Pattern

This pattern is mostly likely evolved from the simplification of the lotus pattern, and is most commonly seen on the exterior wall of bowls or interior wall of plates. Shallowly incised straight or slightly arced lines would act as the chrysanthemum petals, which were thin and long with even distribution (see pictures 2-2-18 and 2-2-19).

C. Floral Scrolls

Floral scrolls most commonly took the shape of peonies, lotuses, or Lingzhi (Auspicious Fungus).

a. Peony Scrolls

These scrolls are most commonly seen on the body section of jars. They include a side view of the peony, with the bud facing upward, and the petals surrounding the stamen. The stamen is composed of crosshatch lines and three petals are on either side (see pictures 2-2-20 and 2-2-21).

b. Lotus Scrolls

These scrolls were most commonly seen on official wares of the Hongwu and Yongle reign periods. They often were used as the primary decoration on Yuhuchun vases, the well of mound bowls, exterior of censers, on jar lids, or even seen as supplementary patterns on the interior and exterior of plates (see pictures 2-2-22—2-2-25).

c. Lingzhi (Auspicious Fungus) Scrolls

These scrolls were most commonly seen on the exterior of bowls (see picture 2-2-26).

D. Floral Sprays

Floral Sprays varieties include: Peony, chrysanthemum, hibiscus, lotus, camellia, Lingzhi, peach blossom, and so forth.

a. Peony Sprays

These sprays are most commonly seen on the body of jars, on lids, or the inner base of plates. On the body of jars, an alternation of a single peony flower and leaf make up the entire spray. The blossom resembles a fingered citron with three petals on either side of an enclosed stamen, which is depicted with crosshatched lines (see picture 2-2-27). On plates, the flower bud is located amongst leaves and stems (see pictures 2-2-28 and 2-2-29). On relatively small depictions, the most common application technique utilized was impression (see pictures 2-2-29 and 2-2-30).

b. Chrysanthemum Sprays

These sprays often present in a grouping of sixteen on the interior or exterior of plates, or an alternation of an independent blossom and leaf on the body of jars. The chrysanthemum petals are depicted in one or two layers with a ring and crosshatched stamen in the center (see pictures 2-2-31 and 2-2-32).

c. Hibiscus Sprays

These sprays most commonly appear on the interior base of plates. The petals are multilayered and are incised with a comb like pattern in the center. The flowers are surrounded by 4 to 5 incised leaves, which have clearly depicted veins (see picture 2-2-33).

d. Lotus Sprays

These sprays most commonly presented on the interior wall of Ming Dynasty Chuzhou Official Kiln Mound bowls (see pictures 2-2-34 and 2-2-35).

e. Camellia Sprays

These sprays most commonly presented on the interior wall of Ming Dynasty Chuzhou Official Kiln Mound bowls (see pictures 2-2-36 and 2-2-37).

f. Lingzhi (Auspicious Fungus) Sprays

These sprays most commonly presented on the interior

2. 缠枝莲纹

缠枝莲纹在洪武、永乐时期的官器中常见，作为主要纹饰装饰在玉壶春瓶和墩式碗的腹部、炉外壁、盖罐盖子上，或作为辅助纹饰装饰于盘的内外壁。（见图2-2-22—图2-2-25）

图2-2-22

图2-2-23

图2-2-24

图2-2-25

3. 缠枝灵芝纹

缠枝灵芝纹常见于碗类外壁。（见图2-2-26）

图2-2-26

（四）折枝花卉纹

折枝花卉纹包括折枝牡丹、折枝菊、折枝芙蓉、折枝莲、折枝山茶花、折枝灵芝、折枝桃花等。

1. 折枝牡丹纹

折枝牡丹纹多见于罐类的腹部、盖子上及盘内底。罐类腹部的折枝牡丹一花一叶独立交替出现，牡丹花瓣三瓣对称，花瓣包裹花蕊。花蕊由交叉斜纹画成（见图2-2-27）；盘内底的折枝牡丹，花朵位于枝叶中间（见图2-2-28、图2-2-29）；较小的图案多以印花方式装饰（见图2-2-29、图2-2-30）。

图2-2-27

图2-2-28

图2-2-29

图2-2-30

wall of Ming Dynasty Chuzhou Official Kiln Mound bowls (see pictures 2-2-38 and 2-2-39).

g. Peach Blossom Sprays

These sprays most commonly appeared on Official Kiln wares of the Ming Dynasty (see picture 2-2-40).

E. Baoxiang Floral Pattern

These patterns most commonly presented on the interior wall of Ming Dynasty Chuzhou Official Kiln Mound bowls. They were depicted with six (see picture 2-2-41), seven (see picture 2-2-42), or eight (see picture 2-2-43) flower petals. They also occurred on Hongwu period official wares in conjunction with honeysuckle pattern on the inner base of plates (see picture 2-2-44).

F. Other Floral Patterns

Other less common floral patterns include: Crabapple blossom, water lily, herbaceous peony, okra, Chinese rose, osmanthus, hawthorn, and so forth.

G. Fruit Pattern

a. Peach Pattern

These patterns were most commonly seen on Early Ming Dynasty official wares.

b. Lychee Pattern

These patterns were most commonly seen on Early Ming Dynasty official wares (see picture 2-2-45).

c. Grape Pattern

These patterns were most commonly seen on Early Ming Dynasty official wares (see picture 2-2-46).

d. Pomegranate Pattern

These patterns were most commonly seen on Early Ming Dynasty official wares (see picture 2-2-47).

e. Loquat Pattern

These patterns were most commonly seen on Early Ming Dynasty official wares (see picture 2-2-48).

H. Pine, Bamboo, and Plum Pattern

Also known as "Three Friends of Winter" (see picture 2-2-49).

I. Pine and Rock Pattern

These patterns were most commonly seen on Early Ming Dynasty official wares (see picture 2-2-50).

J. Lake Rock and Plantain Pattern

These patterns were most commonly seen on Early Ming Dynasty official wares (see picture 2-2-51).

K. Wave Pattern

See picture 2-2-52.

L. Animal Pattern

a. Flying Horse Pattern

These patterns were often seen on the inner base of plates. The horse was life-like, and raring up with four hooves extended and head turned (see picture 2-2-53).

b. Dragon and Cloud Pattern

These patterns were most commonly seen on Hongwu period official wares. They were commonly incised on the inner base of plates. The dragon depiction was a continued style of the previous Yuan Dynasty. Its body was curved in an arc shape, his head bent in a 'Z' shape closely located to its own tail. The Dragon's neck was long and thin, its claws with five talons; it possessed a fearsome strength (see picture 2-2-54).

2. 折枝菊纹

折枝菊纹常以十六组装饰于盘内外壁，或以一花一叶独立交替出现于罐类的腹部。菊花花瓣一层到两层，中间花蕊以圆圈及斜纹表现。（见图2-2-31、图2-2-32）

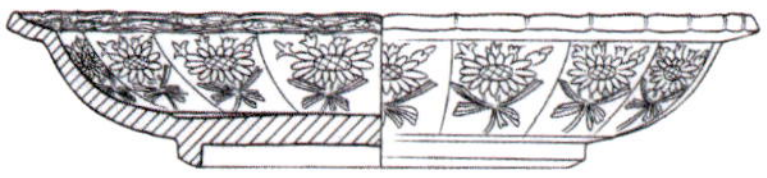

图2-2-31

图2-2-32

3. 折枝芙蓉花纹

折枝芙蓉花纹常见于盘内底心，花瓣多层重叠，花瓣内划致密的篦纹。花朵周围刻划四五片叶子，叶子上有清晰的脉络。（见图2-2-33）

图2-2-33

4. 折枝莲纹

折枝莲纹常见于明代处州官窑的墩式碗内底。（见图2-2-34、图2-2-35）

图2-2-34

图2-2-35

5. 折枝山茶花纹

折枝山茶花纹常见于明代处州官窑的墩式碗内底。（见图2-2-36、图2-2-37）

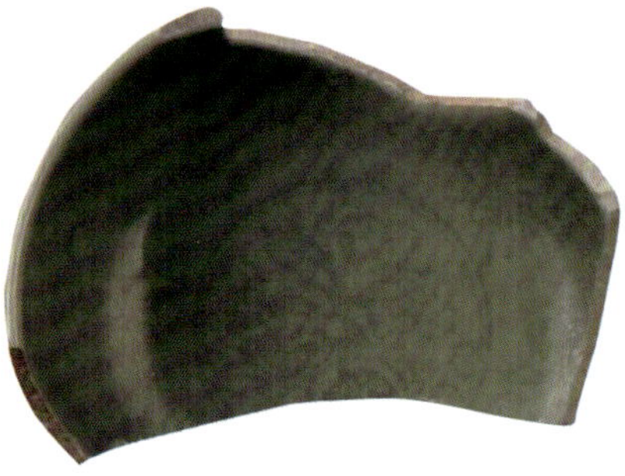

图2-2-36

图2-2-37

6. 折枝灵芝纹

折枝灵芝纹常见于明代处州官窑的墩式碗内底。（见图2-2-38、图2-2-39）

图2-2-38

图2-2-39

c. Deer

See picture 2-2-55.

d. Fish

These patterns were often seen on the inner base of plates. They include double fish pattern or four fish pattern. The fish pairs are back-to-back and surrounded by incised wave pattern (see pictures 2-2-56—2-2-58).

M. Figures

These patterns were relatively popular during the Ming Dynasty. The contents primarily include landscapes with figures, historical stories, or scenes from the twenty-four Filial Exemplars [155] (see pictures 2-2-59 and 2-2-60).

N. Eight Trigrams Pattern

These patterns often occurred on the exterior of censers and were often formed using relief impression technique (see pictures 2-2-61 and 2-2-62).

O. Eight Treasures Pattern

See picture 2-2-63.

P. Waternut Brocade Pattern

See picture 2-2-64.

Q. Ruyi Cloud Pattern

See picture 2-2-65.

R. Golden Staff (Vajra Pestle) Pattern

See picture 2-2-66.

S. Classic Scrolls

See picture 2-2-67.

T. Fretted Scrolls

See picture 2-2-68.

U. Inscriptions

The combination floral patterns and auspicious inscriptions was a popular decoration motif during the Early and Mid Ming Dynasty. The contents included inscriptions wishing prosperity, fortune, and longevity [156] (see pictures 2-2-69—2-2-74).

Aside from this, they could also describe the firing kiln, the name of the kiln master, or the intended use of the vessel. For example, an excavated ware from the Fengdongyan Kiln includes an inscription on the well of the plate designating it for use in a certain family (see picture 2-2-72). "Gu Family" inscribed bowls were created during the Mid Ming Dynasty, this inscription indicates that they were made by the Gu Family Kiln during the Ming Dynasty. Historical records indicate that Mr. Gu was a squire active from the Zhengtong to Chenghua period [157] (see picture 2-2-73).

There are also a very small amount of pieces inscribed with the official language of the Mongolians, "Basiba" Script (see picture 2-2-74).

3. Decorative Techniques of Guangdong Yuli Kiln Celadon

Pieces from the Guangdong Yuli Kiln are primarily undecorated, with only a few decorated pieces discovered. Decoration methods mostly included carving, incising and mold impression. Decoration contents varied according to the method used for decoration. Carving and incising primarily included chrysanthemum patterns, lotus pattern, vine pattern, fretted scrolls, spiral scrolls, and other various floral patterns. Impression primarily included lunar pattern, floral patterns, horse amongst waves pattern, and various types of inscriptions.

7. 折枝桃花纹

折枝桃花纹常见于明早期官窑器上。（见图2-2-40）

图2-2-40

（五）宝相花纹

宝相花纹常见于明代处州官窑的墩式碗内底，花瓣有六片（见图2-2-41）、七片（见图2-2-42）、八片（见图2-2-43）三种；也有在洪武官器上与忍冬纹一同出现在盘内底（见图2-2-44）。

图2-2-41

图2-2-42

图2-2-43

图2-2-44

（六）其他花卉纹

其他花卉纹还包括林檎、荷花、芍药、秋葵、月季、木樨（桂花）、山楂等。

（七）水果纹

1. 桃纹

桃纹常见于明早期官窑器上。

2. 荔枝纹

荔枝纹常见于明早期官窑器上。（见图2-2-45）

图2-2-45

3. 葡萄纹

葡萄纹常见于明早期官窑器上。（见图2-2-46）

图2-2-46

4. 石榴纹

石榴纹常见于明早期官窑器上。（见图2-2-47）

图2-2-47

5. 枇杷纹

枇杷纹常见于明早期官窑器上。（见图2-2-48）

图2-2-48

4. Guangdong Yuli Kiln Celadon Decoration Categories

Following are a few of the most commonly seen patterns on Yuli Kiln Celadon:

A. Lotus Pattern

This pattern is also known as the chrysanthemum pattern, because it is the simplification of the lotus pattern and resembles a chrysanthemum.

This pattern often occurs on the exterior wall of bowls or stem cups, and is relatively narrow. Some of the lotus petals have a pointed tip (see picture 2-2-75), and some petals are depicted free hand with a round tip or a pointed tip (see pictures 2-2-76 and 2-2-77); some of the patterns are separated by a straight line, the tip of the petal drawn with one round line (see pictures 2-2-78 —2-2-80). There are still some short and independent lines that make up lotus petals, and are primarily used on the interior well of plates and saucers (see pictures 2-2-81 and 2-2-82). This type of pattern is the most commonly seen on Yuli Kiln samples and the techniques used were numerous. Some depictions utilized mold impression, some used utilized carving and incising, and others utilized deep carving.

B. Lunar Pattern

These patterns are the evolution floral bouquet patterns, and are often see on the inner base of bowls and plate. They were applied using impression techniques (see pictures 2-2-83—2-2-85).

C. Vine Pattern

These patterns are the collection of densely arranged simple curved lines, and are often seen on the interior wall of open pieces (see picture 2-2-86).

D. Geometrical Scrolls

This is the use of alternating upward and downward slanted lines in continuation to create a pattern [158].

Scrolls found on wares from these samples include triangular scrolls that appear on the interior walls and bases of saucers and bowls. Scrolls found on the interior bases have a rectangular shape (see picture 2-2-87), and scrolls on the interior wall create a "山" shape (see picture 2-2-88).

E. Fretted Scrolls

These patterns normally occur on the exterior wall of bowls and censers, and are often near the rim of the piece. These scrolls occur as independent frets separated by straight lines (see pictures 2-2-89 and 2-2-90).

F. Wave Scrolls

These scrolls are most commonly seen on the outside of wares, and are created with simplistic abstract lines (see pictures 2-2-91 and 2-2-92).

G. Eight Trigrams Pattern

These patterns are most commonly seen on the exterior body of censers and are usually raised in relief from the surrounding surface (see pictures 2-2-93 and 2-2-94).

H. Horse Amongst Waves Pattern

This pattern is one of the more rare animal patterns applied by impressed mold, and is often seen on the inner base of plates (see picture 2-2-95).

I. Inscriptions

Inscriptions are very common on saucers, and present on the middle of the inner base. Most often they include a single word such as "福" (fu, blessing), "寿" (shou, longevity), "宁" (ning, peace), and other auspicious or meaningful words (see pictures 2-2-96—2-2-111). Some of the words are seen written in various fonts and styles and are enclosed with a single or double circle.

（八）松竹梅纹

松竹梅纹又称“岁寒三友”。（见图2-2-49）

图2-2-49

（九）松石纹

松石纹常见于明早期官窑器上（见图2-2-50）。

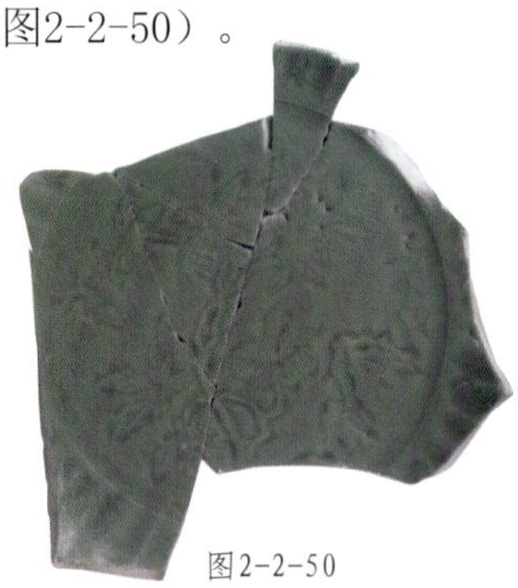

图2-2-50

（十）湖石芭蕉纹

湖石芭蕉纹常见于明早期官窑器上。（见图2-2-51）

图2-2-51

（十一）海涛纹

见图2-2-52。

图2-2-52

（十二）动物纹

1. 飞马纹

飞马纹常见于盘子的内底，马呈现跃起状，四蹄前后伸直，头向后扭转，栩栩如生。（见图2-2-53）

图2-2-53

2. 云龙纹

云龙纹见于明洪武时期的官器。纹饰刻划于盘内底。龙纹基本延续元代龙纹风格，龙整体扭曲呈弧形，头部曲折为“Z”形，与尾部紧靠一起。龙颈细长，龙爪为五爪，刚劲有力。（见图2-2-54）

图2-2-54

3. 鹿

见图2-2-55。

图2-2-55

4. 鱼纹

鱼纹常见于盘内底，有双鱼纹或四鱼纹，鱼相互背对，周围刻划海涛纹。（见图2-2-56—图2-2-58）

图2-2-56

图2-2-57

图2-2-58

Additionally, an inscription indicating time period was found on an unglazed ware (see picture 2-2-112).

5. Conclusion

In relation to decoration technique, Yuli Kiln saw the use of two techniques only: Carving (Incising) and mold impression. These two types of decoration technique were both popular in Longquan during the Yuan and Ming Dynasties, but the other two types of popular decoration technique seen at the same time in Longquan, appliqué and deep carving, were not seen in the Yuli Kiln examples. Additionally, the unglazed decoration and brown glaze spotting techniques that were used during the Ming Dynasty on Longquan Wares were not seen in the Yuli Kiln excavation.

Mold impression was popularly used in Longquan production, a technique which in the Yuan Dynasty, saw the use of a carved out mold that would create a raised pattern on the face of the impressed ware. The Ming Dynasty saw a new innovation in which raised molds were carved and impressed to create indented decorative impression on the clay body, and both indented and raised impression techniques were simultaneously used. In the Yuli Kiln productions, only indented impression decorations occurred, and their content was primarily animals or auspicious inscriptions.

In relation to the decoration motifs, none of the various dragon, fish, floral scrolls, floral sprays, and all types of fruit and garden motifs seen on the Ming Dynasty Longquan Celadon were seen on wares discovered at the Yuli Kiln site. Yuli Kiln items primarily included vegetation decorations such as lotus, lunar, vines, and other various flowers. More rarely occurring were animals including the horse amongst waves. Auspicious inscriptions were also quite popular, such as words and eight trigrams patterns.

In relation to decoration style, Yuli Kiln wares were vastly more simplistic than their Longquan contemporaries.

Yuan and Ming Dynasty Longquan Celadon were commonly decorated with various auspicious inscriptions of blessing, wealth, health, prosperity, longevity, and so forth. Wares discovered at the Fengdongyan Kiln site from the Ming Dynasty saw the popularized use of auspicious inscriptions placed amongst exquisite patterns. Aside from these auspicious inscriptions, there were also a few pieces containing the official "Basiba" script used by the Mongolians during the Yuan Dynasty. Yuli Kiln wares also saw the use of inscriptions adorning the center of bowls, saucers, plates, and so forth. The complexity of such inscriptions was much lower than their Longquan contemporaries, but the auspicious meanings were one in the same. For example, Longquan Wares using four words to signify an auspicious wish of wealth or blessing would be simplified to one word on their Yuli counterparts.

Lotus patterns were common on both Longquan and Yuli Celadon, but the multiplicity of design styles was higher amongst the Longquan variety. They presented with very complex as well as simplified versions, whereas the Yuli lotus patterns were uniformly simplified, some to the extent of just being a simple line.

In general, Zhejiang Longquan Kiln produced celadon had decorations with more abundant content material, more multiplicity in motif representation, and higher refinement in techniques.

（十三）人物纹

人物题材的纹饰在明代较流行，题材主要有山水人物、历史故事、二十四孝等[155]。（见图2-2-59、图2-2-60）

图2-2-59

图2-2-60

（十四）八卦纹

八卦纹常见于香炉的外壁，多采用阳印方式形成。（见图2-2-61、图2-2-62）

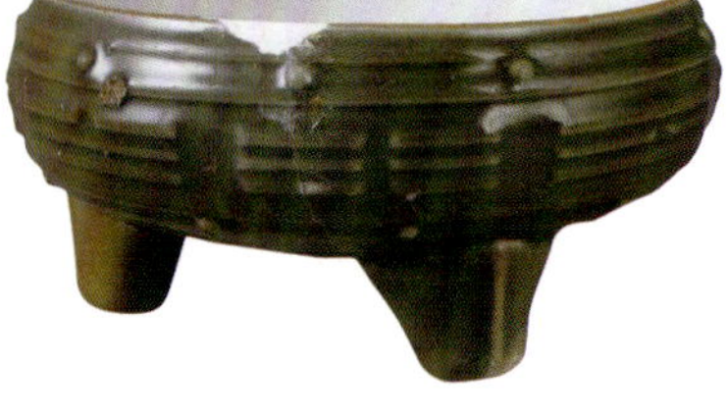

图2-2-61

图2-2-62

（十五）八宝纹

见图2-2-63。

图2-2-63

（十六）菱锦纹

见图2-2-64。

图2-2-64

（十七）如意云纹

见图2-2-65。

图2-2-65

（十八）金刚杵纹

见图2-2-66。

图2-2-66

（十九）卷草纹

见图2-2-67。

图2-2-67

（二十）回纹

见图2-2-68。

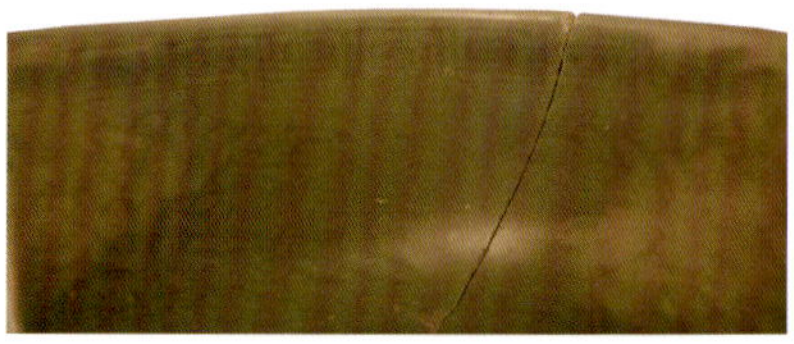

图2-2-68

（二十一）文字

花卉同吉祥文字的纹饰组合在明早中期较流行，常见有“金玉满堂、福如东海、长命富贵”等吉祥语款[156]。（见图2-2-69—图2-2-74）

除此外还有说明窑炉、窑主的姓名和器物用途的，如明代浙江龙泉枫洞岩窑址出土的印有“为□堂记”的折腹盘。（见图2-2-72）明中期出现带有“顾氏”铭文的碗。顾氏碗为明代顾仕成窑场产品，文献记载顾仕成为正统至成化年间活动的乡绅[157]。(见图2-2-73)

更有少数还印有蒙古的官方文字八思巴文。(见图2-2-74)

图2-2-69

图2-2-70

图2-2-72

图2-2-73

图2-2-74

图2-2-71

三、明代广东余里窑青瓷装饰工艺

广东余里窑的器物以光素为主，少数有装饰。装饰手法主要为刻划、戳印两种。装饰的题材因为装饰手法的不同而略有不同，刻划纹饰主要有菊瓣纹、莲瓣纹、草叶纹、回纹、弦纹、花卉纹，戳印纹饰主要有月华纹、花卉纹、海马波涛纹及各式文字等。

四、明代广东余里窑青瓷纹饰类别

下面列举广东余里窑青瓷上常见的一些纹饰。

（一）莲瓣纹

余里窑青瓷上的莲瓣纹已经简易化，形似菊瓣，所以也可以说是菊瓣纹。

莲瓣纹（菊瓣纹）多出现在碗或高足杯的外壁，形状较窄。有的莲瓣纹顶部为尖形（见图2-2-75），有的顶部画得随意，既有尖形又有圆形（见图2-2-76、图2-2-77）；有的以直线间隔，莲瓣顶部统一画一圈弦纹（见图2-2-78—图2-2-80）。也有以短且独立的竖线条组成，多见于盘、碟类内壁。（见图2-2-81、图2-2-82）

莲瓣纹是余里窑青瓷上最常见的纹饰之一，工艺也呈多样性，有用印模，有用刻划，还有的用剔花工艺完成。

图2-2-75

图2-2-76

图2-2-80

图2-2-83

图2-2-77

图2-2-81

图2-2-84

图2-2-78

图2-2-82

图2-2-85

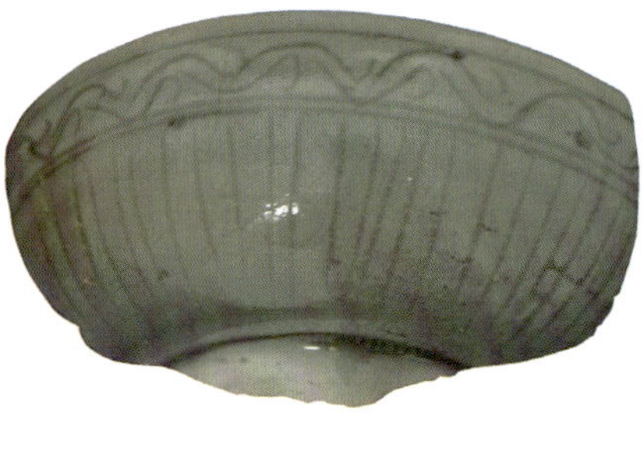

图2-2-79

（二）月华纹

月华纹是由团花纹演变而来的，常见于碗、盘内底，为印花装饰。（见图2-2-83—图2-2-85）

（三）草叶纹

草叶纹为数条密集排列的简易弧线，通常出现在圆器内壁。（见图2-2-86）

图2-2-86

（四）曲折纹

曲折纹是以连续线条曲折而成[158]。

余里窑青瓷的曲折纹由三角折线组成，多出现在碟、碗类的内底及内壁。内底处的曲折纹呈四角形（见图2-2-87），而内壁的曲折纹则呈“山”字形（见图2-2-88）。

图2-2-87

图2-2-88

（五）回纹

回纹多见于碗或炉类的外壁，通常在靠近口沿的位置。回纹单个独立排列，中间有直线隔开。（见图2-2-89、图2-2-90）

图2-2-89

图2-2-90

（六）水波纹

水波纹通常出现在瓷器外壁，纹饰线条简练率性。（见图2-2-91、图2-2-92）

图2-2-91

图2-2-92

（七）八卦纹

八卦纹常见于炉类的腹部，通常以阳纹形式呈现。（见图2-2-93、图2-2-94）

图2-2-93

图2-2-94

（八）海马波涛纹

海马波涛纹是余里窑少数的动物题材的模印装饰纹饰，通常出现在盘内底。（见图2-2-95）

图2-2-95

（九）文字

文字在碟类器物上常见，碗类或杯类器物上少见。常见文字有“福”“寿”“宁”“玉”“安”“然”“富”“禄”“乐”“诚”“德”字等。（见图2-2-96—图2-2-111）其中“福”“寿”“禄”有多种书写形式。文字外以单圈或双圈装饰。单圈为菱花形和圆形；双圈为菱花形在外，圆圈在内。

另外也有纪年文字。在一陶素胎器座上发现有“庚子年□记□”的铭文。（见图2-2-112）

图2-2-96

图2-2-97

图2-2-98

图2-2-99

图2-2-100

图2-2-101

图2-2-102

图2-2-103

图2-2-104

图2-2-105

图2-2-106

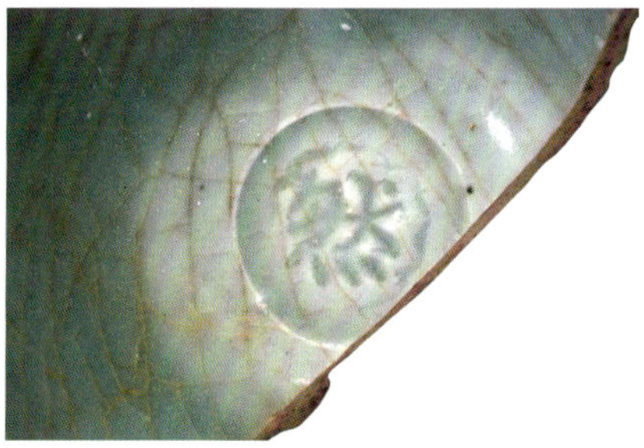

图2-2-107

图2-2-111

图2-2-108

图2-2-112

图2-2-109

图2-2-110

五、总结

就装饰手法而言，余里窑仅有刻划和戳印两种手法，刻划花和戳印都是元明时期龙泉窑很流行的装饰方法，但不见有同时期龙泉窑流行的贴花、剔花等手法。龙泉窑独具特色的青釉露胎装饰和点褐彩装饰也不见于余里窑。

龙泉窑流行戳印装饰，在元代的印模主要为阴刻印模，表现在器物中就是阳纹印花。到明代，新出现阳刻印模，即表现在器物中是阴纹印花；且同时流行阳纹印花和阴纹印花。在余里窑，主要流行阴纹印花，不见阳纹印花；模印纹饰主要为动物纹饰、吉祥文字等。

就装饰题材而言，明代龙泉窑青瓷上的龙纹、鱼纹、缠枝花卉纹、折枝花卉纹以及各类水果纹、湖石芭蕉纹、人物等纹饰均不见于余里窑。余里窑以植物纹饰为主，如莲瓣纹、月华纹、草叶纹、各式花卉纹等；不见或少见动物纹饰，如海马波涛纹；吉祥纹饰也比较流行，如各式文字、八卦纹等。

就装饰风格而言，与龙泉窑青瓷相比，余里窑青瓷上的所有纹饰都趋简。

在元明时期的龙泉窑，还流行在瓷器中刻印文字。有一部分是吉祥语，如“金玉满堂”“长命富贵”“百花朝王”“福如东海”“寿比南山”“福、禄、寿、富、大吉”等等。明代枫洞岩窑就流行在繁复优美的纹饰正中添加吉祥文字。除了吉祥语以外，有少数还印有蒙古的官方文字八思巴文。余里窑盛行在碗、碟、盘等器物上刻印吉祥文字，其寓意和龙泉窑的吉祥语一致，只是都进行了简化，以单字为主，如“玉”寓意“金玉满堂”，“富”寓意“长命富贵”，“福”寓意“福如东海”，“寿”寓意“寿比南山”，“信”寓意“孝悌忠信”等等。

莲瓣纹在龙泉窑青瓷和余里窑青瓷上均较常见，龙泉窑青瓷上的莲瓣纹形式更加多样，有形式复杂的，也有简化成菊瓣纹的；而余里窑的青瓷上莲瓣纹都趋简，有的甚至已简化成竖线。

总体来说，浙江龙泉窑青瓷纹饰题材较广东余里窑纹饰丰富，纹饰表达手法更多样，制作工艺方面更精细。

第三节 明代浙江龙泉窑青瓷与广东余里窑青瓷胎釉比较分析

一、瓷胎比较

（一）瓷胎化学成分

浙江龙泉窑青瓷瓷胎的原料来源于浙江本地。

浙江瓷石是一种含石英—高岭—绢云母类型的伟晶花岗岩风化后的岩石矿物，风化程度较低的含有部分长石，风化程度较高的则含有更多的高岭石矿物。瓷石的Al_2O_3含量为14%—24%，Fe_2O_3含量为0.5%—3%，SiO_2含量为65%—80%。由于这种瓷石已含有制造瓷胎所必需的三种基本矿物成分（石英、高岭石和引入熔剂的绢云母等），所以浙江的工匠们只要用这种瓷土作为主要原料就可以制成瓷胎[159]。

此外，浙江瓷石的Al_2O_3含量比北方黏土低，所以烧成温度较低（多在1200—1270℃烧成），而瓷胎的致密度和瓷化程度则比北方青瓷高。浙江本地的这种优良瓷石为浙江历代出产质量较高的青瓷提供了物质条件基础[160]。

龙泉地区的瓷土含铁量比较低，大多在1%以下，个别的最高也不超过2%。但龙泉青瓷瓷胎的含铁量却比较高，这是因为配方中添加了紫金土的缘故[161]。

紫金土是南方特有的原料，夹杂着石英、长石颗粒和含铁矿物，经淘洗后，可塑性强。紫金土含有较高的铁元素和Al_2O_3、较少的SiO_2，并含有不少碱金属氧化物以及Ti、Cu、Mn、Co、Ni等微量着色元素[162]。

当作为胎用原料时，紫金土中的碱金属氧化物和铁等起着助熔剂和矿化剂作用，使青瓷的烧结温度大大降低；由于紫金土中含有较高的Al_2O_3，因此在胎中添加紫金土可防止坯体高温变形。另一方面，紫金土中的铁离子能使瓷胎着色，使其呈现白中带灰的色调，从而更好地衬托青釉的呈色[163]。

1. 明代浙江龙泉枫洞岩窑址出土青瓷标本瓷胎化学成分

中山大学科人类进化与科技考古实验室给明代浙江龙泉枫洞岩窑址出土青瓷标本瓷胎成分做了能量色散X射线荧光光谱（EDXRF）分析。

成分分析是指通过微观谱图对样品的成分进行分析，是古陶瓷研究中基本的测试方法。它可以分析出样品所含元素的种类及其含量，包括主量元素（含量＞1%）、次量元素（含量0.1%—1%）和微量元素（含量＜0.1%）。其中，主量元素反映出的是陶瓷制作工艺方面的特征，而次量、微量元素则是用于探讨古陶瓷的产地及矿料来源（实验采用仪器为美国EDAX International Inc.的微聚焦X射线荧光光谱仪。实验测试条件为：X光管管压40kV，管流230μA，真空光路，光斑直径为300μm，MnKα处的分辨率137.5eV，deadtime约20%，每个样品选取三个不同的位置测量，每次测量的时间为200s，Version32收谱，Version3.0的解谱软件进行样品的定量分析）[164]。结果见表2-3-1。

Section 3：

Comparative Analysis of Ming Dynasty Longquan Kiln System Celadon: Zhejiang Longquan Kiln and Guangdong Yuli Kiln Celadon Body and Glaze

1. Porcelain Body Comparison

A. Chemical Composition of Porcelain Body

The materials used for Longquan Celadon porcelain clay all came from local sources.

Zhejiang porcelain clay is a type of weathered, large crystal granite, raw mineral containing quartz, kaolin, and mica. Clay with relatively low weathering contains feldspar, and clay with relatively high weathering contains more kaolinite. Porcelain clay contains 14%~24% Al_2O_3, 0.5%~3% Fe_2O_3, and 65%~80% SiO_2. As this raw material contained all the necessary mineral components for making porcelain clay, the local artisans only needed to utilize this clay for the production of the porcelain bodies [159].

Because the Al_2O_3 in Zhejiang porcelain clay was lower than the clays found in Northern China, the firing temperature was also relatively lower (1200℃~1270℃). Additionally, the density and degree to which the porcelain vitrified was higher than the northern celadon varieties. It was the advantages of Zhejiang porcelain clay that provided the material foundation for the comparatively high quality celadon that was produced there [160].

The iron content found in Zhejiang clay was relatively low, predominantly under 1% with only a few examples exceeding 2%. However, one specific quality of Longquan Celadon bodies was that they contained a relatively high amount of iron. This is due to the addition of Zijin clay to the porcelain clay mixture [161].

Zijin clay is a mineral mixture that is exclusive to Southern China and contains quartz, feldspar particles and iron, which after washing has high plasticity. Zijin is relatively rich in elemental iron and Al_2O_3, while relatively low in SiO_2, and contains several alkaline metal oxides, as well as trace amounts of coloring agents in the form of minerals such as Ti, Cu, Mn, Co, Ni [162]. When used in porcelain bodies, the flux and mineralizing properties of alkaline metal oxides and iron within Zijin clay help to greatly decrease the temperature needed to reach agglomeration during celadon firing. Also, the high Al_2O_3 content in Zijin decreased the deformation of clay bodies during firing. Lastly, the iron ions in Zijin clay act as a coloring agent within the porcelain body; giving the body a grey tone which acted as a more suitable background to highlight celadon glaze [163].

a. Chemical Composition of Zhejiang Longquan Fengdongyan Kiln Celadon Body Material

The Hi-tech Archeology Laboratory of Sun Yat-sen University carried out EDXRF analyses on the chemical composition of porcelain body materials of Ming Dynasty Zhejiang Longquan Celadon Fengdongyan Kiln site samples.

Composition analysis refers to the process of utilizing fluorescent light spectrum to analyze the chemical composition of tested specimen, and is a standard procedure of ceramic research. This process has the purpose of finding the chemical compositions and respective amounts of elements within a sample; dividing them into primary elements (containing > 1%), secondary elements (containing 0.1%~1%), and trace elements (containing <0.1%). Of which, the primary elements reveal the characteristics of ceramic production, while the secondary and trace elements reveal the location of production and raw materials [164].

Results see Table 2-3-1.

From the table we can see: The amount of Al_2O_3 in the

表2-3-1 明代浙江龙泉枫洞岩窑址出土青瓷标本瓷胎EDXRF定量分析结果（wt%）

Table 2-3-1 Ming Dynasty Zhejiang Longquan Fengdongyan Kiln Site Celadon Body Chemical Composition EDXRF Analyses Results

编号	Na_2O	MgO	Al_2O_3	SiO_2	K_2O	CaO	TiO_2	Fe_2O_3	MnO	CuO	ZnO	PbO_2	Rb_2O	SrO	Y_2O_3	ZrO_2
LDFDYXRF1	3.39	1.89	19.32	65.91	4.94	0.09	0.12	1.33	0.08	65	18	41	322	42	62	190
LDFDYXRF2	2.23	0.70	19.65	68.20	4.55	0.09	0.15	1.42	0.06	42	102	57	306	8	42	199
LDFDYXRF3	1.88	0.63	20.03	67.45	4.52	0.30	0.19	2.00	0.11	34	106	14	312	32	58	221
LDFDYXRF4	2.05	0.47	19.49	68.47	4.42	0.12	0.16	1.82	0.06	26	151	105	318	-6	54	219
LDFDYXRF5	2.95	1.32	19.44	66.19	5.72	0.09	0.10	1.20	0.04	96	92	11	355	40	50	205
LDFDYXRF6	2.60	0.97	20.74	66.19	5.07	0.06	0.11	1.25	0.05	12	94	89	318	26	55	192
LDFDYXRF7	2.97	1.27	19.18	67.12	4.90	0.08	0.12	1.36	0.07	70	185	47	337	17	72	216
LDFDYXRF8	2.48	0.94	21.01	65.89	4.69	0.09	0.16	1.75	0.05	61	66	43	324	46	40	208
LDFDYXRF9	1.64	0.05	21.65	66.37	5.07	0.15	0.22	1.85	0.06	50	111	110	358	41	48	213
LDFDYXRF10	2.49	1.22	19.78	67.46	4.14	0.15	0.16	1.59	0.07	14	100	95	285	33	33	202
FDY:X	3.60	1.78	21.25	64.18	4.45	0.18	0.11	1.44	0.06	—	89	148	289	31	50	199
FDY:Y	2.23	0.81	19.89	67.76	4.19	0.10	0.21	1.83	0.04	14	99	96	311	41	41	202
LDFDYJ1	3.02	1.96	18.45	66.81	4.70	0.20	0.22	1.64	0.05	40	108	38	279	26	33	209
LDFDYJ2	2.55	1.28	21.25	65.48	4.89	0.04	0.13	1.37	0.04	25	105	30	354	29	57	192
LDFDYJ3	2.45	1.17	20.73	66.41	4.16	0.12	0.15	1.81	0.05	52	115	57	313	29	47	215
LDFDYJ7	2.59	0.98	22.76	64.06	4.33	0.30	0.14	1.83	0.04	53	110	38	312	23	45	209
LDFDYJ12	1.87	0.67	20.38	67.29	4.20	0.10	0.29	2.21	0.05	47	139	39	289	60	35	203
LDFDYJ14	3.12	1.68	20.57	64.84	4.88	0.08	0.19	1.65	0.06	47	109	132	335	22	42	236
LDLBJ13	1.74	0.24	23.27	65.74	3.59	0.10	0.21	2.11	0.03	55	106	49	204	13	56	231
LDLBJ14	1.69	0.63	21.95	66.74	3.61	0.07	0.24	2.07	0.03	59	51	42	188	33	54	223
LDLBJ15	2.32	1.09	22.37	65.49	3.44	0.08	0.18	2.03	0.03	79	101	24	206	30	59	210
LDLBJ16	2.66	1.36	20.97	66.03	3.28	0.17	0.24	2.29	0.04	—	93	96	209	31	38	261
LDLBJ21	1.95	0.87	23.46	63.98	4.35	0.08	0.22	2.09	0.03	—	56	67	297	40	34	199
LDLBJ29	2.27	0.88	24.87	61.72	4.85	0.11	0.21	2.10	0.04	99	166	40	341	38	52	218
LDLBJ31	2.79	1.25	21.24	66.83	2.47	0.07	0.25	2.10	0.04	81	140	11	190	11	41	228

分析结果中主量元素含量为10^{-2}，微量元素含量为10^{-6}

Within the table primary elements are to a factor of 10^{-2} and trace elements are listed to a factor of 10^{-6}

porcelain body ranged from 18.45%-24.87%, SiO_2 ranged from 61.72%-68.47%, Na_2O ranged from 1.64%-3.6%, K_2O ranged from 2.47%-5.72%, CaO ranged from 0.04%-0.3%, and Fe_2O_3 ranged from 1.20%-2.29%.

b. Chemical Composition of Guangdong Yuli Kiln Celadon Body Material

The Hi-tech Archeology Laboratory of Sun Yat-sen University carried out EDXRF analyses on the chemical composition of porcelain body materials of Ming Dynasty Guangdong Yuli Kiln site samples.

Results see Table 2-3-2 [165].

From the table we can see the primary composition elements of Yuli Kiln porcelain body is: Na, Mg, Al, Si, K, Fe, Cu, Zn, Pb, Rb, Sr, Y, Zr. Secondary elements include Ca and Ti. Trace elements include Mn.

The amount of Al_2O_3 in the porcelain body ranged from 16.85%-22.37%, SiO_2 ranged from 68.38%-72.06%, Na_2O ranged from 0.63%-3.25%, K_2O ranged from 3.12%-5.18%, CaO ranged from 0.06%-0.4%, and Fe_2O_3 ranged from 1.11%-2.1%. Of which, sample S_9 had a Al_2O_3 content of 22.37% and SiO_2 content of 66.38%, outside the normal range, and can be hypothesized that the body of this piece underwent more refined clay washing which lowered the SiO_2 and increased the Al_2O_3 content [166].

c. Summary

From the chemical composition analyses we can see that the composition of clay bodied from the two kiln sites, Fengdongyan and Yuli, are extremely similar.

In order to more fully analyze the differences between clay bodies from the two areas, Origin 7.5 software was used to further process the data: The average SiO_2 content of Yuli (69.85%) was higher than that of Longquan (66.325%), and the Al_2O_3 content of Yuli (18.565%) was lower than Longquan (21.98%), presenting with high Silicone low Aluminum characteristics. The Fe_2O_3 content of Yuli samples ranged from 1.51%-1.78%, with an average of 1.62%; lower than the average Fe_2O_3 content of Longquan Wares (1.81%). The K_2O content of Yuli samples ranged from 3.6%-4.4% with an average of 4%, also lower than that of the Longquan sample average (4.5%) [167].

From the above we can see, there is a certain difference in the porcelain body composition of Zhejiang Longquan and Guangdong Yuli Kiln produced wares. These discrepancies are most likely do to the following primary factors [168]:

I. Choice of clay raw material. Both kilns utilized materials from the immediate area for porcelain production. Each location's raw materials have certain differences, and as such produce discrepancies in clay body chemical composition.

II. Raw material processing. In general, raw material (in powder form) is washed before it is used. This process is adopted to wash out the granite granules from the clay. This will decrease the SiO_2 content and increase the Al_2O_3 of the finished porcelain clay. Differences in clay washing processes between the two kiln locations would create discrepancies between the finished porcelain body compositions, affecting the percentages of Si and Al within the respective mixtures.

III. In comparison, the Fe_2O_3 content of Zhejiang Longquan is higher than that of the Yuli Kiln samples. This is due to the addition of Fe_2O_3 rich Zijin clay to increase elasticity and enhance the capability to shape wares more effectively.

B. Porcelain Body Characteristics

Through micro analyses, it has been seen that the clay bodies of the Fengdongyan pieces and Yuli pieces are primarily greyish-white and relatively dense with small needlepoint air pockets (see pictures 2-3-3 and 2-3-4).

In general, the samples from Fengdongyan have a body that is relatively thicker, more pure, and denser. Aside from the relatively thick bodies of the censers, samples from the Yuli kiln site are thinner, the composition less densely compact than the Fengdongyan samples, some samples even have yellow or red coloration, with bigger air pockets [169] (see pictures 2-3-5 — 2-3-7).

The tests mentioned in this section utilized Nikon SMZ1500 Microscope, Nikon C-FLED2 lighting, Nikon DS-Fi2 Lens, and Nikon NIS-Elements D 4.10.00. Tests were carried out by the Hi-tech Archeology Testing Center of Sun Yat-Sen University.

由表2-3-1可知，明代浙江龙泉枫洞岩窑址出土青瓷标本瓷胎中，Al_2O_3的含量集中在18.45%—24.87%，SiO_2的含量基本在61.72%—68.47%，Na_2O的含量在1.64%—3.60%，K_2O的含量集中在2.47%—5.72%，CaO的含量集中在0.04%—0.30%，Fe_2O_3的含量基本在1.20%—2.29%。

2. 明代广东余里窑址出土青瓷标本瓷胎化学成分

中山大学人类进化与科技考古实验室也给明代广东余里窑址出土青瓷标本瓷胎的成分作了能量色散X射线荧光光谱（EDXRF）分析，结果见表2-3-2[165]。

由表2-3-2可知，明代广东余里窑址出土青瓷标本瓷胎中，Al_2O_3的含量集中在16.85%—22.37%，SiO_2的含量基本在68.38%—72.06%，Na_2O的含量在0.63%—3.25%，K_2O的含量集中在3.12%—5.18%，CaO的含量集中在0.06%—0.40%，Fe_2O_3的含量基本在1.11%—2.10%。其中样品S9中Al_2O_3的含量达到22.37%，其SiO_2的含量为66.38%，在均值以下偏低，可以推测此样品的胎料在淘洗程度上更加精细，这会造成SiO_2含量降低，Al_2O_3含量升高[166]。

3. 小结

由标本化学成分表可看出，明代时期龙泉枫洞岩窑址出土青瓷标本的瓷胎成分与广东余里窑址出土青瓷标本非常接近。

为了更好地分析对比两地青瓷标本化学成分组成特征，利用Origin7.5软件对数据进行处理分析：余里窑青瓷胎中的SiO_2含量（69.85%）比浙江龙泉（66.325%）高，而Al_2O_3含量（18.565%）比浙江龙泉（21.98%）低，呈高硅低铝的特征；余里窑青瓷胎中Fe_2O_3含量在1.51%—1.78%，平均含量为1.62%，比浙江龙泉的Fe_2O_3含量（1.81%）低；广东余里窑瓷胎中K_2O含量在3.6%—4.4%，平均含量为4%，比浙江龙泉的K_2O含量（4.5%）低[167]。

综上所述，明代浙江龙泉青瓷瓷胎的化学成分与广东余里窑的有一定的区别。造成这样的差异的主要原因可能包括[168]：

（1）制胎原料的选择。两窑址均为就地取材，受地理环境、地方资源等条件的制约，各地原料的差异，导致两地青瓷胎的化学成分组成不同。

（2）制胎原料的处理。一般制胎是将粉料淘洗后使用，淘洗主要是将部分大颗粒的石英去除。制胎用的瓷石精泥中的SiO_2就会降低，而Al_2O_3就会相对升高。两地陶工对原料的淘洗程序工艺的不同会对两地青瓷胎中硅、铝含量产生一定的影响。

（3）浙江龙泉青瓷胎与广东余里窑青瓷胎化学组成相比，浙江龙泉青瓷胎中Fe_2O_3的含量较高。这主要是由于浙江龙泉在瓷器的制作过程中加入了铁含量较高的紫金土，以增加瓷器的可塑性，有利于成形。

（二）瓷胎特征

通过显微观察得出，大多数枫洞岩窑及余里窑标本瓷胎均白中带灰，胎质较致密，多有针状小气孔。（见图2-3-3、图2-3-4）

总体来说，枫洞岩窑的标本胎质更加厚实、洁白、致密，余里窑的瓷胎除炉类较厚以外，其余器型胎体都比较薄，胎质不如枫洞岩的致密，较为疏松，更有相当一部分标本胎体颜色偏土黄或砖红，有较多大气孔[169]。（见图2-3-5—图2-3-7）

图2-3-3 枫洞岩窑样品瓷胎
Fengdongyan Body

In areas of exposed clay, there is a common phenomenon: reddish-orange appearance on the clay body; often called Huo Shi Hong or Flint Red. Flint red coloration comes from the Iron and dissolvable salts collected on the exposed clay during the drying process. After firing, while the piece cools, second stage oxidation of the Iron occurs, changing Fe^{2+} into Fe^{3+}, resulting in coloration [170]. This feature is seen on samples from both locations.

Flint red can appear at any point on the ware in which the body is exposed, usually including: The interior, mouth, bottom, foot ring, and any point where the glaze meets the exposed clay (see pictures 2-3-8—2-3-15). The color extends from the glaze, dark to light with a natural dwindling, until it disappears. It is possible for large areas of exposed clay to lack even color gradation.

2. Porcelain Glaze Comparison

A. Chemical Composition of Glaze

a. Chemical Composition of Zhejiang Longquan Fengdongyan Kiln Excavated Sample Celadon Glaze

When used in porcelain glazes, the relatively high alkaline metal oxide content in Zijin clay acts as flux during the firing process. Zijin clay also has relatively high Al_2O_3, this had a double benefit for celadon production: First, not only did it raise the high temperature viscosity of the glaze; increasing the temperature limits of glaze vitrifying and giving the glaze an even distribution of tiny air bubbles which produced a soft luster. It also decreased the coefficient of expansion within the glaze, decreasing the tendency of the glaze to crack [171].

The Hi-tech Archeology Testing Center of Sun Yat-sen University carried out EDXRF analyses on the chemical composition of porcelain glaze of Ming Dynasty Zhejiang Longquan Celadon Fengdongyan Kiln site samples. The results are listed in Table 2-3-17.

From the table we can see: The amount of Al_2O_3 in the porcelain glaze ranged from 11.15%-14.12%, SiO_2 ranged from 64.18%-69.46%, Fe_2O_3 ranged from 0.85%-1.88%, TiO_2 ranged from 0.11%-0.26%, Na_2O ranged from 1.10%-4.04%, K_2O ranged from 3.06%-4.92% and CaO ranged from 3.70%-11.67%.

Zhejiang Longquan Samples have a glaze composition that falls within the Calcium-Alkali Glaze family.

b. Chemical Composition of Guangdong Yuli Kiln Excavated Sample Celadon Glaze

The Hi-tech Archeology Testing Center of Sun Yat-sen University carried out EDXRF analyses on the chemical composition of porcelain glaze of Ming Dynasty Guangdong Yuli Kiln site samples. The results are listed in Table 2-3-16 [172].

From the table we can see: The amount of Al_2O_3 in the porcelain glaze ranged from 11.65%-14.48%, SiO_2 ranged from 61.52%-68.91%, Fe_2O_3 ranged from 0.85%-1.88%, TiO_2 ranged from 0.13%-0.29%, Na_2O ranged from 1.25%-4.52%, K_2O ranged from 3.06%-4.92% and CaO ranged from 3.70%-11.67%.

Yuli Kiln samples primarily fall into the Calcium-Alkali Glaze family, while a small portion in the Alkali-Calcium Glaze family.

c. Summary

The average K_2O content of Yuli glaze (4.1%) is lower than that of Longquan glaze (4.6%), and the CaO content is almost the same at approximately 6.9%.

The glaze Fe_2O_3 and TiO_2 content of both kiln sites was very similar. From this we can tell that the Yuli artisans had a firm grasp of the Longquan glaze mixtures, and could find similar raw materials in the surrounding areas [173].

B. Characteristics of Celadon Glaze

a. Scale of Gaze Reflectivity

According to the general sheen or reflectivity of celadon glaze, it can be divided into: Matte, Moist, and Sheen.

I. Matte

Matte glaze, for the most part, has lost all of its reflective

表2-3-2 明代广东余里窑址出土青瓷标本瓷胎EDXRF定量分析结果（wt%）

Table 2-3-2 Ming Dynasty Guangdong Yuli Kiln Site Celadon Body Chemical Composition EDXRF Analyses Results

编号	Na_2O	MgO	Al_2O_3	SiO_2	K_2O	CaO	TiO_2	Fe_2O_3	Mn	Cu	Zn	Pb	Rb	Sr	Y	Zr
S1	1.83	1.30	18.63	69.85	4.15	0.18	0.15	1.78	0.06	38	87	30	253	32	123	205
S2	1.69	0.67	18.02	70.77	4.76	0.34	0.13	1.51	0.04	22	76	40	248	58	170	272
S3	1.08	0.84	19.94	70.27	3.50	0.15	0.13	1.96	0.05	28	87	77	264	32	81	211
S4	1.61	1.11	18.10	70.69	4.54	0.17	0.13	1.53	0.05	9	58	40	260	27	102	199
S5	1.39	0.92	19.57	70.75	3.30	0.28	0.12	1.55	0.03	41	82	103	195	65	83	205
S6	2.22	1.01	19.09	69.76	3.89	0.17	0.12	1.59	0.05	87	84	21	249	39	50	187
S7	2.30	1.45	19.33	68.97	4.04	0.09	0.11	1.56	0.04	92	109	68	255	20	62	219
S8	1.62	0.68	19.08	70.20	4.39	0.12	0.13	1.66	0.04	60	84	60	295	56	70	205
S9	2.36	0.94	22.37	66.38	3.43	0.25	0.15	2.01	0.08	30	22	99	205	29	82	207
S10	1.04	0.77	18.69	71.96	3.37	0.09	0.25	1.68	0.05	168	91	90	235	39	90	206
S11	0.63	0.32	19.45	71.49	3.45	0.07	0.14	1.49	0.06	57	98	29	241	49	107	217
S12	1.07	0.90	19.50	69.72	4.78	0.10	0.15	1.65	0.05	36	56	1	295	61	134	184
S13	1.19	0.31	17.19	72.06	5.18	0.21	0.22	1.52	0.04	9	44	44	224	32	113	214
S14	1.80	1.06	17.54	71.60	4.10	0.17	0.11	1.47	0.05	68	60	65	264	62	293	201
S15	1.09	0.51	20.05	70.11	3.84	0.09	0.15	2.03	0.07	34	100	24	271	47	137	230
S16	3.25	1.22	21.03	67.16	3.23	0.10	0.15	1.73	0.03	105	73	65	234	—	51	166
S17	1.92	1.57	19.85	69.06	3.32	0.12	0.13	1.90	0.05	54	68	108	251	27	104	206
S18	1.54	1.34	18.54	69.07	5.12	0.16	0.15	1.96	0.06	35	93	48	318	69	112	200
S19	1.27	0.49	18.01	71.11	4.92	0.40	0.12	1.58	0.05	20	120	21	238	51	151	180
S20	1.22	0.78	17.87	70.26	5.32	0.27	0.15	2.01	0.06	44	108	32	292	68	132	201
S21	1.17	0.79	19.37	71.35	3.12	0.24	0.12	1.71	0.07	44	50	64	252	7	80	196
T23F1	3.00	1.20	17.52	68.89	4.27	0.17	0.16	1.79	0.05	—	116	104	248	16	68	183
T23F2	2.91	1.72	16.89	69.65	3.81	0.19	0.21	1.62	0.05	13	66	98	232	43	66	198
T23F3	3.20	1.72	18.29	67.75	4.03	0.28	0.14	1.59	0.04	22	43	43	245	50	65	199
T23F4	2.60	1.54	18.51	68.23	4.12	0.20	0.16	1.63	0.04	61	91	86	316	60	71	216
T23F5	2.17	1.51	18.78	68.38	4.19	0.11	0.14	1.73	0.06	76	99	58	279	41	53	202
YA1	3.12	1.77	19.39	67.61	3.43	0.15	0.15	1.38	0.07	54	56	75	250	26	105	227
YA2	2.96	1.38	17.93	69.25	3.95	0.30	0.12	1.11	0.06	15	60	—	224	40	123	186
YC1	2.49	0.69	17.12	70.05	4.69	0.34	0.13	1.48	0.03	70	68	8	269	16	121	192
YC2	1.86	0.77	16.85	71.38	4.25	0.21	0.49	1.18	0.04	49	53	32	257	38	138	205
YC3	2.07	0.15	18.33	70.06	4.49	0.28	0.13	1.48	0.03	22	45	6	268	54	115	200
T23B1	3.06	1.71	17.79	68.91	3.60	0.06	0.16	1.70	0.05	—	64	24	262	—	53	178
T23B2	3.03	1.74	18.20	68.39	3.68	0.10	0.15	1.71	0.05	63	96	74	254	55	64	193
T23B3	2.32	1.10	17.53	70.22	3.92	0.11	0.16	1.64	0.04	33	25	16	240	22	57	183
T23B4	3.09	1.80	17.66	67.91	4.20	0.12	0.13	2.10	0.04	69	71	78	281	8	81	218
T23B5	2.03	0.87	18.05	70.23	3.87	0.06	0.14	1.75	0.03	53	46	5	266	16	63	199
T23B6	2.19	1.11	18.53	69.57	3.60	0.08	0.15	1.78	0.03	55	91	71	241	21	40	183

分析结果中主量元素含量为10^{-2}，微量元素含量为10^{-6}

Within the table primary elements are to a factor of 10^{-2} and trace elements are listed to a factor of 10^{-6}

properties, and has a slightly matted texture, with some pieces even gaining a slightly cloudy appearance (see pictures 2-3-18 and 2-3-19).

Samples from the Yuli Kiln site have a relatively high number of under fired wares, all of which have a muddled or matte glaze (see pictures 2-3-20 and 2-3-21).

II. Moist

Moist glazes have a soft reflective quality, and appear to be wet to the touch (see pictures 2-3-22—2-3-24).

III. Sheen

Sheen glazes have a highly reflective quality, and the surface of the glaze appears to be glossy smooth (see pictures 2-3-25 and 2-3-26).

b. Glaze Color

I. Factors Affecting Glaze Color

During the process of celadon production, there are many complex components that can impact the glaze color. They include:

i. Glaze Composition

Glaze composition is the key deciding factor in determining celadon glaze coloration.

In general, the higher the limestone (CaO) content, the darker the coloration of the glaze. This is because the addition of oxidized calcium decreases the melting point of the glaze, lowering viscosity, which promotes the amalgamation of iron and silicone dioxide, thus deepening the color [174]. Glaze with high CaO content (Limestone Glaze) presents with a relatively low amount of air bubbles and non-dissolved quartz granules; bringing about higher glaze transparency and a sheen glaze surface. However, limestone glaze has a relatively low high-temperature viscosity, allowing the glaze to more easily run, which discouraged thick glaze application.

During the Southern Song Dynasty, glaze production saw the introduction of plant ash to the raw material mixture. Due to the potassium chloride content in plant ash, there was an increase in potassium oxide within the celadon glaze, thus becoming the primary factor that brought about limestone alkali glaze. Limestone alkali glaze has a relatively higher high-temperature viscosity and as such does not easily run during firing. It is more suitable for high temperature firing and produces a sheen glaze surface. The introduction of limestone alkali glaze also allows for thicker glaze application, increasing the desired jade-like quality of the glaze [175]. The development from limestone glaze to limestone alkali glaze was a huge stepping stone in the improvement of ancient glaze application in Zhejiang, Longquan.

The various shades of celadon color are primarily dependent on the iron content of the glaze, ranging from 0.8%-3%. The addition of higher amounts of Zijin clay to the glaze mixture (increasing the iron content), creates a deeper coloration; and similarly a lower amount of Zijin (lower iron content) produces a coloration with lighter shades. When the Zijin content within the clay body is relatively high, the body has higher iron content, which can dissipate into the glaze during firing and increase the iron content of the glaze. During the firing process, a remedial layer is formed between the glaze and clay body. As celadon glaze is transparent, the color of the remedial layer presents through the glaze and thus darkens the perceived color of the glaze [176].

The addition of 1% of titanium oxide produces a yellowish color within the glaze. Similarly, the addition of sulfur produces a yellow hew. The addition of approximately 0.3% of oxidized cobalt, however, will increase the desired blue coloration of celadon glaze.

In addition, the presence of smaller granules within the glaze can produce a darker coloration when fired at a similar temperature. This is due to the fact that the smaller granules are more easily dissolved, and can increase the speed at which ferrous oxide and silicone dioxide react [177].

ii. Firing Temperature

Firing temperature is the primary factor effecting porcelain firing.

Longquan Celadon was fired between 1180℃~1280 ℃. Plum Green and Powder Green were the highest quality and most desirable coloration of celadon glaze, and both were produced with relatively high firing temperatures.

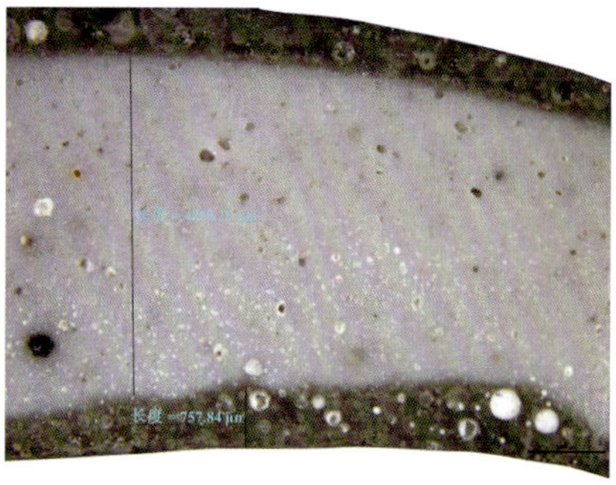

图2-3-4 余里窑样品瓷胎
Yuli Body

本章实验采用日本Nikon公司SMZ1500体视显微镜，照明光源为日本Nikon公司C-FLED2照明用LED光源，镜头为日本Nikon公司DS-Fi2镜头，并用NIS-Elements D 4.10.00软件对其进行显微拍照及图像处理。本章实验于中山大学人类进化与科技考古实验室完成。

图2-3-10

在瓷器露胎部位呈现橘红色或橙色，俗称“火石红”。火石红是由于胎中的铁质和可溶盐类在干燥过程中在露胎处富集，在烧窑结束后的冷却过程中由于二次氧化出现的色调，是Fe^{2+}被氧化成Fe^{3+}的呈色结果[170]。这一现象在两地出土标本中均有发现。

图2-3-5 余里窑S7瓷胎
Yuli Body

图2-3-11

火石红一般在露胎处可见，可以分布在器物口沿、底部、圈足上，以及器物任意一处胎釉结合的地方（见图2-3-8—图2-3-15）。胎釉结合处的火石红通常有颜色的浓淡过渡，通常从胎釉结合线向露胎的方向，颜色由浓到淡，自然过渡，直到消失；大面积露胎处有时不见明显的浓淡过渡。

图2-3-6 余里窑YC1瓷胎
Yuli Body

图2-3-8

图2-3-12

图2-3-7 余里窑T23F1瓷胎
Yuli Body

图2-3-9

图2-3-13

The chemical composition of these glazes were almost identical, but were differentiated only by their firing temperatures and atmospheres. Plum Green was the highest temperature glaze of all Longquan Celadon, ranging from 1250℃-1280 ℃. Powder Green was fired at around 1130 ℃ with variation not straying more than 20℃ in either direction [178].

In general, when using a light reduction atmosphere, the higher the temperature the darker the color of the glaze. This is most likely because the higher the temperature, the higher the ferrous oxide content and the more conducive it is for the formation of silicone dioxide [179].

iii. Firing Atmosphere

Aside from firing temperature, the firing atmosphere also has a direct impact on the coloration of celadon glaze. Simply put, atmosphere control is the control of how much oxygen is in the kiln during firing.

Firing atmosphere can be either a reduction or oxidation environment. Reduction environment refers to a lack of air being allowed to enter into the kiln. A reduction environment causes the Fe_2O_3 in the glaze to reduce to FeO during firing, which brings a more crisp coloration. Powder Green Longquan Celadon utilized a reduction environment for firing. During reduction firing, the following reaction occurs, $Fe_2O_3 + CO_2 \rightleftharpoons 2\ FeO + CO_2$.

From this reaction we can see that there is a movement towards reduced iron oxide. This reduced iron oxide is able to react with silicone dioxide, forming ferric silicate, which when melted within lime glaze, creates green silicate particles. These give the glaze a green coloration. The higher the amount of carbon monoxide within the kiln, the stronger the reduction atmosphere and darker the resulting glaze color [180].

Oxidation refers to the firing environment in which the material being fired has an even and ample amount of oxygen surrounding it during the entire firing process, from heating to cooling. If the air entering the kiln is oxygen saturated, and oxygen is sufficient throughout the entirety of fuel consumption, the kiln interior is considered to be oxidized and there is a higher presence of ferric oxide. Between 1020℃~1180 ℃, glaze begins to melt until it completely seals. If during this time, oxygen is infused into the surrounding environment, ferric oxide content drastically increases, resulting in a color that has a yellow tinge [181].

From the above we can see, iron is an important coloring agent. Oxidized iron includes ferrous oxide and ferric oxide. The relative amounts of each type of oxidized iron determine the outcome color of celadon glaze. In celadon glaze, the relative amount of ferric or ferrous oxide is determined by the use of reduction or oxidation environments while firing.

Powder Green glaze requires a reduction factor of 2~3 which is a moderate intensity reduction environment. Plum Green glaze requires a reduction factor of over 10, which is a strong reduction environment [182].

iv. Glaze Thickness

When glaze is thinner than 0.2 mm, different firing environments do not have a clear effect on the resulting glaze color. Thin glaze color outcomes are relatively invariant and the optimal glaze color cannot be achieved. The thicker the glaze, the deeper the color. When glaze thickness is lower than 0.5 mm, it gradually lacks luminescence and moist luster. As such, glaze application should seek to reach a thickness of around 1 mm [183].

Southern Song Longquan Celadon glaze was generally quite thick, ranging from 0.2-1 mm. Plum Green glaze wares achieved thickness of over 1.5 mm. From the analysis of Plum Green glaze samples we can see, glaze thickness was 0.8 mm at its thinnest, and was most commonly 1.5~1.8 mm; a thickness that was about twice that of the average celadon ware. Due to the running of glaze, the base and interior of wares could see a thickness of as high as 3.5 mm. Areas of thick glaze application would present with a deeper green coloration, and correlating areas of thin glaze would present with lighter coloration [184].

v. Firing Fuel Water Content

Moisture within the wood used to fuel kiln firing can also affect the resulting glaze color.

Wood with higher moisture content would cause deeper coloration in the wares it was used to fire. The reason being: Under high temperatures, steam particles combine with ferric

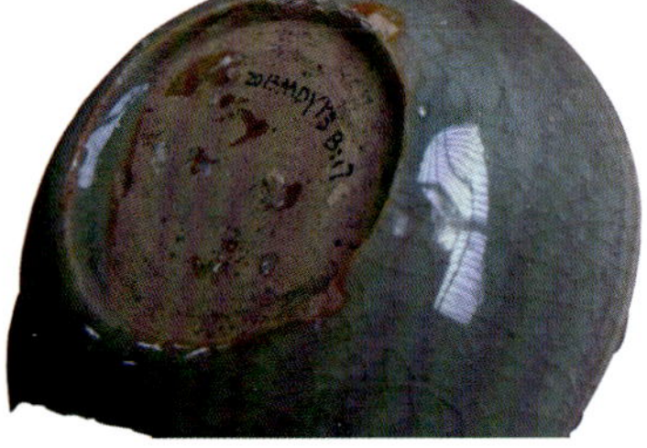

图2-3-14

图2-3-15

二、瓷釉比较

（一）瓷釉化学成分

1.明代浙江龙泉枫洞岩窑址出土青瓷标本瓷釉化学成分

当紫金土作为制釉原料时，紫金土中碱金属氧化物含量较高，在青釉烧成过程中，碱金属氧化物能起助熔剂的作用，同时它又含有较高的Al_2O_3，一方面可提高釉的高温粘度以及增高釉的玻化温度范围，使釉内具有均匀分布的微小气泡，呈现出柔和的光泽；另一方面可以降低釉的膨胀系数，使釉面不开裂[171]。

中山大学人类进化与科技考古实验室给明代浙江龙泉枫洞岩窑址出土青瓷标本瓷釉成分做了能量色散X射线荧光光谱（EDXRF）定量分析，结果见表2-3-17。

瓷釉中Al_2O_3的含量集中在11.15%—14.12%，SiO_2的含量基本在64.18%—69.46%，Fe_2O_3的含量基本在0.85%—1.88%，TiO_2的含量基本在0.11%—0.26%，Na_2O的含量在1.10%—4.04%，K_2O的含量集中在3.06%—4.92%，CaO的含量集中在3.70%—11.67%。

表2-3-16 明代广东余里窑址出土青瓷标本瓷釉EDXRF定量分析结果（wt%）

Table 2-3-16 Ming Dynasty Guangdong Yuli Kiln Site Celadon Glaze Chemical Composition EDXRF Analyses Results

编号	Na_2O	MgO	Al_2O_3	SiO_2	K_2O	CaO	TiO_2	Fe_2O_3	MnO	CuO	ZnO	PbO_2	Rb_2O	SrO	Y_2O_3	ZrO_2
Y23F1-Y	4.21	2.70	12.60	68.79	3.95	3.70	0.21	0.85	0.17	32	108	4	192	171	49	185
Y23F2-Y	3.14	1.93	12.63	68.91	4.09	4.92	0.13	1.25	0.17	15	76	45	195	173	54	195
Y23F3-Y	2.05	1.63	13.74	66.91	4.37	6.55	0.23	1.51	0.18	59	92	58	216	339	49	195
Y23F4-Y	3.66	2.26	13.01	67.25	4.15	5.44	0.14	1.08	0.16	1	78	—	170	200	53	180
Y23F5-Y	3.57	2.77	11.80	65.47	3.84	7.96	0.14	1.46	0.25	24	114	23	155	544	42	204
YA1-Y	3.65	2.37	14.48	65.73	4.81	4.52	0.29	1.16	0.18	23	81	48	245	351	59	202
YA2-Y	3.82	2.86	12.27	65.49	4.54	6.70	0.13	1.19	0.26	—	47	48	207	437	80	204
YC1-Y	2.39	2.49	12.79	61.52	4.52	11.67	0.18	1.45	0.60	46	62	1	225	506	142	215
YC2-Y	3.76	2.82	12.24	66.88	4.60	5.17	0.13	1.41	0.26	15	81	15	188	262	82	203
YC3-Y	4.40	3.08	12.76	65.96	4.92	4.58	0.14	1.17	0.22	0	37	2	211	239	111	186
Y23B1-Y	3.42	2.68	12.46	63.86	3.13	9.74	0.18	1.53	0.25	—	82	3	172	408	49	173
Y23B2-Y	1.25	0.88	12.79	66.65	3.55	9.90	0.15	1.84	0.28	—	129	11	197	195	53	199
Y23B3-Y	1.96	0.93	12.02	68.81	3.56	7.69	0.16	1.88	0.39	27	119	23	181	294	57	193
Y23B4-Y	2.90	1.92	12.61	67.84	4.23	5.97	0.13	1.40	0.27	—	71	97	213	253	61	180
Y23B5-Y	3.62	2.49	11.65	66.65	4.07	7.02	0.13	1.36	0.27	26	79	48	181	370	56	183
Y23B6-Y	4.52	3.00	12.38	64.16	3.06	8.44	0.14	1.31	0.24	36	99	12	158	135	47	182

分析结果中主量元素含量为10^{-2}，微量元素含量为10^{-6}

Within the table primary elements are to a factor of 10^{-2} and trace elements are listed to a factor of 10^{-6}

oxide to produce Fe_3O_4. Additionally, the presence of moisture in a reduction environment can cause carbon deposits on the glaze surface resulting in ashy or dark brown coloration. The use of wet or moist wood during high temperature firing, not only hinders the ability to increase heat, it negatively impacts the coloration of fired celadon glaze[185].

II. CMYK Values of Zhejiang Longquan Fengdongyan Kiln and Guangdong Yuli Kiln Excavated Sample Celadon Glaze Color

In the book *Ceramic Trace Model Research and Material Evidence Authentication: Yuan Dynasty Underglaze Blue Porcelain* there was put forth an innovative way of describing ceramic glaze color, which is to utilize a standard color palette to state the coloration of porcelain.

Standard color palettes are used to express color on digital devices. There are many ways to describe color in digital forms, i.e. the many types of standard color palettes, such as RGB Palette, CMYK Palette, Lab Palette and HSB Palette. Each of which has its own characteristics and range of application.

Currently, the most clear and quantitative way to describe the coloration of porcelain is to employ a more scientific method for color measurement. Using a color detection device, once a standard color panel has been established, the instrument will gather an accurate value of the porcelain coloration.

From a quantitative scientific color measurement stand point, we are still in the early stages. This is a due to a lack in sample pieces, apparatus limitations, and an inability to take measurements at all locations in which Longquan Kiln System Celadon (LKSC) is stored.

Unlike in the book *Ceramic Trace Model Research and Material Evidence Authentication: Yuan Dynasty Underglaze Blue Porcelain* where CMYK analyses was carried out using naked eye evaluation of exhibited Yuan Underglaze Blue pieces, the research team has adopted a new more objective method for color valuation. Using 25 sample pieces from Zhejiang Longquan Kiln and 30 sample pieces from Guangdong Yuli Kiln, analysis was carried out with professional imaging software to establish CMYK values amongst standardized images of each piece.

Note: The CMYK scale is used in printing, CMYK stands for Cyan (Blue), Magenta (Red), Yellow, and Key (Black Ratio). Printers use this scale to adjust the ratio of each ink to be used in relation to black (key) [186]. These are manually observed CMYK values; key factors including the impact of the light and image temperature, as well as the operator discrepancy may have impacted the results.

Using Standard Color Palettes to describe the coloration of LKSC is one type of quantitative color description method that is both more accurate and more easily propagated. Currently, we are still in the early stages of sample collection and color valuation, more quantitative methods and instruments are needed to gradually refine the color valuation methodology.

i. Ming Dynasty Zhejiang Longquan Fengdongyan Kiln Excavated Sample Celadon Glaze Color CMYK Values

See Table 2-3-27.

ii. Ming Dynasty Guangdong Yuli Kiln Excavated Sample Celadon Glaze Color CMYK Values

See Table 2-3-28.

iii. Summary

The use of Standardized CMYK color pallets has shown that Zhejiang Longquan Fengdongyan Kiln samples have a greenish blue coloration that is relatively light. CMYK values are lower across the board. Guangdong Yuli Kiln samples are generally darker green in color. CMYK values have higher values throughout (due to the small size of the sample selection, there is not substantial evidence to put forth a conclusive coloration deduction).

In regards to celadon coloration, excavated samples from Zhejiang Longquan Fengdongyan Kiln include bluish green (see pictures 2-3-29 and 2-3-30), ashen green (see pictures 2-3-31 and 2-3-32), and yellowish green (see pictures 2-3-33 and 2-3-34); of which, ashen green was the most common.

Aside from the aforementioned three common colors, there is also bean green, which is most commonly seen on Early Ming Dynasty official wares, and is considered a classic

表2-3-17 明代浙江龙泉枫洞岩窑址出土青瓷标本瓷釉EDXRF定量分析结果（wt%）

Table 2-3-17 Ming Dynasty Zhejiang Longquan Fengdongyan Kiln Site
Celadon Glaze Chemical Composition EDXRF Analyses Results

编号	Na_2O	MgO	Al_2O_3	SiO_2	K_2O	CaO	TiO_2	Fe_2O_3	MnO	CuO	ZnO	PbO_2	Rb_2O	SrO	Y_2O_3	ZrO_2
LDFDYXRF1	2.13	1.28	12.24	65.86	5.18	8.35	0.16	1.80	0.51	43	45	18	246	411	59	203
LDFDYXRF2	3.00	1.70	12.37	66.46	5.50	6.40	0.14	1.43	0.24	60	91	67	255	579	40	192
LDFDYXRF3	1.97	1.13	14.12	65.71	5.89	6.38	0.17	1.63	0.38	33	34	—	250	343	42	198
LDFDYXRF4	3.30	2.12	11.95	66.91	5.40	5.91	0.15	1.27	0.28	46	74	—	257	506	54	200
LDFDYXRF5	1.62	1.16	11.91	66.07	4.89	10.25	0.16	0.94	0.29	62	607	91	261	432	41	186
LDFDYXRF6	3.85	2.10	11.96	67.61	5.38	4.74	0.17	1.19	0.17	30	162	24	256	379	37	175
LDFDYXRF7	1.73	1.20	13.02	66.38	5.67	7.64	0.16	1.20	0.41	50	165	47	269	596	47	196
LDFDYXRF8	2.85	1.13	12.95	67.53	5.00	6.47	0.17	0.90	0.23	51	140	32	207	573	33	197
LDFDYXRF9	1.99	0.52	12.93	67.43	5.19	6.78	0.21	1.95	0.22	26	62	4	256	588	39	189
LDFDYXRF10	2.50	1.06	11.15	68.93	4.93	6.90	0.13	1.40	0.26	36	85	77	235	500	33	174
FDY:X	3.67	1.62	13.56	67.08	5.21	4.76	0.14	0.96	0.11	2	160	30	257	461	29	177
FDY:Y	2.98	1.45	13.76	66.13	4.74	6.61	0.13	1.21	0.14	19	81	60	253	329	35	188
LDFDYJ1	3.11	1.89	13.73	66.47	5.57	4.42	0.26	1.55	0.26	18	366	12	233	334	32	189
LDFDYJ2	1.69	0.55	12.52	69.46	5.70	5.84	0.15	1.09	0.24	38	140	47	255	559	44	187
LDFDYJ3	4.04	2.09	12.04	65.97	4.45	6.90	0.14	1.38	0.16	2	84	11	234	402	41	198
LDFDYJ7	2.98	1.08	14.09	67.88	4.79	5.21	0.14	0.83	0.17	40	123	11	237	314	38	196
LDFDYJ12	1.70	1.07	13.02	66.53	5.04	7.89	0.20	1.56	0.35	51	137	63	212	698	41	200
LDFDYJ14	1.10	1.11	12.71	66.49	4.91	9.35	0.20	1.13	0.56	47	383	107	218	584	43	189
LDLBJ13	3.39	2.26	12.65	66.50	4.53	6.74	0.15	0.78	0.22	70	1,110	194	202	367	46	184
LDLBJ14	3.00	2.65	12.78	64.18	4.11	9.38	0.18	0.73	0.28	72	179	82	160	787	33	189
LDLBJ15	1.74	0.59	12.66	67.18	3.91	10.02	0.15	0.75	0.47	22	134	20	172	650	36	191
LDLBJ16	1.66	0.83	13.42	65.88	4.02	9.62	0.18	1.39	0.36	53	125	19	165	506	35	192
LDLBJ21	3.62	1.88	12.60	66.21	4.38	7.28	0.13	0.90	0.05	37	105	1	220	636	35	188
LDLBJ29	3.32	1.74	12.22	67.53	4.42	6.71	0.11	0.95	0.06	4	127	48	206	584	29	182
LDLBJ31	1.61	0.51	12.68	69.38	4.61	7.07	0.17	0.98	0.25	46	85	11	235	450	33	187

分析结果中主量元素含量为10^{-2}，微量元素含量为10^{-6}

Within the table primary elements are to a factor of 10^{-2} and trace elements are listed to a factor of 10^{-6}

color of Early Ming Dynasty Official Kiln productions (see picture 2-3-35).

In general, Fengdongyan Kiln wares are relatively milky and mild, with a luster that is soft and deep; glaze crazing and running is not often seen.

The color palette of Yuli Kiln glazes is similar to that of Fengdongyan samples, primarily consisting of three colors: Green (see pictures 2-3-36—2-3-38), Ashen Green (see pictures 2-3-39—2-3-41), and Yellowish Green (see pictures 2-3-42—2-3-44). There is also a select few samples that presented with a bluish green glaze color (see pictures 2-3-45 and 2-3-46).

The largest portion of Yuli samples fall into the ashen green category. Ashen green glazes are almost all fired at high temperatures, and often occur do to over firing. However, ashen qualities can also be brought about by the inherent glaze composition or under firing. In general, the majority of ashen glaze on white body porcelain is because of over firing, and the majority of ashen glaze on red body wares is because of under firing.

The samples at Yuli have a relatively thin layer of glaze. This is because of single glaze application. As such, the coloration is relatively translucent and light. Samples include glaze quality of bright and translucent as well as murky and dull (usually under fired samples present with a murky and dull glaze quality). Crazing and glaze crawling is quite common. Often the internal base or areas of incised pattern have relatively thick collection of glaze, which present with a deeper coloration. As such, a single ware can present with several shades of coloration (see pictures 2-3-47—2-3-50).

Zhejiang Longquan Fengdongyan Kiln samples have a coloration that is more steady and even. Yuli samples; which include complete, incomplete, and under fired pieces; presented with a wide array of glaze discolorations. These glaze color discrepancies between Yuli Kiln wares and Longquan Celadon are primarily due to the differences in quality of glaze materials and production technique. Yuli Kiln glazes contain relatively low amounts of K_2O and Na_2O, which increased the runniness of the glaze.

c. Glaze Crawling

Glaze crawling is a phenomenon cause by the receding of the glaze, and exposing the body beneath (see pictures 2-3-51—2-4-54).

Glaze crawling is formed when the glaze is too thin to cover the body of the glaze in certain areas, and may be caused by the surface tension of the glaze, moisture on the surface of the clay, viscosity of the glaze being too high, and so forth, which causes the glazes inability to cover the body [187].

d. Bristle Pitting

Also called pin-holes, these are small hair follicle-like holes in the surface of the glaze that were caused during the firing process (see Chapter 5 Section 4).

Bristle Pits are observable holes in the glaze, however the porcelain body is not visible to the naked eye (see pictures 2-3-55—2-3-58).

e. Glaze Cracks

Also called crazing, glaze cracks are all of the straight, curved, and sporadic fissures that are disbursed across the glaze formed during the firing process or under the influence of the post-firing environment (see Chapter 5 Section 2 Glaze Cracks heading).

Generally, glaze cracks on celadon are not considered to be intentionally created for aesthetic purposes, have a relatively low occurrence rate, and are considered to be glaze flaws.

Cracks can occur at certain portions on the surface of a piece, or occur across the entire glazed surface. Crazing on aged pieces often has associated color change (see pictures 2-3-59—2-3-62).

f. Scratches

Scratches are the imperfections on celadon glaze that present as lines on the glaze surface that were left by the abrasive force of a solid external object.

Scratches can occur across the entire glaze surface, and varying severities of scratches can coexist or overlap.

枫洞岩窑标本的釉料基本都属于钙—碱釉。

2. 明代广东余里窑址出土青瓷标本瓷釉化学成分

中山大学人类进化与科技考古实验室给广东余里窑址出土青瓷标本瓷釉成分做了EDXRF定量分析，结果见表2-3-16[172]。

其中，瓷釉中Al_2O_3的含量集中在11.65%—14.48%，SiO_2的含量基本在61.52%—68.91%，Fe_2O_3的含量基本在0.85%—1.88%，TiO_2的含量基本在0.13%—0.29%，Na_2O的含量在1.25%—4.52%，K_2O的含量基本在3.06%—4.92%，CaO的含量集中在3.70%—11.67%。

余里窑标本的瓷釉大部分属于钙—碱釉，有少部分样品属于碱—钙釉。

3. 小结

余里窑青瓷样品瓷釉K_2O的含量（4.1%）比浙江龙泉窑（4.6%）低，而CaO的含量相差不大，都在6.9%左右。

余里窑青瓷釉中Fe_2O_3和TiO_2含量与浙江龙泉窑青瓷非常相近。由此可以推测，当时余里窑的窑工在掌握了龙泉窑青瓷的釉料配方的同时，还可能从当地找到了类似的原料[173]。

（二）瓷釉特征

1. 瓷釉光亮特征

青瓷釉的光亮特征可分为三种：哑光、润光及亮光。

（1）哑光

哑光瓷釉有涩感，有的泛白。（见图2-3-18、图2-3-19）

余里窑的标本有相当一部分生烧的陶瓷，釉面均为哑光。（见图2-3-20、图2-3-21）

枫洞岩窑标本：
Fengdongyan Samples:

图2-3-18

图2-3-19

余里窑标本：
Yuli Samples:

图2-3-20

图2-3-21

（2）润光

润光瓷釉泛柔光，给人以莹润之感。（见图2-3-22—图2-3-24）

枫洞岩窑标本：
Fengdongyan Samples:

图2-3-22

图2-3-23

图2-3-24

Scratches can be wide or narrow, long or short, deep or shallow, and can include colorations of yellow, soil, brown, and so forth (see pictures 2-3-63 and 2-3-64).

g. Individual Iron Spots

On occasion, small individual brown iron spots appear on the glaze surface (see pictures 2-3-65—2-3-68).

h. Summary

Longquan and Yuli Kiln Celadon wares both include the aforementioned glaze defects, but as a whole the amount of defects on Longquan Kiln wares is fewer than that of Yuli Kiln wares. This is due to the more matured techniques and higher production quality standards amongst the Longquan Kilns.

（3）亮光

亮光瓷釉整体透亮，瓷釉显得光滑。（见图2-3-25、图2-3-26）

余里窑标本：
Yuli Samples:

图2-3-25

图2-3-26

2. 瓷釉颜色

（1）影响青釉发色的因素

在制作青瓷的过程中，影响青釉呈色的因素较多且复杂。影响其发色的主要因素如下：

① 釉的成分

青瓷的釉料成分是决定青瓷釉色的关键。

通常来说，釉料中石灰石（氧化钙）含量愈高，釉色愈深，因为当氧化钙含量增加时，釉的熔融温度降低，黏度减小，有利于氧化亚铁和二氧化硅的熔解和作用，从而颜色加深[174]。氧化钙含量高的瓷釉（石灰釉）中气泡和未熔石英颗粒很少，因此釉层比较透明，光泽感比较强。但石灰釉在高温下高温黏度较小，易流釉，所以难以施厚釉。

南宋时期开始在制釉原料中加入草木灰，因草木灰中富含钾盐，提高了青釉中氧化钾的含量，这是形成石灰碱釉的主要原因。石灰碱釉的特点是高温黏度比较大，不易流釉，在适当温度烧成时，釉面光泽柔和。石灰碱釉这样的特征允许施釉厚一些，更接近玉质的效果[175]。从石灰釉发展到石灰碱釉，可以说是浙江古代青瓷在配釉技术上的一大进步。

青瓷之所以呈现各种青色，主要是由于釉内含有0.8%—3%铁氧化物的缘故。釉料中紫金土含量愈高（即釉的化学成分中铁的含量愈高），呈色愈深；紫金土含量愈低（即铁的含量愈低），釉色愈浅。当胎料中紫金土含量较高，使得坯料中含铁量比釉料中高时，胎内即可能有一部分铁在高温烧制时扩散到釉中，增加了釉中的铁含量，在烧成时，胎、釉之间形成中间层，青瓷釉具有透明性，使中间层的颜色透映出来，因而加深了釉的色调[176]。

在釉料中加1%的氧化钛时，釉会呈现黄色；硫也会使青釉发黄；在釉料中加0.3%左右的氧化钴时，有益于青瓷釉呈现青色色调。

另外，釉料中的颗粒小，在同一温度下烧成时釉色较深。因为釉料的颗粒度愈小，熔融能力愈强，故可加速釉内氧化亚铁与二氧化硅的反应速度[177]。

② 烧成温度

烧成温度是瓷器烧成的首要条件。

龙泉青瓷的烧成温度约在1180—1280℃之间。龙泉青瓷中以梅子青釉和粉青釉的釉质、釉色最好，这两种釉的烧成温度都很高。梅子青釉与粉青釉的化学成分相差无几，但烧成温度和窑内气氛却不同，梅子青釉的烧成温度在龙泉青瓷各种釉中几乎是最高的，在1250—1280℃之间。粉青釉的烧成温度约在1130℃，上下不超过20℃[178]。

一般来说（采用轻还原焰烧成时），烧成温度越高，釉色越深，可能的原因是：温度越高，氧化亚铁在釉中的比例增高，生成的硅酸盐熔体的熔融程度也就越好[179]。

③ 烧成气氛

除了烧成温度之外，烧成气氛对青釉的呈色也起着决定性的影响。烧成气氛的控制，简单地说，就是控制窑内的空气量。

烧成气氛可以分为还原气氛和氧化气氛。还原气氛是指瓷坯在烧窑时空气供给不充分，燃烧不完全的条件下产生的一种火焰气氛。还原气氛能使青瓷胎釉中的Fe_2O_3还原成FeO，制品的釉色就显得比较青翠。龙泉青瓷釉中的粉青釉一般都采用还原焰烧成。用还原焰烧成时，从$Fe_2O_3 + CO \rightleftharpoons 2FeO + CO_2$的可逆反应中可以看出，反应向生成氧化亚铁的方向移动。氧化亚铁与二氧化硅作用生成偏硅酸铁，并进一步在石灰釉内熔融时，生成具有青绿色的硅酸盐熔体，使釉呈现青绿色。随着窑炉内一氧化碳含量增加，还原性气氛增强而釉色加深[180]。

氧化气氛是指瓷坯在整体烧成过程中，均在充分供给氧气的气氛中加热升温，在燃料完全燃烧时所产生的的一种火焰气氛。如果入窑的空气量多，供燃料充分燃烧后还有多余的氧气时，则窑内处于氧化气氛，氧化铁的相对含量提高。在1020—1180℃时，釉开始熔融至完全密闭时，若采用氧化焰烧成，则氧化铁的相对含量占优势，则成品釉色比较灰黄[181]。

由上文可知，铁是着色剂。铁的氧化物包括氧化亚铁和氧化铁。不同铁氧化物的含量多少决定了青釉的不同色调。在青釉中，氧化亚铁和氧化铁的含量比例取决于烧成时采用还原气氛还是氧化气氛。

粉青釉还原比值约为2—3，要求强弱适中的还原焰；梅子青的还原比值约在10以上，要求强还原焰[182]。

④ 釉层厚度

瓷釉的厚度在0.2毫米以下时，不同的烧成气氛对青瓷釉呈色的影响不十分明显。釉层薄，色调变化较小，但此时釉的色彩欠佳。釉层愈厚，釉色愈深。当釉的厚度在0.5毫米以下时，就逐渐缺乏晶莹滋润的色泽。所以施釉时，釉层的厚度应保持在1毫米左右[183]。

南宋龙泉青釉一般都上得比较厚，约在0.2—1毫米，梅子青釉甚至超过1.5毫米。从梅子青标本分析看，其釉层厚度最薄处为0.8毫米，一般为1.5—1.8毫米，比普通青瓷釉厚一倍左右，器底部分由于流釉厚可达3.5毫米。愈厚之处就显得愈绿；反之，釉层较薄的地方，绿色就显得比较浅[184]。

⑤ 燃料的水分

烧成时木柴的水分对青瓷釉色也有影响。

木柴的含水量越高，烧成后的青瓷釉色就愈深。原因是，在高温时，水蒸气有促进氧化铁离解为四氧化三铁的趋向。同时，在高温还原阶段，水蒸气的存在易造成碳素沉积在器物表面，造成青瓷釉烧成后呈现灰色或暗褐色。高温阶段采用湿木柴做燃料时，不仅烧窑温度不易上升，而且对青瓷釉呈色产生很不好的影响[185]。

（2）明代浙江龙泉枫洞岩窑址出土青瓷标本与广东余里窑址出土青瓷标本釉色CMYK值

在《元青花迹型研究与物证鉴定》一书中，笔者提出了一种对瓷器色彩的创新描述方法——采用色彩表达模式来表述。用色彩表达模式数值来描述瓷器的颜色，旨在量化颜色认知。

色彩表达模式是一种在数字化设备上表达色彩的方式。采用数字化形式来描述色彩更加精确明晰。计算机表达色彩的方式有多种，每一种表达方式都有自己的特点和适用范围，如RGB模式、CMYK模式、Lab模式、HSB模式等等。

目前较精确、科学地确定颜色的方法为，使用颜色探测器，在一定的环境下对准被测物，读出其颜色数值。

在科学量化表述瓷器发色方面，我们尚处初级阶段，由于研究标本的限制和科学仪器的缺乏，我们无法现场测量现存的每一件青瓷标本的颜色数值。

相比在《元青花迹型研究与物证鉴定》一书中所采用的现场目测瓷器颜色，然后比对国家标准色谱后得出它们的CMYK数值，此次研究团队尝试使用更加客观准确的方法，采用明代浙江龙泉枫洞岩窑的25个标本，广东余里窑的30个标本，分别对标本釉色采集拍照，然后通过专业软件识别图片对焦点的CMYK值。

注：CMYK是印刷色彩模型，C代表青色（Cyan），M代表洋红色（Magenta），Y代表黄色（Yellow），K代表黑色比例（Black Ratio）。C、M、Y、K的不同数值代表了印刷色油墨颜色相应的百分比[186]。这里CMYK值为参考值，瓷器实际的颜色受测量时的灯光、温度、仪器及个人等因素影响。

用色彩表达模式来表述瓷器的颜色是一种量化表述颜色的方法，可以使瓷器的颜色表述更加精确，更易传播。目前来说，我们在标本采集及颜色表述上还属初级阶段，需要更多量化的科学方法和仪器，让色彩表述越来越精确。

① 明代浙江龙泉枫洞岩窑址出土青瓷标本釉色CMYK值

见表2-3-27。

② 明代广东余里窑址出土青瓷标本釉色CMYK值

见表2-3-28。

表2-3-27 明代浙江龙泉枫洞岩窑址出土青瓷标本釉色CMYK值

Table 2-3-27 Ming Dynasty Zhejiang Longquan Fengdongyan Kiln Celadon Glaze Color CMYK Values

序号 Reference No.	编号 Record No.	图片 Pictures	CMYK值 CMYK Value
1	11		C=44 M=23 Y=32 K=0
2	6		C=46 M=26 Y=36 K=0
3	9		C=46 M=28 Y=36 K=0
4	23		C=46 M=29 Y=35 K=0
5	20		C=51 M=31 Y=40 K=0
6	21		C=50 M=28 Y=36 K=0
7	22		C=52 M=31 Y=38 K=0
8	16		C=51 M=30 Y=39 K=0
9	24		C=51 M=31 Y=40 K=0
10	12		C=50 M=32 Y=41 K=0
11	19		C=48 M=36 Y=39 K=0
12	10		C=53 M=38 Y=41 K=0
13	25		C=53 M=38 Y=44 K=0
14	3		C=57 M=37 Y=42 K=0
15	8		C=61 M=34 Y=41 K=0
16	17		C=57 M=36 Y=45 K=0
17	5		C=57 M=42 Y=50 K=0
18	2		C=59 M=45 Y=51 K=0
19	14		C=60 M=44 Y=47 K=0
20	15		C=61 M=50 Y=56 K=1
21	4		C=61 M=53 Y=59 K=2
22	1		C=56 M=56 Y=57 K=2
23	13		C=59 M=59 Y=61 K=5
24	7		C=57 M=64 Y=70 K=11
25	18		C=61 M=71 Y=80 K=28

表2-3-28 明代广东余里窑址出土青瓷标本釉色CMYK值

Table 2-3-28 Ming Dynasty Guangdong Yuli Kiln Celadon Glaze Color CMYK Values

序号 Reference No.	编号 Record No.	图片 Pictures	CMYK值 CMYK Value
1	10		C=50 M=39 Y=57 K=0
2	15		C=53 M=43 Y=58 K=0
3	8		C=57 M=43 Y=61 K=0
4	9		C=59 M=47 Y=61 K=1
5	24		C=58 M=46 Y=61 K=1
6	21		C=61 M=47 Y=63 K=1
7	1		C=65 M=44 Y=64 K=1
8	23		C=64 M=48 Y=63 K=2
9	22		C=64 M=50 Y=68 K=4
10	19		C=66 M=49 Y=67 K=4
11	20		C=67 M=50 Y=64 K=4
12	4		C=53 M=32 Y=62 K=0
13	17		C=59 M=40 Y=64 K=0
14	30		C=58 M=59 Y=58 K=0
15	18		C=60 M=42 Y=66 K=1
16	6		C=60 M=43 Y=70 K=1
17	3		C=58 M=44 Y=70 K=1
18	2		C=61 M=44 Y=68 K=1
19	5		C=62 M=51 Y=76 K=5
20	7		C=60 M=47 Y=69 K=2
21	16		C=65 M=47 Y=72 K=3
22	13		C=65 M=50 Y=73 K=5
23	14		C=65 M=50 Y=71 K=4
24	25		C=65 M=52 Y=72 K=6

续表2-3-28
Table 2-3-28 Continued

序号 Reference No.	编号 Record No.	图片 Pictures	CMYK值 CMYK Value
25	26		C=67 M=51 Y=76 K=7
26	11		C=61 M=51 Y=70 K=4
27	12		C=60 M=52 Y=71 K=5
28	28		C=64 M=60 Y=71 K=13
29	27		C=62 M=63 Y=86 K=21
30	29		C=69 M=63 Y=86 K=28

（3）小结

从采集样本对应的CMYK色谱图发现，明代浙江龙泉枫洞岩窑址的青瓷标本发色偏青蓝，颜色较淡，CMYK值大部分较低；明代广东余里窑的青瓷标本发色偏青绿，颜色较深，CMYK值大部分偏高。

注：标本数量不足以做出概括性的对比结论。

在青釉呈色方面，现将浙江龙泉枫洞岩窑的青瓷标本釉色大致分为青蓝（见图2-3-29、图2-3-30）、青灰（见图2-3-31、图2-3-32）、青黄（见图2-3-33、图2-3-34）三种主色调。其中青灰色更常见。

除以上三种主色调以外，还有一种比较少见的豆青色，这种颜色通常出现在明初的官器标本上，属于明初龙泉官窑的典型色。（见图2-3-35）

总的来说，枫洞岩窑的标本釉质都比较乳浊浑厚，光泽柔和深沉，开片、流釉现象不多。

青蓝:
Bluish Green:

图2-3-29

青蓝:
Bluish Green:

图2-3-30

青灰:
Ashen Green:

图2-3-31

图2-3-32

余里窑的釉色分类与枫洞岩窑的类似，大致分为青绿（见图2-3-36—图2-3-38）、青灰（见图2-3-39—图2-3-41）、青黄（见图2-3-42—图2-3-44）三种主色调。还有一种青蓝的釉色，但不多见。（见图2-3-45、图2-3-46）

余里窑标本的釉色主要为青灰。灰色釉基本都是高温下形成的，常因过烧才能显现。但也有釉料本身就含呈灰色的成分，或者在欠烧状态下也能产生。一般来看，白胎青釉器多半是因过烧而呈现灰色调，红胎青釉器多半是因欠烧而呈现灰色调。

青黄:
Yellowish Green:

图2-3-33

图2-3-34

豆青:
Bean Green:

图2-3-35

青绿:
Green:

图2-3-36

图2-3-37

图2-3-38

青灰:
Ashen Green:

图2-3-39

图2-3-40

图2-3-41

青黄:
Yellowish Green:

图2-3-42

图2-3-46

图2-3-48

图2-3-43

余里窑址出土实物器身釉层一般较薄，为一次施釉，因此釉色显透明，颜色浅淡。标本中既有釉质透明清亮的，也有乳浊的（一般生烧的标本釉质都属于乳浊类），开片、流釉现象常见。器内底或刻印纹饰低洼处常因积釉较厚而显得色深，所以常有同一件器物上好几种颜色的现象。（见图2-3-47—图2-3-50）

浙江龙泉枫洞岩窑的标本呈色更加稳定，而余里窑存在成品和半成品甚至生烧品混杂，各种釉色器物并存现象。余里窑的釉色之所以不如浙江龙泉窑，主要是因为其釉料成分和工艺的不足。

图2-3-49

图2-3-44

图2-3-50

青蓝:
Bluish Green:

图2-3-45

图2-3-47

3. 缩釉

缩釉是瓷器釉表面向周边滚缩，导致中间缺釉露出胎体。（见图2-3-51—图2-3-54）

造成缩釉的原因有很多，如釉表面张力的作用、坯胎潮湿、釉的黏度过大，都可能会造成缩釉[187]。

枫洞岩窑标本:
Fengdongyan Samples:

图2-3-51

图2-3-52

余里窑标本:
Yuli Samples:

图2-3-53

图2-3-54

4. 鬃眼

鬃眼是在瓷器烧制过程中形成的釉层小孔(参见第五章第四节)。

鬃眼是瓷器釉表面的缺陷，凭肉眼可见，但用肉眼通过小孔观察不到胎体。（见图2-3-55—图2-3-58）

枫洞岩窑标本:
Fengdongyan Samples:

图2-3-55

图2-3-56

余里窑标本:
Yuli Samples:

图2-3-57

图2-3-58

5. 釉裂纹

釉裂纹是瓷器在烧制过程中和在后天环境影响下形成的，以直线、曲线等不规则线条形貌分布在釉表面的开裂纹路(参见第五章第二节釉裂纹部分)。

通常来说，龙泉窑青瓷上的釉裂纹不属于因审美要求而刻意造成的，而且较少出现，如果有釉裂现象，都属于瓷器缺陷。余里窑青瓷也是这样。釉裂纹既可以局部存在，也可以遍布全器，通常有一定年份的釉裂纹都会有变色现象。（见图2-3-59—图2-3-62）

枫洞岩窑标本:
Fengdongyan Samples:

图2-3-59

图2-3-60

余里窑标本:
Yuli Samples:

图2-3-61

图2-3-62

6. 划痕

划痕是龙泉窑系青瓷釉表面与硬物碰划留下的破坏性纹路。

划痕通常随机无序地分布在釉表面，深浅交织共存，有粗有细，有长有短，颜色有无色、黄色、褐色等。（见图2-3-63、图2-3-64）

枫洞岩窑标本:
Fengdongyan Samples:

图2-3-63

余里窑标本:
Yuli Samples:

图2-3-64

7. 独立铁斑

有时青瓷上会随机出现个别褐色的独立铁斑。（图2-3-65—图2-3-68）

枫洞岩窑标本:
Fengdongyan Samples:

图2-3-65

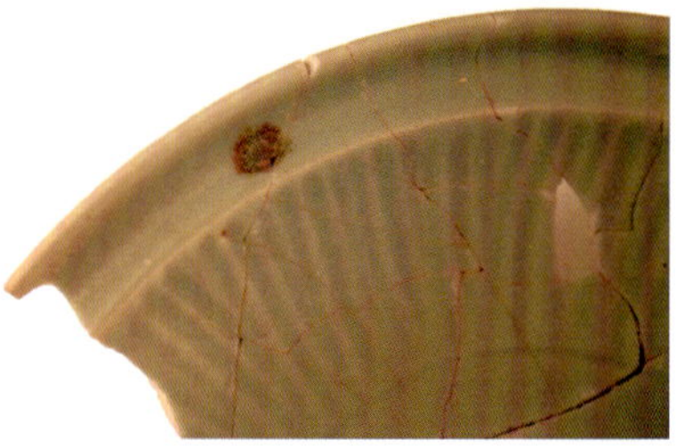

图2-3-66

余里窑标本:
Yuli Samples:

图2-3-67

图2-3-68

8. 小结

在龙泉窑及余里窑的标本中都能发现以上列举的瓷釉缺陷，但总体而言龙泉窑的标本的缺陷要少很多。这离不开龙泉窑更成熟的工艺及对产品更高的要求。

第四节
明代浙江龙泉窑青瓷与广东余里窑青瓷制作工艺比较分析

一、浙江龙泉窑青瓷制作工艺

浙江龙泉青瓷传统的制作工艺流程有原料预备、成形、装饰、素烧、施釉、装烧、烧成等几个重要工序。

（一）原料预备

制作浙江龙泉青瓷所需的原料来自当地，原料的预备包括胎料配制和釉料配制[188]。

1. 胎料配制

青瓷坯胎的原料组成主要有瓷土和紫金土。原料经过粉碎、淘洗、脱水、练泥、陈腐的步骤，才能成为制瓷坯的胎料[189]。

2. 釉料配制

制作青瓷釉的原料有瓷土、紫金土、石灰石、植物灰。配制过程是将原料煅烧、粉碎、淘洗后按一定的比例混合制成釉浆。

（二）成形

成形工艺主要包括制坯前的器型设计、制坯和制坯后的阴干、补水等阶段[190]。

1. 器型设计

器型设计是由专人负责出图样。如果烧制贡瓷或者官用瓷器，还要按照宫廷或者官府的来样或者实物进行设计。

明代初期官窑龙泉青瓷就是按照朝廷提供的官样烧制的。

2. 制坯

制坯是决定瓷器质量的重要环节。龙泉窑主要采用拉坯、模制和捏塑三种方式[191]。

《菽园杂记》中有关于龙泉窑制坯工艺的记载："匠作先以钧运成器，或模范成形。候泥干，则蘸油涂饰。"[192]

（1）拉坯

《菽园杂记》中的"钧"即辘轳（辘轳是一种靠人力制动的拉坯工具）。工匠将坯泥放在辘轳的圆轮上，依靠圆轮转动的惯性拉坯成形[193]。

（2）模制

"模范"是按照陶瓷所需器型或纹样制作的模具。龙泉窑模具采用黏土制作，经低温焙烧而成[194]。

（3）捏塑

捏塑工艺通常用于制作人物、动物和器物局部的饰件。对某些拉坯和模制方式都难以成形的器物或饰件，就需要采用捏塑工艺。一些琢器上的动物捏塑、动物盖钮还有各类塑像和饰件等器物，都是工匠用手捏制而成的。

（4）琢器成形

琢器是指不能仅靠陶车一次拉坯成形，而需要多种工序加工成形的器物[195]。一般包括瓶、罐、觚、炉、壶之类的"立件"。

龙泉器物中的琢器基本采用了多次拉坯、分段黏结的先进成形工艺。分段拉坯的部位因年代及窑场而异，一般分为两段或者三段，最多可达四段。通常在器物的颈、肩、腹、底等部位可见接胎痕迹[196]。

这种分段拉坯、再黏结节坯的成形工艺提高了制作大型或者复杂器物的成功率，减少了器物开裂变形的情况。像凤尾尊等器型高大、腹部曲折的器物，都是分段拉坯，然后镶接成形；方瓶、琮式瓶、六角杯、八角杯和部分爪形壶，则用模具印节坯，再黏合接固修整而成[197]。

（5）圆器成形

圆器是指能够直接在陶车上拉坯或用陶模成形的器物[198]。一般包括碗、盘、杯、碟、盏等圆形的日用器皿。在龙泉各地窑址中，发现了很多辘轳遗迹。

Section 4：

Comparative Analysis of Ming Dynasty Longquan Kiln System Celadon: Zhejiang Longquan Kiln and Guangdong Yuli Kiln Celadon Manufacturing Technique

1. Zhejiang Longquan Kiln Celadon Manufacturing Technique

Traditional Longquan Celadon production primarily consist of the following important manufacturing processes: Raw material preparing, shaping, decorating, clay body firing, glazing, kiln outfitting, and firing.

A. Raw Material Preparing

All the raw materials used in the production of Longquan Celadon come from local sources, and preparations are carried out on body and glaze material [188].

a. Body Material Preparation

The primary composition of celadon clay consists of porcelain clay and Zijin clay. The raw materials must undergo pulverizing, washing, draining, kneading, and aging before it can be used for the celadon body [189].

b. Glaze Material Preparation

The primary composition of celadon glaze consists of porcelain clay, Zijin clay, limestone, and plant ash. Material burning, pulverizing, and washing must all take place before the elements can be mixed together in certain proportions to form the glaze.

B. Shaping

The shape formation process primarily consists of three stages: Pre-production shape design, shape formation, and post-production drying and wetting [190].

a. Shape Design

Shape design consists of a professional designer producing a shape pattern. If the piece is for official or imperial use, it is designed according to a preapproved pattern or model passed down from the official or imperial court.

Early Ming Dynasty Official Kiln Longquan Celadon was fired in accordance with the models prescribed by the imperial court.

b. Body Formation

Body formation is an important deciding factor in the quality of the ceramic ware. Longquan Kilns primarily used the following three type of body formation: Pulling, Molding, and Pressing [191].

Ancient texts record the process of Longquan body shaping as such, “First, the artisan forms the shape on the wheel or models the piece. Second, the body is dried then glaze is applied.” [192]

I. Body Pulling

Pulling, in the above-mentioned text, refers to the potter’s wheel. The potter would place a lump of clay on the center of a potter’s wheel and use the centrifugal forces of the spinning wheel to slowly pull the piece into the desired shape. This is also referred to as throwing the piece [193].

II. Body Modeling

“Modeling” is the process of shaping a piece in accordance with a model or desired pattern. Models used in the Longquan

龙泉窑生产的圆器基本上都是采用拉坯方式制作的，即上文陆容所说的：“钧运成器”。工匠们用手在辘轳上拉坯，制成粗坯。

3. 成形后工序

坯体成形后还只是粗坯，属于半成品，经过自然干燥，再修坯、挖足和补水，使胎壁厚薄适当，表面光滑[199]。

4. 明代浙江龙泉窑青瓷成形特征

（1）琢器成形特征

相比元代琢器而言，明代琢器外壁的接痕表现不明显。

罐类通常是隐圈足，小件罐类则继承元代的平沙底。

玉壶春瓶圈足外撇，圈足底平切处理。

执壶圈足较深，通常外撇，圈足底平切处理（见图2-4-1、图2-4-2）。

高足杯的高足上有的有一节凸棱（见图2-4-3），有的刻划几道弦纹，如竹节（见图2-4-4），有的刻划简易纹饰（见图2-4-5），也有的素面（见图2-4-6）。高足为平切底，足内实心（见图2-4-7）。

樽式炉有饼底也有平底，有的底心有洞，有的没有（见图2-4-8—图2-4-12）。

图2-4-2

图2-4-6

图2-4-3

图2-4-7

图2-4-4

图2-4-8

图2-4-1

图2-4-5

图2-4-9

Kilns were made of low-temperature fired clay [194].

III. Shape Pinching

Shape pinching was a process normally reserved for the shaping of people and animal figures or portions of wares to be affixed later. For parts of pulled or modeled pieces that were difficult to form, or added as decorative fixtures, pinching was utilized. Animals and handles on closed wares, fixtures on lids, and all types of statues and decorative figures would all have been hand pinched by a potter.

IV. Closed Shape Formation

Closed shapes refer to pieces that cannot be formed in one throw on the potter's wheel, but need to be formed from two or more shaping processes [195]. These include: Vases, jars, beakers, censers, kettles, and so forth "standing wares".

Longquan Kiln closed wares almost all utilized multiple thrown shapes, and then the conjoining of these sections by adhering the separate pieces together. The break down of sections was different amongst each local kiln, but was primarily done in two or three sections, with as many as four sections per pieces used. Often in areas such as the neck, shoulder, body, and foot of the pieces, a noticeable joint is visible [196].

This type of section and joint shaping improved the ability of the kilns to produce larger and more complex pieces, as well as decrease the number of pieces that cracked during firing. Phoenix Tail Zun vases and other large pieces with rotund bodies were all formed with conjoined pulled sections; while pieces with straight edges such as square vases, hexagonal vases, octagonal vases, and a portion of gourd shaped wares were formed using the conjoining of molded sides [197].

V. Open Shape Formation

Open shaping refers to the process of creating a piece by throwing it once on the potter's wheel or using only one mold to complete the shape [198]. They primarily include round daily use wares such as bowls, plates, cups, saucers and so forth. Many potter's wheels have been discovered amongst the Longquan Kiln area.

Almost all the open wares produced in the Longquan area utilized a pulling shape method.

c. Body Formation Post Production

The freshly formed clay body is merely a coarse unfinished product, and must undergo natural drying, reworking, footing, and water application to make the thickness uniform and surface smooth [199].

d. Ming Dynasty Zhejiang Longquan Celadon Shaping Characteristics

I. Closed Shape Characteristics

Compared to wares from the Yuan Dynasty, Ming Dynasty closed wares have less distinctive joints.

Jars often have a round foot ring, but jarlettes continue the Yuan tradition of flat bottom shape.

The foot rings of Yuhuchun vases are outwardly slanted, and the inner base has been carved flat.

The feet of kettles are deep and often outward slanting, and the base has been carved flat (see pictures 2-4-1 and 2-4-2).

Stem cups present a with a single ribbed ring on the stem of the piece (see picture 2-4-3); with several carved rings, similar to bamboo joints (see picture 2-4-4); with simple pattern (see picture 2-4-5); or with a plain face (see picture 2-4-6). The stem has a flat base, and is not hollow (see picture 2-4-7).

Zun style censers can have cake bases or flat bases, some with a hole in the center and some without (see pictures 2-4-8—2-4-12).

II. Open Shape Characteristics

Small closed shape wares almost all have a foot ring, which is small but relatively deep and either outward slanting or vertical (see pictures 2-4-13—2-4-16).

Some bowls are gradually thicker from mouth to base, but the gradation is not drastic (see pictures 2-4-17—2-4-20), and some pieces have a uniform thickness (see pictures 2-4-21 and 2-4-22).

Plate bodies are relatively thick and have shallow foot

图2-4-10

图2-4-11

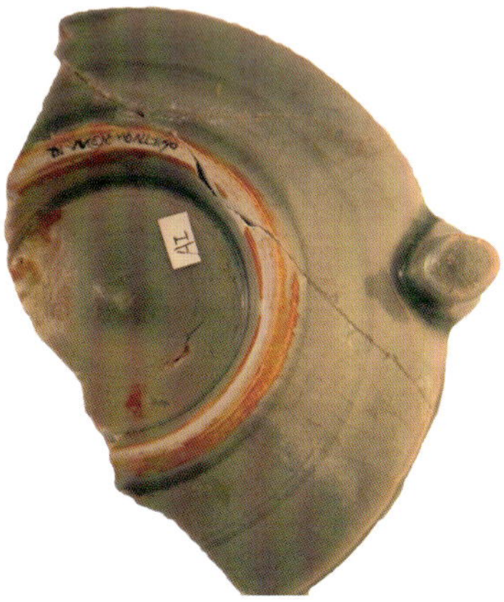

图2-4-12

（2）圆器成形特征

小件圆器几乎都有圈足，圈足小但较深，外撇或垂直。（见图2-4-13—图2-4-16）

图2-4-13

图2-4-14

图2-4-15

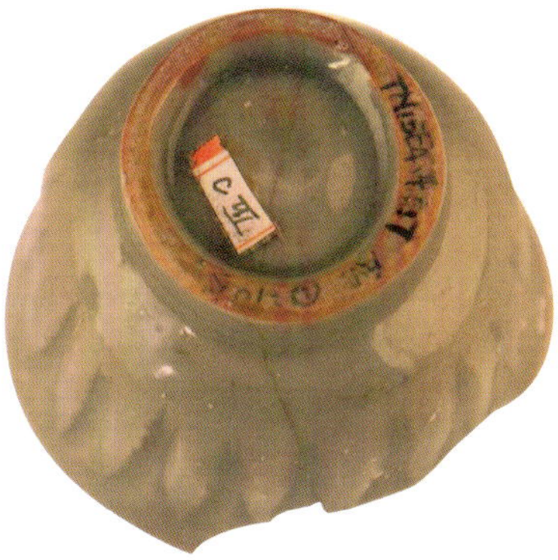

图2-4-16

碗类由口沿到底部逐渐变厚，但过渡不明显（见图2-4-17—图2-4-20）；也有的厚度基本一致（见图2-4-21、图2-4-22）。

图2-4-17

图2-4-18

图2-4-19

图2-4-20

rings that are straight or trapezoidal in shape, and are thinner than the foot rings of bowls (see pictures 2-4-23 and 2-4-27).

C. Decorating

Once shaped, the body could undergo the process of decoration.

D. Body Firing

Once the raw clay body had been decorated and air-dried, it could be baked, a process that is called body firing.

Baking can elevate the strength of the clay body and illiminate the possibility of deformation during glazing. It also allows for the application of more glaze, which is desirable for the thick glaze application seen in Longquan. Body firing normally is conducted at a temperature lower than normal firing and can be carried out at around 800℃ [200].

E. Glazing

During the Ming Dynasty, glaze application at Longquan was carried out in primarily two ways: Dunking and Swaying. Dunking was the process of dipping the clay body directly into a glaze mixture and pulling it out. Swaying refers to the process of pouring glaze liquid into the interior of a vessel and slightly swaying the piece to uniformly cover the interior wall of the ware and pouring out the excess.

Bowls, plates and so forth wares would employ dunking for exterior and then swaying for the interior walls.

As early as the Southern Song Dynasty, Longquan Wares began to present with fully glazed pieces, and this carried into the Yuan Dynasty. By the Late Southern Song Dynasty, Longquan glazing reached its peak. The complex process of multiple glazing and multiple firing brought about the successful emergence of Plum Green glaze porcelain. By the Yuan Dynasty, multiple glaze applications gradually ceased, and common wares of the Ming Dynasty were almost exclusively single glazed. Large wares increased during the Ming Dynasty, and some of the larger pieces began to incorporate a glaze pouring technique for application. Medium and small pieces continued to utilize dunking and swaying.

Longquan Celadon also utilized spotting and exposed body techniques when glazing. Spotting is the process of adding irregular dots of Zijin glaze to the surface of the glazed vessel, the end result is iron brown spots on the surface of the glaze [201]. Exposed body decorated Longquan Celadon refers to pieces that have an intentionally unglazed portion or portions of exposed clay body.

a. Open Shape Glazing Characteristics

Open pieces can present with several different characteristics: Some open pieces can have a ring of scraped away glaze on the base, with a glazed foot ring (see pictures 2-4-28—2-4-31); some bases are unglazed, but the foot ring is glazed (see picture 2-4-32); some bases and foot rings can have irregular glazing, in which the circular scraped glaze on the bottom of the pieces is relatively spontaneous (see pictures 2-4-33—2-4-35); some pieces have a completely unglazed base and foot ring (see picture 2-4-36); and sometimes only the foot ring is unglazed (see pictures 2-4-37 and 2-4-38).

b. Closed Shape Glazing Characteristics

Jars often have glaze scraped from the mouth and foot ring with a ring on the interior of scraped glaze as well; small jars have a flat unglazed base.

Yuhuchun vases have only an unglazed foot ring.

Kettles have only an unglazed foot ring, some with an irregularly glazed base (see pictures 2-4-39 and 2-4-40).

The bases of stem cups are glazed, with the foot rings scraped (see picture 2-4-41).

Zun censers are sometimes unglazed on the inner and outter base, and sometimes only the foot ring is unglazed (see pictures 2-4-42—2-4-44).

F. Kiln Outfitting

Before a piece can be fired, an artisan must scrape away glaze for the placement of setter cakes or rings to avoid kiln sticking.

Because of the variety of wares that were fired in

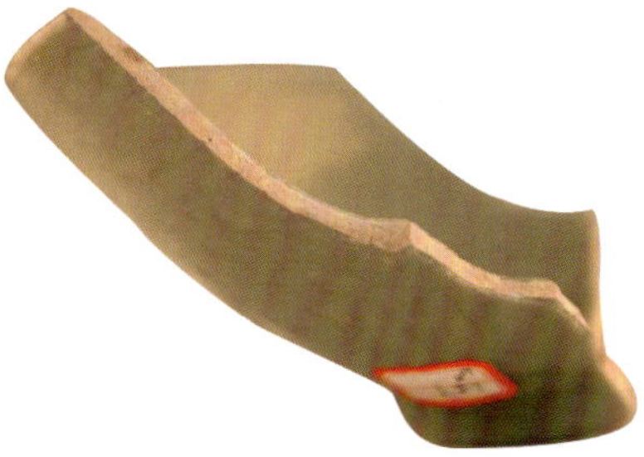

图2-4-21

图2-4-22

盘类胎体比较厚，圈足有垂直或呈倒梯形，较浅，足壁不及碗类的厚。（见图2-4-23—图2-4-27）

图2-4-23

图2-4-24

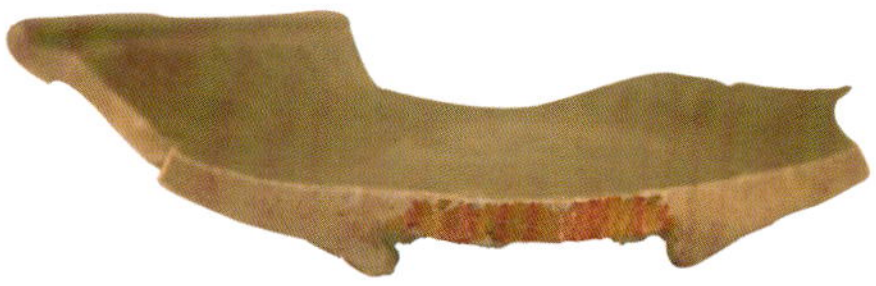

图2-4-25

图2-4-26

图2-4-27

（三）装饰

制作好瓷器坯体后，便可以开始装饰。

（四）素烧

晾干后的坯体可在施釉前进行焙烧，这种工艺称为素烧。

素烧可以提高坯体的强度，施釉时坯体不会变形；素烧过后的坯件可施釉更多，对烧制厚釉产品有利。素烧温度一般要低于正式烧成的温度，控制在800℃左右[200]。

（五）施釉

明代浙江龙泉窑常见的施釉方法包括浸釉和荡釉。浸釉是将坯件浸没于釉浆中，然后取出。荡釉是将釉浆导入坯体内部，稍微震荡，使釉浆均匀覆盖内壁，然后倒出多余的釉浆。

碗、盘等器物为外部浸釉，内部荡釉。

早在南宋时期，龙泉窑就出现瓷器的满釉装饰，并在元明时期继续流行。在南宋晚期，龙泉窑的施釉工艺达到顶峰，形成多次上釉多次素烧的复杂技艺，成功烧制“梅子青”瓷器。到了元代，多次上釉多次素烧的技艺逐渐消失，明代的龙泉民窑多为一次施釉。明代时期的大件产品增多，有的大件产品改用浇釉的方法施釉。中小件产品仍沿用浸釉和荡釉法施釉。

龙泉窑青瓷还有点彩及露胎两种装饰手法。在施釉完成的瓷器上点加不规则的斑块称之为点彩，点彩采用是紫金土釉，出窑后呈赭色[201]。露胎装饰的龙泉青瓷，露胎部分不施釉浆。

1. 圆器施釉特征

圆器有时外底刮釉一圈，圈足裹釉（见图2-4-28—图2-4-31）；有时外底无釉，圈足裹釉（见图2-4-32）；有时外底或圈足不规则挂釉，外底刮釉圈也比较随意（见图2-4-33—图2-4-35）；有时圈足及外底都无釉（见图2-4-36）；有时仅圈足端无釉（见图2-4-37、图2-4-38）。

Longquan Kilns, outfitting into saggars utilized many methods, including encased firing, stacked firing, and so forth. Flat based saggars would hold vases, censer, kettles, and so forth relatively tall standing vessels or smaller pieces such as bird feeding jarlettes, washers, or cups. Each saggar, depending on size, could hold one to four vessels until it was filled. Lidded items were usually fired with their matching lid in place.

a. Ming Dynasty Kiln Outfitting Methods

I. Early Ming Dynasty

Early Ming Dynasty saw a wide variety of kiln outfitting methods; different types of vessels called for different types of outfitting.

In general, items such as bowls, plates, washers, and the like would have a ring of glaze scraped away from the bottom before they were fitted with setter cakes. Large items such as jars, vases, kettles, stem cups, and the like had unglazed foot rings fitted with a setter cake. Items such as censers and small bowls had an unglazed base fitted with a setter cake.

At this time, it was common for pieces with foot rings to have a ring of scraped glaze for firing setter placement. The scraped glaze ring relatively broad and separated from the foot ring.

Larger items saw the use of high quality saggars, with a saggar mouth that was comparatively pointed; smaller pieces would use lower quality saggars, and used clay setter cakes or rings [202].

II. Mid Ming Dynasty

During the Mid Ming Dynasty, aside from the continued use of setter cakes and rings seen during the Early Ming Dynasty, there was also an induction of concave setter cakes that allowed for the central glaze spots seen on the bottom of bowls, plates, and similar wares from that period.

It was during this time that encased firing techniques first emerged. For example, censers of different sizes could be encased in one another and fired as a set, or stem cups could be encased inside cylindrical censers [203].

III. Late Ming Dynasty

Outfitting utilized setters, aside from a few continuations of early and mid period kiln tools, most bowls and plates used clay setter cakes and rings [204].

G. Firing

Firing is the last step of the ceramic making process, and determines the success or failure of the final product.

Pieces from the same glaze batch applied at the same time; under different firing conditions, atmosphere, and cooling conditions; can all produce discrepancies in glaze quality and color.

Historical records help to give us a glimpse into the firing process. They state that wood and bamboo would be added around a fully packed kiln of saggar-outfitted porcelain. Once fired to a state of no visible smoke, the kiln would be closed off to disallow oxygenated air to enter, preventing the second oxidation of the celadon glaze. This would continue until the completely cooled kiln was opened [205].

Longquan Kilns, from Southern Song through to the Yuan Dynasty, utilized dragon kilns of various lengths. The uphill slant of the kiln body created a natural draft, pulling the smoke up the mountainside and out of the top of the kiln. The elongated body of the kiln resembled the body of a dragon stretched up the mountain slope, earning it the name "dragon kiln" [206].

The Ming Dynasty saw the introduction of separated room dragon kilns, such as the Y6 Kiln at the Dayao Site. The Y6 structure appears similar to a standard dragon kiln with the firing furnace to the front and chimney at the aft. However, the kiln interior is separated into 5-6 meter rooms with two doors per room, one for kiln loading one for unloading. Separate room dragon kilns have benefits to standard dragon kilns in that they transformed even kiln flame into inverted kiln flames, achieving more even firing temperature. This allowed for a more constant firing atmosphere, beneficial for firing larger items and helping to fire uniform glaze color [207].

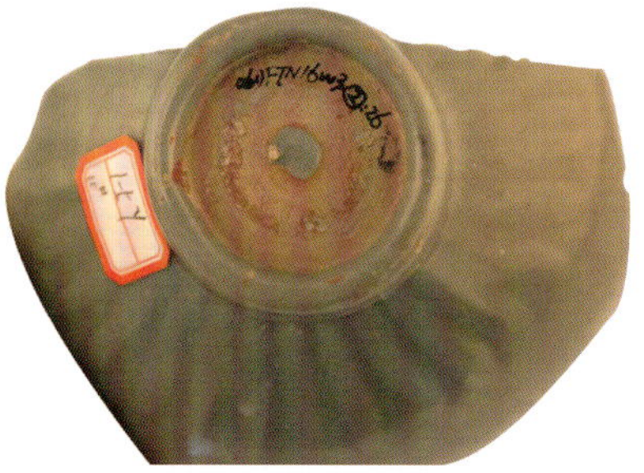
图2-4-28

图2-4-32

图2-4-36

图2-4-29

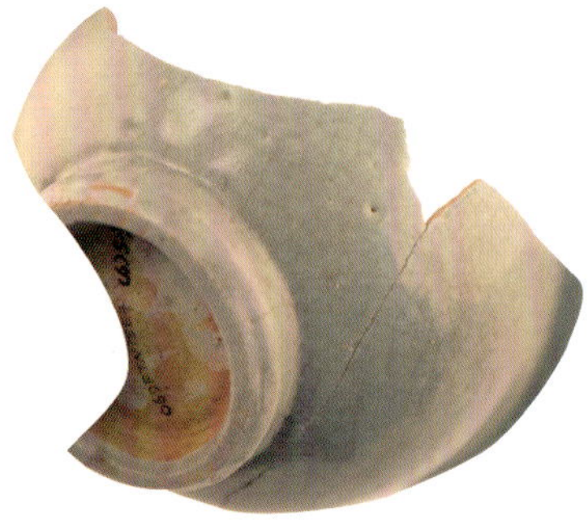
图2-4-33

图2-4-37

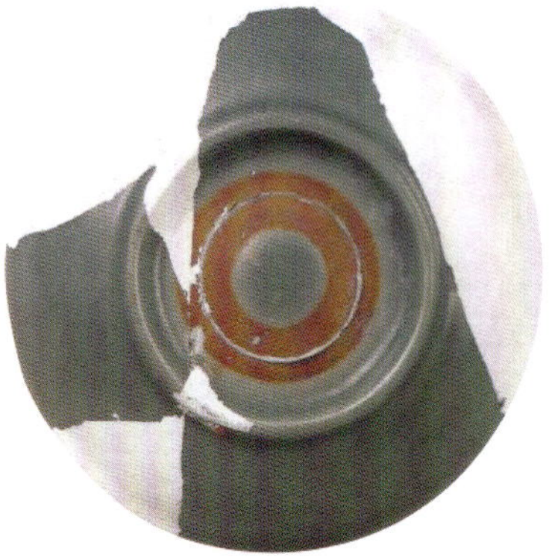
图2-4-30

图2-4-34

图2-4-38

图2-4-31

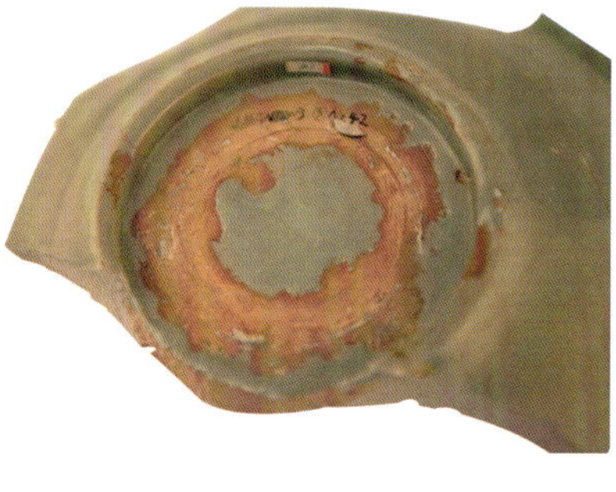
图2-4-35

2. 琢器施釉特征

罐类通常口沿和足端刮釉，内底刮釉一圈；小件罐类平沙底无釉。

玉壶春瓶仅足端无釉。

执壶仅圈足端无釉，有时外底不规则挂釉。（见图2-4-39、图2-4-40）

高足杯的高足底部施釉，足端无釉。（见图2-4-41）

H. Kiln Tools/Furniture

Kiln furniture are elements and tools used for the outfitting or packing of the kiln before firing. Longquan Kilns primarily used the following two types of kiln furniture: Saggars and Setters.

a. Saggars

Saggars are firing cases used to protect and stack ceramics during the firing process. They are often made of heat resistant clay and are a cylindrical or conical shape (see pictures 2-4-45—2-4-47). Saggars are not only highly heat resistant but can also hold heavy loads, allowing for the vertical stacking of many pieces within the kiln interior without collapsing, increasing the kiln usage. Clay vessels outfitted inside saggars during firing avoid direct contact with flames and falling grit, as well as reduced the impact of hot spots. This allows for uniform temperature and protects the clarity of the glaze, increasing the quality of the finished product [208].

b. Setters

Setter cakes and setter rings are firing tools that are used as spacers between wares and other wares or wares and saggars during the firing process. Setter cakes are circular flat tablets of heat resistant clay that are larger, equal to, or smaller than the diameter of the foot of the pieces they were made to hold. Most are made to be used between a vessel and its saggar [209] (see pictures 2-4-48—2-4-50).

Setter rings were a circular ring of heat resistant clay with a flat surface, equal to, or smaller than the diameter of the foot of the pieces they made to hold [210] (see picture 2-4-51).

Aside from the aforementioned more common setters, there are many other shapes and varieties of setters used (see pictures 2-4-52—2-4-59).

During the Late Southern Song Dynasty, kiln artisans began to apply a layer of yellow-brown paint to the bottom of saggars in order to prevent falling grit, increasing the clarity of the encased glaze. At the same time, they moved the placement of the setter cakes from the vessel base to the foot ring, allowing for glaze to cover the entire piece except for the foot ring, increasing the quality of the finished porcelain. These setter firing techniques continued into the Yuan and Ming Dynasties, and as such fully glazed pieces with only the foot ring remaining unglazed was commonly seen. With innovations to the firing tools, new styles of vessels with a ring of glaze scraped off the base emerged. Pieces with unglazed bases were rarely seen during the Early and Mid Ming Dynasty, and it wasn't until the Late Ming Dynasty that Longquan saw a return to the wide spread use of setter cakes.

2. Ming Dynasty Guangdong Yuli Kiln Celadon Manufacturing Technique

The manufacturing process of Gunagdong Yuli Kiln was very similar to that of Zhejiang Longquan Celadon. Below is a description of the main components of celadon production at the Yuli Kiln Site: Shaping, Glazing, Kiln Tools, Outfitting and Firing.

A. Shaping Characteristics

The primary shapes found at the Yuli Kiln site are bowls, plates, and so forth open wares. As such, the main shaping tool was the potter's wheel. Of the open wares, some have foot rings (see pictures 2-4-60 and 2-4-61) and some have flat bases (see pictures 2-4-62 and 2-4-63). Visible base scraping lines sometimes appear on open wares with unglazed bases (see pictures 2-4-64 and 2-4-65).

Bowls can present with a clear thickness discrepancy from mouth to base or without a clear difference (see pictures 2-4-66—2-4-69).

Lampstands most often have a flat sandy bottom (see picture 2-4-70).

Stem cup stems can present with ridges (see pictures 2-4-71 and 2-4-72), or with a smooth surface (see picture 2-4-73). The stem is solid with a flat base (see pictures 2-4-74 and 2-4-75).

Zun censers are almost all cake based, some with holes some without (see pictures 2-4-76 and 2-4-77).

樽式炉有时内底外底无釉，有时仅圈足端无釉（见图2-4-42—图2-4-44）。

图2-4-39

图2-4-40

图2-4-41

图2-4-42

图2-4-43

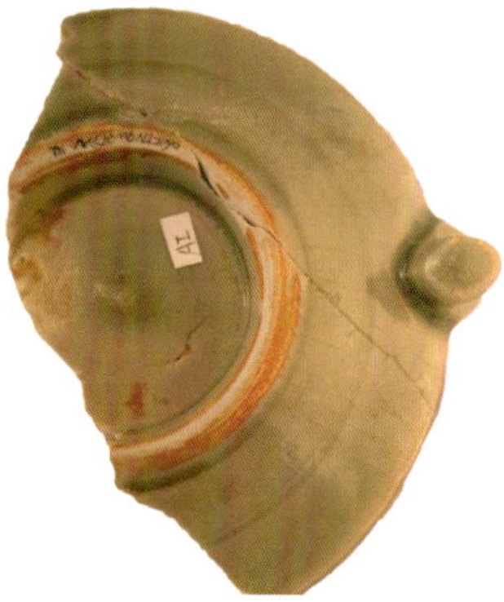

图2-4-44

（六）装烧

陶瓷在装烧前，工匠会在外底心刮掉一圈釉，露出胎，用来放置垫圈或垫饼等垫具，避免发生窑粘。

龙泉窑因烧制器物种类多样，在装匣烧制时会采用套烧、叠烧等方式。平底匣钵装瓶、炉、壶等较高的器物或鸟食罐、洗、把杯等较小的坯件，一个匣钵装一至四件不等，装满为止。盖罐、盖碗一般采用合烧法。

明代时期的装烧方式

1. 明早期

明代早期装烧方式多样，器类不同，装烧方式也不同。

一般碗、盘、洗等圈足器外底刮釉一圈垫烧，大型盖罐、瓶、壶、高足杯等仍是足端垫烧，炉、小碗则外底垫烧。

此时期圈足器外底刮釉一圈垫烧已成为主流，刮釉部分较宽，刮釉部位相对距足壁较远。

较大的器物仍使用瓷质的钵状托具，但其钵口部位多数较尖；较小的器物有的使用粗瓷质的钵状托具，另外还使用辅助用的泥质垫饼和垫圈等[202]。

2. 明中期

明中期除沿用早期垫具外，碗、盘等更多地使用一种带凹洞的泥质垫饼，这也是某些器物底心有点釉的原因所在。

这一期出现器物套烧，比如炉按大小不同逐个套烧，筒式炉里套烧高足杯等[203]。

3. 明晚期

装烧用垫具，除少部分沿用早中期垫具外，碗、盘类等更多地使用泥质垫饼和垫圈[204]。

（七）烧成

陶瓷的烧成是生产中最后一道工序，决定着产品的成败。

同一釉料配方，同次施釉的坯体在不同烧成条件、窑内气氛和冷却环境下，烧制出的釉质、釉色都会有差异。

《菽园杂记》有一段关于龙泉窑瓷器装窑焙烧的记叙："……用泥筒盛之。置诸窑内，端正排定，以柴筱日夜烧变。候火色红焰无烟，即以泥封闭火门，火气绝而后启。"即将装有瓷器坯体的匣钵整齐地排列于窑

B. Glazing

Ming Dynasty Yuli Celadon glazing techniques were the same as Longquan Celadon; primarily dunking exterior and swaying interior. Similar to common wares of the Longquan area, Yuli Kiln wares only underwent one round of glazing. The glazing was relatively spontaneous, with glaze running common. A very small number of samples had an unglazed mouth rim, and only one sample presented with an unglazed ring on the interior base.

Double handle vases have a glazed base with unglazed foot ring (see pictures 2-4-78 and 2-4-79), and straight neck vase interiors only have glaze within the upper portion of the neck interior, the rest is unglazed (see pictures 2-4-80 and 2-4-81).

Small jars have a glazed interior, but the mouth rim, base, and foot ring remained unglazed (see pictures 2-4-82 and 2-4-83).

Zun censers are unglazed on the interior and exterior base (see pictures 2-4-84 and 2-4-85).

Open ware bases often are unglazed (see pictures 2-4-86—2-4-91), some have an unglazed foot ring (see pictures 2-4-86 and 2-4-87), and some have a glazed foot ring (see pictures 2-4-88 and 2-4-89).

Lampstands were often very casually glazed, the exterior near the base often presenting with exposed clay (see pictures 2-4-92 and 2-4-93).

C. Kiln Outfitting

The outfitting techniques employed at the Yuli Kilns are essentially the same as the firing techniques used in the Longquan Kilns during the Yuan and Ming Dynasties. For pieces such as bowls, saucers, plates, and so forth large quantity items, Yuli Kilns employed a one piece per saggar and saggar stacking method for kiln outfitting (see pictures 2-4-94 and 2-4-95). Lidded jars are a common ware seen in the Yuli Kilns, and were fired fitted with one another. Irregular shaped items such as vases, cups, and censers utilized an encasing outfitting method in which larger pieces would encase smaller pieces (see picture 2-4-96)

Outfitting techniques changed according to the differences in vessels.

When outfitting wares, the saggar rim would be inverted and the concave well would face upward allowing for round wares such as bowls, plates, and so forth to be placed within the well of the saggar. Once it was placed properly, another similar shaped saggar could be stacked on top and the next vessel placed inside. This continued until the stack reached the roof of the kiln. During firing, there was one piece per saggar and each piece would be fitted with a setter cake or ring between the vessel base and the saggar well.

D. Firing

Four kiln furnaces have been found at the Yuli Kiln site, of which Y3 has been the best preserved. Y3 is a stepped dragon kiln with five separate kiln rooms of two-meter length and three-meter width. Each room is fitted with a door on the South-East edge, and a fire-stoking vent is fitted on the West side of each room. Each room has separating walls, fire stoking vent, kiln door, kiln bed, and chimney to the aft. The kiln bed was filled with sand, and the saggars would be placed directly on the sandy floor.

From the preserved structures of Y1 and Y3 we can see that the stepped dragon kiln structure used at the Yuli Kiln site is very similar to that of the Ming Dynasty Longquan Kiln area. The Kilns at Yuli were operated on a 19-degree slope, similar to that in Longquan. The kiln structure was essentially the same as that of their Longquan counterparts, slightly smaller than the Dayao Y6, and with one kiln door per room instead of two (see Appendix 2).

E. Kiln Tools/Furniture

a. Saggars

Both "M" shaped and flat based saggars have been found at the Yuli Kiln site, with "M" shaped the most common (see pictures 2-4-97— 2-4-99). The two saggar styles found at the Yuli Kiln site had already been commonly used at Longquan during the Early Southern Song Dynasty.

The majority of Yuli wares utilized the "M" shape

室内，用木柴和竹子为燃料焙烧，烧到高温无烟时（即达到既无不完全燃烧的烟雾，又不是空气过量的近中性焰或者轻微还原焰的清火阶段），然后封住窑门不让空气二次进入窑内，以防釉面的重新氧化，直至冷却后再开窑[205]。

龙泉窑自南宋至元均使用龙窑。龙窑依山而建，长度不等，窑身斜度产生自然抽力，取代了烟囱的部分功用；狭长的窑身像一条伏在山坡上的龙，故得名“龙窑”[206]。

明代出现了分室龙窑，如大窑岙底牛头颈山Y6。Y6的结构与龙窑相似，前有火膛，后设排烟坑，窑内每隔五六米筑两堵墙，把窑分成多室。每室开两个窑门，分别用作装窑和出窑。分室龙窑与龙窑相比的优越之处，是火焰由平焰变成倒焰，使室内温度更加均匀，烧成气氛一致，利于烧大件瓷器，烧成釉色也比较统一[207]。

（八）窑具

窑具是陶瓷装烧过程中必需的用具。龙泉窑的窑具主要包括匣钵和垫具等。

1. 匣钵

匣钵是陶瓷焙烧时置放坯件并对其起保护作用的匣状窑具，以耐火黏土制作，一般呈筒形或漏斗形。（见图2-4-45—图2-4-47）匣钵不仅耐高温，承重力也很强，可以叠置而不倒塌，节省烧制空间。坯件装在匣钵里焙烧，避免了窑内烟火与坯件直接接触和砂尘落粘的影响，使坯件受热均匀，釉表面洁净，提高陶瓷烧制质量[208]。

图2-4-45

图2-4-46

图2-4-47

2. 垫具

垫饼和垫圈都属于垫具，是在陶瓷焙烧时器物与器物、器物与匣钵之间起间隔作用的。

垫饼以耐火黏土制作，呈圆饼状，直径大于、略等于或小于所承托器物的足（底径）。多见用于器物与匣钵之间[209]。（见图2-4-48—图2-4-50）

垫圈以耐火黏土制作，呈环形，上、下面较平整，直径等于或者小于所承托的器物的足径[210]。（见图2-4-51）

除以上两种以外，还有其他各种形制的垫具。（见图2-4-52—图2-4-59）

在南宋后期，龙泉窑的工匠们开始在匣钵内施一层黄褐色涂料，以防落砂，从而陶瓷釉面得以保持光洁；同时把垫具由置于外底改成置于圈足上，仅圈足下端放垫饼处一圈无釉，实现了陶瓷通体施釉的可能，提高了陶瓷质量。这一垫烧技艺在元明时期继续传承，所以这个时段仅圈足下端无釉的满釉瓷器仍很常见。由于窑具的创新，又新出现了外底刮釉一圈垫烧的器物。明代外底无釉的瓷器较少见，直至明代中晚期，龙泉窑才大量恢复使用圆形垫饼。

图2-4-48

图2-4-49

saggar during firing, with a small portion of large wares such as censers using flat-based saggars. "M" shape saggars were primarily used in the outfitting of bowls, plates, saucers, cups, stands, stem cups, and so forth. According to the size and shape of each piece, different size and styles of "M" shape saggars were made to fit the wares, of which, the saggars made to fit stem cups have a drastically more concave inner well to fit the shape of the cup.

b. Setters

Yuli Kiln primarily used two styles of setters: Cake and Ring, the former the most common.

The cake setters were circular and mostly flat with a small concavity in the center. They were coarsely constructed of rough porcelain clay, and varied in size according to the piece they were formed to hold (see picture 2-4-100).

Setter rings are donut shaped with a hollow center. The base is flat and the walls slant up to a point creating a triangular cross section (see picture 2-4-101).

Due to the widespread use of setter cakes, the majority of samples excavated from the Yuli Kiln site have an unglazed base (see pictures 2-4-102 and 2-4-103). Kiln furniture used at the Yuli Kiln shows that local kiln outfitting was not as refined as the contemporary Longquan Kilns.

图2-4-50

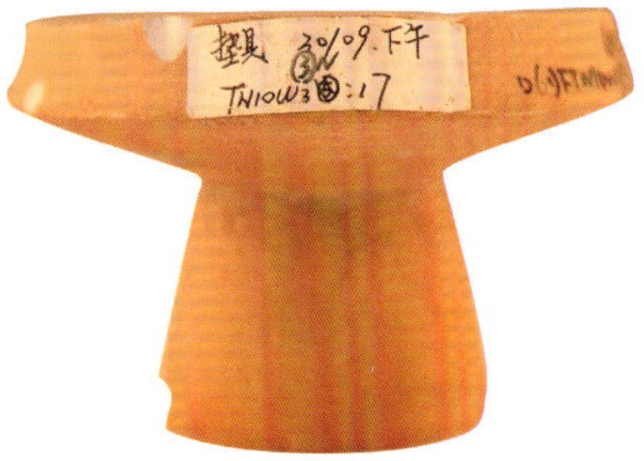
图2-4-54

图2-4-59

图2-4-51

图2-4-55

图2-4-52

图2-4-56

图2-4-57

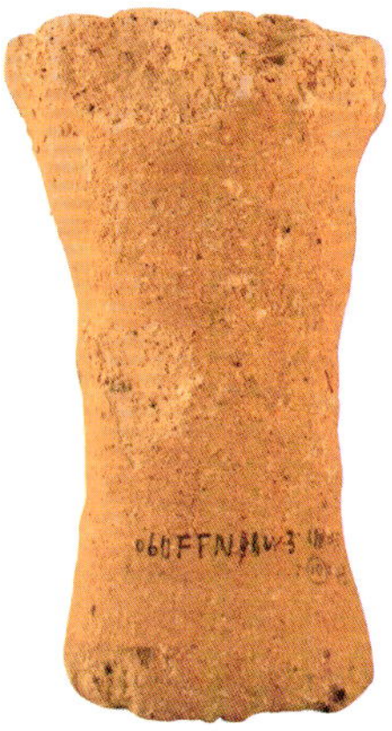
图2-4-53

图2-4-58

二、广东余里窑青瓷制作工艺

明代广东余里窑的青瓷制作过程与浙江龙泉窑青瓷类似，现就成形、施釉、窑具、装烧、烧成等几个重要工序进行讨论。

（一）成形特征

余里窑的器物以碗、盘等圆器为主，所以其成形工具主要是使用辘轳。圆器有的为圈足（见图2-4-60、图2-4-61），有的为卧足（见图2-4-62、图2-4-63）。外底无釉的圆器，在圈足内壁及外底有时可见挖足时留下的旋削纹。（见图2-4-64、图2-4-65）

碗类由口沿到底部厚度逐渐增加，也有的厚度过渡不明显。（见图2-4-66—图2-4-69）

灯盏通常为平沙底。（见图2-4-70）

高足杯的高足上有的有凸棱（见图2-4-71、图2-4-72），也有的素面（见图2-4-73）。高足为平切底，实心。（见图2-4-74、图2-4-75）

樽式炉基本上是饼底，底部有的有洞，有的无洞。（见图2-4-

76、图2-4-77）

图2-4-60

图2-4-64

图2-4-68

图2-4-61

图2-4-65

图2-4-69

图2-4-62

图2-4-66

图2-4-70

图2-4-63

图2-4-67

图2-4-71

图2-4-72

图2-4-76

圆器通常外底无釉（见图2-4-86—图2-4-91），有的圈足也无釉（见图2-4-86、图2-4-87），有的圈足裹釉（见图2-4-88、图2-4-89）。

灯盏施釉较随意，外壁靠近底部常常无釉露胎。（见图2-4-92、图2-4-93）

图2-4-78

图2-4-73

图2-4-77

（二）施釉

明代余里窑址的施釉方法与明代浙江龙泉窑的一样，基本上都是外壁浸釉，内壁荡釉。与龙泉窑民窑器物一样，余里窑器物通常仅一次施釉。施釉较随意，流釉现象普遍。少数口沿一周不施釉，内底有涩圈的仅有一件标本。

双耳瓶外底施釉，足端无釉；（见图2-4-78、图2-4-79）直颈瓶，瓶内部仅颈部分施釉，其余部分无釉。（见图2-4-80、图2-4-81）

小罐内部也施釉，口部一圈，外底和圈足无釉。（见图2-4-82、图2-4-83）

樽式炉内底外底无釉。（见图2-4-84、图2-4-85）

图2-4-74

图2-4-75

图2-4-79

图2-4-80

图2-4-81

图2-4-82

图2-4-83

图2-4-84

图2-4-85

图2-4-86

图2-4-87

图2-4-88

图2-4-89

图2-4-90

图2-4-91

图2-4-92

图2-4-93

（三）装烧

余里窑的装烧方式与元明时期的龙泉窑的装烧方式相同。对于碗、碟、盘等器型规整且烧制量大的器物，余里窑采用一器一匣钵且进行叠烧的装烧方式。（见图2-4-94、图2-4-95）盖罐是余里窑址常见的一种器物，烧制时是盖、罐合烧的。而杯、炉、瓶等不规则器型的器物，则采用大小相套的套烧方式。（见图2-4-96）

图2-4-94

图2-4-95

图2-4-96

器物不同，其装烧方式也略有不同。

装坯时，匣钵口朝下，凹底向上，将碗、盘等坯件仰置在匣钵的外底上，放妥后，再覆盖匣钵，装坯件，如此一个个地叠装到窑顶。烧制时多一器一匣钵，足底垫一圆形垫饼或垫圈。

（四）烧成

在余里窑共发现了四座窑炉，其中Y3保存相对较好。Y3是一座阶级龙窑，共五个窑室，窑室长两米多，宽三米多，每个窑室东壁南端开有窑门，向西有一条火道。各窑室有隔墙、火道、窑门、窑床、窑尾烟道。窑床底部为沙质填土，上面直接落满匣钵。

从Y1和Y3保存的结构看，余里窑的窑炉主要是分室龙窑，与明代龙泉窑类似。余里窑址的窑炉坡度为19°，与龙泉窑的龙窑坡度相差不多；窑炉结构与龙泉窑的基本一致，其窑室比大窑岙底Y6的窑址规模略小，窑门仅开一个。（详见附录2）

（五）窑具

1. 匣钵

在余里窑址发现有“M”形匣钵和平底匣钵两种，以“M”形匣钵为主。（见图2-4-97—图2-4-99）余里窑址发现的这两种匣钵早在南宋时期就是浙江龙泉窑使用的主要匣钵类型。

余里窑的器物多采用“M”形匣钵装烧，少数大型器物如炉等用平底匣钵装烧。“M”形匣钵主要装烧的器物有碗、盘、碟、杯、盏、高足杯等，根据瓷器的大小不同，配有各种大小、规模形制不同的“M”形匣钵，其中烧制高足杯的匣钵内底凹陷明显呈杯型。

图2-4-97

图2-4-98

图2-4-99

2. 垫具

余里窑的垫具有两种——垫饼和垫圈，以前者为主。

垫饼为圆形，上下皆平，略内凹，粗砂瓷土捏制，制作随意粗糙。垫饼根据垫烧器物的大小不同有各种尺寸。（见图2-4-100）

垫圈呈圆形，中空，底平，上部内凹，顶部尖圆，截面为三角形。（见图2-4-101）

由于垫饼的普遍使用，余里窑址出土的瓷器基本都是外底无釉。（见图2-4-102、图2-4-103）可见从窑具垫烧的技术来看，余里窑不如龙泉窑精细。

图2-4-102

图2-4-103

图2-4-100

图2-4-101

第三章

龙泉窑系青瓷釉层的化学成分、性质与形貌

阅读提示：

本章将对龙泉窑系青瓷釉的化学成分、性质与形貌做理论性论述与阐明。

主要论述问题：

1. 龙泉窑系青瓷釉层的化学成分有哪些？它们各自的作用是什么？
2. 龙泉窑系青瓷釉层为什么会风化？
3. 龙泉窑系青瓷釉层的形貌是怎样的？

Chapter 3

Chemical Composition, Nature, and Appearance of Longquan Kiln System Celadon Glaze

Text Note:

This chapter theorizes the chemical composition, nature and appearance of Longquan Kiln System Celadon (LKSC) glaze in order to fully discuss and depict its characteristics.

第一节 龙泉窑系青瓷瓷釉化学成分

一、青瓷瓷釉的概念

瓷釉是施于青瓷坯体表面，利用天然矿物原料按比例配合，在高温作用下熔融而覆盖在坯体表面的玻璃质层[211]。

二、青瓷瓷釉的构成

青瓷瓷釉主要由网络形成剂、助熔剂和着色剂组成。

（一）网络形成剂

玻璃相是釉层的主相，形成玻璃相的主要氧化物是二氧化硅（SiO_2），它在釉层中以四面体的形式相互结合成不规则网络，所以SiO_2又称为网络形成剂[212]。

（二）助熔剂

在青瓷釉料熔化过程中，助熔剂能促进高温分解反应，加速高熔点晶体（如SiO_2）化学键的断裂和生成低共熔物。助熔剂还起着调整釉层物理化学性质（如力学性质、膨胀系数、黏度、化学稳定性等）的作用[213]。常用的助熔剂化合物有氧化钠（Na_2O）、氧化钾（K_2O）、氧化钙（CaO）等。

（三）着色剂

着色剂是在陶瓷的胎、釉中起呈色作用的物质[214]。着色剂包括氧化亚铁（FeO）、三氧化二铁（Fe_2O_3）、氧化钴（CoO）和氧化锰（MnO）等氧化物。龙泉窑系青瓷釉色呈青色，是Fe^{2+}在釉中所呈现的颜色。如窑中氧化还原气氛掌握不好，可能呈黄色，是Fe^{3+}在釉中所呈现的颜色。瓷釉中Fe^{2+}和Fe^{3+}的比值决定了瓷釉的呈色。

（四）其他成分

青瓷瓷釉中还含有三氧化二铝（Al_2O_3）和其他成分。Al_2O_3是一种重要成分，适量的Al_2O_3能与SiO_2形成网络，可增强釉层的强度及化学稳定性。

三、青瓷瓷釉化学成分

龙泉窑系青瓷通常是在1150℃以上的温度烧成的，属高温釉瓷器。

熊樱菲等对历代龙泉青瓷瓷釉成分做了分析[215]。（见表3-1-1）

由以上研究结果可得出，龙泉青瓷瓷釉的化学成分主要有：SiO_2、Al_2O_3、Fe_2O_3、TiO_2、CaO、MgO、K_2O、Na_2O、MnO、P_2O_5等。

为了方便描述，我们将青瓷瓷釉中影响其釉层结构的主要成分归纳成一个系统，所以龙泉窑系青瓷瓷釉可归于Na_2O-K_2O-CaO-MgO-Al_2O_3-SiO_2系统。

四、龙泉青瓷瓷釉的配方

龙泉青瓷瓷釉的配方主要由瓷石加草木灰或釉灰配制而成[216]。古代龙泉青瓷大体可分钙釉和钙碱釉。北宋中期和南宋初期的釉中CaO含量达13%—16%，钾、钠含量合计仅3.8%。所以基本上属于钙釉，南宋中晚期开始，釉中CaO含量较前大为降低，而K_2O和Na_2O的含量则提高到4.8%—6.2%，元、明更是提高到6.6%—7.6%，所以它们都属于钙碱釉[217]。

Section 1 :

Chemical Composition of Longquan Kiln System Celadon Glaze

1. The Definition of Celadon Glaze

A specifically mixed set of natural and mineral raw materials for application to the surface of clay body that when fired, melts and then cools to become a glass phase layer over the body [211].

2. The Components of Celadon Glaze

Celadon glaze primarily consists of: Networking Agents, Flux, and Coloring Agents.

A. Networking Agents

Glass is the main phase of the celadon glaze level; composed primarily of Silicone Dioxide (SiO_2) in tetrahedron shapes, mutually interlocking to create an irregular network; thus being slated as networking agents [212].

B. Flux

During the melting of celadon glaze, these solvents promote high temperature split reactions and accelerate the splitting of high-melting-point crystals (such as SiO_2) into eutectic solutions. Fluxes also bring rise to changes in the physical chemical properties of the glaze (Such as mechanics, coefficient of expansion, viscosity, and chemical stability) [213].

Commonly used fluxes are: Sodium Oxide (Na_2O), Potassium Oxide (K_2O), Calcium Oxide (CaO), and so forth.

C. Coloring Agents

Coloring Agents are substances that act to add color to a ceramic piece [214]. They include: Iron Oxide (FeO), Ferric Oxide (Fe_2O_3), Cobaltous Oxide (CoO), Manganese Oxide (MnO), and so forth various metal oxides.

Celadon glaze has a green appearance. This green coloration is due to the presence of Fe^{2+} ions in the glaze level. If the reduction atmosphere within the kiln is not controlled properly, yellowish coloration can also occur, which is the presence of Fe^{3+} ions affecting the glaze color.

D. Other Components

Celadon Glaze also contains Aluminum Oxide (Al_2O_3) and other elements. Aluminum Oxide is a more instrumental component in that, with the proper quantities, it can network with Silicone Dioxide to increase the strength and chemical stability of the glaze level.

3. The Chemical Composition of Celadon Glaze

Longquan Kiln System Celadon (LKSC) glazes are formed in temperatures over 1150℃, and are considered High-Temperature Glazes.

Xiong Ying Fei et al undertook analytical research of the compositions of the Longquan Kiln Celadon glazes from different time periods, results are shown below [215] (see Table 3-1-1).

From the table we can see the primary chemical components of LKC glazes are: SiO_2, Al_2O_3, Fe_2O_3, TiO_2,

表3-1-1 历代龙泉青瓷瓷釉成分表

Table 3-1-1 Chemical Composition of Longquan Kiln Celadon Glaze Throughout History

年代 Period	样品名称 Record No.	Na_2O	MgO	Al_2O_3	SiO_2	K_2O	CaO	TiO_2	MnO	Fe_2O_3	P_2O_5
宋早期 Early Song	Lq3-y	0.04	1.23	12.56	65.2	2.13	15.3	0.21	0.37	2.5	0.4
	SZQ-1	0.33	1.74	14.73	60.57	2.14	17.3	0.31	0.7	1.51	0.64
	SZQ-2	0.23	1.2	13.62	61.9	1.49	18.3	0.37	0.69	1.8	0.43
	SZQ-3	0.2	1.64	13.26	61.95	1.75	18	0.35	0.55	1.77	0.51
	SZQ-8	0.4	2.01	14.68	60.49	2.59	16.3	0.32	0.78	1.4	0.92
南宋黑胎 Southern Song Black Body	wyy1-qy	0	0.69	13.18	66.99	3.64	13.9	0.07	0.17	0.93	0.45
	wyy2-qy	0.05	0.68	13.4	67.97	3.55	12.5	0.05	0.12	1.24	0.47
	wyy6-qy	0	0.89	14.7	62.12	3.34	17	0.08	0.16	1.32	0.4
	wyy7-hy	0.49	0.77	14.23	64.84	3.73	14.2	0.07	0.1	1.33	0.2
	wyy9-qy	0.7	0.83	15.27	66.26	3.97	11.7	0.07	0.22	0.74	0.23
	wyy10-qy	0.57	1.18	14.51	65.7	4.37	12.2	0.07	0.24	0.81	0.29
	wyy20-qy	0.4	0.95	14.34	65.47	3.8	13.4	0.09	0.09	1.19	0.19
	wyy22-wy	0.49	0.96	14.14	65.13	3.78	14.3	0.08	0.12	0.75	0.25
	wyy24-wy	0.18	0.99	14.43	64.61	4.02	13.9	0.09	0.14	1.32	0.36
	wyy30-wy	0.66	0.99	15.96	63.6	4.16	12.7	0.09	0.25	1.28	0.33
	wyy32-wy	0.03	0.81	13.23	64.47	3.85	16	0.08	0.19	1.01	0.34
	Ckp-2-ly	0.49	1.04	13.99	63.18	3.45	16.16	0.14	0.21	1.12	0.12
	Ckp-2-hy	0.46	1.07	13.94	64.33	3.45	15.42	0.12	0.22	0.78	0.25
南宋白胎 Southern Song White Body	lq5-2	0.17	0.44	12.67	72.35	4.53	7.95	0.07	0.11	1.54	0.09
	swt1-fq	0.28	0.54	12.11	72.56	4.12	9.21	0.06	0.17	0.82	0.12
	swt4-qy	0.51	0.62	13.83	68.56	4.25	10.7	0.06	0.11	1.29	0.12
	swt12	0.03	0.49	12.44	72.32	4.5	8.6	0.07	0.09	1.34	0.11
	STT8	0.5	0.57	13.56	68.49	4.27	10.4	0.09	0.2	1.79	0.13

CaO, MgO, K_2O, Na_2O, MnO, and P_2O_5.

For ease of description, we systemize high-temperature glaze based upon the primary elements that are acting on the composition of the glaze level. Therefore, the system for categorizing the high-temperature glazes used in LKSC is based on a chemical composition of the Na_2O-K_2O-CaO-MgO-Al_2O_3-SiO_2 system.

4. The Formulation of Longquan Kiln Celadon Glaze

Longquan Kiln Celadon (LKC) glazes were primarily formulated using porcelain clay, and added plant ash or glaze ash [216].

The CaO found in LKC glaze comes primarily from plant ash or glaze ash. Ancient Longquan Celadon glazes can be primarily split into two categories: Calcium Glaze and Alkaline Calcium Glaze. The CaO content of the glaze from the Mid Northern Song to Early Southern Song Dynasty was 13%-16%, and the combined content of Potassium and Sodium was just 3.8%. As such, it was essentially a Calcium Glaze. From the Mid to Late Southern Song Dynasty, the Calcium content within the glaze began to decrease and the K_2O and Na_2O contents saw an increase to between 4.8%-6.2%. The Ming Dynasty saw a continued increase to between 6.6%-7.6%, and as such the celadon glaze from this period can be classified as Alkaline Calcium Glaze [217].

续表3-1-1
Table 3-1-1 Continued

年代 Period	样品名称 Record No.	Na_2O	MgO	Al_2O_3	SiO_2	K_2O	CaO	TiO_2	MnO	Fe_2O_3	P_2O_5
南宋白胎 Southern Song White Body	STT12	0.41	0.52	12.67	72.52	4.34	7.93	0.1	0.15	1.19	0.14
	STT17	0.61	0.51	14.98	68.88	4.47	8.36	0.11	0.13	1.76	0.18
	STT18	0.83	0.81	14.79	67.44	4	9.99	0.08	0.17	1.68	0.15
元 Yuan	hm9	0.72	0.71	12.84	70.02	4.81	9.27	0.08	0.25	1.14	0.15
	hm10	0.24	0.91	14.05	69.03	4.84	8.85	0.11	0.38	1.31	0.26
	hm14	0.74	0.9	14.12	68.65	4.77	9.03	0.14	0.28	1.12	0.24
	STT3-fqy	0.66	0.6	13.35	69.14	4.88	9.56	0.07	0.17	1.43	0.09
	STT4-fqy	0.28	0.54	12.85	70.65	4.89	9.32	0.09	0.18	1.05	0.11
	STT5-fqy	0.24	0.34	13.48	71.34	4.81	8.25	0.1	0.19	1.13	0.09
	STT9	0.46	0.42	14.16	70.13	4.88	7.25	0.08	0.13	1.47	0.15
明 Ming	lq7-y	0.53	0.83	13.22	66.62	5.47	10.6	0.11	0.43	1.88	0.32
	hm8-qy	0.43	1.14	14	67.01	5.27	8.89	0.14	0.60	2.04	0.42
	ming2-wy	1.00	1.7	13.76	64.35	5.37	10.6	0.13	0.05	1.87	0.74
	ML1*	0.20	0.78	15.00	67.57	6.48	6.28	0.00	0.00	1.44	0.00
现代 Modern	fgc-dl	0.77	1.55	13.44	69.82	3.89	9.46	0.04	0.07	0.9	0.04
	fgc-xwl	0.19	1.12	12.89	71.14	4.23	8.96	0.08	0.09	1.11	0.18
	fgc3-wy	0.54	0.7	13.06	69.39	3.88	10.8	0.09	0.05	1.37	0.09
	fgc4-h	0.12	0.79	13.6	69.49	4.07	10.4	0.06	0.06	1.2	0.04
	fgc5-h	0.53	0.74	13.6	67.9	3.93	11.8	0.08	0.08	1.36	0.01

第二节
龙泉窑系青瓷瓷釉各化学成分的作用

在第一节我们了解到青瓷釉层是各类氧化物在高温作用下被熔化，然后冷却形成的玻璃体。但并不是所有的氧化物都能形成玻璃体，只有在氧化物的分子结构能形成特定的网络结构时，才能形成玻璃体。

一、网络形成剂作用

网络形成剂主要由SiO_2构成。SiO_2的基本结构是硅氧四面体（简写为$[SiO_4]$四面体），Si与O通过硅氧键（Si—O）相连，一个硅原子与四个氧原子相连接形成四面体（见图3-2-1）。为了便于书写，将其简化成≡Si—。

氧原子通过与两个硅原子相连将四面体连接起来，连接这四面体的氧原子称为桥氧。它们以顶角相连而构成连续的架状三维硅氧网络（见图3-2-2[218]）。

为了便于书写，将其简化成≡Si—O—Si≡（中间的O为桥氧）。≡Si—O—Si≡的连接角度是不定的，也就是说，图3-2-2中的α_1、α_2和β角的度数是可变化的，故就整体而言，形成的是不规则的硅氧网络。通过这样的连接形成的SiO_2三维网络（也就是玻璃体），是没有对称性和周期性的，它是最简单的单组分硅酸盐玻璃。

由于SiO_2是一种能相互连接形成三维空间网络的氧化物，我们称之为网络形成体氧化物。SiO_2是釉层的主要成分，机械强度及化学稳定性都比较好，所以釉层有保护瓷器的作用。

二、助熔剂作用

龙泉窑系青瓷釉料配方中的石英熔点较高，达到1750℃，而当代瓷窑最高的烧成温度也不过1400℃。由第一节可知，碱金属氧化物Na_2O和K_2O以及碱土金属氧化物CaO、MgO都可在龙泉窑系青瓷瓷釉中充当助熔剂的角色，它们可以降低石英的熔点，从而降低青瓷的烧结温度。

当在SiO_2熔体中加入碱金属（R_2O，R在此指Na、K）或碱土金属氧化物（RO，R在此指Ca、Mg）时，由于R—O是离子键为主，其键强比Si—O键弱得多，因此，Si—O键中的Si^{4+}能把R—O键上的O^{2-}吸引到自己的周围，使≡Si—O—R中的≡Si—O键比≡Si—O—Si≡中的≡Si—O键还要强，结果是使原来

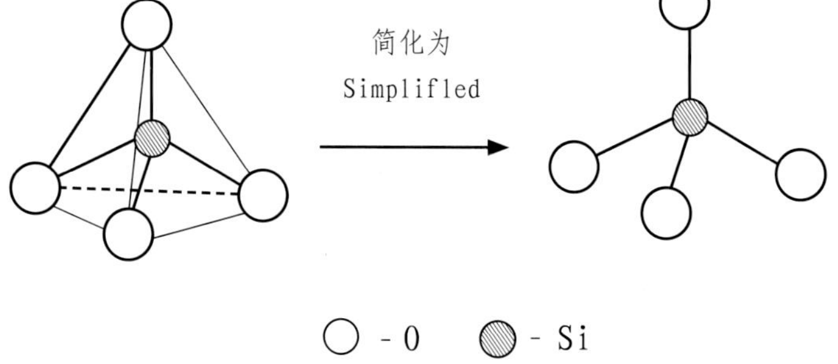

图3-2-1

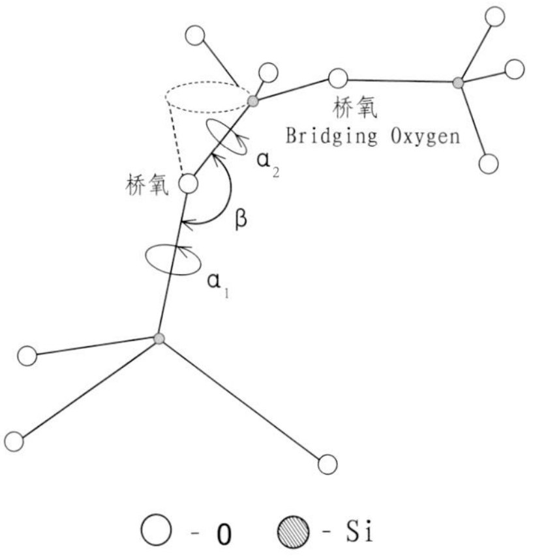

图3-2-2

Section 2：

The Functions of Longquan Kiln System Celadon Glaze Chemical Components

According to Section 1, celadon glaze is a fusion of certain oxidized components, melded under high temperatures, and cooled to form a glass-like coating. However, not all oxidized compounds have the ability to form glass; only those that have set networking construction are able to arrange as such.

1. The Function of Networking Agents

Networking agents are comprised primarily of Silica SiO_2. The foundational construction of SiO_2 is a Silicone and Oxygen tetrahedron (Simplified as $[SiO_4]$ tetrahedron) in which one Si atom is combined with four O atoms to form the shape illustrated in Picture 3-2-1. Hereafter to be simplified as ≡Si—.

An Oxygen atom that links two Silicone atoms is called a bridging Oxygen. They affix in static angles to form a three dimensional silica network structure illustrated in 3-2-2 [218]. Hereafter to be simplified as ≡Si—O—Si≡ (the central O as the bridging Oxygen).

Because of the unfixed angle of attachment of the ≡Si—O—Si≡ we can see in Picture 3-2-2 that angles α_1, α_2, and β can vary. It is due to this that SiO_2 molecules fuse to form an irregularly shaped network structure that lacks symmetry and periodicity; this structure is generically called silicate glass. This irregular construction of SiO_2 is the main building block of celadon glaze. Because SiO_2 is able to interconnect and form a three-dimensional network structure, we call it a networking oxide. This glaze level geometric structure is relatively strong with a good chemical stability, creating an inherent functionality of protecting the porcelain body.

2. The Function of Flux

Quartz, used in LKSC glaze, has a very high melting point, as high as 1750℃; and currently the highest temperature used in firing ceramics is around 1400℃. Because of this, alkaline metal oxides Na_2O and K_2O as well as alkaline earth metal oxides CaO and MgO are added to LKSC glazes to act as a flux, effectively lowering the melting temperature of quartz and allowing for a lower firing temperature.

During the fusion of SiO_2, if alkaline metal oxides (R_2O, where R represents Na, K) or alkaline earth metal oxides (RO where R represents Ca, Mg) are added, the bond of the R—O is primary and much weaker than that of Si—O. This is to say that the Si^{4+} ions in Si—O can attract the O^{2-} ions of the R—O creating a bond of ≡Si—O—R that has a ≡Si—O bond that is stronger than that of the ≡Si—O bond found in ≡Si—O—Si≡. The result is the breaking away of the bridging O (≡Si…O—Si≡). Thus, the bridging Oxygen becomes a non-bridging Oxygen and a new ≡Si—O—R bond is formed. After the breakdown of ≡Si—O—Si≡, the ≡Si—O bond's strength, length, and angle all undergo change [219] (see picture 3-2-3).

Therefore, the network experiences several locations of breakdown where Si and O are no longer conjoined on both sides, but rather an O and R bond takes its place.

SiO_2 silicone dioxide has a Si:O ratio of 1:2. With the addition of R_2O or RO, this Si:O ratio can increase to 1:3 or 1:4, from which the three-dimensional $[SiO_4]$ tetrahedron network is split into stratified, chain, and toroidal structures until the entire network is spilt into island structured $[SiO_4]$ tetrahedrons. During the breaking down process, chains of SiO_4 come together to form low polymers, under the right

的桥氧键（≡Si…O—Si≡）从虚线处断开，桥氧成为非桥氧，同时形成新的≡Si—O—R键。

≡Si—O—Si≡断裂后，Si—O键的键强、键长和键角都会发生变化[219]（见图3-2-3）。

这样，硅氧网络中许多地方会出现断点，即O不是与两个Si相连，而是其中一端与R相连。

SiO_2的硅氧比（Si/O）为1:2。随着Na_2O、K_2O、CaO的加入，Si/O可由原来的1:2上升到1:3或1:4，从而使$[SiO_4]$四面体的架状三维网络发生断裂，连接方式随着硅氧比的不同会由架状变为层状、链状、环状，直至最后桥氧全部断裂形成岛状的$[SiO_4]$四面体。在这个过程中，许多断裂的$[SiO_4]$四面体短链会聚集，形成低聚物。这种低聚物不断增多，在一定条件下会产生相互作用，形成高聚物，直至平衡。所以，釉层的结构会因Na_2O、K_2O、CaO、MgO的加入而发生变化。

这些碱金属氧化物（Na_2O、K_2O）和碱土金属氧化物（CaO、MgO）的加入，并没有参与到硅氧网络中去，而是使网络断裂，从而使其熔点降低。它们改变了硅氧网络的性质，我们称它们为网络外体氧化物。（注：MgO只有在碱金属氧化物较多而且不存在Al_2O_3及B_2O_3等氧化物时，才可进入硅氧网络。）

三、着色剂作用

龙泉窑系青瓷瓷釉的青色，实质上是釉层中铁元素的呈色。铁并没有参加网络，不会对网络结构产生直接的影响。当铁元素主要以+2价形式熔在釉层中时，呈色为青色；当其以+3价形式熔在釉层中时，呈色为黄色；如以氧化物形式出现时，通常在釉层中或釉表面以黄褐色斑块形式出现，成分通常为Fe_2O_3及Fe_3O_4，它们与玻璃相（主要为Si_2O）相比，更易与外部物质（酸或碱等）发生反应，产生风化作用。

由第二章第三节的内容可知，烧成气氛对青釉的呈色起着决定性的作用，烧制时是氧化气氛还是还原气氛决定了Fe^{2+}或Fe^{3+}的数量，所以控制好烧成气氛非常重要。

四、其他成分作用

龙泉窑系青瓷瓷釉中除了网络形成剂、助熔剂、着色剂以外，还有其他成分，如三氧化二铝（Al_2O_3），这是一个重要成分。

在硅酸盐玻璃中，Al_2O_3中的Al^{3+}有4、6两种配位状态，即位于四面体或八面体中。当摩尔比$R_2O/Al_2O_3>1$时，Al^{3+}位于四面体中，以$[AlO_4]$四面体形式将一些$[SiO_4]$四面体的断点连接起来，与$[SiO_4]$组成统一的网络，使玻璃结构趋向紧密，对硅氧网络起补网作用，提高釉层结构的稳定性；当摩尔比$R_2O/Al_2O_3<1$时，碱金属离子不足以使Al^{3+}离子形成$[AlO_4]$四面体时的化合价平衡，超出的Al^{3+}离子只能在玻璃中以六配位的形式[220]，作为网络外体存在于八面体之中，从而使玻璃结构趋向于松散，使硅氧网络的紧密程度下降，化学稳定性也随之下降[221]。

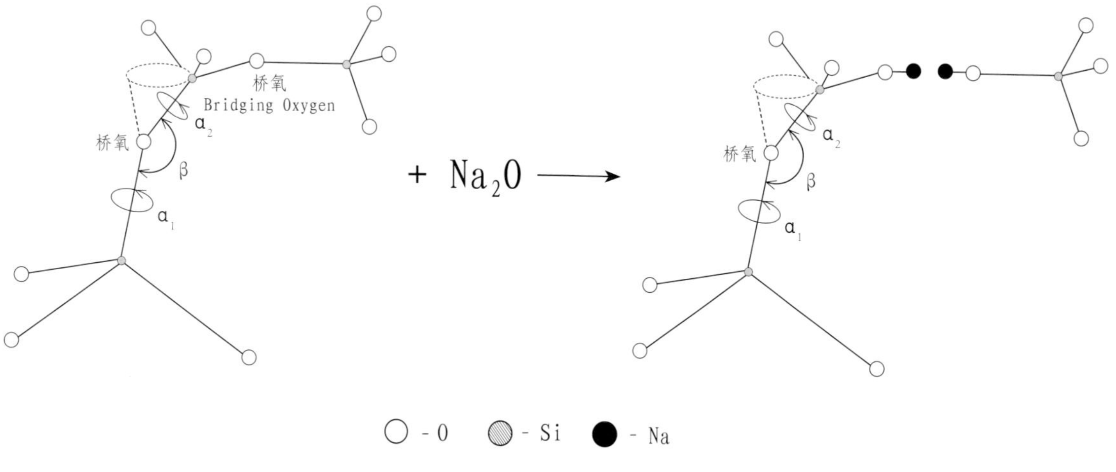

图3-2-3

circumstances these low polymers begin to interact and form high polymers until equilibrium is reached. Therefore because of the addition of Na_2O, K_2O, CaO, MgO, the structure of the glaze undergoes change.

These alkaline metal oxides and alkaline earth metal oxides do not enter into the silicate network, but only assist in the network breakdown and bringing down the melting point. As such, they only work to change the structural characteristics of the silicate network, so we call them external oxides (note: Without the presence of Al_2O_3, B_2O_3 or other Oxides, and with large amounts of alkaline metal oxides present, MgO can enter into the silica network).

3. The Function of Coloring Agents

The celadon, or green, coloration of Longquan Kiln System Celadon Glaze is essentially due to the presence of elemental iron within the glaze level. The iron does not take part in the glaze network, and as such does not directly impact its structure. When the primary elemental pairing is +2 ions, the coloration is green; when presenting as +3 ions, the coloration is yellow, and if it presents in an oxidized state, it primarily presents as a yellowish brown mottle and consist of Fe_2O_3 and Fe_3O_4. These oxides, compared to the glass phase of the glaze (primarily SiO_2), more easily undergo reaction with external materials (acids or alkali) and produce weathering.

From Chapter 2 Section 3 we can see, the firing atmosphere has a direct impact on the coloration of the celadon glaze. The oxidation or reduction atmosphere dictates the amount of Fe^{2+} or Fe^{3+} within the glaze, and as such, firing atmosphere control is very important.

4. The Function of Other Components

Apart from networking agents, flux, and coloring agents; LKSC glaze contains a few other inclusions, such as Aluminum Oxide (Al_2O_3), which is a critical component.

Within silicate glass, positive Al^{3+} ions of Al_2O_3 have two types of coordinate pairs; 4 and 6 arranged into tetrahedron and hexahedron shapes respectively. When the Molar Ratio $R_2O/ Al_2O_3>1$, Al^{3+} ions match to the $[SiO_4]$ tetrahedron as a $[AlO_4]$ tetrahedron network. This tightly woven network improves the stability of the silica glass. However, when the Molar Ratio $R_2O/Al_2O_3<1$ the amount of alkaline metal ions are less than the Al^{3+} ions, and the Al^{3+} ions exceed chemical equilibrium and are pushed into hexahedron pairing with the silicate glass network rather than the tetrahedron shape [220]. This creates a more loosely woven network with lower density of silicate glass and thus a lower physical chemical stability [221].

Al_2O_3 can network together with SiO_2 as well as remain outside the glass network; because of this we call them intermediate oxides.

5. The Relationship Between Longquan Kiln System Celadon Glaze Composition and Glaze Stability

In order to maintain ionic neutrality, alkaline metal ions and alkaline earth metal ions will disperse evenly but without order throughout the naturally occurring spaces within the silica tetrahedron network of LKSC glaze. These ions and atoms that have weaker bonds with the Si—O can collect and move throughout the glaze level. For example: H^+, Li^+, Na^+, K^+, Rb^+, Cs^+, Ag^+, Cu^+, and other monovalent ions can network and enter into, without breaking down, the glaze level. Even under normal temperatures, they can continue to move within the silicate glass. Additionally, small molecules such as Hydrogen and water can also move throughout the glaze level [222]. According to the above stated, the introduction of alkaline metal oxides breaks down the tetrahedron $[SiO_4]$ network. At the same time, the presence of alkaline metal ions increases the likelihood of the glaze level receiving corrosion caused by reaction with air, water, acids, and bases. Therefore, the higher the concentration of alkaline metal oxides within the glaze, the lower the resistance the glaze has to weathering and decay, as well as having a weakened mechanical strength.

Moreover, the addition of Al_2O_3 into the $[SiO_4]$ network increases the strength and chemical stability of the glaze level. However, if the amount of Al_2O_3 becomes too high, the network density decreases and with it the strength and chemical stability [223].

Al_2O_3既可以与SiO_2形成网络，也可处于网络外，所以它是一种中间体氧化物。

五、龙泉窑系青瓷瓷釉的化学成分与釉层结构稳定性的关系

在龙泉窑系青瓷瓷釉中，由于[SiO_4]四面体间隙的存在，碱金属或碱土金属离子会均匀而无序地分布在某些[SiO_4]四面体之间的空隙中，以维持网络中局部的电中性。

与Si—O连接较弱的原子、离子或原子团在釉层中可以移动，如H^+、Li^+、Na^+、K^+、Rb^+、Cs^+、Ag^+、Cu^+等一价离子可以不破坏釉层网络而进入釉层之中，即使在常温下，也较易在玻璃中移动；此外，H_2、H_2O等小分子也可以在釉层中通过[222]。由前述得知，碱金属氧化物的介入，打断了原有[SiO_4]四面体的网络连接；同时，碱金属离子的移动，使釉层易于与空气、水、酸、碱发生反应，从而釉层遭到腐蚀。所以碱金属氧化物含量越高，釉层抗腐蚀能力越差，机械强度也会越弱。

此外，中间体氧化物Al_2O_3的加入可使[SiO_4]网络加强，釉层化学稳定性提高；但如果Al_2O_3含量过高，反而会使网络紧密程度下降，化学稳定性也会下降[223]。

六、总结

龙泉窑系青瓷釉层是玻璃体（Na_2O-K_2O-CaO-MgO-Al_2O_3-SiO_2），它是由[SiO_4]四面体为基础结构的三维空间网络所组成的非晶体固体。

龙泉窑系青瓷釉层的抗风化能力与碱金属、碱土金属氧化物含量有关，这些氧化物含量越高，釉层抗风化能力越差。

龙泉青瓷瓷釉中，北宋中期和南宋初期钾、钠含量较低，而南宋中晚期开始至元、明，逐步提高，所以越往后釉层结构稳定性相对越差。

所以，在相同生存环境的前提下，陶瓷迹型风化强度的高低与陶瓷瓷釉的化学成分密切相关，与其所属年代久远并不一定是正比例关系。

6. Conclusion

LKSC glaze level is in glass phase (Na_2O-K_2O-CaO-MgO-Al_2O_3-SiO_2), it is a non-crystalline solid formed on the foundation of a three-dimensional [SiO_4] tetrahedron network.

The resistance to weathering of LKSC glaze is related to the amount of alkaline metal and alkaline earth metal oxides within the glaze level, with the higher the amount of these oxides, the lower the resistance. LKSC glaze, with relatively lower Na_2O and K_2O, has a higher chemical stability and resistance to weathering.

Longquan Celadon glaze, in the Mid Northern Song to Early Southern Song Dynasty, had relatively lower amounts of potassium and sodium and these levels increased gradually from the Mid Southern Song Dynasty through to the Yuan and Ming Dynasties. As such, the stability of the glaze structure was increasingly volatile.

This is to say, of pieces within the same weathering environment, the degree to which ceramic glaze weathers depends more so on the chemical composition (its stability) than upon the relative age of the piece.

第三节
龙泉窑系青瓷釉表面活性

一、龙泉窑系青瓷釉表面活性概念

龙泉窑系青瓷釉表面活性是龙泉窑系青瓷釉表面与外部环境中的物质发生反应的能力。

二、龙泉窑系青瓷釉表面活性产生原因

龙泉窑系青瓷釉表面具有活性的产生原因主要有：

第一，青瓷釉料在高温熔融后形成玻璃体，由于高温与助熔剂的作用，玻璃熔体中会有很多断键，不完全配位。在釉料冷却时断键应该合拢，但由于釉表面冷却速度比内部快，断键来不及合拢，键角也不容易恢复，从而在釉表面存在着更多断键。因为釉表面的断键，釉表面会产生极性，从而会在大气中吸收羟基，这些羟基可以吸附水或与其他化合物反应。

第二，有研究指出：在玻璃熔体中，Al_2O_3挥发量为0.5%－5%，B_2O_3为1%－5%，Na_2O和K_2O的挥发量可达5%。釉表面成分的挥发会造成空位，这些空位迁移聚集，会在釉表面形成多个孔隙，使其具有多孔性[224]。

第三，釉裂纹的存在。

三、总结

龙泉窑系青瓷釉表面具有活性，易于吸附和积聚水分，从而便于釉表面的离子交换。这样的瓷器釉表面容易与酸、碱、盐溶液发生反应，造成釉表面的风化。

Section 3 :

Active Nature of the Longquan Kiln System Celadon Glaze Surface

1. The Active Nature of the LKSC Glaze Surface Defined

This is the ability of the LKSC glaze surface to undergo physical and chemical changes with materials within the external environment.

2. Causes of the Glaze Surface Activity

Causes of activity on the glaze surface are roughly split into three types:

A. During the high temperature firing of LKSC glaze, it forms a molten glass. Due to high temperature and the presence of flux, the glass body has many broken bonds and is not completely coordinated evenly. During the cooling of the glaze, these broken bonds should join together; but because the surface of the glaze cools faster than the center of the glaze, not all broken bonds are able to join together and the bonding angles are difficult to repair. Because of this, the glaze surface presents with numerous bond separations.

Glaze surface bond separations gives rise to chemical polarity, which absorbs hydroxyls from the surrounding atmosphere. These hydroxyls absorb water and react with other chemical compounds, leaving the face of the glaze chemically activated.

B. Research shows: Within molten glass, with a volatized Al_2O_3 quantity of 0.5-5% and B_2O_3 1-5%; volatized Na_2O and K_2O quantity can reach 5%. This volatized composition can create empty space, these empty spaces, in turn, migrate and assemble to create small holes which effectively bring about a porous glaze surface [224].

C. The presence of glaze cracks.

3. Conclusion

The glaze surface is active; prone to attracting and absorbing surrounding water that partakes in ion swapping across the face of the glaze. These characteristics make the surface of the glaze susceptible to weathering due to the ease of physical and chemical reactions with acids, bases, and salt solutions.

第四节
龙泉窑系青瓷釉层形貌

一、龙泉窑系青瓷釉层概念

龙泉窑系青瓷釉层是由玻璃相、气相、晶相及少量原料残留颗粒构成的覆盖在青瓷坯体上的玻璃体[225]。

二、龙泉窑系青瓷釉层形貌

（一）龙泉窑系青瓷釉层形貌概念

龙泉窑系青瓷釉层形貌是龙泉窑系青瓷釉层在一定观察角度下的三维可视状况。

（二）龙泉窑系青瓷釉层形貌特征

用肉眼观察青瓷釉表面，非常平滑，但它在显微成像下却凹凸不平，主要可分为两种特征：凸形特征及凹形特征。

1. 凸形特征

龙泉窑系青瓷釉层形貌大部分呈凸形特征，类似星球表面（见图3-4-1、图3-4-2[226]、图3-4-3[227]）。

凸形特征的形成原因参见本章本节玻璃相形成及特征部分及图3-4-9。

釉表面凸起处通常也是一些析晶存在的地方，如C形、O形纹（简称CO纹）。CO纹是存在于釉层的析晶或分相，它们与玻璃相结合处的组织结构稳定性较差，通常风化从这里开始。

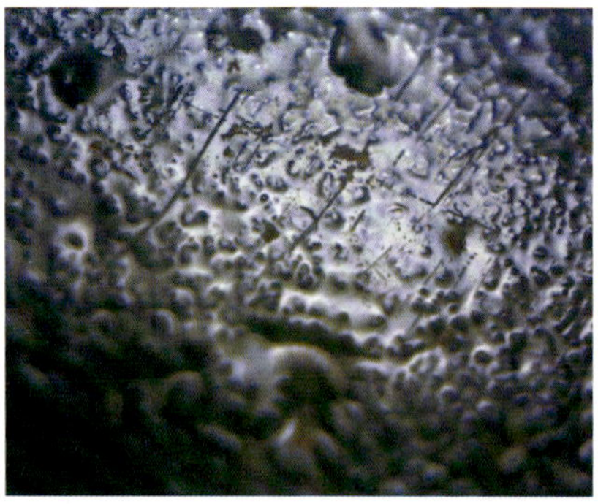

图3-4-1

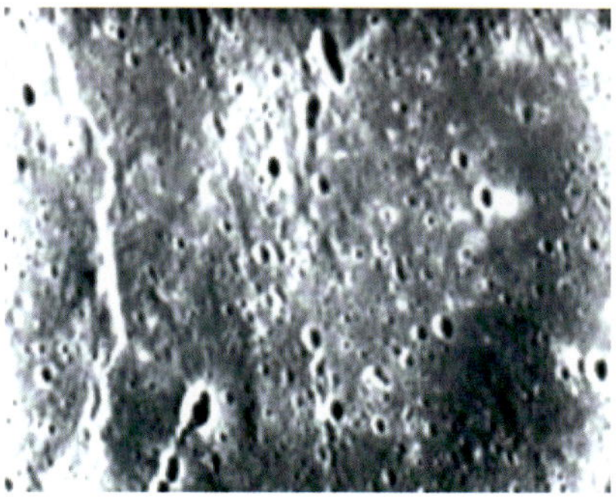

图3-4-2

美国国家航空航天局公布的水星表面照片
Photo taken by NASA of the surface of Mercury

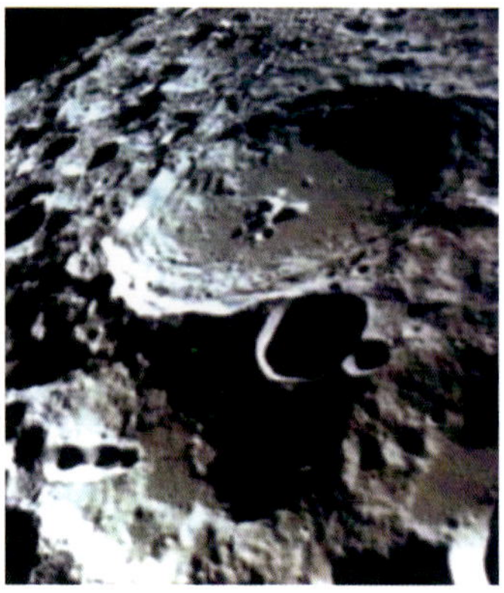

图3-4-3

阿波罗11号飞船在1969年绕月飞行时拍摄的月球背面环形山
Picture taken in 1969 of the Moon by Apollo 11

2. 凹形特征

龙泉窑系青瓷釉层形貌的凹形特征如同弹坑（见图3-4-5箭头所指处）。凹形特征的形成原因参见本章本节玻璃相形成及特征部分及图3-4-8。

釉表面凹陷处易于集聚沉积外界物质，易于吸附水及空气。所以，风化往往先从凹陷处开始，如壁变泡的形成（见图3-4-4、图3-4-5，二者为同一器物同一位置图片，图3-4-4为二维图片，图3-4-5为三维图片）。

Section 4：

Longquan Kiln System Celadon Glaze Level Appearance

1. LKSC Glaze Level Defined

The LKSC glaze level is composed of glass, gas, crystals and trace amounts of other raw materials left over after forming into a vitreous body. Essentially, it is a layer of glass of varying thickness that covers all or a certain portion of the porcelain body [225].

2. LKSC Glaze Level Appearance

A. LKSC Glaze Level Appearance Defined

Describes the three-dimensional state of the glaze surface; including the micro-topography of the glaze.

B. LKSC Glaze Level Appearance Characteristics

To the naked eye, glaze appears smooth and level; but under 500X microscopic magnification the surface appears uneven with humps and pits, and can be split into two primary types of glaze surface: Bumpy Surface and Pitted Surface.

a. Bumpy Surface Characteristics

The majority of LKSC glaze surfaces present with bumpy characteristics, similar to that of celestial bodies (compare pictures 3-4-1, 3-4-2 [226], 3-4-3 [227]). For the causes of these characteristics please refer to the Glass Phase Formation and Characteristics of this chapter as well as picture 3-4-9.

The raised portions of the bumpy surface generally are areas in which crystallization exists, such as C and O striae. C and O striae occur at these points of crystallization or split phase within the glaze level because the connection point with the glass phase at these points is less structurally stable, thus weathering can first occur.

b. Pitted Surface Characteristics

The LKSC pitted surface resembles that of a bullet crater (see the point indicated by the arrow in picture 3-4-5). For the causes of these characteristics please refer to the Glass Phase Formation and Characteristics of this chapter as well as picture 3-4-8.

The pits on the surface of the glaze often collect foreign materials, as well as water and air from the surrounding environment. The effects of weathering present first at these pits. They include traces such as textured bubbles (see pictures 3-4-4 and 3-4-5, where 3-4-4 is the two-dimensional, and 3-4-5 is the three-dimensional image of the same location).

C. LKSC Glaze Appearance Types

a. Glass Phase

I. Glass Phase Defined

Refers to all the non-crystalline composite materials that emerged from a series of physical and chemical reactions during the firing of LKSC that solidify when cooled [228].

II. Glass Phase Formation and Characteristics

During the firing of LKSC, gaseous bodies are formed (see Gas Phase Formation of this section). When the glaze is in a molten state, a portion of gasses from within the body or the glaze level escape, while the remainder remain within the

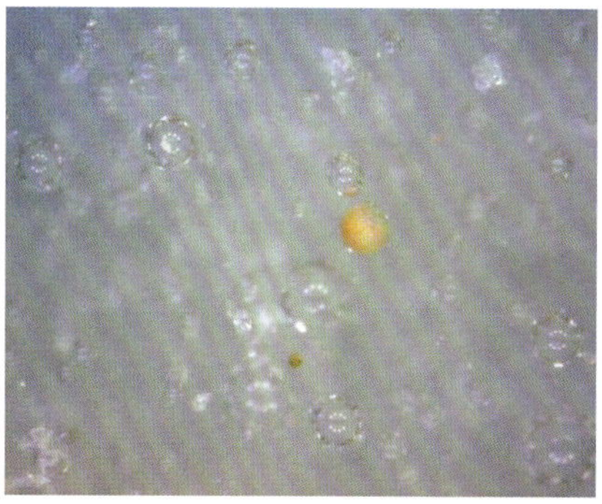

图3-4-4

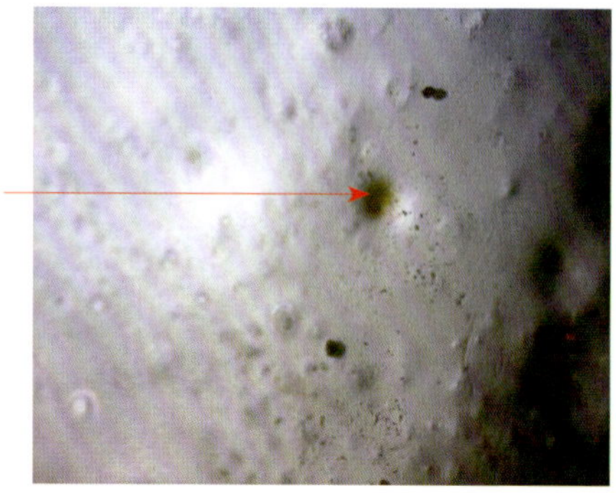

图3-4-5

（三）龙泉窑系青瓷釉层形貌分类

1. 玻璃相

（1）玻璃相概念

玻璃相是青瓷高温烧制时各组成物质产生一系列物理变化、化学反应后冷却凝固形成的一种非晶态物质[228]。

（2）玻璃相形成及特征

青瓷在烧制过程中产生气体（参见本章本节气相形成部分），当釉料熔化时，一部分气体从胎面（胎釉结合处）或釉层中逸出，一部分则留在釉层中形成气泡。由于气泡在熔融釉层中的运动而产生的扰动效应及胎面不平，烧制好的瓷器釉表面会有凹凸不平的现象（见图3-4-6，图中箭头所指处为釉表面同一处在烧制过程中的变化）。

有些气孔由于降温较快或釉层黏度较大而没有闭合，从而使釉表面出现微小的孔洞。不过这些孔洞过于微小，用500倍显微镜一般是观察不到的（见图3-4-7，图中箭头所指处为釉表面同一处在烧制过程中的变化）。

当气泡接近釉表面，温度下降时，气体体积缩小，待釉表面冷却凝固后，气泡上方的釉表面就会形成凹坑（见图3-4-8，图中箭头所指处为釉表面同一处在烧制过程中的变化）。

如果气泡高出釉表面，温度下降时，气体体积缩小，高出釉表面的气泡上方会有凹坑出现，如同月球上的环形山，气泡周围较低的地方则形成沟壑（见图3-4-9，图中箭头所指处为釉表面同一处在烧制过程中的变化）。

2. 气相

（1）气相概念

气相是存在于烧制好的青瓷釉层中的气体。

（2）气相形成

气相的形成有以下几个原因[229]：

① 青瓷胎釉本身反应形成气泡

青瓷胎体中存在开口气孔和闭口气孔。温度升高时，气体体积膨胀，经开口气孔进入釉层；熔融的釉层将坯体润湿，釉对坯体的溶解作用可以打开一些闭口气孔，使气体进入釉层。青瓷胎釉中含有Fe_3O_4、Fe_2O_3、$CaCO_3$、Pb_3O_4等，它们在高温下发生化学反应，产生气体，形成气泡。

部分反应方程式如下：

$CaCO_3 \rightarrow CaO + CO_2\uparrow$

（600—1050℃）

$MgCO_3 \rightarrow MgO + CO_2\uparrow$

（400—900℃）

$FeCO_3 \rightarrow FeO + CO_2\uparrow$

（>200℃）

$2Fe_2O_3 \rightarrow 4FeO + O_2\uparrow$

（1250—1370℃）

$Fe_2O_3 + CO \rightarrow 2FeO + CO_2\uparrow$

（1000—1100℃）

$CaSO_4 \rightarrow CaO + SO_3\uparrow$

（1250—1370℃）

$Na_2SO_4 \rightarrow Na_2O + SO_3\uparrow$

（1200—1370℃）

青瓷胎釉中的矿物质在高温下排出结晶水，也会形成气泡被排出。

熔块中的水分在高温下形成气泡。

② 碳素形成气泡

在青瓷烧制过程中，CO在高温下裂解产生CO_2和C，同时C沉积在釉表面，在高温下氧化生成CO_2，形成气泡。

③ 工艺影响形成气泡

在施釉时将一部分气体封闭在釉层中，烧制时膨胀形成气泡。在烧制时，窑炉中的燃烧产物会被夹带进入釉层形成气泡。

④ 小结

青瓷烧制过程中，由上述原因生成的气体进入釉层，部分气体逸出釉面，部分留在釉层中形成气

glaze level. Due to the turbulent motion of the formation and movement of these air bubbles within the molten glaze level as well as the unevenness of the porcelain body, the post-firing glaze surface is topographically uneven. From illustration 3-4-6 we can see the progression of one point on the glaze surface as indicated by the red arrow.

There are some air holes, due to the rapid cooling or viscous nature of the glaze, that were unable to close and leave behind microscopic pits across the glaze surface (see picture 3-4-7). However, there are some pits that are microscopically invisible (while using a 500X magnification microscope, they are usually unobservable).

When air bubbles approach the surface, while the glaze is cooling, the gas within the bubble contracts; this creates a small depression on the surface of the glaze over the top of the air pocket once the glaze hardens (see picture 3-4-8) .

If an air bubble extrudes above the surface level while the glaze is cooling, the gas within the bubble still contracts; these bubbles create an extruding crater on the surface of the glaze (similar to that of moon craters, see picture 3-4-9). The area surrounding the air bubble is slightly lower, forming a trough.

b. Gas Phase

I. Gas Phase Defined

Gas phase is the gaseous materials left within the glaze level of fired LKSC.

II. Gas Phase Formation

Gas phases are formed due to the following reasons [229]:

i. Celadon Body-Glaze Reaction Formed Air Bubbles

(a) The celadon body presents with open and closed air pockets, when temperatures increase, these gaseous bodies expand. Open air pockets eject air directly into the glaze level. Molten glaze also moistens the porcelain body; dissolving some of the clay and opening up closed air pockets, which allows gas to enter into the glaze.

(b) Celadon clay and glaze have trace amounts of CO_3^{2-}, SO_4^{2-}, NO_3^-, Fe_2O_3, $CaCO_3$, Pb_3O_4, and so forth, which under high temperatures react and form gasses that create air bubbles. Some of the above-mentioned reactions are listed below:

$CaCO_3 \rightarrow CaO + CO_2$ (600℃ - 1050℃)

$MgCO_3 \rightarrow MgO + CO_2$ (400℃ - 900℃)

$FeCO_3 \rightarrow FeO + CO_2$ (200℃)

$2Fe_2O_3 \rightarrow 4FeO + O_2$ (1250℃ - 1370℃)

$Fe_2O_3 + CO \rightarrow 2FeO + CO_2$ (1000℃ - 1100℃)

$CaSO_4 \rightarrow CaO + SO_3$ (1250℃ - 1370℃)

$Na_2SO_4 \rightarrow Na_2O + SO_3$ (1200℃ - 1370℃)

(c) The minerals within the ceramic body and glaze, under high temperatures, discharge water of crystallization that can form air bubbles.

(d) Water particles in the molten bodies, under high temperatures, create air bubbles.

ii. Carbon Formed Air Bubbles

During the firing process, CO undergoes decomposition, splitting to form C and CO_2. At the same time, Carbon deposits on the surface of the glaze oxidize to form CO_2, creating air bubbles.

iii. Air Bubbles Formed By Technical Influences

During the glazing process, a small portion of air can become trapped within the glaze level; these expand while firing to form air bubbles. Additionally, during the firing process, combustion products within the kiln furnace can also become dislodged into the glaze level and create air bubbles.

iv. Summary

During the firing of celadon, because of the aforementioned reasons, gasses can enter into the glaze level; some of which seep out of the glaze surface, while others remain to create air bubbles. The possible gasses within air bubbles are: O_2, H_2, H_2O, N_2, CO, CO_2, and SO_2.

While air bubbles are moving throughout the molten glaze, some small bubbles converge with other bubbles to create larger bubbles. Additionally, the coarseness and refinement of the porcelain clay has a direct impact on the size of the bubbles within the glaze. The distribution and size of air bubbles are affected by the following: Firing heat

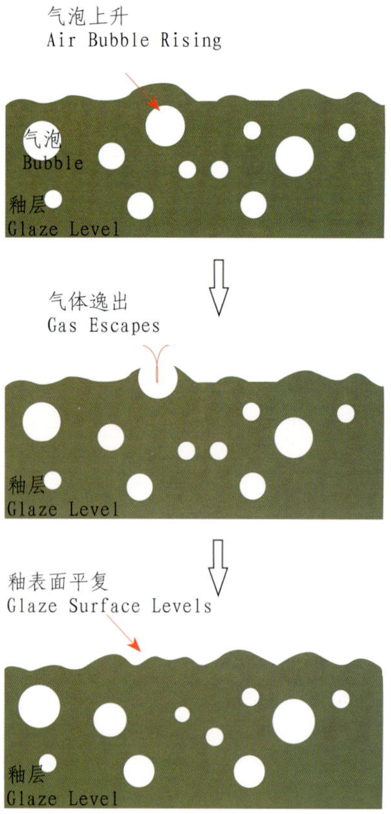

图3-4-6

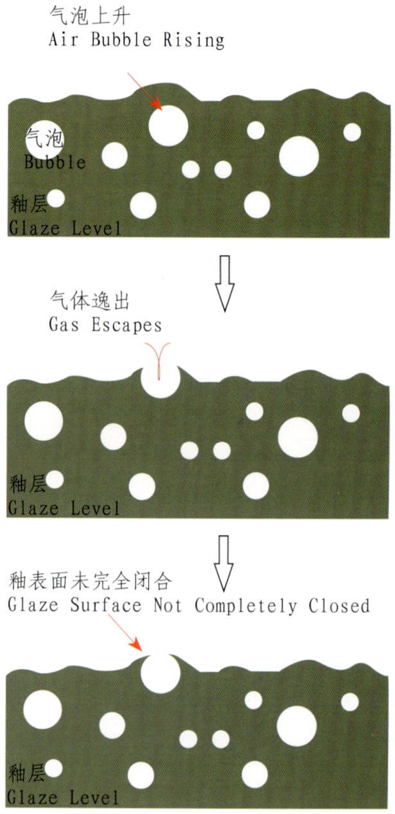

图3-4-7

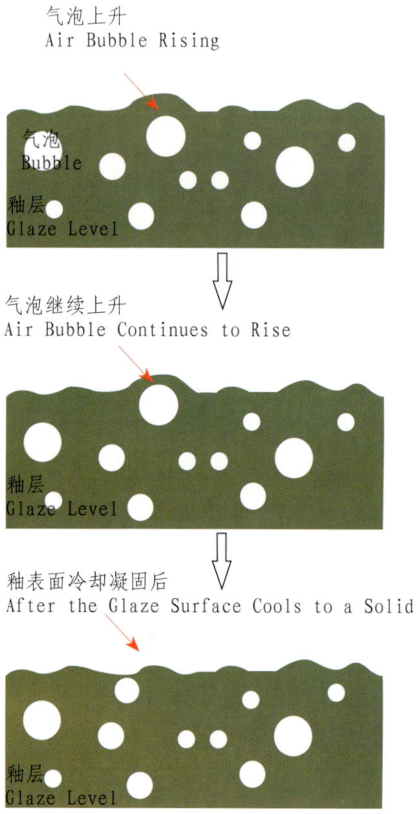

图3-4-8

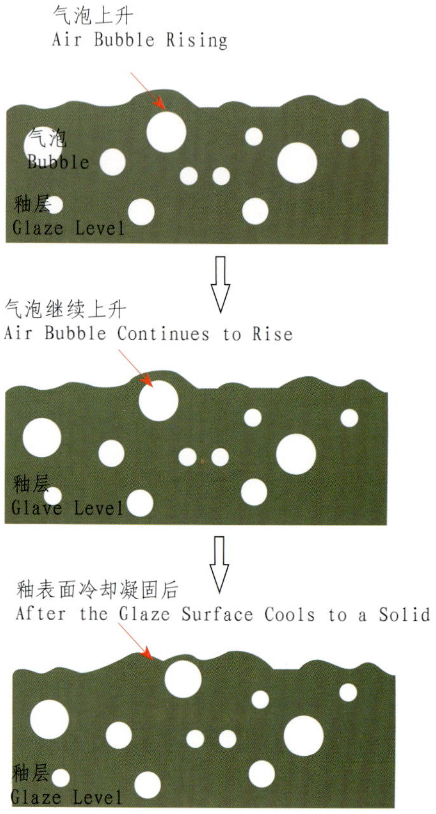

图3-4-9

distribution, forming techniques, body and glaze chemical composition, glaze thickness, and so forth.

III. Gas Phase Characteristics

Most bubbles occur with sparse distribution (see pictures 3-4-10, 3-4-11) or dense distribution (see pictures 3-4-12, 3-4-13); occasionally, random distribution of independent large bubbles present (see pictures 3-4-10, 3-4-11).

c. Crystal Phase

I. Crystal Phase Defined

Crystal phase refers to the crystallized formations, with certain shape and color, which have formed within the LKSC glaze level or on the glaze surface.

The primary crystal phases found in Longquan Celadon include leftover quartz granules and its variants as well as mullite. Also included are various metal, primarily iron, oxides that appears as mottles or striae.

II. Crystal Phase Formation

From a thermodynamics perspective, when any specific state of matter cools (or heats) to a point of phase change, it will undergo phase change and a new phase is formed. This is precisely the process of crystal phase formation during the cooling of melted glaze.

Crystallization has two processes, first is nucleation into crystal nuclei and the second is crystal growth into mature crystals. However, it is not all crystal nuclei that can grow crystals, it is only nuclei that have achieved critical mass that can stabilize to form crystals.

Nucleation occurs in two different ways, homogeneously distributed and heterogeneously distributed nucleation.

Homogeneously distributed nucleation occurs in well dispersed base solvents, having nothing to do with structural flaws of the solution. It is brought on by the undulation caused by heat induction, and causes a change from the high Gibbs free energy state (i.e. liquid) into the low Gibbs free energy state (i.e. solid). Heterogeneously distributed nucleation occurs at the interface point of two phases, i.e. a liquid and its containing vessel, liquid and foreign material grains, or liquid and air interfaces. It also often occurs at points of structural flaw within the solution. As the required compiled energy needed for heterogeneously distributed nucleation is lower than that of homogeneously distributed, the vast majority of crystal nucleation is of the heterogeneously distributed variety.

During the firing of celadon, glaze gradually transitions into a molten state. Due to the buoyancy, surface tension, and movement of the air bubbles within the glaze level, the Oxidized Iron and Manganese within the glaze collect around the edges of gaseous bodies within the glaze and rise with these bubbles to the surface of the glaze, forming heterogeneously distributed nuclei crystallizations.

As the glaze cools, more crystallization happens. Crystal types are dictated by the chemical composition of the glaze. According to their composition, their density, and differences in surface tension of the glaze; these crystallizations present with different appearances, colors, and amounts of mottles (blotches) and striae (lines).

As the glaze cools to a solid, iron ions (Primarily Fe^{3+}) dissolved within the glaze level form flowing mottles or flowing striae.

Other crystallization within the LKSC glaze level could include non-melted quartz granules in the form of mullite and anorthite crystallizations formed during the cooling process. They can also occur on the glaze surface.

III. Crystal Phase Characteristics

Crystal phases within the glaze level of LKSC primarily consisting of quartzite, mullite, and anorthite or other predominantly iron metal oxides present as mottles and striae.

i. Mottles

Mottles include Flowing Mottles, Radiating Mottles and Blotch Mottles (see Chapter 5 Flowing Mottles, Radiating Mottles and Blotch Mottles sections).

Flowing mottles on the surface of the glaze have a relatively high ability to soak the surface of the glaze, allowing for an even distribution between the mottle and the surrounding glass phase (see pictures 3-4-14 and 3-4-15, where 3-4-14 is the two-dimensional, and 3-4-15 is the three

泡。气泡中的气体可以是O_2、H_2、H_2O、N_2、CO、CO_2、SO_2等。在气泡的运动过程中，一些小气泡会在熔融的釉层中相聚变成大气泡。另外，胎泥的粗与精，对气泡大小的生成有直接关系。烧制火力分布不均匀、工艺参数不同、胎釉的化学组成不同以及釉层的厚度不同等因素，都会影响釉层中气泡的分布和大小。

（3）气相特征

气相即气泡，有分布舒朗（见图3-4-10、图3-4-11），也有分布密集（见图3-4-12、图3-4-13）。偶尔随机可见独立大气泡分布（见图3-4-10、图3-4-11）。

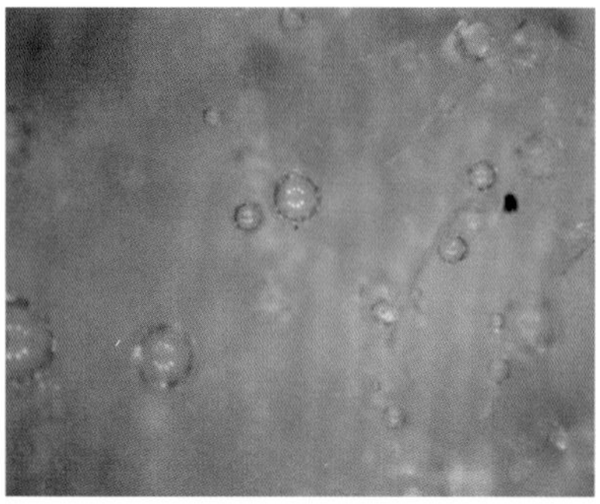

图3-4-10

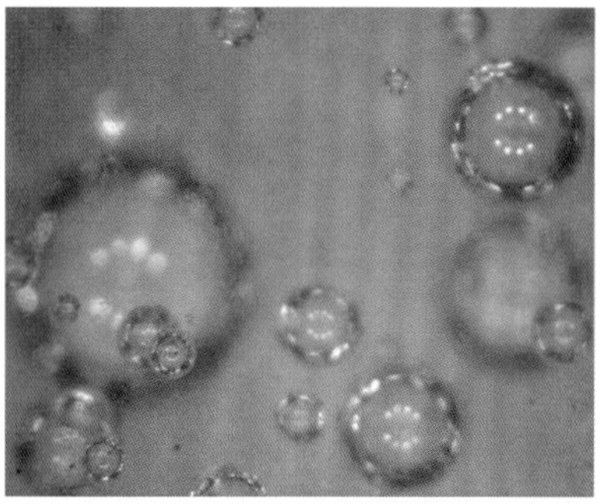

图3-4-11

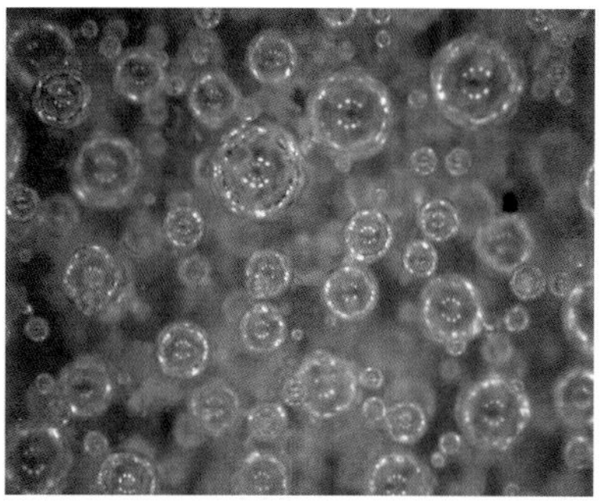

图3-4-12

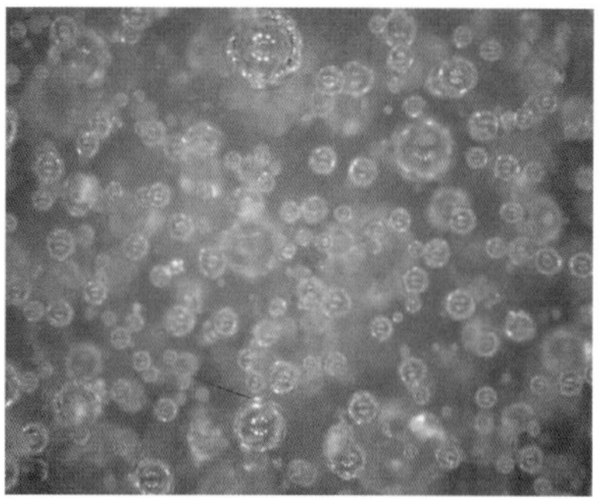

图3-4-13

3. 晶相

（1）晶相概念

晶相是龙泉窑系青瓷釉表面或釉层中析出的有一定形状和颜色的结晶体。

（2）晶相形成

从热力学的观点来看，将一定状态的物体冷却（或加热）到相变温度，就会发生相转变而产生新相。在熔融釉中晶体析出便是产生新相的过程。

析晶有两个过程：一是形成稳定晶核的成核过程，二是晶核成长为晶体的晶体长大过程。但并非所有的晶核都能长成晶体，只有超过临界尺寸的晶核才有可能稳定成长而形成晶体。

形成晶核的成核过程又分为均匀成核与非均匀成核两种。

均匀成核发生于均匀基质内部，与相界结构缺陷无关。它是由于热运动引起组织和结构上的起伏，使得部分质点从高的吉布斯自由能状态（如液相）转变为低的吉布斯自由能状态（如晶体）形成的。

非均匀成核，发生于系统中两相的界面处，如液相与容器的界面、液相与杂质颗粒的界面或液相与气相的界面，也常常发生在液体中结构缺陷处。由于非均匀成核所须克服的能垒比均匀成核所须克服的能垒要小，实际上大多数析晶相变的成核都属于非均匀成核。

青瓷在高温烧制时，釉料会逐渐熔化成熔融态，在浮力、表面张力及气泡搅动的作用下，釉料中的铁氧化物及锰氧化物等易在气泡边缘积聚，也可能再形成分相，部分会随气泡升至釉表面，形成非均匀成核析晶。在降温过程中，会有更多的结晶在釉表面析出。结晶的种类取决于釉层的化学组成。根据它们的成分、密度、表面张力不同，这些晶体表现为不同形貌、不同颜色和不同层次的斑块或纹路。

龙泉窑系青瓷釉层中的晶相还可能是未熔的残留石英颗粒及其变体以及在冷却时析出的莫来石、钙长石等。它们也可以存在于釉表面。

（3）晶相特征

龙泉窑系青瓷釉层中的晶相，主要成分包括残留石英颗粒及其变体以及莫来石、钙长石等，或是以铁为主的金属氧化物，出现形式有斑块或纹路。

dimensional image of the same location).

When radiating mottle crystallizations form on the glaze surface during the firing of LKSC, due to the continued rising of the firing temperature and the reduction of viscosity of the glaze, some crystallizations meld into the molten glass and can easily move and become covered by the glaze level. However, the composition of the glass phase above these radiating mottles has already achieved a different composition from than that of the primary glass phase surrounding the mottle. Thus the interface between the mottle and the surrounding glass phase becomes the border of the mottle (see pictures 3-4-16 and 3-4-17).

Radiating mottles can achieve multiple colorations in a maple leaf or irregular shape crystallization distributed along the glaze surface and within the glaze level (see pictures 3-4-18—3-4-22, picture 3-4-18 is the two-dimensional, and 3-4-19 is the three dimensional image of the same location).

Blotch mottles are those crystallized formations on the glaze surface and within the glaze level that have assembled into a clustered group but do not possess a radiating shape (see picture 3-4-23).

ii. Striae

When crystallization amounts are relatively low, unable to form mottles, they will be forced into striae by the surrounding glass phase, creating flowing striae (see pictures 3-4-24 and 3-4-25). When they are even lower in number, they can occur all across the glaze surface as C and O shaped striae (see pictures 3-4-26 and 3-4-27).

IV. Summary

The crystallization within the glaze level of LKSC is directly impacted by the composition and compound ratios of the glaze as well as the firing techniques (temperature and reduction control).

From a thermodynamics perspective, glaze cooling into a solid does not achieve perfect equilibrium, but remains in a metastable state in which crystallization has a tendency to still occur. However, from a kinetics perspective, as the molecules in the solidified glaze have difficulty in continued movement, crystallization has essentially stopped, and as such, a vitrified glaze level is in a relatively stable state.

① 斑块

斑块包括流淌斑、放射斑及团状斑（见第五章第一节流淌斑、放射斑及团状斑部分）。

位于釉表面的流淌斑，其析出的晶体能润湿釉表面，通常斑块与玻璃相之间过渡均匀（见图3-4-14、图3-4-15，二者为同一器物同一位置图片，图3-4-14为二维图片，图3-4-15为三维图片）。

图3-4-16

图3-4-19

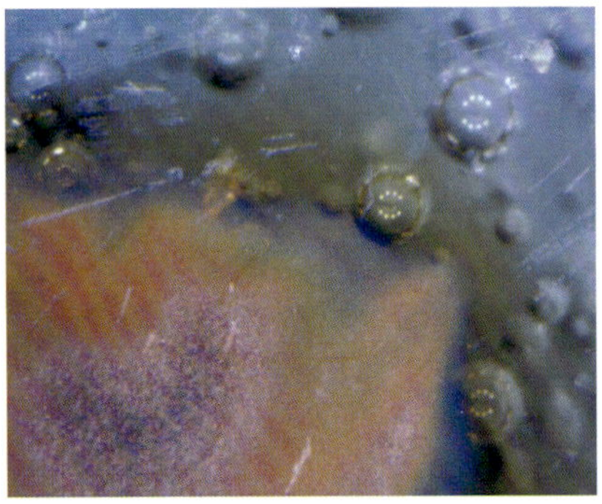

图3-4-14

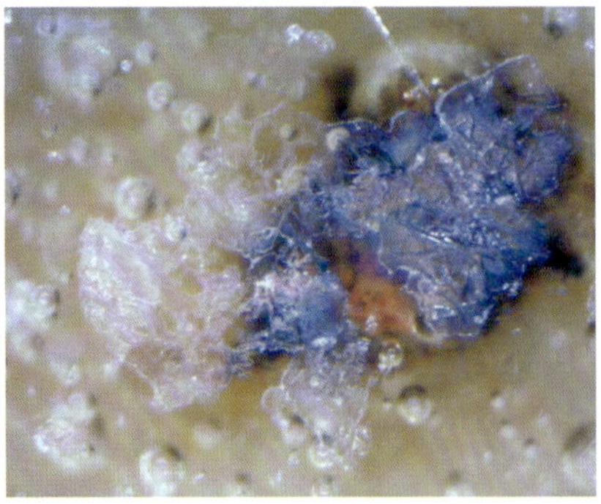

图3-4-17

图3-4-20

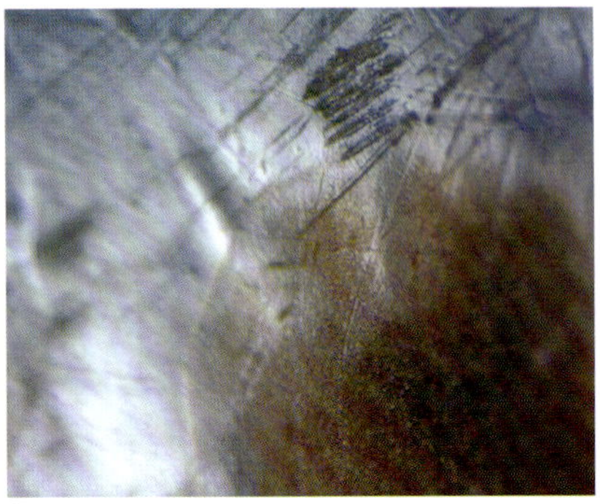

图3-4-15

放射斑还以不同颜色、呈不规则形状分布在釉表面及釉层中（见图3-4-18—图3-4-22，图3-4-18、图3-4-19为同一器物同一位置图片，图3-4-18为二维图片，图3-4-19为三维图片）。

图3-4-21

在青瓷的烧制过程中，当放射斑晶体在釉表面析出时，由于烧制温度继续升高，部分晶体又会被熔解在玻璃相中；同时釉的黏度降低，相对易流动，以至晶体又被玻璃相覆盖，但这时覆盖于放射斑上的玻璃相的成分已与主玻璃相有差异，所以这两相的界面就表现为放射斑的边线（见图3-4-16、图3-4-17）。

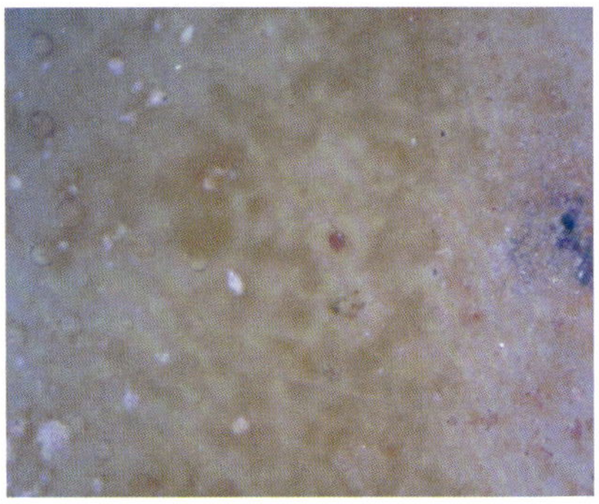

图3-4-18

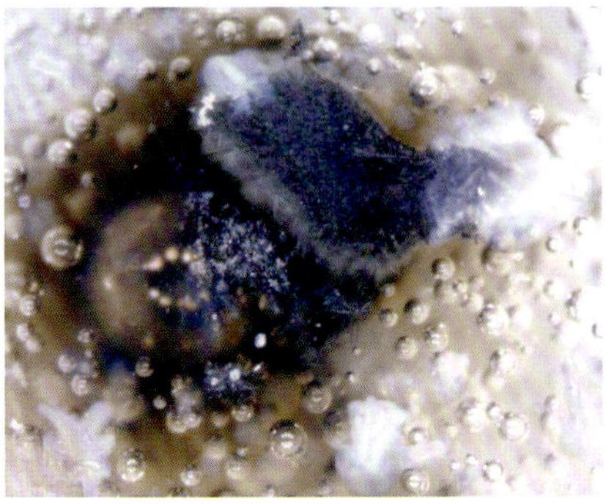

图3-4-22

团状斑是釉表面及釉层中聚集成一团、没有放射感的析晶斑块。（见图3-4-23）

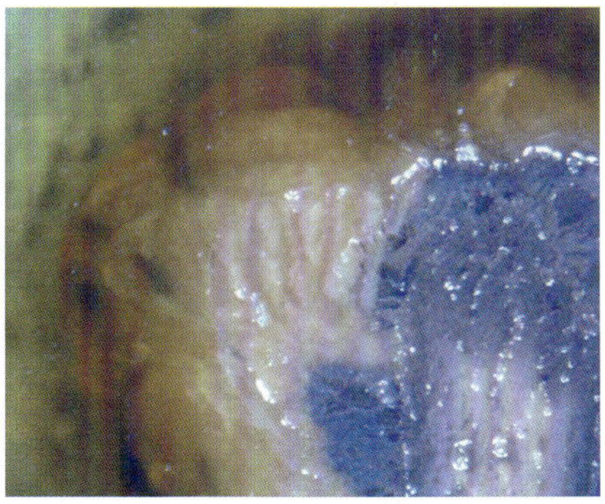

图3-4-23

② 纹路

当析出的晶体数量较少，不足以形成斑块时，会被其周围的玻璃相排挤形成流淌纹（见图3-4-24、图3-4-25），数量更少的时候，在釉表面任何地方都可以形成C形、O形纹。（见图3-4-26、图3-4-27）

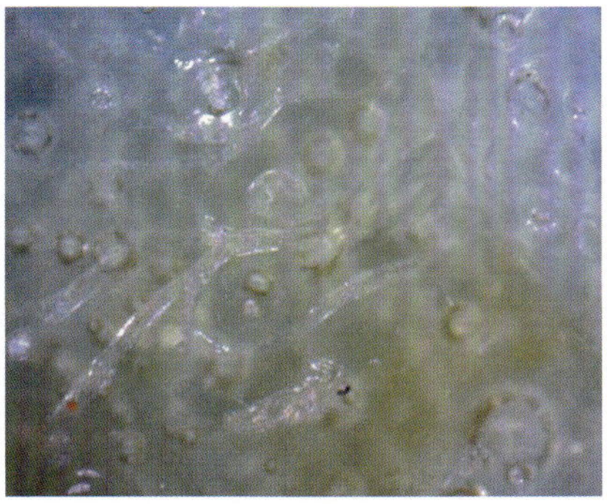

图3-4-24

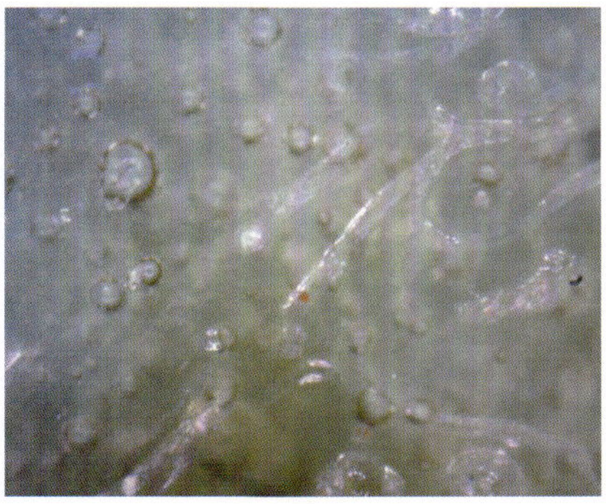

图3-4-25

（4）小结

龙泉窑系青瓷釉层析晶与釉料的成分及含量有关，而烧制工艺（温度控制、氧化和还原气氛控制等）也是重要的影响因素。

从热力学的观点来看，冷却凝固了的釉层并未达到平衡，处于介稳状态，仍有继续析出结晶的趋势。但从动力学的观点来看，由于釉层降温固化，分子运动较为困难，析晶几乎停止。所以，冷却凝固了的釉层应处于一个相对稳定的状态。

图3-4-26

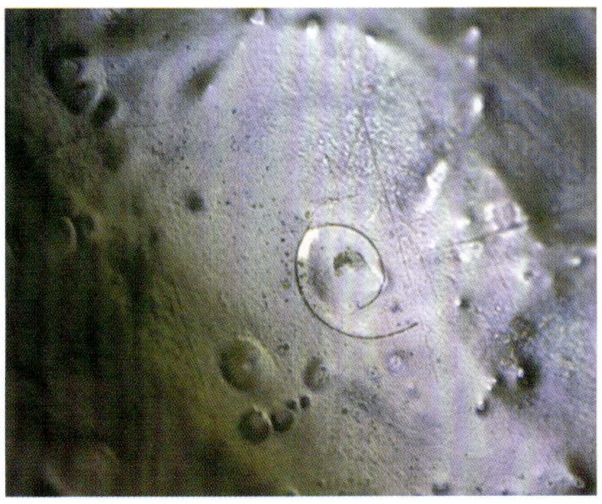

图3-4-27

第五节 总结

龙泉窑系青瓷釉层的性质是由釉层的成分及其含量决定的。

釉层不同的成分，会形成不同结构的网络，形成釉层不同的性质；相同的釉层构成成分，但各成分含量的差异，也会造成釉层网络结构的差异，形成不同性质的釉层。

此外，工艺参数如烧制温度、烧制气氛等也会对青瓷釉层的性质产生影响。

不同性质的釉层会有不同的先天迹型表现，继而在后天的环境中也会出现不同的风化迹型特征。

一般来说，釉层的风化都从釉层结构稳定性较差（如釉层本身存在的一些裂纹、孔隙）或釉层成分物理化学性质相对较活跃的地方开始（如铁氧化物聚集暴露处）。釉层在经过几百年的风化作用后产生的迹型特征是缓慢量变的结果。现代人为制假做旧，在短时间内以质变、突变的方式制造出的迹型特征，与长期自然风化的迹型特征有本质的区别。

龙泉窑系青瓷釉层性质的不同是先天性的。釉料配方、工艺参数的差异表现出不同的迹型特征，加上后天环境变化的差异，最终形成釉层迹型风化作用强度快慢的差异和风化强度高低的不同。这样就形成了迹型风化的多样性及复杂性。这是观察、认识和了解龙泉窑系青瓷的迹型变化现象以及迹型变化规律的理论基础。

Section 5:
Conclusion

The characteristics of LKSC glaze are determined by the different chemical compositions and respective amounts of individual components.

The different compositions of glaze create different glaze network constructions, and thus different glaze characteristics. Even though the chemical components of two certain glazes are the same, differences in characteristics can arise from using different amounts of associated components.

According to the differences in LKSC glaze composition, they can be divided into calcium glaze, calcium alkaline glaze, and alkaline calcium glaze.

Additionally, the technological parameters under which a piece is fired, such as the firing temperature and atmosphere, also have an impact on the characteristics of the glaze.

Different glaze qualities bring about varied inherent traces, which under the influences of the post firing environment, create different weathered trace characteristics.

Usually, weathering first takes place where defects in the glaze level are present; namely cracks and openings or areas in the glaze level with a relatively active nature (i.e. exposed Iron Oxide). Corrosion caused by external materials start at these defects. The trace characteristic changes within the LKSC glaze level, after hundreds of years of weathering, are the result of slow quantitative changes. Modern methods of aging ceramics utilize a qualitative change over a very short period of time and create trace characteristics that are innately differentiated from natural weathering changes.

The differences in glaze characteristics are intrinsic, and these innate differences form unique traces. Additionally, various post-firing environments ultimately bring forth dissimilarities in weathering intensity, and as such, disparities in weathering severity. This brings about complexity and multiplicity in LKSC trace weathering. This is the theoretical foundation for observing, recognizing, and understanding the appearance of trace changes and the laws that govern them.

第四章

龙泉窑系青瓷釉层变化

阅读提示：

本章主要阐述龙泉窑系青瓷釉层变化机理，论述釉层变化与环境的关系，并列举龙泉窑系青瓷釉层风化的迹型特征。

主要论述问题：

1. 龙泉窑系青瓷釉层在外界环境中会有哪些物理变化和化学反应？
2. 龙泉窑系青瓷釉层的变化与其所处环境有什么关系？
3. 龙泉窑系青瓷釉层迹型的风化特征是什么？

Chapter 4

Longquan Kiln System Celadon Glaze Level Changes

Text Note:

This chapter explains the mechanics of LKSC glaze level change, discusses the relationship between the post-firing environment and LKSC glaze level change, and presents the characteristics of weathered LKSC traces.

第一节
龙泉窑系青瓷釉层变化机理

一、龙泉窑系青瓷釉层与水的反应

由于青瓷釉表面的活性，易于吸附水分子，会形成单羟基、双羟基团，单羟基之间会通过氢键键合形成闭合羟基团[230]，反应如下（氢键用虚线表示）：

$\equiv$Si— + $OH^-\rightarrow\equiv$Si— OH 单羟基

$\equiv$Si—$O^-+H_2O\rightarrow$=Si<(OH)(OH) 双羟基团

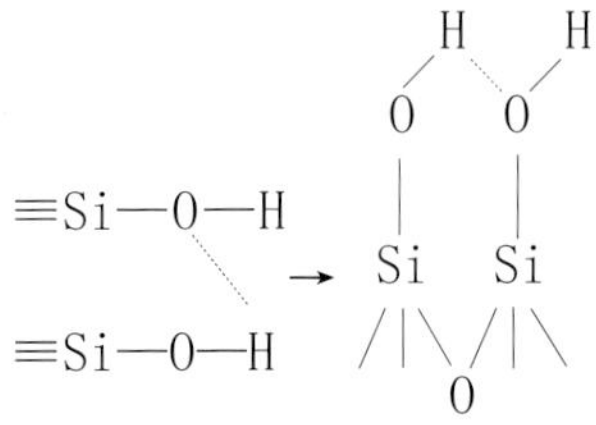

闭合羟基团

通过羟基的氢键再进一步物理吸附水分子，在釉层表面形成水膜。

对龙泉窑系青瓷瓷釉（Na_2O-K_2O-CaO-MgO-Al_2O_3-SiO_2系统）来说，釉层中的碱金属离子和碱土金属离子没有参加硅氧网络，均为网络外离子，具有较大的可迁移性。它们会和吸附在釉表面的水分子中的H^+进行离子交换，生成碱（ROH）（见反应①）。

$\equiv$Si—O—R^+ + H^+OH^- $\rightarrow$
$\equiv$Si—O—H + ROH ①

接着又有下列反应：

$$\equiv Si—O—H+\frac{3}{2}H_2O\rightarrow Si(OH)_4 \quad ②$$

水分子（H_2O）也能与硅氧网络直接反应：

$\equiv$Si—O—Si$\equiv$ + H_2O $\rightarrow$
2[$\equiv$Si—O—H] ③

随着反应③的继续，Si原子周围原有的4个桥氧全部变成—OH，形成$Si(OH)_4$，这是水对硅氧网络的直接破坏[231]。

以上反应的产物$Si(OH)_4$是一种极性分子，它能使周围的水分子极化，然后吸附在自己周围，成为$Si(OH)_4\cdot nH_2O$，通常称为硅酸凝胶[232]。这种硅酸凝胶除了有一部分溶于水之外，大部分都会附着在釉表面，形成一层薄膜。它具有较强的抗水和抗酸能力。

反应①中，由于R^+比H^+要大，它们交换后，H^+代替R^+，使釉层产生空位，结构变疏松，稳定性下降，所以易受到风化侵蚀。

二、龙泉窑系青瓷釉层与碱的反应

碱的来源有两个方面：一是来自反应①，水与釉表面作用生成的，它取决于H^+和R^+交换的速度；二是外部环境提供的。

碱（ROH）可溶解硅酸凝胶$Si(OH)_4\cdot nH_2O$（见反应④），使釉表面失去保护，风化得以继续进行。

$Si(OH)_4$+ROH$\rightarrow$[$Si(OH)_3O$]$^-R^+$+H_2O ④

ROH也可以直接与硅氧网络反应，使Si—O键断裂，网络解体，产生$\equiv$Si—O^-粒子群，使SiO_2溶于碱液中，因而破坏釉表面（见反应⑤）：

$\equiv$Si—O—Si$\equiv$ + $OH^-\rightarrow$
$\equiv$Si—OH + $\equiv$Si—O^- ⑤

而断裂一端的$\equiv$Si—O-又能与H_2O反应：

$\equiv$Si—O^-+$H_2O\rightarrow\equiv$Si—OH+OH^- ⑥

反应⑥产生的碱可使反应⑤继续发生，从而溶解SiO_2。

对于龙泉窑系青瓷瓷釉（Na_2O-K_2O-CaO-MgO-Al_2O_3-SiO_2系统）而言，随着R^+（R在此指Na、K）的不断迁出，Ca^{2+}的含量相对增多，Ca^{2+}会对R^+产生“抑制效应”，使得H^+和R^+的离子交换变得缓慢，碱（ROH）的生成速度变慢（反应①速度变慢），从而反应⑤也变得缓慢。这样对釉层的侵蚀就

Section 1：

Mechanics of Longquan Kiln System Celadon Glaze Level Change

1. LKSC Glaze Level Reactions with Water

The active nature of the LKSC glaze surface and its high absorption allows for the formation of single and double hydroxyls, as well as the hydrogen bonding between single hydroxyls forming closed hydroxyl groups [230]. The reactions are shown below (Hydrogen bonding is represented with a dotted line):

$\equiv Si- + OH^- \rightarrow \equiv Si-OH$ Single Hydroxyl

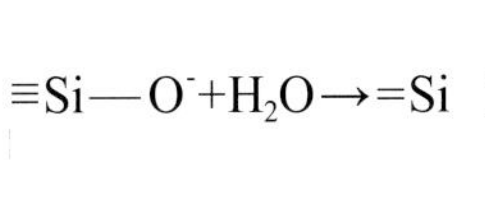

Double Hydroxyls

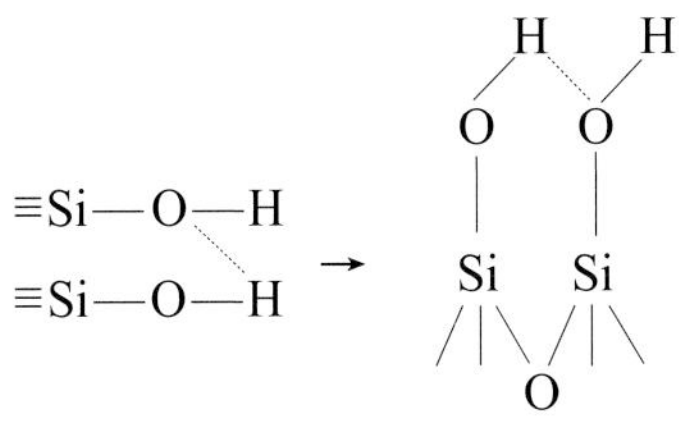

Hydroxyl Group

The Hydrogen bonds of these hydroxyls physically attract water molecules, forming a film of water over the surface of the glaze.

As the alkaline metal and alkaline earth metal ions in LKSC (Na_2O-K_2O-CaO-MgO-Al_2O_3-SiO_2 System) glazes do not take part in the silica network, they retain a relatively high ability to migrate throughout the glaze level. This allows them to partake in ion exchange with the H^+ ion of the water that has been absorbed to the glaze surface, creating alkali (ROH) (see reaction ①).

$$\equiv Si-O-R^+ + H^+OH^- \rightarrow \equiv Si-O-H + ROH \quad ①$$

Additionally there are the following reactions:

$$\equiv Si-O-H + \frac{3}{2}H_2O \rightarrow Si(OH)_4 \quad ②$$

Water particles can also react directly with the silica network:

$$\equiv Si-O-Si\equiv + H_2O \rightarrow 2[\equiv Si-O-H] \quad ③$$

The continuation of reaction ③ is the four bridging oxygen surrounding the Si atom becoming —OH particles, forming $Si(OH)_4$. This is the direct breakdown effect water has on the silica network [231].

The $Si(OH)_4$ created in the above reaction is a polarized molecule that can also polarize the surrounding water molecules, attracting them to itself creating $Si(OH)_4 \cdot nH_2O$, often called silicic acid gel [232]. Aside from a small portion that dissolves in water, this silicic acid gel can absorb to the glaze surface, forming a thin layer or film. This film, in turn, has a relatively high resistance to water and other acids.

In reaction ①, the location left by the R^+ ion, being larger than the H^+ ion with which they change places, leaves voids in the glaze level. This in turn, loosens the structure, decreases the stability, and increases the susceptibility to corrosion.

2. LKSC Glaze Level Reactions with Alkali

The introduction of alkali occurs in two different ways: The first being the aforementioned reaction ① water-glaze reaction, depending on the speed of R^+ and H^+ ion exchange.

变得非常缓慢，甚至几乎停止了。但如果外部环境是碱性的，风化作用会继续进行。由于碱（ROH）的作用，硅氧网络遭到破坏后（见反应⑤），以≡Si—O⁻粒子群的形式溶解下来，和釉表面游离的R^+、R^{2+}等阳离子结合成硅酸盐。这些风化产物不断堆积，在釉表面形成一个壳层。当这一壳层达到一定厚度时，会令釉表面失去光泽，严重时呈不透明状。此壳层是疏松多孔的，吸水性也很强，它提供了一个有高浓度的碱性水溶液的环境，使釉表面无法形成保护膜，原有的硅酸凝胶薄膜也会遭到破坏。因此，这种壳层的形成会大大加剧外界对釉层的侵蚀[233]。

三、龙泉窑系青瓷釉层与酸的反应

龙泉窑系青瓷釉层与酸的反应跟其与水的反应相似，除氢氟酸外，一般的酸并不直接与釉发生反应，而是通过水起作用。氢氟酸对玻璃的作用是直接破坏硅氧网络（见反应⑦）：

$$\equiv Si—O—Si\equiv + H^+F^- \rightarrow$$
$$\equiv Si—O—H + \equiv Si—F \qquad ⑦$$

对龙泉窑系青瓷瓷釉（Na_2O-K_2O-CaO-MgO-Al_2O_3-SiO_2系统）来说，酸溶液中的H^+浓度比水中的H^+浓度要大，所以H^+与R^+的离子交换速度在酸中比在水中快，即反应①有较快的速度，生成的碱（ROH）会侵蚀釉表面。如果R_2O含量低或有Ca^{2+}的“抑制效应”，反应①就会减缓速度或停止。$Si(OH)_4$不溶于酸，在酸性溶液中溶解度减小，即减慢了反应④的反应速度，从而能够减缓釉表面的侵蚀。

在高碱釉中，R_2O含量较高时，R^+的浓度较高，反应①是主要的，有碱不断生成，侵蚀釉表面；在高硅釉中，SiO_2含量较高时，反应④的速度会变得缓慢，也就是说硅酸凝胶被溶解的速度减慢，风化得以减缓。所以，高碱釉的耐酸性小于耐水性，而高硅釉的耐酸性大于耐水性。

四、龙泉窑系青瓷釉层与CO_2的反应

CO_2会与釉表面的碱反应生成碳酸盐（Na_2CO_3或$NaHCO_3$）（见反应⑧⑨）：

$$NaOH + CO_2 \rightarrow NaHCO_3 \qquad ⑧$$

$$2NaOH + CO_2 \rightarrow Na_2CO_3 + H_2O \qquad ⑨$$

它们在釉表面会进一步吸附水分子，形成随机分布的白色雾状斑点，属于可溶盐[234]。当水分蒸发后，这些盐便析出，它能稳定存在于空气中。由于CO_2与碱反应生成盐，降低了釉表面的R^+和OH^-的浓度，这更有利于反应①中的离子交换。而釉表面的碱被中和成盐，减缓了碱对釉层的直接侵蚀，有利于硅酸凝胶的形成与保持。但是，当釉表面吸附水分子时，处于釉表面的碳酸盐结晶颗粒（Na_2CO_3或$NaHCO_3$）又会水解生成碱（ROH），ROH溶解硅酸凝胶（见反应④），侵蚀釉表面。CO_2还会与析出到釉表面的游离Ca^{2+}等作用形成碳酸盐晶体，属于难溶盐（见反应⑩）：

$$Ca^{2+} + CO_3^{2-} \rightarrow CaCO_3\downarrow \qquad ⑩$$

五、龙泉窑系青瓷釉层与盐溶液的反应

釉层中迁出的金属离子会与盐溶液的酸根（如CO_3^{2-}, SO_4^{2-}, SiO_3^{2-}, PO_4^{3-}）发生反应，生成可溶盐或难溶盐。部分反应如下：

$$Na^+ + CO_3^{2-} \rightarrow Na_2CO_3$$
$$Ca^{2+} + CO_3^{2-} \rightarrow CaCO_3\downarrow$$
$$Pb^{2+} + SO_4^{2-} \rightarrow PbSO_4\downarrow$$
$$Ca^{2+} + SO_4^{2-} \rightarrow CaSO_4\downarrow$$
$$Pb^{2+} + CO_3^{2-} \rightarrow PbCO_3\downarrow$$

在干湿交替的环境中，可溶盐如Na_2CO_3、$NaHCO_3$可能流失，也可能渗入釉裂纹中，当水分蒸发后便结晶析出。难溶盐会附着于釉表面或沉积于釉裂纹中。

六、总结

青瓷釉层的风化过程是一个漫长、复杂的物理变化和化学反应的综合过程，上述的各种化学反应并非是一个单一过程，可能会有几种反应同时进行。如当H^+与R^+产生交换的同时，也有ROH与釉层的反应，ROH还可能同时与CO_2发生反应；同时也有物理变化发生，如盐溶液中的晶体析出，温度变化使釉层产生裂纹等。由于青瓷所存在的后天环境是复杂多样的，风化的产物也多种多样，所以，青瓷的迹型也呈现出多样性。

The second is the introduction via external environment.

Alkali (ROH) can dissolve silicic acid gel (see reaction ④); this destroys the glaze surface protection, and starts the weathering process.

$$Si(OH)_4 + ROH \rightarrow [Si(OH)_3O]^- R^+ + H_2O \quad ④$$

ROH can also react directly with the silica network, breaking down the Si—O bonds, creating ≡Si—O- grains, dissolving the SiO_2 in alkali solution, and breaking down the glaze surface (see reaction ⑤):

$$\equiv Si—O—Si\equiv + OH^- \rightarrow \equiv Si—OH + \equiv Si—O^- \quad ⑤$$

The other side of the ≡Si—O^- split is able to react with water:

$$\equiv Si—O^- + H_2O \rightarrow \equiv Si—OH + OH^- \quad ⑥$$

The alkali formed in reaction ⑥ can facilitate the continuation of reaction ⑤, and break down the glaze surface.

In reference to the continuous migrating out of R^+ ions (where R represents Na and K) in LKSC (Na_2O-K_2OCaO-MgO-Al_2O_3-SiO_2 System), Ca^{2+} ions in relatively high numbers can act as reaction inhibitors; slowing the H^+ and R^+ ion exchange, slowing the creation of alkali (ROH) (reaction ① slows), and slowing the occurrence of reaction ⑤. This drastically reduces the speed at which the glaze surface corrodes, almost bringing it to a stop. However, if the external environment has an alkaline nature, weathering can proceed. With the introduction of alkali (ROH), after the silica network encounters breakdown (see reaction ⑤), ≡Si—O^- grains dissolve down together with the free R^+ and R^{2+} ions on the surface and join to create silicate salts. This weathering causes continuous sedimentation, forming a sort of shell over the glaze level. As this shell reaches a certain thickness, it depletes the sheen of the glaze surface and decreases its translucency. This shell is loosely porous and highly water absorbent; creating a strong alkali solvent liquid covering, disallowing the glaze to form its protective film, and destroying the silicic acid gel film originally present. Because of this shell, the corrosion to the glaze surface by the external environment is drastically increased [233].

3. LKSC Glaze Level Reactions with Acid

The LKSC glaze level and acid reactions are very similar to that of reactions with water. Aside from hydrofluoric acid, normal acids do not directly react with the glaze surface, but rely on water to react.

The effect of hydrofluoric acid on glass is direct destruction to the silica network (see reaction ⑦).

$$\equiv Si—O—Si\equiv + H^+F^- \rightarrow \equiv Si—O—H + \equiv Si—F \quad ⑦$$

For LKSC (Na_2O-K_2O-CaO-MgO-Al_2O_3-SiO_2 System) glazes, the amount of H+ ions in acid solutions is much higher than that of water, therefore the R+ and H+ ion exchange rate is much higher than that of water; accelerating reaction ① and creating glaze-corrosive alkali (ROH). If the amount of R_2O is low, or the Ca^{2+} ions' inhibiting effect is present, reaction ① slows or even stops.

$Si(OH)_4$ is not acid soluble, therefore its solubility in acid solution is very slow, which can slow reaction ④ and slow glaze surface corrosion.

In high alkaline glazes, R_2O is relatively high and R^+ ions are abundant. Reaction ① is predominant, and the continuous formation of alkali corrodes the glaze surface. In high Silicone glazes, SiO_2 is relatively high. This slows reaction ④; which is to say the dissolving of the silicic acid gel slows, thus slowing the weathering process. Therefore, high alkaline glazes are more water-resistant than acid-resistant, and high Silicone glazes are more acid-resistant than water-resistant.

4. LKSC Glaze Level Reaction with Carbon Dioxide

Carbon Dioxide can react with the alkali on the glaze surface creating carbonates (Na_2CO_3 or $NaHCO_3$) (see reactions ⑧ and ⑨).

$$NaOH + CO_2 \rightarrow NaHCO_3 \quad ⑧$$

$$2NaOH + CO_2 \rightarrow Na_2CO_3 + H_2O \quad ⑨$$

Carbonates act to absorb water on the glaze surface forming randomly distributed, foggy-white blotches, which are soluble salts that crystallize as the water evaporates and stabilize in open air [234]. As the Carbon Dioxide and alkali form salts, the amount of R^+ and OH^- ions decrease, fostering the ion exchange in reaction ①. The neutralization of alkali into salt on the glaze surface slows its ability to directly corrode the glaze surface, and promotes the formation of the protective silicic acid gel.

However, once the glaze surface absorbs water, surface level crystallized salts (Na_2CO_3 or $NaHCO_3$) again dissolve into alkali (ROH); which in turn dissolves the silicic acid gel (see reaction ④) and corrodes the glaze surface.

Carbon Dioxide can also join with surface level free ions such as Ca^{2+} and form carbonate crystals which are partially soluble salts (see reaction ⑩).

$$Ca^{2+} + CO_3^{2-} \rightarrow CaCO_3\downarrow \quad ⑩$$

5. LKSC Glaze Level Reaction with Salt Solutions

The migrating metal ions on the glaze surface can react with the acid radicals (i.e. CO_3^{2-}, SO_4^{2-}, SiO_3^{2-}, PO_4^{3-}) in salt solutions to form soluble and partially soluble salts. Sample reactions:

$$Na^+ + CO_3^{2-} \rightarrow Na_2CO_3$$
$$Ca^{2+} + CO_3^{2-} \rightarrow CaCO_3\downarrow$$
$$Pb^{2+} + SO_4^{2-} \rightarrow PbSO_4\downarrow$$
$$Ca^{2+} + SO_4^{2-} \rightarrow CaSO_4\downarrow$$
$$Pb^{2+} + CO_3^{2-} \rightarrow PbCO_3\downarrow$$

In environments of alternating moisture, soluble salts such as Na_2CO_3 and $NaHCO_3$ can dissolve away. It is also possible that they permeate into glaze cracks and crystallize when the water evaporates. Partially soluble salts can become absorbed by the glaze surface or deposit into glaze cracks.

6. Conclusion

LKSC glaze level weathering is the accumulation of lengthy, complicated physical change and chemical reaction processes. The above mentioned physical changes and chemical reactions are not entirely independent processes, but rather a series of simultaneously occurring events: For example, as the R+ and H+ ions exchange, the ROH and glaze level reaction is taking place; ROH could also be reacting with Carbon Dioxide. Meanwhile, physical changes can be occurring: For example the crystallization of salt solutions or temperature changes creating glaze cracks.

Due to the multi-faceted and complex characteristics of post-firing environments in which LKSC wares pass time, the materialization of weathering is not limited to the aforementioned reactions, but can contain other byproducts. Therefore, LKSC traces present with multiple variations.

第二节
龙泉窑系青瓷釉层变化与环境的关系

一、地上环境

（一）地上环境概念

地上环境是指青瓷所处的自然大气情况。

（二）地上环境组成

组成大气的主要成分是氮N_2（78.08%）、氧O_2（20.95%）、氩Ar（0.934%）和CO_2（0.034%）。大气中也含有水，但水的含量是一个可变化的数值，在不同的时间、不同的地点及不同的气候条件下，水的含量是不一样的，其数值一般在1%－3%的范围内发生变化。此外，大气中还有很多痕量组分，如H_2、CH_4、CO、SO_2、NH_3、N_2O、NO_2、O_3[235]。地上环境中还有细小的灰尘，它们会被吸附或沉积在釉表面上。

（三）地上环境的风化

青瓷釉表面在地上环境中的风化实质是水、CO_2、SO_2等在釉表面作用的总和。釉表面灰尘积聚处易吸附大气中的水分，有利于风化的进行。

由第一节可知，青瓷釉表面会吸附空气中的水分子，在釉表面形成水膜；通过H^+和R^+离子交换等一些反应，釉表面会产生硅酸凝胶薄膜（见反应①②③）。如果釉层的R_2O含量少，这种薄膜的形成及发展非常缓慢；如果R_2O含量较高，迁出的R^+则形成ROH（见反应①），ROH会溶解附在釉表面的硅酸凝胶薄膜（见反应④），接着直接与釉表面的硅氧网络反应，使网络解体（见反应⑤），破坏釉表面。风化后，通常有雾状或颗粒状白斑，自然分布在釉表面或深入釉层中。

二、地下环境

（一）地下环境概念

地下环境是指青瓷所处的土壤情况。

（二）地下环境组成

土壤是由固体、液体和气体三相共同组成的多相体系。固相是指矿物质和有机质，矿物质约占90%以上，有机质占1%－10%。液相是指土壤中的水分及其水溶物。气相是指充斥在土壤无数孔隙中的空气。

不同于在大气中，土壤中的水是具有一定酸碱性的。我国土壤的pH值大多在4.5—8.5范围内，并有由南向北pH值递增的规律性：如华南、西南地区大多为pH值4.5－5.5，有少数低至3.6－3.8；华中、华东地区为5.5－6.5；长江以北的土壤多为中性或碱性，如华北、西北的土壤大多含$CaCO_3$，pH值一般在7.5－8.5，少数强碱性土壤的pH值高达10.5[236]。

深圳职业技术学院的林峰教授对广东余里窑址附近的土壤进行了检测，检测结果为偏酸性。（见表4-2-1，无结果的系土壤样品量太少，无法测定）

（三）地下环境的风化

1. 液相产生的风化作用

在土壤中由液相产生的风化作用是以水溶液的形式与釉表面进行的。风化作用可以是H^+与碱金属离子交换，其结果是釉层产生空位，结构变疏松（见反应①），也可以是碱直接破坏硅氧网络（见反应②），或者是生成难溶盐沉积在釉表面，或生成可溶盐流失。水溶液中的可溶盐可渗入釉裂纹、孔

Section 2:

Relationship Between Environment and LKSC Glaze Level Change

1. Above Ground Environment

A. Above Ground Environment Defined

Above Ground Environment indicates a positioning situation in which a LKSC piece is exposed to open air.

B. Above Ground Environmental Components

Atmosphere (or open air) consists primarily of N_2 (78.08%), O_2 (20.95%), Ar (0.934%), and CO_2 (0.034%). Open air also includes a certain amount of water, but to varying degrees. Due to humidity changing over time and different weather conditions, water usually compiles 1~3% of the atmosphere. In addition, open air often includes trace amounts of the following compounds: H_2, CH_4, CO, SO_2, NH_3, N_2O, NO_2, O_3 [235]. The above ground environment also includes minute dust particles, which can be absorbed by or deposited in to the glaze surface.

C. Above Ground Environment Weathering

Above ground weathering of LKSC glaze is the accumulation of the interaction between the glaze level and water, CO_2, SO_2 and so forth. Glaze areas that have dust deposits tend to absorb water; creating a starting point for weathering.

From Section 1, we know that LKSC glaze surfaces absorb water, creating a sort of wet film across the surface.

Through $H^+$and R^+ ion exchange, the surface can present with a thin silicic acid gel covering (see reactions ①②③). If the amount of R_2O is relatively low, the formation of this film is extremely slow. If the amount of R_2O is relatively high, free R^+ ions separate out to form ROH (see reaction ①), which in turn dissolves the silicic acid gel film (see reaction ④). The result is direct contact between ROH and the silica network, and the breaking down and corrosion of the glaze surface (see reaction ⑤).

After weathering, it is common to see foggy-white and grainy-white mottles naturally occurring across the glaze surface, and entering in to the glaze level.

2. Underground Environment

A. Underground Environment Defined

Underground Environment indicates a positioning situation in which a LKSC piece is under the surface of the earth.

B. Underground Environmental Components

Soil is a multi-phase body that consists of a conglomeration of gas, liquid, and solid phases. Solids consist of primarily +90% minerals and 1~10% organics. Liquids are a combination of water and hydrotropes. Gasses are comprised of a combination of any air components that exist in the numerous cavities within the soil.

Unlike open-air moisture, the water within soil has certain acidic or basic properties. Chinese soil, for example,

表4-2-1 广东余里窑址附近土壤pH值测定结果

样品名称	pH（水中）	pH（1mol/L KCl溶液）
1号窑泥土	5.03	3.81
2号窑泥土	6.21	4.98
1号窑与2号窑之间路边泥土（一）	5.30	4.23
1号窑与2号窑之间路边泥土（二）	5.15	4.07
3号窑泥土	5.21	2.98
1号窑瓷土	6.47	—
2号窑瓷土	6.18	4.98
1号窑与2号窑之间路边瓷土（一）	6.11	4.48
1号窑与2号窑之间路边瓷土（二）	5.42	4.46
3号窑瓷土	5.68	—

隙等釉层的疏松结构中，水分蒸发后，可溶盐结晶析出。在干湿交替的过程中，溶解、结晶反复进行，产生的应力会使釉表面开裂，甚至出现剥釉。

土壤中的及釉表面的阴阳离子（Ca^{2+}、Mg^{2+}、Fe^{3+}、Mn^{2+}、Pb^{4+}、CO_3^{2-}、SO_4^{2-}、OH^-、SiO_3^{2-}、PO_4^{3-}）会发生反应，形成不同颜色的难溶盐沉积物。难溶盐在沉积过程中还可胶结土壤颗粒，在釉表面形成坚硬的垢层。

水溶液侵蚀釉表面，从而使釉层变成疏松的多孔层，这时，如果有土壤细小颗粒进入釉层中，待水分蒸发时，便会形成土沁，颜色与周围土壤接近。土壤中各种矿物质颗粒并非均匀分布，而由于土壤颗粒表面的吸附力和微细孔隙的毛细管作用，水分被保持在土壤中不流动，这使土壤中各处的水溶液成分及干湿程度有差异。所以，龙泉窑系青瓷釉表面各处被风化侵蚀的方式和程度就有所不同。

2. 气相产生的风化作用

土壤中的空气组成与大气基本相似，主要成分都是N_2、O_2、CO_2。

其差异是：

（1）土壤空气存在于相互隔离的土壤孔隙中，是一个不连续的体系。

（2）在O_2和CO_2含量上有很大差别。土壤空气中的CO_2含量比大气中高得多，大气中CO_2含量仅为0.02%－0.03%，而土壤空气中CO_2含量一般在0.15%－0.65%，甚至高达5%，它主要是由生物呼吸作用和有机物分解产生；土壤中的氧气含量低于大气，而水蒸气的含量比大气中高得多；土壤空气中还含有少量还原性气体，如CH_4、H_2S、H_2、NH_3等[237]。土壤中的CO_2和水的含量比大气中要高得多，存在于土壤中的陶瓷风化强度比大气中的要高很多。需要注意的是有些墓室和窖藏环境密封较好，基本隔绝了其内部与外界的物质交换，使墓室和窖藏环境长期处于一个较稳定的状态。在这种保存情况下的青瓷，其釉层的风化强度往往比较低，甚至比在大气环境中保存得还要好。

（四）小结

地下环境的复杂性及不均匀性，造成青瓷釉表面风化的随机性：有的地方风化严重，有的地方保存相对完好。潮湿的土壤比干燥的土壤腐蚀性强，干湿交替的土壤比湿度恒定的土壤腐蚀性强，酸性或碱性土壤比中性土壤腐蚀性强。

primarily ranges from 4.5-8.5 pH, with the pH generally increasing as you move toward northern latitudes: Southern and Southwestern China soil primarily ranges between 4.5~5.5 pH, with a small portion between 3.6~3.8 pH; Central and Eastern China soil ranges from 5.5~5.6 pH; soil north of the Yangtze River is primarily neutral or basic, North and Northwestern China ranges from 7.5~8.5 pH and presents with high amounts of $CaCO_3$; the highest recorded pH reached as much as 10.5 [236].

Professor Lin Feng, from Shenzhen Polytechnic conducted test on soil and clay samples in and around the Guangdong Yuli Kiln Site area. Results showed that the soil was slightly acidic (see Table 4-2-1, unlisted results are due to limited sample size, and test was not able to be conducted).

C. Underground Environment Weathering

a. Weathering Caused By Liquids

Hydro-solutions reacting with the LKSC glaze surface are the primary causes of liquid weathering within the soil.

The forms of weathering include: The H^+ and alkali metal ion exchange, producing voids and weakened glass structural integrity (see reaction ①); direct decomposition of the silica network by alkali bases (see reaction ②); or the deposit of partially soluble salts and dissolving of soluble salts. Water-soluble salts can enter into cracks, openings, and other glaze imperfections. As water evaporates, these salts crystallize. The repetitive dissolving and crystallization during the process of alternating moisture creates tension, and can crack the glaze, or even cause glaze erosion.

Both the soil and the LKSC glaze level contain many positive and negative particles (Ca^{2+}, Mg^{2+}, Fe^{3+}, Mn^{2+}, Pb_4+, CO_3^{2-}, SO_4^{2-}, OH^-, SiO_3^{2-}, PO_4^{3-}), which can react with each other, creating varying colors of partially soluble salt deposits. It is possible for these partially soluble salts to become cemented to the surrounding soil, forming a hard dirt layer on the surface of the glaze.

Water solutions corrode the glaze surface, and develop a loosely porous geography across its face. At this time, if the surrounding soil particles enter into the glaze level, as the water evaporates, it leaves behind dirt deposits. The deposits' colors reflect the surrounding soil.

Due to the absorptive and porous capillary qualities of soil; water remains within the soil without flowing away. The mineral particles of soil are unevenly distributed, leading to

Table 4-2-1 Guangdong Yuli Kiln and Surrounding Area Soil pH Test Results

Sample Name	pH (In Water)	pH (1mol/L KCl Solution)
#1 Kiln Soil	5.03	3.81
#2 Kiln Soil	6.21	4.98
Soil Sample 1 Between #1 Kiln and #2 Kiln	5.30	4.23
Soil Sample 2 Between #1 Kiln and #2 Kiln	5.15	4.07
#3 Kiln Soil	5.21	2.98
#1 Kiln Porcelain Clay	6.47	——
#2 Kiln Porcelain Clay	6.18	4.98
Porcelain Clay Sample 1 Between #1 Kiln and #2 Kiln	6.11	4.48
Porcelain Clay Sample 2 Between #1 Kiln and #2 Kiln	5.42	4.46
#3 Kiln Porcelain Clay	5.68	——

与地上风化形貌最大的差异是，由于有难溶盐及土壤小颗粒的存在，地下环境的风化产物可以是黄色、褐色或其他颜色。

三、水中环境

（一）水中环境概念

水中环境是指青瓷所处的水下情况。

（二）水中环境风化

当青瓷处在水中时，釉层中的网络外的金属离子（如Na^+、K^+等）与H^+交换，生成碱。一般情况下，碱会被水稀释，因而不能进一步腐蚀釉表面。但如果R_2O含量较高，则R^+与H^+的交换会继续进行，使釉表面变得疏松多孔。当水偏碱性时，则会对釉表面进一步产生腐蚀作用，碱性增强时反应会加快。

（三）龙泉窑系青瓷釉层在水中环境不同覆盖物下的表现

当青瓷在水下环境中时，其表面覆盖的沉积物大致可分为两种：致密的沉积物和疏松的沉积物。致密的沉积物通常为颗粒细小的黏土软泥，疏松的沉积物为砾石、沙、贝壳、珊瑚碎片等。由于致密的沉积物层隔断了陶瓷与外界的物质交换，水也难以渗透，所以釉表面的风化作用难以进行，在这种情况下，陶瓷保存得较好。而在疏松的沉积物下，由于水流涌动带动沙粒等与釉面不断发生摩擦，对釉表面造成损害，同时，水对釉层的腐蚀在不同程度下进行，使釉层孔隙扩大，向纵深发展，甚至致使釉层剥落。

例如，南海Ⅰ号沉船掩埋于珠江口海域一米以下的黏土质软泥中，该船所出瓷器光亮如新，而南海西沙和渤海湾中沉船的陶瓷，因其沉船遗址在粉砂以及砂与珊瑚碎屑交错的沉积物上，海水易渗透，加之海水涌动带动大量粉砂及珊瑚碎屑，与沉积层中的陶瓷不断发生摩擦，致使釉表面风化强度较高[238]。

（四）龙泉窑系青瓷釉层出水后的变化

青瓷长期处于水下环境中，胎及釉的疏松部分均有水及可溶盐溶液渗入。当陶瓷出水后，原有的平衡被打破，析出的可溶盐结晶会对周围釉层产生压力，可能会导致釉表面发生开裂，甚至釉层剥落。

陶瓷釉层主要是由玻璃相、气相和晶相构成的，在风化过程中，玻璃相、气相和晶相各自都会发生不同的变化（各迹型类别的详细风化特征描述参见第五章）。

different solutions and moisture in different areas. Therefore, a LKSC piece can present with varying severities and types of weathering across the glaze.

b. Weathering Caused By Gasses

Air within soil is composed of essentially the same gasses as open air, with the main differences being:

I. Soil air exists in mutually isolated spaces within the soil; it is not a continuous system.

II. O_2 and CO_2 levels in soil are vastly different, with CO_2 being much higher than open air. Open air consists of 0.02%~0.03%, whereas the amount in soil is 0.15%-0.65% and as high as 5%. This is due primarily to the presence of organism respiration and the breakdown of organic materials. The amount of O_2 in soil is lower than that of open air, and moisture is much higher. Soil also contains trace amounts of reduced gasses such as: CH_4, H_2S, H_2, NH_3 and so forth [237].

Because of the heightened amounts of CO_2 and water in soil, associated weathering severity is drastically higher.

Special attention must be paid to the fact that some underground burial chambers and cellars are relatively well sealed; essentially isolating the internal content from the outside environment. Thus burial chambers and cellars represent a long-term stable environment. In most cases, celadon found in these types of locations have a lower glaze weathering severity, even lower than pieces stored in open air.

D. Summary

As the underground environment is complex and heterogeneous, glaze corrosion is randomly distributed, with areas of severe weathering and areas retaining relatively innate characteristics.

Moist soil corrodes more severely than dry soil. Soils of alternating moisture corrode more severely than soils of consistent moisture. Acidic and basic soils corrode more than soils of pH neutrality. Differing from open-air weathering, the presence of partially soluble salts and soil particles in underground weathering can materialize as yellow, brown, black and so forth discolorations.

If a piece is present within a relatively sealed and dry underground environment the weathering severity is lower than that of pieces that come into direct contact with soil.

3. Underwater Environment

A. Underwater Environment Defined

Underwater Environment indicates a positioning situation in which a LKSC piece becomes submerged in a body of water.

B. Underwater Environment Weathering

When a LKSC piece becomes submerged in water, the metallic ions (i.e. Na^+, K^+, Pb^{2+}) that are outside of the silica network enter into H^+ ion exchange, however the alkali formed become diluted in the water and cannot further corrode the glaze surface. If R_2O is relatively high, ion exchange continues, therefore persistently increasing glaze surface porosity. Water with alkalinity can move forward in glaze surface corrosion, with higher alkalinity increasing reaction speed.

C. LKSC Glaze Level Under Different Underwater Material Covering

The material deposits that present on underwater LKSC wares can be divided into two main categories: Compact sediments and loose sediments. Compact sediments are clay and silt, while loose sediments are gravel, sand, shell fragments, and pieces of coral. Compact sediments can act as a partition, inhibiting exchange between the glaze and external elements, as well as water permeation; because of this, it is difficult for weathering to proceed, and under this type of situation, the glaze is protected from corrosion. Whereas with loose sediments, the continuous contact of sand and other hard particles with the glaze face can cause damage. Additionally, water can continue corrosion, to a certain degree, broadening and deepening glaze openings, even causing glaze corrosion. An example of this is the Nanhai No. 1 shipwreck, which was buried under one meter of silt at the mouth of the Pearl River.

The pieces excavated have a like-new sheen.

Alternatively, in Xisha and Bohai Bay of the South China Sea, shipwreck pieces that were located among sand and coral debris, due to the contact with salt-water and constant friction caused by sand movement in underwater currents, presented with a much higher weathering severity [238].

D. Changes To Glaze Level After Water Excavation

Water and soluble salt solutions enter into the loosened glaze and body of LKSC that have spent a long period of time underwater. After excavation, the original equilibrium is disturbed, soluble salts crystallize, and stress is placed on the surrounding glaze. This can possibly cause glaze cracks, leading to glaze corrosion.

LKSC glaze consists of glass, gas, and crystal phase components. During the process of weathering, these components begin to experience different types of changes (for detailed characteristics of trace categories please see Chapter 5).

第三节
龙泉窑系青瓷釉层迹型风化特征

一、玻璃相迹型风化特征

由于龙泉窑系青瓷釉层玻璃相先天的凹凸不平以及釉层结构稳定性的差异，釉层经风化后，会在釉表面及釉层中的玻璃相上形成斑块和纹路两大迹型类别。

（一）斑块

1．针眼斑

针眼斑是大小较均匀、深浅大致相同、疏密不定的独立微孔，以聚集形式呈不规则形貌出现的斑块。它是龙泉窑系青瓷在后天环境影响下，在釉表面随机形成的。

2．坑点斑

坑点斑是深浅不一、大小不一、形貌不一的不规则凹形斑块。它是龙泉窑系青瓷在后天环境影响下，在釉表面形成的。

3．物盖斑

物盖斑是龙泉窑系青瓷在后天环境影响下，釉表面被外界物质覆盖而形成的斑块。

4．泡根斑

泡根斑是龙泉窑系青瓷在后天环境影响下，由破口泡发展形成，内有沉积物的凹形斑块。

5．絮状斑

絮状斑是以白色为主，呈无序状，具有流淌、渗透、漫延趋势的不规则斑块。它是龙泉窑系青瓷在后天环境影响下，在釉层中由可溶盐、难溶盐和灰尘等物质沉积形成的。

（二）纹路

1．釉裂纹

釉裂纹是龙泉窑系青瓷在烧制过程中和在后天环境影响下形成的，以直线、曲线等不规则线条形貌分布在釉表面的开裂纹路。

2．划痕

划痕是龙泉窑系青瓷釉表面与硬物碰划留下的破坏性纹路。

二、气相迹型风化特征

（一）色变泡

色变泡是龙泉窑系青瓷在后天环境影响下，釉层中透明气泡的颜色发生了变化，但仍具透影性的气泡。

（二）壁变泡

壁变泡是龙泉窑系青瓷在后天环境影响下，釉层中的气泡内壁质地发生了风化现象，被风化处失去了透影性的气泡。

三、晶相迹型风化特征

（一）针眼斑出现在流淌斑上

流淌斑含铁较高，比较容易风化。瓷器烧制成后，流淌斑上无釉层保护的部分最先风化，形成针眼斑。有釉层保护的，在后天釉层受到侵蚀后也以针眼斑形式开始风化。

（二）针眼斑出现在放射斑上

放射斑含一定量的铁氧化物，比较容易风化。瓷器烧制成后，无釉层保护的放射斑最先风化，形成针眼斑。有釉层保护的，在后天釉层受到侵蚀后也以针眼斑形式开始风化。

（三）针眼斑出现在流淌纹上

流淌纹含一定量的铁氧化物，

Section 3:
Characteristics of Weathered Longquan Kiln System Celadon Glaze Level Traces

1. Characteristics of Weathered Glass Phase Traces

After weathering, due to the innate uneven topography of the LKSC glaze level glass phase and differences in glaze level structural stability, the following two main categories: Mottles (Blotches) and Striae (Lines), can appear in the glass phase across the glaze surface, or within the glaze level.

A. Mottles

a. Needlepoint Mottles

Needlepoint Mottles are acquired pits formed under post-firing surroundings with a limited variation of size and depth, either accumulated or independent, randomly dispersed on the LKSC glaze surface.

b. Pit Mottles

Pit Mottles (also called Pitting) are the irregularly shaped small depressions or pits on the LKSC glaze surface, caused by external post-firing conditions, with non-uniform depth, size, and appearance.

c. Overlay Mottles

Overlay Mottles are acquired in the post-firing environment, and are the result of corrosion brought on by the coverage of LKSC glaze by a foreign material.

d. Bubble Roots

A Bubble Root (mottle) is a depressed shaped mottle with internal sediments, formed by the progression of a broken mouth bubble on the surface of LKSC glaze under the influences of post-firing factors.

e. Floccus Mottles

Floccus Mottles are primarily white colored appearances within the LKSC glaze level brought about under post-firing conditions; with irregular, free flowing, and disorderly shapes that were formed by the depositing of soluble and partially soluble salts, dust particles, and so forth materials.

B. Striae

a. Glaze Cracks

Also called crazing, Glaze Cracks are any appearance of straight, round, or irregular lines splitting the glaze surface or glaze level of LKSC, which was caused either during firing or under the influence of the post-firing environment.

b. Scratches

Scratches are the LKSC glaze-damage lines left on the glaze surface because of contact with abrasive forces of hardened external objects.

2. Characteristics Of Weathered Gas Phase Traces

A. Color Change Bubbles

Color Change Bubbles are the appearance of air bubbles within the LKSC glaze level that have undergone a coloration change under the influences of the post-firing environment,

比较容易风化。瓷器烧制成后，没有被釉层保护的流淌纹以针眼斑形式开始风化，表现为针眼型阴纹。

（四）C形纹、O形纹

C形纹、O形纹是龙泉窑系青瓷在烧制过程中及后天环境影响下，以铁氧化物等金属氧化物为主，以字母C、O形貌分布在釉表面的线形纹路。C形纹、O形纹是龙泉窑系青瓷上的先天性迹型，但通常要经过风化后其二维成像才能用显微镜观察到。

but have retained their original translucency.

B. Textured Bubbles

Textured Bubbles are the appearance of LKSC glaze bubbles in which the interior has undergone weathering brought on by the post-firing environment; gaining texture and losing their inherent translucency.

3. Characteristics Of Weathered Crystallized Traces

A. Needlepoint Mottling On Flowing Mottles

Flowing mottles consist primarily of Iron Oxide, which exposed to air is easily weathered. After firing, the areas without glaze protection are the first to undergo weathering and form needlepoint mottles. Areas receiving protection from a thin glaze covering, when the glaze level encounters corrosion, can also present with needlepoint style weathering patterns.

B. Needlepoint Mottling On Radiating Mottles

Radiating mottles contain trace amounts of Iron Oxide, which exposed to air are easily weathered. After firing, the areas without glaze protection are the first to undergo weathering and form needlepoint mottles. Areas receiving protection from a thin glaze covering, when the glaze level encounters corrosion, can also present with needlepoint style weathering patterns.

C. Needlepoint Mottling On Flowing Striae

Flowing striae consist primarily of Iron Oxide, which exposed to air are easily weathered. After firing, the areas without glaze protection undergo weathering and form needlepoint mottling.

D. C and O Shaped Striae

C and O shaped lines in areas of structurally weakened LKSC glaze, acquired under the influence of the post-firing environment.

LKSC C and O shaped striae are formed during the firing process, but need to undergo weathering in order to be observable through two-dimensional microscopic imaging.

第四节
总结

龙泉窑系青瓷釉层的变化是釉层风化的结果，是釉层与多种物质发生物理变化、化学反应的综合结果。

在不同的存放环境中，无论是物理变化还是化学反应，其结果都会使青瓷釉层迹型发生变化。龙泉窑系青瓷存放环境的变化，会使其釉层的风化作用强度产生快慢的差异，从而导致釉层迹型风化强度有高有低。

这些迹型现象从一定程度上能够帮助我们推断青瓷在后天存放环境的简单性或复杂性。在长时间的风化过程中，风化产物在釉层的物理堆积方式和釉层被溶蚀的形貌，一定与短时间人为的物理堆积和化学溶蚀结果有根本的区别。

Section 4:
Conclusion

LKSC glaze level change is the total accumulated outcome of the physical changes and chemical reactions between the glaze level and various materials.

Regardless of physical change or chemical reaction, the results are glaze level trace changes with varying characteristics. These weathering trace changes are heterogeneous. Changes in the post-firing environment bring forth differences in the weathering intensity, thus the weathering severities experienced by the glaze level traces are similarly varied.

These trace change characteristics reflect the complexity of LKSC post-firing environments.

The aforementioned glaze level byproducts of physical amassing and chemical corrosion created over a long period of time have fundamental differences to those resulting from immediate man-made physical amassing and chemical corrosion caused by forged weathering.

第五章

明代龙泉窑系青瓷典型迹型类别

阅读提示：

明代龙泉窑系青瓷釉层在烧制过程中及后天环境影响下，会表现出各种迹型特征。这些不同的迹型特征主要是因不同的釉料配方、烧制工艺以及在不同环境中风化作用造成的。通过观察与研究，可将明代龙泉窑系青瓷迹型归纳总结出不同的类别。本章主要介绍明代龙泉窑系青瓷迹型中最典型的四大类别：斑块、纹路、气泡和鬃眼。

主要论述问题：

1. 明代龙泉窑系青瓷釉层中有哪些斑块种类？它们各自有什么特征？
2. 明代龙泉窑系青瓷釉层中有哪些纹路种类？它们各自有什么特征？
3. 明代龙泉窑系青瓷釉层中有哪些气泡种类？它们各自有什么特征？
4. 明代龙泉窑系青瓷鬃眼的主要特征是什么？

Chapter 5

Ming Dynasty Longquan Kiln System Celadon Typical Trace Categories

Text Note:

During the firing process and in the post-firing environment, Longquan Kiln System Celadon (LKSC) glazes present with several different varieties of traces. Due to differences in glaze recipes, craftsmanship, as well as the variances in weathering caused by the post-firing environment, several typical trace categories become evident. Through observation and research, we have been able to surmise and classify the different categories of typical LKSC traces. The purpose of this chapter is to introduce the four typical categories of LKSC traces: Mottles, Striae, Air Bubbles, and Bristle Pits.

第一节
龙泉窑系青瓷斑块类别

一、龙泉窑系青瓷斑块概念

龙泉窑系青瓷斑块是龙泉窑系青瓷在烧制过程中和后天环境影响下形成的，以不规则形貌分布在釉表面及釉层中的迹型类别。

二、龙泉窑系青瓷斑块类型

如果将在烧制过程中形成的龙泉窑系青瓷斑块称为先天性斑块，在后天环境影响下形成的斑块称为后天性斑块，那么龙泉窑系青瓷斑块就可以分成两大类型。

（一）先天性龙泉窑系青瓷斑块

1. 先天性龙泉窑系青瓷斑块概念

先天性斑块是龙泉窑系青瓷在烧制过程中形成的，以不规则形貌分布在釉表面及釉层中的各类斑块。

2. 先天性龙泉窑系青瓷斑块种类

先天性龙泉窑系青瓷斑块按照其形貌特征可分成三个种类：流淌斑、放射斑和团状斑。

（1）流淌斑

①流淌斑概念

流淌斑是含铁和锰为主，具有流淌感和不规则形貌的片状斑块。它是龙泉窑系青瓷在烧制过程中，在其釉表面及釉层中形成的。

②流淌斑形成

青瓷在高温烧制时，釉料会逐渐熔化成熔融态。在浮力、表面张力及气泡搅动的作用下，釉料中的铁氧化物和锰氧化物易在气泡边沿积聚，部分会随气泡升至釉表面，顺着凹凸不平的釉表面向四周扩散，流动铺展，并结晶析出，也可能产生分相。当温度下降时，会有更多结晶析出，这就是一个润湿过程。由于结晶的成分、密度和表面张力不同，会在釉表面形成不同形貌、不同颜色的流淌斑。熔解在釉层中的铁离子（主要是Fe^{3+}），当釉层冷却凝固时在釉层中形成流淌斑。

③流淌斑分类

流淌斑可分为碘酒斑和沙滩斑两种。

A. 碘酒斑概念

碘酒斑是釉层中呈褐色的流淌斑。

B. 沙滩斑概念

沙滩斑是釉表面呈褐色的流淌斑。

④流淌斑分布

一般来说，流淌斑所在处就是肉眼可见的独立铁斑。（参见第二章第三节独立铁斑部分）

⑤流淌斑特征

A. 碘酒斑

碘酒斑二维特征

见图5-1-1—图5-1-4。

a. 碘酒斑颜色有深有浅。

b. 由于碘酒斑已经和玻璃相融为一体，较难受到侵蚀，所以基本保持刚烧制出来的原态。

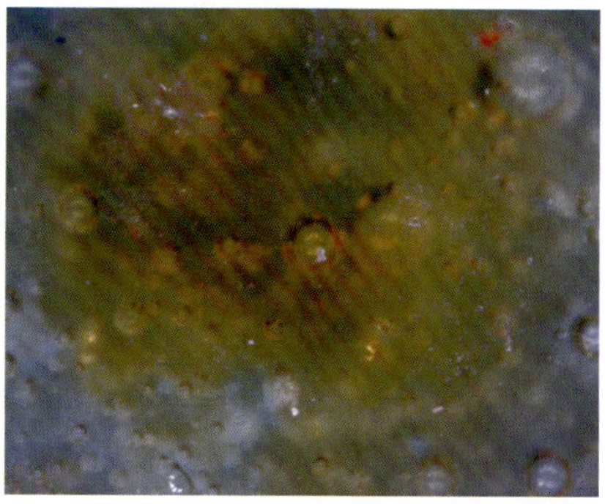

图5-1-1

Section 1：

Longquan Kiln System Celadon Mottle Category

1. LKSC Mottles Defined

LKSC Mottles (spots and blotches) are a category of irregularly shaped appearances, created during the firing process and acquired under the post-firing environment, that are unevenly disbursed across the glaze surface and within the glaze level of LKSC.

2. LKSC Mottle Classes

Mottles created during the firing process are called Innate Mottles. For those formed under the influences of the post-firing environment, the term Acquired Mottles is used. These are the two main classes of LKSC Mottles.

A. Innate LKSC Mottles

a. Innate LKSC Mottles Defined

Innate LKSC Mottles are mottles of irregular shape and distribution on the glaze surface and within the glaze level of LKSC that were formed during the firing process.

b. Innate LKSC Mottle Types

According to the appearance characteristics of Innate Mottles, they can be split into three types: Flowing Mottles, Radiating Mottles, and Blotch Mottles.

I. Flowing Mottle

i. Flowing Mottle Defined

Primarily consisting of Iron and Manganese, Flowing Mottles are the irregular blotch-shaped appearances across the glaze surface and within the glaze level which have a free flowing shape and were formed during the firing of LKSC.

ii. Formation of Flowing Mottles

During the firing of LKSC, glaze gradually transitions into a molten state. Due to the buoyancy, surface tension and movement of the air bubbles within the glaze level, the Iron and Manganese Oxides within the glaze collect around the edges of gaseous bodies within the glaze. A portion of these oxides rise with these bubbles to the surface of the glaze. According to the uneven topography of the surface, these compounds diffuse and flow across the glaze surface and crystallize, some producing split phases. When the temperature drops, more crystallization can occur. This flowing dispersion is a fluid process. According to their composition, density, and surface tension differences, they present with alternate appearances and colors of flowing mottles across the surface of the glaze. When the glaze cools and solidifies, Iron ions (mainly Fe^{3+}) diffused within the glaze level form flowing mottles.

iii. Types of Flowing Mottles

There are two types of flowing mottles: Iodine Mottles and Beach Mottles.

(a) Iodine Mottle Defined

Iodine Mottles are brown colored flowing mottles that exist within the glaze level.

(b) Beach Mottle Defined

Beach Mottles are flowing mottles with brown coloration located on the surface of the glaze.

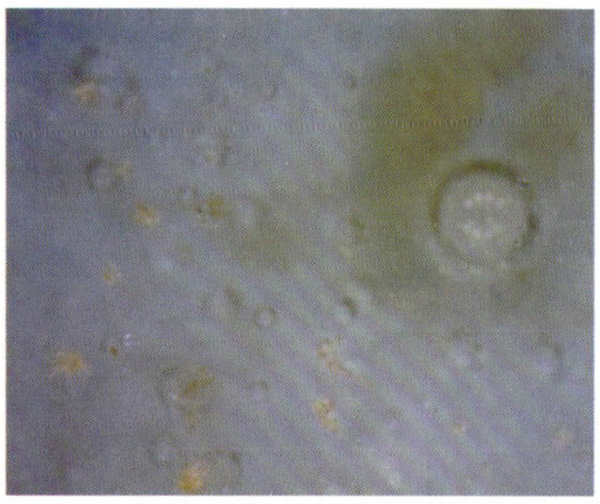

图5-1-2

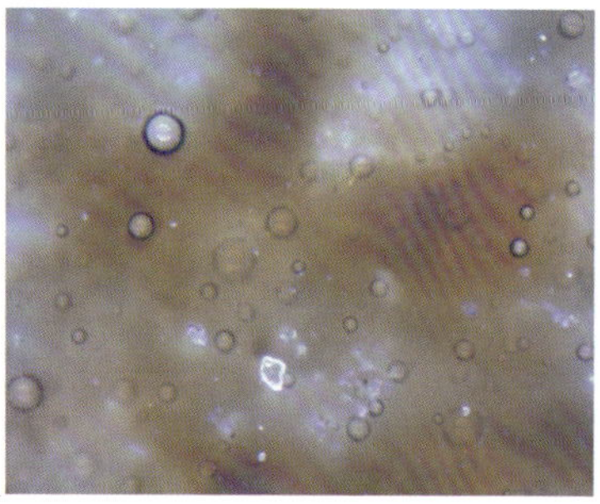

图5-1-3

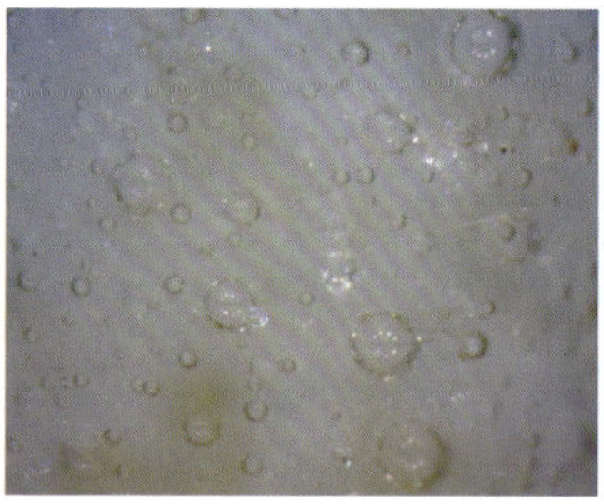

图5-1-4

B．沙滩斑

沙滩斑在龙泉系青瓷上不常见。

a. 沙滩斑二维特征

I. 有的沙滩斑边沿呈火焰形，这种火焰形沙滩斑通常外围釉层中会延展出较明显的碘酒斑（见图5-1-5、图5-1-6）。

II. 有的沙滩斑边沿呈荷叶形，这类斑块在流淌铺展时，表面张力比火焰形沙滩斑大（见图5-1-7、图5-1-8）。

III. 由于釉表面凹凸不平，沙滩斑在流淌润湿时无法完全覆盖釉表面，会造成沙滩斑上出现不规则圆孔的现象，圆孔分布如同筛网（见图5-1-9、图5-1-10）。

IV. 偶尔可见含铁量较低的沙滩斑，呈橘红色（见图5-1-11、图5-1-12）。

V. 由于受釉层保护程度较低，铁含量较高的沙滩斑较易风化，沙滩斑上会出现针眼斑。（参见本章本节针眼斑部分）

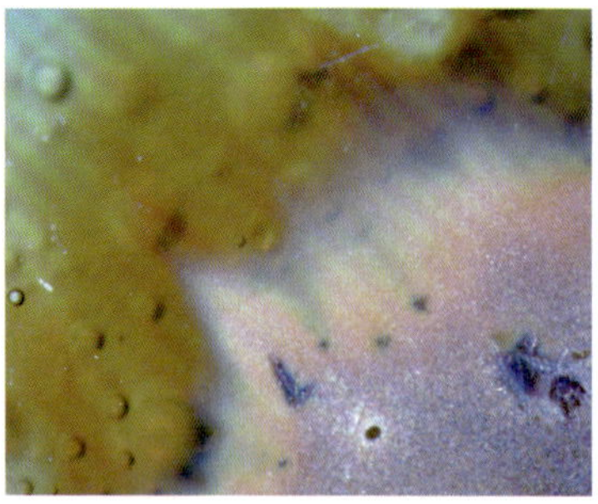

图5-1-5

图5-1-6

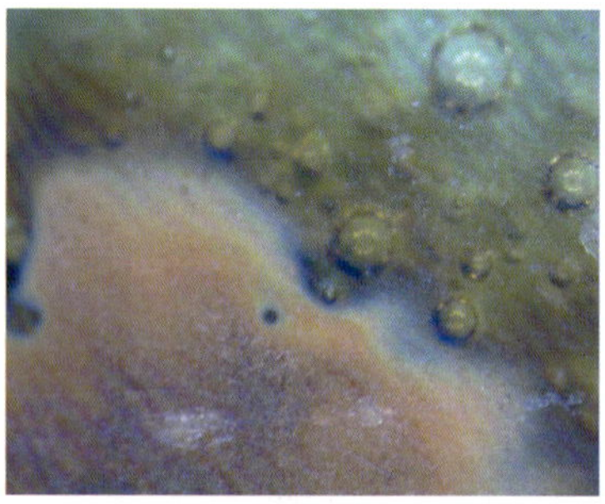

图5-1-7

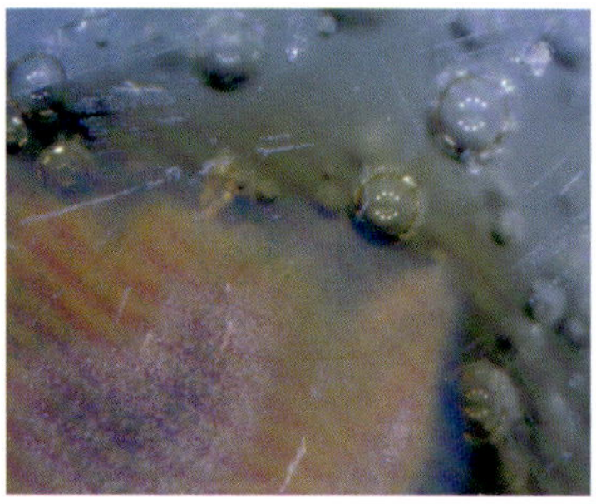

图5-1-8

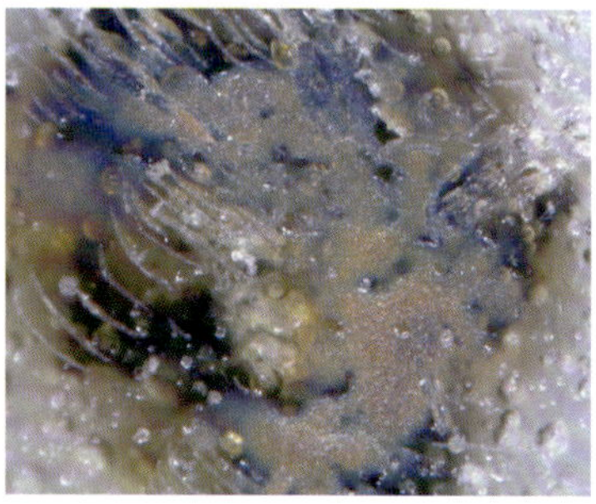

图5-1-9

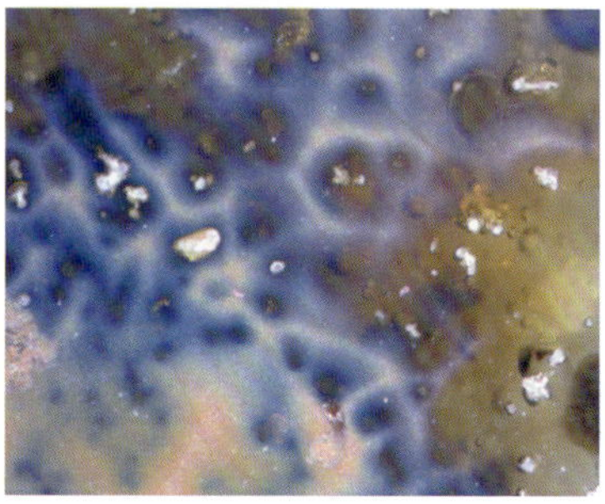

图5-1-10

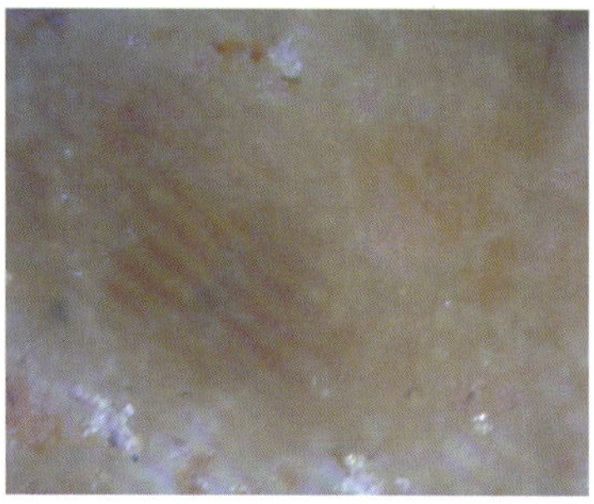

图5-1-11

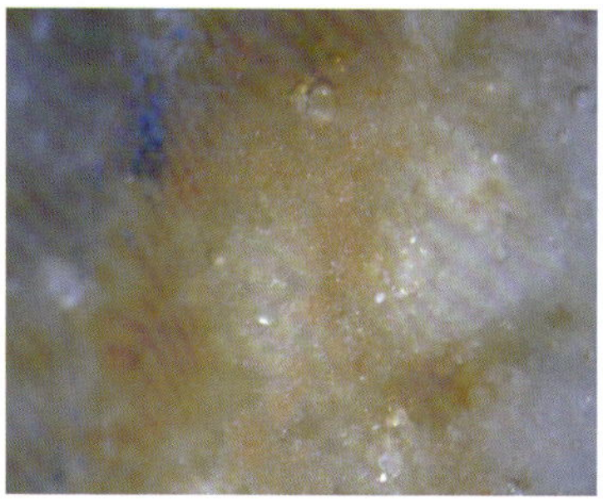

图5-1-12

iv. Distribution of Flowing Mottles

In General, Flowing Mottles appear in areas of visible individual iron spots (See Chapter 2 Section 3 Individual Iron Spots).

v. Characteristics of Flowing Mottles

(a) Iodine Mottle

Two-dimensional Characteristics of Iodine Mottles

See pictures 5-1-1—5-1-4.

(1) Iodine mottles have dark and light coloration.

(2) As iodine mottles are diffused within the glaze, it is difficult for them to receive corrosion, thus they retain their original inherent characteristics.

(b) Beach Mottle

Beach Mottles are not often seen on Longquan Kiln System Celadon.

(i) Two-dimensional Characteristics of Beach Mottles

(1) Beach mottles can appear with flame-like edges. Often the outer edges of these flame shaped mottles have relatively evident iodine mottles within the glaze level surrounding them (see pictures 5-1-5 and 5-1-6).

(2) Beach mottles can also appear with lotus leaf-like edges. This classification of beach mottle occurs due to a higher surface tension during the mottles flowing formation stage (see pictures 5-1-7 and 5-1-8).

(3) Due to the topographical unevenness of the glaze surface, during the fluid state of the mottle, the mottle is not able to completely cover the glaze surface, leaving irregularly shaped openings, resembling a sieve (see pictures 5-1-9 and 5-1-10).

(4) Occasionally seen relatively low iron Beach Mottles, with a reddish orange coloration (see pictures 5-1-11 and 5-1-12).

(5) Due to the relatively low protection received from glaze, beach mottles are easily weathered, and as such the mottle surface presents with needlepoint mottling (see Needlepoint Mottle heading of this section).

(ii) Three-dimensional Characteristics of Beach Mottles

(1) Needlepoint mottling on beach mottles is clearly evident, and presents as pin points. In general, the more congested the distribution of needlepoint mottling, the more evident its pitting and darker its coloration.

(2) The irregularly shaped openings in the beach mottle are glass phase, which is clearly higher than the surrounding beach mottle.

(3) The gradation between the mottle edge and the surrounding glass phase is uniform.

See pictures 5-1-13 and 5-1-14, where 5-1-13 is the two-dimensional and 5-1-14 is the three-dimensional image of the same location.

See pictures 5-1-15 and 5-1-16, where 5-1-15 is the two-dimensional and 5-1-16 is the three-dimensional image of the same location.

The brown beach mottle in picture 5-1-13 is the light colored area of 5-1-14. The portion indicated by Arrow A, which has little or no needlepoint mottling, is relatively smooth and clean. The white frosted needlepoint mottling in pictures 5-1-13 and 5-1-15 are the dark colored areas of 5-1-14 and 5-1-16. The needlepoint mottling indicated by Arrows B and C forms pin points of crowded distribution resembling cinder.

The gradation from the edge of the mottle to the glass phase is uniform (see pictures 5-1-14 and 5-1-16)。

See pictures 5-1-17 and 5-1-18, where 5-1-17 is the two-dimensional and 5-1-18 is the three-dimensional image of the same location.

The brown colored beach mottle in picture 5-1-17 is not clearly visible in picture 5-1-18. The distribution of needlepoint mottling on the beach mottle is not obvious, and the needlepoints do not form pits.

See pictures 5-1-19 and 5-1-20, where 5-1-19 is the two-dimensional and 5-1-20 is the three-dimensional image of the same location.

The orange beach mottle in picture 5-1-19 is not clearly visible in picture 5-1-20, and is relatively smooth. As such, it can be theorized that the mottle is present within the glaze level. Aside from this, the needlepoint mottling on the beach

b. 沙滩斑三维特征

I.沙滩斑上有针眼斑，表现为独立的点状凹坑。一般来说，针眼斑分布越密集，凹坑越明显，颜色越深。

II.沙滩斑中心的玻璃相圆孔高于沙滩斑，二者有明显的高度差。

III.沙滩斑边沿与玻璃相过渡平润。

见图5-1-13、图5-1-14，二者为同一器物同一位置图片，图5-1-13为二维图片，图5-1-14为三维图片。

见图5-1-15、图5-1-16，二者为同一器物同一位置图片，图5-1-15为二维图片，图5-1-16为三维图片。

图5-1-13中的褐色沙滩斑在图5-1-14中呈浅色，成像清晰。沙滩斑上无针眼斑或针眼斑较稀疏处显得干净细腻（见箭头A所指处）。图5-1-13及图5-1-15中的白色磨砂针眼斑在图5-1-14及5-1-16中呈深色，成像清晰。针眼斑呈独立的点状凹坑，分布密集处形貌如微小细碎的煤渣（见箭头B、C所指处）。

沙滩斑边沿与玻璃相过渡平润（见图5-1-14、图5-1-16）。

见图5-1-17、图5-1-18，二者为同一器物同一位置图片，图5-1-17为二维图片，图5-1-18为三维图片。

图5-1-17中的褐色沙滩斑在图5-1-18中可见斑块轮廓。沙滩斑上针眼斑分布并不明显，不见

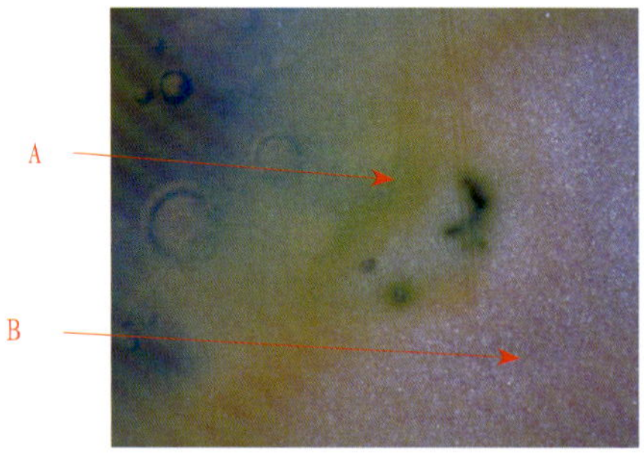

图5-1-13

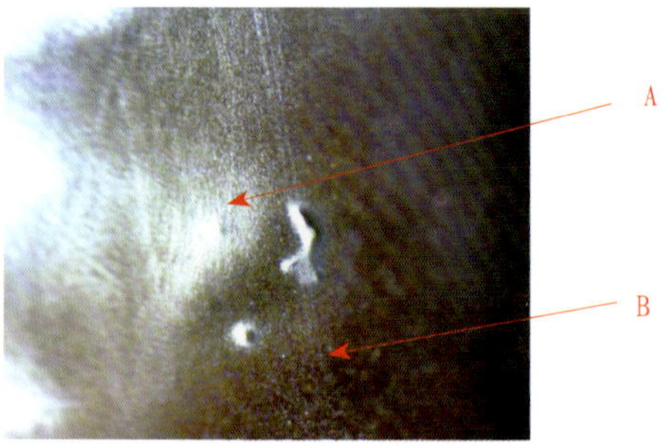

图5-1-14

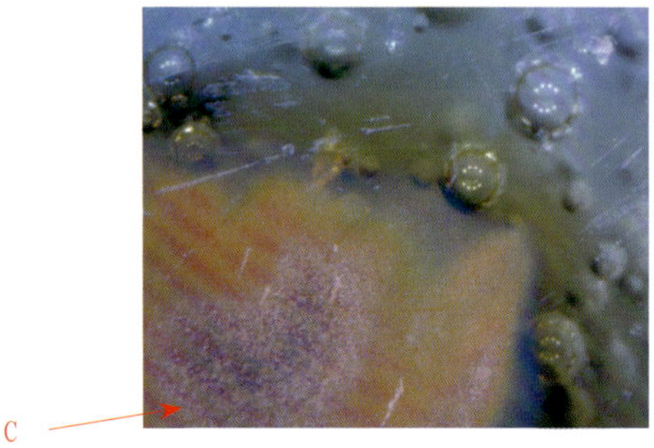

图5-1-15

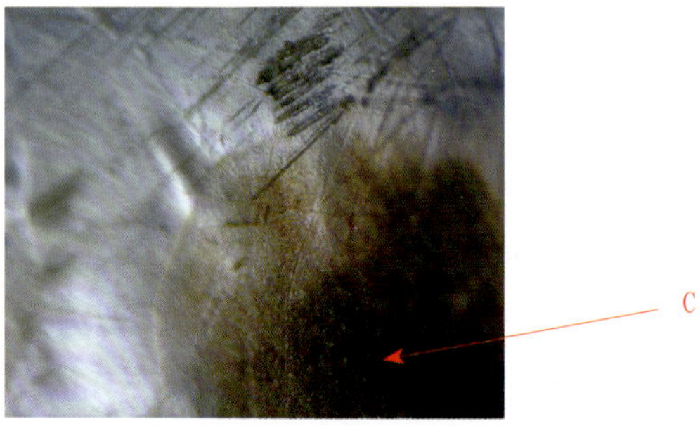

图5-1-16

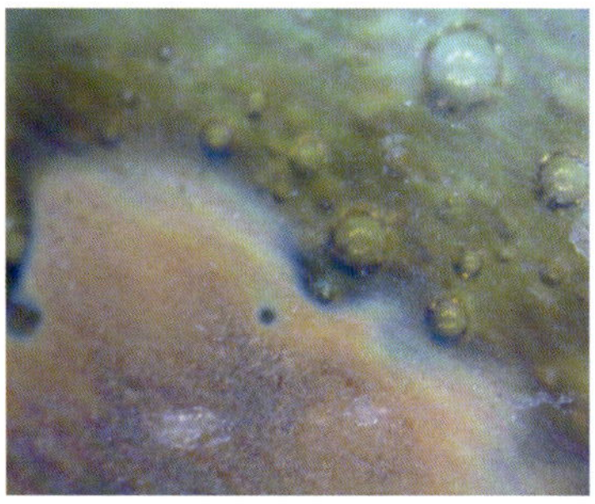
图5-1-17

图5-1-18

mottle is very sparse. Because the needlepoint mottling is not widespread, only the area indicated by Arrow D is relatively visible.

II. Radiating Mottle

i. Radiating Mottle Defined

Formed during the firing of LKSC, Radiating Mottles are the irregular shaped appearances across the glaze surface and within the glaze level, which have a crystallized, radiating form.

ii. Formation of Radiating Mottles

During the firing of LKSC, glaze gradually transitions into a molten state. Due to the buoyancy, surface tension and movement of the air bubbles within the glaze level, the Iron and Manganese Oxides (or mullite, feldspar and so forth compounds) within the glaze collect around the edges of gaseous bodies within the glaze. A portion of these Oxides rise with these bubbles to the surface of the glaze, crystalize, and can form into spilt phases. As the temperature drops, more crystallization occurs. According to their composition, density, and surface tension differences, they present with alternate appearances and colors of radiating mottles across the surface of the glaze or within the glaze level. Additionally, the firing atmosphere within the kiln can also affect the composition of the radiating mottle. In a relatively strong reduction atmosphere, Iron Oxides form as Fe_3O_4 crystallizations, with black coloration. When there is a high amount of these crystallizations and their surface areas extends across the surface of the glaze, there is a gunmetal coloration observable by the naked eye. In an oxidation atmosphere or relatively weak reduction atmosphere environment, Iron Oxides crystallize as Fe_2O_3 and have a brown or yellow coloration.

iii. Types of Radiating Mottles

Radiating mottles can be divided into five color series: white series, red series, yellow series, brown series and black series.

Almost all radiating mottles have certain amounts of Iron and Manganese Oxides, white series being the exception with little or none. Due to the differences in Iron and Manganese valance, composition, and density, as well as the degree to which they receive glaze protection, these mottles present with various colors and appearances.

iv. Characteristics of Radiating Mottles

(a) White Series Radiating Mottles

White series radiating mottles have a primarily white coloration, and can be split into the following groups: Chrysanthemum Shape, Pine Needle Shape and Irregular Shape.

(i) Two-dimensional Characteristics of Chrysanthemum Shape Radiating Mottles

Shape similar to that of a chrysanthemum flower, with a radiating feel. The petals can appear sparsely intersecting (see pictures 5-1-21 and 5-1-22), or with full overlapping (see pictures 5-1-23 and 5-1-24).

(ii) Three-dimensional Characteristics of Chrysanthemum Radiating Mottles

See pictures 5-1-25 and 5-1-26, where 5-1-25 is the two-dimensional and 5-1-26 is the three-dimensional image of the same location.

See pictures 5-1-27 and 5-1-28, where 5-1-27 is the two-dimensional and 5-1-28 is the three-dimensional image of the same location.

Chrysanthemum radiating mottles can present on the glaze surface with clear radiating properties (see picture 5-1-26), or present within the glaze level (see picture 5-1-28).

(iii) Two-dimensional Characteristics of Pine Needle Radiating Mottles

The mottles' pine needle widths are not consistent, and can intermingle and overlap (see pictures 5-1-29 and 5-1-30).

(iv) Three-dimensional Characteristics of Pine Needle Radiating Mottles

(1) Pine Needle radiating mottles have distinct three-dimensional characteristics.

(2) They have a dense distribution creating a stacked effect.

See pictures 5-1-31 and 5-1-32, where 5-1-31 is the two-

针眼斑形成的点状凹坑。

见图5-1-19、图5-1-20，二者为同一器物同一位置图片，图5-1-19为二维图片，图5-1-20为三维图片。

图5-1-19中的橘红色沙滩斑在图5-1-20中三维成像不明显，斑块较光滑，由此可推测斑块基本存于釉层中。此外，沙滩斑上少见针眼斑形成的点状凹坑，因针眼斑分布不广，只有箭头D所指处较明显。

（2）放射斑

① 放射斑概念

放射斑是具有放射感的析晶斑块。它是龙泉窑系青瓷在烧制过程中，在其釉表面及釉层中形成的。

② 放射斑形成

青瓷在高温烧制时，釉料会逐渐熔化成熔融态，在浮力、表面张力及气泡搅动的作用下，釉料中的铁氧化物和锰氧化物（或莫来石、长石等物质）易在气泡边沿积聚，部分会随气泡升至釉表面，并结晶析出，也可能产生分相。当温度下降时，会有更多结晶析出。由于放射斑的成分、密度和表面张力不同，会在釉表面、釉层中形成不同形貌、不同颜色的放射斑。此外，窑内的烧制气氛也会影响放射斑的成分。在较强的还原气氛下，铁氧化物大都会形成Fe_3O_4晶体，颜色为黑色，当析出的Fe_3O_4晶体较大，且晶面大多平行于釉表面时，用肉眼就可以看见锡光。在氧化气氛或弱还原气氛下，铁氧化物形成的晶体大都为Fe_2O_3晶体，颜色有褐色或黄色等。

③ 放射斑分类

放射斑可分成五大色系：白色系、红色系、黄色系、褐色系及黑色系。

除白色系放射斑不含或含极少铁氧化物和锰氧化物之外，大部分放射斑都一定程度地含有铁氧化物和锰氧化物。由于铁和锰的价位、结构及含量的不同，加之受釉层保护程度不同，这些放射斑呈现颜色及形貌差异。

④ 放射斑特征

A. 白色系放射斑

白色系放射斑颜色主要为白色。白色系放射斑主要有菊花形、松针形及不规则形。

a. 菊花形放射斑二维特征

菊花形放射斑形状像菊花，具有放射感。花瓣有的稀疏交错（见图5-1-21、图5-1-22），有的饱满重叠（见图5-1-23、图5-1-24）。

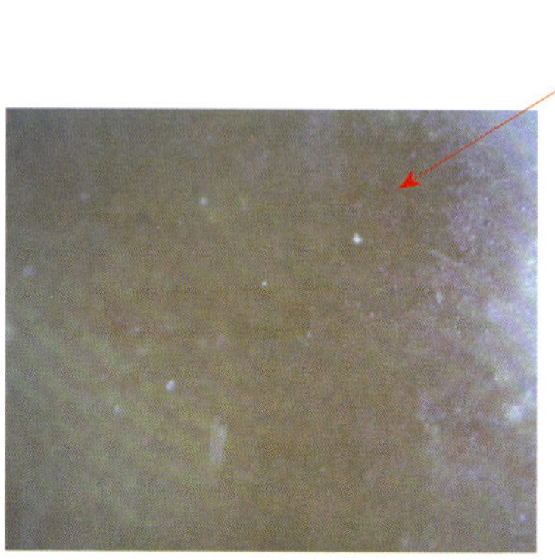

图5-1-19

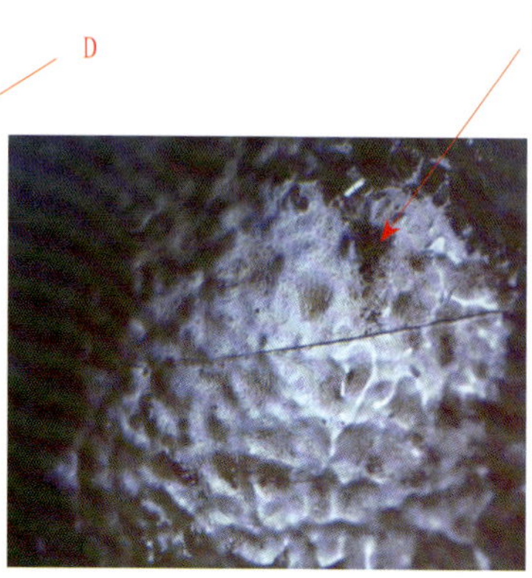

图5-1-20

图5-1-21

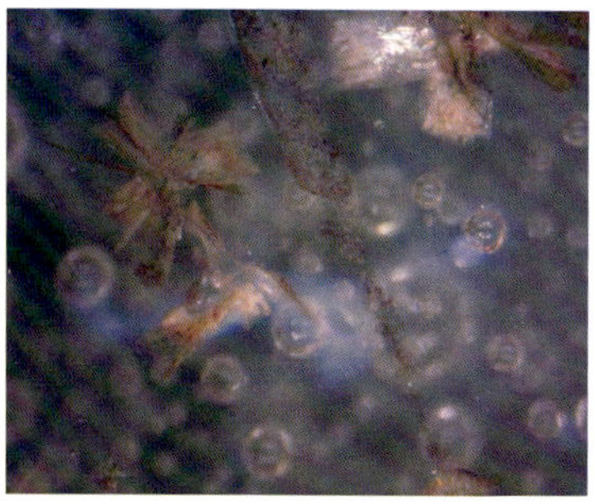
图5-1-22

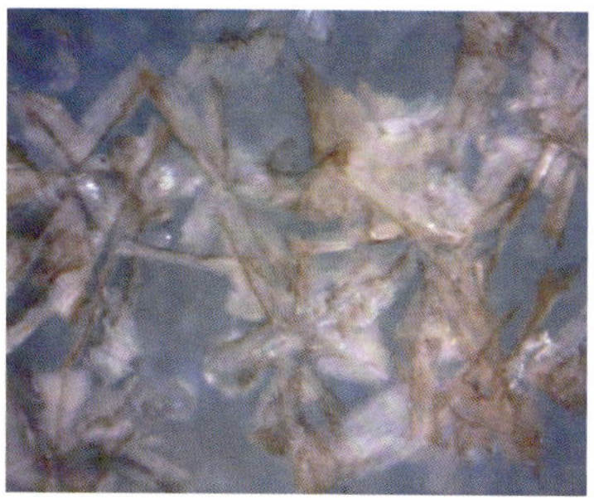
图5-1-23

图5-1-24

dimensional and 5-1-32 is the three-dimensional image of the same location.

See pictures 5-1-33 and 5-1-34, where 5-1-33 is the two-dimensional and 5-1-34 is the three-dimensional image of the same location.

Pine needle radiating mottles can appear on the glaze surface or within the glaze level. Mottles appearing on the surface can have a relatively sparse distribution, with radiating properties that have clear three-dimensional visibility (see picture 5-1-32); or be densely distributed with a stacked appearance (see picture 5-1-34).

(v) Two-dimensional Characteristics of Irregular Radiating Mottles

See pictures 5-1-35—5-1-38.

(1) Irregular Radiating Mottles have various shapes and are primarily white in color. As the coloration is quite light, careful inspection is required to observe them (see pictures 5-1-35 Arrow E and 5-1-36 Arrow F).

(2) Some of these mottles can come up to the surface of the glaze, and partially present with yellow or brown coloration (see pictures 5-1-37 and 5-1-38).

(vi) Three-dimensional Characteristics of Irregular Radiating Mottles

(1) Clear three-dimensional appearance.

(2) Some protruding and some inverted in shape, they have a rough surface.

(3) Some mottles present with white deposits.

(4) Clear delineation from the surrounding glass phase.

See pictures 5-1-39 and 5-1-40, where 5-1-39 is the two-dimensional and 5-1-40 is the three-dimensional image of the same location.

See pictures 5-1-41 and 5-1-42, where 5-1-41 is the two-dimensional and 5-1-42 is the three-dimensional image of the same location.

See pictures 5-1-43 and 5-1-44, where 5-1-43 is the two-dimensional and 5-1-44 is the three-dimensional image of the same location.

See pictures 5-1-45 and 5-1-46, where 5-1-45 is the two-dimensional and 5-1-46 is the three-dimensional image of the same location.

See pictures 5-1-47 and 5-1-48, where 5-1-47 is the two-dimensional and 5-1-48 is the three-dimensional image of the same location.

This type of radiating mottle can appear on the glaze surface (see pictures 5-1-39—5-1-46), or within the glaze level (see pictures 5-1-47 and 5-1-48). Regardless of the two-dimensional color depth, the three-dimensional visibility is clear, with delineation between the mottle and the surrounding glass phase.

Some mottles located on the glaze surface have a depressed shape with a rough interior (see picture 5-1-40); some have a raised shape with a rough surface and encompassing border (see picture 5-1-42); and some have clearly visible white crystallizations (see pictures 5-1-44 and 5-1-46).

Some mottles are partially within the glaze and partially on the glaze surface (see picture 5-1-48).

(b) Red Series Radiating Mottles

(i) Two-dimensional Characteristics of Red Series Radiating Mottles

(1) Colors primarily range within rust, blood orange, and tangerine, and have a clear radiating shape (see pictures 5-1-49—5-1-52).

(2) Receiving a relatively low amount of glaze protection, they are relatively easily weathered, allowing for needlepoint mottling over the mottle (see Needlepoint Mottle heading of this section).

(ii) Three-dimensional Characteristics of Red Series Radiating Mottles

(1) Mottle borders clearly delineated.

(2) Some mottle surfaces present with fine texturized striations.

(3) Most of the radiating mottles are higher than that of the surrounding beach mottle, and there is a clearly delineated border between the two.

See pictures 5-1-53 and 5-1-54, where 5-1-53 is the two-dimensional and 5-1-54 is the three-dimensional image of the same location.

b.菊花形放射斑三维特征

见图5-1-25、图5-1-26，二者为同一器物同一位置图片，图5-1-25为二维图片，图5-1-26为三维图片。

见图5-1-27、图5-1-28，二者为同一器物同一位置图片，图5-1-27为二维图片，图5-1-28为三维图片。

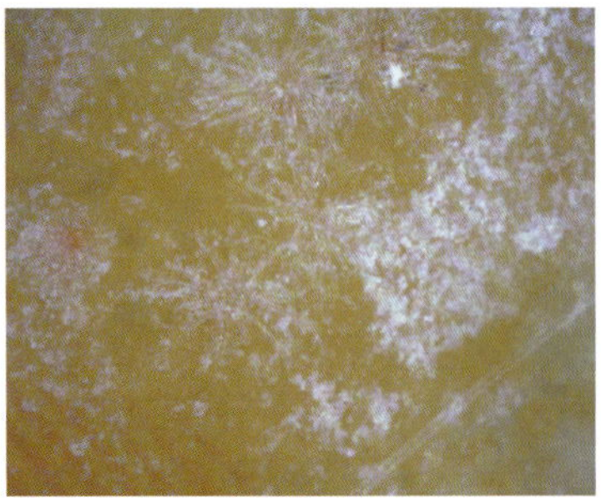

图5-1-25

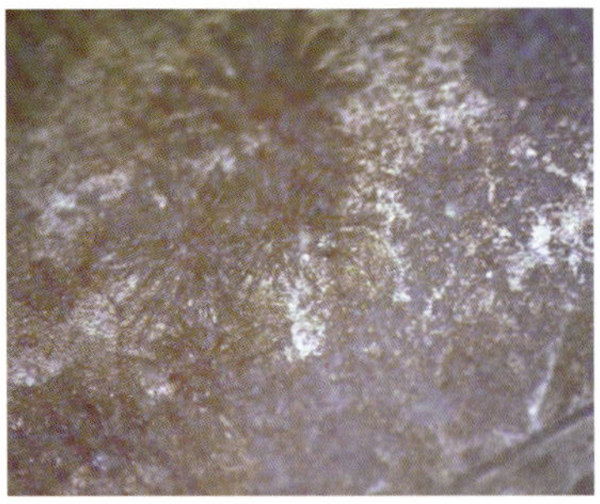

图5-1-26

图5-1-27

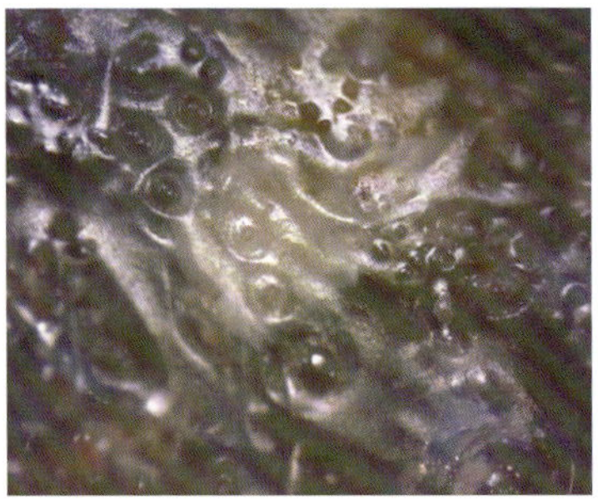

图5-1-28

菊花形放射斑有的分布于釉表面，放射形貌明显（见图5-1-26），也有的分布于釉层中（见图5-1-28）。

c.松针形放射斑二维特征

松针形放射斑的“松针”粗细不一，互叠交错（见图5-1-29、图5-1-30）。

图5-1-29

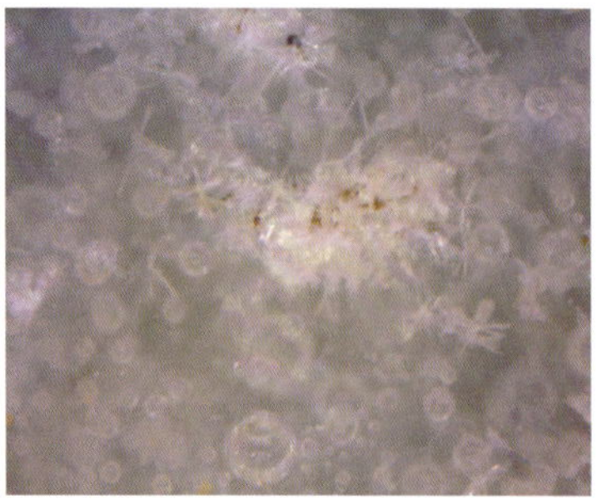

图5-1-30

d.松针形放射斑三维特征

I.松针形放射斑三维放射形貌清晰。

II.分布密集处呈堆积状。

见图5-1-31、图5-1-32，二者为同一器物同一位置图片，图5-1-31为二维图片，图5-1-32为三维图片。

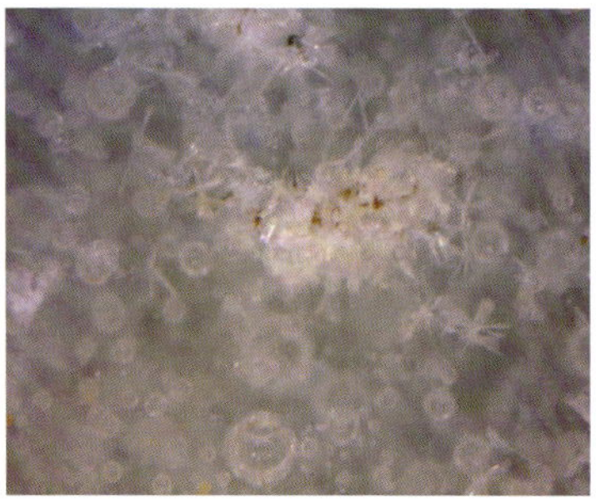

图5-1-31

见图5-1-33、图5-1-34，二者为同一器物同一位置图片，图5-1-33为二维图片，图5-1-34为三维图片。

松针形放射斑既可以位于釉表面，也可以位于釉层中。位于釉表面的松针形放射斑，分布较稀疏的，可见清晰的放射三维形貌（见图5-1-32）；分布较密集的，三维形貌呈堆积状（见图5-1-34）。

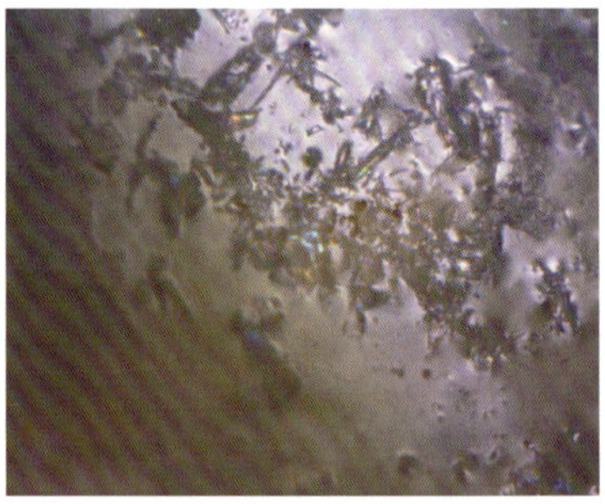

图5-1-32

图5-1-33

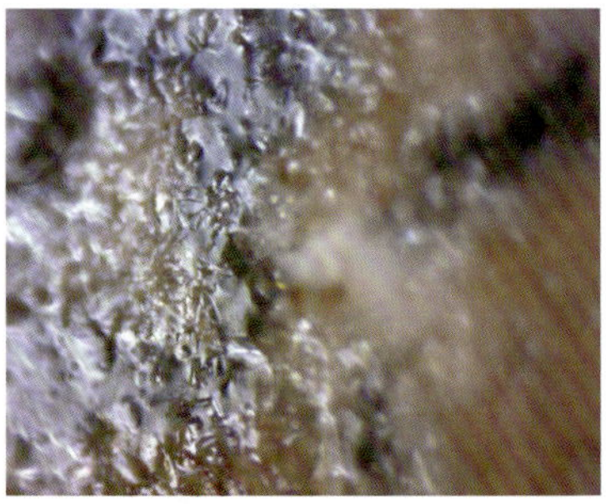

图5-1-34

The red radiating mottle in picture 5-1-53 appears to be light-colored in picture 5-1-54, clearly delineated with surface striations of crowded distribution. The mottles protrude form the glaze surface, and have a clear delineation from the surrounding glass phase.

See pictures 5-1-55 and 5-1-56, where 5-1-55 is the two-dimensional and 5-1-56 is the three-dimensional image of the same location.

The red-orange mottle in picture 5-1-55 is clearly visible in picture 5-1-56. It has an uneven surface and color variation.

(c) Yellow Series Radiating Mottles

(i) Two-dimensional Characteristics of Yellow Series

(1) Colorations fall within the bright to dark yellow spectrum (see pictures 5-1-57—5-1-63).

(2) Most are of irregular shape and appearance (see pictures 5-1-57—5-1-63).

(3) The mottle edge often has a lined border. The borders are usually thin and delicate in appearance and rarely attain any relative thickness, but all retain clear distinction. The border retains a certain distance from the edge of the mottle and the glass phase can be seen between the mottle and its lined border (see picture 5-1-57).

(4) They can present in conjunction with white (see pictures 5-1-59—5-1-61), brown (see picture 5-1-62) and red series radiating mottles (see picture 5-1-63).

(5) These mottles receive a relatively high amount of glaze protection, and as such are not easily weathered, and can retain their original post-firing characteristics. However, it is possible for the glass phase surrounding these mottles to present with needlepoint mottling (see Needlepoint Mottle heading of this section).

(d) Brown Series Radiating Mottles

(i) Two-dimensional Characteristics of Brown Series

(1) Coloration primarily consists of a coffee-like color with fern shape (see pictures 5-1-64 and 5-1-65) or irregular shape (see pictures 5-1-66 and 5-1-67).

(2) Some mottles have a lined border. The border is usually thin and delicate in appearance and rarely attains any relative thickness, but still retain clear distinction. The border often retains a certain distance from the edge of the mottle and the glass phase can be seen between the mottle and its lined border (see picture 5-1-66).

(3) Due to a relatively low amount of glaze protection, they are easily weathered and can present with needlepoint mottling on the mottle itself (see Needlepoint Mottle heading of this section).

(ii) Three-dimensional Characteristics of Brown Series

(1) The surface of these mottles are distinctly coarse, and some have a clear radiation effect.

(2) In general, these mottles are higher than the surrounding glaze level or flowing mottles, and present with clearly delineated borders between them.

See pictures 5-1-68 and 5-1-69, where 5-1-68 is the two-dimensional and 5-1-69 is the three-dimensional image of the same location.

See pictures 5-1-70 and 5-1-71, where 5-1-70 is the two-dimensional and 5-1-71 is the three-dimensional image of the same location.

The brown series radiating mottles in pictures 5-1-68 and 5-1-70 are the lighter colored mottles in picture 5-1-69 and 5-1-71. The mottles are clearly higher than the surrounding glaze. The surface of the radiating mottle in picture 5-1-69 is distinctly coarse, and the mottle in picture 5-1-71 has a pine needle appearance. Both have clearly delineated border with the surrounding glass phase.

(e) Black Series Radiating Mottles

(i) Two-dimensional Characteristics of Black Series

(1) Coloration is primarily black and the shape is irregular.

(2) Some mottles present with radiating edges (see picture 5-1-72).

(3) Some mottles can have a granulated appearance (see picture 5-1-73).

(4) They can present in conjunction with white (see picture 5-1-72) and brown series radiating mottles (see

e.不规则形放射斑二维特征

见图5-1-35—图5-1-38。

I.不规则形放射斑形貌各异，主要颜色为白色，颜色较浅的放射斑需要仔细观察才能看见。（见图5-1-35箭头E所指处、图5-1-36箭头F所指处）

II.有的斑块冲出釉表面，部分呈黄色或褐色。（见图5-1-37、图5-1-38）

f. 不规则形放射斑三维特征

I. 不规则形放射斑三维成像清晰。

II. 有的呈凹陷状，有的呈凸起状，斑块表面都显得粗糙。

III. 有的斑块形似白色堆积物。

IV. 与周围玻璃相界线分明。

见图5-1-39、图5-1-40，二者为同一器物同一位置图片，图5-1-39为二维图片，图5-1-40为三维图片。

见图5-1-41、图5-1-42，二者为同一器物同一位置图片，图5-1-41为二维图片，图5-1-42为三维图片。

见图5-1-43、图5-1-44，二者为同一器物同一位置图片，图5-1-43为二维图片，图5-1-44为三维图片。

见图5-1-45、图5-1-46，二者为同一器物同一位置图片，图5-1-45为二维图片，图5-1-46为三维图片。

见图5-1-47、图5-1-48，二者为同一器物同一位置图片，图5-1-47为二维图片，图5-1-48为三维图片。

这类放射斑，既有存在于釉表面的（见图5-1-39—图5-1-46），也有存在于釉层中的（见图5-1-47、图5-1-48）。无论二维成像颜色深浅与否，其三维成像都比较清晰，并与周围玻璃相界线分明。

位于釉表面的斑块，有的斑块略微凹陷，内部粗糙（见图5-1-40）；有的斑块凸起，表面粗糙，外围有一圈包边（见图5-1-42）；有的斑块上可见白色析晶（见图

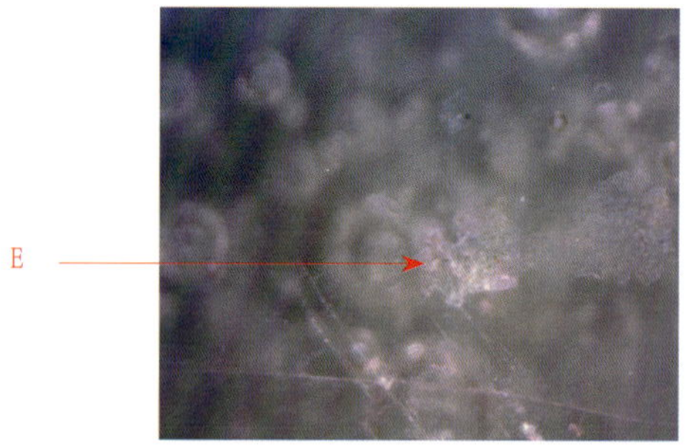

图5-1-35

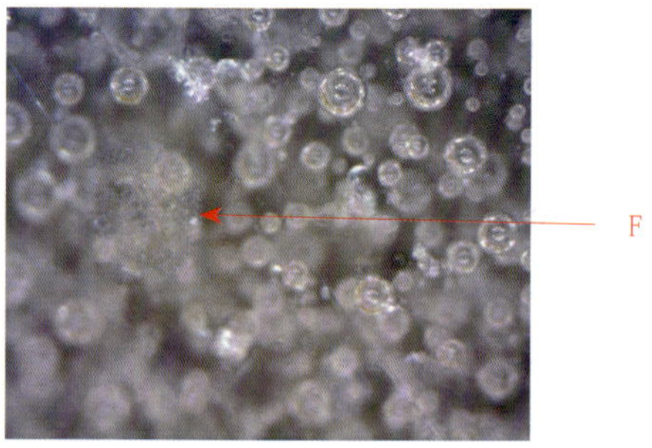

图5-1-36

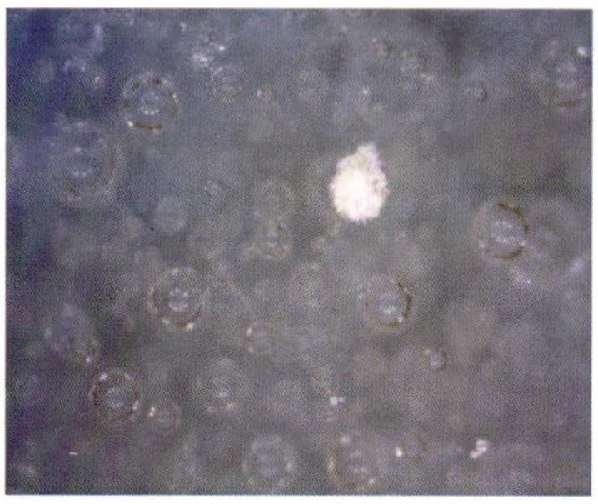

图5-1-37

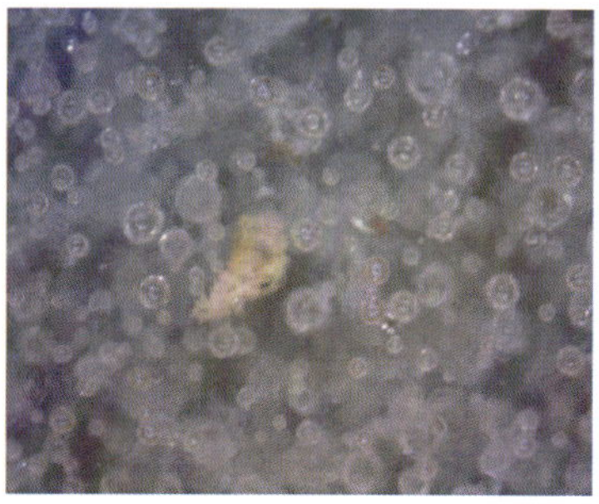

图5-1-38

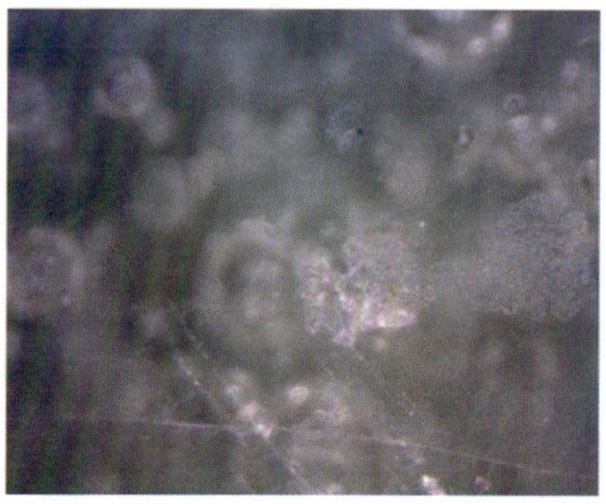

图5-1-39

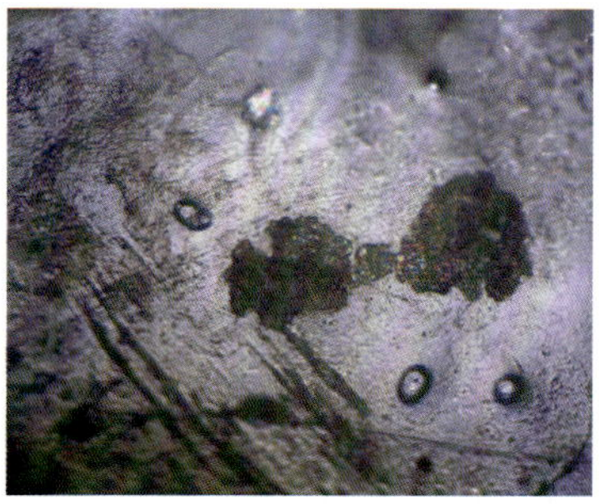

图5-1-40

图5-1-41

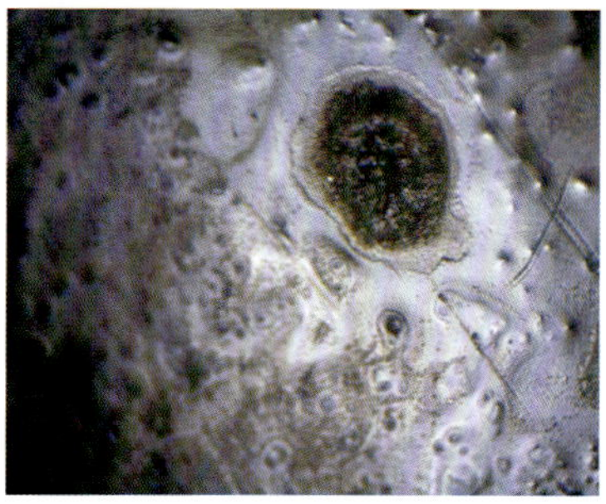

图5-1-42

pictures 5-1-73 and 5-1-74).

(5) Most mottles are at the surface of the glaze, receiving little glaze level protection, and are relatively easily weathered thus present with needlepoint mottling (see Needlepoint Mottle heading of this section).

(ii) Three-dimensional Characteristics of Black Series

See pictures 5-1-75 and 5-1-76.

(1) These mottles occur on the glaze surface, and have an irregular shape.

(2) Some mottles have a clear radiating property, some look like particle deposits on the glaze surface.

III. Blotch Mottle

i. Blotch Mottle Defined

Formed during the firing of LKSC, Blotch Mottles are those crystallized formations across the glaze surface and within the glaze level that have assembled into a clustered group but do not possess a radiating shape.

ii. Formation of Blotch Mottles

Blotch mottles are similar to the white series radiating mottles discussed earlier in that they are both formed by the crystallization of mullite (or feldspar and so forth compounds).

Since mullite crystallization is directly impacted by firing temperature and the amount of Al_2O_3, its presence indicates a firing temperature of over 1000℃ [239], as well as higher amount of Al_2O_3.

iii. Characteristics of Blotch Mottles

Two-dimensional Characteristics of Blotch Mottles

See pictures 5-1-77 and 5-1-78.

(i) Blotch mottles appear in the shape of smooth stones, with coloration of white, yellow, or brown.

(ii) Portions of mottles can present as translucent, while others are not translucent.

(iii) Some blotch mottles present with a single color while some present with a color spectrum.

IV. Summary

During the high temperature firing of LKSC; according to differences in composition, density, and glaze surface tension; various forms of flowing, radiating, and blotch mottles within the glaze level and on the glaze surface. These sometime occur simultaneously, for example: the combination of beach mottle and radiating mottle (see pictures 5-1-79 and 5-1-80). The LKSC body and glaze both have certain amounts of elemental Iron and Manganese. There are different types and appearances of crystallization mottles; some spilling over onto the glaze surface and some existing only within the glaze level, with the majority containing a certain amount of Iron and Manganese Oxides. The multiplicity of appearances and colorations of crystallizations within mottles are dependent on the viscosity and thickness of the glaze as well as the surface tension, density, and valence of elemental Iron and Manganese within crystallizations or split phase components.

Note: All microscopic pictures of innate characteristics on LKSC samples have undergone weathering; all of the observable qualities of innate mottles have experienced hundreds of years of history. Even the most protected pieces of porcelain have undergone certain amounts of weathering. As we do not have the capability of entering back into the unique LKSC firing environment, we can only use the pictures gained through microscopic observation in addition to current scientific knowledge to postulate the appearance and characteristics of the original inherent qualities.

B. Acquired LKSC Mottle

a. Acquired LKSC Mottle Defined

Acquired LKSC Mottles are mottles of irregular shape and distribution on the glaze surface and within the glaze level of LKSC that were formed under the influences of the post firing environment.

b. Acquired LKSC Mottle Types

I. Needlepoint Mottle

i. Needlepoint Mottle Defined

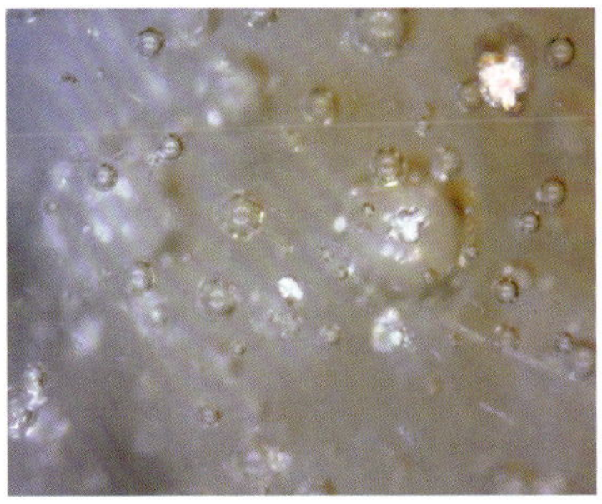
图5-1-43

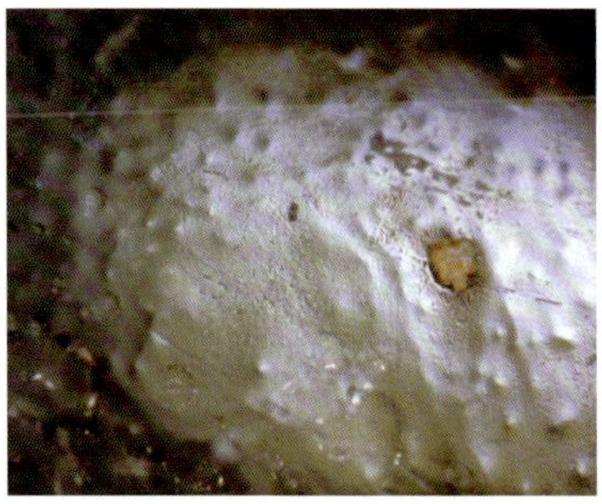
图5-1-44

图5-1-45

图5-1-46

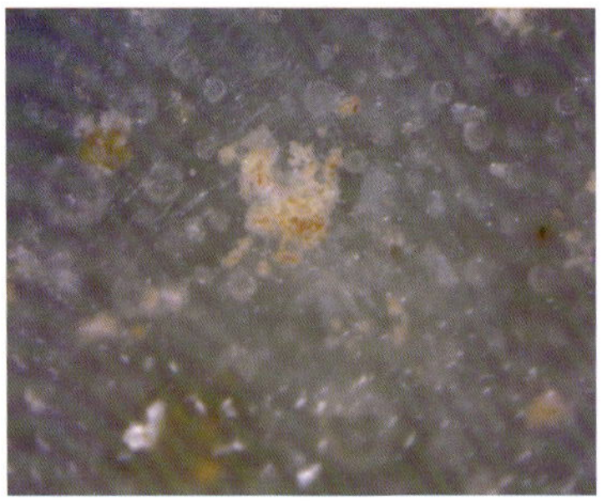
图5-1-47

图5-1-48

5-1-44、图5-1-46）。

有的斑块部分存在于釉层中，部分存在于釉表面（见图5-1-48）。

B. 红色系放射斑

a. 红色系放射斑二维特征

I. 红色系放射斑的颜色包括铁红、橘红色和橘黄色，形貌呈明显放射状（见图5-1-49—图5-1-52）。

II. 受釉层保护程度较低的红色系放射斑较易风化，有的放射斑上会出现针眼斑。（参见本章本节针眼斑部分）

b. 红色系放射斑三维特征

I. 红色系放射斑形状轮廓清晰。

II. 有的放射斑表面有细密纹路。

III. 放射斑大部分呈凸起状，与周围沙滩斑有高度差，界线分明。

见图5-1-53、图5-1-54，二者为同一器物同一位置图片，图

图5-1-49

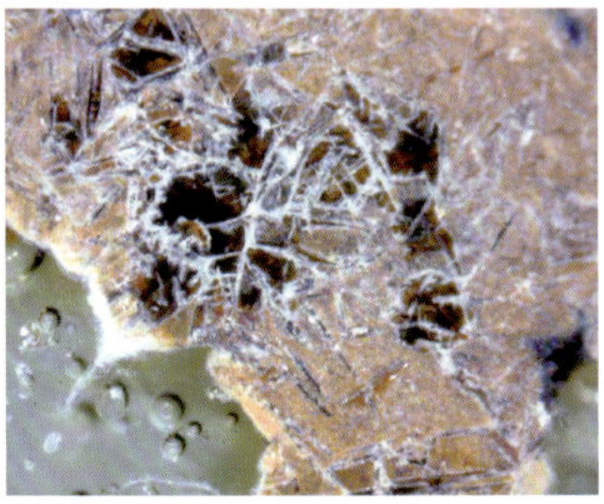
图5-1-50

图5-1-51

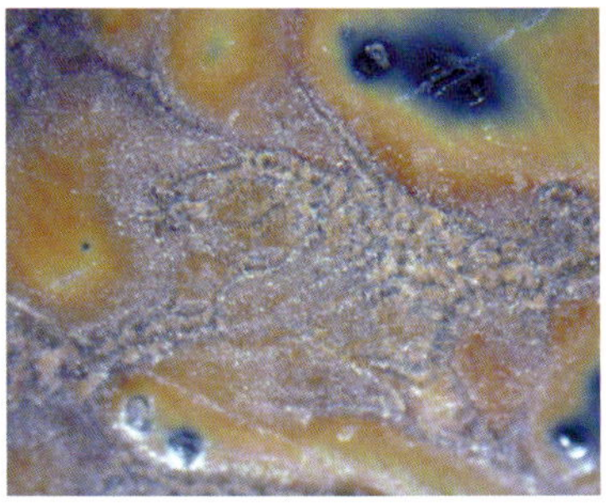
图5-1-52

Needlepoint Mottles are a collection of relatively unified variation of size and depth, either amassed or independent, and randomly dispersed pits on the LKSC glaze surface, formed under post-firing environment.

Generally, needlepoint mottles are first formed in areas on crystallization mottles without glaze coverage, in areas of glaze defect, or areas covered by soil or sand.

ii. Types of Needlepoint Mottles

Needlepoint mottles occur with random distribution, and can occur anywhere on the glaze surface; they can be divided into two types of appearances: Foggy and Frosted.

(a) Foggy Needlepoint Mottle

(i) Two-dimensional Characteristics of Foggy Needlepoint Mottles

See pictures 5-1-81 and 5-1-82.

(1) They present with a fine, white, and evenly distributed foggy appearance.

(2) They often occur on areas of transition from beach mottle to glass phase, the distribution of foggy needlepoint mottling becomes denser towards the center of beach mottles and the coloration more white. Even though there is not a clear delineation with the surrounding glass phase, there is a clear gradation from sparse to dense.

(3) Foggy needlepoint mottling can also occur independently on the glaze surface (see pictures 5-1-83 and 5-1-84).

(ii) Three-dimensional Characteristics of Foggy Needlepoint Mottles

See pictures 5-1-85 and 5-1-86, where 5-1-85 is the two-dimensional and 5-1-86 is the three-dimensional image of the same location.

(1) The foggy needlepoint mottling has even density gradation.

(2) Areas of sparse distribution have unobvious characteristics; areas of denser distribution have uniform, fine, dense distribution, like sand.

(b) Frosted Needlepoint Mottle

Frosted Needlepoint Mottles can be further divided into two types:

The first type is the progression from foggy needlepoint mottles, with a higher density and severity of weathering, but also presenting on areas of exposed Iron or Manganese Oxide.

The second type occurs in areas where Overlay Mottles have been cleaned away from the glaze surface, leaving frosted needlepoint mottles. For clarity sake, this is referred to as overlay frosted needlepoint mottling.

(i) Two-dimensional Characteristics of Frosted Needlepoint Mottles

(1) These mottles have a white coloration similar to sandblasted or frosted glass with pits larger than that of foggy needlepoint mottling. The weathering severity is higher than that of foggy needlepoint mottling.

(2) Frosted needlepoint mottles in general, have a less dense to sparse gradation, this mottling can present with very crowded density, or with widely sparse distribution, allowing visibility of the brown flowing mottle below, and retains clear delineation on the beach mottle (see pictures 5-1-87 and 5-1-88).

(3) Frosted Needlepoint mottling on radiating mottles occur in conjunction with the dense radiating crystallization distribution of the associated mottle, and are not likely to extend beyond the border of the underlying mottle (see pictures 5-1-89 and 5-1-90).

(ii) Three-dimensional Characteristics of Frosted Needlepoint Mottles

See pictures 5-1-91 and 5-1-92, where 5-1-91 is the two-dimensional and 5-1-92 is the three-dimensional image of the same location.

Frosted needlepoint mottling appears as individual points. The edges of the mottling closely follow the general contour of the underlying beach mottle.

II. Pit Mottle

i. Pit Mottle Defined

Pit Mottles (also called Pitting) are the irregularly shaped small depressions or pits on LKSC glaze, caused by

5-1-53为二维图片，图5-1-54为三维图片。

图5-1-53中的红色放射斑在图5-1-54中呈浅色，形貌清晰，上面分布有密集的线条，在斑块上形成皱褶般的纹路。斑块整体凸起，并且与周围沙滩斑界线分明。

见图5-1-55、图5-1-56，二者为同一器物同一位置图片，图5-1-55为二维图片，图5-1-56为三维图片。

图5-1-55中的橘红色放射斑在图5-1-56中成像清晰，斑块表面纹理凹凸不平，可见颜色变化。

C．黄色系放射斑

a．黄色系放射斑二维特征

I．黄色系放射斑有淡黄、深黄等颜色（见图5-1-57—图5-1-63）。

II．大多数都属于不规则形貌一类（见图5-1-57—图5-1-63）。

III．放射斑边沿通常有一条包边，包边整体纤细、精致，少量的稍粗，但总体都是清晰的，与放射斑轮廓保持一致，放射斑与包边之间可见玻璃相（见图5-1-57）。

IV．黄色系放射斑可以与白色系（见图5-1-59—图5-1-61）、褐色系（见图5-1-62）或红色系放射斑同时存在（见图5-1-63）。

V．黄色系放射斑受釉层保护程度较高，不易风化，所以基本保持刚烧制出来的原态。但有时在黄色系放射斑所在处及周边的玻璃相上会出现针眼斑。（参见本章本节针眼斑部分）

D．褐色系放射斑

a．褐色系放射斑二维特征

I．褐色系放射斑主要是咖啡色，包括蕨叶形（见图5-1-64、图5-1-65）及不规则形貌（见图5-1-66、图5-1-67）。

图5-1-53

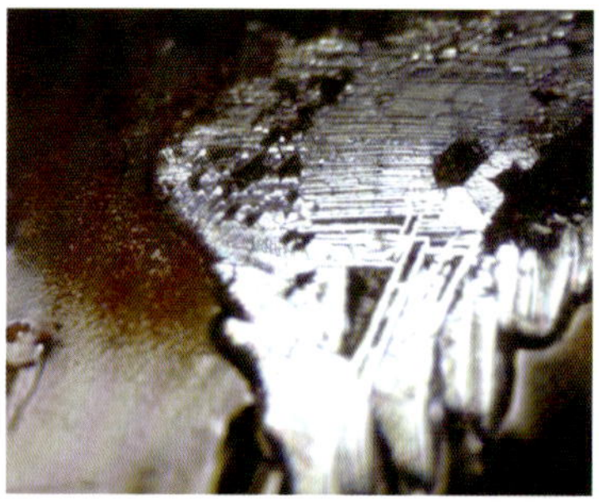
图5-1-54

图5-1-55

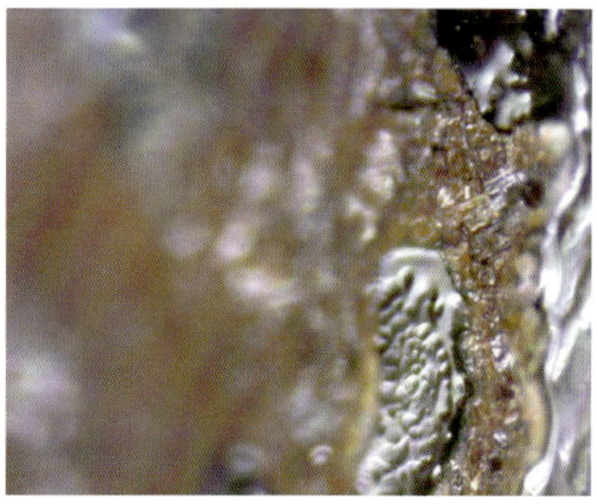
图5-1-56

图5-1-57

图5-1-58

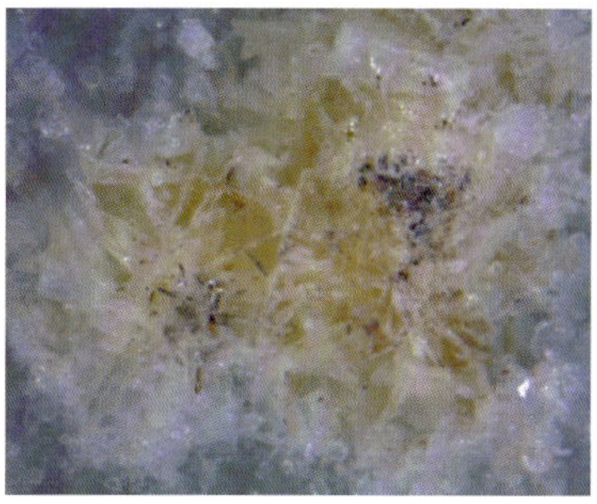
图5-1-59

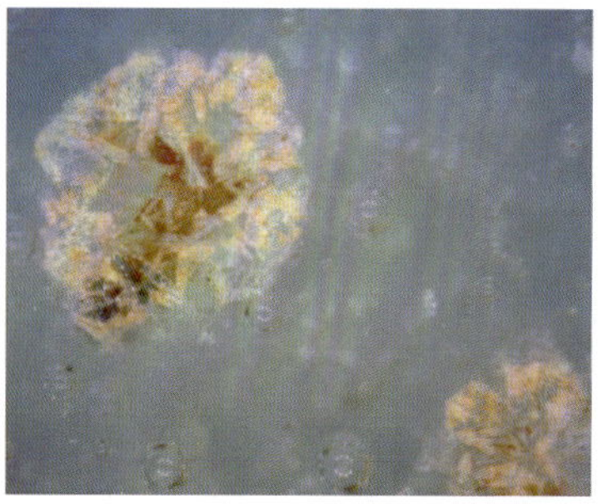
图5-1-60

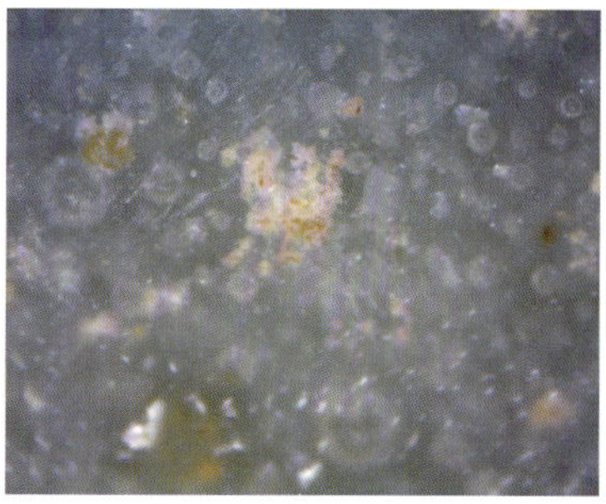
图5-1-61

the post-firing environment, with non-uniform depth, size, and appearance.

ii. Formation of Pit Mottles

There are five main causes of Pit Mottles:

(a) The progression of C and O shaped striae: C and O striae are crystallizations or split phases on the glaze surface. Their point of contact with the surrounding glass phase is structurally unstable; and as such, are easily weathered (see C and O Shaped Striae heading of this section). As these C and O shaped striae continue to be weathered, they form pit mottles. These are referred to as CO Type Pit Mottles (see C and O Striae heading in Section 2 of this chapter).

(b) The progression of needlepoint mottling: The further weathering of needlepoint mottles changes into pitting. These are referred to as Needlepoint Type Pit Mottles.

(c) Damage caused by external collision: This type of pitting is usually larger in surface area. These are referred to as Damage Type Pit Mottles.

(d) Overlay Material Corrosion: Once foreign materials are washed away, pitting can present. These are referred to as Overlay Type Pit Mottles.

(e) Long-term Underwater Submersion: Sustained underwater environments, such as shipwrecks, can cause glaze surface pitting. These are referred to as Underwater Type Pit Mottles.

iii. Characteristics of Pit Mottles

(a) CO type Pitting

(i) Two-dimensional Characteristics of CO Type Pitting

(1) Within one image, pits can have alternating size, depth, and distance of separation from surrounding pits (see pictures 5-1-93—5-1-101).

(2) C and O shaped striae are visible in conjunction with pits. These primarily appear in two forms: The first is amongst or in the close vicinity of C and O striae (see pictures 5-1-93—5-1-96), these shapes often retain clear delineation. The second is overlapping with C and O striae; both are clearly present, and sometimes the outline of the C and O striae are still observable (see pictures 5-1-97—5-1-101).

(3) Coloration is primarily white or light yellow. It is possible for the pits to have the same coloration as the C and O striae or different coloration (see pictures 5-1-93—5-1-101).

(4) C and O shaped pits can have white coloration extending into the glaze level (see picture 5-1-100).

(5) Initially, these pits are independently distributed, but as weathering continues pits can become interlocked in a chain-like fashion (see pictures 5-1-99—5-1-101).

(6) C and O shaped pits retain clear delineation from the surrounding glass phase and other traces (see pictures 5-1-93—101).

(ii) Three-dimensional Characteristics of CO Type Pitting

(1) This type of pitting occurs primarily in areas of convex glaze surface.

(2) It is possible to only observe small, fine, reserved C and O striae on the glaze surface.

(3) It is also possible to observe C and O striae as well as pit openings on the glaze surface with a smaller area than that of the two-dimensionally observable pit. They are clearly delineated, and the pit is reserved and not dispersing.

(4) C and O shaped pits have a clear delineation from the surrounding glass phase or other trace types.

See pictures 5-1-102 and 5-1-103 where 5-1-102 is the two-dimensional and 5-1-103 is the three-dimensional image of the same location.

The pit indicated by the arrow in picture 5-1-102 is only observable as a C shaped striation and has a much smaller three-dimensional appearance (see Arrow A) in picture 5-1-103. The striae are fine and reserved, the mottle is reserved and lacking dispersive qualities, and retains independent delineation with the surrounding glass phase.

These pits are the result of weathering development of the C shaped striae, and extend down into the glaze level. Three-dimensional imaging is unable to observe the pit within the glaze level, therefore the observable opening is smaller than the size of the pit observable by two-dimensional imaging.

See pictures 5-1-104 and 5-1-105, where 5-1-104 is the

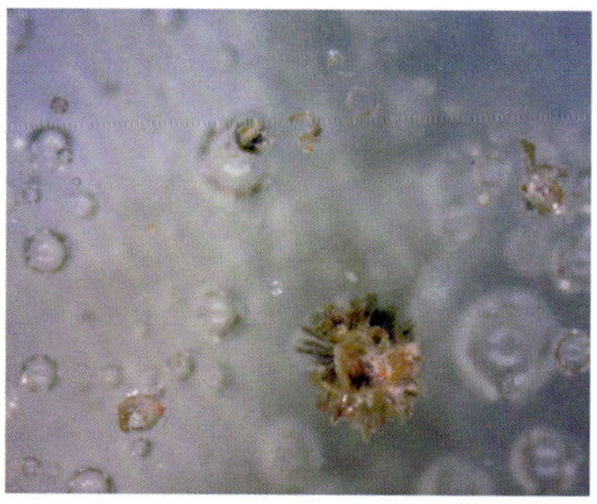
图5-1-62

图5-1-63

图5-1-64

图5-1-65

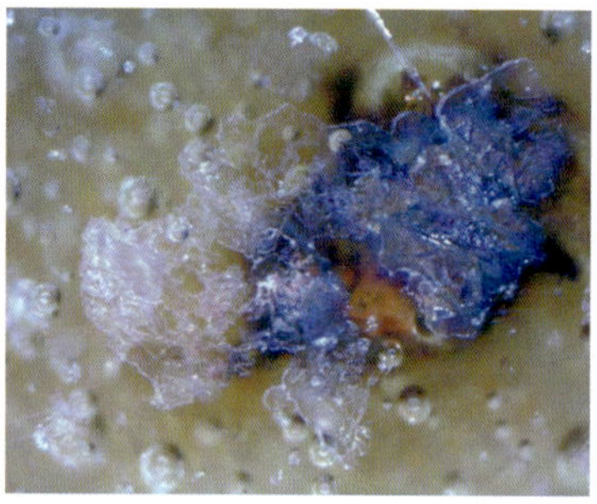
图5-1-66

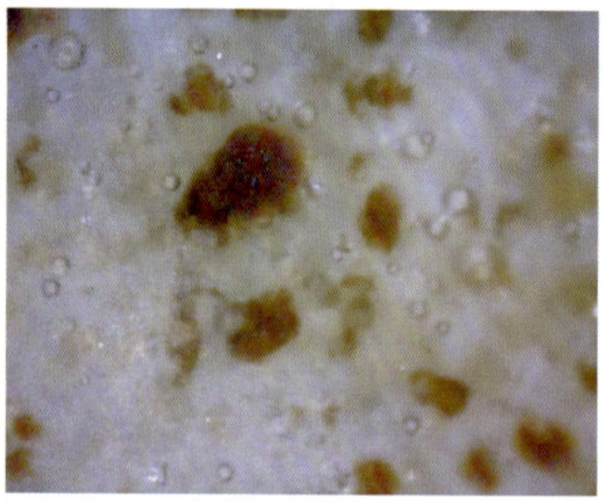
图5-1-67

II. 有的褐色系放射斑边沿有包边，包边整体纤细、精致，少量的稍粗，但总体都是清晰的，放射斑与包边之间大部分时候可见玻璃相。（图5-1-66）

III. 由于受釉层保护程度较低，褐色系放射斑较易风化，褐色系放射斑上会出现针眼斑。（参见本章本节针眼斑部分）

b. 褐色系放射斑三维特征

I. 有的褐色系放射斑表面纹理粗糙，有的有明显放射感。

II. 一般来说，褐色系放射斑所处位置较周边玻璃相或流淌斑明显要高，彼此界线分明。

见图5-1-68、图5-1-69，二者为同一器物同一位置图片，图5-1-68为二维图片，图5-1-69为三维图片。

见图5-1-70、图5-1-71，二者为同一器物同一位置图片，图5-1-70为二维图片，图5-1-71为三维图片。

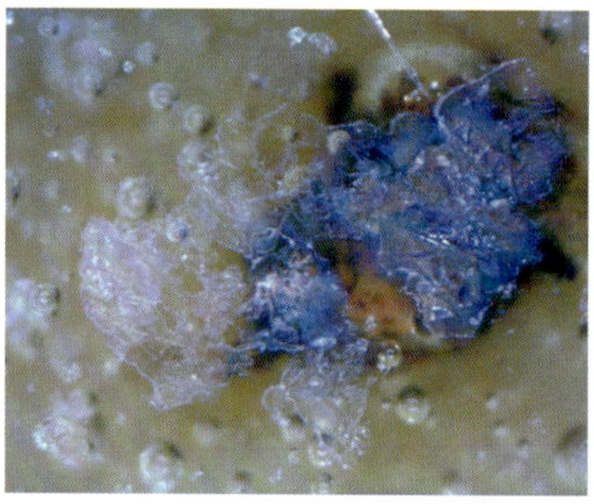
图5-1-68

图5-1-69

two-dimensional and 5-1-105 is the three-dimensional image of the same location.

The pitting visible in picture 5-1-104 is the conjunction of C and O striae and pit mottles, but is only visible as a comparatively large C shaped striation (see Arrow B) and three smaller O striae that all appear smaller three-dimensionally (see Arrow C) in picture 5-1-105. The striae are fine and reserved, lacking dispersive qualities, and retaining independent delineation with the surrounding glass phase.

See pictures 5-1-106 and 5-1-107, where 5-1-106 is the two-dimensional and 5-1-107 is the three-dimensional image of the same location.

The pit indicated by the arrow in picture 5-1-106 is right next to a C shaped striation. The pit in picture 5-1-106 is only observable as a C shaped striation and a small dark pit, smaller than that of picture 5-1-106 on the glaze surface (see Arrow D). The striae are fine and reserved, lacking dispersive qualities, and both are clearly independent and delineated from the surrounding glass phase.

The pits indicated by Arrow D are the continued weathering of a C shaped striation. The continuation of weathering gradually extends the pit into the glaze level creating a CO type pit. Three-dimensional imaging does not allow for the observation of the pit below the glaze surface, and as such the observable opening is smaller than the size of the pit observable by two-dimensional imaging.

See pictures 5-1-108 and 5-1-109, where 5-1-108 is the two-dimensional and 5-1-109 is the three-dimensional image of the same location.

The pits in picture 5-1-108 are the area of dark coloration in picture 5-1-109, the three-dimensionally visible size are smaller than two-dimensionally visible (see Arrow E), Mottle E is reserved and clearly independent, and retains delineation with the surrounding glass phase.

The pits in picture 5-1-109 are the continued weathering development of CO shaped striations. Weathering gradually extended the pit into the glaze level. Three-dimensional imaging does not allow for the observation of the pit below the glaze surface, and as such the observable opening is smaller than the size of the pit observable by two-dimensional imaging.

Generally, CO type pitting occurs on areas of convex glaze. The two-dimensionally observable pitting in picture 5-1-108 is directly correlated with the small hills observable with three-dimensional microscopic imaging in picture 5-1-109. Portions of the glaze without protruding formations remain clean and smooth. As the areas of pitting are points of relatively unstable composition within the glass phase, weathering easily occurs. On the other hand, areas of smooth glass phase are relatively stable, and weathering severity is lower, thus it is able to retain a clean and smooth surface.

(b) Damage Type Pitting

Two-dimensional Characteristics of Damage Type Pitting

(1) Pits present with irregular shapes and often present with coloration (see pictures 5-1-110—5-1-115).

(2) Pits with a larger area often present with needlepoint mottling or material deposits in the internal cavity of the pit (see pictures 5-1-110—5-1-114).

(c) Immersion Type Pitting

(i) Two-dimensional Characteristics of Immersion Type Pitting

See pictures 5-1-116 and 5-1-117.

(1) Pits can present at any location on the glaze with random distribution.

(2) Immersion pits can have a circular, ovular, or irregular shape. Pit interiors present with frosted needlepoint mottling or deposits.

(3) Pits retain clear delineation with the surrounding glass phase.

(ii) Three-dimensional Characteristics of Immersion Type Pitting

See pictures 5-1-118 and 5-1-119.

Immersion type pits are clearly visible depressions of circular, ovular, or irregular shape on the glaze surface. Sometimes it is possible to observe deposits within the pit.

图5-1-68及图5-1-70中的褐色系放射斑在图5-1-69及图5-1-71中均呈浅色，成像清晰。斑块明显高于釉表面，图5-1-69中的放射斑表面纹理粗糙，图5-1-71中的放射斑有松针形放射形貌，二者均与周围玻璃相界线分明。

E. 黑色系放射斑

a. 黑色系放射斑二维特征

I. 黑色系放射斑中主要是黑色，属于不规则形貌一类。

II. 有的黑色系放射斑边沿有放射感（见图5-1-72）。

III. 有的黑色系放射斑呈颗粒状（见图5-1-73）。

IV. 黑色系放射斑可以与白色系（见图5-1-72）或褐色系放射斑同时存在（见图5-1-73、图5-1-74）。

V. 黑色系放射斑大都位于釉表面，受釉层保护程度较低，较易风化，斑块上分布的针眼斑明显。（参见本章本节针眼斑部分）

b. 黑色系放射斑三维特征

见图5-1-75、图5-1-76。

I. 黑色系放射斑位于釉表面，呈不规则形貌。

II. 有的斑块呈明显放射状，有的呈颗粒状堆积。

（3）团状斑

① 团状斑概念

团状斑是聚集成一团、没有放射感的析晶斑块。它是龙泉窑系青瓷在烧制过程中，在其釉表面及釉层中形成的。

② 团状斑形成

团状斑与放射斑中的白色系放射斑类似，应是莫来石（或长石类）的析晶。莫来石结晶与烧造温度以及Al_2O_3的含量有关。有莫来石结晶出现说明瓷器的烧结温度至少达1000℃[239]，并且Al_2O_3

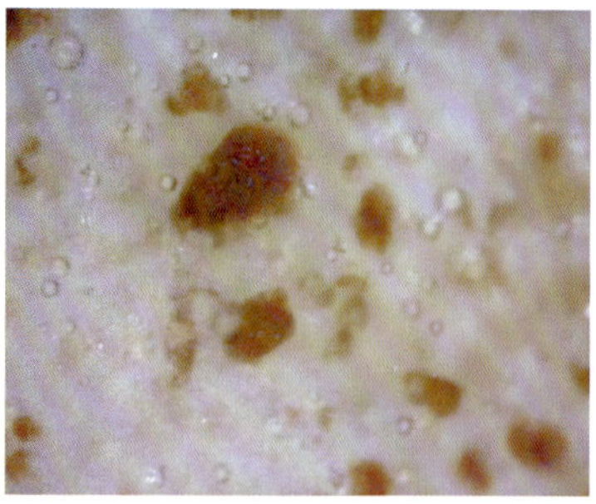

图5-1-70

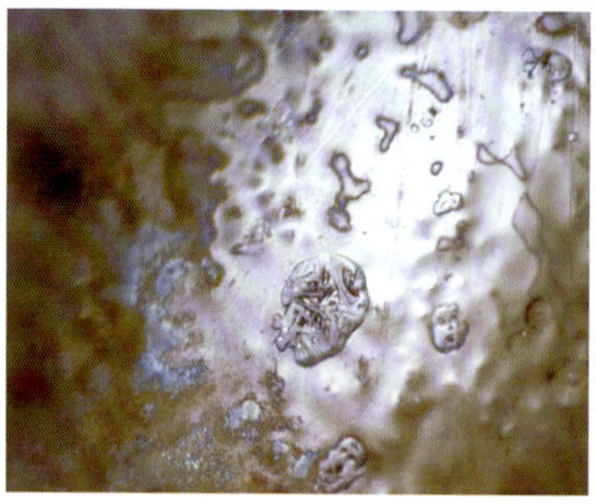

图5-1-71

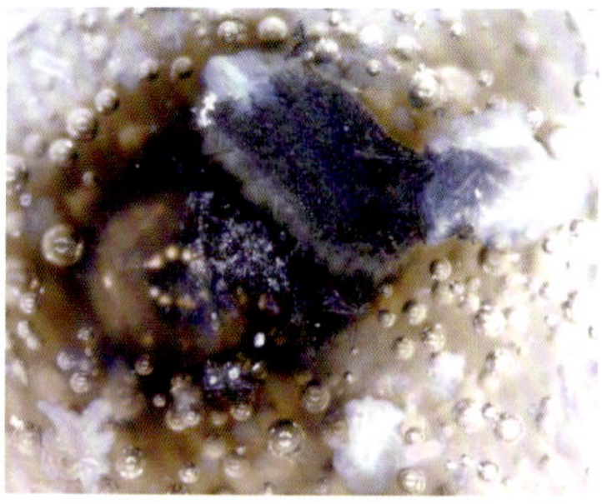

图5-1-72

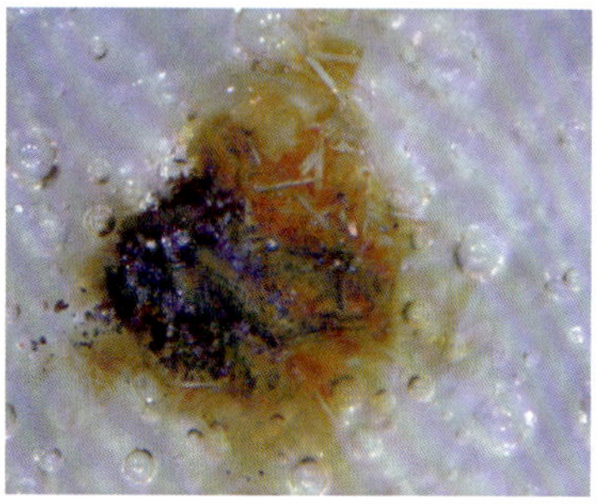

图5-1-73

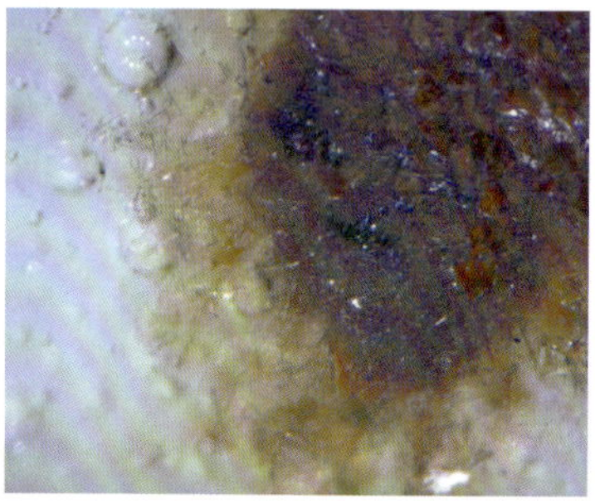

图5-1-74

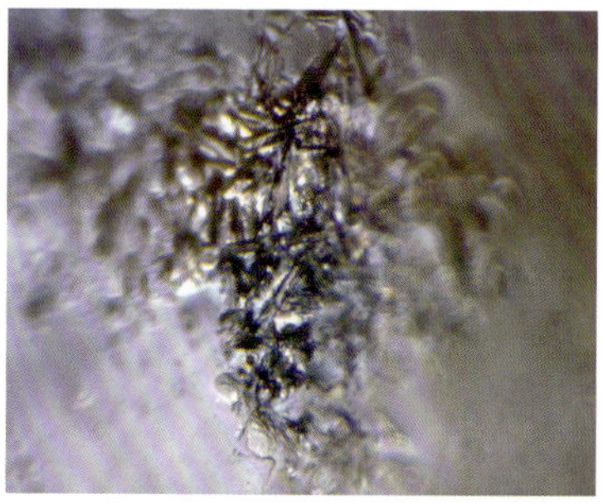

图5-1-75

图5-1-76

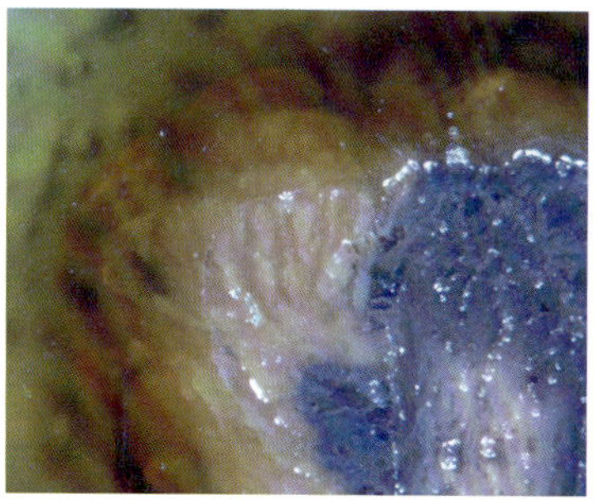

图5-1-77

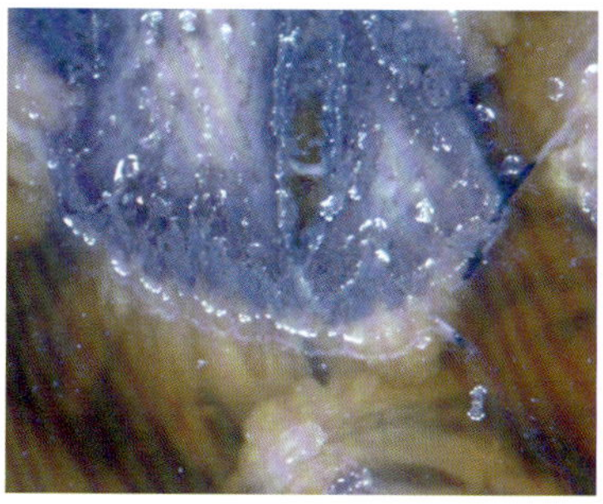

图5-1-78

III. Overlay Mottle

i. Overlay Mottle Defined

Overlay Mottles are acquired under the effect of the post-firing environment, and are the result of coverage of a foreign material over LKSC glaze.

ii. Formation of Overlay Mottles

Majority of LKSC overlay mottles are formed by the coverage of dirt and other materials on the surface of the porcelain, as well as any man-made or foreign materials added to repair or restore the piece.

iii. Characteristics of Overlay Mottles

Two-dimensional Characteristics of Overlay Mottles

(i) The primary colors of overlay mottles are yellow, brown, or greyish-white (see pictures 5-1-120—5-1-127).

(ii) Mottles are clearly delineated from the surrounding glass phase and can have straight or irregular edges (see pictures 5-1-120—5-1-127).

(iii) Mottles can have distinct layers, presenting as flaky skin (see pictures 5-1-121—5-1-127).

(iv) It is common to see scratches across the mottle (see picture 5-1-120).

(v) Due to the several different chemical components used in the restoration of ceramics, the characteristics of overlay mottles created by these materials can be widely varying. It is very difficult to tell the difference between glue, natural overlay mottles, and needlepoint mottles. As such, there is a need for naked-eye inspection to tell whether or not an observed item has undergone repair.

IV. Bubble Root

i. Bubble Root Defined

A Bubble Root (mottle) is a concave mottle which is the progression of a broken mouth bubble on the surface of LKSC glaze with internal sedimentation, formed under the influences of the post-firing environment.

ii. Formation of Bubble Roots

After LKSC glaze undergoes corrosive weathering, small portions of bubbles within the glaze level become flayed, leaving a deep depressed pit on the glaze surface, also called a bubble root. Completely exposed to the elements, foreign materials are easily accumulated within the pit leaving deposited sediments on the internal wall, thus creating a bubble root mottle.

Generally, the mouth or rim portion of the porcelain piece presents with bubble roots. On shipwrecked pieces with normally more severe weathering, it is also common for bubble roots to present.

iii. Characteristics of Bubble Roots

Two-dimensional Characteristics of Bubble Roots

(i) The majority of bubble roots retain their inherent round shape, with a small portion also having ovular or irregular shape (see pictures 5-1-128—5-1-139).

(ii) Commonly seen colors in bubble roots are: White, yellow, brown, and black (see pictures 5-1-128—5-1-139).

(iii) Some bubble roots can present with multiple types of sedimentation, and as such, a spectrum of colors (see pictures 5-1-138 and 5-1-139).

(iv) Neighboring bubble roots can have color discrepancy (see pictures 5-1-137— 5-1-139).

V. Floccus Mottle

i. Floccus Mottle Defined

Floccus Mottles are primarily white colored appearances within the LKSC glaze level and on the glaze surface brought about by the post-firing environment; they have indistinct, free flowing, and irregular shapes that were formed by the depositing of soluble and partially soluble salts, dust particles, and other materials.

ii. Formation of Floccus Mottles

The fired LKSC glaze surface has randomly distributed cracks and openings. Additionally, as soil contains acidic and alkaline solutions that corrode the glaze surface, small cracks and openings in the glaze surface can be further created. It is through these small cracks and openings that foreign material can enter into the glaze level, forming soluble and partially soluble salts.

含量较高。

③ 团状斑特征

团状斑二维特征

见图5-1-77、图5-1-78。

I. 团状斑形貌如石块，颜色有白色、黄色、褐色。

II. 部分斑块具备透影性，部分不具备透影性。

III. 部分斑块颜色单一，部分有色阶变化。

（4）小结

龙泉窑系青瓷在烧制过程中，根据各处的成分、密度、表面张力的不同，会在釉表面及釉层中形成形貌各异的流淌斑、放射斑或团状斑，它们有时会组合出现。比如：沙滩斑和放射斑的组合（见图5-1-79、图5-1-80）。龙泉窑系青瓷的胎和釉中均含有铁元素和锰元素，不同种类、不同形貌的析晶斑，有的溢出釉表面，有的存在于釉层中，大部分都含一定量的铁氧化物和锰氧化物。这些析晶斑形貌和颜色的多样性，与釉的黏度及厚度有关，与结晶或分相物质的张力、密度、铁元素和锰元素的价位都有关。

注：在现今采集的龙泉窑系标本的显微成像图片上，我们能看到所有的先天性斑块特征都已经过了相当一段年月，即使是保存再好的瓷器也会有一定程度的风化。我们无法回到古代探索龙泉青瓷先天斑块的原貌，只能在迹型风化的绝对时间内，根据图片情况，运用科学知识加以推理，想象龙泉青瓷先天性斑块的本来面目。

（二）后天性龙泉窑系青瓷斑块

1. 后天性龙泉窑系青瓷斑块概念

后天性龙泉窑系青瓷斑块是龙泉窑系青瓷在后天环境影响下形成的，以不规则形貌分布在釉表面及

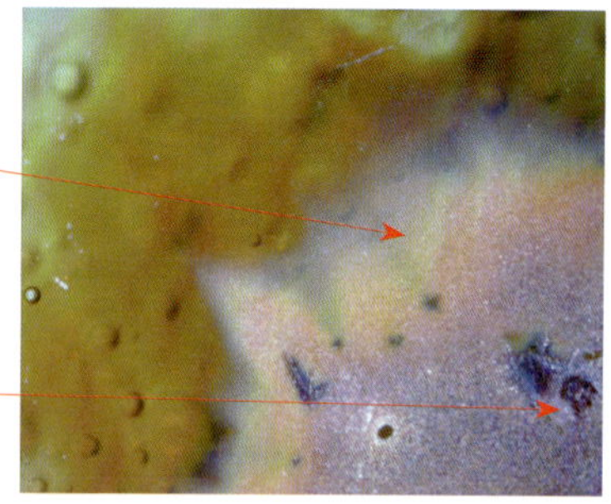

图5-1-79

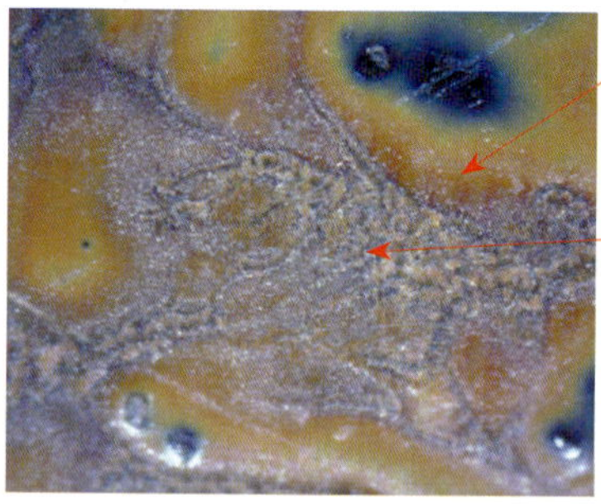

图5-1-80

图5-1-81

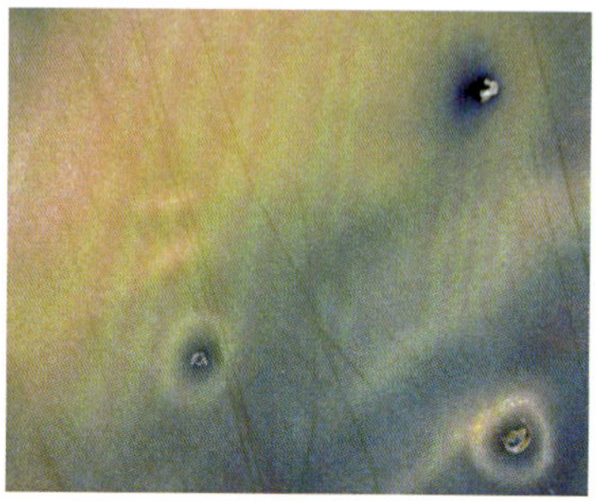

图5-1-82

图5-1-83

图5-1-84

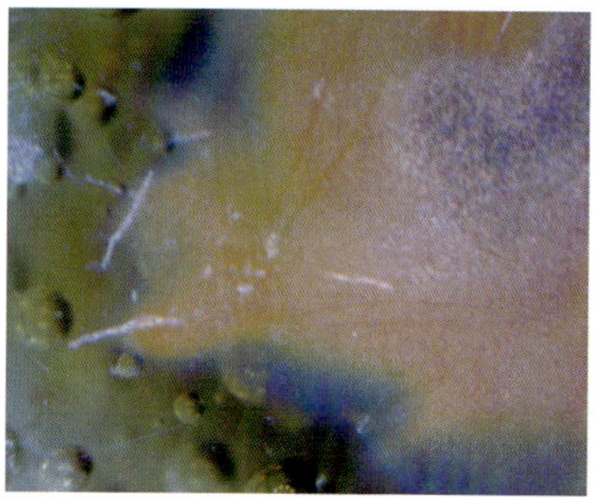

图5-1-85

图5-1-86

When the water in the soil evaporates, the soluble salts crystalize. However, due to the solubility of these salts, surface level water can dissolve and wash them away. Therefore, the rate of floccus mottling is relatively low across the surface, but common within the glaze level.

In environments of alternating moisture, it is difficult for partially soluble salts to be dissolved away from the glaze level. Soluble salts dispersed within the glaze level crystalized after the evaporation of water and trap with them microscopic dust particles within the glaze level; these sedimentations form floccus mottles.

Soil and the glaze surface also contain positive and negative ions that, in reaction with each other, create partially soluble salt deposits of varying colors.

iii. Characteristics of Floccus Mottles

(a) Two-dimensional Characteristics of Floccus Mottles

See pictures 5-1-140—5-1-145.

(i) Floccus Mottles are primarily white in color. Within the glaze level, these mottles mainly assume irregular blotch and spot shapes, similar to wisps of clouds.

(ii) Mottles occur in conjunction with areas of relatively unstable glaze composition or glaze flaw. For example under pitting, under overlay mottles, under glaze cracks, under C and O striae, under scratches, around bristle pits, and under areas of other glaze defect.

(iii) The mottle forms at the location of glaze flaw and permeates down into the glaze level. The center of the mottle is non-transparent and milky white, and the edges feather out like goose down.

(b) Three-dimensional Characteristics of Floccus Mottles

(i) Under the glaze floccus mottling is not visible, and the glaze surface defect (i.e. pit, crack) is much smaller than the defect and floccus mottling observable through two-dimension microscopic imaging of the same location.

(ii) Aside from glaze defect, the glaze surface remains smooth without any other large area flaws.

See pictures 5-1-146 and 5-1-147, where 5-1-146 is the two-dimensional and 5-1-147 is the three-dimensional image of the same location.

The white floccus mottling indicated by Arrow A in picture 5-1-146 is not visible in picture 5-1-147. The glaze crack is the only evident glaze flaw without any large area glaze flaws in the vicinity, demonstrating that the floccus mottle is present under the glaze surface.

3. Conclusion

LKSC Mottles can be divided into two categories: Innate and Acquired.

The multiplicity of LKSC innate mottles is primarily due to differences in glaze and firing techniques; and as such, to some extent reflects the materials and techniques used in that day. Acquired mottles are formed because of the post firing environments, and changes and differences in those environments. The multiplicity of acquired mottles reflects the corresponding relationship between the formation of LKSC traces and their post-firing environments. The characteristics of these mottles are in accordance with the quantitative change and passage of time principles of ceramic traces, and embody the various laws that govern ceramic trace formation and change.

釉层中的各类斑块。

2. 后天性龙泉窑系青瓷斑块种类

（1）针眼斑

① 针眼斑概念

针眼斑是大小较均匀、深浅大致相同、疏密不定的独立微孔，以聚集形式呈不规则形貌出现的斑块。

它是龙泉窑系青瓷在后天环境影响下，在釉表面随机形成的。通常情况下，在析晶斑无釉覆盖处、釉表面组织结构稳定性较差处，或曾有泥沙等异物覆盖处，会较先以针眼斑形式开始风化。

② 针眼斑分类

针眼斑的形貌主要分为雾状针眼斑和磨砂针眼斑。

A．雾状针眼斑

a．雾状针眼斑二维特征

见图5-1-81、图5-1-82。

I. 雾状针眼斑呈白色雾状，均匀细腻，像雾化的喷漆均匀地喷在釉表面。

II. 雾状针眼斑通常存在于沙滩斑与玻璃相过渡的区域，越往沙滩斑中心部分雾状针眼斑分布越密集，颜色越白；越往沙滩斑边沿处雾状针眼斑分布越稀疏，颜色越趋淡，呈玻璃相的颜色。尽管与玻璃相之间没有明显的边界线，但有一个从浓到淡的均匀过渡。

III. 也有的雾状针眼斑单独出现在玻璃相上（见图5-1-83、图5-1-84）。

b．雾状针眼斑三维特征

见图5-1-85、图5-1-86，二者为同一器物同一位置图片，图5-1-85为二维图片，图5-1-86为三维图片。

I. 雾状针眼斑表现出均匀的过渡。

II. 雾状针眼斑分布稀疏处特征不明显；雾状针眼斑分布密集的地方如同均匀铺展的细沙。

B．磨砂针眼斑

磨砂针眼斑的成因主要分为两种：

第一种磨砂针眼斑属于雾状针眼斑的发展，是风化强度更高的表现，分布密集，存在于无釉覆盖的铁氧化物及锰氧化物暴露处。

第二种磨砂针眼斑的主要成因为，物盖物侵蚀釉表面，清除物盖物后暴露出磨砂针眼斑。为了区别，我们称这一类为物盖磨砂针眼斑。

a．磨砂针眼斑二维特征

I．磨砂针眼斑呈白色，有磨砂感，针眼较雾状针眼斑粗粝，风化强度大于雾状针眼斑。

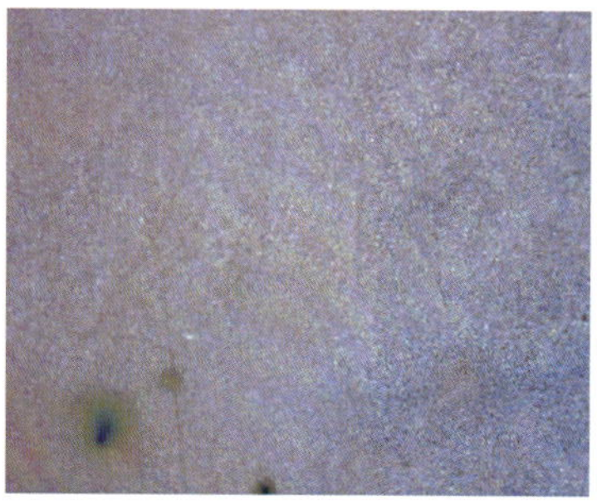
图5-1-87

图5-1-88

图5-1-89

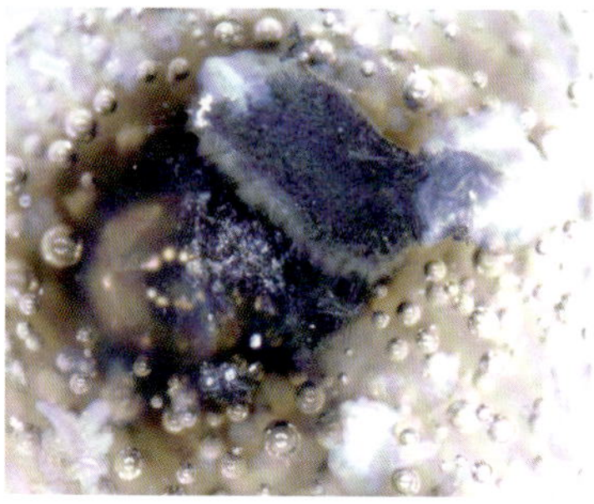
图5-1-90

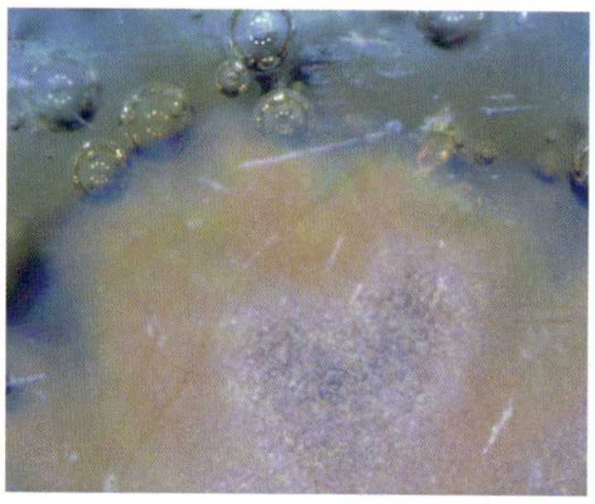
图5-1-91

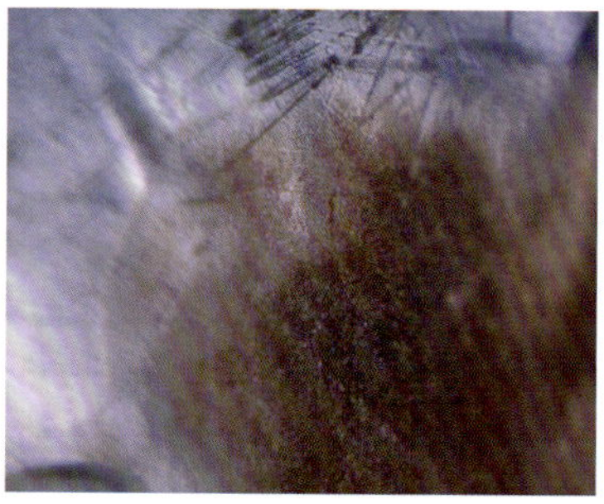
图5-1-92

II.磨砂针眼斑在沙滩斑上一般没有浓淡过渡，有的地方分布密集，有的地方几乎没有，露出褐色的沙滩斑。磨砂针眼斑在沙滩斑上的边界感较强（见图5-1-87、图5-1-88）。

III. 放射斑上的磨砂针眼斑随放射斑的析晶形状密集分布，一般不超出放射斑的范围（见图5-1-89、图5-1-90）。

b. 磨砂针眼斑三维特征

见图5-1-91、图5-1-92，二者为同一器物同一位置图片，图5-1-91为二维图片，图5-1-92为三维图片。

磨砂针眼斑表现为独立点状凹坑，在沙滩斑上则随着沙滩斑的轮廓走势分布。

（2）坑点斑

① 坑点斑概念

坑点斑是深浅不一、大小不一、形貌不一的不规则凹形斑块。它是龙泉窑系青瓷在后天环境影响下，在其釉表面形成的。

② 坑点斑形成

坑点斑的形成原因主要有五种，不同成因的坑点斑可以共存：

A. 由C形、O形纹发展而成。C形、O形纹路（以下简称CO纹）是釉层的析晶或分相，它们与玻璃相结合处的组织结构稳定性较差，易风化。CO纹继续风化就会形成坑点斑。我们称这类坑点斑为CO型坑点斑。（参见本章第二节C形纹、O形纹部分）

B. 由针眼斑发展而成。针眼斑进一步风化后，形成坑点斑。我们称这类坑点斑为针眼型坑点斑。

C. 外界磕碰或磨损形成。釉表面被磕碰或磨损后，形成坑点斑。我们称这类坑点斑为外伤型坑点斑。

D. 物盖物侵蚀釉表面，清除

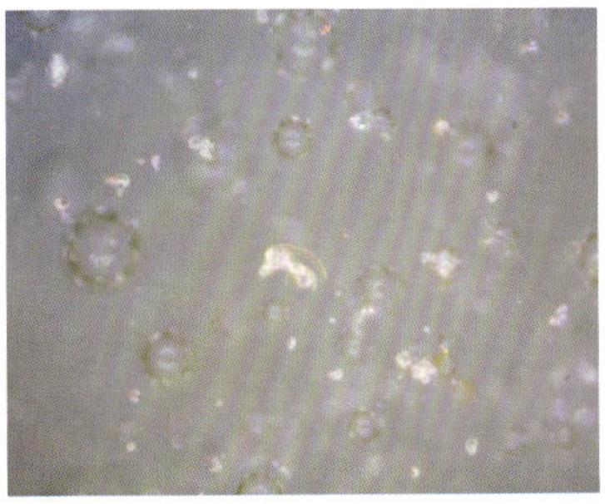
图5-1-93

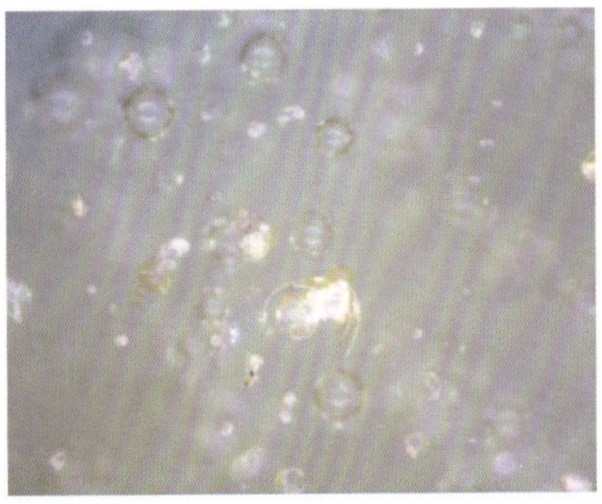
图5-1-94

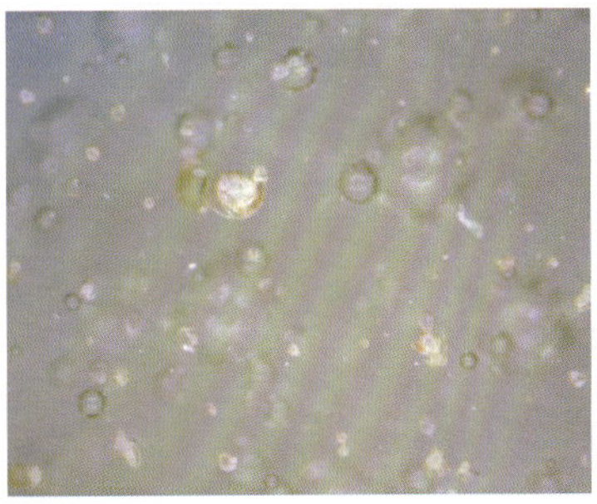
图5-1-95

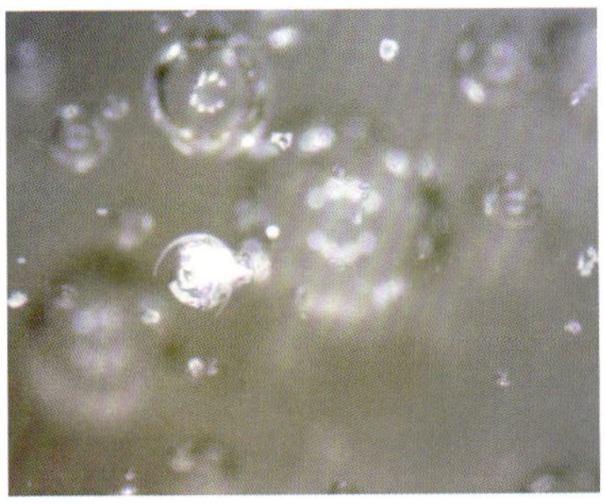
图5-1-96

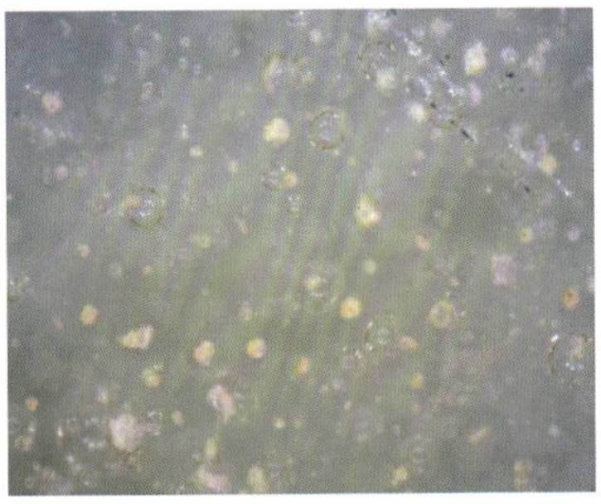
图5-1-97

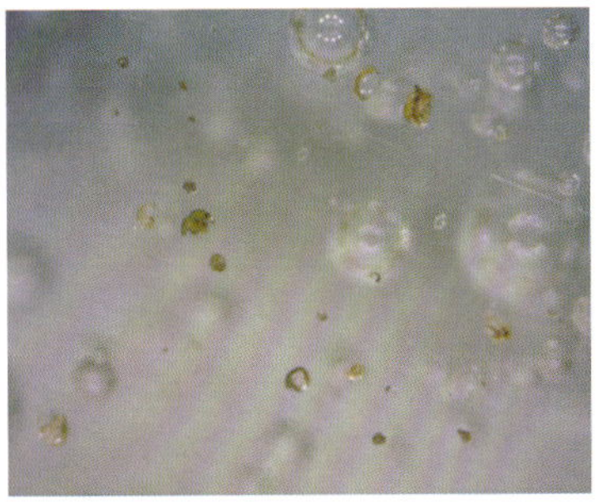
图5-1-98

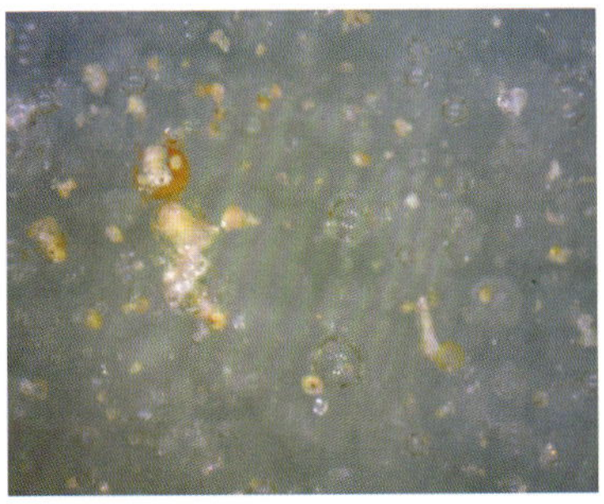
图5-1-99

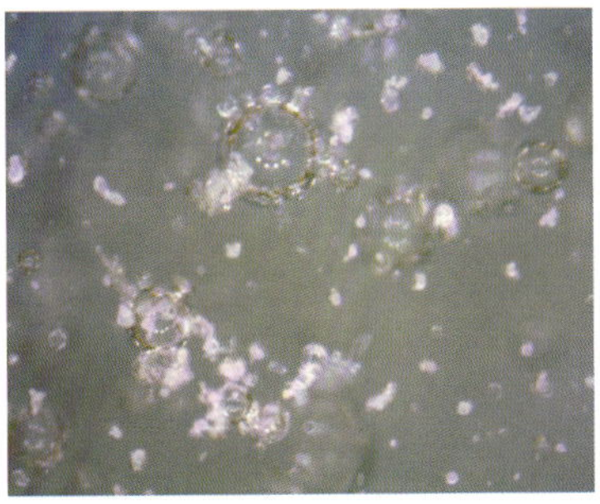
图5-1-100

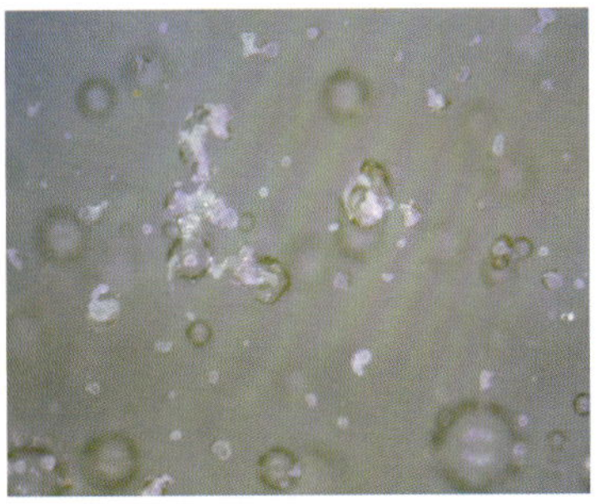
图5-1-101

物盖物后，暴露出坑点斑。我们称这类坑点斑为物盖型坑点斑。

E. 由于长期浸泡在水中，釉表面风化形成坑点斑。这类坑点斑通常出现在海捞瓷上。我们称这类坑点斑为浸水型坑点斑。

③ 坑点斑特征

A. CO型坑点斑

a. CO型坑点斑二维特征

I. 单位图片中CO型坑点斑大小不一、深浅不一，各个坑点斑之间距离不等（见图5-1-93—图5-1-101）。

II. 坑点斑与CO纹伴生的现象，主要有两种形式：一种是坑点斑与CO纹紧挨或邻近（见图5-1-93—图5-1-96），通常二者界线清晰分明；一种是坑点斑与CO纹重叠，二者皆清晰，有时可见CO纹纹路轮廓（见图5-1-97—图5-1-101）。

III. CO型坑点斑通常呈白色或淡黄色，伴生的CO型坑点斑大部分时候颜色与C形纹或O形纹一致，有时二者颜色不一致（见图5-1-93—图5-1-101）。

IV. CO型坑点斑有沿着其轮廓向外呈白雾状蔓延的趋势（见图5-1-100）。

V. 一开始CO型坑点斑独立零星分布，如果风化继续，坑点斑之间相连贯通，就变成连环状、有螺旋感的坑点斑群（见图5-1-99—图5-1-101）。

VI. CO型坑点斑与周围玻璃相或其他迹型种类界线分明（见图5-1-93—图5-1-101）。

b. CO型坑点斑三维特征

I. CO型坑点斑大都分布在釉表面凸起处。

II. CO型坑点斑所在处釉表面只见纤细收敛的C形纹或O形纹，清晰独立。

III. CO型坑点斑所在处釉表面通常只见纤细收敛的C形纹或O形纹，以及面积小于或等于坑点斑二

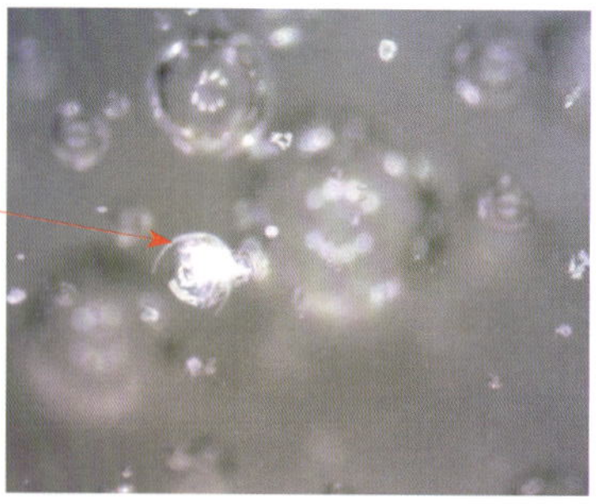

图5-1-102

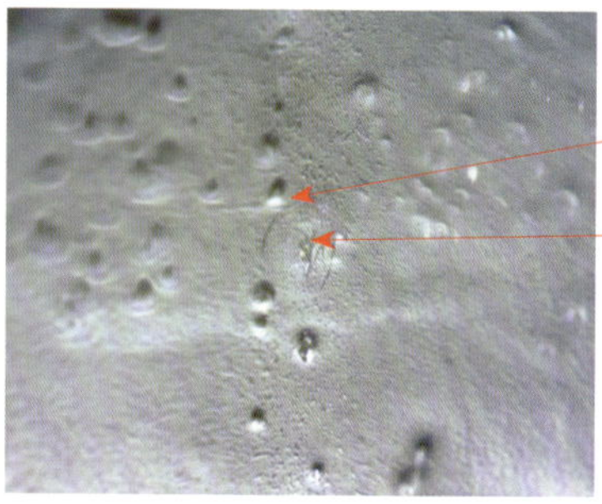

图5-1-103

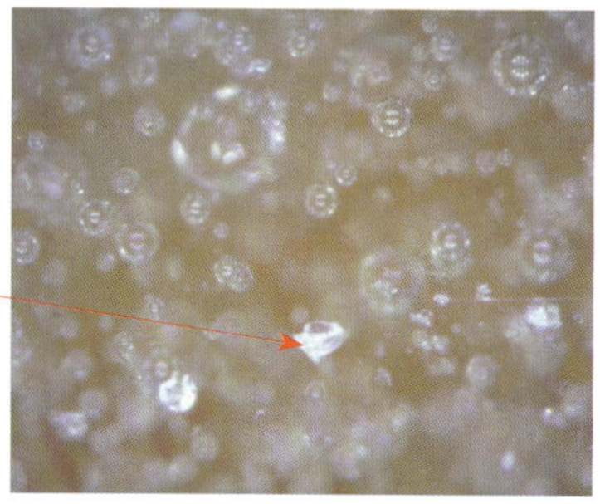

图5-1-104

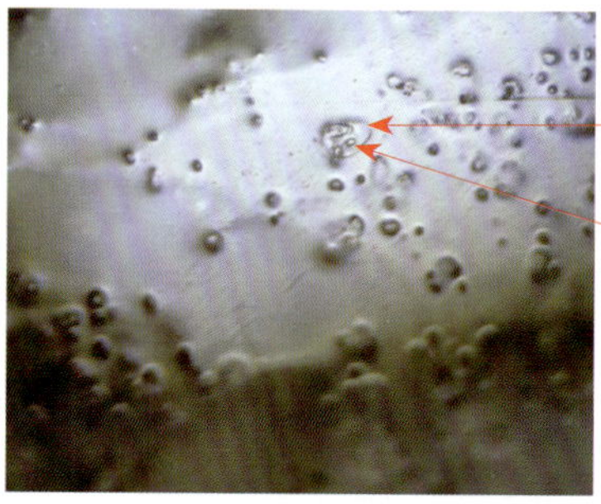

图5-1-105

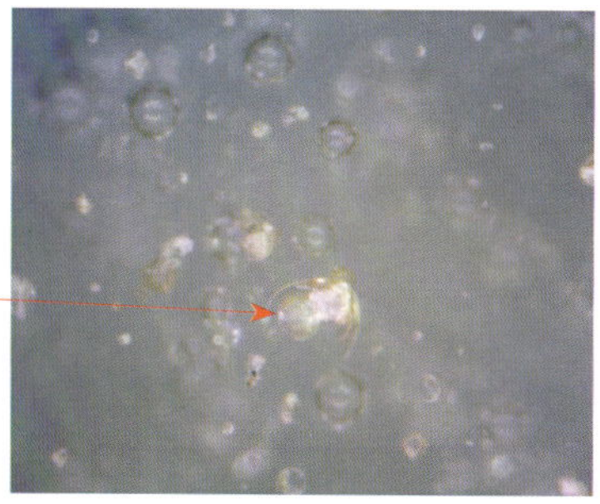

图5-1-106

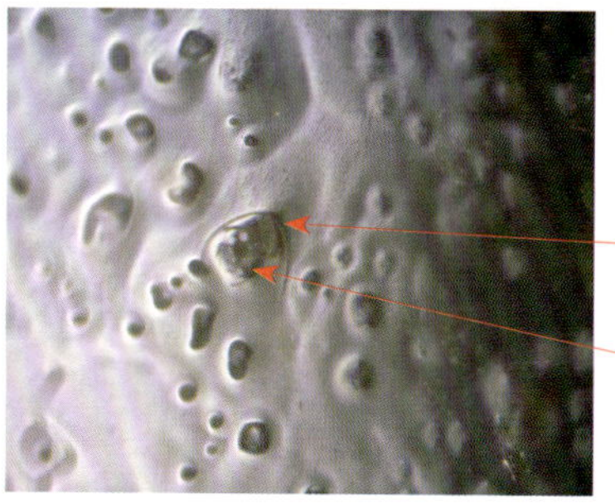

图5-1-107

维面积的风化斑块，斑块收敛，无扩张感，彼此界线分明。

IV.CO型坑点斑与周围玻璃相或其他迹型种类界线分明。

见图5-1-102、图5-1-103，二者为同一器物同一位置图片，图5-1-102为二维图片，图5-1-103为三维图片。

图5-1-102中箭头所指的CO型坑点斑，坑点斑紧挨C形纹，但在图5-1-103中只见C形纹及一处三维成像面积远远小于二维的深色斑块（见箭头A所指处），C形纹纹路纤细、收敛、清晰，斑块收敛，无扩张感。二者均与周围玻璃相界线分明。

箭头A所指的深色斑块是由C形纹继续风化发展而形成的风化斑块，风化斑块继续向釉层中发展，就逐渐形成深入釉层的CO型坑点斑，三维成像无法全面观察到深入釉层的坑点斑，所以面积显得比二维成像要小。

见图5-1-104、图5-1-105，二者为同一器物同一位置图片，图5-1-104为二维图片，图5-1-105为三维图片。

图5-1-104中的CO型坑点斑属于坑点斑与CO纹重叠，但在图5-1-105中仅见一条较大的C形纹（见箭头B所指处）及三处三维成像面积远远小于二维的较小CO纹（见箭头C所指处），C形纹纹路纤细、收敛、清晰，无扩张感。二者均与周围玻璃相界线分明。

见图5-1-106、图5-1-107，二者为同一器物同一位置图片，图5-1-106为二维图片，图5-1-107为三维图片。

图5-1-106中箭头所指的CO型坑点斑，坑点斑紧挨C形纹，但在图5-1-107中只见C形纹及一处三维成像面积小于二维的深色斑块（见箭头D所指处），C形纹纹路纤细、收敛、清晰，斑块收敛，无扩张感。二者均与周围玻璃相界线分明。

箭头D所指的深色斑块是由C

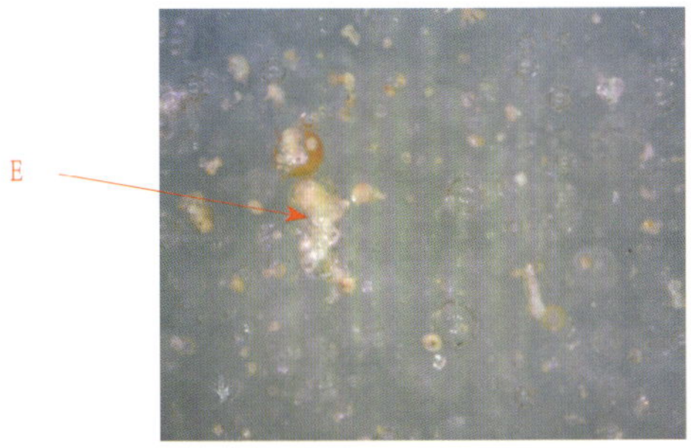

图5-1-108

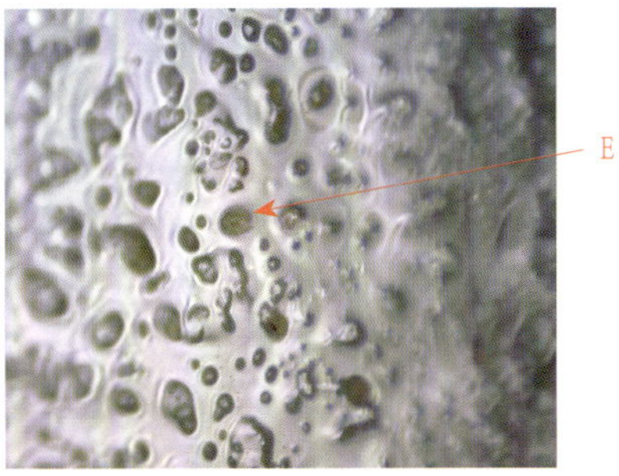

图5-1-109

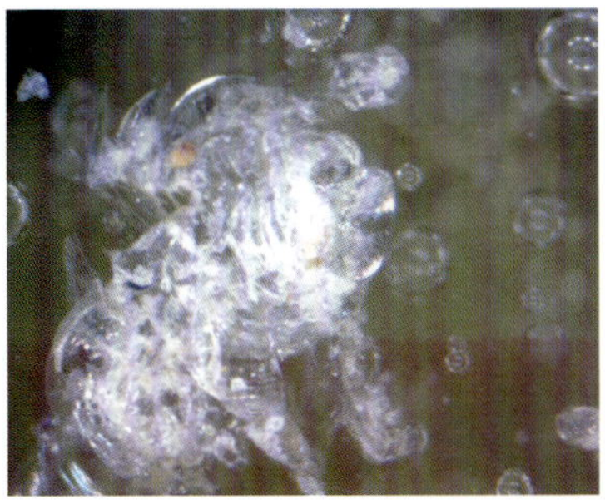
图5-1-110

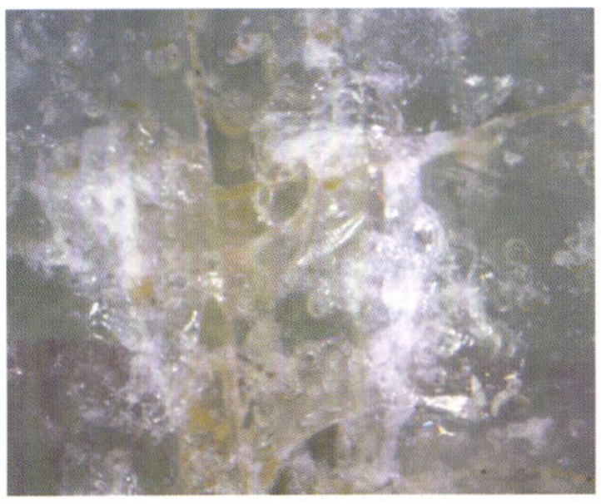
图5-1-111

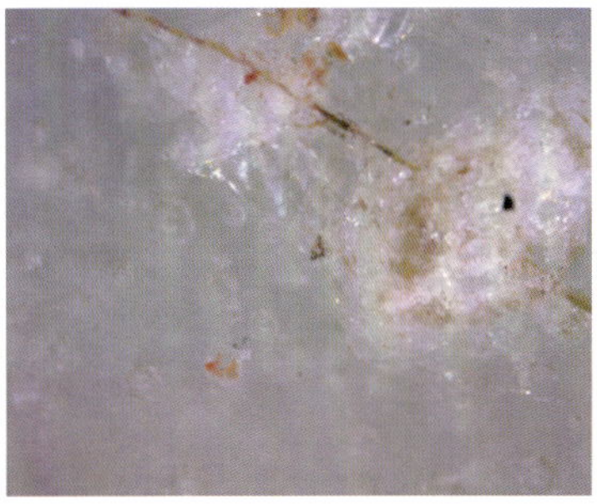
图5-1-112

图5-1-113

图5-1-114

图5-1-115

形纹继续风化发展而形成的风化斑块，风化斑块继续向釉层中发展，就逐渐形成深入釉层的CO型坑点斑，三维成像无法全面观察到深入釉层的坑点斑，所以面积显得比二维成像要小。

见图5-1-108、图5-1-109，二者为同一器物同一位置图片，图5-1-108为二维图片，图5-1-109为三维图片。

图5-1-108中的浅色CO型连环坑点斑群在图5-1-109中呈深色，三维成像面积明显比图5-1-108中的二维要小（见箭头E所指处），斑块E三维成像收敛，无扩张感，与周围玻璃相界线分明。

图5-1-109中的CO型连环坑点斑群是由C形纹、O形纹纵向往釉层中发展的结果，三维成像无法全面观察到深入釉层的坑点斑群，所以面积显得比二维成像要小。

一般来说，CO型坑点斑大都分布在釉表面凸起处。在图5-1-108和图5-1-109中，二维成像的CO型坑点斑，与三维成像中一个个凸起的“小山包”一一对应，釉表面没有凸起的地方光滑洁净。这是由于CO型坑点斑与玻璃相结合处的组织结构稳定性较差，容易风化；釉表面较平滑处组织结构稳定性较好，风化强度低，表现光滑洁净。

B. 外伤型坑点斑

外伤型坑点斑二维特征

I. 外伤型坑点斑通常形状不规则，大都有颜色变化（见图5-1-110—图5-1-115）。

II. 面积较大的坑点斑还能够观察到斑块内的针眼斑和沉积物（见图5-1-110—图5-1-114）。

C. 浸水型坑点斑

a. 浸水型坑点斑二维特征

见图5-1-116、图5-1-117。

I. 浸水型坑点斑可以出现在釉表面任何地方，分布随机。

图5-1-116

图5-1-117

图5-1-118

图5-1-119

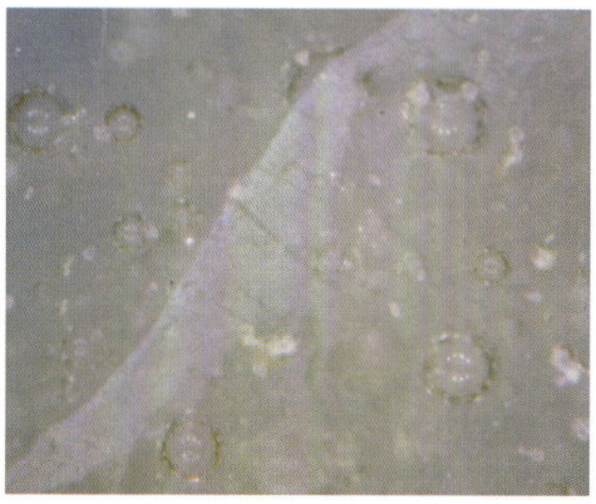
图5-1-120

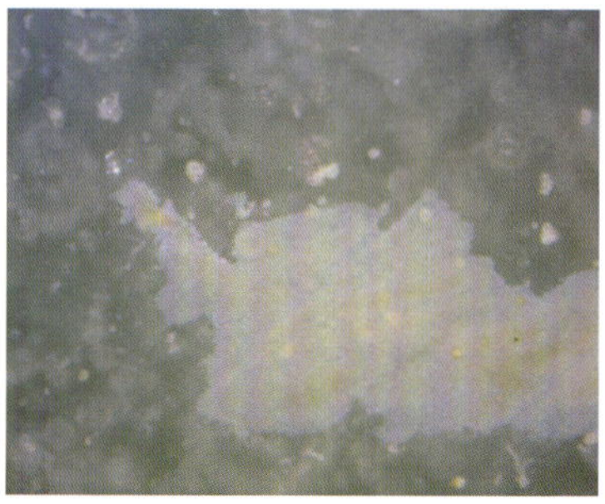
图5-1-121

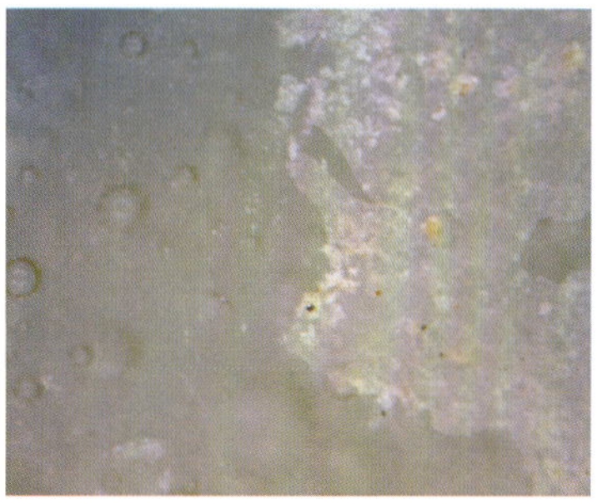
图5-1-122

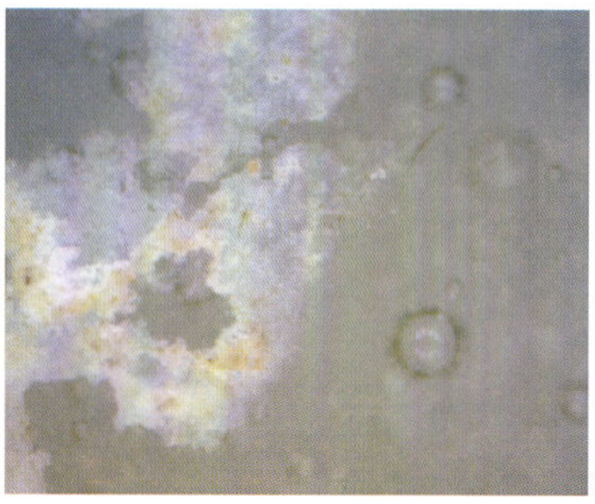
图5-1-123

图5-1-124

II. 浸水型坑点斑有的呈圆形或椭圆形，也有的呈不规则形状。有时坑点斑内可见磨砂针眼斑或沉积物。

III. 浸水型坑点斑与周围玻璃相界线分明。

b. 浸水型坑点斑三维特征

见图5-1-118、图5-1-119。

I. 浸水型坑点斑三维显微特征为明显凹陷的凹坑，形状有圆形或椭圆，也有不规则形，凹坑边沿圆滑。

II. 有时凹坑内可见沉积物。

（3）物盖斑

① 物盖斑概念

物盖斑是龙泉窑系青瓷在后天环境影响下，釉表面被外界物质覆盖而形成的斑块。

② 物盖斑形成

龙泉窑系青瓷上的物盖斑大都是后天环境中的泥沙等物质长期覆盖在瓷器表面形成的，也有后来人们对瓷器修补时留下的黏合剂印记。

③ 物盖斑特征

物盖斑二维特征

a. 物盖斑颜色主要有黄色、褐色及灰白色（见图5-1-120—图5-1-127）。

b. 物盖斑与周围未被覆盖的底板界线是分明的，边界有直线、有曲线（见图5-1-120—图5-1-127）。

c. 物盖斑有层次，有的呈起皮状（见图5-1-121—图5-1-127）。

d. 有的物盖斑上有划痕（见图5-1-120）。

e. 修补瓷器留下的印记根据使用的化学用剂的不同，其物盖斑形貌也不同。有时黏合剂形成的物盖斑与针眼斑形貌相近，难以区分，必要时需要结合肉眼来观察瓷器。

（4）泡根斑

① 泡根斑概念

泡根斑是龙泉窑系青瓷在后天

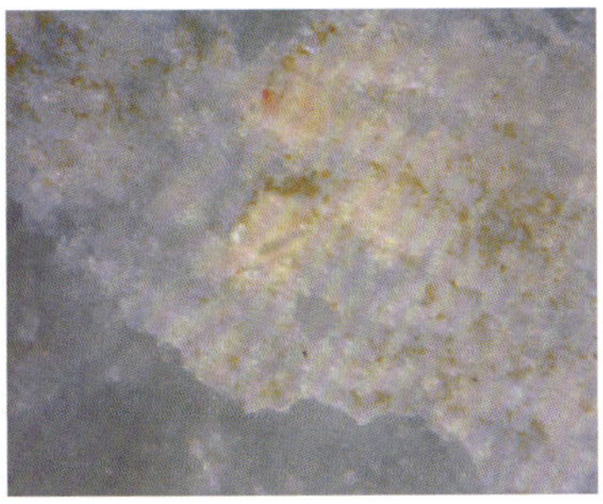
图5-1-125

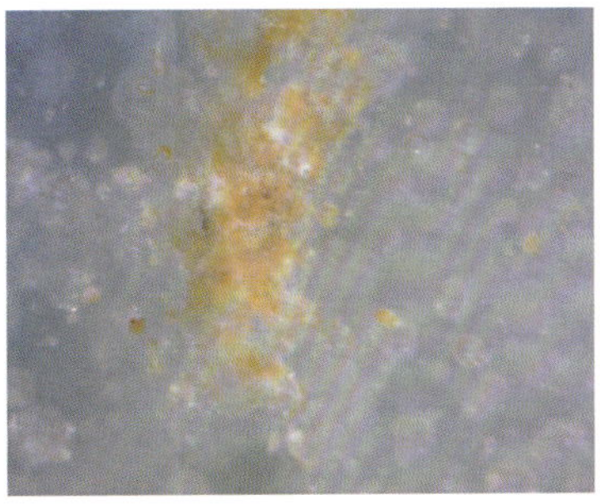
图5-1-126

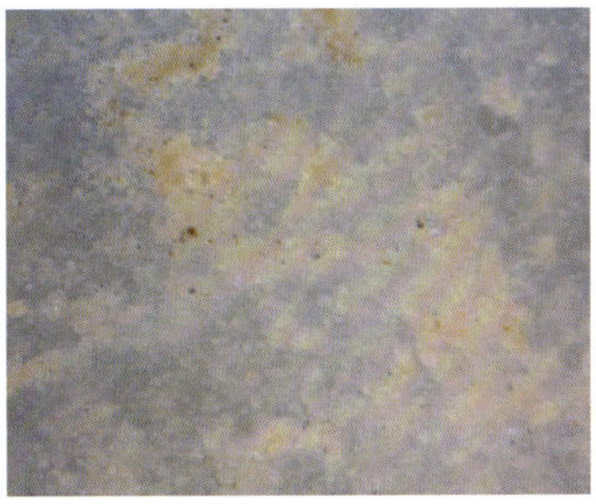
图5-1-127

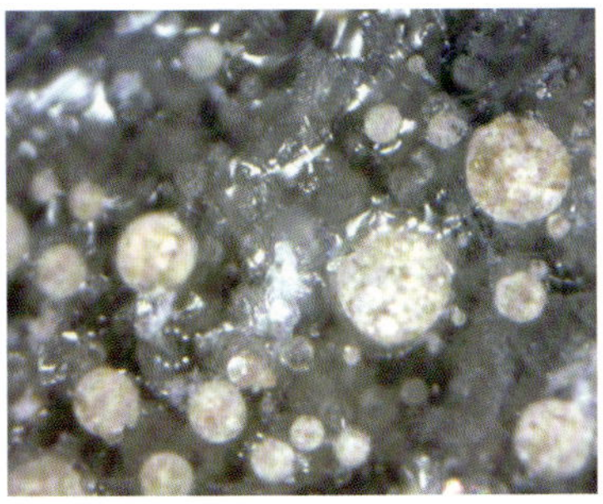
图5-1-128

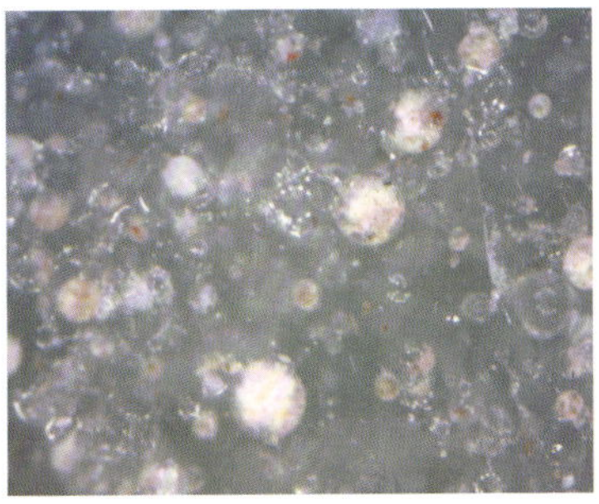
图5-1-129

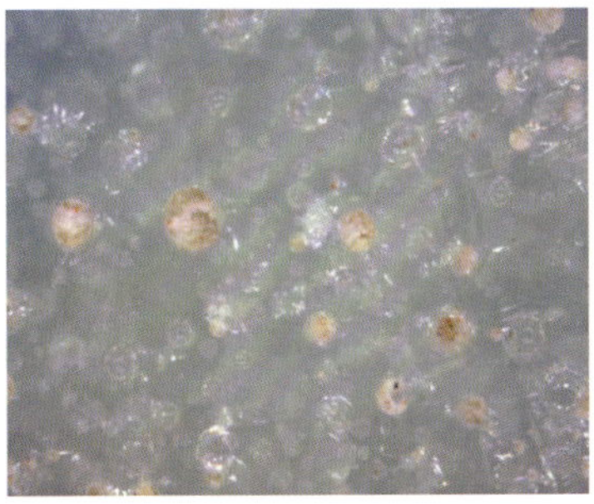
图5-1-130

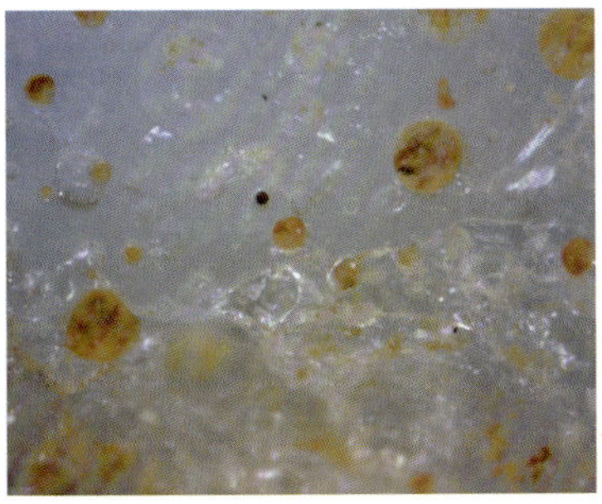
图5-1-131

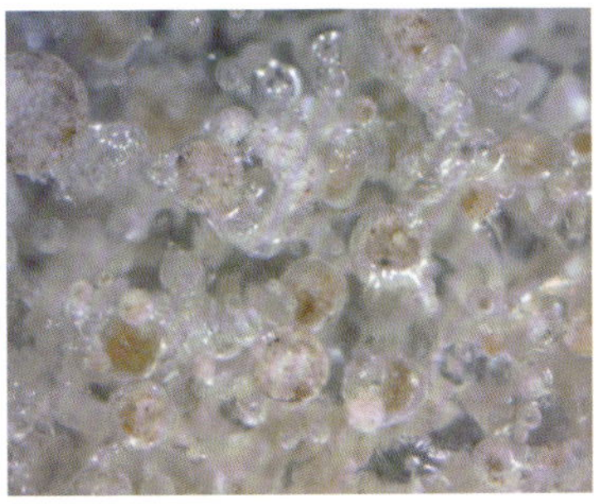
图5-1-132

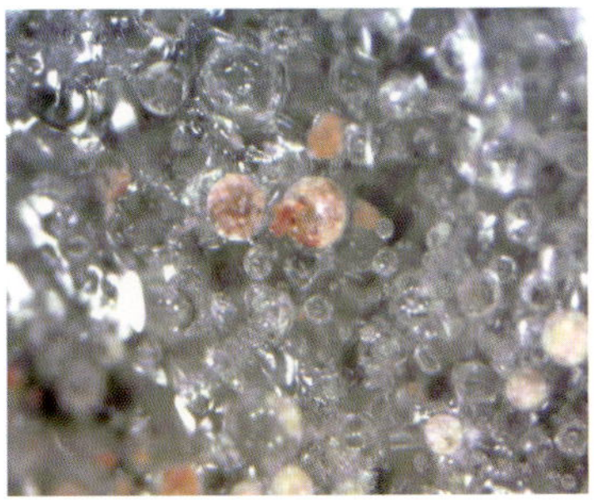
图5-1-133

环境影响下，由破口泡发展形成，内有沉积物的凹形斑块。

② 泡根斑形成

青瓷的釉表面被风化侵蚀或磨损后，存在于釉层中的部分气泡无釉层包裹，完全暴露在外界环境中，变成泡根，形成深浅不一的凹坑，外界物质长期在泡根内沉积形成泡根斑。一般来说，瓷器的口沿处易形成泡根斑。在风化强度普遍比较高的海捞瓷上，泡根斑在瓷器上各处都可以出现。

③ 泡根斑特征

泡根斑二维特征

a. 泡根斑大部分是圆形，也有椭圆形和不规则形貌（见图5-1-128—图5-1-139）。

b. 泡根斑颜色有白色、黄色、褐色及黑色等（见图5-1-128—图5-1-139）。

c. 有的同一泡根斑有色阶变化（见图5-1-138、图5-1-139）。

d. 邻近的泡根斑有色差变化（见图5-1-137—图5-1-139）。

（5）絮状斑

① 絮状斑概念

絮状斑是以白色为主，呈无序状，具有流淌、渗透、漫延趋势的不规则斑块。它是龙泉窑系青瓷在后天环境影响下，在其釉表面及釉层中，由可溶盐、难溶盐和灰尘等物质沉积形成的。

② 絮状斑形成

青瓷釉表面随机分布有裂纹或

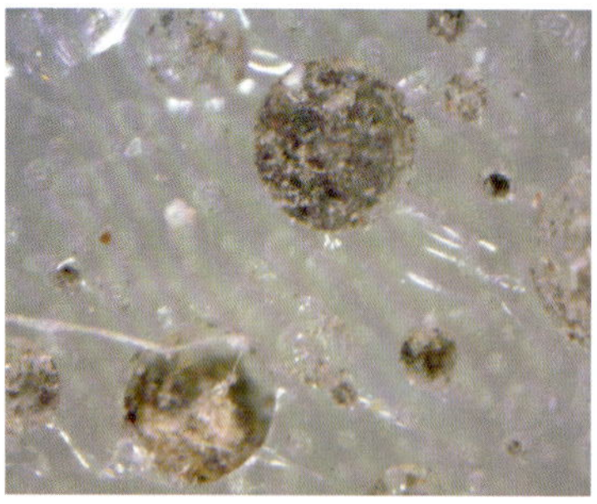
图5-1-134

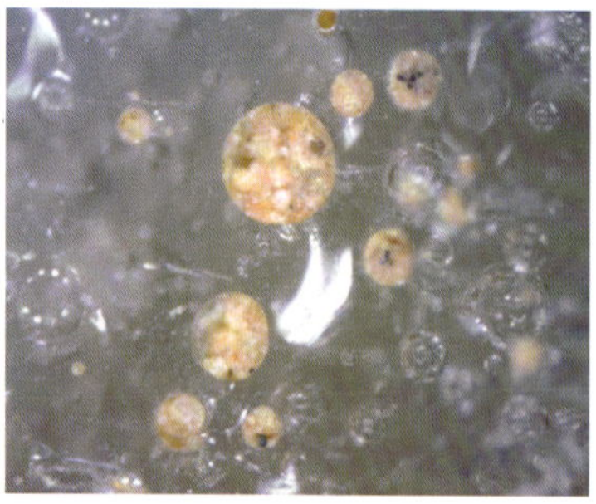
图5-1-135

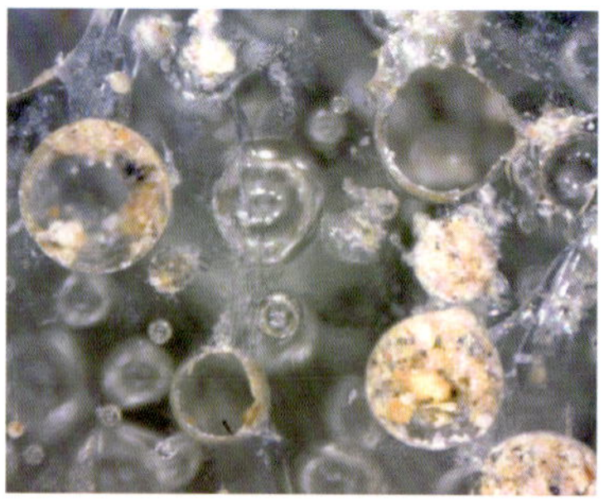
图5-1-136

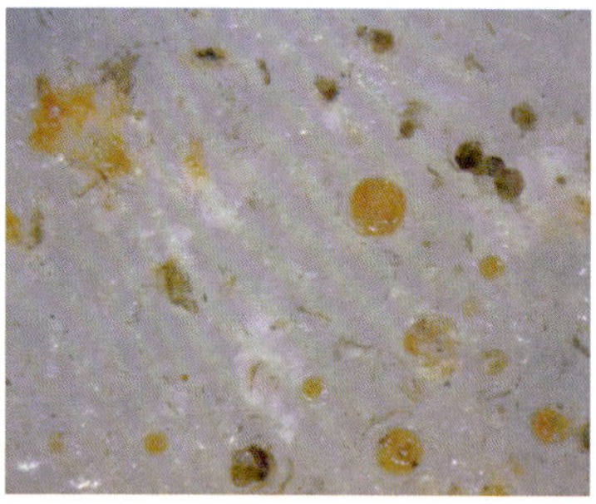
图5-1-137

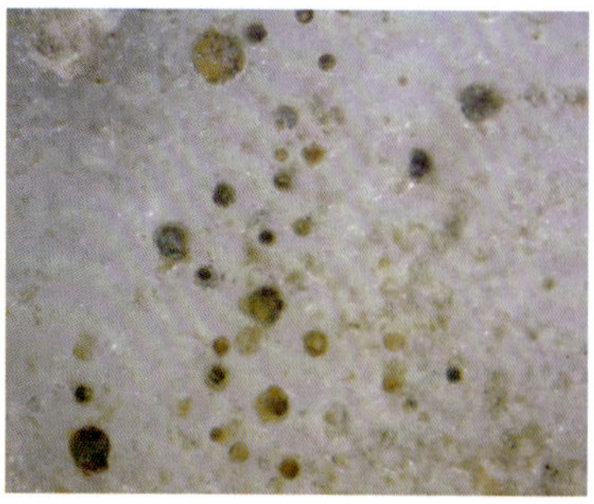
图5-1-138

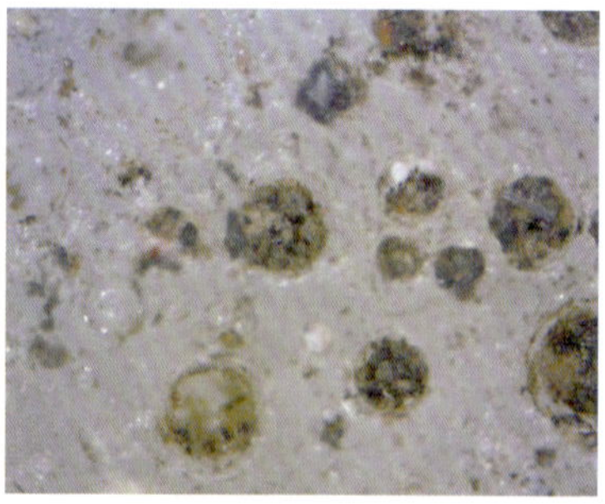
图5-1-139

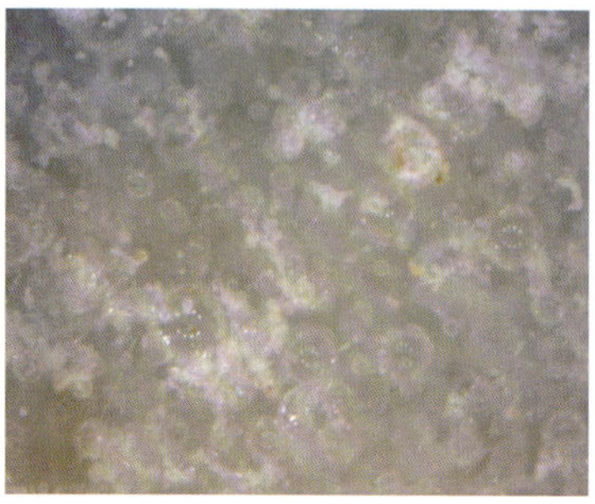
图5-1-140

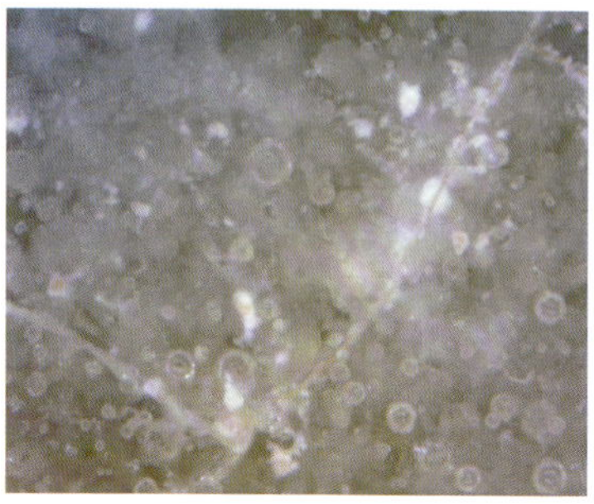
图5-1-141

图5-1-142

孔隙。此外，大气及土壤中具有一定酸性或碱性的水溶液会侵蚀青瓷釉表面，在釉表面形成新的裂纹或孔隙。外界物质通过这些裂纹和孔隙进入釉层，在釉层中形成可溶盐及难溶盐。当土壤中水分蒸发，可溶盐在釉表面及釉层中析出。在釉表面的可溶盐易因溶于水而流失，难溶盐也易掉落，所以絮状斑在釉表面存在的概率较小，普遍存在于釉层中。在干湿交替的环境中，渗入釉层中的难溶盐难以流失，可溶盐会在水分蒸发后的釉层中形成结晶，它们连同一些细小灰尘在釉层中叠加沉积形成絮状斑。土壤中的及釉表面的阴阳离子会发生反应，形成不同颜色的难溶盐沉积物。

③ 絮状斑特征

A. 絮状斑二维特征

见图5-1-140—图5-1-145。

a. 絮状斑以白色为主，一般都以块状、片状等不规则形貌分布在釉层中，大小不一。

b. 絮状斑一般在釉层组织结构稳定性较差处或破损处出现，如坑点斑下方、物盖斑下方、釉裂纹下方、C形、O形纹下方、划痕下方、鬃眼下方和其他釉损处下方等。

c. 絮状斑由釉损处呈梯度向周边的釉下扩散。斑块中心色白如牛奶，不透明；斑块边沿呈绒状，半透明，有向四周蔓延的趋势。

B. 絮状斑三维特征

a. 絮状斑在釉表面不可见，釉表面釉损处（如坑点斑、釉裂纹）的面积远远小于釉损处与絮状斑二维成像面积的总和。

b. 釉表面釉损处以外的地方光滑洁净，无其他明显的大面积损伤。

见图5-1-146、图5-1-147，二者为同一器物同一位置图片，图5-1-146为二维图片，图5-1-147为三维图片。

图5-1-146中的白色絮状斑在图5-1-147中难以观察到，釉表面只见釉裂纹，无其他明显损伤，说明絮状斑存在于釉层中（见箭头A所指处）。

三、总结

龙泉窑系斑块分为先天性斑块和后天性斑块两大类型。

龙泉窑系先天性斑块的多样性，主要是由釉料及烧制工艺的不同所致。所以龙泉窑系先天性斑块从一定程度上能够反映当时制作龙泉窑系青瓷的用材及烧制工艺。龙泉窑系后天性斑块，主要是由其后天的存放环境和环境变化的差异造成的。龙泉窑系青瓷上后天性斑块呈现出多样性，能够说明龙泉窑系青瓷的迹型生成与环境变化的相关性，它们的特征符合陶瓷迹型变化的量变原理及时间过程性原理，也体现了陶瓷迹型形成与变化的诸规律。

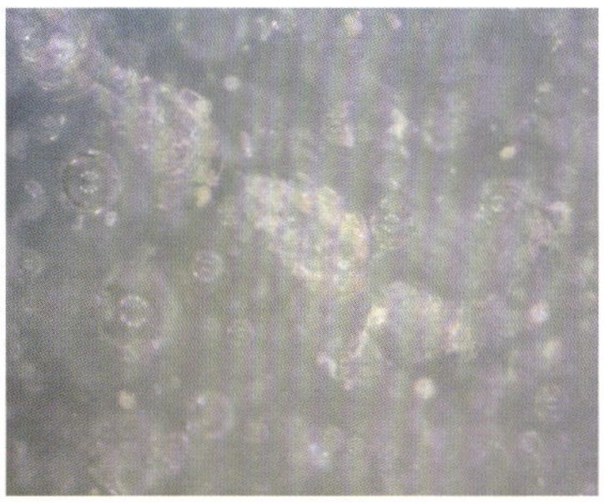

图5-1-143

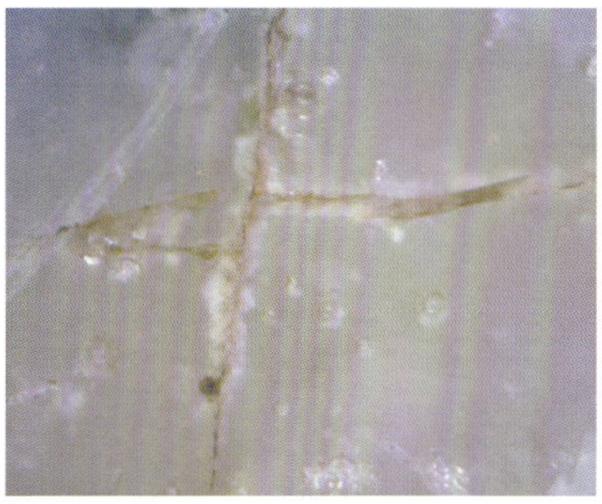

图5-1-144

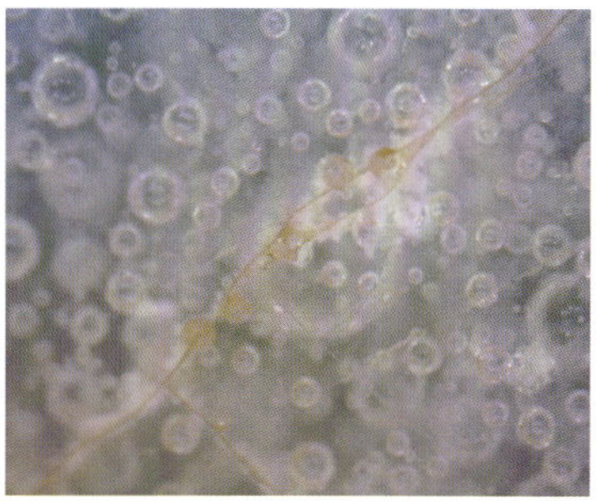

图5-1-145

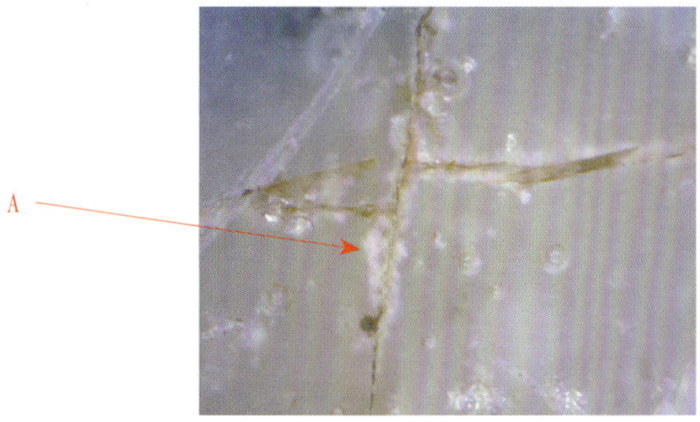

图5-1-146

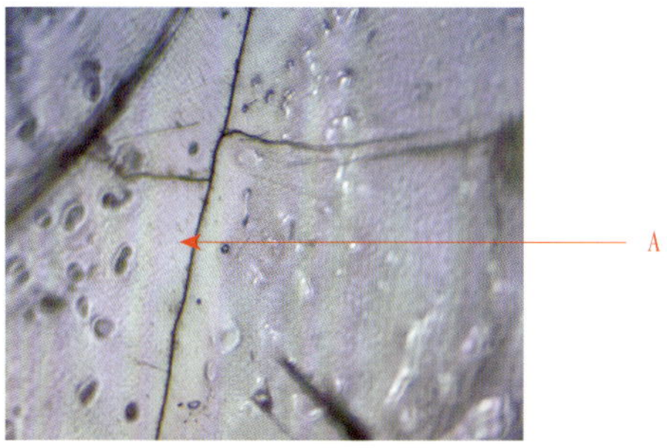

图5-1-147

第二节 龙泉窑系青瓷纹路类别

一、龙泉窑系青瓷纹路概念

龙泉窑系青瓷纹路是龙泉窑系青瓷在烧制过程中和后天环境影响下形成的，是以线状、条状、网状等形貌分布在釉表面和釉层中的迹型类别。

二、龙泉窑系青瓷纹路种类

（一）流淌纹

1. 流淌纹概念

流淌纹是以线状、条状、网状等形貌分布在龙泉窑系青瓷釉表面和釉层中的纹路。它的主要成分有铁氧化物及锰氧化物等，是在龙泉窑系青瓷烧制过程中和后天环境影响下形成的。

2. 流淌纹形成

青瓷在高温烧制时，釉料会逐渐熔化成熔融态。在浮力、表面张力及气泡搅动的作用下，釉料中的铁氧化物和锰氧化物易在气泡边沿积聚，部分会随气泡升至釉表面，顺着凹凸不平的釉表面向四周扩散，流动铺展，并结晶析出，也可能产生分相。当温度下降时，会有更多结晶析出，铁氧化物及锰氧化物数量多的形成斑块，铁氧化物及锰氧化物少的形成纹路，就是流淌纹。

釉层中未升至釉表面的铁离子在高温下熔融在釉料中，釉层冷却凝固时在釉层中形成碘酒纹。

位于釉表面，铁氧化物及锰氧化物含量较高的流淌纹形貌为凹槽，更易风化，就是阴纹。这些阴纹呈现不同形貌。

釉表面SiO_2含量较高的流淌纹相对凸起，不易被风化，为阳纹。

3. 流淌纹分类

龙泉窑系青瓷上的流淌纹主要可分为三类：碘酒纹、阴纹、阳纹。

（1）碘酒纹

碘酒纹概念

碘酒纹是龙泉窑系青瓷在烧制过程中形成的，存在于釉层中的褐色流淌纹。

（2）阴纹

① 阴纹概念

阴纹是龙泉窑系青瓷在烧制过程中及后天环境影响下形成的凹形流淌纹。

② 阴纹种类

阴纹可分成中空型阴纹及针眼型阴纹。

A. 中空型阴纹概念

中空型阴纹是纹路未被针眼斑完全覆盖的阴纹。

B. 针眼型阴纹概念

针眼型阴纹是纹路被针眼斑完全覆盖的阴纹。

③ 阴纹分布

阴纹主要出现在流淌斑处。中空型阴纹通常不会出现在沙滩斑上，大都出现在玻璃相上。针眼型阴纹主要出现在流淌斑上。

④ 阴纹特征

A. 中空型阴纹特征

a. 中空型阴纹二维特征

见图5-2-1—图5-2-3。

I. 中空型阴纹有粗有细，一般都有两条白色细边，细边夹住的中间部分主要成分为玻璃相，风化作用不明显，未完全被针眼斑覆盖，所以纹路内部像是“中空”的。

II. 中空型阴纹的两条细边若隐若现，明暗度有差异。

Section 2 :

Longquan Kiln System Celadon Striae Category

1. LKSC Striae Defined

LKSC Striae are the category of line, stripe, and web shaped appearances, created during the firing process and acquired under the influences of the post-firing environment, that are disbursed across the glaze surface and within the glaze level of LKSC.

2. Types of LKSC Striae

A. Flowing Striae

a. Flowing Striae Defined

Flowing Striae are line, stripe, and web shaped appearances across the surface and within the glaze level of LKSC, created during the firing process or acquired under the influences of the post-firing environment, that consist primarily of Iron and Manganese Oxide.

b. Formation of Flowing Striae

During the firing of LKSC, glaze gradually transitions into a molten state. Due to the buoyancy, surface tension and movement of the air bubbles within the glaze level, the Iron and Manganese Oxides in the glaze collect around the edges of gaseous bodies within the glaze, and rise with these bubbles to the surface of the glaze. According to the uneven topography of the surface, these compounds diffuse and flow across the glaze surface and crystallize, some producing split phases. When the temperature drops, more crystallization can occur. Areas of higher Iron and Manganese amounts culminate to form mottles, and areas of lower amounts accumulate into channels, called flowing striae.

Iron ions that remained within the molten glaze level, when the glaze cools and solidifies, can pull together to form iodine striae.

On the surface of the glaze, flowing striae with relatively high Iron and Manganese form concave troughs, called depressed striae. These depressed striae can assume a variety of appearances.

Surface level flowing striae in which the amount of SiO_2 is relatively high, are not easily weathered and form convex furrows, called raised striae.

c. Types of Flowing Striae

As per above, there are three types of Flowing Striae: Iodine Striae, Depressed Striae and Raised Striae.

I. Iodine Striae

Iodine Striae Defined

Formed during the firing of LKSC, these striae are present within the glaze level and are brown colored flowing striae.

II. Depressed Striae

i. Depressed Striae Defined

Concave flowing striae formed during firing and under the influences of the post-firing environment of LKSC.

ii. Types of Depressed Striae

Empty Striae and Needlepoint Striae are the two types of Depressed Striae.

(a) Empty Striae Defined

Depressed Striae that have not become completely

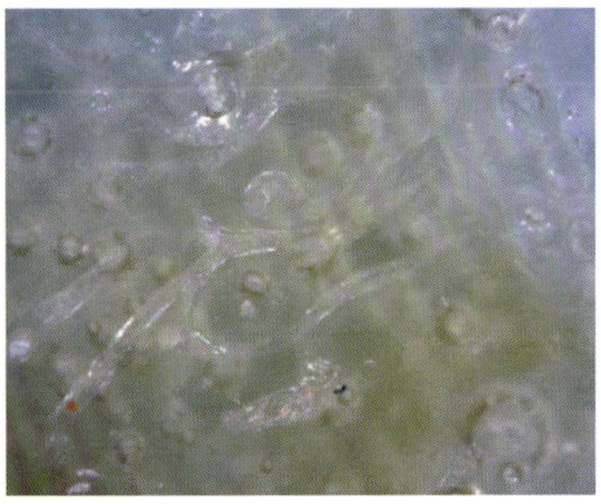
图5-2-1

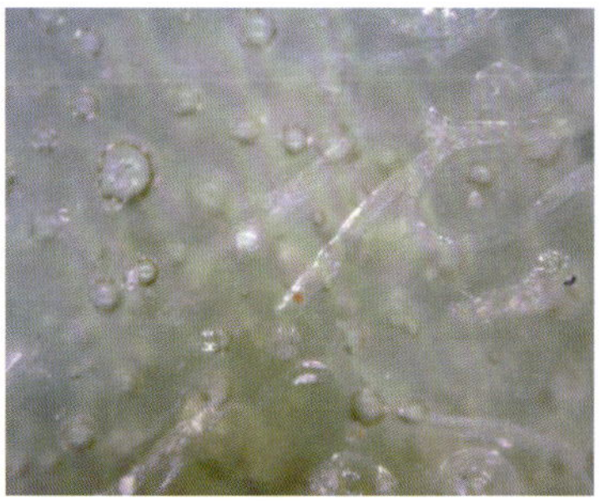
图5-2-2

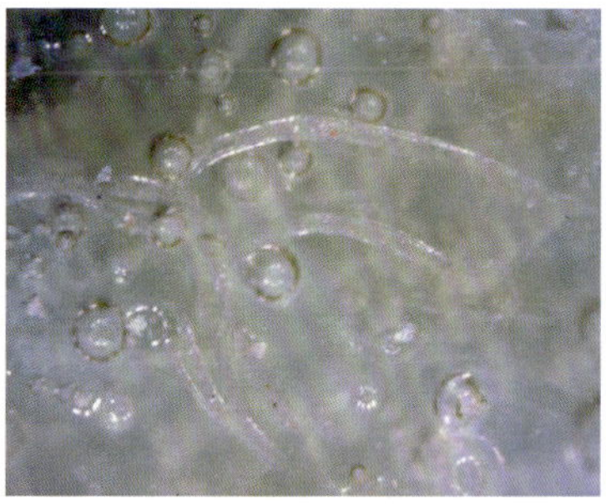
图5-2-3

b. 中空型阴纹三维特征

I. 中空型阴纹纹路剖面一般都呈“W”形（见图5-2-4）。

II. 中空型阴纹三维成像不明显，与釉层颜色相近，纹路脊部光滑洁净（见图5-2-5）。

B. 针眼型阴纹特征

a. 针眼型阴纹二维特征

见图5-2-6、图5-2-7。

针眼型阴纹通常与沙滩斑一起出现，纹路内的针眼斑大部分呈白色或橘黄色。

b. 针眼型阴纹三维特征

I. 龙泉窑系青瓷上的针眼型阴纹剖面大部分属于“U”形（见图5-2-8）。

II. 纹路凹槽内呈铁红色，内部可见针眼斑堆积。

III. 纹路与周围玻璃相界线分明。

见图5-2-9、图5-2-10，二者为同一器物同一位置图片，图5-2-9为二维图片，图5-2-10为三维图片。

图5-2-9中的浅色纹路在图5-2-10中呈深色，成像清晰。纹路呈凹陷状，进入釉层一定深度，与周围玻璃相界线分明（见箭头A所指处）。

图5-2-4

图5-2-8

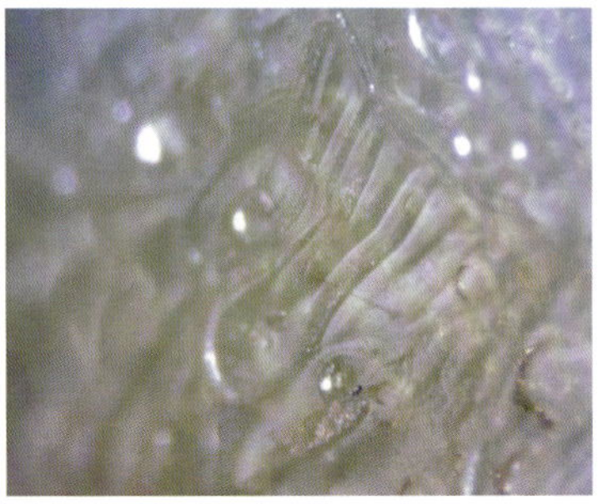
图5-2-5

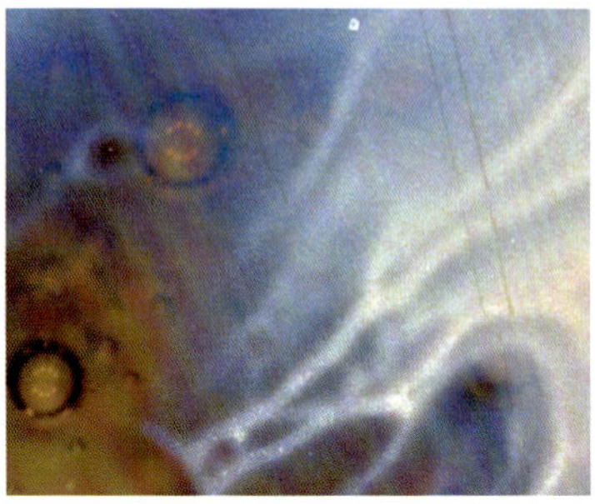
图5-2-6

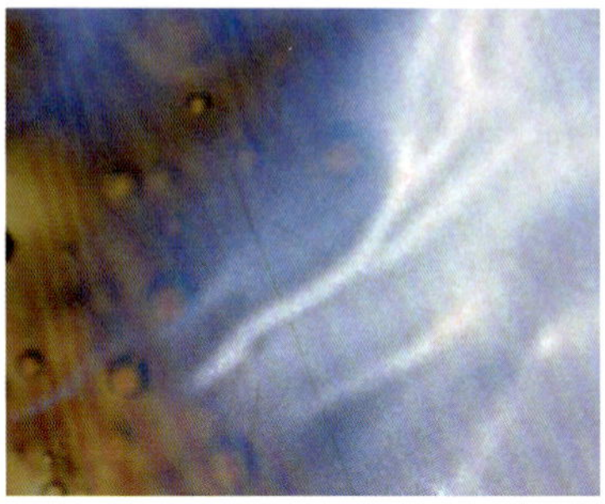
图5-2-7

covered by needlepoint mottling.

(b) Needlepoint Striae Defined

Depressed striae that have become covered by needlepoint mottling.

iii. Distribution of Depressed Striae

Depressed striae primarily present on areas of flowing mottles, they very rarely extend beyond the borders of said areas.

Empty striae do not occur over beach mottles, but rather areas of lower Iron Oxide to glass phase ratio.

Needlepoint striae generally occur in association with flowing mottles.

iv. Characteristics of Depressed Striae

(a) Characteristics of Empty Striae

(i) Two-dimensional Characteristics of Empty Striae

See pictures 5-2-1—5-2-3.

(1) Striae can be of varied width, usually occurring with two white outlines. The area between the outlines is primarily glass phase, thus resistant to weathering, allowing it to stay uncovered by needlepoint mottling, giving it an empty effect.

(2) Empty striae have two fine, lined edges with variation in clarity of appearance.

(ii) Three-dimensional Characteristics of Empty Striae

(1) Striae cross-section has an approximate W shape (see picture 5-2-4).

(2) Empty striae do not have clear depressed qualities, and retain similar coloration to the surrounding glaze. The interior troughs of the striae are usually smooth and clean (see picture 5-2-5).

(b) Characteristics of Needlepoint Striae

(i) Two-dimensional Characteristics of Needlepoint Striae

See pictures 5-2-6 and5-2-7.

Needlepoint Striae often occur in conjunction with beach mottles, needlepoint mottling within the striae often presents as white or yellowish-orange.

(ii) Three-dimensional Characteristics of Needlepoint Striae

(1) Striae cross-sections have approximate U shape (see picture 5-2-8).

(2) The striae trough usually presents with an iron-red coloration, and with needlepoint mottling visible within the interior.

(3) There is delineation between the striae and the surrounding glass phase.

See pictures 5-2-9 and 5-2-10, where 5-2-9 is the two-dimensional and 5-2-10 is the three-dimensional view of the same location.

The light colored striation indicated by Arrow A in picture 5-2-9 is the clearly depicted darker area in picture 5-2-10. The striation is concave and extends a certain depth into the glaze level, but retains delineation from the surrounding glass phase.

B. C and O Shaped Striae

a. C and O Shaped Striae Defined

C and O shaped lines consisting primarily of Iron, Manganese, and so forth metal Oxides; disbursed across the surface of LKSC glaze; that are acquired during the firing process and under the influence of the post-firing environment (simplified as CO Striae).

b. Formation of C and O Shaped Striae

During the firing of LKSC, the glaze slowly transitions into a molten state. Due to the buoyancy, glaze surface tension and movement of the air bubbles within the glaze level, Iron and Manganese Oxides within the glaze easily collect around the edges of gaseous bodies within the glaze, and rise with these bubbles to the surface of the glaze. According to the uneven topography of the surface, these compounds diffuse and flow across the glaze surface and crystallize, some producing split phases. When the temperature drops, more crystallization can occur. Under the influence of surface

A
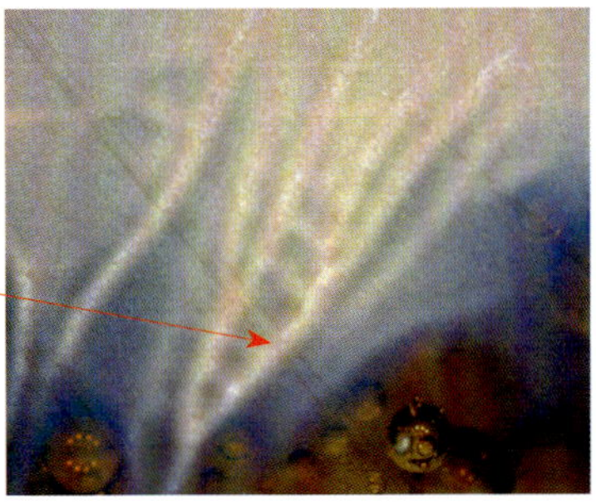

图5-2-9

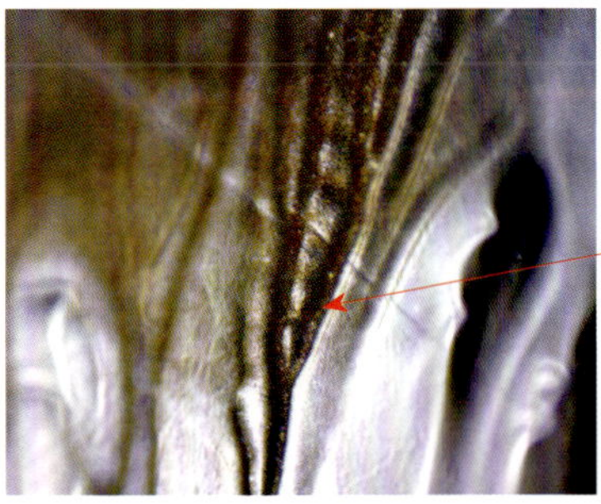
A

图5-2-10

（二）C形纹、O形纹

1. C形纹、O形纹概念

C形纹、O形纹是龙泉窑系青瓷在烧制过程中及后天环境影响下，以铁氧化物、锰氧化物等金属氧化物为主，以字母C、O形貌分布在釉表面的线形纹路。

2. C形纹、O形纹形成

龙泉窑系青瓷在高温烧制时，釉料会逐渐熔化成熔融态。在浮力、表面张力及气泡搅动的作用下，釉料中的铁氧化物和锰氧化物易于在气泡边沿积聚，部分会随气泡升至釉表面，并结晶析出，也可能产生分相。当温度下降时，会有更多结晶析出，在表面张力的作用下，析晶主要以环状形式存在于釉表面及釉层中。一般情况下，它们的化学稳定性不及玻璃相，而且两相结合处组织结构有缺陷，易风化，从而逐渐形成可被观察到的C形纹、O形纹。

另一方面，高温烧制龙泉窑系青瓷时，产生的气泡在熔融的釉料中不断上升，有的冲出釉表面。当釉料冷却凝固下来时，气泡冲出釉表面时留下的环状凹槽便会留在釉表面上，外界物质容易在釉表面的这些环状凹槽处沉积，逐渐风化形成C形纹、O形纹。

3. C形纹、O形纹分布

C形纹、O形纹一般都出现在玻璃相上。大都出现在釉表面凸起处（见图5-2-11箭头A所指处），也会在不明显凸起的地方出现（见图5-2-12箭头B所指处）。

通常龙泉窑系青瓷上的C形纹、O形纹二维成像不易被观察到。

4. C形纹、O形纹特征

（1）C形纹、O形纹二维特征

① C形纹、O形纹的基本形状以C形和O形为主：C形纹是半圆形貌的纹路，O形纹是圆形、椭圆形貌的纹路。（以下简称CO纹）

② CO纹纹路清晰，粗细不一，有的在同一条纹路上有粗细变化（见图5-2-13—图5-2-31）。

③ CO纹的颜色以白色和黄色居多，也可出现红褐色和黑灰色。有的单项CO纹有色阶变化，单位图片内邻近的CO纹有色差（见图5-2-13—图5-2-33）。

④ 单位图片内，CO纹通常分布稀疏，密集分布的情况较少（见图5-2-13—图5-2-33）。

⑤ CO纹继续风化，纹路线条逐渐变粗，C形弧线内或O形圈有白雾状蔓延，由透影发展至不透影，逐渐往坑点斑发展，最后形成CO纹与坑点斑共存的现象（见图5-2-23—图5-2-33）。

（2）C形纹、O形纹三维特征

① CO纹大都分布在釉表面凸起处。

A
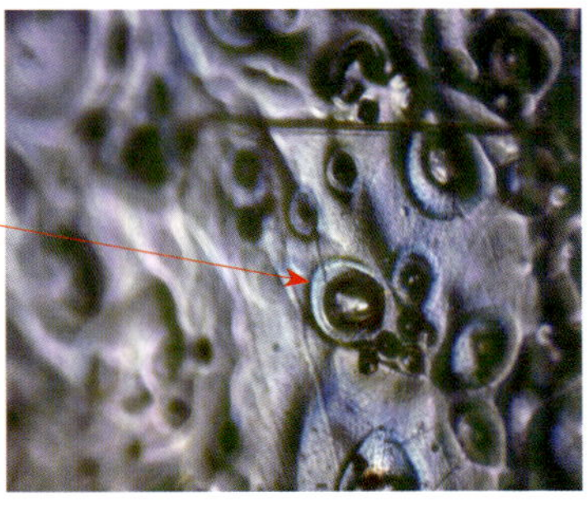

图5-2-11

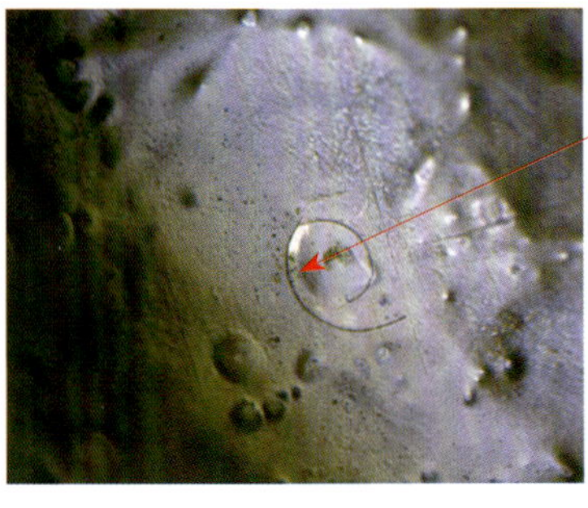
B

图5-2-12

tension of the glaze, some crystallizations form ring shapes on the glaze surface and within the glaze level. In general, these deposits are less chemically stable than the surrounding glass phase, and the areas where these two phases meet have structural integrity flaws; thus allowing for easier weathering, and as such form C and O shaped striae.

Additionally, during the firing of LKSC, gaseous bodies that rise up and erupt upon the surface of the molten glaze can leave a circular traces on the glaze surface. Foreign materials are easily deposited within the grooves present across the glaze surface, and these areas weather to become C and O shaped striae.

c. Distribution of C and O Shaped Striae

These striae all occur on the glass phase. The majority occur on areas of raised glaze surface (see area indicated by Arrow A in picture 5-2-11), but can also occur on areas of indistinct unevenness (see Arrow B in picture 5-2-12)

Often, the C and O shaped Striae on LKSC are not easily observed using two-dimensional imaging.

d. Characteristics of C and O Shaped Striae

I. Two-dimensional Characteristics of C and O Shaped Striae

i. C and O shaped striae primarily occur in C and O shapes: C shaped striae are semi-circle lines, and O shaped striae are circular and ovular lines.

ii. C and O shaped striae are clearly visible, with variations in thickness; some with thickness disparity occurring within a single striation (see pictures 5-2-13—5-2-31).

iii. Coloration is primarily white and yellow, but reddish-brown and ashen grey are also possible. Color variation within a single striation is possible, as well as color discrepancy between neighboring striae (see pictures 5-2-13—5-2-33).

iv. Distribution is often sparse, with dense distribution very rarely observed (see pictures 5-2-13—5-2-33).

v. As weathering continues, the striae gradually broaden, the interior of the C arc or O ring presents with white foggy coloration that disperses in to the glaze level. It gradually develops into a pit mottle, and finally presents as the aggregation of CO striae and pit mottles (see pictures 5-2-23—5-2-33).

II. Three-dimensional Characteristics of C and O Shaped Striae

i. Most CO striae occur at points of raised glaze surface.

ii. The striae are thin and reserved, markedly independent.

iii. It is common to observe white foggy coloration in association with C and O shaped striae with two-dimensional imaging, but the associated three-dimensional image only presents with a fine C or O shaped striation and mottle on the glaze surface; their observable size smaller than that which is visible in the two-dimensional image. The mottle is reserved and lacks dispersive qualities. There is clear delineation with the surrounding glass phase.

iv. Clear delineation between the striae and surrounding glass phase.

See pictures 5-2-34 and 5-2-35, where 5-2-34 is the two-dimensional and 5-2-35 is the three-dimensional view of the same location.

The C shaped striation in picture 5-2-34 is clearly visible in picture 5-2-35. The three-dimensionally visible striation is even more thin and reserved, and has clear delineation from the surrounding glass phase.

See pictures 5-2-36 and 5-2-37, where 5-2-36 is the two-dimensional and 5-2-37 is the three-dimensional view of the same location.

The C shaped striation indicated by Arrow D in picture 5-2-36 appears darker at the points of raised glaze surface in picture 5-2-37. Its end is forked, and is more fine and reserved than in picture 5-2-36. The three-dimensionally observable size is smaller than that of the two-dimensional weathered mottle, and it is reserved and lacking dispersive qualities.

See pictures 5-2-38 and 5-2-39, where 5-2-38 is the two-dimensional and 5-2-39 is the three-dimensional view of the same location.

The C shaped striation in picture 5-2-38 has associated white coloration, and appears in picture 5-2-39 as two clearly independent C shaped striae (see Arrow E).

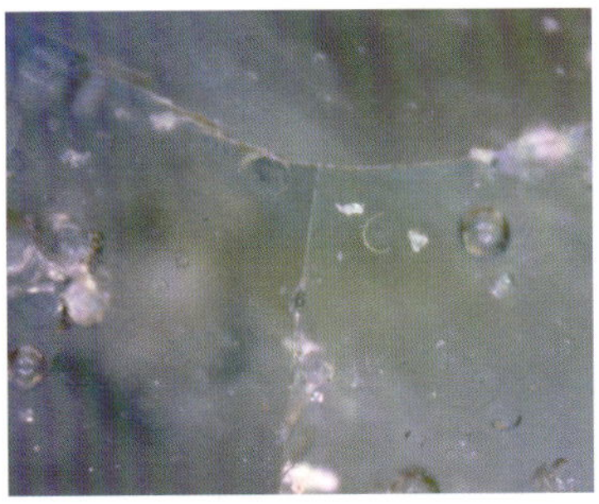
图5-2-13

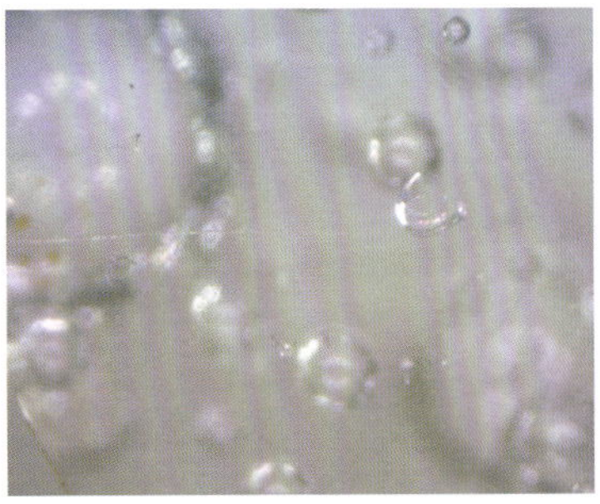
图5-2-14

图5-2-15

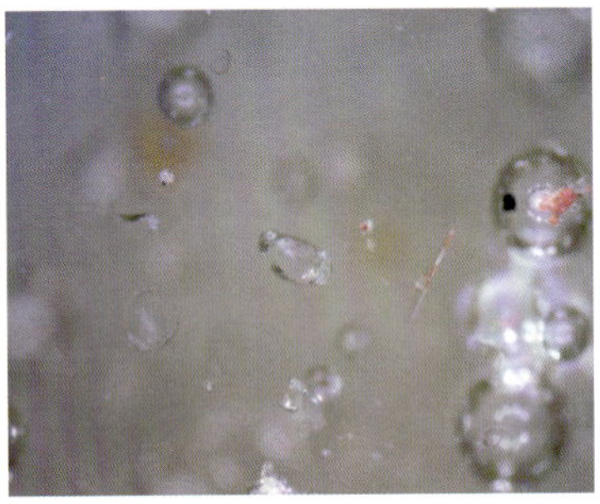
图5-2-16

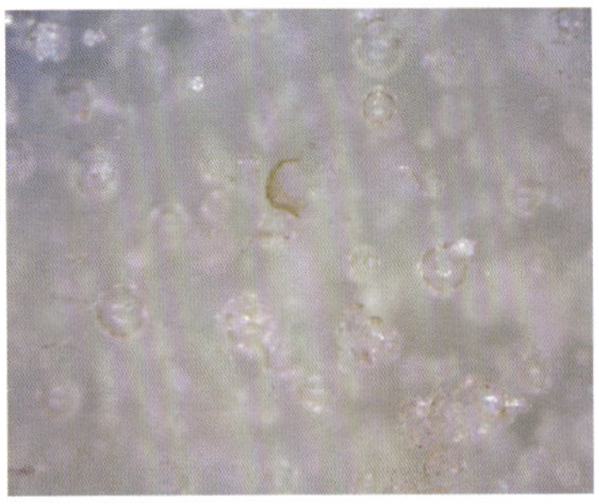
图5-2-17

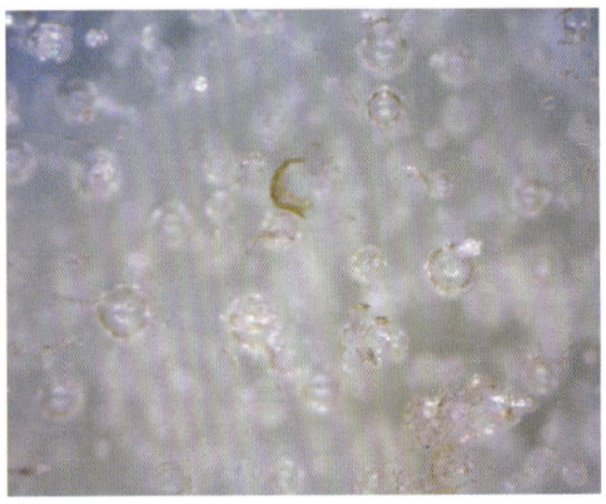
图5-2-18

图5-2-19

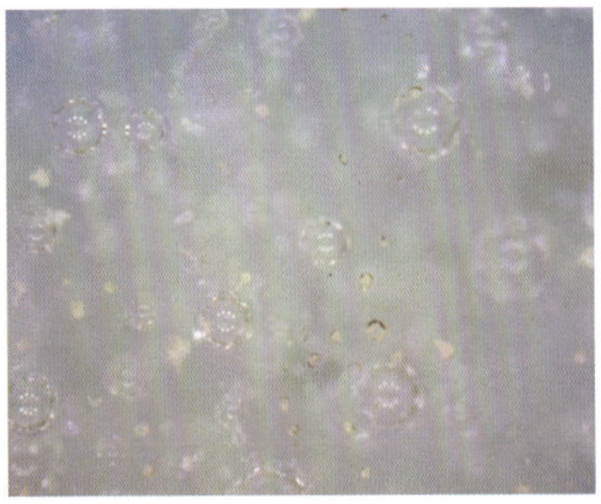
图5-2-20

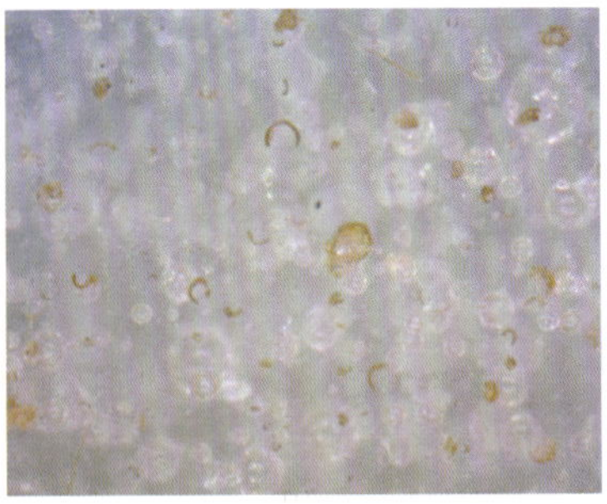
图5-2-21

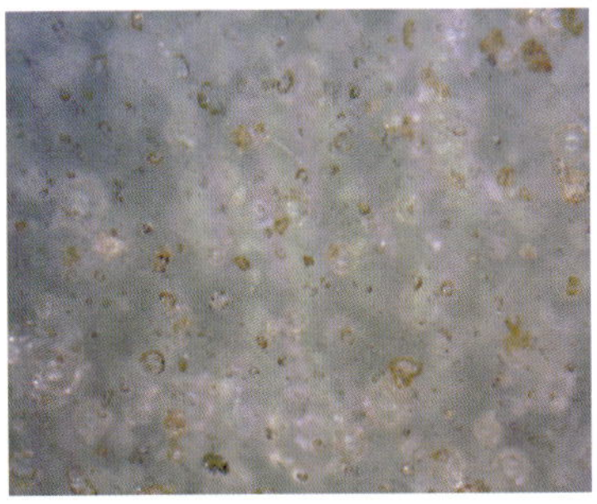
图5-2-22

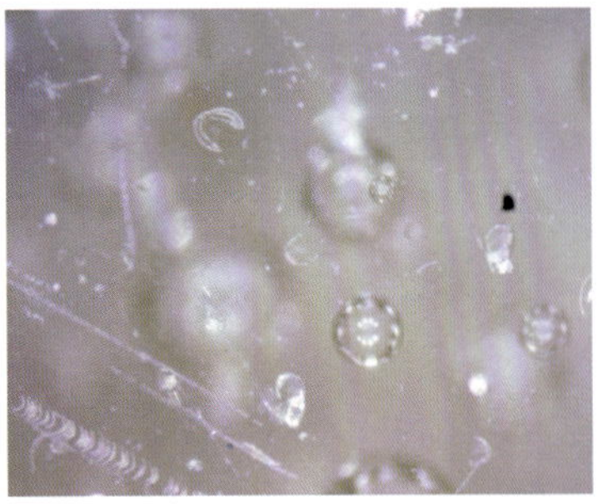
图5-2-23

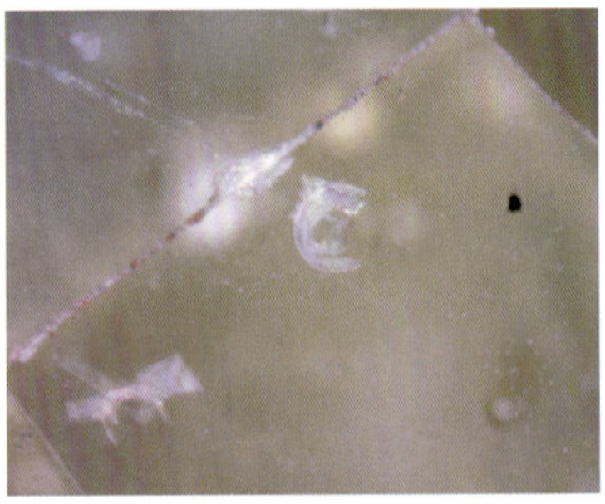
图5-2-24

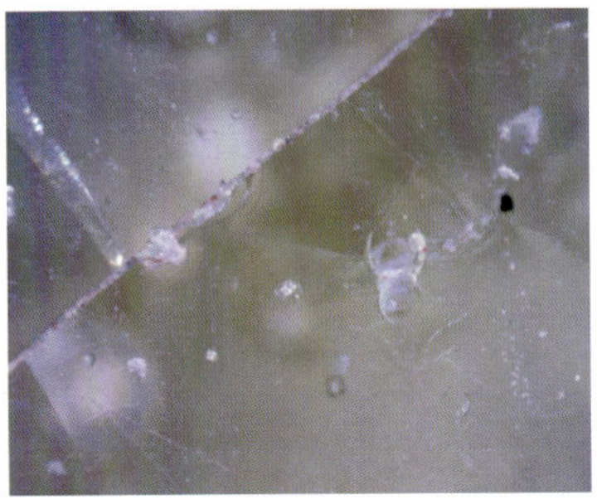
图5-2-25

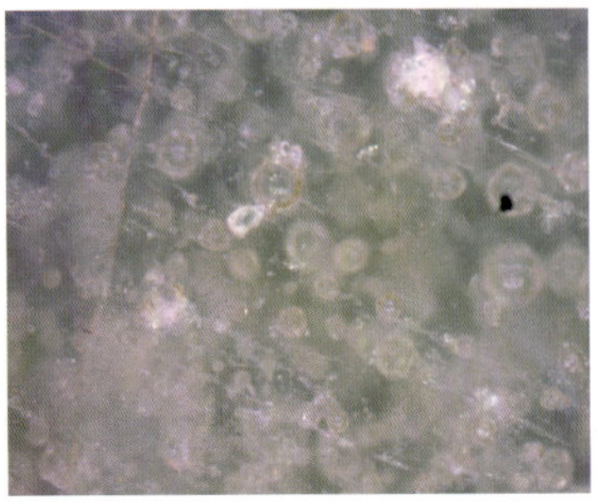
图5-2-26

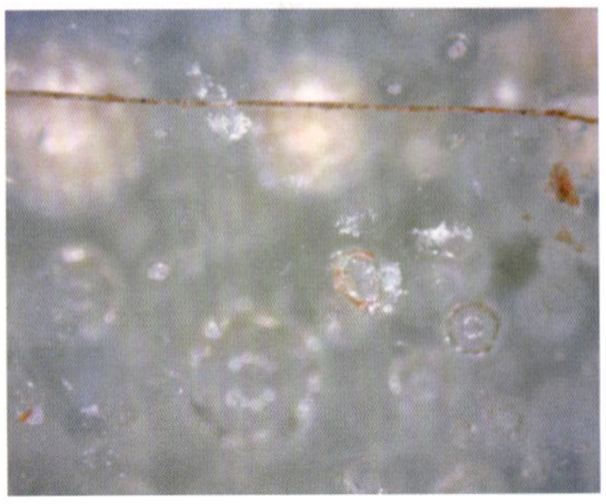
图5-2-27

They are clearly delineated from one another and from the surrounding glass phase.

C. Glaze Cracks

a. Glaze Cracks Defined

Also called crazing, Glaze Cracks are any appearance of straight, curved, or irregular lines splitting the glaze surface of LKSC that was caused either during firing or under the influence of the post-firing environment.

b. Formation of Glaze Cracks

Glaze cracks can be caused by any number of the following reasons:

i. During the firing process, the components of the glaze volatilize and create empty spaces. Due to the stress caused by the accumulation of these spaces into gaps, the glaze cracks.

ii. If the micro phases within the glaze expand at different rates, cracks in the glaze can occur.

iii. The stress tension caused by the R^+ and H^+ ion exchange of ≡Si—O—R, because of the H^+ ion being relatively smaller than the R^+ ion, can create glaze cracks [240].

iv. The composition of glaze and clay body being different, their expansion rates are also different. As the porcelain cools, stress is created, which the thicker glaze body can absorb, but the glaze reaches a breaking point at which it cracks.

v. Glaze lacks malleability. As such, when hard external forces collide with the glaze, the inability to absorb the blow can result in cracking.

Cracks are not necessarily a direct result of weathering; some are caused inherently during the firing process but some are indeed acquired under the influence of the post-firing environment. Additionally, not all cracks are visible under microscopic observation. If, after firing, the glaze encounters drastic temperature changes or the stress imposed by the crystallization of soluble salt or partially soluble salt deposits, the glaze cracks can become broadened.

There is a type of glaze crazing that is intentionally man-made, in the pursuit of aesthetic beauty, by utilizing the differences in body-glaze expansion rates. However, the crazing that presents on LKSC was not intentionally created with this sort of artistic outcome in mind. Therefore, crazing that presents is considered to be a glaze flaw.

c. Characteristics of Glaze Cracks

I. Two-dimensional Characteristics of Glaze Cracks

i. Cracks can occur as straight or curved lines (see pictures 5-2-40—5-2-60).

ii. Some cracks can occur with several cracks branching off of it (see pictures 5-2-40 and 5-2-41).

iii. Glaze cracks often present in association with white foggy coloration, and some have coloration of their own (see picture 5-2-42).

iv. Crack width spectrums have the following characteristics:

(a) No clear width spectrum (see pictures 5-2-43 and 5-2-44).

(b) With width spectrum (see picture 5-2-45).

v. Crack colorations have the following characteristics:

(a) No evident coloration (see pictures 5-2-46 and 5-2-47).

(b) Complete coloration but no evident color spectrum (see pictures 5-2-48 and 5-2-49).

(c) Color spectrum, colors include: White, yellow, brown, black and so forth (see pictures 5-2-40, 5-2-44, 5-2-45, 5-2-50 and 5-2-51).

vi. Crack surroundings characteristics include:

(a) Appearance of color change or textured bubbles (see pictures 5-2-52—5-2-55).

(b) Under the glaze coloration (see pictures 5-2-56 and 5-2-57).

(c) Deposits within the glaze crack (see pictures 5-2-45, 5-2-50, 5-2-58, 5-2-59).

(d) There is floccus mottling beneath the glaze crack (see picture 5-2-60).

II. Three-Dimensional Characteristics of Glaze Cracks

i. The three-dimensionally observable size is often smaller than the associated two-dimensional image.

ii. The three-dimensionally observable size of

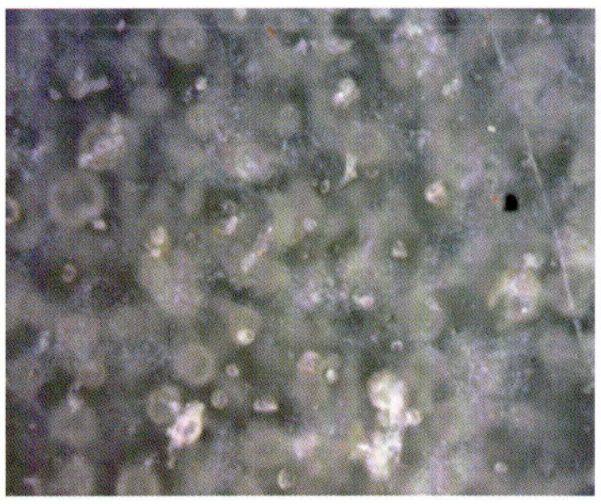
图5-2-28

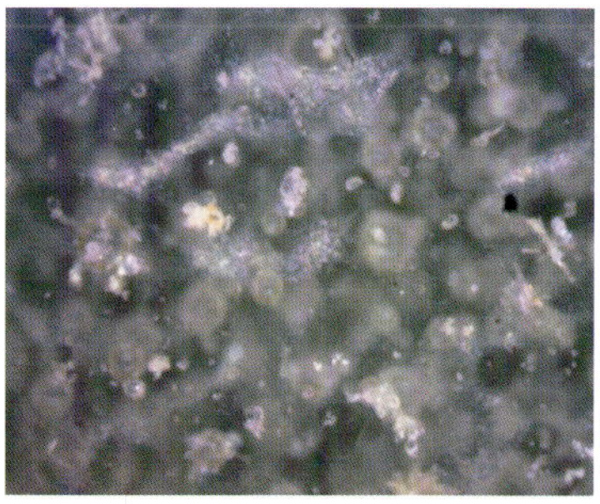
图5-2-29

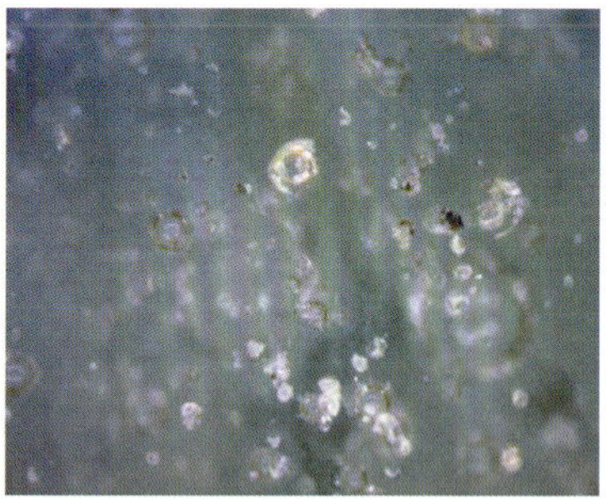
图5-2-30

图5-2-31

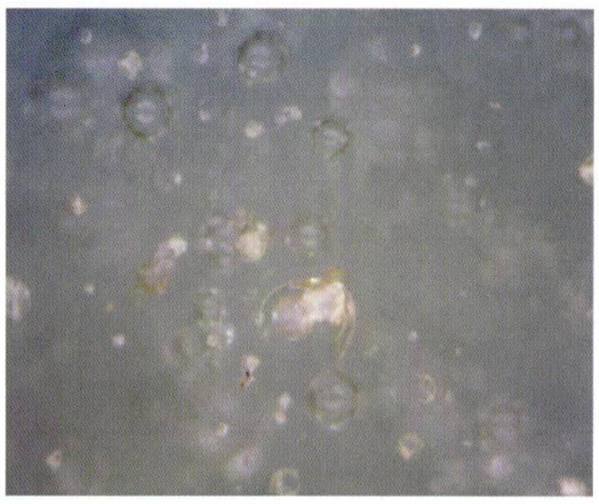
图5-2-32

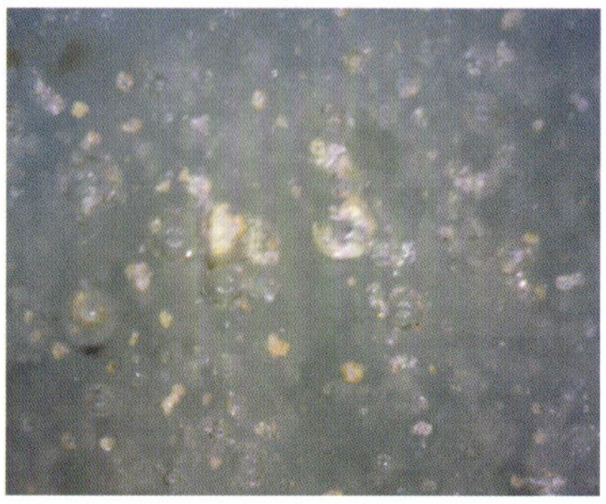
图5-2-33

② CO纹所在处釉表面只见纤细收敛的C形纹或O形纹，清晰独立。

③ 二维成像有呈白雾状蔓延趋势的CO纹，其所在处釉表面三维成像通常只见纤细收敛的C形纹或O形纹，以及面积小于或等于二维成像面积的风化斑块，斑块收敛，无扩张感，彼此界线分明。

④ CO纹与周围玻璃相界线分明。

见图5-2-34、图5-2-35，二者为同一器物同一位置图片，图5-2-34为二维图片，图5-2-35为三维图片。

图5-2-34中箭头C所指的C形纹在图5-2-35中成像清晰，而且纹路三维成像更加纤细收敛，与周边玻璃相界线分明。

见图5-2-36、图5-2-37，二者为同一器物同一位置图片，图5-2-36为二维图片，图5-2-37为三维图片。

图5-2-36中箭头D所指的C形纹在图5-2-37中分布在釉表面凸起处，末端可见分叉，纹路三维成像更纤细收敛，还有三维成像面积小于二维的风化斑块，斑块收敛，无扩张感。

见图5-2-38、图5-2-39，二者为同一器物同一位置图片，图5-2-38为二维图片，图5-2-39为三维图片。

图5-2-38中的C形纹二维成像有呈白雾状蔓延的趋势，其在图5-2-39中的三维成像为两条纤细收敛、清晰独立的C形纹（见箭头E所指处），与周围玻璃相也界线分明。

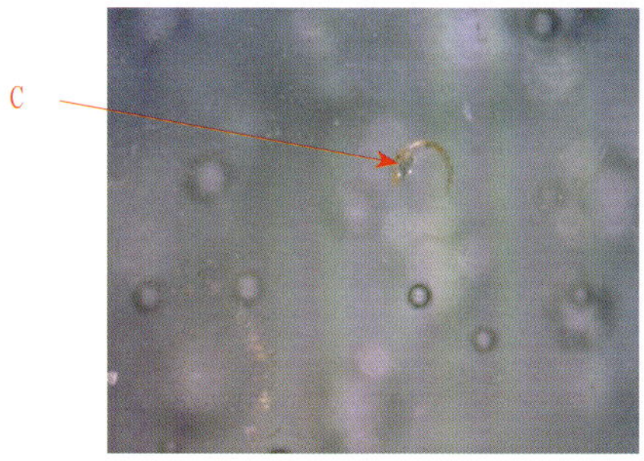

图5-2-34

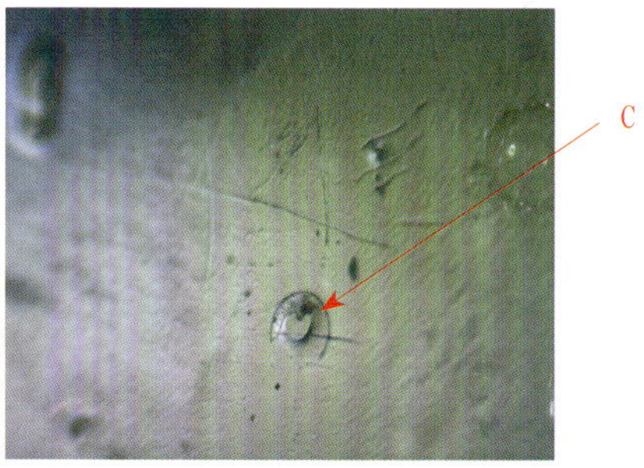

图5-2-35

surrounding needlepoint or pit mottles is often smaller than the associated two-dimensional image.

iii. The edges of the cracks are rounded and smooth.

iv. Clear delineation between the glaze crack and surrounding glass phase.

See pictures 5-2-61 and 5-2-62, where 5-2-61 is the two-dimensional and 5-2-62 is the three-dimensional view of the same location.

See pictures 5-2-63 and 5-2-64, where 5-2-63 is the two-dimensional and 5-2-64 is the three-dimensional view of the same location.

The glaze cracks in pictures 5-3-61 and 5-2-63 are clearly visible in pictures 6-2-62 and 6-2-64, respectively. The glaze cracks have width variation, but the size observable in the three-dimensional image is smaller than the associated two-dimensional image. The needlepoint and pit mottles also have an observably smaller size in the three-dimensional images (see Arrows A and B). The glaze cracks retain clear delineation between themselves and the surrounding glass phase.

See pictures 5-3-65 and 5-2-66, both are three-dimensional images.

The glaze cracks in both pictures are both clearly visible, and the edges are smooth and rounded. The glaze cracks retain clear delineation with the surrounding glass phase.

D. Scratches

a. Scratches Defined

Scratches are the imperfections on LKSC glaze that present as lines on the glaze surface that were left by the abrasive force of a solid external object.

b. Formation of Scratches

During post-firing use, and due to coming into contact with hard objects in the surrounding environment, the glaze surface can become scratched.

c. Characteristics of Scratches

I. Two-dimensional Characteristics of Scratches

i. Scratches can be broad or thin, long or short, deep or shallow, solid or intermittent, straight or curved (see pictures 5-2-67—5-2-90).

ii. Some scratches look like centipedes (see pictures 5-2-67—5-2-70).

iii. Some scratches have irregular shapes (see pictures 5-2-71—5-2-90).

iv. Scratch colorations include white, yellow, brown and so forth (see pictures 5-2-67—5-2-90).

v. Generally scratches occur randomly and without regularity. They can occur with several directions, depths, lengths, and colors in conjunction (see pictures 5-2-71, 5-2-72, 5-2-75—5-2-77, 5-2-79—5-2-88).

vi. Deep scratches have an evident concavity, over time they are easily filled with foreign material deposits and can weather to present with needlepoint mottling (see pictures 5-2-69, 5-2-70, 5-2-74—5-2-78, 5-2-85—90).

vii. As scratches are an area of glaze flaw, they are commonly a location of floccus mottling (see pictures 5-2-71 and 5-2-72).

II. Three-dimensional Characteristics of Scratches

i. Scratches can appear as tiny evenly distributed pits, centipede feet, tiny directionless ox hair, larger concavities, and so forth.

ii. It is possible for deposits to present in the interior of scratches.

iii. The three-dimensional image of scratches that present with white foggy coloration in association with them appear smaller than the accompanying two-dimensional image.

iv. The edges of the scratch are rounded.

v. Scratches retain clear delineation with the surrounding glass phase.

See pictures 5-2-91 and 5-2-92, both are three-dimensional images.

Often short and thin scratches are unobservable using two-dimensional imaging; it is necessary to use three-dimensional imaging to observe them. Ox-hair scratches are blunt and short, with variable directions, depths, and distribution densities. They retain clear delineation from the surrounding glass phase.

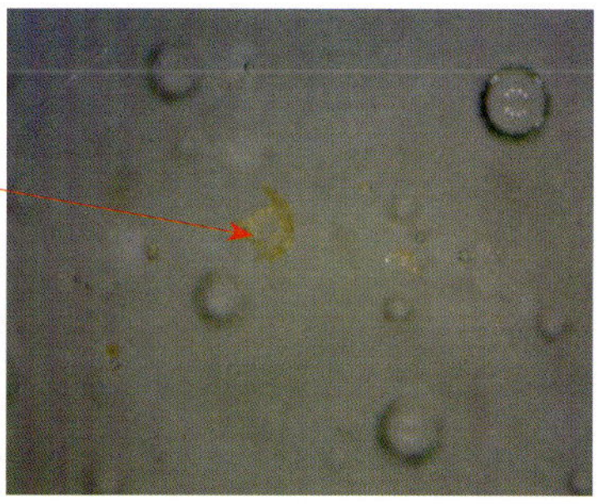

图5-2-36

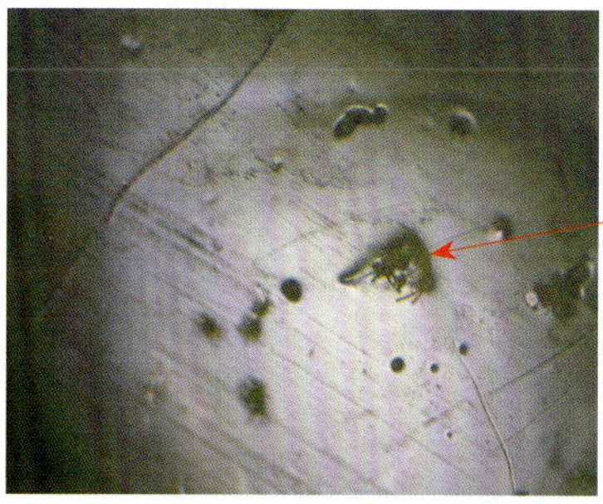

图5-2-37

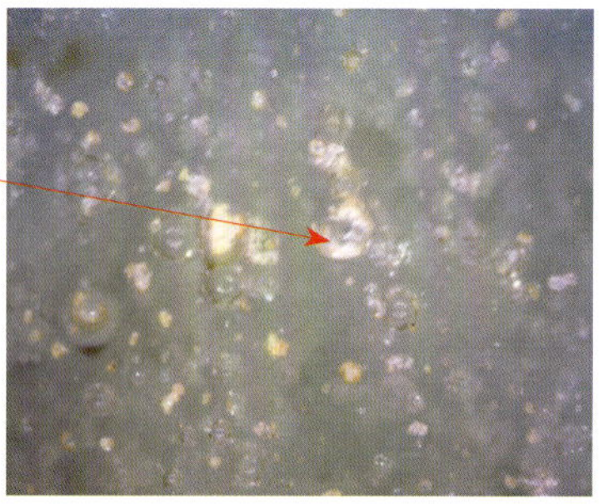

图5-2-38

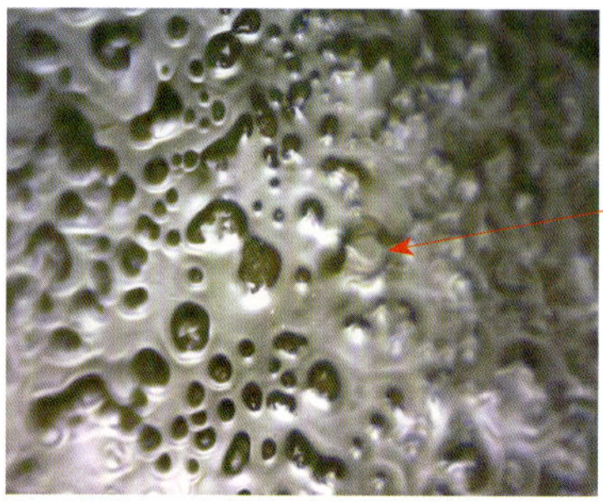

图5-2-39

（三）釉裂纹

1. 釉裂纹概念

釉裂纹是龙泉窑系青瓷在烧制过程中和后天环境影响下形成的，以直线、曲线等不规则线条形貌分布在釉表面的开裂纹路。

2. 釉裂纹形成

釉裂纹的形成主要有以下几种原因：

（1）龙泉窑系青瓷在高温烧制时，釉表面的成分挥发会造成空位，这些空位集聚成为空隙，因应力形成釉裂纹。

（2）釉层与微相之间膨胀不一可形成釉裂纹。

（3）由于$\equiv Si-O-R$中R^+和H^+的离子交换，H^+离子取代R^+位置，而H^+又比R^+小，因而产生应力，形成釉裂纹[240]。

（4）釉层与胎的膨胀系数不同，当温度变化时，胎釉之间会产生应力，由于胎较厚，承受应力的能力比釉层强，当应力大到一定程度时，釉层不能承受，便形成釉裂纹。

（5）釉层没有延展性，当外力打击超过其承受能力时，釉层便开裂形成釉裂纹。

釉裂纹未必与风化作用有直接的因果关系，有些釉裂纹是烧制过程中形成的，有的是后天环境影响下形成的。不是所有釉裂纹在显微成像下都能被观察到。在后天环境中，当温度发生变化或有可溶盐或难溶盐渗入而又析出时，产生的应力会使釉裂纹逐渐扩大。

陶瓷的釉表面出现裂纹，有时是人们利用胎与釉膨胀系数的差异，刻意追求的艺术效果。龙泉窑系青瓷的釉裂现象不属于人们刻意追求的艺术效果，而且较少出现，如果有釉裂现象，都属于瓷器缺陷。

3. 釉裂纹特征

（1）釉裂纹二维特征

① 釉裂纹有直线形貌，也有曲线形貌（见图5-2-40—图5-2-60）。

② 釉裂纹上会延伸出多条裂纹，像人参须一样（见图5-2-40、图5-2-41）。

③ 釉裂纹两边呈现白雾状蔓延趋势，有时与釉裂纹本身有颜色差异（见图5-2-42）。

④ 釉裂纹的粗细变化特征有：

A. 粗细变化不明显的（见图5-2-43、图5-2-44）。

B. 粗细有变化的（见图5-2-45）。

⑤ 釉裂纹的颜色变化特征有：

A. 颜色没有明显变化的（见图5-2-46、图5-2-47）。

B. 全部变色但无明显色阶变化（见图5-2-48、图5-2-49）。

See pictures 5-2-93 and 5-2-94, where 5-2-93 is the two-dimensional and 5-2-94 is the three-dimensional view of the same location.

The light colored centipede scratches in picture 5-2-93 are the clearly depicted darker areas of centipede feet in picture 5-2-94. The centipede feet are fine yet clearly visible, and have a certain observable separation in which the glass phase is visible. As a whole, the scratches retain clear delineation from the surrounding glass phase.

See pictures 5-2-95 and 5-2-96, where 5-2-95 is the two-dimensional and 5-2-96 is the three-dimensional view of the same location.

The scratch indicated by Arrow A in picture 5-2-95 is relatively unclear and has associated white foggy coloration. However, the three-dimensional perspective in picture 5-2-96 shows clearly independent saw-tooth like small scratches that are smaller in size than their associated two-dimensional counterpart. They also retain clear delineation from the surrounding glass phase.

See pictures 5-2-97 and 5-2-98, where 5-2-97 is the two-dimensional and 5-2-98 is the three-dimensional view of the same location.

The three-dimensionally observable scratch is smaller than that of the two-dimensional image. However, it has an area that is relatively large, and its interior is a concave pit shape with visible deposits and coarse unevenness. There is a visible color disparity and the edges of the scratch are smooth and rounded, while it retains clear delineation from the surrounding glass phase.

See pictures 5-2-99—5-2-102, all are three-dimensional images.

One image can present with several different kinds of scratches with variation in width, length, depth, curvature, and direction. Their edges are smooth and rounded and they retain clear delineation from the surrounding glass phase.

3. Conclusion

LKSC striae can be innate or acquired.

The formation of flowing striae occurs during the firing of LKSC glaze, but many flowing striae require years of weathering in order to be observable through two-dimensional microscopic imaging. The cross section of flowing striae can be divided as W and U shaped. It is possible for the interior of striae to present with needlepoint mottling or granulation, the edges are reserved and rounded, and there is a clear delineation between the striae and the surrounding beach mottle or glass phase.

LKSC CO striae are also formed during the firing process, but need to undergo weathering in order to be observable through two-dimensional microscopic imaging. The majority of CO striae occur on portions of raised glaze, and are finely minute under three-dimensional observation. CO striae can occur in conjunction with CO type pit mottles, but as a whole, the surface area of the striae under three-dimensional observation is smaller than that observable through two-dimensional microscopic imaging.

Scratches are all acquired damage striae that have come about in the post-firing environment. Scratch appearances are numerous. They can present with internal needlepoint mottling, and round edges can be observed through three-dimensional microscopic imaging.

Glaze cracks can be formed during the firing process or can be acquired, and are considered as a glaze structural flaw. Over time they allow for the gradual formation of other acquired traces such as color change bubbles, texturized bubbles, floccus mottles, and so forth. These striae and the multiplicity of their appearances and characteristics reflect the quantitative change and passage of time principles of ceramic traces, and embody the various laws that govern ceramic trace formation and change.

C. 有色阶变化，颜色有白色、黄色、褐色、黑色等（见图5-2-40、图5-2-44、图5-2-45、图5-2-50、图5-2-51）。

⑥ 釉裂纹周边的特征包括：

A. 色变泡或壁变泡的出现（见图5-2-52—图5-2-55）。

B. 釉下变色（见图5-2-56、图5-2-57）。

C. 釉裂纹下有堆积物（见图5-2-45、图5-2-50、图5-2-58、图5-2-59）。

D. 釉裂纹下有絮状斑（见图5-2-60）。

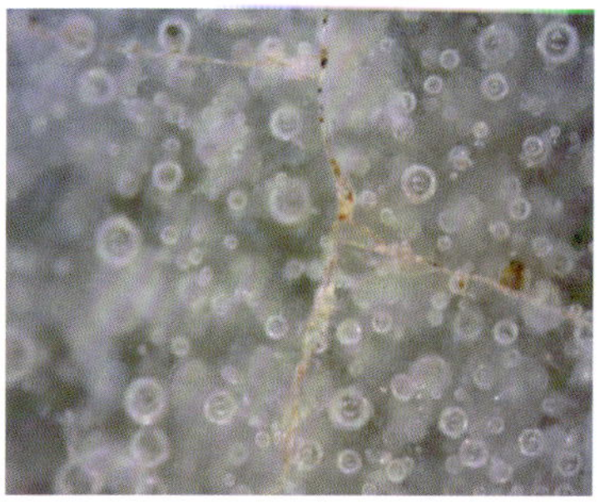

图5-2-40

图5-2-41

图5-2-42

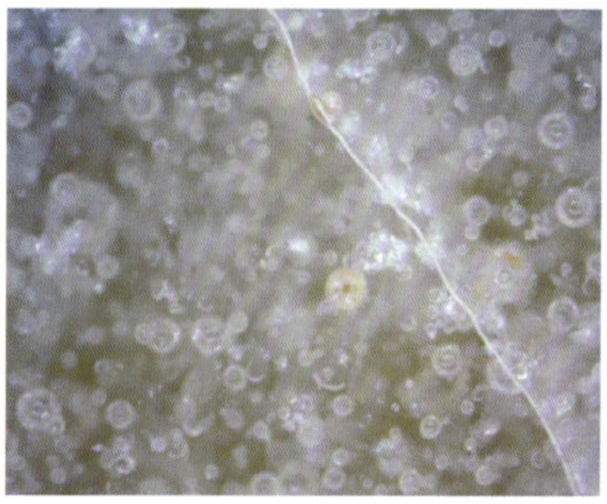

图5-2-43

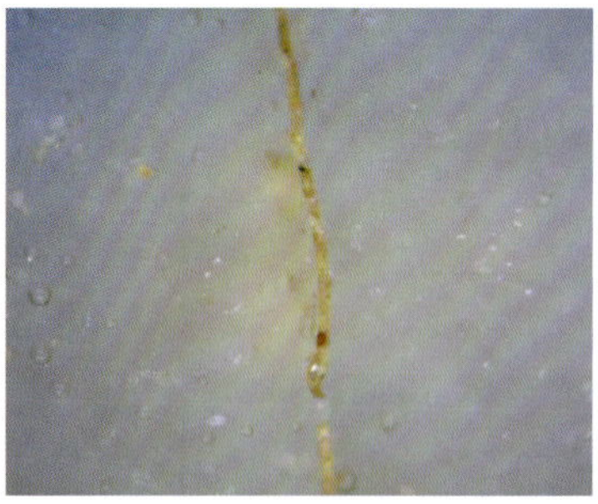

图5-2-44

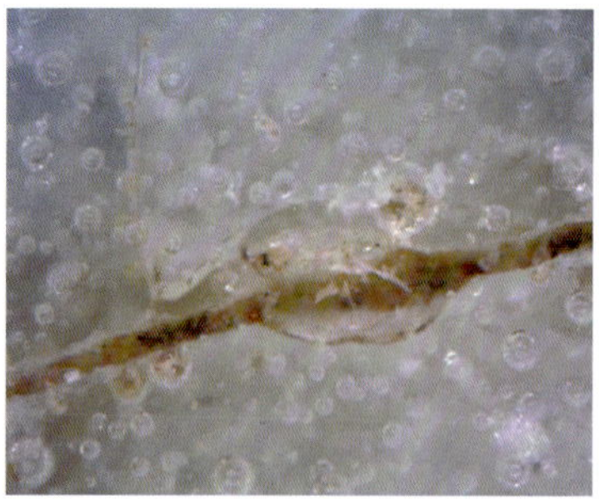

图5-2-45

图5-2-46

图5-2-47

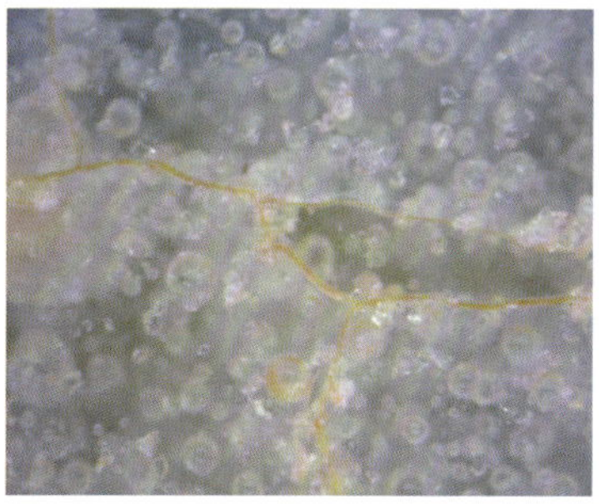

图5-2-48

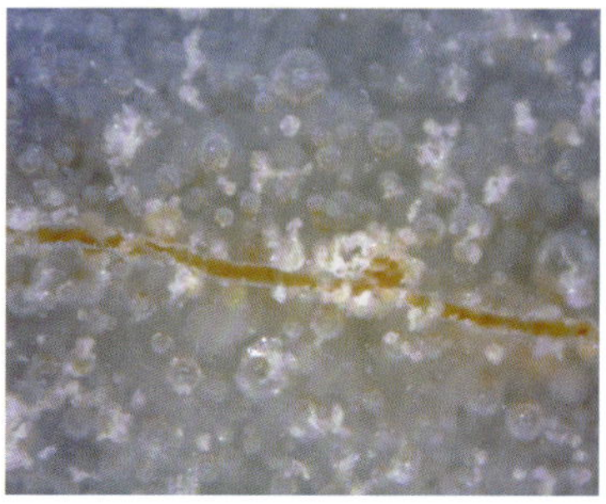

图5-2-49

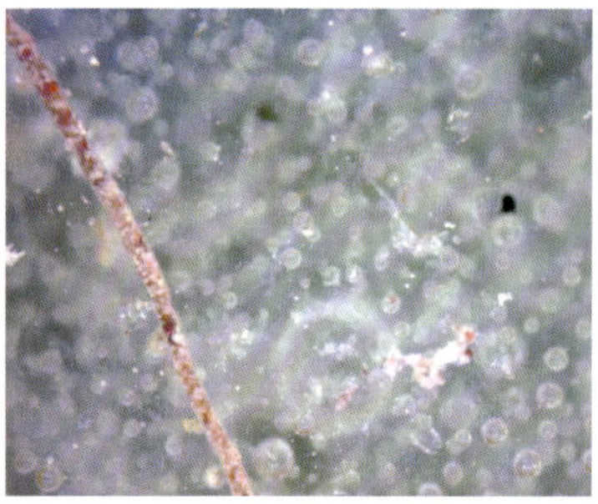

图5-2-50

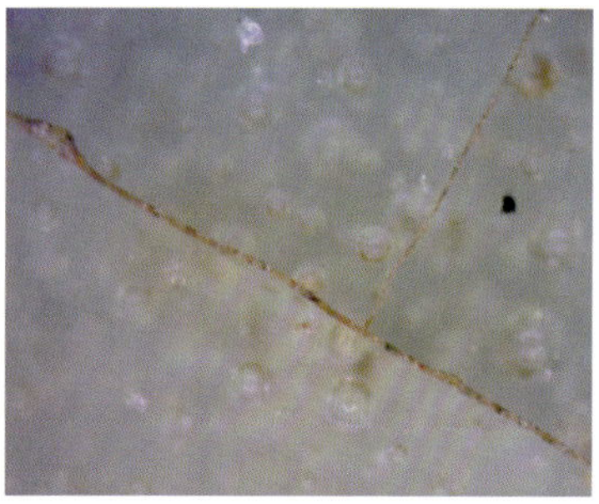

图5-2-51

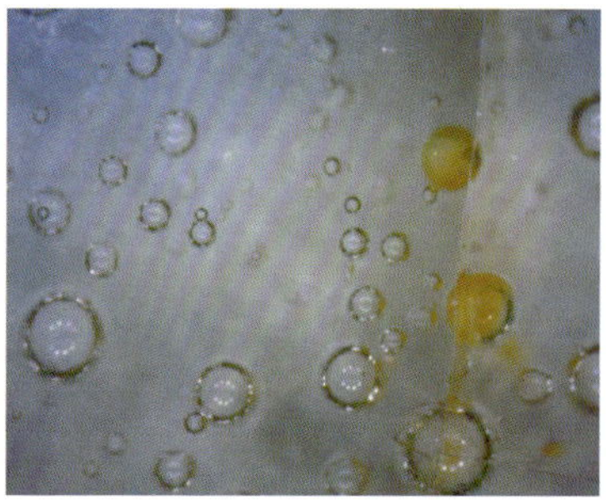

图5-2-52

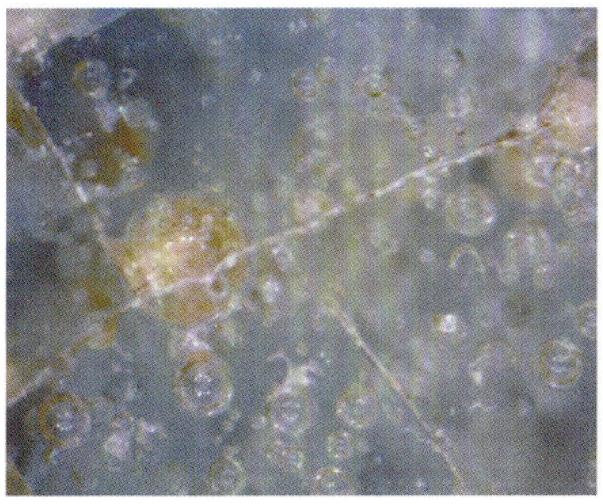

图5-2-53

图5-2-54

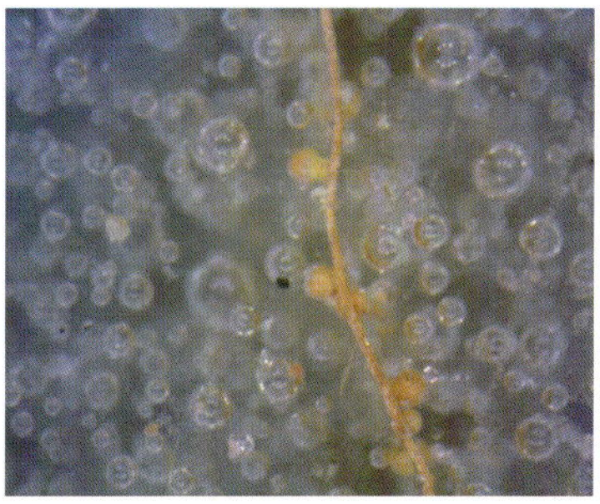

图5-2-55

（2）釉裂纹三维特征

① 釉裂纹的三维成像面积通常小于或等于二维成像。

② 釉裂纹周围出现的针眼斑或坑点斑三维成像面积要小于二维。

③ 釉裂纹边沿圆滑。

④ 釉裂纹与周围玻璃相界线分明。

见图5-2-61、图5-2-62，二者为同一器物同一位置图片，图5-2-61为二维图片，图5-2-62为三维图片。

见图5-2-63、图5-2-64，二者为同一器物同一位置图片，图5-2-63为二维图片，图5-2-64为三维图片。

图5-2-61及图5-2-63中的釉裂纹在图5-2-62及图5-2-64中成像清晰，釉裂纹有粗有细，其三维成像面积均小于二维成像。釉裂纹周围出现的坑点斑在图5-2-62及图5-2-64中三维成像面积要小于图5-2-61及图5-2-63中的二维成像面积（见箭头A、B所指处）。釉裂纹与周围玻璃相界线分明。

见图5-2-65、图5-2-66，二者均为三维图片。

图5-2-65及图5-2-66中的釉裂纹三维成像清晰，边沿显得圆滑。釉裂纹与周围玻璃相界线分明。

（四）划痕

1. 划痕概念

划痕是龙泉窑系青瓷釉表面与硬物碰划留下的破坏性纹路。

2. 划痕形成

龙泉窑系青瓷在后天长期使用中或存在环境中与硬物碰划，在釉表面会留下划痕。

3. 划痕特征

（1）划痕二维特征

① 划痕有粗有细，有长有

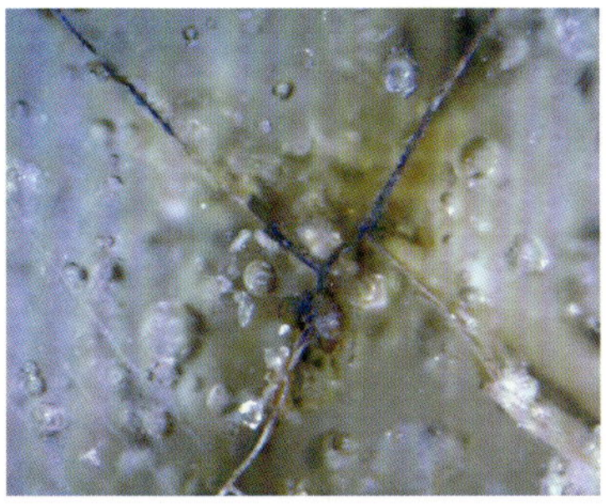

图5-2-56

图5-2-57

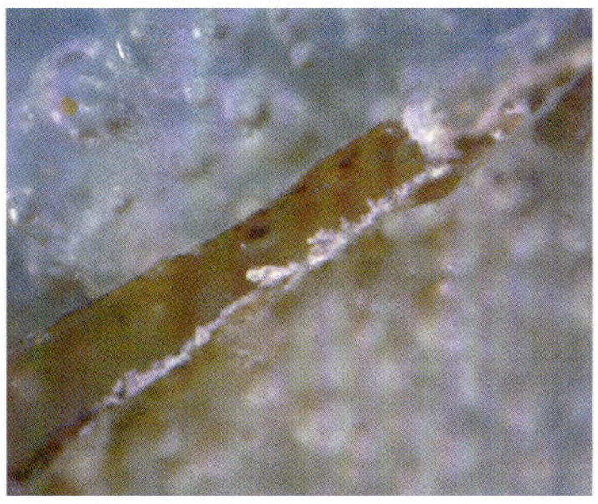

图5-2-58

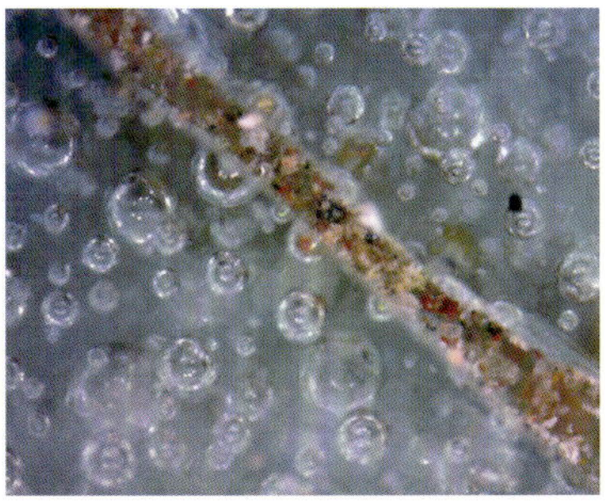

图5-2-59

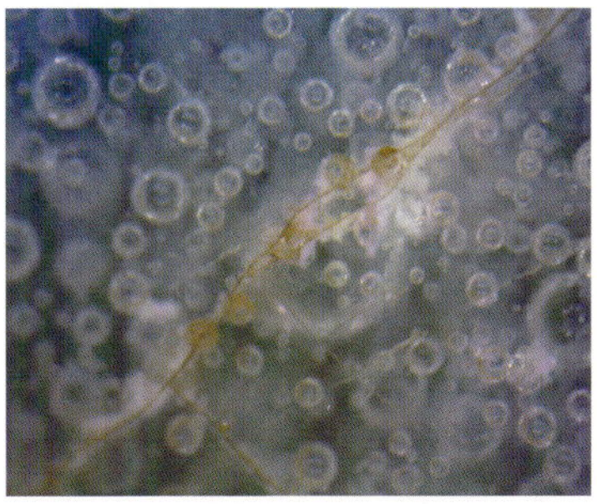

图5-2-60

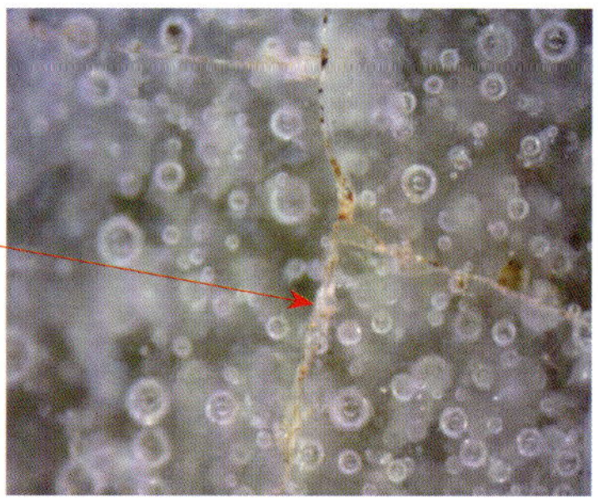

图5-2-61

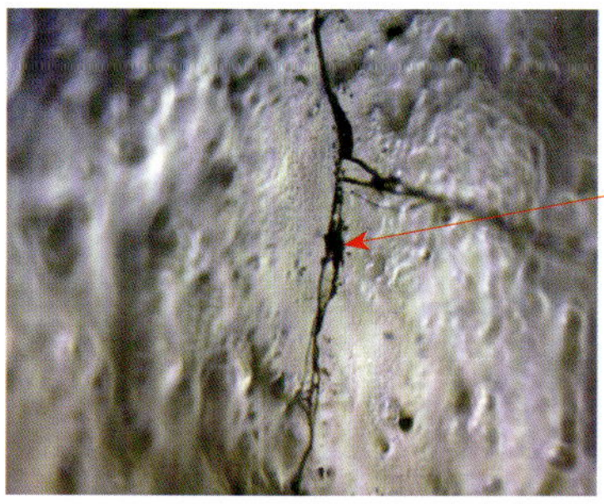

图5-2-62

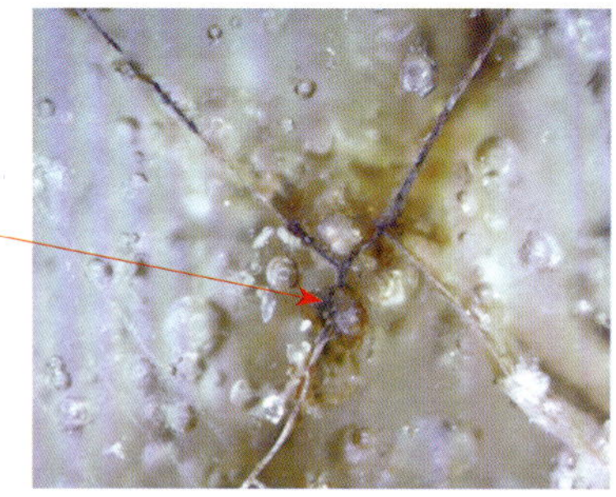

图5-2-63

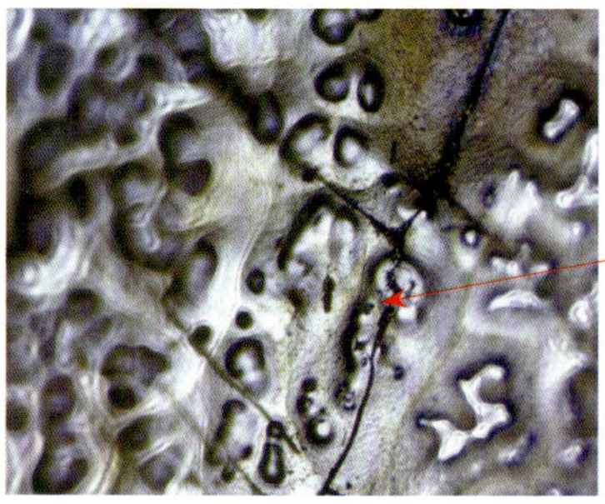

图5-2-64

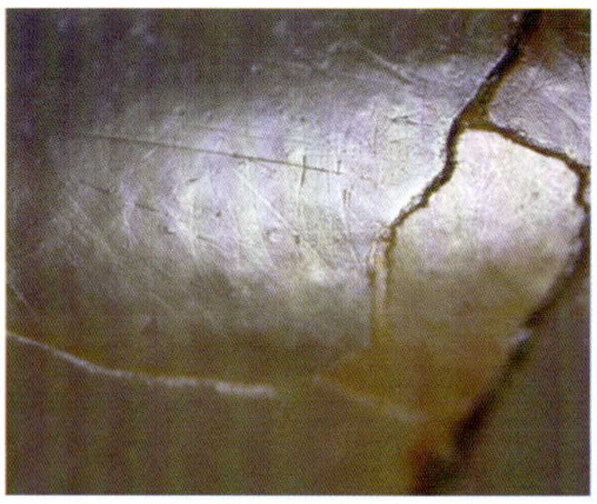

图5-2-65

图5-2-66

短，有深有浅，有连有断，有直线有曲线（见图5-2-67—图5-2-90）。

② 有的划痕形如蜈蚣（见图5-2-67—图5-2-70）。

③ 有的划痕呈不规则形貌（见图5-2-71—图5-2-90）。

④ 划痕颜色有白色、黄色、褐色等（见图5-2-67—图5-2-90）。

⑤ 划痕通常随机无序地分布在釉表面，深浅交织共存。在同一张图片上可以同时存在不同形貌、不同颜色的划痕（见图5-2-71、图5-2-72、图5-2-75—图5-2-77、图5-2-79—图5-2-88）。

⑥ 划痕入釉较深，形成一定的凹槽，长期易积聚外来物质风化形成针眼斑（见图5-2-69、图5-2-70、图5-2-74—图5-2-78、图5-2-85—图5-2-90）。

⑦ 由于划痕属于釉层结构缺陷，划痕凹槽内容易形成絮状斑（见图5-2-71、图5-2-72）。

（2）划痕三维特征

① 划痕有多种表现形式：间隔均匀的小凹坑、清晰的“蜈蚣脚”、细小且杂乱无章的牛毛划痕及面积较大的凹坑等。

② 划痕的凹坑内可见堆积物。

③ 二维成像有雾状蔓延趋势的划痕，其三维成像面积要小于二维。

④ 划痕边沿圆滑。

⑤ 划痕与周围玻璃相界线分明。

见图5-2-91、图5-2-92，二者均为三维图片。

通常细短的划痕二维成像难以观察到，需要借用三维成像法观察。牛毛状划痕粗细、长短、方向不一，有深有浅，距离有疏有密，划痕与周围玻璃相界线分明。

见图5-2-93、图5-2-94，二者为同一器物同一位置图片，图5-2-93为二维图片，图5-2-94为三维图片。

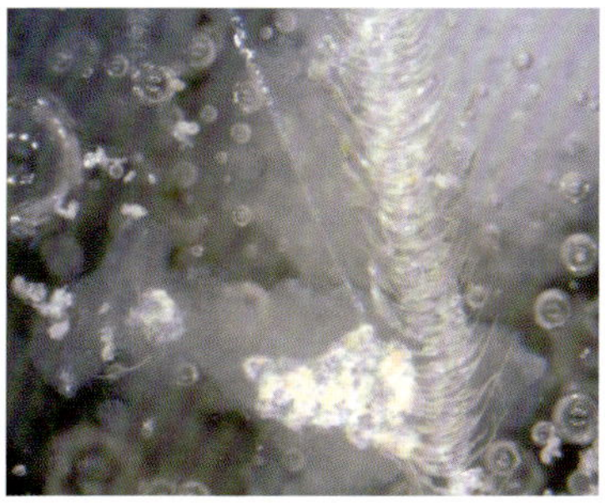
图5-2-67

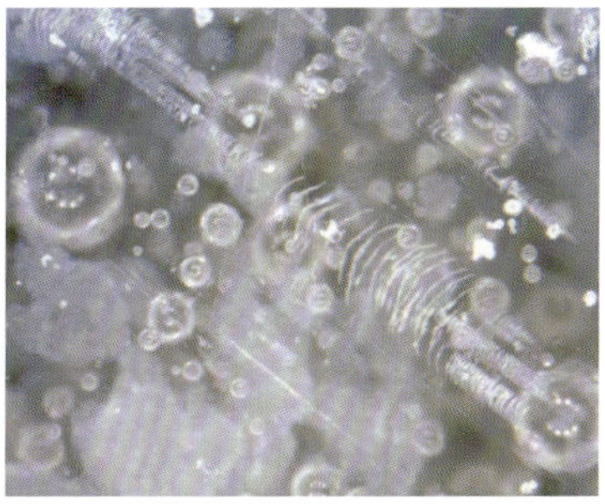
图5-2-68

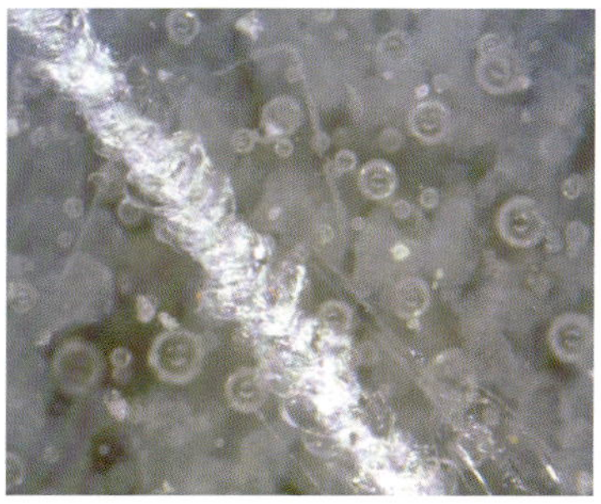
图5-2-69

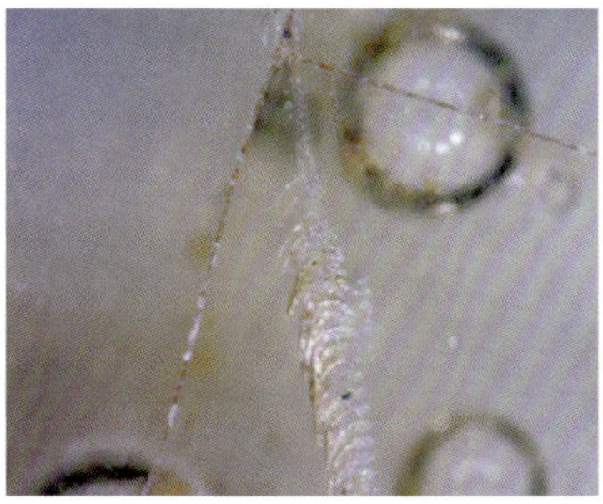
图5-2-70

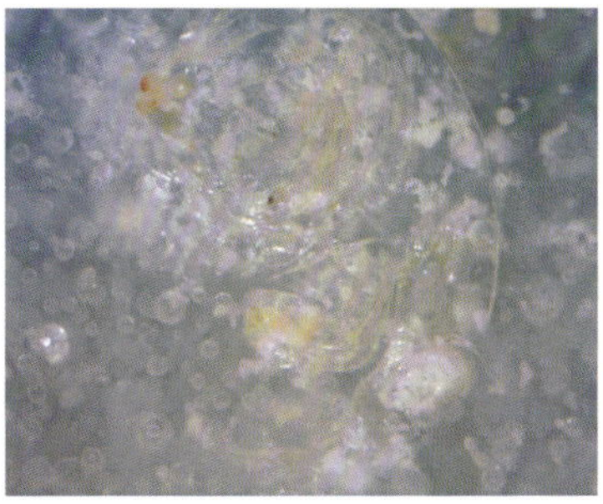
图5-2-71

图5-2-72

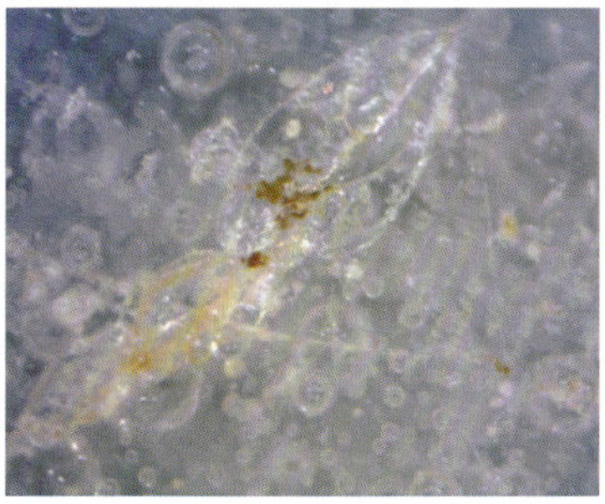
图5-2-73

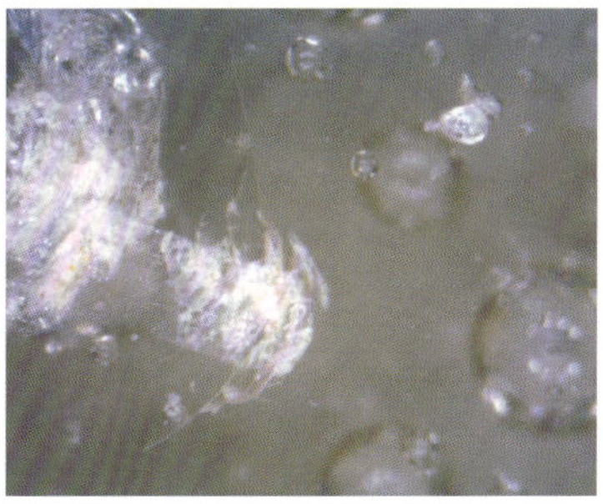
图5-2-74

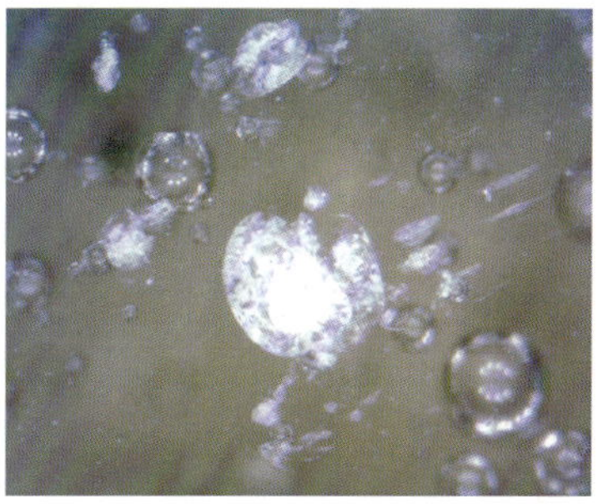
图5-2-75

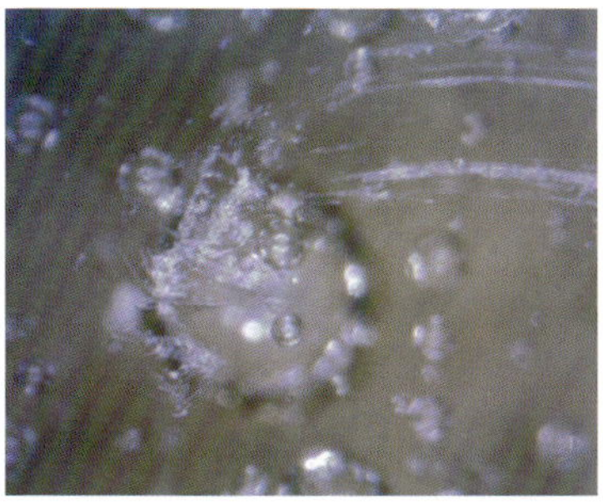
图5-2-76

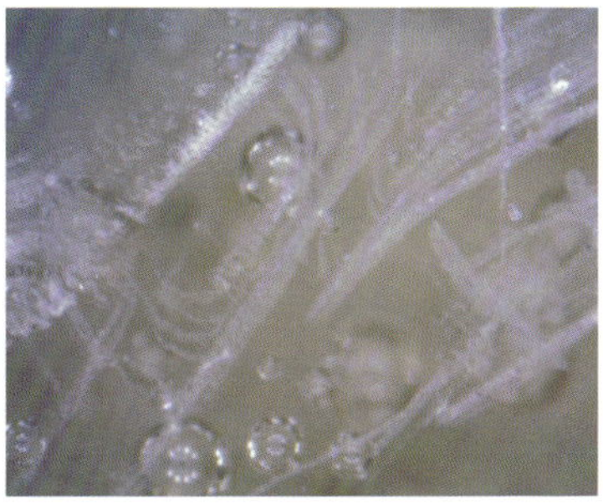
图5-2-77

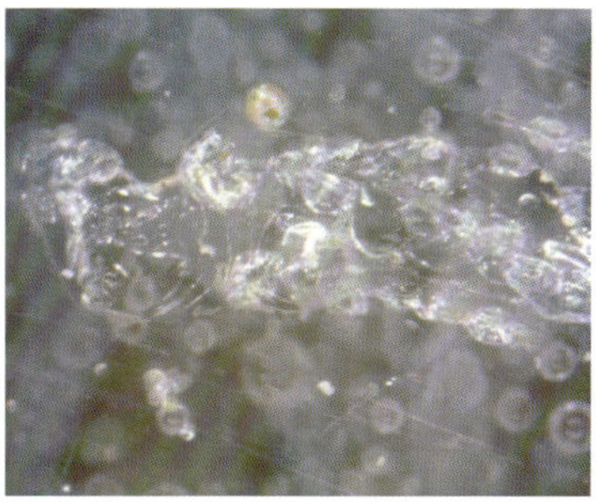
图5-2-78

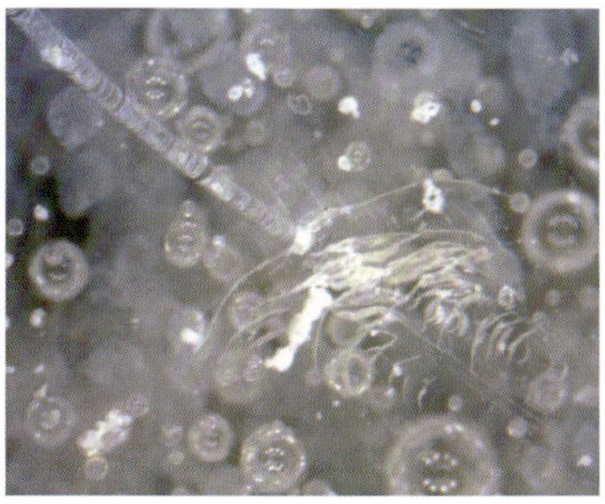
图5-2-79

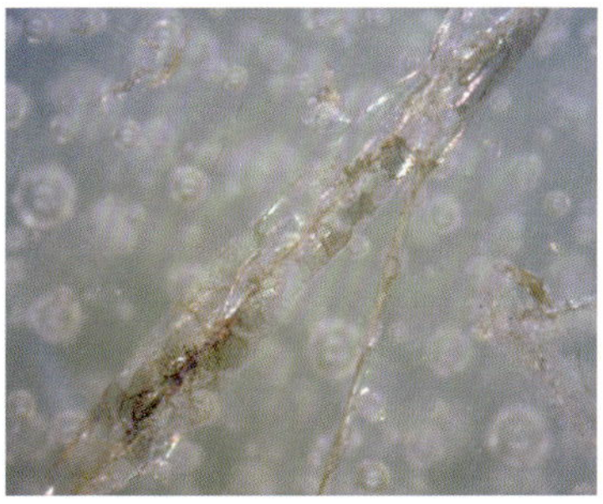
图5-2-80

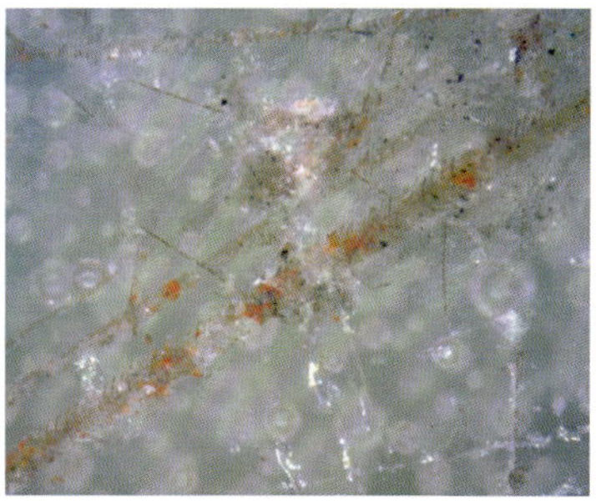
图5-2-81

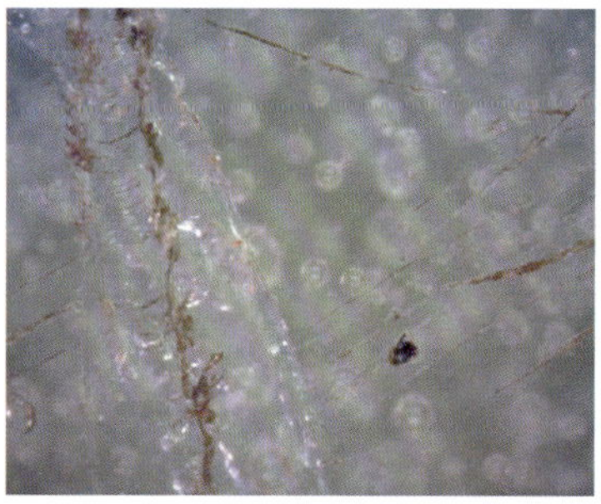
图5-2-82

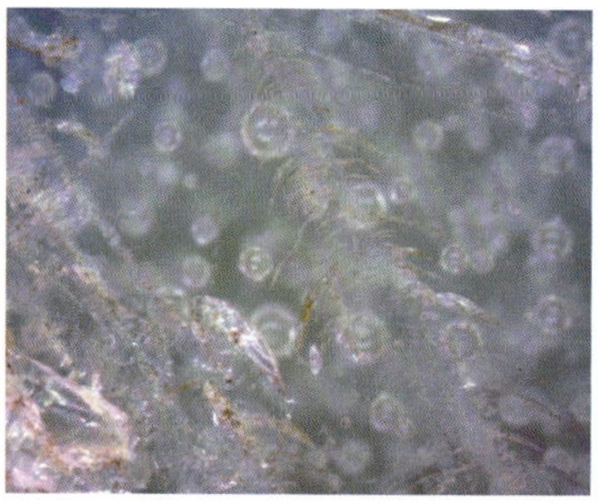
图5-2-83

图5-2-84

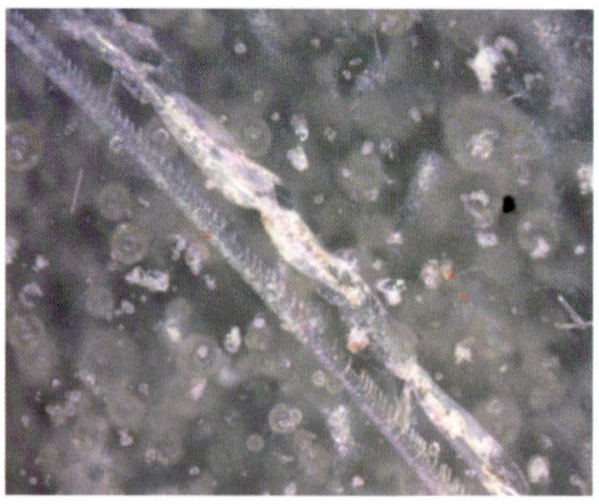
图5-2-85

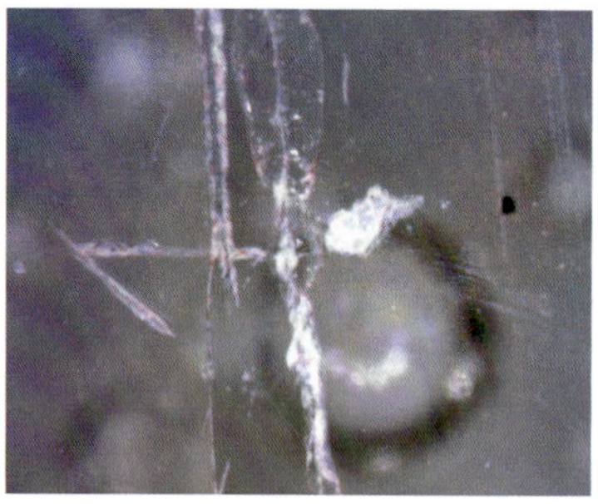
图5-2-86

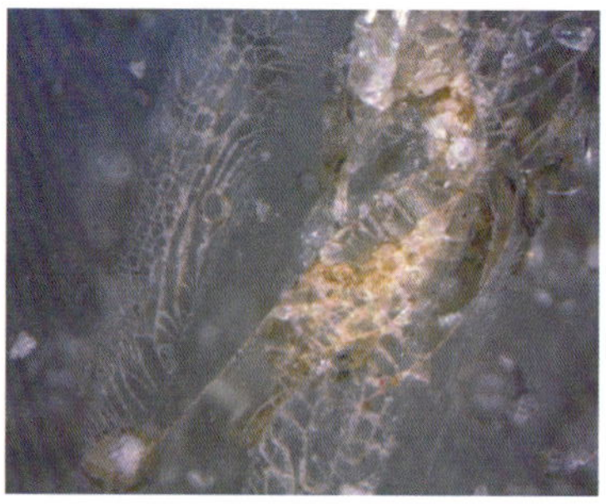
图5-2-87

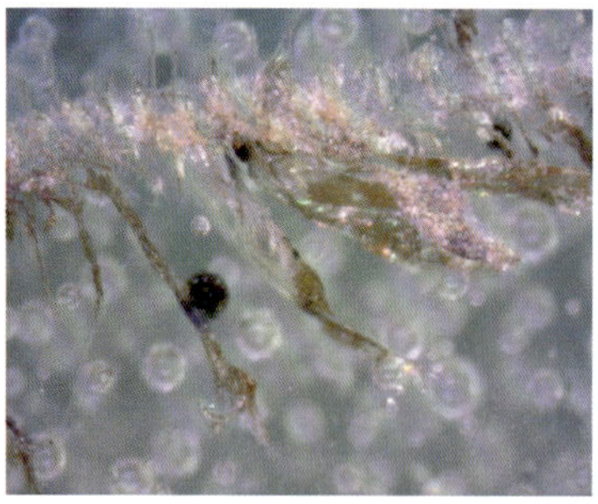
图5-2-88

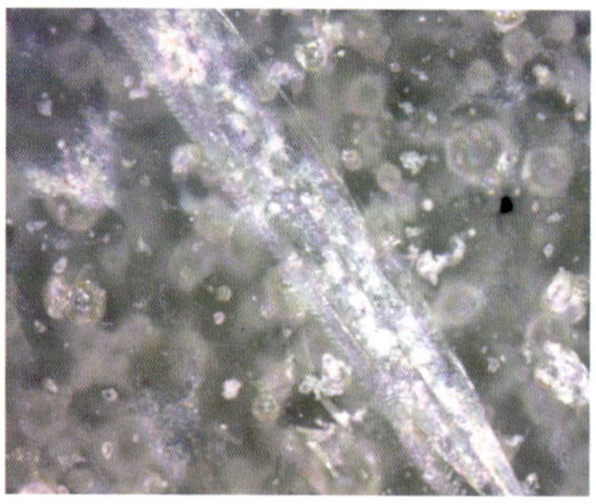
图5-2-89

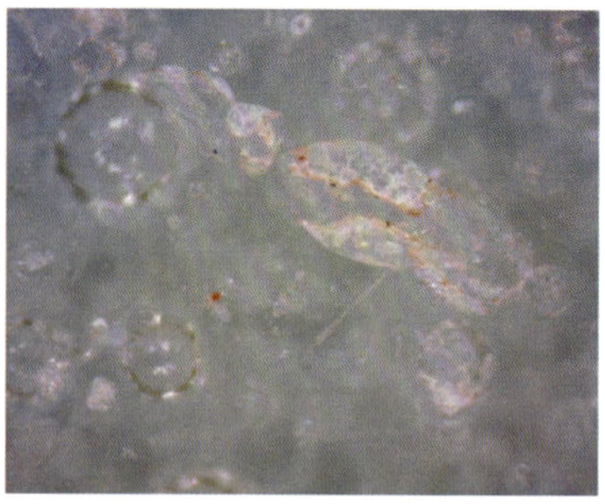
图5-2-90

图5-2-93中的浅色蜈蚣形划痕在图5-2-94中呈深色，“蜈蚣脚”更加纤细而且清晰，“蜈蚣脚”之间的玻璃相也非常清晰。划痕整体与周围玻璃相界线分明。

见图5-2-95、图5-2-96，二者为同一器物同一位置图片，图5-2-95为二维图片，图5-2-96为三维图片。

图5-2-95中箭头A所指的划痕二维成像较模糊，有白雾状蔓延趋势，但其三维成像在图5-2-96中却可见一个个独立清晰的锯齿状小划痕，三维成像面积小于二维，而且与周围玻璃相界线分明。

见图5-2-97、图5-2-98，二者为同一器物同一位置图片，图5-2-97为二维图片，图5-2-98为三维图片。

图5-2-97中划痕的三维成像面积小于图5-2-98中的二维成像面积，划痕面积较大，呈凹坑状，可见内部堆积物，还可见色阶变化，划痕边沿圆滑，与周围玻璃相界线分明。

见图5-2-99—图5-2-102，四者均为三维图片。

同一图片中存在多个形貌各异的划痕，有粗有细，有长有短，有深有浅，有直线有曲线，方向不一，边沿圆滑，与周围玻璃相界线分明。

三、总结

龙泉窑系青瓷纹路也有先天形成与后天形成之分。

龙泉窑系青瓷流淌纹的形貌先天就已形成，但有的流淌纹往往要经历长久的风化后其二维成像才能在显微镜下被观察到。流淌纹剖面可以是“W”形或“U”形。纹路内部有时可见针眼斑或颗粒，边沿收敛圆滑，与周围玻璃相和沙滩斑界线分明。

龙泉窑系青瓷CO纹的形貌也是先天形成的，但通常也是要经过风化后其二维成像才能用显微镜观察到。CO纹大都出现在釉表面凸起处，三维成像纤细紧致，有时CO纹与坑点斑伴生，但整体三维面积都要小于二维。

划痕属于在后天环境影响下形成的破坏性纹路，形貌多变，有时划痕内部可见堆积物，三维成像边沿圆滑。

釉裂纹既可以是先天形成的也可以是后天形成的，它属于釉层结构的缺陷，长期存在会导致其周边逐渐形成一些后天性风化迹型，如色变泡、壁变泡及絮状斑等。龙泉窑系青瓷上的这些纹路种类和特征能够反映陶瓷迹型变化的量变原理及时间过程原理，也能够体现陶瓷迹型形成及变化的诸规律。

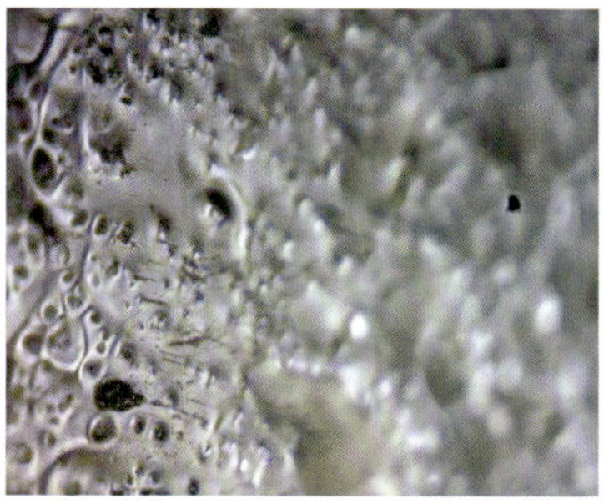

图5-2-91

图5-2-92

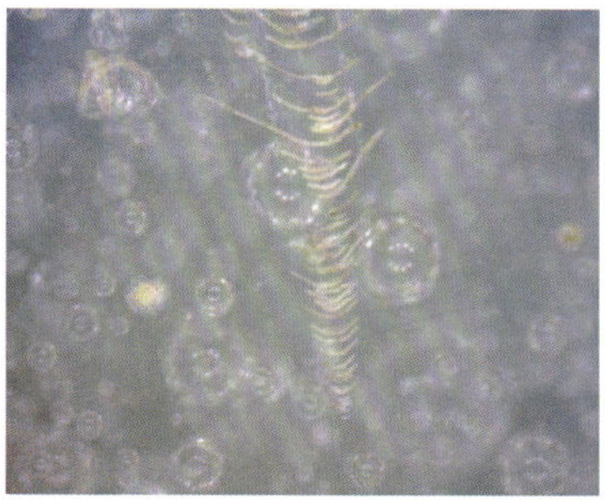

图5-2-93

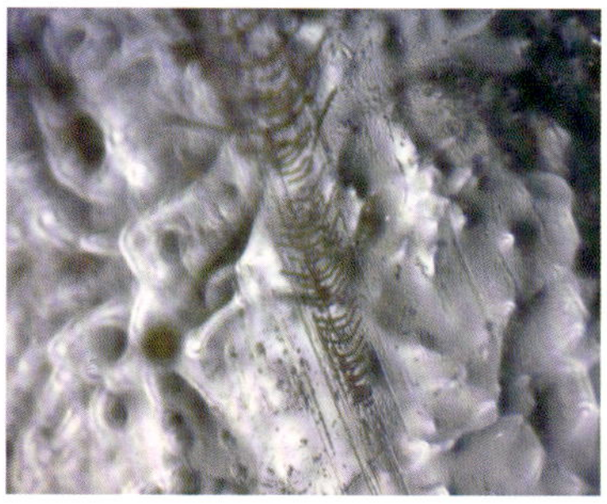

图5-2-94

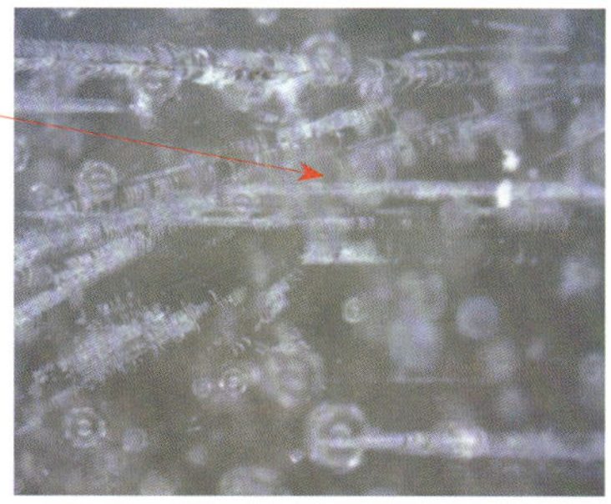

图5-2-95

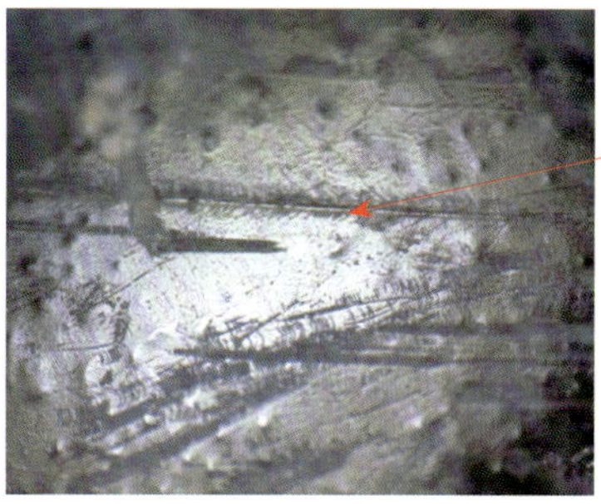

图5-2-96

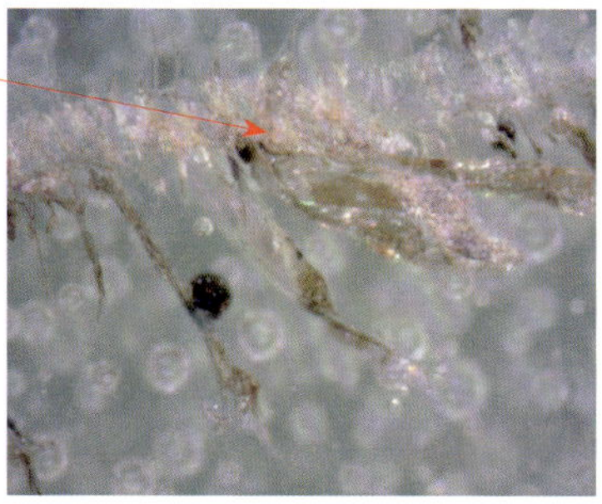

图5-2-97

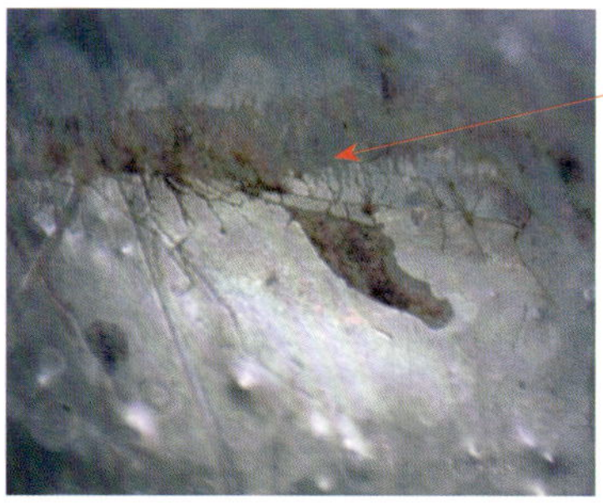

图5-2-98

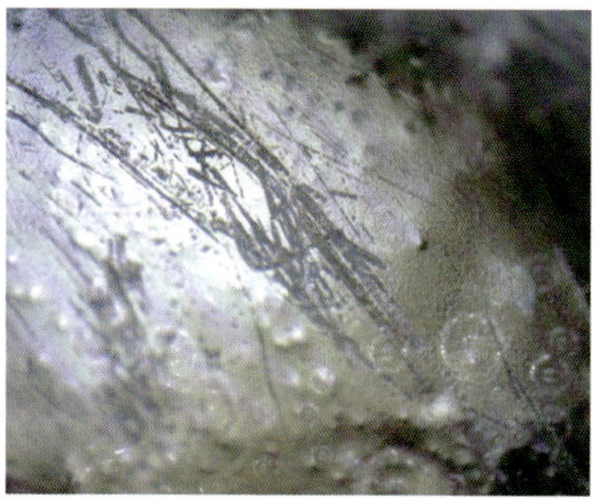

图5-2-99

图5-2-100

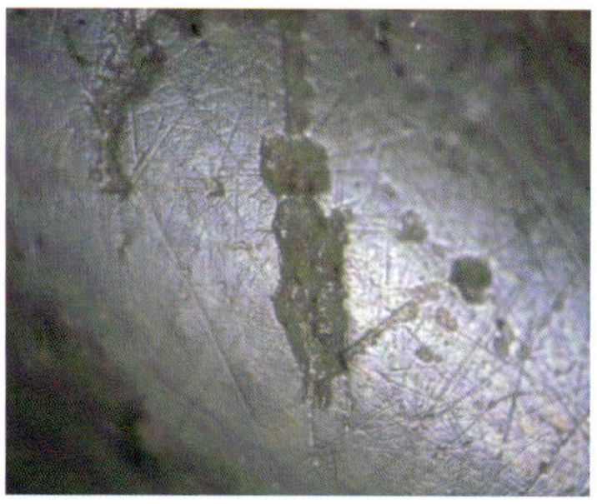

图5-2-101

图5-2-102

第三节
龙泉窑系青瓷气泡类别

一、龙泉窑系青瓷气泡概念

龙泉窑系青瓷气泡是在龙泉窑系青瓷烧制过程中，在釉层中形成的气相迹型类别。

釉层中的气泡在烧制产生时，绝大多数都是透明无色的。

二、龙泉窑系青瓷气泡种类

按气泡颜色变化与气泡内壁质地变化的特征，可将龙泉窑系青瓷气泡分为色变泡与壁变泡两大种类。

（一）色变泡

1. 色变泡概念

色变泡是龙泉窑系青瓷在后天环境影响下，釉层中透明气泡的颜色发生了变化，但仍具透影性的气泡（即半透明状态）。

2. 色变泡形成

无色透明的气泡变成有色气泡需要以下条件：

（1）有一定量的铁元素

气泡从无色变成有色，是气泡内一定量的铁元素发生反应的结果。刚烧制出来的龙泉窑系青瓷，釉层中的气泡绝大多数是无色透明的，在这些无色透明的气泡中，只有部分气泡内壁含有铁元素，这些气泡随机分布在釉层中。在后天环境的影响下，外界的铁元素也可经通道进入气泡内，使气泡变色。

（2）有一定量的水分

气泡从无色变成有色，离不开水的作用，水既可以是输送外界元素进入气泡的媒介，也可以参与反应使气泡变色。

（3）有连接外界环境的通道

釉层通往气泡内的通道可以有两种：

①烧制过程中形成的

在烧制过程中形成的，有以下两种情况：

A.青瓷高温烧制时，在熔融釉层冷却平复的过程中，釉未能将气泡冲出釉表面时产生的破口完全填满，使釉表面留有微小孔隙，这些微小孔隙构成了连接气泡与外界环境的通道。

B.青瓷烧制时形成的釉裂纹成为通道。

②后天环境影响下形成的

釉层长期风化受到侵蚀，形成新的裂纹或孔隙，成为通道。这些通道会随着时间的推移逐渐变大。由于通道的存在，气泡与外界环境相通，外界环境中的各类物质可进入气泡内。通道存在是气泡变色的关键因素，它可以使部分含铁元素的气泡变色，也可以让不含铁元素的气泡变色。

（4）经一定时间反应

气泡从无色变成有色的自然风化是一个较长时间的过程，因为通道极为细小。统计观察大量民国瓷器与“文革”瓷器的结果表明，部分存放在大气环境中的瓷器，至少经过40年的时间才有色变泡产生。40年之内的瓷器除了在烧制过程中产生的极个别灰泡之外，很少能观察到黄色、褐色等色变泡现象。

3. 色变泡种类

（1）非破口色变泡

①非破口色变泡概念

非破口色变泡是用500倍显微镜观察到的完整无破口的色变泡。

②非破口色变泡特征

A.非破口色变泡二维特征

a.龙泉窑系青瓷上的非破口色变泡颜色有黄色、褐色、黑色及绿色等（见图5-3-1—图5-3-16）。

b.有的气泡局部变色，有的气泡全部变色（见图5-3-1—图5-3-

Section 3:
Longquan Kiln System Celadon Air Bubble Category

1. LKSC Air Bubble Defined

LKSC Air Bubbles (also simplified as bubbles) are the trace category of gas phase appearances, formed during the firing process, within the glaze level of LKSC.

Almost all bubbles formed during the firing process are clear and colorless.

2. LKSC Air Bubble Types

The color and internal texture change properties of air bubbles to divide LKSC air bubbles into two types: Color Change Bubble and Textured Bubble.

A. Color Change Bubbles

a. Color Change Bubbles Defined

Color Change Bubbles are the appearance of air bubbles within the glaze level that have undergone a coloration change under the influences of the post-firing environment, but have retained their translucency.

b. Formation of Color Change Bubbles

For a bubble to change from clear transparency to having coloration, it must fulfill the following criterion:

I. Certain Amount of Iron

The change from a non-colored to colored bubble is primarily due to the reaction of Iron. The vast majority of bubbles are clear directly after firing, and only a few of them randomly distributed throughout the glaze level contain trace amounts of elemental Iron. It is also possible, under the influence of the post-firing environment, for Iron to enter through channels into the glaze level and create colored bubbles.

II. Certain Amount of Water

Coloration is dependent on the presence of moisture.

Not only can moisture help to carry foreign materials into the bubble, but it also aids in the reactions that cause coloration.

III. Contact with the Outside Surroundings

Channels through the glaze level into the bubble interior can be:

i. Formed during the firing process:

(a) When cooling from a molten state, the glaze is unable to fully recede over the mouth of an air bubble's escape passage, leaving a microscopic opening in the surface of the glaze. This opening acts as a channel between the bubble and the outside world.

(b) The Firing process creates glaze cracks that act as channels.

ii. Formed under the influences of the post-firing environment:

Over long periods of corrosive weathering, the glaze can present with new cracks and holes, these act as channels.

Some channels can gradually become larger over time.

Due to the presence of channels, some air bubbles are in contact with the external elements. This allows for the entrance of foreign materials into the bubble interior.

The presence of these channels is necessary for the formation of color change bubbles; they allow for bubbles inherently containing Iron to change color, as well as allow external Iron to enter in and color the bubbles, post-firing.

16）。

c. 有的单项气泡有颜色差异，有的地方颜色浓重，有的地方颜色浅淡，色浓处通常就是通道所在处（见图5-3-1—图5-3-3、图5-3-11—图5-3-13）。

d. 有的气泡色变较均匀，通道不明显（见图5-3-4—图5-3-8）。

e. 有的气泡仅仅是泡壁外沿一圈改变了颜色，像土星光环围绕，气泡内颜色未变或部分变色。通常这类气泡都是泡壁外沿一圈的颜色较浓，越往气泡中心方向的颜色越淡（见图5-3-9、图5-3-10）。

f. 气泡变色部分与未变色部分界线分明，没有渐变的形式。形成这种现象主要有两种原因：一是气泡内壁出现裂纹，泡壁发生错位，形成气泡内壁风化的屏障；二是气泡内壁是凹凸不平的，凹凸不平的表面会形成气泡内壁风化的屏障

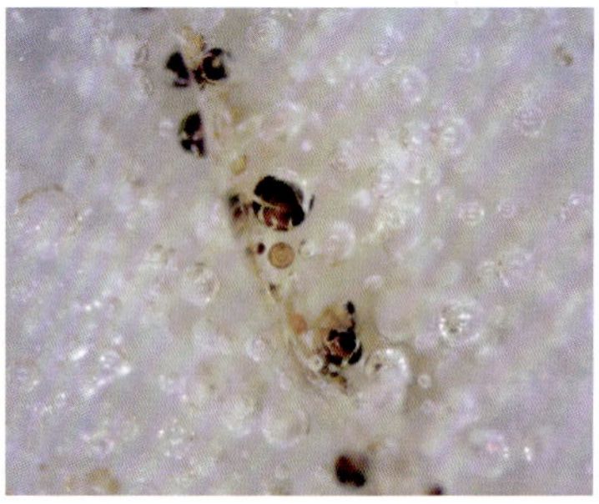
图5-3-1

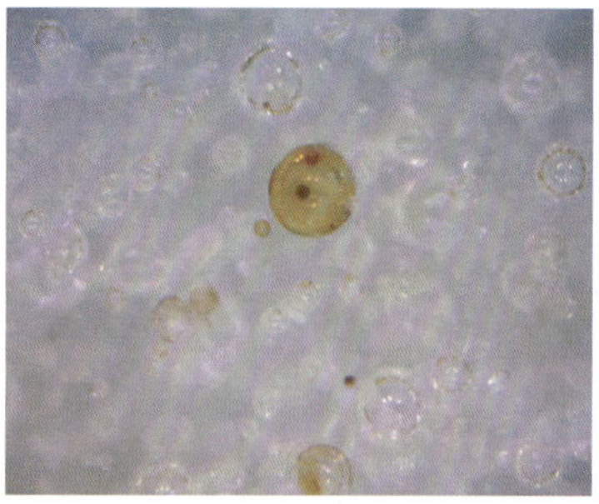
图5-3-2

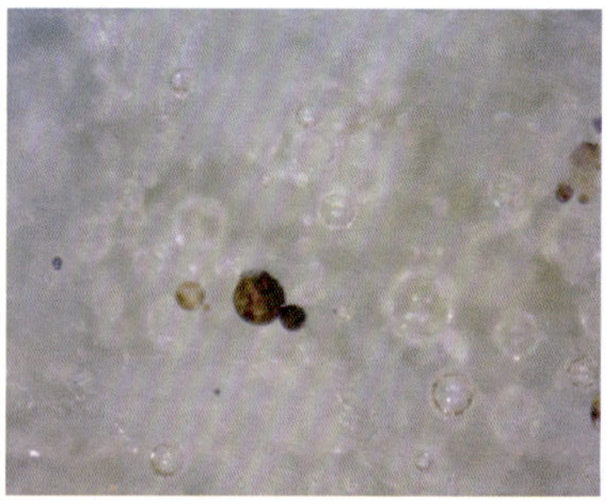
图5-3-3

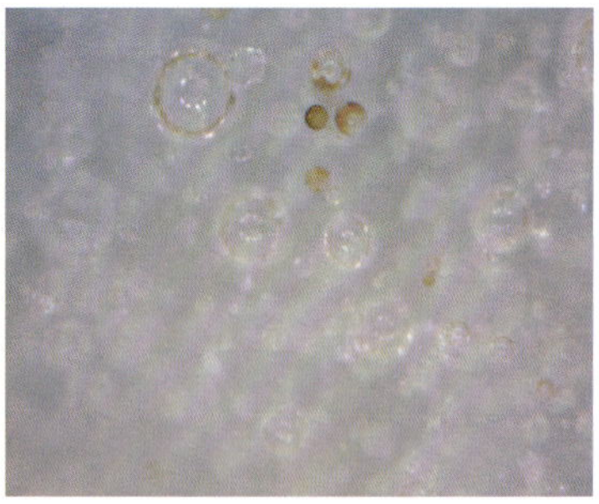
图5-3-4

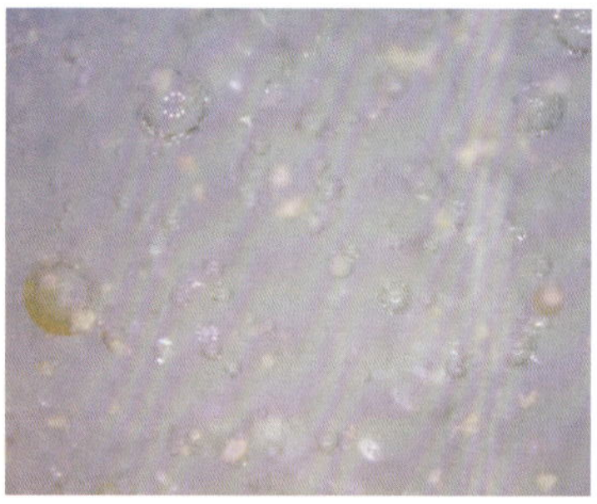
图5-3-5

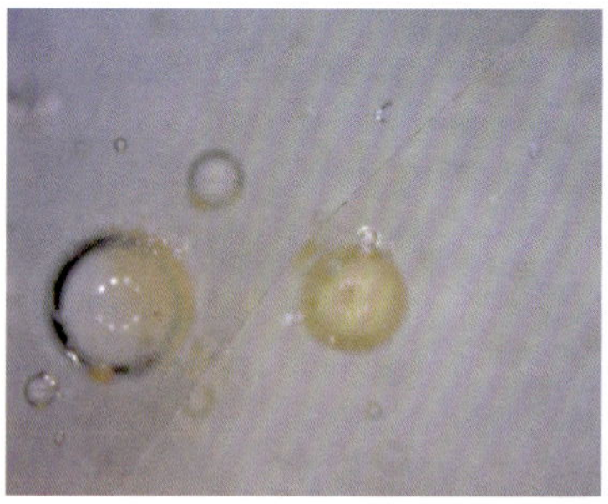
图5-3-6

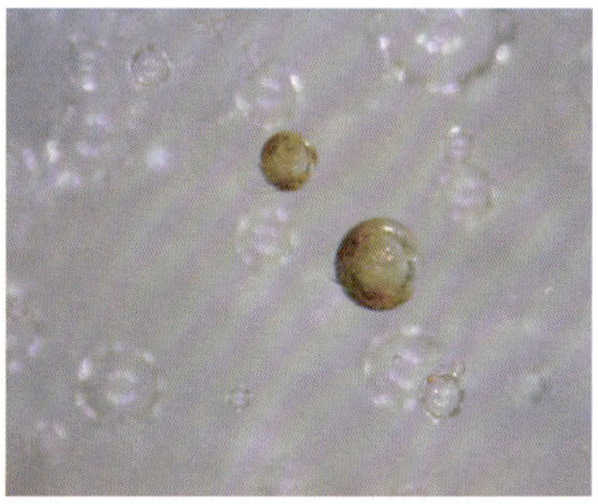
图5-3-7

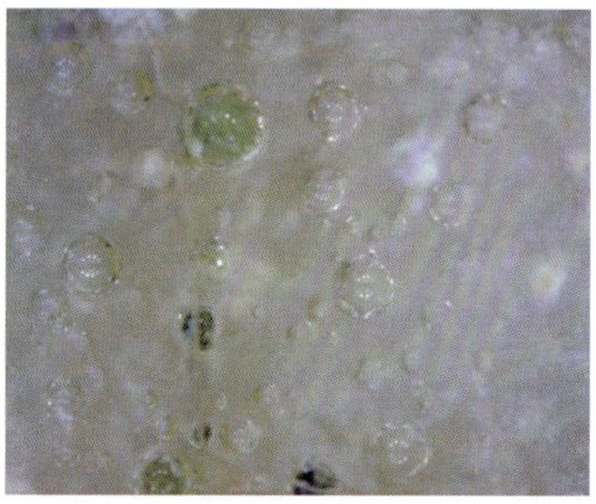
图5-3-8

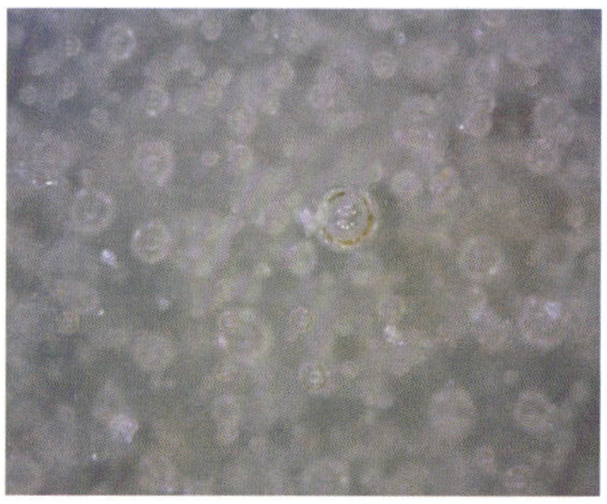
图5-3-9

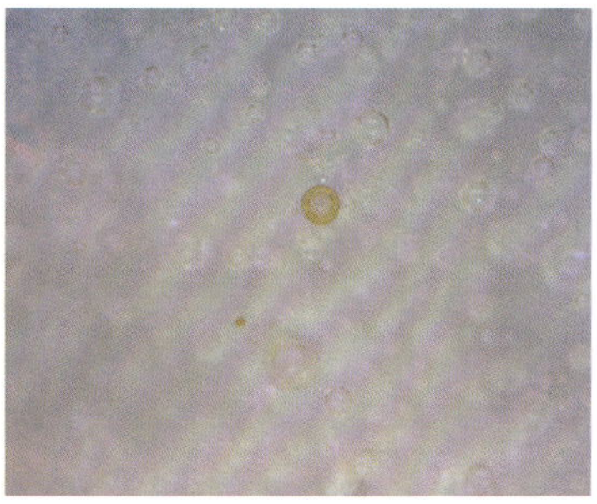
图5-3-10

图5-3-11

图5-3-12

IV. Certain Amount of Reaction Time

The coloration of air bubbles through natural weathering is a relatively long process due to the minute size of the channels. Through several controlled observations, it has been found that pieces sitting in an open air environment take approximately forty years to naturally develop color change bubbles. On pieces less than forty years of age, it is extremely rare to find yellow, brown, and so forth colored bubbles appearing (except for a trace amount of ashen colored bubbles sometimes created during the firing process).

c. Color Change Bubble Types

I. Unbroken Mouth Color Change Bubbles

i. Unbroken Mouth Color Change Bubbles Defined

Color change bubbles without an observable mouth under 500X magnification.

ii. Characteristics of Unbroken Mouth Color Change Bubbles

(a) Two-dimensional Characteristics of Unbroken Mouth Color Change Bubbles

(i) Coloration can include: Yellow, Brown, Black, and Green (see pictures 5-3-1—5-3-16).

(ii) Coloration can occur partially or completely (see pictures 5-3-1—5-3-16)。

(iii) Within a single bubble, color disparity can occur; with areas of lighter and darker coloration, the areas of darker coloration are often the weathering channels (see pictures 5-3-1—5-3-3, 5-3-11—5-3-13);

(iv) Some bubble coloration is more even, without clear coloration channels (see pictures 5-3-4—5-3-8).

(v) Some bubbles present with external coloration, resembling a halo, the interior of the bubble can also undergo partial coloration; Often the coloration is darker towards the outside of the bubble, and gradually grades to a lighter color in the center (see pictures 5-3-9 and 5-3-10).

(vi) Semi-Changed Bubbles with Clear Delineation: Clearly delineated borders between the colored portion and uncolored portion with no gradation evident is primarily caused by two types of factors: First, the interior wall of the bubble cracks, creating a displaced surface, blocking the progression of weathering along the bubble interior. Second, the interior of the bubble is topographically uneven, these concave and convex distortions act as barriers to weathering along the bubble interior (see pictures 5-3-11—5-3-16).

(b) Three-dimensional Characteristics of Unbroken Mouth Color Change Bubbles

(i) Some bubbles have clearly visible coloration channels observable on the glaze surface.

(ii) The channel surface area is usually much smaller than the underlying bubble.

(iii) The glaze surface surrounding the channel retains its smooth reflective nature.

(iv) Some bubbles do not present with visible channels, and the overlying glaze retains smooth reflective nature.

See pictures 5-3-17 and 5-3-18, where 5-3-17 is the two dimensional and 5-3-18 is the three-dimensional view of the same location.

Bubble A in picture 5-3-17 is not visible, but indicated by the red circle in picture 5-3-18. There are no clear scratches or damage to the glaze surface above Bubble A, thus the two spots of darker coloration are most likely the area of coloration channel (see Arrow B).

See pictures 5-3-19 and 5-3-20, where 5-3-19 is the two dimensional and 5-3-20 is the three-dimensional view of the same location.

Bubble C in picture 5-3-19 is not visible, but indicated by the red circle in picture 5-3-20. There are multiple scratches and mottles on the surface indicated by Arrow D, that may offer direct contact between the bubble and the external environment, acting as the coloration channel with the underlying bubble.

See pictures 5-3-21 and 5-3-22, where 5-3-21 is the two dimensional and 5-3-22 is the three-dimensional view of the same location.

Bubble E in picture 5-3-21 is not visible, but indicated

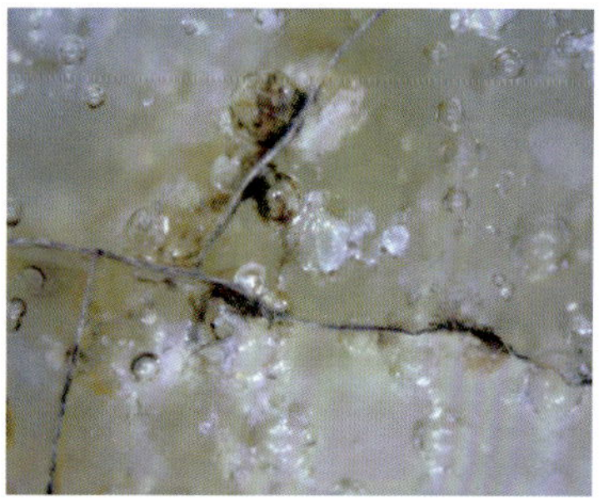
图5-3-13

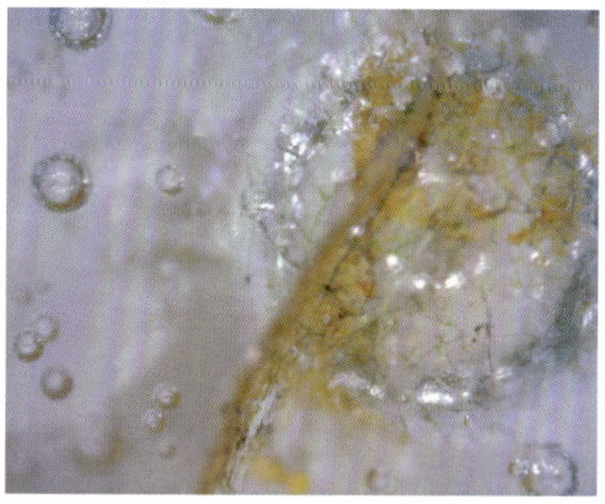
图5-3-14

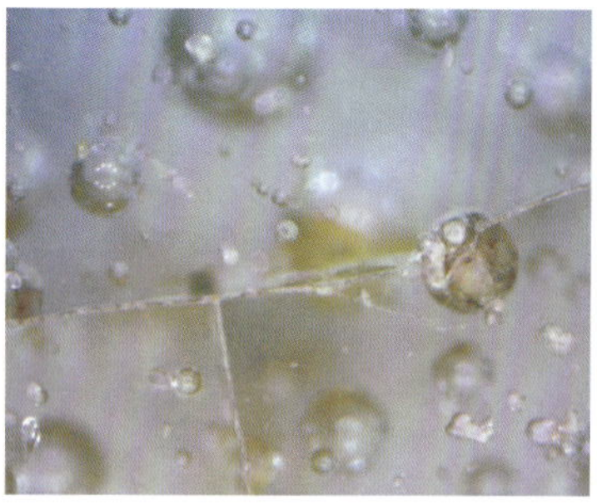
图5-3-15

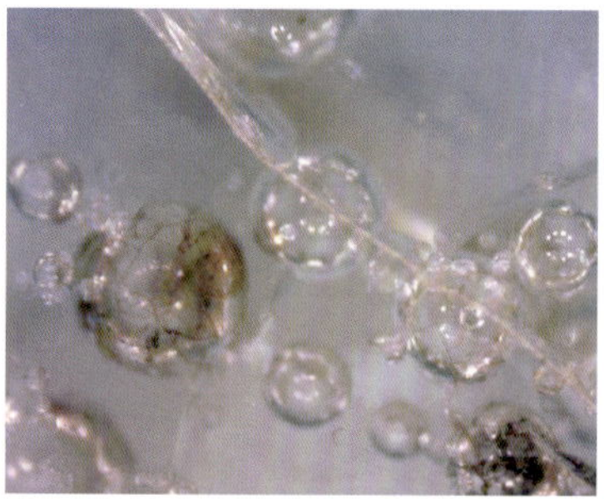
图5-3-16

（见图5-3-11—图5-3-16）。

B. 非破口色变泡三维特征

a. 有的气泡所在处釉表面可见清晰独立的通道。

b. 通道的面积通常远远小于气泡面积。

c. 通道周围的釉表面保持光滑洁净。

d. 有的气泡所在处釉表面不可见明显通道，釉表面光滑洁净。

见图5-3-17、图5-3-18，二者为同一器物同一位置图片，图5-3-17为二维图片，图5-3-18为三维图片。

图5-3-17中气泡A在图5-3-18中位于红圈釉下处，不可见。气泡A所在处的釉表面无明显划痕或损伤，但有两处颜色较浓（见箭头B所指处），这应该是外界连接气泡内的通道所在处。

见图5-3-19、图5-3-20，二者为同一器物同一位置图片，图5-3-19为二维图片，图5-3-20为三维图片。

图5-3-19中气泡C在图5-3-20中位于红圈釉下处，不可见。气泡C所在处的釉表面存在划痕及斑块（见箭头D所指处），应该是外界连接气泡内的通道。

见图5-3-21、图5-3-22，二者为同一器物同一位置图片，图5-3-21为二维图片，图5-3-22为三维图片。

图5-3-21中气泡E在图5-3-22中位于红圈釉下处，不可见。气泡E所在处的釉表面有一条明显的C形纹，应该是外界连接气泡内的通道。

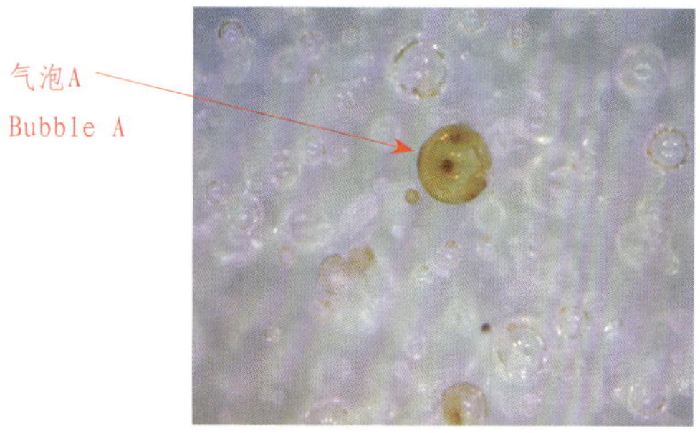

图5-3-17

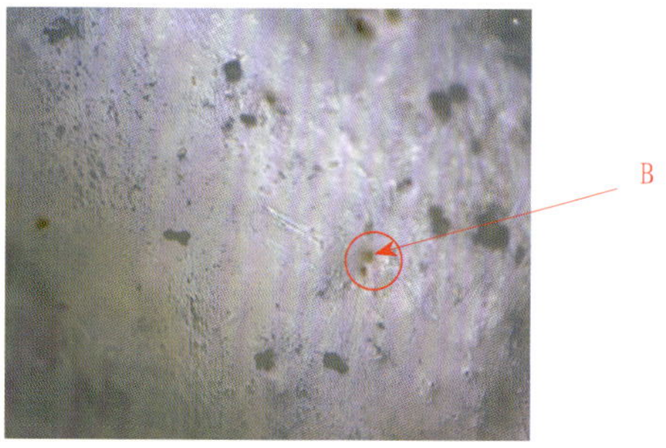

图5-3-18

by the red circle in picture 5-3-22. There is a clear C shaped striae on the glaze surface above Bubble E, which is most likely to be the area of the coloration channel.

See pictures 5-3-23 and 5-3-24, where 5-3-23 is the two dimensional and 5-3-24 is the three-dimensional view of the same location.

Bubble F in picture 5-3-23 is faintly visible beneath the glaze surface in picture 5-3-24 as indicated by the red circle. The overlying glaze surface is smooth and reflective, and no clear channel is evident. This is likely due to the minute size of the channel, as such it is unable to be observed under 500X magnification.

See pictures 5-3-25 and 5-3-26, where 5-3-25 is the two dimensional and 5-3-26 is the three-dimensional view of the same location.

Bubble G in picture 5-3-25 is faintly visible in picture 5-3-26, and the multiple small scratches presenting act as the coloration channels (see Arrow H).

Foreign materials are able to slowly pass through channels into the glaze surface and gradually create coloration within the bubbles, while the surface of the glaze is able to retain its smooth reflectivity.

B. Textured Bubbles

a. Textured Bubbles Defined

Textured Bubbles are the appearance of LKSC bubbles in which the interior has undergone weathering under the influence of the post-firing environment; gaining texture and losing their inherent translucency.

The determining factor as to whether a bubble can be considered textured is whether or not it has lost its translucency. If the bubble has a portion that has lost translucency, it can be considered a textured bubble.

b. Types of Textured Bubbles

I. Unbroken Mouth Textured Bubbles

i. Unbroken Mouth Textured Bubbles Defined

These are textured bubbles that do not have an opening observable under 500X magnification.

ii. Unbroken Mouth Textured Bubble Formation

Porcelain glazes present with a random distribution of cracks and openings. Additionally, acidic and alkaline solutions within soil can act to corrode the LKSC glaze surface, creating new cracks and openings on the glaze surface.

Foreign materials are able to pass through these channels and enter into the glaze bubbles, forming soluble and partially soluble salts. In environments of changing moisture, it is difficult for these materials to dissolve away. When water evaporates, salts and other particles can adhere and accumulate on the bubble interior, creating a textured bubble.

Ions within the soil and the glaze level react to form colored, partially soluble salt deposits, thus textured bubble can present with multiple colors.

Similar to the coloration patterns of colored bubbles, the area of darkest coloration indicates a channel to the external environment. These channel entry points are the first to experience weathering change, and coloration is most dense.

iii. Characteristics of Unbroken Mouth Textured Bubbles

(a) Two-dimensional Characteristics of Unbroken Mouth Textured Bubbles

See pictures 5-3-27—5-3-37.

(i) Colorations include: White, Yellow, Reddish-brown, Brown, and Black.

(ii) Some of the bubbles are completely changed, with the entire interior undergoing a change in texture; some are only partially changed, with only a portion of the interior texturized.

(iii) Some bubbles present without obvious color spectrum and some do not.

(iv) Due to the topographically uneven interior surface of the bubbles and various weathering forces, unbroken mouth textured bubbles present with a wide array of appearances.

(b) Three-dimensional Characteristics of Unbroken Mouth Textured Bubbles

(i) Bubbles have clearly visible coloration channels

见图5-3-23、图5-3-24，二者为同一器物同一位置图片，图5-3-23为二维图片，图5-3-24为三维图片。

图5-3-23中的气泡F，在图5-3-24中位于红圈釉下处，隐约可见轮廓。气泡F所在处的釉表面光滑洁净，通道不明显，可能是因为通道较小，用500倍显微镜难以观察到。

见图5-3-25、图5-3-26，二者为同一器物同一位置图片，图5-3-25为二维图片，图5-3-26为三维图片。

图5-3-25中的气泡G在图5-3-26中隐约只见淡淡轮廓，气泡所在处的釉表面有一处颜色较浓（见箭头H所指处），除此外釉表面还存在许多细小划痕，这些都应该是外界连接气泡内的通道。

外界物质通过釉表面的这些通道进入釉层中的气泡内，使气泡变色，形成色变泡。通道周围的釉表面保持光滑洁净。

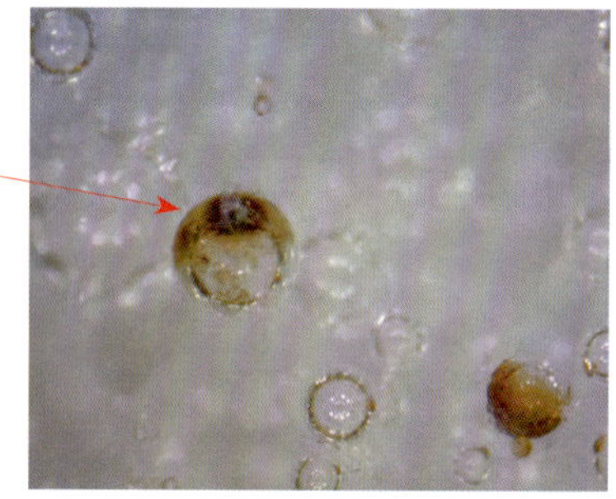

图5-3-19

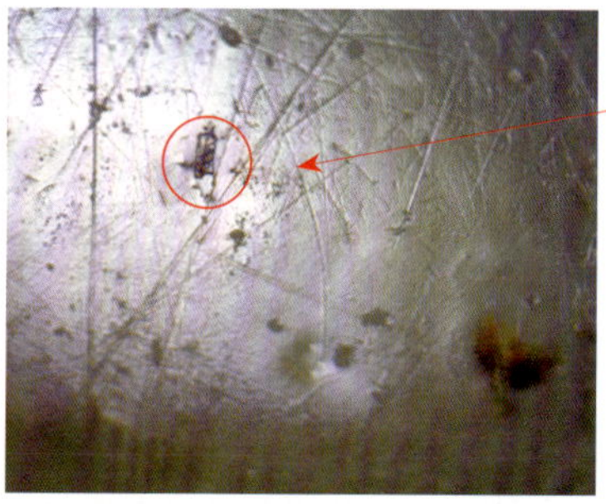

图5-3-20

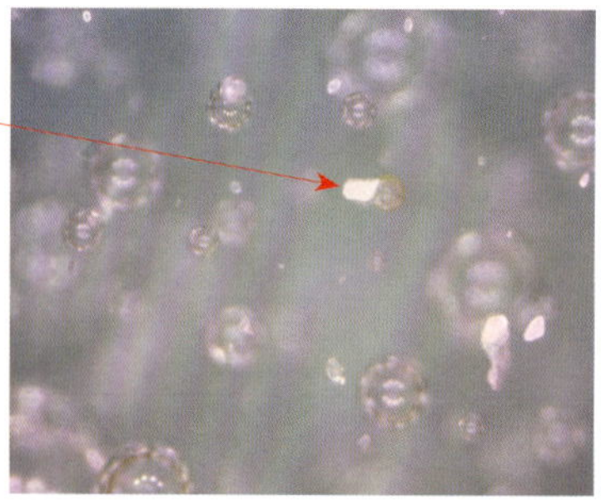

图5-3-21

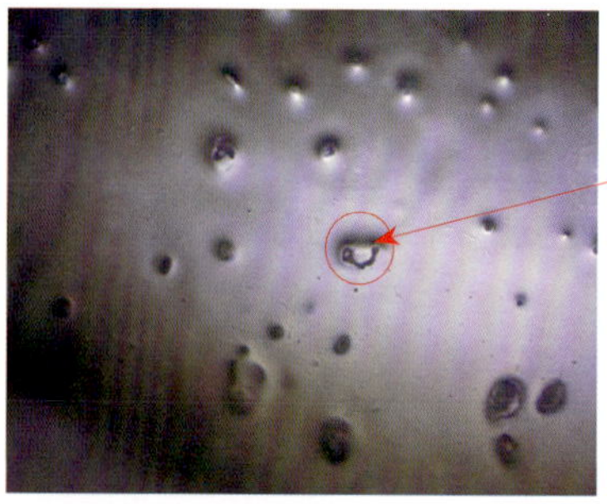

图5-3-22

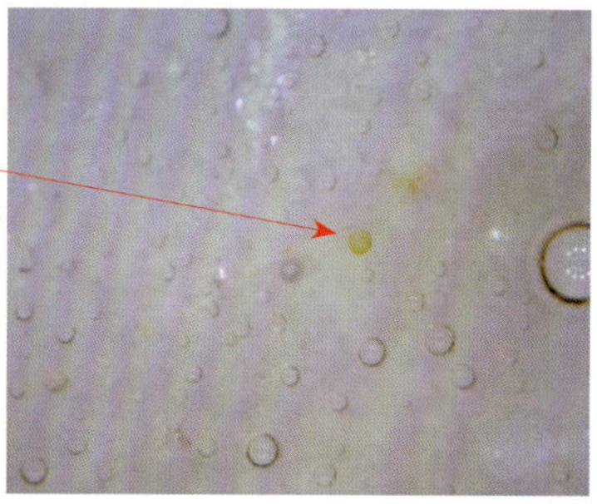

图5-3-23

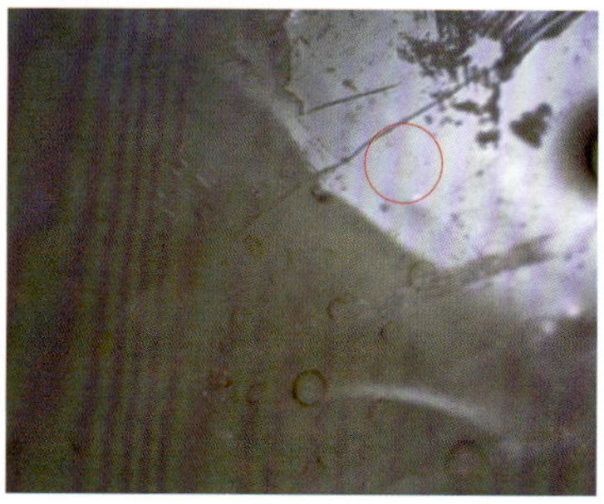
图5-3-24

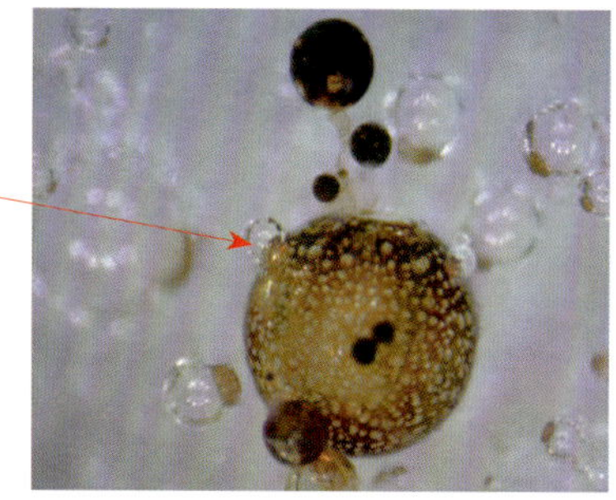

图5-3-25

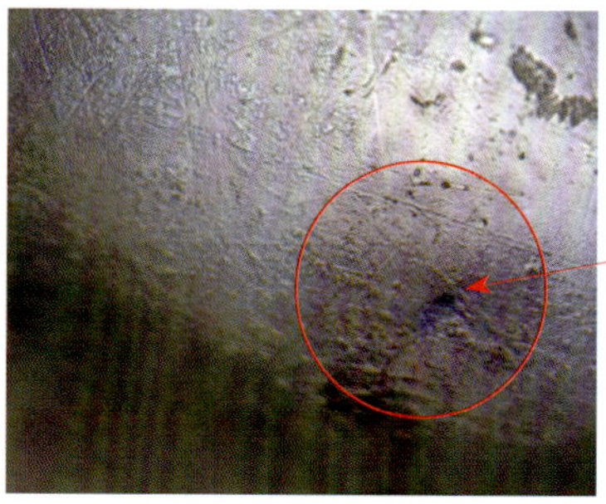

图5-3-26

observable on the glaze surface.

(ii) The channel size is usually much smaller than the underlying bubble.

(iii) The glaze surface surrounding the channel retains its smooth reflective nature.

See pictures 5-3-38 and 5-3-39, where 5-3-38 is the two dimensional and 5-3-39 is the three-dimensional view of the same location.

The surface area of Bubble I in picture 5-3-39 is smaller than that of the two-dimensional depiction in picture 5-3-38, the darker area on Bubble I in picture 5-3-39 is most likely the channel between the bubble and the external environment. The surface of the glaze retained its smooth reflectivity.

See pictures 5-3-40 and 5-3-41, where 5-3-40 is the two dimensional and 5-3-41 is the three-dimensional view of the same location.

Bubble J in picture 5-3-40 is not visible, but indicated by the red circle in picture 5-3-41. There is a scratch, a glaze crack, and an irregular distribution of pits on the surface of the glaze surrounding the weathered bubble. These are most likely the channels between the bubble and the external environment, while the remaining surface of the glaze retained its smooth reflectivity.

See pictures 5-3-42 and 5-3-43 where 5-3-42 is the two dimensional and 5-3-43 is the three-dimensional view of the same location.

Bubble K in picture 5-3-42 is faintly visible beneath the glaze surface in picture 5-3-43 as indicated by the red circle. There are multiple scratches and mottles on the surface, which may offer direct contact with the external environment, acting as the weathering channel with the underlying bubble. The surface of the glaze retained its smooth reflectivity.

II.Broken Mouth Textured Bubbles

i. Broken Mouth Textured Bubbles Defined

Broken mouth bubbles have an opening diameter, observable under 500X magnification, which does not exceed the largest diameter of the bubble.

Note: Conceptually, some bubble mouths are minute, unobservable under 500X magnification. These are unobservable-broken-mouth broken mouth bubbles. For the time being, these are classified as the unbroken mouth bubble type.

ii. Formation of Broken Mouth Textured Bubbles

The formation of broken mouth textured bubbles is similar to that of color change and unbroken mouth textured bubbles (See Formation of Color Change Bubbles and Formation of Unbroken Mouth Textured Bubbles headings of this section).

The weathering occurring in the bubble interior corrodes the internal glaze level; additionally, the weathering occurring on the glaze surface can also work to corrode towards the bubble. Thus, the formation of broken mouth bubbles can be divided into two types:

(a) Single Direction

(i) During the firing of LKSC, as molten glaze cools, if air bubbles come near to the surface of the glaze without breaking and the temperature cools relatively quickly, the air within the bubble contracts. This causes a small crater on the surface of the glaze, lower than the surrounding glaze surface (see picture 5-3-44), or higher than the surrounding glaze surface (see picture 5-3-45). This indention tends to collect sediments, which corrode the glaze.

(ii) During the firing of LKSC, as molten glaze cools, if air bubbles burst through the surface of the glaze and the temperature drops relatively quickly or the glaze is relatively viscous, the mouth of the bubble is unable to close, and a tiny hole in the surface of the glaze forms. However, these openings are often unobservable under 500X magnification. Over a long period of weathering, the glaze surface corrodes, and the mouth of the bubble progressively enlarges (see picture 5-3-46).

Under the above stated two types of glaze surface corrosion, the final result is a break in the bubble apex; creating a broken mouth bubble. Once a bubble mouth has opened, materials from the external environment can enter even more easily and weather the bubble, forming a broken mouth textured bubble.

(b) Double Direction

Similar to single direction, while one of the two types

（二）壁变泡

1. 壁变泡概念

壁变泡是龙泉窑系青瓷在后天环境影响下，釉层中的气泡内壁质地发生风化现象，被风化处失去了透影性的气泡。区分气泡内壁是否发生质变的依据就是气泡是否失去了透影性。如果气泡有部分风化处不具有透影性，气泡就属于壁变泡。

2. 壁变泡种类

（1）非破口壁变泡

①非破口壁变泡概念

非破口壁变泡是用500倍显微镜能观察到的完整无破口的壁变泡。

②非破口壁变泡形成

瓷器釉表面随机分布有裂纹或孔隙。此外，土壤中具有一定酸性或碱性的水溶液会侵蚀瓷器釉表面，使釉表面形成新的裂纹或孔隙。外界物质通过这些裂纹和孔隙进入气泡内，在气泡内生成可溶盐及难溶盐。在干湿交替的环境中，气泡中的难溶盐难以流失，可溶盐及一些细小灰尘在水蒸发后的气泡中形成结晶，它们在气泡内壁叠加沉积，形成壁变泡。

土壤中的及釉层中的阴阳离子会在气泡内发生反应，形成不同颜色的难溶盐沉积物，所以壁变泡有多种颜色。

与色变泡颜色变化规律类似，通常壁变泡哪个部位颜色浓，说明哪个部位很可能有连接外界的通道存在。所以，通道在壁变泡内的出口处，一般就是颜色最早变化和颜色较浓的地方。

③非破口壁变泡特征

A. 非破口壁变泡二维特征

见图5-3-27—图5-3-37。

a. 颜色有白色、黄色、红棕色、褐色及黑色等。

b. 有的气泡为全变，即整个内壁质地发生变化；有的为局变，即仅局部发生变化。

c. 有的气泡没有明显色阶变化，有的有色阶变化。

d. 由于气泡内壁的凹凸不平，风化作用多样，非破口壁变泡质地也呈现多种不同的形貌。

B. 非破口壁变泡三维特征

a. 气泡所在处釉表面可见清晰独立的通道。

b. 通道的面积通常远远小于气泡面积。

c. 通道周围的釉表面保持光滑

图5-3-27

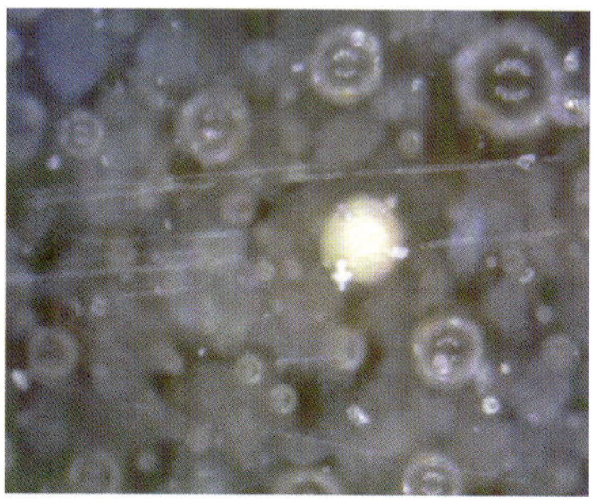

图5-3-28

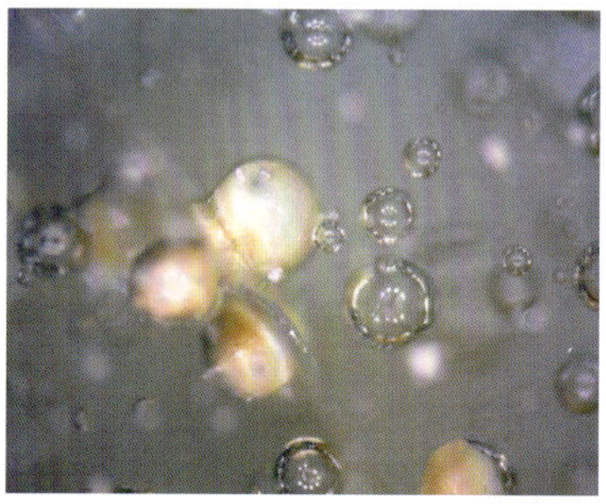

图5-3-29

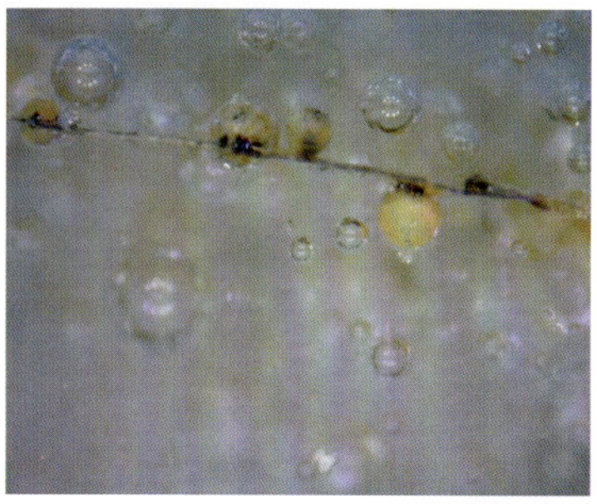

图5-3-30

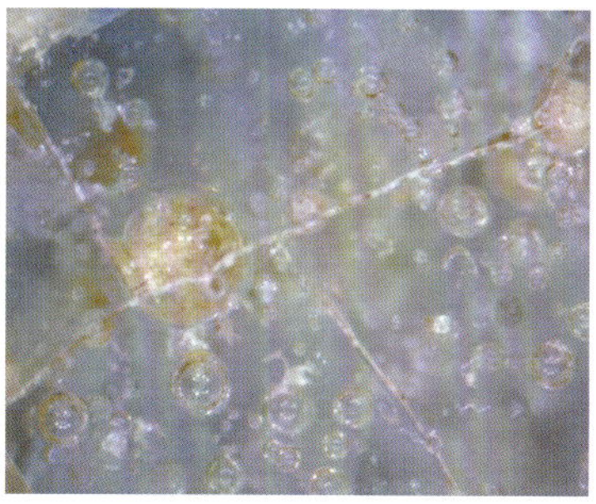

图5-3-31

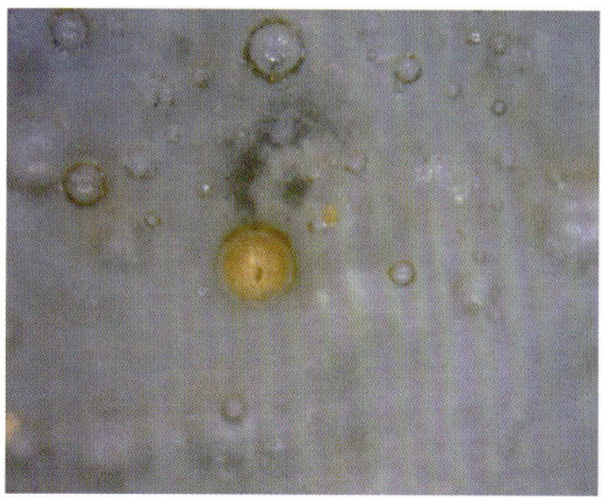

图5-3-32

of glaze surface level corrosion is occurring; simultaneously, because of alternate existing channels, internal weathering also occurs. Internal and external double directional corrosion thins the bubble wall and eventually creates a bubble mouth.

At the same time, the interior of the bubble is undergoing textural changes; the result is a broken mouth textured bubble.

iii. Broken Mouth Textured Bubble Types

(a) Characteristics of Broken Mouth Textured Bubbles

(i) Two-dimensional Characteristics of Broken Mouth Textured Bubbles

(1) The mouth portion of the bubble has a general circular shape (see pictures 5-3-47—5-3-54), or irregular shape (see pictures 5-3-55—5-3-63). The edges smooth; sometimes materials are observable beneath the mouth opening (see pictures 5-3-48—5-3-52, 5-3-55—5-3-62).

(2) Some appear with color spectrum (see pictures 5-3-49—5-3-57, 5-3-63), some are a single color (see pictures 5-3-47, 5-3-48, 5-3-58—5-3-62).

(3) Some bubbles become fully textured (see pictures 5-3-47—5-3-49, 5-3-56—5-3-61), and some become only partially textured, with the glass phase still visible (see pictures 5-3-50—5-3-55, 5-3-62 and 5-3-63).

(ii) Three-dimensional Characteristics of Broken Mouth Textured Bubbles

(1) The mouth edge is round and smooth.

(2) There are no other obvious channels other than the bubble mouth.

(3) It is possible to see other surface level channels other than the bubble mouth.

(4) The channel size is smaller than that of the bubble.

(5) The glass phase surrounding the channel retains clearly smooth reflectivity.

See pictures 5-3-64 and 5-3-65, where 5-3-64 is the two dimensional and 5-3-65 is the three-dimensional view of the same location.

Bubble L in picture 5-3-64 is faintly visible in picture 5-3-65. The edge of the mouth of Bubble L is round and smooth. There are no other obvious channels other than the broken mouth. The glass phase surrounding the bubble mouth is clean and smooth.

See pictures 5-3-66 and 5-3-67, where 5-3-66 is the two-dimensional and 5-3-67 is the three-dimensional view of the same location.

Bubble M in picture 5-3-66 is faintly visible in picture 5-3-67 and is indicated by the red circle. The mouth of Bubble M is clearly visible in picture 5-3-67; its edge round and smooth. Other than the CO striae and pit mottles indicated by Arrow N, the glass phase surrounding the bubble mouth is clean and smooth. The bubble mouth, CO striae and pit mottles are all possible channels between the bubble and the external environment.

Foreign materials are able to pass through these channels into the underlying bubble, creating a change to the bubble, causing it to lose its translucency, becoming a textured bubble.

See pictures 5-3-68 and 5-3-69, where 5-3-68 is the two dimensional and 5-3-69 is the three-dimensional view of the same location.

Bubble O in picture 5-3-68 has a visible broken mouth in picture 5-3-69. Bubble O has a black ring circling the broken mouth, which is also faintly visible three-dimensionally in picture 5-3-69. The broken mouth is rounded and smooth.

III. Summary

On a single piece of LKSC, round and irregular mouth bubbles can present simultaneously. The majority of the mouth edges present with a certain smoothness; the higher percentage of smooth openings being a quantitative trace change characteristic.

The phenomenon of broken mouth bubble weathering is a gradual process of material accumulation on the internal bubble wall, and not the complete filling of the bubble cavity. Coloration begins at the bubble mouth, where the coloration is darker. This is due to the fact that the open mouth is the channel to the external environment, and coloration begins at this point.

Aside from the bubble mouth, dark discolorations can also present over the bubble. These spots are the location of channels. Three-dimensional imaging can sometimes show

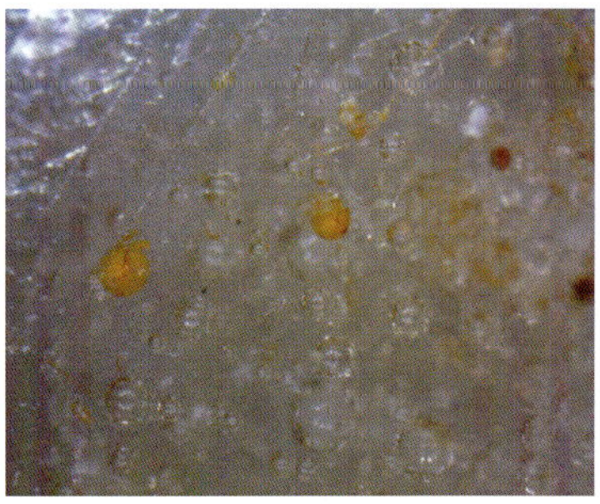
图5-3-33

图5-3-34

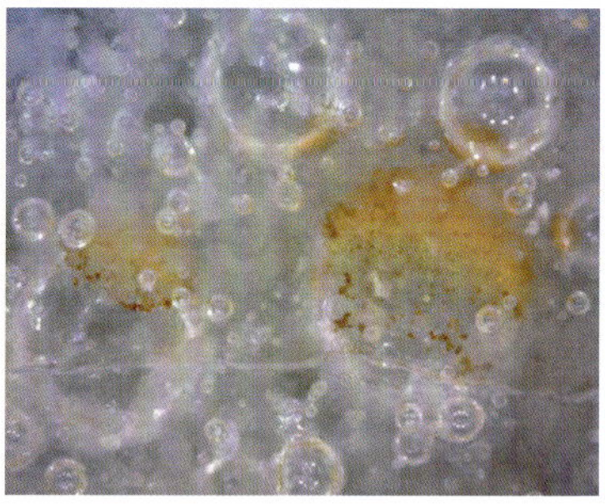
图5-3-35

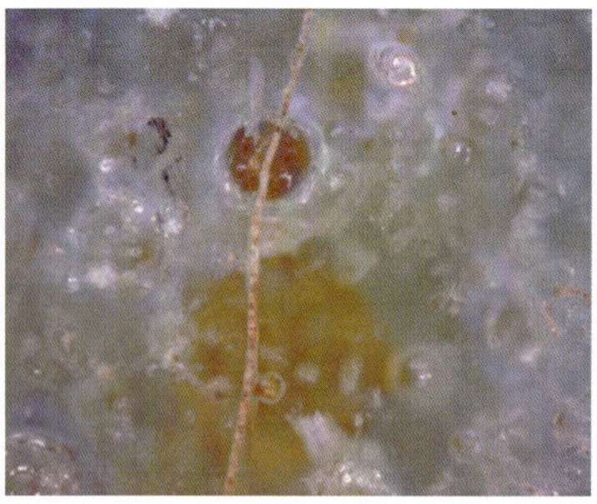
图5-3-36

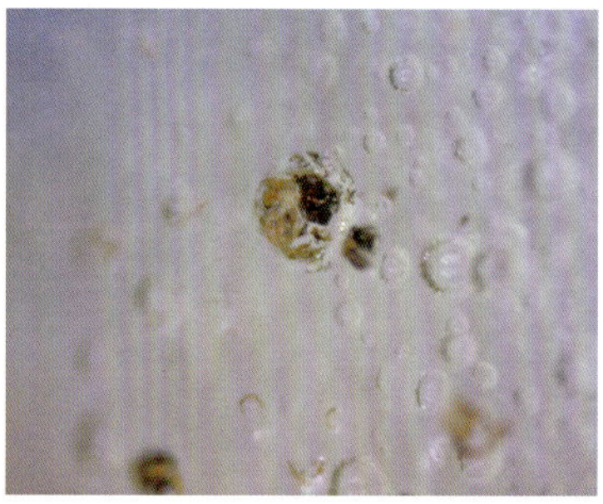
图5-3-37

洁净。

见图5-3-38、图5-3-39，二者为同一器物同一位置图片，图5-3-38为二维图片，图5-3-39为三维图片。

气泡I在图5-3-38中的釉表面三维成像面积小于在图5-3-39中的二维成像面积，气泡I在图5-3-39中颜色较深的地方，应该是外界连接气泡内的通道。通道周围的釉表面保持光滑洁净。

见图5-3-40、图5-3-41，二者为同一器物同一位置图片，图5-3-40为二维图片，图5-3-41为三维图片。

图5-3-40中的气泡J在图5-3-41中位于红圈釉下处，几乎不可见，气泡所在处的釉表面存在一条釉裂纹和一些不规则分布的坑点斑，它们应该都是外界连接气泡内的通道。这些通道周围的釉表面还

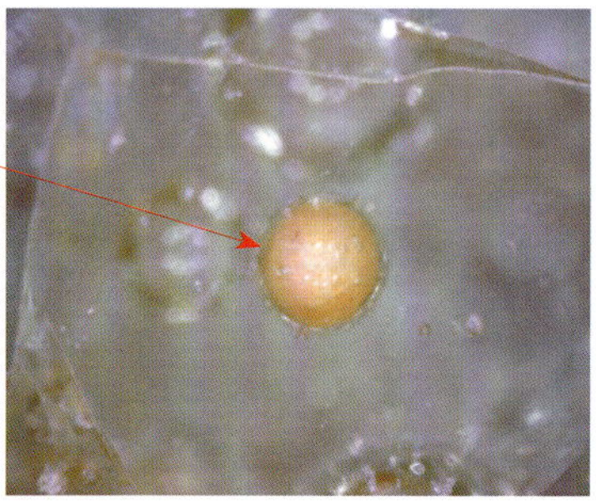

图5-3-38

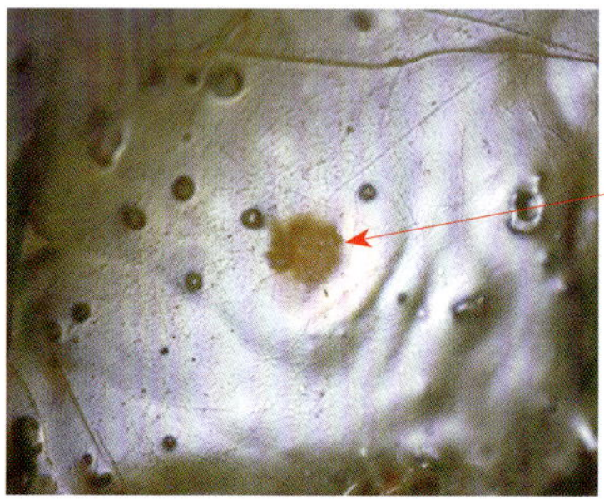

图5-3-39

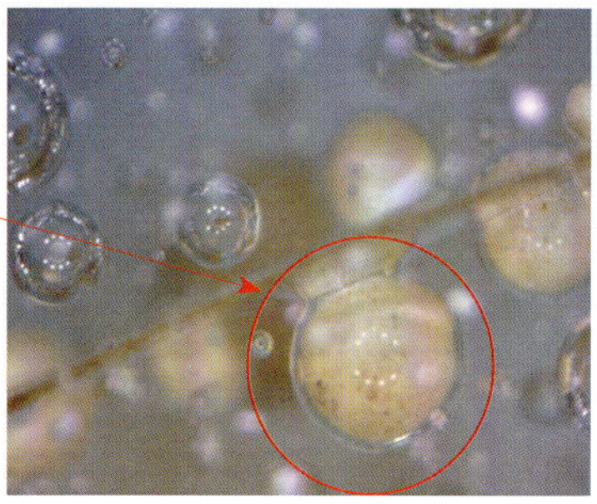

图5-3-40

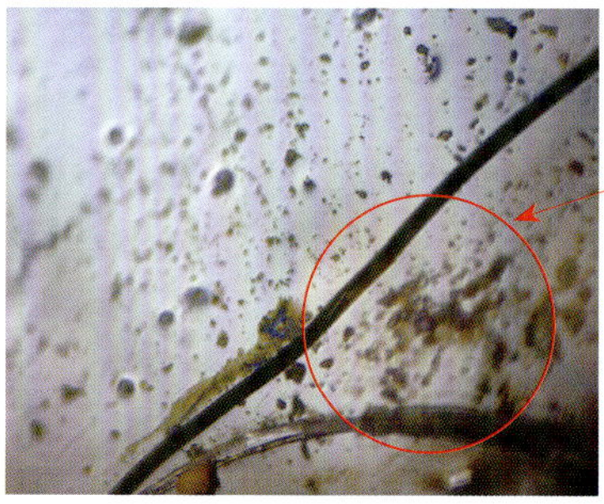

图5-3-41

channels clearly (i.e. scratches, mottles, etc.), and sometimes these channels are not evident. The surrounding glaze surface is clean and smooth.

On a single piece of LKSC, it is possible for there to be a congruent appearance of unbroken mouth and broken mouth textured bubbles. The weathering severity on the inside of unbroken mouth textured bubbles is usually less than that of broken mouth bubbles, which embodies the ceramic trace weathering passage of time principle.

3. Conclusion

Directly after the firing of LKSC, the air bubbles in the glaze are colorless and transparent, but under the influences of the post-firing environment, these bubbles can gradually weather to form colored and textured bubbles.

Some bubbles present with an even gradation of light to dark color spectrum.

Some bubbles can present with clearly darker areas of coloration that indicate the coloration channels, and represent the areas that first weathered. Through three-dimensional microscopic observation, some of these channels are visible (i.e. scratches, mottles, etc.) and some are not. The surrounding glaze surface retains clearly smooth reflectivity.

Color disparity between color change bubbles is also possible. Textured bubbles include foggy, frosted, and grainy needlepoint mottling, which represent differences in weathering severity. Textured bubbles can present with color spectrum, as well as a color disparity between bubbles.

It is sometimes possible to observe areas that have a clearly darker coloration on textured bubbles, these spots indicate locations of channels. Through three-dimensional microscopic observation, some of these channels are visible (i.e. scratches, mottles, etc.) and some are not. The surrounding glaze retains clearly smooth reflectivity.

The large majority of broken mouth bubble mouths are rounded and smooth.

The weathering characteristics of the bubble category on LKSC are consistent with the quantitative change and passage of time principles of ceramic traces, and embody the laws of ceramic trace formation and change.

是保持光滑洁净。

见图5-3-42、图5-3-43，二者为同一器物同一位置图片，图5-3-42为二维图片，图5-3-43为三维图片。

图5-3-42中的气泡K在图5-3-43中隐约只见淡淡的轮廓，气泡所在处的釉表面存在坑点斑及划痕，它们应该都是外界连接气泡内的通道。

（2）破口壁变泡

① 破口壁变泡概念

破口壁变泡是用500倍显微镜能观察到的，其破口直径小于气泡直径的壁变泡。

② 破口壁变泡形成

破口壁变泡的形成原因与色变泡以及非破口壁变泡的形成原因相似（参见本章本节色变泡形成及非破口壁变泡形成）。

气泡内壁的风化会对气泡内壁的釉层造成侵蚀，而气泡所在处釉表面的风化也会对釉层造成侵蚀，所以我们可将破口壁变泡的形成分成两类：

A．单向侵蚀

a. 青瓷高温烧制时，在熔融釉层冷却平复的过程中，当气泡升至釉表面而又未冲破釉表面时，如果降温较快，气体体积缩小，气泡上方的釉表面会形成凹槽，或低于釉表面（见图5-3-44）或高出釉表面（见图5-3-45）。凹槽易长期积垢从而侵蚀釉表面。

b. 青瓷高温烧制时，在熔融釉层冷却平复的过程中，有些升至釉表面的气泡，由于降温较快或釉层黏度较大而没有闭合，从而使釉表面出现微小的孔洞。不过这些孔洞过于微小，用500倍显微镜一般是观察不到的。长期的风化作用侵蚀釉表面，使孔洞逐渐变大（见图5-3-46）。

B．双向侵蚀

双向侵蚀，一方面同单向侵蚀的情况类似，另一方面，气泡内壁因通道存在也会产生风化作用。内外双向的风化作用会侵蚀气泡壁，从而产生破口；同时，气泡内壁的风化也使气泡内壁的质地发生改变，最终形成破口壁变泡。

两种形式的风化作用不断侵蚀釉表面，最终导致气泡上方的釉表面出现较大破口，形成破口泡，外界物质更易进入产生风化作用，形成破口壁变泡。

③ 破口壁变泡特征

A．破口壁变泡二维特征

a. 气泡破口既有较规整的圆形（见图5-3-47—图5-3-54），也有不规则形状（见图5-3-55—图5-3-63），但边沿都比较圆滑，有时破口下方可见物质存在（见图5-3-48—图5-3-52、图5-3-55—图5-3-

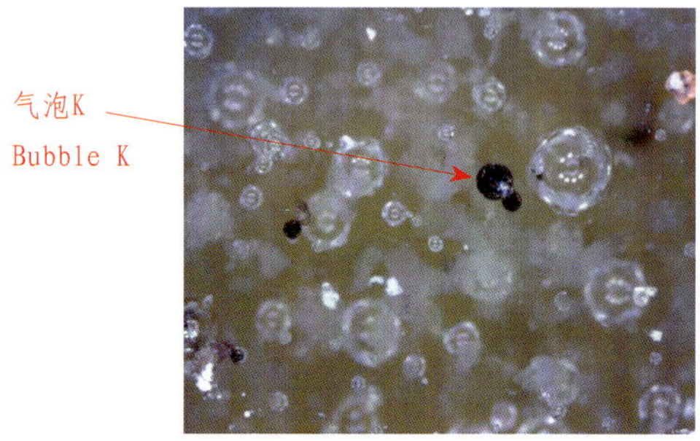

图5-3-42

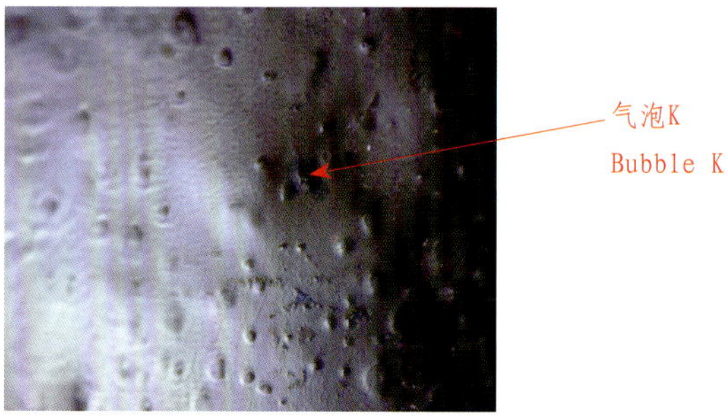

图5-3-43

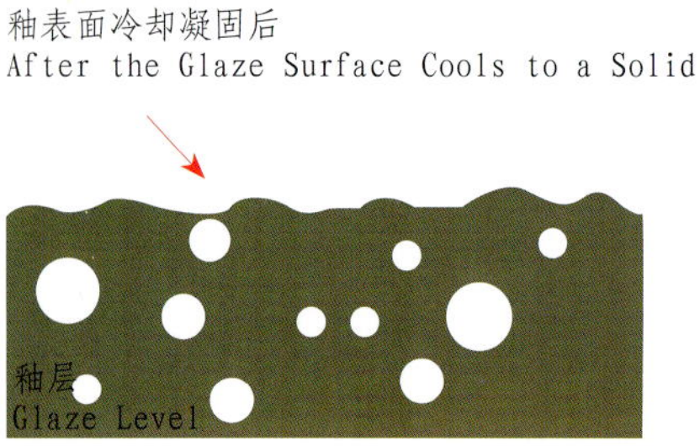

图5-3-44

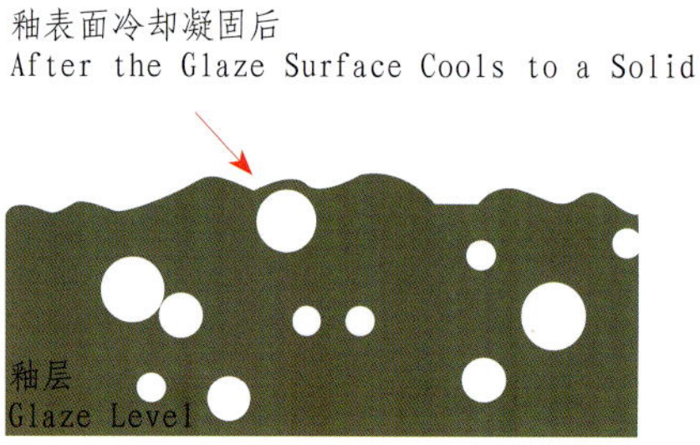

图5-3-45

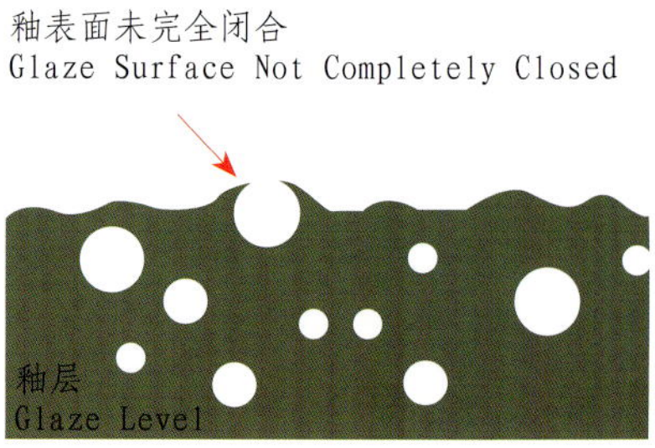

图5-3-46

62）。

b. 有的气泡内壁有色阶变化（见图5-3-49—图5-3-57、图5-3-63），有的没有明显色阶变化（见图5-3-47、图5-3-48、图5-3-58—图5-3-62）。

c. 有的气泡为全变破口壁变泡（见图5-3-47—图5-3-49、图5-3-56—图5-3-61），有的为局变，能见玻璃相（见图5-3-50—图5-3-55、图5-3-62、图5-3-63）。

B. 破口壁变泡三维特征

a. 气泡破口边沿圆滑。

b. 气泡所在处釉表面除破口外无其他明显通道。

c. 气泡所在处釉表面可见除破口以外的通道。

d. 通道的面积通常小于气泡面积。

e. 通道周围的釉表面保持光滑

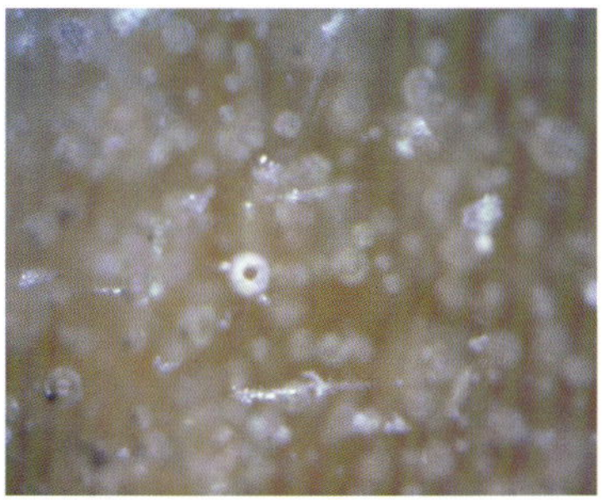

图5-3-47

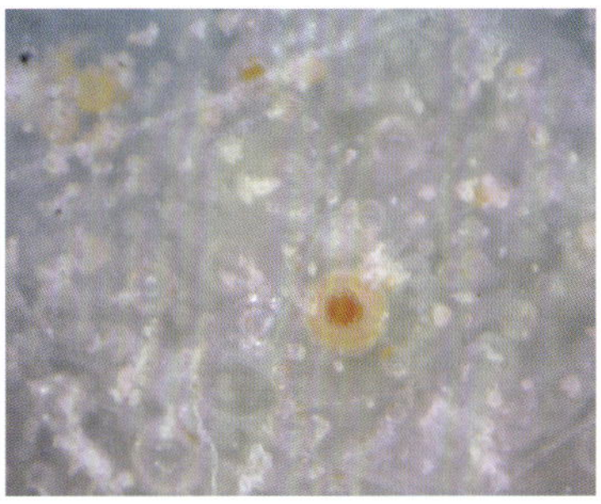

图5-3-48

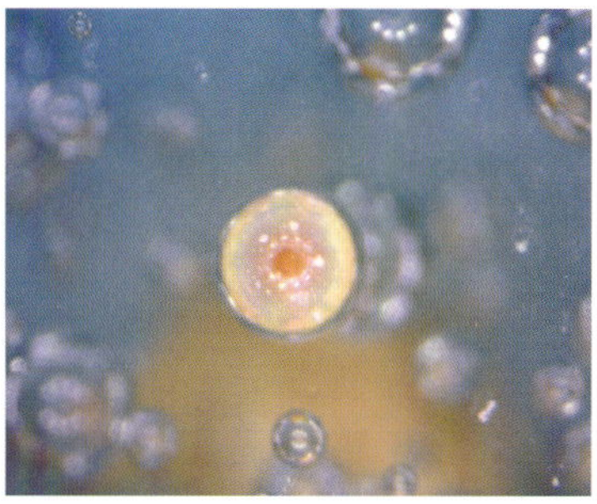

图5-3-49

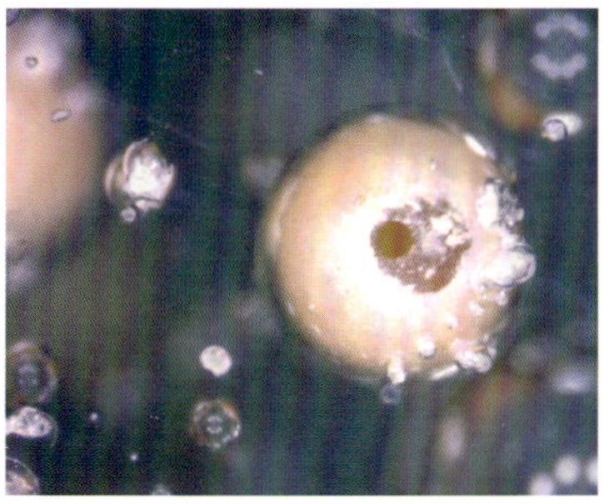

图5-3-50

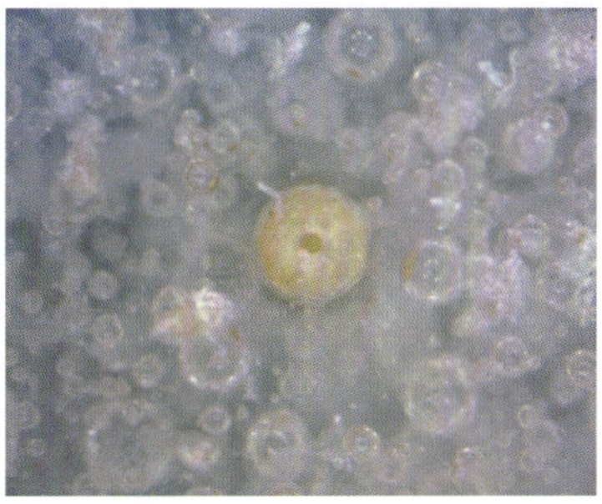

图5-3-51

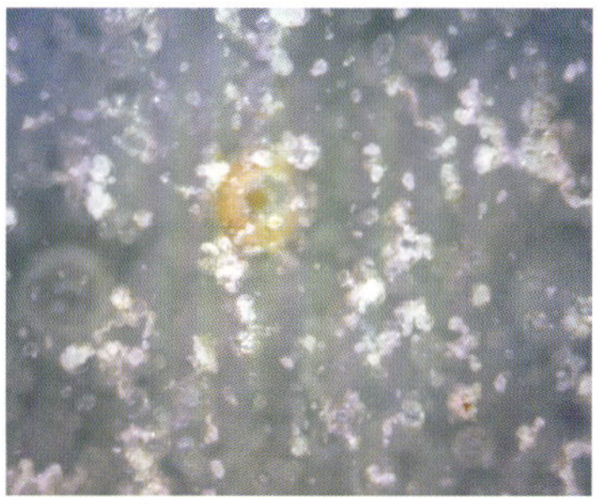

图5-3-52

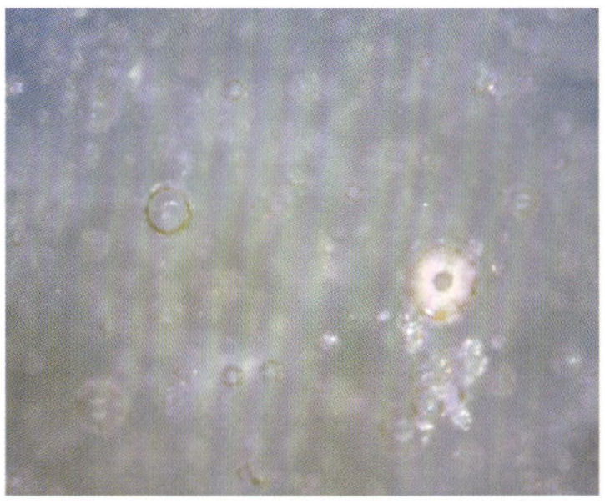

图5-3-53

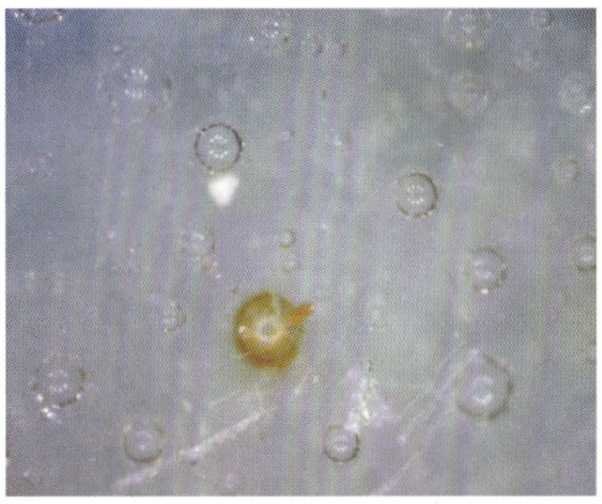

图5-3-54

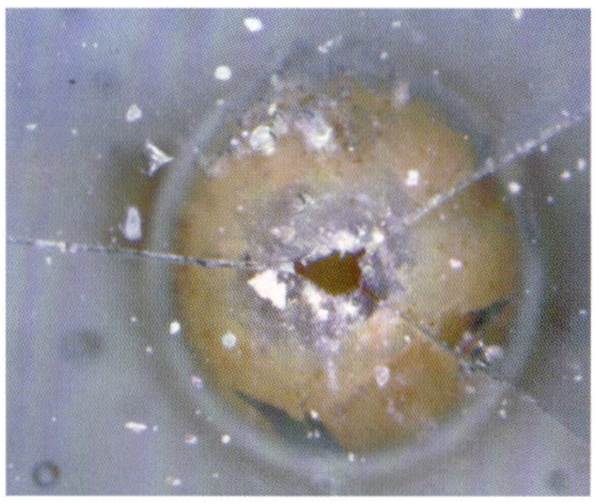

图5-3-55

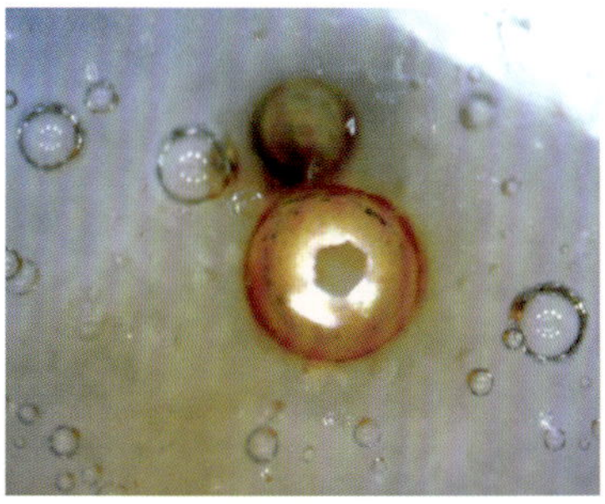

图5-3-56

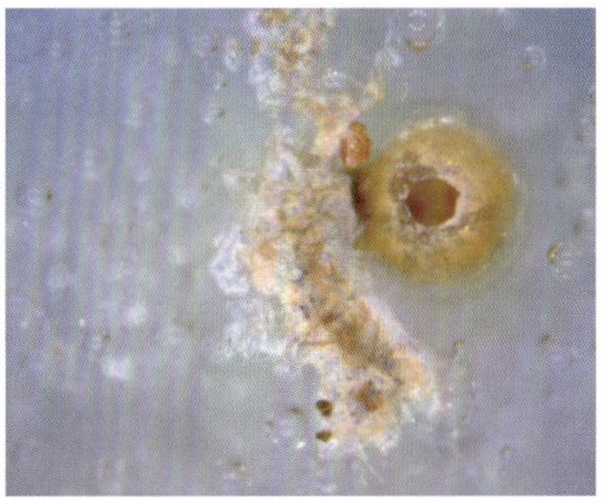

图5-3-57

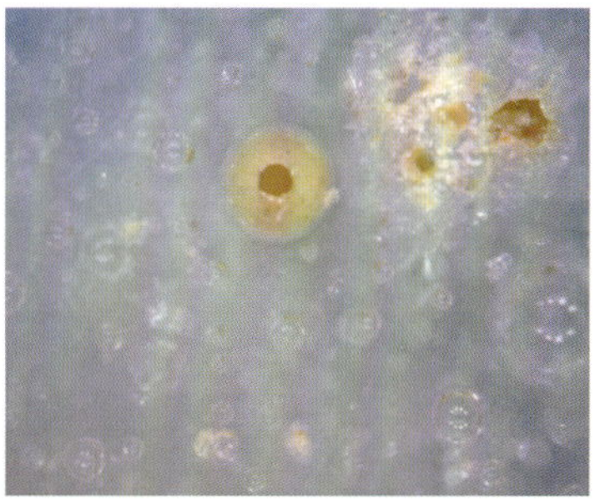

图5-3-58

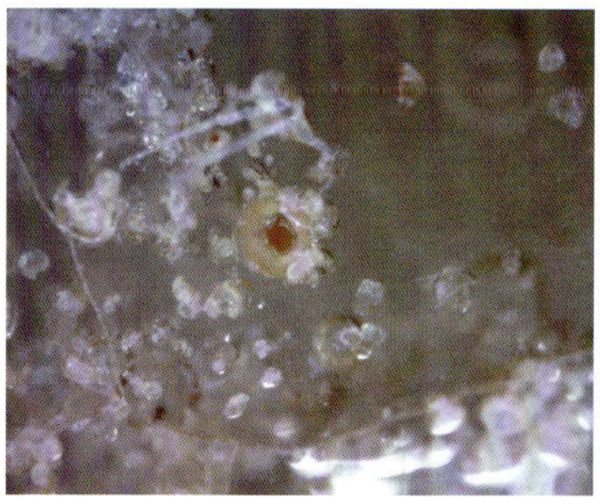

图5-3-59

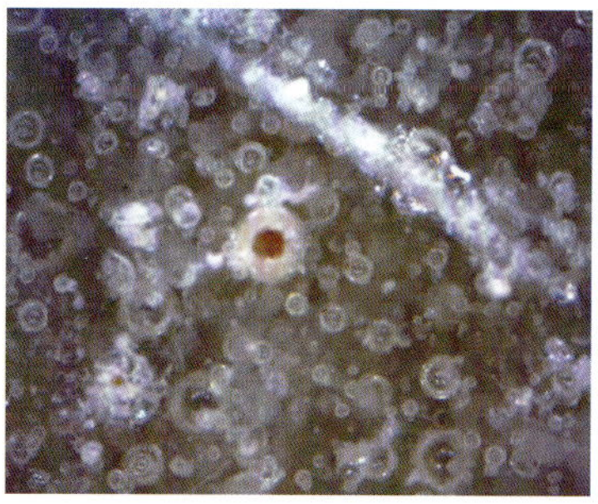

图5-3-60

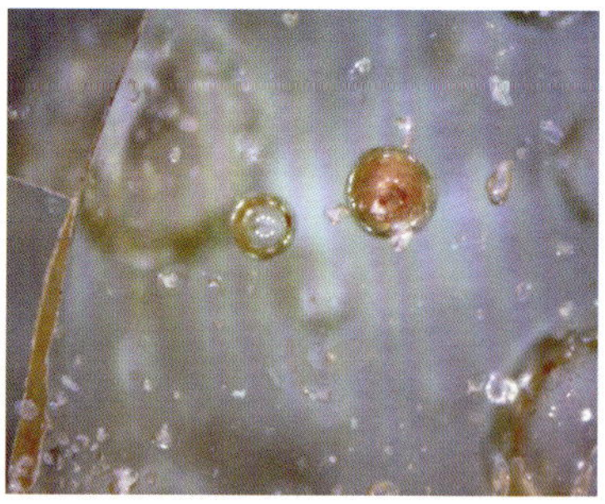

图5-3-61

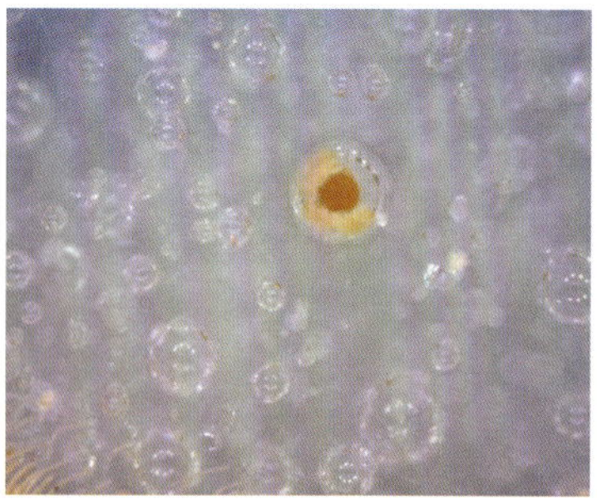

图5-3-62

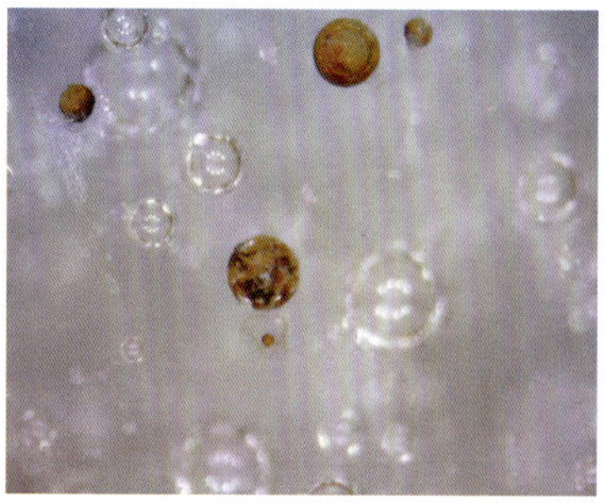

图5-3-63

洁净。

见图5-3-64、图5-3-65，二者为同一器物同一位置图片，图5-3-64为二维图片，图5-3-65为三维图片。

图5-3-64中的气泡L在图5-3-65中隐约只见淡淡的轮廓，破口边沿圆滑。除破口外，不见其他明显通道。气泡所在处的釉表面都保持光滑洁净。

见图5-3-66、图5-3-67，二者为同一器物同一位置图片，图5-3-66为二维图片，图5-3-67为三维图片。

图5-3-66中的气泡M在图5-3-67中位于红圈釉下处，隐约可见。气泡M的破口在图5-3-67中清晰可见，破口圆滑。破口周围有CO纹及坑点斑（见箭头N所指处），除此以外釉表面光滑洁净。CO纹、坑点斑和气泡破口都可以是外界连接气泡内的通道所在处。

外界物质通过釉表面的这些通道进入釉层中的气泡内，使气泡内壁发生质地变化，失去了透影性，形成壁变泡。通道周围的釉表面保持光滑洁净。

见图5-3-68、图5-3-69，二者为同一器物同一位置图片，图5-3-68为二维图片，图5-3-69为三维图片。

图5-3-68中的气泡O在图5-3-69中只见破口，气泡O的二维成像中，破口边缘一圈已变黑，这现象在图5-3-69的三维成像中，也隐约可见，另外还可见破口边缘圆滑。

（3）小结

在同一青瓷上，圆口破口壁变泡与非圆口破口壁变泡可以同时存在。它们中绝大部分破口边沿是圆滑的。同一器物上，破口圆滑率越高越能体现迹型的量变特征。破口壁变泡内的风化现象是侵蚀物紧贴气泡的内壁，以积累的模式渐进

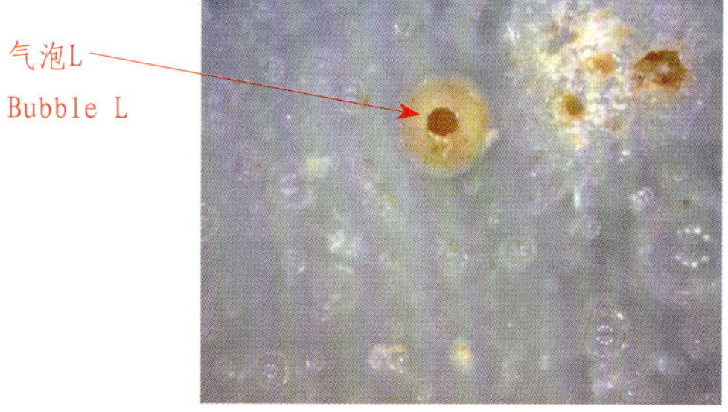

图5-3-64

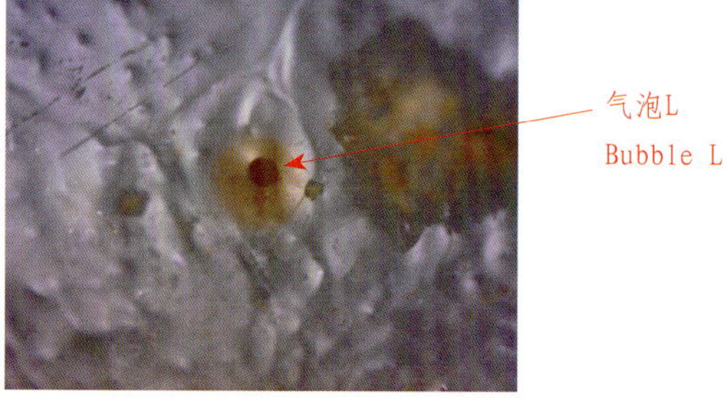

图5-3-65

风化，而不是弥漫在空间风化。气泡破口周围往往是颜色最早变化和颜色较浓的地方，因为破口是气泡连接外界的通道。除破口以外，破口壁变泡上还会有其他颜色明显较浓的地方，这些地方往往就是通道所在处。三维成像有时可观察到清晰的通道（如划痕、风化斑块等），有时通道不明显，釉表面光滑洁净。

在同一青瓷上，非破口壁变泡与破口壁变泡可以同时存在。非破口壁变泡内壁的风化程度一般要比破口壁变泡低，体现了陶瓷迹型风化的时间过程性原理。

三、总结

龙泉窑系青瓷釉层中的气泡，在刚烧制出来时基本上都是无色透明的，在后天环境的影响下，部分无色气泡会逐渐风化成色变泡和壁变泡。

有时色变泡呈现具有色阶浓淡的均匀过渡。

有时在色变泡上可观察到颜色明显较浓的地方，这些地方往往就是通道所在处，也是气泡最早开始变色的地方。三维成像有时可观察到清晰的通道（如划痕、风化斑块等），有时通道不明显，釉表面光滑洁净。色变泡之间也会有色差变化。

壁变泡有不同风化强度的表现。壁变泡内有时有色阶变化，壁变泡之间有色差变化。

有时在壁变泡上可观察到颜色明显较浓的地方，这些地方往往就是通道所在处，三维成像有时可观察到清晰的通道（如划痕、风化斑块等），有时通道不明显，釉表面光滑洁净。壁变泡破口大都比较圆滑。龙泉窑系青瓷上气泡类别的风化特征符合陶瓷迹型量变原理和时间过程性原理，体现了陶瓷迹型形成及变化的诸规律。

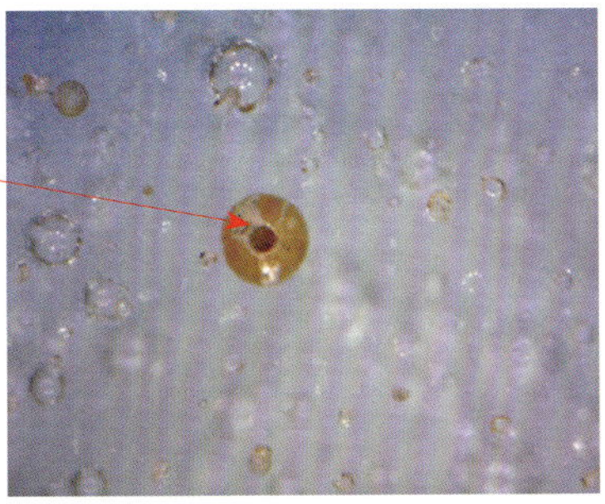

图5-3-66

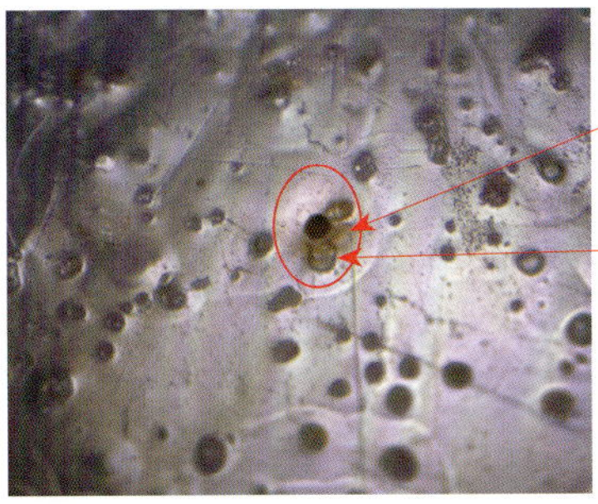

图5-3-67

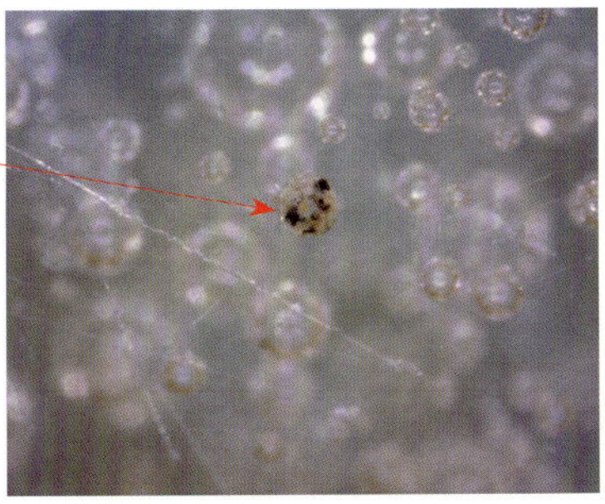

图5-3-68

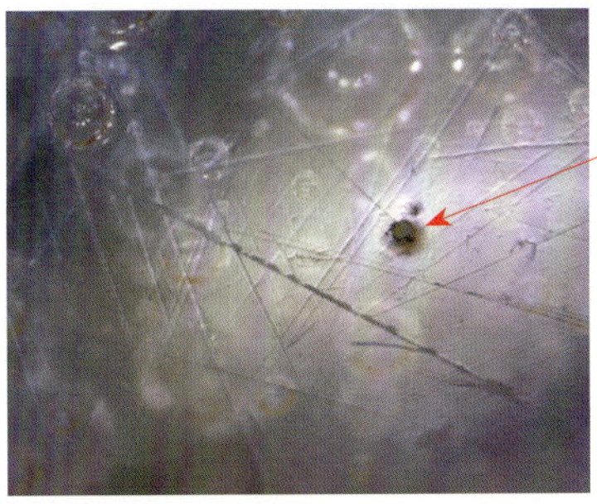

图5-3-69

第四节
龙泉窑系青瓷鬃眼类别

一、龙泉窑系青瓷鬃眼概念

龙泉窑系青瓷鬃眼是在龙泉窑系青瓷烧制过程中形成的釉层小孔。鬃眼是瓷器釉表面的缺陷，凭肉眼可见，但用肉眼通过小孔观察不到胎体。

二、龙泉窑系青瓷鬃眼形成与分布

龙泉窑系瓷器高温烧制过程中产生气泡，产生的气泡冲出釉表面后，会在釉表面留下小孔。当釉的黏度较高时，流动性差，加上瓷器胎质疏松等缺陷，会导致胎中有较多气体排出。在熔融釉层恢复的过程中，有些小孔不能被釉层覆盖，成为鬃眼。鬃眼现象与瓷器坯胎质地有直接关系，与釉料配方及釉层厚薄也有关系。鬃眼随机分布在瓷器有釉处。

三、龙泉窑系青瓷鬃眼特征

（一）鬃眼口部形状特征

1. 大多数鬃眼口部为不规则形状（见图5-4-1—图5-4-5），少数口部形状近似圆形或椭圆（见图5-4-6—图5-4-11）。

2. 有的鬃眼口部圆滑（见图5-4-1、图5-4-2、图5-4-6、图5-4-7、图5-4-9、图5-4-12），有的呈锯齿状（见

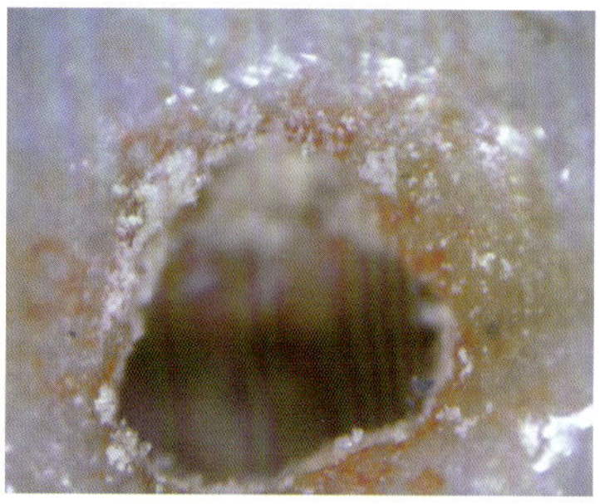
图5-4-1

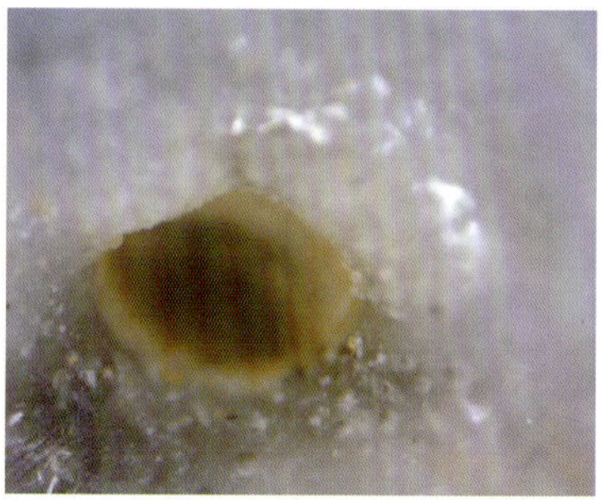
图5-4-2

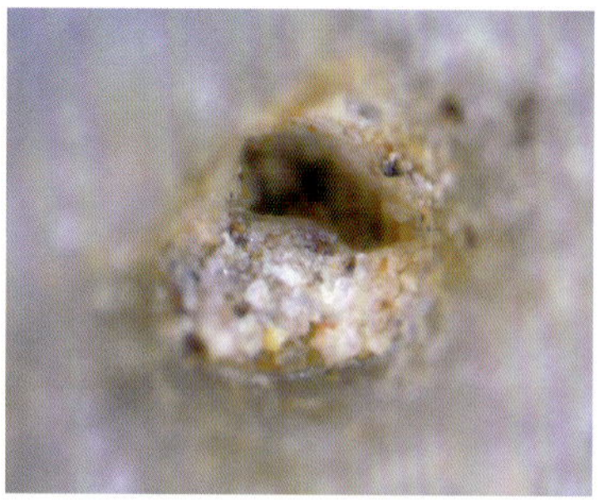
图5-4-3

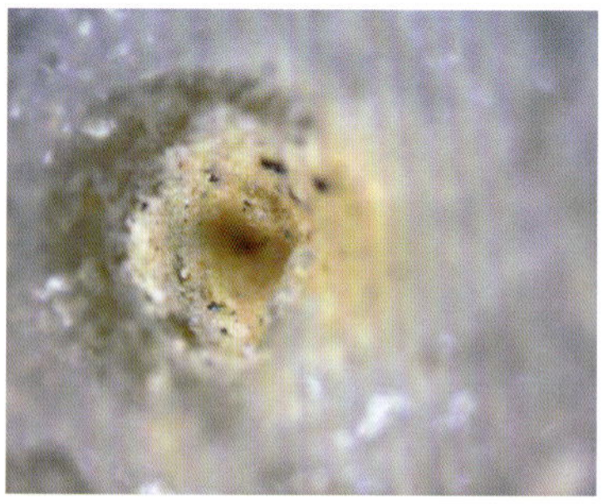
图5-4-4

图5-4-5

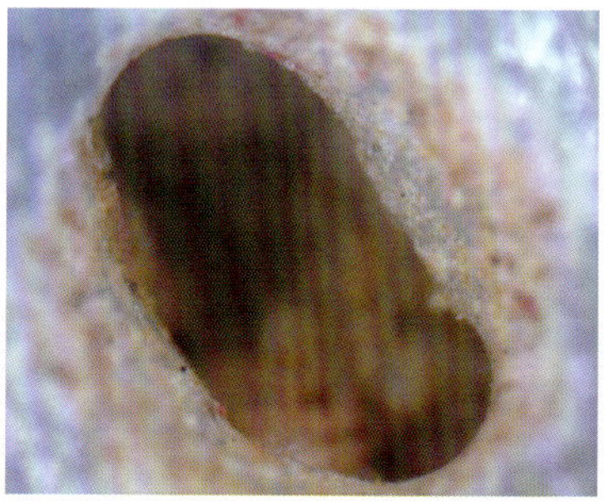
图5-4-6

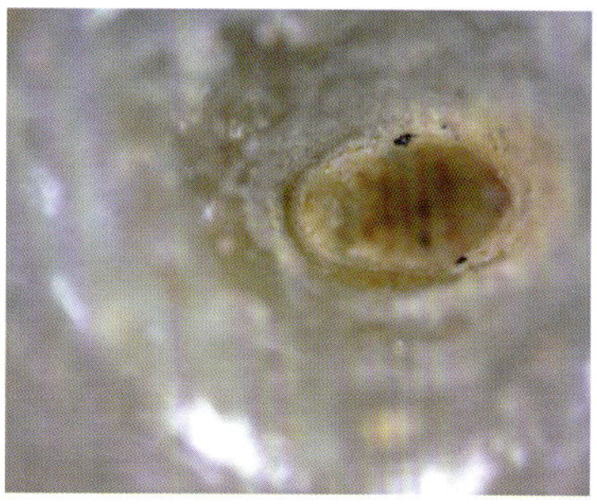
图5-4-7

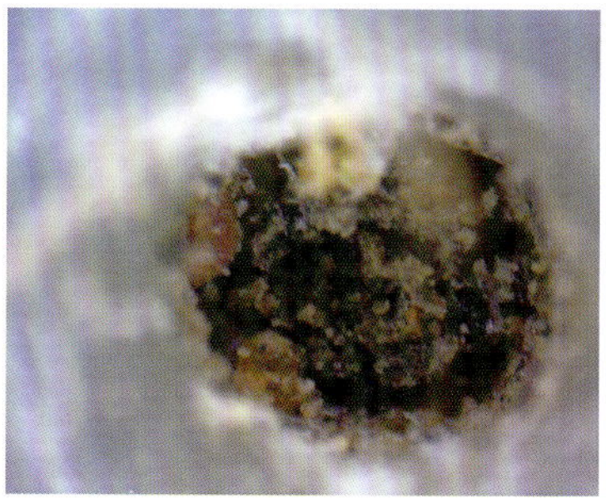
图5-4-8

Section 4:

Longquan Kiln System Celadon Bristle Pit Category

1. LKSC Bristle Pits Defined

Bristle Pits are the holes in the glaze level that were formed during the firing process of LKSC.

Bristle Pits are glaze flaws visible to the naked eye, however the ceramic body is not observable by the naked eye.

2. LKSC Bristle Pit Formation and Distribution

During the firing of LKSC, air bubbles are formed that can burst through the glaze level leaving small openings in the glaze surface. When the viscosity of the glaze is relatively high, its fluidity low, in addition to the looseness or other flaws of the ceramic body, larger amounts of gaseous bodies are expelled from the body. There are some openings that are not able to be completely covered by the molten glaze, forming bristle pits. The bristle pit phenomenon has a direct relationship with the qualities of the ceramic clay as well as the recipe and thickness of the glaze. Bristle pitting occurs randomly across the glaze of the porcelain.

3. LKSC Bristle Pit Characteristics

A . LKSC Bristle Pit Mouth Shape Characteristics

I. The majority of bristle pits present with irregularly shaped mouth openings (see pictures 5-4-1—5-4-5), a portion can also present as circular or ovular (see pictures 5-4-6 and 5-4-11).

II. Bristle pits mouths can present as round and smooth (see pictures 5-4-1, 5-4-2, 5-4-6, 5-4-7, 5-4-9 and 5-4-12), and can also present with saw-like teeth (see pictures 5-4-3—5-4-5, 5-4-11).

B. LKSC Bristle Pit Mouth Surroundings Characteristics

I. Coloration

Some bristle pit mouths can present with coloration, these include white, yellow, reddish-orange, brown, black and so forth (see pictures 5-4-13—5-4-18).

II. Presence of Other Traces

a. Floccus mottling under the glaze surrounding the pit mouth (see picture 5-4-19).

b. Colored bubbles can occur in conjunction with bristle pits (see picture 5-4-20).

III. Presence of Other Materials

a. Bristle pit mouths can present with filaments, primarily white in color. They can be long or short, thick or thin, independent or networked (see pictures 5-4-21—5-4-30).

b. It is possible for granulated materials to become covered by glaze surrounding the bristle pit mouth, colors include white, yellow, brown, and so forth (see pictures 5-4-31—5-4-35).

C. LKSC Bristle Pit Interior Characteristics

I. Coloration

Bristle pit interiors can undergo coloration, colors include white, yellow, reddish-orange、brown, black and so forth (see pictures 6-5-36—5-4-42).

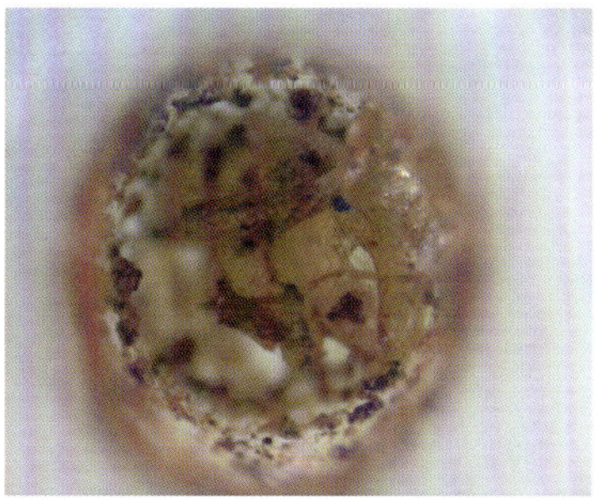

图5-4-9

图5-4-10

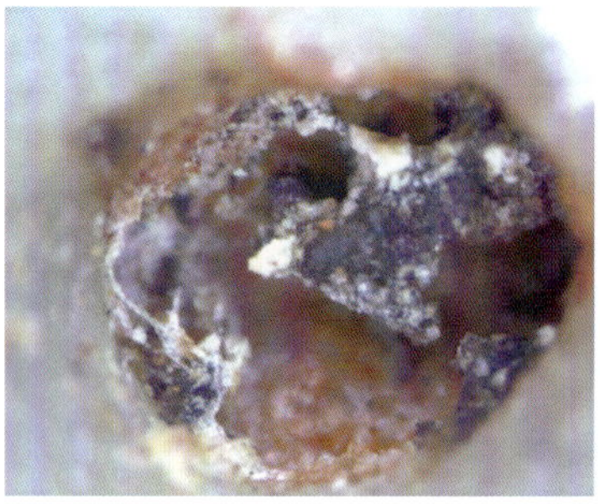

图5-4-11

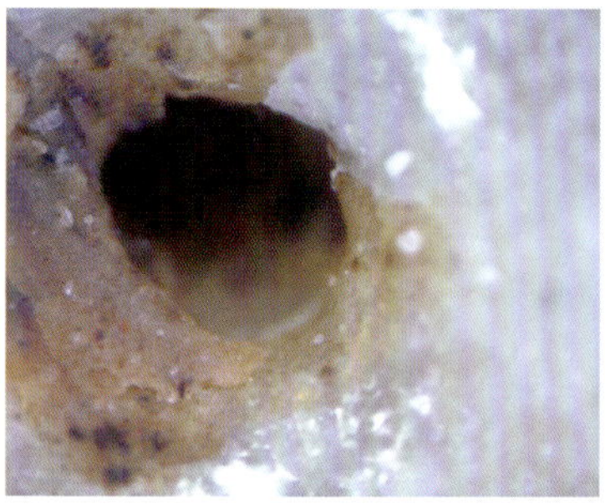

图5-4-12

图5-4-3—图5-4-5、图5-4-11）。

（二）鬃眼口部周围特征

1. 颜色变化特征

部分鬃眼口部周围的釉表面会有颜色变化，包括白色、黄色、橘红色、褐色及黑色等（见图5-4-13—图5-4-18）。

2. 其他迹型出现特征

（1）鬃眼口部周围釉下出现絮状斑（见图5-4-19）。

（2）鬃眼口部周围釉下存在色变泡（见图5-4-20）。

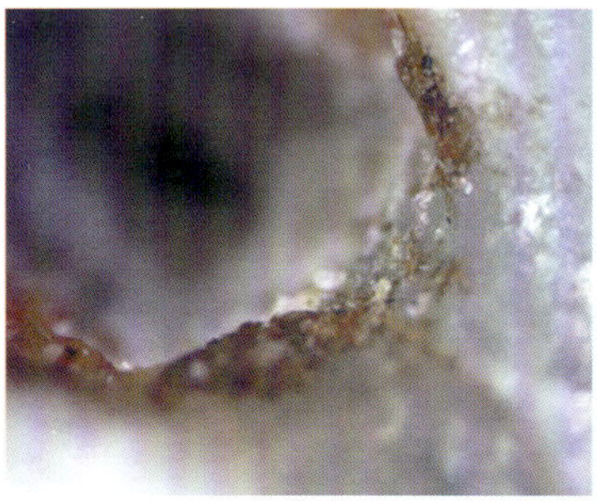

图5-4-13

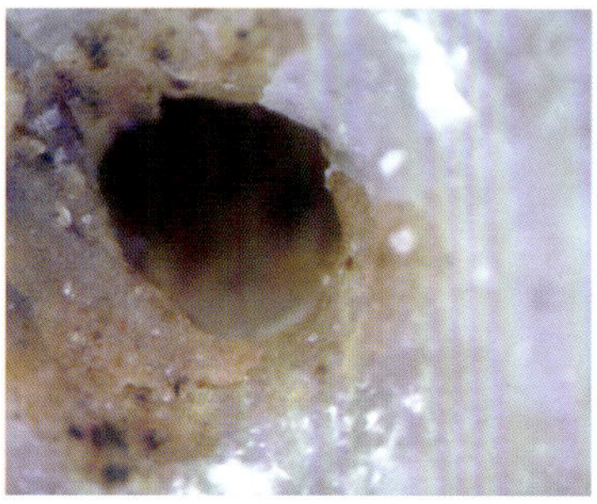

图5-4-14

图5-4-15

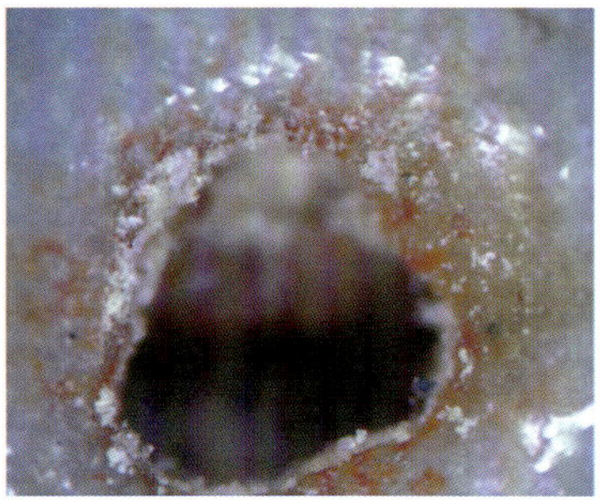

图5-4-16

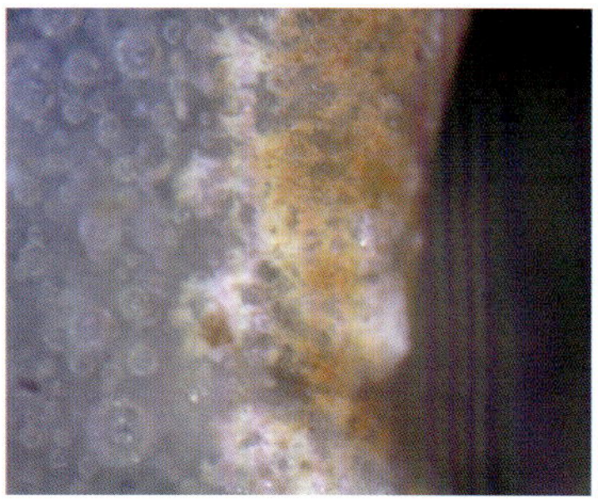

图5-4-17

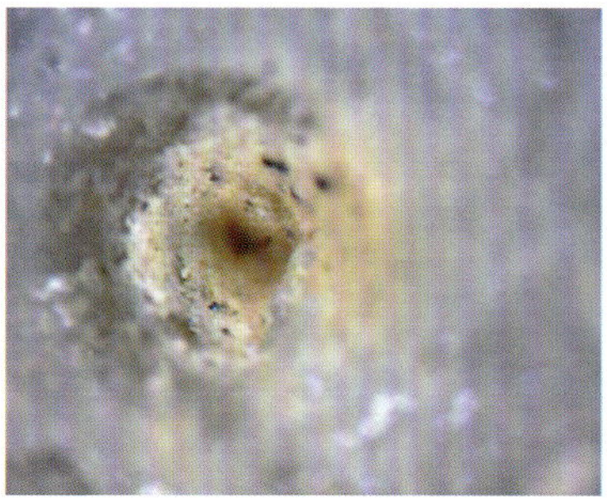

图5-4-18

II. Presence of Other Materials

a. Bristle pit interiors can also present with filaments, such characteristics are similar to those listed above (see pictures 5-4-43—5-4-48).

b. Bristle pit interiors can present with granulated material deposits. Granules can be large or small, independent or in clusters, and colors include white, yellow, brown, black, and so forth (see pictures 5-4-49—5-4-55).

4. Conclusion

Bristle pits are a common appearance in the LKSC glaze level. Pieces smaller in size or with relatively thin glaze rarely present with bristle pits.

The pit interior and mouth area often present with granule deposits and filaments. They can also present with color variation, and a portion of bristle pits present with floccus mottling or colored bubbles around the pit mouth.

Bristle pits reflect the glaze and clay composition as well as firing techniques characteristic to LKSC. Their weathering characteristics are in conjunction with the quantitative change and passage of time principles of ceramic traces and embody the laws of ceramic trace formation and change.

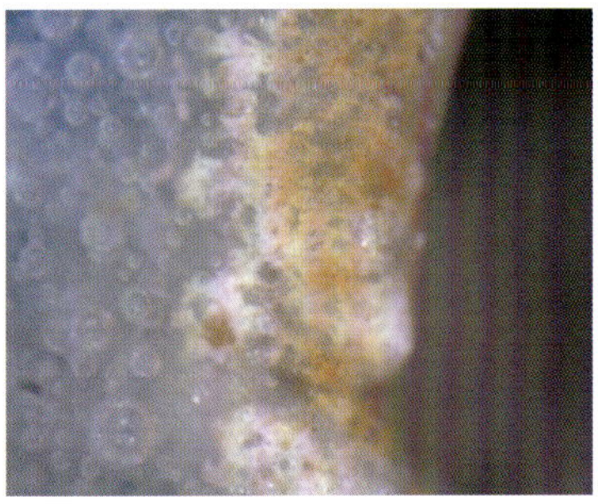
图5-4-19

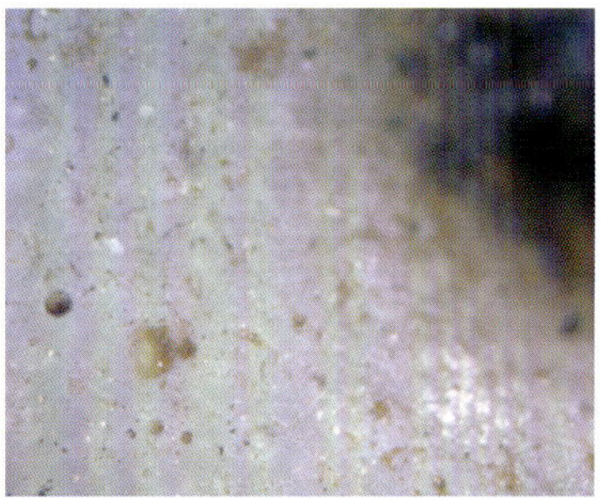
图5-4-20

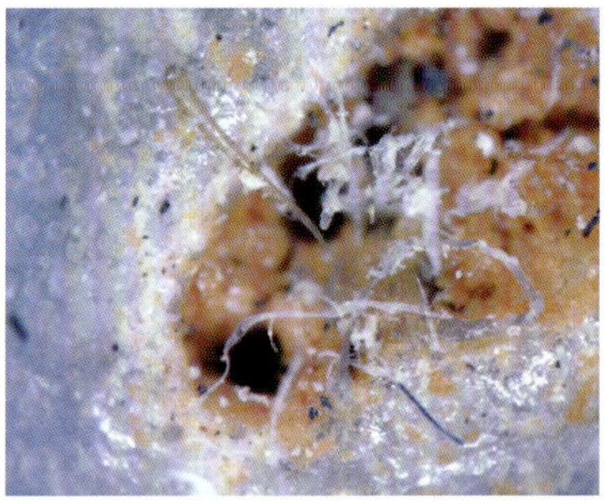
图5-4-21

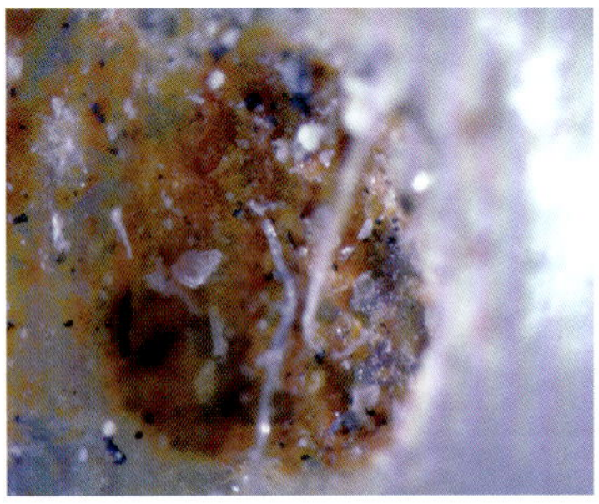
图5-4-22

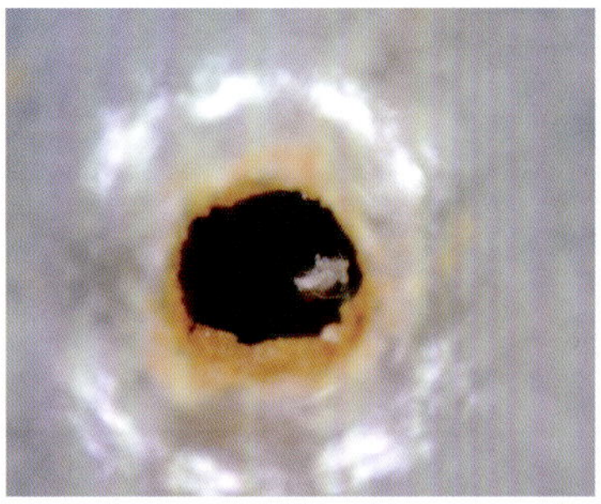
图5-4-23

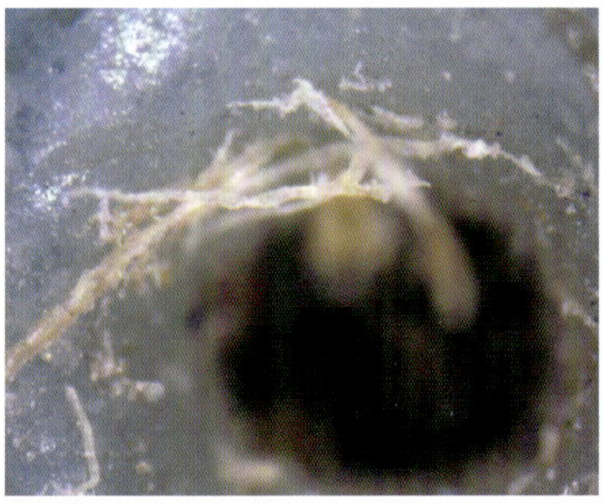
图5-4-24

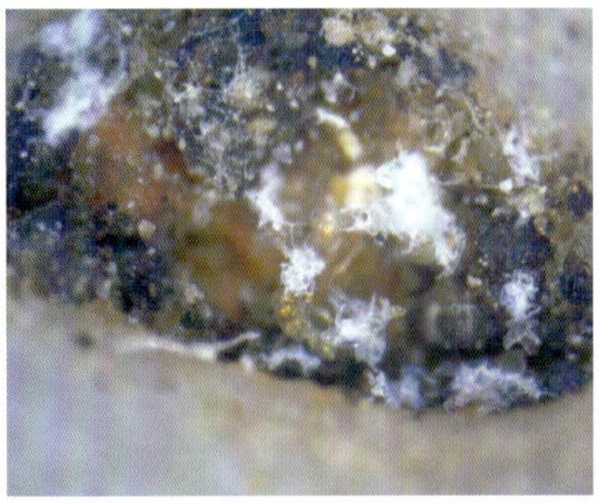
图5-4-25

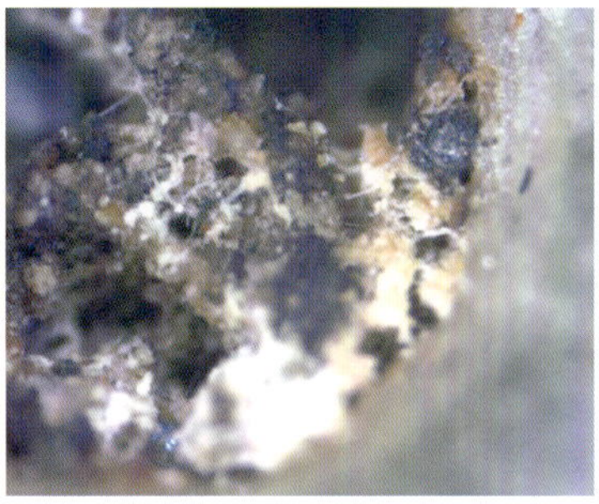
图5-4-26

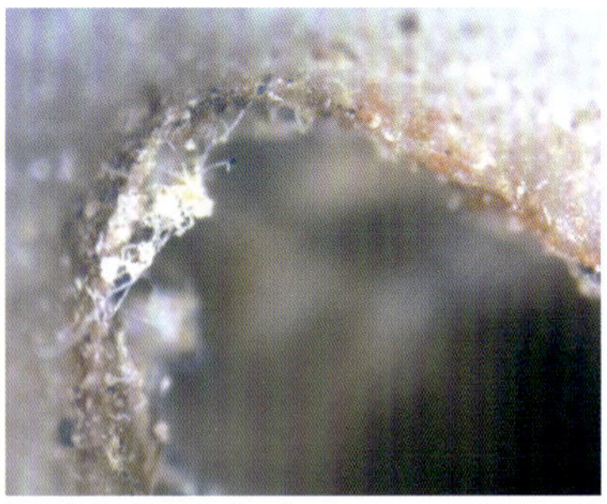
图5-4-27

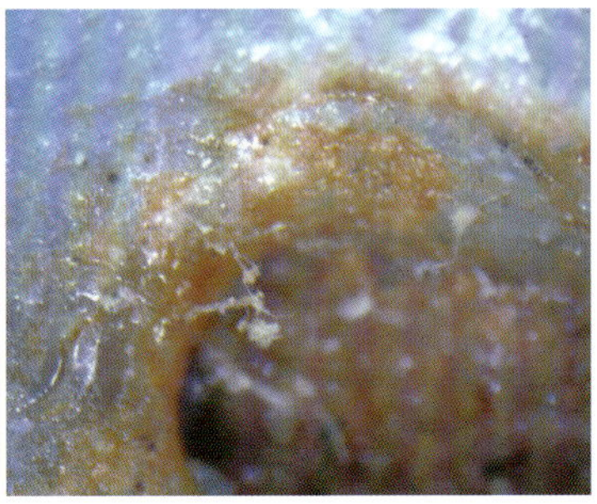
图5-4-28

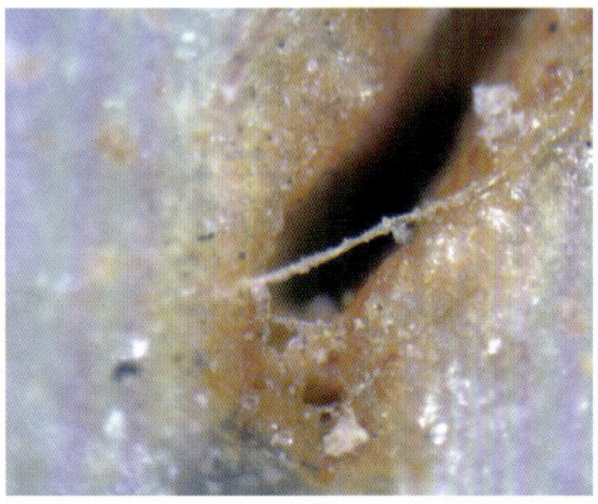
图5-4-29

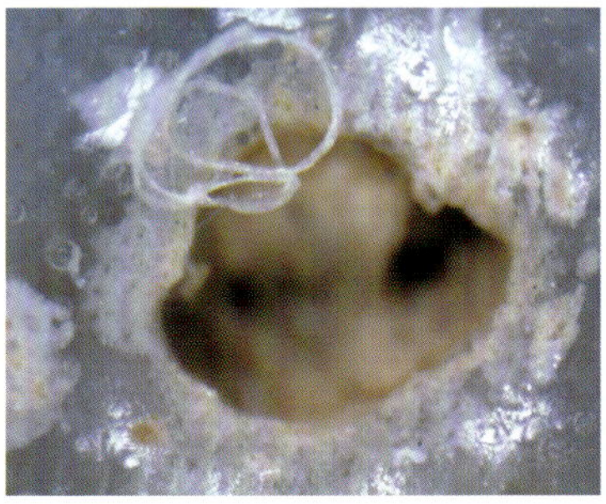
图5-4-30

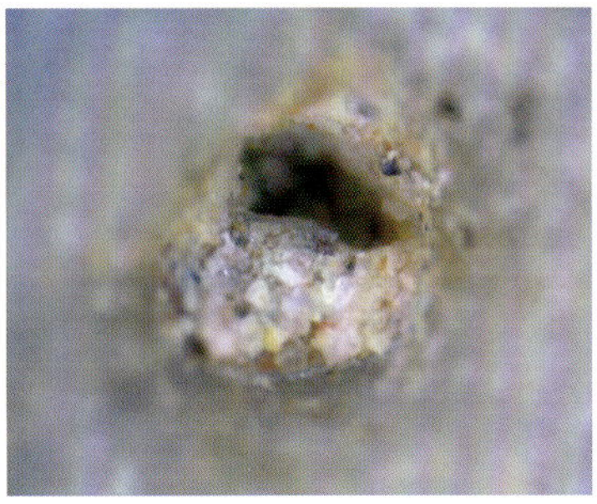
图5-4-31

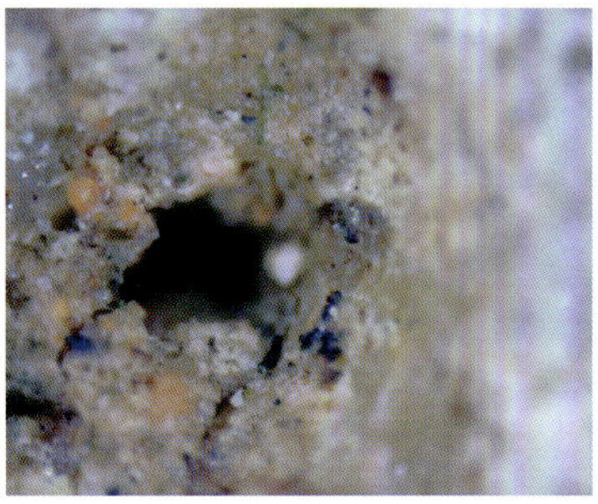
图5-4-32

图5-4-33

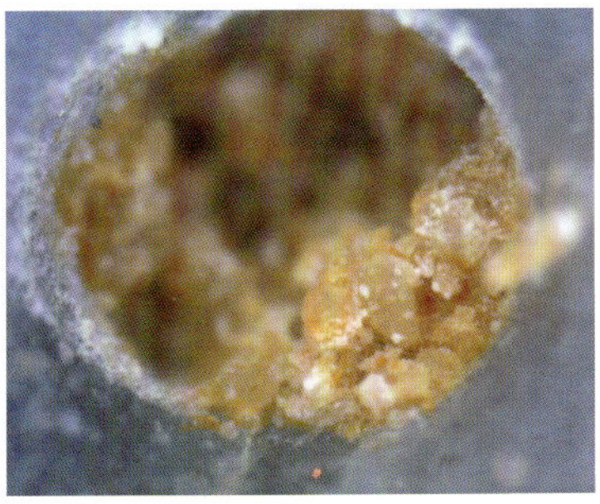
图5-4-34

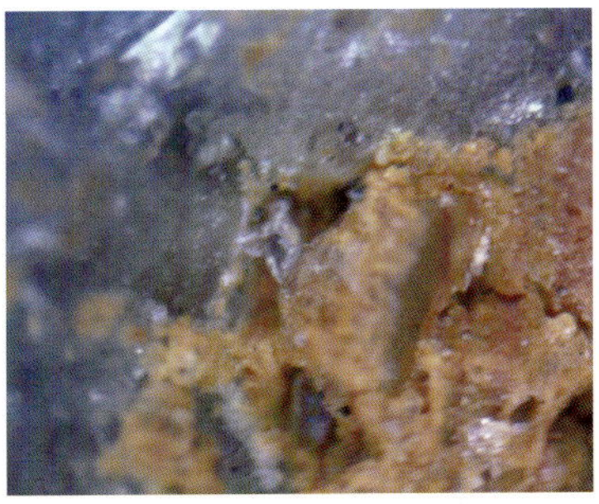
图5-4-35

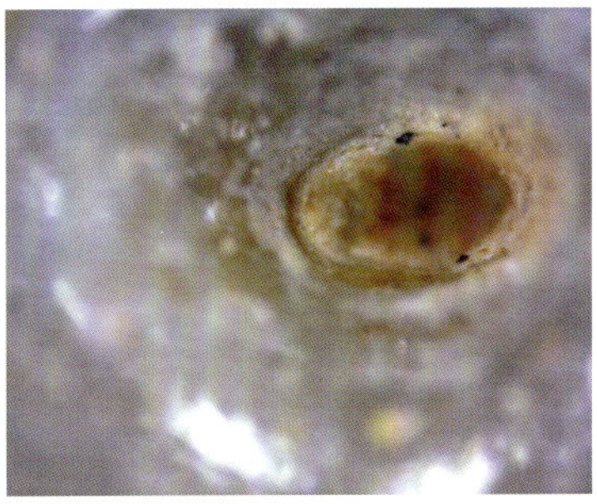
图5-4-36

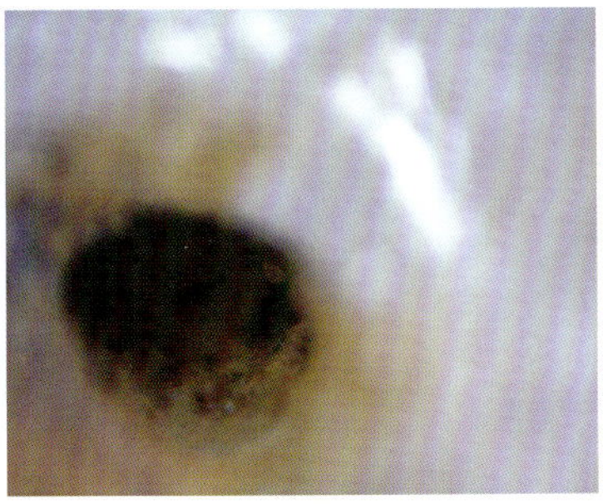
图5-4-37

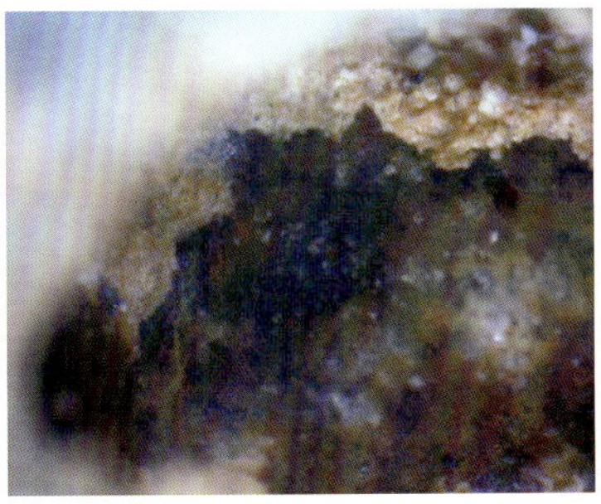
图5-4-38

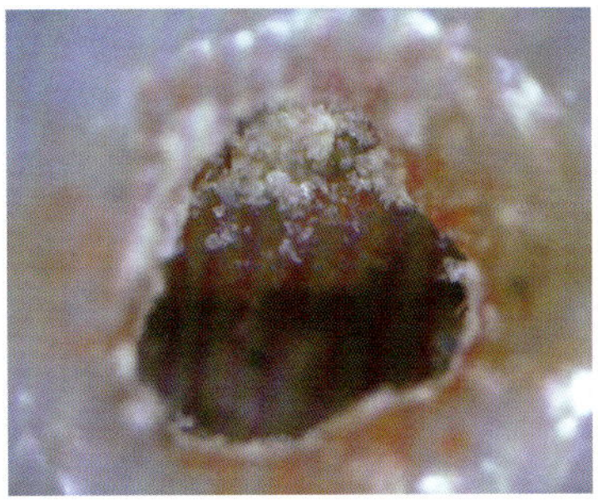
图5-4-39

3. 其他物质出现特征

（1）鬃眼口部周围釉表面上存在纤丝，主要是白色。纤丝有粗有细，有长有短，有的单一出现，有的错综出现（见图5-4-21—图5-4-30）。

（2）鬃眼口部周围釉表面存在颗粒物质，颜色包括白色、黄色及褐色等，覆盖部分釉表面（见图5-4-31—图5-4-35）。

（三）鬃眼内部特征

1. 颜色变化特征

有时鬃眼内部可见颜色变化，如白色、黄色、橘红色、褐色及黑色等（见图5-4-36—图5-4-42）。

2. 其他物质出现特征

（1）鬃眼内部有纤丝现象，纤丝有粗有细，有长有短，有细微颜色变化，包括白色、黄色等。纤丝有的单一出现，有的错综出现（见图5-4-43—图5-4-48）。

（2）鬃眼内部有颗粒沉积，颗粒物有大有小，有的独立存在，有的以团簇形式存在，颜色包括白色、黄色、褐色及黑色（见图5-4-49—图5-4-55）。

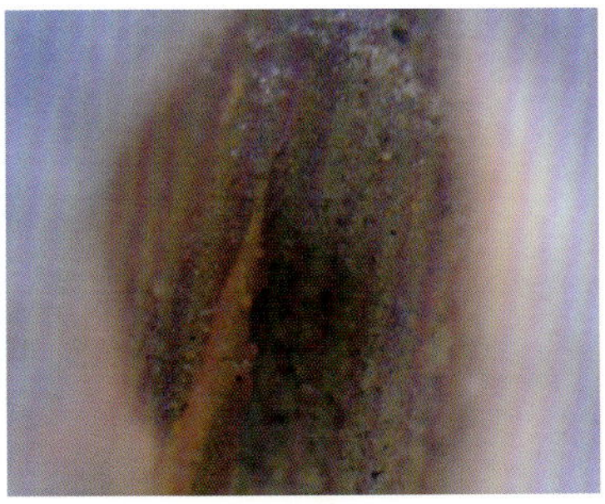
图5-4-40

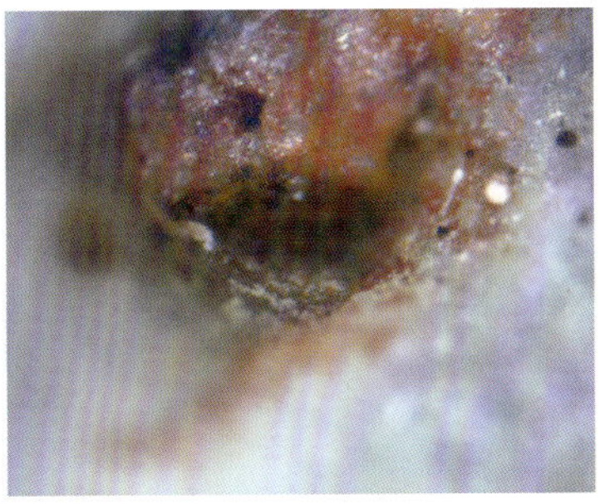
图5-4-41

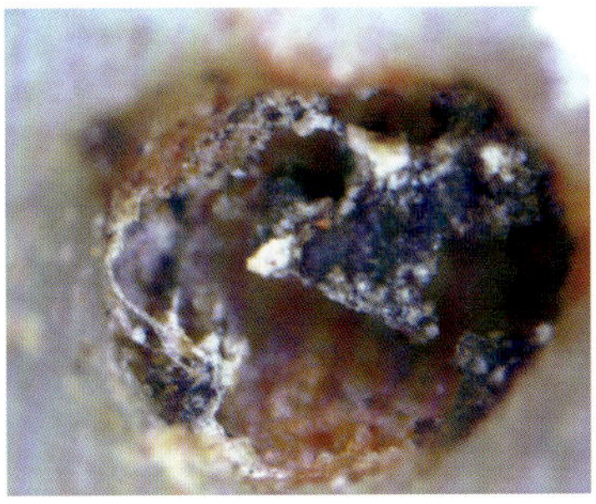
图5-4-42

图5-4-43

图5-4-44

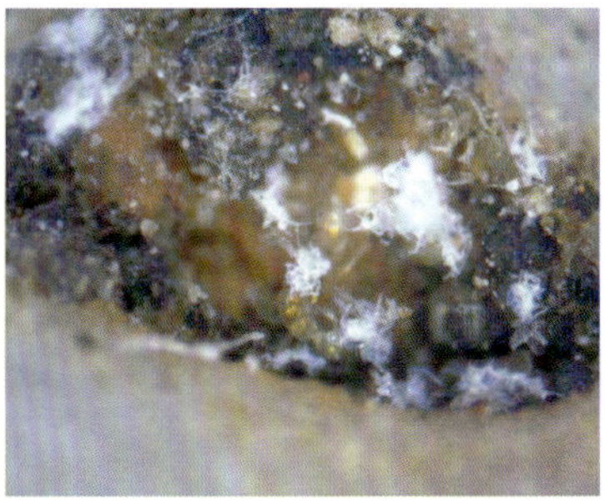
图5-4-45

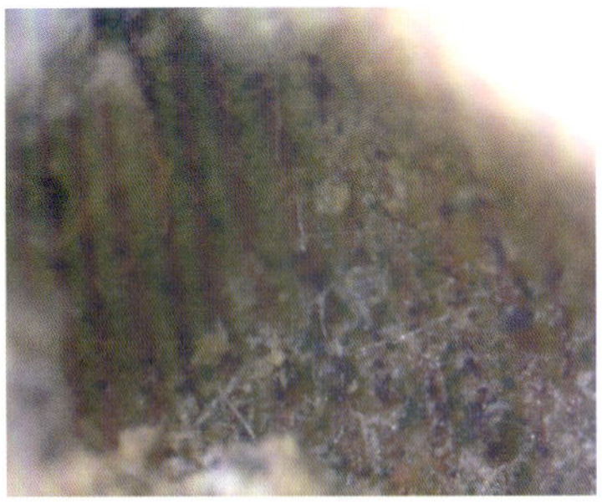
图5-4-46

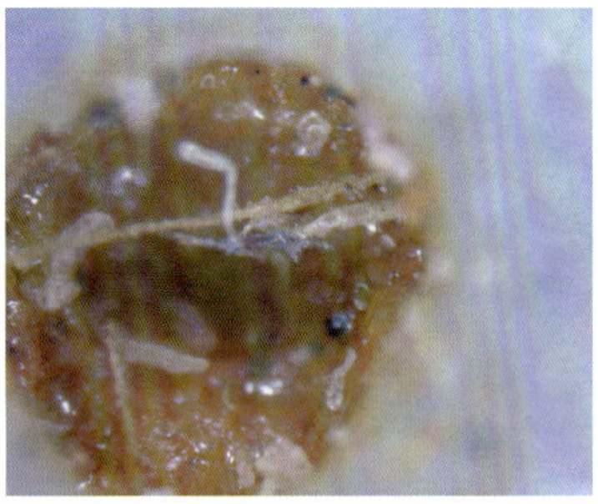
图5-4-47

图5-4-48

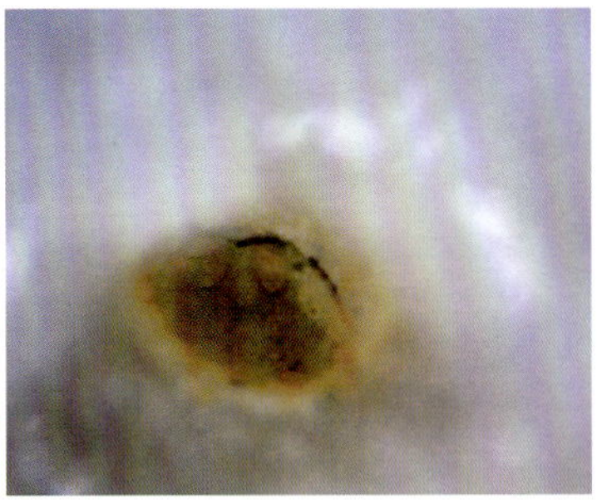
图5-4-49

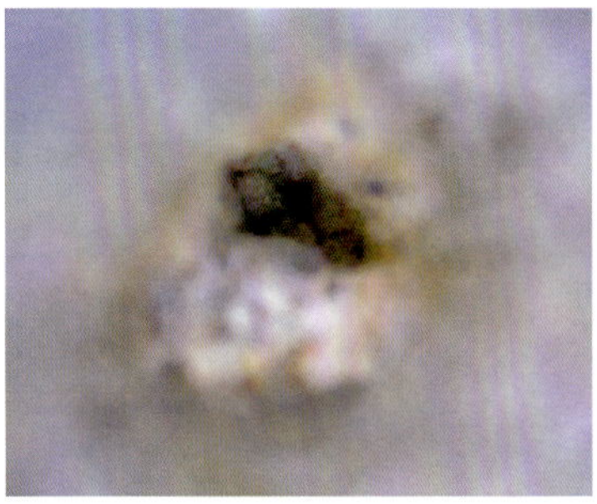
图5-4-50

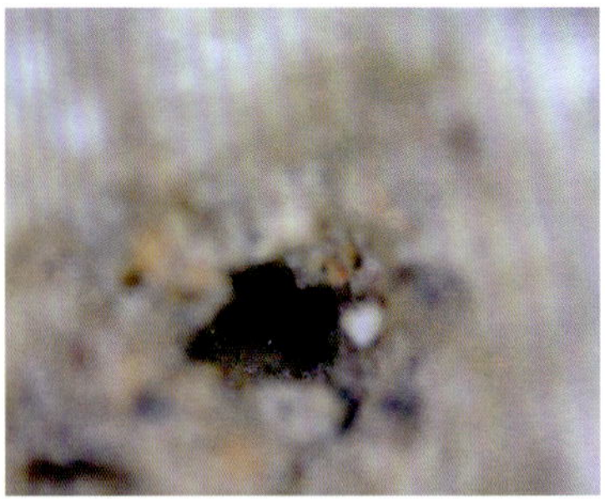
图5-4-51

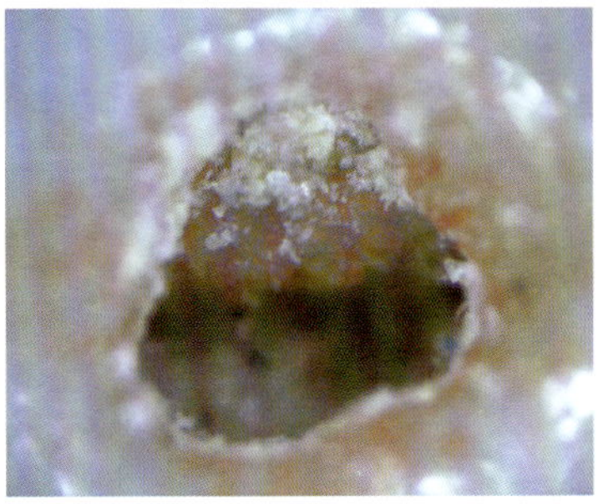
图5-4-52

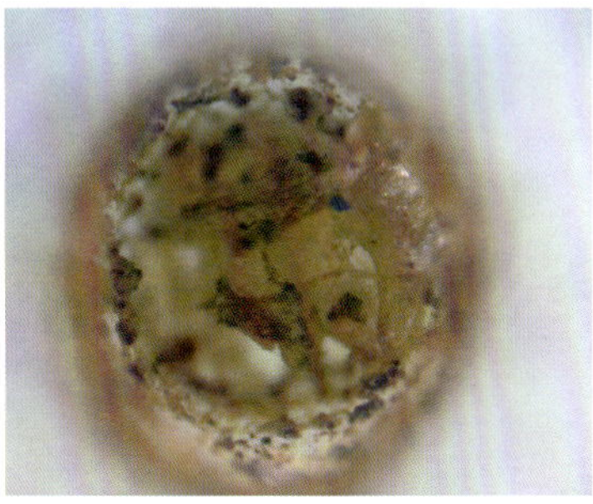
图5-4-53

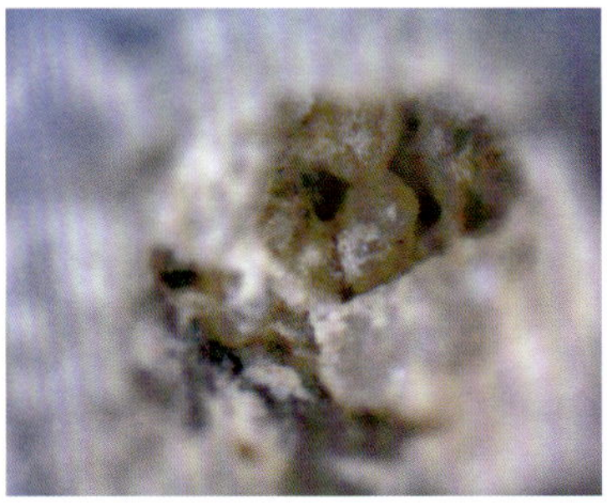
图5-4-54

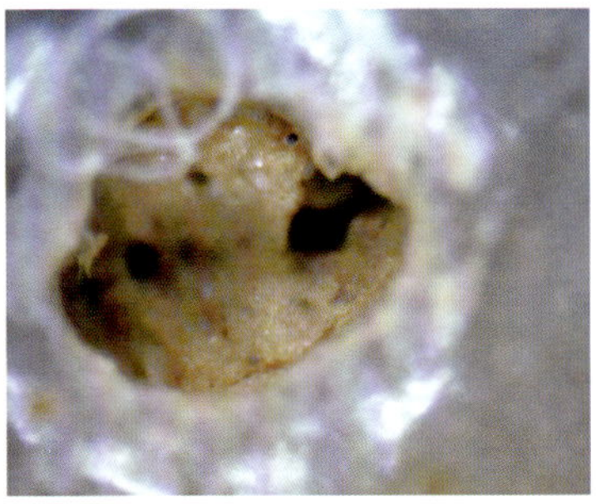
图5-4-55

四、总结

鬃眼是龙泉窑系青瓷釉层存在的普遍现象，在体积较小或釉层较薄的器物上一般比较少见。鬃眼内部及口部周围的釉表面常会发现有颗粒物质及纤丝的存在，还会有颜色变化，部分鬃眼口部周围釉下会出现絮状斑或色变泡。

鬃眼现象反映了龙泉窑系青瓷的胎釉特征和烧制工艺特征，其风化特征符合陶瓷迹型的量变原理与时间过程性原理，也反映了陶瓷迹型形成及变化的诸规律。

第六章

陶瓷迹型原理及规律

阅读提示：

本章阐述了陶瓷迹型的两个基本原理、七大规律以及其出现位置的合理性和变化的同步性。

主要论述问题：

1. 陶瓷迹型的基本原理有哪两个？
2. 陶瓷迹型有哪七大规律？
3. 陶瓷迹型出现位置的合理性和变化的同步性是怎样的？

Chapter 6

Principles and Laws of Ceramic Traces

Text Note:

This chapter explains the two principles and seven laws of ceramic traces, as well as trace location rationality and change congruency.

第一节
陶瓷迹型基本原理

一、陶瓷迹型量变原理

陶瓷迹型的量变原理是：陶瓷迹型的风化强度是在绝对风化时间内，以缓慢、渐变的形式形成的（其中包含无数个在相对风化时间内形成的风化强度），具有细腻、精致、分明等特征。量变原理的具体迹型表现见本章第二节陶瓷迹型量变规律部分。

二、陶瓷迹型时间过程性原理

陶瓷迹型的时间过程性原理是，在绝对风化时间内，陶瓷迹型特征反映了其生成、发展的时间过程。以下是龙泉窑系青瓷迹型反映陶瓷迹型时间过程性原理的举例说明：

（一）CO纹与CO型坑点斑伴生现象

单位图片中CO纹、CO型坑点斑及坑点斑群同时存在，彼此界线分明。

（二）釉损处所在的釉层中存在絮状斑

釉损处如坑点斑、裂纹等所在处的釉层中存在絮状斑。

Section 1:
The Principles of Ceramic Traces

1. The Quantitative Change Principle

The Quantitative Change Principle states: The weathering severity of ceramic traces occurs within an absolute weathering time. It is a slow, gradual formation that is the accumulation of weathering severities formed during innumerable variable weathering time periods, it has minute, fine, and distinct characteristics.

For the specifics of the Quantitative Change Principle see Ceramic Trace Law of Quantitative Change in Section 2 of this Chapter.

2. The Passage of Time Principle

The Passage of Time Principle states: Throughout the absolute weathering time, the ceramic trace generation and transformation processes, within numerous variable weathering time periods, form the multiplicity and complexity of trace weathering severities throughout the ceramic glaze level. The following are two specific examples that illustrate the passage of time principle as seen in LKSC traces.

A. CO Striae and CO Type Pits Accompaniment

There are clearly delineated CO striae, CO type pits, and pit groups all presenting within a unit image.

B. Floccus Mottling in Association with Areas of Glaze Damage

Areas of glaze damage such as pits, cracks, and so forth; present with floccus mottling within the glaze level.

第二节 陶瓷迹型规律

龙泉窑系青瓷上的一系列迹型特征体现了陶瓷迹型形成及发展的七大规律。下面将选取一些典型的青瓷迹型现象加以说明。

一、陶瓷迹型随机性规律

陶瓷迹型随机性规律是在烧制过程中和后天环境影响下形成的，分布在釉表面及釉层中的陶瓷迹型具有不可预测性、非人为设定性的现象。

（一）先天性迹型的随机性

青瓷上的放射斑可以出现在任何一处，比如在一件青瓷盘的内壁和外壁都可能观察到随机出现的同一种类的放射斑。

（二）后天性迹型的随机性

青瓷上的色变泡和壁变泡可以随机出现在瓷器釉层的任何一处。

二、陶瓷迹型色差规律

陶瓷迹型色差规律是在烧制过程中和后天环境影响下形成的，分布在釉表面及釉层中的同一陶瓷迹型种类表现出颜色差异的现象。

（一）色阶变化

1. 青瓷上同一流淌斑上可观察到色阶变化。

2. 青瓷上同一釉裂纹上可观察到色阶变化。

3. 青瓷上同一色变泡上可观察到色阶变化。

（二）色差变化

1. 青瓷上的CO纹路群中可观察到色差变化。

2. 青瓷上的多个色变泡之间可观察到色差变化。

三、陶瓷迹型量变规律

陶瓷迹型量变规律是分布在陶瓷釉表面及釉层中的迹型在后天的风化过程中，有着缓慢性、渐变性、细腻性、精致性、分明性等特征的现象。

（一）细腻性特征

青瓷上雾状针眼斑在沙滩斑上的分布，有从浓到淡的均匀过渡，显得细腻。

（二）内敛性特征

青瓷上C形纹、O形纹的三维成像纤细、紧致且收敛，没有发散的毛边。

（三）精致性特征

青瓷上放射斑周围的包边纤细精致。

四、陶瓷迹型层次性规律

陶瓷迹型层次性规律是陶瓷迹型不同类别之间和同一类别之间迹型风化强度的差异，通过它们在釉层（釉表面或釉层中）纵向垂直的位置表现出来的现象。

（一）就某一迹型单项而言

流淌斑分布于釉表面及釉层中，受釉层保护的程度不一，这使它们各处风化强度有差异。针眼斑在流淌斑上疏密不一的分布，就是流淌斑风化强度不一的表现。流淌斑的分布特征以及覆盖在上面的针眼斑分布特征使其有了层次感。

（二）就同一类别中相邻的两个或多个迹型单项而言

坑点斑形成后成为连接外界物质与釉层内部的通道之一，长期存放于干湿交替的环境中，釉下絮状斑会在坑点斑下的釉层

Section 2 :

Ceramic Trace Laws

The series of trace characteristics on LKSC embodies the seven laws of ceramic trace change and development. Below are a few typical examples of LKSC trace phenomenon.

1. Ceramic Trace Law of Randomness

The Ceramic Trace Law of Randomness states: The distribution of trace appearances across the glaze surface and within the glaze level, created during firing and under the influence of the post-firing environment, is unpredictable and a non-human-controlled phenomenon.

A. Inherent Trace Randomness

Radiating mottles can appear at any point on the porcelain glaze, for example a plate interior or exterior can both present with the random distribution of the same type of radiating mottle.

B. Acquired Trace Randomness

Color change bubbles or textured bubbles can appear at any point on the porcelain glaze.

2. Ceramic Trace Law of Chromatic Aberration

The Ceramic Trace Law of Chromatic Aberration states: Within a single trace type; distributed across the glaze surface and within the glaze level, both innate and acquired; the phenomenon of chromatic aberration (differences in color) can be present.

A. Color Spectrum

a. A color spectrum presenting on a single flowing mottle.

b. A color spectrum presenting in a single glaze crack.

c. A color spectrum presenting in a single color change bubble.

B. Color Disparity

a. A color disparity presenting in a CO Striae group.

b. A color disparity presenting across several color change bubbles.

3. Ceramic Trace Law of Quantitative Change

The Ceramic Trace Law of Quantitative Change states: The innate and acquired trace appearances distributed across the glaze surface and within the glaze level have all undergone slow, gradual, and minute processes, and appear with fine and distinct characteristics.

A. Minute Characteristics

Foggy needlepoint mottling distribution on beach mottles, appears with a dark to light even progression.

B. Restrained Characteristics

C and O shaped striae edges are tightly constrained instead of roughly dispersed.

中及坑点斑周围的釉层中逐渐形成，坑点斑与釉层中存在的絮状斑就有了层次关系。

（三）就不同类别中相邻的两个或多个迹型单项而言

由C形纹、O形纹发展而来的坑点斑，这两种不同类别之间的迹型种类也可表现出层次性。从存在于釉表面的C形纹、O形纹发展到深入釉层中的坑点斑，由浅到深，富有层次。

五、陶瓷迹型多样性规律

陶瓷迹型多样性规律是陶瓷在后天环境影响下，在釉表面及釉层中，因风化而形成的迹型，比其先天形成的迹型类别或种类数量增加的现象。

六、陶瓷迹型差异性规律

陶瓷迹型差异性规律是陶瓷迹型类别或迹型种类的风化强度，与其邻近的相同或不同迹型类别、迹型种类不一致的现象。如破口壁变泡周围是干净清晰的玻璃相，螺旋叠加的坑点斑周围是干净清晰的玻璃相。

七、陶瓷迹型分明性规律

陶瓷迹型分明性规律是陶瓷在后天环境影响下形成的，分布在釉表面及釉层中的迹型类别或种类之间保持界线清晰，各自独立的现象。

如针眼型阴纹与周围玻璃相的界线清晰分明，放射斑与其周围的流淌斑之间界线清晰分明，伴生的C形纹与坑点斑之间界线清晰分明。

注：关于陶瓷迹型规律更详细的论述，请参阅《陶瓷迹型学概论》。

C. Fine Characteristics

The finely exquisite thin border of radiating mottles.

4. Ceramic Trace Law of Gradation

The Ceramic Trace Law of Gradation (Layering) states: The weathering severity, whether inter or intra-trace category has variation; a phenomenon resulting due to their positioning throughout the glaze level (across the glaze surface or within the glaze level).

A. In reference to a single trace

Flowing mottles are located above and below the surface of the glaze and receive different degrees of glaze protection allowing a range of weathering severity. Therefore, the differences in density of needlepoint mottling are a direct result of differences in weathering severity. The characteristics of flowing mottles and associated overlaid needlepoint mottling appear with a feeling of layers or gradation.

B. In reference to two or more adjacent individual traces (belonging to the same category)

After the formation of pit mottles, these mottles act as channels between the external environment and the glaze level. After a long period of time in an environment of alternating moisture, floccus mottling can present under the overlaid pit mottle and disperse down into the glaze level. The pit mottle and floccus mottling have a layered relationship.

C. In reference to two or more adjacent individual traces (belonging to different categories)

The progression from C and O shaped striae into pit mottles represents the layered relationship between different trace categories. The temporal process of progression from C to O shaped striae, then to pit mottles gives varying depths and a feeling of gradation.

5. Ceramic Trace Law of Variegation

The Ceramic Trace Law of Variegation describes the phenomenon of an increase in appearances of trace categories and types distributed across the glaze surface and throughout the glaze level due to weathering incurred in the post-firing environment.

Statistical observation has shown that the vast majority of LKSC samples present with at least five types of acquired traces.

6. Ceramic Trace Law of Disparity

The Ceramic Trace Law of Disparity describes the phenomenon of two similar or dissimilar ceramic trace categories or types within the same vicinity appearing with differences in weathering severity.

For example:

The clean and clear glass phase surrounding a broken mouthed textured bubble and the clean and clear glass phase surrounding a CO pit group.

7. Ceramic Trace Law of Distinction

The Ceramic Trace Law of Distinction describes the phenomenon of trace categories and types distributed across the glaze surface and within the glaze level, formed within the post-firing environment, retaining clear delineation and respective independence from one another.

For example:

The boundary between needlepoint striae and the surrounding glass phase is clearly distinct. The boundary between radiating and flowing mottles is clearly distinct. The boundary between textured bubbles and the surrounding glass phase is clearly distinct.

Note: For a more detailed description of The Ceramic Trace Laws, please refer to *Survey of Ceramics Trace Model Study.*

第三节 迹型出现位置的合理性与变化的同步性

一、陶瓷迹型出现位置的合理性

陶瓷迹型出现位置的合理性关注的是陶瓷迹型出现的位置是否符合陶瓷迹型风化的原理及规律。以龙泉窑系青瓷上的迹型为例：

（一）CO型坑点斑出现在釉表面凸起处

青瓷上的CO型坑点斑通常都出现在釉表面凸起处，釉表面其他地方通常光滑洁净。

（二）针眼斑在沙滩斑上的分布

青瓷上的针眼斑在沙滩斑上的分布有一定规律，一般来说，在沙滩斑中心部分针眼斑以磨砂针眼斑形式出现，在沙滩斑与玻璃相过渡的地方，针眼斑通常以雾状针眼斑形式出现。

二、陶瓷迹型变化的同步性

陶瓷迹型变化的同步性关注的是同一件器物上的各迹型风化强度是否同步。

（一）晶相与玻璃相的同步性

通常来说，同一件器物上，金属氧化物的晶相与玻璃相的风化强度具有同步性，当一件器物上的玻璃相有一定风化强度，其釉表面金属氧化物的晶相应表现出更高的风化强度。

（二）同一迹型单项的同步性

对于同一迹型单项而言，其二维成像与三维成像的风化强度应该是同步的。

Section 3 :

Ceramic Trace Location Rationality and Change Congruency

1. Ceramic Trace Location Rationality

Ceramic Trace Location Rationality focuses on whether or not the locations where ceramic traces appear fit the principles and laws of the weathered ceramic traces. The following examples of LKSC traces illustrate this principle:

A. CO Type Pit Mottles Present on Areas of Raised Glaze

CO type pit mottles usually present on areas of raised glaze, the surrounding glaze level remains smooth and clean.

B. Needlepoint Mottling on Flowing Mottle

The distribution of needlepoint mottling on flowing mottle has regularity. The center of beach mottles usually presents with frosted needlepoint mottling, and the borders between the beach mottle and glass phase usually present with foggy needlepoint mottling.

2. Ceramic Trace Change Congruency

The concept of Ceramic Trace Change Congruency refers to whether or not there is a congruency in trace weathering severity according to their respective weathering resistance.

A. Congruency between Crystallization Phase and Glass Phase

Usually, the weathering severity of crystallized metal oxide and glass phase on the same piece of ceramic should be congruent. This is to say that if a piece's glass phase displays a certain weathering severity, the adjacent crystallization on the glaze surface should even more so display such weathering severity.

B. Congruency of a Single Trace

For a single trace, its two and three-dimensional appearances of weathering severity should be congruent.

第七章

明代龙泉窑系青瓷迹型标准图谱模型建构

阅读提示：

本章展示了明代浙江龙泉枫洞岩窑址青瓷及广东余里窑青瓷迹型标准图谱模型的部分图片，阐述了在建构此两套标准图谱模型时其标本的选择标准及来源，并论述了标准图谱模型的可靠性及自证性。

主要论述问题：

1. 选择建构明代浙江龙泉枫洞岩窑址青瓷及广东余里窑青瓷标准图谱模型的标本有哪些标准？

2. 明代浙江龙泉枫洞岩窑址青瓷及广东余里窑青瓷迹型标准图谱模型各有什么重要特征？

Chapter 7

Ming Dynasty Longquan Kiln System Celadon Standard Trace Atlas Model Construction

Text Note:

This chapter introduces a portion of images that compose The Ming Dynasty Zhejiang Longquan Fengdongyan Kiln Celadon and Ming Dynasty Guangdong Yuli Kiln Celadon Standard Trace Atlas Models, elaborates on the selection and origin of these images, and expounds upon the reliability and self-evidence of these models.

第一节
标本选择与来源

一、标本选择

明代浙江龙泉大窑枫洞岩窑址青瓷标本以及明代广东大埔余里窑青瓷标本的真实可靠性，决定了二者迹型标准图谱模型的真实可靠性。

标本选取正确与否，决定了比对鉴定的结论准确与否。因此，为了确保标本的真实性、可靠性和代表性，在标本选取的过程中，研究团队特赴浙江丽水龙泉大窑枫洞岩窑址和广东大埔余里窑窑址，确保选取标本有明确的发掘时间、发掘地点及年代依据。

二、标本来源

建构明代浙江龙泉大窑枫洞岩窑址青瓷迹型标准图谱模型的标本来源于浙江丽水龙泉枫洞岩窑址；建构明代广东大埔余里窑青瓷迹型标准图谱模型的标本来源于广东大埔余里窑窑址。

三、研究合作单位

除了用于建构迹型标准图谱模型的标本以外，本书研究所使用的其他青瓷标本分别来自国内外多家博物馆、研究机构及私人收藏，它们分别是：

（一）广州东方博物馆

（二）金乐轩

（三）泰国曼谷大学东南亚陶瓷博物馆

（四）印度尼西亚国立博物馆

（五）新加坡国立大学博物馆

（六）新加坡国立大学考古研究中心

（七）英国巴斯亚洲艺术博物馆

（八）英国格拉斯哥博物馆

（九）美国洁蕊堂

（十）美国波士顿艺术博物馆

（十一）美国印第安纳波利斯艺术博物馆

Section 1:
Selection and Origin of the Samples

1. Sample Selection

The veracity and reliability of samples establishes the veracity and reliability of The Ming Dynasty Zhejiang Longquan Fengdongyan Kiln Celadon and Ming Dynasty Guangdong Yuli Kiln Celadon Standard Trace Atlas Models.

The genuineness of the samples decides the accuracy of conclusions in comparative authentication. Because of this, in order to guarantee the veracity, reliability, and representativeness of these samples, when selecting samples, the research team went directly to the associated kiln sites and used samples of recorded excavation time, location, and known age.

2. Sample Origins

The Ming Dynasty Zhejiang Longquan Fengdongyan Kiln Celadon Standard Trace Atlas Model was constructed using samples from the Zhejiang Longquan Dayao Fengdongyan Kiln site; and The Ming Dynasty Guangdong Yuli Kiln Celadon Standard Trace Atlas Model was constructed using samples from the Guangdong Yuli Kiln site.

3. Research Partner Organizations

Other sample images listed in the book come from International and Domestic Museums, Research Institutions, and Private Collections, they are:

1. Guangzhou Oriental Museum
2. The Jinlexuan Collection
3. Southeast Asian Ceramics Museum, Bangkok University
4. National Museum of Indonesia
5. National University of Singapore Museum, Singapore
6. National University of Singapore Archeology Research Center, Singapore
7. Museum of Oriental Art, Bath U.K.
8. The Burrell Collection, Glasgow U.K.
9. The Stamen Collection
10. Museum of Fine Art, Boston U.S.A.
11. Indianapolis Museum of Art, Indianapolis U.S.A

第二节
明代浙江龙泉枫洞岩窑青瓷和明代广东余里窑青瓷迹型标准图谱模型

一、明代浙江龙泉枫洞岩窑青瓷和明代广东余里窑青瓷迹型标准图谱模型说明

（一）明代浙江龙泉枫洞岩窑青瓷和明代广东余里窑青瓷迹型标准图谱模型的可靠性

明代浙江龙泉枫洞岩窑青瓷和明代广东余里窑青瓷迹型标准图谱模型选取了在浙江丽水龙泉枫洞岩窑址和在广东余里窑窑址出土的青瓷标本，这两批标本有明确的发掘时间、发掘地点及年代依据。所以，在这些标本迹型图片中提炼出来的青瓷迹型标准图谱模型，可靠性是毋庸置疑的。

（二）明代浙江龙泉枫洞岩窑青瓷和明代广东余里窑青瓷迹型标准图谱模型的自证性

由于标本均有可靠的发掘时间、发掘地点及年代依据，在此基础上提炼出来的迹型标准图谱模型具有自证性。标本的迹型图片就是证据，在此基础上建构的两个明代青瓷迹型标准图谱模型是明代龙泉窑系比对鉴定的客观物证系统。

Section 2: Ming Dynasty Zhejiang Longquan Fengdongyan Kiln Celadon Standard Trace Atlas Model and Ming Dynasty Guangdong Yuli Kiln Celadon Standard Trace Atlas Model

1. Ming Dynasty Zhejiang Longquan Fengdongyan Kiln Celadon Standard Trace Atlas Model and Ming Dynasty Guangdong Yuli Kiln Celadon Standard Trace Atlas Model Explanation

A. Reliability of the Two Standard Trace Atlas Models

The two Standard Trace Atlas Modes are composed of excavated samples from Zhejiang Province Lishui Dayao Fengdongyan Kiln site and Guangdong Province Dabu Yuli Kiln site, which both have clear excavation date, excavation location, and age foundation. As such, the trace atlas model founded on the extraction of these trace sample images leaves no uncertainty.

B. Self-Evidence of the two Standard Trace Atlas Models

As the samples are all of established excavation record, there is a self-evidence nature to the Trace Atlas Model built on their foundation. The two Standard Trace Atlas Models, constructed with these sample images, are the objective material evidence system for Ming Dynasty Longquan Kiln System Celadon Trace Model Material Evidence Authentication.

二、明代浙江龙泉枫洞岩窑青瓷迹型标准图谱模型

2. Ming Dynasty Zhejiang Longquan Fengdongyan Kiln Celadon Standard Trace Atlas Model

沙滩斑
Beach Mottles

二维 Two-dimensional		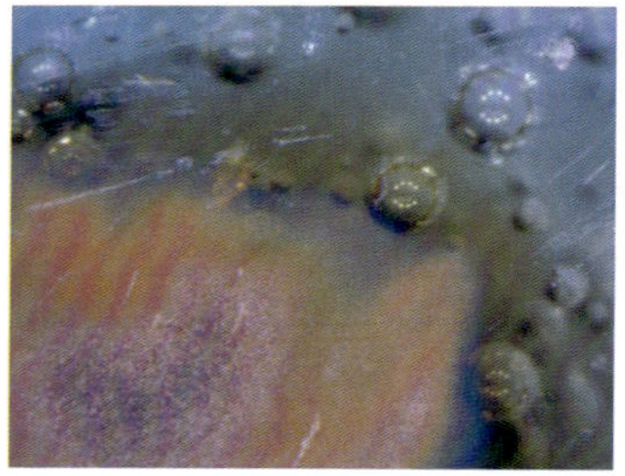	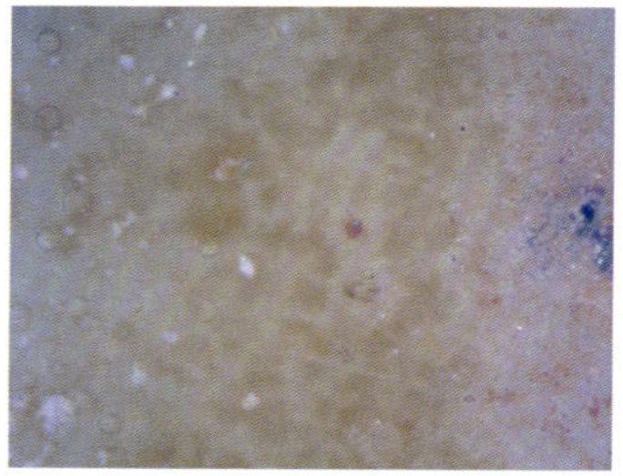	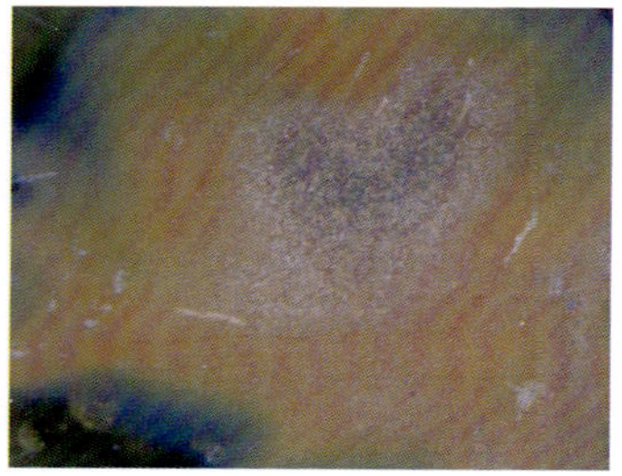
三维 Three-dimensional	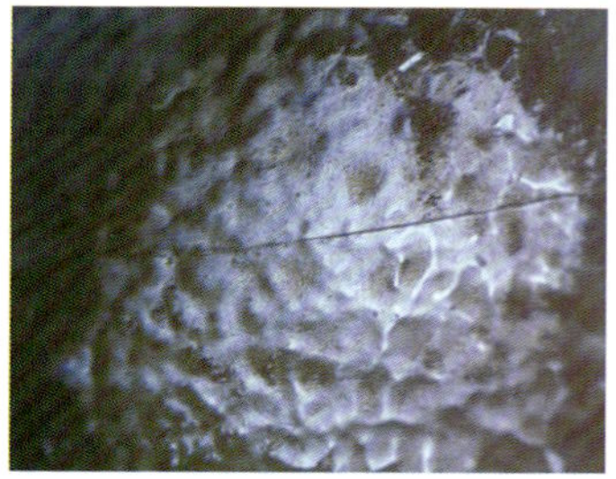	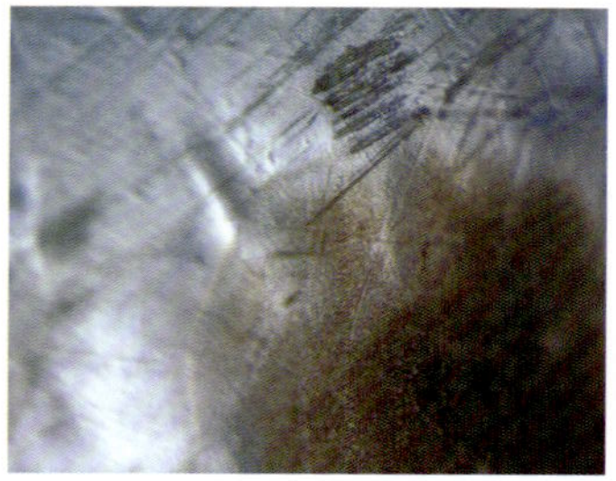	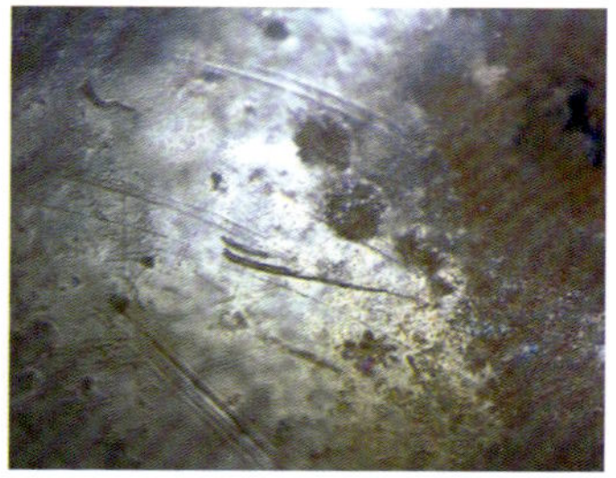	

放射斑
Radiating Mottles

二维 Two-dimensional		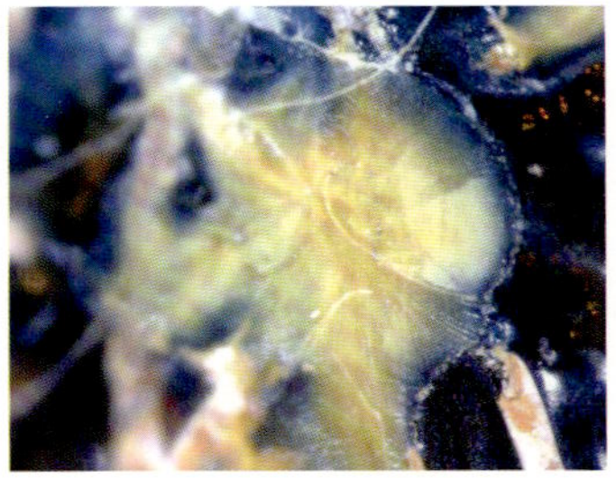	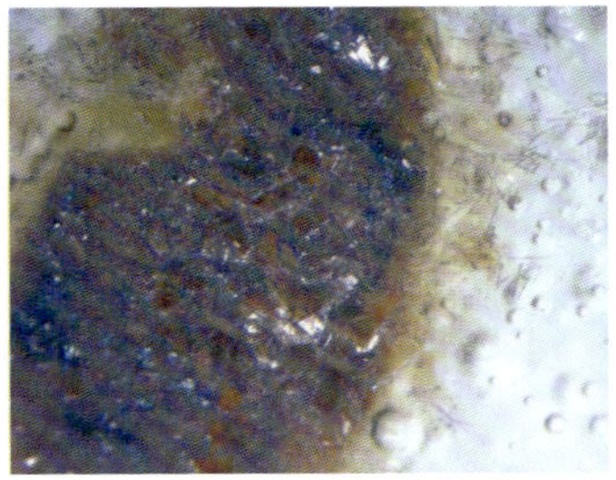	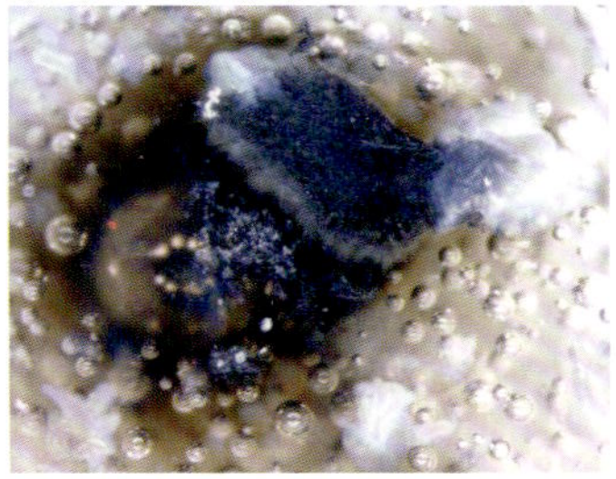
三维 Three-dimensional	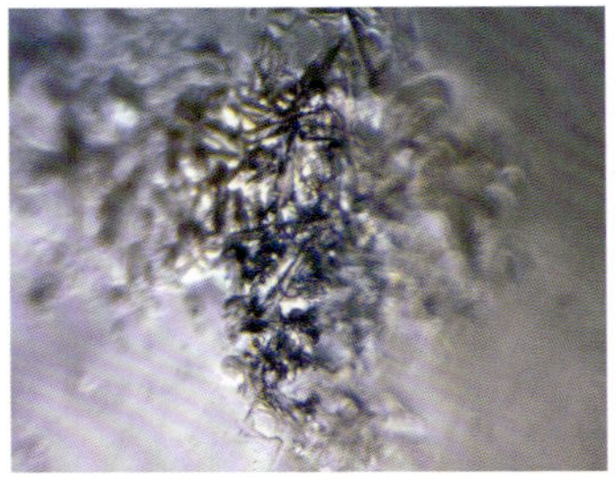	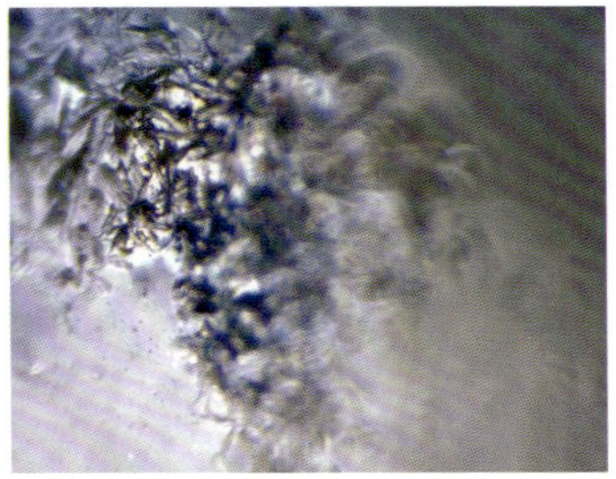	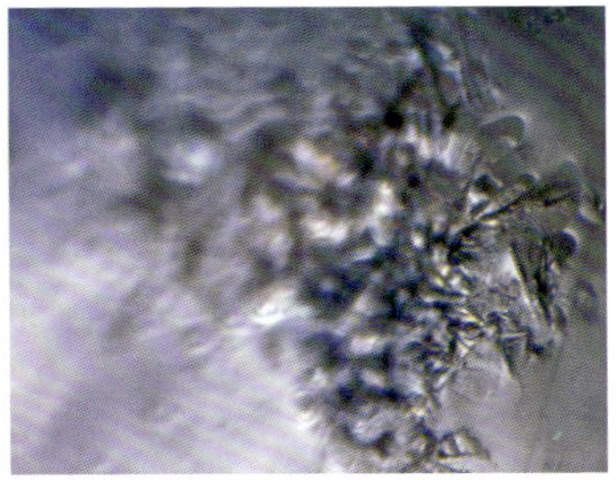	
二维 Two-dimensional	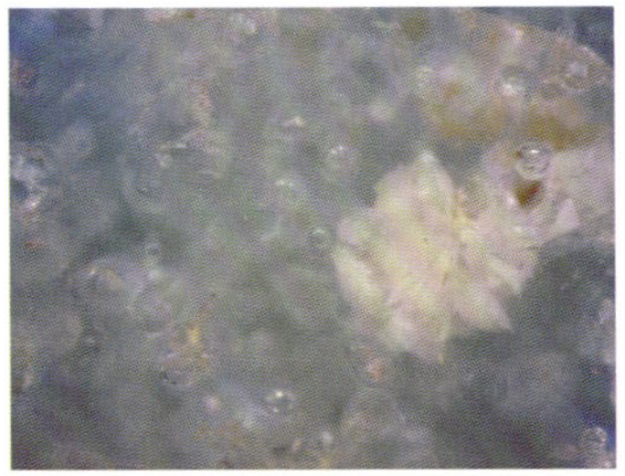	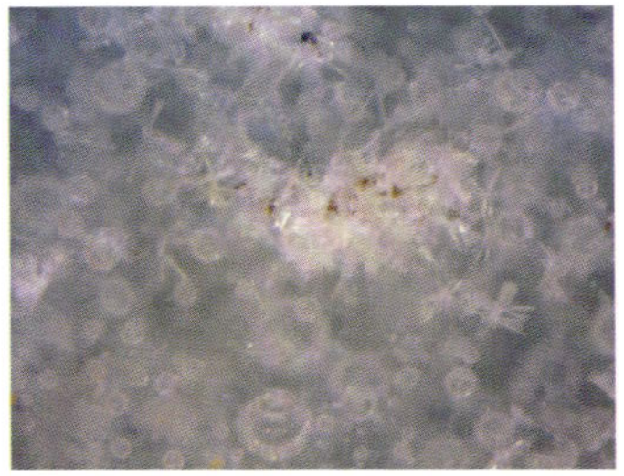	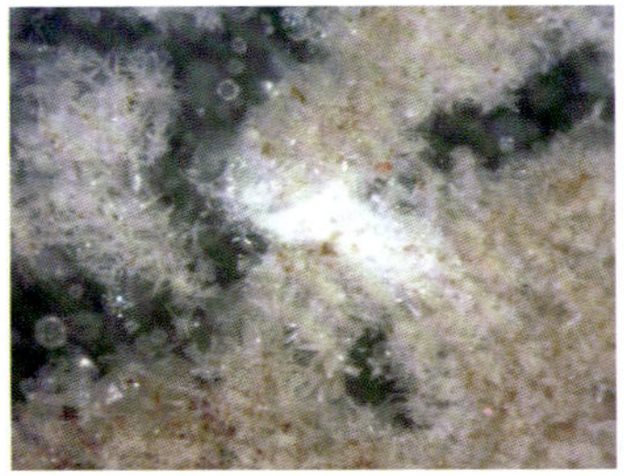	
三维 Three-dimensional	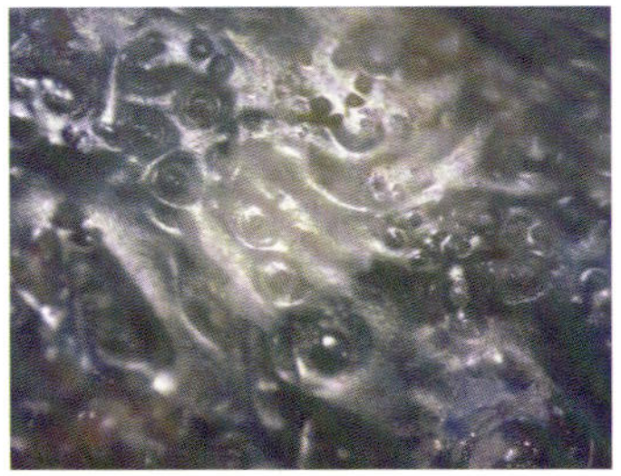	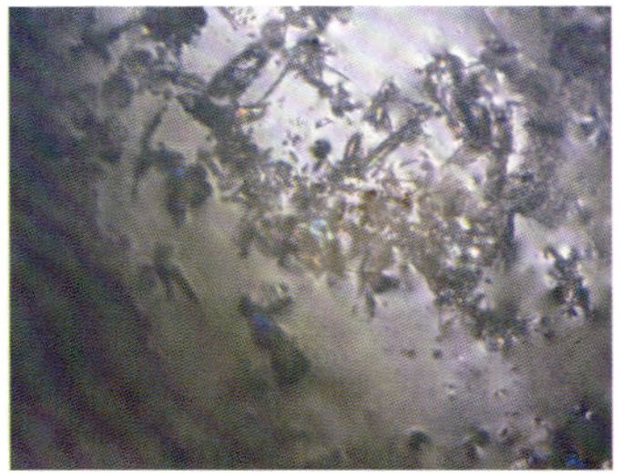	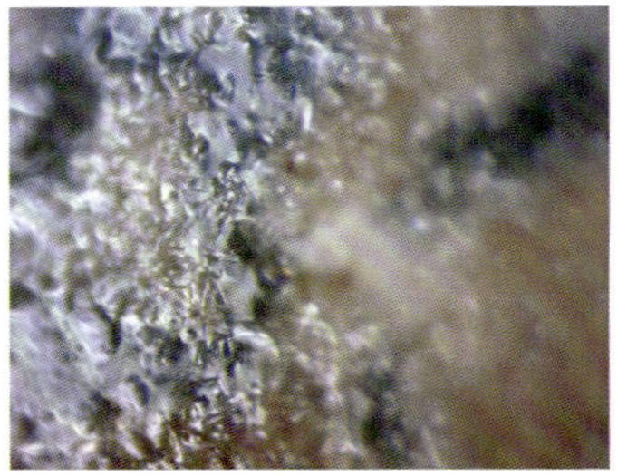	

（续图）
(Continued)

二维 Two-dimensional	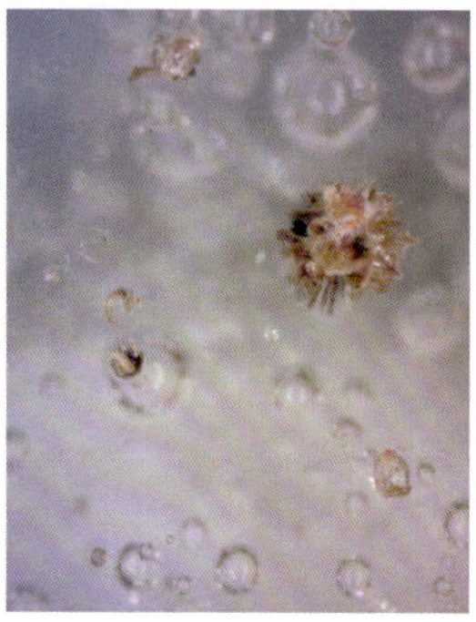	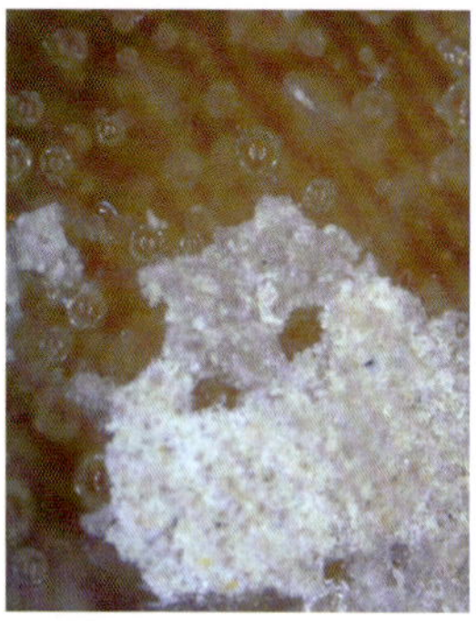	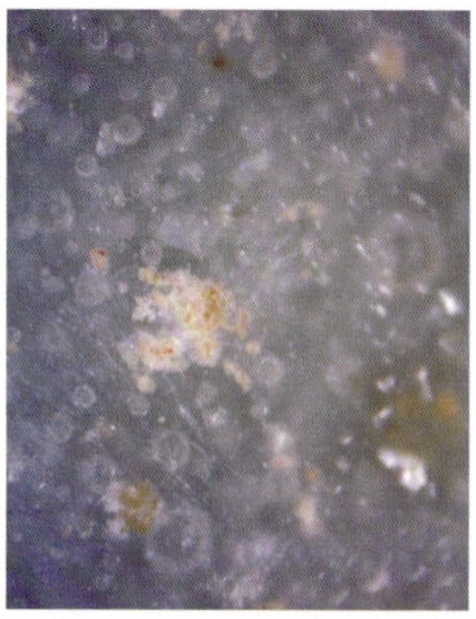	
三维 Three-dimensional	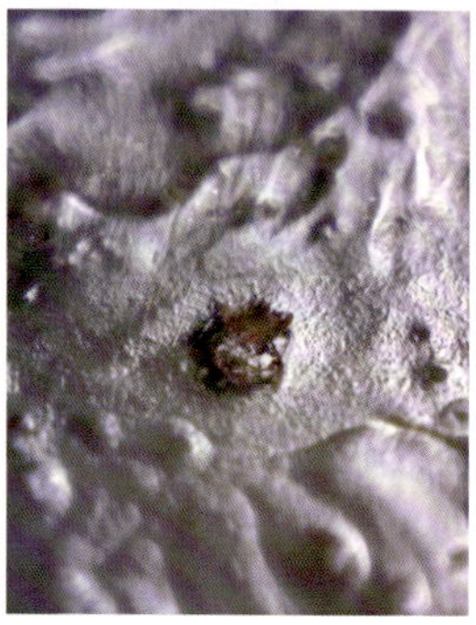		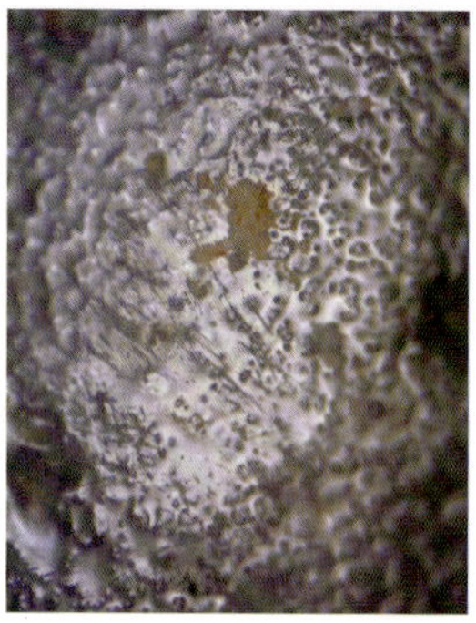	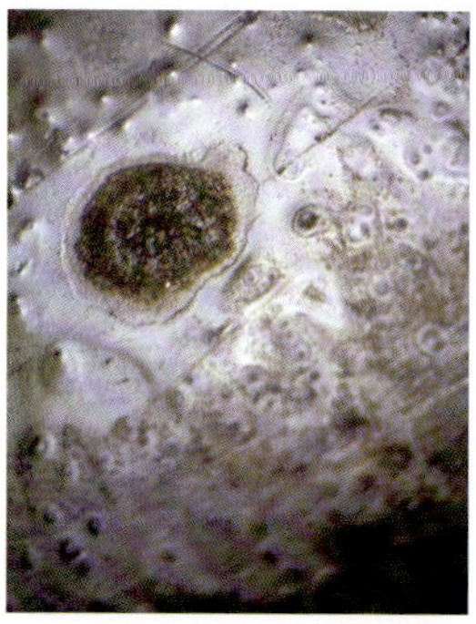
二维 Two-dimensional	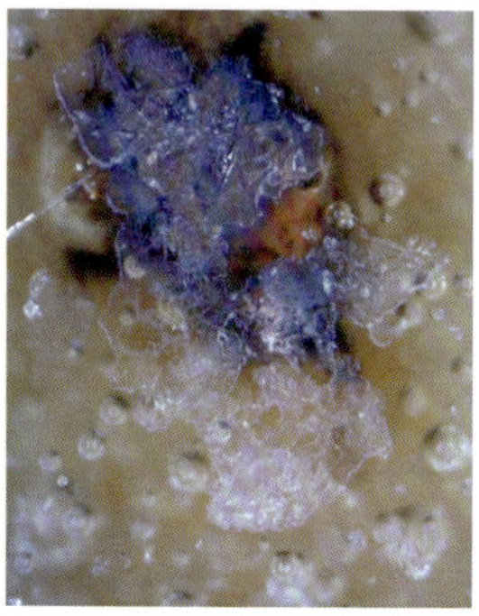	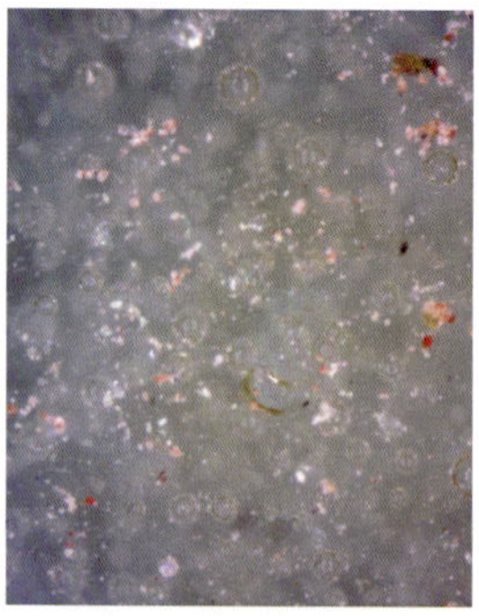		
三维 Three-dimensional	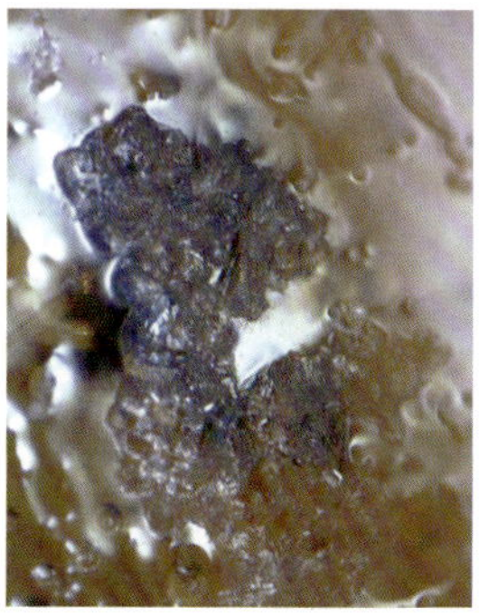	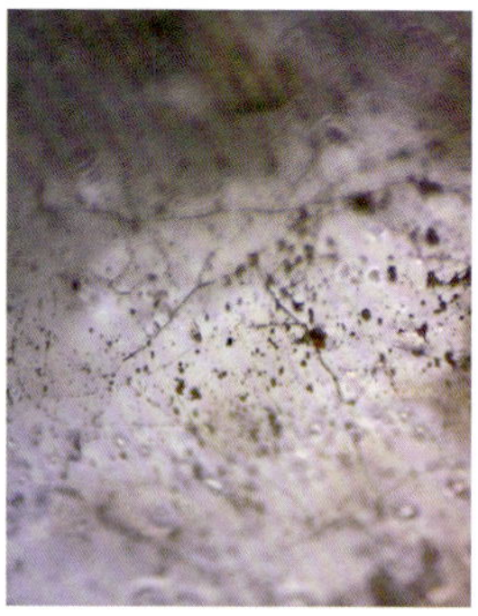		

CO型坑点斑
CO Type Pit Mottles

二维 Two-dimensional	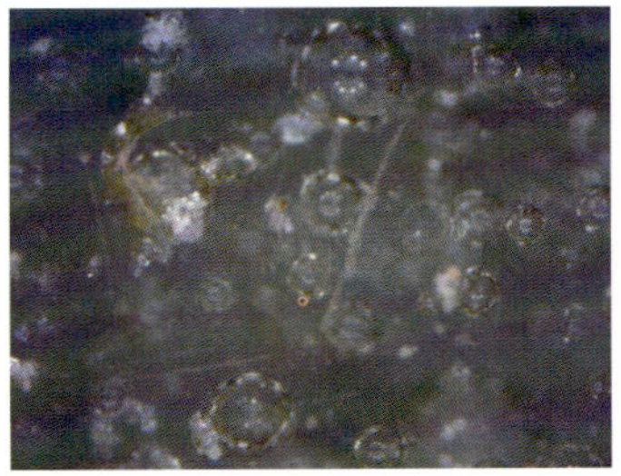	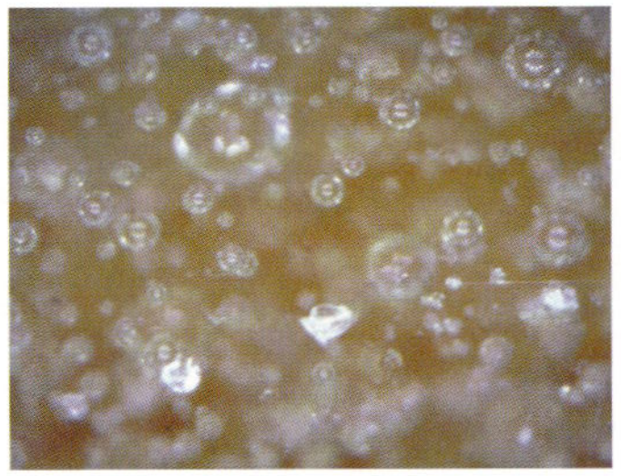	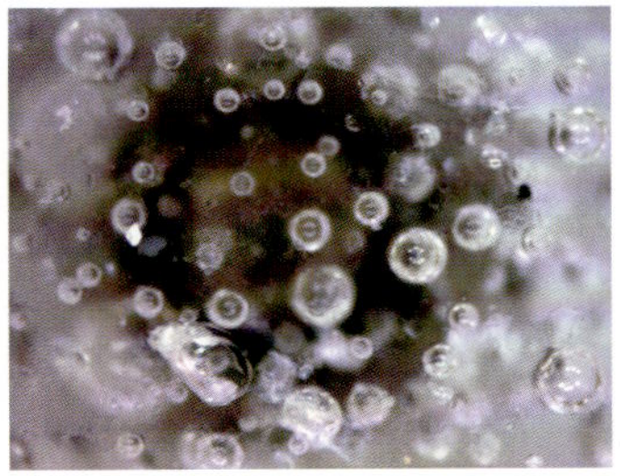	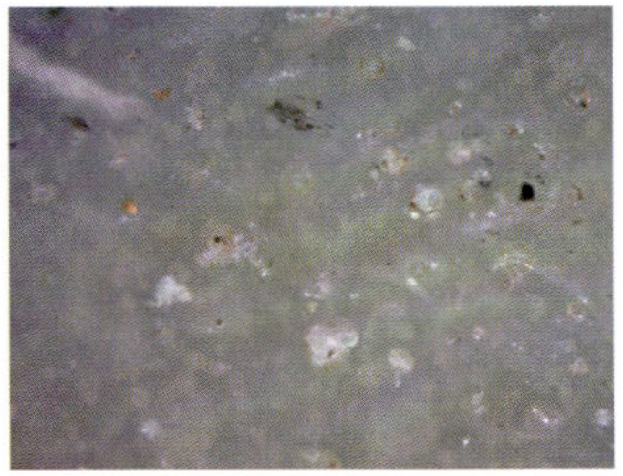
三维 Three-dimensional		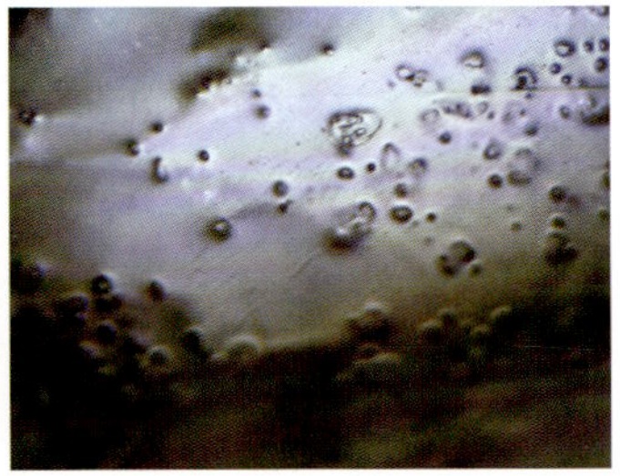		
二维 Two-dimensional	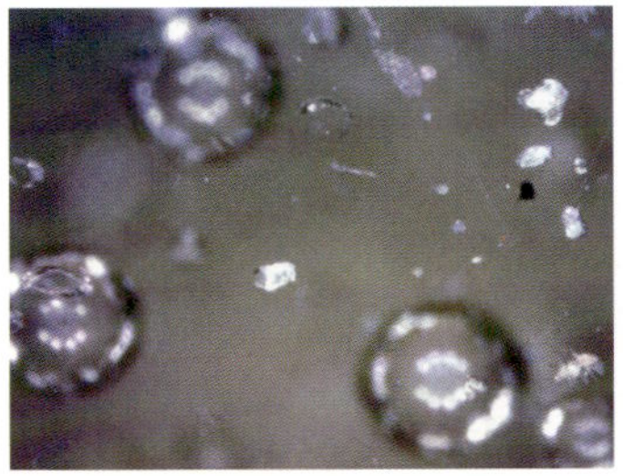	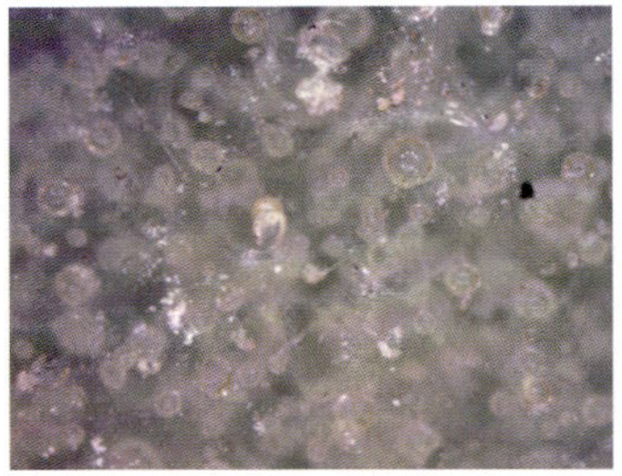	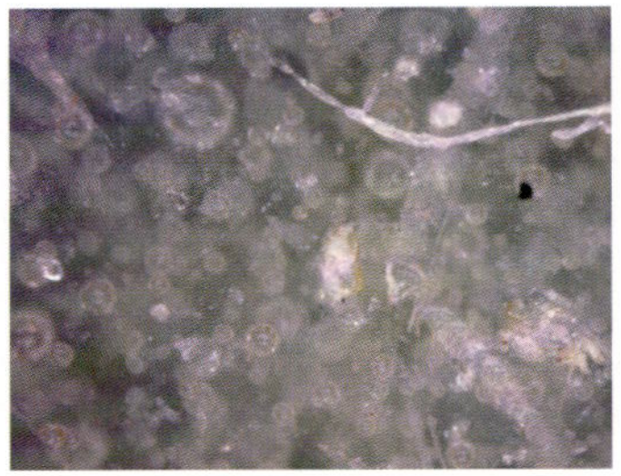	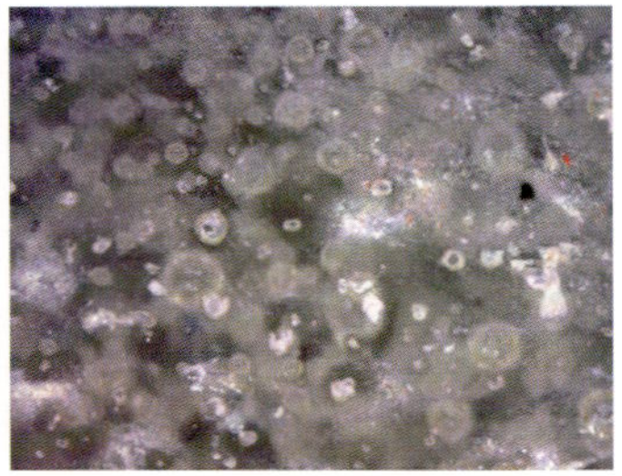

外伤型坑点斑
Damage Type Pit Mottles

二维 Two-dimensional			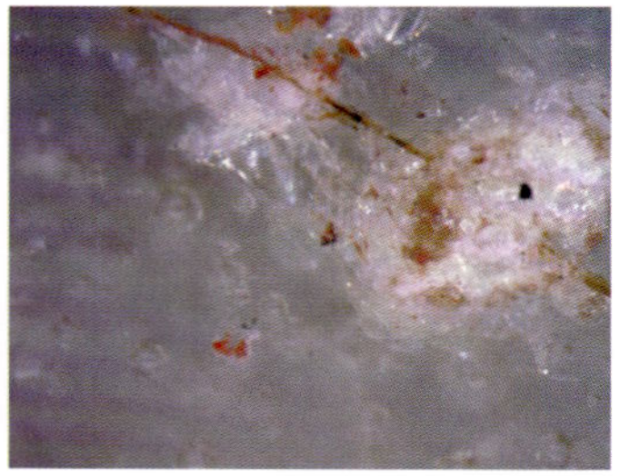	
三维 Three-dimensional	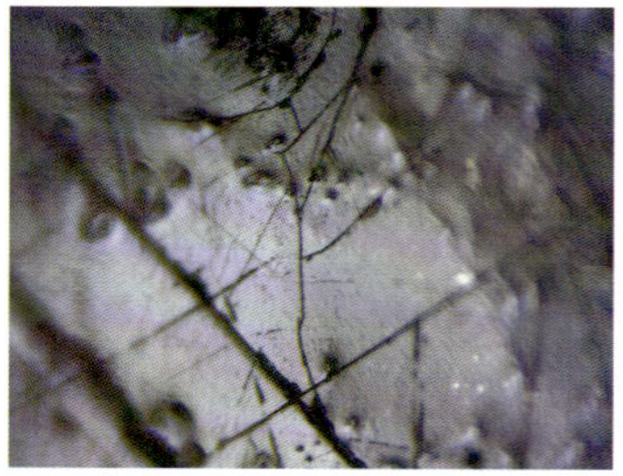			

泡根斑
Bubble Roots

二维 Two-dimensional	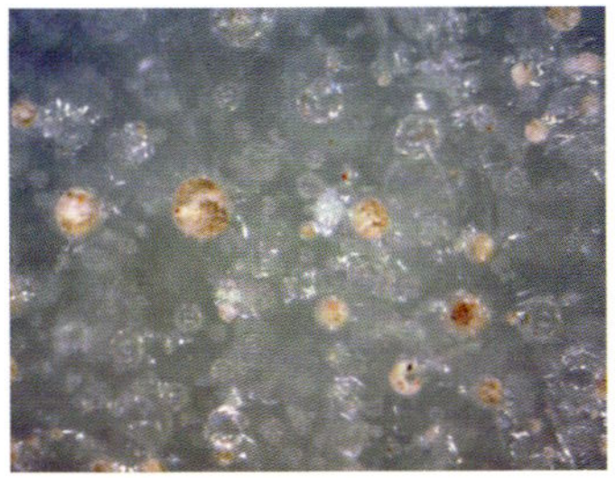	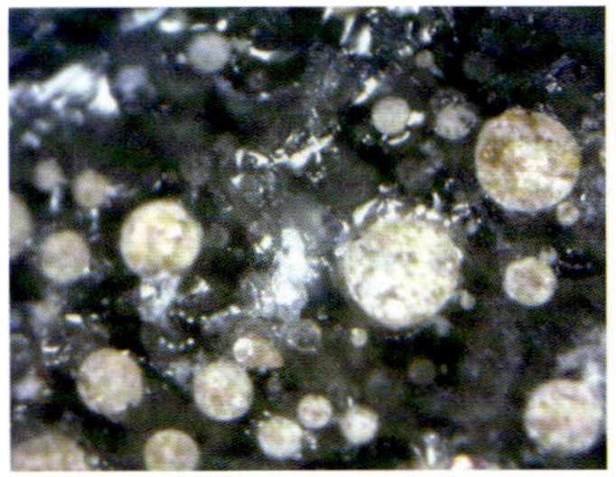		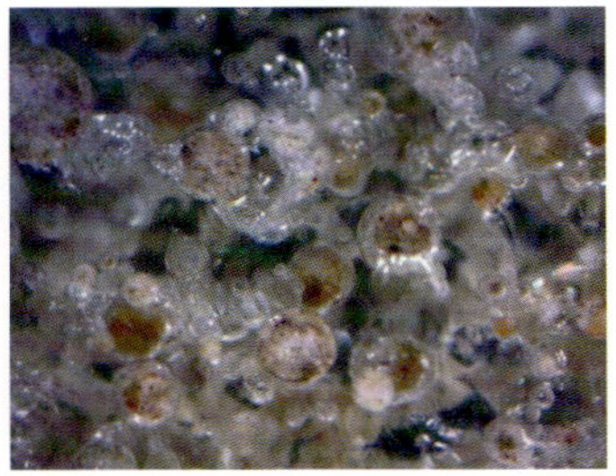
	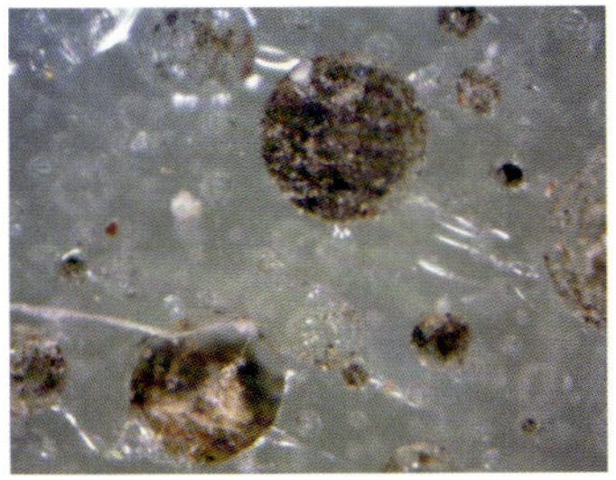	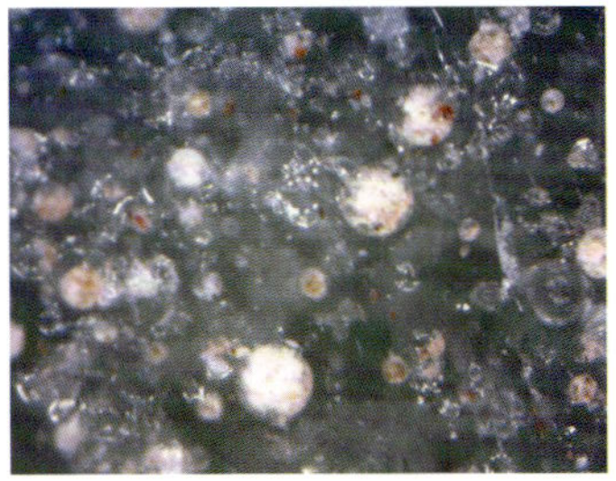		

流淌纹
Flowing Striae

二维 Two-dimensional	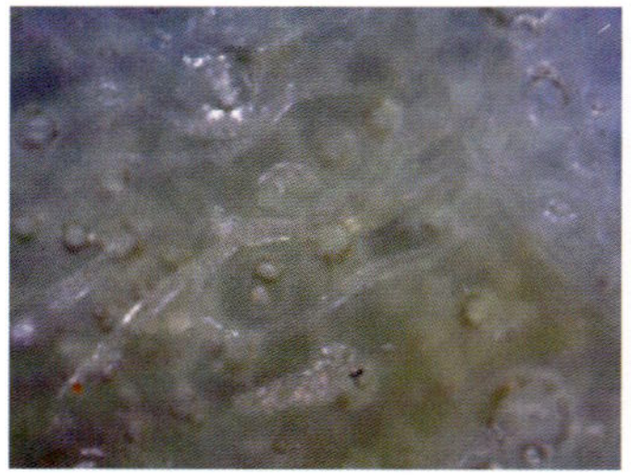	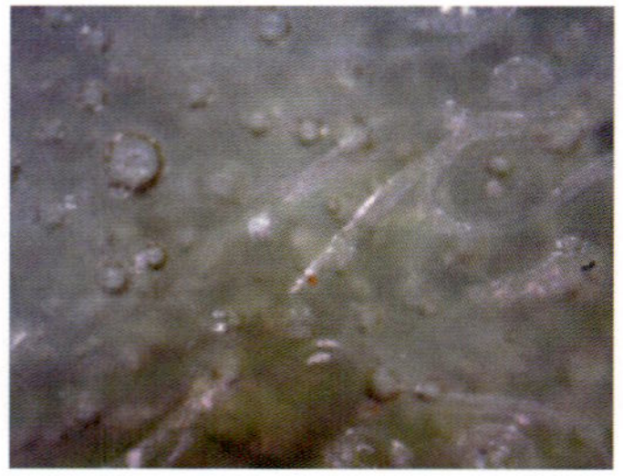	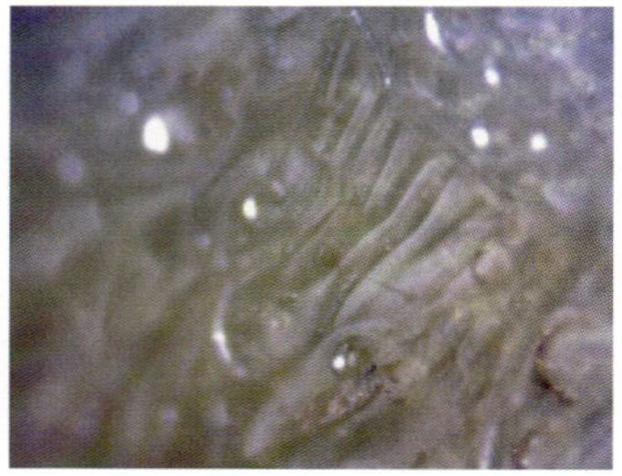	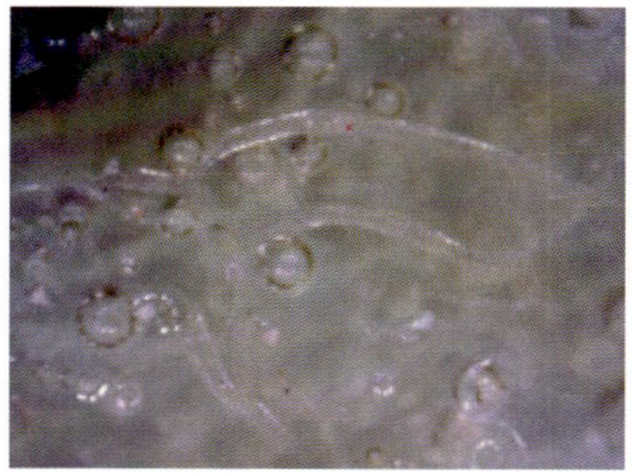

C形、O形纹
C and O Shaped Striae

二维 Two-dimensional	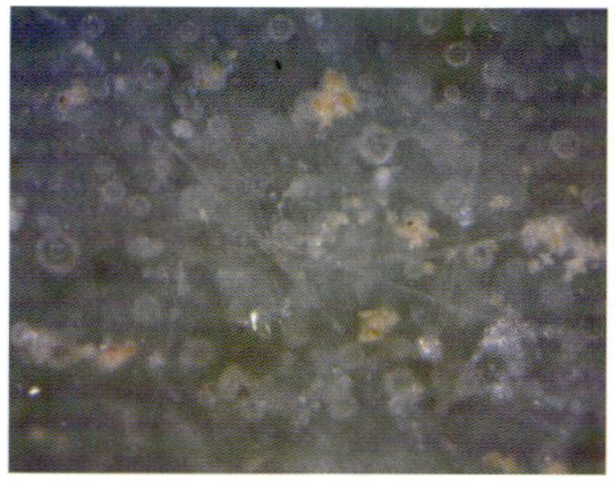	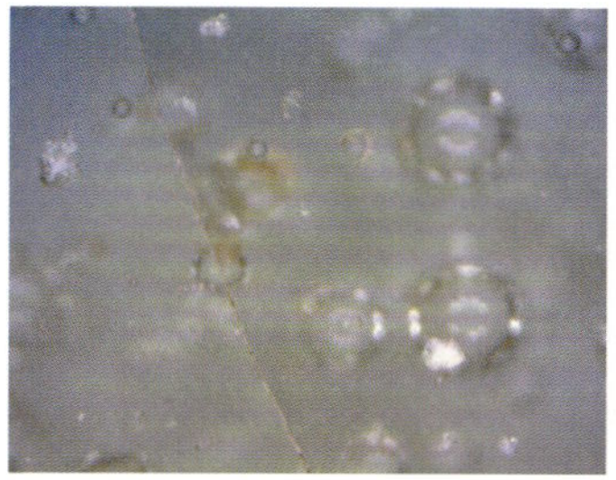	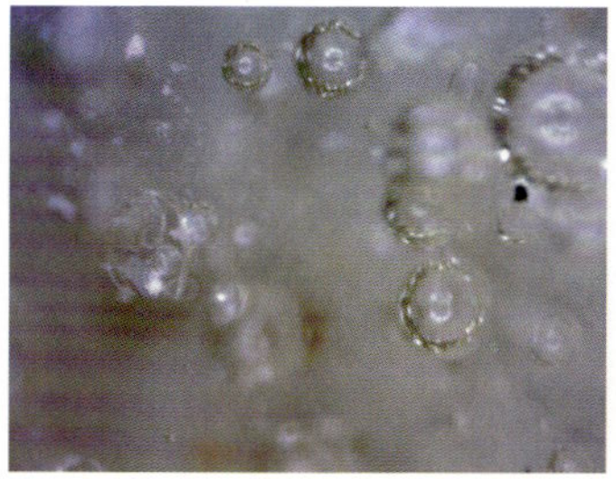	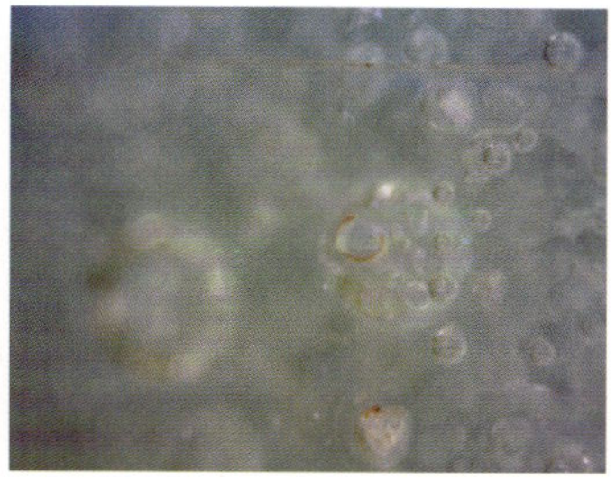
三维 Three-dimensional		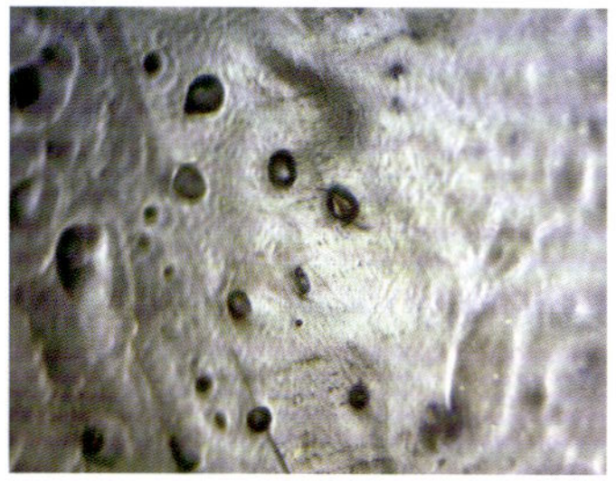	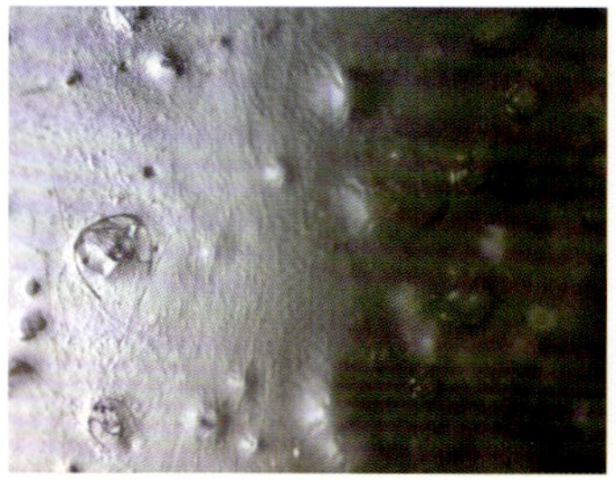	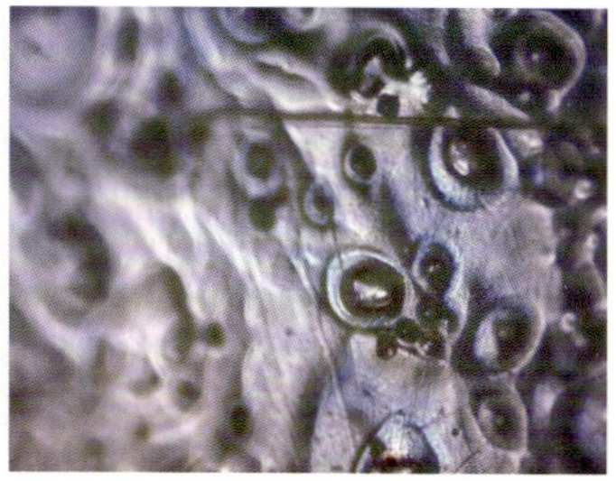
二维 Two-dimensional	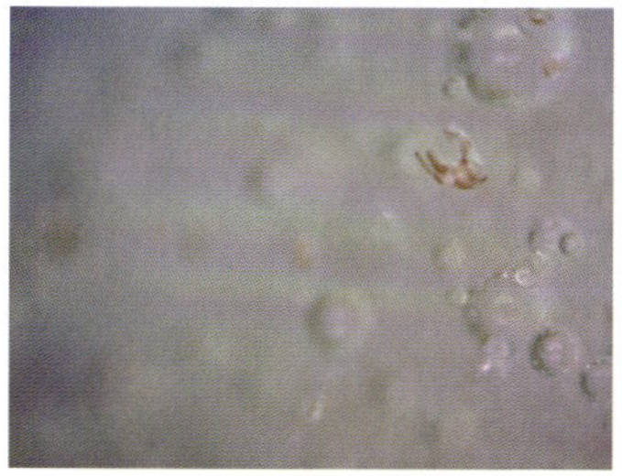	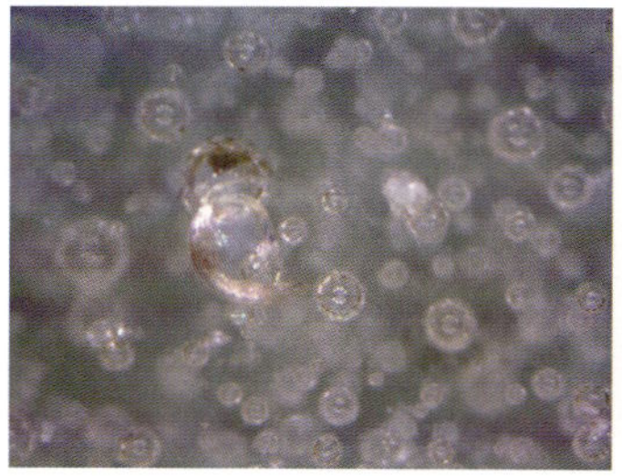	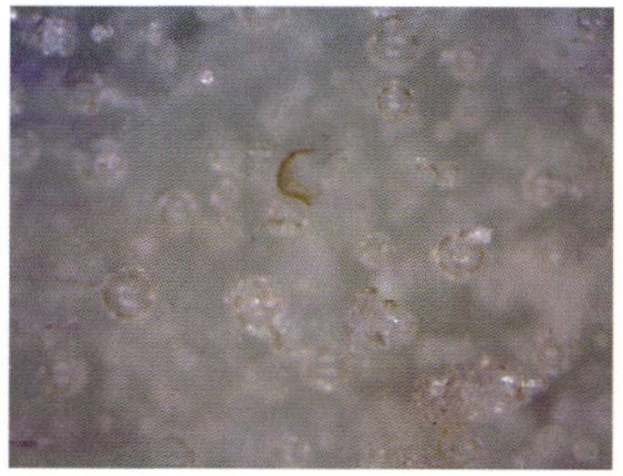	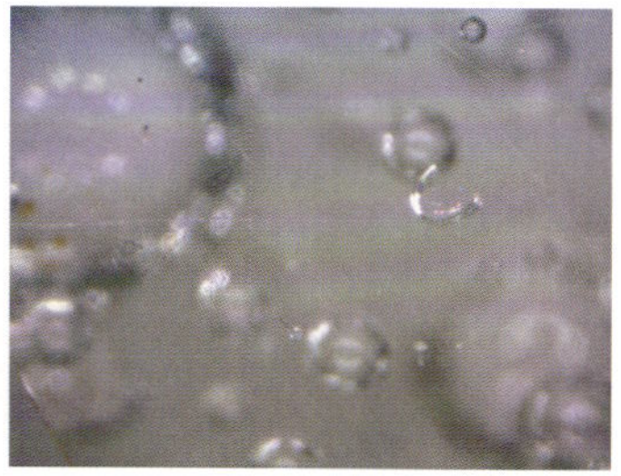
三维 Three-dimensional	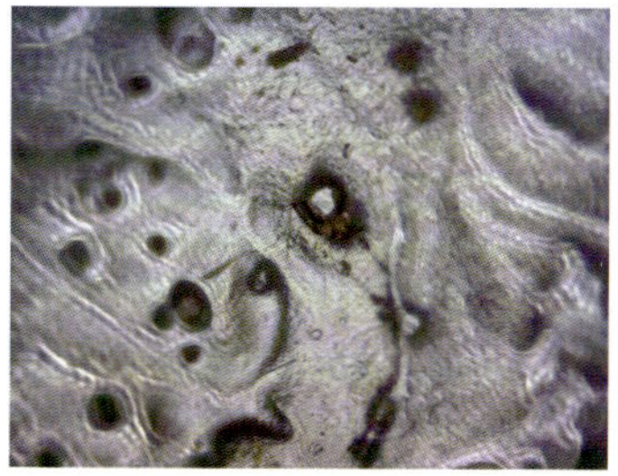	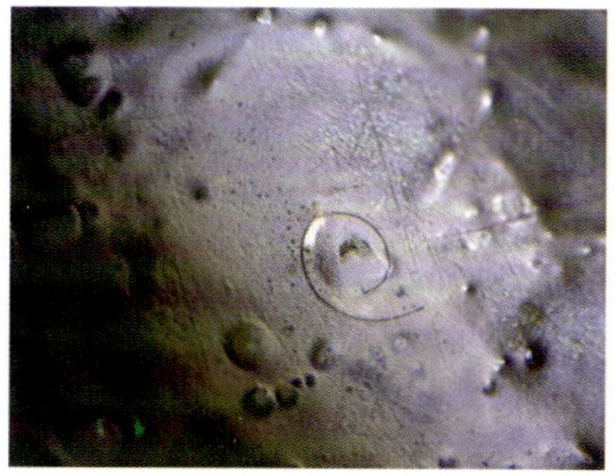	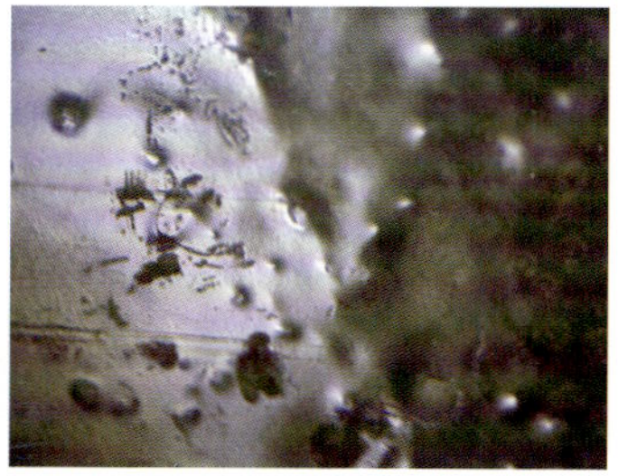	

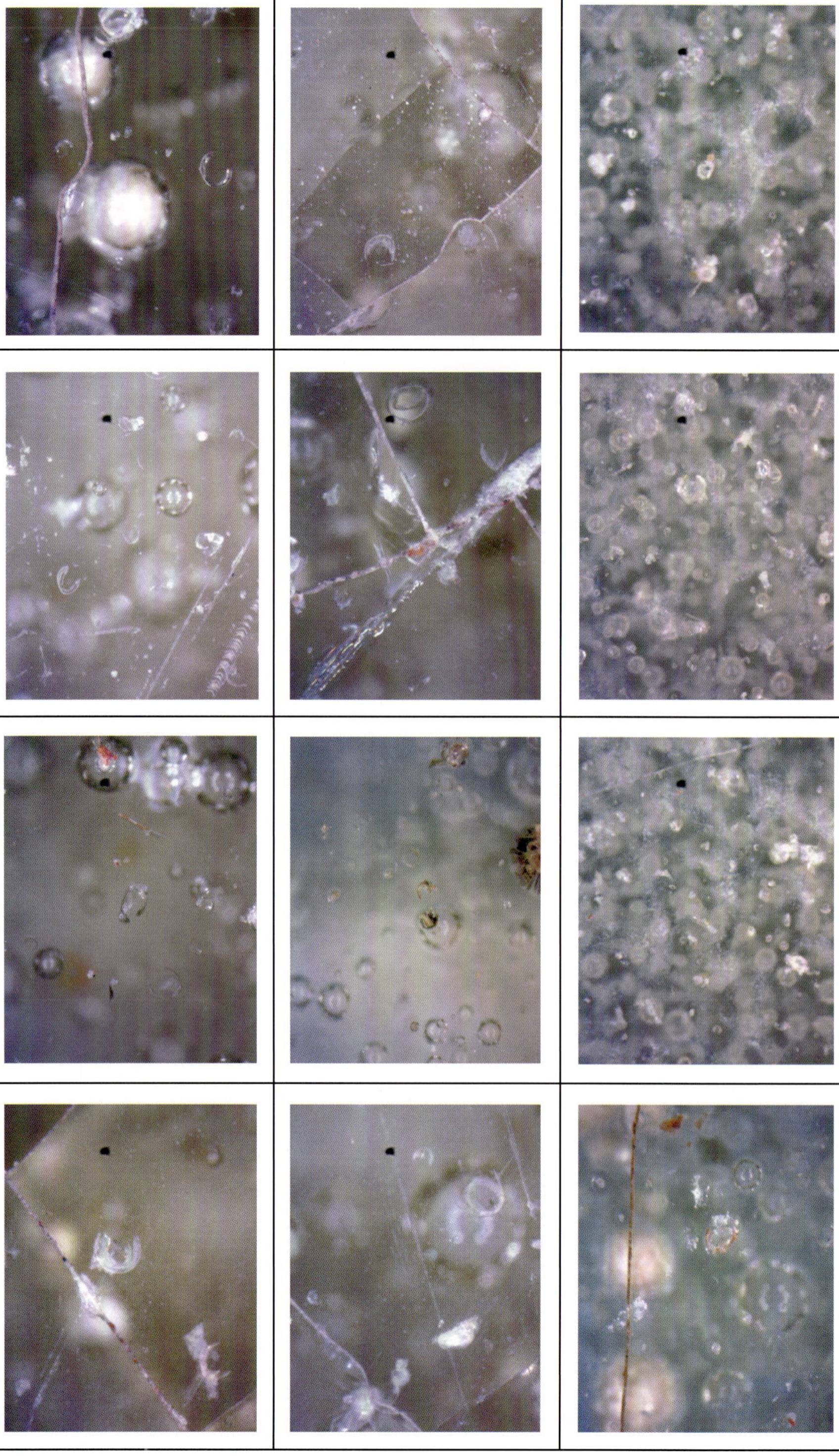

二维
Two-dimensional

（续图）
（Continued）

釉裂纹 Glaze Cracks

二维 Two-dimensional	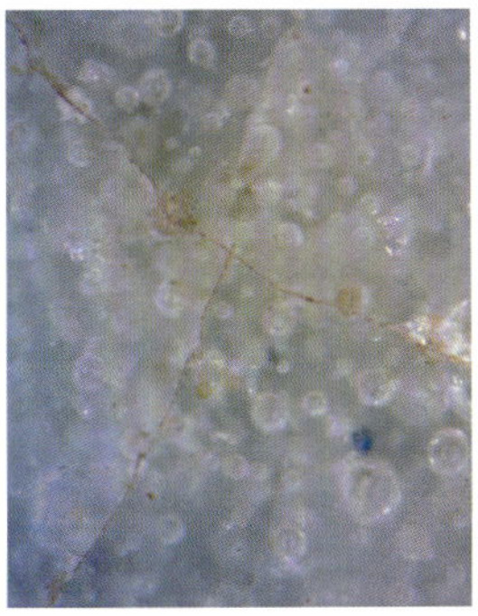	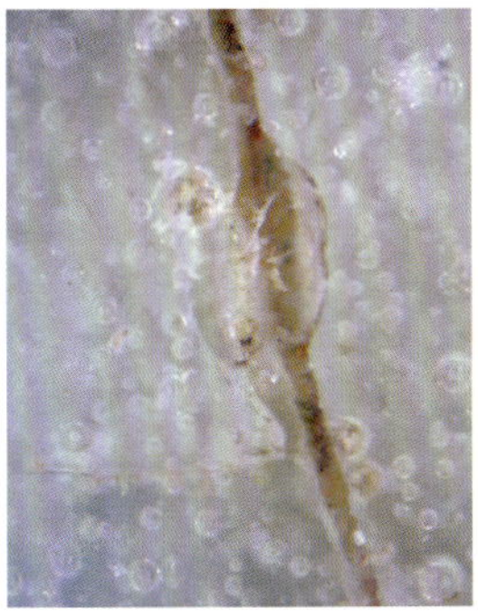	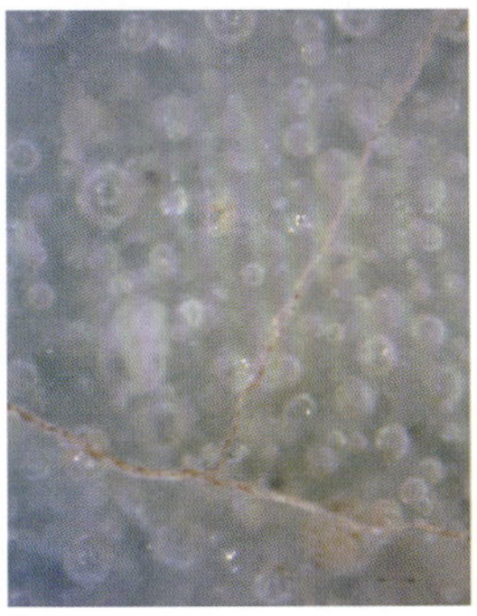	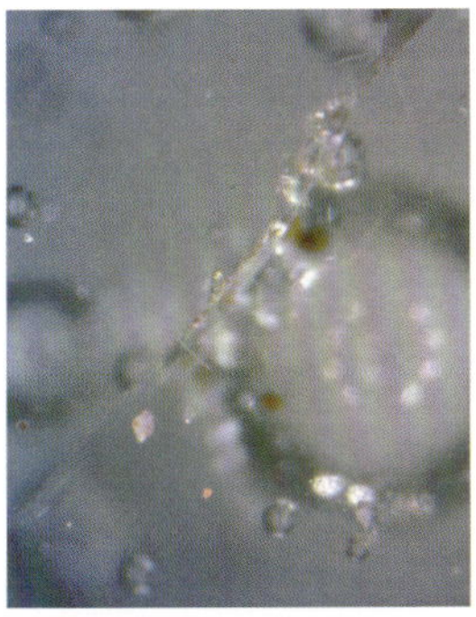
三维 Three-dimensional		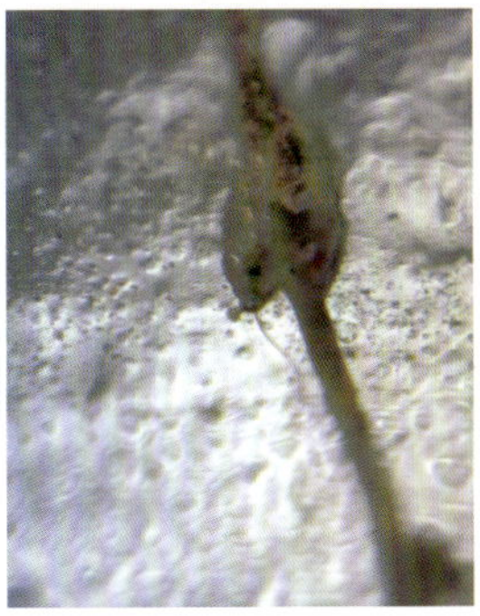	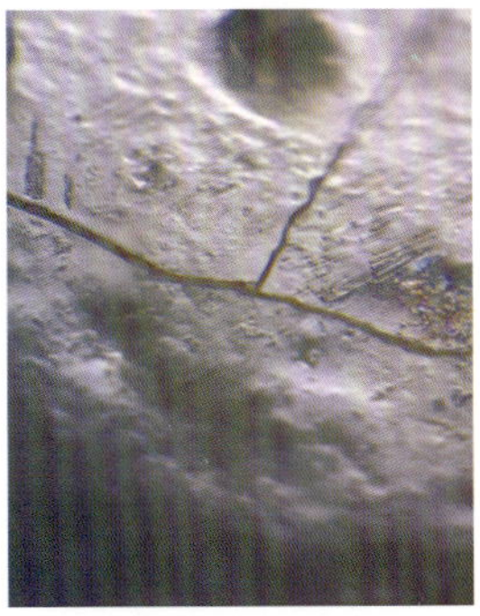	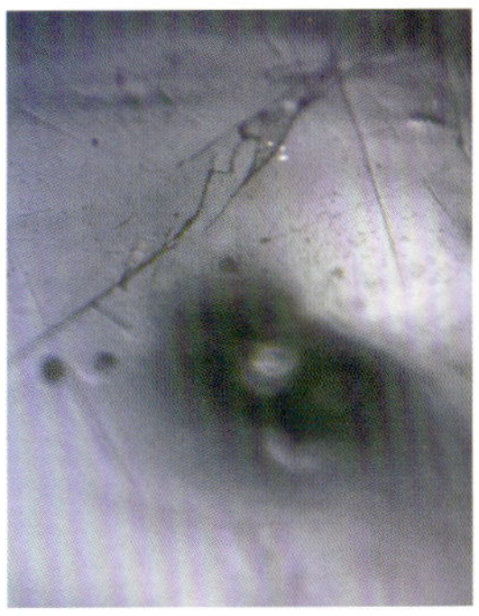
二维 Two-dimensional	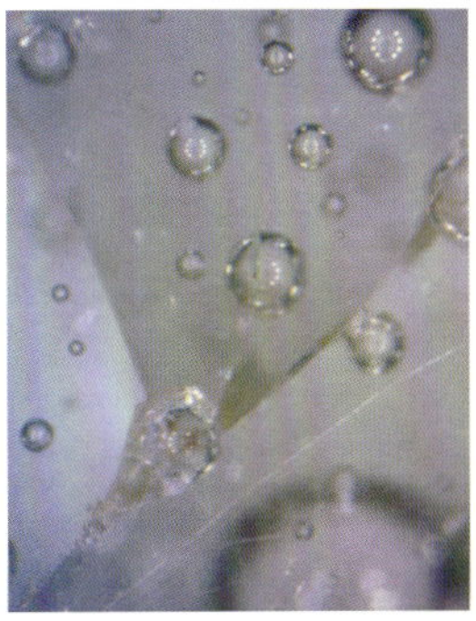	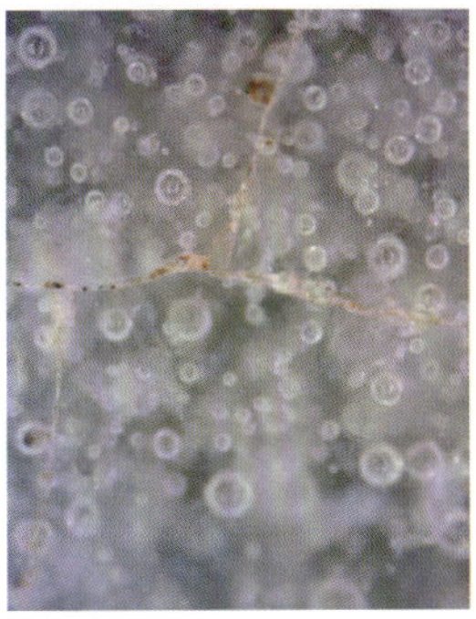	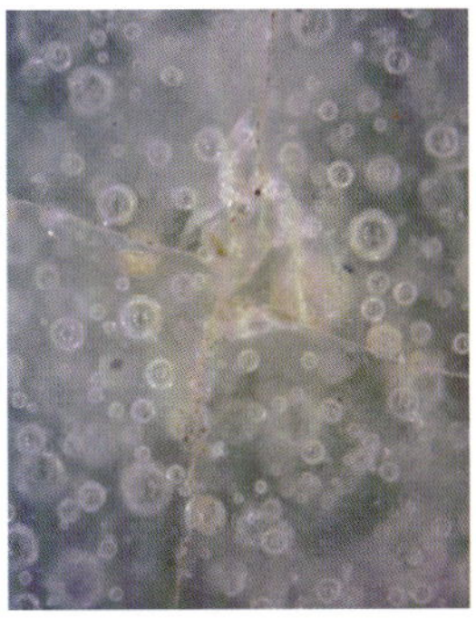	
三维 Three-dimensional	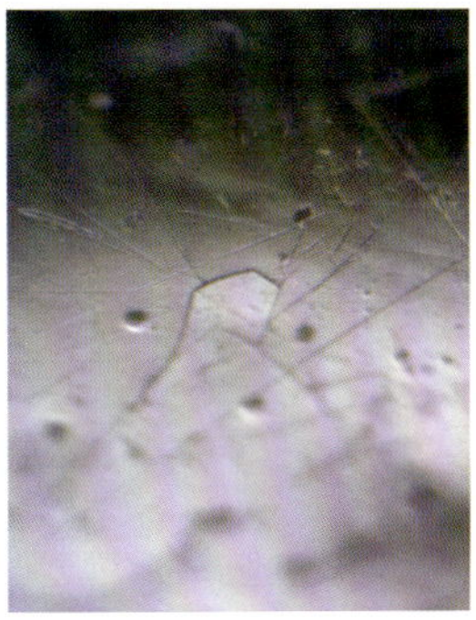	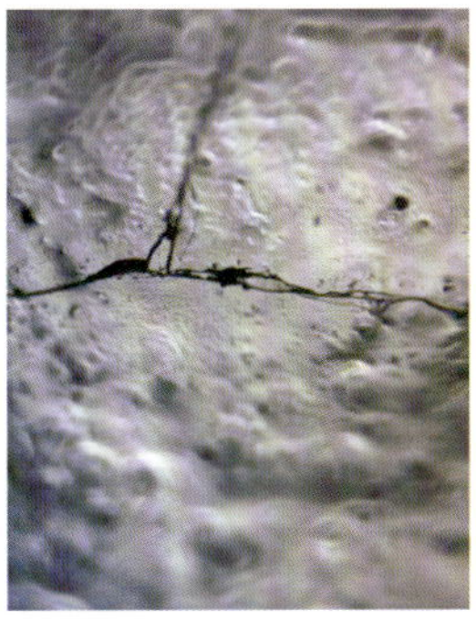	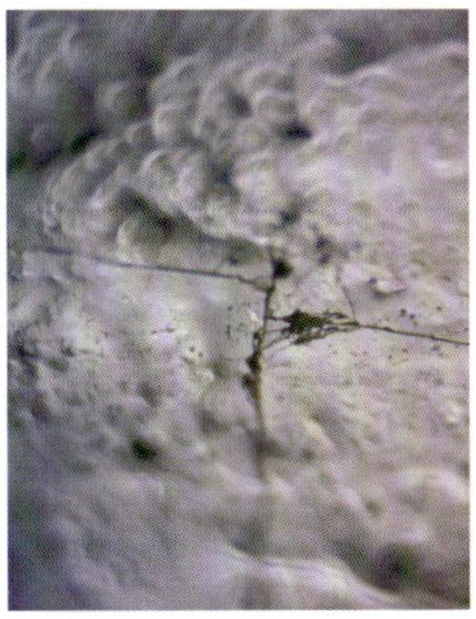	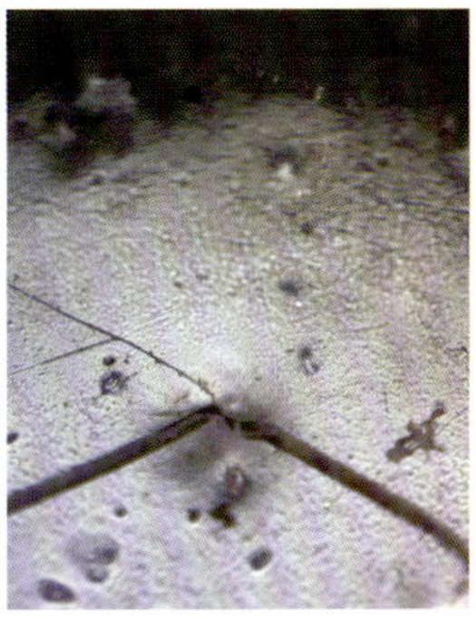

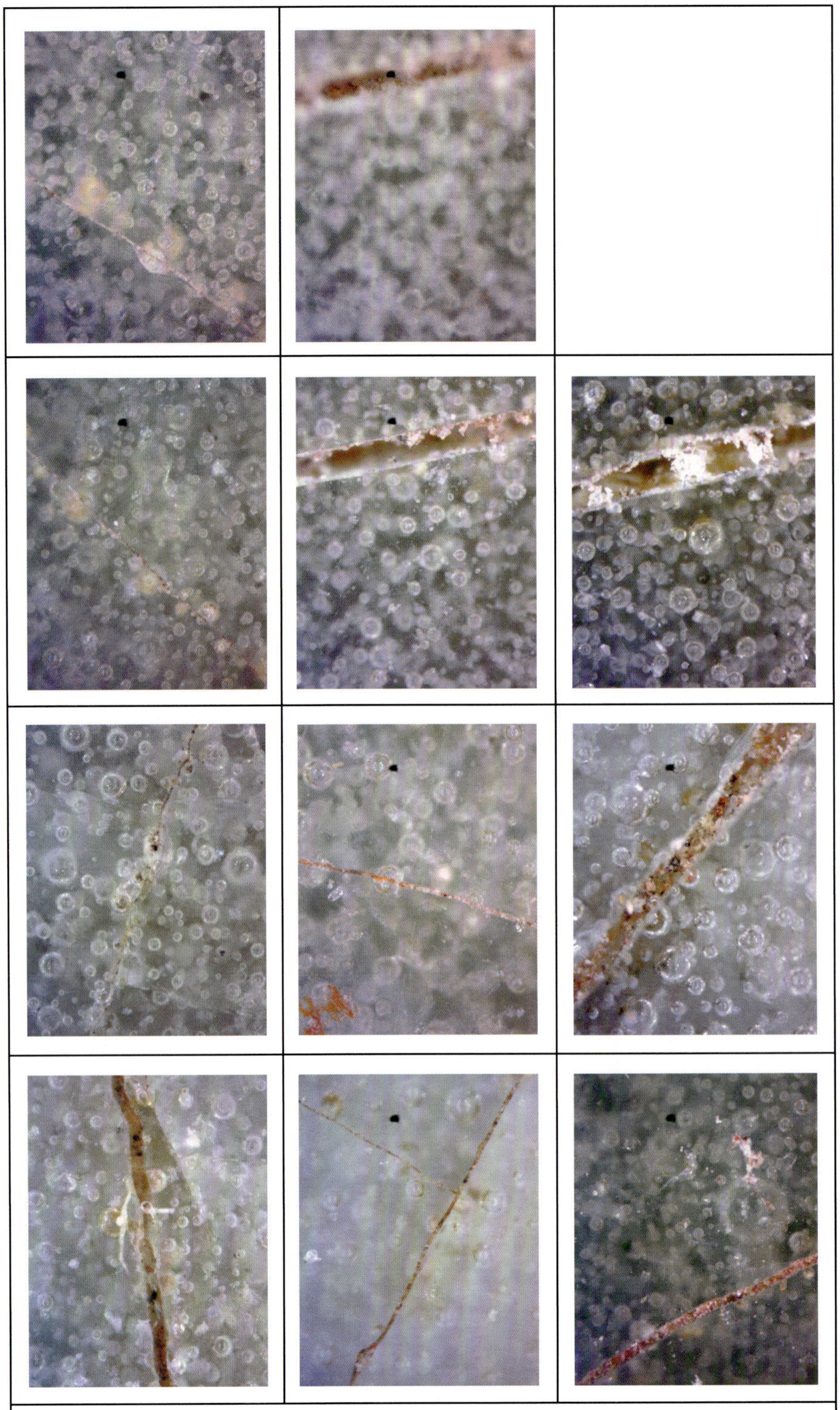

二维
Two-dimensional

（续图）
（Continued）

划痕
Scratches

二维 Two-dimensional	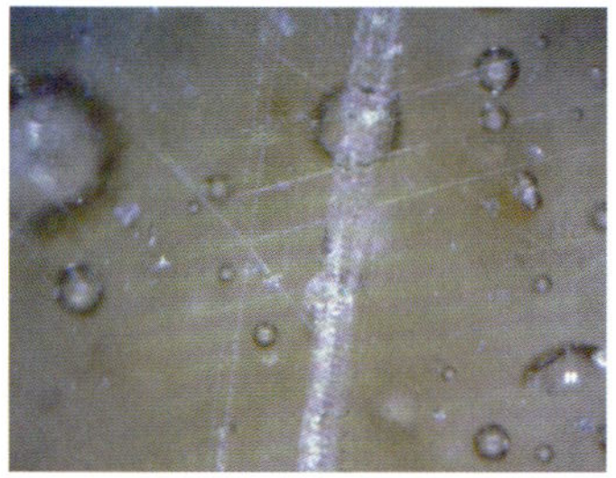	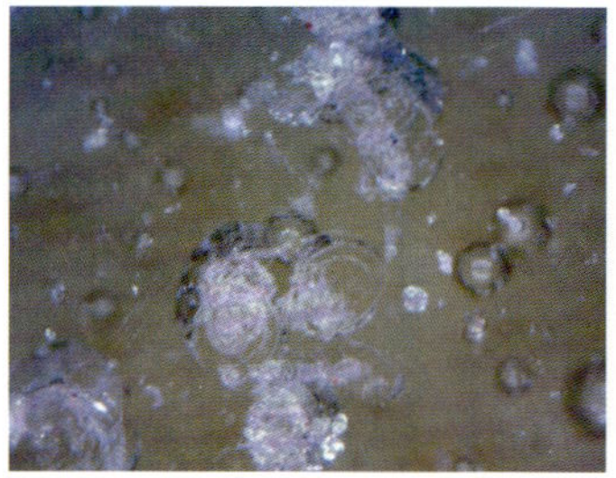		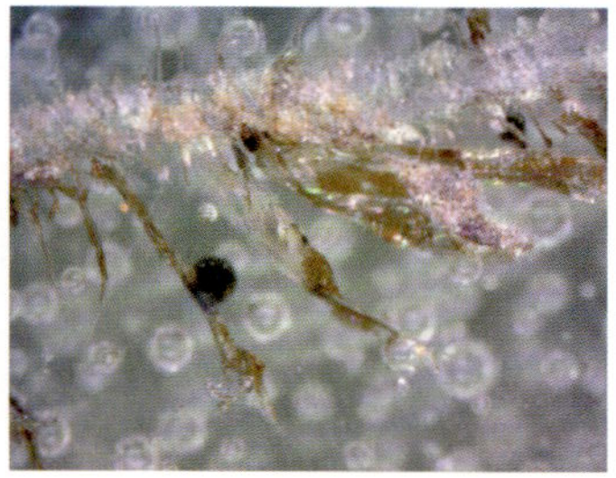
三维 Three-dimensional	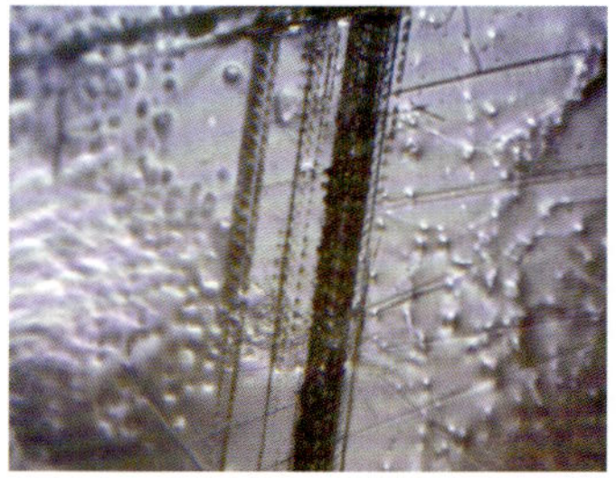	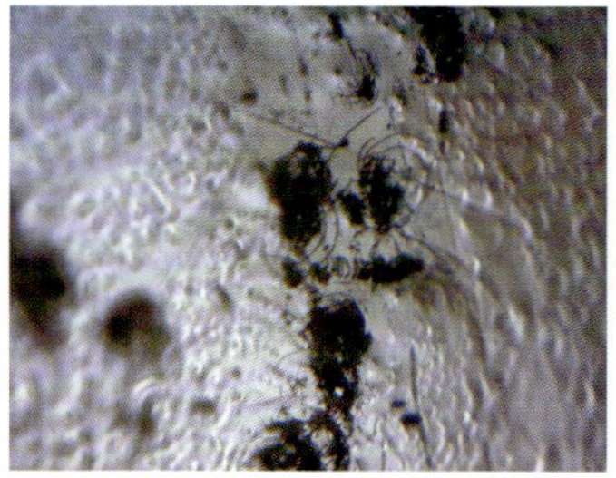	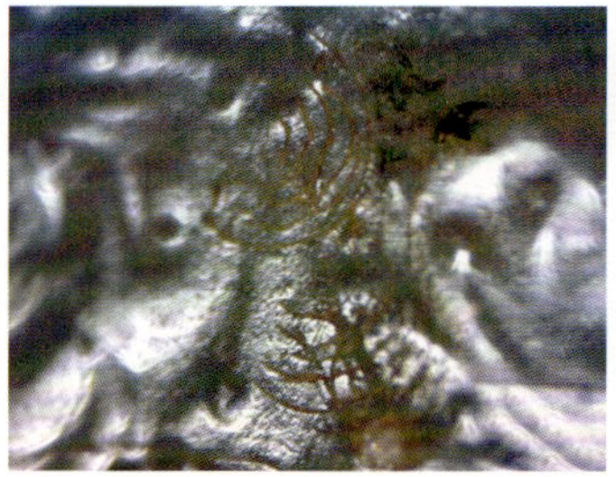	
二维 Two-dimensional	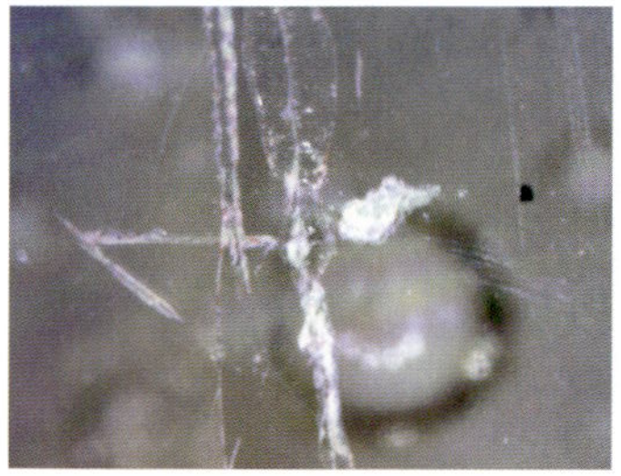	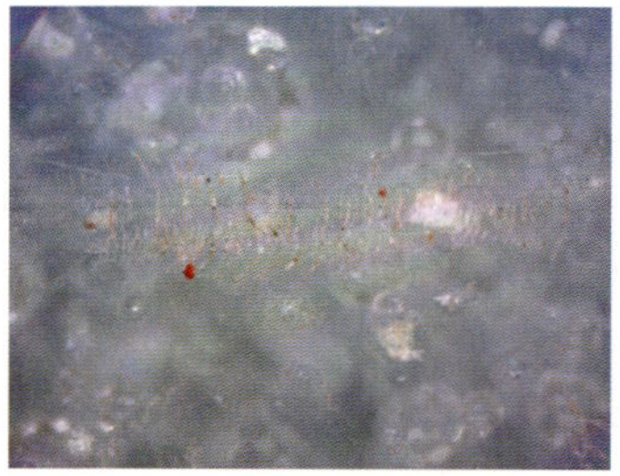	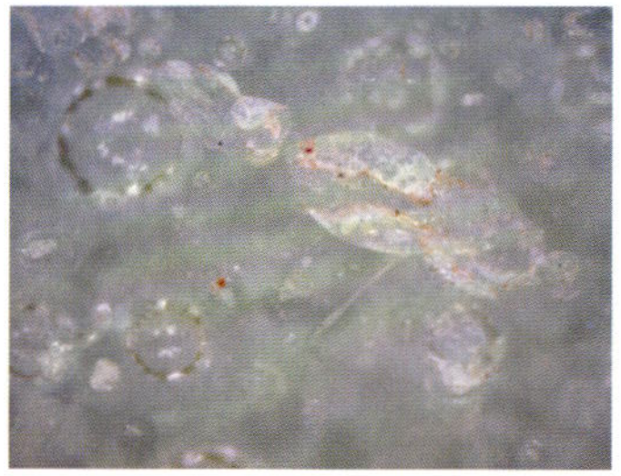	
	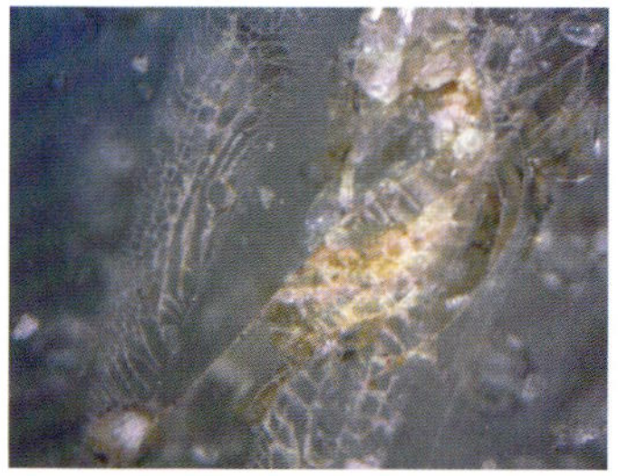	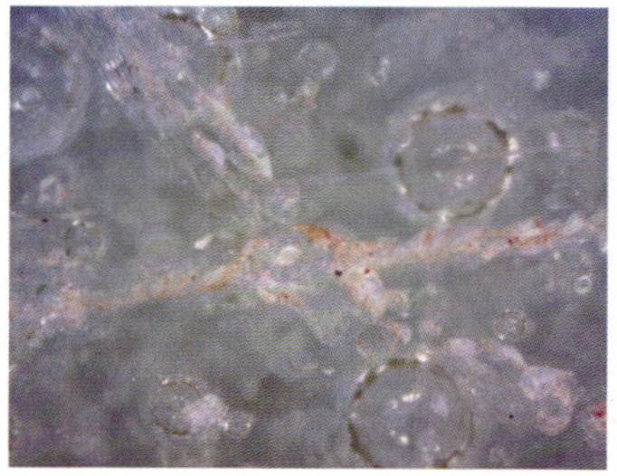	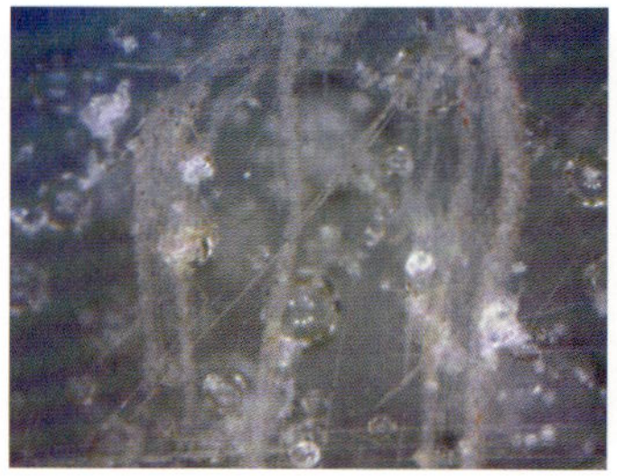	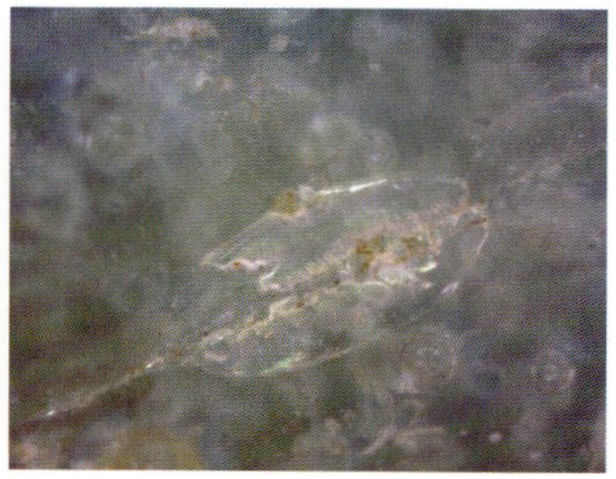

（续图）
(Continued)

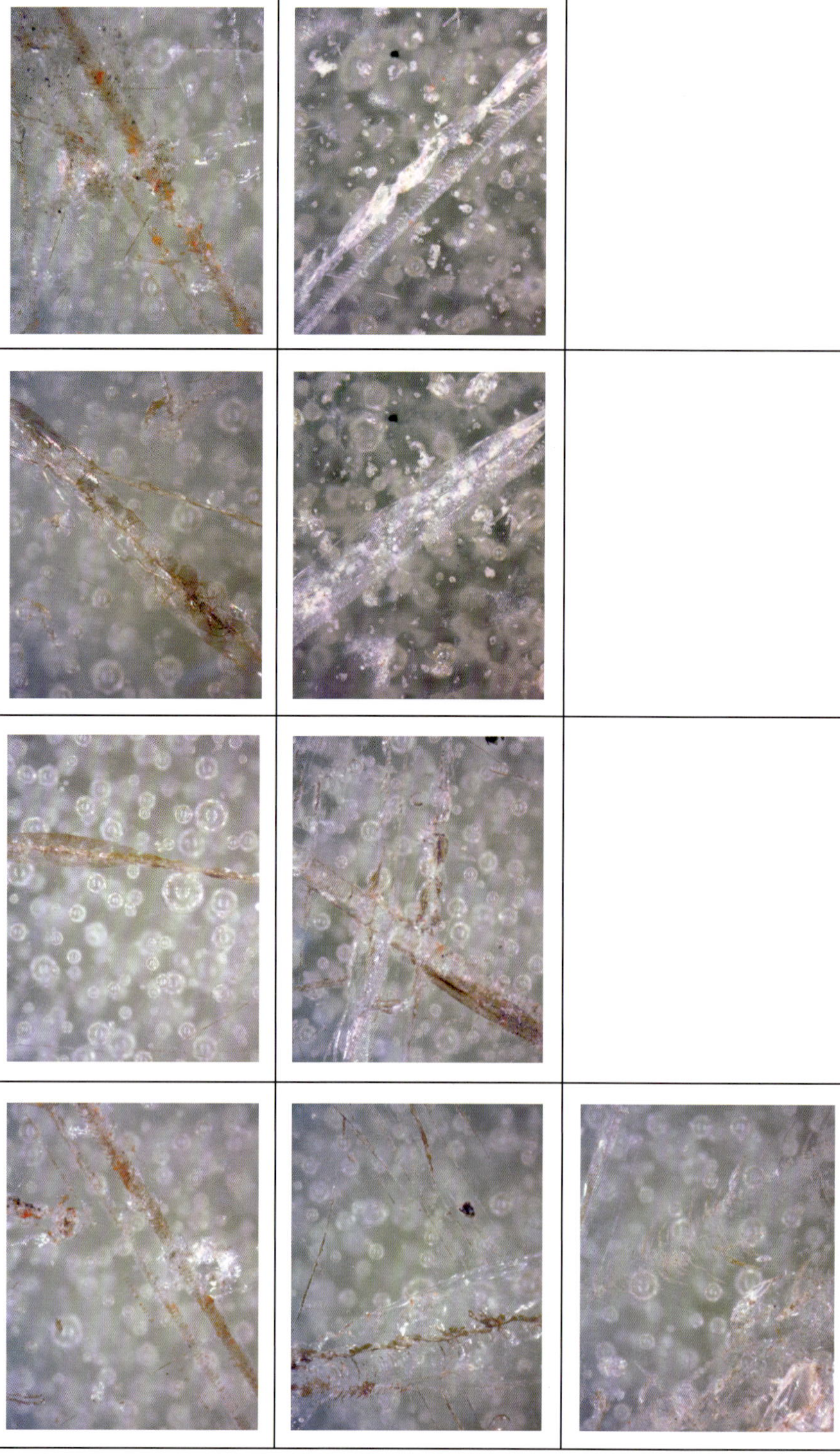

二维
Two-dimensional

(续图)
(Continued)

三维
Three-dimensional

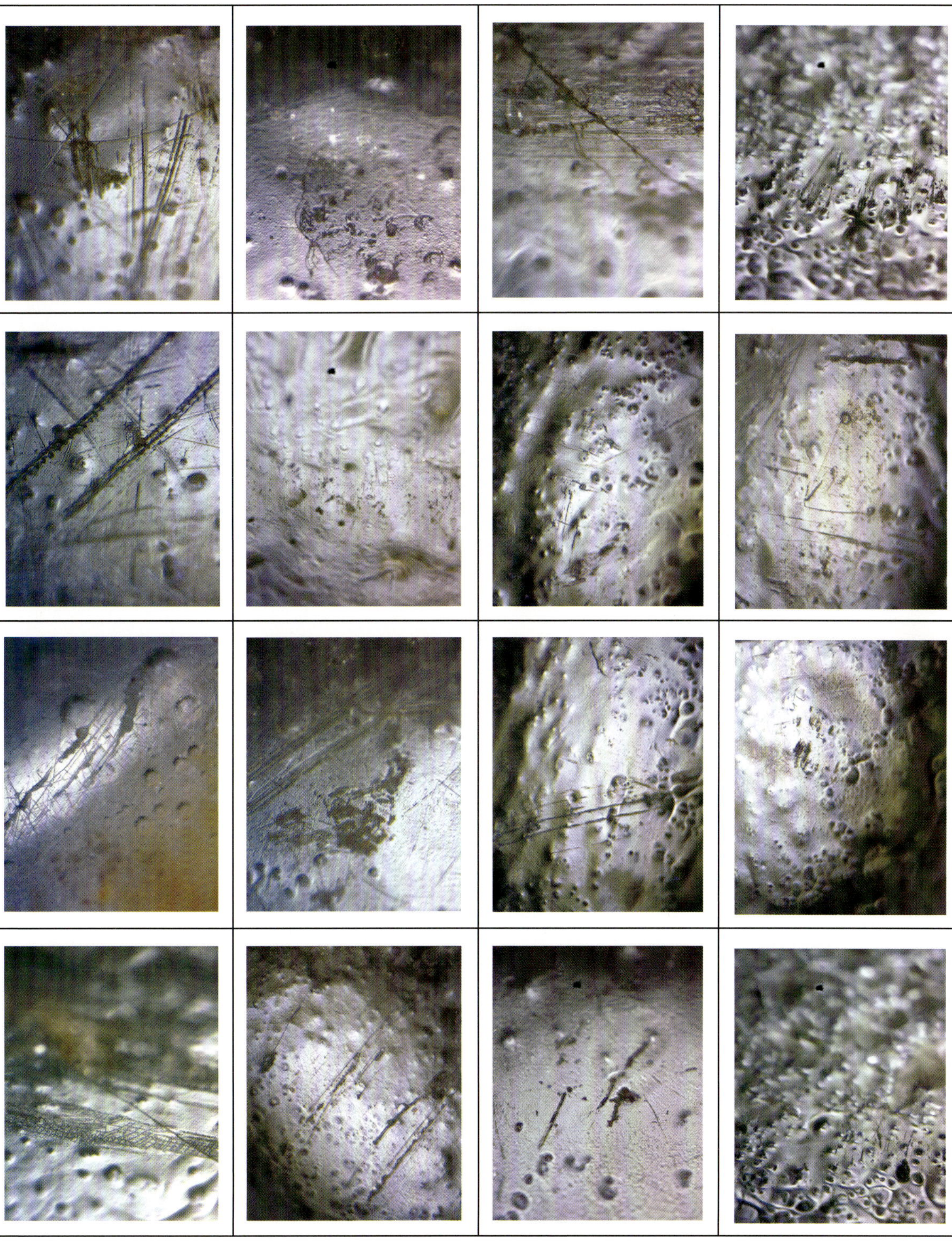

色变泡
Color Change Bubbles

二维 Two-dimensional	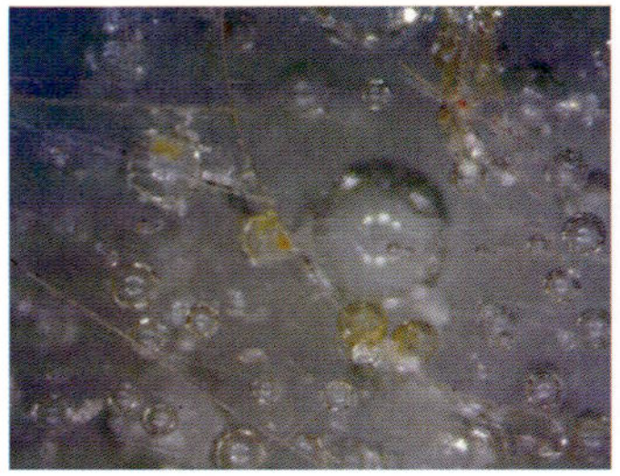	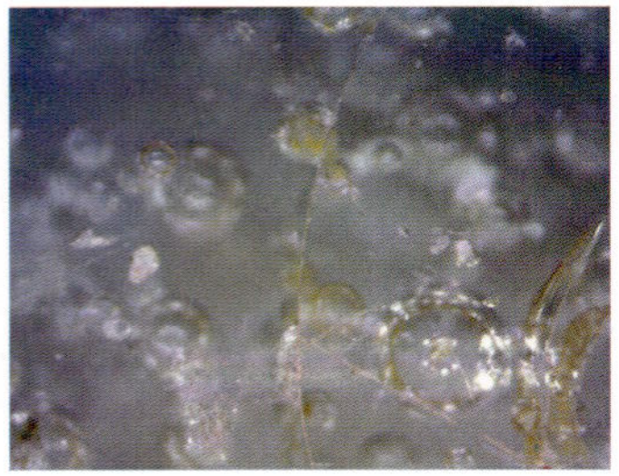	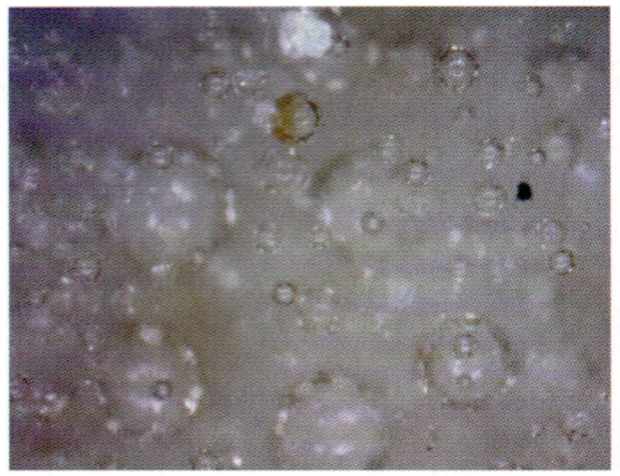	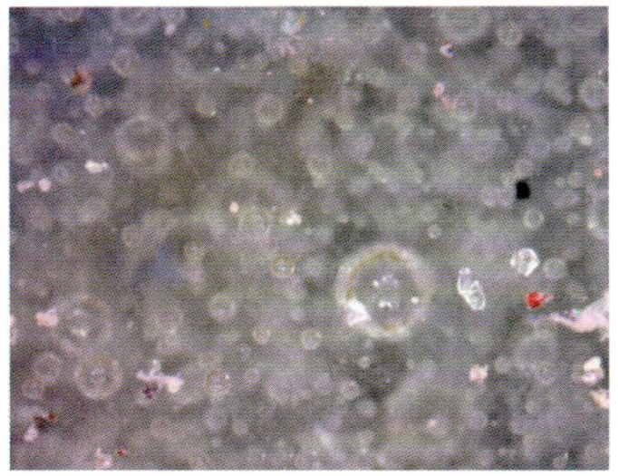
	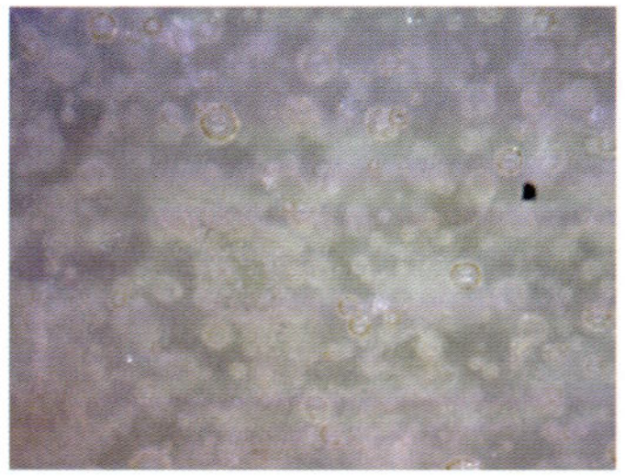	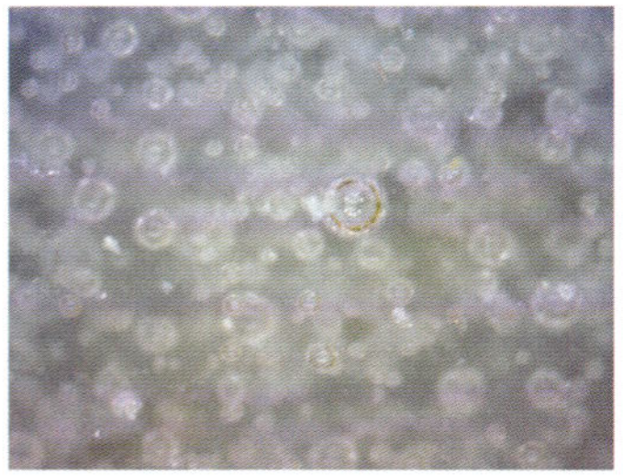	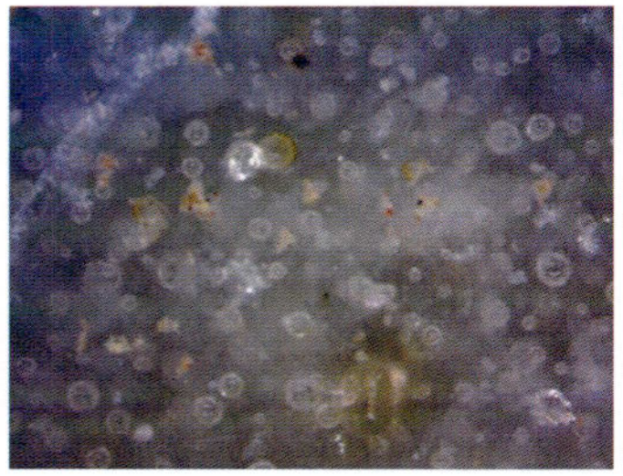	

壁变泡
Textured Bubbles

二维 Two-dimensional	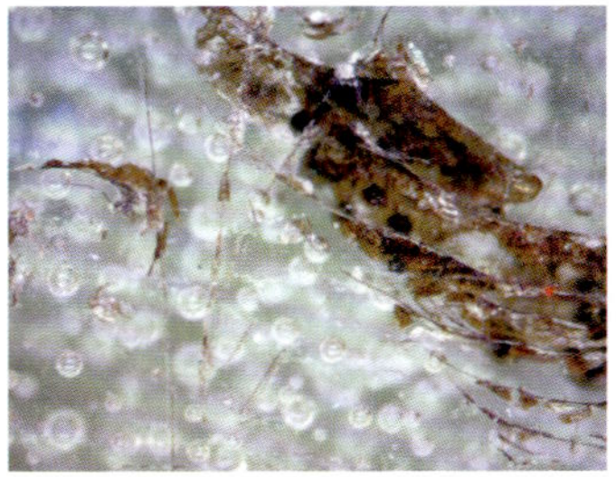	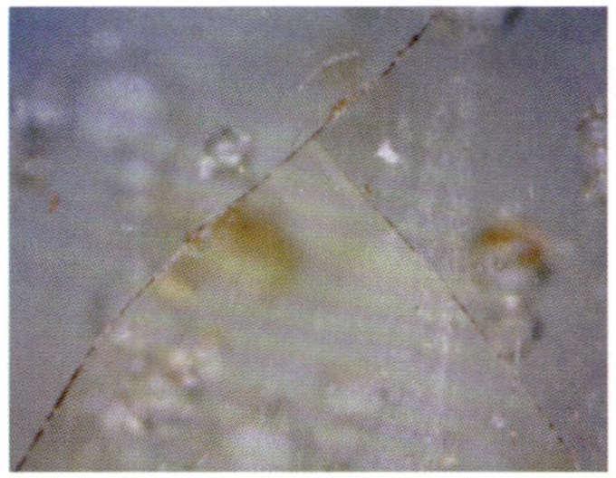	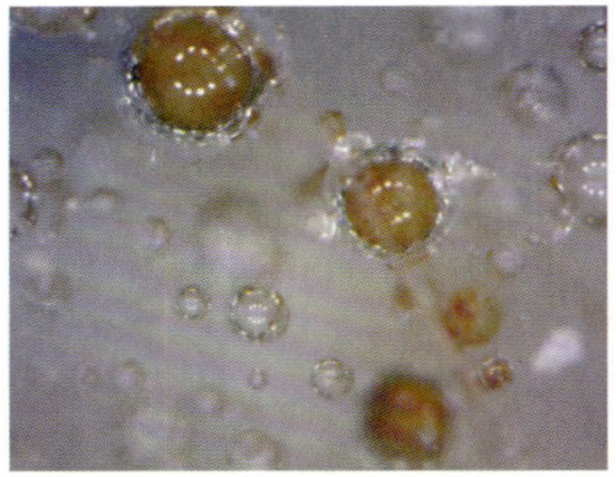	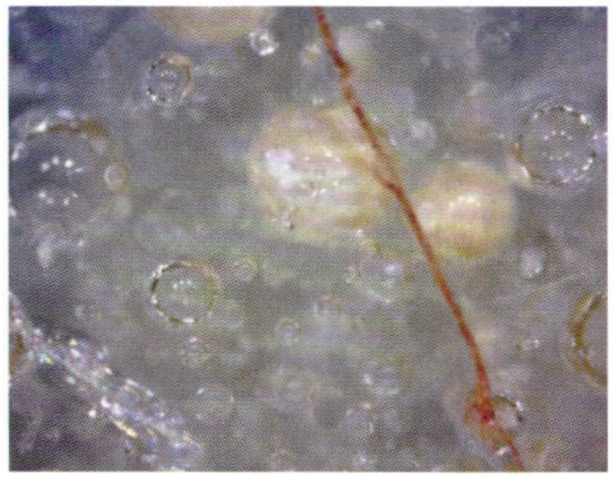
三维 Three-dimensional	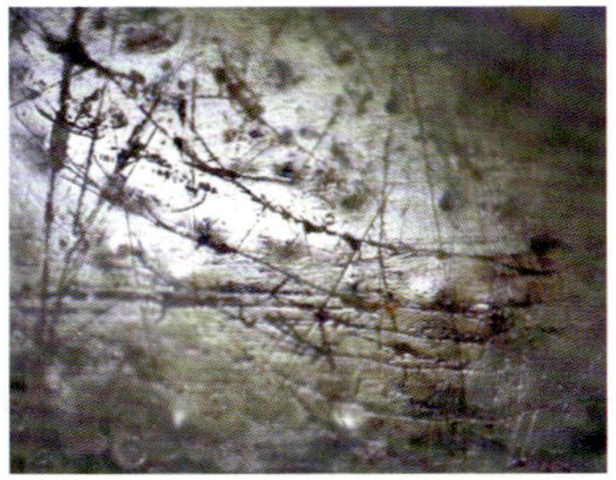	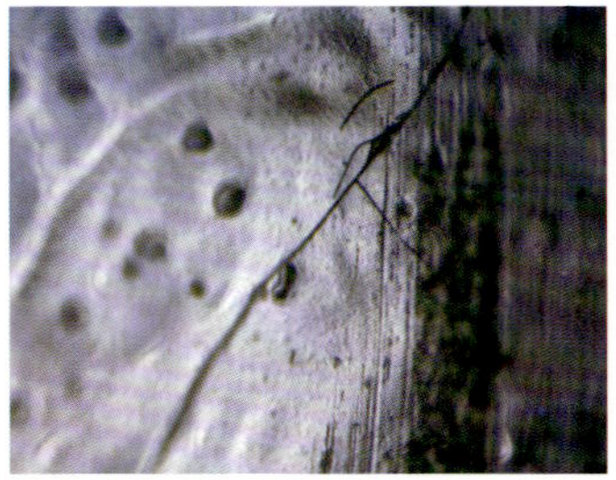	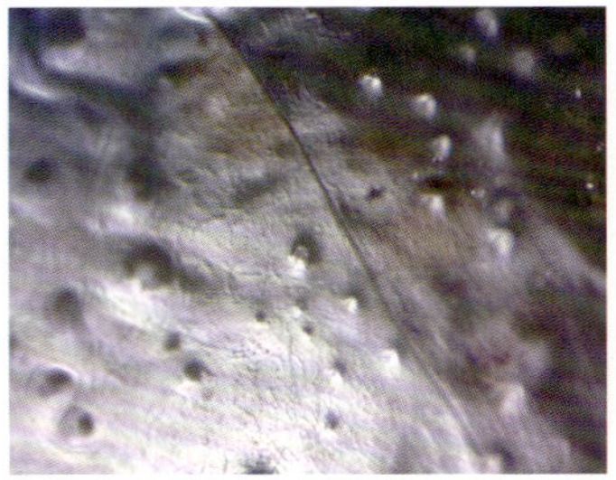	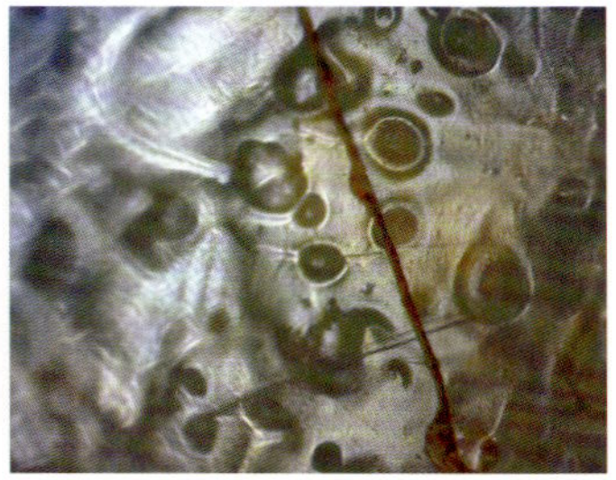
二维 Two-dimensional	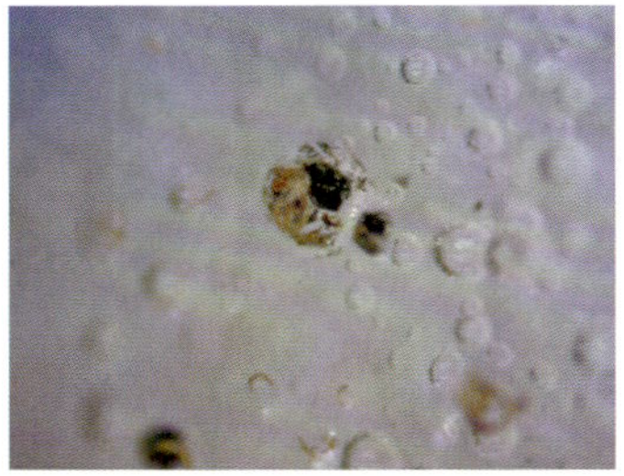		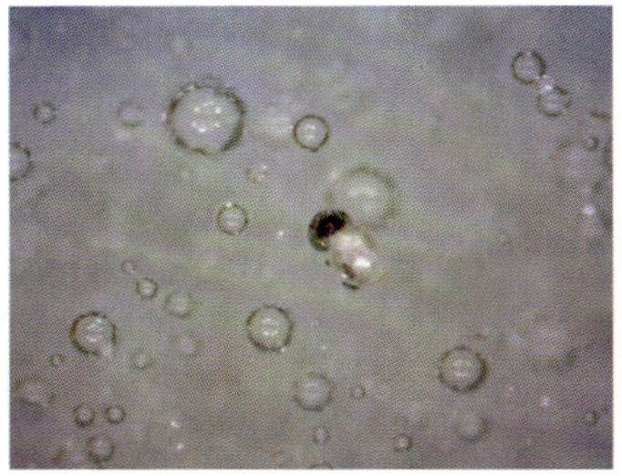	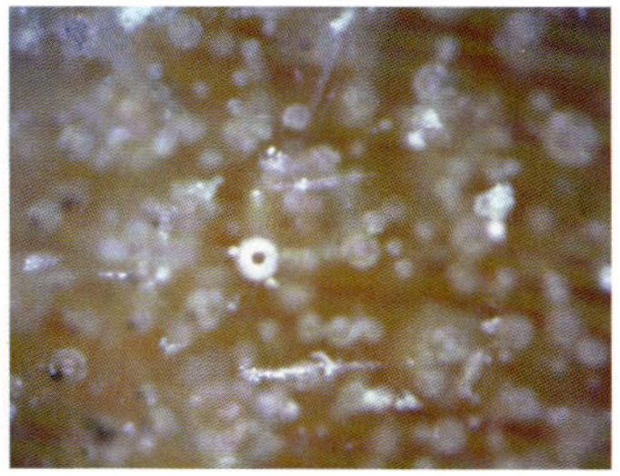
三维 Three-dimensional	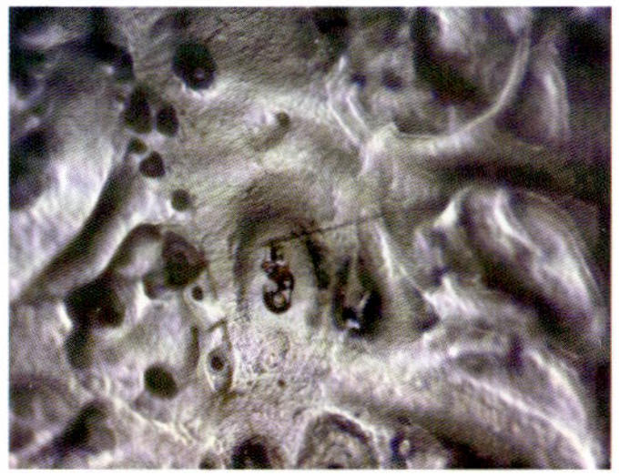	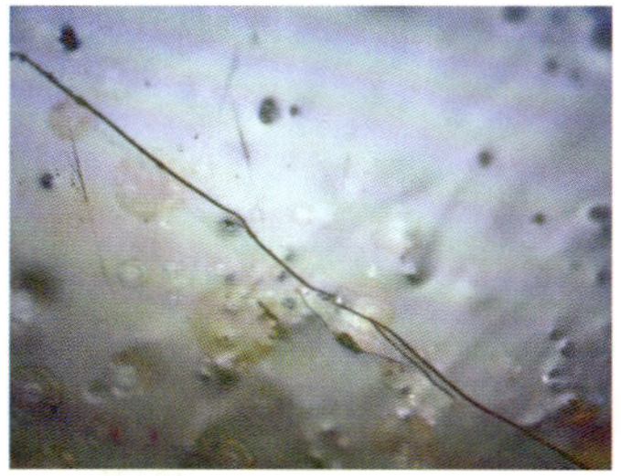	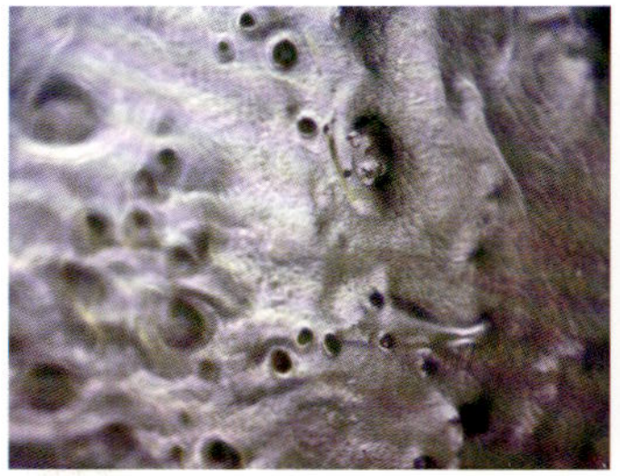	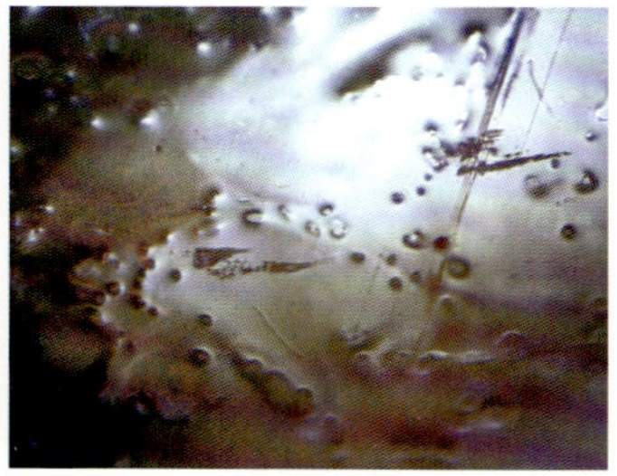

（续图）
（Continued）

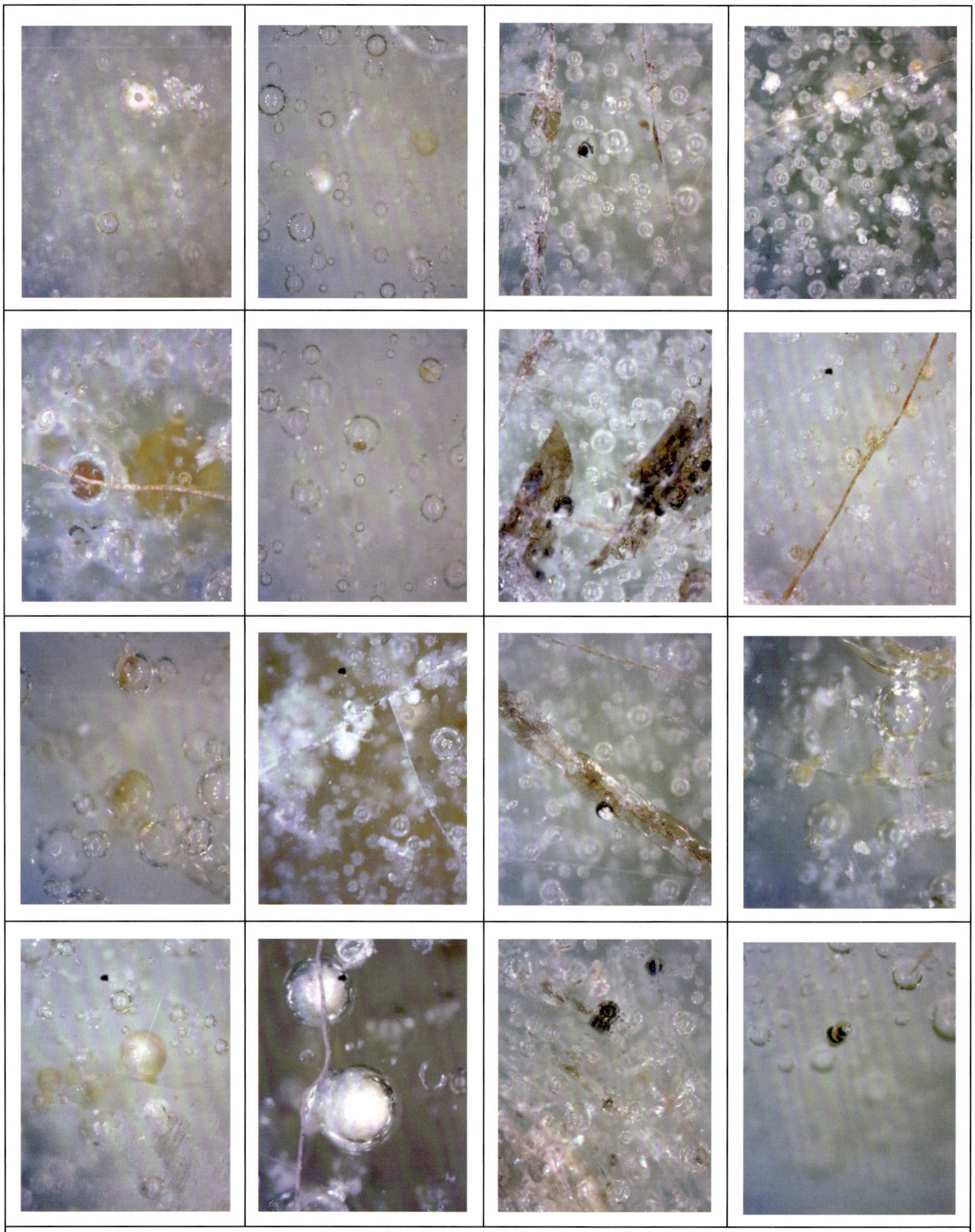

二维
Two-dimensional

玻璃相
Glass Phase

二维
Two-dimensional

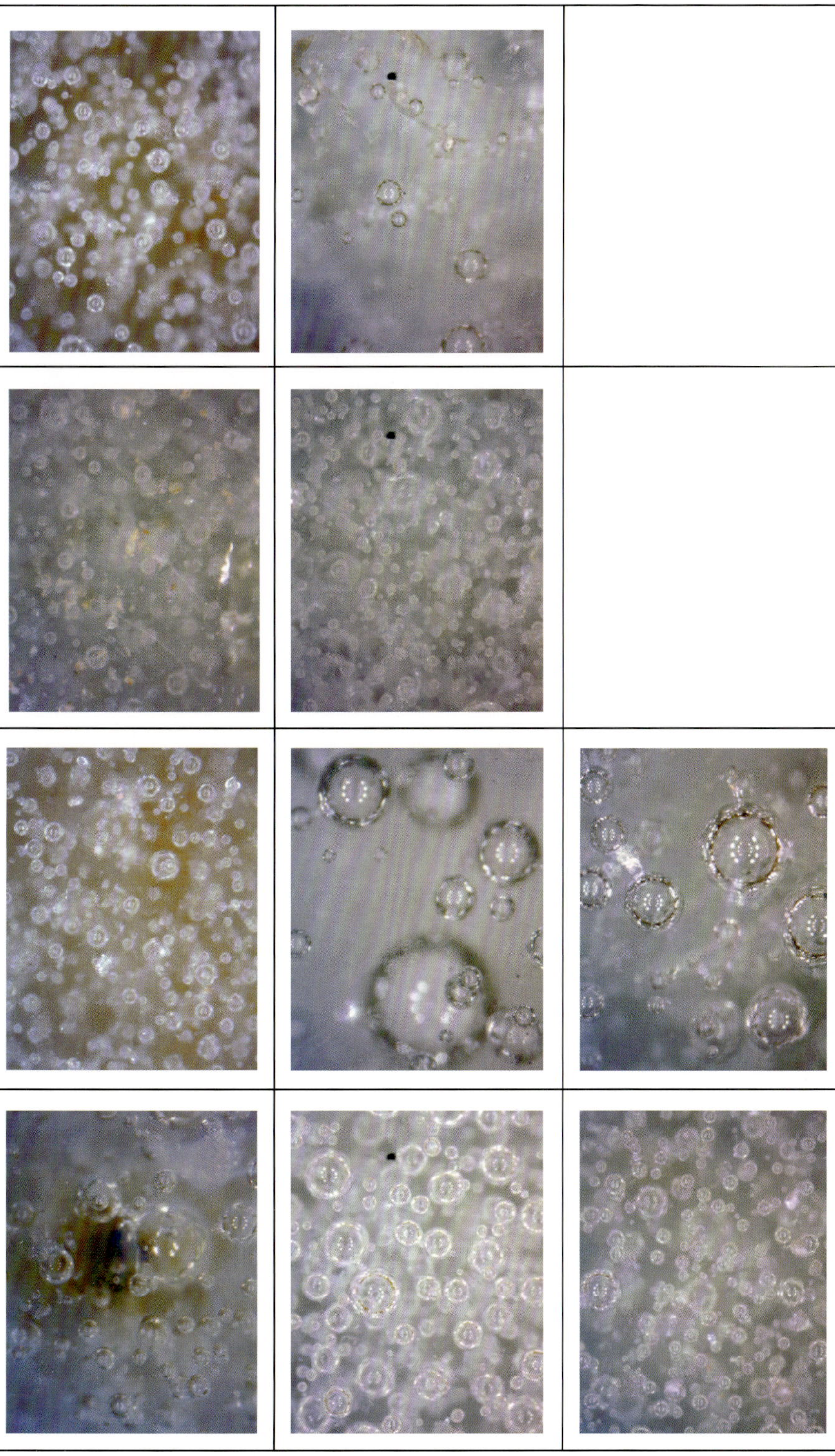

（续图）
（Continued）

三维
Three-dimensional

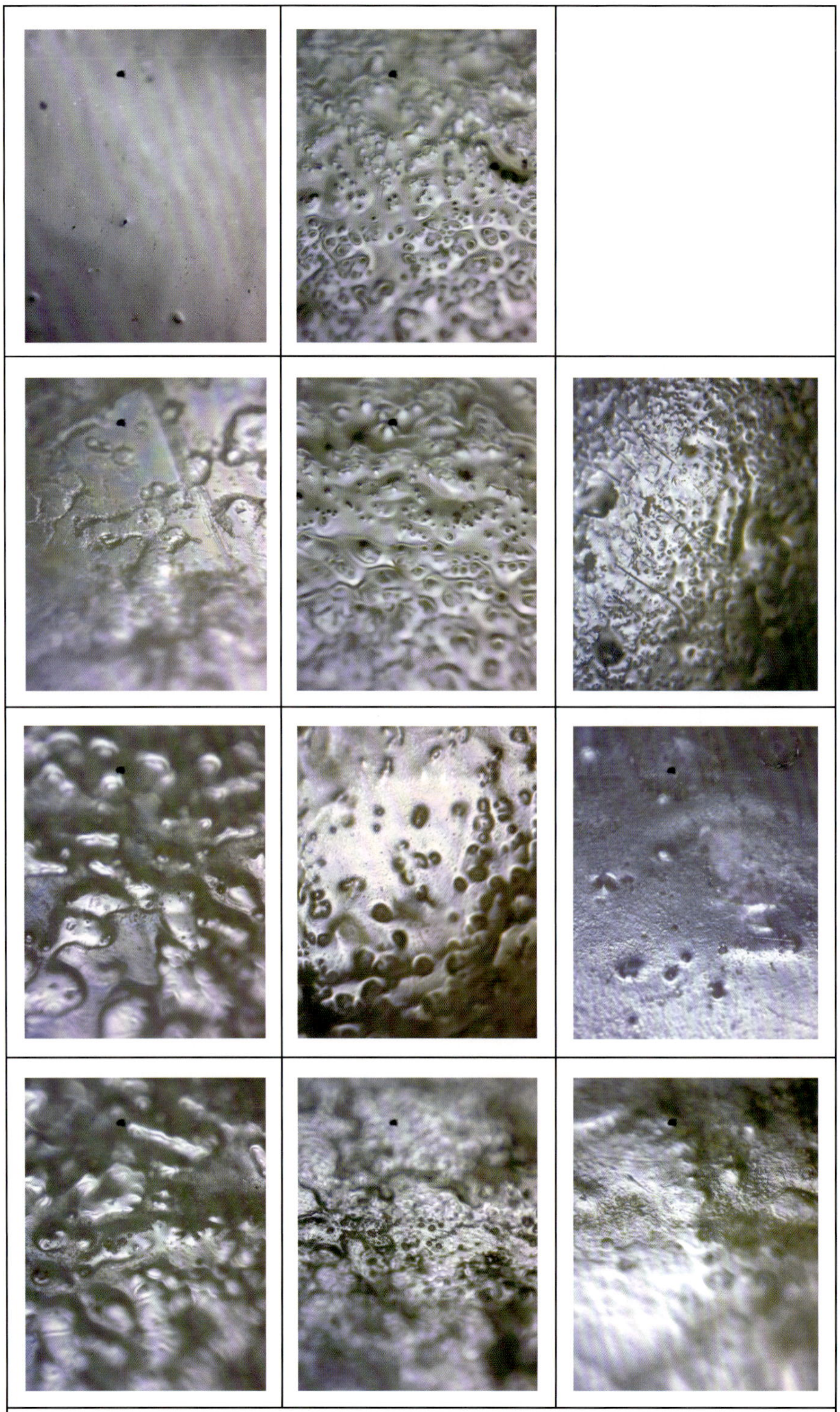

鬃眼
Bristle Pits

二维
Two-dimensional

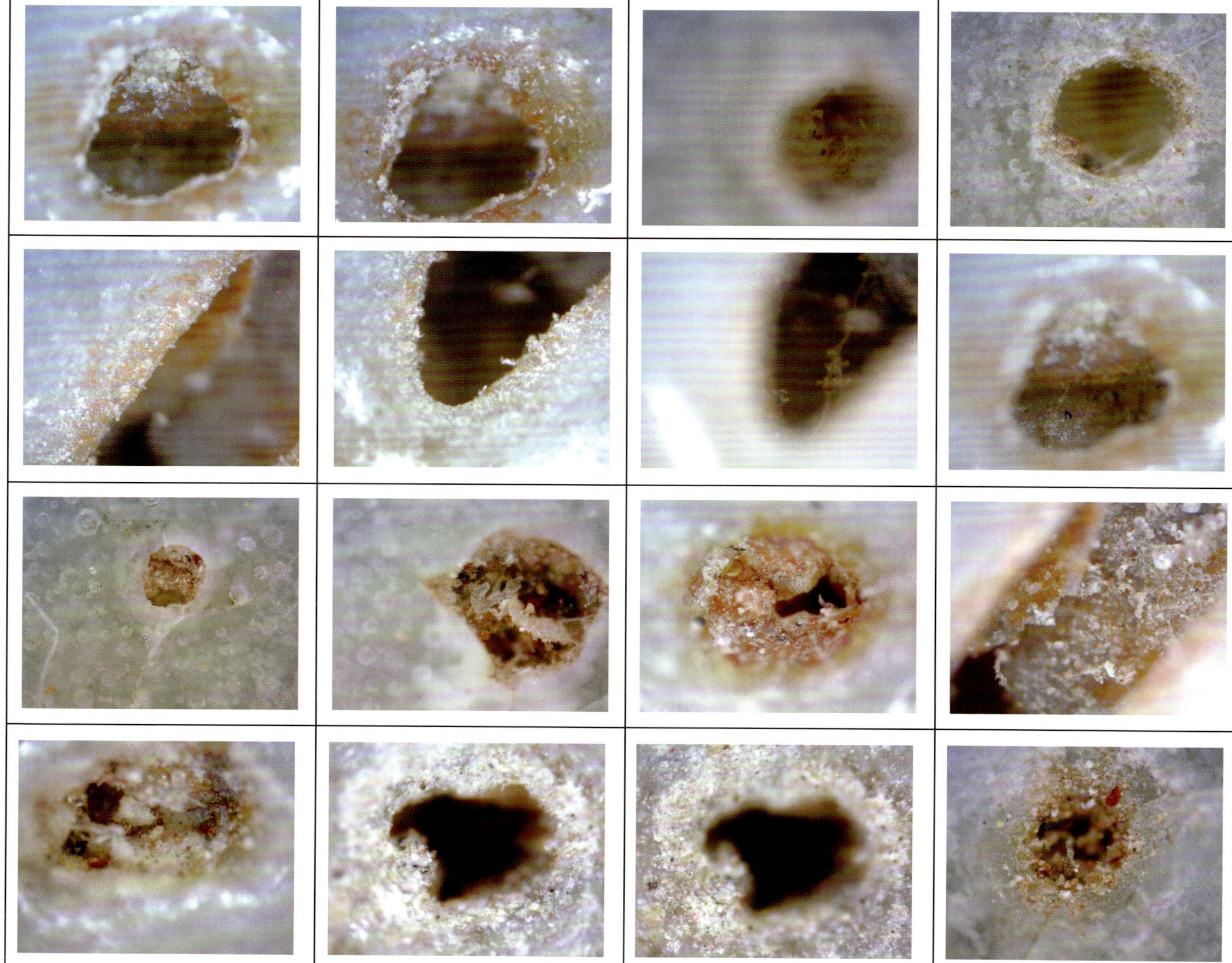

（续图）

（Continued）

二维 Two-dimensional	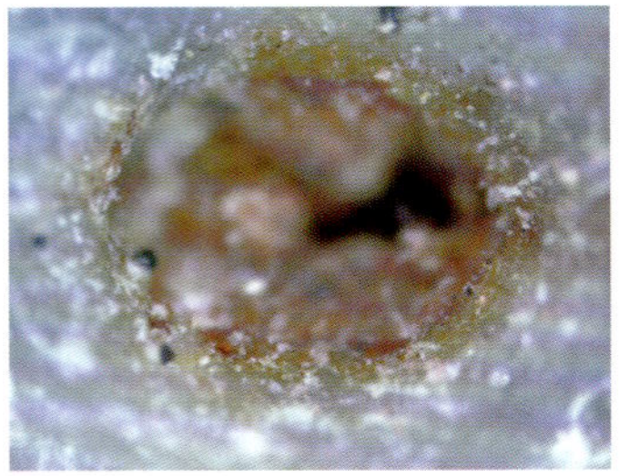	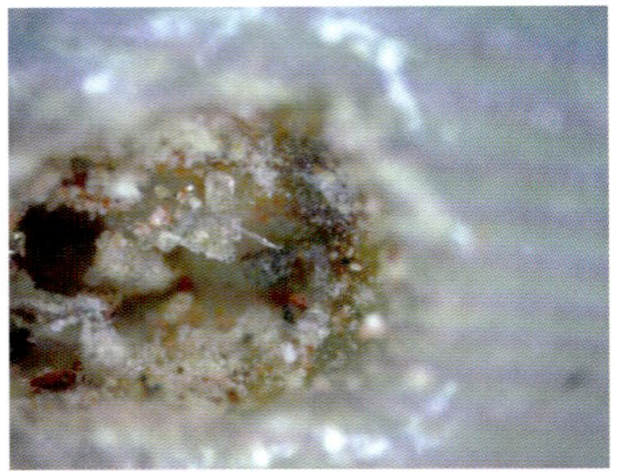	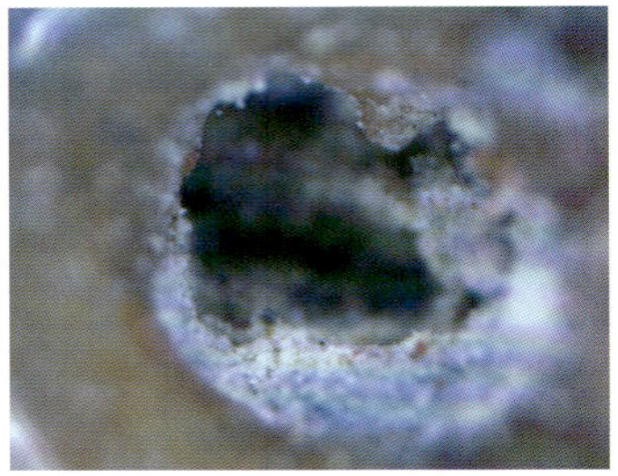	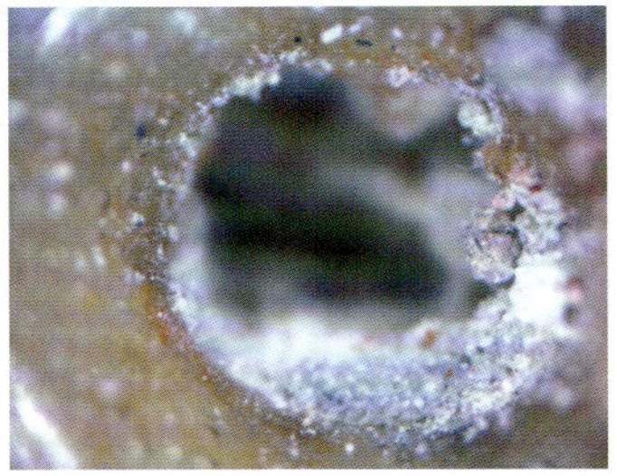

三、明代广东余里窑青瓷迹型标准图谱模型

3. Ming Dynasty Guangdong Yuli Kiln Celadon Standard Trace Atlas Model

沙滩斑
Beach Mottles

二维 Two-dimensional			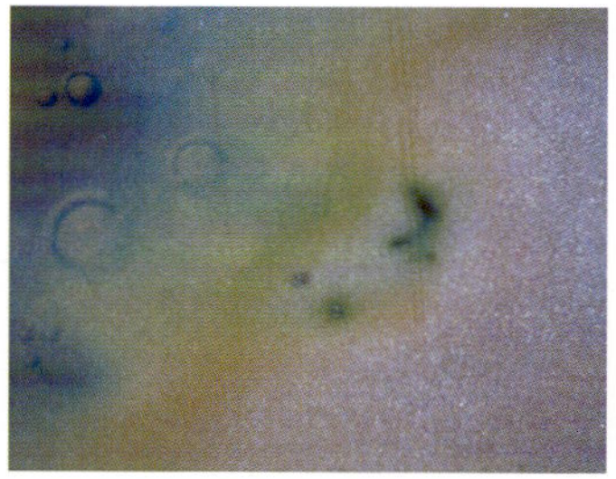	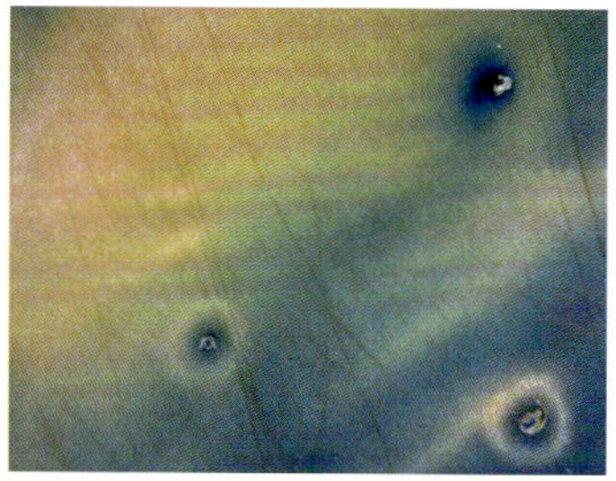
三维 Three-dimensional	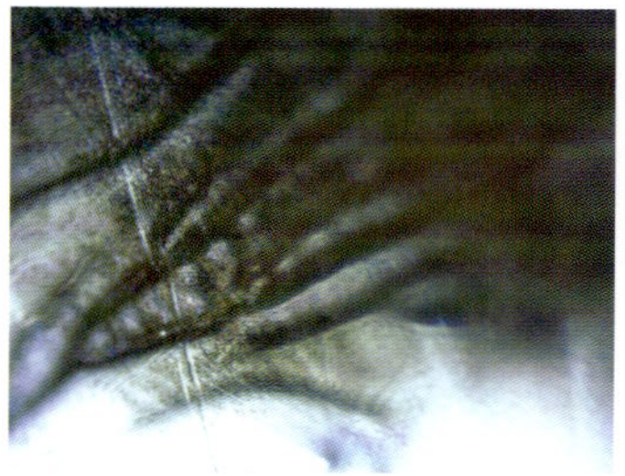	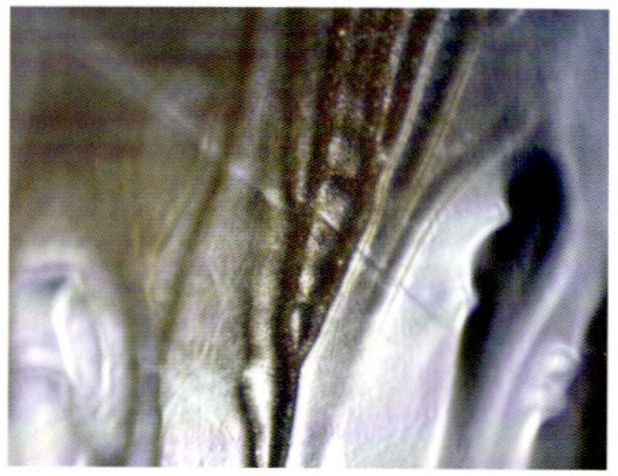	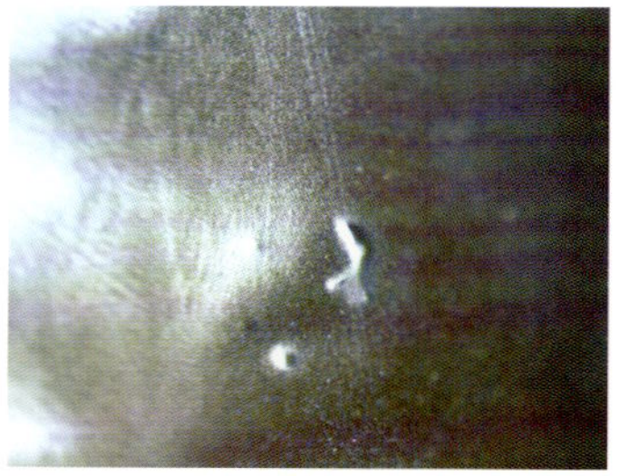	
二维 Two-dimensional	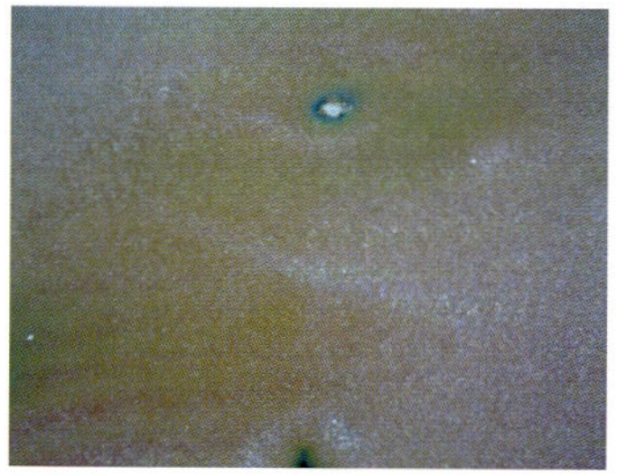			

放射斑
Radiating Mottles

二维 Two-dimensional			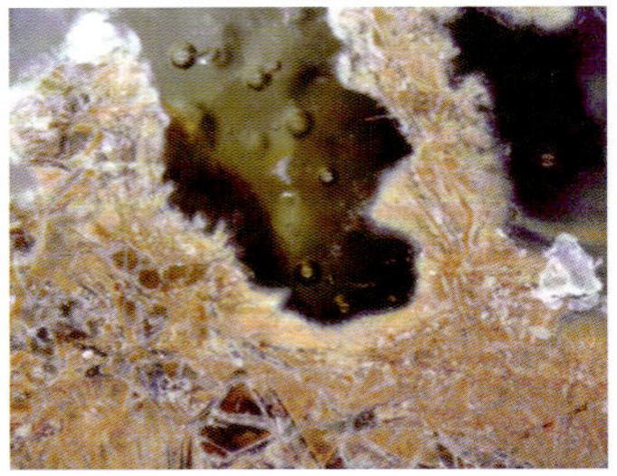	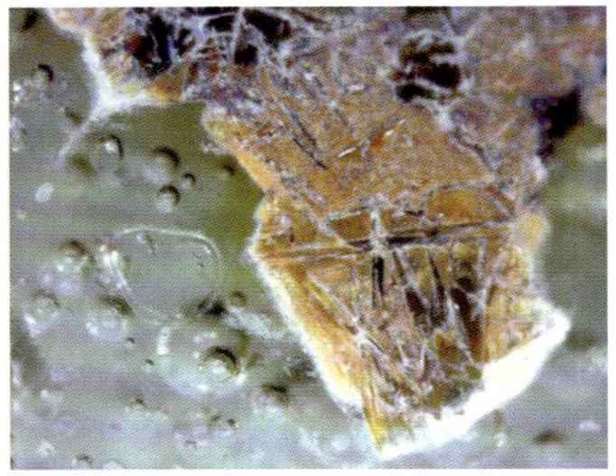
三维 Three-dimensional		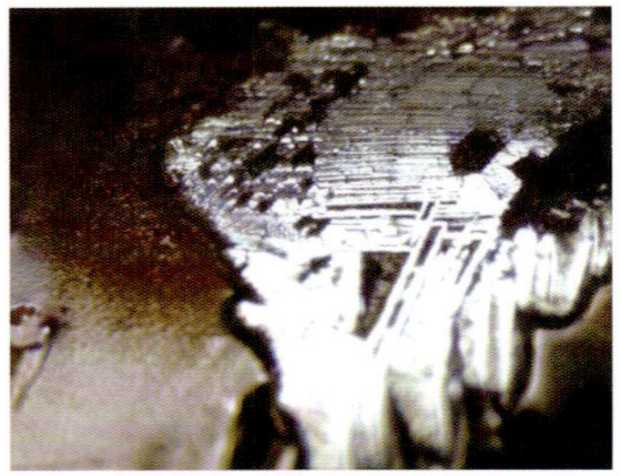		
二维 Two-dimensional	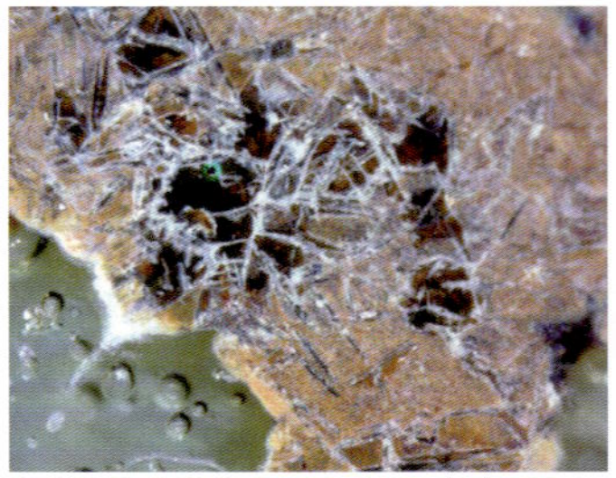	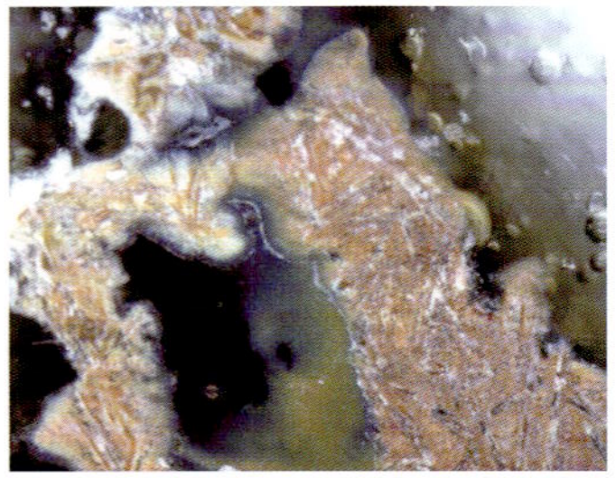		

（续图）

（Continued）

二维 Two-dimensional	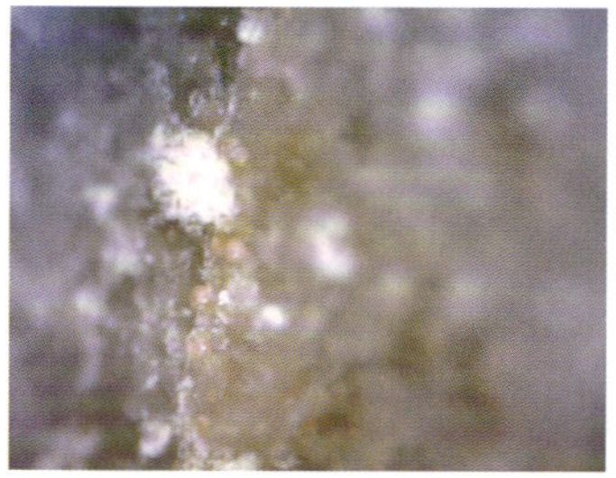		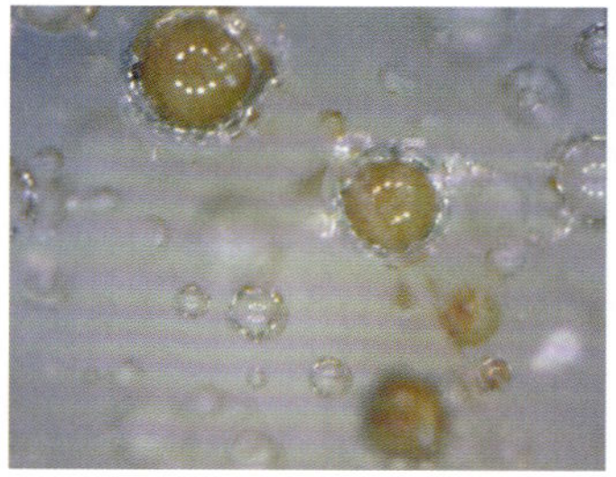	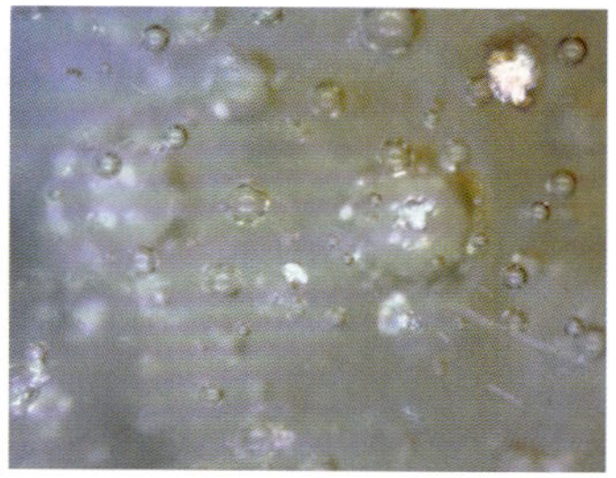
三维 Three-dimensional	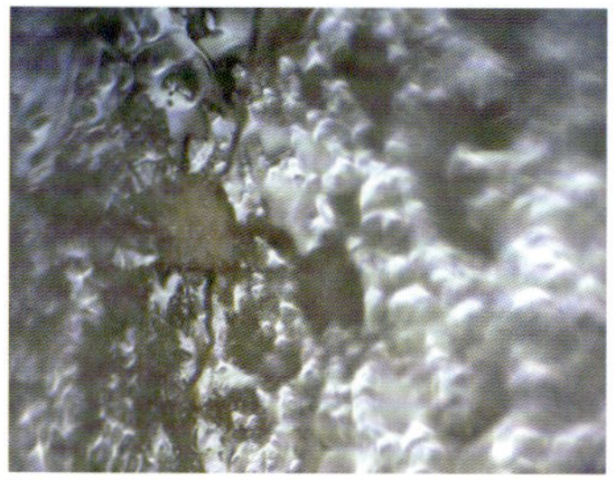	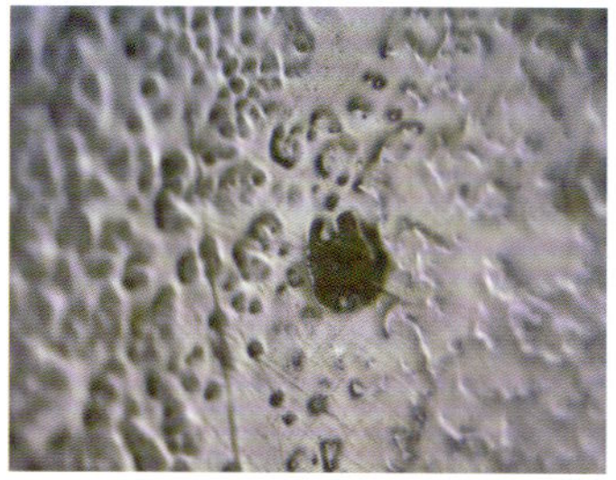	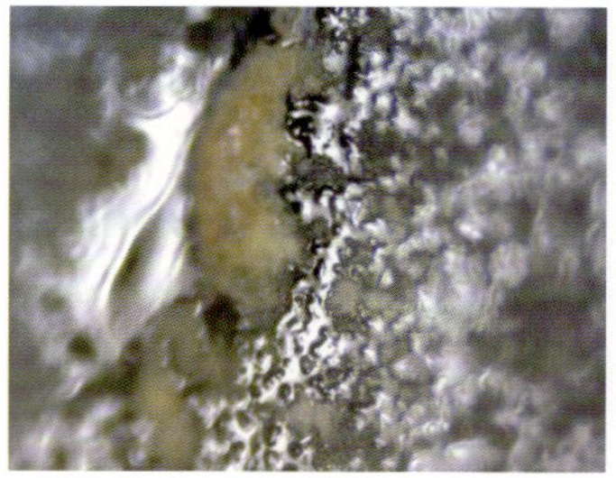	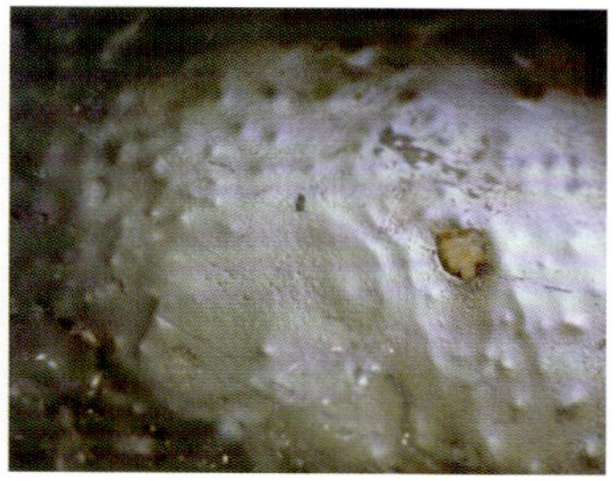
二维 Two-dimensional	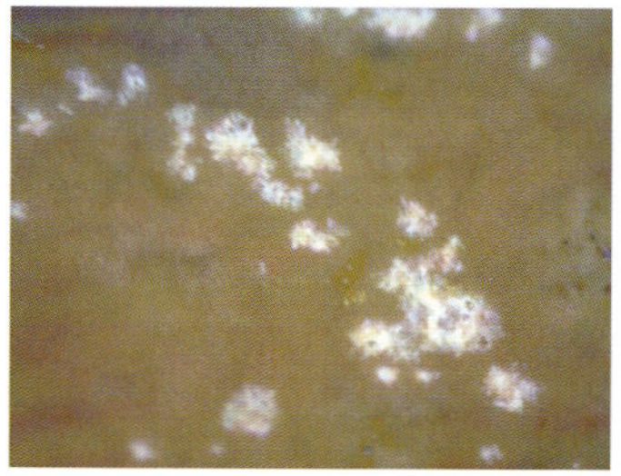	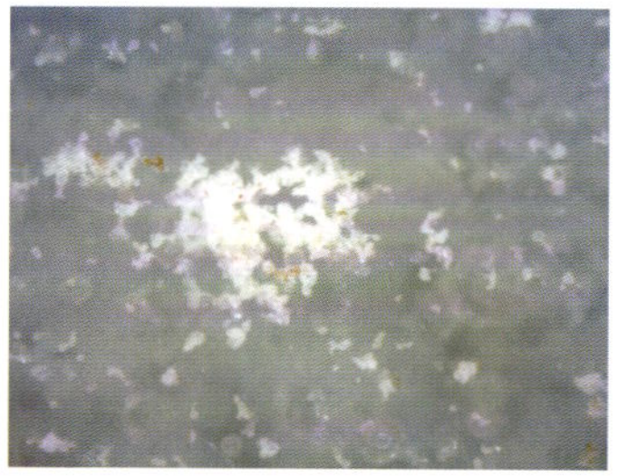		
三维 Three-dimensional	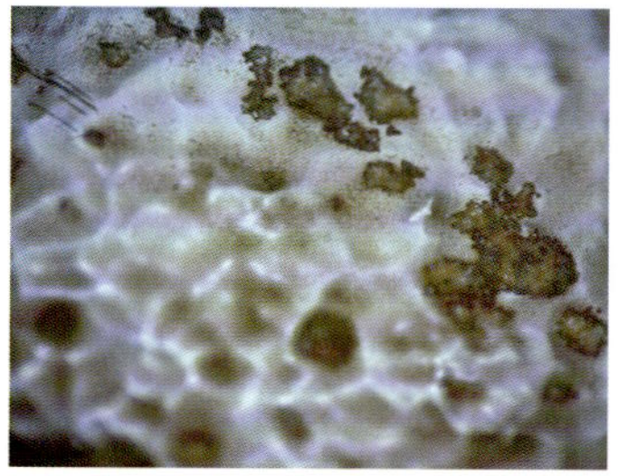	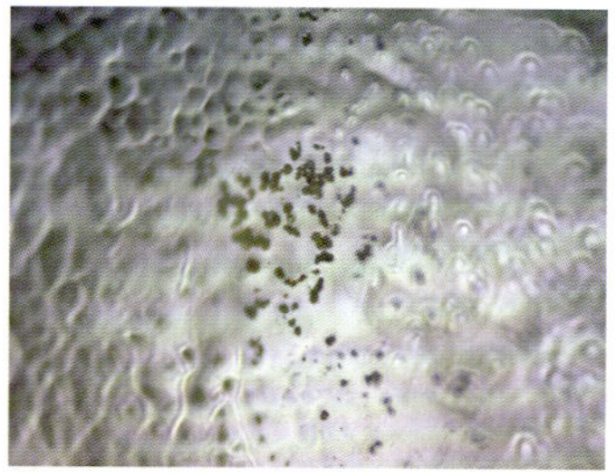		

团状斑
Blotch Mottles

二维 Two-dimensional	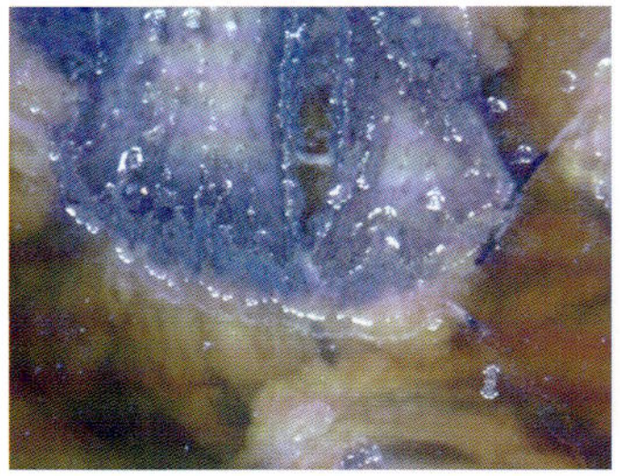	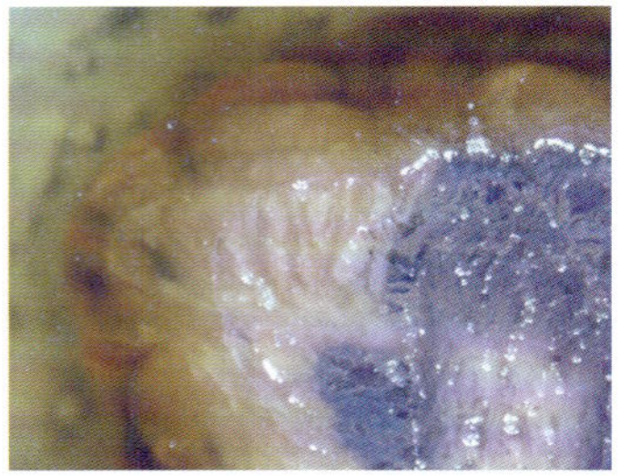		

混合斑
Mixed Mottles

二维 Two-dimensional		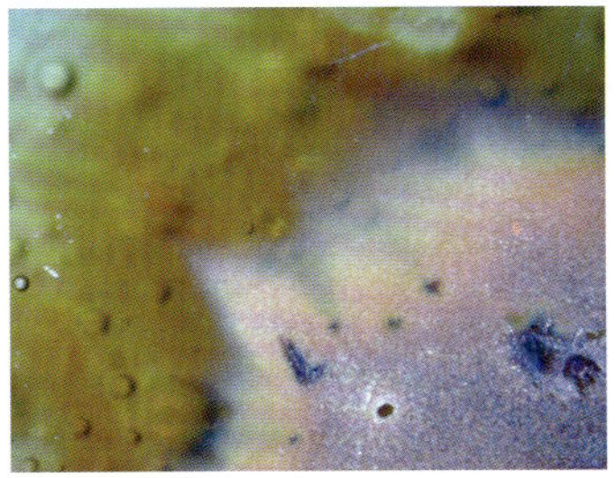		
三维 Three-dimensional	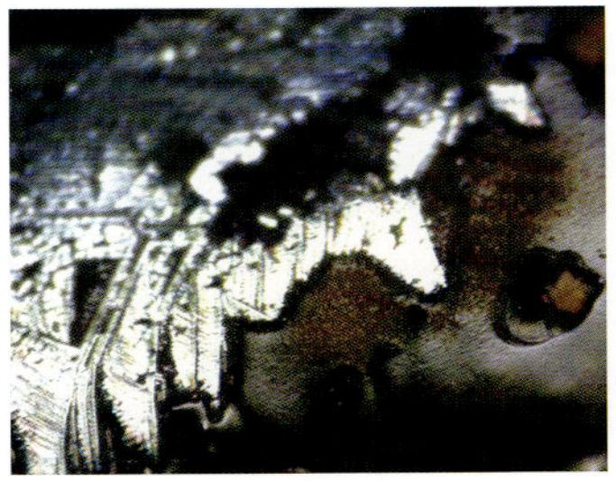	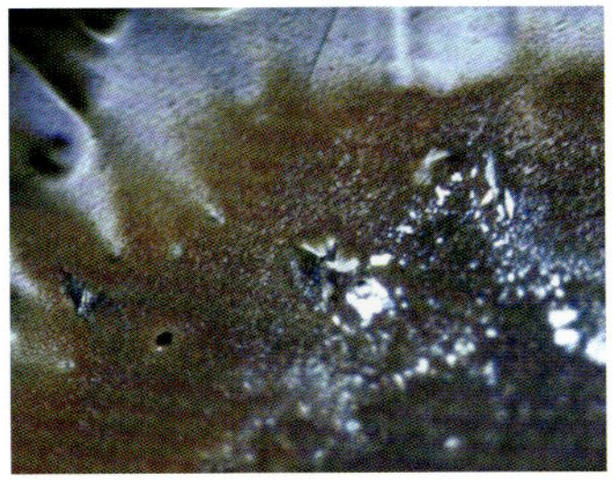		

CO型坑点斑
CO Type Pit Mottles

二维 Two-dimensional	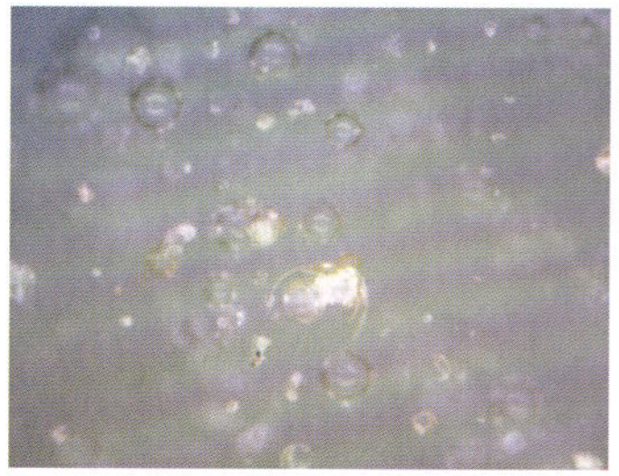	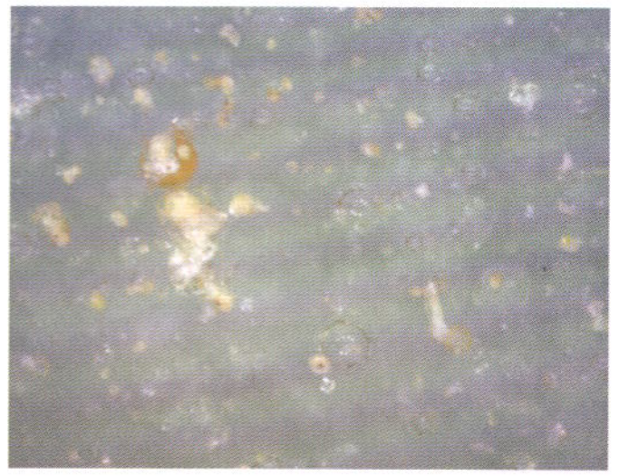	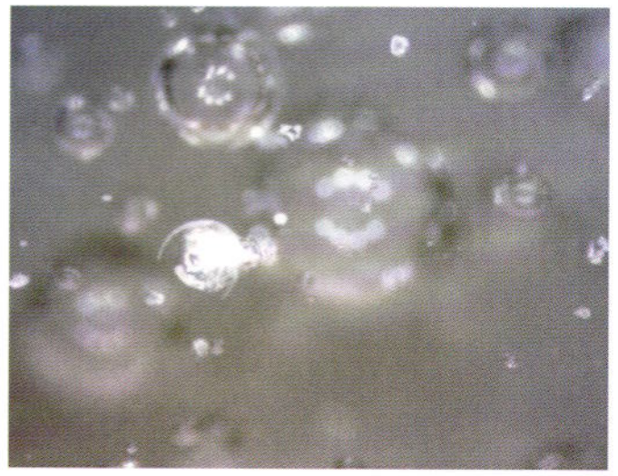	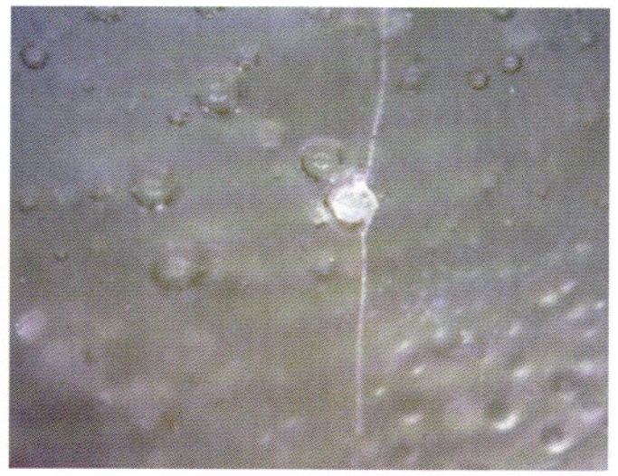
三维 Three-dimensional	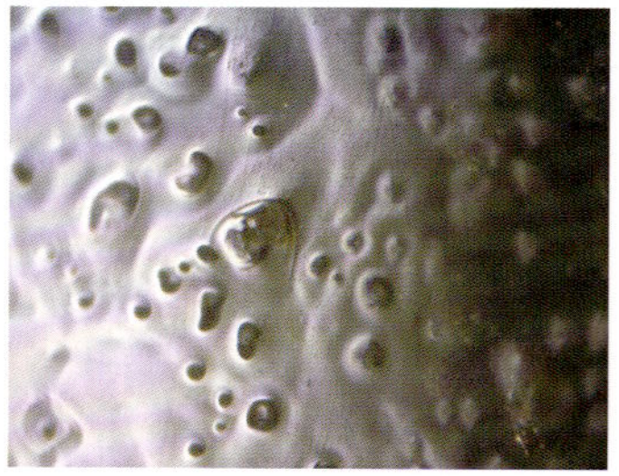	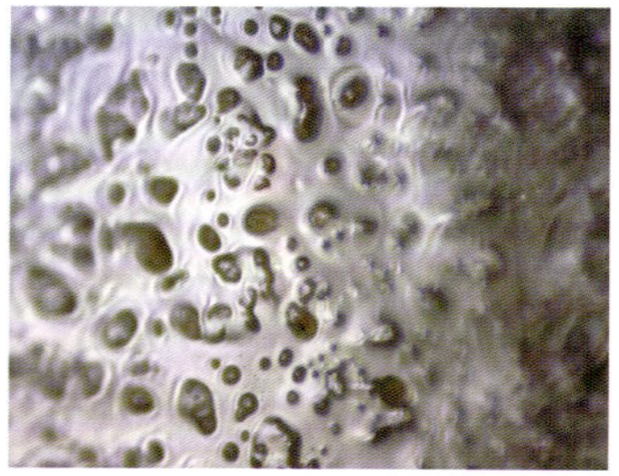	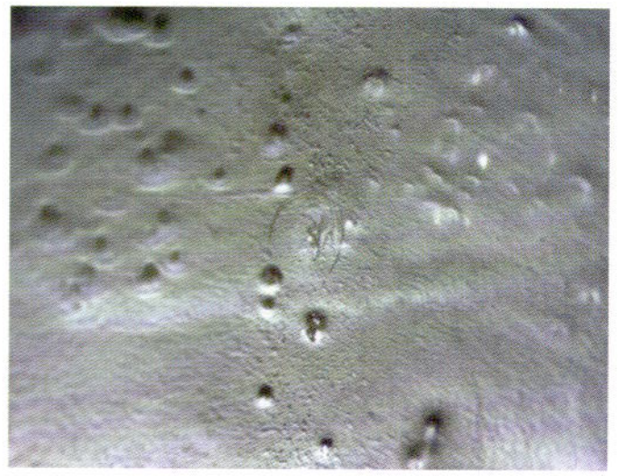	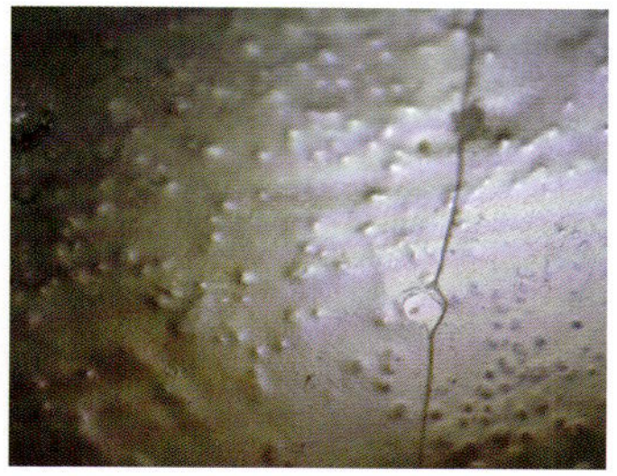
二维 Two-dimensional	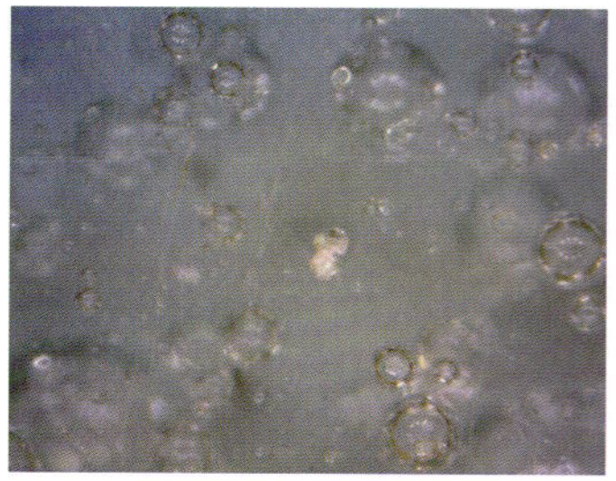	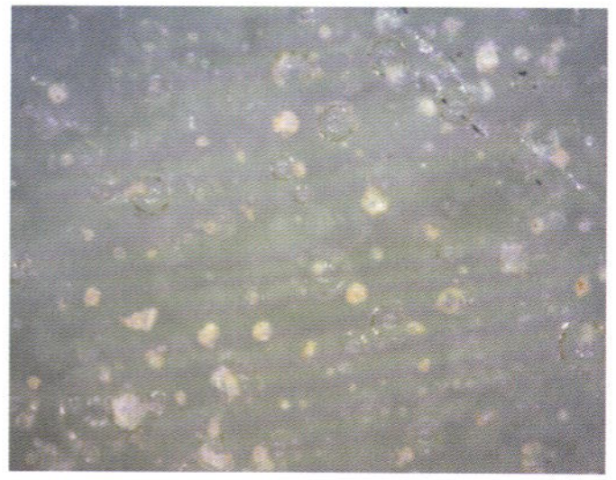	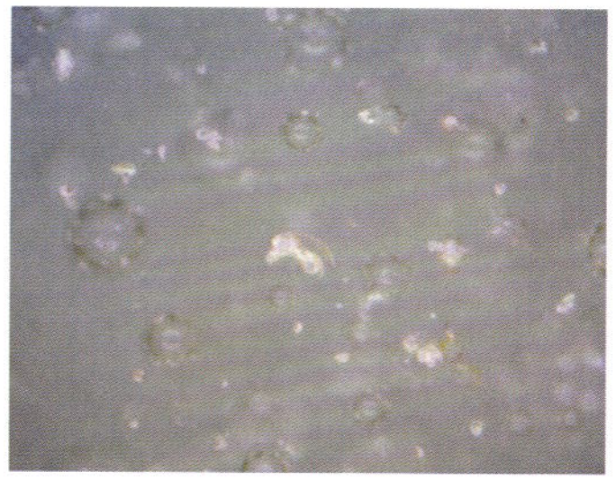	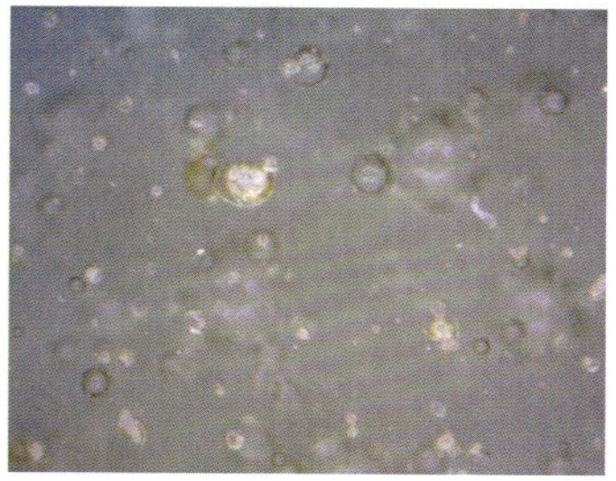
三维 Three-dimensional	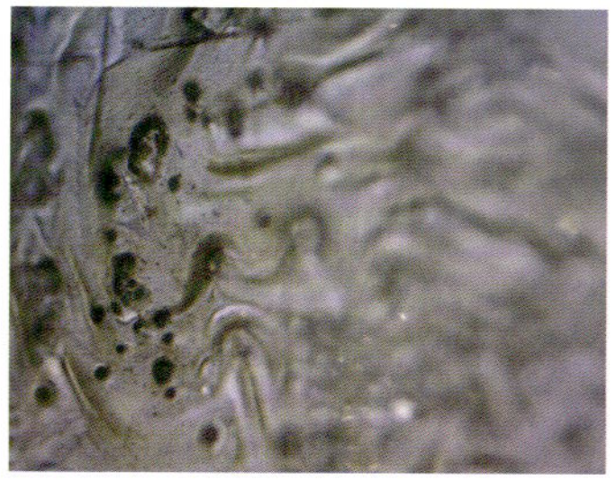			

（续图）
（Continued）

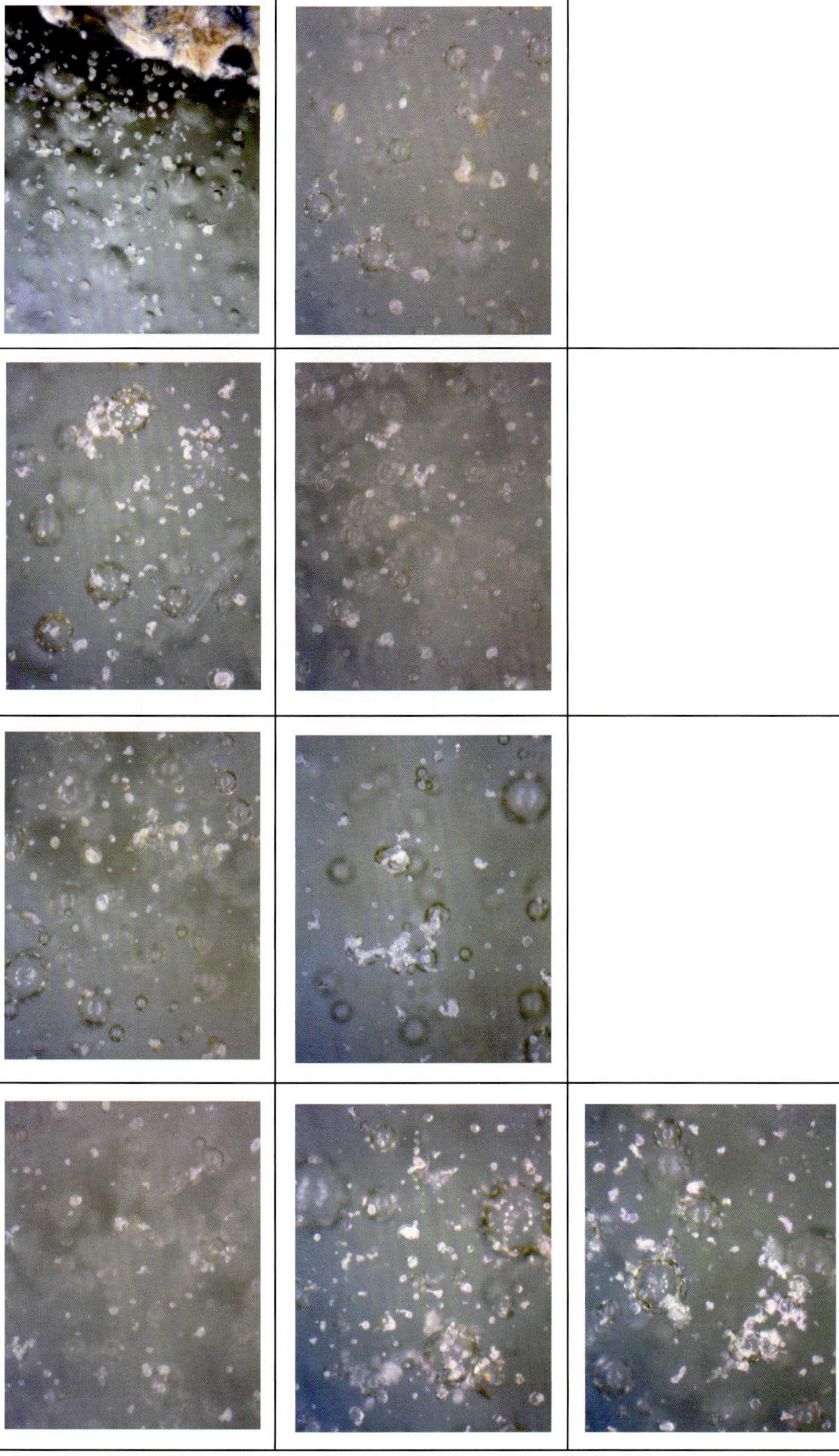

二维
Two-dimensional

物盖斑
Overlay Mottles

二维 Two-dimensional		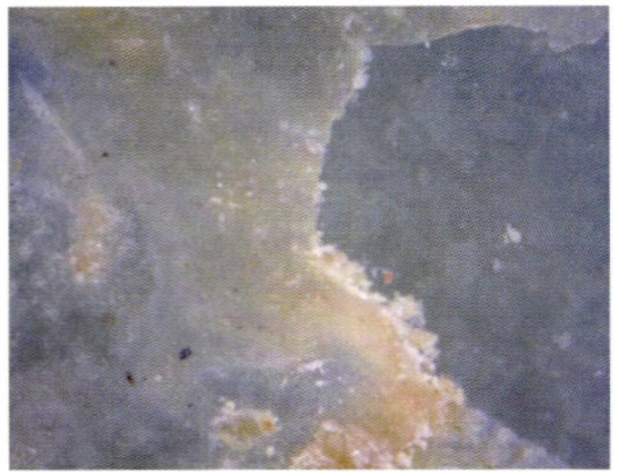	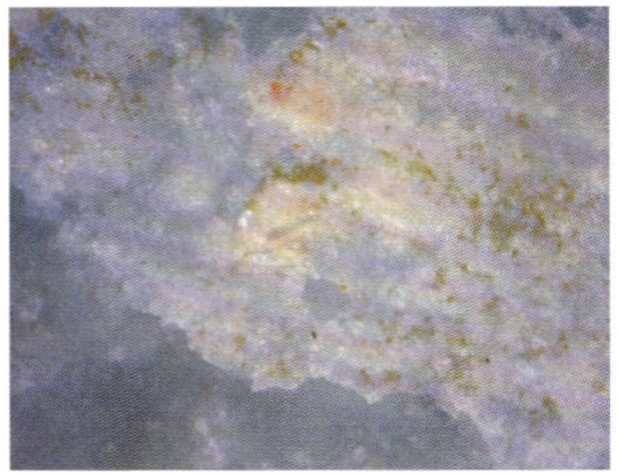	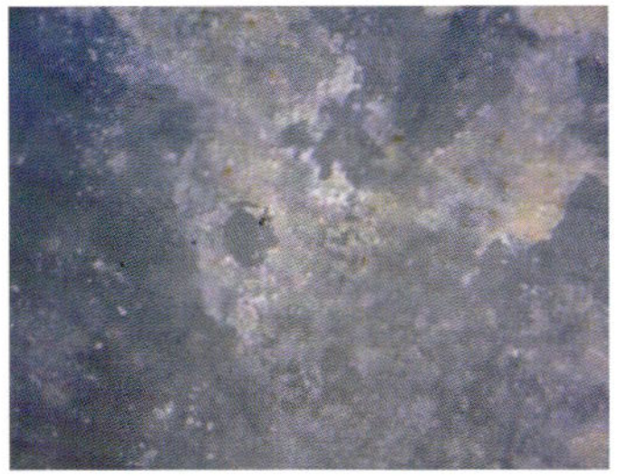
三维 Three-dimensional	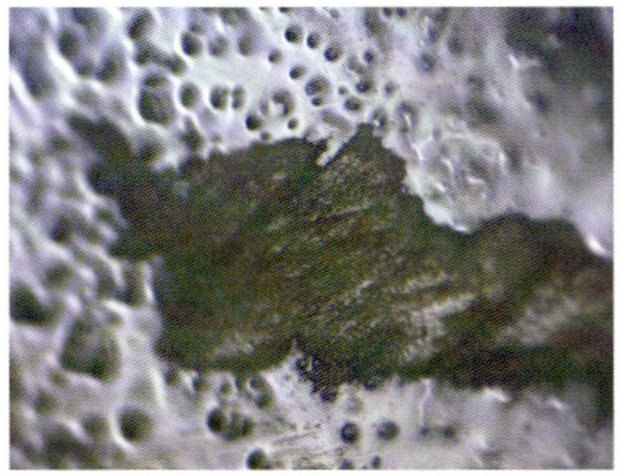			
二维 Two-dimensional	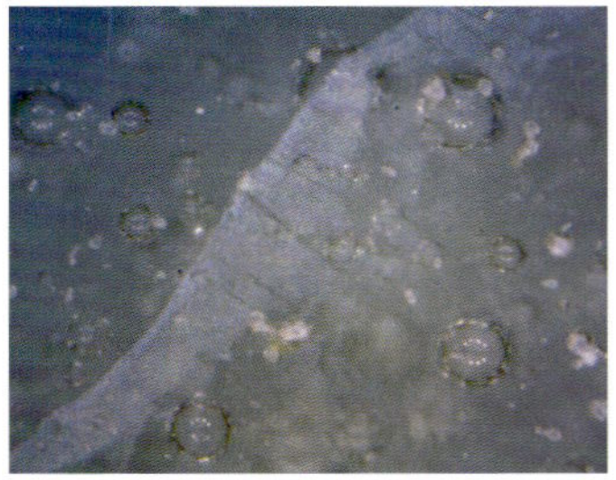	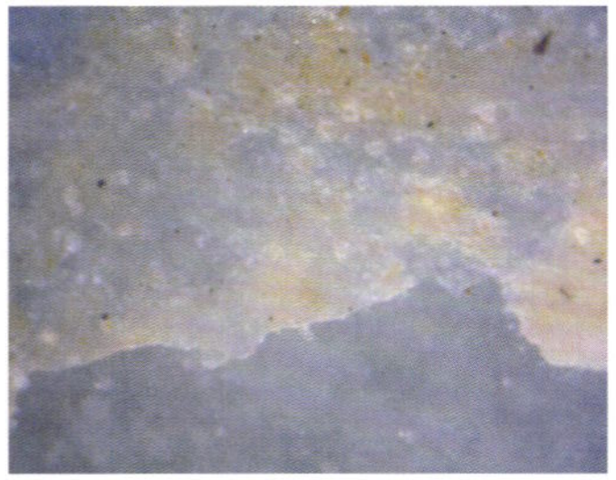	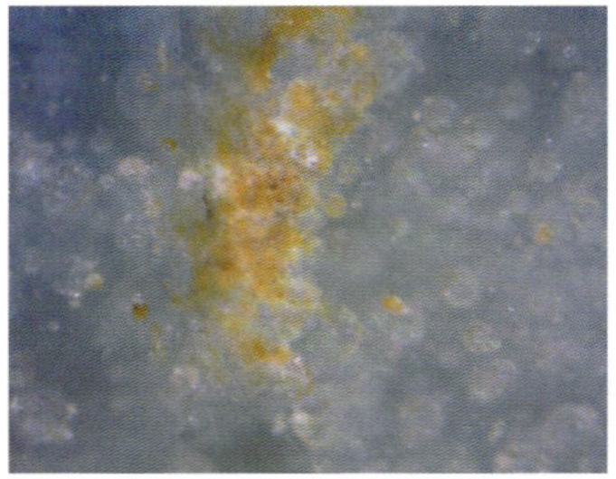	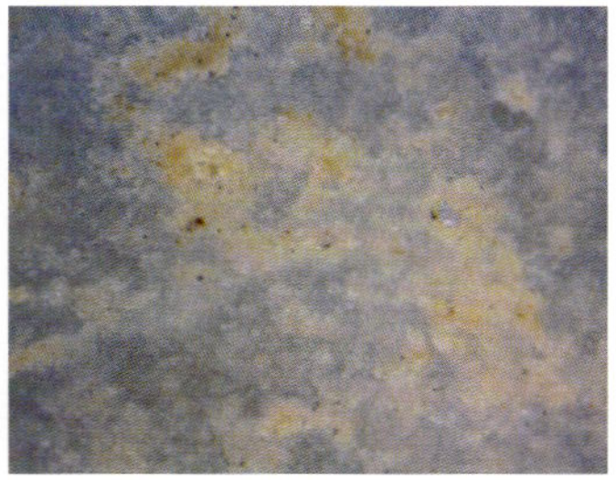
	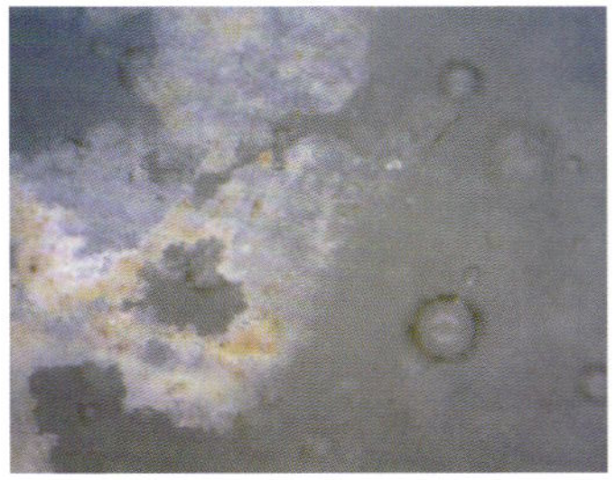	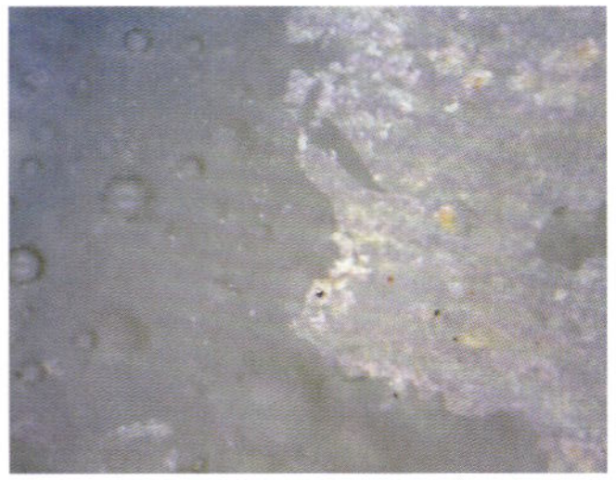		

泡根斑
Bubble Roots

二维 Two-dimensional	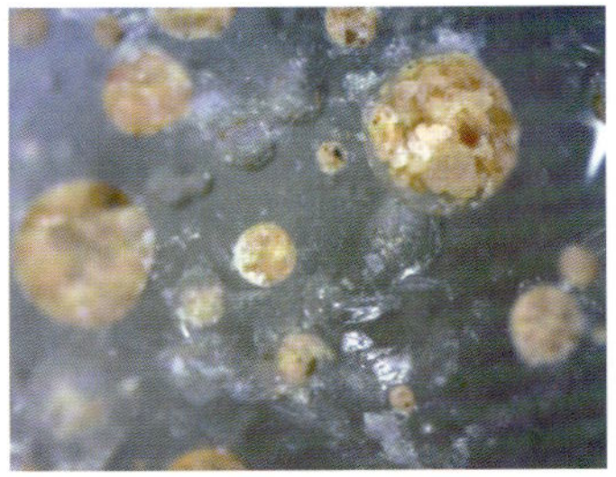	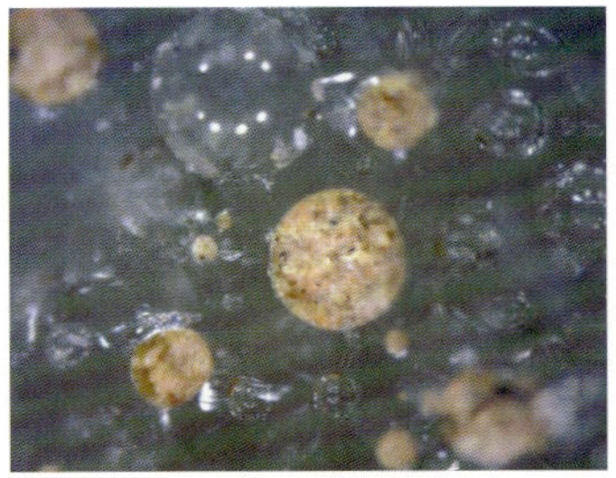		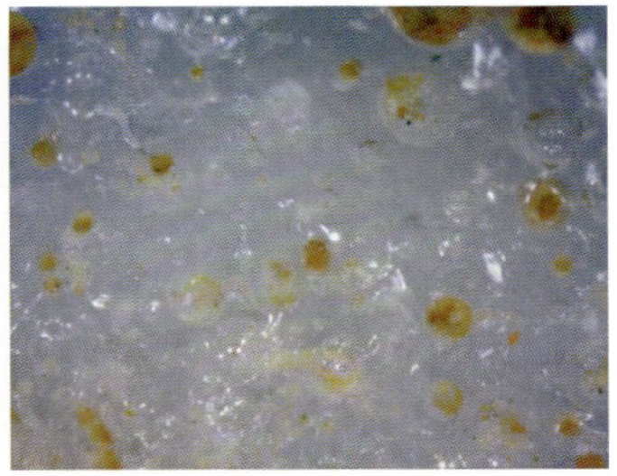
		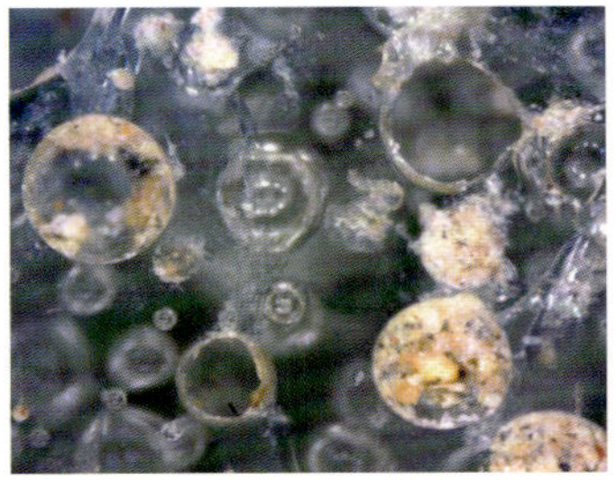	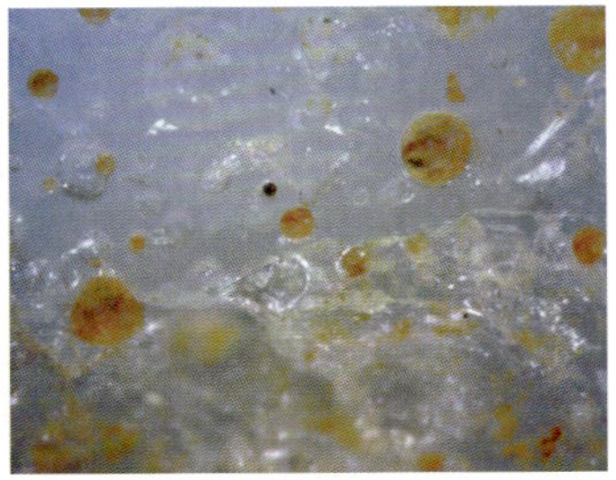	

二维 Two-dimensional	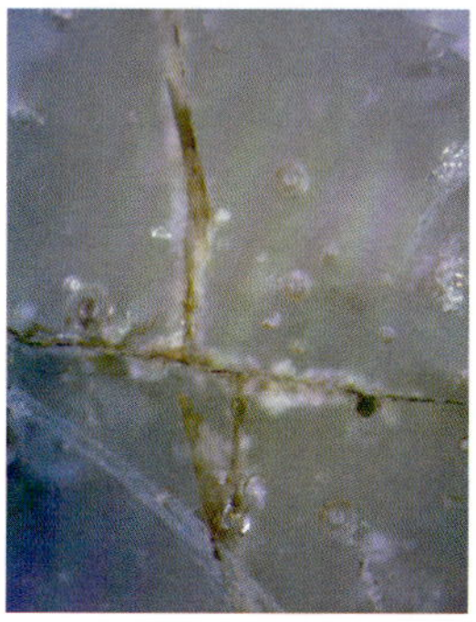	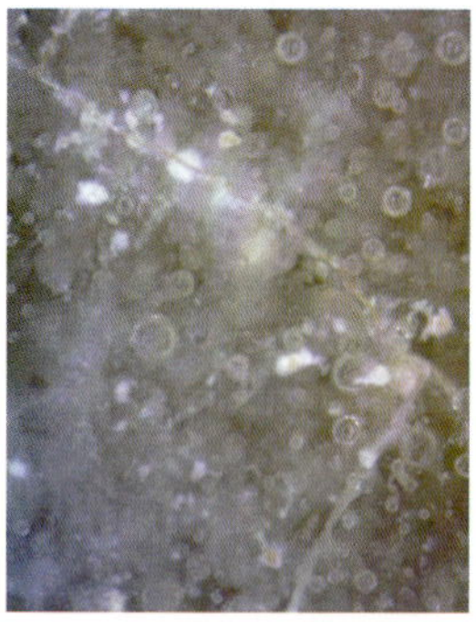	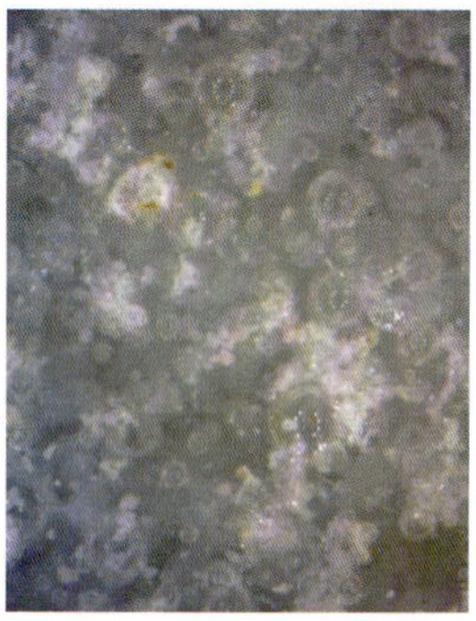	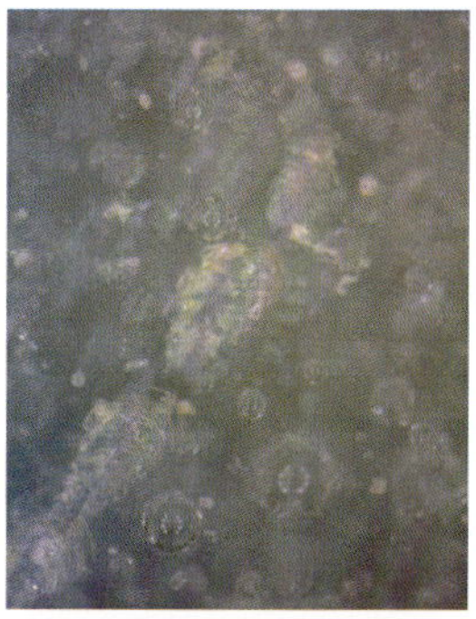
三维 Three-dimensional	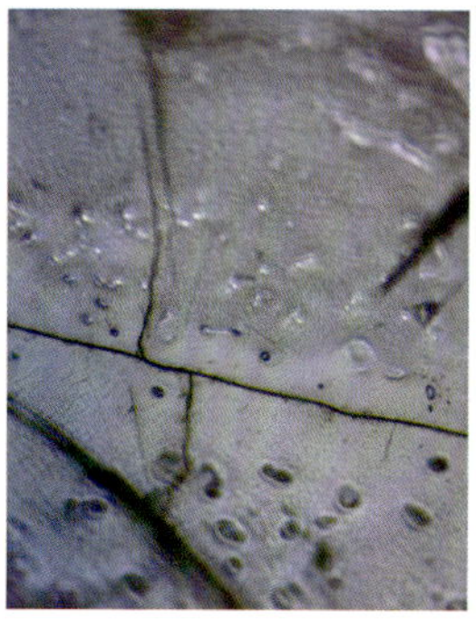			
二维 Two-dimensional	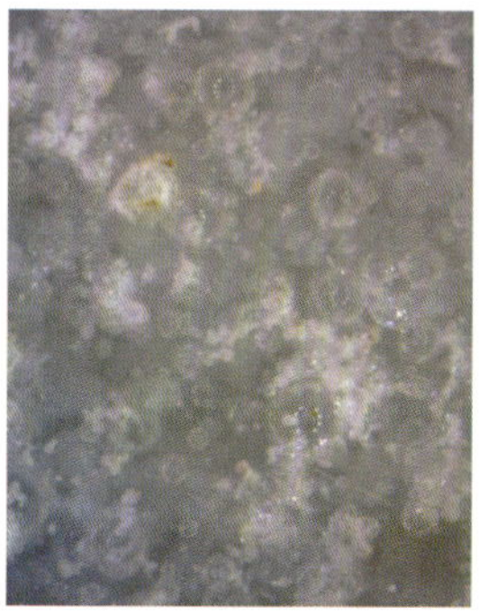			

C形、O形纹
C and O Shaped Striae

二维 Two-dimensional	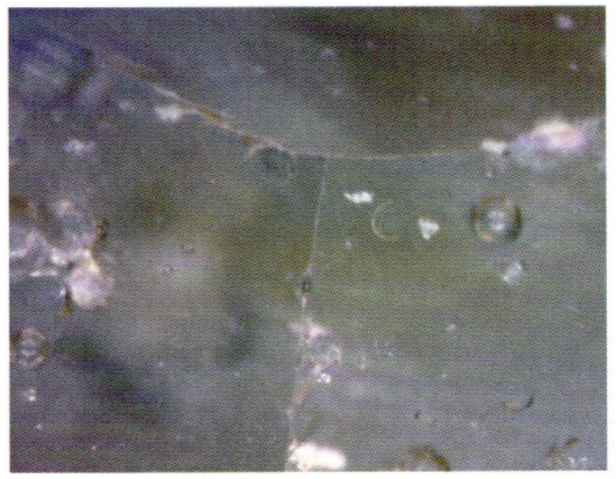	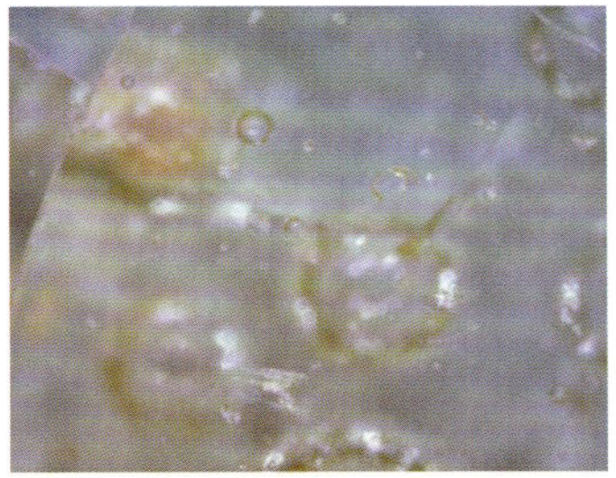	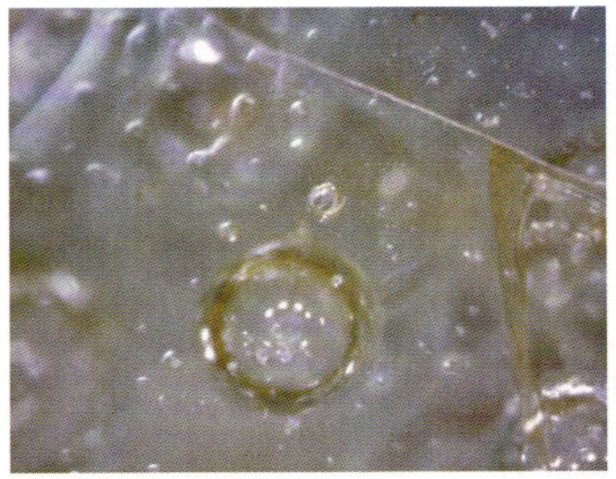	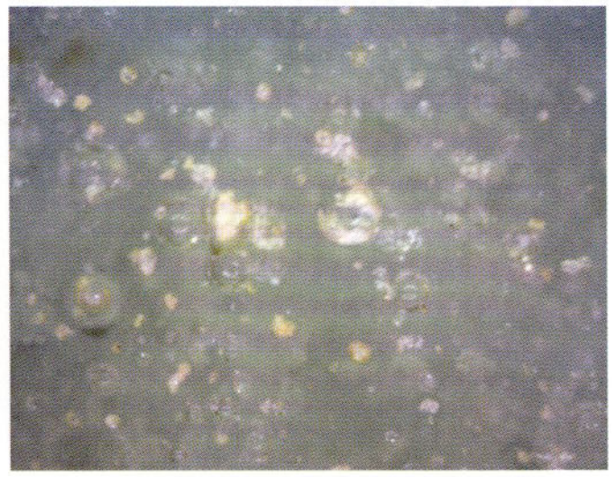
三维 Three-dimensional		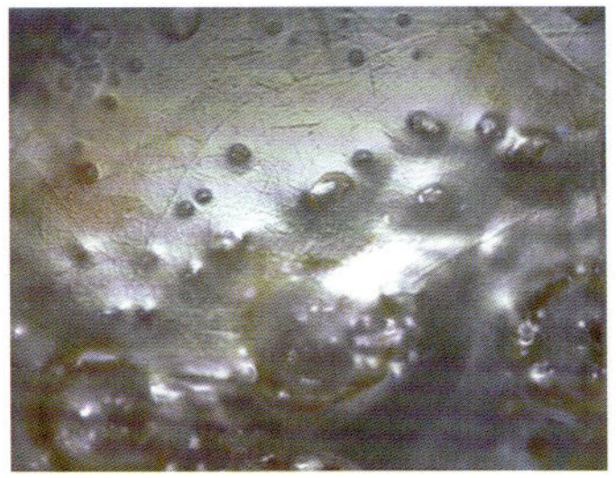	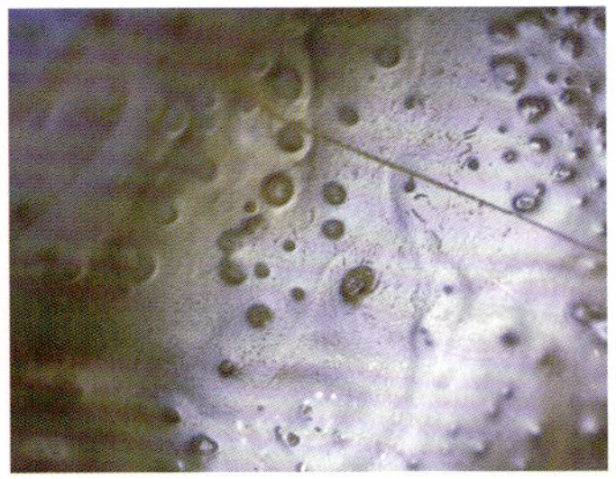	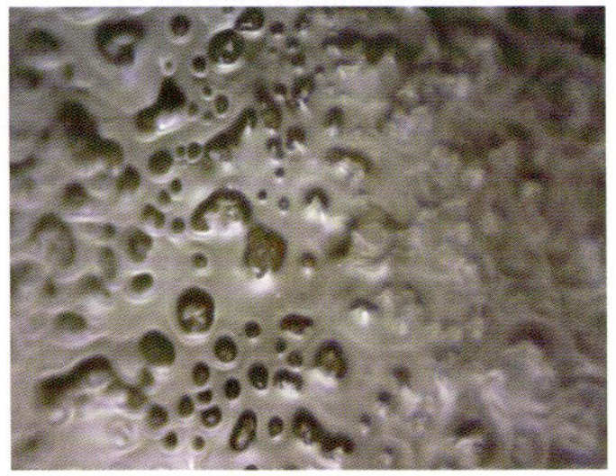
二维 Two-dimensional	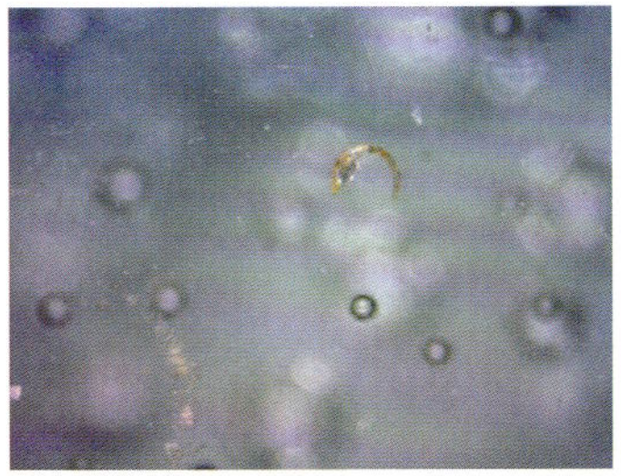	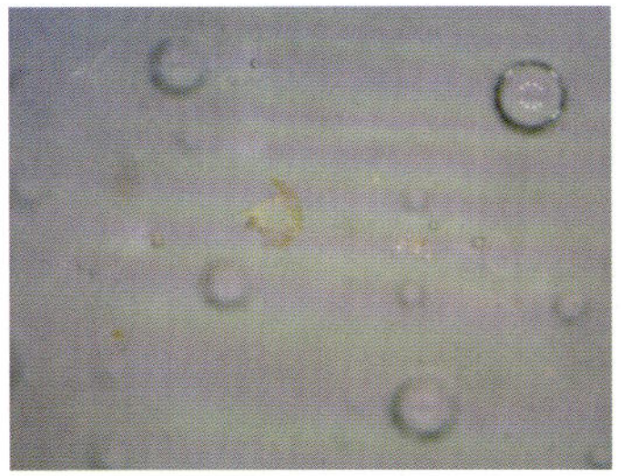	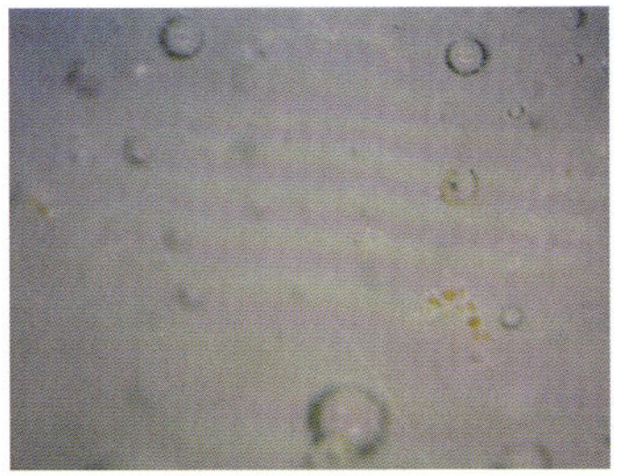	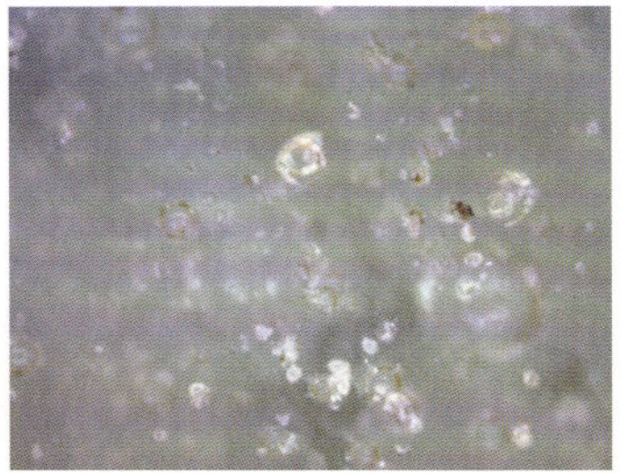
三维 Three-dimensional	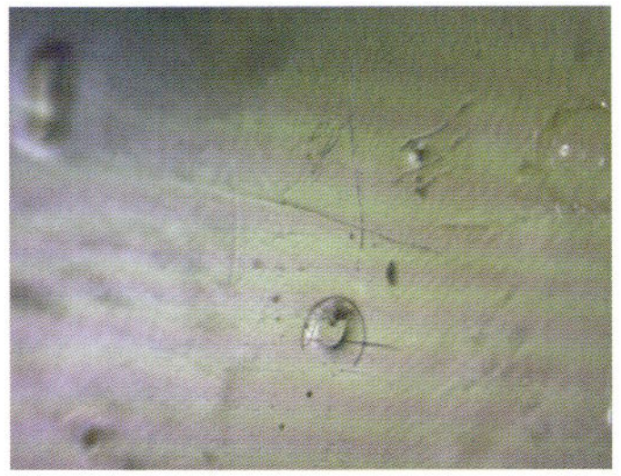	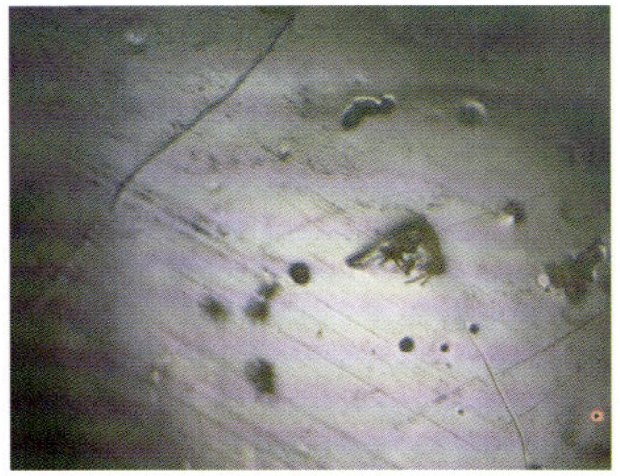		

（续图）
（Continued）

二维 Two-dimensional	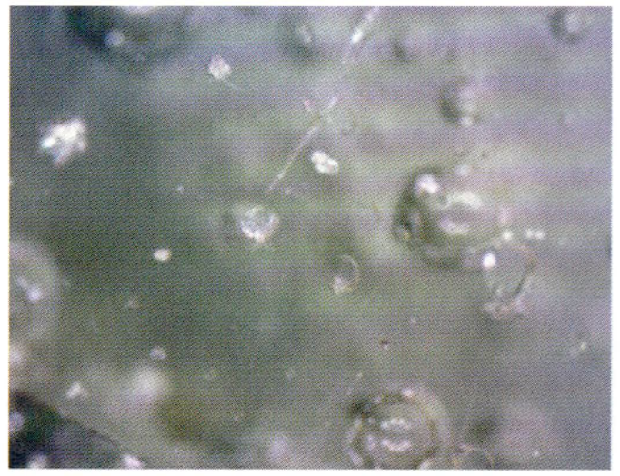	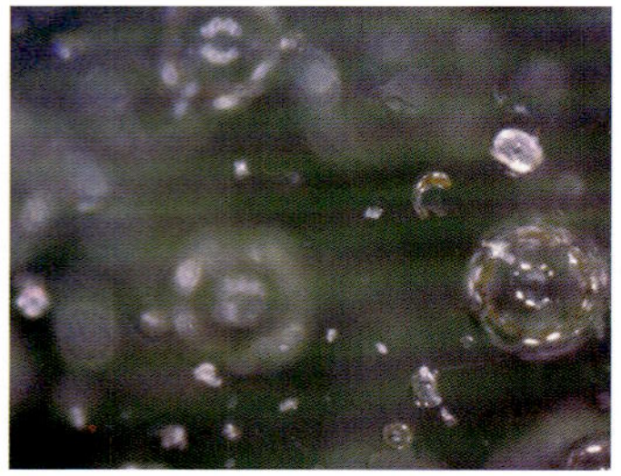	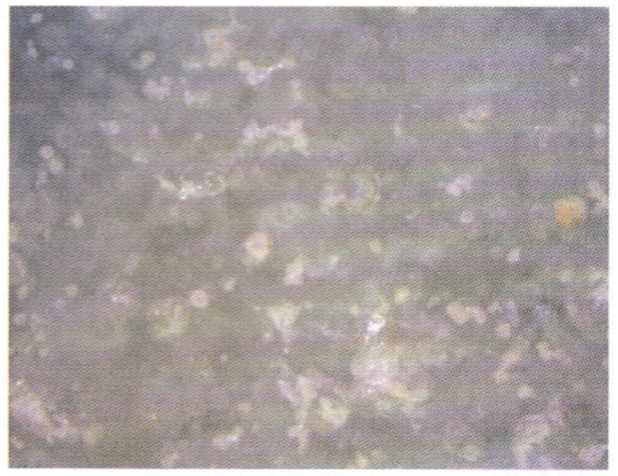	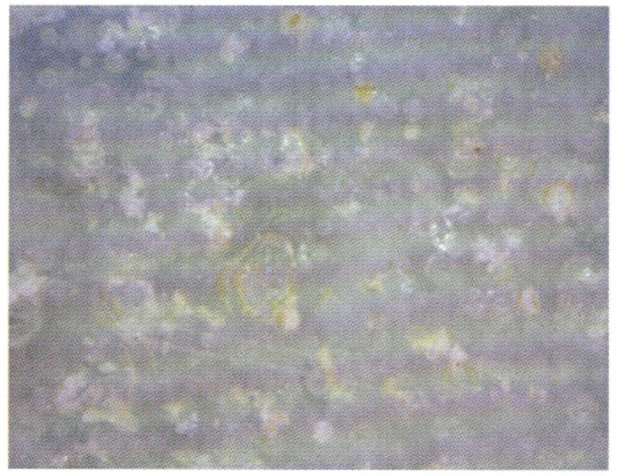
	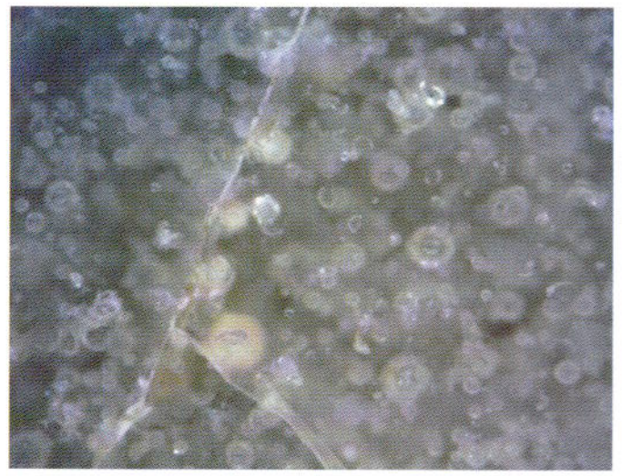			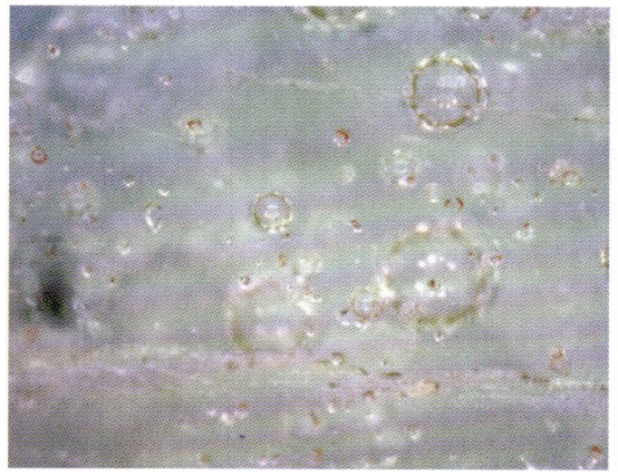

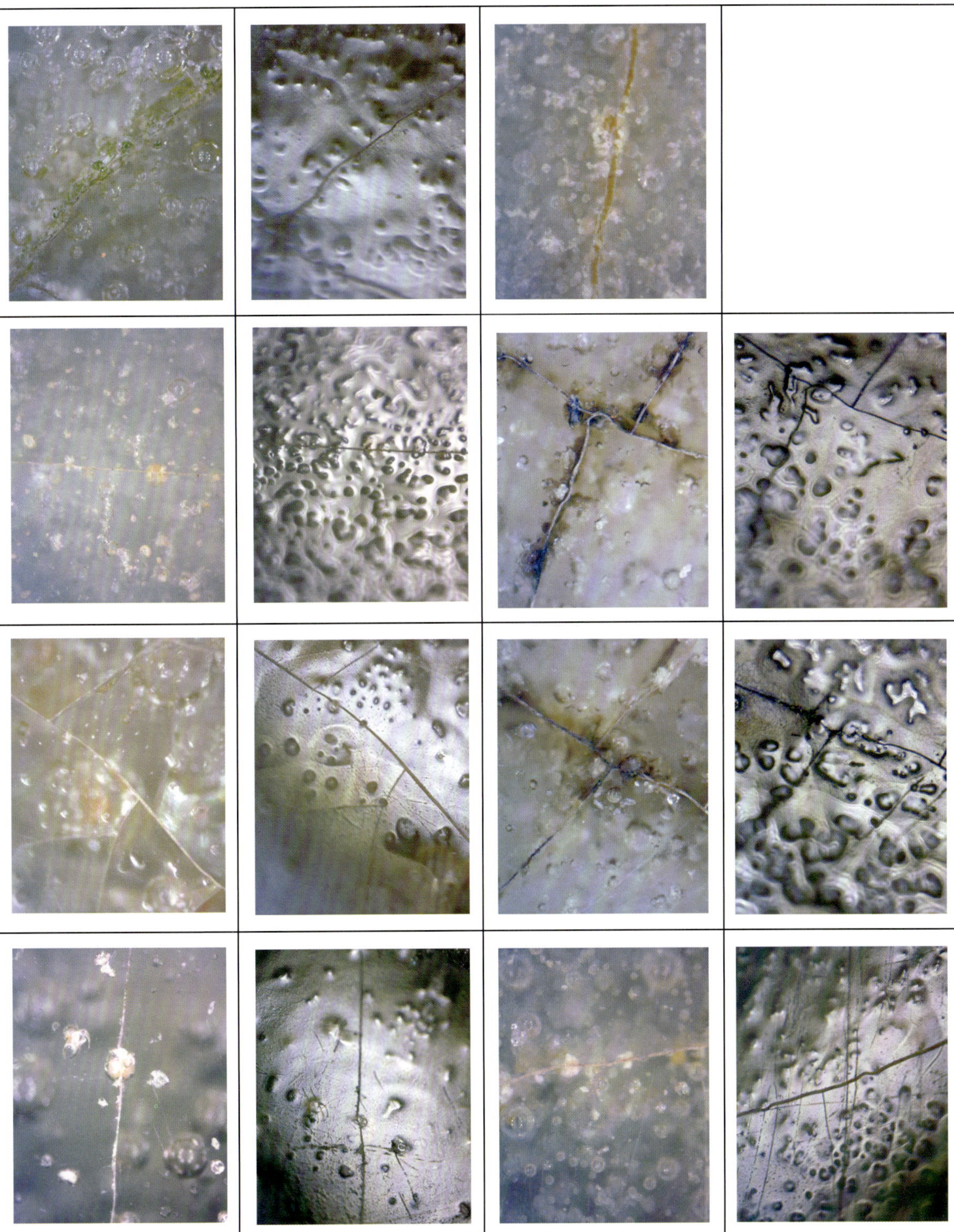

二维 Two-dimensional

三维 Three-dimensional

二维 Two-dimensional

三维 Three-dimensional

（续图）
(Continued)

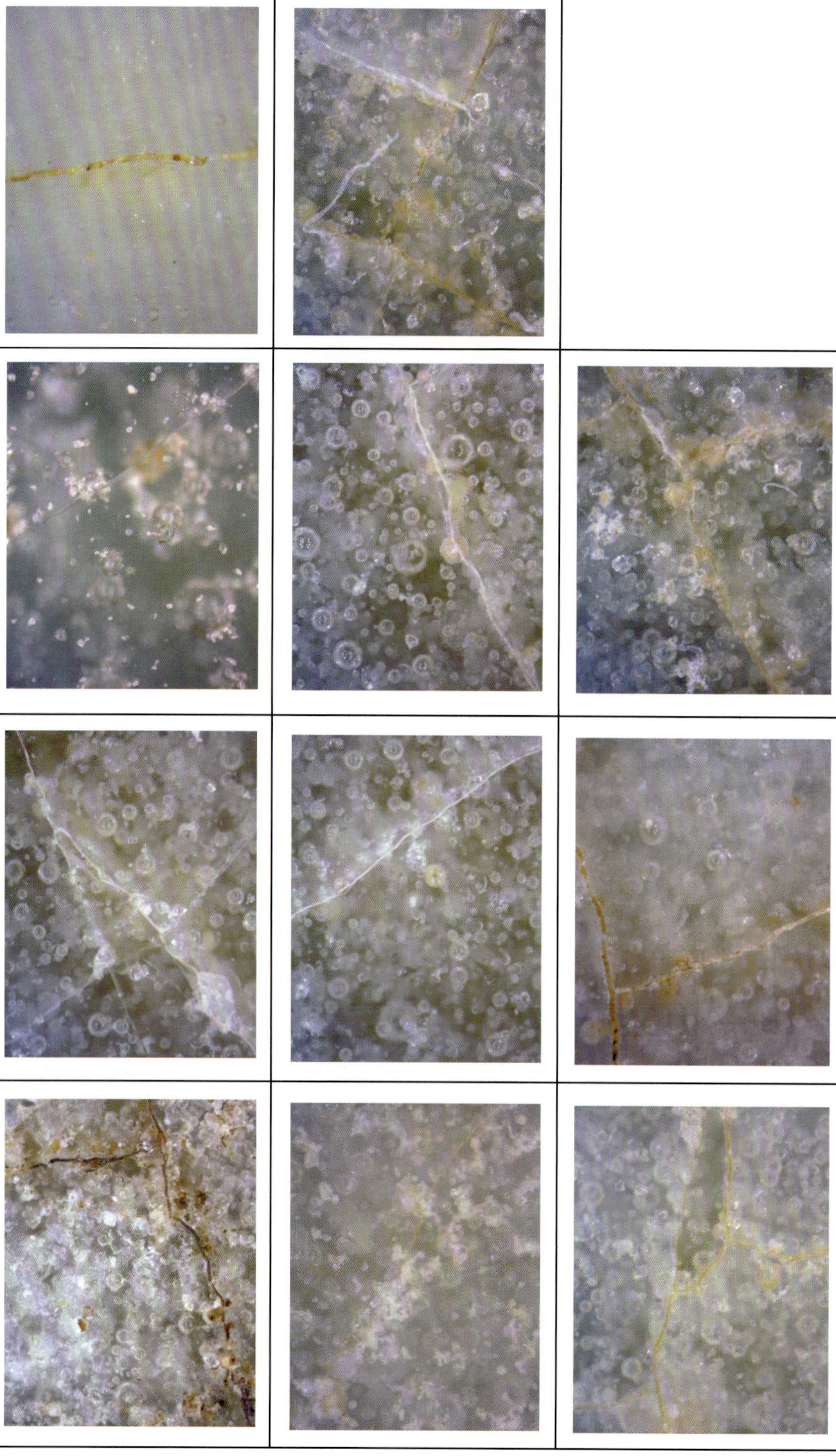

二维
Two-dimensional

划痕
Scratches

二维 Two-dimensional	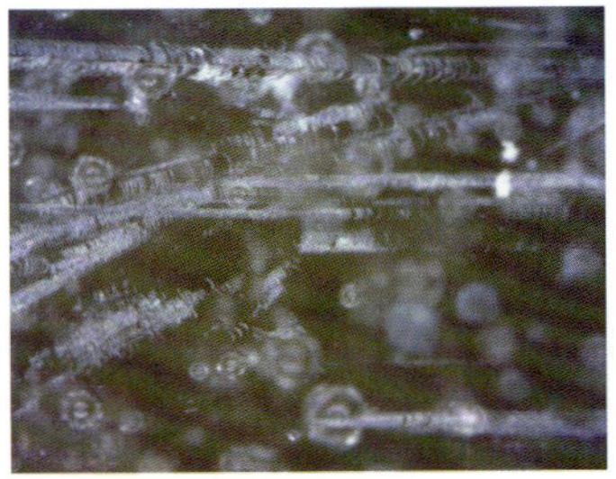	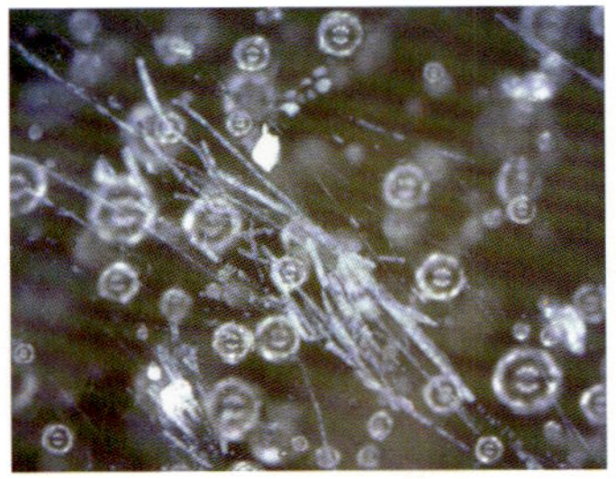	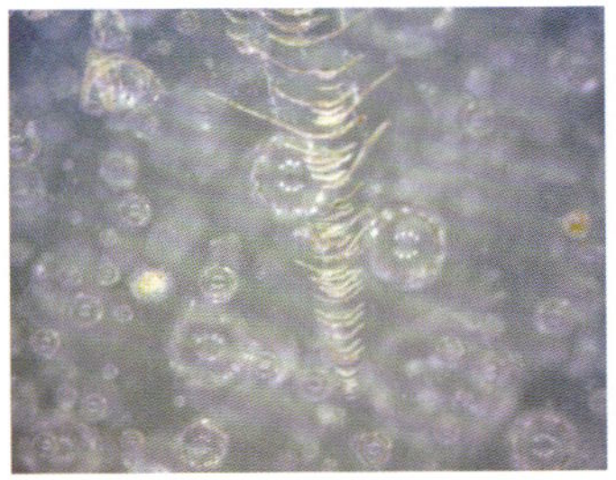	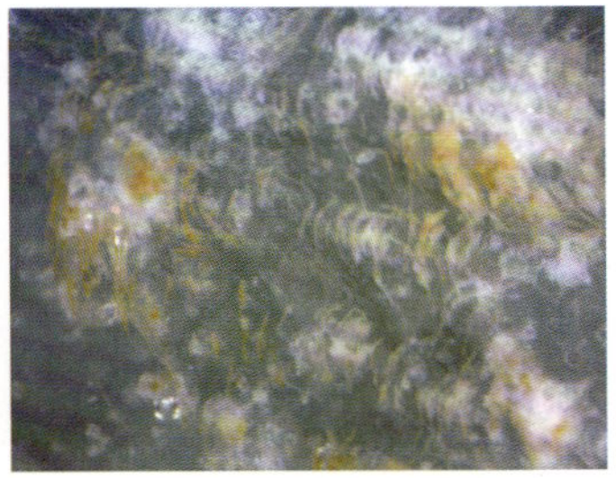
三维 Three-dimensional		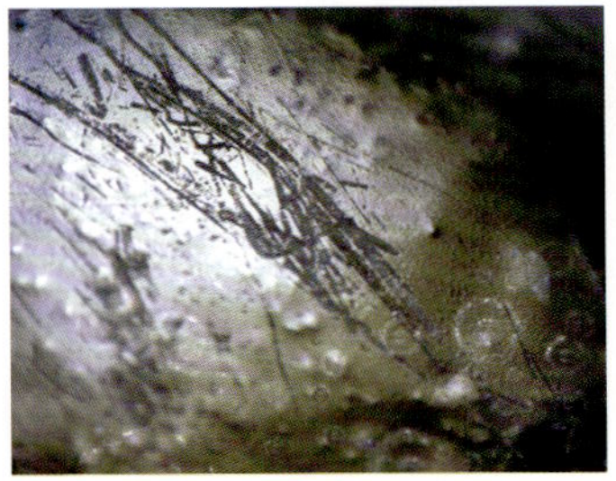	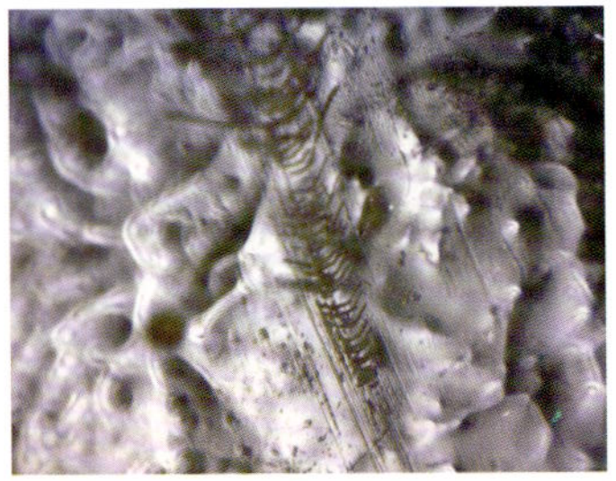	
二维 Two-dimensional	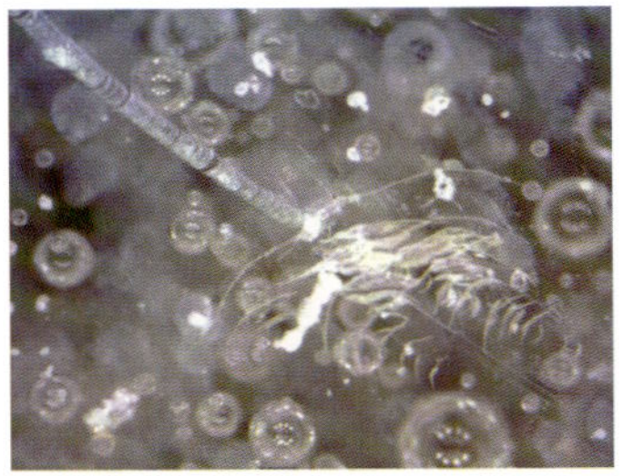	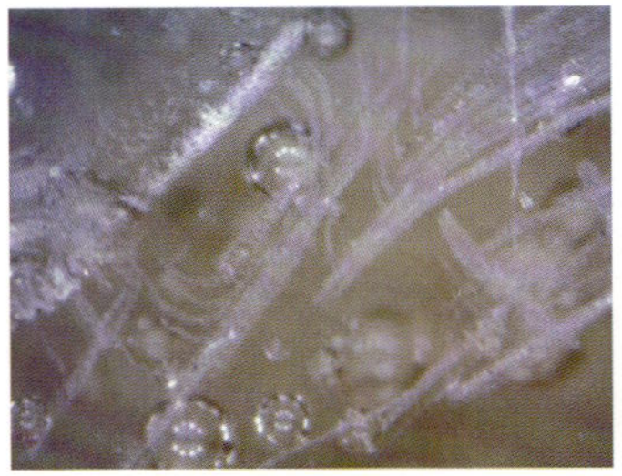	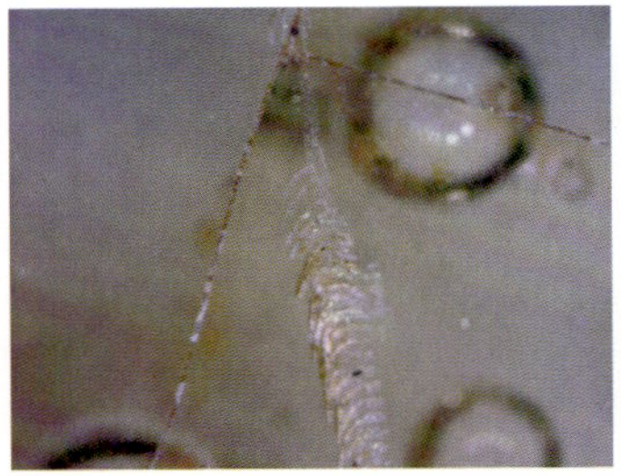	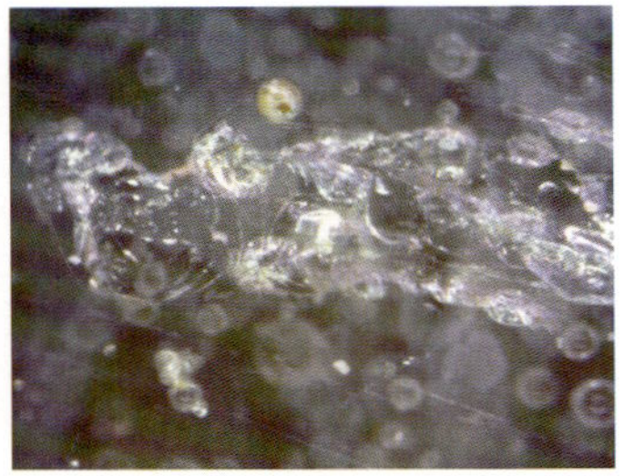
	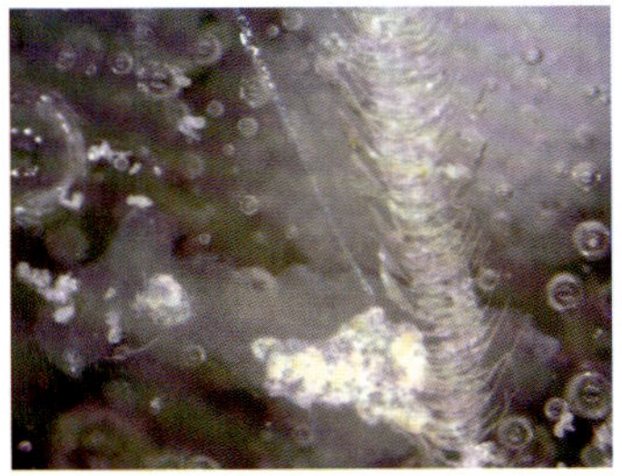	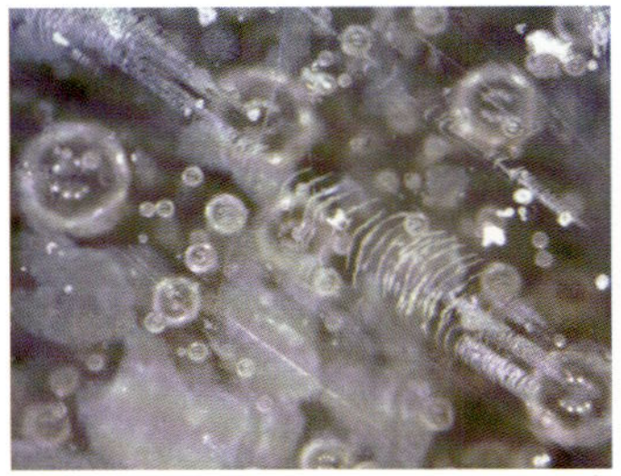	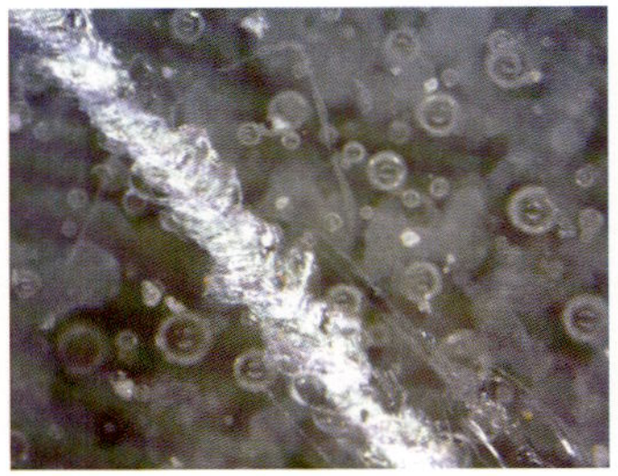	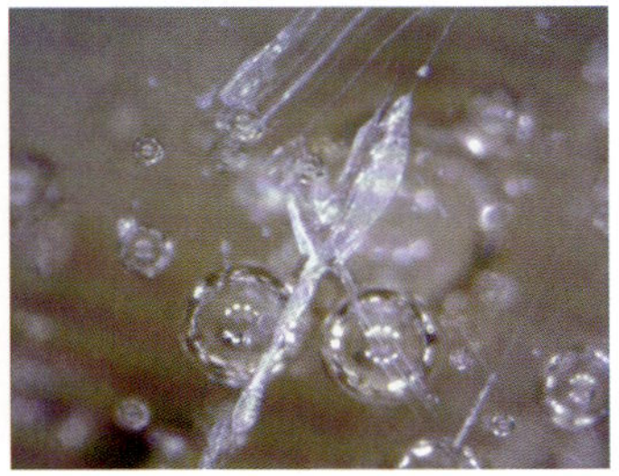

（续图）
(Continued)

三维
Three-dimensional

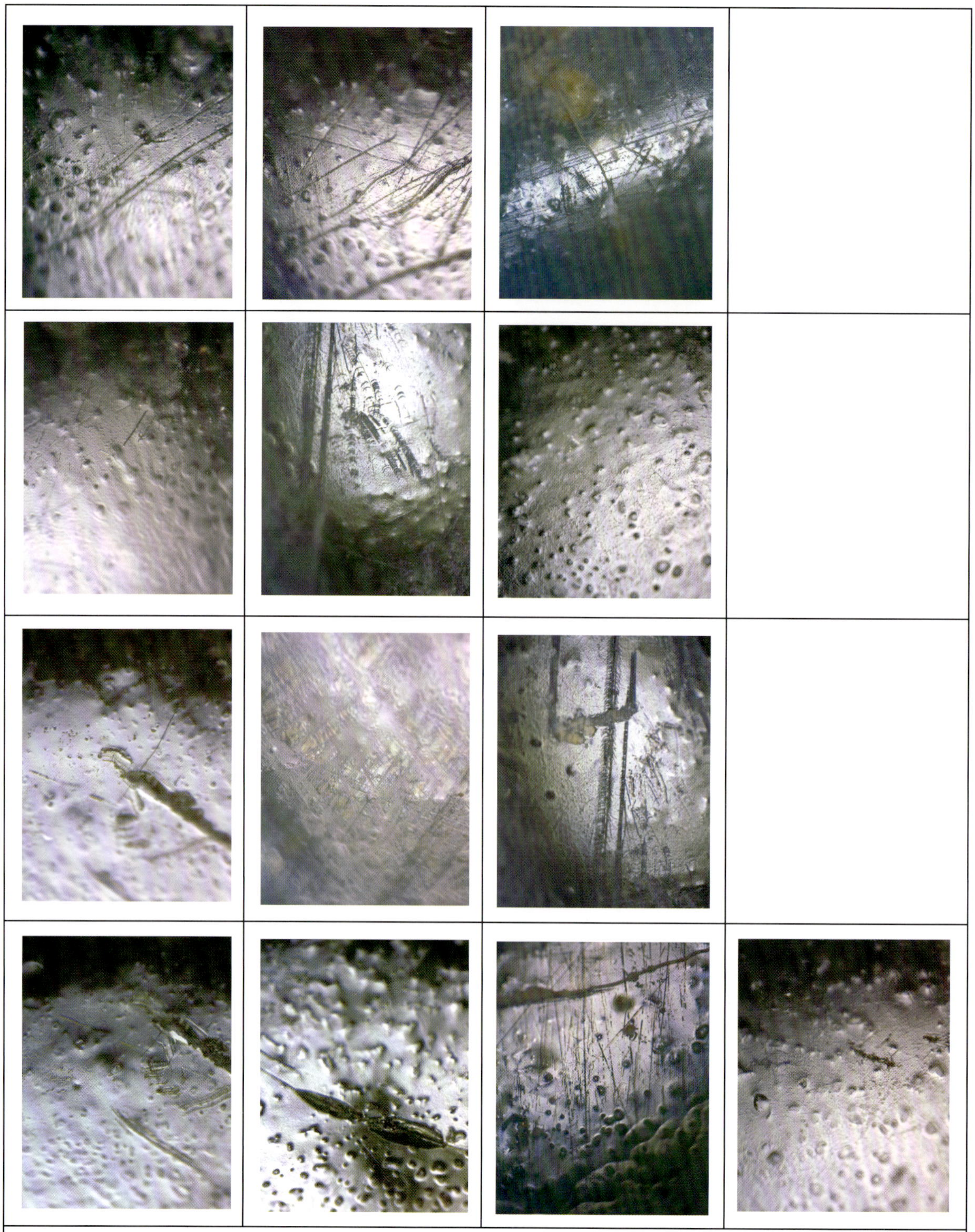

色变泡
Color Change Bubbles

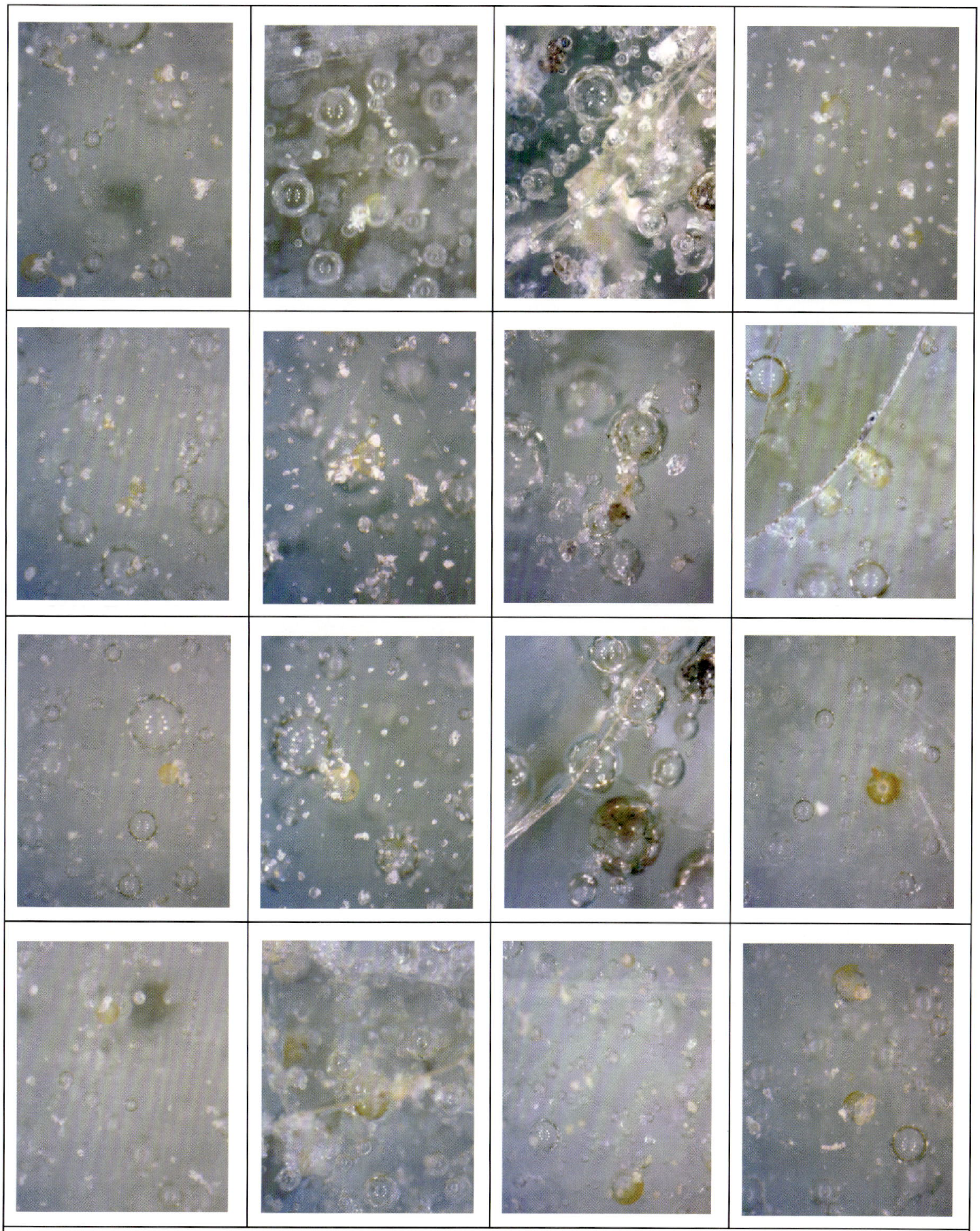

二维
Two-dimensional

（续图）
（Continued）

二维 Two-dimensional	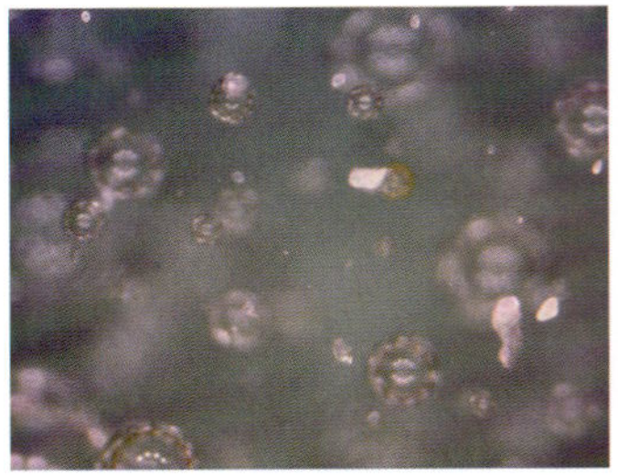	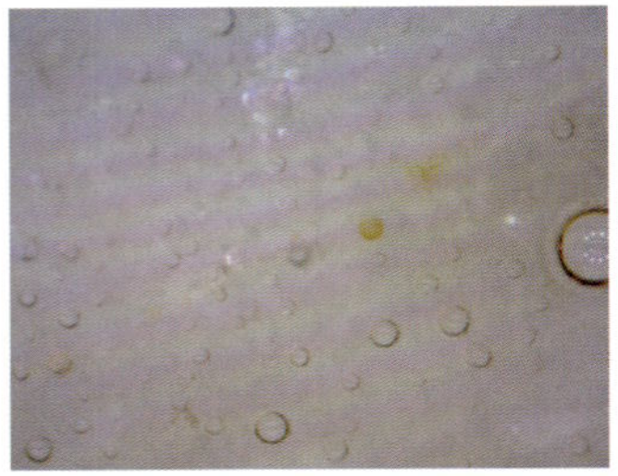	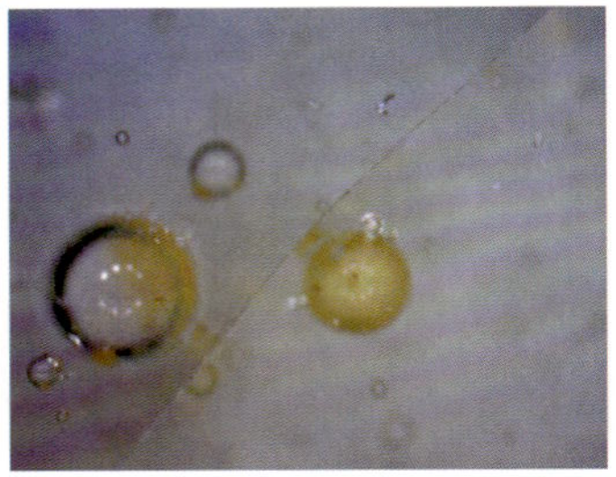	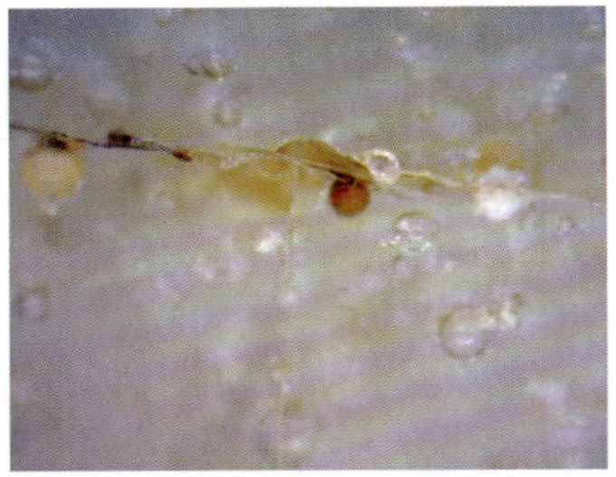
三维 Three-dimensional	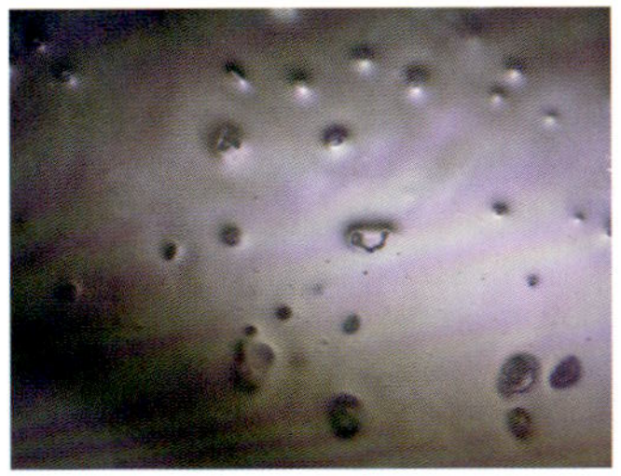			
二维 Two-dimensional	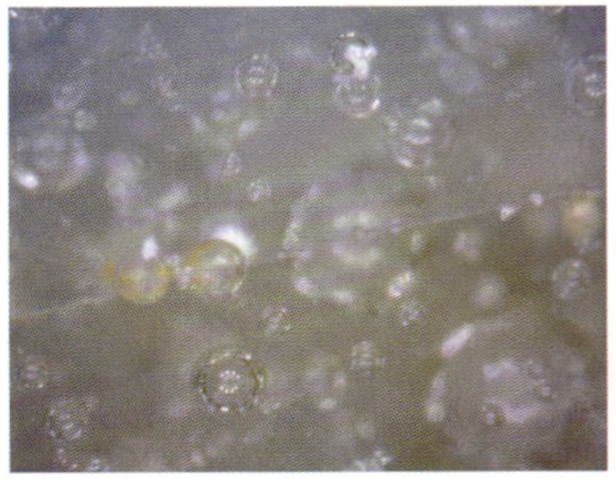	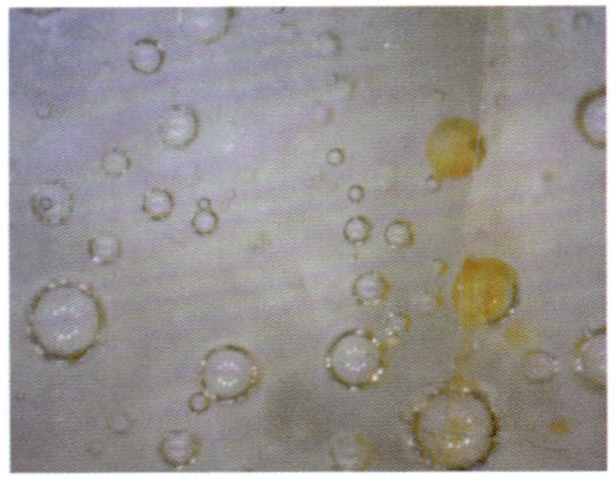	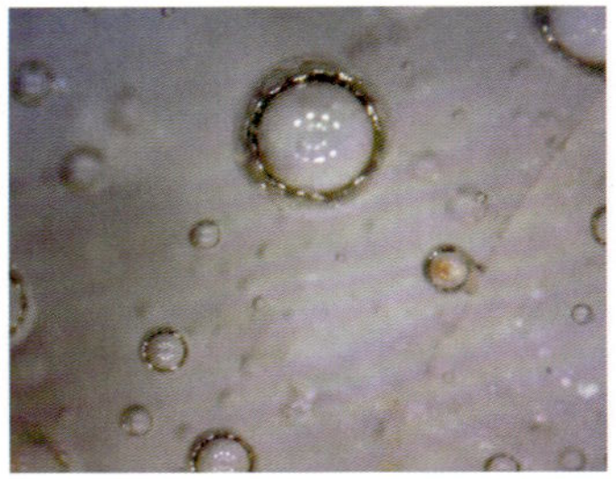	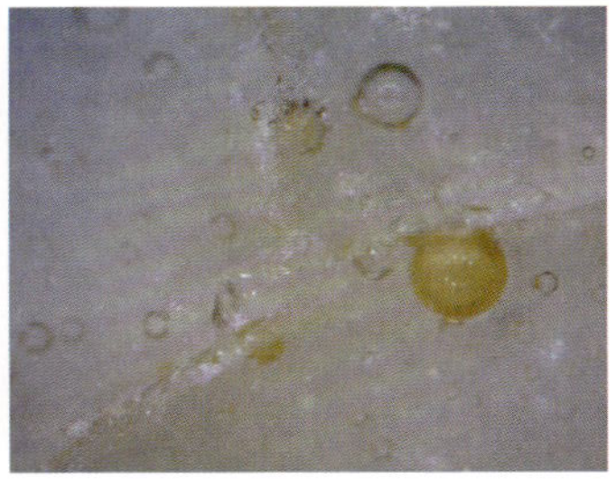

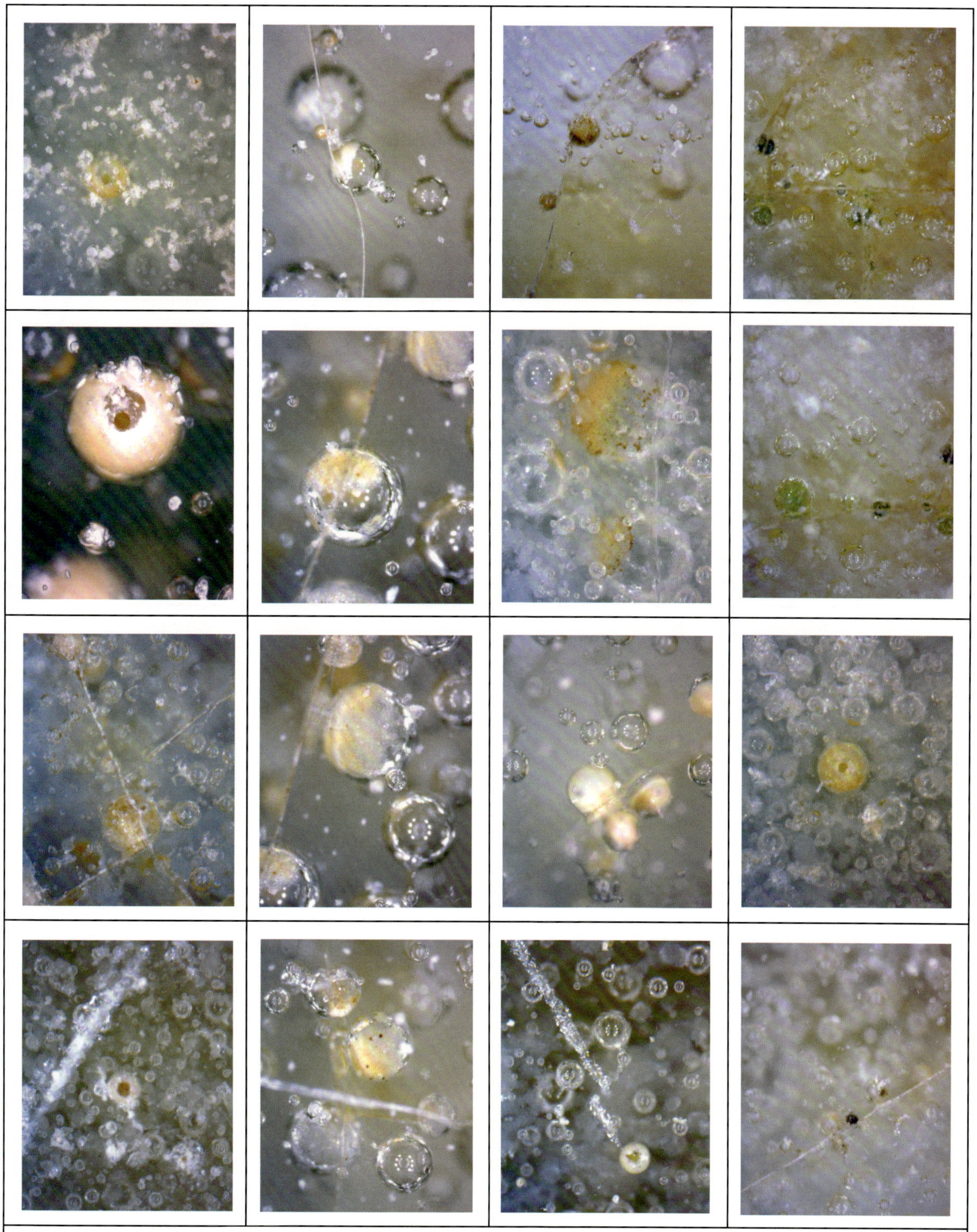

二维
Two-dimensional

壁变泡
Textured Bubbles

（续图）
(Continued)

二维 Two-dimensional		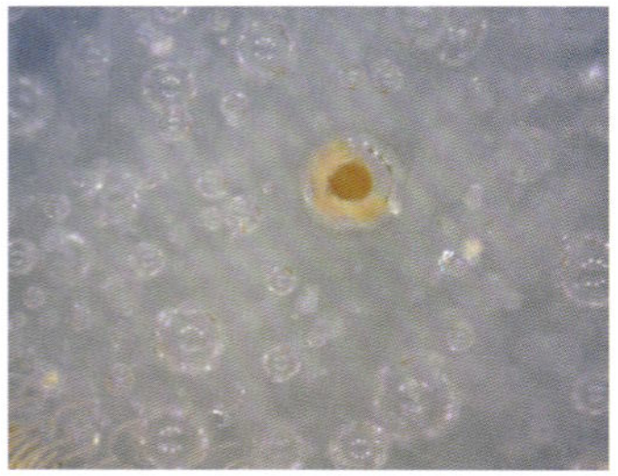	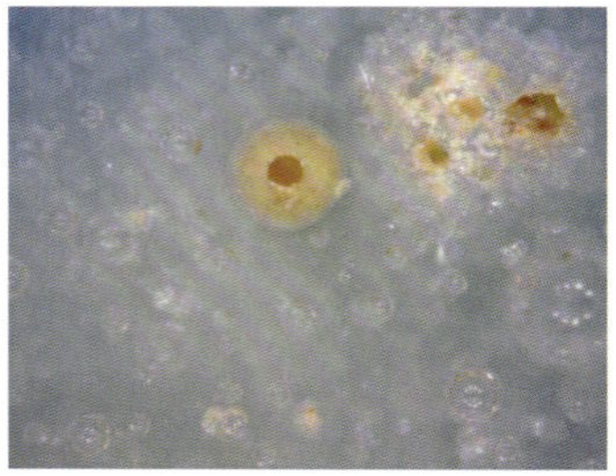	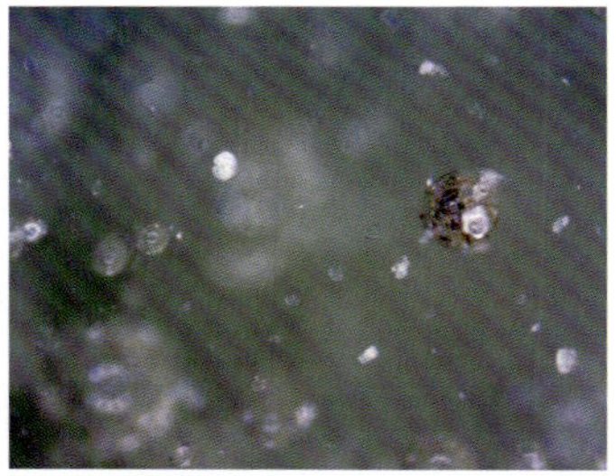
三维 Three-dimensional	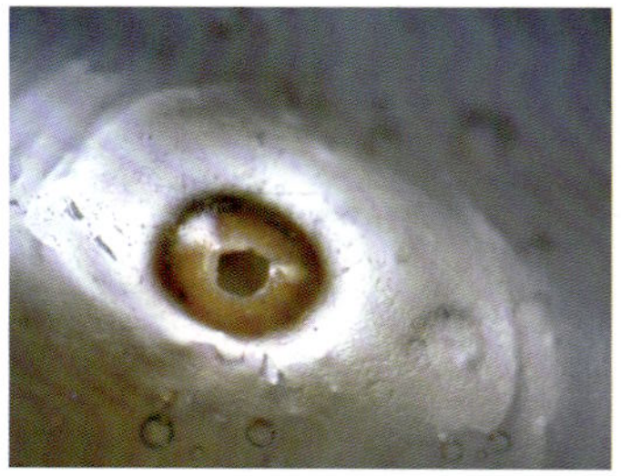	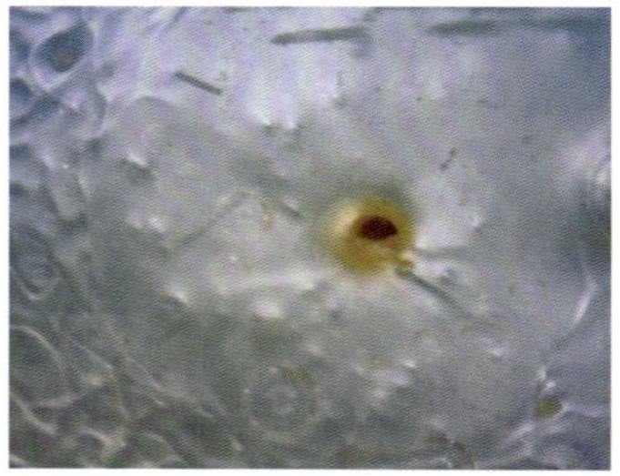	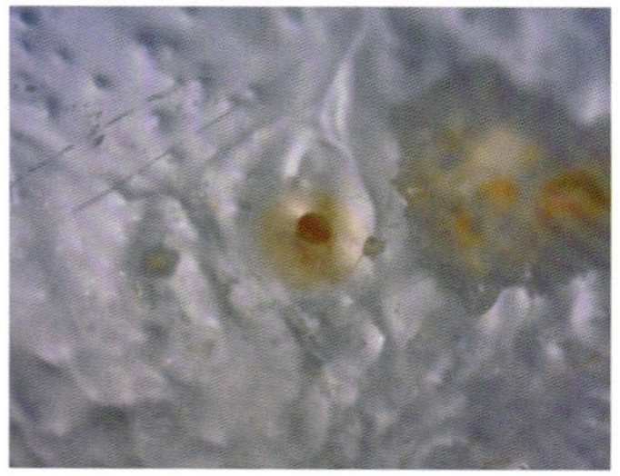	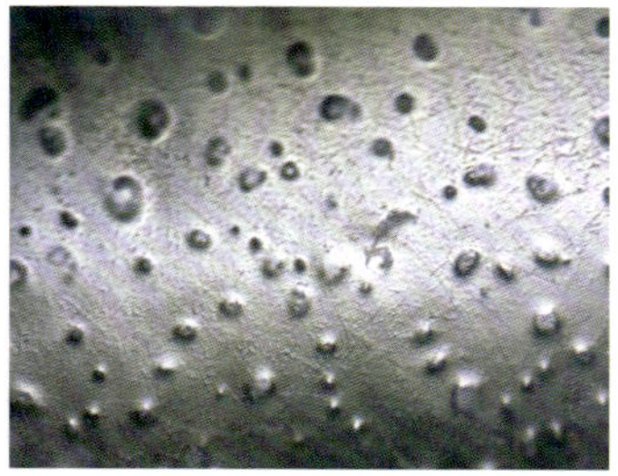
二维 Two-dimensional	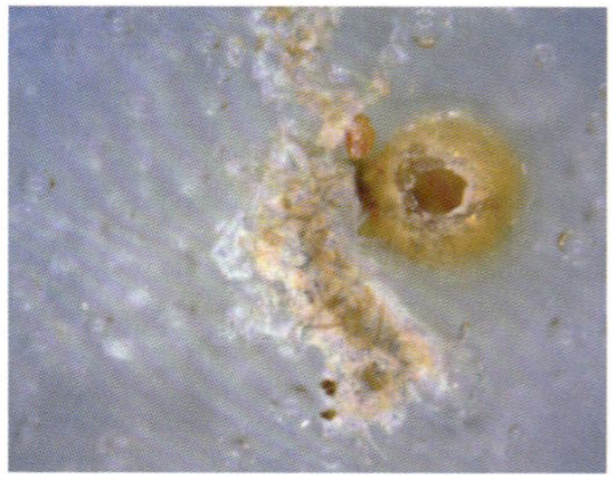	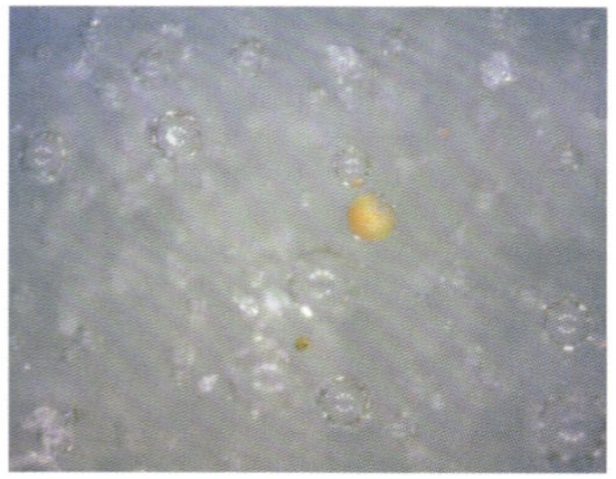	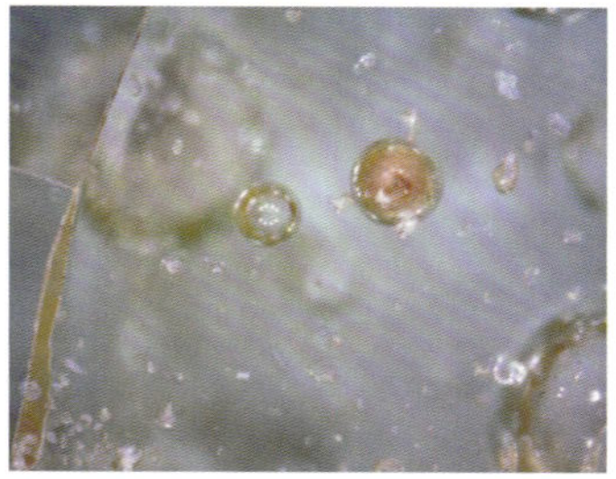	
三维 Three-dimensional		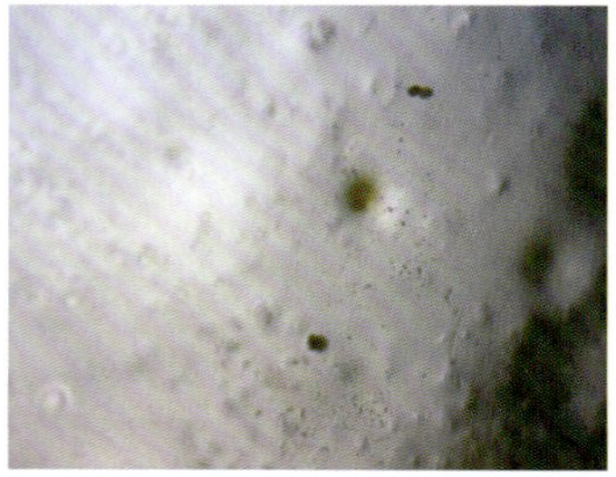	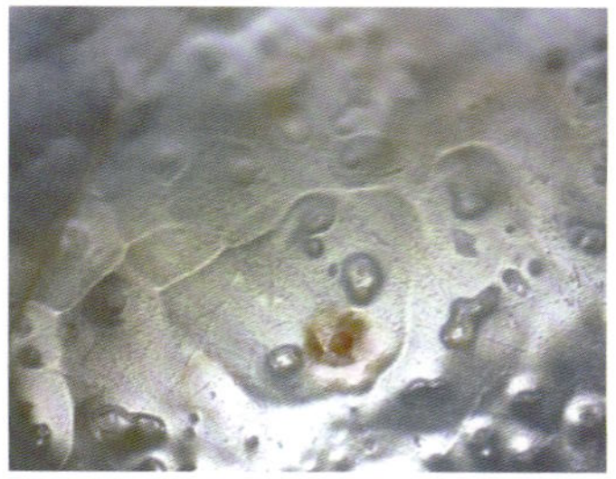	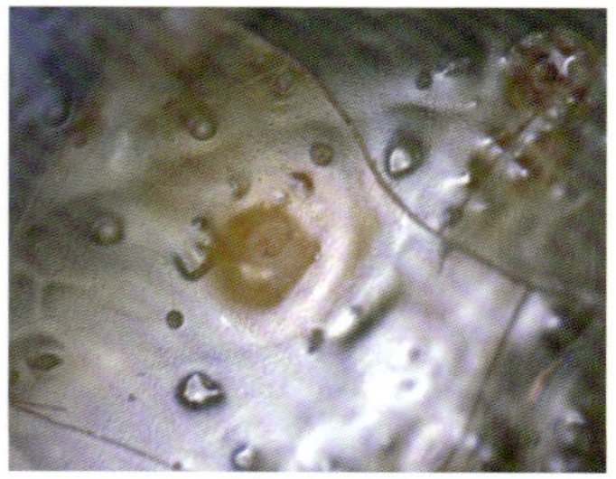

（续图）
（Continued）

二维 Two-dimensional	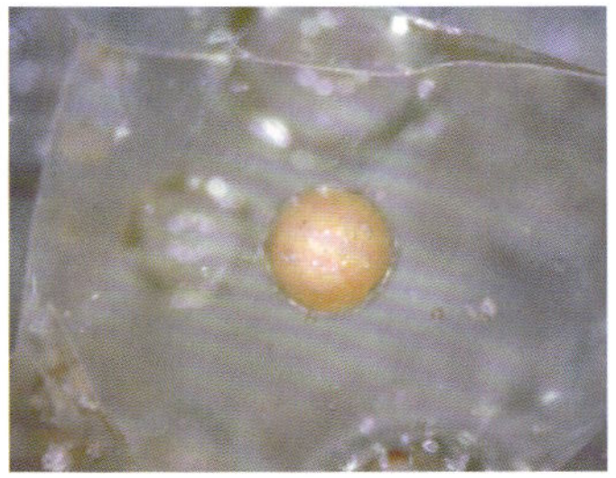	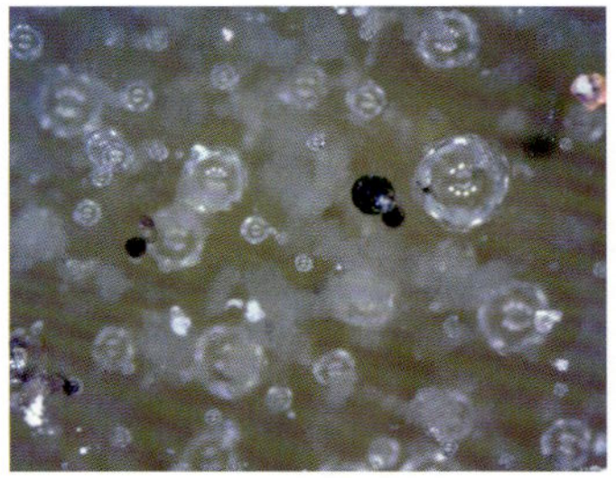	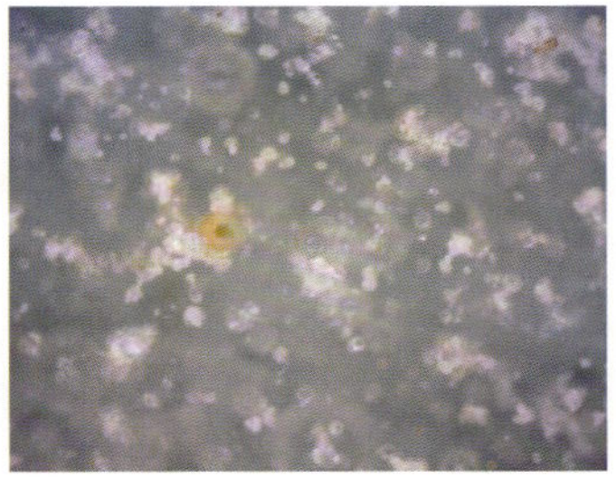	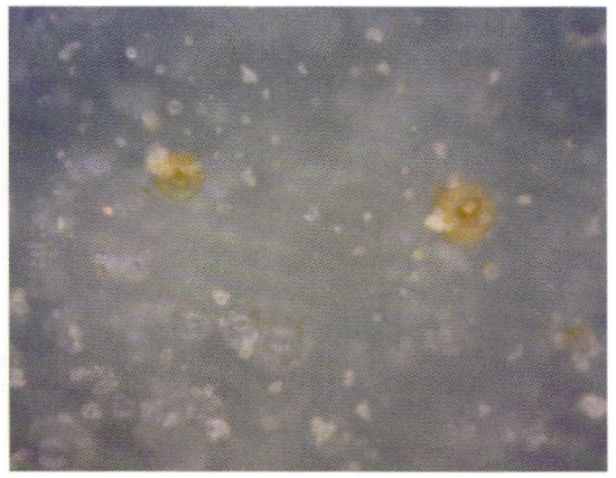
三维 Three-dimensional	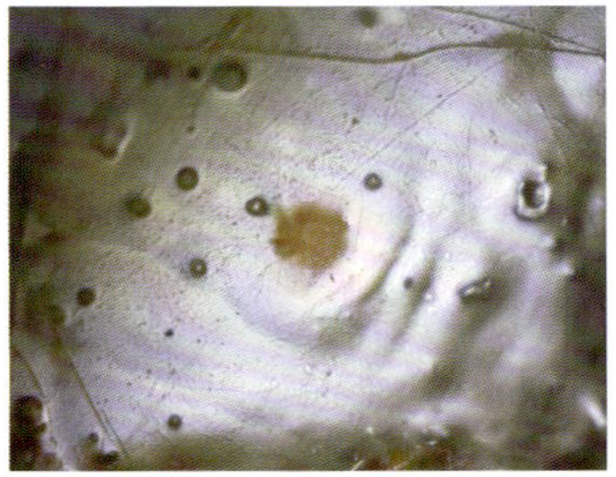	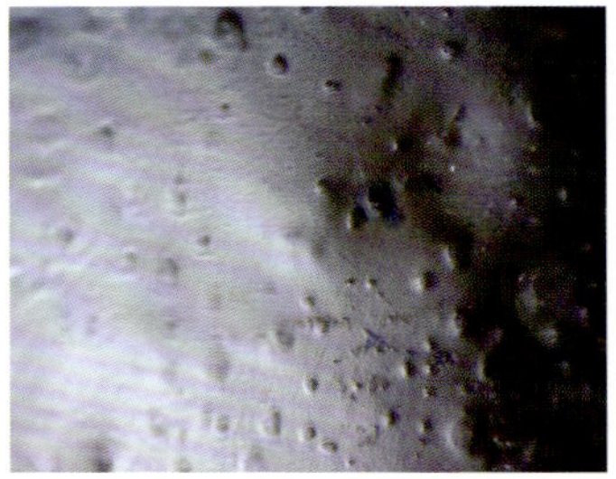	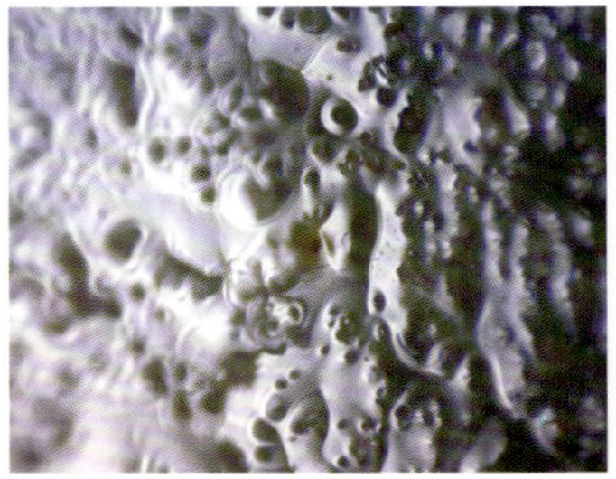	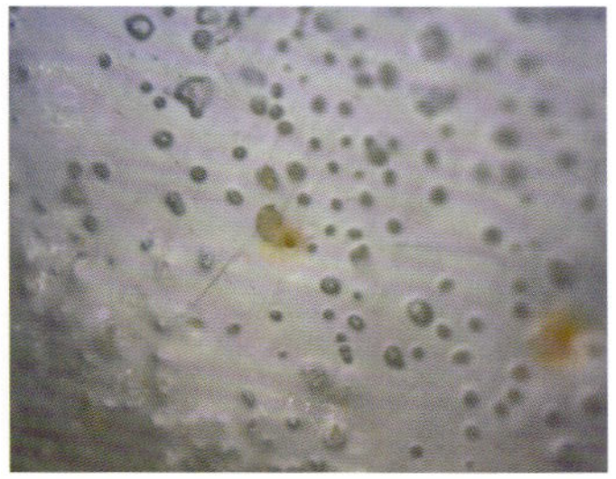
二维 Two-dimensional		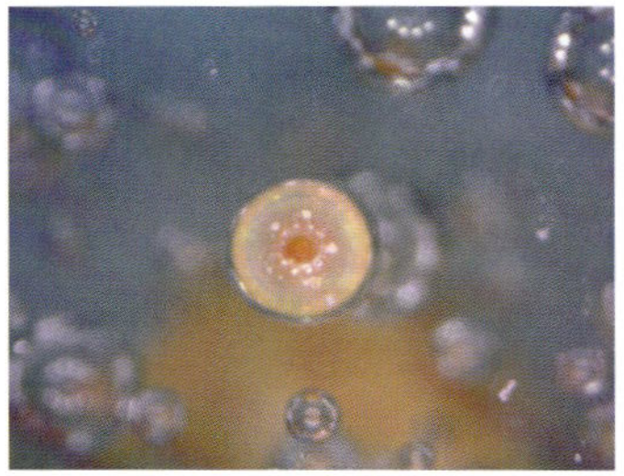	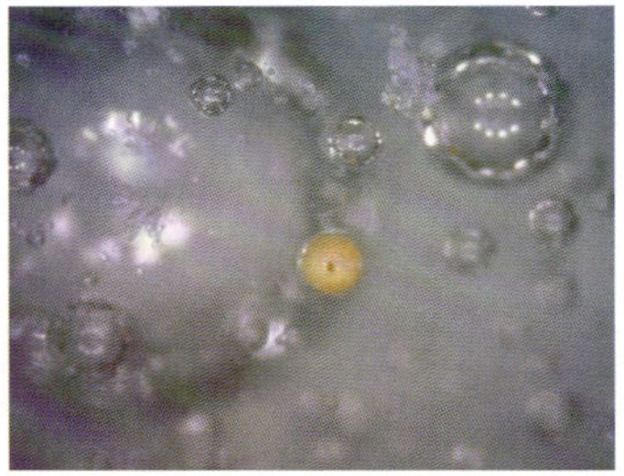	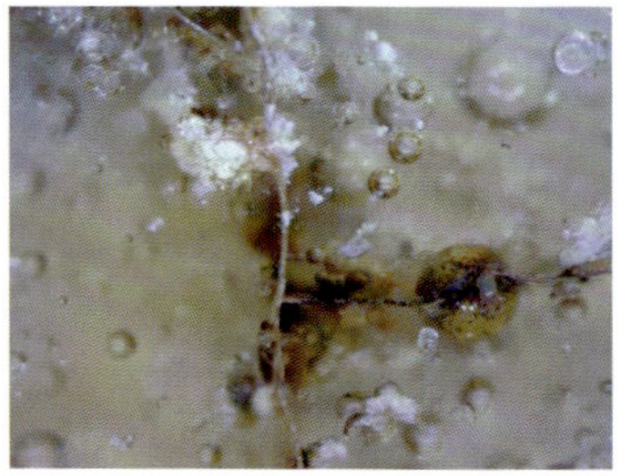
三维 Three-dimensional		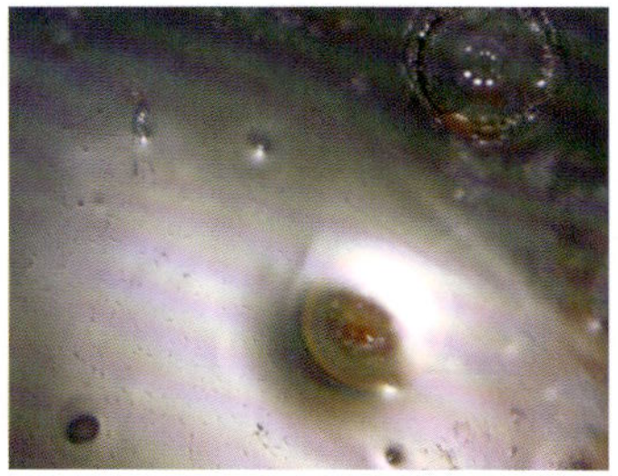	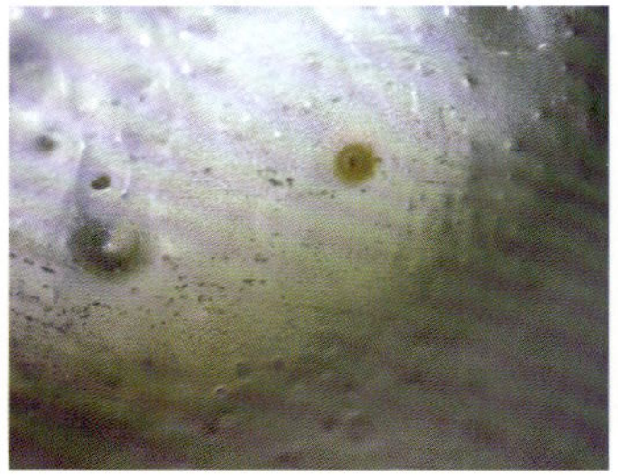	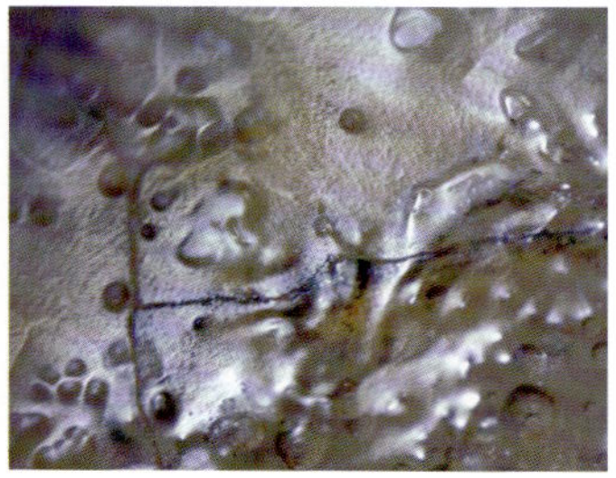

（续图）
（Continued）

		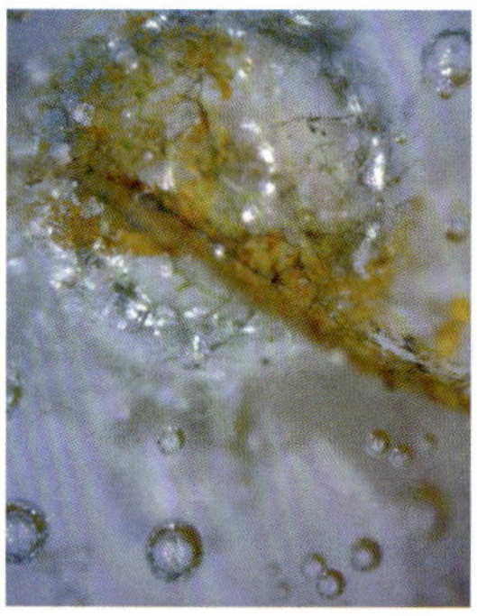	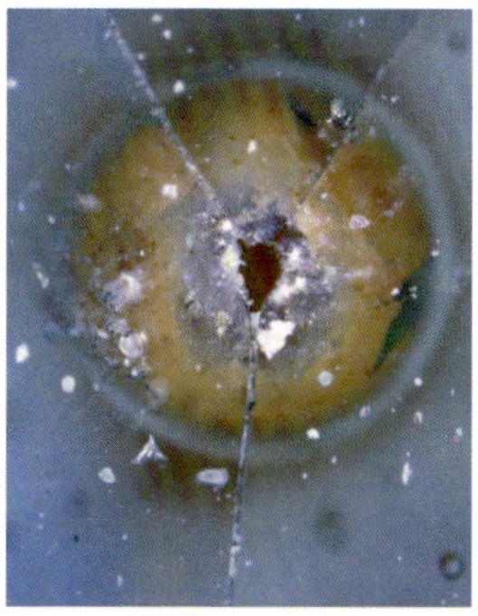
	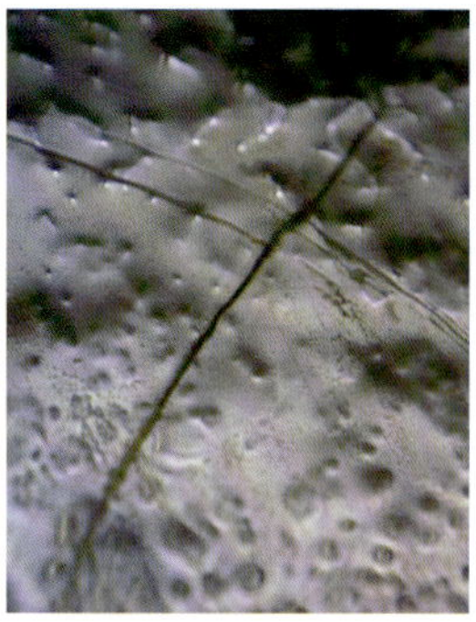	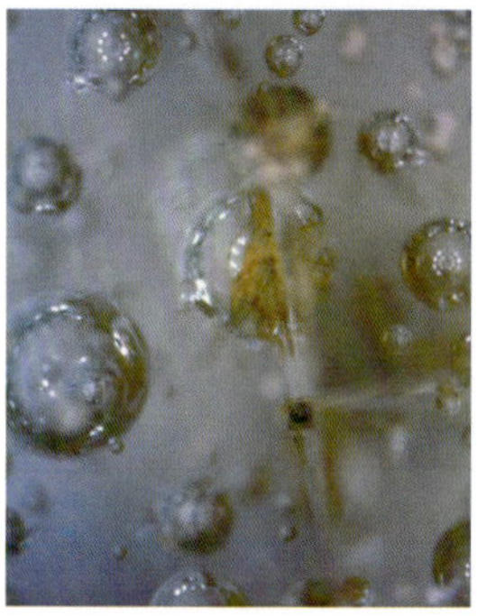	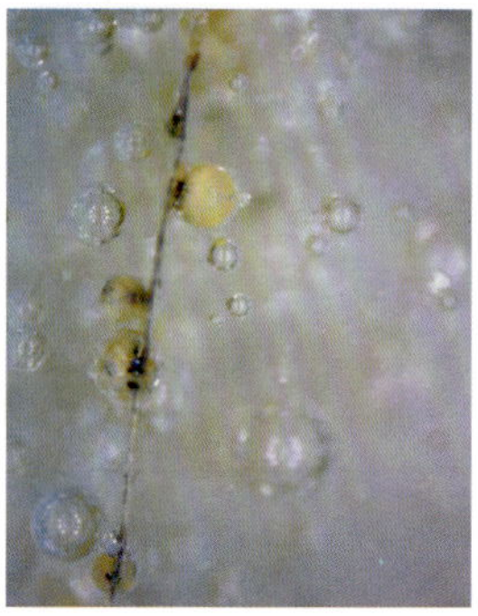
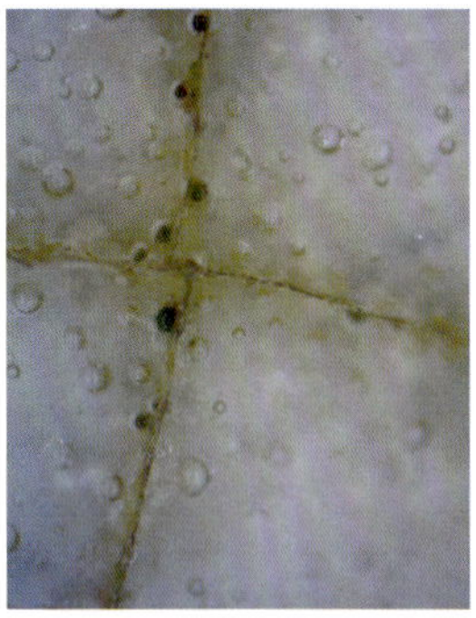			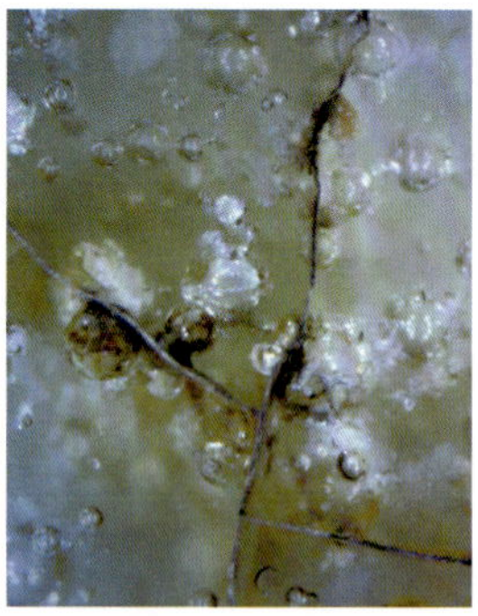
	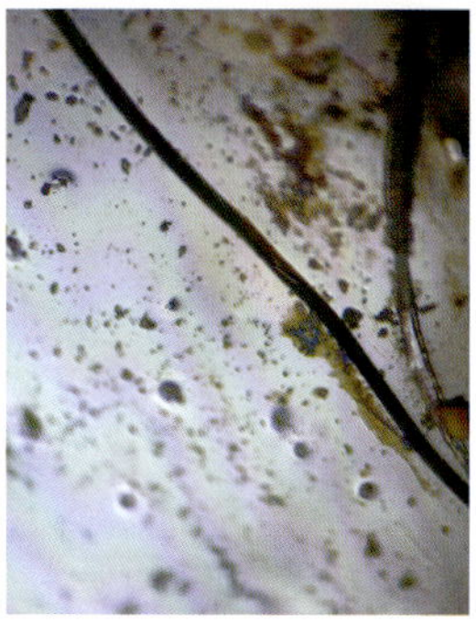	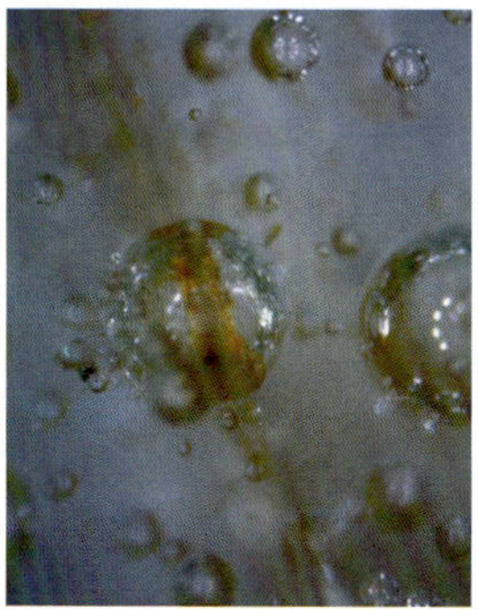	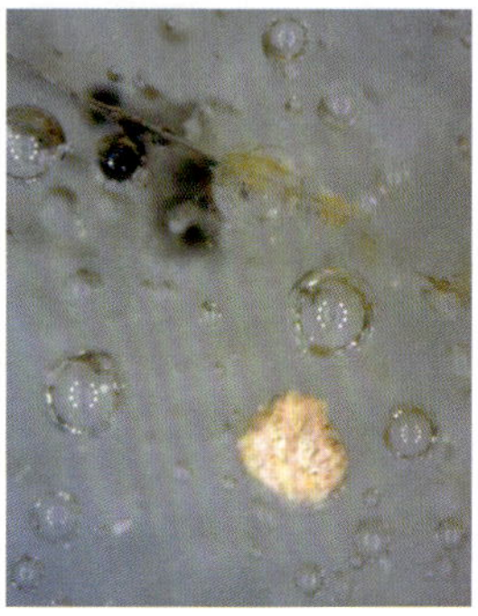
二维 Two-dimensional	三维 Three-dimensional	二维 Two-dimensional	

玻璃相
Glass Phase

二维 Two-dimensional	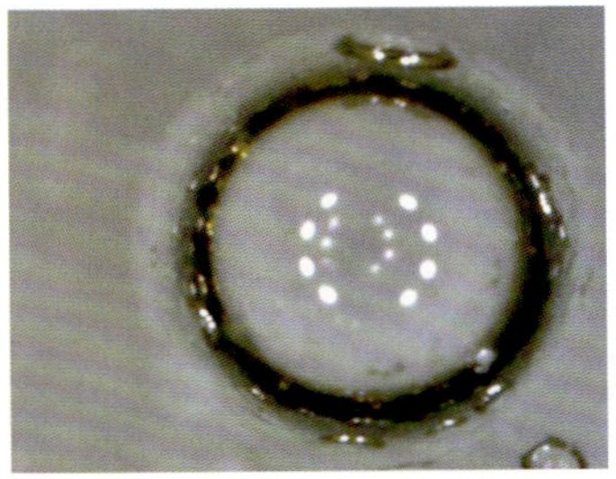	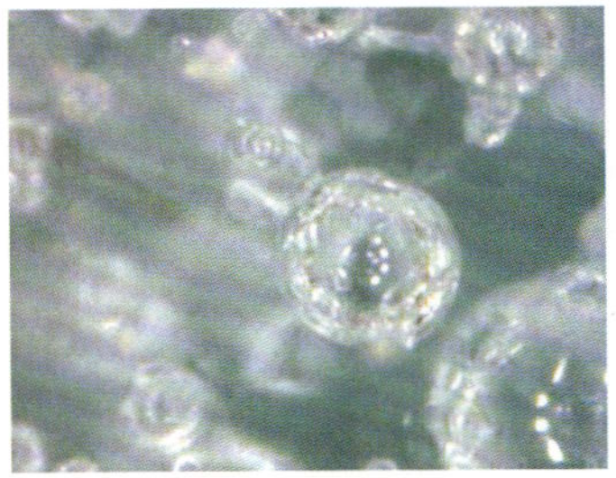	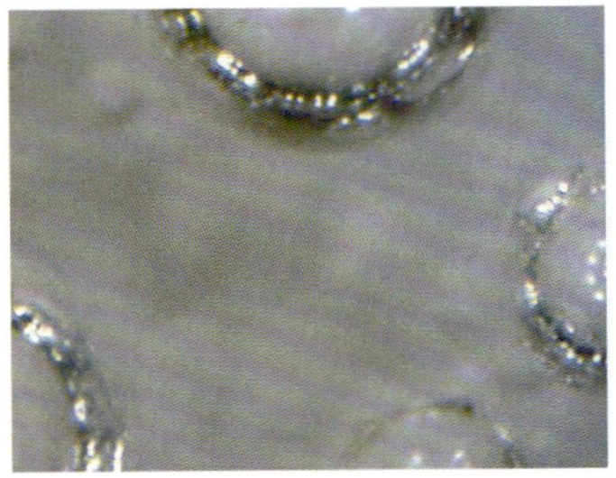	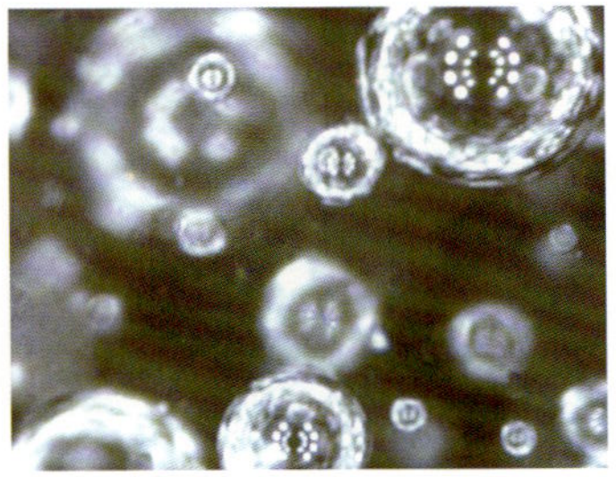
三维 Three-dimensional	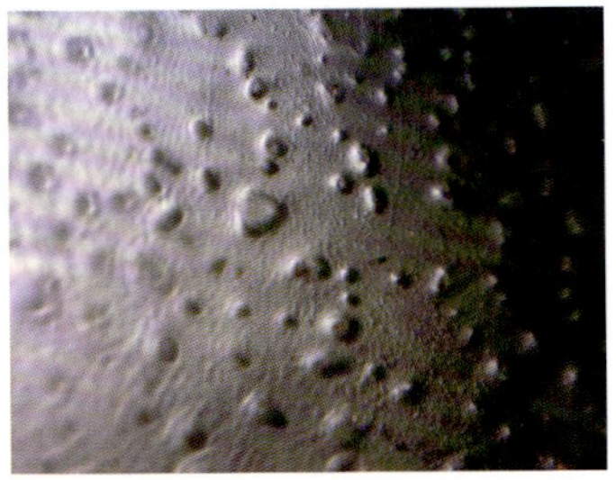	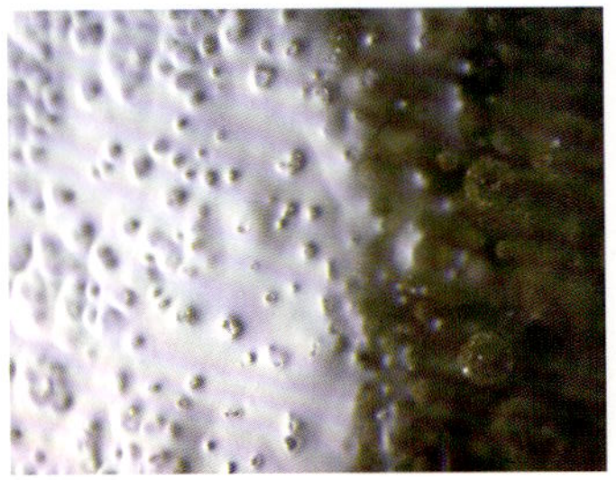	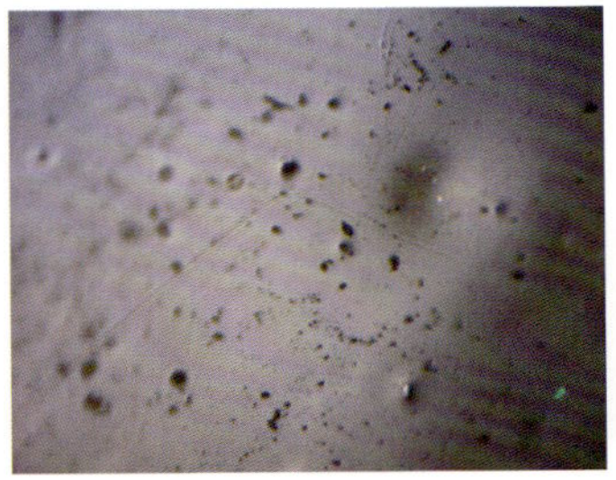	

鬃眼
Bristle Pits

二维
Two-dimensional

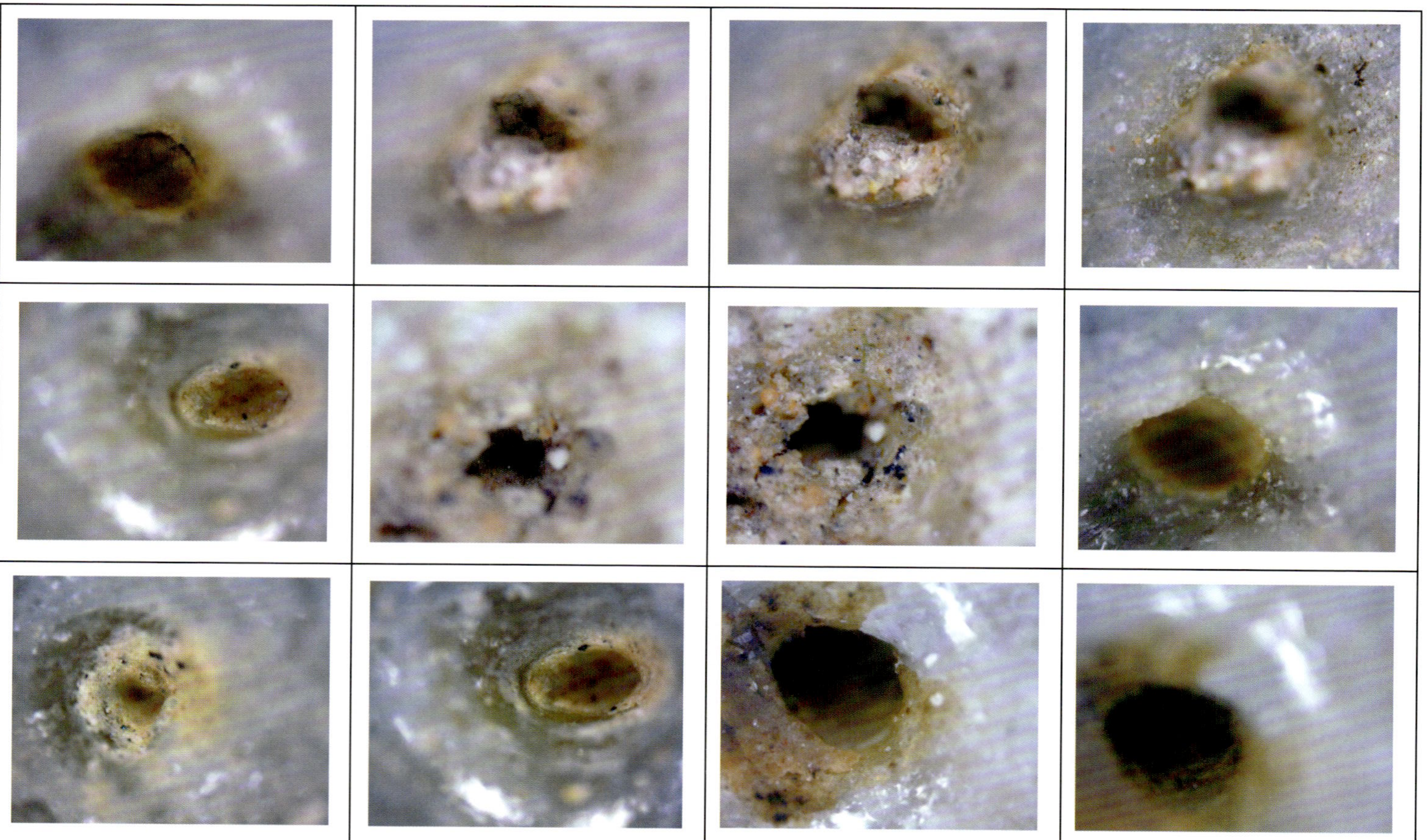

第八章

明代龙泉窑系青瓷迹型真品与赝品比对分析

阅读提示：

本章将明代龙泉窑系青瓷真品与赝品上的四大迹型类别（斑块、纹路、气泡及鬃眼）及釉层三维形貌进行深入的比对描述及分析。

主要论述问题：

1. 明代龙泉窑系青瓷真品与赝品上的各斑块种类有什么区别？
2. 明代龙泉窑系青瓷真品与赝品上的各纹路种类有什么区别？
3. 明代龙泉窑系青瓷真品与赝品上的各气泡种类有什么区别？
4. 明代龙泉窑系青瓷真品与赝品上的鬃眼有什么区别？
5. 明代龙泉窑系青瓷真品与赝品上的釉层三维形貌有什么区别？

Chapter 8

Ming Dynasty Genuine and Forged Longquan Kiln System Celadon Trace Comparative Analysis

Text Note:

This chapter enters into the deep comparative description and analysis of the four trace categories (Mottles, Striae, Bubbles, and Bristle Pits) as well as three-dimensional appearance of Ming Dynasty genuine and forged Longquan Kiln System Celadon (LKSC).

科学研究的目的是对自然现象进行探索。研究取得的成果能提高人们对自然现象及规律的认识，具有认识论的意义。文物保护的目的就是传承中华民族的文化。传承民族文化首先要识真驱假，文物以真为贵，只有真，才有传承的必要，才能彰显民族文化的价值与特色。

文物鉴定识真驱假，于过去而言，是使真正的民族文化得以传承；于未来而言，既是对子孙后代负责，又是对国家与民族负责。

文物鉴定识真驱假，有利于倡导社会诚信、维护市场公平、繁荣文化市场，使民族文化发扬光大。

当代陶瓷造假技术已经可以蒙骗不少眼学专家。当代假鉴、乱鉴藏品，也蒙骗了不少藏家。

如果我们再用肉眼与高仿技术抗衡，那无疑是螳臂当车，心有余而力不足。所以，必须借助科学仪器，延伸我们的观测器官，这样才能有效识破陶瓷迹型假象，提高陶瓷鉴定水平。

陶瓷生产出来以后，就会产生风化现象。长期的自然风化，会在陶瓷表面留下痕迹。古陶瓷上存在着的这些风化迹型，正等待我们去观察和发现。从来不缺少迹型物证，缺的是判别迹型真假的眼力。利用科学仪器观察陶瓷迹型，识破人为做旧迹型的假象，是一门慢工出细活的学问。研究者必须坚持不懈、扎扎实实地去观察大量的真品标本上的迹型，才能领悟到“真迹与假迹”的微妙区别，才能从相似的真假迹型中辨识出它们的“不似”之处。

“真迹与假迹”在500倍显微成像下，至今尚存真假难辨的情况。研究者要继续深入研究，在这些真假难辨的迹型中找出差异，并综合分析器物整体迹型特征及规律，有效地识真驱假。

本章比对分析时选用的真品龙泉窑系青瓷均已被证实为真品，赝品均为研究团队定制的高仿龙泉青瓷。

The purpose of Scientific Research is the exploration of natural phenomenon. The fruits of research elevate our understanding of natural phenomenon and laws, and are meaningful to the theory of knowledge. The goal of relic conservation is the preservation of [Chinese] culture, but in order to preserve culture we must ensure the authenticity of such relics. Only when relics are authentic are they worth conservation, and only then is there a clearer depiction of a culture's values and characteristics.

Cultural relic authentication is the preservation of culture, and carries a responsibility to our future generations, our country, and our people.

Cultural relic authentication can initiate society's trust, ensure market equality, proliferate the cultural market, and carry forward national culture.

Currently, forgery techniques and false authentication have pulled the wool over the eyes of many experienced professionals and collectors.

If we continue forward with using the naked eye to contend with forgery technology, even though there may be a will, there is no capacity to keep up. Thus, we must draw support from scientific instruments to enhance our observation ability, and effectively cut through the false appearance of ceramic traces and elevate our authentication standard.

From the firing of ceramics onwards, the weathering phenomenon takes place. A long period of weathering leaves traces on the surface of ceramics. The traces left on the face of antique ceramics are just waiting for our observation and discovery. Ceramics have never lacked material evidence, there has only been a lack of vision to differentiate true and false ceramic traces.

The use of scientific instruments cuts through the false trace appearances of man-made forgeries. However, it is a slow work of systematic learning that yields fine results.

The microscopic observation of ceramic traces is a laborious project that requires unending patience and determination to observe huge amounts of authentic samples in order to discover the fine dissimilarities between genuine and forged traces, as well as comprehensively analyse a whole piece's trace characteristics and laws. Only then are we able to decipher the seemingly indistinguishable, and separate real from fake.

Under the current limitation of 500X magnification observation, difficulty still presents when distinguishing real and fake traces. Researchers must relentlessly continue to deepen research, dig out the differences in these seemingly indistinguishable traces, and bring forth effective authentication means.

The genuine samples used in this chapter for comparative analysis are all LKSC of known authenticity, and the forgeries are high-end fakes purchased by the research team for the purpose of research.

第一节
龙泉窑系青瓷斑块真品与赝品比对分析

一、坑点斑

（一）CO型坑点斑

1. 真品二维特征

（1）单位图片中CO型坑点斑有大小及深浅的差异（见图8-1-1—图8-1-8）。

（2）单位图片中CO型坑点斑之间的距离有疏有密（见图8-1-1—图8-1-8）。

（3）单位图片中CO型坑点斑与CO纹伴生，CO纹纤细精致，二者都独立清晰，有时二者有色差（见图8-1-1—图8-1-4）。

（4）CO型坑点斑有沿着其轮廓向外呈白雾状蔓延的趋势（见图8-1-7）。

（5）单位图片中CO型坑点斑与CO纹或连环坑点斑群同时存在，各自独立清晰，彼此界线分明（见图8-1-3—图8-1-8）。

（6）CO型坑点斑与周围玻璃相或其他迹型种类界线分明（见图8-1-1—图8-1-8）。

（7）CO型坑点斑周围玻璃相干净清晰（见图8-1-1—图8-1-8）。

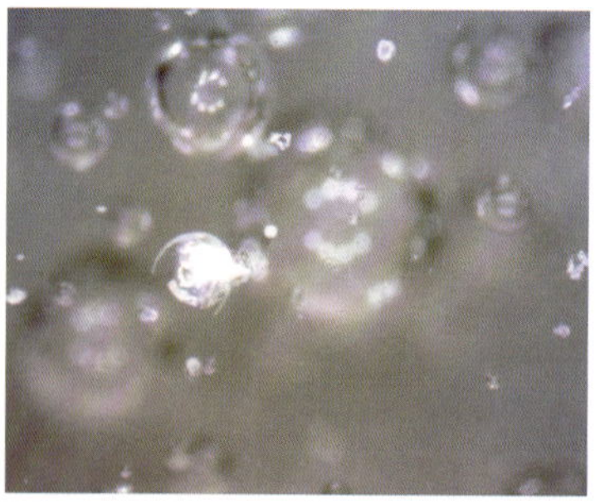

图8-1-1

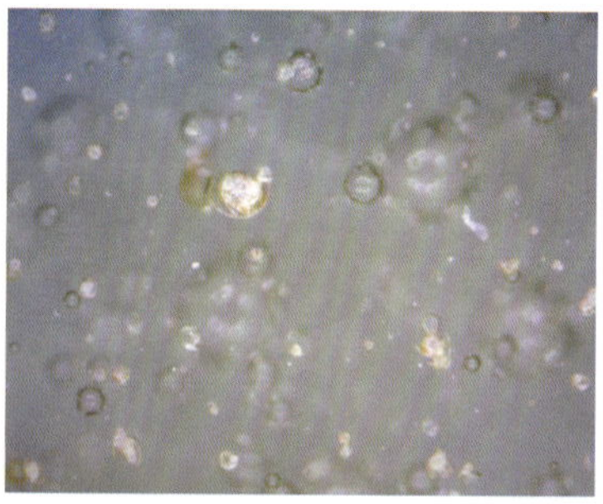

图8-1-2

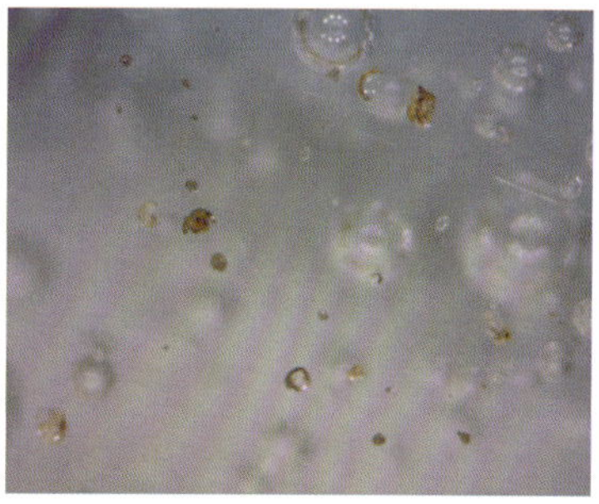

图8-1-3

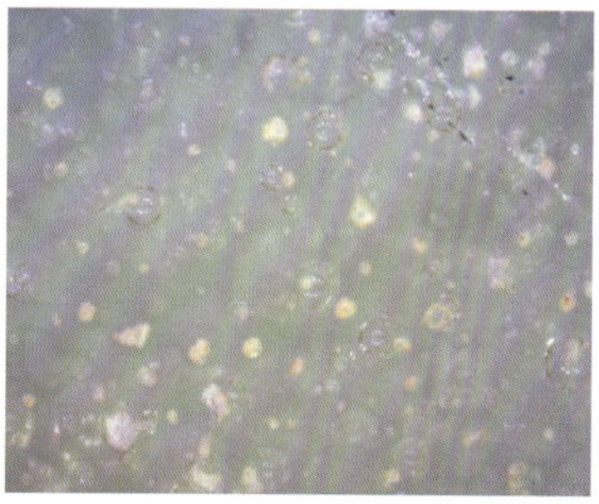

图8-1-4

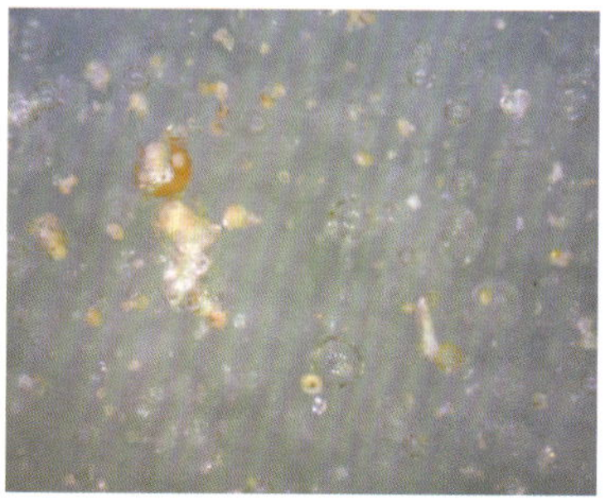

图8-1-5

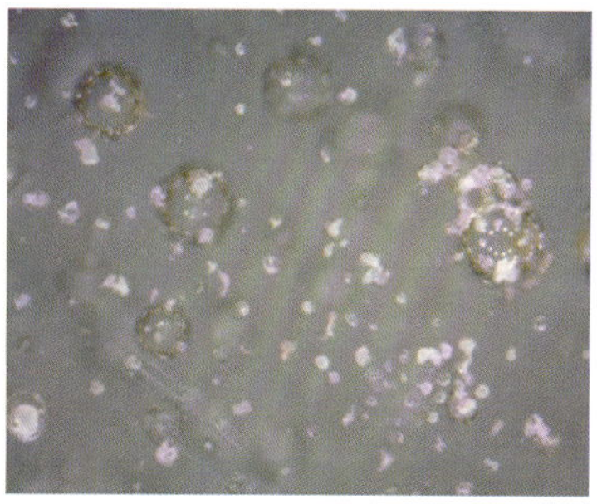

图8-1-6

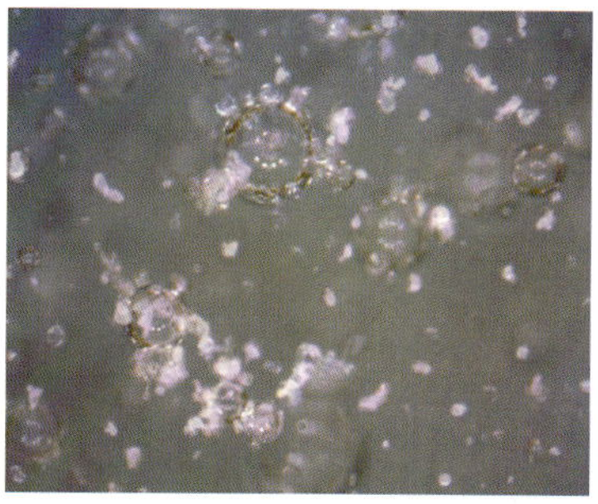

图8-1-7

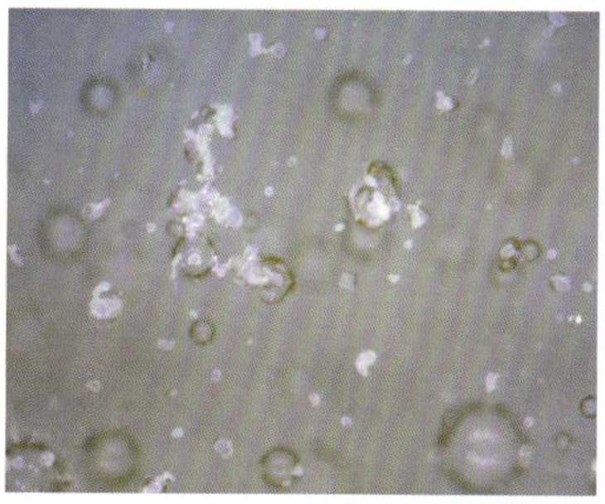

图8-1-8

Section 1:
Genuine and Forged Longquan Kiln System Celadon Mottle Comparison

1. Pit Mottles

A. CO Type Pit Mottles

a. Two-Dimensional Characteristics of Genuine Article

I. CO type pit mottles have alternating size and depth within one unit image (see pictures 8-1-1—8-1-8).

II. CO type pit mottles have disparate density within one unit image (see pictures 8-1-1—8-1-8).

III. A unit image can present with CO type pit mottles as well as CO striae. CO striae are fine and reserved and have clear delineation. Striae can present with color disparity, and are mutually delineated (see pictures 8-1-1—8-1-4).

IV. CO type pits can have white coloration extending into the glaze level (see picture 8-1-7).

V. A unit image can present with CO type pit mottles, CO striae, and CO pit groups. They are independent and mutually delineated (see pictures 8-1-3—8-1-8).

VI. CO type pits retain clear delineation from the surrounding glass phase and other traces (see pictures 8-1-1—8-1-8).

VII. The glass phase surrounding the pits is clean and clear (see pictures 8-1-1— 8-1-8).

b. Three-Dimensional Characteristics of Genuine Article

I. CO type pitting generally occurs in areas of raised glaze surface.

II. Only finely reserved CO striae are present on the glaze surface, they are clear and independent.

III. CO type pits presenting on the protrusions of the glaze surface often have a higher amount of weathering, and as such, darker coloration around the base of the protrusion, while its surface remains smooth (lighter coloration).

IV. Only finely reserved CO striae and mottles are present on the glaze surface. The surface area of visible CO striae and mottle is much smaller than that of the two-dimensionally visible mottle; they are mutually delineated, the mottle is reserved and lacking dispersive qualities.

V. CO type pits retain clear delineation from the surrounding glass phase and other traces.

VI. Some of the glass phase is clean and clear.

VII. Some of the glass phase presents with an aged feel.

See pictures 8-1-9 and 8-1-10, where 8-1-9 is the two-dimensional and 8-1-10 is the three-dimensional view of the same location.

The CO type pit mottle in picture 8-1-9 is only observable as a C shaped striation and has a much smaller three-dimensional appearance (see Arrow A) in picture 8-1-10. The striation is fine and reserved, the mottle is reserved and lacking dispersive qualities and retains independent delineation with the surrounding glass phase.

The surrounding glass phase also has clear and mutually independent CO type pit mottles, all showing a base that is more weathered than the raised center. The mottles are reserved and clearly delineated. The surrounding glass phase also presents with densely distributed weathered striae and a relatively evident aged feel.

See pictures 8-1-11 and 8-1-12, where 8-1-11 is the two-dimensional and 8-1-12 is the three-dimensional view of the same location.

See pictures 8-1-13 and 8-1-14, where 8-1-13 is the two-dimensional and 8-1-14 is the three-dimensional view of the same location.

The CO type pit mottles in pictures 8-1-11 and 8-1-

2. 真品三维特征

（1）CO型坑点斑大都分布在釉表面凸起处。

（2）CO型坑点斑所在处釉表面只见纤细收敛的C形纹或O形纹，清晰独立。

（3）存在于釉表面凸起处的CO型坑点斑，通常都是根部风化程度较高，颜色较深，顶部风化程度较低，颜色较浅。

（4）CO型坑点斑所在处釉表面通常只见纤细收敛的C形纹或O形纹，以及面积小于或等于坑点斑二维面积的风化斑块，斑块收敛，无扩张感，彼此界线分明。

（5）CO型坑点斑与周围玻璃相或其他迹型种类界线分明。

（6）有的玻璃相干净清晰。

（7）有的玻璃相有明显陈旧感。

见图8-1-9、图8-1-10，二者为同一器物同一位置图片，图8-1-9为二维图片，图8-1-10为三维图片。

图8-1-9中的CO型坑点斑在图8-1-10中只见C形纹及一处三维成像面积远远小于二维的深色斑块（见箭头A所指处），C形纹纹路纤细、收敛、清晰，斑块收敛，无扩张感。二者均与周围玻璃相界线分明。

周围玻璃相上还有其他各自独立清晰的CO型坑点斑，均为根部风化程度较顶部高，颜色比顶部深，斑块收敛，彼此界线清晰，玻璃相其余地方布满细密的风化纹路，有比较明显的陈旧感。

见图8-1-11、图8-1-12，二者为同一器物同一位置图片，图8-1-11为二维图片，图8-1-12为三维图片。

见图8-1-13、图8-1-14，二者为同一器物同一位置图片，图8-1-13为二维图片，图8-1-14为三维图片。

图8-1-11及图8-1-13中的CO型坑点斑在图8-1-12及图8-1-14

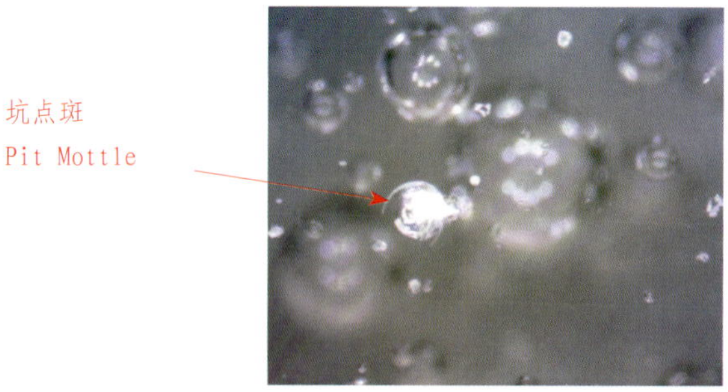

图8-1-9

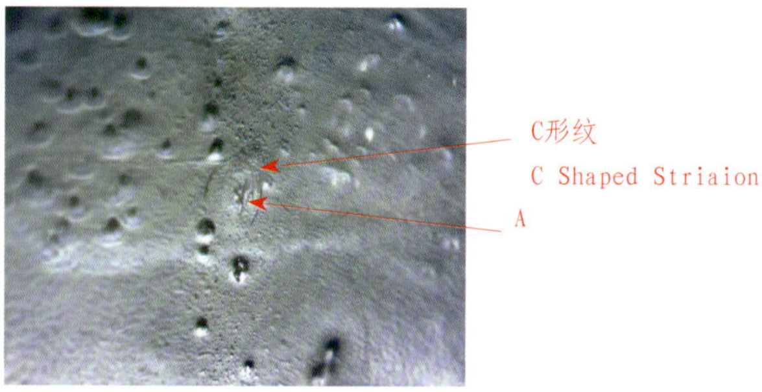

图8-1-10

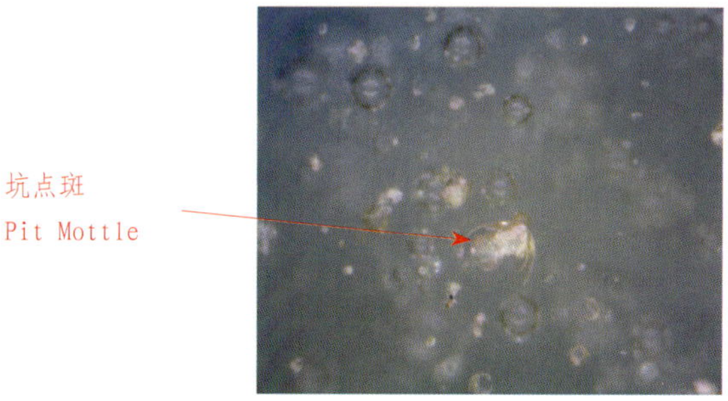

图8-1-11

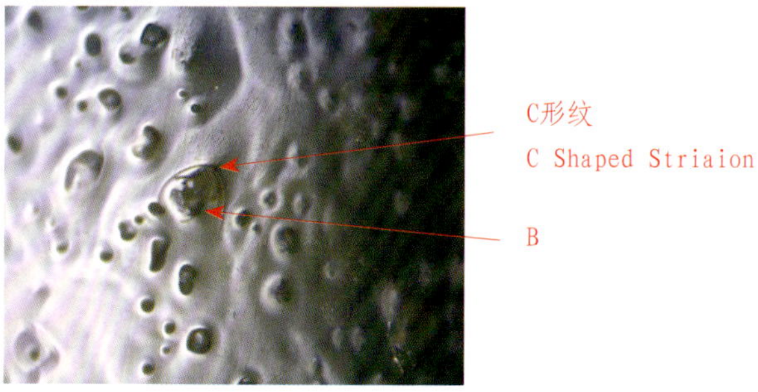

图8-1-12

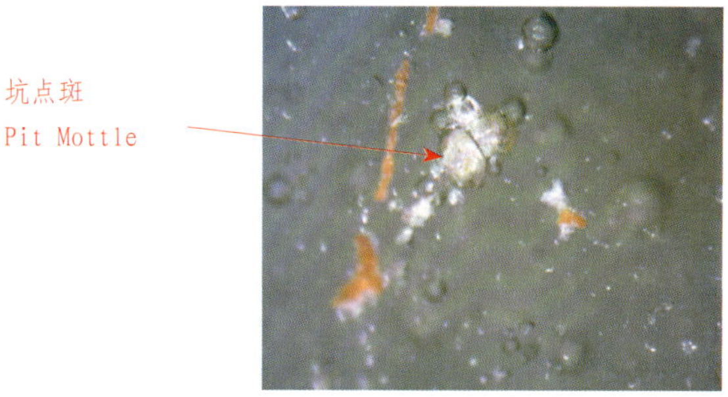

图8-1-13

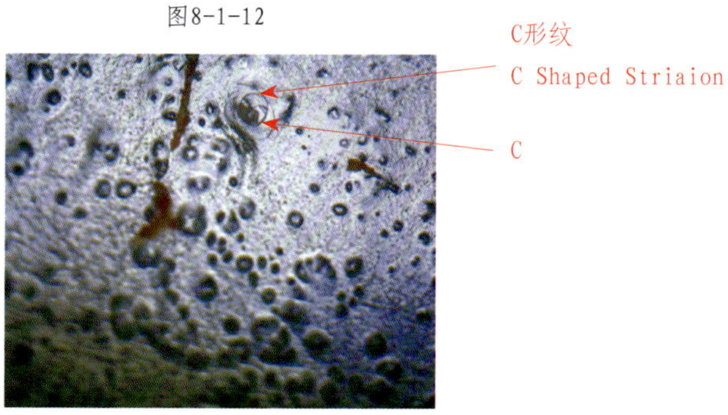

图8-1-14

13 are only observable as C shaped striae and have a much smaller three-dimensional appearance (see Arrows B and C) in pictures 8-1-12 and 8-1-14. The striae are fine and reserved, the mottle is reserved and lacking dispersive qualities, and retains independent delineation from the surrounding glass phase.

The surrounding glass phase also has clear and mutually independent CO type pit mottles, all showing a base that is more weathered than the raised center. The mottles are reserved and clearly delineated. The surrounding glaze surface is clean and clear.

The glass phase in picture 8-1-14 presents with densely distributed weathered striae and a relatively evident aged feel.

See pictures 8-1-15 and 8-1-16, where 8-1-15 is the two-dimensional and 8-1-16 is the three-dimensional view of the same location.

The pit group indicated by Arrow D in picture 8-1-15 has a much smaller three-dimensional appearance in picture 8-1-16, The surrounding glass phase also has clear and mutually independent CO type pit mottles, all presenting on areas of glaze protrusion and showing a base that is more weathered than the raised center. The mottle is reserved and lacking dispersive qualities, and retains independent delineation from the surrounding glass phase. Other portions of the glass phase are similarly clean and clear.

c. Two-Dimensional Characteristics of Forged Article

See pictures 8-1-17—8-1-20 (this piece has undergone treatment with aging reagent).

I. The size and depths of the CO type pits lack variation.

II. Coloration is monotonous and often the same as CO striae. They lack clear delineation and there is no clear evidence of a causal relationship.

III. The pits can present with fuzzy edges, creating an unclear appearance.

IV. These pits often have highly reflective properties, and are relatively obvious.

V. The pits often cover and entire piece, and are densely distributed within one unit image.

VI. Within one unit image, CO type pit mottles and other traces are densely distributed across the glaze surface and there is no clear delineation between them. They lack clear delineation from the surrounding glass phase.

VII. The image as a whole is coarsely muddled.

d. Three-Dimensional Characteristics of Forged Article

I. In general the glaze surface does not have CO striae, or the CO shape is unclear.

II. The three-dimensionally observable CO type pit mottle surface area is the same or larger than the two-dimensional view. The observably larger pits have rough surfaces and fuzzy edges that disperse across the glaze surface.

III. Within one unit image, all CO type pit mottles have similar corrosion on the protrusion as well as base of the mottle, there is no weathering regularity to speak of.

IV. Within one unit image, areas of relatively smooth glaze surface present with randomly dispersed pits and scrapes with fuzzy edges and a dispersive feel. Some present as coarsely dispersed small dots, some larger pits have an internal surface that is coarse.

V. Within one unit image, CO type pit mottles and other traces are densely distributed across the glaze surface and there is no clear delineation between them. They lack clear delineation from the surrounding glass phase (glaze surface).

VI. Some glass phase lacks aged feel, and presents with pristine smoothness.

VII. Some glass phase, as a whole, is coarsely muddled.

See pictures 8-1-21 and 8-1-22, where 8-1-21 is the two-dimensional and 8-1-22 is the three-dimensional view of the same location (this piece has undergone treatment with aging reagent).

Mottle A' in picture 8-1-21 is visibly larger in picture 8-1-22. The mottle edges are fuzzy and dispersive, lacking clear distinction from the surrounding glass phase.

The pit mottles in picture 8-1-22 have equally corroded protrusions and bases without and weathering regularity (see Arrow B' and Arrow C'). Additionally, the relatively flat areas of the glaze surface also present with random coarsely dispersed pits.

中只见C形纹及一处三维成像面积小于二维的深色斑块（见箭头B、C所指处），C形纹纹路纤细、收敛、清晰，斑块收敛，无扩张感。C形纹以及深色斑块均与玻璃相界线分明。

周围玻璃相上还有其他各自独立清晰的CO型坑点斑，均为根部风化程度较顶部高，颜色比顶部深，彼此界线清晰，玻璃相其余地方干净清晰。

图8-1-14中的玻璃相上布满细密的风化纹路，有明显陈旧感。

见图8-1-15、图8-1-16，二者为同一器物同一位置图片，图8-1-15为二维图片，图8-1-16为三维图片。

图8-1-15中箭头D所指的CO型连环坑点斑群，其三维成像面积小于其在图8-1-16中的二维面积，周围玻璃相上还有其他各自独立清晰的CO型坑点斑，均出现在釉表面凸起处，根部风化程度较顶部高，颜色比顶部深，斑块收敛，无扩张感，界线清晰。玻璃相其余地方干净清晰。

3. 赝品二维特征

见图8-1-17—图8-1-20。（该器物釉表面曾被腐蚀剂腐蚀）

（1）单位图片中CO型坑点斑大小及深浅差异不大，比较一致。

（2）CO型坑点斑颜色单一，通常与CO纹一致，二者界线不清晰分明，伴生关系不清晰。

（3）CO型坑点斑边沿起毛刺，形貌杂乱、模糊不清。

（4）CO型坑点斑通常反光更甚，比较刺眼。

（5）CO型坑点斑通常遍布整器，而且在单位图片中分布密集。

（6）单位图片中CO型坑点斑与其他迹型种类分布密集，彼此界线不分明，与周围的玻璃相界线也不清晰。

（7）图片整体模糊不清，凌乱涂污。

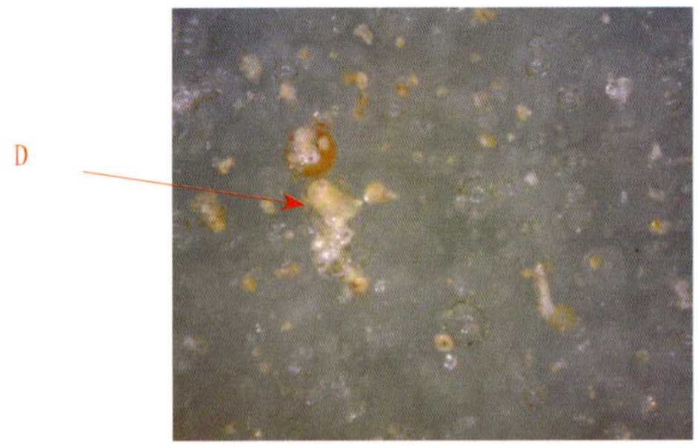

图8-1-15

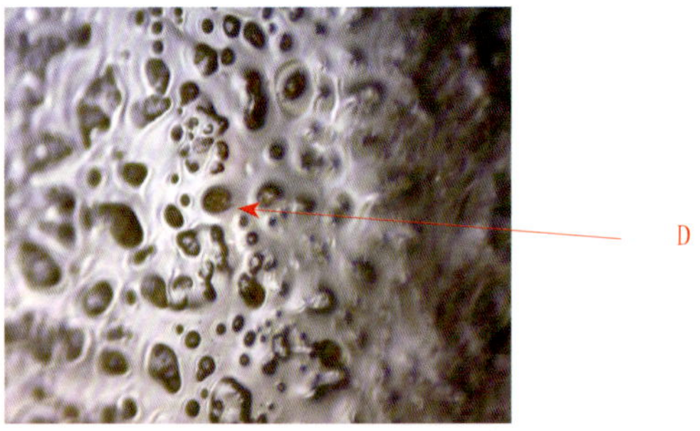

图8-1-16

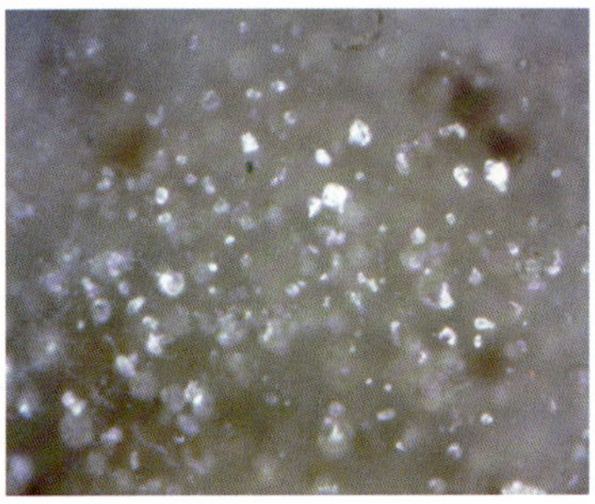

图8-1-17

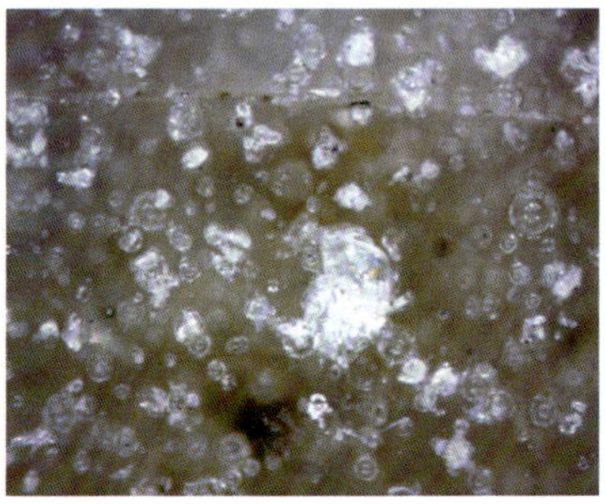

图8-1-18

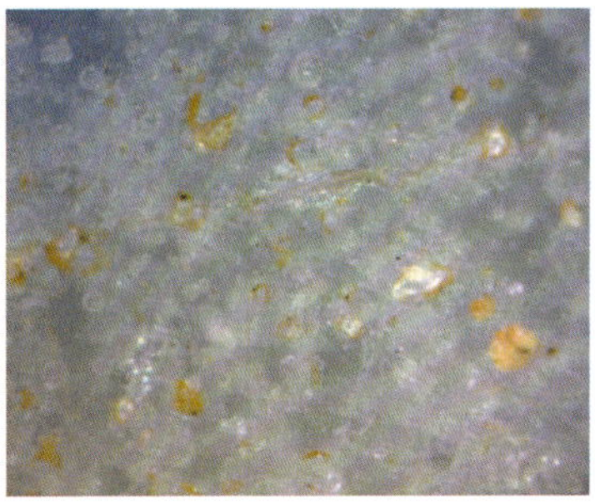

图8-1-19

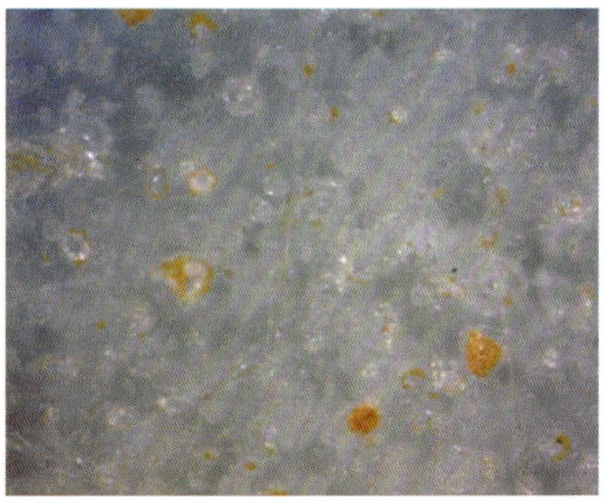

图8-1-20

The glaze surface lacks an aged feel, but instead is generally coarse and muddled in appearance.

See pictures 8-1-23 and 8-1-24, where 8-1-23 is the two-dimensional and 8-1-24 is the three-dimensional view of the same location (this piece has undergone treatment with aging reagent).

Pit mottle D' in picture 8-1-24 appears larger than the two-dimensional pit in picture 8-1-23.

The glaze surface is thoroughly damaged with coarsely dispersed pit mottles and scrapes with a relatively large surface area and fuzzy dispersive edges that lack clear distinction from the surrounding glass phase. The glaze surface lacks an aged feel, and as a whole, is coarsely muddled.

2. Floccus Mottles

A. Two-Dimensional Characteristics of Genuine Article

See pictures 8-1-25 and 8-1-26.

a. Floccus mottles are primarily white in coloration, presenting in all different sizes.

b. Floccus mottling usually occurs in areas of structural instability or damage on the glaze surface; such as in conjunction with scratches (see picture 8-1-27) and glaze cracks (see picture 8-1-28); and disperse down into the glaze level.

c. Beneath cracks, mottling can have various widths and densities.

d. The center of the mottle is non-transparent and milky white, and the edges feather out similar to goose down.

B. Three-Dimensional Characteristics of Genuine Article

a. Floccus mottling is not visible on the surface of the glaze, only the entry point on the glaze surface is visible (i.e. pitting, crack, etc.). The three-dimensional surface area of the entry point is much smaller than the underlying flaw and floccus mottles observable with two-dimensional imaging.

b. The glass phase surrounding the entry point remains clean and smooth, without any other visibly large surface flaws.

c. Some glass phase retains a clean clarity.

d. Some glass phase presents with a clear aged feel.

See pictures 8-1-27 and 8-1-28, where 8-1-27 is the two-dimensional and 8-1-28 is the three-dimensional view of the same location.

The floccus mottle indicated by Arrow A in picture 8-1-27 is not visible in picture 8-1-28. Only a glaze crack is visible, making it clear that the floccus mottling is within the glaze level. Aside from the crack, there is no visible damage to the glaze surface, and the glass phase is relatively clean and clear.

C. Two-Dimensional Characteristics of Forged Article

See pictures 8-1-29—8-1-32 (this piece has undergone treatment with aging reagent).

a. Aside from white coloration, the mottle presents with yellow as well, clearly indicating human dyeing (see pictures 8-1-29—8-1-31).

b. The mottle present in a grainy manner lacking density gradation and downward dispersion from glaze damage.

c. Mottling also occurs in areas of no glaze damage (see pictures 8-1-30—8-1-32).

d. Mottling can occur across an entire piece, lacking any regularity.

D. Three-Dimensional Characteristics of Forged Article

a. Mottles not only present within the glaze level, but across the glaze surface.

b. They are innately formed crystallization mottles, and not caused by natural weathering.

See pictures 8-1-33 and 8-1-34, where 8-1-33 is the two-dimensional and 8-1-34 is the three-dimensional view of the same location.

The mottle demarked by Arrow A' in picture 8-1-33 is

4. 赝品三维特征

（1）釉表面难以观察到CO纹或CO纹不清晰。

（2）CO型坑点斑三维成像的面积通常大于或等于二维，面积较大的坑点斑可见粗糙的表面，边沿粗糲，呈毛刺状，有扩张感。

（3）单位图片中出现的所有CO型坑点斑，顶部及根部都出现腐蚀现象，没有规律可言。

（4）单位图片内，釉表面较平的地方多处随机出现坑点斑及划痕，边沿粗糲，呈毛刺状，有扩张感。有的坑点斑似小麻点杂乱分布，面积较大的可见底部粗糙。

（5）单位图片中CO型坑点斑与其他迹型种类分布密集，彼此界线不分明，与周围的玻璃相界线也不清晰。

（6）有的玻璃相呈现新瓷光滑，无陈旧感。

（7）有的玻璃相整体显得粗糙涂污。

见图8-1-21、图8-1-22，二者为同一器物同一位置图片，图8-1-21为二维图片，图8-1-22为三维图片。（该器物釉表面曾被腐蚀剂腐蚀）

图8-1-21中箭头A’所指坑点斑在图8-1-22中的三维成像的面积大于二维，坑点斑三维成像边沿粗糲，呈毛刺状，有扩张感，与周围玻璃相界线不分明。

图8-1-22中的CO型坑点斑，顶部及根部都出现腐蚀现象，没有规律可言（见箭头B’和C’所指处）。而且釉表面较平的地方也随机出现不规则坑点斑，坑点斑杂乱分布。

周围釉表面无陈旧感，整体显得粗糙涂污。

见图8-1-23、图8-1-24，二者为同一器物同一位置图片，图8-1-23为二维图片，图8-1-24为三维图片。（该器物釉表面曾被腐蚀剂腐蚀）

图8-1-24中坑点斑D’的三维成像面积大于图8-1-23中的二维面积。

周围釉表面破坏严重，杂乱无章地分布着坑点斑、划痕，面积都比较大，表面粗糙，边沿粗糲，呈毛刺状，有扩张感，与周围玻璃相界线不分明。未被破坏的玻璃相无陈旧感。釉表面整体显得粗糙涂污。

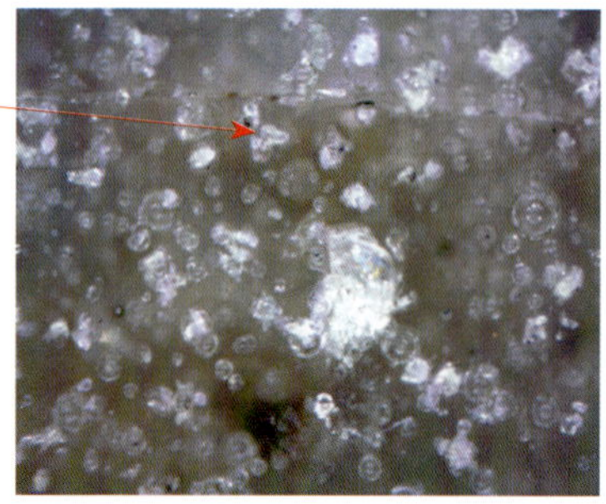

图8-1-21

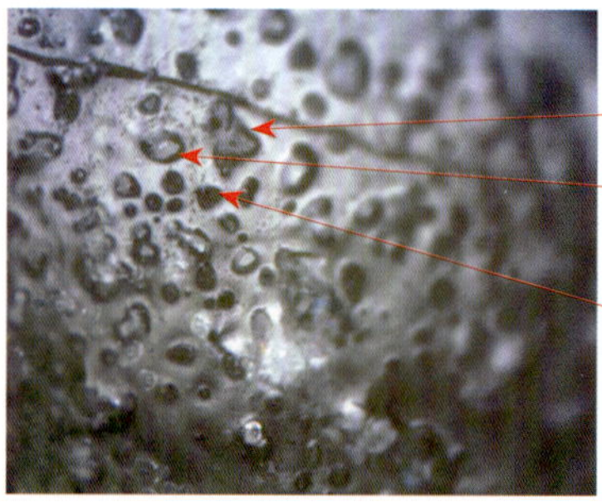

图8-1-22

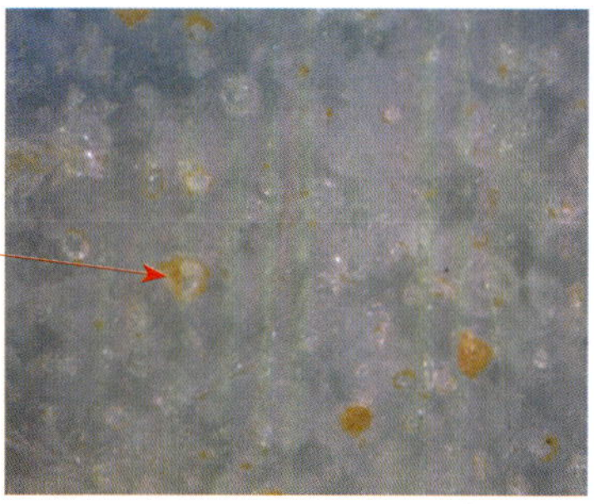

图8-1-23

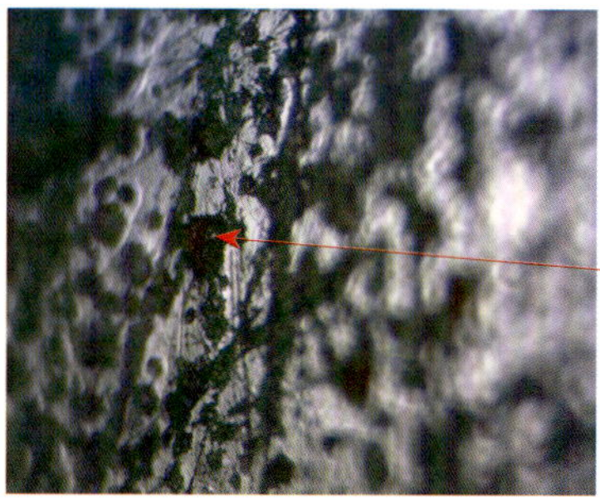

图8-1-24

clearly visible on the surface of the glaze in picture 8-1-34, and is not a true floccus mottle. The mottle is granular without density gradation and does not disperse down and outward from an area of glaze damage.

See pictures 8-1-35 and 8-1-36, where 8-1-35 is the two-dimensional and 8-1-36 is the three-dimensional view of the same location.

The mottle in picture 8-1-35 is located on the glaze surface, and is not a true floccus mottle. The area of mottling lacks any clear glaze damage.

二、絮状斑

（一）真品二维特征

见图8-1-25、图8-1-26。

1. 絮状斑以白色为主，大小不一。

2. 絮状斑一般在釉层组织结构稳定性较差处或破损处出现，如划痕下（见图8-1-27）、釉裂纹下（见图8-1-28），由釉损处呈梯度向周边的釉下扩散。

3. 釉裂纹下的絮状斑宽窄不一，浓淡有别。

4. 絮状斑中心色白如牛奶，不透明；斑块边沿呈绒状，半透明，有向四周蔓延的趋势。

（二）真品三维特征

1. 絮状斑在釉表面不可见，釉表面釉损处（如坑点斑、釉裂纹）的三维面积远远小于釉损处与絮状斑二维成像面积的总和。

2. 釉表面釉损处以外的地方无其他明显的大面积损伤。

3. 有的玻璃相干净清晰。

4. 有的玻璃相有明显陈旧感。

见图8-1-27、图8-1-28，二者为同一器物同一位置图片，图8-1-27为二维图片，图8-1-28为三维图片。

图8-1-27中的白色絮状斑在图8-1-28中难以观察到，釉表面只见釉裂纹，说明絮状斑存在于釉层中（见箭头A所指处）。釉表面无其他明显的大面积损伤，玻璃相比较干净清晰。

（三）赝品二维特征

见图8-1-29—图8-1-32。（该器物釉表面曾被腐蚀剂腐蚀）

1. “絮状斑”除白色外，还呈现黄色，人为染色痕迹明显（见图8-1-29—图8-1-31）。

2. “絮状斑”呈颗粒状，没有

图8-1-25

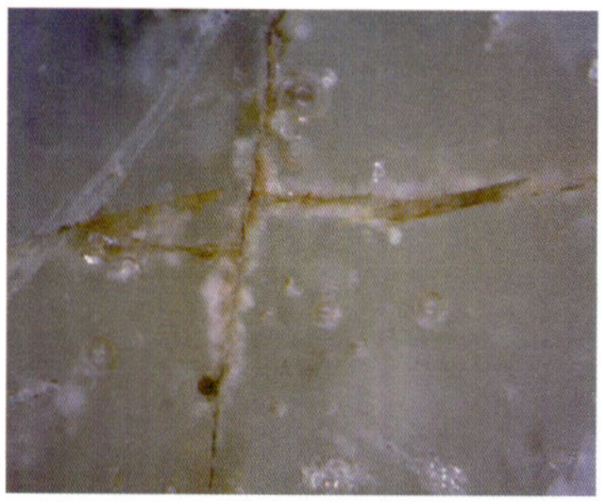

图8-1-26

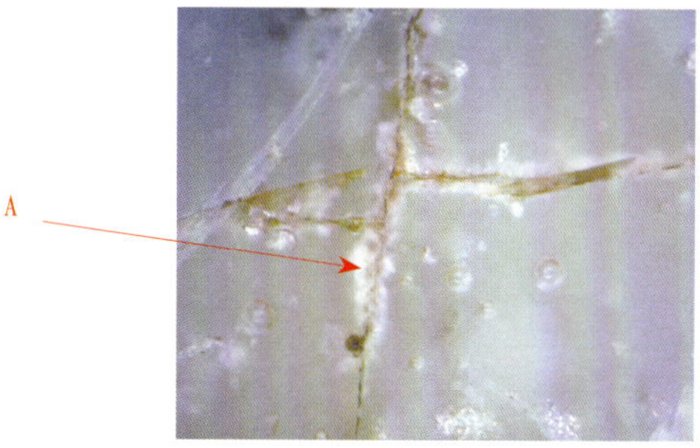

图8-1-27

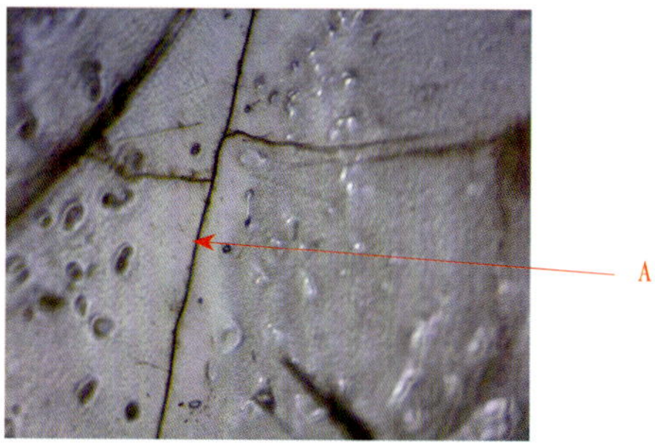

图8-1-28

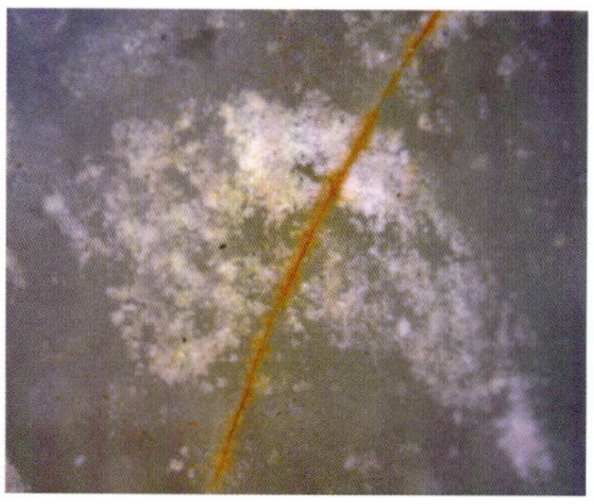

图8-1-29

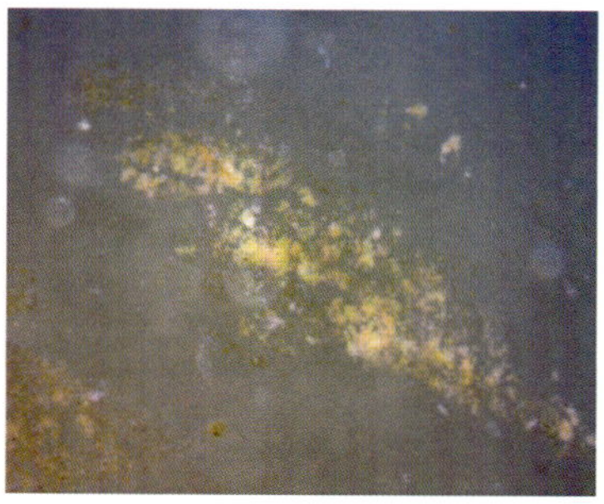

图8-1-30

浓淡过渡，没有沿着釉损处呈梯度向四周蔓延的趋势。

3.“絮状斑”在非釉损处也出现（见图8-1-30、图8-1-32）。

4.“絮状斑”整器都是，出现毫无规律。

（四）赝品三维特征

1. 所谓的“絮状斑”不仅存在于釉层中，也在釉表面。

2. 属于先天性的析晶斑块，而非后天风化形成。

见图8-1-33、图8-1-34，二者为同一器物同一位置图片，图8-1-33为二维图片，图8-1-34为三维图片。

图8-1-33中箭头A’所指的“絮状斑”在图8-1-34中位于釉表面，并非真正的絮状斑。斑块呈颗粒状，没有浓淡过渡，也并非沿着釉损处（釉裂纹）呈梯度蔓延。

见图8-1-35、图8-1-36，二者为同一器物同一位置图片，图8-1-35为二维图片，图8-1-36为三维图片。

图8-1-35中的“絮状斑”呈颗粒状，位于釉表面，并非真正的絮状斑。斑块所在处釉表面并无其他明显损伤。

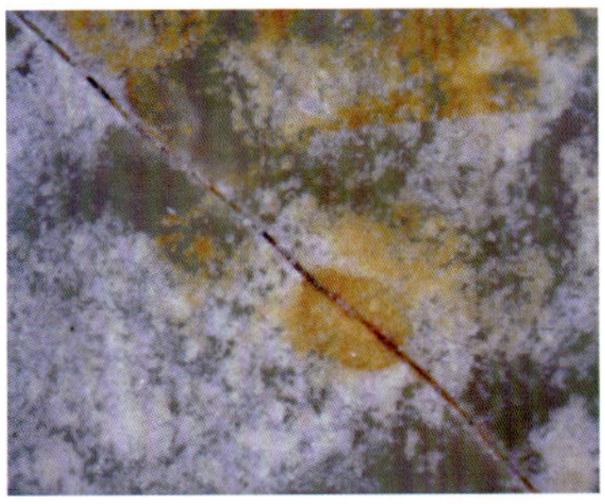

图8-1-31

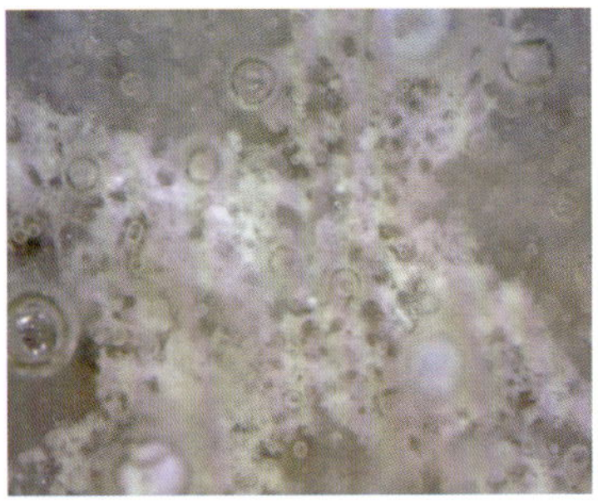

图8-1-32

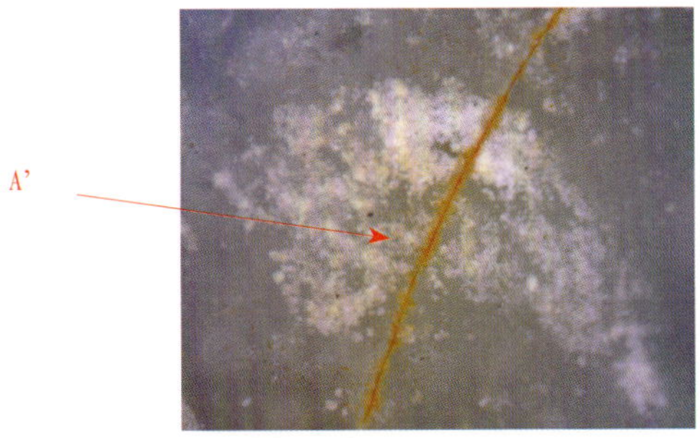

图8-1-33

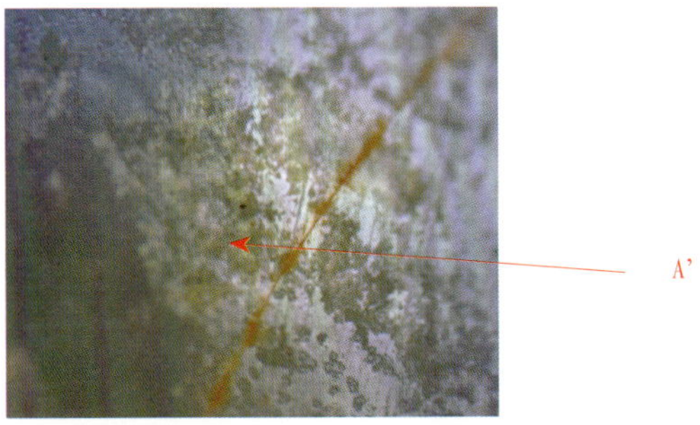

图8-1-34

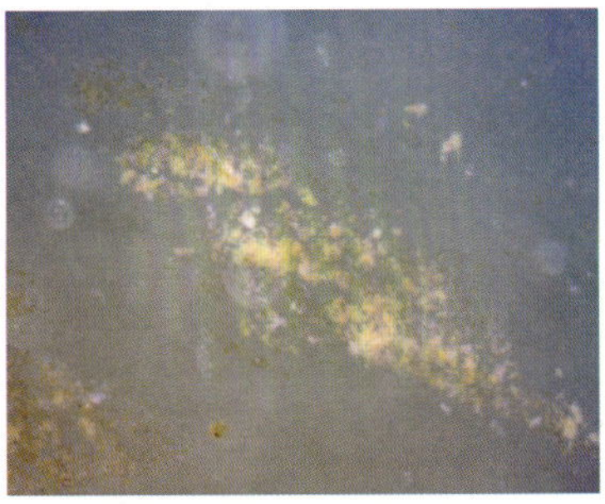

图8-1-35

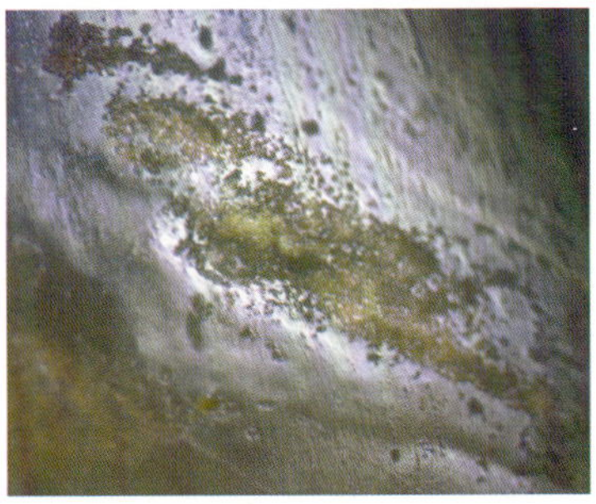

图8-1-36

第二节

龙泉窑系青瓷纹路真品与赝品比对分析

一、C形纹、O形纹

（一）真品二维特征

1.C形纹、O形纹（以下简称CO纹）纹路清晰，有的纤细，有的较粗，有的在同一条纹路上有粗细变化（见图8-2-1—图8-2-13）。

2.有的单项CO纹有色阶变化，单位图片内邻近的CO纹有色差（见图8-2-4—图8-2-6）。

3.有时有两条C形纹紧挨邻近，各自独立清晰，界线分明（见图8-2-7、图8-2-8）。

4.单位图片内，CO纹通常分布稀疏，密集分布较少（见图8-2-1—图8-2-11）。

5.有的沿着CO纹轮廓向外有呈白雾状蔓延的趋势，与呈现黄色的CO纹形成对比（见图8-2-9—图8-2-14）。

6.单位图片中，CO纹与CO型坑点斑或连环坑点斑群同时存在，各自独立清晰，彼此界线分明（见图8-2-12、图8-2-13）。

7.CO纹与周围玻璃相或其他迹型种类界线分明（见图8-2-1—图8-2-14）。

8.周围的玻璃相干净清晰（见图8-2-1—图8-2-14）。

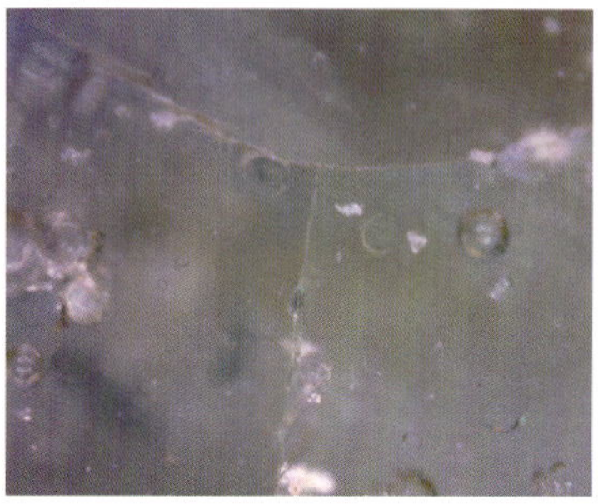
图8-2-1

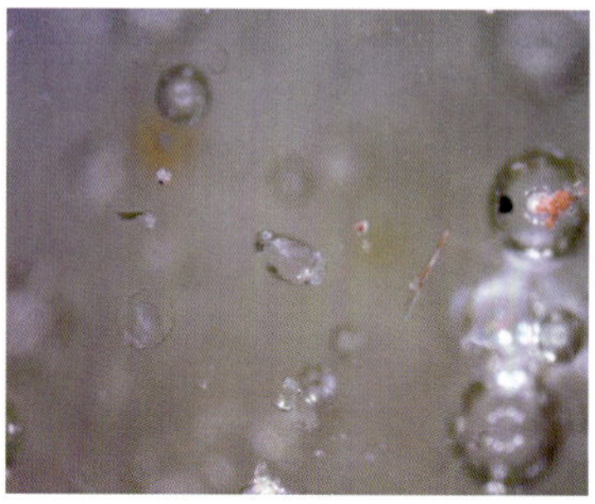
图8-2-2

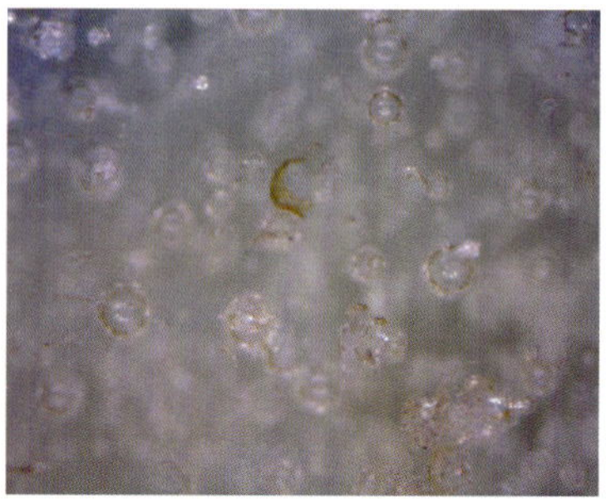
图8-2-3

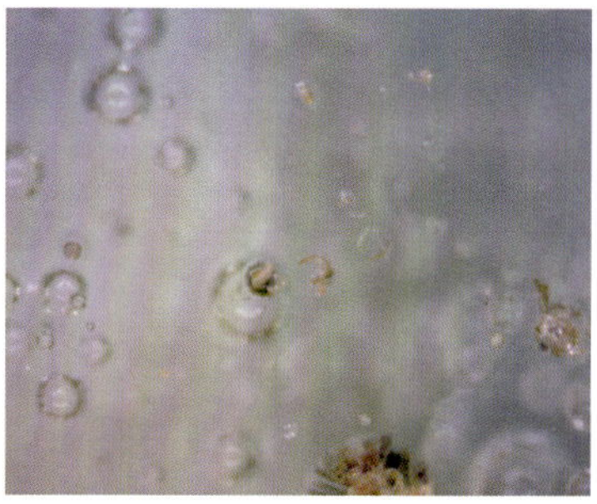
图8-2-4

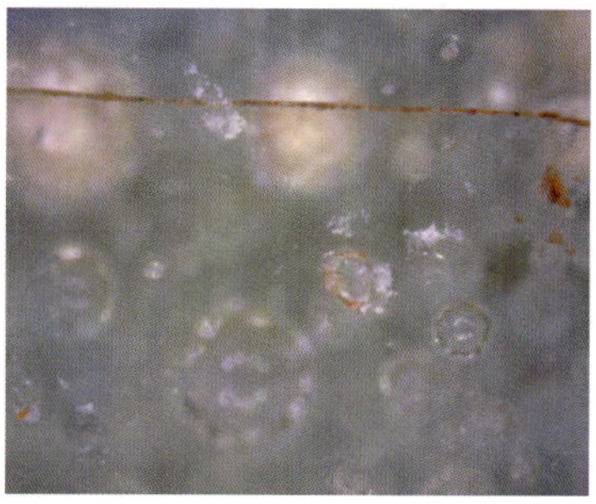
图8-2-5

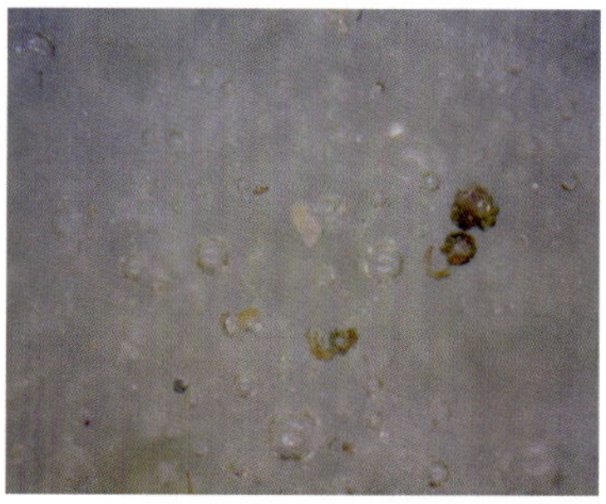
图8-2-6

Section 2:

Genuine and Forged Longquan Kiln System Celadon Striae Comparison

1. C and O Shaped Striae

A. Two-Dimensional Characteristics of Genuine Article

a. C and O shaped striae (CO Striae) present clearly, some can present with varying widths (see pictures 8-2-1—8-2-13).

b. A single striation can present with a color spectrum, and color disparity between different striae within one unit image is common (see pictures 8-2-4—8-2-6).

c. At times, two C shaped striae can occur in conjunction with one another, they are independent and clearly delineated (see pictures 8-2-7 and 8-2-8).

d. Within one unit image, CO striae are generally sparsely distributed, dense distribution is uncommon (see pictures 8-2-1—8-2-11).

e. Some CO striae can have white foggy coloration extending into the surrounding glaze level, creating a contrast with the yellow CO striae (see pictures 8-2-9—8-2-14).

f. A unit image can present with CO type pit mottles, CO striae, and CO pit groups. They are independent and mutually delineated (see pictures 8-2-12 and 8-2-13).

g. CO striae retain clear delineation from the surrounding glass phase and other traces (see pictures 8-2-1—8-2-14).

h. The surrounding glass phase is clean and clear (see pictures 8-2-1—8-2-14).

B. Three-Dimensional Characteristics of Genuine Article

a. CO striae generally occur in areas of raised glaze surface.

b. Only finely reserved CO striae are present on the glaze surface, they are clear and independent.

c. CO striae that have white foggy coloration extending from the striae visible two-dimensionally, present as finely reserved CO striae, and mottles are not present on the glaze surface three-dimensionally. The surface area of visible CO striation is much smaller than that of the two-dimensionally visible striation and mottle. They are mutually delineated, and the mottle is reserved and lacking dispersive qualities.

d. CO striae retain clear delineation from the surrounding glass phase and other traces.

e. Some of the glass phase is clean and clear.

f. Some of the glass phase presents with an aged feel.

See pictures 8-2-15 and 8-2-16, where 8-2-15 is the two-dimensional and 8-2-16 is the three-dimensional view of the same location.

The C striation indicated by Arrow A in picture 8-2-15 presents clearly as a dark thin line, and is more reserved in picture 8-2-16. It is clearly delineated from the surrounding glass phase. The glaze surface surrounding the striation also presents multiple forms of clearly independent scratches and densely distributed weathered striae. It has a relatively evident aged feel.

See pictures 8-2-17 and 8-2-18, where 8-2-17 is the two-dimensional and 8-2-18 is the three-dimensional view of the

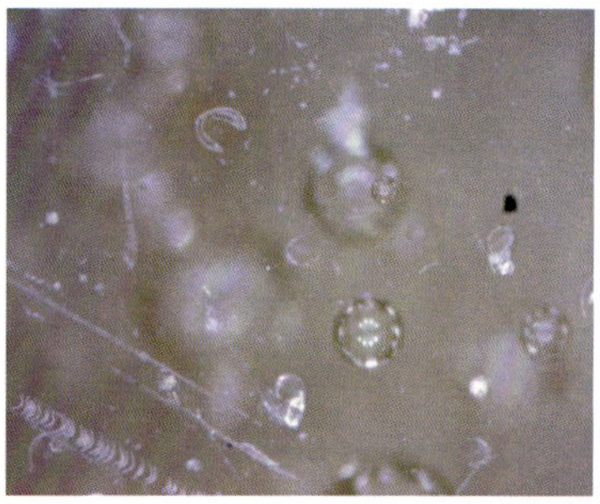

图8-2-7

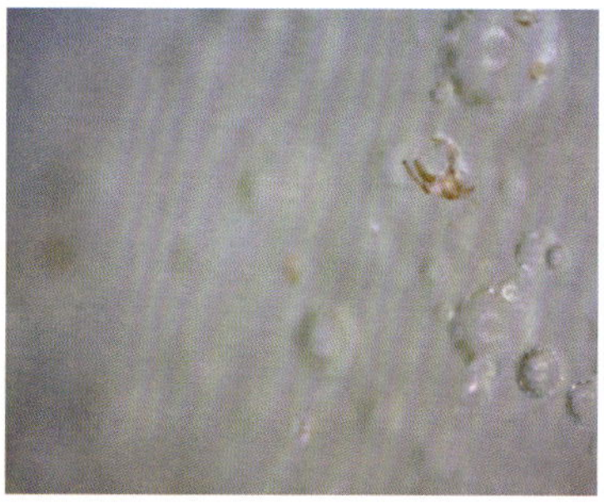

图8-2-8

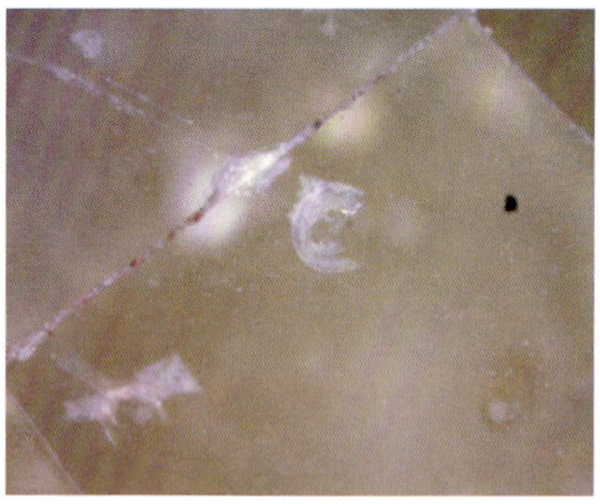

图8-2-9

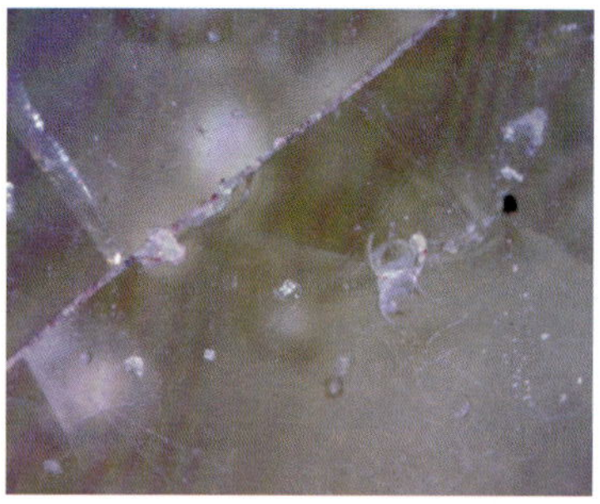

图8-2-10

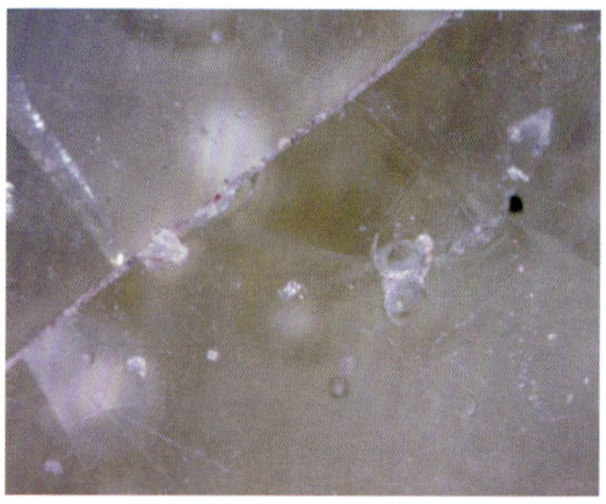

图8-2-11

图8-2-12

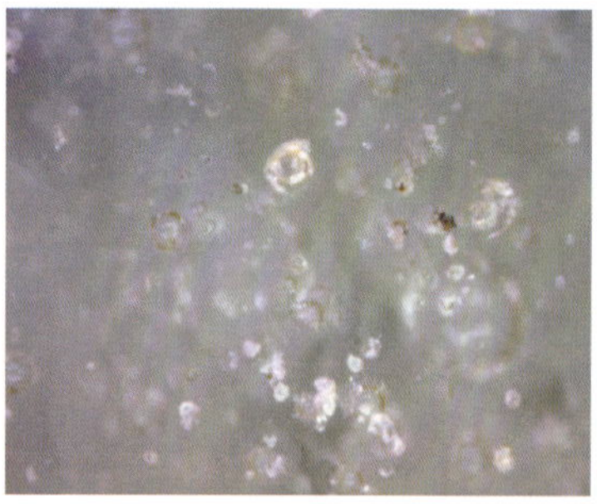

图8-2-13

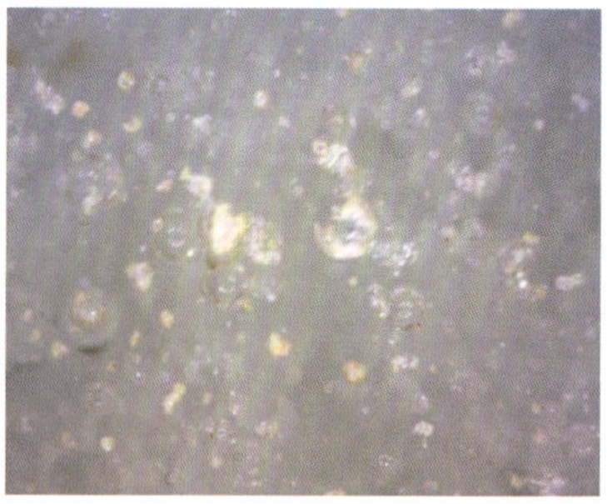

图8-2-14

（二）真品三维特征

1. CO纹大都分布在釉表面凸起处。

2. CO纹所在处釉表面只见纤细收敛的C形纹或O形纹，清晰独立。

3. 二维成像有白雾状蔓延的CO纹，其所在处釉表面三维成像通常只见纤细收敛的C形纹或O形纹，以及面积小于或等于二维面积的风化斑块，斑块收敛，无扩张感，彼此界线分明。

4. CO纹与周围玻璃相界线或其他迹型种类界线分明。

5. 有的玻璃相干净清晰。

6. 有的玻璃相表现出明显陈旧感。

见图8-2-15、图8-2-16，二者为同一器物同一位置图片，图8-2-15为二维图片，图8-2-16为三维图片。

图8-2-15中箭头A所指的C形纹在图8-2-16中分布在釉表面凸起处，成像清晰，而且纹路三维成像更纤细收敛，与周围玻璃相界线分明。周围玻璃相除C形纹外还有独立清晰、形貌各异的划痕，彼此界线分明。玻璃相其余地方布满细密的风化纹路，有比较明显的陈旧感。

见图8-2-17、图8-2-18，二者为同一器物同一位置图片，图8-2-17为二维图片，图8-2-18为三维图片。

图8-2-17中箭头B所指的C形纹在图8-2-18中分布在釉表面凸起处，末端可见分叉，纹路三维成像更纤细收敛，还有三维成像面积小于二维的风化斑块，斑块收敛，无扩张感，彼此界线分明。周围玻璃相除C形纹外还有独立清晰的坑点斑和划痕，彼此界线分明。玻璃相其余地方干净清晰。

见图8-2-19、图8-2-20，二者为同一器物同一位置图片，图8-2-

same location.

The C striation indicated by Arrow B in picture 8-2-17 appears in areas of glaze protrusions. Its end is forked. The tip of the striation presents with clear splitting and is more fine and reserved in picture 8-2-18. The three-dimensional visibility of the striation and mottle is smaller than the two-dimensional; the mottle is reserved and lacking dispersive qualities. Aside from the C striation, there are also independent pits and scratches, all clearly delineated. The rest of the glass phase is clean and clear.

See pictures 8-2-19 and 8-2-20, where 8-2-19 is the two-dimensional and 8-2-20 is the three-dimensional view of the same location.

The C striation in picture 8-2-19 has white foggy coloration extending down into the surrounding glaze level, but appears in picture 8-2-20 as fine and reserved, clearly independent C shaped striae (see Arrow C). It has clear delineation from the surrounding glass phase, and the rest of the glass phase is clean and clear.

There are also independent pits, lacking dispersive qualities, all clearly delineated. The rest of the glass phase is clean and clear.

See pictures 8-2-21 and 8-2-22, where 8-2-21 is the two-dimensional and 8-2-22 is the three-dimensional view of the same location.

The C striation in picture 8-2-21 has white foggy coloration extending down into the surrounding glaze level, but appears in picture 8-2-22 as two fine and reserved, clearly independent C shaped striae (see Arrow D). It has clear delineation from the surrounding glass phase.

Aside from the C striation, there are also independent pits and scratches, lacking dispersive qualities, all clearly delineated. The glass phase presents with densely distributed weathered striae and a relatively evident aged feel.

C. Two-Dimensional Characteristics of Forged Article

See pictures 8-2-23—8-2-26 (this piece has undergone treatment with an aging reagent).

a. CO striae are uniform, lacking clear width discrepancy.

b. The striae can present with fuzzy edges, and dispersive nature.

c. The coloration is uniform, and lacks color spectrum or disparity.

d. CO striae are densely distributed within one unit image.

e. There is no white foggy coloration extending down into the surrounding glaze level.

f. CO striae have no clear delineation from the surrounding glass phase and other traces.

g. The glaze surface as a whole is generally muddled.

D. Three-Dimensional Characteristics of Forged Article

a. In general the glaze surface does not have CO striae, or the CO shape is unclear.

b. The three-dimensionally observable CO striae surfaces area are usually the same or larger than the two-dimensional view. They usually have fuzzy edges that disperse onto the glaze surface.

c. Within one unit image, areas of relatively smooth glaze surface present with randomly dispersed pits and scrapes with fuzzy edges and a dispersive feel. Some present as coarsely dispersed small dots, some larger pits have an internal surface that is coarse.

d. Within one unit image, CO type pit mottles and other traces are densely distributed across the glaze surface and there is no clear delineation between them. They lack clear delineation from the surrounding glass phase.

e. Most glaze surfaces lack aged feel, and some present with pristine smoothness.

f. Some pieces have a glass phase that, as a whole, is coarsely muddled.

See pictures 8-2-27 and 8-2-28, where 8-2-27 is the two-dimensional and 8-2-28 is the three-dimensional view of the same location (this piece has undergone treatment with an aging reagent).

The three-dimensional view of the striation (indicated by Arrow A') is much thicker than the two-dimensional view,

19为二维图片，图8-2-20为三维图片。

图8-2-19中的C形纹二维成像有呈白雾状蔓延的趋势，其在图8-2-20中的三维成像为纤细收敛、清晰独立的C形纹（见箭头C所指处），与周围玻璃相也界线分明。

周围玻璃相上还有其他各自独立清晰的坑点斑，斑块收敛，彼此界线清晰，玻璃相其余地方干净清晰。

见图8-2-21、图8-2-22，二者为同一器物同一位置图片，图8-2-21为二维图片，图8-2-22为三维图片。

图8-2-21中的C形纹二维成像有呈白雾状蔓延的趋势，其在图8-2-22中的三维成像为两条纤细收敛、清晰独立的C形纹（见箭头D所指处），与周围玻璃相也界线分明。

周围玻璃相上还有其他各自独立清晰的坑点斑及划痕，斑块收敛，彼此界线清晰，玻璃相其余地方布满细密的风化纹路，有比较明显的陈旧感。

（三）赝品二维特征

见图8-2-23—图8-2-26。（该器物釉表面曾被腐蚀剂腐蚀）

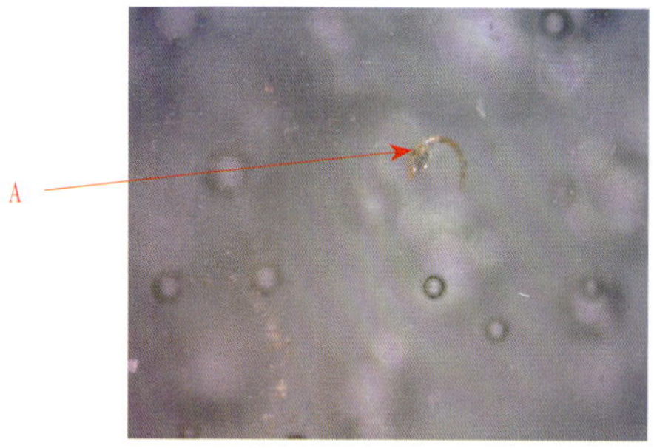

图8-2-15

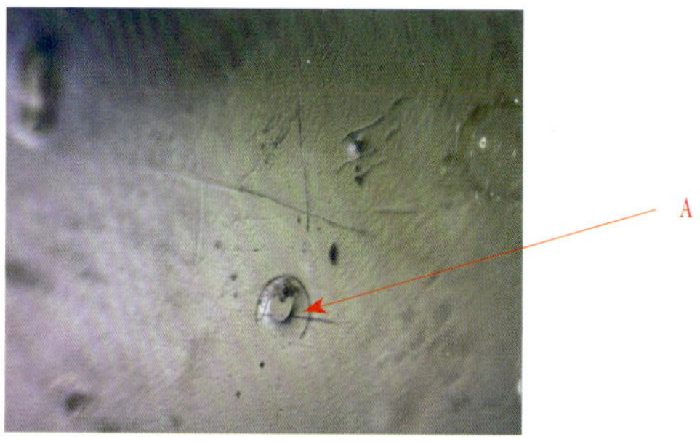

图8-2-16

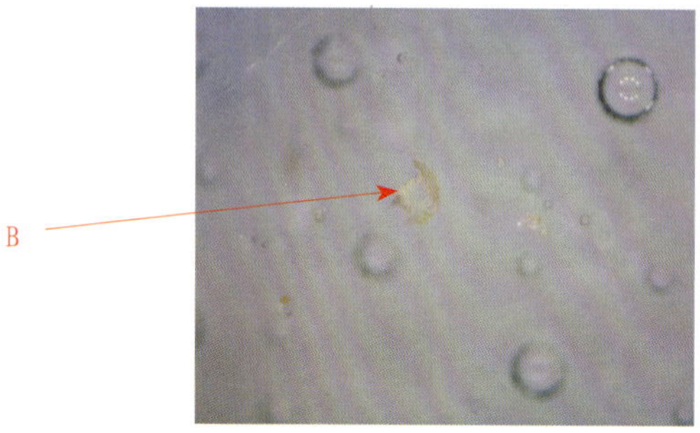

图8-2-17

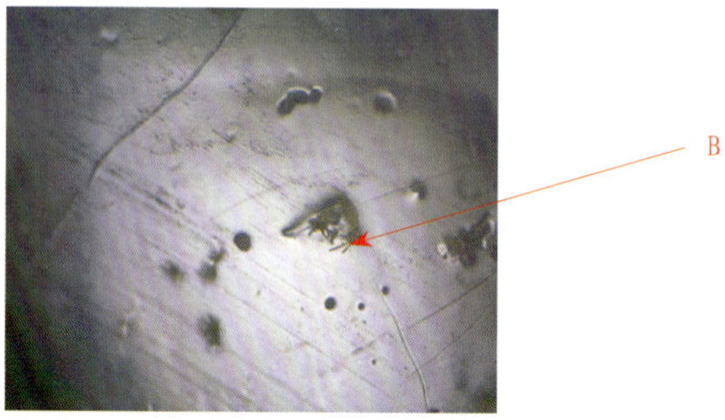

图8-2-18

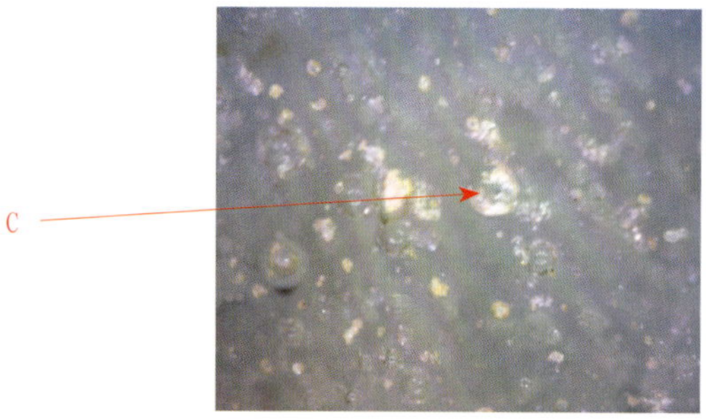

图8-2-19

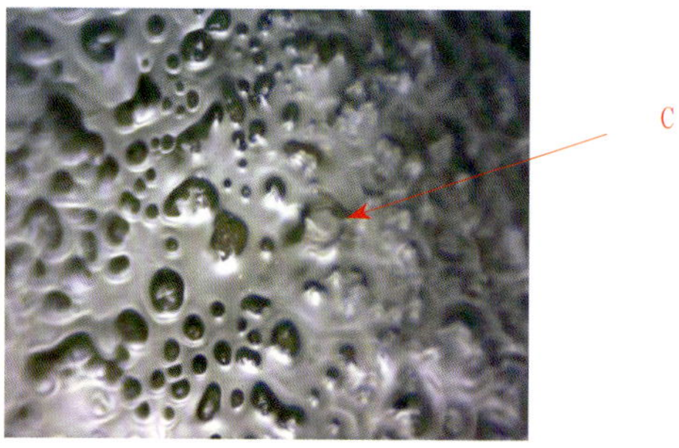

图8-2-20

and generally coarse. Striation A' has fuzzy dispersive edges.

In picture 8-2-28, all CO striae have similar corrosion on the glaze protrusions as well as base of the mottle; there is no weathering regularity to speak of. The striae also have fuzzy dispersive edges.

The glaze surface lacks an aged feel, but instead is generally coarse and muddled in appearance.

See pictures 8-2-29 and 8-2-30, where 8-2-29 is the two-dimensional and 8-2-30 is the three-dimensional view of the same location (this piece has undergone treatment with an aging reagent).

The CO striae visible in picture 8-2-29 are not clearly visible in image 8-2-30. The entire glaze surface is coarsely damaged with general pitting and unidirectional scratches. The traces are dispersive and the glaze level as a whole is coarse and muddled.

See pictures 8-2-31 and 8-2-32, where 8-2-31 is the two-dimensional and 8-2-32 is the three-dimensional view of the same location (this piece has undergone treatment with an aging reagent).

The CO striation indicated by Arrow B' in picture 8-2-31 is visibly larger in picture 8-2-32 and presents amongst a large area of corroded glaze pitting.

The glaze level damage is severe, with sporadically disbursed pits and scratches that all are relatively large with coarse fuzzy edges that are dispersive and lack clear delineation from the surrounding glass phase. The undamaged glaze surface lacks an aged feel, and is generally coarse and muddled.

2. Glaze Cracks

A. Two-Dimensional Characteristics of Genuine Article

a. Within a single unit image, a glaze crack can present with different colorations (see pictures 8-2-33—8-2-36).

b. Within a single unit image, neighboring glaze cracks can present with different colorations (see picture 8-2-36).

c. Within a single unit image, glaze cracks can have different coloration from the coloration of the surrounding glaze (see picture 8-2-36).

d. Within a single unit image, glaze cracks and surrounding pit mottles can have color disparity (see picture 8-2-37).

e. White foggy coloration dispersing downward into the surrounding glaze level on either side of the glaze crack can occur, at times with coloration different to the glaze crack (see pictures 8-2-38 and 8-2-40).

f. Colored bubbles and texturized bubbles can occur beneath or around the glaze crack; the crack remaining uncolored or having color disparity from said bubble (see pictures 8-2-39—8-2-42).

g. It is possible to observe deposits within the interior of relatively wide cracks (see pictures 8-2-43 and 8-2-44).

h. Glaze cracks can occur in conjunction with floccus mottling, with color disparity between the two (see pictures 8-2-45 and 8-2-46).

B. Three-Dimensional Characteristics of Genuine Article

a. The three-dimensional visibility of glaze cracks are often smaller than two-dimensional.

b. Glaze cracks can occur in conjunction with needlepoint and pit mottling.

c. The edges of glaze cracks are rounded and smooth.

d. Glaze cracks retain clear delineation from the surrounding glass phase.

e. The surrounding glass phase is clean and clear.

f. Some of the surrounding glass phase presents with an aged feel.

See pictures 8-2-47 and 8-2-48, where 8-2-47 is the two-dimensional and 8-2-48 is the three-dimensional view of the same location.

The glaze cracks in picture 8-2-47 are clearly visible in picture 8-2-48. The cracks have varying width, but are all three-dimensionally smaller (see Arrow A). Glaze cracks retain clear delineation from the surrounding glass phase. The surrounding glass phase is clean and clear.

See pictures 8-2-49 and 8-2-50, both are three-

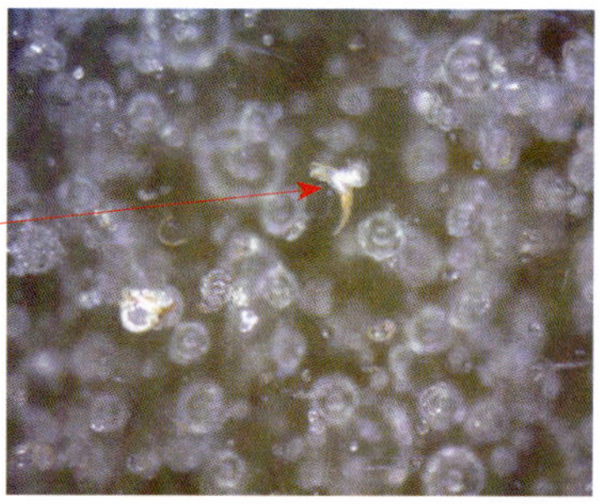

图8-2-21

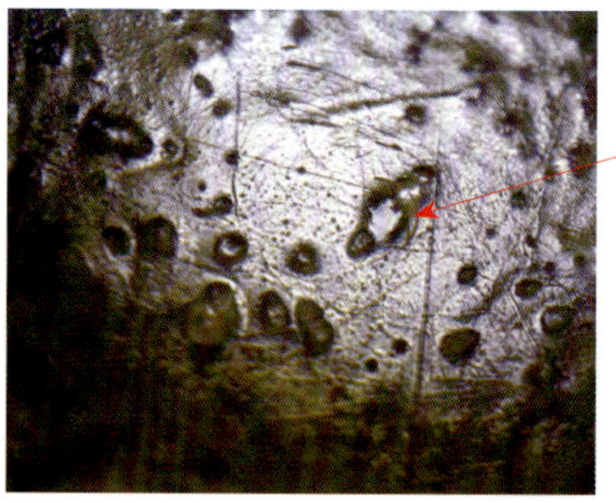

图8-2-22

1. CO纹形貌一致，粗细变化不明显。

2. CO纹边沿粗糙，有毛刺。

3. CO纹颜色一致，没有色阶或色差变化。

4. CO纹在单位图片中分布密集。

5. CO纹没有白雾状蔓延。

6. CO纹与玻璃相或其他迹型种类界线不清晰。

7. 图片整体模糊不清，凌乱涂污。

（四）赝品三维特征

1. 釉表面难以观察到CO纹或CO纹不清晰。

2. CO纹三维成像的面积通常大于或等于二维，大部分都边沿粗糙，呈毛刺状，有扩张感。

3. 单位图片内，釉表面较平的地方多处随机出现坑点斑及划痕，边沿粗糙，呈毛刺状，有扩张感。有的坑点斑似小麻点杂乱分布，面

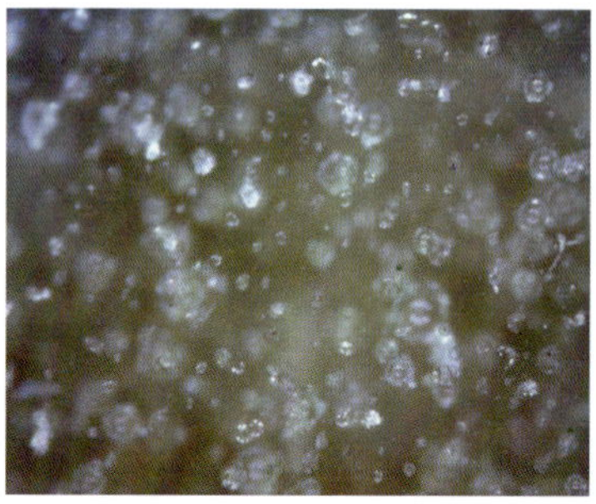

图8-2-23

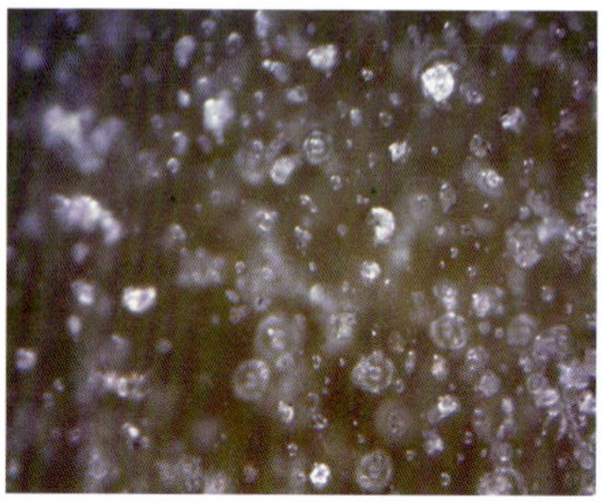

图8-2-24

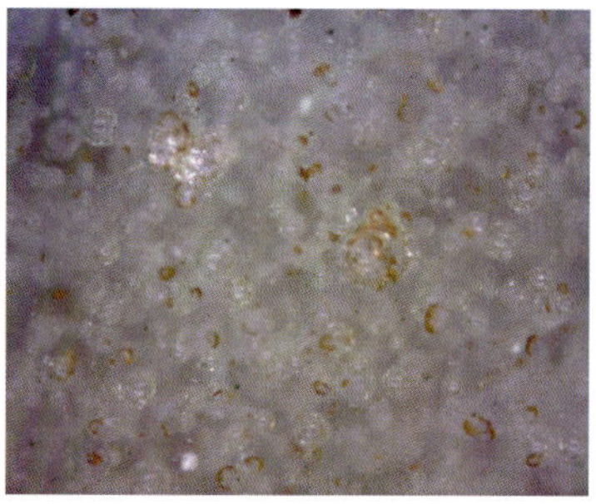

图8-2-25

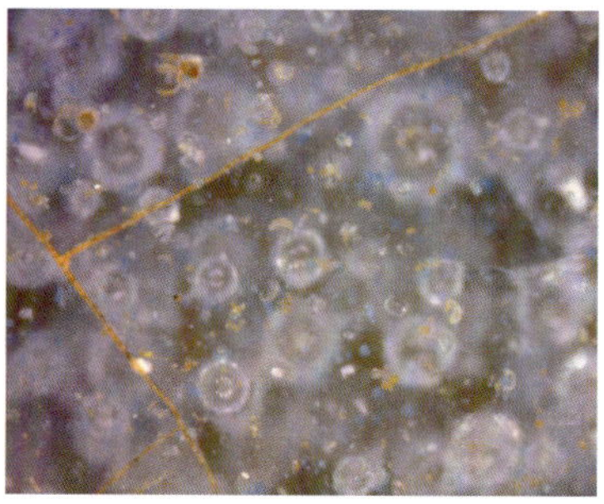

图8-2-26

dimensional pictures.

The glaze cracks in pictures 8-2-49 and 8-2-50 are three-dimensionally very clear, with rounded and smooth edges, clearly delineated from surrounding glass phase. The surrounding glass phase is mostly clean, with a distribution of short multidirectional scratches, the edges of which are also rounded and smooth. The rest of the glass phase presents with densely distributed weathered striae and a relatively evident aged feel.

C. Two-Dimensional Characteristics of Forged Article

See pictures 8-2-51—8-2-56 (this piece has undergone treatment with an aging reagent).

a. Often glaze cracks over an entire piece, and within a single unit image, lack width disparity

b. Coloration within a single unit image is uniform. Often an entire piece has uniformly colored glaze cracks.

c. On glaze cracks that have been intentionally dyed, the coloration is fuzzy and disperses into the surrounding glaze level (see picture 8-2-51).

d. Often on dyed pieces, one unit image presents with uniform coloration between the glaze crack and surrounding glaze level (see pictures 8-2-53 and 8-2-54).

e. The coloration of associated colored bubbles and the glaze crack are uniform (see pictures 8-2-55 and 8-2-56).

f. Because of dying, the glaze cracks have similar coloration with the surrounding crystalized mottles on the glaze surface (see picture 8-2-55).

g. The surrounding glaze level lacks white foggy coloration dispersing away from the glaze crack.

D. Three-Dimensional Characteristics of Forged Article

See pictures 8-2-57—8-2-59 (this piece has undergone treatment with an aging reagent).

a. As forged articles are relatively new, the glaze crack edges are relatively acute.

b. As the result of human forced aging, some glaze cracks have fuzzy edges, giving it a coarse appearance.

c. Most glaze surfaces lack an aged feel, and some present with pristine smoothness.

d. Some surrounding glaze surfaces have a random distribution of pitting; these pit edges are coarse, fuzzy, and dispersive.

3. Scratches

A. Two-Dimensional Characteristics of Genuine Article

a. Within one unit image, scratches can appear in varying widths, lengths, depths, directions, appearances, and colorations; their distribution can be sparse or dense (see pictures 8-2-60—8-2-74).

b. A single scratch can present with color variation (see pictures 8-2-60—8-2-64).

c. Scratches can present with white foggy coloration dispersing down into the glaze level (see pictures 8-2-64—8-2-74).

d. Relatively large scratches can present with needlepoint mottling on the interior, but not extending beyond the scratch edges (see pictures 8-2-65, 8-2-67—8-2-72).

e. Scratches retain clear delineation from the surrounding glass phase and other traces.

f. The surrounding glass phase is clean and clear.

B. Three-Dimensional Characteristics of Genuine Article

a. The scratch can present with uniform waves of indentions clearly appearing as 'centipede' feet, tiny multidirectional oxen hairs, relatively large surface intrusions, and so forth.

b. Relatively large and deep scratches can present with deposits on the interior.

c. Scratches with white foggy coloration extending down into the surrounding glaze level have a larger two-dimensional visibility than three-dimensional.

积较大的可见底部粗糙。

4. 单位图片中CO纹与其他迹型种类分布密集，彼此界线不分明，与周围的玻璃相界线也不清晰。

5. 有的玻璃相呈现新瓷光滑，无陈旧感。

6. 有的玻璃相整体显得粗糙涂污。

见图8-2-27、图8-2-28，二者为同一器物同一位置图片，图8-2-27为二维图片，图8-2-28为三维图片。（该器物釉表面曾被腐蚀剂腐蚀）

图8-2-27中箭头A'所指的CO纹，在图8-2-28中三维成像模糊，比二维成像要大，边沿粗粝，有扩张感。

图8-2-28中的CO型坑点斑，顶部及根部都出现腐蚀现象，没有规律可言，而且斑块边沿粗粝，呈毛刺状，有扩张感。

周围釉表面无陈旧感，整体显得粗糙涂污。

见图8-2-29、图8-2-30，二者为同一器物同一位置图片，图8-2-29为二维图片，图8-2-30为三维图片。（该器物釉表面曾被腐蚀剂腐蚀）

图8-2-29中的CO纹在图8-2-30中三维成像难以观察到，釉表面整体破坏严重，遍布坑点斑及方向一致的划痕，有扩张感，整体显得粗糙涂污。

见图8-2-31、图8-2-32，二者为同一器物同一位置图片，图8-2-31为二维图片，图8-2-32为三维图片。（该器物釉表面曾被腐蚀剂腐蚀）

图8-2-31中箭头B'所指的CO纹，在图8-2-32中三维成像的黄色纹路比二维成像要粗，且纹路所在处已被腐蚀成一大片坑点。

周围釉表面破坏严重，杂乱无章地分布着坑点斑、划痕，面积都比较大，表面粗糙，边沿粗粝，呈毛刺状，有扩张感，与周围玻璃相界线不分明。未被破坏的玻璃相无陈旧感。釉表面整体显得粗糙涂污。

二、釉裂纹

（一）真品二维特征

1. 单位图片中同一条釉裂纹呈现不同颜色（见图8-2-33—图8-2-36）。

2. 单位图片中邻近的釉裂纹呈现不同颜色（见图8-2-36）。

3. 单位图片中釉裂纹颜色与其所在处釉层颜色不同（见图8-2-36）。

4. 单位图片中釉裂纹与坑点斑有颜色差异（见图8-2-37）。

5. 釉裂纹两边呈现白雾状蔓延趋势，有时与釉裂纹本身有颜色差异（见图8-2-38、图8-2-40）。

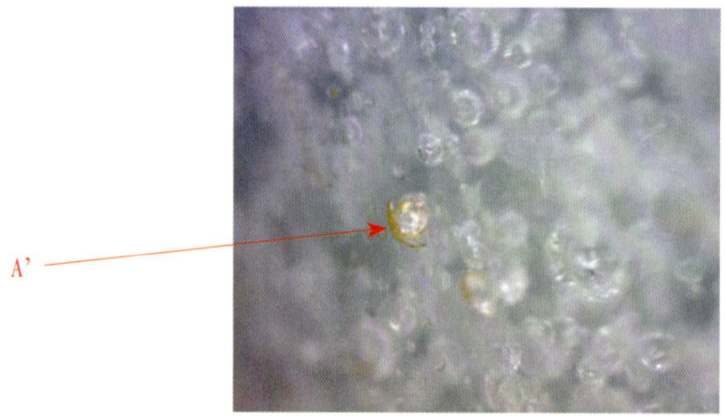

图8-2-27

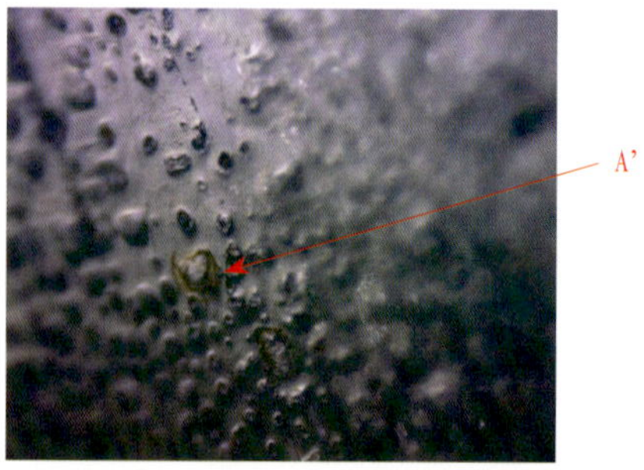

图8-2-28

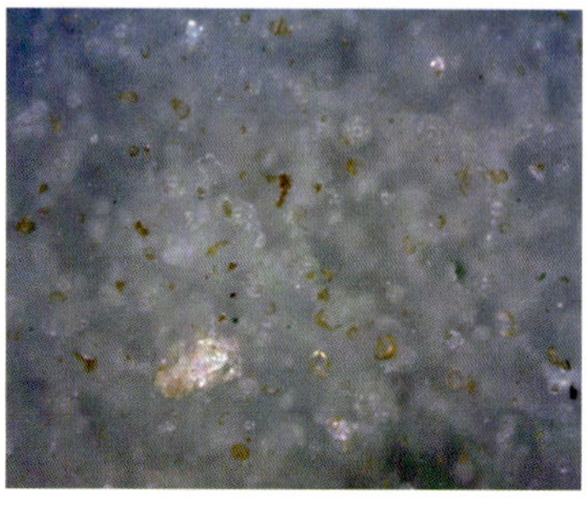

图8-2-29

图8-2-30

d. The edges of large scratches are rounded and smooth.

e. There is clear delineation between the scratches.

f. The scratches retain clear delineation from the surrounding glass phase and other traces.

g. Some of the glass phase is smooth and clean.

h. Some of the glass phase presents with an aged feel.

See picture 8-2-75 (three-dimensional picture).

The oxen hair scratches in picture 8-2-75 have varied width, length, direction, depth, and distribution density.

The surrounding glaze protrusions present with reserved, clearly delineated CO striae.

The rest of the glass phase presents with densely distributed weathered striae and a relatively evident aged feel.

See pictures 8-2-76 and 8-2-77, where 8-2-76 is the two-dimensional and 8-2-77 is the three-dimensional view of the same location.

The scratch indicated by Arrow A in picture 8-2-76 is not clearly visible two-dimensionally, but has white foggy coloration dispersing downward into the surrounding glaze level. The three-dimensional image, picture 8-2-77, shows clearly visible independent saw-tooth-like scratches that are smaller three-dimensionally, and have clear delineation from the surrounding glass phase.

The rest of the glass phase presents with densely distributed weathered striae and a relatively evident aged feel.

See pictures 8-2-78 and 8-2-79, where 8-2-78 is the two-dimensional and 8-2-79 is the three-dimensional view of the same location.

Some of the scratches in picture 8-2-78 have white foggy coloration dispersing down into the surrounding glaze level (see Arrow B), and it is smaller in the three-dimensional image, picture 8-2-79. The scratch is relatively large, intruding into the glaze level. Then interior of the scratch presents with deposits and color variation; and the edges are rounded and smooth, retaining clear delineation from the surrounding glass phase.

The scratch indicated by Arrow B also has many independently clear scratches extending off either side. The surrounding glass phase is clean and clear.

See pictures 8-2-80 and 8-2-81, both are three-dimensional pictures.

Both pictures 8-2-80 and 8-2-81 have scratches of multiple width, length, depth, angle, and direction. Their edges are rounded and smooth, they are distinctly independent, and they retain clear delineation from the surrounding glass phase.

The rest of the glass phase presents with densely distributed weathered striae and a relatively evident aged feel.

C. Two-Dimensional Characteristics of Forged Article

See pictures 8-2-82 and 8-2-85 (this piece has undergone treatment with aging reagent).

a. If scratches lack coloration, they are not very visible two-dimensionally.

b. The scratches are often uniform, their size large, and directional changes uncommon.

c. Scratch coloration across a piece or within a unit image is relatively uniform.

d. Larger scratches lack evident needlepoint mottling.

e. Scratches do not present with white foggy coloration dispersing down into the glaze level.

f. Scratches lack clear delineation from the surrounding glass phase and other traces.

g. There are also other traces occurring in association with the scratches, but the glass phase is generally muddled and unclear.

D. Three-Dimensional Characteristics of Forged Article

a. Oxen hair scratches are very uncommon.

b. The scratch is coarse and muddled; edges are not rounded but diffused.

c. The three-dimensional image of the scratch is larger than the two-dimensional.

d. Scratches are not distinctly independent.

e. Scratches and the surrounding glass phase or other trace types are not clearly delineated.

f. The surrounding glass phase is sporadically littered with pitting. Edges of the pits are fuzzy and dispersive, and

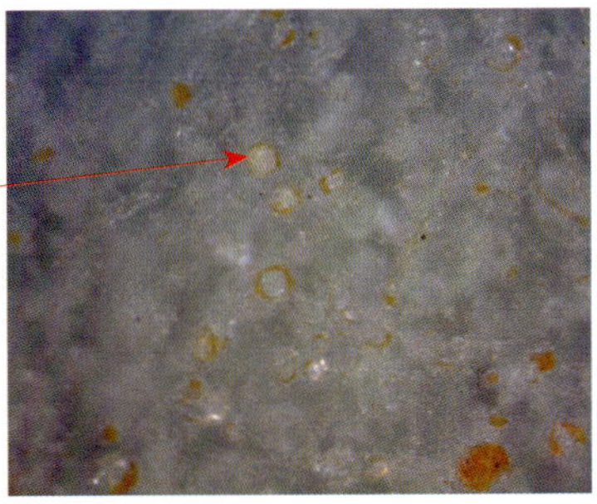

图8-2-31

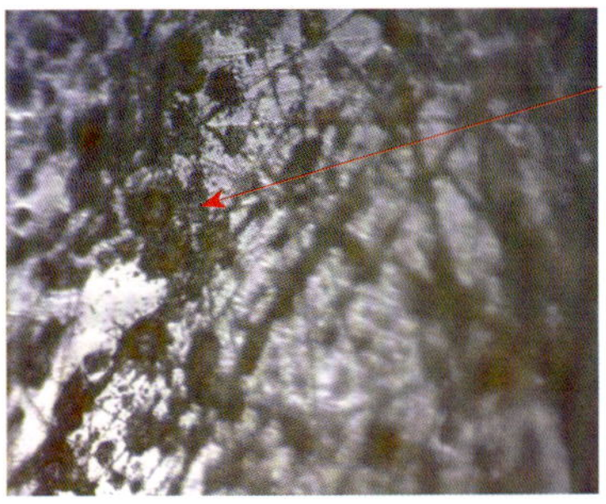

图8-2-32

6. 釉裂纹下有色变泡和壁变泡，但釉裂纹不变色，或者颜色与泡有差异（见图8-2-39—图8-2-42）。

7. 釉裂纹较宽的，可见裂纹中的堆积物（见图8-2-43、图8-2-44）。

8. 釉裂纹下有絮状斑，单位图片中白色絮状斑与釉裂纹有颜色差异（见图8-2-45、图8-2-46）。

（二）真品三维特征

1. 釉裂纹的三维成像面积通常小于或等于二维。

2. 釉裂纹周围出现的针眼斑或坑点斑三维成像面积要小于二维。

3. 釉裂纹边沿圆滑。

4. 釉裂纹与周围玻璃相界线分明。

5. 周围玻璃相干净清晰。

6. 有的玻璃相表现出明显陈旧感。

见图8-2-47、图8-2-48，二者为同一器物同一位置图片，图8-2-47为二维图片，图8-2-48为三维图片。

图8-2-47中的釉裂纹在图5-2-48中成像清晰，釉裂纹有粗有细，其三维成像面积均小于二维。（见箭头A所指处）。釉裂纹与周围玻

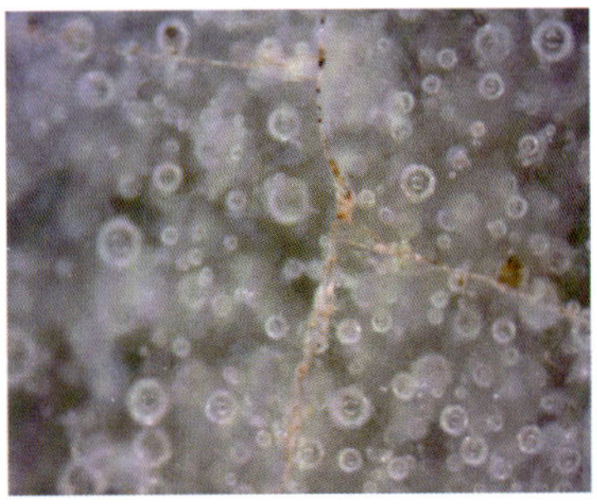

图8-2-33

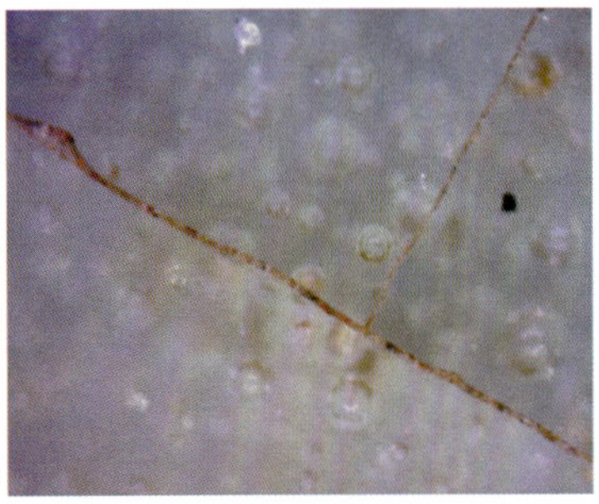

图8-2-34

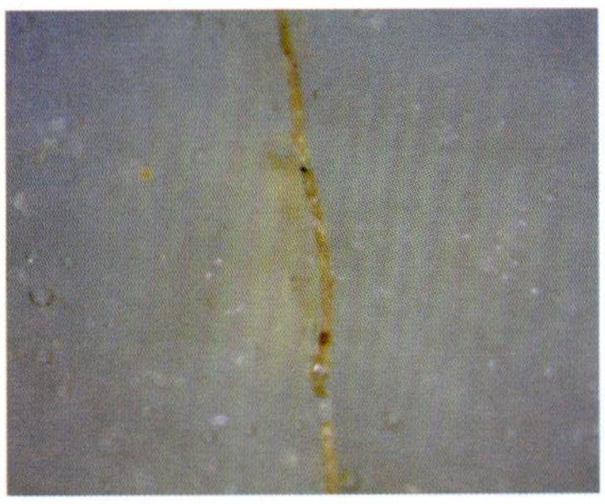

图8-2-35

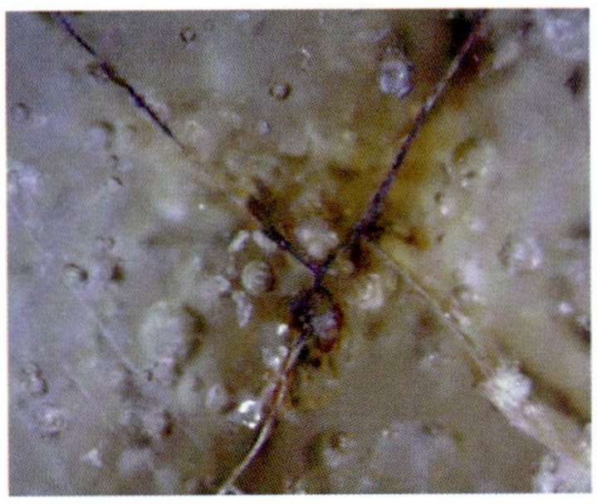

图8-2-36

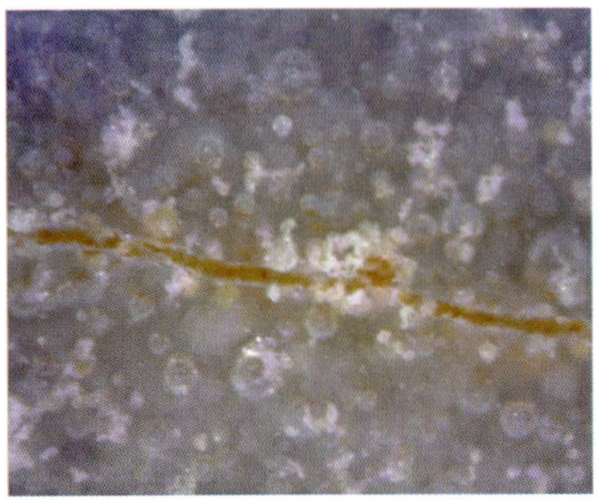

图8-2-37

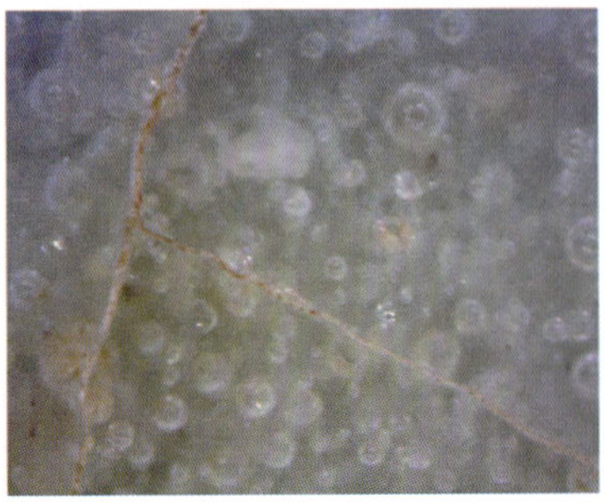

图8-2-38

the general appearance is muddled.

See pictures 8-2-86 and 8-2-87, where 8-2-86 is the two-dimensional and 8-2-87 is the three-dimensional view of the same location (this piece has undergone treatment with an aging reagent).

See pictures 8-2-88 and 8-2-89, where 8-2-88 is the two-dimensional and 8-2-89 is the three-dimensional view of the same location (this piece has undergone treatment with an aging reagent).

See Scratch A’ in picture 8-2-86 and Scratch B’ in picture 8-2-88. Their three-dimensional appearance is larger than the two-dimensional. The scratch indicated by Arrow A’ in picture 8-2-87 is an indention on the glaze surface and has rigid coloration. Scratch A’ and B’ are both coarse and rigid with jagged edges and a dispersed feel.

The surrounding glass phase is severely damaged with coarsely disbursed pits and large scratches across the surface. The scratches are rough and jagged with dispersive edges that lack clear delineation from the surrounding glass phase. There is no evident aged feel to the glaze surface, and the glaze is generally coarse and muddled.

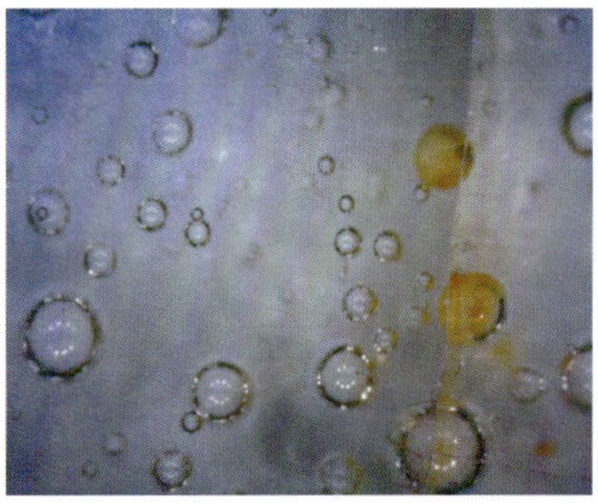
图8-2-39

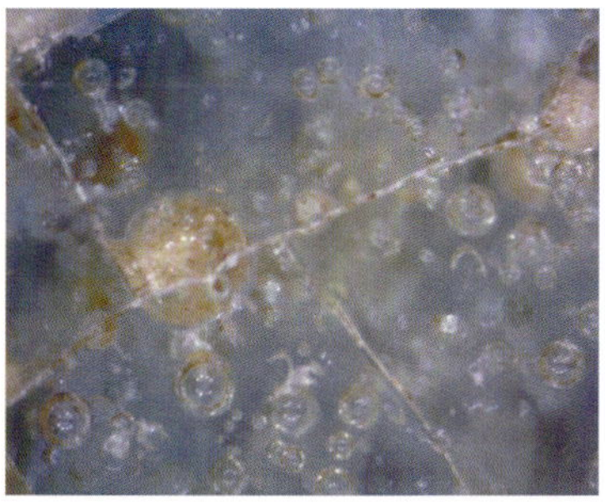
图8-2-40

图8-2-41

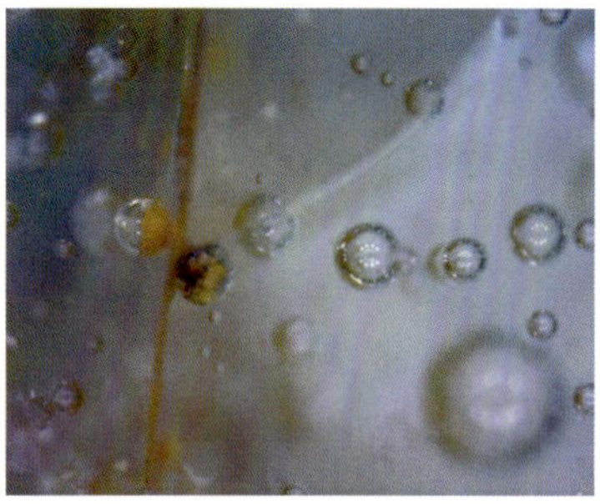
图8-2-42

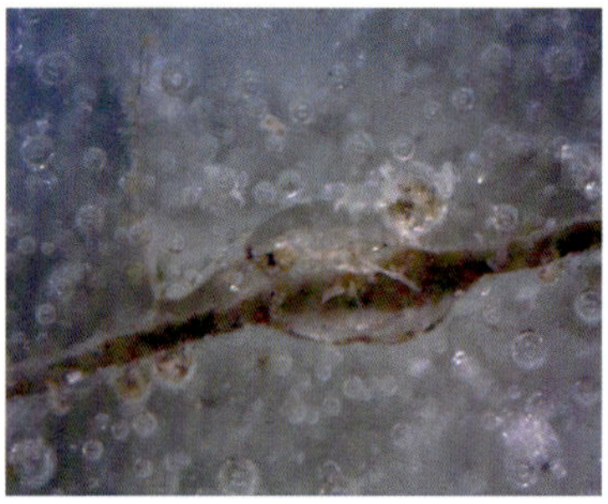
图8-2-43

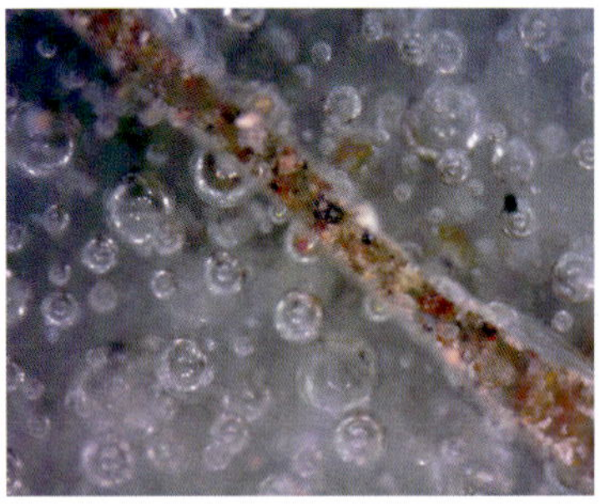
图8-2-44

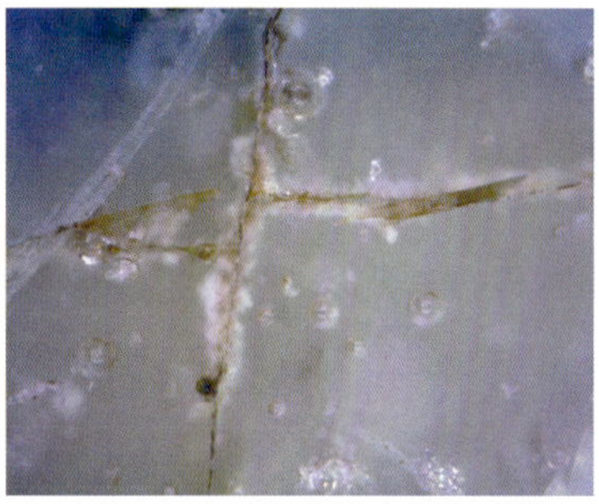
图8-2-45

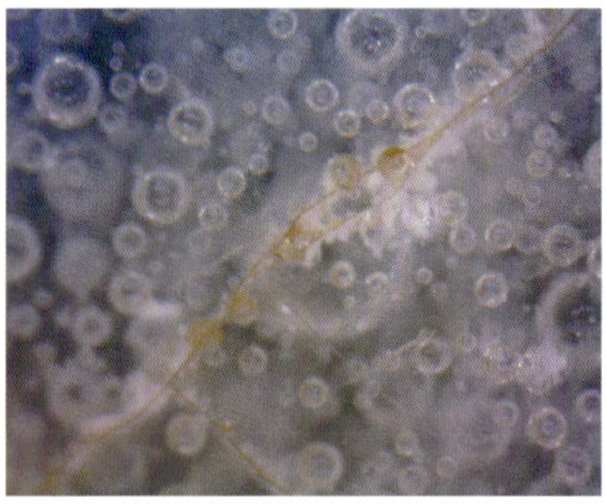
图8-2-46

璃相界线分明。周围玻璃相干净清晰。

见图8-2-49、图8-2-50，二者均为三维图片。

图8-2-49、图8-2-50中的釉裂纹三维成像清晰，边沿显得圆滑。釉裂纹与周围玻璃相界线分明。周围玻璃相清晰，玻璃相其余地方布满长短、方向不一的细密划痕，划痕边沿显得圆滑。玻璃相其余地方布满细密的风化纹路，有比较明显的陈旧感。

（三）赝品二维特征

见图8-2-51—图8-2-56。（该器物釉表面曾被腐蚀剂腐蚀）

1. 通常无论是单位图片中还是整件器物，釉裂纹的粗细变化都不大。

2. 单位图片中釉裂纹颜色单一，有时整器的釉裂纹都是同一颜色。

3. 人为染色的釉裂纹，颜色如毛刺向釉裂纹两边蔓延（见图8-2-51）。

4. 通常人为染色的器物，单位图片中釉裂纹颜色与其所在处釉层颜色一样（见图8-2-53、图8-2-54）。

5. 釉裂纹下的色变泡或壁变泡与釉裂纹颜色相同（见图8-2-55、图8-2-56）。

6. 釉裂纹周围釉表面的析晶斑，因人为染色与釉裂纹同一颜色（见图8-2-55）。

7. 釉裂纹两边没有呈现白雾状蔓延趋势。

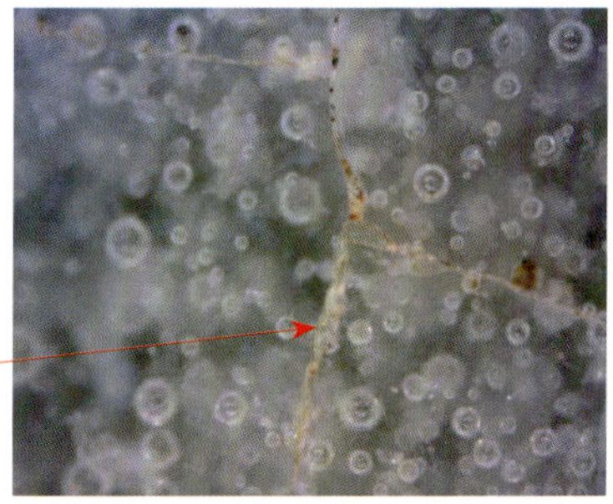

图8-2-47

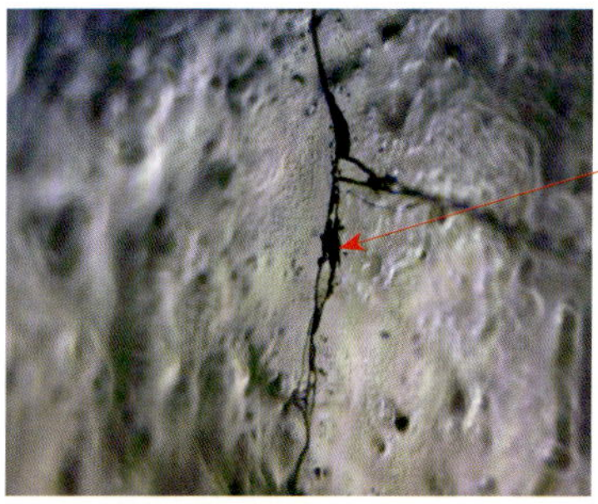

图8-2-48

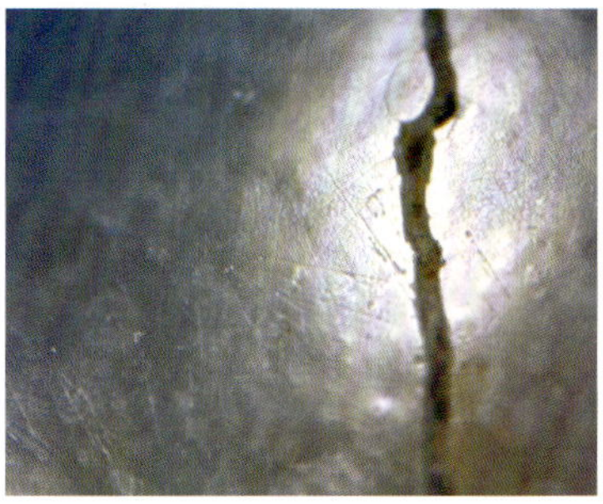

图8-2-49

图8-2-50

（四）赝品三维特征

见图8-2-57—图8-2-59。（该器物釉表面曾被腐蚀剂腐蚀）

1. 因为赝品存世时间较短，釉裂纹边沿显得较锋利。

2. 有时因人为做旧的缘故，釉裂纹边沿有毛刺，显得粗糙。

3. 有的玻璃相呈现新瓷光滑，无陈旧感。

4. 有的釉表面不规则地分布有坑点斑，斑块边沿粗粝，呈毛刺状，有扩张感。

三、划痕

（一）真品二维特征

1. 单位图片中有粗细、长短、深浅、方向、形貌、颜色不一的多个划痕，分布有疏有密（见图8-2-60—图8-2-74）。

2. 同一划痕上有颜色变化（见图8-2-60—图8-2-64）。

3. 划痕有呈白雾状蔓延的趋势（见图8-2-64—图8-2-74）。

4. 面积较大的划痕上有针眼斑，针眼斑不超出划痕范围（见图8-2-65、图8-2-67—图8-2-72）。

5. 划痕与周围玻璃相或其他迹型种类界线分明。

6. 周围玻璃相干净清晰。

（二）真品三维特征

1. 划痕可以表现为间隔均匀的小凹坑、清晰的“蜈蚣脚”、细小且杂乱无章的牛毛划痕及面积较大的凹坑等。

2. 凹坑状面积较大的划痕内部可见堆积物。

3. 二维成像有白色雾状蔓延趋

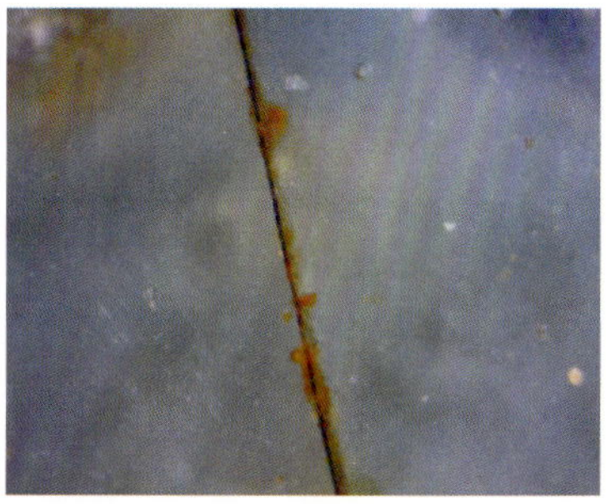

图8-2-51

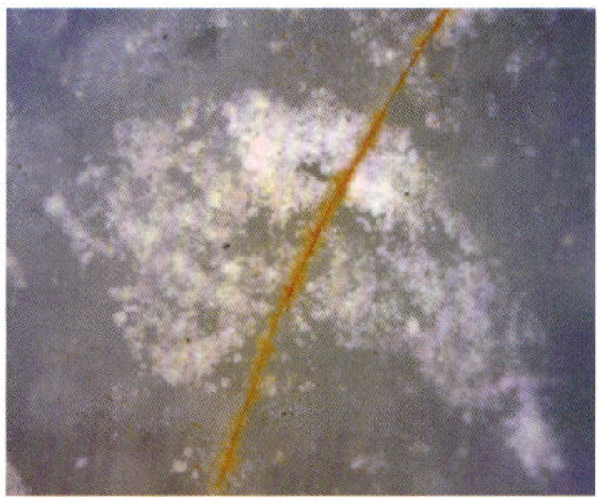

图8-2-52

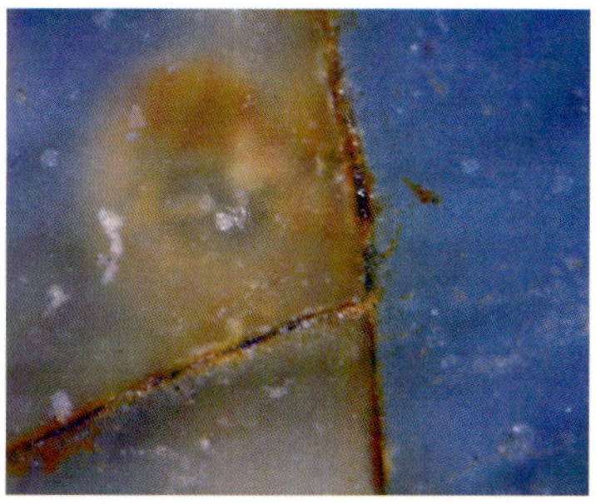

图8-2-53

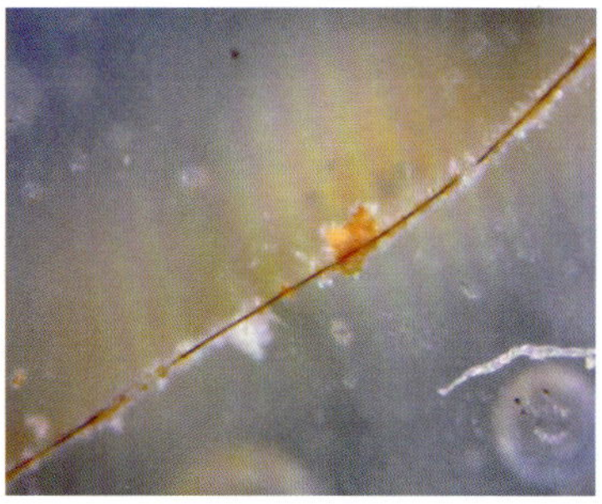
图8-2-54

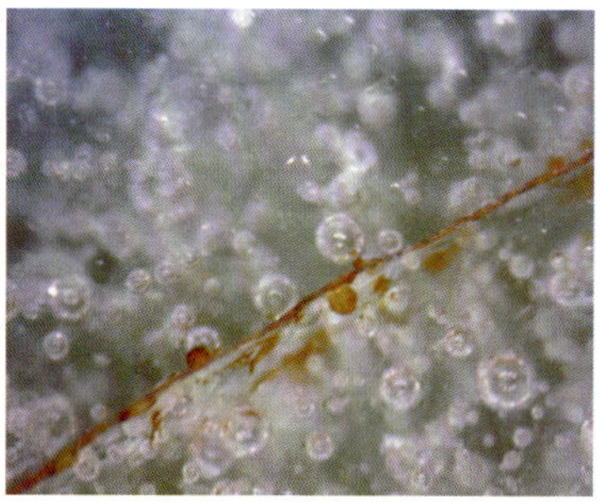
图8-2-55

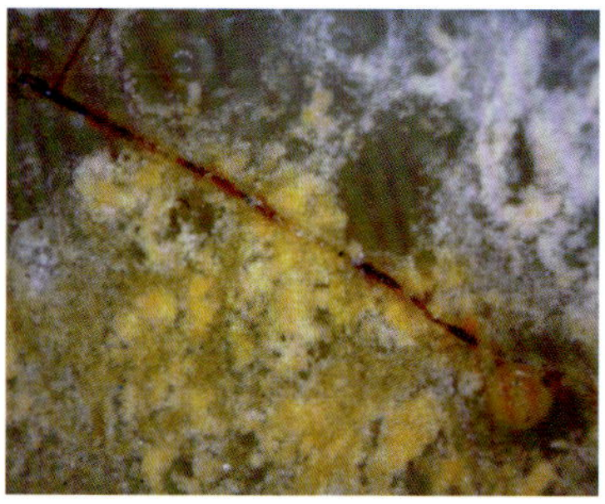
图8-2-56

势的划痕，其三维成像面积通常小于二维。

4. 划痕边沿圆滑。

5. 划痕之间界线分明，各自独立。

6. 划痕与周围玻璃相或其他迹型种类界线分明。

7. 有的玻璃相光滑洁净。

8. 有的玻璃相表现出明显陈旧感。

见图8-2-75（为三维图片）。

图8-2-75中牛毛状划痕粗细、长短、方向不一，有深有浅，距离有疏有密。

周围釉表面凸起处的CO型坑点斑，通常都是根部风化程度较高，颜色较深，顶部风化程度较低，颜色较浅。斑块收敛，彼此界线清晰。

玻璃相其余地方布满细密的风化纹路，有比较明显的陈旧感。

见图8-2-76、图8-2-77，二者为同一器物同一位置图片，图8-2-76为二维图片，图8-2-77为三维图片。

图8-2-76中箭头A所指的划痕二维成像较模糊，有白雾状蔓延趋势，但其三维成像在图8-2-77中却可见一个个独立清晰的锯齿状小划痕，三维成像面积小于二维成像面积，而且与周围玻璃相界线分明。

玻璃相其余地方布满细密的风化纹路，有比较明显的陈旧感。

见图8-2-78、图8-2-79，二者为同一器物同一位置图片，图8-2-78为二维图片，图8-2-79为三维图片。

图8-2-78中的划痕部分有白雾状蔓延趋势（见箭头B所指处），其在图8-2-79中的三维成像面积小于图8-2-78中的二维，划痕面积较大，呈凹坑状，可见内部堆积物，还可见色阶变化。划痕边沿圆滑，

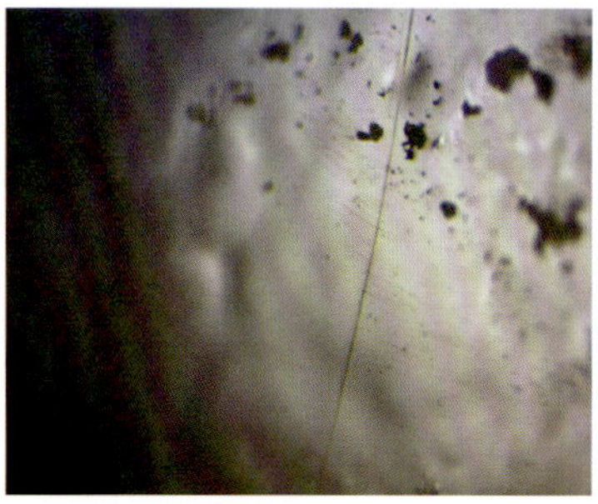
图8-2-57

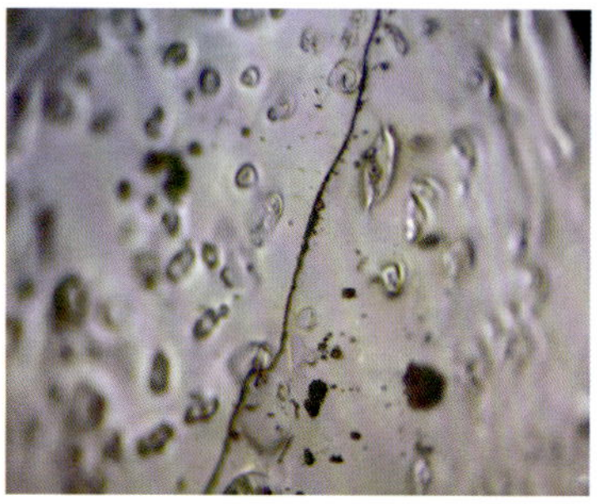
图8-2-58

图8-2-59

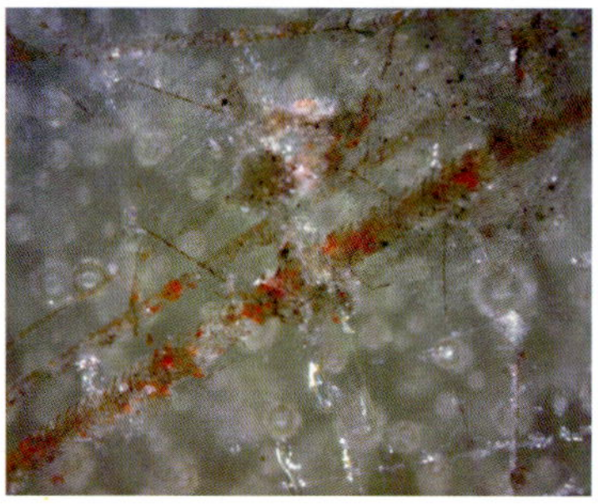
图8-2-60

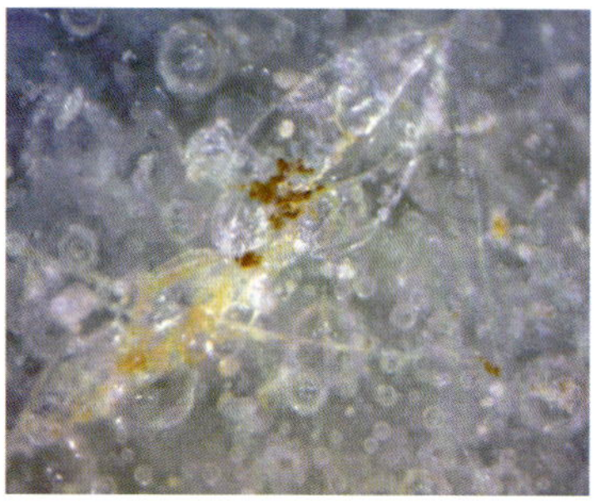
图8-2-61

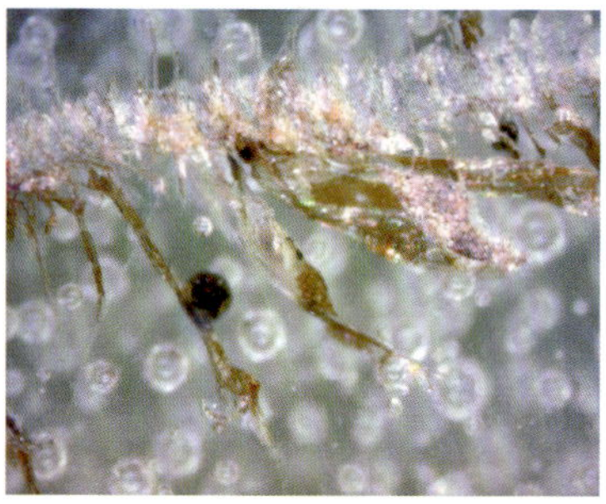
图8-2-62

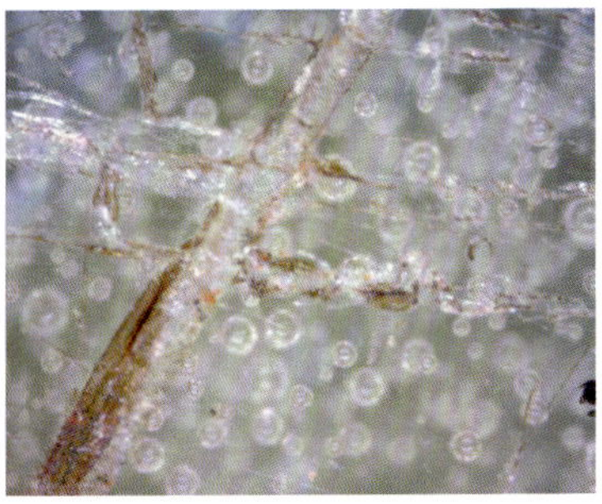
图8-2-63

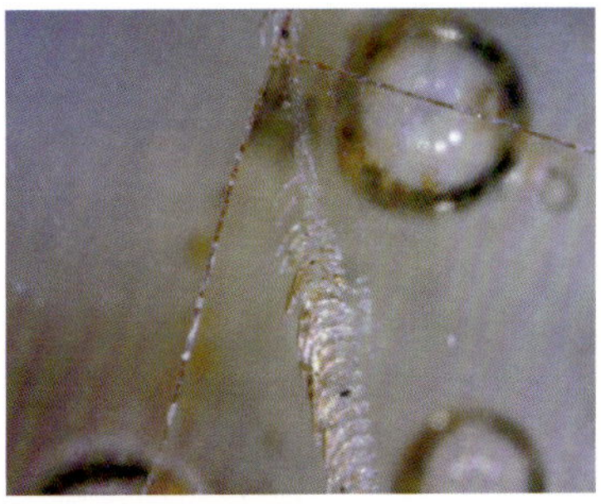
图8-2-64

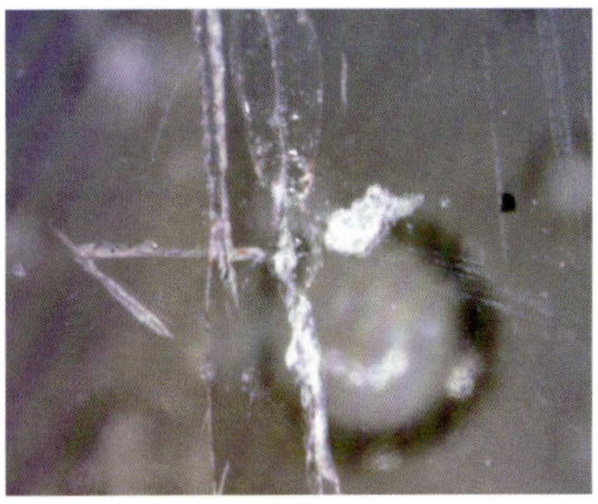
图8-2-65

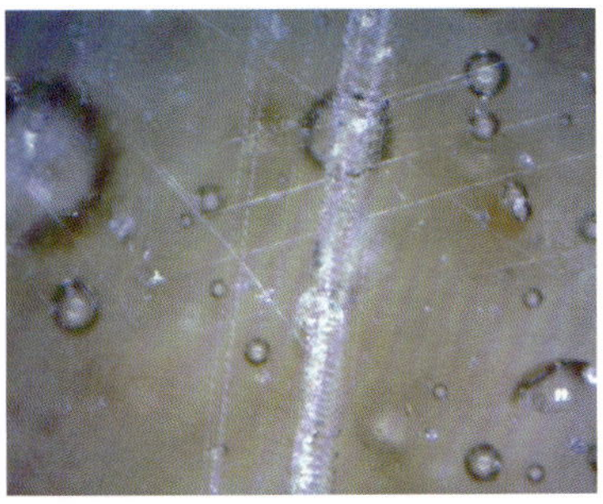
图8-2-66

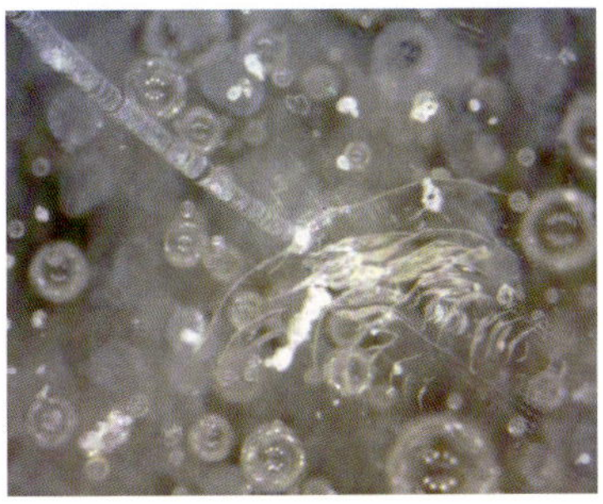
图8-2-67

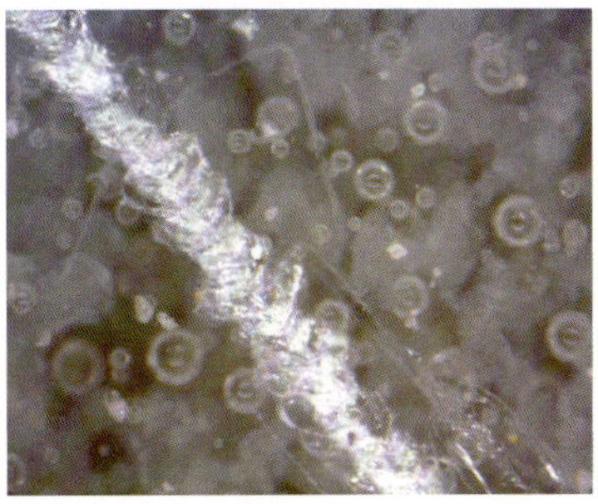
图8-2-68

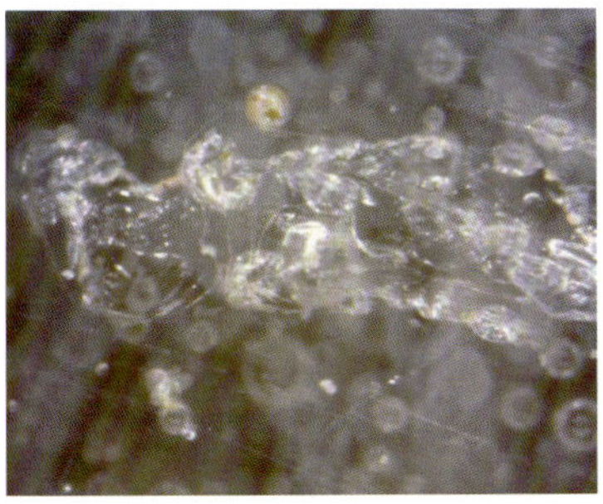
图8-2-69

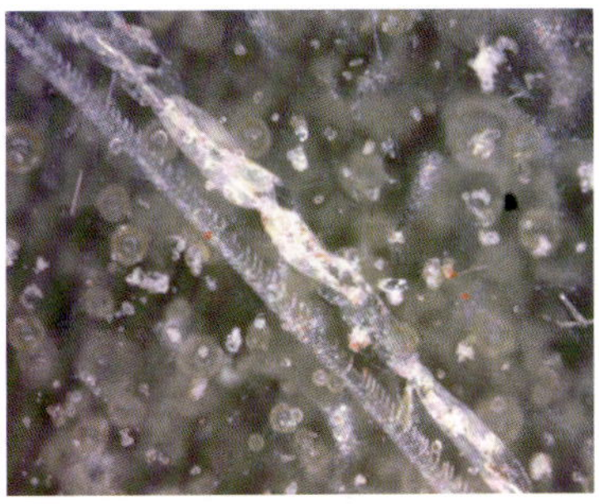
图8-2-70

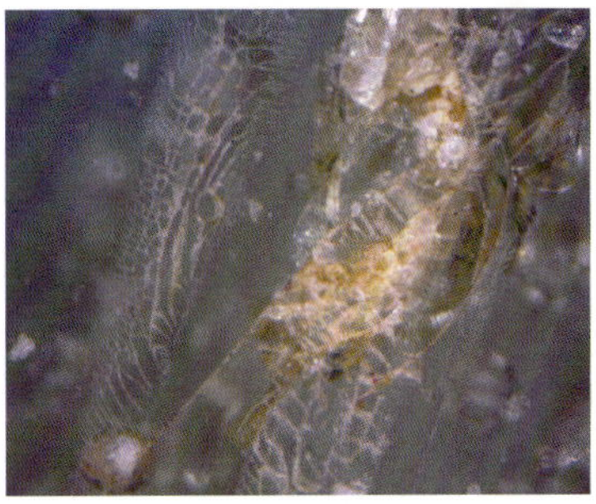
图8-2-71

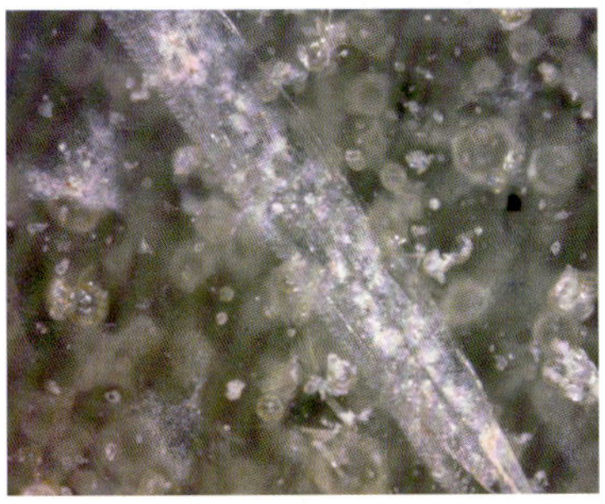
图8-2-72

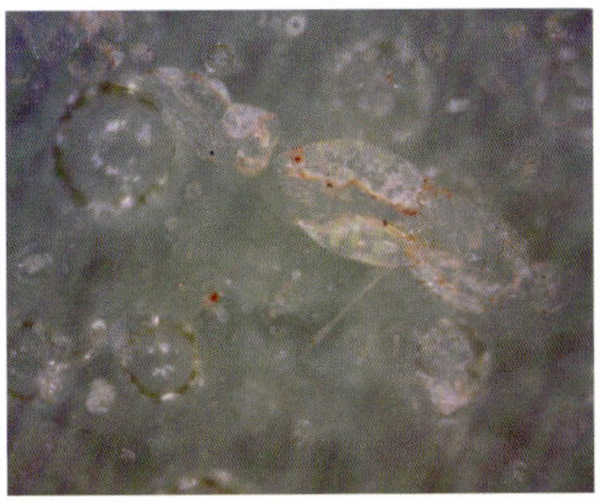
图8-2-73

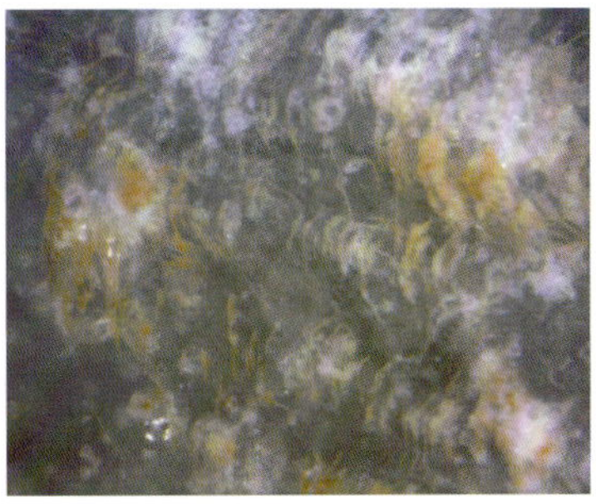
图8-2-74

与周围玻璃相界线分明。

箭头B所指的划痕两边还延伸出许多小划痕，独立清晰。周围玻璃相干净清晰。

见图8-2-80、图8-2-81，二者均为三维图片。

图8-2-80及图8-2-81中的划痕有粗有细，有长有短，有深有浅，有直线有曲线，方向不一，边沿圆滑，各自独立清晰，与周围玻璃相界线分明。

玻璃相其余地方布满细密的风化纹路，有比较明显的陈旧感。

（三）赝品二维特征

见图8-2-82—图8-2-85。（该器物釉表面曾被腐蚀剂腐蚀）

1. 如划痕没有颜色，其二维成像通常很难观察到。

2. 划痕形貌单一，通常面积都比较大，方向变化较少。

3. 整器上或单位图片内的划痕颜色都比较一致。

4. 面积较大的划痕，划痕上针眼斑不明显。

5. 划痕不见有白雾状蔓延。

6. 划痕与周围玻璃相或其他迹型种类界线不分明。

7. 玻璃相上除划痕以外还有其他迹型，但彼此界线模糊，整体显得混乱涂污。

（四）赝品三维特征

1. 少见牛毛纹。

2. 划痕粗糙生硬，边沿粗粝，呈毛刺状，具有扩张感。

3. 划痕的三维成像面积通常比二维大。

4. 划痕之间界线不分明。

5. 划痕与周围玻璃相或其他迹型种类界线不分明。

6. 周围玻璃相上杂乱无章地分布有坑点斑，斑块边沿粗粝，呈毛刺状，具有扩张感。整体显得粗糙涂污。

见图8-2-86、图8-2-87，二者为同一器物同一位置图片，图8-2-86为二维图片，图8-2-87为三维图片。（该器物釉表面曾被腐蚀剂腐蚀）

见图8-2-88、图8-2-89，二者为同一器物同一位置图片，图8-2-88为二维图片，图8-2-89为三维图片。（该器物釉表面曾被腐蚀剂腐蚀）

图8-2-86及图8-2-88中的划痕A’和划痕B’，三维成像面积比二维要大，图8-2-87中划痕A’呈一凹坑，内有颜色变化，但色块生硬。划痕A’及划痕B’粗糙生硬，边沿呈毛刺状，具有扩张感。

周围釉表面破坏严重，杂乱无章地分布着坑点斑、划痕，面积都比较大，表面粗糙，边沿粗粝，呈毛刺状，有扩张感，与周围玻璃相界线不分明。未被破坏的玻璃相无陈旧感。釉表面整体显得粗糙涂污。

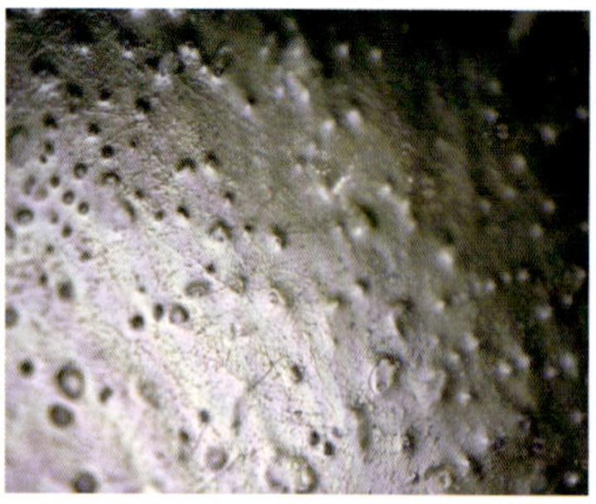

图8-2-75

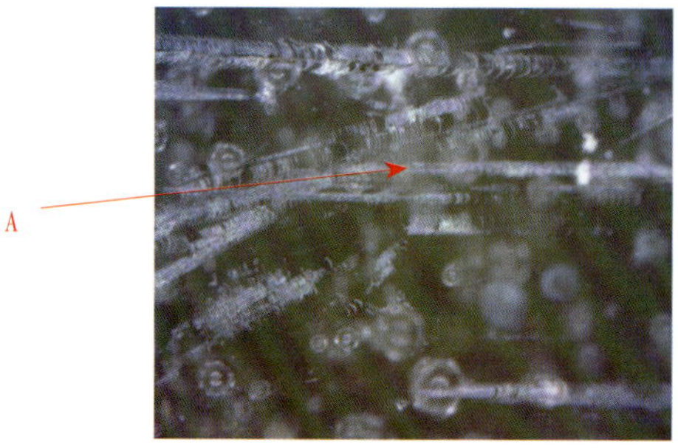

图8-2-76

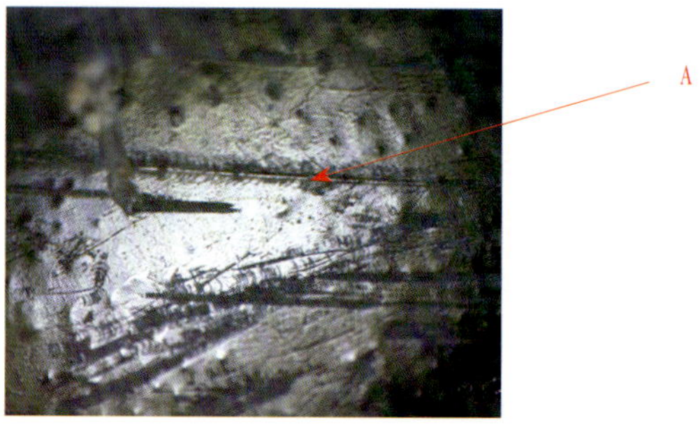

图8-2-77

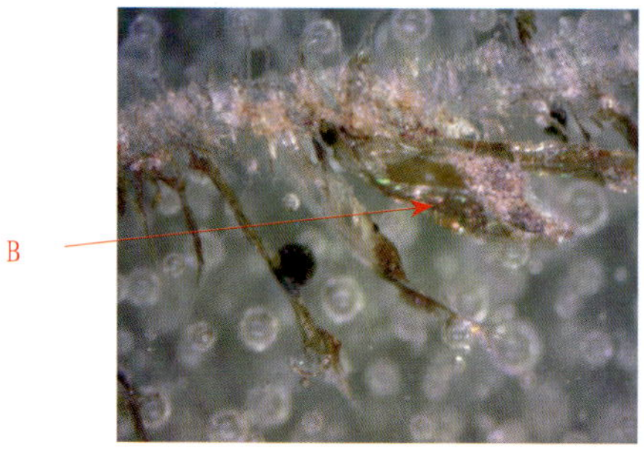

图8-2-78

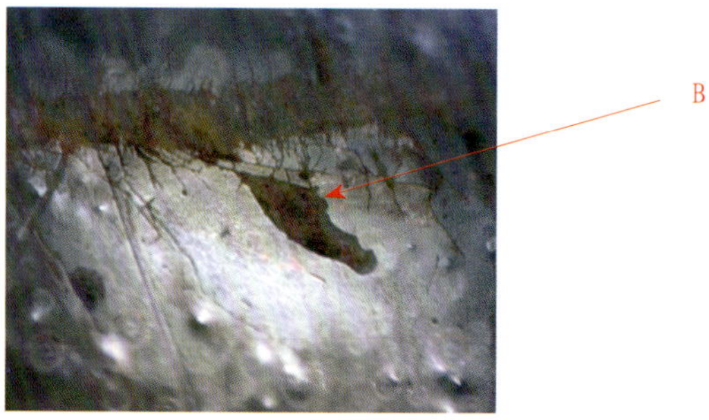

图8-2-79

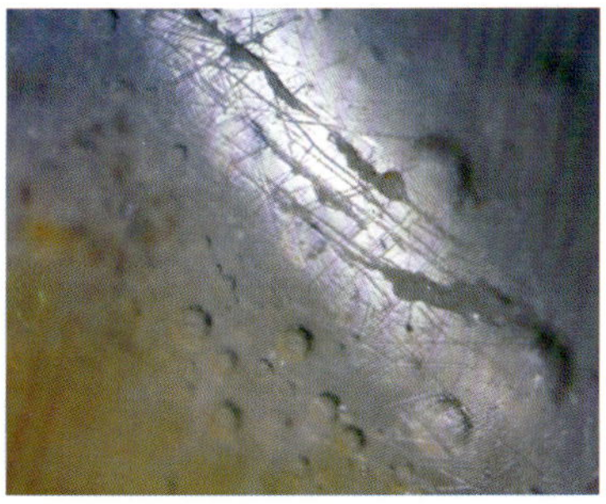
图8-2-80

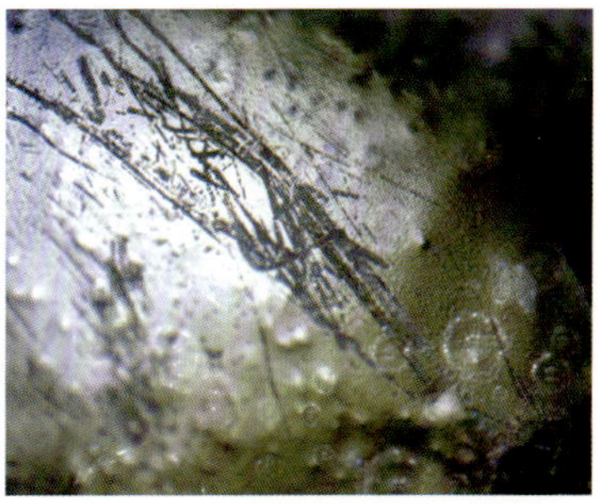
图8-2-81

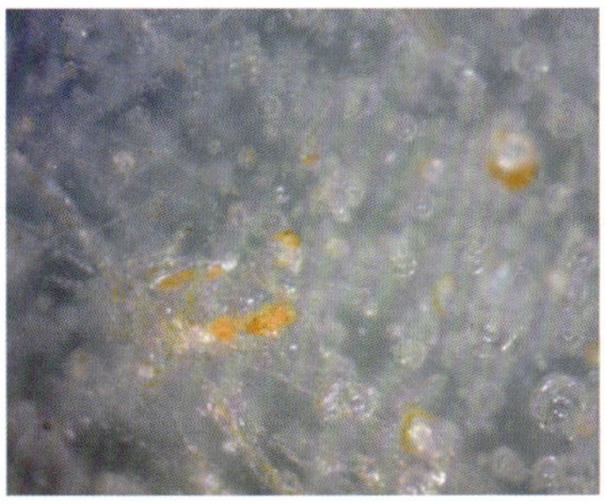
图8-2-82

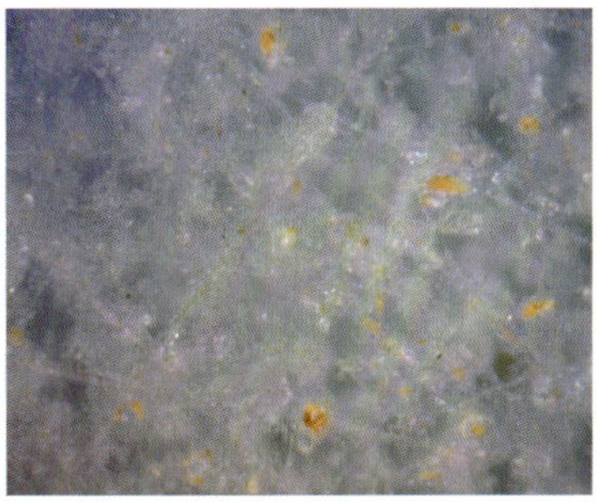
图8-2-83

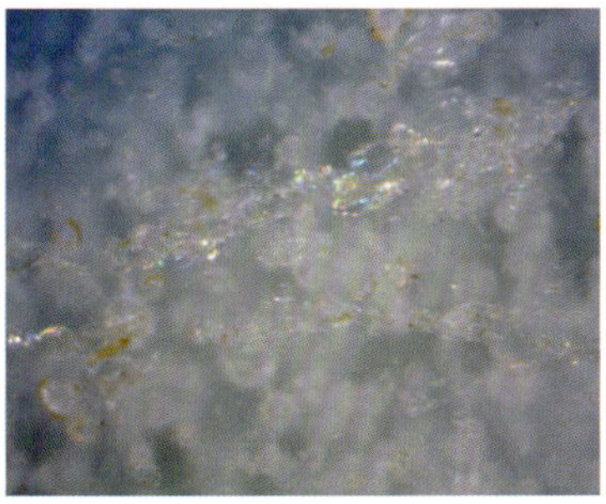
图8-2-84

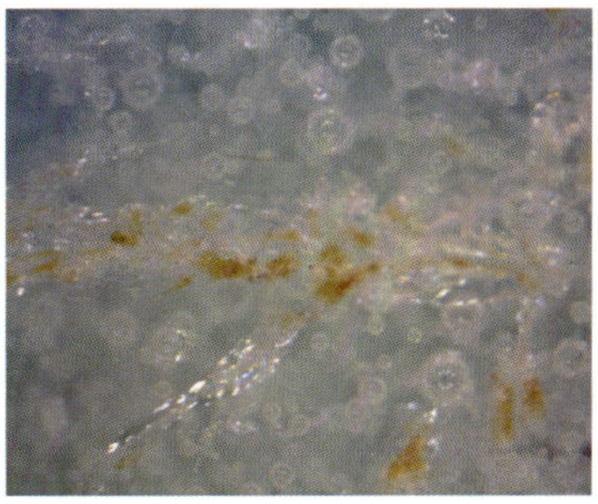
图8-2-85

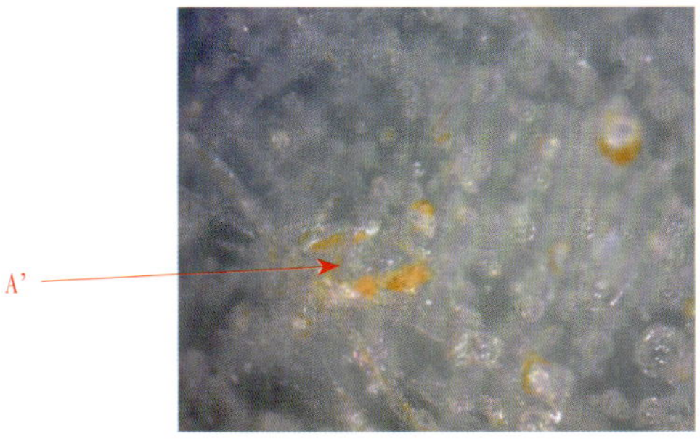

图8-2-86

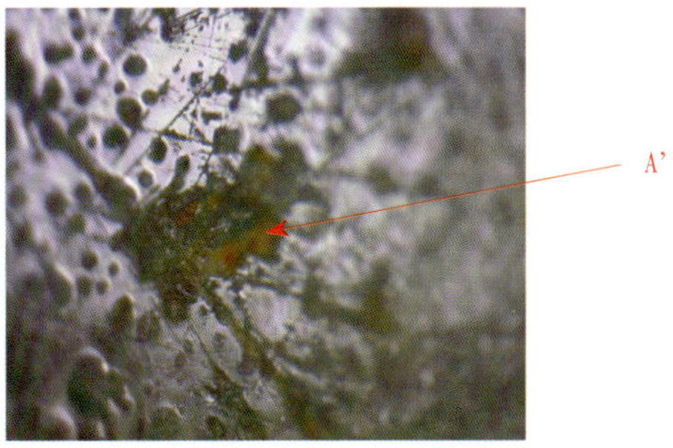

图8-2-87

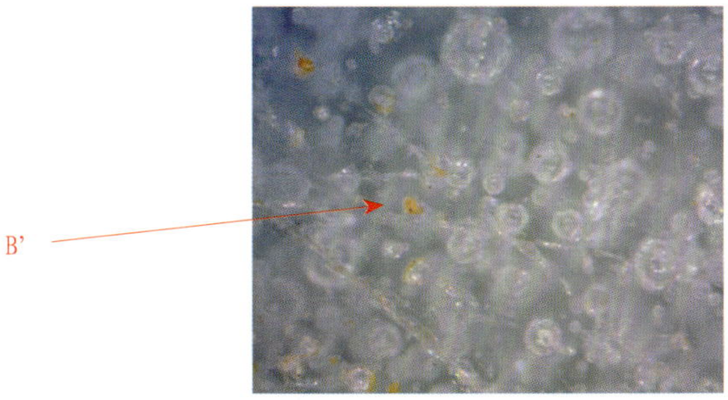

图8-2-88

图8-2-89

第三节
龙泉窑系青瓷气泡真品与赝品比对分析

一、色变泡

（一）真品二维特征

见图8-3-1—图8-3-11。

1. 单位图片中有色变泡群，包括全变泡和局变泡。

2. 单项色变泡中有色阶变化。

3. 气泡内壁有的地方颜色浓重，有的地方颜色浅淡。

4. 气泡变色的轮廓沿着泡壁，很少出界。

5. 单位图片中泡与泡之间有色差变化。

6. 色变泡群中的色变泡，通常彼此界线分明。

7. 色变泡与周围玻璃相界线分明。

8. 周围玻璃相干净清晰。

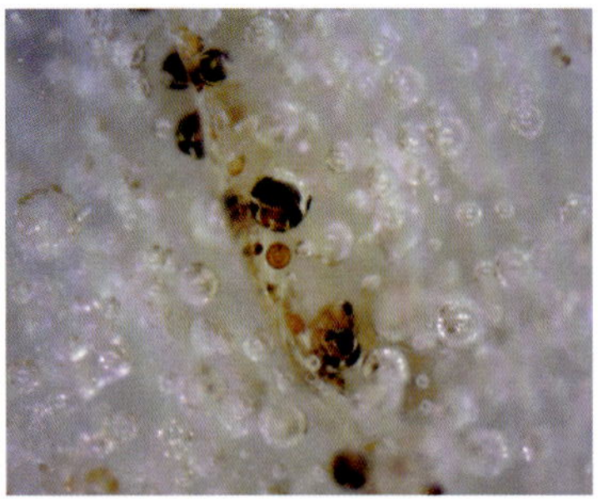
图8-3-1

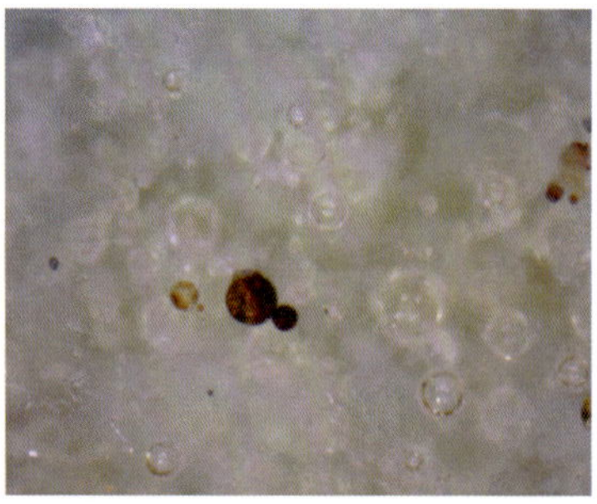
图8-3-2

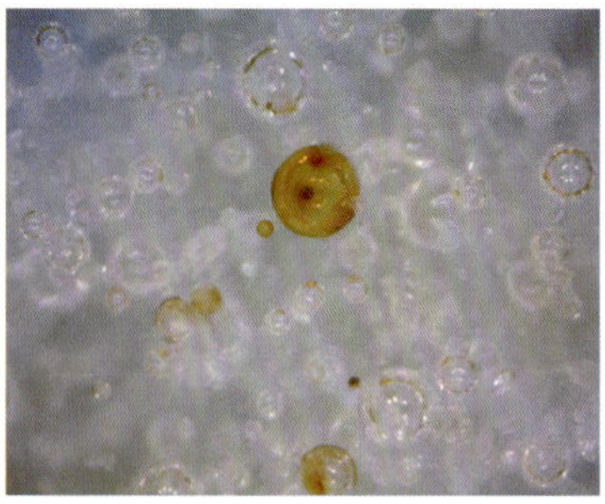
图8-3-3

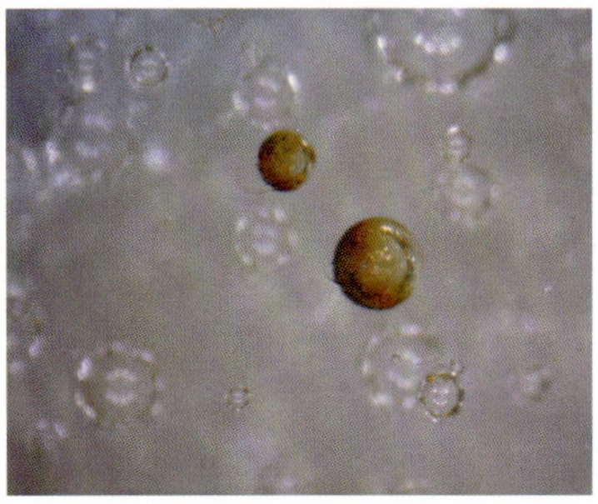
图8-3-4

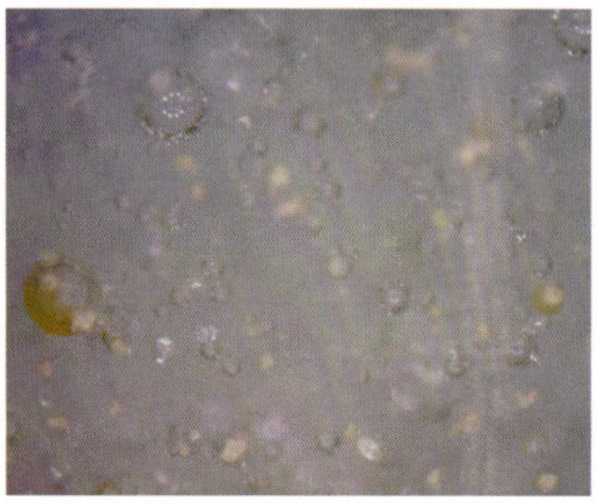
图8-3-5

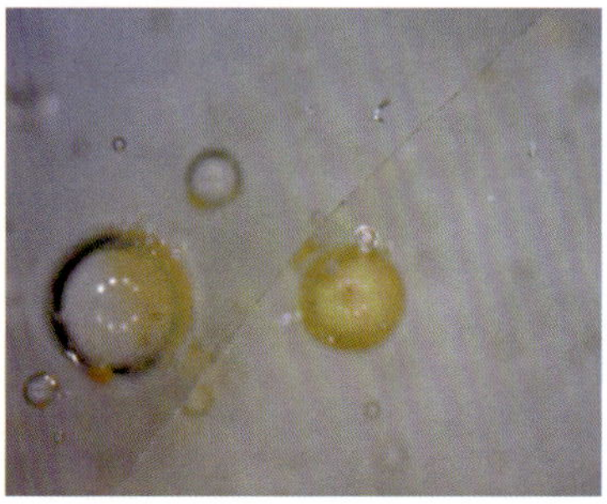
图8-3-6

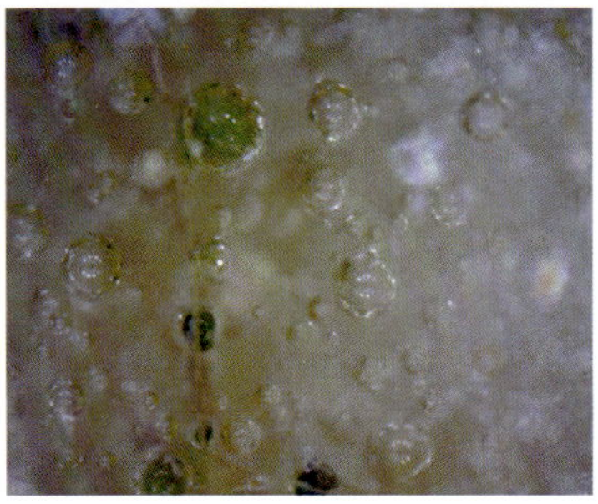
图8-3-7

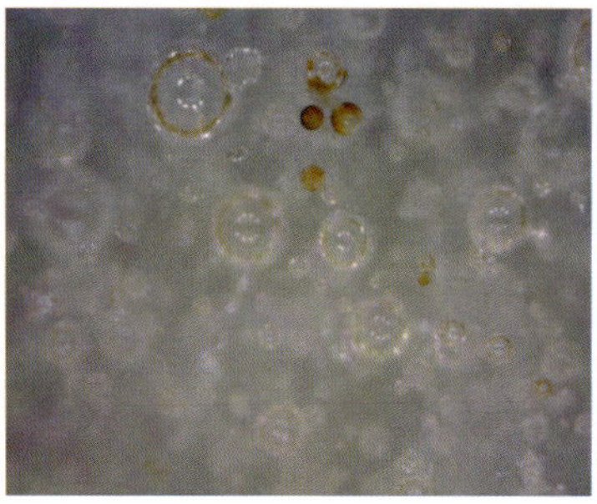
图8-3-8

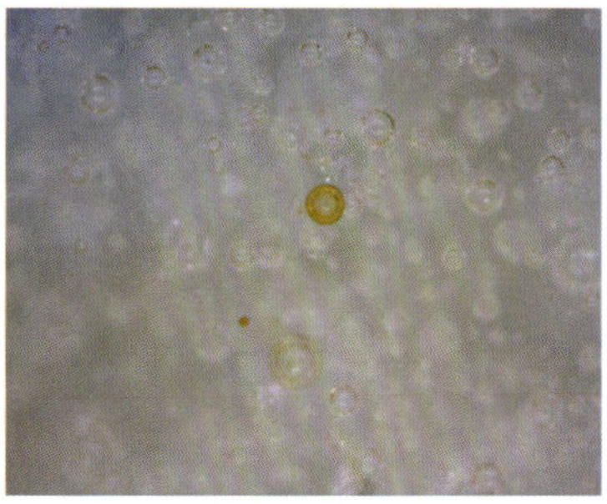
图8-3-9

Section 3:

Genuine and Forged Longquan Kiln System Celadon Bubble Comparison

1. Color Change Bubbles

A. Two-Dimensional Characteristics of Genuine Article

See pictures 8-3-1—8-3-11.

a. A unit image can present with color change bubble groups; with semi and fully changed bubbles both present.

b. A single color change bubble can present with color spectrum.

c. There is color density disparity within a single bubble, with areas of darker and lighter coloration.

d. Coloration occurs within the bubble interior, and rarely diffuses into the surrounding glaze.

e. There is color disparity among bubbles.

f. Colored bubbles within a colored bubble group retain clear delineation.

g. The color change bubbles retain clear delineation from the surrounding glass phase.

h. The surrounding glass phase is clean and clear.

B. Three-Dimensional Characteristics of Genuine Article

a. Clearly visible coloration channel presents on the glaze surface near the color change bubble.

b. The coloration channel is much smaller than the underlying bubble.

c. The glaze surface surrounding the channel is smooth and clean.

d. In areas where a coloration channel is not evident, the glaze surface remains smooth and clean.

e. Some of the glass phase is clean and clear.

f. Some of the glass phase presents with an aged feel.

See pictures 8-3-12 and 8-3-13, where 8-3-12 is the two-dimensional and 8-3-13 is the three-dimensional view of the same location.

Bubble A is faintly visible under the red ring in picture 8-3-13. There are no evident scratches or damage on the glaze surface, but two spots are darker than the rest (indicated by Arrow B), which are most likely the coloration channels. The surrounding glaze surface retains a smooth and clean nature.

See pictures 8-3-14 and 8-3-15, where 8-3-14 is the two-dimensional and 8-3-15 is the three-dimensional view of the same location.

Bubble C is invisible under the red ring in picture 8-3-15. The glaze surface has a C shaped striation, which can act as the coloration channel.

The surrounding glass phase presents with several independent, reserved, clearly delineated CO type pits. Aside from this, the glass phase is clean and clear.

See pictures 8-3-16 and 8-3-17, where 8-3-16 is the two-dimensional and 8-3-17 is the three-dimensional view of the same location.

Bubble D is faintly visible under the red ring in picture 8-3-17. There are no evident scratches or damage on the glaze surface. Possibly due to the small size of the coloration channel, it is not observable under 500X magnification. The surrounding glaze surface presents with clear and independent scratches and pitting. The rest of the glass phase is clean and clear.

C. Two-Dimensional Characteristics of Forged Article

See pictures 8-3-18—8-3-21 (the piece has undergone

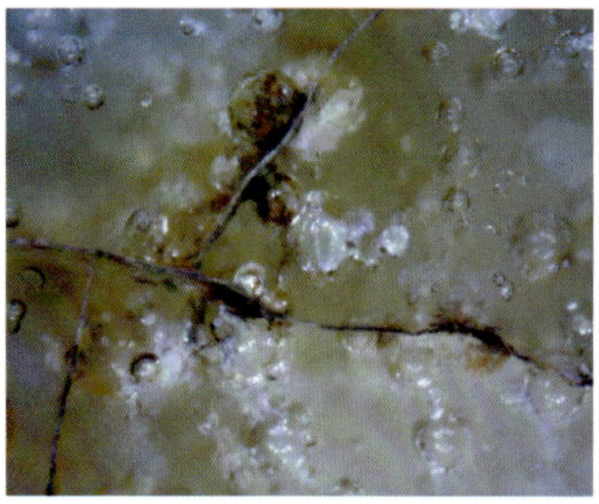

图8-3-10

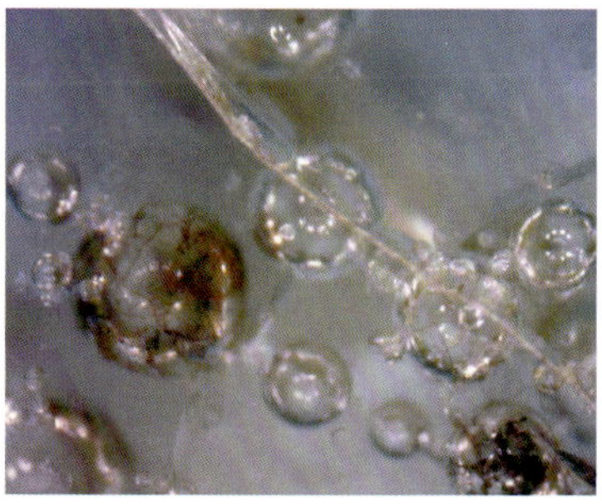

图8-3-11

（二）真品三维特征

1. 有的气泡所在处釉表面可见清晰独立的通道。

2. 通道的面积通常远远小于气泡面积。

3. 通道周围的釉表面保持光滑洁净。

4. 有的气泡所在处釉表面不可见明显通道，釉表面光滑洁净。

5. 有的玻璃相干净清晰。

6. 有的玻璃相表现出明显陈旧感。

见图8-3-12、图8-3-13，二者为同一器物同一位置图片，图8-3-12为二维图片，图8-3-13为三维图片。

图8-3-12中气泡A在图8-3-13中位于红圈釉下处，气泡A所在处的釉表面无明显划痕或损伤，但有两处颜色较浓（见箭头B所指处），这应该是外界连接气泡内的通道所在处。周围玻璃相比较干净清晰。

见图8-3-14、图8-3-15，二者为同一器物同一位置图片，图8-3-14为二维图片，图8-3-15为三维图片。

图8-3-14中气泡C在图8-3-15中位于红圈釉下处，不可见。气泡C所在处的釉表面有一条明显的C形纹，应该是外界连接气泡内的通道。

周围玻璃相上还有其他各自独立清晰的CO型坑点斑，斑块收敛，彼此界线清晰，玻璃相其余地方干

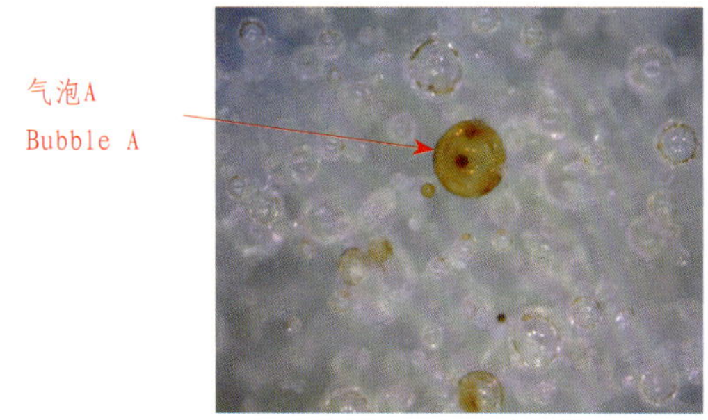

图8-3-12

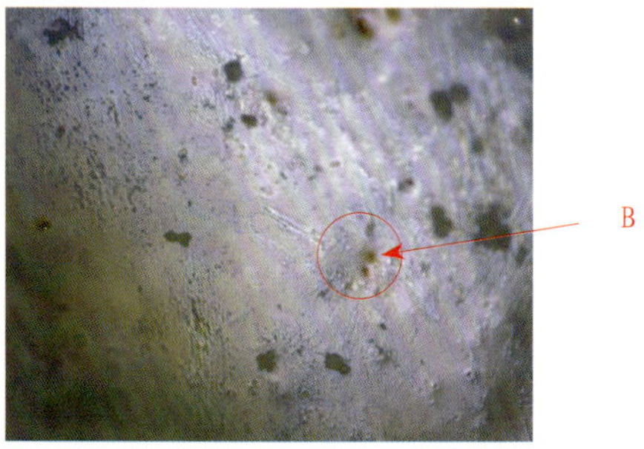

图8-3-13

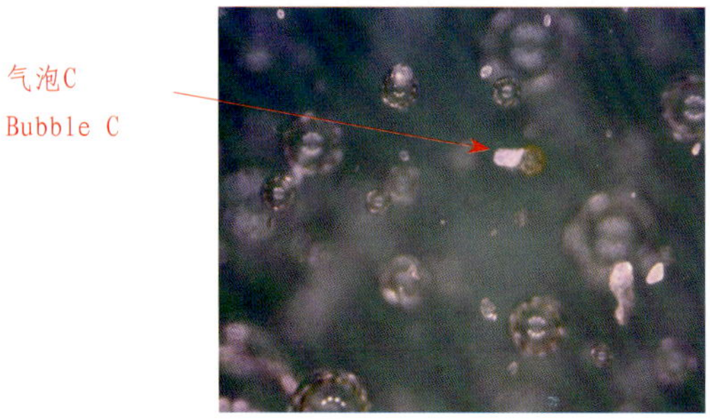

图8-3-14

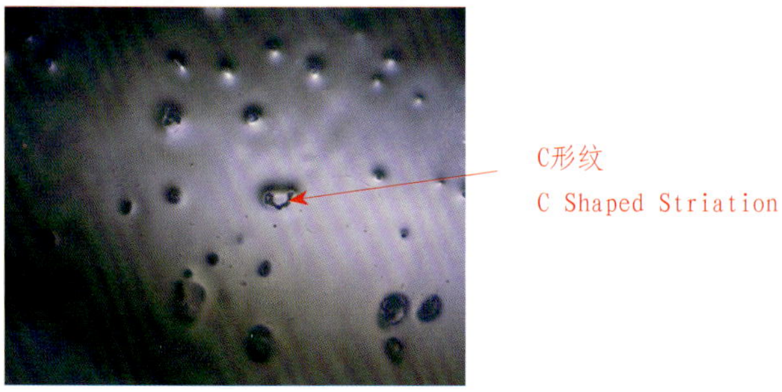

图8-3-15

treatment with aging reagent).

a. Forged pieces often present with general distribution of colored bubbles across the entire piece. The coloration of bubbles is essentially uniform and lacking color disparity.

b. If a piece has glaze cracks, colored bubbles often occur in close association with these cracks; their coloration consistent with that of the crack and surrounding glaze area (see pictures 8-3-18 and 8-3-19).

c. Colored bubble groups present, coloration threads often conjoin them and their delineation is not clear. This is due to the use of human forced dying materials (see pictures 8-3-20 and 8-3-21).

D. Three-Dimensional Characteristics of Forged Article

a. The glaze surface is littered with relatively large and diffused corrosion mottles.

b. The glaze surface near colored bubbles occurring in conjunction with glaze cracks is coarse and dispersive.

c. The surrounding glaze surface has a sporadic dispersion of pitting, and the general appearance is muddled.

See pictures 8-3-22 and 8-3-23, where 8-3-22 is the two-dimensional and 8-3-23, is the three-dimensional view of the same location (this piece has undergone treatment with aging reagent).

Bubble A' is faintly visible under the red ring in picture 8-3-23, but is overlaid with a coarsely diffused corrosion mottle. The surrounding glaze surface is densely covered in sporadic pitting with uniform appearances.

See pictures 8-3-24 and 8-3-25, where 8-3-24 is the two-dimensional and 8-3-25 is the three-dimensional view of the same location (this piece has undergone treatment with aging reagent).

Bubble B' is faintly visible under the red ring in picture 8-3-25, and is overlaid with a coarsely diffused corrosion mottle (see Arrow C' in picture 8-3-25). The surrounding glaze surface is densely covered in sporadic pitting with uniform appearances.

2. Textured Bubbles

A. Unbroken Mouth Textured Bubbles

a. Two-Dimensional Characteristics of Genuine Article

See pictures 8-3-26—8-3-36.

I. Semi-changed textured bubbles are relatively common.

II. The bubble interior presents with foggy, frosted, and grainy needlepoint mottling. The texture change rarely extends beyond the perimeter of the bubble itself.

III. Foggy needlepoint mottling is fine and evenly distributed (see pictures 8-3-26—8-3-29).

IV. Grainy needlepoint mottling can be seen in relatively large bubbles and occurs with a color spectrum (see pictures 8-3-34 and 8-3-35).

V. The bubble retains clear delineation from the surrounding glass phase.

VI. The surrounding glass phase is clean and clear.

b. Three-Dimensional Characteristics of Genuine Article

I. A channel is clearly visible on the glaze surface in the vicinity of the bubble.

II. The channel is clearly independent, its surface area is much smaller than the underlying bubble.

III. The surrounding glaze surface is smooth and clean.

IV. Some of the surrounding glass phase is clean and clear.

V. Some of the surrounding glass phase presents with an aged feel.

See pictures 8-3-37 and 8-3-38, where 8-3-37 is the two-dimensional and 8-3-38 is the three-dimensional view of the same location.

The coloration present in Bubble A in picture 8-3-38 is within the bubble, similar to 2D image, but lighter. The coloration area is smaller than the bubble area.

The surrounding glass phase also has clear and mutually independent scratches and CO type pit mottles. The CO

净清晰。

见图8-3-16、图8-3-17，二者为同一器物同一位置图片，图8-3-16为二维图片，图8-3-17为三维图片。

图8-3-16中的气泡D，在图8-3-17中位于红圈釉下处，隐约可见轮廓。气泡D所在处的釉表面光滑洁净，通道不明显，可能是因为通道较小，用500倍显微镜难以观察到。周围釉表面有独立清晰的划痕和坑点斑，彼此界线分明。玻璃相其余地方干净清晰。

（三）赝品二维特征

见图8-3-18—图8-3-21（该器物釉表面曾被腐蚀剂腐蚀）。

1. 赝品通常整个器物上布满色变泡，而且气泡颜色比较一致，没有色差变化。

2. 如果一件器物上遍布釉裂纹，色变泡通常都出现在釉裂纹所在处，与釉裂纹颜色一致，釉裂纹周边釉层也有变色现象，且颜色一致（见图8-3-18、图8-3-19）。

3. 有时出现色变泡群，泡与泡之间有色块或色丝粘连，界线不分明。疑是人为做旧用有色液体染色形成的现象（见图8-3-20、图8-3-21）。

（四）赝品三维特征

1. 气泡所在处的釉表面可见面积较大的粗糙的腐蚀斑块，具有扩张感。

2. 色变泡所在处的釉裂纹，三维成像边沿粗粝，有扩张感。

3. 周围釉表面有腐蚀性坑点斑密集分布，整体显得混乱涂污。

见图8-3-22、图8-3-23，二

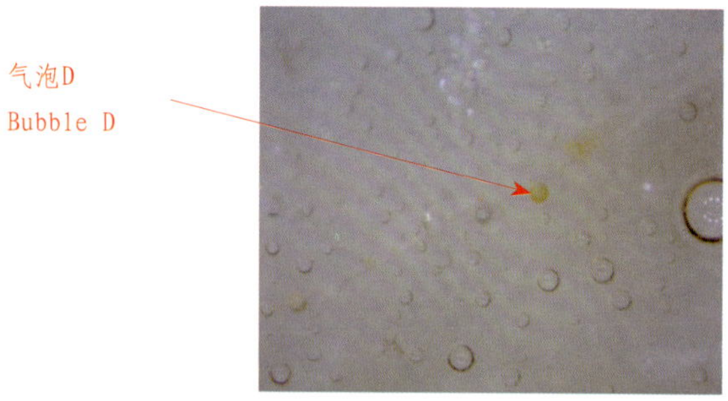

图8-3-16

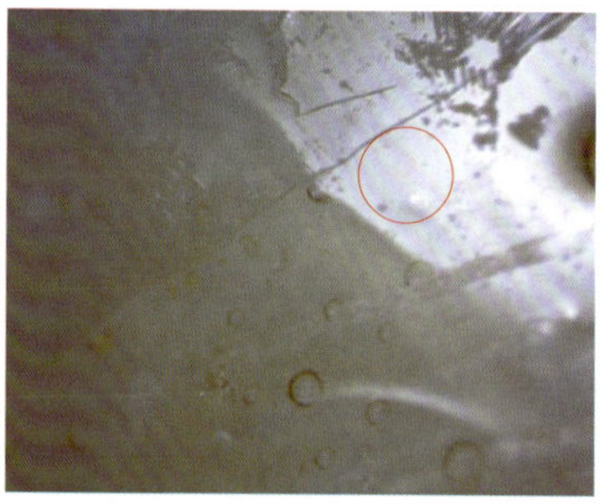

图8-3-17

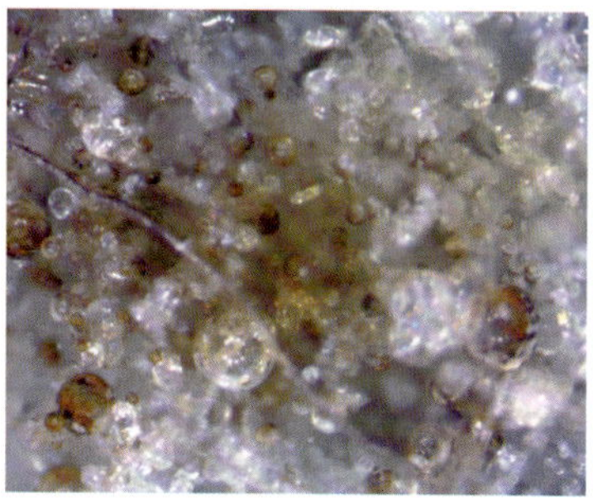

图8-3-18

图8-3-19

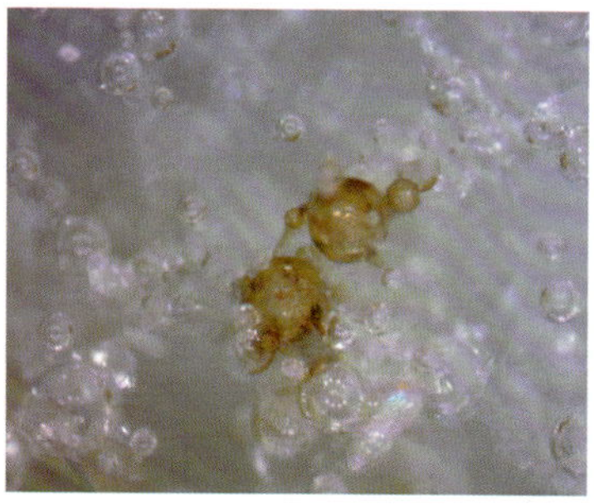

图8-3-20

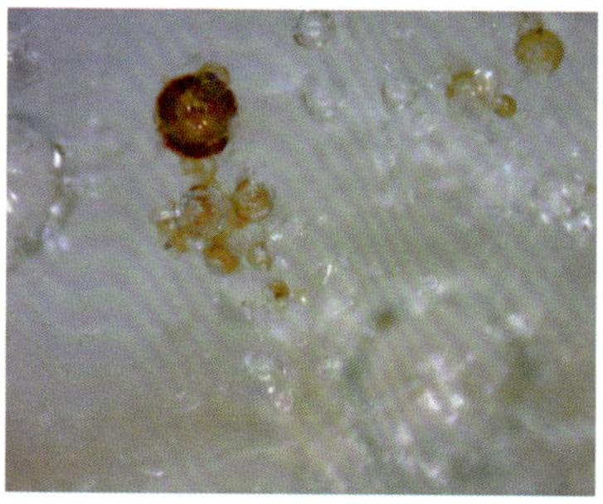

图8-3-21

pits all show a base that is more weathered than the raised center. The mottles are reserved and clearly delineated. The surrounding glass phase also presents with densely distributed weathered striae and a relatively evident aged feel.

See pictures 8-3-39 and 8-3-40 where 8-3-39 is the two-dimensional and 8-3-40 is the three-dimensional view of the same location.

Bubble B is faintly visible in picture 8-3-40. The glaze surface surrounding the textured bubble presents with pits and scratches, these are most likely the channels through which weathering has occurred.

The surrounding glass phase also has clear and mutually independent scratches and pit mottles. The mottles are reserved and clearly delineated. The surrounding glass phase also presents with densely distributed weathered striae and a relatively evident aged feel.

c. Two-Dimensional Characteristics of Forged Article

See pictures 8-3-41 and 8-3-44.

I. The deposits materials on the bubble interior are blurry and muddled.

II. Often all the textured bubbles on a forged piece are similar in nature, lacking disparity.

III. At times, textured bubble groups occur. Coloration threads often conjoin them and their delineation is not clear. This is due to the use of human forced dying materials (see pictures 8-3-43—8-3-44).

IV. No clear delineation with the surrounding glass phase.

V. Surrounding glass phase littered with sporadically distributed pitting or scratches, its general appearance muddled.

d. Three-Dimensional Characteristics of Forged Article

I. The glaze surface above the bubble has become grossly damaged and presents with coarse and diffused corrosion mottles.

II. The corrosion mottle has a surface area larger than the underlying bubble, indicating that the bubble is a faux textured bubble.

III. The surrounding glaze level is littered with sporadically distributed pitting; these pits or scratches are fuzzy and dispersive, giving it a generally muddled appearance.

See pictures 8-3-45 and 8-3-46, where 8-3-45 is the two-dimensional and 8-3-46 is the three-dimensional view of the same location (this piece has undergone treatment with an aging reagent).

Bubble A' is not visible in picture 8-3-46 and as such is indicated with a red ring. The overlying glaze surface has become damaged, covered by the coarsely diffused corrosion mottles.

The surrounding glass phase is severely damaged, with a coarse distribution of pitting and scratches of a relatively large size with coarse surfaces, rough edges, and fuzzy and dispersive qualities that muddle their delineation from the surrounding glass phase. Undamaged areas of glass phase lack a clear aged feel, and the surface in general is coarsely muddled.

See pictures 8-3-47 and 8-3-48, where 8-3-47 is the two-dimensional and 8-3-48 is the three-dimensional view of the same location (this piece has undergone treatment with an aging reagent).

Bubble B' is not visible in picture 8-3-48 and as such is indicated with a red ring. The overlying glaze surface has become damaged, and the coarsely diffused corrosion mottle is larger than the underlying bubble. This is a faux textured bubble. The surrounding glaze surface resembles newly fired porcelain with the exception of being covered in unidirectional scratches.

B. Broken Mouth Textured Bubbles

a. Two-Dimensional Characteristics of Genuine Article

I. The mouth of the bubble is rounded with smooth

者为同一器物同一位置图片，图8-3-22为二维图片，图8-3-23为三维图片。（该器物釉表面曾被腐蚀剂腐蚀）

图8-3-22中的气泡A’在图8-3-23中位于红圈釉下处，不可见。其所在处釉表面一大部分已被破坏，可见腐蚀性坑点斑密集分布，显得粗糙涂污。

见图8-3-24、图8-3-25，二者为同一器物同一位置图片，图8-3-24为二维图片，图8-3-25为三维图片。（该器物釉表面曾被腐蚀剂腐蚀）

图8-3-24中的气泡B’在图8-3-25中隐约可见轮廓，其所在处釉表面比较粗糙，可见一处腐蚀斑块（见图8-3-25箭头C’所指处），具有扩张感。周围釉表面可见腐蚀性坑点斑密集分布，显得粗糙涂污。

二、壁变泡

（一）非破口壁变泡

1. 真品二维特征

见图8-3-26—图8-3-36。

（1）局变壁变泡较常见。

（2）非破口壁变泡内壁的风化以雾状针眼斑、磨砂针眼斑或颗粒针眼斑等形式呈现，质地变化的轮廓沿着泡壁，很少出界。

（3）雾状针眼斑分布细腻均匀（见图8-3-26—图8-3-29）。

（4）较大的气泡中其颗粒针眼斑可见色阶变化（见图8-3-34、图8-3-35）。

（5）壁变泡与周围玻璃相界线分明。

（6）周围玻璃相干净清晰。

图8-3-22

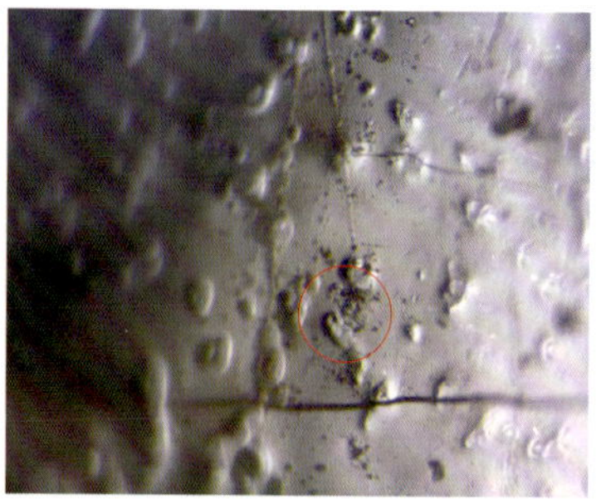

图8-3-23

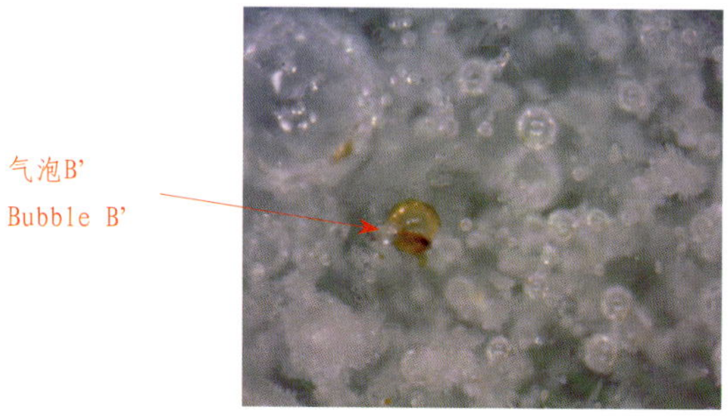

图8-3-24

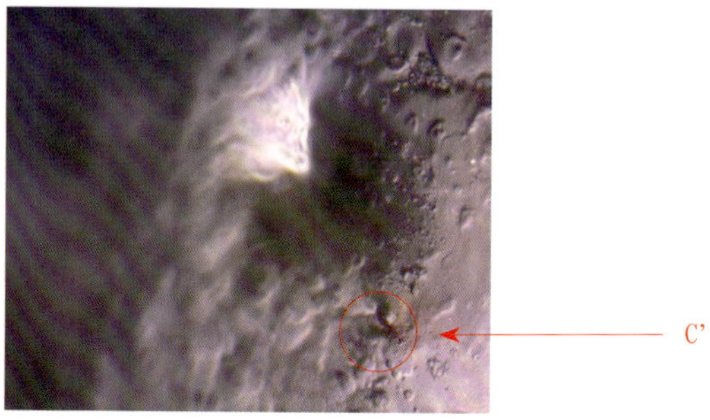

图8-3-25

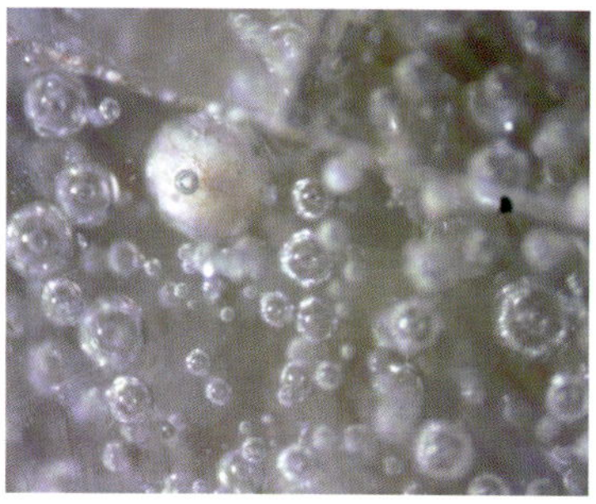

图8-3-26

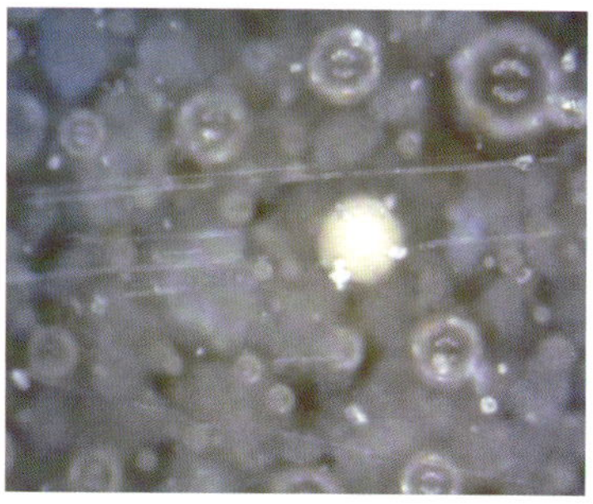

图8-3-27

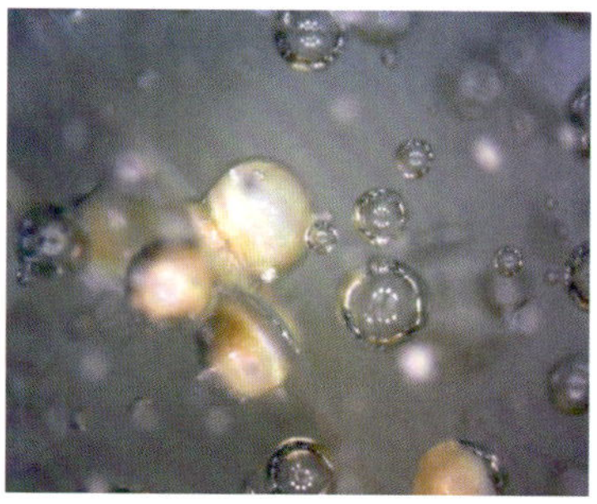

图8-3-28

edges (see pictures 8-3-49—8-3-51).

II. At times, foreign materials present beneath the bubble opening (see pictures 8-3-50, 8-3-52—8-3-54).

III. Some bubbles present with internal color spectrum (see pictures 8-3-51, 8-3-56 and 8-3-57).

IV. Some broken mouth bubbles present with CO type pitting (see Arrow E) in close conjunction with the bubble mouth. The bubble and pits can present with coloration, they are independent and clearly delineated (see pictures 8-3-54 and 8-3-55).

V. The bubble retains clear delineation from the surrounding glass phase.

VI. The glass phase is clean and clear.

b. Three-Dimensional Characteristics of Genuine Article

I. The bubble mouth is rounded and smooth.

II. It is possible for the surrounding glaze surface to present with channels other than the broken mouth.

III. The channel is clearly independent, its area is smaller than the underlying bubble.

IV. The glass phase surrounding the bubble opening remains smooth and clean.

V. Some of the glass phase presents with an aged feel.

See pictures 8-3-58 and 8-3-59, where 8-3-58 is the two-dimensional and 8-3-59 is the three-dimensional view of the same location.

Bubble C is not visible in picture 8-3-59, and as such is indicated with a red ring. The mouth opening of Bubble C is clearly visible in picture 8-3-59, rounded and smooth. There are two independently clear CO type pit mottles next to the mouth opening. Aside from these, the glaze surface is smooth and clean. This shows that at least some of the weathering occurring on Bubble C in picture 8-3-59 is on the bubble's interior surface. The pit mottles and mouth opening can all act as channels between the bubble and the external environment.

The surrounding glass phase also has clear and mutually independent scratches and CO type pit mottles. The mottles are reserved and clearly delineated.

See pictures 8-3-60 and 8-3-61, where 8-3-60 is the two-dimensional and 8-3-61 is the three-dimensional view of the same location.

The bubble is not visible in picture 8-3-61, and as such is indicated with a red ring. The mouth of Bubble C is clearly depicted with rounded smooth edges.

The surrounding glass phase also has clear and mutually independent scratches and CO type pit mottles. The mottles are reserved and clearly delineated. The surrounding glass phase also presents with densely distributed weathered striae and a relatively evident aged feel.

c. Two-Dimensional Characteristics of Forged Article

See pictures 8-3-62 and 8-3-63.

I. Broken mouths are usually not round and smooth.

II. The entire piece presents with uniform broken mouth bubbles.

III. The interior nature of the bubble has unclear depiction.

IV. The bubble and surrounding glass phase are not clearly delineated.

V. The surrounding glass phase is littered with needlepoint mottling and pitting, and is generally muddled.

d. Three-Dimensional Characteristics of Forged Article

I. The surrounding glaze surface presents with corrosion mottles with relatively large surface areas. The mottle edges are fuzzy and dispersive.

II. The surrounding glaze surface presents with corrosion mottles with surface areas larger than the underlying bubbles, indicating faux broken mouth bubbles.

III. The surrounding glaze surface has sporadic distribution of pitting or scratches, giving it a general muddled appearance.

See pictures 8-3-64 and 8-3-65, where 8-3-64 is the two-dimensional and 8-3-65 is the three-dimensional view of the same location (this piece has undergone treatment with aging reagent).

Bubble A' is not visible in picture 8-3-64 and as such is indicated with a red ring. The mouth of the bubble is clearly depicted, but has rough jagged edges. The glaze surface has

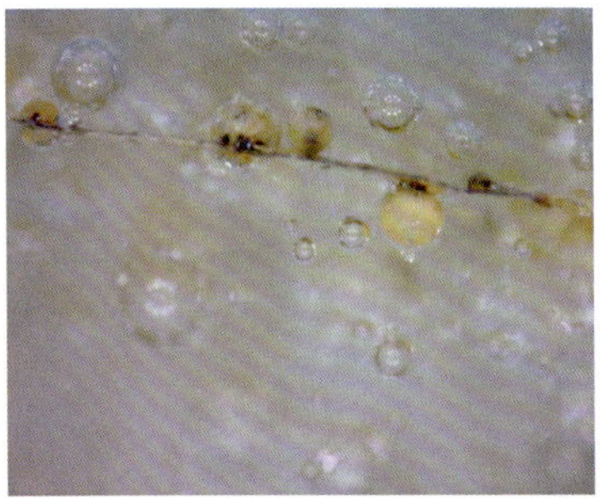
图8-3-29

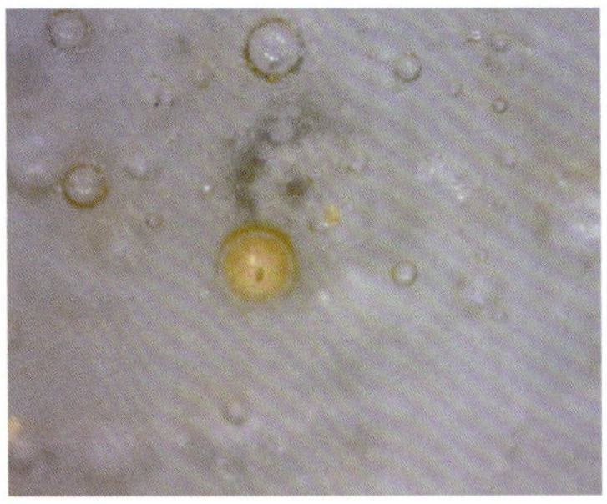
图8-3-30

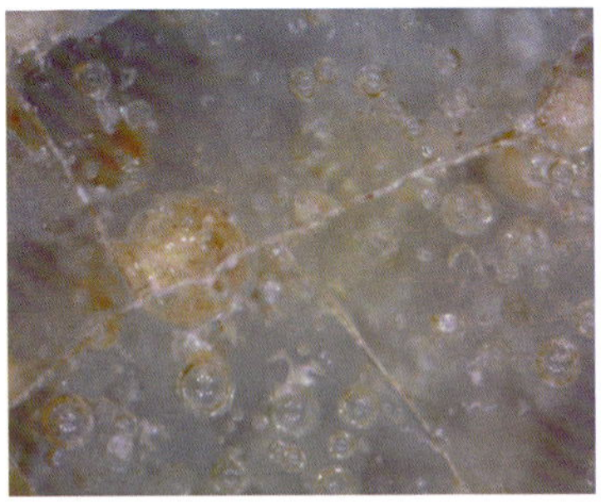
图8-3-31

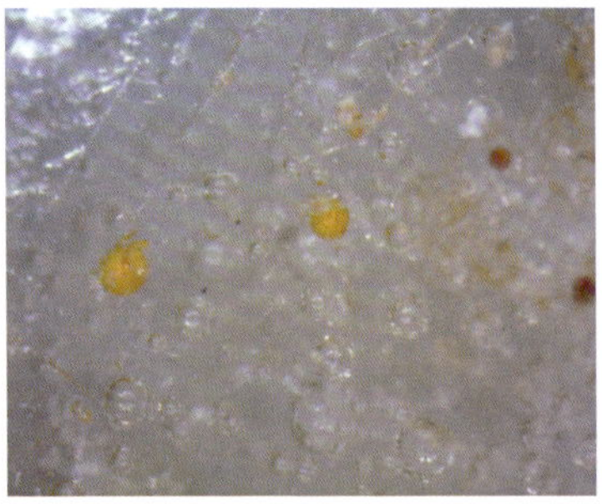
图8-3-32

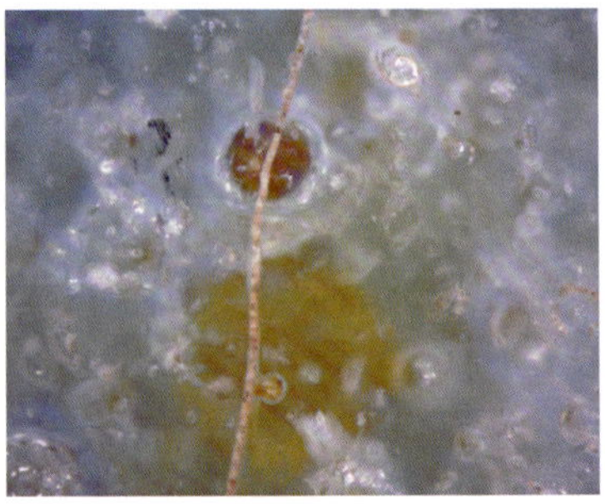
图8-3-33

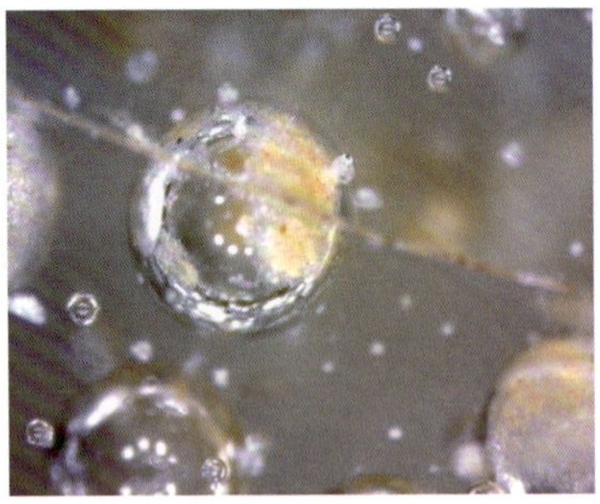
图8-3-34

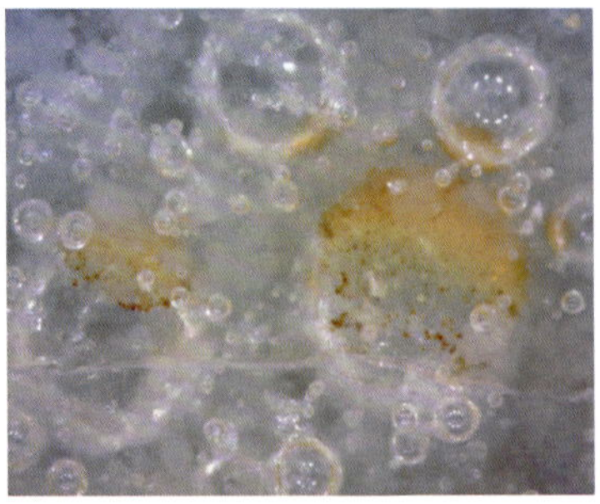
图8-3-35

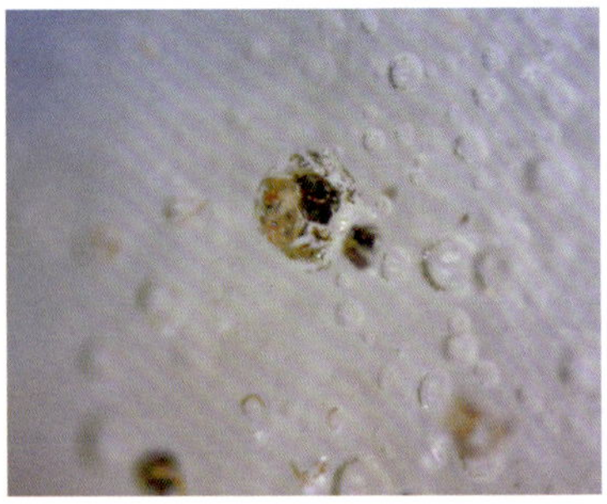
图8-3-36

2. 真品三维特征

（1）气泡所在处釉表面可见通道。

（2）通道清晰独立，面积远远小于气泡面积。

（3）通道周围的釉表面保持光滑洁净。

（4） 有的玻璃相干净清晰。

（5） 有的玻璃相表现出明显陈旧感。

见图8-3-37、图8-3-38，二者为同一器物同一位置图片，图8-3-37为二维图片，图8-3-38为三维图片。

图8-3-38中气泡A所在处釉表面有颜色变化，是由釉层中透出来的。颜色与其二维成像颜色相近，但显得更淡。颜色变化面积小于气泡最大直径。

周围玻璃相上还有其他各自独立清晰的划痕及CO型坑点斑，坑点斑均出现在釉表面凸起处，根部风化程度较顶部高，颜色比顶部深，斑块收敛，无扩张感，彼此界线清晰。玻璃相其余地方布满细密的风化纹路，有比较明显的陈旧感。

见图8-3-39、图8-3-40，二者为同一器物同一位置图片，图8-3-39为二维图片，图8-3-40为三维图片。

图8-3-39气泡B在图8-3-40中隐约只见淡淡的轮廓，气泡所在处的釉表面存在坑点斑及划痕，它们应该都是外界连接气泡内的通道。

周围玻璃相上还有其他各自独立清晰的坑点斑及划痕，斑块收敛，无扩张感，界线清晰。玻璃相其余地方布满细密的风化纹路，有比较明显的陈旧感。

coarsely diffused corrosion mottles, one of which completely covers the underlying bubble and extends beyond its surface area. This is a broken mouth bubble with faux texture.

The surrounding glaze surface is severely damaged, with a coarse distribution of pitting and scratches of a relatively large size with coarse surfaces, rough edges, and fuzzy and dispersive qualities that muddle their delineation from the surrounding glass phase. Undamaged areas of glass phase lack a clear aged feel, and the surface in general is coarsely muddled.

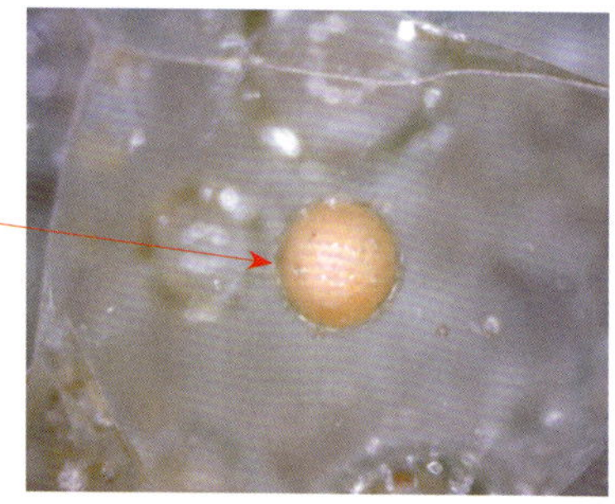

图8-3-37

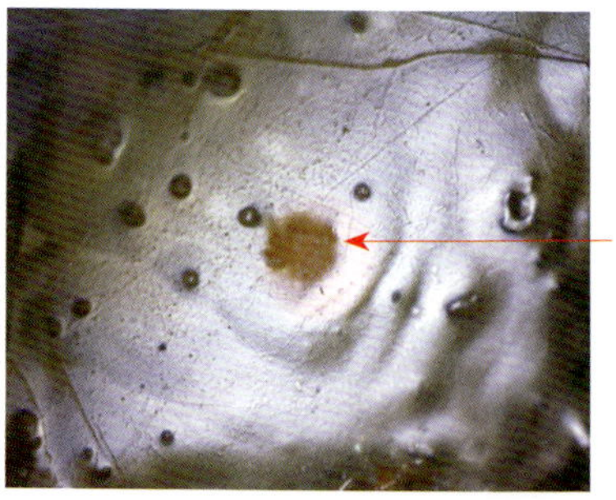

图8-3-38

图8-3-39

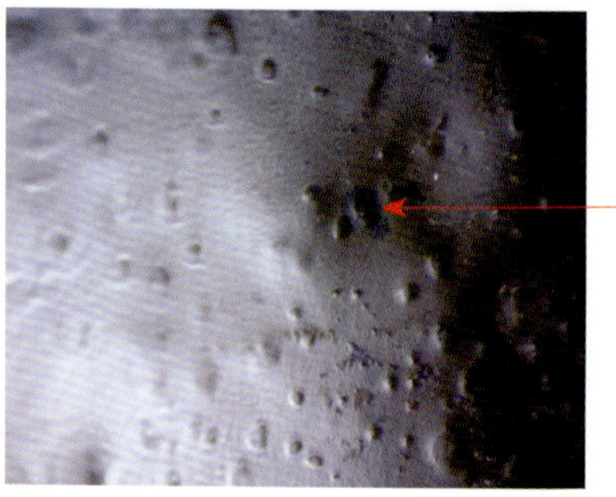

图8-3-40

3. 赝品二维特征

见图8-3-41—图8-3-44。

（1）赝品上的非破口壁变泡成像模糊。

（2）通常赝品上通器都是形貌类似的壁变泡，缺乏变化。

（3）有时出现壁变泡群，泡与泡之间有色块或色丝粘连，界线不分明。疑是人为做旧用有色液体染色形成的现象（见图8-3-43、图8-3-44）。

（4）壁变泡与周围玻璃相界线不分明。

（5）周围玻璃相上分布有坑点斑或划痕，具有扩张感，整体显得涂污模糊。

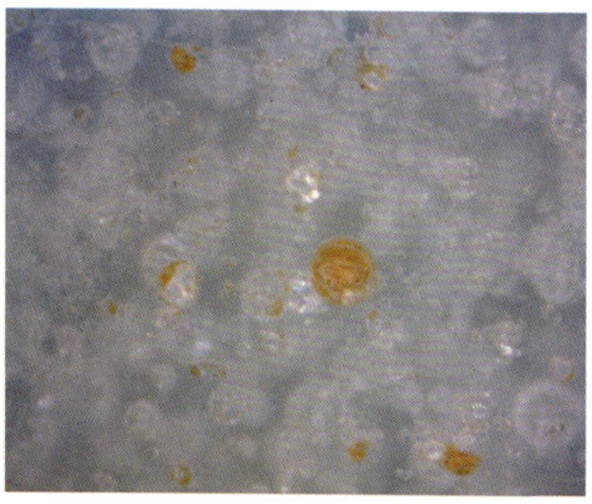

图8-3-41

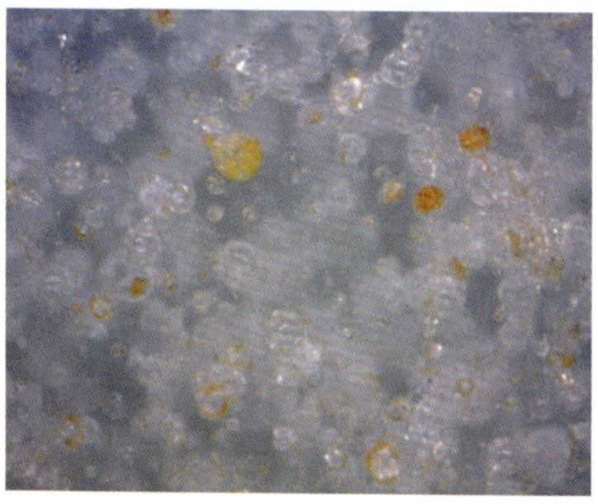

图8-3-42

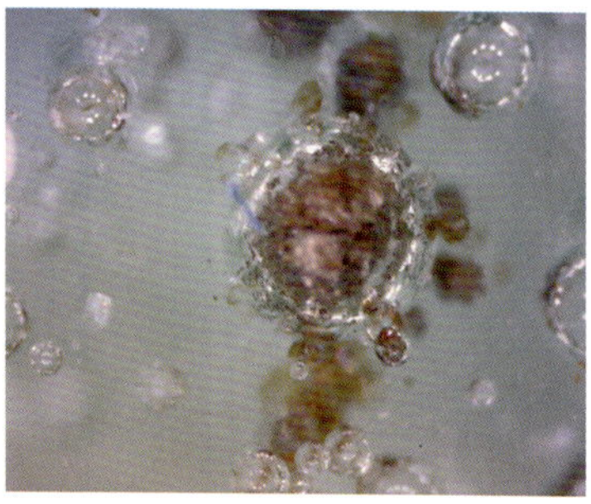

图8-3-43

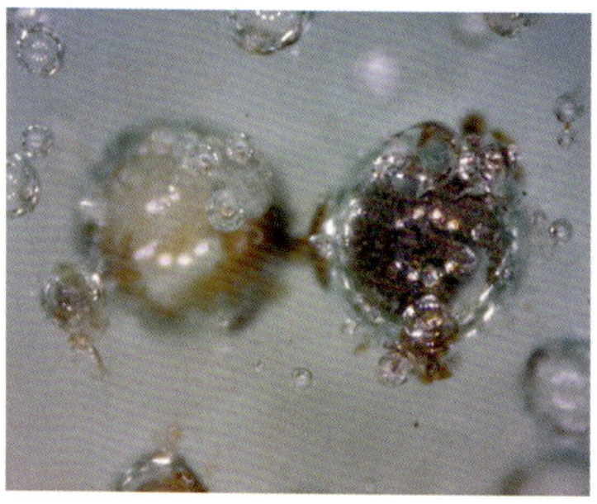

图8-3-44

4. 赝品三维特征

（1）有的壁变泡所在处的釉表面大部分被腐蚀性斑块覆盖，斑块具有扩张感。

（2）有的壁变泡所在处的釉表面存在腐蚀斑块，斑块最大直径甚至超过气泡最大直径，所谓的非破口壁变泡实际是假象壁变泡。

（3）周围玻璃相有腐蚀性坑点斑或划痕密集分布，斑块或划痕边沿呈毛刺状，具有扩张感，整体显得混乱涂污。

见图8-3-45、图8-3-46，二者为同一器物同一位置图片，图8-3-45为二维图片，图8-3-46为三维图片。（该器物釉表面曾被腐蚀剂腐蚀）

图8-3-45的气泡A’在图8-3-46中位于红圈釉下处，其所在处釉表面大部分被腐蚀性斑块覆盖，斑块具有扩张感。

周围釉表面破坏严重，杂乱无章地分布着坑点斑、划痕，面积都比较大，表面粗糙，边沿粗粝，呈毛刺状，有扩张感，与周围玻璃相界线不分明。未被破坏的玻璃相无陈旧感。釉表面整体显得粗糙涂污。

见图8-3-47、图8-3-48，二者为同一器物同一位置图片，图8-3-47为二维图片，图8-3-48为三维图片。（该器物釉表面曾被腐蚀剂腐蚀）

图8-3-47中的气泡B’在图8-3-48中位于红圈釉下处，其所在处釉表面已被破坏，腐蚀斑块的最大直径甚至超过气泡最大直径，具有扩张感，所谓的非破口壁变泡实际是假象壁变泡。周围釉表面呈现新瓷的光滑，还有整齐、方向一致的刷痕。

（二）破口壁变泡

1. 真品二维特征

（1）气泡破口呈较规整的圆形，边沿圆滑（见图8-3-49—图8-3-51）。

（2）有时破口下方可见物质存在（见图8-3-50、图8-3-52—图8-3-54）。

（3）有的气泡内壁有色阶变化（见图8-3-51、图8-3-56、图8-3-57）。

（4）有时破口壁变泡所在处及邻近的釉表面存在CO型坑点斑（如图8-3-55箭头所指处）。坑点斑与壁变泡有时有色差变化，各自独立清晰，界线分明（见图8-3-54、图8-3-55）。

（5）破口壁变泡与周围玻璃相界线分明。

（6）周围玻璃相干净清晰。

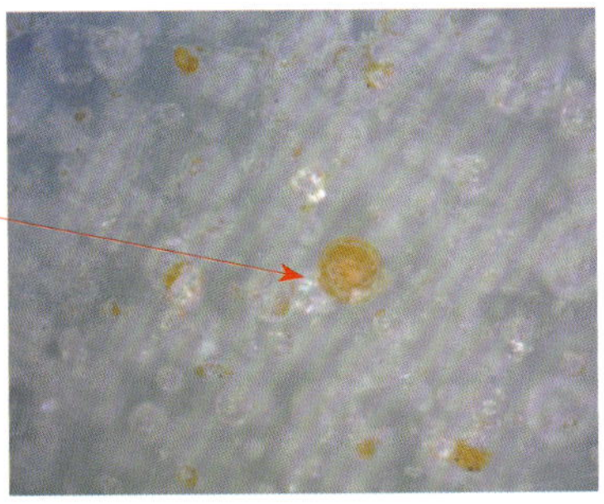

图8-3-45

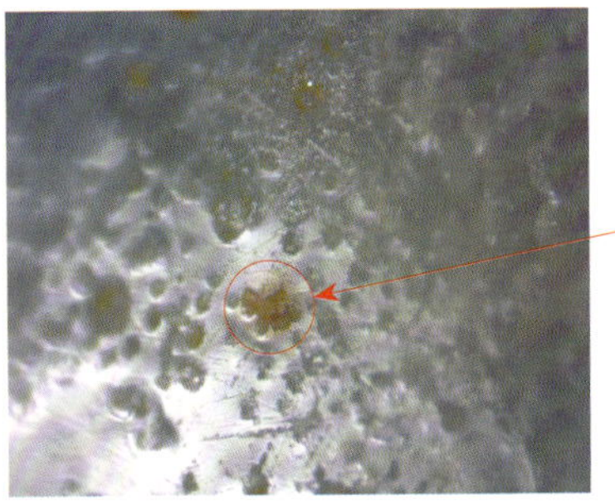

图8-3-46

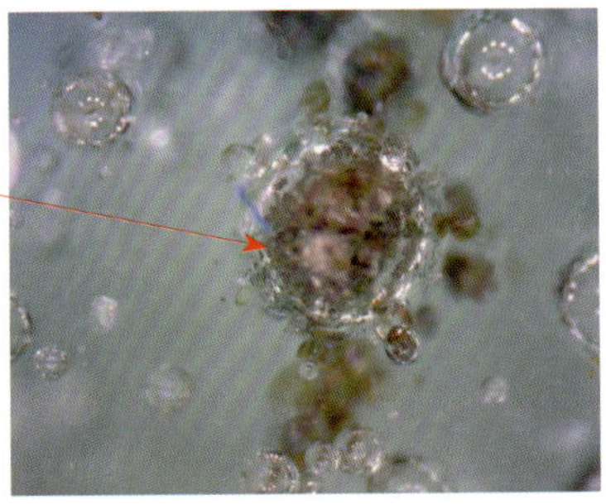

图8-3-47

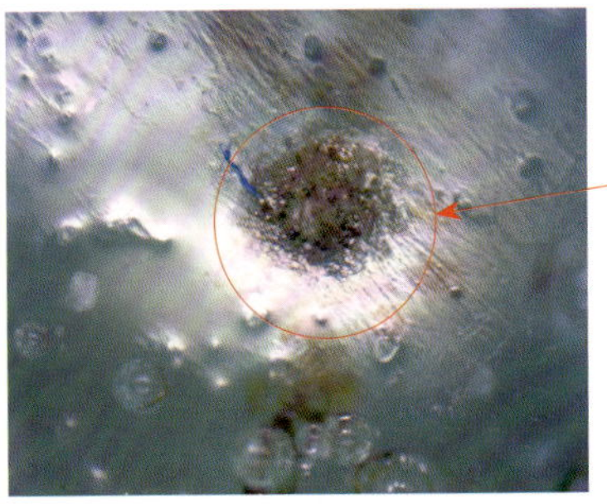

图8-3-48

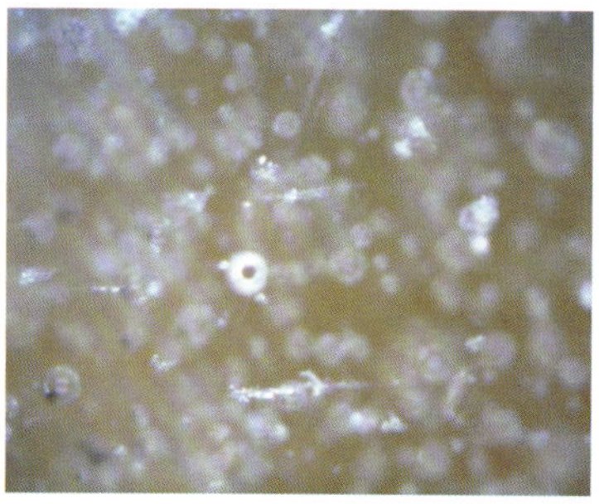

图8-3-49

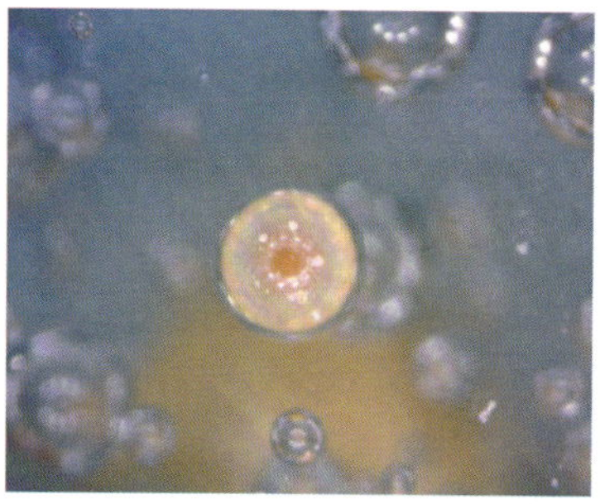

图8-3-50

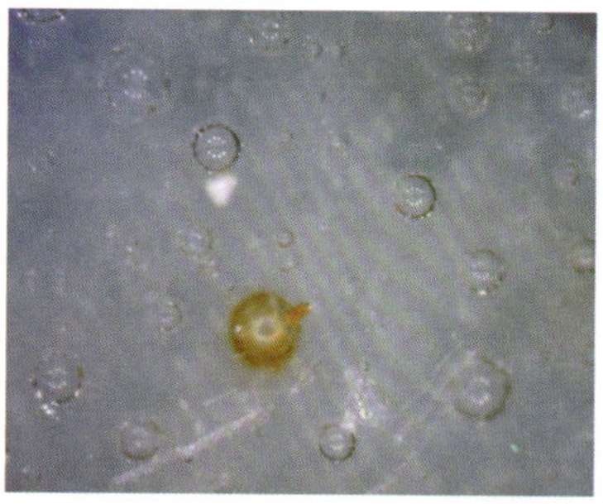

图8-3-51

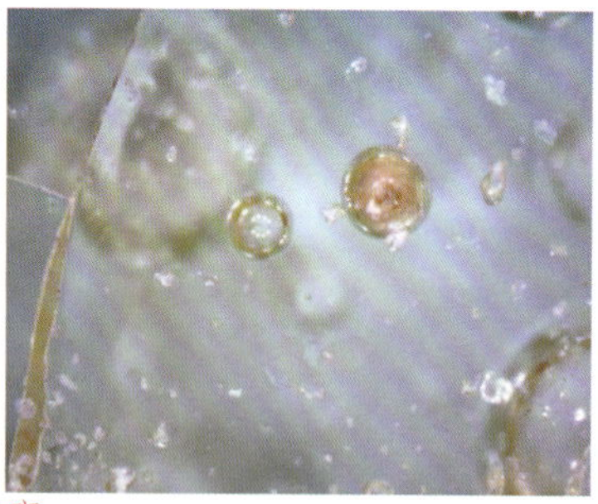

图8-3-52

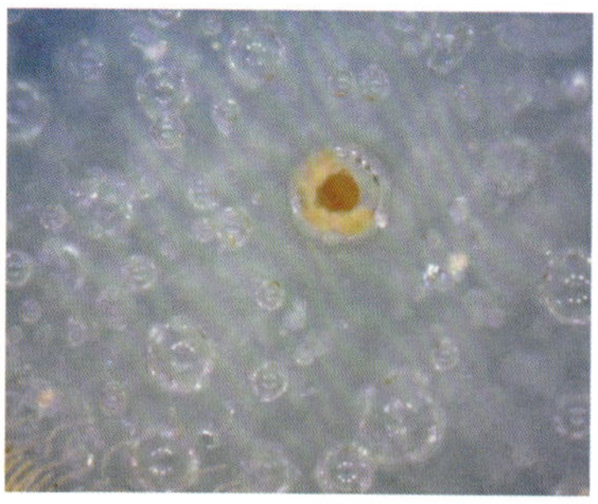

图8-3-53

CO型坑点斑
CO Type Pit Mottle

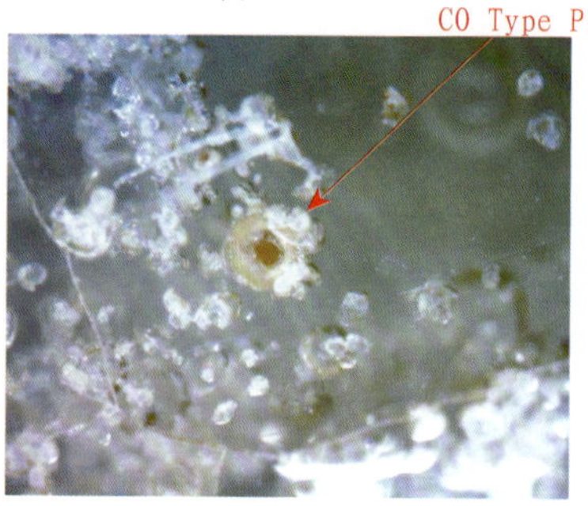

图8-3-54

CO型坑点斑
CO Type Pit Mottle

图8-3-55

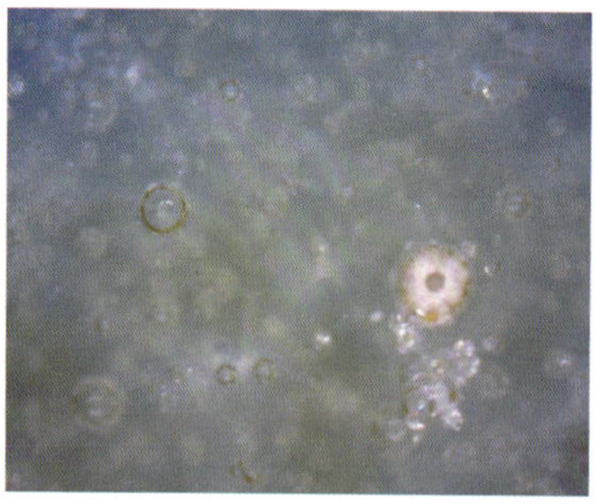

图8-3-56

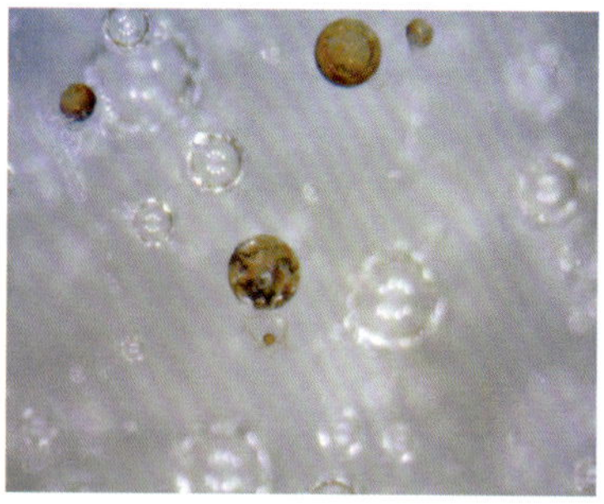

图8-3-57

2. 真品三维特征

（1）气泡破口边沿圆滑。

（2）气泡所在处釉表面可见除破口以外的通道。

（3）通道清晰独立，面积小于气泡面积。

（4）通道周围釉表面保持光滑洁净。

（5）有时玻璃相表现出明显陈旧感。

见图8-3-58、图8-3-59，二者为同一器物同一位置图片，图8-3-58为二维图片，图8-3-59为三维图片。

图8-3-58中的气泡C在图8-3-59中位于红圈釉下处，不可见。气泡C的破口在图8-3-59中清晰可见，破口圆滑。破口周围可见两处颜色较深的CO型坑点斑，清晰独立。除此以外釉表面光滑洁净。这说明图8-3-59中气泡C的风化斑块大部分处于气泡内壁。坑点斑及破口都可以是外界连接气泡内的通道所在处。

周围玻璃相上还有其他各自独立清晰的坑点斑及划痕，斑块收敛，彼此界线清晰。

见图8-3-60、图8-3-61，二者为同一器物同一位置图片，图8-3-60为二维图片，图8-3-61为三维图片。

图8-3-60中的气泡D在图8-3-61中位于红圈釉下处，不可见。气泡D的破口在图8-3-61中清晰可见，破口圆滑。

周围玻璃相上还有其他各自独立清晰的坑点斑及划痕，斑块收敛，彼此界线清晰，玻璃相其余地方布满细密的风化纹路，有比较明显的陈旧感。

3. 赝品二维特征

见图8-3-62、图8-3-63。

（1）破口大多不圆滑。

（2）器物通器都是形貌相似的破口壁变泡。

（3）破口壁变泡成像不清晰。

（4）破口壁变泡与周围玻璃相界线不分明。

（5）周围玻璃相上分布有针眼斑和坑点斑等迹型，整体显得涂污模糊。

4. 赝品三维特征

（1）有的破口壁变泡所在处的釉表面存在腐蚀斑块，腐蚀斑块面积较大，斑块粗粝，呈毛刺状，具有扩张感。

（2）有的破口壁变泡所在处的釉表面存在腐蚀斑块，斑块最大直径甚至超过气泡最大直径，所谓的破口壁变泡实际是破口假象壁变泡。

（3）周围玻璃相上分布有坑点斑或划痕等迹型，整体显得粗糙涂污。

见图8-3-64、图8-3-65，二者为同一器物同一位置图片，图8-3-64为二维图片，图8-3-65为三维图片。（该器物釉表面曾被腐蚀剂腐蚀）

图8-3-64中的破口壁变泡在图8-3-65中红圈下，其所在处釉表面已被破坏，腐蚀斑块粗糙，呈毛刺状，最大直径甚至超过气泡最大直径，具有扩张感，所谓的破口壁变泡实际是破口假象壁变泡。

周围釉表面破坏严重，杂乱无章地分布着坑点斑、划痕，面积都比较大，表面粗糙，边沿粗粝，呈毛刺状，有扩张感，与周围玻璃相界线不分明。未被破坏的玻璃相无陈旧感。釉表面整体显得粗糙涂污。

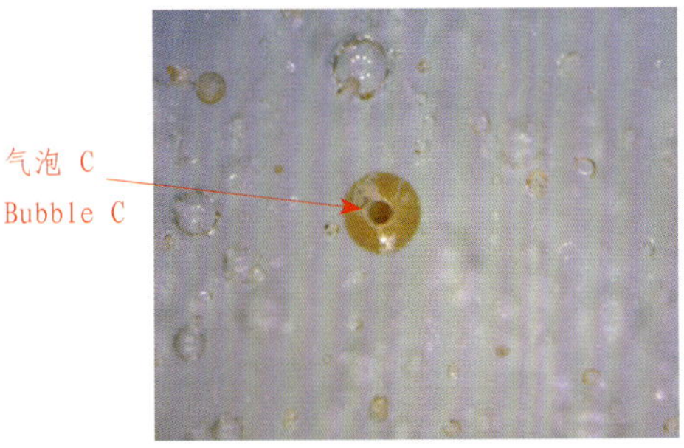

图8-3-58

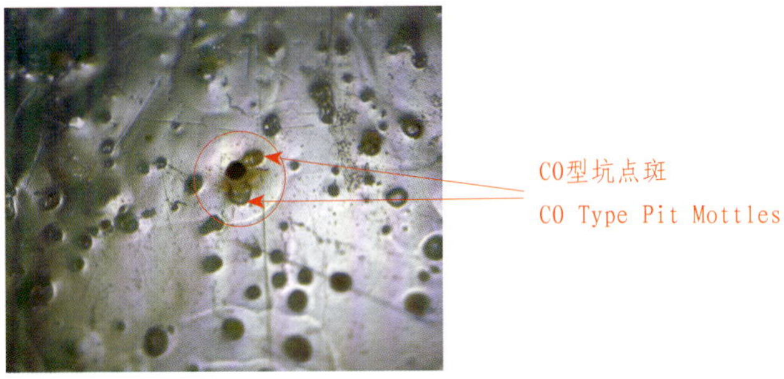

图8-3-59

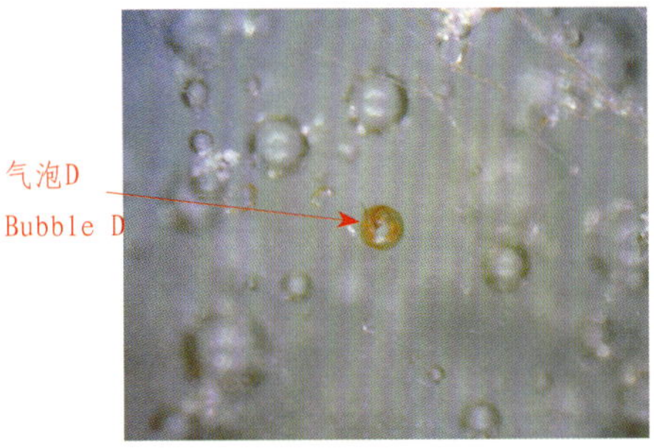

图8-3-60

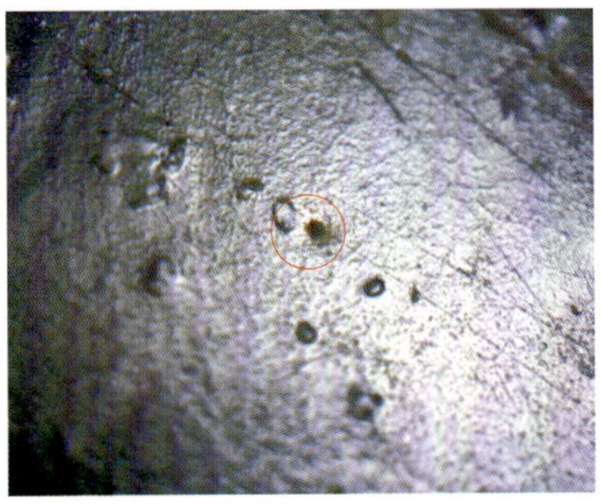

图8-3-61

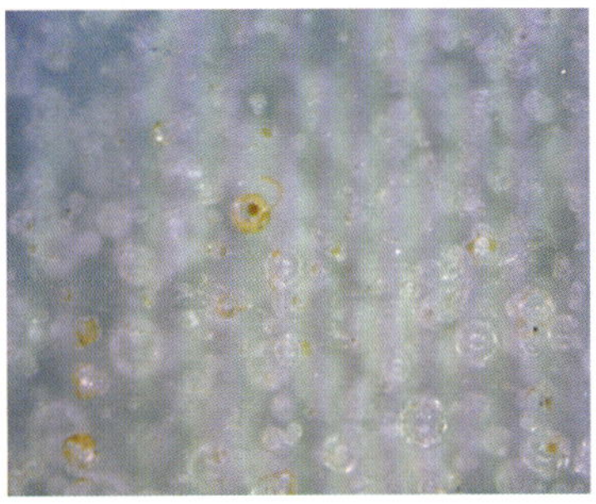

图8-3-62

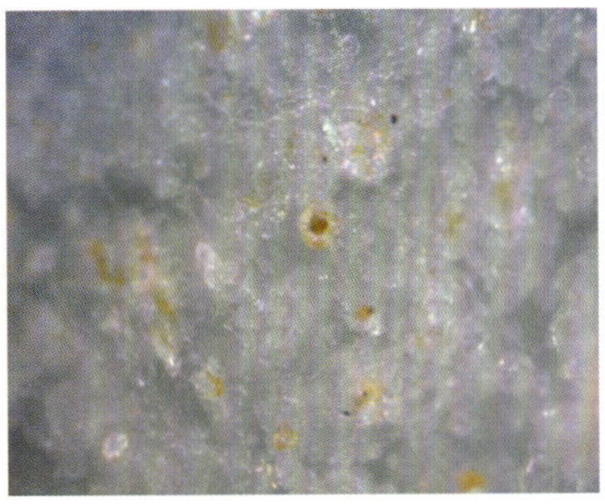

图8-3-63

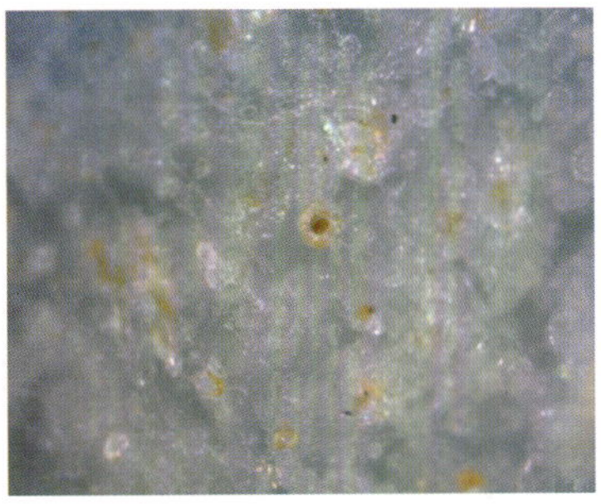

图8-3-64

图8-3-65

第四节
龙泉窑系青瓷鬃眼真品与赝品比对分析

一、真品二维特征

（一）鬃眼内部及口部周围的釉表面存在颗粒物质（见图8-4-1—图8-4-8）。

（二）鬃眼内部及口部周围的釉表面存在纤丝（见图8-4-9—图8-4-11）。

（三）鬃眼内部及口部周围的釉表面会有颜色变化（见图8-4-12—图8-4-23）。

（四）部分鬃眼口部周围釉下出现絮状斑或色变泡（见图8-4-24、图8-4-25）。

二、赝品二维特征

见图8-4-26—图8-4-31。

（一）鬃眼内部沉积堆积物很少（见图8-4-26、图8-4-27）。

（二）鬃眼内部及口部周围大部分都未变色，少见色阶变化。

（三）鬃眼内部及口部周围偶尔可见纤丝，但数目很少（见图8-4-28、图8-4-29）。

（四）鬃眼口部周围的釉表面反光非常明显（见图8-4-30、图8-4-31）。

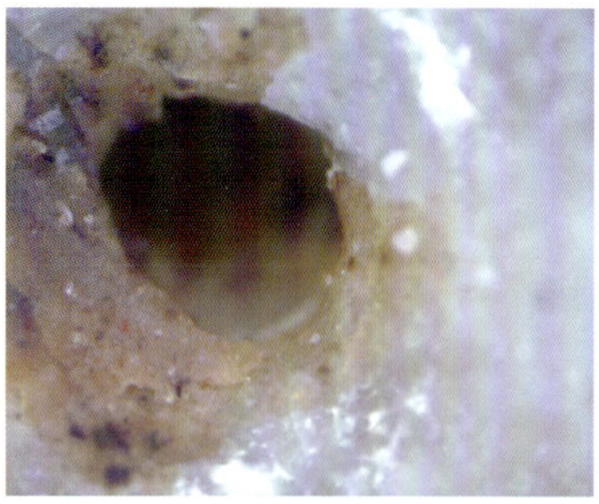
图8-4-1

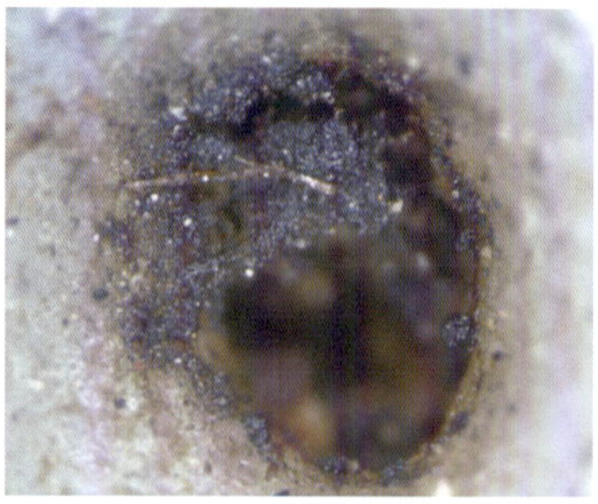
图8-4-2

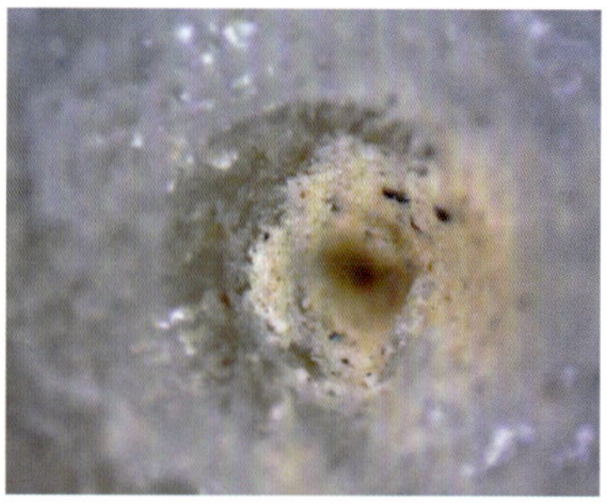
图8-4-3

图8-4-4

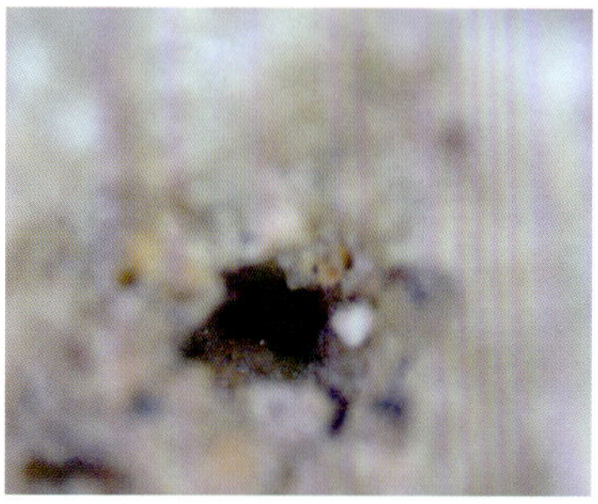
图8-4-5

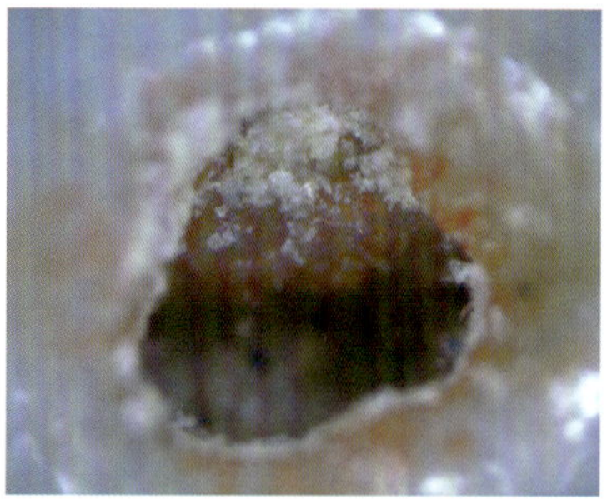
图8-4-6

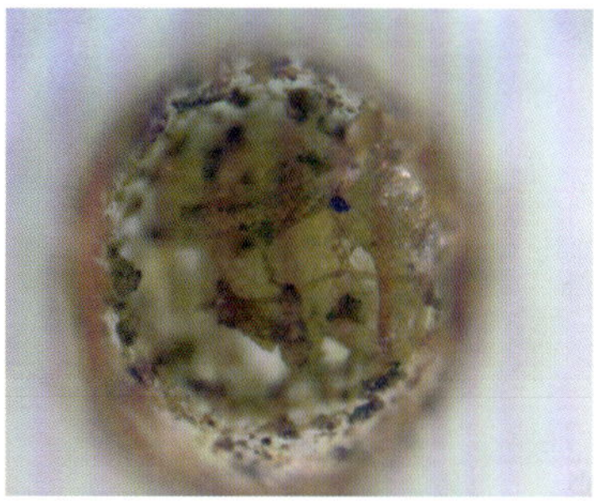
图8-4-7

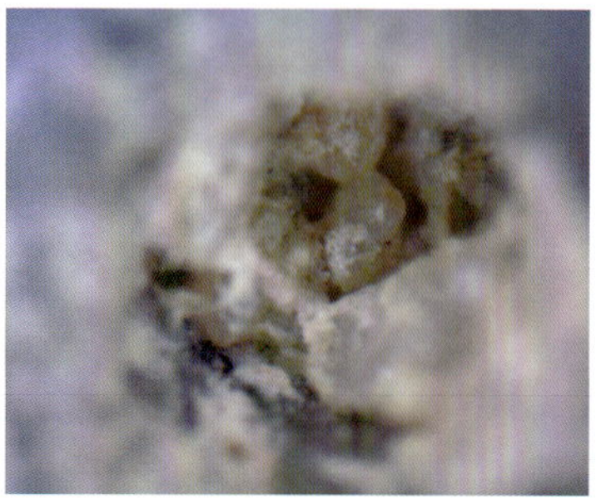
图8-4-8

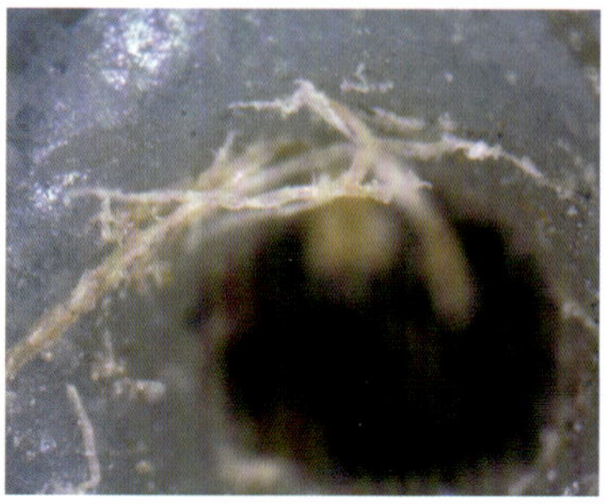
图8-4-9

Section 4:

Genuine and Forged Longquan Kiln System Celadon Bristle Pit Comparison

1. Two-Dimensional Characteristics of Genuine Article

A. The pit interior and mouth surroundings can present with granulated materials (see pictures 8-4-1—8-4-8).

B. The pit interior and mouth surroundings can present with filaments (see pictures 8-4-9—8-4-11).

C. The pit interior and mouth surroundings can present with color change (see pictures 8-4-12—8-4-23).

D. Some pits present with colored bubbles or floccus mottling in the glaze level surrounding the pit mouth (see pictures 8-4-24 and 8-4-25).

2. Two-Dimensional Characteristics of Forged Article

See pictures 8-4-26—8-4-31.

A. Relatively few material deposits within the pit interior (see pictures 8-4-26 and 8-4-27).

B. The pit interior and mouth surroundings present without coloration or limited color change.

C. The pit interior and mouth surroundings can present with filaments, however they are limited in number (see pictures 8-4-28 and 8-4-29).

D. The trumpet shaped mouth surrounding the pit has a glossy reflectivity (see pictures 8-4-30 and 8-4-31).

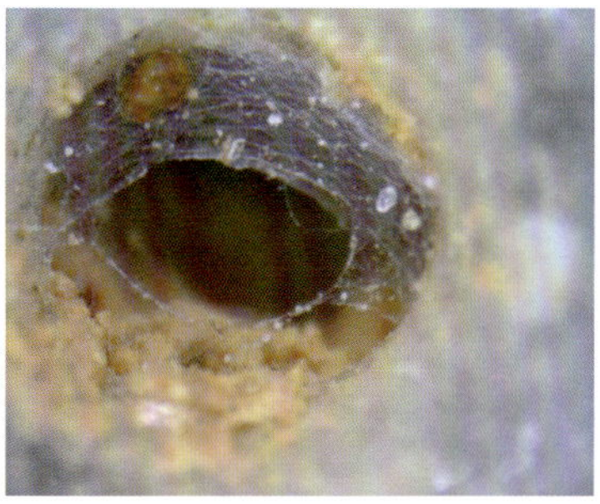
图8-4-10

图8-4-11

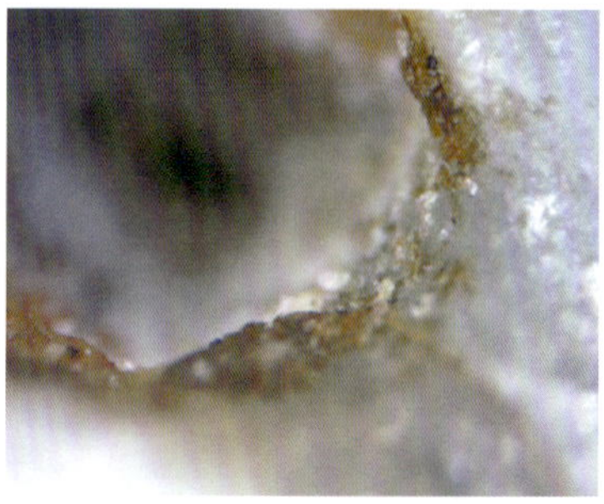
图8-4-12

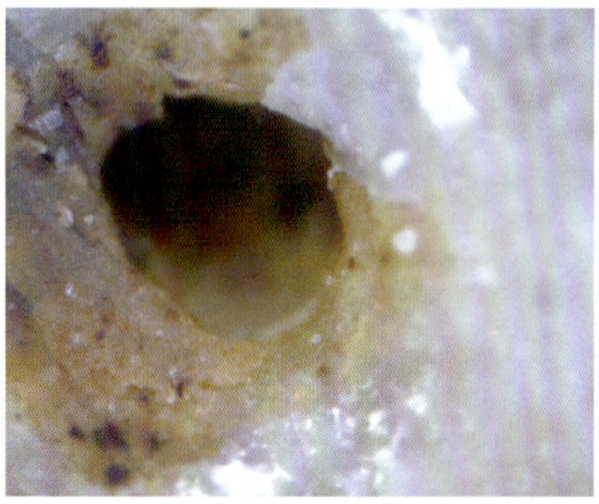
图8-4-13

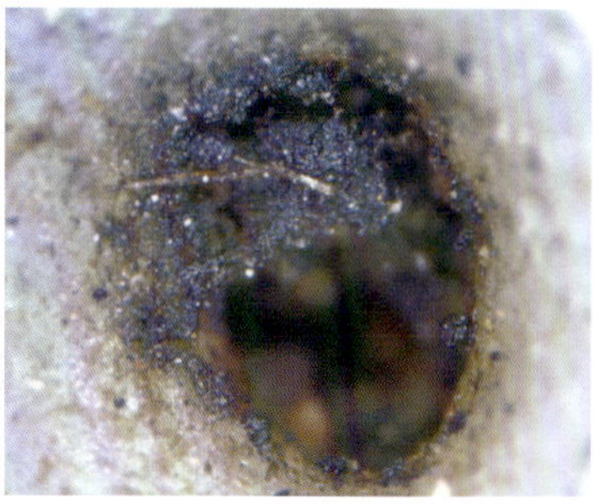
图8-4-14

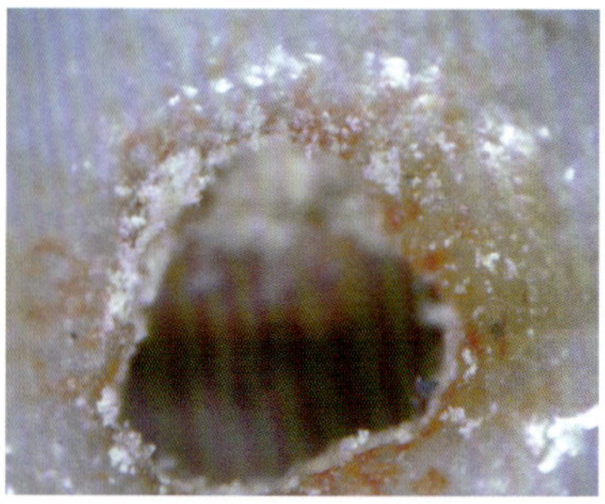
图8-4-15

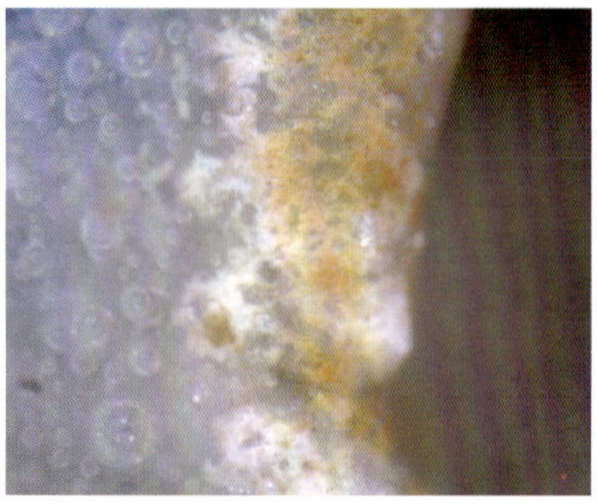
图8-4-16

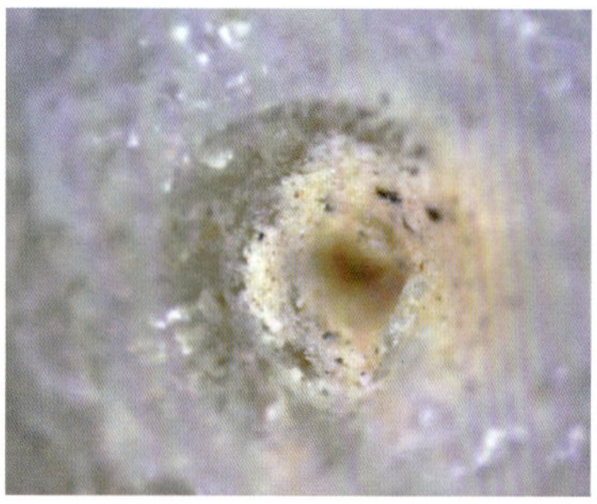
图8-4-17

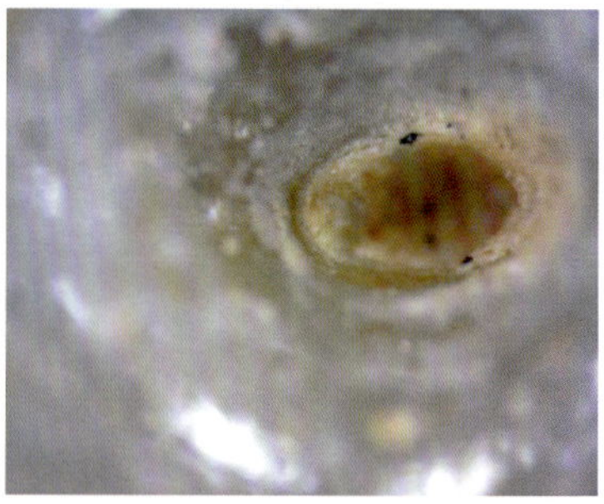
图8-4-18

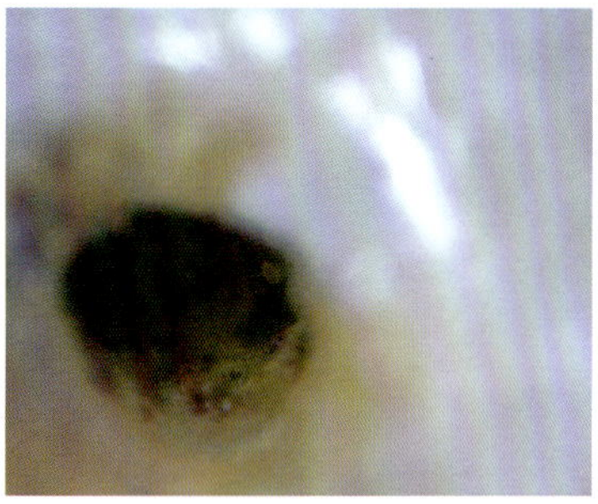
图8-4-19

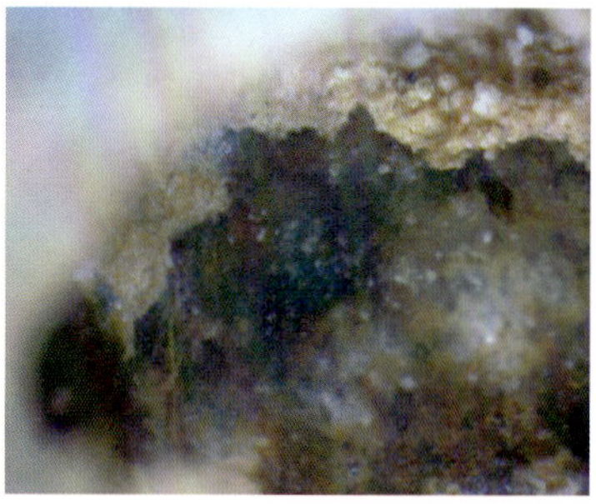
图8-4-20

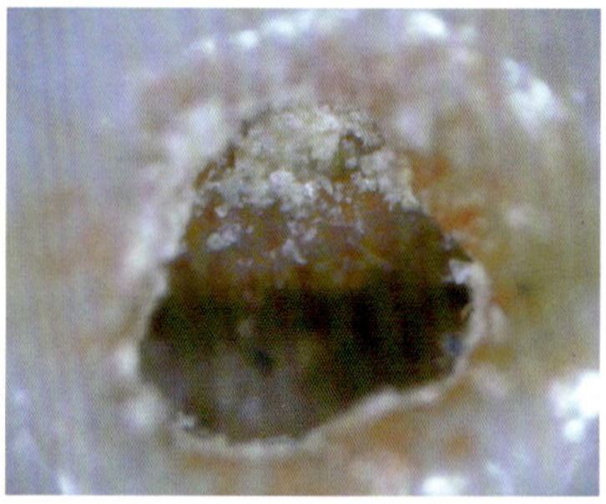
图8-4-21

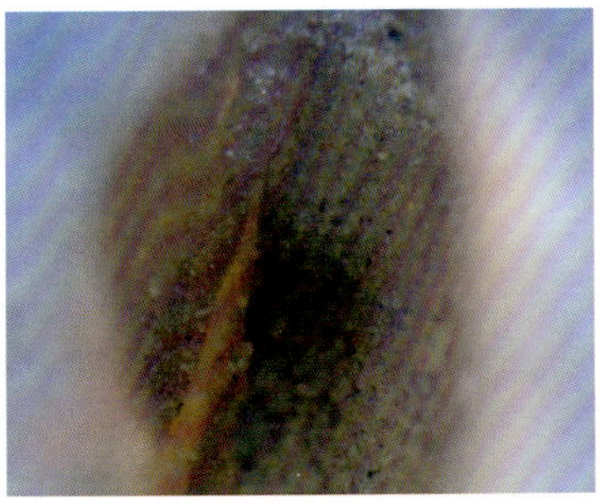

图8-4-22

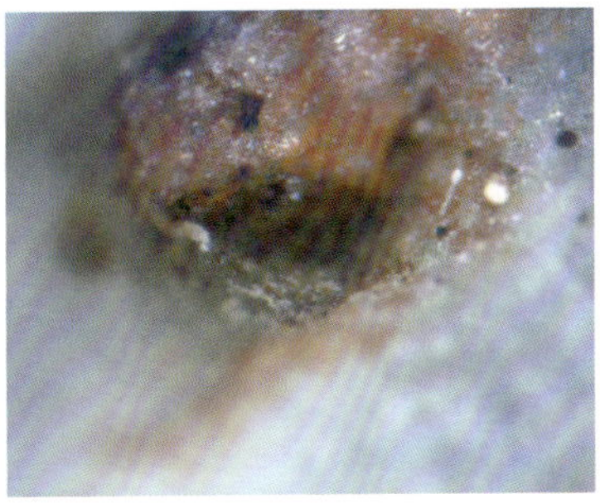

图8-4-23

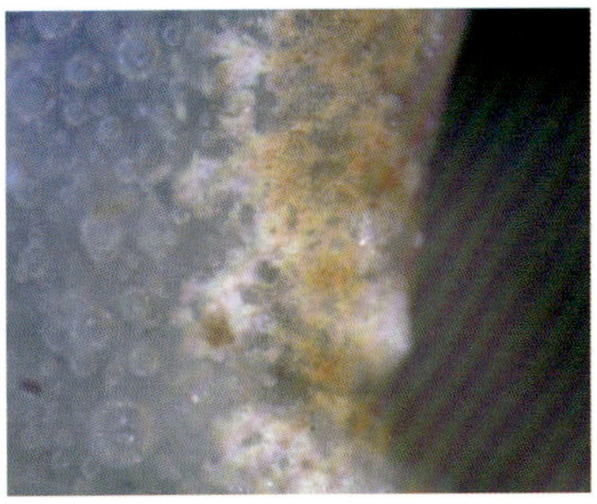

图8-4-24

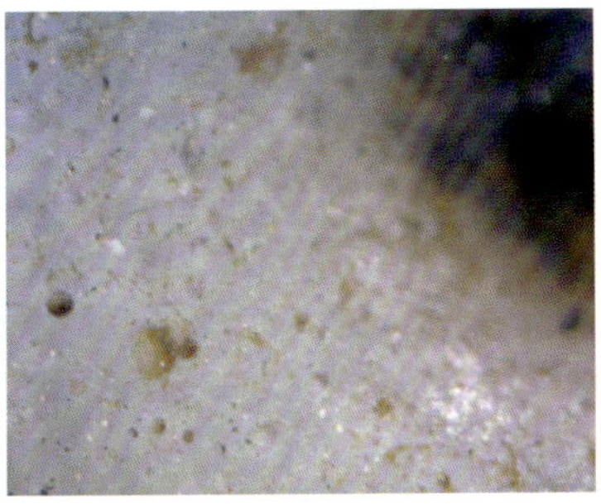

图8-4-25

图8-4-26

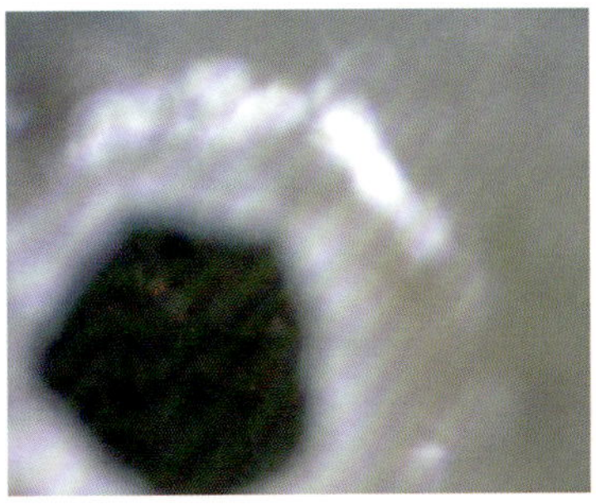

图8-4-27

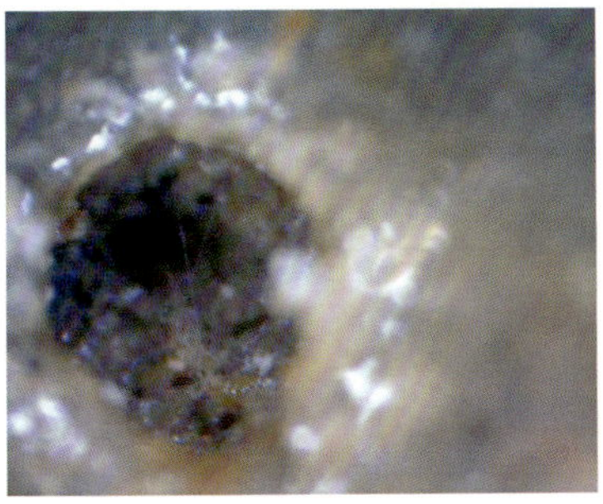

图8-4-28

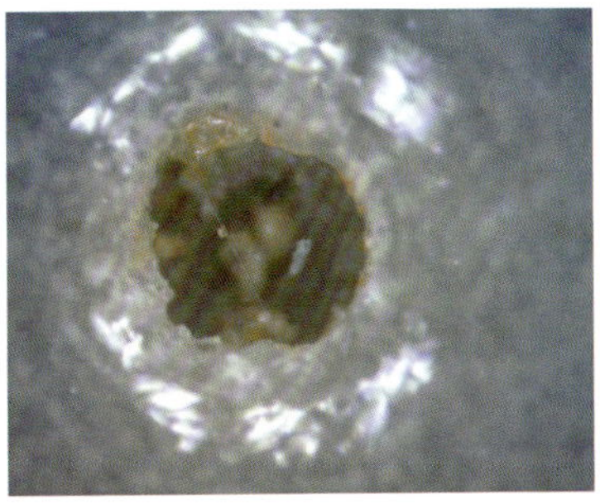

图8-4-29

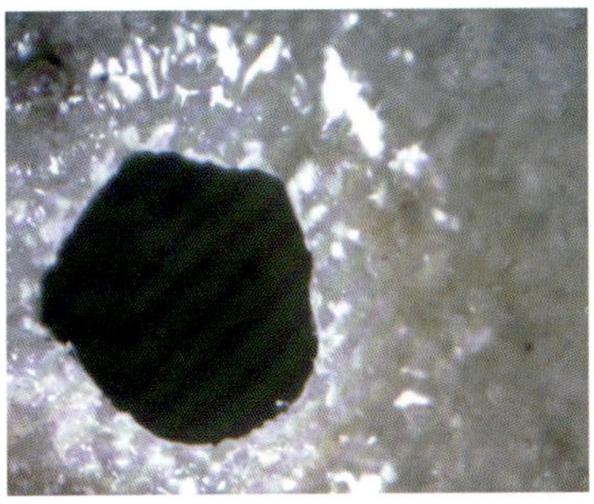

图8-4-30

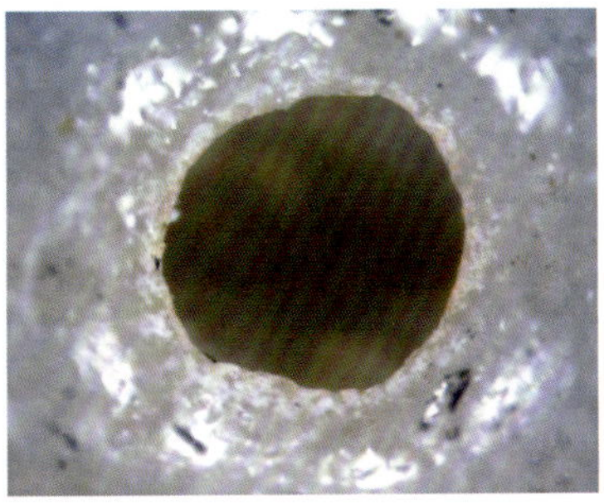

图8-4-31

第五节
龙泉窑系青瓷釉层形貌真品与赝品比对分析

一、真品三维特征

（一）有的釉表面布满划痕或坑点斑，纹路及斑块边沿都显得圆滑（见图8-5-1—图8-5-6）。

（二）有的釉表面CO型坑点斑分布较多，通常CO型坑点斑的风化形貌都是根部风化程度更高，所以颜色更暗，顶部较浅（见图8-5-7—图8-5-10）。

（三）有的釉表面整体布满细密的风化纹路，就像陈旧的硬币表面（见图8-5-10—图8-5-14[241][242]）。

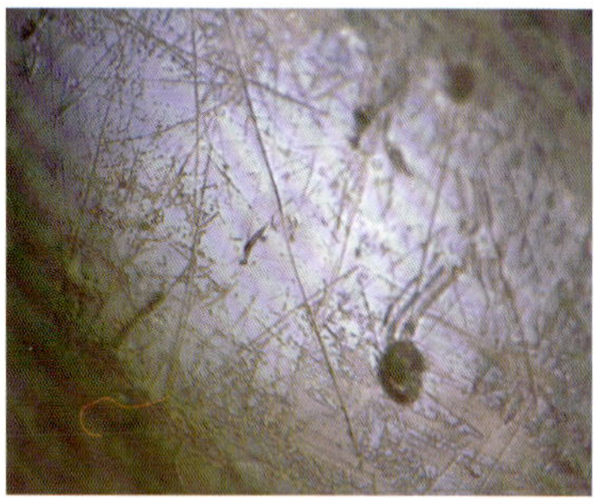
图8-5-1

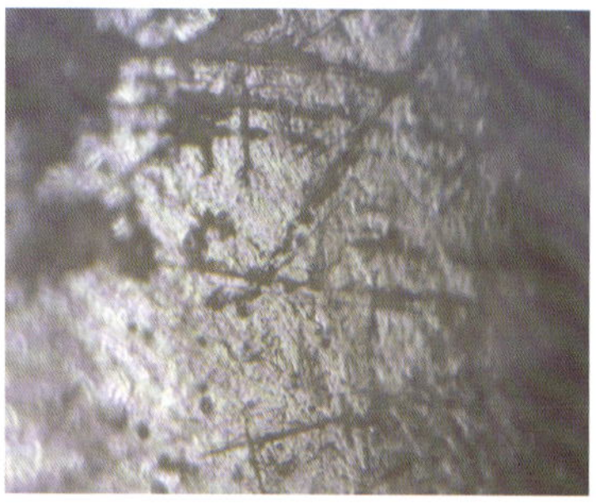
图8-5-2

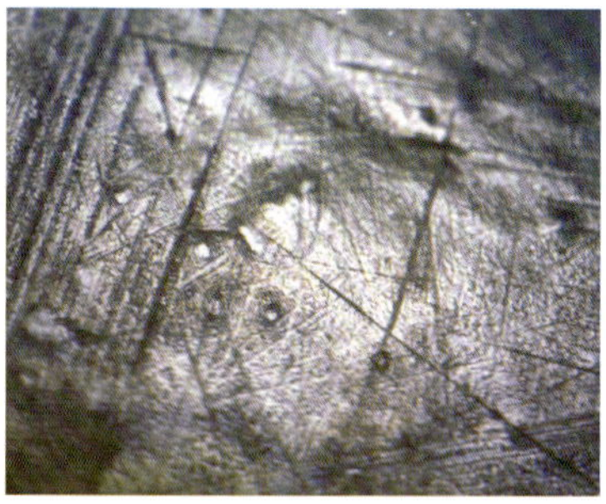
图8-5-3

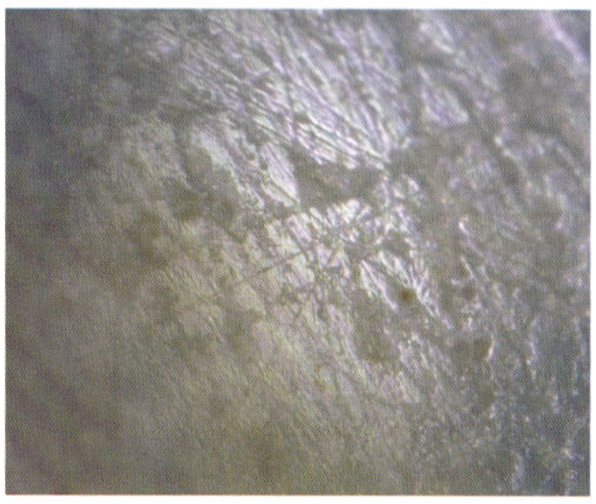
图8-5-4

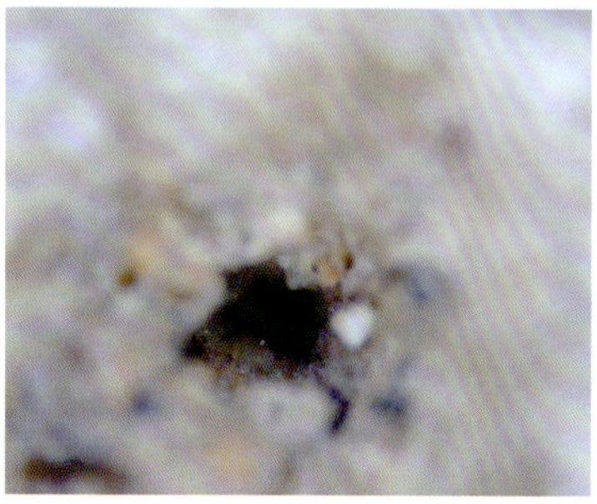
图8-5-5

图8-5-6

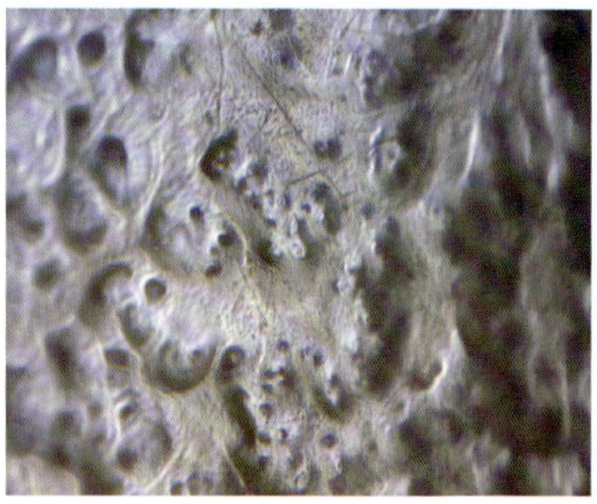
图8-5-7

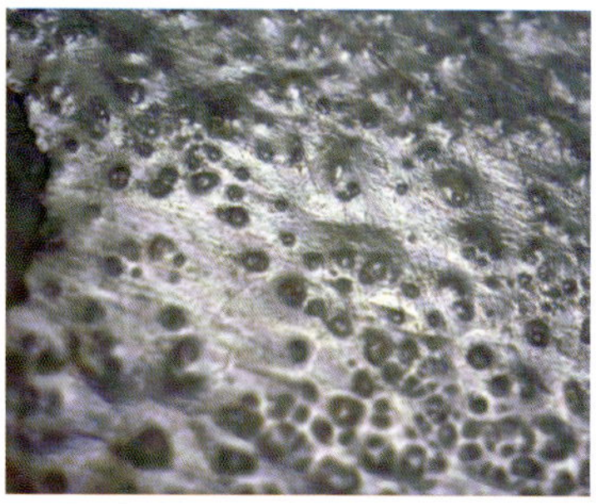
图8-5-8

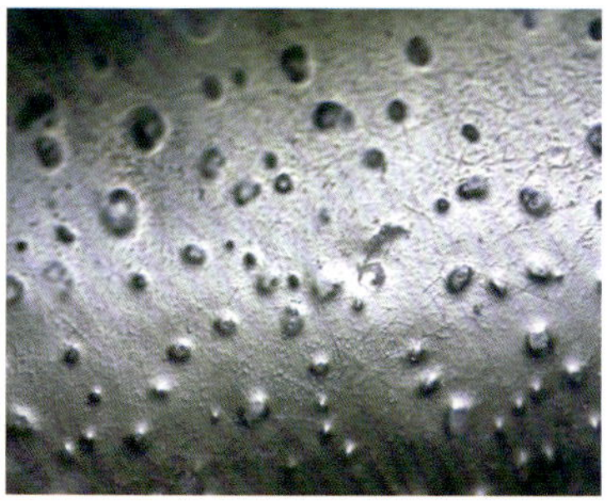
图8-5-9

Section 5:
Genuine and Forged Longquan Kiln System Celadon Glaze Surface Appearance Comparison

1. Three-Dimensional Characteristics of Genuine Article

A. Some glaze surfaces present with a relatively full distribution of scratches or pits. The edges of said traces appear rounded and smooth (see pictures 8-5-1—8-5-6).

B. Some glaze surfaces present with a relatively high distribution of CO type pitting. These CO type pits most commonly present on areas of glaze protrusion, with the higher weathering severity occurring at the base of the protrusion (darker coloration) while the peak of the protrusion retains a smooth quality (lighter coloration) (see pictures 8-5-7—8-5-10).

C. Some glaze surfaces present with a relatively full distribution of finely dense weathering striae, similar to that of an old coin, giving it an aged feel (see pictures 8-5-10—8-5-14 [241][242]).

2. Three-Dimensional Characteristics of Forged Article

A. Some glaze surfaces are smooth and clean, lacking any signs of weathering traces (see pictures 8-5-15 and 8-5-16).

B. Some glaze surfaces present with a relatively full distribution of CO type pits, their weathered appearance uniform. Within one unit image, protrusions can present with both dark colored bases as well as peaks. This is due to human forced aging in which an entire piece has undergone unnatural corrosion (see pictures 8-5-17—8-5-20).

C. Aside from these CO type pits, the surrounding glass phase can present with a sporadic distribution of pits or scratches with coarse surfaces, rough edges, and fuzzy dispersive qualities (see pictures 8-5-17—8-5-20). The surface in general is coarsely muddled.

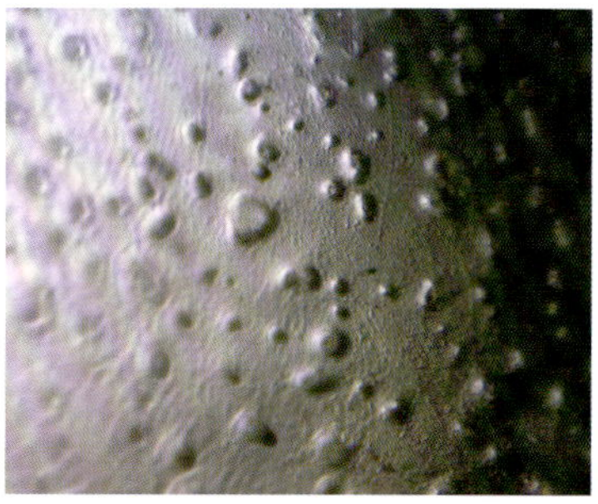

图8-5-10

图8-5-11

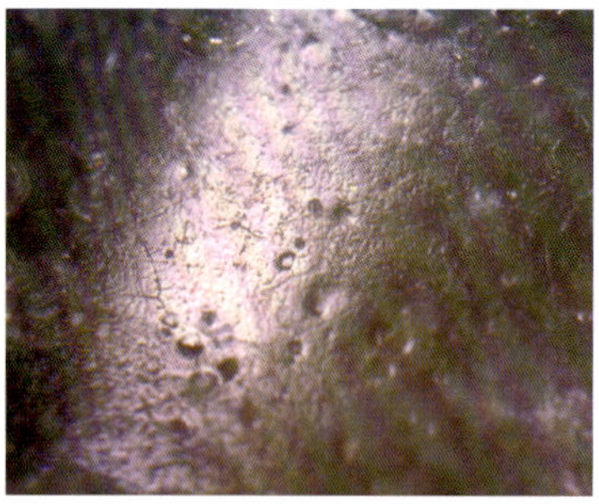

图8-5-12

图8-5-13

图8-5-14

二、赝品三维特征

（一）有的釉表面光滑干净，没有明显风化痕迹（见图8-5-15、图8-5-16）。

（二）有的釉表面CO型坑点斑分布较多，CO型坑点斑的风化形貌不一致，单位图片中既有根部颜色较暗的，也有顶部较暗的，疑是人为做旧以后，整体无规律地破坏了釉表面的结果（见图8-5-17—图8-5-20）。

（三）除CO型坑点斑以外，玻璃相上其余的地方杂乱无章地分布有坑点斑或划痕，边沿粗糙，呈毛刺状，具有扩张感。整体显得粗糙涂污（见图8-5-17—图8-5-20）。

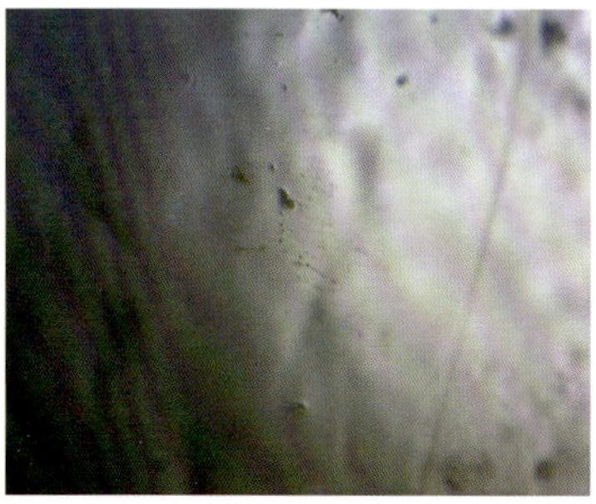

图8-5-15

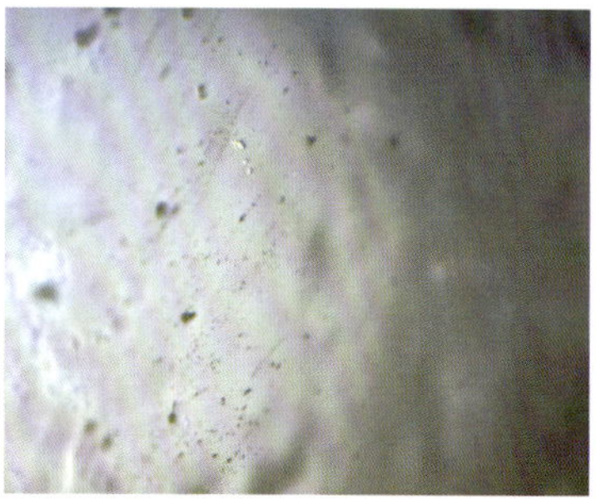

图8-5-16

图8-5-17

图8-5-18

图8-5-19

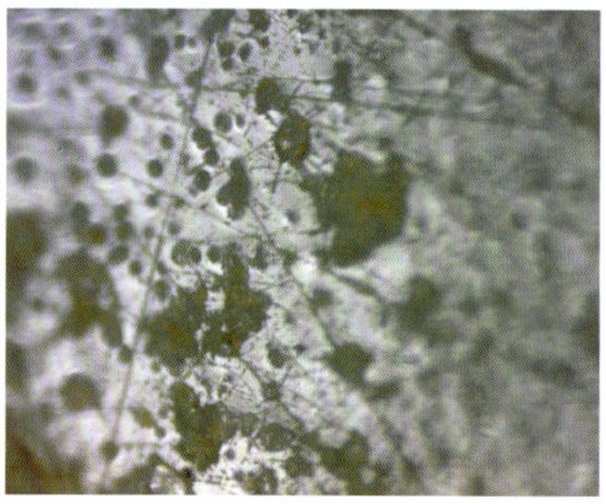

图8-5-20

第九章

建立龙泉窑系青瓷迹型物证的实际操作

阅读提示：

本章主要阐述了龙泉窑系青瓷迹型物证建立的方法要点和鉴定操作程序，并展示龙泉窑系青瓷物证建立的操作案例。

主要论述问题：

1. 龙泉窑系青瓷迹型物证建立主要包括哪些步骤？
2. 论证龙泉窑系青瓷迹型本质充分吻合的要素有哪几点？

Chapter 9

Trace Model Material Evidence Establishment: Longquan Kiln System Celadon Methodology and Operation

Text Note:

This chapter describes the key operation points of the Longquan Kiln System Celadon (LKSC) Trace Model Material Evidence Establishment Method as well as offers an operational authentication case study in the form of a LKSC Material Evidence Establishment Report.

第一节

建立龙泉窑系瓷器迹型物证的方法

鉴定陶瓷的传统方法主要是眼学，包括用肉眼看器型、看胎质、看纹饰、看款识、看底足。相对于眼学的“五看”，龙泉窑系迹型物证研究在此基础上，强调利用显微镜观察瓷器迹型的“五看”：看斑块、看纹路、看气泡、看鬃眼、看玻璃相。此“五看”就是：

1. 通过观察、比对和分析被研究器物的迹型与图谱的迹型，发现二者迹型之间的高度相似性；

2. 在被研究器物迹型与图谱迹型高度相似的基础上，深入论证迹型的本质吻合。

这两个部分具有内在联系和因果关系。迹型比对是龙泉窑系瓷器迹型物证建立的前提，而迹型本质论证则是物证建立的核心。

这种迹型物证建立的方法能够减少非客观因素对物证建立的影响，让鉴定结果更加准确、真实。熟练掌握方法并且正确操作，以便实现鉴定的客观实在性。

一、迹型物证建立的特性

在迹型物证的建立过程中，比对的对象是陶瓷釉层的显微迹型，使用的标准是标准图谱模型中的迹型图片，这些图片就是物证系统。总的来说，迹型物证的建立过程主要有三个特性：

（一）标准可靠性

作为建立迹型物证比对时使用的标准，龙泉窑系瓷器迹型标准图谱模型是可靠的。

龙泉窑系瓷器迹型标准图谱模型是观察研究一定量的确切龙泉窑系窑址发掘出来的有明确发掘时间、发掘地点、年代依据的龙泉窑系瓷器标本后，按其迹型现象提炼概括出来的物证系统。

可靠的标本来源是建构龙泉窑系瓷器迹型标准图谱模型的基础和前提。

（二）证据现实性

陶瓷迹型物证能够增加陶瓷鉴定的说服力。

陶瓷迹型比对过程就是观察过程，就是寻找、提取物证的过程。陶瓷迹型的物证更强调眼见为实。建立物证时所使用的龙泉窑系瓷器迹型标准图谱模型是现实可见的。

在陶瓷迹型比对的过程中，标准图谱模型中的龙泉窑系瓷器迹型图片会与被研究器物的迹型图片同时被展示出来，二者之间的共同点及差异一目了然。

（三）比对客观性

眼学比对是依据个人记忆中的表象进行判断，这个表象记忆的准确性是存在偏差的。眼学比对的判断过程还会受到诸多因素的影响与制约，如其人的学识水平、身体状况、外部环境，甚至道德品质等等。而迹型比对是根据现实中可视的标准图谱模型，即物证要素来进行比对判断，这就减少了许多人为因素的干扰，具有不以人的意志为转移的客观属性，因此也更具公正性。

二、迹型比对

在龙泉窑系瓷器迹型物证比对中，应该如何把握比对的高度相似性？究竟有多么相似，才能通过迹型比对这一关？我们要关注两点：

（一）器物的整体迹型现象

要判断一件龙泉窑系瓷器的整体迹型现象是否具备龙泉窑系瓷器的普遍性特征，必须综合观察器物的先天性迹型及后天性迹型。

先天性迹型包括流淌斑、放射斑、团状斑、流淌纹等。后天性迹型包括针眼斑、坑点斑、泡根斑、

Section 1:

Longquan Kiln System Celadon Trace Model Material Evidence Establishment Method

Traditional ceramic authentication is mainly centered on experience-based naked-eye appraisal methods. It utilizes the naked-eye check of the shape, clay, decoration, marking, and base.

In contrast to the Five Checks of naked-eye appraisal, Trace Model Material Evidence Establishment of LKSC builds on this foundation and emphasizes comprehensive microscopic observation, bringing about Five New Checks:

Mottles, Bubbles, Striae, Bristle Pits, and Glass Phase. These Five New Checks mean:

1. Through observation, comparison, and analysis of the traces on the authenticated item and Standard Trace Atlas Model, we can determine the degree of their similarities.

2. On the foundation of their similarities, we can deeply expound upon the nature of these traces.

These two parts have an inherent connection as well as a cause and effect relationship. Trace comparison is the premise of Trace Model Material Evidence Establishment and Nature of Trace Proofs are the core of evidence establishment.

This type of Trace Model Material Evidence Establishment Method can decrease the impact of nonobjective factors, and allow for higher accuracy and veracity in authentication. Proper grasp of these methods, in addition to precise operation, will greatly increase the accuracy of authentication.

1. Trace Model Material Evidence Establishment Characteristics

Trace Model Material Evidence Establishment uses ceramic glaze level traces for comparison, and the standard used is the trace images from the Standard Trace Atlas Model, which represents the material evidence system. Generally speaking, Trace Model Material Evidence Establishment has three main characteristics:

A. Sample Reliability

As the standard for Trace Model Material Evidence Establishment, the LKSC Standard Trace Atlas Model is reliable.

The LKSC Standard Trace Atlas Model is the material evidence system that represents the series of trace appearances extracted and condensed from the observation of LKSC samples of known excavation date, location, period, and provenance.

The reliable source of samples is the foundation and premise of the LKSC Standard Trace Atlas Model construction.

B. Evidence Transparency

Trace Model Material Evidence increases the cogency of ceramic authentication.

This comparative trace process is the process of observing and searching for material evidence. Thus, Trace Model Material Evidence emphasizes what is actually observable.

While carrying out Trace Model Material Evidence Establishment, the images of the LKSC Standard Trace Atlas Model and images of the piece being evaluated are available for side-by-side comparison; their similarities and differences tangibly observable.

C. Comparison Objectivity

As experience-based authentication relies on the

絮状斑、CO纹、划痕、色变泡、壁变泡及鬃眼风化的多样性等（见表9-1-1）。

首先要了解一件龙泉窑系瓷器上一共包含了哪些迹型种类，这些迹型种类是否是那个时代迹型普遍应有的。

例如，在清代的瓷器上通常是找不到絮状斑的，所以絮状斑就不属于清代的普遍性迹型种类。

（二）迹型的具体特征

在掌握了一件龙泉窑系瓷器的普遍性迹型特征后，我们需要观察比对每一个迹型种类的具体特征。比对时需要重点观察比较的一系列迹型特征，请参考表9-1-1。

三、迹型本质论证

龙泉窑系瓷器迹型物证建立除了迹型比对之外，还需要对迹型形成本质进行逻辑论证。迹型形成本质论证实质就是对迹型比对的结果进行论述及分析。

通过观察比对被研究器物的迹型与标准图谱模型的迹型，将最终结果的本质吻合程度用逻辑方式阐明。

可以说，任何证据都难以起到100%的证明作用。亲子鉴定比对DNA也不可能达到100%吻合，只能是高度相似。同样，在迹型物证建立过程中，迹型现象也没有绝对完全的相似，只有本质的充分吻合。

在迹型高度相似的基础上，论证迹型形成本质充分吻合需要包含如下几个因素：

（一）被研究器物迹型现象是否与图谱一样反映了当时的制瓷用材及烧制工艺；

（二）被研究器物上后天性迹型的多样性；

（三）被研究器物上迹型的变化是否具有同步性；

（四）被研究器物上迹型出现的位置是否具有合理性；

（五）被研究器物迹型现象是否具有量变特征；

（六）被研究器物迹型现象是否能够反映时间过程性原理；

（七）被研究器物迹型现象是否体现了迹型形成与发展的诸规律。

以上七点是被研究器物迹型本质吻合的充分理由。迹型高度相似仅仅是迹型本质吻合的现象，即迹型表现特征的静态理由，还要综合论证与迹型本质吻合的其他因素，即能反映迹型形成过程特征的动态理由，这样才能得到最终的充分物证证明，才能切实显示迹型物证的“鹰眼”作用。

memory of the authenticator to offer proof; the accuracy of these memories presents with bias. Additionally, the process of authentication meets with other key influences and restrictions of the authenticator, i.e. their ability, their health, external factors, moral character, and so forth. Trace Model Material Evidence Establishment, on the other hand, utilizes the material evidence of the Standard Trace Atlas Model, limiting the disturbance of human factors, and increasing the objectivity of authentication.

Ceramic traces are objective material evidence, and Trace Model Material Evidence Establishment is the progression from subjective experience-driven human witness towards more scientific, objective, and concrete material evidence. This type of comparative technique and comparison process places more emphasis on resolute truth and decreases the impact of subjective factors. Because of this, it is inherently less biased.

2. Trace Comparison

During the process of Trace Model Material Evidence Establishment of LKSC, how can we grasp the degree of similarity in comparison? Just how similar do traces need to be to pass the test of trace comparison? To answer this we need to focus on two points:

A. Holistic Trace Appearance

In order to determine whether a LKSC piece's holistic trace appearance is or is not consistent with the Typical LKSC Trace Characteristics, we must comprehensively observe a piece's innate and acquired traces.

Innate traces include flowing mottles, radiating mottles, blotch mottles, flowing striae, and bristle pits. Acquired traces include needlepoint mottles, pit mottles, bubble roots, floccus mottles, CO striae, scrapes, color change bubbles, textured bubbles, and multiplicity of bristle pit weathering (see table 9-1-1).

Thus when authenticating, we first need to discover what trace categories are included on the piece, and understand if these are the Typical Trace Types of the said period. For example, floccus mottling is not known to occur on Qing Dynasty porcelain, thus floccus mottling is not a Typical Trace Type of Qing Dynasty porcelain.

B. Specific Trace Characteristics

After grasping a piece's typical trace characteristics, we must observe and compare each of the specific trace characteristics. During comparison we must emphasize the comparative observation of the series of trace characteristics listed in table 9-1-1.

3. Nature of Trace Proofs

Aside from Trace Comparison, Trace Model Material Evidence Establishment of LKSC must present logical proofs of the nature of the traces.

Essentially, Nature of Trace Proofs are the discussion and analysis of the results of Trace Comparison. Through the comparative observation of the authenticated piece's traces and those of the Trace Atlas Model, we must use logic to clearly explain the degree of similarity between the natures of the resultant traces.

We can say that any form of evidence has difficulty in reaching a one hundred percent match. Even DNA testing cannot reach a one hundred percent match, but can only attain a high degree of certainty. Similarly, trace appearances cannot be identical; they can only have a fully matched nature. On the foundation of high similarity, to prove the fully matched trace nature, the following criteria must be met:

1. The traces reflect the same materials and techniques as the Trace Atlas Model;

2. The acquired traces present with multiplicity;

3. The trace changes occur with proper congruency;

4. The traces present in rational locations;

5. The traces have quantitative change characteristics;

6. The traces reflect the passage of time principle;

7. The traces embody the Ceramic Trace Laws.

The above-listed criteria are the Nature of Trace Grounds for Full Match. The high similarity of trace appearances is only one portion of the grounds for full trace nature match. It is the static grounds of the trace appearance characteristics. Thus, we must further comprehensively prove the other factors in play for a trace nature match. In this way we can reflect the dynamic grounds of the trace formation process. Only then can we reach a final material evidence based conclusion and act as the 'Hawkeye' authority in Trace Model Evidence.

表 9-1-1

反映青瓷材料、工艺的迹型特征			反映量变原理的迹型特征		反映时间过程性原理的迹型特征		反映迹型出现位置合理性的迹型特征		反映迹型变化同步性的迹型特征	
先天迹型种类			二维成像	三维成像	二维成像	三维成像	二维成像	三维成像	二维成像	三维成像
流淌斑	沙滩斑	火焰形及荷叶形	有色阶变化	颜色有由浅至深的变化		沙滩斑呈凹陷状，与玻璃相圆孔有明显高度差				
			沙滩斑上的玻璃相圆孔干净清晰，与沙滩斑界线分明	沙滩斑上的玻璃相圆孔光滑洁净，与沙滩斑界线分明						
			与周围玻璃相及其他迹型各自独立清晰，界线分明							
			周围玻璃相干净清晰	周围玻璃相光滑洁净						
放射斑	白色系									
	红色系		形貌轮廓清晰，有清晰的色阶变化（橘红、橘黄等等）	形貌轮廓清晰						
			与周围玻璃相及其他迹型各自独立清晰，界线分明							
	黄色系		形貌轮廓清晰	所在处的釉表面光滑洁净						
			放射斑与其表面的分相（黑色系放射斑）各自独立清晰，界线分明	放射斑位于釉下，其所在釉表面光滑洁净，其表面的分相（黑色系放射斑）独立清晰						
			外围有精致细腻的包边	放射斑与周围釉表面有高度差						
			包边内外的玻璃相干净清晰	包边内外的玻璃相光滑洁净						
			与周围玻璃相及其他迹型各自独立清晰，界线分明							

（续表）

反映青瓷材料、工艺的迹型特征		反映量变原理的迹型特征		反映时间过程性原理的迹型特征		反映迹型出现位置合理性的迹型特征		反映迹型变化同步性的迹型特征	
先天迹型种类		二维成像	三维成像	二维成像	三维成像	二维成像	三维成像	二维成像	三维成像
放射斑	褐色系	形貌轮廓清晰	有的表面较粗粝；有的表面有细密纹路，但总体还是比较平滑细腻						
		外围有精致细腻的包边	与周围釉表面有高度差						
		包边内外的玻璃相干净清晰	包边内外的玻璃相光滑洁净						
		与周围其他迹型各自独立清晰，界线分明							
		放射斑与其表面的分相（黑色系放射斑）各自独立清晰，界线分明	放射斑位于釉表面，其表面的分相（黑色系放射斑）独立清晰						
	黑色系	形貌轮廓清晰	位于釉层中的放射斑所在釉表面光滑洁净						
			位于釉表面的放射斑形貌轮廓清晰						

（续表）

反映青瓷材料、工艺的迹型特征			反映量变原理的迹型特征		反映时间过程性原理的迹型特征		反映迹型出现位置合理性的迹型特征		反映迹型变化同步性的迹型特征	
先天迹型种类			二维成像	三维成像	二维成像	三维成像	二维成像	三维成像	二维成像	三维成像
流淌纹	阴纹	中空型	纹路边线清晰精致	W形纹路凹槽较浅者脊部洁净，呈哑光						
			纹路内部清晰，可见一条或多条连续或错综的细线	W形纹路凹槽较深者，脊部反光部分断续						
			与周围玻璃相及其他迹型各自独立，界线分明							
		针眼型	U形纹路内针眼斑密实，无虚空，有时可见白色、橘黄色等的色阶变化	纹路凹槽内可见颗粒风化物质，有时可见白色及橘黄色的色阶变化		U形纹路有一定宽度和深度			U形纹路内针眼斑密实，无虚空	U形纹路有一定宽度和深度，有时纹路内可见风化物及色阶变化
			U形纹路与周围玻璃相界线分明，周围玻璃相干净清晰	U形纹路边沿圆滑，与周围玻璃相界线分明，周围玻璃相光滑洁净						
			U形纹路与周围的沙滩斑界线分明，沙滩斑有量变特征			U形阴纹在沙滩斑上呈凹陷状，与沙滩斑有高度差				
			V形纹路内针眼斑有时蔓延到周围玻璃相上，浓淡过渡均匀	针眼斑三维成像面积小于二维面积						
			纹路与周围玻璃相及其他迹型各自独立，界线分明							

（续表）

反映青瓷材料、工艺的迹型特征		反映量变原理的迹型特征		反映时间过程性原理的迹型特征		反映迹型出现位置合理性的迹型特征		反映迹型变化同步性的迹型特征	
先天迹型种类		二维成像	三维成像	二维成像	三维成像	二维成像	三维成像	二维成像	三维成像
流淌纹	阳纹	粗的纹路边沿呈锯齿状	粗的纹路边沿呈锯齿状，光滑有细密纹路						
		纹路与沙滩斑上的针眼斑界线分明			纹路凸起，高出周围沙滩斑				
			纹路周围沙滩斑上的磨砂针眼斑呈独立点状凹坑						
鬃眼		口部周围有颜色变化		周围釉下有絮状斑					
		口部周围呈炭黑色		周围釉下有色变或壁变泡					
		口部有纤丝或颗粒物质		内部沉积多种物质					
		内部有针眼斑							
		内部有颜色变化							
		口部及内部纤丝有色阶变化							
		口部及内部纤丝有粗有细，错综交杂							
		周围玻璃相呈哑光，反光较弱							

（续表）

后天风化迹型			反映量变原理的迹型特征		反映时间过程性原理的迹型特征		反映迹型出现位置合理性的迹型特征		反映迹型变化同步性的迹型特征	
迹型种类			二维成像	三维成像	二维成像	三维成像	二维成像	三维成像	二维成像	三维成像
针眼斑	在流淌斑上	雾状针眼斑	由浓到淡，过渡均匀细腻				通常出现在沙滩斑与玻璃相交界处		由浓到淡，过渡均匀细腻	
		磨砂针眼斑	有的地方密集，有的地方稀疏，边界感强	呈独立凹坑状密集分布，有明显边界感			一般出现在沙滩斑中部		有的地方密集，有的地方稀疏，边界感强	呈独立点状凹坑密集分布，有明显边界感
	在放射斑上	磨砂针眼斑	分布于放射斑形貌范围内，边界感强	呈独立点状凹坑，边界感强			一般出现在釉表面放射斑形貌范围内			
坑点斑	CO型坑点斑		与周围玻璃相及其他迹型各自独立清晰，界线分明		有C形、O形纹伴生	釉表面只可见清晰纤细的C形、O形纹		CO型坑点斑通常都出现在釉表面凸起处		
					CO型坑点斑有沿着其轮廓向外呈白雾状蔓延的趋势	除CO纹以外，还可见面积比CO型坑点斑二维成像面积要小的斑块		釉表面其余地方光滑洁净		
					大小不一、深浅不一的坑点斑群	釉表面只见面积比坑点斑群二维成像面积要小的风化斑块				
					单位图片中CO型坑点斑与CO纹或坑点斑群同时存在，各自独立清晰，彼此界线分明	同上三项				
			周围玻璃相干净清晰	周围玻璃相光滑洁净	与色变或壁变泡伴生	见色变泡及壁变泡部分				

（续表）

后天风化迹型		反映量变原理的迹型特征		反映时间过程性原理的迹型特征		反映迹型出现位置合理性的迹型特征		反映迹型变化同步性的迹型特征	
迹型种类		二维成像	三维成像	二维成像	三维成像	二维成像	三维成像	二维成像	三维成像
坑点斑	CO型坑点斑			坑点斑所在处釉下有絮状斑	通常只见坑点斑，坑点斑有量变特征，不见絮状斑		坑点斑根部风化程度较高，颜色较深，顶部风化程度较低，颜色较浅		
	外伤型坑点斑	有色阶变化		可见针眼斑及沉积物					
		内有针眼斑	呈独立凹坑，边沿圆滑			针眼斑不超过坑点斑范围			
	浸水型坑点斑	有的形貌为上下各一半圆弧	呈独立近圆凹坑，边沿圆滑						
		有的坑点斑内可见磨砂斑	呈独立凹坑，边沿圆滑，坑点斑内凹凸不平			针眼斑不超过坑点斑范围			
		与周围玻璃相及其他迹型各自独立，界线分明							
		周围玻璃相干净清晰							

（续表）

后天风化迹型	反映量变原理的迹型特征		反映时间过程性原理的迹型特征		反映迹型出现位置合理性的迹型特征		反映迹型变化同步性的迹型特征	
迹型种类	二维成像	三维成像	二维成像	三维成像	二维成像	三维成像	二维成像	三维成像
泡根斑	同一泡根斑内有色阶变化		面积较大的泡根斑可见沉积物					
	单位图片中邻近的多个泡根斑之间有色差变化							
	与周围玻璃相及其他迹型各自独立清晰，界线分明							
絮状斑		釉损处以外地方光滑洁净，无其他明显大面积损伤	斑块中心色白如牛奶，不透明；斑块边沿呈绒状，半透明，有向四周蔓延的趋势	釉表面通常只见釉损处，釉损处有量变特征，不见絮状斑				
			在釉损处（如坑点斑、釉裂纹等）周围釉下，絮状斑呈梯度扩散状					
玻璃相				釉表面整体布满细密的风化纹路，就像陈旧的硬币表面				

（续表）

<table>
<tr><th>后天风化迹型</th><th colspan="2">反映量变原理的迹型特征</th><th colspan="2">反映时间过程性原理的迹型特征</th><th colspan="2">反映迹型出现位置合理性的迹型特征</th><th colspan="2">反映迹型变化同步性的迹型特征</th></tr>
<tr><th>迹型种类</th><th>二维成像</th><th>三维成像</th><th>二维成像</th><th>三维成像</th><th>二维成像</th><th>三维成像</th><th>二维成像</th><th>三维成像</th></tr>
<tr><td rowspan="6">CO纹</td><td>单位图片内的CO纹粗细及大小都不一致，彼此之间清晰独立</td><td></td><td>有C形、O形纹伴生（见CO型坑点斑部分）</td><td>见CO型坑点斑部分</td><td rowspan="6" colspan="2"></td><td rowspan="6" colspan="2"></td></tr>
<tr><td colspan="2">CO纹纤细</td><td>与色变或壁变泡伴生</td><td>见色变及壁变泡部分</td></tr>
<tr><td>C形纹有清晰分叉</td><td>C形纹精致收敛，分叉清晰</td><td rowspan="2">C形弧线内或O形圈有白雾状蔓延</td><td>釉表面只可见清晰纤细的C形、O形纹</td></tr>
<tr><td>单项C形或O形纹上有色阶变化</td><td></td><td>除CO纹以外，还可见面积比CO型坑点斑二维成像面积要小的斑块</td></tr>
<tr><td>单位图片中CO纹有色差变化</td><td></td><td>周围釉下有絮状斑</td><td>通常只见CO纹，CO纹有量变特征，不见絮状斑</td></tr>
<tr><td colspan="2">与周围的玻璃相及其他迹型各自独立，界线分明</td><td></td><td></td></tr>
<tr><td rowspan="3">釉裂纹</td><td></td><td>釉裂纹边沿圆滑</td><td>釉裂纹周围釉下出现絮状斑</td><td>釉表面只见釉裂纹，不见絮状斑</td><td>釉裂纹与其周围釉下出现絮状斑有色差</td><td></td><td rowspan="3" colspan="2"></td></tr>
<tr><td>釉裂纹本身及其周边釉下颜色与周围色变及壁变泡有差异</td><td rowspan="2">釉裂纹周围釉表面光滑洁净</td><td rowspan="2" colspan="2">釉裂纹下有堆积物</td><td rowspan="2" colspan="2"></td></tr>
<tr><td>釉裂纹本身及其周边釉下未变色或变色不明显，但釉裂纹周边出现零星色变或壁变泡</td></tr>
</table>

（续表）

后天风化迹型	反映量变原理的迹型特征		反映时间过程性原理的迹型特征		反映迹型出现位置合理性的迹型特征		反映迹型变化同步性的迹型特征	
迹型种类	二维成像	三维成像	二维成像	三维成像	二维成像	三维成像	二维成像	三维成像
划痕	单位图片内：形貌方向不一致，粗细长短不一致，有交叉	划痕边沿圆滑，与玻璃相界线分明，面积小于或等于二维面积	划痕有呈白雾状蔓延的趋势	三维成像面积小于二维				
	有“牛毛纹”划痕	划痕边沿圆滑，面积小于或等于二维面积	划痕所在处釉下有絮状斑	釉表面只见划痕，不见絮状斑				
	有“蜈蚣”划痕	“蜈蚣”的“足”清晰可见，彼此独立，面积小于或等于二维面积	划痕内部有针眼斑	划痕内部粗糙				
	单项划痕上有色阶变化		划痕有部分与沙滩斑重叠，被沙滩斑上的针眼斑覆盖					
	单位图片中各个划痕有色差变化							
	与周围的玻璃相及其他迹型各自独立，界线分明							

（续表）

后天风化迹型			反映量变原理的迹型特征		反映时间过程性原理的迹型特征		反映迹型出现位置合理性的迹型特征		反映迹型变化同步性的迹型特征	
迹型种类			二维成像	三维成像	二维成像	三维成像	二维成像	三维成像	二维成像	三维成像
气泡	色变泡		单项色变泡中有色阶变化	色变泡所在处釉表面通道不明显						
			单位图片中多个色变泡有色差变化	色变泡所在处釉表面有一个或多个明显通道，通道收敛，清晰独立，且与周围迹型界线分明						
			色变泡上可明显观察到颜色明显较深的色块（即通道所在处）							
			周围玻璃相干净清晰	周围玻璃相光滑洁净						
	壁变泡	非破口壁变泡	单项壁变泡中有色阶变化	气泡所在处釉表面通道不明显						
			单位图片中多个壁变泡有色差变化	气泡釉表面有一个或多个明显通道，通道收敛，清晰独立，且与周围迹型界线分明						
			气泡内的物质有堆积感，有时斑块之间可见玻璃相	气泡所在处釉表面有颜色变化，是由釉层中透出来的。颜色与壁变泡二维成像颜色相近，但显得更淡。颜色变化面积小于气泡最大直径						
			气泡内风化颗粒不在同一平面上							
		破口壁变泡	破口圆滑，接近正圆	气泡所在釉表面除破口外无其他明显通道，破口清晰独立，与周围迹型界线分明						
			破口下方可见块状物质存在							
			气泡内壁风化情况可参考非破口壁变泡情况	气泡所在釉表面除破口外还可见其余通道，但彼此各自独立分明，与周围迹型界线分明						

Table 9-1-1

Reflects Celadon Materials and Techniques			Reflects Quantitative Change Principle		Reflects Passage of Time Principle		Reflects Trace Location Rationality		Reflects Trace Change Congruency	
Inherent Trace Category			2D Image	3D Image	2D Image	3D Image	2D Image	3D Image	2D Image	3D Image
Flowing Mottle	Beach Mottle	Flame Shape & Lotus Leaf Shape	Color Spectrum	Light to dark color gradation		Beach mottle is depressed, clear height discrepancy with glaze openings				
			Glaze openings on the beach mottle are clean and clear, delineated from surrounding beach mottle	Glaze openings on the beach mottle are smooth and clean, delineated from surrounding beach mottle						
			Mutually independent from surrounding glass phase and other traces, clearly delineated							
			Surrounding glass phase is clean and clear	Surrounding glass phase is smooth and clean						
Radiating Mottle	White Series									
	Red Series		Clearly defined border, clear color spectrum	Clearly defined border						
			Mutually independent from surrounding glass phase and other traces, clearly delineated							
	Yellow Series		Clearly defined border	Glaze surface is smooth and clean						
			Mottle and other split phases mutually independent, clearly delineated	Mottle is below the glaze suface, which is smooth and clean, surface split phases are clearly independent						
			Surrounded by a fine lined border	Mottle has height discrepancy with surrounding glaze surface						
			Glass phase within the border is clear and clean	Glass phase within the border is smooth and clean						
			Mutually independent from surrounding glass phase and other traces, clearly delineated							

（Continued）

Reflects Celadon Materials and Techniques		Reflects Quantitative Change Principle		Reflects Passage of Time Principle		Reflects Trace Location Rationality		Reflects Trace Change Congruency	
Innate Trace Category		2D Image	3D Image	2D Image	3D Image	2D Image	3D Image	2D Image	3D Image
Radiating Mottle	Brown Series	Clearly defined border	Some surfaces are grainy; some striated, but generally smooth and refined						
		Surrounded by a fine lined border	Mottle has height discrepancy with surrounding glaze surface						
		Glass phase within the border is clear and clean	Glass phase within the border is smooth and clean						
		Mutually independent from surrounding glass phase and other traces, clearly delineated							
		Mottle and other split phases mutually independent, clearly delineated	Mottle is on the glaze surface, other split phases mutually independent, clearly delineated						
	Black Series	Clearly defined border	Presenting within the glaze level, the glaze surface is smooth and clean						
			Presenting on the glaze surface, clearly evident radiating mottle shape						

(Continued)

Reflects Celadon Materials and Techniques			Reflects Quantitative Change Principle		Reflects Passage of Time Principle		Reflects Trace Location Rationality		Reflects Trace Change Congruency	
Innate Trace Category			2D Image	3D Image	2D Image	3D Image	2D Image	3D Image	2D Image	3D Image
Flowing Striae	Depressed Striae	Empty Striae	Striae border clear and refined	Shallow W shaped striae, interior is clean and matte						
			Striae interior has clear single or multi-line. Continuous or intermittent fine line	Deep W shaped striae, interior is intermittently reflective						
			Mutually independent from surrounding glass phase and other traces, clearly delineated							
		Needlepoint Striae	Densly filled needlepoint mottling in U shaped striae interior, with white or orange color spectrum	U shaped striae is coarse, interior presents with grainy material with white and orange spectrum		U shaped striae have a certain depth and width			Densly filled needlepoint mottling in U shaped striae interior	U shaped striae have a certain depth and width, interior presents with weathering materials and color spectrum
			U shaped striae clearly delineated from surrounding glass phase, which is clear and clean	U shaped striae edges are rounded, clearly delineated from surrounding glass phase, which is smooth and clean						
			U shaped striae clearly delineated from surrounding beach mottle			U shaped striae are depressed into beach mottle and have a clear height discrepancy				
			V shaped striae needlepoint mottling has gradual dispersion onto the surrouding glass phase, the gradation is gradual	3D needlepoint mottling surface area smaller than 2D						
			Mutually independent from surrounding glass phase and other traces, clearly delineated							

（Continued）

Reflects Celadon Materials and Techniques		Reflects Quantitative Change Principle		Reflects Passage of Time Principle		Reflects Trace Location Rationality		Reflects Trace Change Congruency	
Innate Trace Category		2D Image	3D Image	2D Image	3D Image	2D Image	3D Image	2D Image	3D Image
Flowing Striae	Rasied Striae	Thick striae present with saw-like border	Thick striae present with saw-like border, smooth with striated feel						
		Striae clearly delineated from needlepoint mottling on the beach mottle			Striae higher than surrounding beach mottles				
			Frosted needlepoint mottling surrounding striae are independent pits						
Bristle Pits		Color changed around mouth		Associated under the glaze floccus mottles					
		Charcoal black around mouth		Associated under the glaze color change or textured bubbles					
		Mouth presents with filaments or granulated materials		Multiple types of internal deposits					
		Internal needlepoint mottling							
		Internal coloration							
		Filaments have color spectrum							
		Filaments have girth disparity, multi-directional							
		Surrounding glass phase is matte with relatively low refelctivity							

(Continued)

Acquired Traces			Reflects Quantitative Change Principle		Reflects Passage of Time Principle		Reflects Trace Location Rationality		Reflects Trace Change Congruency	
Trace Categories			2D Image	3D Image	2D Image	3D Image	2D Image	3D Image	2D Image	3D Image
Needlepoint Mottle	On Flowing Mottle	Foggy	Density disparity, even and fine				Presents at the border of beach mottle and glass phase		Density disparity, even and fine	
		Frosted	Some places dense, some places sparse, strong border feel	Dense independent pit distribution, clearly defined border			Presents within the center of the beach mottle		Some places dense, some places sparse, strong border feel	Dense independent pit distribution, clearly defined border
	On Radiating Mottle	Frosted	Dispersed within radiating mottle border, strong border feel	Independent pit points, strong border feel			Presents within the radiating mottles that are on the glaze surface			
Pit Mottle	CO Type Pit Mottle		Mutually independent from surrounding glass phase and other traces, clearly delineated		In association with CO striae	Fine CO stirae clearly visble on the glaze surface		Present on areas of raised glaze		
					CO pits have white foggy coloration extending into the glaze level	Aside from CO striae, pits with smaller area than 2D image visible		Surrounding glaze level smooth and clean		

(Continued)

Acquired Traces		Reflects Quantitative Change Principle		Reflects Passage of Time Principle		Reflects Trace Location Rationality		Reflects Trace Change Congruency	
Trace Categories		2D Image	3D Image	2D Image	3D Image	2D Image	3D Image	2D Image	3D Image
Pit Mottle	CO Type Pit Mottle			Size and depth disparate pit mottle group	Visible weathered mottles with smaller area than 2D image				
				Clearly delineated CO pits, CO stirae or pit groups within a unit image					
		Surrounding glass phase is clean and clear	Surrounding glass phase is smooth and clean	In association with color change or textured bubbles	See color change and textured bubbles				
				In assosiction with under the glaze floccus mottle	Pit has quantitative change characteristics, floccus mottle not visible		Higher amount of weathering (darker color) around the base of the protrusion, while its surface retains smoothness (lighter coloration)		

(Continued)

Acquired Traces		Reflects Quantitative Change Principle		Reflects Passage of Time Principle		Reflects Trace Location Rationality		Reflects Trace Change Congruency	
Trace Categories		2D Image	3D Image	2D Image	3D Image	2D Image	3D Image	2D Image	3D Image
Pit Mottle	Damage Type Pit Mottle	Color Spectrum		Visible needlepoint mottling and material deposits					
		Interior has needlepoint mottling	Independent pits, rounded edges			Needlepoint mottling does not exceed boundary of pit mottle			
	Underwater Type Pit Mottle	Present with disconnected semi-circles, interior without needlepoint mottling	independent half sphere pits, smooth edges						
		Interior has needlepoint mottling	Independent pits with coarse interior and rounded edges			Needlepoint mottling does not exceed boundary of pit mottle			
		Mutually independent from surrounding glass phase and other traces, clearly delineated							
		Surrounding glass phase is clean and clear							

(Continued)

Acquired Traces	Reflects Quantitative Change Principle		Reflects Passage of Time Principle		Reflects Trace Location Rationality		Reflects Trace Change Congruency	
Trace Categories	2D Image	3D Image	2D Image	3D Image	2D Image	3D Image	2D Image	3D Image
Bubble Root	Color spectrum within single root		Larger roots present with deposits and color spectrum					
	Bubble root color disparity within a unit image							
	Mutually independent from surrounding glass phase and other traces, clearly delineated							
Floccus Mottle		Area surrounding glaze flaw smooth and clean, no other large glaze flaws	The center of the mottle is non-transparent and milky white, and the edges feather out like goose down	Only glaze flaw visible and has quantitative change characteristics, floccus mottle not visible				
			Present in areas beneath glaze flaw i.e. pits, cracks, and so forth					
			Floccus mottle disperses out and into the glaze level surrounding the glaze flaw					
Glass Phase				Relatively full distribution of finely dense weathering striae, similar to that of an old coin				

(Continued)

Acquired Traces	Reflects Quantitative Change Principle		Reflects Passage of Time Principle		Reflects Trace Location Rationality		Reflects Trace Change Congruency	
Trace Categories	2D Image	3D Image	2D Image	3D Image	2D Image	3D Image	2D Image	3D Image
CO Striae	Clearly delineated CO stirae with width and size disparity within a unit image		In association with CO style pits (See CO Type Pit section)	See CO Type Pit section				
	CO Striae thin and refined		In association with color change or textured bubbles	See color change and textured bubbles				
	C striae have clear split ends	C striation is reserved, split is clear	CO Striae have white foggy coloration extending into the surrounding glaze level	Fine CO stirae clearly visble on the glaze surface				
	Color spectrum on a single C or O striation			Aside from CO striae, pits with smaller area than 2D image visible				
	Color disparity within a unit image		In association with under the glaze floccus mottling	CO striae presents with quantitative change characteristics, floccus mottle not visible				
	Mutually independent from surrounding glass phase and other traces, clearly delineated							

(Continued)

Acquired Traces	Reflects Quantitative Change Principle		Reflects Passage of Time Principle		Reflects Trace Location Rationality		Reflects Trace Change Congruency	
Trace Categories	2D Image	3D Image	2D Image	3D Image	2D Image	3D Image	2D Image	3D Image
Glaze Crack		The edges of glaze cracks are rounded and smooth	In association with under the glaze floccus mottling	Only crack visible, floccus mottle not visible	Color discrepancy between glaze crack and floccus mottles			
	Coloration of glaze crack and associated color change under the glaze or textured bubbles are disparate	Surrounding glaze surface is smooth and clean	Deposits within the glaze crack					
	Coloration of glaze crack and associated color change under the glaze is not present or obvious, but surrounding color change or textured bubbles are present							
Scratches	Within One Unit Image: direction width and length disparity, intersecting scratches	Scratch edge is rounded and smooth, clearly delineated from surrounding glass phase, area smaller or same as 2D image	Scratches have white foggy coloration extending into the surrounding glaze level	3D smaller than 2D				
			In association with under the glaze floccus mottling	Only scratch visible, floccus mottle not visible				

(Continued)

Acquired Traces	Reflects Quantitative Change Principle		Reflects Passage of Time Principle		Reflects Trace Location Rationality		Reflects Trace Change Congruency	
Trace Categories	2D Image	3D Image	2D Image	3D Image	2D Image	3D Image	2D Image	3D Image
Scratches	"Ox Hair" Scratches present	Scratch edge is rounded and smooth, area smaller or same as 2D image	Scratch interior has needlepoint mottling	Scratch interior coarse				
	"Centipede" Scratches present	"Centipede" feet are visible, clearly independent, area smaller or same as 2D image	In areas of scratches intersecting beach mottle, beach mottle covers over scratch					
	Color spectrum within a single scratch							
	Color dispraity within a unit image							
	Mutually independent from surrounding glass phase and other traces, clearly delineated							

(Continued)

Acquired Traces			Reflects Quantitative Change Principle		Reflects Passage of Time Principle		Reflects Trace Location Rationality		Reflects Trace Change Congruency	
Trace Categories			2D Image	3D Image	2D Image	3D Image	2D Image	3D Image	2D Image	3D Image
Air Bubbles	Color Change Bubbles		Color spectrum within a single bubble	Coloration channel not clear						
			Color disparity amongst bubbles within a unit image	One or several clear channels which are reserved, clearly independent from the surrounding glaze surface						
			Clearly observable areas of darker coloration (Coloration channel)							
			Surrounding glass phase is clean and clear	Surrounding glass phase is smooth and clean						
	Textured Bubble	Unbroken Mouth Textured Bubble	Color spectrum within a single bubble	Coloration channel not clear						
			Color disparity amongst bubbles within a unit image	One or several clear channels which are reserved, clearly independent, and delineated from the surrounding traces						
			Weathered granules have a material deposit feel, some have color spectrum, glass phase visible between granules	Coloration present is from within bubble, similar to 2D image, but lighter. Coloration area smaller than bubble area.						
			Weathered granules within the bubble occur at different levels							

(Continued)

Acquired Traces		Reflects Quantitative Change Principle		Reflects Passage of Time Principle		Reflects Trace Location Rationality		Reflects Trace Change Congruency	
Trace Categories		2D Image	3D Image	2D Image	3D Image	2D Image	3D Image	2D Image	3D Image
Air Bubbles	Broken Mouth Textured Bubble	Mouth is smooth, almost a perfect circle	No visible channels aside from the bubble mouth, mouth is clearly independent and delineated from surrounding traces						
		Material deposits visible beneath bubble mouth							
		For internal weathering characteristics see Unbroken Mouth Textured Bubbles	Visible channels aside from the bubble mouth present, but they are mutually independent and delineated from surrounding traces						

第二节
龙泉窑系青瓷迹型物证建立操作

一、迹型观察记录

（一）全面扫描记录

在获取被研究器物迹型图片时，无论是整器或残片，都要求对其整个面积进行全方位扫描式观察记录。

从口沿、器身至器底，不要遗漏，同时要做好观察不同部位的标记记录。被研究的陶瓷，只要观察工具能够做到，都要进行观察。所以，观察的过程是全向扫描，尽量做到无死角的观察记录。全向扫描法就是利用500倍的数码显微镜，快速对被研究器物按由上至下、由里至外的顺序全面扫视，拍摄记录器物上各种迹型种类（斑块、纹路、气泡、鬃眼等）的图片。全面扫描记录后，能够让我们大致了解器物的整体迹型现象是否具备该年代及该类型陶瓷的普遍性，做到心中有数。

（二）重点记录

重点记录就是对一些典型迹型进一步归类遴选，建构被研究器物的显微图谱模型，以便接下来与龙泉窑系瓷器标准图谱模型进行比对。在对被研究器物全向扫描记录的基础上，对某些需要更仔细、深入观察比较的迹型种类，可以重点记录，就是拍摄记录多张该迹型种类不同位置、不同表现的二维成像及三维成像图片，以获取翔实的数据和迹型特征。同时也要留意该迹型出现的位置与其各迹型特征之间的联系。

二、迹型形成本质论证

在完成迹型比对后，还要完成迹型本质的逻辑论证。论证时可从以下七个方面进行论证：

（一）被研究器物迹型现象是否与图谱一样反映了当时的制瓷用材及烧制工艺；

（二）被研究器物上后天性迹型的多样性；

（三）被研究器物上迹型的变化是否具有同步性；

（四）被研究器物上迹型出现的位置是否具有合理性；

（五）被研究器物迹型现象是否具有量变特征；

（六）被研究器物迹型现象是否能够反映时间过程性原理；

（七）被研究器物迹型现象是否体现了迹型形成与发展的诸规律。

三、龙泉窑系青瓷迹型标准图谱模型的局限性

目前已建构有明代浙江龙泉青瓷迹型标准图谱模型以及明代广东大埔余里窑青瓷迹型标准图谱模型。这两个标准图谱模型仅限于作为这两个明代窑口的参考比对标准，有一定局限性。

由于青瓷上先天性具特色的迹型种类较少，在反映当时的制瓷用材及烧制工艺方面特征不明显，所以在逻辑论证时暂不包括这一方面。

青瓷属于单色釉，有一定的特殊性。釉中的铁元素主要以硅酸盐形式存在，少量以氧化物形式存在，迹型的风化特征不明显。龙泉枫洞岩窑和大埔余里窑，总的来说各自有一定的特征，这与其所在年代、后天的生存环境以及工艺都有关系，但由于各自特征都不明显，所以，不能仅仅根据显微迹型所提供的信息，在青瓷的年代及窑口两方面下决定性结论。

四、总结

在物证建立的实际操作过程中，一定要综合分析器物整体迹型现象和迹型之间的关系，根据瓷器迹型各方面的特征表现做出判断，这样才能减少失误，提高鉴定的客观性和准确性。

陶瓷迹型物证的建立方法，是在传统眼学鉴定的基础上发展而来的。传统的眼学鉴定，是人本身对物的认识，而迹型的物证鉴定，是

Section 2:

Longquan Kiln System Celadon Trace Model Material Evidence Authentication Operation

1. Trace Recording Process

A. Comprehensive Scanning

Regardless of whether it is a complete ware or just a shard, a full-scan observation record of the entire piece needs to be completed when collecting images for authentication.

Comprehensive scanning from the mouth, to the body, and down to the foot is needed. Meanwhile, taking observation recordings in the process. Simply put, any portion of the piece that is technically practical to do so, should undergo observation. As such, the authentication observation utilizes a holistic scanning technique in order to offer a complete observation record.

Currently, comprehensive scanning utilizes a 500X magnification digital microscope to effectively scan a ware from top to bottom, inside to outside, in a pre-determined flow, whilst taking image recordings of each type of trace (mottles, striae, bubbles, bristle pits) on the piece. After comprehensive scanning and image recording, we can have a better, more general understanding as to whether or not the piece in question is in accordance with the typical characteristics of a LKSC ware.

B. Emphasized Recording

Emphasized recording is essentially a more specific image taking process, with certain typical traces as the focus, in order to construct a Trace Atlas Model for the piece in question that can be later compared against the LKSC Standard Trace Atlas Model. On the foundation of the comprehensive scan record, we can further develop imaging for trace categories that need specific attention or deeper observation (i.e. taking several images at different locations of a single trace type). This also includes two and three-dimensional corresponding imaging in order to offer more robust proof of the characteristics of a certain trace category.

At the same time, special attention can be paid to the location of traces and the inter-trace relationships.

2. Nature of Trace Proofs

After completing the Trace Comparison phase, it is time to move on to the Nature of Trace Proofs. Proofs need to be carried out from the following seven perspectives:

1. Do the traces reflect the same materials and techniques as the Standard Trace Atlas Model?
2. Do the acquired traces present with multiplicity?
3. Do the trace changes occur with proper congruency?
4. Do the traces present in rational locations?
5. Do the traces have quantitative change characteristics?
6. Do the traces reflect the Passage of Time Principle?
7. Do the traces embody the Ceramic Trace Laws?

3. LKSC Standard Trace Atlas Model Limitations

Currently, Standard Trace Atlas Models have been constructed for Ming Dynasty Zhejiang Longquan Fengdongyan Kiln and Ming Dynasty Guangdong Yuli Kiln Celadon. These models are the comparative standards for two Ming Dynasty kilns, and as such are limited.

Due to the relatively low amount of trace characteristics as well as inherent trace properties, that is to say the firing technique characteristics are not clearly indicative of a specific

人借助科学仪器对物的认识。科学仪器延伸了人类的观察器官，提高了人类的认识能力，使得人们对陶瓷的鉴定从感性认识上升到了理性认识，从认识的低级阶段走向了认识的高级阶段，这也是社会与科技进步使然。

陶瓷迹型物证的方法能够帮助我们对陶瓷做出更接近真实的判断，决不是说这种方法已经绝对证明了真实。任何证明都不可能做到100%。所以，我们决不能用形而上学的眼光将迹型物证的鉴定方法绝对化。

新的陶瓷迹型物证的建立，是在眼学基础上的发展与优化。但是，科学的研究探索是无止境的，我们深信这种建立在学科基础上的迹型物证能够在未来陶瓷科学鉴定的路上走得更远！

period; these characteristics are not included in logical proofs.

Celadon is a monochrome glaze, and has particular characteristics. Iron within the glaze primarily occurs within silicic acid, and rarely occurs in its oxidized form. As such, trace weathering characteristics are less evident. Longquan Dayao and Dabu Yuli Kiln celadon do have specific characteristics. These arise do to the period, external environment, and firing technique similarities. As such, they are not distinctly different, and using only microscopic observation does not provide sufficient evidence to distinguish between firing period or kiln site.

4. Conclusion

During the process of testing this evidence establishment method, it was found impractical to only include small amounts of atlas model-like images in order to hastily assign the conclusion "Authentic". It is imperative to comprehensively analyze the holistic trace characteristics and inter-trace relationships, in order to decrease error and improve authentication accuracy.

Trace Model Material Evidence Establishment of LKSC has been developed on the foundation laid by experience based authentication. Traditional experience-based authentication utilizes our own understanding of objects, while Trace Model Material Evidence Authentication utilizes the help of scientific instruments. These are instruments that help to broaden our observation and heighten our understanding. This marks our movement from perceptual knowledge to conceptual knowledge in ceramic authentication, and a shift from low to high understanding, and is the result of societal and technological advancement.

Trace Model Material Evidence Authentication can help us get closer to certainty about ceramics; it does not mean that we have reached full assurance. No proof is able to attain 100% certainty, and as such we must be careful not to haplessly rest on our laurels in Trace Model Material Evidence Authentication.

Trace Model Material Evidence Authentication is the development and optimization established on the foundation of solely naked-eye based authentication. However, scientific research is never ending, and we strongly believe that this new material evidence establishment method, rooted within science, can continue to develop and improve for many years to come.

附录1：青釉莲瓣纹碗迹型分析报告

一、送检器物基本情况

（一） 送检器物名称：青釉莲瓣纹碗。

（二） 送检器物尺寸：通高7.5厘米，口径15.7厘米，底径5.7厘米。

（三） 送检器物实图：

二、检验性质

迹型物证分析。

三、条件

（一）工具：500倍数码光学显微镜和其他辅助工具。

（二）指标：送检器物的斑块、纹路、气泡、鬃眼等迹型类别。

四、方法

（一）送检器物迹型现象与标准图谱模型比对。

（二）送检器物迹型形成本质论证。

五、操作流程

（一）送检器物全方位扫描检测。

（二）送检器物重点区域检测。

（三）送检器物迹型二维成像记录。

（四）送检器物迹型三维成像记录。

六、送检器物迹型与龙泉窑系青瓷迹型标准图谱模型比对

由于送检器物从中观工艺及纹饰特征上具备明代初期龙泉窑系青瓷的特征，所以物证分析过程中将使用明代龙泉窑系青瓷迹型标准图谱模型进行比对。

（一）反映青瓷材料、工艺的迹型特征

◆ 二维特征

1. 送检器物上存在松针形白色系放射斑（见检图1）。
2. 送检器物上存在红色系、褐色系及黑色系放射斑（见检图2）。

送检器物二维成像　　标准图谱模型二维成像

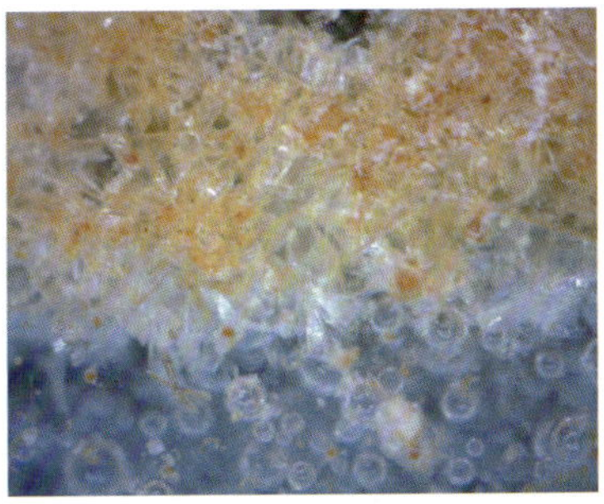

检图1

标图1

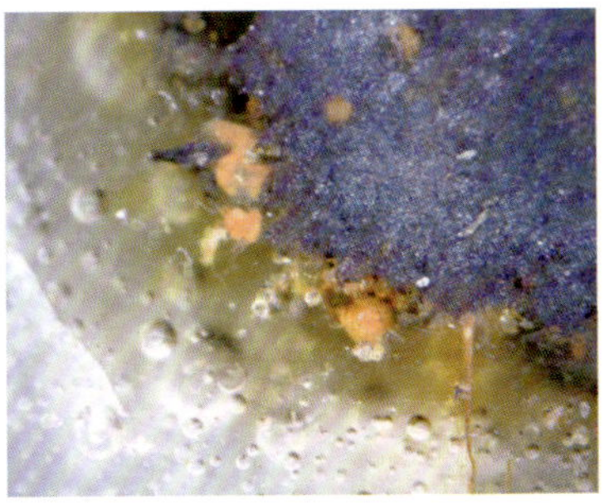

检图2

标图2

◆ 迹型本质论证

送检器物上存在上述类型放射斑，均符合明代龙泉窑系标本特点，但由于青瓷迹型的特殊性，这些反映青瓷材料、工艺的迹型特征并不能直接作为判断年代、窑口的依据，所以在此不做进一步分析讨论。

（二）反映量变原理的迹型特征

陶瓷迹型的量变原理是：陶瓷迹型的风化强度是在绝对风化时间内，以缓慢、渐变的形式形成的（其中包

含无数个在相对风化时间内形成的风化强度），具有细腻、精致、分明等特征。

送检器物二维成像

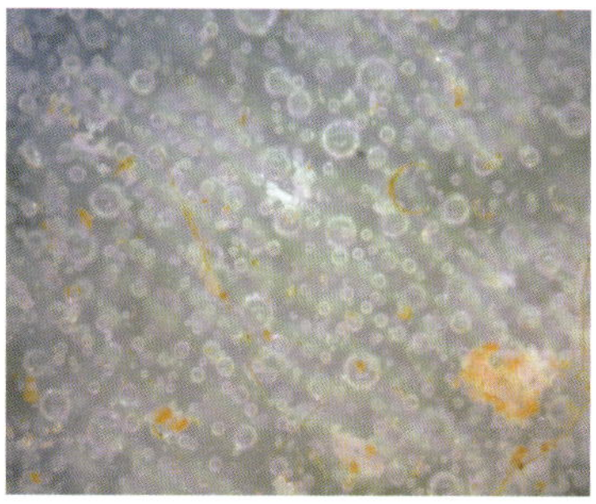

检图3

标准图谱模型二维成像

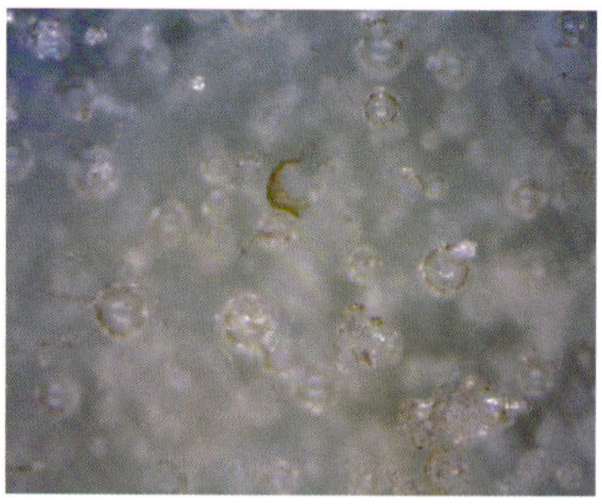

标图3

◆ 二维特征

见检图3。

1. C形纹纤细清晰。
2. C形纹与周围玻璃相界线分明。

送检器物三维成像

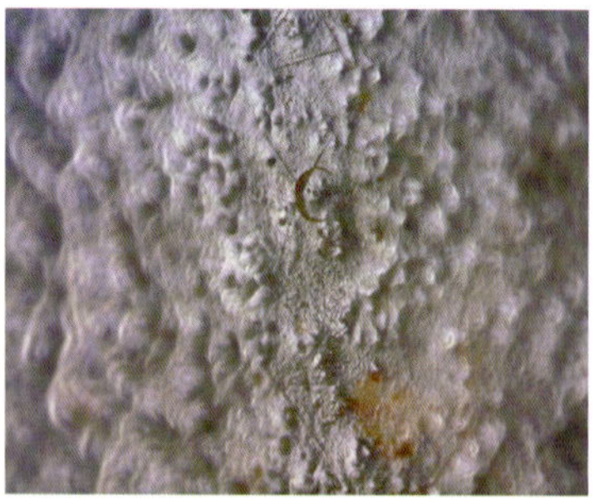

检图4

标准图谱模型三维成像

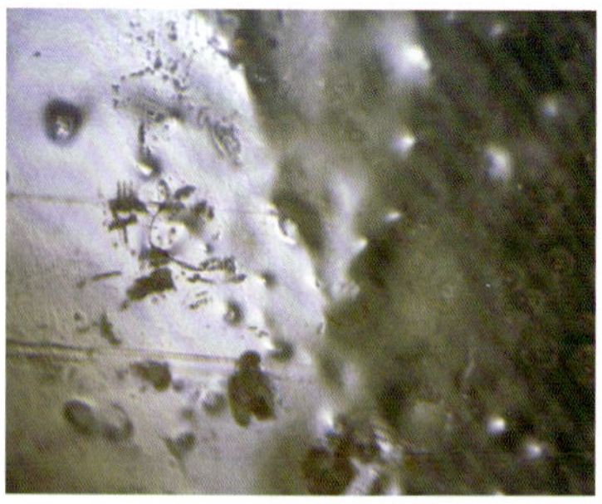

标图4

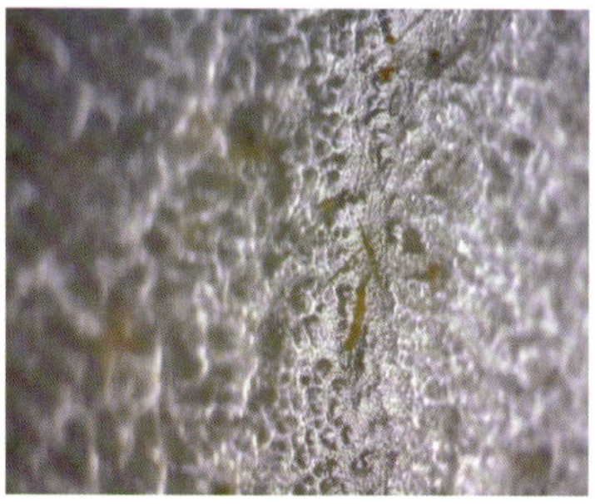

检图5

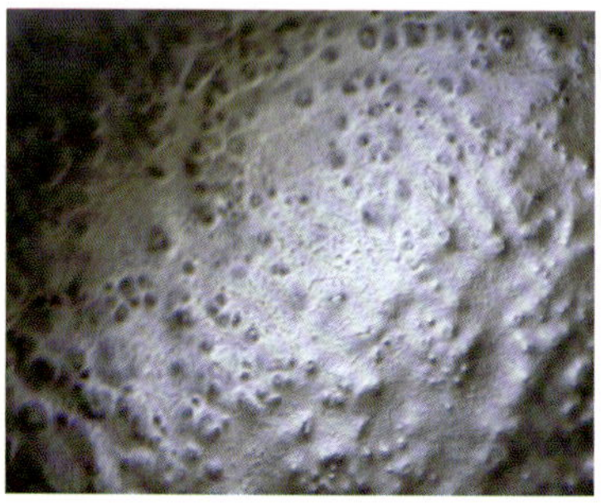

标图5

送检器物二维成像

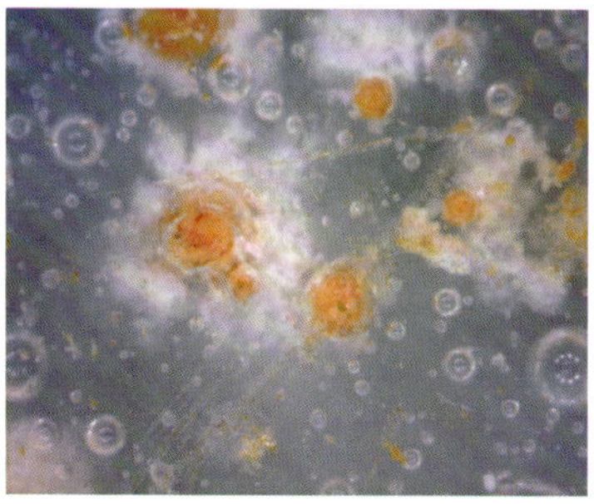

检图6

标准图谱模型二维成像

标图6

送检器物三维成像

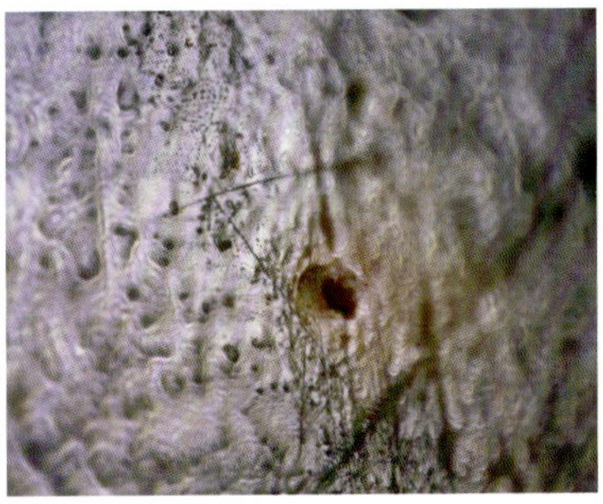

检图7

标准图谱模型三维成像

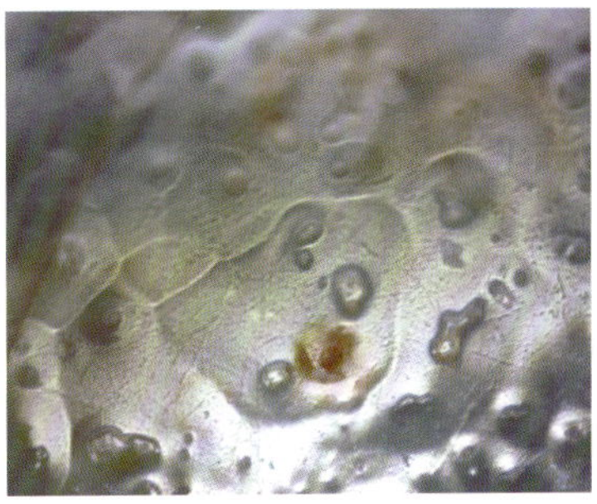

标图7

◆ 三维特征

1. 可见C形纹及紧挨着C形纹的风化斑块，纹路和斑块都清晰收敛，无扩张感，二者均与周围玻璃相界线分明。（见检图3、检图4。二者为同一器物同一位置图片，图3为二维图片，图4为三维图片）

2. 釉表面除几道较大、较明显的划痕以外，整体布满细密的风化纹路，就像陈旧的硬币表面（见检图5）。

3. 破口壁变泡所在釉表面除破口外还有其他坑点斑及划痕，但彼此各自独立分明，与周围玻璃相也界线分明。（见检图6、检图7。二者为同一器物同一位置图片，图6为二维图片，图7为三维图片）

◆ 迹型本质论证

1. 上述送检器物上的各个迹型表现特征与明代龙泉窑系青瓷迹型标准图谱模型本质相符。

2. 检图中的C形纹，无论是二维还是三维成像都十分清晰，且纹路收敛；三维成像除C形纹本身以外，可见清晰收敛的风化斑块，符合陶瓷迹型的量变原理。

3. 釉表面整体的细腻的风化特征符合陶瓷迹型的量变原理。

4. 破口壁变泡三维成像特征符合陶瓷迹型的量变原理。

(三) 反映时间过程性原理的迹型特征

陶瓷迹型的时间过程性原理是：在绝对风化时间内，陶瓷迹型特征反映了其生成、发展的时间过程。

送检器物三维成像

检图8

标准图谱模型三维成像

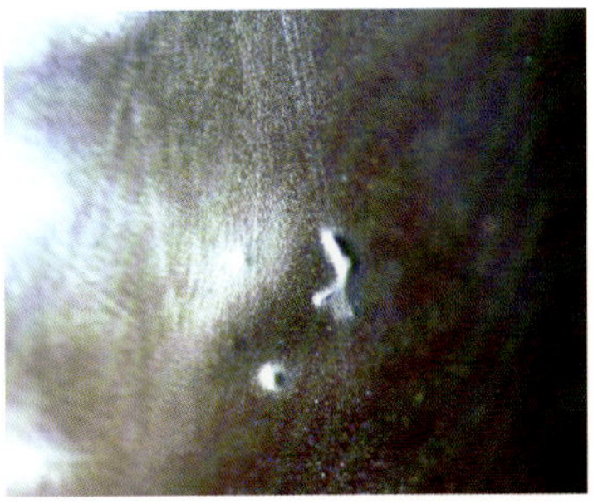

标图8

◆ 三维特征

见检图8。

放射斑三维成像可见部分放射斑明显呈凹陷状。

◆ 迹型本质论证

1. 送检器物上析晶斑的表现特征与明代龙泉窑系青瓷迹型标准图谱模型本质相符。

2. 标图中流淌斑整体明显低于釉表面，及检图中放射斑明显呈凹陷状，均是因为金属氧化物风化后不易附着，逐渐脱落所致，符合陶瓷迹型的时间过程性原理。

（四）陶瓷迹型的分明性规律

陶瓷迹型分明性规律是陶瓷在后天环境影响下形成的，分布在釉表面及釉层中的迹型类别或种类之间保持界线清晰，各自独立的现象。

送检器物二维成像

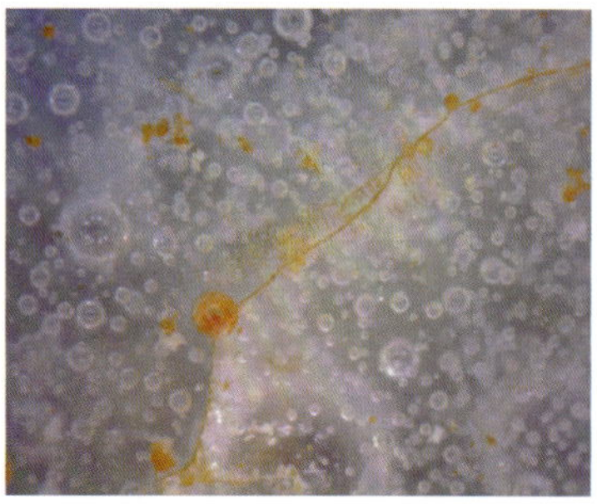

检图9

标准图谱模型二维成像

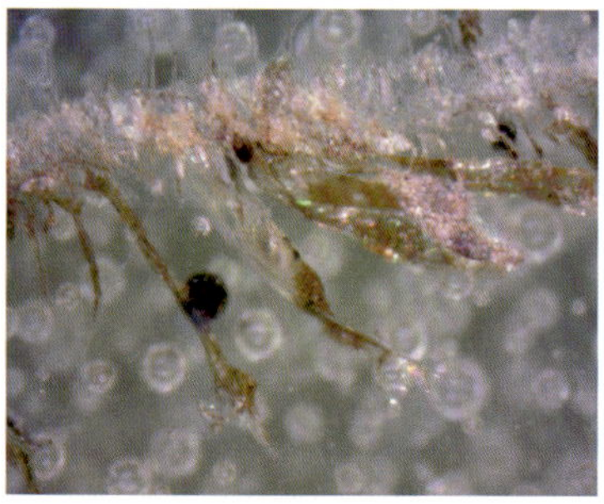

标图9

送检器物三维成像

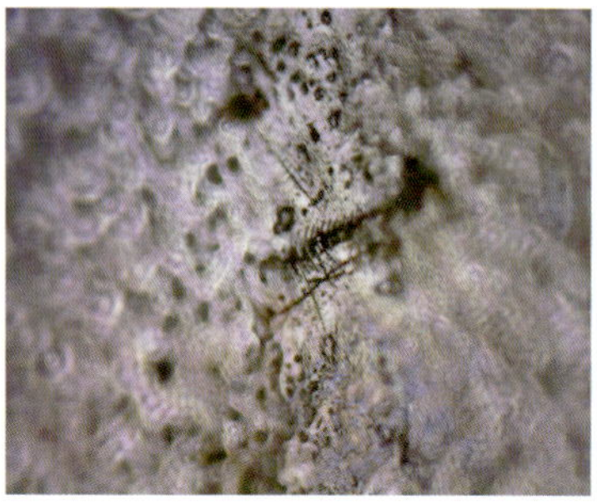

检图10

标准图谱模型三维成像

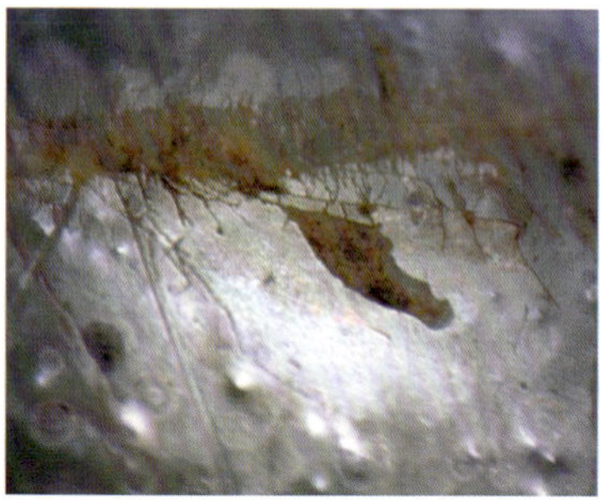

标图10

◆ 二维特征及三维特征

见检图9、检图10。

单位图片中有坑点斑、划痕、釉裂纹、壁变泡等多个种类的迹型，各自独立，界线分明。

◆ 迹型本质论证

1. 上述送检器物上各个迹型的表现特征与明代龙泉窑系青瓷迹型标准图谱模型本质相符。

2. 分布在釉表面的某个迹型与玻璃相之间，以及多个迹型种类之间各自独立，界线清晰，体现了陶瓷迹型的分明性规律。

（五）反映陶瓷迹型变化的同步性原理

陶瓷迹型变化的同步性原理关注的是同一件器物上的各迹型风化强度是否同步。

送检器物二维成像

检图11

标准图谱模型二维成像

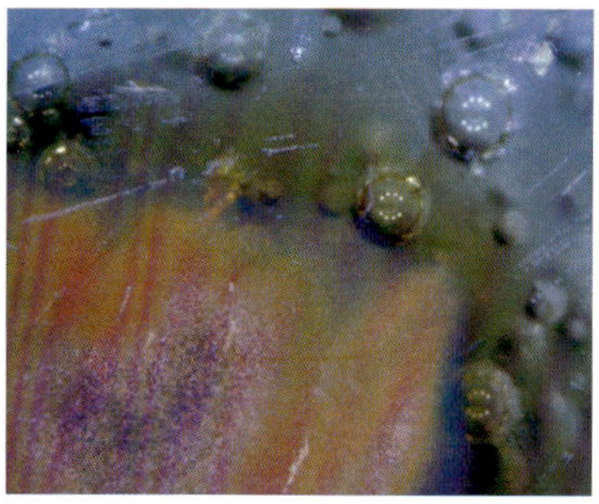

标图11

送检器物三维成像

检图12

标准图谱模型三维成像

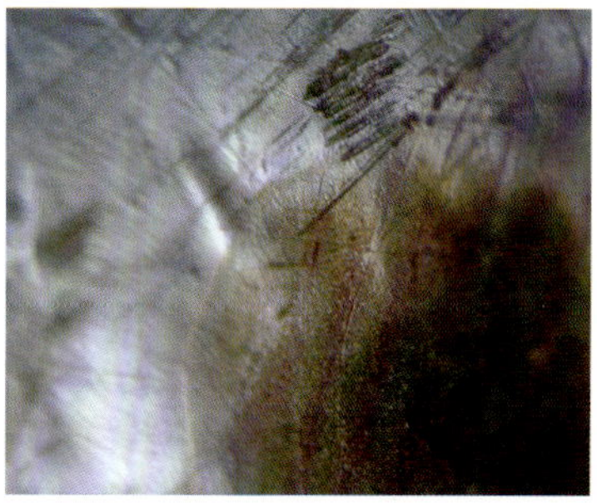

标图12

送检器物二维成像

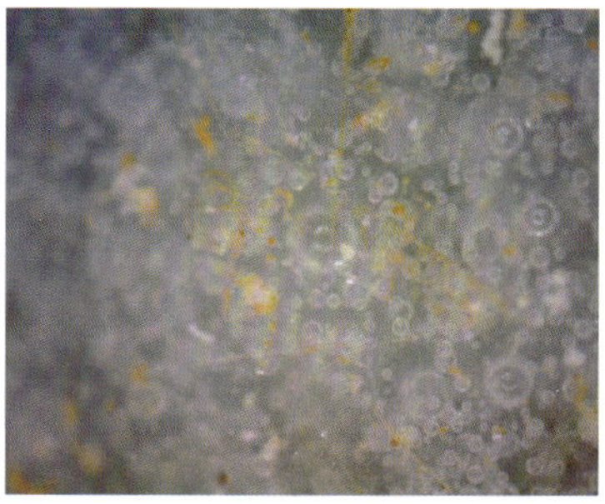

检图13

标准图谱模型二维成像

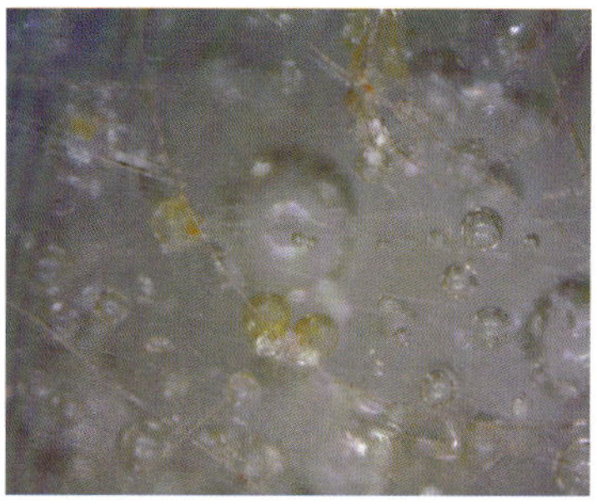

标图13

送检器物三维成像

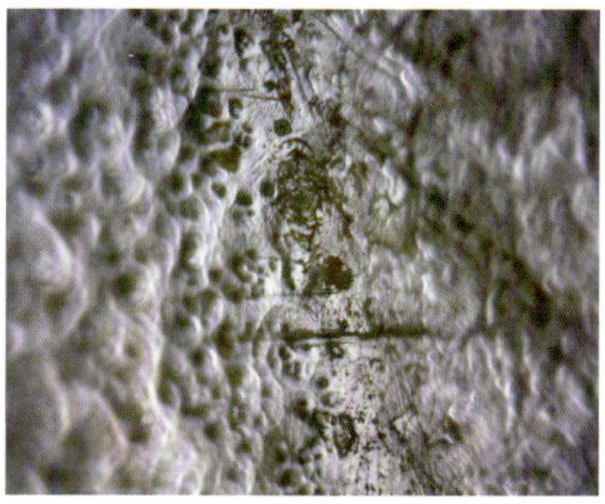

检图14

标准图谱模型三维成像

标图14

◆ 二维特征

1. 晶相：针眼型阴纹（晶相），边线清晰明亮，纹路内有针眼斑，有一定风化强度（见检图11）。
2. 玻璃相：釉表面（玻璃相）可见划痕及坑点斑，有一定的风化强度（见检图13）。

◆ 三维特征

1. 晶相：针眼型阴纹（晶相），纹路内有针眼斑，有一定风化强度。纹路内针眼斑密实，三维成像体现的风化强度与二维成像匹配（见检图11、检图12，检图11、检图12为同一器物同一位置图片，图11为二维图片，图12为三维图片）。
2. 玻璃相：釉表面（玻璃相）可见形貌各异、方向不一的划痕及坑点斑，三维成像体现的风化强度与二维成像匹配（见检图14）。

◆ 迹型本质论证

1. 送检器物上釉表面的金属氧化物晶相与玻璃相风化强度的表现特征与明代龙泉窑系青瓷迹型标准图谱模型本质相符。
2. 通常来说，同一件器物上金属氧化物的晶相与玻璃相的风化强度具有同步性，当一件器物上釉表面的玻璃相有一定风化强度，其釉表面的金属氧化物的晶相应该表现出更高的风化强度。标准图谱模型的晶相图片以及玻璃相图片均来自同一件标本，晶相与玻璃相的风化程度具有同步性。送检器物上的玻璃相上出现较多坑点斑及划痕，且有陈旧感，具备一定的风化强度，其金属氧化物晶相的表现特征也体现相应的风化强度，符合陶瓷迹型的同步性原理。
3. 对于同一迹型单项而言，其二维成像与三维成像的风化强度应该是同步的。比如检图11、检图12以及检图13、检图14的二维三维对应图，它们所表现出来的风化强度也具有同步性，符合陶瓷迹型的同步性原理。

（六）陶瓷迹型多样性规律

陶瓷迹型多样性规律是陶瓷在后天环境影响下，在釉表面及釉层中，因风化而形成的迹型，比其先天形成的迹型类别或种类数量增加的现象。

送检器物二维成像

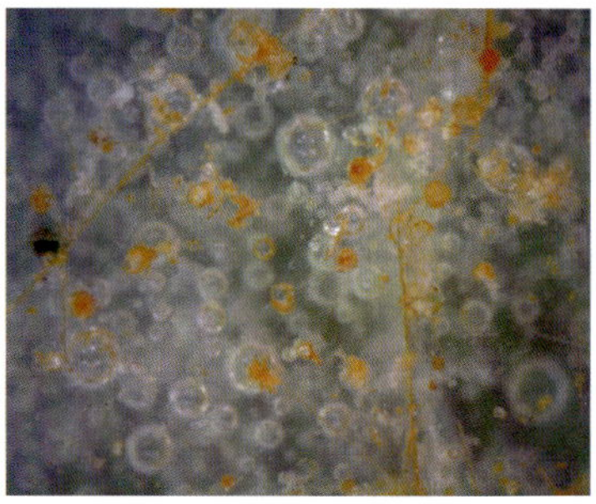

检图15

标准图谱模型二维成像

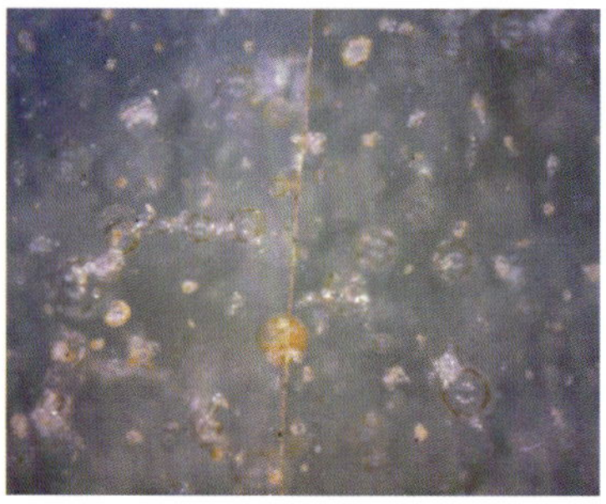

标图15

送检器物二维成像　　　　标准图谱模型二维成像

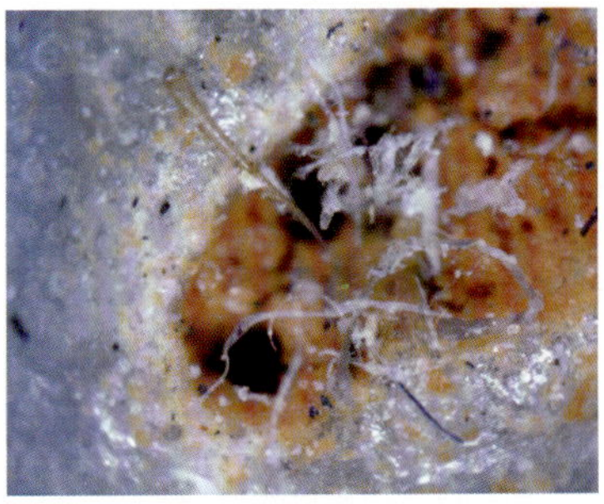

检图16

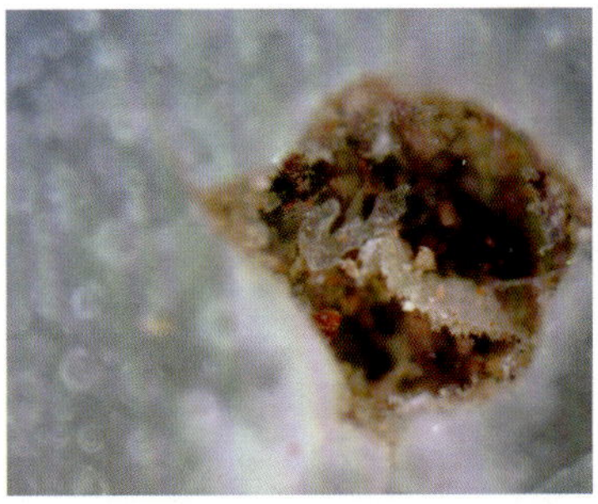

标图16

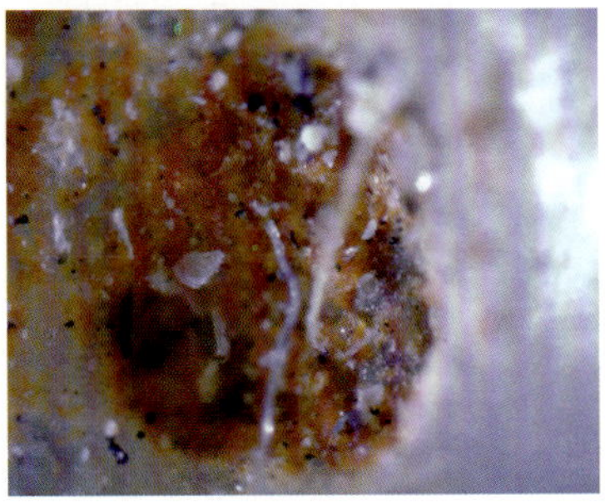

检图17

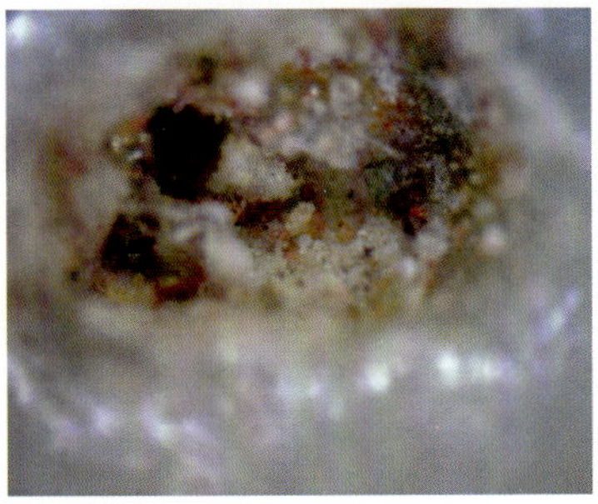

标图17

◆ 二维特征

1. 单位图片中可见多种迹型种类的迹型存在：坑点斑、CO纹、釉裂纹、划痕等（见检图15）。
2. 鬃眼口沿及内部有多处纤丝及风化沉积物（见检图16、检图17）。
3. 送检器物整体迹型具有多样性。

送检器物三维成像　　　　标准图谱模型三维成像

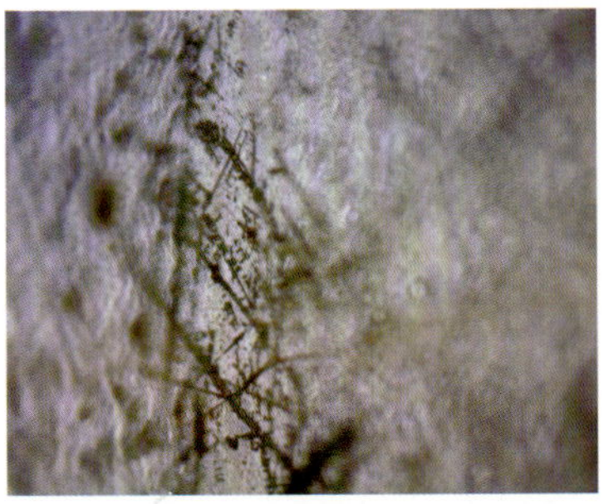

检图18

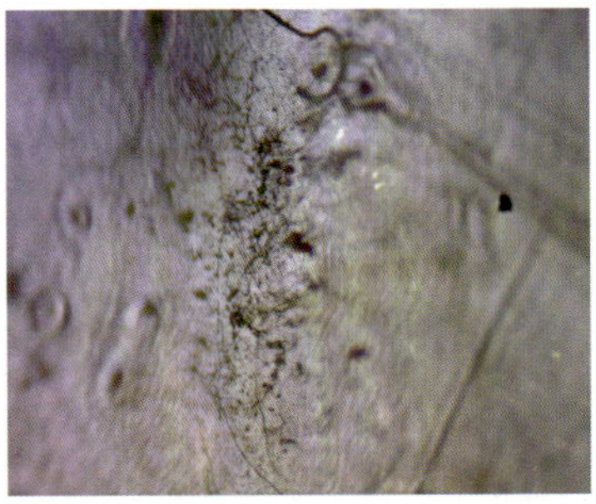

标图18

◆ 三维特征

见检图18。
1. 单位图片中可见多种迹型种类的迹型存在，如坑点斑及划痕等形貌各异。
2. 送检器物整体迹型具有多样性。

◆ 迹型本质论证

1. 上述送检器物上的各个迹型表现特征与明代龙泉窑系青瓷迹型标准图谱模型本质相符。
2. 单位图片中，器物整体的迹型多样性及鬃眼口沿及内部的风化特征都体现了陶瓷迹型的多样性规律。

（七）陶瓷迹型的色差规律

陶瓷迹型色差规律是在烧制过程中和后天环境影响下形成的，分布在釉表面及釉层中的同一陶瓷迹型种类表现出颜色差异的现象。

送检器物二维成像	标准图谱模型二维成像
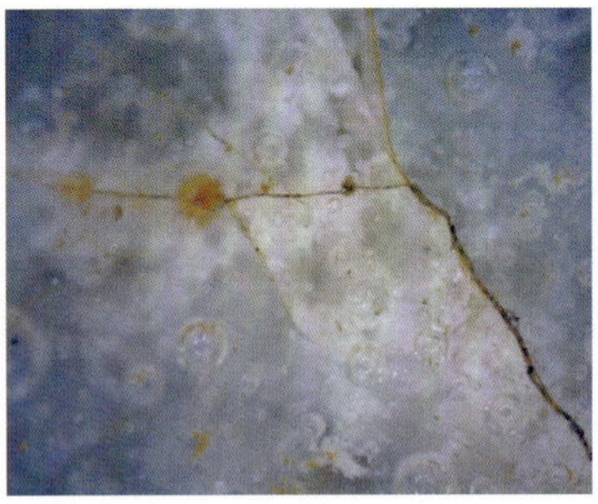 检图19	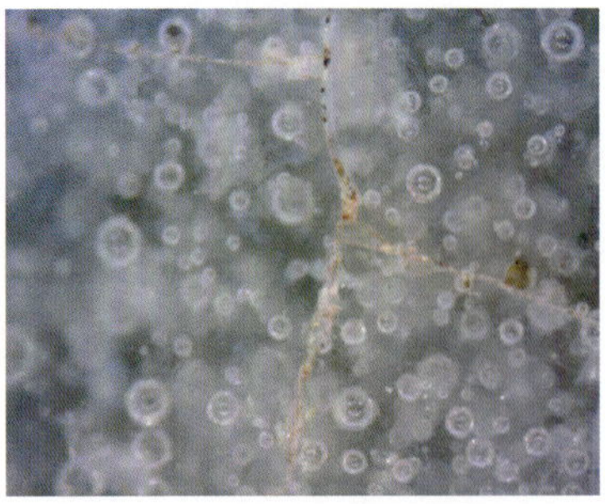 标图19
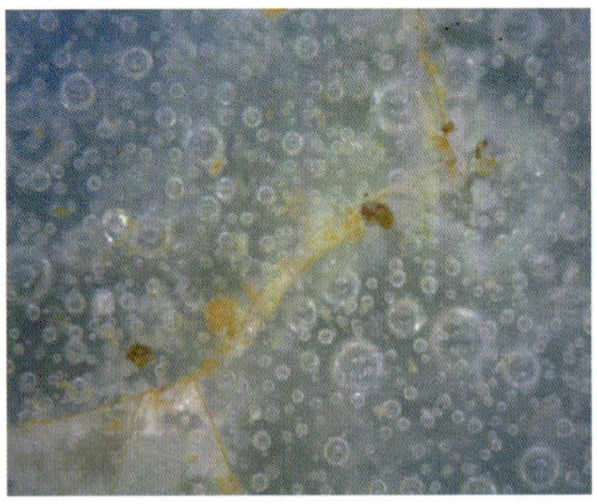 检图20	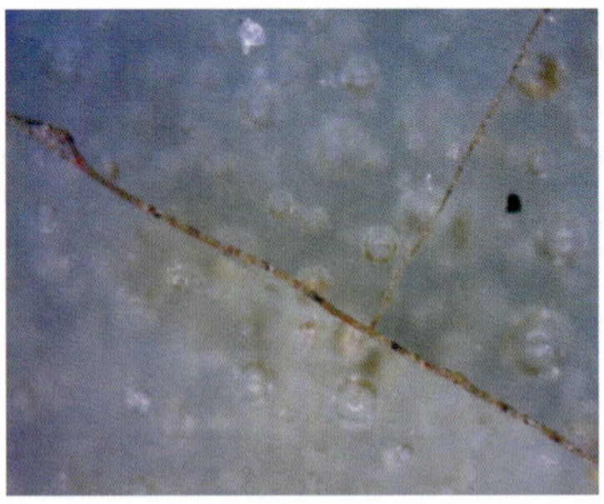 标图20
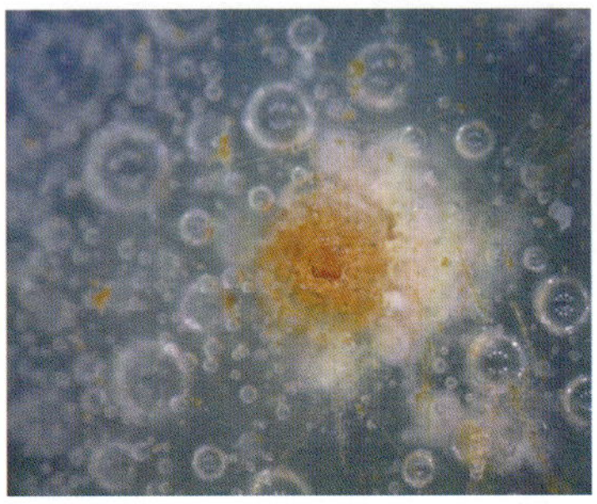 检图21	 标图21
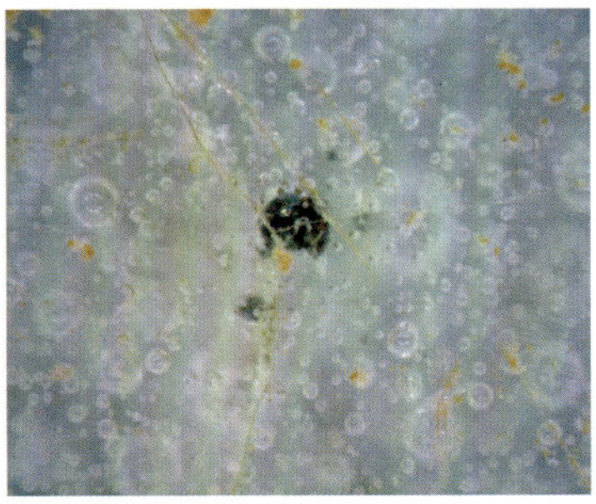 检图22	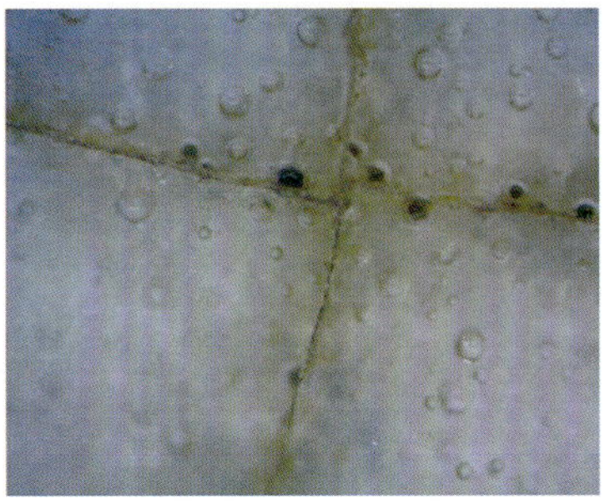 标图22

◆ 二维特征

1. 单位图片中各个单项迹型或多个迹型之间存在色差（见检图19、检图20）。
2. 送检器物上，同一迹型种类也存在色差（见检图21、检图22）。

◆ 迹型本质论证

1. 上述送检器物上的各个迹型表现特征与明代龙泉窑系青瓷迹型标准图谱模型本质相符。
2. 单位图片中，器物整体的各个单项迹型及多个迹型之间的颜色差异都体现了陶瓷迹型的色差规律。

（八）陶瓷迹型的层次性规律

陶瓷迹型层次性规律是陶瓷迹型不同类别之间和同一类别之间迹型风化强度的差异，通过它们在釉层（釉表面或釉层中）纵向垂直的位置表现出来的现象。

◆ 二维特征

见检图23。
CO纹有沿着其轮廓向外呈白雾状蔓延的趋势。

◆ 三维特征

见检图23、检图24。（二者为同一器物同一位置图片，检图23为二维图片，检图24为三维图片）
三维成像只见纤细收敛的C形纹。

送检器物二维成像

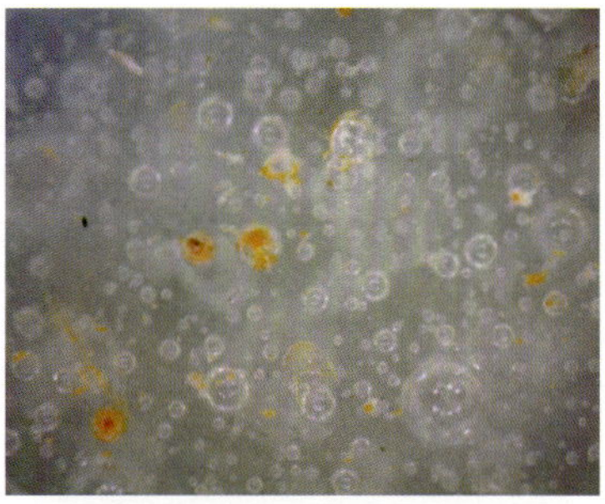

检图23

标准图谱模型二维成像

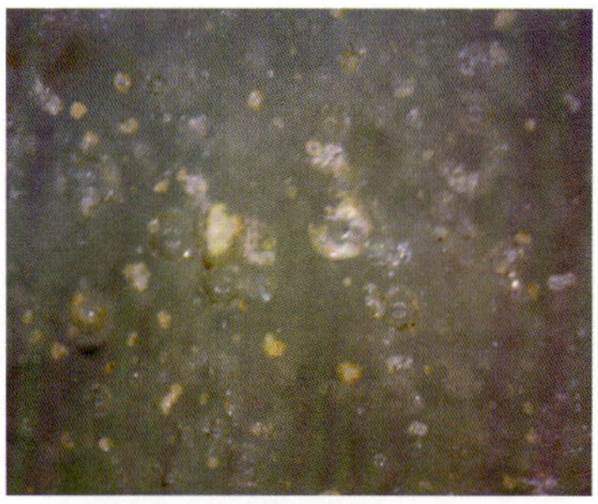

标图23

送检器物三维成像

检图24

标准图谱模型三维成像

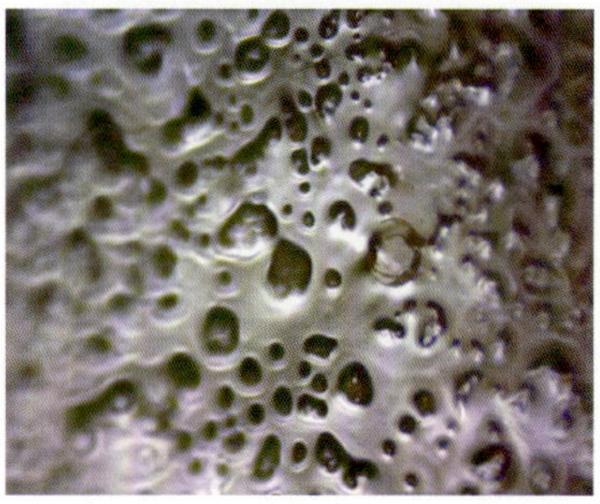

标图24

◆ 迹型本质论证

1. 送检器物上CO纹的表现特征与明代龙泉窑系青瓷迹型标准图谱模型本质相符。

2. CO纹的二维成像有沿着其轮廓向外呈白雾状蔓延的趋势，三维成像却只见纤细收敛的C形纹，说明风化是纵向深入釉层中的，符合陶瓷迹型的层次性规律。

（九）反映迹型出现位置合理性的迹型特征

陶瓷迹型出现位置的合理性，关注的是陶瓷迹型出现的位置是否符合陶瓷迹型风化的原理及规律。

◆ 二维特征及三维特征

见检图25、检图26。（二者为同一器物同一位置图片，检图25为二维图片，检图26为三维图片）
图中箭头所指的C形纹三维成像所在位置为釉表面凸起处。

送检器物二维成像

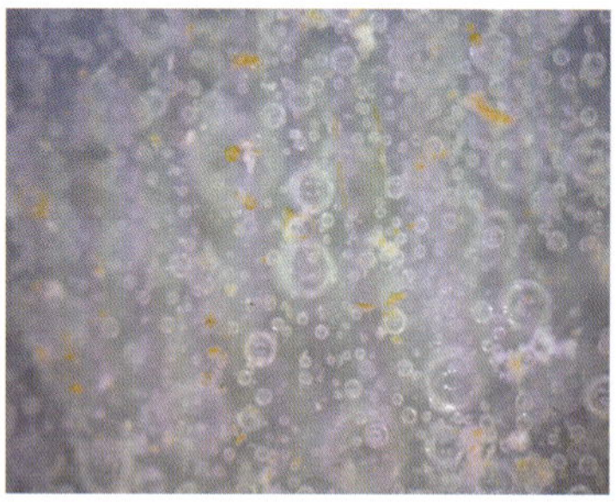

检图25

标准图谱模型二维成像

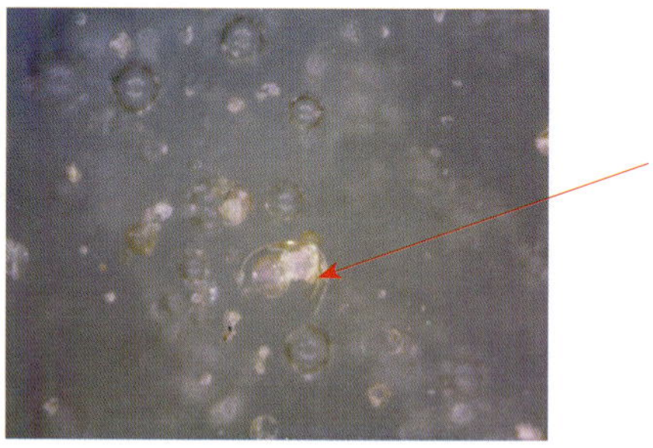

标图25

送检器物三维成像

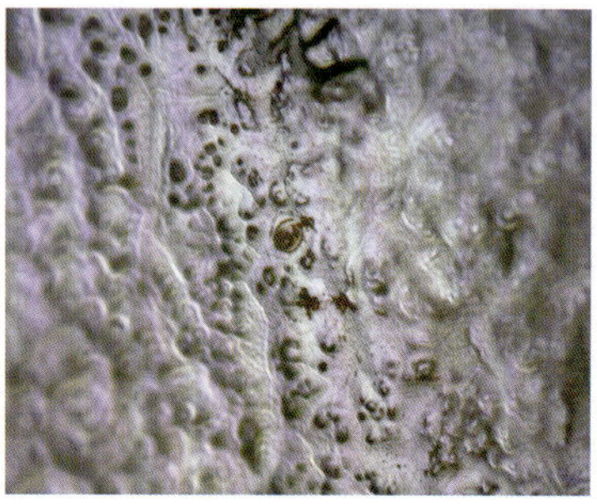

检图26

标准图谱模型三维成像

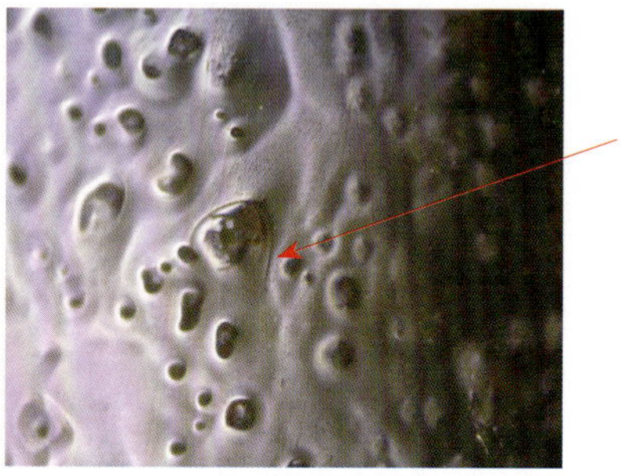

标图26

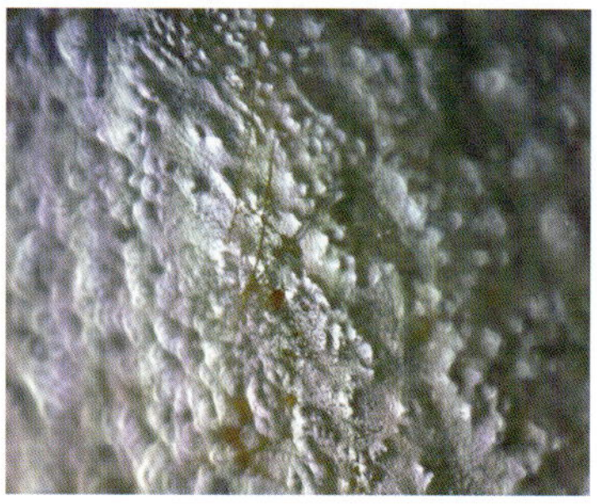

检图27

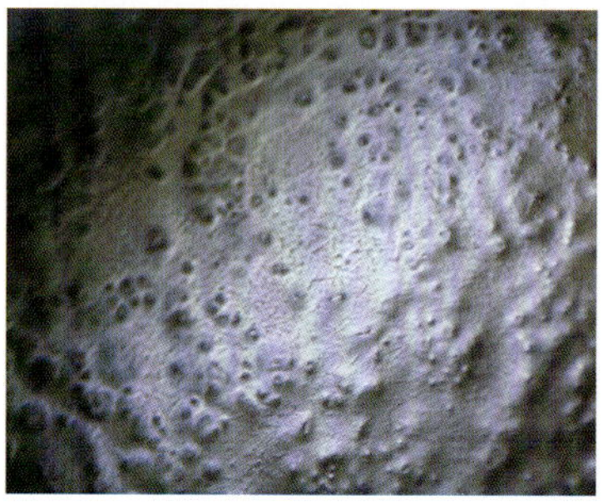

标图27

◆ 三维特征

见检图27。

所有釉表面凸起处都是根部风化程度较高，颜色较深，顶部风化程度较低，颜色较浅。

◆ 迹型本质论证

1. 上述送检器物上的各个迹型表现特征与明代龙泉窑系青瓷迹型标准图谱模型本质相符。
2. 送检器物上的CO纹、CO型坑点斑，具有迹型出现位置的合理性。

七、迹型现象比对结果综述

◆ 经显微仪器检测发现，送检器物共有放射斑、针眼斑、坑点斑、流淌纹、CO纹、釉裂纹、划痕、色变泡、壁变泡、鬃眼等十种迹型，其中后天性迹型达八种（包括针眼斑、坑点斑、CO纹、多样性釉裂纹、划痕、色变泡、壁变泡及多样性鬃眼）。

◆ 经与龙泉窑系青瓷迹型标准图谱模型比对后发现，送检器物在能够反映龙泉窑系青瓷用材、烧制工艺、量变原理、时间过程性原理及其他陶瓷迹型规律的重要迹型上，不管是二维还是三维成像，都与明代龙泉窑系青瓷迹型标准图谱模型本质相符，具备明代龙泉窑系青瓷迹型的普遍性特征。除此之外，送检器物上后天性风化迹型的种类数量体现了迹型的多样性，迹型出现的位置及表现特征也与图谱迹型一样，具有迹型出现位置的合理性及迹型变化的同步性。因此从迹型现象表现特征和迹型形成原理及规律来看，送检器物的迹型特征与明代龙泉窑系青瓷迹型标准图谱模型本质相符。

八、送检器物物证分析

送检器物存在与龙泉窑系青瓷迹型标准图谱模型本质相符的迹型，同时，送检器物上的迹型特征符合且反映了陶瓷迹型量变原理、时间过程性原理、同步性原理、分明性规律、多样性规律及色差规律。

因此送检器物上的显微迹型可作为鉴定其年代所需的物证依据。

Appendix 1: Longquan Celadon Bowl with Lotus Petal Pattern: Trace Model Material Evidence Analysis Report

1. General Information of Test Piece

A. Name: Longquan Celadon Bowl with Lotus Petal Pattern

B. Measurements: Height ~ 7.5 cm; Mouth ~ 15.7cm; Base Width ~ 5.7cm

C. Whole Piece Image:

2. Nature of Test

Trace Model Material Evidence Analysis.

3. Evidence Collection Requirements:

A. Evidence Collection Equipment: Digital 500X magnification optical microscope and associated tools.

B. Evidence Collection Focus: Mottles, Striae, Bubbles, Bristle Pits and Glaze Level Trace Categories.

4. Evidence Collection Method:

A. Trace comparison with the LKSC Standard Trace Atlas Model

B. Trace Nature Proofs

5. Evidence Collection Operating Procedure

A. Holistic Scan and Sampling

B. Focused Area Sampling

C. Two-Dimensional Record Taking

D. Three-Dimensional Record Taking

6. Trace Comparison with the Longquan Kiln System Celadon Standard Trace Atlas Model

Due to the observable production and decorative characteristics of the tested piece being consistent with Early Ming Dynasty Longquan Kiln System Celadon, the tested piece will be compared against the Ming Dynasty Longquan Kiln System Celadon Standard Trace Atlas Model to analyze its material evidence.

A. Reflects Celadon Materials and Techniques

Two-Dimensional Sample Images

Two-Dimensional LKSCSTAM Images

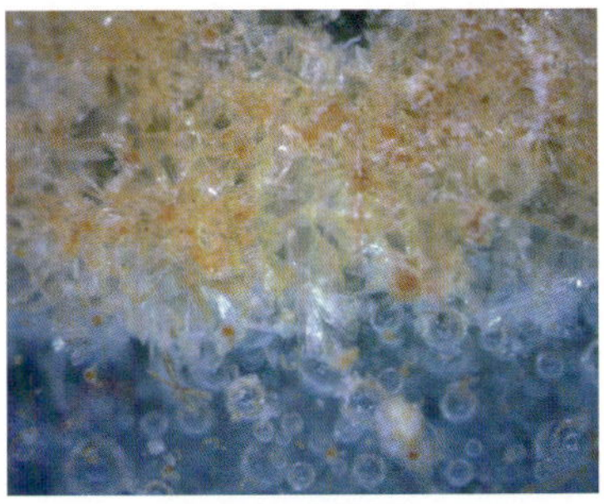

Sample Image 1

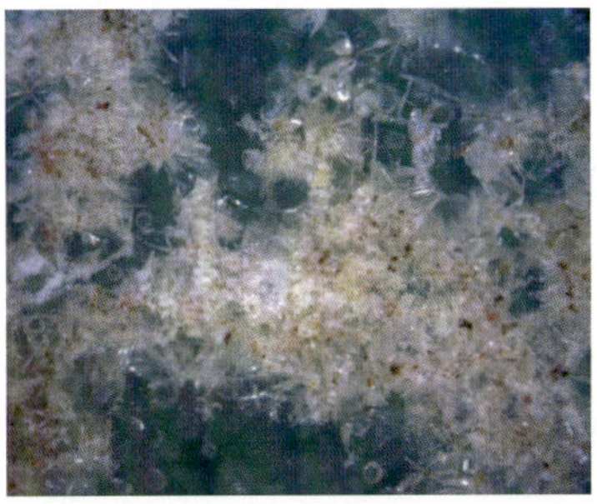

LKSCSTAM Image 1

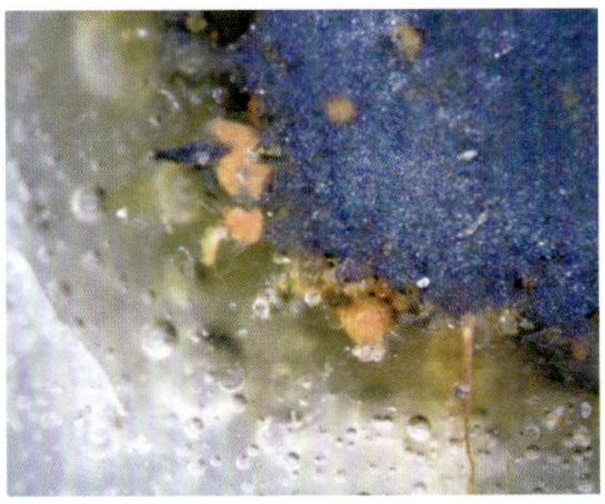

Sample Image 2

LKSCSTAM Image 2

◆ Two-Dimensional Characteristics

1) The test piece has white series pine needle shaped radiating mottles (see Sample Image 1).

2) The test piece has red series, brown series and black series radiating mottles (see Sample Image 2).

◆ Trace Nature Proofs

The tested piece presents with the aforementioned radiating mottles, both of which are consistent with LKSC sample characteristics. However, due to the special nature of celadon glazes, this can not be used to specifically determine its date or production location. As such, no further discussion will be carried out here.

B. Reflects Quantitative Change Principle

The Quantitative Change Principle states: The weathering severity of ceramic traces occurs within an absolute weathering time. It is a slow, gradual formation that is the accumulation of weathering severities formed during innumerable variable weathering time periods, it has minute, fine, and distinct characteristics.

Two-Dimensional Sample Image

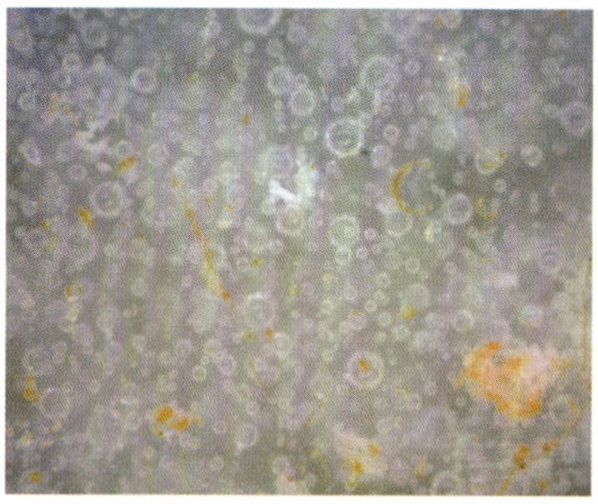

Sample Image 3

Two-Dimensional LKSCSTAM Image

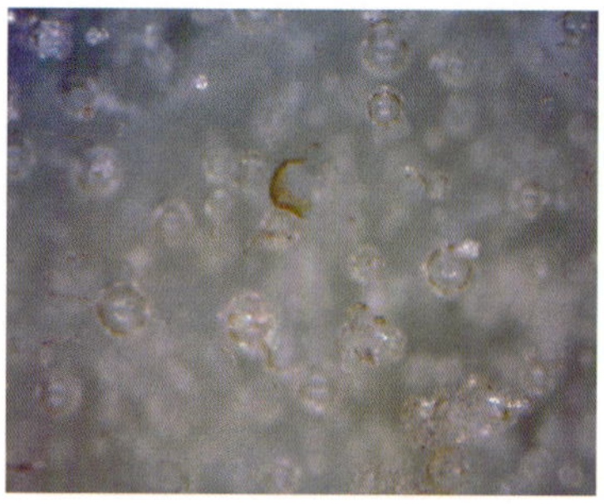

LKSCSTAM Image 3

◆ Two-Dimensional Characteristics

See Sample Image 3.

1) C Striation is clearly fine and reserved.

2) C Striation retains clear delineation from the surrounding glass phase.

Three-Dimensional Sample Images

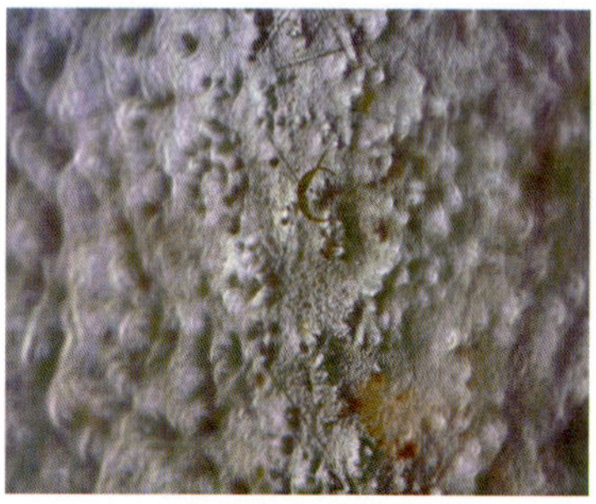

Sample Image 4

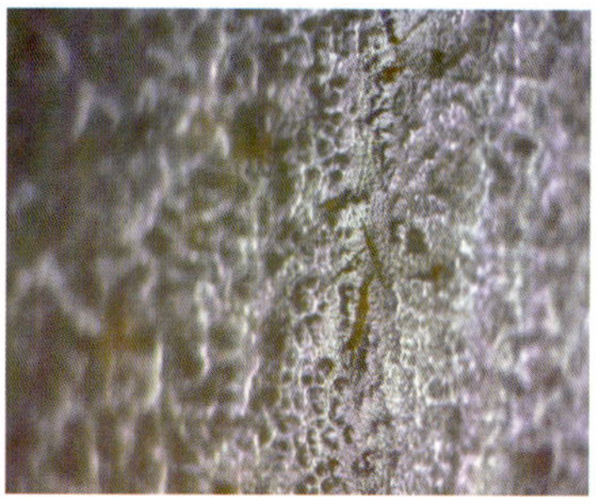

Sample Image 5

Three-Dimensional LKSCSTAM Images

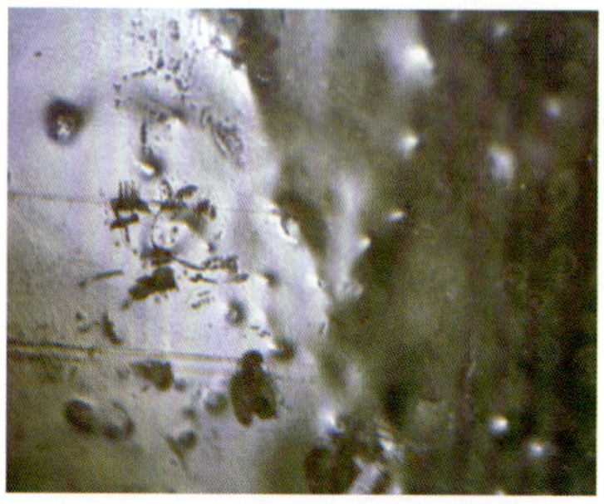

LKSCSTAM Image 4

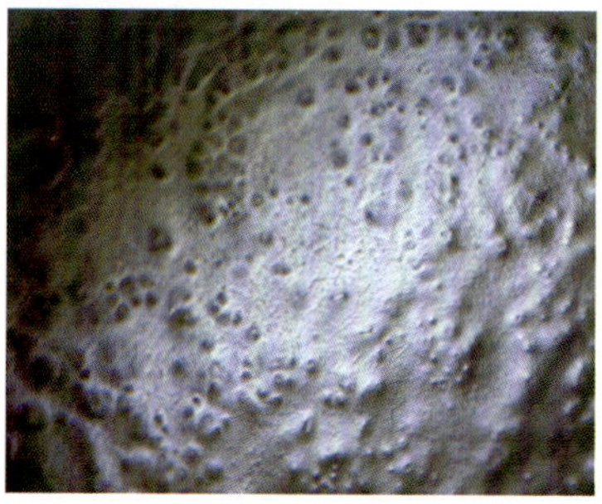

LKSCSTAM Image 5

Two-Dimensional Sample Image

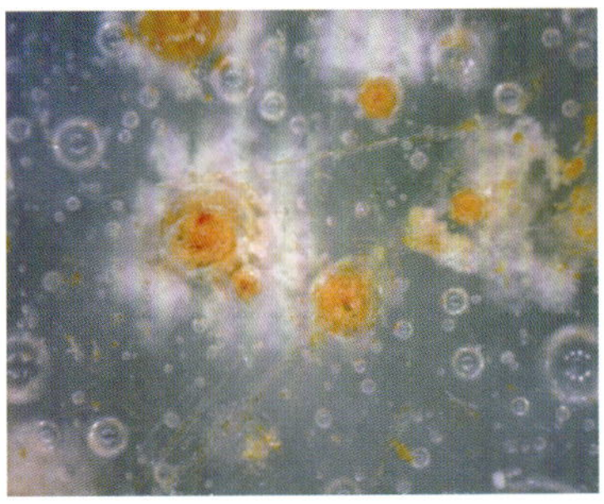

Sample Image 6

Two-Dimensional LKSCSTAM Image

LKSCSTAM Image 6

Three-Dimensional Sample Image

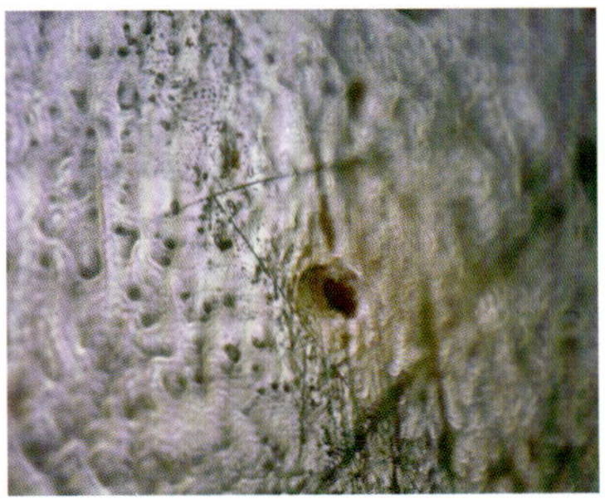

Sample Image 7

Three-Dimensional LKSCSTAM Image

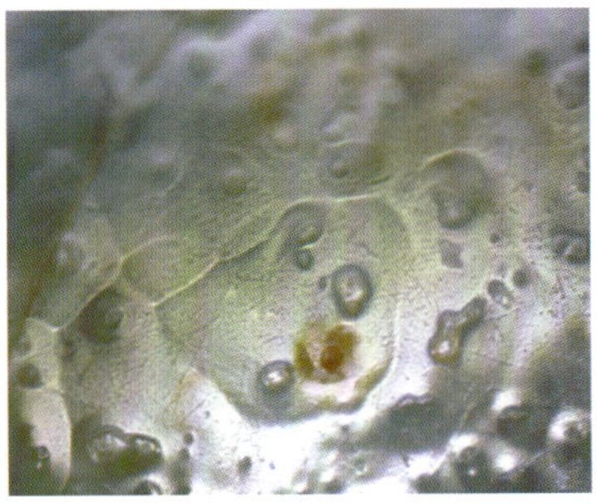

LKSCSTAM Image 7

◆ Three-Dimensional Characteristics

1) A C striation and associated weathering mottle are apparent. The striation and mottle are clear and reserved. They lack dispersive properties, and both are clearly delineated from the surrounding glass phase (see Sample Images 3 and 4, where 3 is the two-dimensional and 4 is the three-dimensional view of the same location).

2) The glaze surface, aside from a few relatively large and clear scratches, presents with a relatively full distribution of finely dense weathering striae, similar to that of an old coin, giving it an aged feel (see Sample Image 5).

3) Pits and scratches appear on the glaze surface surrounding the broken mouth textured bubbles. However, they are clearly independent, and retain delineation from the surrounding glass phase (see Sample Images 6 and 7, where 6 is the two-dimensional and 7 is the three-dimensional view of the same location).

◆ Trace Nature Proofs

1) The characteristics of the test piece's traces and those of the LKSC Standard Trace Atlas Model are matching in nature.

2) The C shaped striae, regardless of two or three-dimensional image, are perfectly clear and reserved. Aside from the three-dimensional C shaped striae, other clearly delineated weathering mottles also appear, which are in accordance with the CeramicTrace Quantitative Change Principle.

3) The glaze surface weathering characteristics are generally refined, which is in accordance with Ceramic Trace Quantitative Change Principle.

4) The three-dimensional characteristics of the broken mouth textured bubbles are in accordance with the Ceramic Trace Quantitative Change Principle.

C. Reflects Passage of Time Principle

The Passage of Time Principle states: Throughout the absolute weathering time, the ceramic trace generation and transformation processes, within numerous variable weathering time periods, form the multiplicity and complexity of trace weathering severities throughout the ceramic glaze level.

Three-Dimensional Sample Image

Sample Image 8

Three-Dimensional LKSCSTAM Image

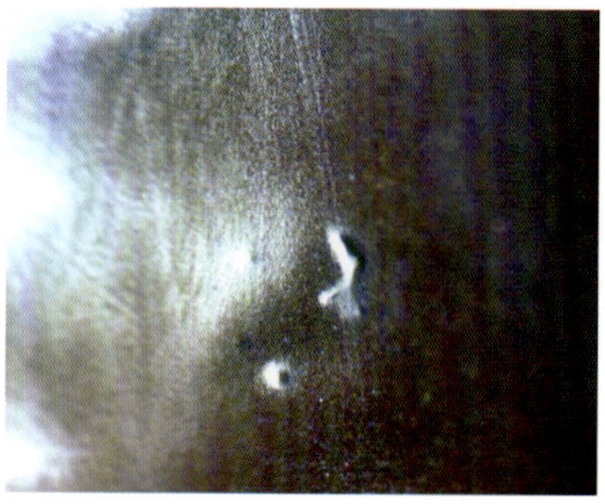

LKSCSTAM Image 8

◆ Three-Dimensional Characteristics

See Sample Image 8.
Three-dimensional imaging of radiating mottles shows that a portion of radiating mottles have distinct depressed shape.

◆ Trace Nature Proofs

1) The characteristics of the crystalized mottles on the test piece and those of the LKSC Standard Trace Atlas Model are matching in nature.
2) The flowing mottles on the standard images are clearly lower than the surrounding glaze surface. Similarly, the images of the sample piece's radiating mottles have a depressed shape. This is due to the fact that they both depict metal oxides present on the glaze surface, which after weathering, do not hold fast to the surface, and as such are easily detached. This is consistent with the Ceramic Trace Passage of Time Principle.

D. Ceramic Trace Law of Distinction

The Ceramic Trace Law of Distinction describes the phenomenon of trace categories and types distributed across the glaze surface and within the glaze level, formed within the post-firing environment, retaining clear delineation and respective independence from one another

Two-Dimensional Sample Image

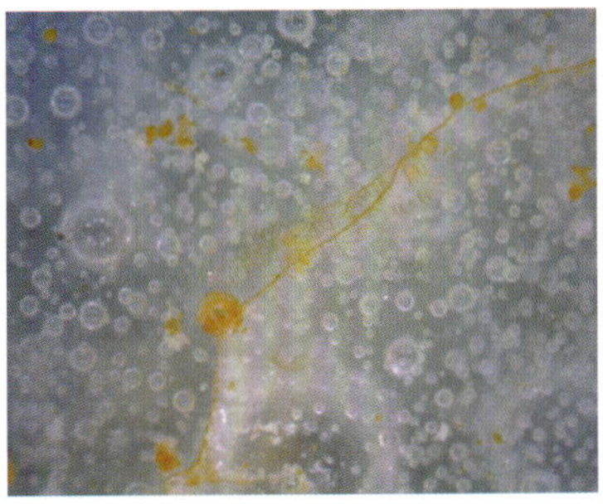

Sample Image 9

Two-Dimensional LKSCSTAM Image

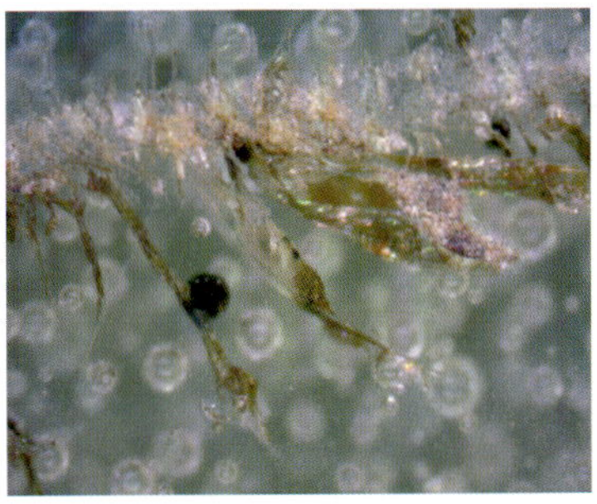

LKSCSTAM Image 9

Three-Dimensional Sample Image

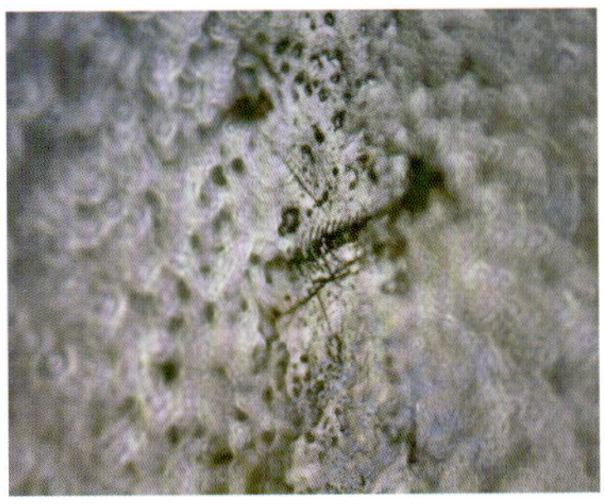

Sample Image 10

Three-Dimensional LKSCSTAM Image

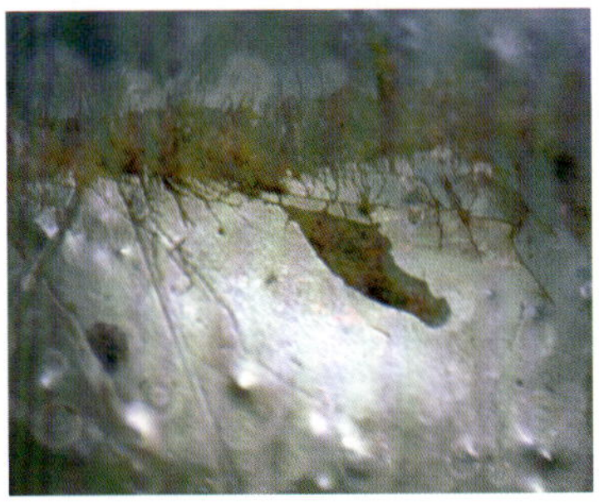

LKSCSTAM Image 10

◆ Two-Dimensional and Three-Dimensional Characteristics

See Sample Images 9 and 10.

Within a single unit image: Pits, scratches, glaze cracks, textured bubbles, and so forth categories of traces appear in conjunction; they are independent and clearly delineated.

◆ Trace Nature Proofs

1) The characteristics of the above mentioned traces on the test piece and those of the LKSC Standard Trace Atlas Model are matching in nature.

2) The traces distributed across the glaze surface retain clear independence and delineation from the surrounding glass phase as well as other traces. This reflects the Ceramic Trace Law of Distinction.

E. Reflects Trace Change Congruency

The concept of Ceramic Trace Change Congruency refers to whether or not there is a congruency in trace weathering severity according to their respective weathering resistance.

Two-Dimensional Sample Image

Sample Image 11

Two-Dimensional LKSCSTAM Image

LKSCSTAM Image 11

Three-Dimensional Sample Image

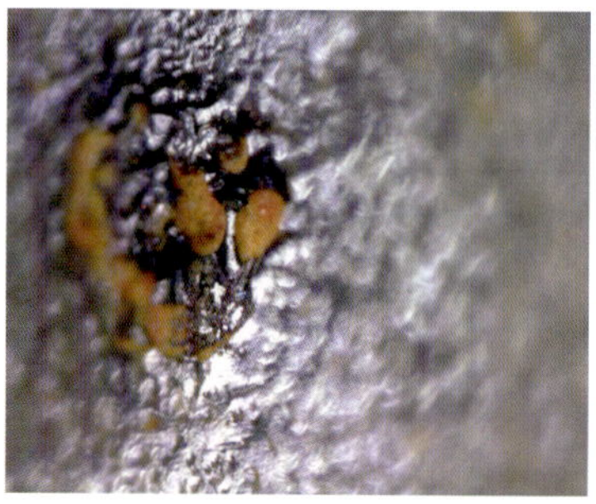

Sample Image 12

Three-Dimensional LKSCSTAM Image

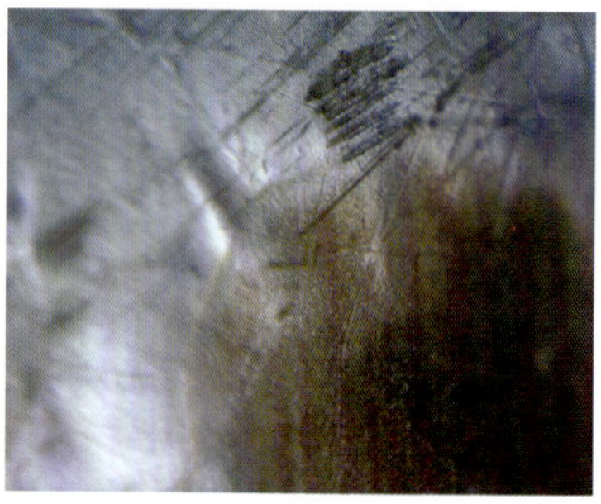

LKSCSTAM Image 12

Two-Dimensional Sample Image

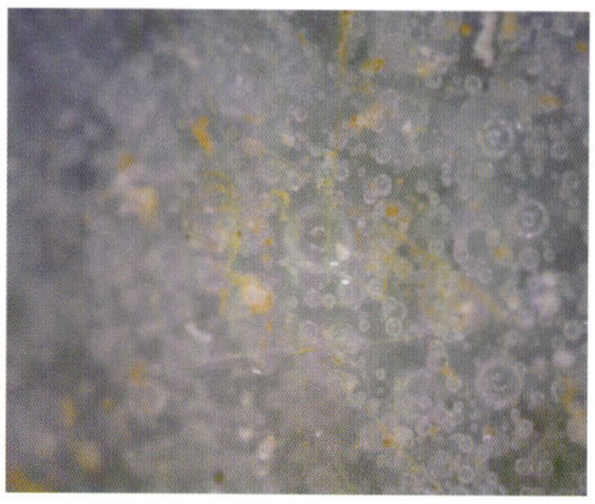

Sample Image 13

Two-Dimensional LKSCSTAM Image

LKSCSTAM Image 13

Three-Dimensional Sample Image

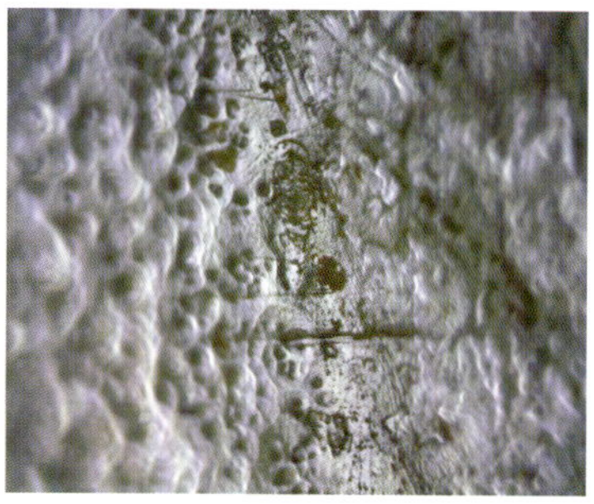

Sample Image 14

Three-Dimensional LKSCSTAM Image

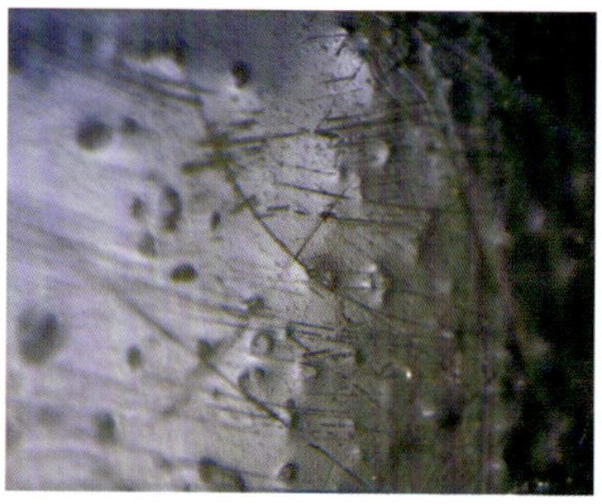

LKSCSTAM Image 14

◆ Two-Dimensional Characteristics

1) Crystal Phase: Needlepoint depressed striae (crystal phase), has a brightly clear boundary with needlepoint mottling presenting within the striae interior; reflecting a certain amount of weathering (see Sample Image 11).
2) Glass Phase: The glaze surface (glass phase) presents with pitting and scratches; indicating a certain amount of weathering (see Sample Image 13).

◆ Three-Dimensional Characteristics

1) Crystal Phase: Needlepoint depressed striae (crystal phase) present with needlepoint mottling within the striae interior, indicating a certain amount of weathering. The needlepoint mottling within the striae are dense, and the three-dimensionally observable weathering is consistent with weathering two-dimensionally observable (see Sample Images 11 and 12, where 11 is the two-dimensional and 12 is the three-dimensional view of the same location).
2) Glass Phase: The glaze surface (glass phase) presents with scratches of disparate appearance and direction as well as pitting; the three-dimensionally observable weathering is consistent with two-dimensionally observable weathering (see Sample Image 14).

◆ Trace Nature Proofs

1) The characteristics of the metal oxide crystallization on the glaze surface and glass phase weathering on the test piece and those of the LKSC Standard Trace Atlas Model are matching in nature.
2) Often, the crystal and glass phase on the glaze surface of a single piece have weathering congruency. When a piece presents with a certain amount of glass phase weathering, the associated metal oxide crystallizations reflect a relatively higher amount of weathering. The LKSCSTAM images of glass and crystal phase weathering all come from a single piece, and as such reflect weathering congruency. The sample piece's glass phase presents with a relatively high amount of pitting and scratches, as well as a glaze surface with an aged feel, reflecting a certain amount of weathering. Similarly, the metal oxide crystallizations also reflect a characteristically related amount of weathering, and as such are consistent with the Ceramic Trace Change Congruency Principle (Part A).
3) Additionally, in regards to a single trace, its two and three-dimensionally observable weathering severity are congruent. Sample Images 11—14, where each pair are corresponding two and three-dimensional images, present with congruent trace weathering severity, and as such this piece is consistent with the Ceramic Trace Change Congruency Principle (Part B)

F. Ceramic Trace Law of Variegation

The Ceramic Trace Law of Variegation describes the phenomenon of an increase in appearances of trace categories and types distributed across the glaze surface and throughout the glaze level due to weathering incurred in the post-firing environment.

Two-Dimensional Sample Images	Two-Dimensional LKSCSTAM Images

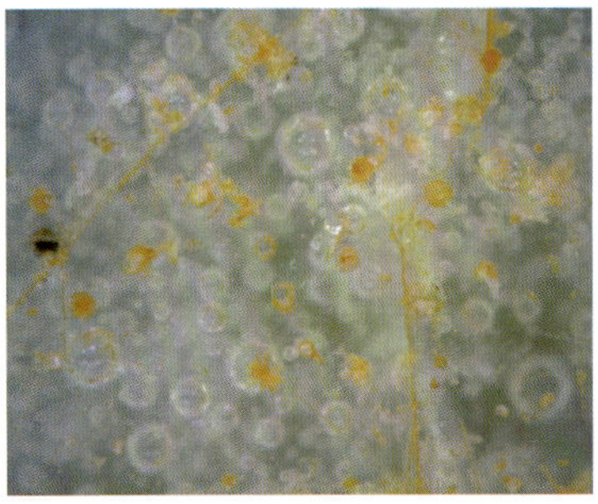
Sample Image 15

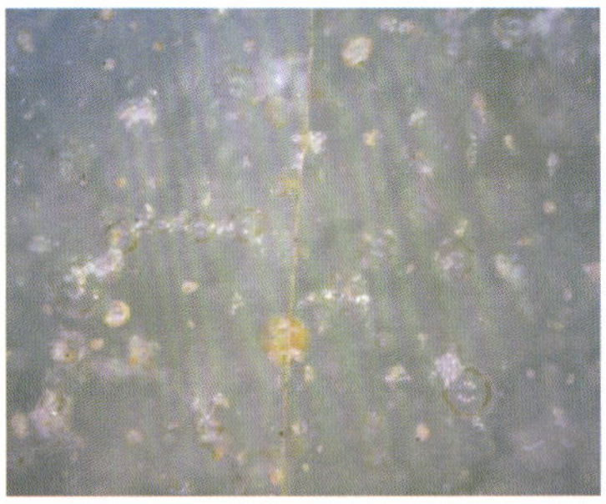
LKSCSTAM Image 15

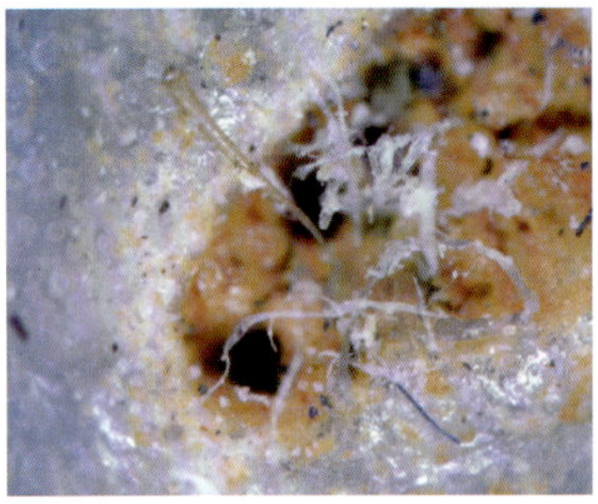
Sample Image 16

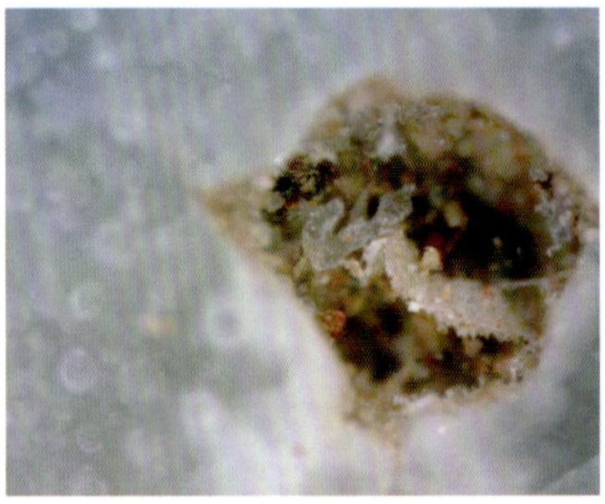
LKSCSTAM Image 16

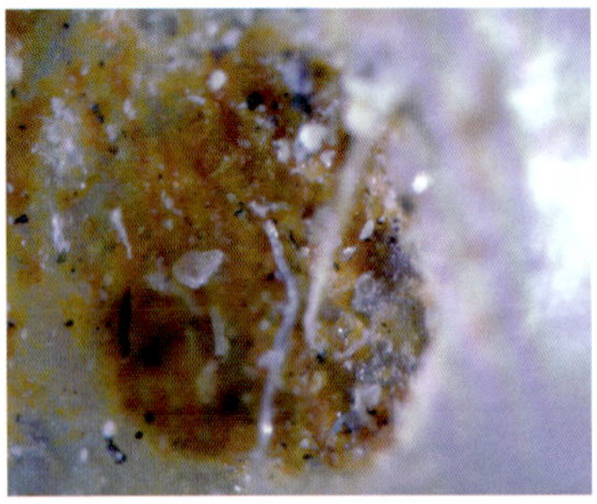
Sample Image 17

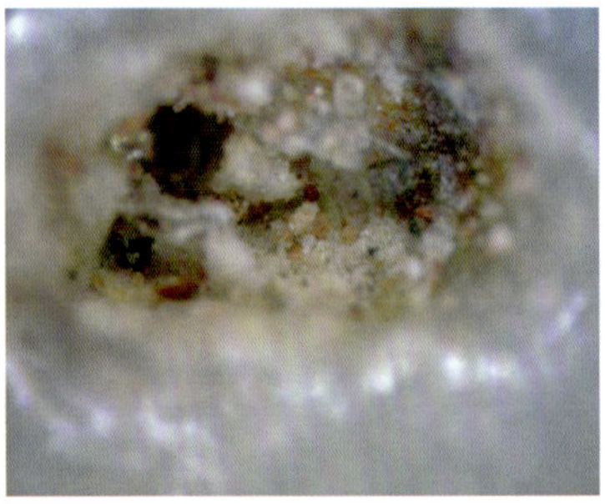
LKSCSTAM Image 17

◆ Two-Dimensional Characteristics

1) Within a single unit image, multiple trace types can be observed: Pits, C and O striae, glaze cracks, scratches, and so forth (see Sample Image 15).

2) The edges and interior of the bristle pits present with multiple filaments and weathering deposits (see Sample Images 16 and 17).

3) The sample piece generally presents with trace multiplicity.

Three-Dimensional Sample Image	Three-Dimensional LKSCSTAM Image

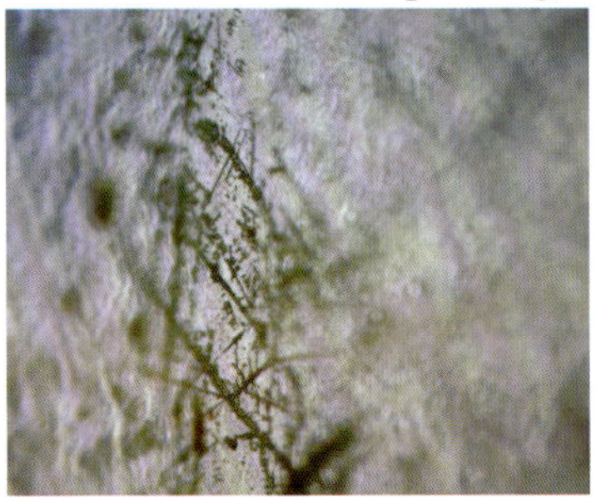
Sample Image 18

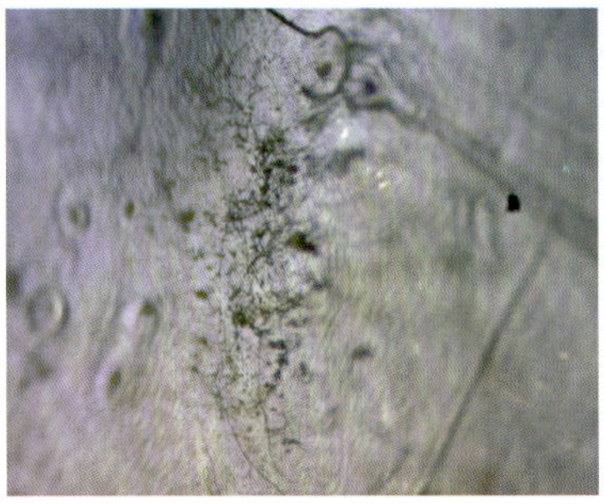
LKSCSTAM Image 18

◆ Three-Dimensional Characteristics

See Sample Image 18.

1) Within one unit image, multiple trace types can be observed. For example, pit mottles and scratches, all with different appearances.

2) The sample piece generally presents with trace multiplicity.

◆ Trace Nature Proofs

1) The characteristics of the above mentioned traces on the test piece and those of the LKSC Standard Trace Atlas Model are matching in nature.

2) Within one unit image, the presence of trace multiplicity and weathering characteristics within bristle pit interiors are consistent with the Ceramic Trace Law of Multiplicity.

G. Ceramic Trace Law of Chromatic Aberration

The Ceramic Trace Law of Chromatic Aberration states: Within a single trace type, distributed across the glaze surface and within the glaze level, both innate and acquired, the phenomenon of chromatic aberration (differences in color) can be present.

Two-Dimensional Sample Images | Two-Dimensional LKSCSTAM Images

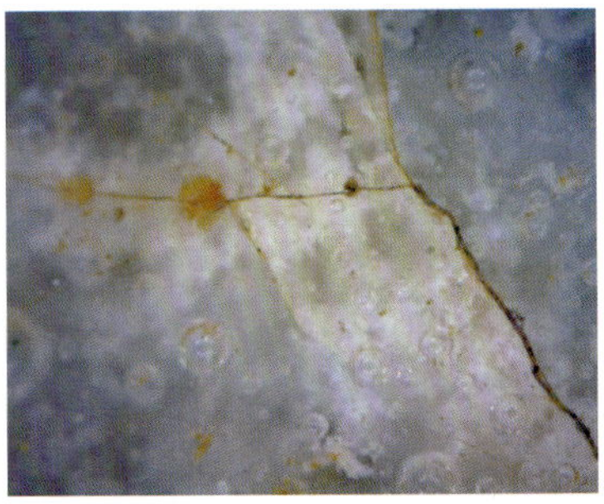

Sample Image 19

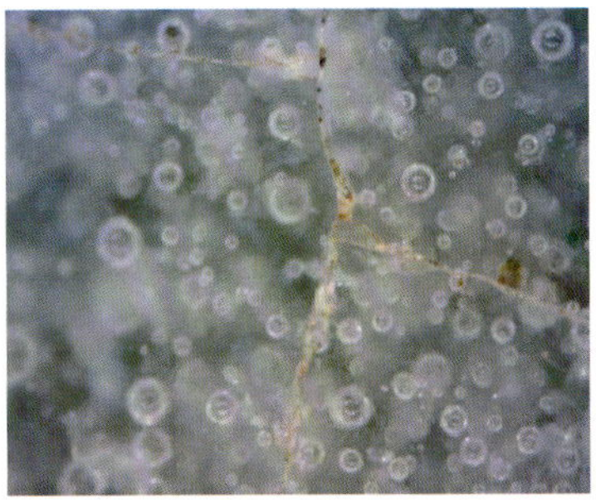

LKSCSTAM Image 19

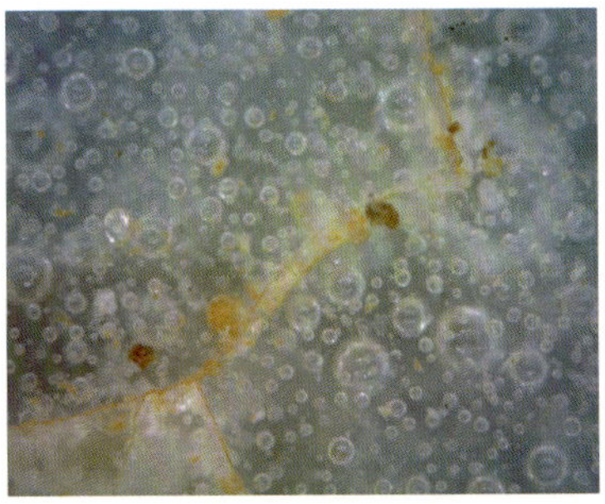

Sample Image 20

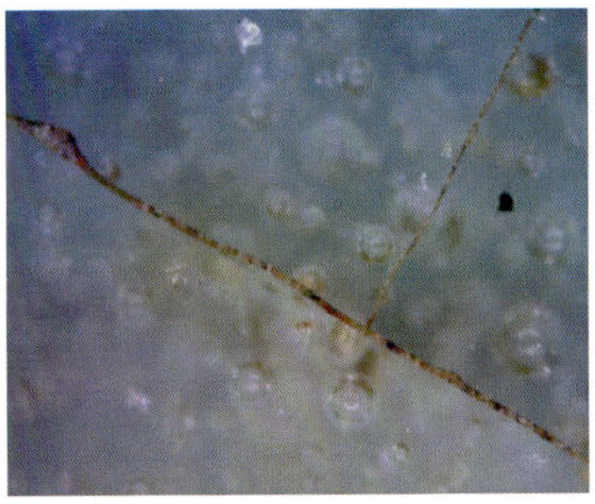

LKSCSTAM Image 20

Two-Dimensional Sample Images	Two-Dimensional LKSCSTAM Images

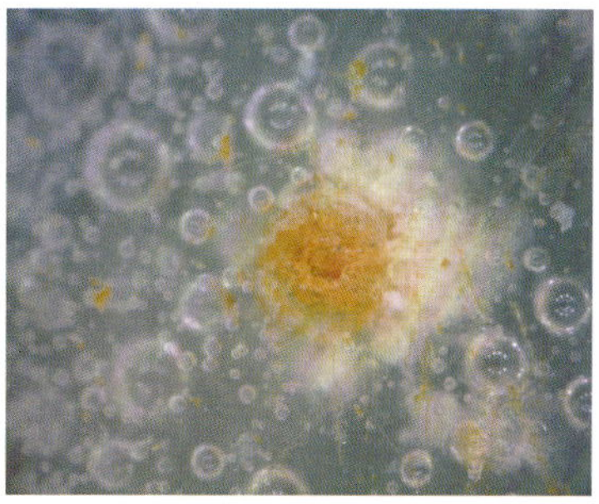
Sample Image 21

LKSCSTAM Image 21

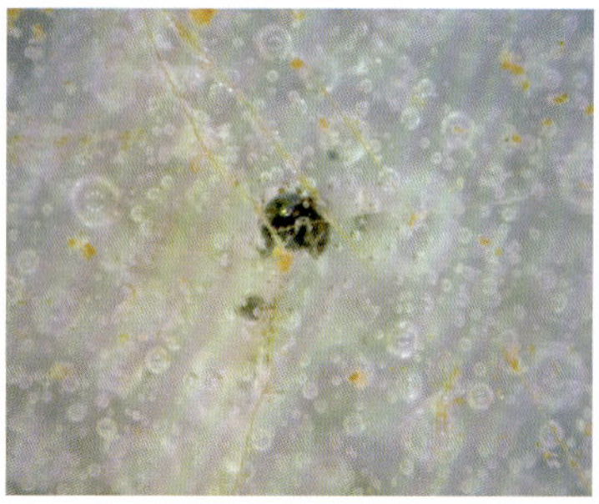
Sample Image 22

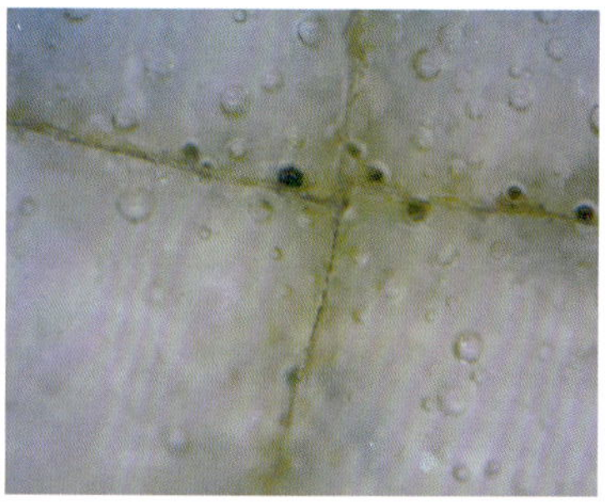
LKSCSTAM Image 22

◆ Two-Dimensional Characteristics

1) Within one unit image, color variation presents within a single trace or between different traces (see Sample Images 19 and 20).
2) On the sample piece, color disparity presents within a single trace (see Sample Image 21 and 22).

◆ Trace Nature Proofs

1) The characteristics of the above mentioned traces on the test piece and those of the LKSC Standard Trace Atlas Model are matching in nature.
2) Within one unit image, the color disparity within a single trace or between traces is consistent with the Ceramic Trace Law of Chromatic Aberration.

H. Ceramic Trace Law of Gradation

The Ceramic Trace Law of Gradation (Layering) states: The weathering severity, whether inter or intra-trace category has variation; a phenomenon resulting due to trace positioning throughout the glaze level (across the glaze surface or within the glaze level).

Two-Dimensional Sample Image | Two-Dimensional LKSCSTAM Image

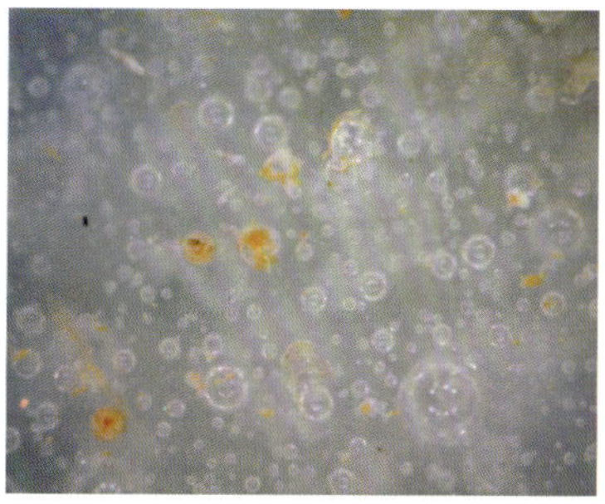

Sample Image 23

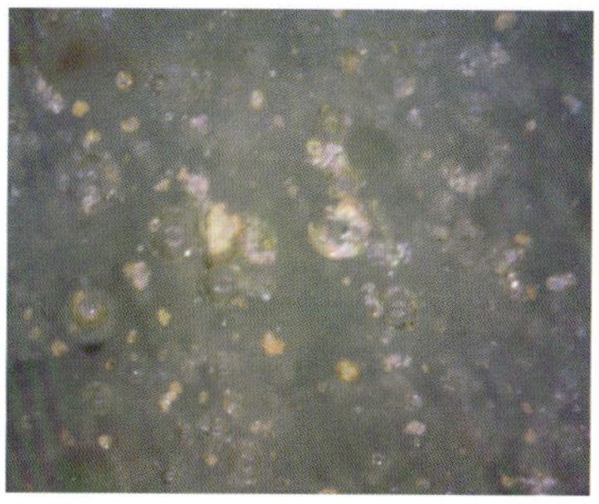

LKSCSTAM Image 23

◆ Two-Dimensional Characteristics

See Sample Image 23.

There is white foggy dispersion extending out from the borders of the C and O shaped striae.

Three-Dimensional Sample Image | Three-Dimensional LKSCSTAM Image

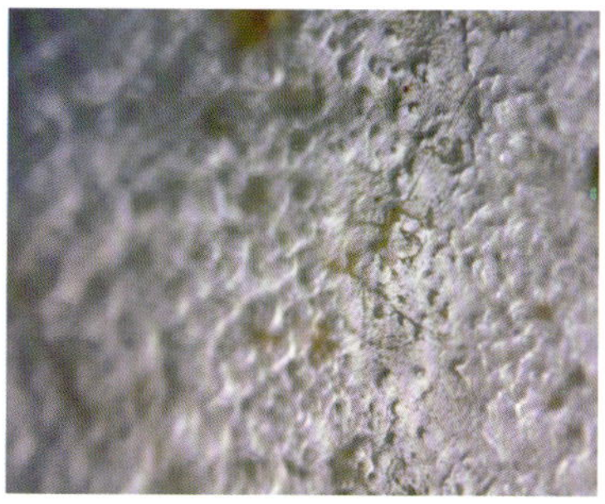

Sample Image 24

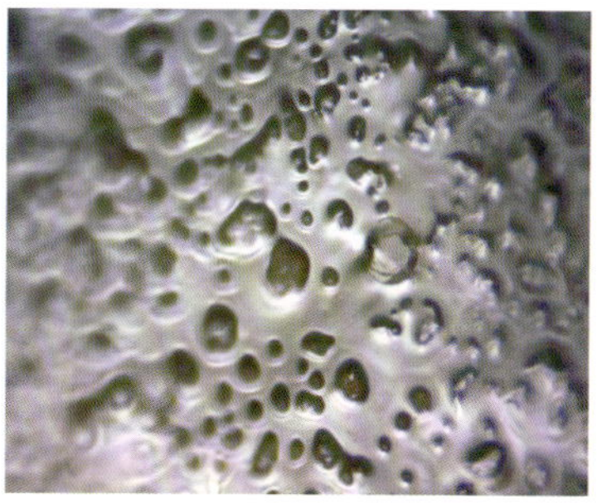

LKSCSTAM Image 24

◆ Three-Dimensional Characteristics

See Sample Images 23 and 24 (where 23 is the two-dimensional and 24 is the three-dimensional view of the same location). The C shaped striation in the three-dimensional image presents as a small fine line.

◆ Trace Nature Proofs

1) The characteristics of the above mentioned C and O striae on the test piece and those of the LKSC Standard Trace Atlas Model are matching in nature.

2) White foggy dispersions extend out from the borders of the C and O shaped striae, and the C shaped striation presents three-dimensionally as a small fine line. This goes to show that weathering has occurred from the surface downward into the glaze level; this is in accordance with the Ceramics Trace Law of Gradation.

I. Ceramic Trace Location Rationality

Ceramic Trace Location Rationality focuses on whether or not the locations where ceramic traces appear fit the principles and laws of weathered ceramic traces.

Two-Dimensional Sample Image   Two-Dimensional LKSCSTAM Image

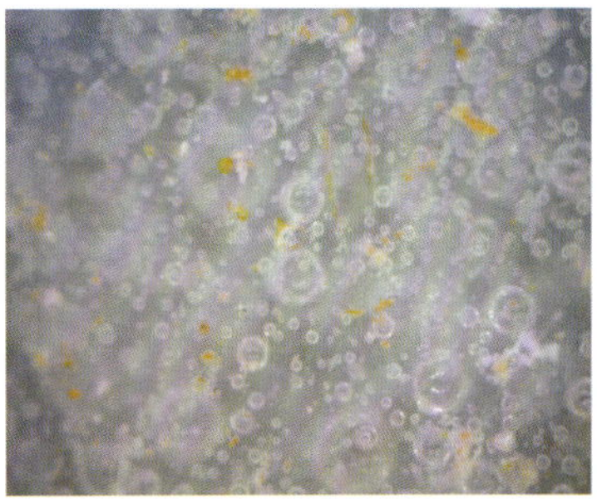

Sample Image 25

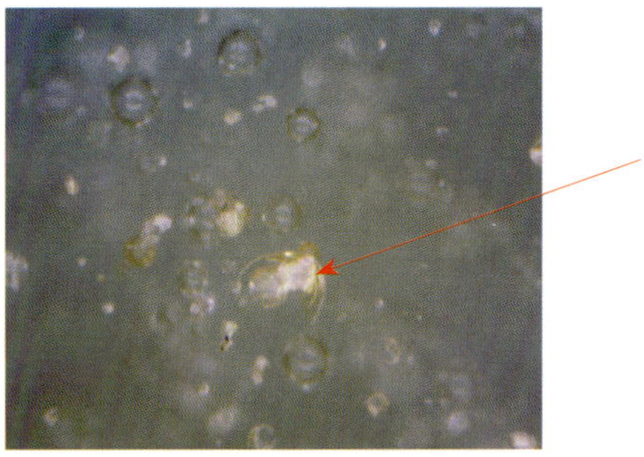

LKSCSTAM Image 25

◆ Two-Dimensional and Three-Dimensional Characteristics

See Sample Images 25 and 26 (where 25 is the two-dimensional and 26 is the three-dimensional view of the same location).

The C shaped striation, as indicated by the arrow, is clearly depicted in the three-dimensional image at an area of glaze level protrusion.

Three-Dimensional Sample Images   Three-Dimensional LKSCSTAM Images

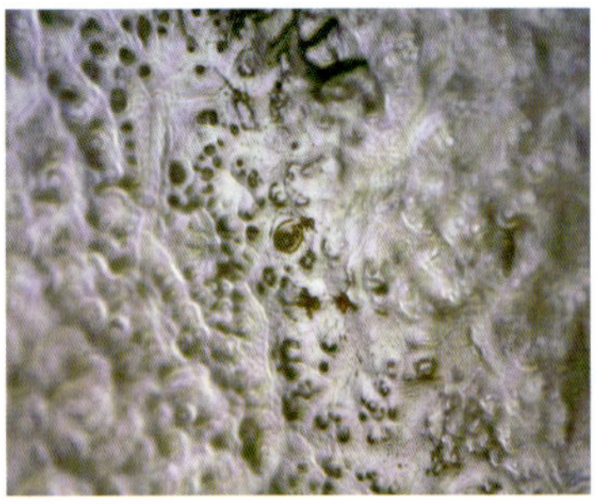

Sample Image 26

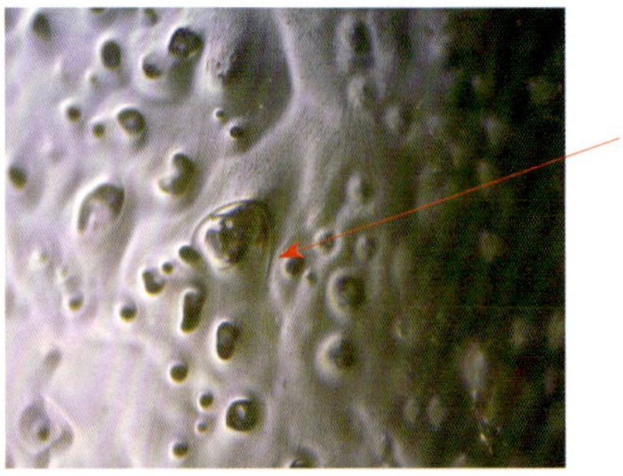

LKSCSTAM Image 26

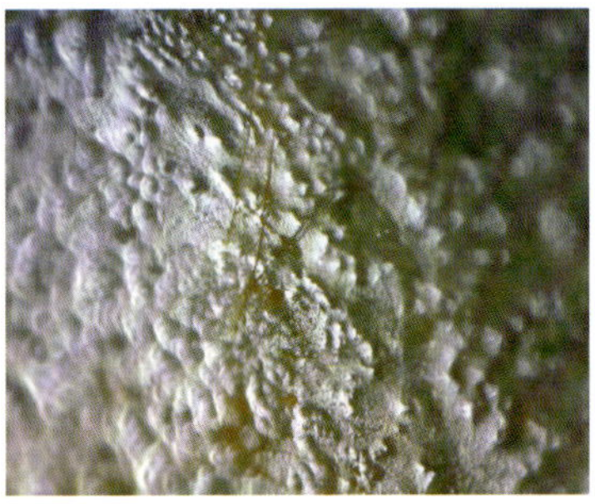

Sample Image 27

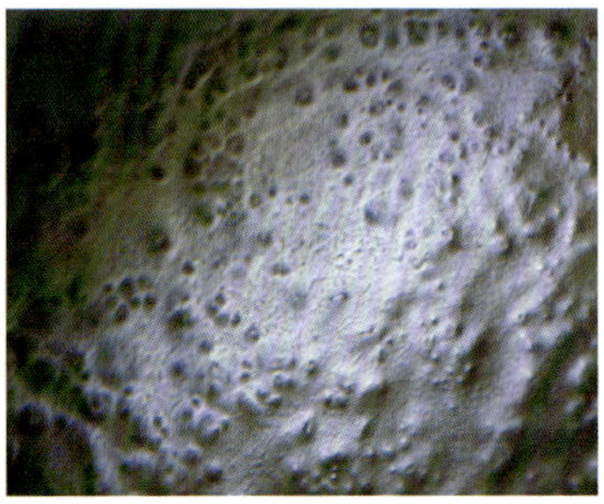

LKSCSTAM Image 27

◆ Three-Dimensional Characteristics

See Sample Image 27

All protrusions across the glaze surface present with relatively high weathering at the base, dark coloration, and relatively low weathering on the apex, with light coloring.

◆ Trace Nature Proofs

1) The characteristics of the above mentioned traces on the test piece and those of the LKSC Standard Trace Atlas Model are matching in nature.
2) The C and O striae as well as C and O type pit mottles on the sample piece all reflect the Ceramic Trace Location Rationality Principle.

7. Trace Appearance Comparison Comprehensive Results

◆ By using microscopic observation, it has been found that the tested piece has ten traces: radiating mottles, needlepoint mottles, pit mottles, flowing striae, CO striae, glaze cracks, scratches, color change bubbles, textured bubbles, and bristle pits; of which eight are acquired traces (including needlepoint mottles, pit mottles, CO striae, scratches, glaze cracks with trace multiplicity, color change bubbles, textured bubbles, and bristle pits with trace multiplicity).
◆ After comparison with the LKSC Standard Trace Atlas Model it has been found that the piece's primary traces display material and firing technique characteristics consistent with LKSC samples. This is in accordance with Quantitative Change and Passage of Time Principles, and embodies the Ceramic Trace Laws. Regardless of two or three-dimension, images possess a matching nature to the LKSC Standard Trace Atlas Model, and have typical characteristics of LKSC. Aside from this, the acquired trace quantity displays trace change multiplicity. Additionally, the trace locations are consistent with those of the LKSC Standard Trace Atlas Model, and as such the locations of traces have rationality and traces occur with congruency. Therefore, from a trace appearance characteristics and trace nature principles and laws perspective, the tested piece and the LKSC Standard Trace Atlas Model are a close match in nature.

8. Trace Valuation and Evidence Collection Result

The test sample shows trace consistency with the LKSCSTAM. At the same time, the traces on the test image are consistent with and reflect the Ceramic Trace Principles and Laws including: Quantitative Change, Passage of Time, Change Congruency, Distinction, Variegation, and Chromatic Aberration.

As such, the microscopically observable traces on the test piece are sufficient to act as material evidence to substantiate its date.

附录2：2013年度广东大埔余里窑址发掘概况

一、地理位置

大埔县位于广东省东北部、韩江中上游，东北紧靠福建省平和县、永定县，东南连接潮州饶平县，西依梅县，南邻丰顺县。该县有磷、水晶石、长石、石英石、瓷土、紫砂陶土等非金属矿。其中瓷土储量4.2亿吨，紫砂陶土储量超1亿吨，有700多年制作陶瓷的历史，号称“中国青花瓷之乡”。

三河镇位于该县中部偏西，距县府14公里，古为粤、闽交通要津，是该县境内的汀江、梅江、梅潭河三水汇合成韩江的起点，故当地客家居民和其他地方的客家人通常都称之为三河坝。余里窑址地处韩江东侧，位于三河镇南部余里村下村小盆地中东侧的一个称山尾睡的小山坳，中心地理坐标为N24° 22.827′、E116° 35.679′，海拔178米。山坳内外曾有过农田耕作，但已荒芜多年，现繁林密布杂草丛生。山尾睡三面环山，西面正对余里村下村，其间一条南北向村道横穿而过，连通村里村外，往西直达韩江东岸的碗窑口。碗窑口有古码头，早期余里窑生产瓷器皆由里往外挑往此处再用船运达四方。

二、发掘经过

2013年10月底，经国家文物局批准，广东省文物考古研究所联合中国客家博物馆、大埔县文化广电新闻出版局、大埔县博物馆等单位对其进行了考古发掘。本次发掘领队为刘成基研究员，主要工作人员还有广东省文物考古研究所肖达顺，中国客家博物馆陈靖云，大埔县文广新局彭日韵，大埔县博物馆刘洪伟、罗皎明、罗志坚，三河镇文化站陈尚国等。2014年1月9日，把现场出土遗物转移到大埔县博物馆保管，等待下一步室内整理工作。至此，田野发掘工作告一段落。

此次工作共布5米×5米探方九个，探沟一条，发掘总面积约350平方米。发现并揭露了龙窑四座、房址两间、土灶一座、辘轳坑四个、灰坑九个、灰沟两条，同时出土大批窑具和瓷器标本。现将该窑址发掘清理的主要情况介绍如下：

三、文化堆积

发掘前该窑址地表虽已被浓密的杂草、灌木丛等覆盖，仍可见散落满地的陶瓷片、匣钵残件等，还有十余个大小不等的盗洞盗坑。我们在文化层堆积较厚，且相对平坦的，应是早期平整过的台地上先布置四个探方，然后根据文化层堆积分布及所现的遗迹情况再向东扩了三个，向北另一块位置较高的小平地上也布了两个。

我们根据地层包含物、性质和成因等，把整个工地文化层分成七大层，再根据各大层形成时间和包含物不同而继续细分。现将堆积最厚、文化层最多的TN1E1、TN1E2、TN1E3三个探方的北壁以及TN1E1西壁地层情况介绍如下：

第①层：为现代耕土层或回填堆积。前者厚15—22厘米，主要分布在平整过的台地上，均匀分布。为灰色粉沙土，土质疏松，沙性大，含大量草根、藤等植物根系。基本不见瓷片等文化遗物。后者因盗掘活动破坏形成的回填堆积，土色很驳杂，土质疏松，非常杂乱，含较多瓷片、匣钵、垫饼等窑渣堆积。将该坑可复原的、具有特色的瓷片均收集。瓷片均为青瓷，釉色以青釉为主，少量天青釉、粉青釉、青灰釉、青黄釉等。器型有碗、碟、灯盏、盘、折腰碟、炉、器盖、高足杯等，碗、碟内底多印有“安”“然”“福”等。

第②层：为晚期垫土层，主要分布在台地上。内有数个小层，均十分平整、分布均匀，且包含物少，基本不见瓷片等文化遗物。可细分为以下几层：

②A层：深15—22厘米，厚10—15厘米，在台地上均匀分布。为灰黄土，土质板结致密，含沙量少，很纯净，无包含物。

②B层：深25—40厘米，厚30—40厘米，在台地上均匀分布。为灰白土，土质板结硬实，含沙量

少，很纯净，无包含物。

②C层：深65—75厘米，厚5—12厘米，在台地上均匀分布。为黄色黏土层，土质板结致密，含沙量少，很纯净，无包含物。

②D层：深75—77厘米，厚5—7厘米，在台地上均匀分布。为青灰色沙土层，土质疏松，含沙量大，纯净，无包含物。

②E层：深75—85厘米，厚5—7厘米，在台地上均匀分布。为黄色沙土层，含沙量大，土质疏松，底部有褐色铁锈斑，部分质地坚硬，很纯净。基本无包含物，但该层下陆续出土大量瓷片、匣钵残片等。

本次发掘发现的大部分遗迹都是②E层下开口，其中有房址F1、F2，灰坑H6、H7、H8、H9，灰沟G1，土灶Z1，辘轳坑L1、L2、L3、L4，柱洞ZD5等等。

此外，TN1E1、TN2E2两探方有一大盗坑，把东西两边③A层上的文化层隔断，在该盗坑的西侧有几个文化层仅见于TN1E1西部，又与上述②层有区别，因此用小写后缀加以区别，编号如下：

②a层：深60—100厘米，厚5—10厘米，仅探方西北侧有分布，且往西壁延伸，余皆被现代坑打破。为红砂土，疏松，沙性大，夹有烧土粒等。出土瓷片很少很碎，未收集。

②b层：深65—105厘米，厚10—30厘米，仅探方西北侧有分布，且往西壁延伸，余皆被现代坑打破。为黑砂土，致密，含沙量大，夹有红砖、烧土粒、匣钵残片、瓷片。出土瓷片较少较碎，未收集。

②c层：深75—120厘米，厚10—30厘米，仅探方西北侧有分布，且往西壁延伸，余皆被现代坑打破。为黄土，致密，黏性大，含吉奥多匣钵碎片、瓷片、碎砖。出土瓷片较碎，未收集。

②d层：深120—145厘米，厚0—20厘米，仅探方西北侧有分布，且往西壁延伸，余皆被现代坑打破。为黄土，致密，黏性大，夹有大量的匣钵、红砖等。出土的瓷片有碗、碟等。碟多内底印“福”字。

第③层：为窑渣堆积，可细分为数层，堆积状况每小层略有不同，各层具体情况如下：

③A层：深90—125厘米，厚10—65厘米，主要分布在TN1E1和TN1E2，向南还有延伸。窑渣堆积层，有大量匣钵、瓷片，含一定泥土，呈灰色，黏性大，夹有瓦片、碳粒、碎砖。出土遗物主要为瓷片、匣钵残片、垫饼等，其中生烧器占一定比例。瓷片有盘、碟、碗、杯等，纹饰以素面的为主，少量有“福”“宁”“玉”和菊瓣纹等纹饰。较完整的瓷器比较多。

③B层：深155—175厘米，厚10—80厘米，主要分布在TN1E1东南和TN1E2西部，堆积自西北向东南倾斜，且西北薄，东南厚。为纯粹的窑渣堆积层，疏松，流动性大。出土主要为瓷片、匣钵残片等，瓷器主要有碗、小碗、盘、碟、折腰碟等，且完整盘比较多。纹饰以素面为主，少量有刻划纹。

③C层：深175—240厘米，厚35—40厘米，主要分布在TN1E1东南和TN1E2西部，堆积自西北向东南倾斜，厚薄均匀。为红砂土层，含较多红砖碎块，沙性大，西侧有散落的窑砖。不见瓷片等遗物出土。

③D层：深175—280厘米，厚20—205厘米，主要分布在TN1E1东南和TN1E2西部，堆积自西北向东南倾斜。为较纯粹的窑渣堆积层，疏松，流动性大。出土主要为瓷片、匣钵残片等，瓷器主要有碗、盘，少量碟、杯、小碗等，且完整盘比较多。纹饰以素面为主，少量有刻划纹。该层出土的瓷片烧制火候高、质量好。

③E层：深370—372厘米，厚10—50厘米，主要分布在TN1E1东南和TN1E2西部，堆积自西北向东南倾斜，厚薄均匀。为红砂土层，含较多红砖碎块，沙性大。不见瓷片等遗物出土。

③F层：深345—420厘米，厚30—55厘米，主要分布在TN1E1东南和TN1E2西部，堆积自西北向东南倾斜，厚薄较均匀。为较纯粹的窑渣堆积层，疏松，流动性大。出土主要为瓷片、匣钵残片等，瓷器主要有碗、盘、碟，少量杯、小碗、高足杯等。出土较多带“宁”字的碟，其次是花卉纹碟。

第④层：深120—420厘米，厚5—10厘米，仅TN1E1东北部有分布，为红色砂土夹层，较为疏松，堆积自西北向东南倾斜，厚薄较均匀。

第⑤层：仅见于TN1E1北部，其中第④层与第⑥层之间又可见东西两侧不同的堆积，但未见相互叠压打破，因此区分为⑤A和⑤B两个文化层。

⑤A层：深120—175厘米，厚10—25厘米，仅见于TN1E1西北部，为黄褐色砂土，砂粒较大，土质坚硬，较为纯净，包含物较少。堆积自北向南倾斜，厚薄较均匀。

⑤B层：深135—175厘米，

厚5—10厘米，仅见于TN1E1东北部，为红褐色砂土，土质坚硬较细腻，砂粒较细，较为纯净，包含物较少。堆积自北向南倾斜，厚薄较均匀。

第⑥层：深125—455厘米，厚度不明，主要分布在TN1E1全方和TN1E2西部，堆积自西北向东南倾斜，呈坡状。为黑色黏土层，较为纯净，黏性大，基本不见其他包含物。因各层窑渣堆积疏松无法切壁，故此层可清理空间太小而无法继续往下清理。

第⑦层：深135—？厘米，厚度不明，只在TN1E1西北部有暴露，堆积自西北向东南倾斜。为纯净的黄土，无包含物。

四、主要遗迹

现已揭露的龙窑都有不同程度破坏。其中Y3是一座阶梯龙窑，保存相对较好，除窑口、窑顶部分被破坏严重外，左右两侧窑壁及各窑室隔墙、火道、窑门、窑床、窑尾烟道等结构都较为清楚。Y1仅存三个窑室，Y2和Y4则仅存一个窑室。

Y3位于山尾睡西侧小山坡上，地理坐标为N24°22.842′、E116°35.669′，海拔176米。残长14.86米，方向211度，整体坡度19度。窑壁厚约0.3—0.4米，外侧为红烧土层，内侧多砌一层0.2米厚的砖墙，残存的砖墙内壁一般都抹泥硬面，北部第五窑室的硬面还有青绿色的窑汗面。Y3除前部窑口外，共五个窑室，第五窑室北部还有一条烟道。

窑口破坏严重，残长1.27米，宽2—2.55米，由北至南渐收小。窑口底面为灰黄色的烧结层，表面较为平滑；窑口与第一窑室间由于地形倾斜导致烧结层间有断裂。

第一窑室南北长2米，宽2.95米，坡度25度；窑室两侧砖墙还残存少量壁砖，内壁局部还保存部分硬面；东壁南端开有窑门，宽约0.4米，向西有一条火道，底部较平且有一层黑灰，宽也是0.4米左右；窑床底部为沙质填土，上面还落满残存的匣钵，个别还保存较为完好；窑门外东侧南北两端各有一个柱洞，开口直径0.28—0.32米，深0.26—0.28米；柱洞以东为约1.6米宽的活动面，一直到东面断崖，被山下冲沟破坏前应是向东部作坊区延伸。与第二窑室间有一道隔墙，中部保存较好，残高0.72米，宽约0.3米，略向南面山下倾倒，底部有烟道口15个。

第二窑室南北长2.3米，宽3.38米，坡度27度；窑室两侧砖墙还残存少量壁砖，西壁局部还保存硬面较为大片；东壁南端开有窑门，宽约0.54米，向西有一条火道，底部较平且有一层黑灰，宽0.34—0.62米；窑床底部为沙质填土，上面还落满残存的匣钵，个别还保存较为完好；窑门外东侧南北两端各有一个柱洞，开口直径0.26—0.28米，深0.34—0.46米；柱洞以东为成片的活动面，一直到东面断崖，被山下冲沟破坏前也应是向东部作坊区延伸。与第三窑室间有一道隔墙，保存较差，仅存底部，残高0.48米，宽约0.34米，从底部残存痕迹看有烟道口19个。

第三窑室南北长2.23米，宽3.6米，坡度28度；窑室两侧砖墙还残存少量壁砖，西壁局部还保存硬面较为大片；东壁南端开有窑门，宽约0.61米，向西有一条火道，底部较平且有一层黑灰，宽0.3—0.61米；火道北面有一条土坎，宽0.2—0.36米，最厚处约0.22米，西侧还有一小堆匣坡残堆积；窑床底部仅存沙质填土层，窑床上的匣坡大多无存。考虑到保护与展示各方面因素，第三窑室窑门东侧外填土未清理。与第四窑室间的隔墙已无存，仅存一道0.4—0.6宽的黄色硬土面。

第四窑室南北长约2.36米，坡度28度；两侧窑壁大部分无存，东北部被Y4叠压，东西宽残存约2.5米；南部被破坏严重，北部窑床残存南北最长约1.67米；窑床底部仅存沙质填土层，窑床上的匣坡大多无存。与第五窑室间有一道隔墙，东部被Y4打破，保存较差，仅存底部，残高0.31米，宽约0.29米，东西残长1.87米，从底部残存痕迹看残存烟道口11个。

第五窑室南北长约2.14米，坡度20度；西侧窑壁还保存较好，内壁还有窑汗硬面，东侧窑壁则无存，东南部被Y4叠压，东北角则为断崖，东西宽不明；除被Y4叠压外的窑床底部尚存部分沙质填土层，窑床上的匣坡大多无存；窑床北部部分还露出黄色细沙层。北部与烟道有一墙之隔。烟道南北宽约0.31米，东西残长0.24米，北壁多为残砖堆砌，底部为整砖平铺，砖上为红褐色细沙。

Y1位于山尾睡东侧小山坡上，地理坐标为N24°22.811′、E116°35.693′，海拔212米。残长6.26米，方向240度，整体坡度19.5度。窑壁厚约0.4—0.45米，外侧为红烧土层，内侧多砌一层0.2米厚的砖墙，残存的砖墙内壁一般都有抹泥硬面。Y1南北两端都被破坏，残存共三个窑室。最南端为一道倾斜变形的隔墙。南面第一窑室南北长约2.2米，东西宽2.4米；窑床上填土基本无存，只剩下黄色硬层，北部还残存若干匣钵；东壁南端开有窑门，宽约0.4米，向西隐约能辨认土质发黑的火道，向东还有活动面。第二窑室与第一窑室间有一道隔墙，仅存底部一层铺砖，其余不详。第二窑室南北长约2.1米，东西宽2.86米；窑床上填土基本无存，只剩下黄色硬层；东壁南端开有窑门，宽约0.41米，向西隐约能辨认土质发黑的火道，向东还有活动面。第三窑室与第二窑室间也有一道隔墙，仅存底部一层铺砖，其余不详。第三窑室北部大部已被破坏，南北残长约0.8米，东西宽2.86米；窑床上填土基本无存，只剩下黄色硬层，东部还残存若干匣钵；东壁开有窑门，宽约0.61米；考虑未来保护与展示等因素，东部未进一步清理。

Y2位于山尾睡东北面的山坡上，　地理坐标为N24° 22.853′、E116° 35.692′，海拔220米。残长3米，方向325度。仅存一个窑室，后壁依山体修成，坡度26度。两侧窑壁厚约0.24—0.46米，外侧为红烧土层，内侧多砌一层0.2米厚的砖墙，残存的砖墙内壁一般都有抹泥硬面。窑床底部为灰褐色硬土层，后壁下还有一个小平台，宽约0.4米，疑是烟道。后壁依山体抹平烧成，表层也成硬面，外侧则为厚约0.24米的红色烧土。Y2北侧还发现有一小片活动面，山体边上还保存有少量早期堆放的匣钵残件。

Y4位于山尾睡西侧小山坡上，断崖边上，打破Y3后面两个窑室。南北残长3米，方向191度。仅存一个窑室，坡度23度。仅存西侧窑壁，厚约0.4米，外侧为红烧土层，内侧多砌一层0.2米厚的砖墙，残存的砖墙内壁一般都有抹泥硬面。窑床底部为沙质填土，局部还保存若干匣钵。东部为断崖，被破坏严重，东西残宽约2米。

该遗址发现的房址砖墙遗迹应是当时窑业作坊隔墙。F1和F2仅一墙之隔，两者方向大致为45度，砖墙多为残砖斜砌，残存多为一层或两层，多则不过三层。其中F1东北至西南向长5米，西北至东南向宽4.5米。F2东北至南北向长3.5米，已露出的西北至东南向宽度达4.5米。其中F1西墙与F2西墙间有1米的过道。此外F1北面还有一条向北露出长3.7米，宽1.1米的残砖铺砌的过道。

房内还有与制瓷有关的辘轳坑等迹象。房外发现一座土灶，灶边紧挨两灰坑和两灰沟。其中一个灰坑底部有红色烧面，一条灰沟的填土是草木灰。灶边几个迹象应与灶有关。

五、遗物概况

该窑址出土大量青釉瓷器残件，主要器型有碗、盘、杯、碟、瓶、炉、砚台、盖罐、灯盏、烛台等十余种日常用瓷，以及印模和窑具匣钵、窑垫等生产工具。我们还采集大量有刻画文字或符号的匣钵，如“大”“二”等式样。各类器型素面为主，但也有一些菊瓣纹等花纹。碗和碟上则多印有汉字，如“福”“禄”“寿”“安”“德”“宁”“玉”“用”等吉语。另外，还发现一件刻有“庚子年记□”的纪年陶器座。

余里山尾睡远景

碗窑口古码头远眺

发掘工地全景

Y1全景

Y2全景

Y3和Y4全景

F1和F2全景

F1隔墙内外的柱洞和辘轳坑等

参考文献
References

[1] 朱伯谦，王士伦．浙江省龙泉青瓷窑址调查发掘的主要收获[J].文物，1963(1)：27-40.

[2] 朱伯谦.龙泉青瓷简史[C]．龙泉青瓷研究．北京：文物出版社，1989：1-37.

[3] 同[2].

[4] 任世龙.论龙泉窑的空框架和文化结构[C]．龙泉窑研究．北京：故宫出版社，2011：7-15.

[5] 任世龙，汤世婴．龙泉窑瓷鉴定与鉴赏[M]．南昌：江西美术出版社，2004.

[6] 李刚，龙泉窑纵笔[J]．东方博物，2004(1)：29-40.

[7] 庄绰.鸡肋编:卷上[M]．北京：中华书局，1983.

[8] 同[1].

[9] 同[1].

[10] 同[1].

[11] 王帆.五代至北宋早期的龙泉窑瓷器及鉴定[J]．艺术市场，2007(7)：86-87.

[12] 同[1].

[13] 同[1].

[14] 蔡小辉．试论龙泉的衰落[J]．东方博物，2014(7)：66-74.

[15] 同[6].

[16] 李宝平．浙江龙泉宋元时期瓷器手工业遗存初步研究[J].东方博物，2002(7).

[17] 蔡和璧．由文献资料看龙泉窑[C]．和泉市文保纪念美术馆、文保几年文化财团东洋美术研究所纪要．京都：写真印刷株式会社，1998.

[18] 同[2].

[19] 申献友．读龙泉窑笔录[C]．龙泉窑研究．北京：故宫出版社，2011：179-190.

[20] 周丽丽.有关龙泉窑两个问题的再认识[C]．龙泉窑研究．北京：故宫出版社，2011：17-31.

[21] 顾文荐.负暄杂录[M]．上海：上海古籍出版社，2013.

[22] 同[20].

[23] 邓白．略谈古代龙泉青瓷的艺术成就[C]．龙泉青瓷研究．北京：文物出版社，1989：92-101.

[24] 叶维德，张磊．龙泉窑瓷业历史浅析[J]．美术大观，2013(11)：74.

[25] 同[24].

[26] 同[23].

[27] 同[23].

[28] 同[2].

[29] 沈琼华，孙秋珍．龙泉窑盛衰述略[J]．东方博物，2008(27)：106-110.

[30] 同[29].

[31] 中国硅酸盐学会．中国陶瓷史[M]．北京：文物出版社，1982.

[32] 同[31].

[33] 陈孟龙．略谈龙泉青瓷的装饰方法[J]．江西文物，1991(4)：73-75.

[34] 同[31].

[35] 朱伯谦．龙泉窑青瓷[M]．台北：台湾艺术家出版社，1998.

[36] 徐军．从枫洞岩窑址的发掘试析元明龙泉青瓷分期和特征[C]．龙泉大窑枫洞岩窑址出土瓷器．北京：文物出版社，2009：11-18.

[37] 同[14].

[38] 叶文程．宋元时期龙泉青瓷的外销及其有关问题的探讨[C]．叶文程．中国古外销瓷研究论文集．北京：紫禁城出版社，1988：46-52.

[39] 黄挺．海禁政策对明代潮州社会的影响[J]．海交史研究，1996(1)：40-51.

[40] 同[14].

[41] 青柳洋治．东南亚发掘的中国外销瓷器[J]．南方文物，2000(2)：104-107.

[42] 同[14].

[43] 周勇，周强．元青花迹型研究与物证鉴定[M]．广州：南方日报出版社，2013.

[44] 王光尧．明代宫廷陶瓷史[M]．北京：紫禁城出版社，

2010.
[45] 同[14].
[46] 同[14].
[47] 项坤鹏. 浅析东南亚地区出土（水）的龙泉青瓷:遗址概况、分期及相关问题分析[J]. 东南文化, 2012(2): 85-95.
[48] 同[14].
[49] 徐兢.宣和奉使高丽图经:卷三十二:器皿[M].北京: 商务印书馆，1937.
[50] 叶文程, 罗立华. 中国古外销陶瓷的年代[J]. 江西文物, 1991(4): 109-113.
[51] 庄良有. 浅谈龙泉窑对东南亚青瓷的影响[J].东方博物,1999(3).
[52] 同[51].
[53] 马文宽, 孟凡人. 中国古瓷在非洲的发现[M]. 北京: 紫禁城出版社, 1987.
[54] 同[47].
[55] 同[14].
[56] 项坤鹏. 龙泉窑研究综述[J]. 东方博物，2008(26): 38-46.
[57] 明书:卷八三[M].
[58] 浙江通志:卷八:地理志:处州[M]. 上海: 上海古籍出版社，1991.
[59] 清谷应泰.影印文渊阁四库全书:史部:纪事本末类:明史纪事本末:卷三一[M].北京: 北京出版社，2003.
[60] 明实录. 英宗实录[M].
[61] 高濂. 遵生八笺:卷十四:燕闲清赏笺:论诸品窑器[M]. 太原: 山西科学技术出版社，2014.
[62] 龙泉县志:卷三:赋役志:物产[M]. 上海: 汉语大词典出版社，1994.
[63] 陈雨前, 朱浙安. 宋代景德镇青白瓷“尚玉” 审美意蕴研究[J]. 中国陶瓷, 2006(12)：58-62.
[64] 同[23].
[65] 同[23].
[66] 龙泉县志:卷十二[M]. 上海: 汉语大词典出版社，1994..
[67] 同[24].
[68] 同[23].
[69] 同[24].
[70] 同[7].
[71] 项坤鹏. 龙泉青瓷在中国古代宫廷中使用的相关问题[J]. 华夏考古, 2013(3): 115-123.
[72] 同[71].
[73] 刘兴, 肖梦龙. 江苏溧阳竹箦北宋李彬夫妇墓[J]. 文物，1980(5): 34-45.
[74] 同[71].
[75] 杭州市文物考古研究所. 南宋太庙遗址[M]. 北京: 文物出版社, 2008.
[76] 同[29].
[77] 靳远风,王家民. 龙泉青瓷的装饰艺术演变研究[J]. 中国校外教育, 2012(21): 155-156.
[78] 同[33].
[79] 同[29].
[80] 施静菲. 蒙元宫廷瓷器使用初探[C]. 美术史研究集刊, 2003(15): 169-194.
[81] 陶宗仪. 南村辍耕录[M]. 北京: 中华书局, 2004.
[82] 宋濂. 元史[M]. 北京: 中华书局, 1976.
[83] 李知宴. 故宫元代皇宫地下出土陶瓷资料初探[J]. 中国历史博物馆馆刊, 1986(00): 73-80.
[84] 同[2].
[85] 王霞. 元代集宁路古城遗址出土瓷器解读[J]. 北方文物, 2008(3): 54-57.
[86] 贾洲杰. 元上都调查报告[J]. 文物, 1977(5): 65-76.
[87] 同[31].
[88] 同[31].
[89] 大明会典:第一百九十四卷[M]. 北京: 国家图书馆出版社，北京图书馆出版社，2009.
[90] 沈岳明.龙泉大窑枫洞岩窑址出土瓷器:枫洞岩窑址发掘的主要收获和初步认识[C]. 北京: 文物出版社, 2009: 1-10.
[91] 明宪宗实录[M]. 学识斋, 1868.
[92] 同[71].
[93] 钟琦. 龙泉窑的下限年代考[J]. 收藏界, 2006(6): 74-76.
[94] 叶佩兰. 清代龙泉窑系青瓷[J]. 故宫博物院院刊, 1982(2).
[95] 周绍达. 龙泉青瓷宋元明时期的对外输出[J]. 中国陶瓷, 1988(6).
[96] 同[31].
[97] 刘晓斌. 宋元龙泉青瓷外销探析[J]. 江西文物, 1991(4): 114-117.
[98] 同[2].
[99] 同[5].
[100] 同[31].

[101] 同[47].
[102] 同[31].
[103] 同[95].
[104] 申浚. 浅谈西亚与南亚地区发现的元明龙泉窑瓷器[J]. 故宫博物院院刊, 2013(6): 68-77.
[105] 同[29].
[106] 同[29].
[107] 同[47].
[108] 同[29].
[109] 吴越滨. 中国龙泉青瓷考论[J]. 装饰, 2004(7): 63.
[110] 同[47].
[111] 同[50].
[112] 同[95].
[113] 同[47].
[114] 叶文程. 试述浙江青瓷的对外输出[J]. 江西文物, 1989(3): 23-33.
[115] 汪梅, 米朝辉. 浙江龙泉青瓷海外流传历史及风格演变研究[J]. 中国建筑装饰装修, 2013(2): 220-223.
[116] 同[115].
[117] 同[47].
[118] 同[47].
[119] 雷国强. 托普卡帕皇宫珍藏龙泉青瓷鉴赏[J]. 文物鉴定与鉴赏, 2011(9): 58-63.
[120] 同[119].
[121] 同[115].
[122] 同[36].
[123] 叶英挺, 华雨农. 发现：大明处州龙泉官窑[M]. 杭州: 西泠印社出版社, 2005.
[124] 徐军. 明代早期龙泉青瓷官器[C]. 中国古陶瓷协会.龙泉窑研究. 北京: 故宫出版社, 2011: 129-137.
[125] 同[123].
[126] 冯先铭. 中国古陶瓷图典[M]. 北京: 文物出版社,1998.
[127] 许之衡. 饮流斋说瓷[M]. 济南: 山东画报出版社, 2010: 13.
[128] 同[126].
[129] 任志录. 玉壶春瓶略论[J]. 故宫学刊, 2009(5): 754-799.
[130] 同[126].
[131] 同[126].
[132] 叶英挺. 元明龙泉窑“牡丹瓶”[J]. 东方收藏, 2014(3): 42-45.
[133] 同[132].
[134] 同[132].
[135] 同[126].
[136] 同[126].
[137] 同[126].
[138] 上海博物馆. 幽蓝神采元代青花瓷器特集[M]. 上海: 上海书画出版社, 2012.
[139] 同[23].
[140] 陈扬.龙泉窑研究:试论龙泉窑的时代风格与变迁[C].北京: 故宫出版社, 2011: 191-204.
[141] 同[36].
[142] 同[36].
[143] 同[36].
[144] 同[36].
[145] 同[36].
[146] 同[36].
[147] 胡小平. 明代龙泉青瓷产品类型和特征[J]. 收藏界, 2009(9): 58-62.
[148] 同[36].
[149] 同[36].
[150] 同[36].
[151] 同[123].
[152] 同[123].
[153] 同[123].
[154] 同[123].
[155] 周觉民. 龙泉青瓷造型与装饰[J]. 景德镇陶瓷, 2002, 12(2): 14-20.
[156] 冯素阁. 龙泉窑瓷器的装饰艺术[J]. 收藏家, 2000(11): 7-11.
[157] 同[36].
[158] 同[126].
[159] 叶宏明, 曹鹤鸣, 程朱海. 浙江古代青瓷工艺发展过程的研究[J]. 硅酸盐, 1980(3): 6-38.
[160] 同[159].
[161] 周仁, 张福康, 郑永圃. 龙泉历代青瓷烧制工艺的科学总结[J]. 考古学报, 1973(1): 131-155.
[162] 李家治. 中国科学技术史: 陶瓷卷[M]. 北京: 科学出版社, 2007.
[163] 同[162].
[164] 同[161].
[165] 吴枫. 广东大埔余里窑工艺初探[J].
[166] 同[165].
[167] 同[165].
[168] 同[165].
[169] 同[165].
[170] 同[165].
[171] 张福康. 中国古陶瓷的科学[M]. 上海：上海人民美术出版社, 2000.
[172] 同[165].
[173] 同[165].
[174] 杨程, 吴龙伟.龙泉青瓷传

统烧制技艺数字保护研究[M]. 杭州: 浙江大学出版社, 2013.
[175] 同[174].
[176] 同[174].
[177] 同[174].
[178] 同[19].
[179] 同[174].
[180] 同[159].
[181] 同[174].
[182] 同[19].
[183] 同[174].
[184] 同[174].
[185] 同[174].
[186] 陈治戈, 蒋孝锋, 鲁虹. 服装设计的计算机方法[M]. 南京: 江苏科学技术出版社, 2005.
[187] 同[126].
[188] 同[174].
[189] 同[174].
[190] 杨寒桥, 马骋. 龙泉窑[M]. 上海: 上海大学出版社, 2012.
[191] 同[190].
[192] 陆容. 菽园杂记:卷十四[M]. 北京: 中华书局, 1985.
[193] 同[190].
[194] 同[190].
[195] 同[126].
[196] 同[190].
[197] 同[2].
[198] 同[126].
[199] 同[2].
[200] 同[174].
[201] 同[161].
[202] 同[36].
[203] 同[36].
[204] 同[36].
[205] 同[190].
[206] 同[190].
[207] 朱伯谦.龙泉青瓷研究:龙泉大窑古瓷窑遗址发掘报告[C].北京: 文物出版社, 1989: 38-67.
[208] 同[126].
[209] 同[126].
[210] 同[126].
[211] 李家驹. 陶瓷工艺学[M]. 北京: 中国工业出版社, 2010.
[212] 同[211].
[213] 同[211].
[214] 同[211].
[215] 熊樱菲, 何文权, 李戈扬, 历代龙泉青瓷釉的初步研究[J]. 文物保护与考古科学, 2004, 16(2): 45-50.
[216] 同[171].
[217] 同[161].
[218] 田英良, 孙诗兵. 新编陶瓷工艺学[M]. 北京: 中国轻工业出版社, 2009.
[219] 李丽霞, 贾茹. 硅酸盐物理化学[M]. 天津: 天津大学出版社, 2010.
[220] 曹志峰, 赵志强. 重火石光学玻璃化学稳定性的研究[J]. 长春光学精密机械学院学报, 1987, 31 (2): 59-65.
[221] 赵彦钊, 殷海荣. 玻璃工艺学[M]. 北京: 化学工业出版社, 2006.
[222] 冯明良. 玻璃表面之组成，结构与特性[J] . 玻璃,1986(2): 39-42.
[223] 王承遇, 陶瑛. 玻璃的表面结构和性质[J]. 硅酸盐通报,1982(1): 24-34.
[224] 同[211].
[225] 同[211].
[226] http://www.flickr.com/photos/nasacommons/7544559478/sizes/l/in/photostream/.
[227] http://www.cnsa.gov.cn/n1081/n7619/n7905/45514.html.
[228] 张金升, 张银燕, 王美婷, 等. 陶瓷材料显微结构与性能[M]. 北京: 化学工业出版社, 2007.
[229] 同[211].
[230] 王承遇, 陶瑛. 硅酸盐玻璃的风化[J]. 硅酸盐学报, 2003, 31(1): 78-85.
[231] 同[221].
[232] 杭州南宋官窑博物馆. 南宋官窑文集[M]. 北京: 文物出版社, 2004.
[233] 同[230].
[234] 同[232].
[235] 戴树桂. 环境化学[M] . 北京: 高等教育出版社, 2006.
[236] 同[235].
[237] 同[235].
[238] 马燕如. 我国水下考古发掘陶瓷器的脱盐保护初探[J]. 博物馆研究, 2007, 97(1): 85-89.
[239] 吴隽. 古陶瓷科技研究与鉴定[M]. 北京: 科学出版社, 2009.
[240] 同[230].
[241] http://coins.thefuntimesguide.com/files/closeup-quarter-with-wear-by-shoothead.jpg.
[242] https://24carat.co.uk /images/1699halfpennyobv400.jpg.

后记
Afterword

《明代龙泉窑系青瓷迹型研究与物证鉴定》历经两年，已付梓。

在广东省文物考古研究所、广州番禺博物馆、广州番禺职业技术学院、广东大埔县博物馆、广东客家博物馆及龙泉市博物馆的领导及专家们直接支持与参与下，该项目的科研工作得以顺利展开。

衷心感谢龙泉市博物馆及广东大埔县博物馆无偿提供此次科研项目所需的陶瓷标本，确保了建构龙泉窑系青瓷迹型标准图谱模型的真实性及公正性。此外还感谢其他无偿提供陶瓷样本的来自国内外的多家博物馆、研究机构及私人收藏。最后，感谢中山大学人类进化与科技考古实验室及深圳职业技术学院在技术方面提供的支持。

作为陶瓷迹型物证鉴定的技术支持，广州东方博物馆研究人员发明的陶瓷迹型“马士宁三维成像法”，已正式取得国家知识产权局颁发的技术发明专利。

本书第二章中关于大埔余里窑址出土器物相关介绍研究摘录自陈靖云（现就职于东莞可园博物馆）未发表文章，有改动。

鉴于此项研究是课题的阶段性成果，尚有不成熟的地方，还望专家及读者批评指正。

特向为本书出版付出辛勤和智慧的南方日报出版社同仁，尤其是责任编辑和美编，表示由衷谢意。

作者

2016年9月7日于广州

After two years of work, this text *Trace Model Research and Material Evidence Authentication: Ming Dynasty Longquan System Celadon Porcelain* is now headed to print.

The support and participation of leaders and experts from Guangdong Provincial Cultural Relic Archeology Department, Guangzhou Panyu Museum, Guangzhou Panyu Polytechnic, Guangdong Dabu Museum, Guangdong Hakka Museum, and Longquan Provincial Museum made this project possible.

A heartfelt thanks is owed to Longquan Provincial Museum and Guangdong Dabu Museum for offering shard samples used during this research, free of charge. This contribution enabled the establishment of a veritable and just Longquan Kiln System Standard Celadon Trace Atlas Model. Additionally, special thanks to all foreign and domestic museums, research institutions, and private collections that offered sample pieces to be used in this project. Lastly, gratitude is owed to the Sun Yat-sen University Human Evolution and Technology Archeology Laboratory and Shenzhen Polytechnic, for their technical support.

As technical support for Trace Model Material Evidence Authentication, “The Bunney Three-Dimensional Imaging Method”, developed by researchers at Guangzhou Oriental Museum, has now formally received a Technological Invention Patent from the National Intellectual and Property Rights Bureau.

The relevant research excerpts introducing the Dabu Yuli Kiln Sites were revised from an unpublished article by Chen Jin Yun (currently at Dongguan Keyuan Museum).

As this research project is in its formative stages, there are still areas not fully developed. We welcome criticism and comments from experts and readers alike.

We would also like to offer deep gratitude to the hardworking editors and designers at China Southern Daily Press, who offered their industrious talents and wisdom during the publishing of this book.

Author’s Note

September 7th, 2016 Guangzhou